Library and Book Trade Almanac™

The Bowker Annual

2008 | 53rd Edition

Library and Book Trade Almanac™

The Bowker Annual

2008 | 53rd Edition

Editor Dave Bogart
Consultant Julia C. Blixrud

 Information Today, Inc.

Published by Information Today, Inc.
Copyright © 2008 Information Today, Inc.
All rights reserved

International Standard Book Number 978-1-57387-321-5
International Standard Serial Number 0068-0540
Library of Congress Catalog Card Number 55-12434

Information Today, Inc.
143 Old Marlton Pike
Medford, NJ 08055-8750
Phone: 800-300-9868 (customer service)
         800-409-4929 (editorial queries)
Fax: 609-654-4309
E-mail (orders): custserv@infotoday.com
Web Site: http://www.infotoday.com

Printed and bound in the United States of America

US $199.95

ISBN 13: 978-1-57387-321-5

19995>

9 781573 873215

Contents

Part 1
Reports from the Field

Special Reports

Federal Agency and Federal Library Reports

National Association and Organization Reports

International Reports

Part 2
Legislation, Funding, and Grants

Legislation

Funding Programs and Grant-Making Agencies

Part 3
Library/Information Science
Education, Placement, and Salaries

Part 4
Research and Statistics

Part 5
Reference Information

Part 6
Directory of Organizations

Directory of Library and Related Organizations

Directory of Book Trade and Related Organizations

Preface

Welcome to this 53rd edition of the *Bowker Annual,* a compilation of informed analysis and practical information for the worlds of librarianship and publishing.

It has been another year of change and adjustment in the information industry, presenting new challenges in a continually evolving environment.

Our Special Reports highlight areas of particular interest:

- Harold Relyea of the Congressional Information Service examines the numerous ways in which the federal executive branch has continued to limit access to government information.
- Nancy John and Edward Valauskas look at the effect the open access campaign is having on scholarly publishing.
- Ken Haycock chronicles the noteworthy growth of the world's biggest MLIS program and how it has achieved that distinction.
- In two copyright-related reports, Sarah K. Wiant reviews developments in this ever-changing field and Jonathan Band details three recent appellate court decisions affecting "fair use" in an academic setting.

Part 1 continues with reports on the activities of federal agencies and federal libraries, and of national and international library and publishing organizations. Among these is probably the last report from the National Commission on Libraries and Information Science (NCLIS), which is being forced to close its doors after nearly four decades of performing valuable services to the library field.

Legislation and regulations affecting libraries and publishing are explained in detail in Part 2, along with the activities of funding programs and major grant-making agencies.

Part 3 provides professional information for librarians and aspiring librarians, ranging from guides to employment and studies of salaries to a complete listing of the year's major scholarship and award winners.

Part 4 offers a wealth of statistics and research—book and periodicals prices, library acquisitions expenditures, and a detailed examination of the United States' export and import trade in published products.

Reference information fills Part 5, including lists of recommended books and other media, an examination of the year's bestsellers, and an expanded rundown of the year's major literary prize winners.

Part 6 is our directory of library and publishing organizations at the state, national, and international levels, plus a calendar of major upcoming conferences, book fairs, and other events.

Many people are involved in the production of each edition of the *Bowker Annual,* and we are grateful to all who provided reports, assembled statistics, and responded to our requests for information. Once again, special thanks are due to Consultant Editor Julia C. Blixrud and Contributing Editor Catherine Barr.

We are confident that you will find this edition a valuable and frequently consulted resource. As always, we welcome your comments and suggestions for future editions.

Dave Bogart
Editor

Part 1
Reports from the Field

Special Reports

Access to Federal Government Information: A New Status Report

Harold C. Relyea

Specialist in American National Government
Congressional Research Service, Library of Congress

As the administration of President George W. Bush moves into its final year of governance, recent critical assessments of the policies and actions of this regime have taken issue with its constitutional interpretations, aggrandizement of executive powers, and penchant for secrecy.[1] Among these, Pulitzer prize-winning reporter Charlie Savage of the *Boston Globe,* while doubting that the expanded executive authority established by the Bush-Cheney administration will be successfully reduced by the next president or Congress, is seemingly less certain about the future of another aspect of the current regime's legacy, commenting only that the "zone of secrecy surrounding the executive branch has been dramatically widened."[2] Indeed, efforts at narrowing this existing "zone of secrecy" were already under way in the 110th Congress, which, while scrutinizing and questioning secrecy policies and practices, is also being asked to build upon the statutory bequest of its predecessors to ensure better information access and transparency.

The origins of that statutory bequest can be traced to the creation of the Special Subcommittee on Government Information, which was established in the House of Representatives in 1955. When it commenced exploratory hearings, the panel's immediate focus was on the availability of unpublished departmental and agency records to journalists and the public. Later, assertions of "executive privilege"—or constitutional separation of powers privilege—throughout the executive branch and claims of "national security" for information protection would also garner subcommittee attention. These hearings continued until April 1959; they were paralleled, and succeeded, by subcommittee staff investigations and reports, which continued until the enactment of the Freedom of Information Act (FOIA) in 1966.[3] The statute was designed to enable any person—individual or corporate, regardless of citizenship—to request, without explanation or justification, presumptive access to existing, identifiable, unpublished, executive branch agency records on any topic. It specified nine categories of information that might be permissibly exempted from the rule of disclosure. Disputes over the accessibility of requested records could be ultimately settled in court.

Thereafter, the House subcommittee and its successors worked with counterpart Senate panels to strengthen FOIA through amendments in 1974, 1976, 1986, 1996, and 2007. FOIA was soon joined by other open-government laws providing presumptive access to advisory and policy deliberation meetings and to one's personally identifiable records, chief among these being the Federal Advisory Committee Act of 1972,[4] the Privacy Act of 1974,[5] and the Government in the Sunshine Act of 1976.[6]

Federal information access and open-government law and policy were, of course, much affected by the September 11, 2001, terrorist attacks on the World Trade Center and the Pentagon. These events prompted rethinking, as well as continuing concern, about various aspects of the internal security—or homeland security—of the United States, not the least of which included the public availability of information of potential value to terrorists for either the commission of their acts or forewarning them of ways of their being detected.

Information access retrenchment in response to the terrorist attacks, however, was not the only factor contributing to secrecy permeating the executive branch. While President Bush has professed belief in open government, he also cloaked some of his policies, decision making, and actions in secrecy supposedly as a matter of military necessity because, as he often stresses, the United States is engaged in a war.[7] For example, he secretly ordered the National Security Agency (NSA) to conduct warrantless electronic surveillance of United States persons outside of the framework of the Foreign Intelligence Surveillance Act (FISA) that was established to authorize such monitoring.[8] Although it was later discovered that NSA had initially acted on its own authority in the weeks after the September 11 terrorist attacks to pursue such surveillance operations[9]—and was capturing purely domestic communications in some cases[10]—President Bush, in remarks at a December 19, 2005, press conference reacting to the revelation of this activity in the *New York Times,*[11] justified it in terms of "defending the country against an enemy that declared war against the United States." Continuing, he said:

> As President and Commander-in-Chief, I have the constitutional responsibility and the constitutional authority to protect our country. Article II of the Constitution gives me that responsibility and that authority necessary to fulfill it. And after September the 11th, the United States Congress also granted me additional authority to use military force against al Qaeda.[12]

His reliance upon Article II authority and the congressional joint resolution of September 18, 2001, authorizing the use of all necessary and appropriate force against those responsible for the terrorist attacks of the previous week, while ignoring the FISA arrangements, has been called into question in various quarters. Regarding the secrecy surrounding his order to NSA and its expanded surveillance effort, the president said: "My personal opinion is it was a shameful act for someone to disclose this very important program in a time of war. The fact that we're discussing this program," he maintained, "is helping the enemy." Concerning the leak, the president commented: "We're at war, and we must protect America's secrets. And so the Justice department, I presume, will proceed forward with a full investigation." Secrecy also figured prominently in his consideration to modify FISA to accommodate the kind of expanded surveillance he had ordered NSA to perform. He appeared to reject the constitutionally prescribed legislative process in this regard with the comment that "an open debate about law would say to the enemy, here is what we are going to do. And this is an enemy which adjusts." Reiterating this view in a response to another question, he added: "This is a war."[13]

Contributing, as well, is the president's view of the "unitary executive." In one regard, this means that the president has managerial control over all executive branch information. In another, President Bush and Vice President Richard B. Cheney, from the outset of their tenure, have justified taking certain actions in secret and otherwise declining to respond to congressional demands for information as part of a broader effort to reassert powers of the presidency that they believe had been dangerously eroded in the years after the Vietnam conflict and the Watergate fiasco. In remarks at a March 13, 2002, White House press conference when the General Accounting Office (GAO—since July 2004 the Government Accountability Office) was initially seeking records concerning the deliberations of the vice president's energy task force, President Bush, indicating he was "not going to let Congress erode the power of the Executive Branch," said: "I have a duty to protect the Executive Branch from legislative encroachment. I mean, for example, when the GAO demands documents from us, we're not going to give them to them." He then reiterated that he had "an obligation to make sure that the presidency remains robust and the Legislative Branch doesn't end up running the Executive Branch."[14]

With less than one year of governance remaining, the Bush-Cheney administration leaves a multifaceted legacy—information access conditions being the subject of this report. Some aspects of the withdrawal of information from public availability in the aftermath of the September 11, 2001, terrorist attacks were examined in a special report appearing in the 2003 edition of the *Bowker Annual*.[15] A follow-up report on access to federal government information was offered in the 2006 edition.[16] The report provided here assesses the status of public access to government information at the close of 2007.

Freedom of Information

The Bush administration's FOIA policy, which had been in formulation before the September 11 terrorist attacks, was expressed in an October 12, 2001, memorandum from Attorney General John Ashcroft to the heads of all federal departments and agencies.[17] While appearing to ignore the statute's presumptive right of records access and to regard the application of its exemptions to the rule of disclosure to be mandatory rather than permissive, the memorandum apprised readers that the Department of Justice and "this Administration," in addition to being "committed to full compliance with the Freedom of Information Act," were "equally committed to protecting other fundamental values that are held by our society," including "safeguarding our national security, enhancing the effectiveness of our law enforcement agencies, protecting sensitive business information and, not least, preserving personal privacy." The attorney general encouraged each agency "to carefully consider the protection of all such values and interests when making disclosure determinations under the FOIA." Furthermore, the agencies were advised, when "making these decisions, you should consult with the Department of Justice's Office of Information and Privacy when significant FOIA issues arise, as well as with our Civil Division on FOIA litigation matters." They were also assured that "the Department of Justice will defend your decisions unless they lack a sound legal basis or present an unwarranted risk of adverse impact on the ability of other agencies to protect other important records."

Historically, the statute generally was neither supported as legislation nor enthusiastically received as law by the federal departments and agencies. Initially, many of them had been far less than faithful in their administration of it, which contributed significantly to the 1974 remedial amendments that the House and the Senate crafted and approved in the face of a presidential veto.[18] Indeed, it was Congress that championed FOIA and had continued to perfect it to overcome bureaucratic resistance. Consequently, congressional reaction to the FOIA policy of the Bush administration was not surprising. The House Committee on Government Reform, in its March 2002 version of *A Citizen's Guide on Using the Freedom of Information Act,* pointedly noted that "the statute requires Federal agencies to provide the fullest possible disclosure of information to the public." Continuing, it said:

> The history of the act reflects that it is a disclosure law. It presumes that requested records will be disclosed, and the agency must make its case for withholding in terms of the act's exemptions to the rule of disclosure. The application of the act's exemptions is generally permissive— to be done if information in the requested records requires protection—not mandatory. Thus, when determining whether a document or set of documents should be withheld under one of the FOIA exemptions, an agency should withhold those documents only in those cases where the agency reasonably foresees that disclosure would be harmful to an interest protected by the exemption. Similarly, when a requestor asks for a set of documents, the agency should release all documents, not a subset or selection of those documents. *Contrary to the instructions issued by the Department of Justice on October 12, 2001, the standard should not be to allow the withholding of information whenever there is merely a "sound legal basis" for doing so.*[19]

What was surprising was the notable waning of congressional oversight not only regarding FOIA, but also generally during the 107th, 108th, and 109th Congresses. The watchdogs were asleep, and, as a result, the administration of FOIA suffered. According to a July 2006 survey by the Coalition of Journalists for Open Government, delays in agency responses to FOIA requests in fiscal year (FY) 2005 increased by 11 percent over those in FY 2004, and the backlog of unprocessed FOIA requests grew from 20 percent in FY 2004 to 31 percent in FY 2005, despite a drop in the total number of requests.[20]

There were some legislative attempts in 2005 to improve the situation, some with bipartisan support, and with one modest proposal receiving Senate approval. Late in the year President Bush issued E.O. (Executive Order) 13392 on improving agency disclosure of information.[21] The order required each agency to designate, from existing personnel, a "chief FOIA officer" by mid-January 2006. While many agencies already had an official who was responsible, in whole or in part, for FOIA administration, they were not at the assistant secretary or equivalent level prescribed for the new chief FOIA officers. Officials at the assistant secretary or equivalent level, however, were likely to be presidential appointees and could serve a brief tenure. Also, those designated as the chief FOIA officer likely would have other duties that would compete for attention.

The new chief FOIA officers were directed to conduct a review of their agencies' FOIA operations and draft a plan for improvement with concrete milestones for FY 2006 and FY 2007. By mid-June 2006, each chief FOIA officer was to submit to the Department of Justice, with a copy to the Office of Management and Budget (OMB) and another posted on the agency's Web site, a summary of the agency review and FOIA improvement plan. Follow-up reports in February 2007 and 2008 were to include information on the agency's performance in meeting the milestones of its FOIA improvement plan. Finally, the order directed each agency to establish one or more FOIA Requester Service Centers to enable those seeking information pursuant to the statute to learn about the status of their request and the agency's response, and to place contact information for the center on the agency's Web site. The chief FOIA officer for each agency was also to designate at least one public liaison to serve as a supervisory official to whom a FOIA requester could pose concerns about the service received from the center.

Some critics of existing FOIA administrative conditions regarded the reforms mandated by E.O. 13392 as an attempt by the Bush administration to preclude legislative attempts to improve the situation. A July 2006 assessment of a sample of agency plans for improving FOIA operations found it "surprising how many of the improvement areas were either not addressed or rated as poorly addressed, especially for the non-Cabinet agencies."[22] Seven months later, a GAO representative, testifying at a House subcommittee hearing, discussed a sample of agency "improvement plans that mostly included goals and timetables addressing the four areas of improvement emphasized by the Executive Order."

> Out of 25 plans, 20 provided goals and timetables in all four areas. In some cases, agencies did not set goals for a given area because they determined that they were already strong in that area. For the first area of improvement, reducing backlog, all agencies with reported backlog planned activities aimed at such reduction, and (with minor exceptions) all included both measurable goals and milestones for the other areas of improvement emphasized by the Executive Order (that is, increasing public dissemination, improving status communications, and increasing public awareness of FOIA processing); for example, to increase public awareness, agencies generally planned to ensure that their FOIA reference guides were comprehensive and up to date. The exception was the Department of the Treasury, whose review and plan addressed only activities to reduce backlog, omitting the other three areas of improvement.[23]

Such revelations did not satisfy congressional watchdogs, once again galvanized into action to seek statutory improvements in FOIA administration at the beginning of the 110th Congress. A reform bill, H.R. 1309, was introduced in the House with bipartisan support on March 5, 2007; subcommittee consideration, markup, and forward to the full committee occurred the following day; committee consideration, markup, and report took place on March 8.[24] The House considered the bill and, under a suspension of the rules, approved it on March 14.[25]

A counterpart Senate bill, S. 849, was introduced with bipartisan support on March 13; a hearing on the bill was held by the Committee on the Judiciary on March 14;[26] and the panel approved the measure on a voice vote on April 12, with a report on the measure filed and ordered to be printed on April 30.[27] The bill was held up for floor consideration and a final vote due to concerns arising from Department of Justice objections, which were resolved just before the

Senate adjourned for the August recess. The bill came before the Senate by unanimous consent on August 3, was amended, and passed by unanimous consent.[28]

Negotiations to resolve differences between H.R. 1309 and S. 849 continued through the fall. One of the more contentious issues concerned the Senate bill's failure to specify the source for the payment of attorney fees to FOIA requesters, who would be entitled to payments if an agency changed its position concerning the release of records after a requester challenged an agency denial in court. While the House bill provided that such payments would come from annually appropriated agency funds, the lack of such specificity in the Senate bill posed the strong possibility that it would trigger "pay-as-you-go" objections in the House. On December 6, a revised version of S. 849 was introduced with bipartisan support as S. 2427, which contained the language of the House bill concerning the source of attorney fees payments.[29] A slightly revised version of this bill, addressing other House concerns, was introduced with 17 bipartisan cosponsors on December 14 as S. 2488. That same day, the Senate considered the bill, and approved it without amendment by unanimous consent.[30] As adopted by the Senate, the bill amends FOIA as follows:

- Defines "representative of the news media" and "news" for purposes of request processing fees, and regards a freelance journalist as working for a news media entity if the journalist can demonstrate a solid basis for expecting publication through that entity

- Provides that, for purposes of awarding attorney fees and litigation costs, a FOIA complainant has substantially prevailed in a legal proceeding to compel disclosure if such complainant obtained relief through either (1) a judicial order or an enforceable written agreement or consent decree, or (2) a voluntary or unilateral change in position by the agency if the complainant's claim is not substantial

- Prohibits the Treasury Claims and Judgment Fund from being used to pay reasonable attorney fees in cases where the complainant has substantially prevailed, and requires fees to be paid only from funds annually appropriated for authorized purposes for the federal agency against which a claim or judgment has been rendered

- Directs the attorney general to (1) notify the special counsel of civil actions taken for arbitrary and capricious rejections of requests for agency records, and (2) submit annual reports to Congress on such civil actions, while also directing the special counsel to submit an annual report on investigations of agency rejections of FOIA requests[31]

- Requires the 20-day period during which an agency must determine whether to comply with a FOIA request to begin on the date the request is received by the appropriate component of the agency, but no later than ten days after the request is received by any component that is designated to receive FOIA requests in the agency's FOIA regulations; and prohibits the tolling of the 20-day period by the agency, except (1) that the agency may make one request to the requester for clarifying information and toll the 20-day period while awaiting such information, or (2) if necessary to clarify with the requester issues regarding fee assessment, and ends the tolling period on the agency's receipt of the requester's response

- Prohibits an agency from assessing search or duplication fees if it fails to comply with time limits, provided that no unusual or exceptional circumstances apply to the processing of the request, and requires each agency to make available its FOIA Public Liaison (see below), who shall assist in the resolution of any disputes between the agency and the requester
- Requires agencies to establish (1) a system to assign an individualized tracking number for each FOIA request received that will take longer than ten days to process, and (2) a telephone line or Internet service that provides information on the status of a request
- Revises annual reporting requirements on agency compliance with the FOIA to require information on (1) FOIA denials based upon particular statutory provisions, (2) response times, and (3) compliance by the agency and by each principal component thereof; and requires agencies to make the raw statistical data used in reports electronically available to the public upon request
- Redefines "record" under FOIA to include any information maintained by an agency contractor
- Establishes within the National Archives and Records Administration (NARA) an Office of Government Information Services (OGIS) to (1) review compliance with FOIA policies, (2) recommend policy changes to Congress and the president, and (3) offer mediation services between FOIA requesters and agencies as a nonexclusive alternative to litigation; and authorizes OGIS to issue advisory opinions if mediation fails to resolve a dispute
- Requires each agency to designate a chief FOIA officer, who shall (1) have responsibility for FOIA compliance, (2) monitor FOIA implementation, (3) recommend to the agency head adjustments to agency practices, policies, personnel, and funding to improve implementation of FOIA, and (4) facilitate public understanding of the purposes of the FOIA's statutory exemptions; and requires agencies to designate at least one FOIA public liaison, who shall be appointed by the chief FOIA officer to (1) serve as an official to whom a FOIA requester can raise concerns about service from the FOIA Requester Center, and (2) be responsible for assisting in reducing delays, increasing transparency and understanding of the status of requests, and assisting in the resolution of disputes
- Requires the Office of Personnel Management to report to Congress on personnel policies related to FOIA
- Requires the identification of the FOIA exemption(s) relied upon to redact information from records provided in response to a FOIA request

The Senate-approved bill was received in the House on December 17 and was referred to the Committee on Oversight and Government Reform. The following day the measure was considered by the House under a suspension of the rules, agreed to by voice vote, and cleared for the president.[32] The legislation was signed into law by President Bush on December 31, 2007, without a statement.[33]

Less than a month later, Sen. Patrick Leahy (D-Vt.), the principal Senate proponent of the FOIA reform legislation, complained to his colleagues that OMB officials had indicated that all of the funding authorized by the new law for the OGIS within the National Archives and Records Administration would be placed within the Department of Justice budget for FY 2009. This arrangement was viewed as seemingly giving the department control over OGIS, perhaps to the point of euthanizing it, or allocating the OGIS funds to its own Office of Information and Privacy, which oversees FOIA compliance by federal agencies. In creating OGIS, legislators had deliberately located it outside of the Department of Justice, which represents agencies sued by FOIA requesters. Calling the OMB tactic "not only contrary to the express intent of the Congress, but . . . also contrary to the very purpose of this legislation," Leahy expressed hope "that the administration will reconsider this unsound decision and enforce this law as the Congress intended."[34] OMB declined to comment on the matter prior to the formal presentation of the president's budget to Congress on February 4.

What the president's budget offered regarding OGIS was the following section proposed for enactment as part of Title V, General Provisions, of the Commerce, Justice, Science, and Related Agencies Appropriations legislation for FY 2009:

> Sec. 519. The Department of Justice shall carry out the responsibilities of the office established in 5 U.S.C. 552(h), from amounts made available in the Department of Justice appropriation for "General Administration Salaries and Expenses." In addition, subsection (h) of section 552 of title 5, United States Code, is hereby repealed, and subsections (i) through (l) are redesignated as (h) through (k).[35]

The office established in 5 U.S.C. 552(h) is OGIS. The Department of Justice, which would be vested with carrying out the responsibilities of that office, would be authorized to utilize funds from its general administration appropriation to do so. Congressional acceptance of this section seems most unlikely.

Security Classification

Initially authorized by armed services regulations, security classification policy and practice assumed a presidential character in a 1940 executive order, and later came to be prescribed in broadly discretionary terms for most departments and agencies in the early years of the Cold War, prompting an adverse reaction from Congress, the press, and the public. Beginning in 1953, reforms by President Dwight D. Eisenhower, followed by those of Presidents Richard M. Nixon, Jimmy Carter, and William Clinton, successively narrowed the bases and discretion for the security classification of executive branch records and documents. President Ronald Reagan briefly reversed this trend in 1982 with E.O. 12356,[36] as did President George W. Bush in 2003 with E.O. 13292.[37] Moreover, heightened official secrecy in the aftermath of the September 11 terrorist attacks and in conjunction with American military operations in Afghanistan and Iraq contributed, as well, to the greater resort to security classification during the Bush tenure. The *New York Times* observed editorially in July 2005 that the "Bush Administration is classifying the documents to be kept from public scrutiny at the rate of 125 a minute. The move toward greater secrecy," it continued, "has nearly doubled the number of documents annually hidden from public view—to well more than 15 million last year, nearly twice the number classified in 2001."[38] Until recently, as the number of classification actions has been increasing, the volume of declassified material has been decreasing, as the data in Table 1 below indicate.[39]

Table 1 / Information Moving In and Out of Classified Status

Fiscal Year	New Classification Actions	Declassified Pages
2001	8,650,735	100,104,990
2002	11,271,618	44,365,711
2003	14,228,020	43,093,233
2004	15,645,237	28,413,690
2005	14,206,773	29,540,603
2006	20,556,445	37,647,993

Of course, these activities have related costs. Security classification expenses—which include personnel security, physical security, education and training, and management and planning—have largely far exceeded expenditures for declassification, which are reflected in Table 2.[40]

Table 2 / Cost Estimates for Information Security Activities

Fiscal Year	Classification	Declassification
2001	$4.5 billion	$232 million
2002	5.5 billion	113 million
2003	6.4 billion	54 million
2004	7.1 billion	48.3 million
2005	7.7 billion	57 million
2006	8.2 billion	44 million

President Bush signed E.O. 13292 amending the Clinton order, E.O. 13292, on security classification policy and practice on March 25, 2003. The product of a review and reassessment initiated in the summer of 2001, the directive, among other changes, eliminated the Clinton order's standard that information not be classified if there is "significant doubt" about the need to do so; treated information obtained in confidence from foreign governments as classified; and authorized the vice president, "in the performance of executive duties," to classify information originally. It also added "infrastructures" and "protection services" to the categories of classifiable information; eased the reclassification of declassified records; postponed the automatic declassification of protected records 25 or more years old from beginning on April 17, 2003, to beginning on December 31, 2006; eliminated the requirement that agencies prepare plans for declassifying records; and permitted the director of central intelligence to block declassification actions of the Interagency Security Classification Appeals Panel (ISCAP), unless overruled by the president.

Created by the Clinton order, ISCAP is composed of senior-level representatives of the secretary of state, secretary of defense, attorney general, director of central intelligence, archivist of the United States, and assistant to the president for national security affairs. The president selects the panel's chair from among its members. The director of the Information Security Oversight Office (ISOO), which is the government-wide overseer of the security classification program, serves as the ISCAP executive secretary. The panel makes final determinations on classification challenges appealed to it; approves, denies, or amends exemptions from automatic declassification sought by agencies; makes final determinations on mandatory declassification review requests appealed to it; and generally advises and assists the president in the discharge of his discretionary authority to protect the national security of the United States. The recent review activities of ISCAP are detailed in Table 3.[41]

Table 3 / ISCAP Decisions

Year	Documents Reviewed	Declassified in Full	Declassified in Part	Affirmed Classification
2001	34 (100%)	8 (23%)	21 (62%)	5 (15%)
2002	49 (100%)	9 (18%)	17 (35%)	23 (47%)
2003	106 (100%)	3 (3%)	80 (75%)	23 (22%)
2004	159 (100%)	11 (7%)	30 (19%)	118 (74%)
2005	81 (100%)	21 (26%)	44 (54%)	16 (20%)
2006	675 (100%)	139 (21%)	294 (43%)	242 (36%)

As suggested by these data, the trend generally appears to be that, as more documents are reviewed, fewer are being declassified in whole or in part.

ISOO, established by E.O. 12958, as amended by E.O. 13292, is responsible, according to Section 5.2 of the order, for overseeing agency actions to ensure compliance with the order and related implementing directives, and for reporting at least annually to the president on the implementation of the order. In its oversight capacity, ISOO obtains management information from agencies that originate or handle classified information. Section 6.1 of the order defines such agencies as (1) "any 'Executive agency,' as defined in 5 U.S.C. 105"; (2) "any 'Military department' as defined in 5 U.S.C. 102"; and (3) "any other entity within the executive branch that comes into the possession of classified information." The third prong of this definition seemingly could cover a host of executive branch components possessing classified information.

Initially, the office of the vice president during the Bush administration provided information to ISOO on its management of classified information, and the ISOO FY 2001 annual report to the president reflected this compliance.[42] While the FY 2002 annual report was silent regarding the receipt of managerial information from the office of the vice president, the ISOO executive director has confirmed that such information was provided.[43] In the aftermath of the amendment of E.O. 12958 by E.O. 13292 in March 2003, the office of the vice president failed to provide management data to ISOO.[44] Footnotes in the FY 2003, FY

2004, FY 2005, and FY 2006 ISOO annual reports indicated that the office of the vice president did not report management data for each of the respective reporting periods.[45] In early January 2007 the ISOO executive director, pursuant to Section 6.2(b) of E.O. 12958, as amended, requested the attorney general to render an interpretation as to whether or not the office of the vice president was an agency, as defined in Section 6.1(b) of the order, and thus responsible for submitting reports to ISOO regarding its security classification management activities.

In June 2007 the House Committee on Oversight and Government Reform publicly released correspondence regarding the failure of the office of the vice president to file security classification management reports with ISOO. Related press stories revealed that, in 2004, the office of the vice president had rebuffed an on-site inspection by ISOO, and it was also disclosed that aides to the vice president had proposed amending E.O. 12958 to abolish ISOO.[46] The vice president's chief of staff, without citing specific language from the order, argued that it treated the vice president the same as the president and distinguished them both from "agencies" subject to the reporting requirements.[47] Near the end of the month, the White House indicated that the vice president did not have to cooperate with ISOO because he is a member of the executive branch with power vested in him by the president.[48] A few weeks later, the ISOO director received a letter from Steven G. Bradbury, principal deputy assistant attorney general, office of legal counsel, Department of Justice, advising him that the office of the vice president was not an "agency" for purposes of E.O. 12958.

In early January 2008 the Public Interest Declassification Board (PIDB) issued *Improving Declassification,* its first report.[49] Statutorily established in 2000, the board was a response to the work of the Commission on Protecting and Reducing Government Secrecy, chaired by Sen. Daniel P. Moynihan (D-N.Y.) during 1995–1997.[50] The nine-member PIDB was to (1) advise the president and other executive branch officials "on the systematic, thorough, coordinated, and comprehensive identification, collection, review for declassification . . . of declassified records and materials (including donated historical materials) that are of archival value"; (2) "promote the fullest possible public access to a thorough, accurate, and reliable documentary record of significant United States national security decisions and significant United States national security activities"; (3) "provide recommendations to the President for the identification, collection, and review for declassification of information of extraordinary public interest that does not undermine the national security of the United States, to be undertaken in accordance with a declassification program that has been established or may be established by the President by Executive order"; and (4) advise the president and other executive branch officials "on policies deriving from the issuance by the President of Executive orders regarding the classification and declassification of national security information."[51]

Its charter was amended in late 2004 after congressional committees experienced problems with the timely vetting of security classified information that had been used in reports they wanted to publish. Such difficulties had arisen, for instance, when the House Permanent Select Committee on Intelligence and the Senate Select Committee on Intelligence prepared to publish the findings from their joint inquiry into intelligence community activities prior to, and after, the September 11, 2001, terrorist attacks.[52] "It took more than six months of wrangling," according to a *Washington Post* editorial, "for the congressional joint committee investigating the Sept. 11 attacks to extract approval to publish its report—and even then it had to black out an entire section involving Saudi Arabia."[53] A similar experience occurred with the July 9, 2004, release of the Senate Intelligence Committee's report on the intelligence community's prewar intelligence assessments on Iraq.[54] According to one account, an estimated 20 percent of the draft report was deleted at the request of the Central Intelligence Agency (CIA) prior to its publication.[55] "It could have been worse, though," editorialized the *Washington Post*: "If intelligence officials had their way, nearly half of the 511-page report would have been redacted, rather than the 15 percent or so that was excised in the final version."[56]

These developments prompted calls for the creation of an independent panel for the impartial and expeditious resolution of disputes over whether or not to declassify portions of the sensitive content of official reports prior to their publication. In a July 2004 editorial on the matter, the *Washington Post* said:

> No one wants to insist on the release of information that could aid terrorists or other enemies of the United States. Clearly, some information reviewed by lawmakers or other investigators must remain secret. But the way the system is structured, no one can have confidence that the judgments to keep information classified are being made on the basis of national security alone—and there is ample evidence to the contrary. The reports already produced have offered a powerful, even chastening demonstration of the importance of outside oversight and review; it's hard to see what the arguments for classifying parts of those documents would have been. Among other effects, this undermines the credibility of the classifiers when it comes to protecting real secrets.[57]

To remedy the situation, Sen. Ron Wyden (D-Ore.) offered legislation creating a three-member board that would, prior to publication, review official reports containing information in dispute regarding its need to be classified and render a final decision regarding the matter.[58] Several weeks later he proposed amending omnibus intelligence reform legislation, then under consideration in the Senate, with the language of his bill.[59] The floor manager for the intelligence reform bill noted that "the administration has expressed grave reservations about the amendment as it is now drafted," and suggested that some reconciliation of it with other points in the bill might be in order. She proposed some staff-level adjustment of the amendment.[60]

Two days later Sen. Wyden offered a revised version of his original amendment. It sought to empower PIDB to review, at the request of the leaders of congressional armed services, foreign policy, and intelligence committees, existing or proposed classification actions, and to make recommendations to the president regarding the continued need for such classification. Not later than 60 days after receiving the board's recommendations, the president, if he did not accept and implement them, would be required to transmit to Congress a written justification for his decision. The Wyden amendment, as modified, was agreed to by the Senate,[61] and remained in the intelligence reform bill given Senate approval on a 96–2 vote on October 6, and was subsequently sent to conference.[62] The conferees further modified the amendment, rewriting it to indicate that the board was authorized to "review and make recommendations to the president in a timely manner with respect to any congressional request, made by the committee of jurisdiction, to declassify certain records or to reconsider a declination to declassify specific records," and that, if requested by the president, the board "shall review in a timely manner certain records or declinations to declassify specific records, the declassification of which has been the subject of specific congressional request." While the board was obligated to advise a requesting congressional committee as to whether or not it intended to conduct a declassification review, it was not required to inform the committee of the results of such a review, which was left to the president's discretion.[63] These modifications appeared to strengthen the president's control over the board's conduct of declassification reviews requested by congressional committees and the findings resulting from such reviews as were conducted. On December 7, the House, on a 336–75 vote, agreed to the conference committee report; the Senate gave its approval the following day on an 89–2 vote, clearing the intelligence reform legislation for the president's signature on December 17, 2004.[64] At that time, however, PIDB was inactive. After being mandated in 2000 in the closing weeks of the Clinton administration, the board did not have members until September 2004, when President Bush named five nominees; the other four members being designated by congressional leaders, but only two had been selected by the end of 2005. Furthermore, the board did not receive an appropriation until the end of 2005, when $1 million was allocated for its operations in the Department of Defense appropriations act for FY 2006.[65] As indicated in the letter transmitting *Improving Declassification* to the president, the board met for the first time in February 2006. PIDB's charter was amended a second time in August 2007 when Congress clarified that, upon receiving a congressional committee request to review and make recommendations to the president to declassify records or to reconsider a disinclination to declassify specific records, PIDB may conduct the review and make its recommendation regardless of whether such a review was requested by the president, and that any such recommendations submitted to the president shall be submitted, as well, to the chairman and ranking minority member of the committee requesting the review.[66]

Preparation of *Improving Declassification* began shortly after PIDB's initial February 2006 meeting. For the remainder of the year and into 2007, the board, on a nearly monthly basis, took testimony on declassification matters from representatives of the departments and agencies with the largest declassification programs, the National Archives and Records Administration, including the presidential libraries, and from knowledgeable members of the public.[67] Its overall finding might be found in the following comments.

> Though the Government is committed, as a matter of policy, to making historically significant information available to the public as soon as it can safely do so, there is no common understanding among the agencies of what "historically significant" information is, nor any common understanding of how such information will be treated once identified as such. Rather, it becomes part of the "queue," lost in the shuffle of automatic declassification reviews, FOIA requests, specially mandated searches, and the like. What of historical significance is actually being declassified is unclear both to the public and to the Government.
>
> Making matters worse, declassification does not necessarily mean that information will be available to the public any time soon. Once declassified, documents undergo archival processing, which includes determining whether they should be withheld for reasons other than security classification, conducting archival description (which may include indexing the

documents), and conducting any necessary preservation activities. The National Archives lacks sufficient resources to keep pace with agency declassification reviews, resulting in enormous backlogs. It will likely take years for hundreds of millions of pages of materials declassified over the past 12 years to become available to the public. Moreover, many declassified documents will continue to be withheld from the public because they contain other types of controlled, unclassified information, such as investigative or personal information. Many more years are likely to pass before this protected information is allowed into the public domain.[68]

Recognizing that "manpower is not the sole key to success" in the declassification effort, the PIDB report proffers that declassification "can and must be done in a smarter way," "needs to be better focused with greater uniformity among departments and agencies," and "needs to use technology to a greater extent to accomplish its mission and institute better strategic planning to address the needs of the future, especially the declassification of information stored in existing as well as emerging digital, optical, and other nontextual formats."[69] It is with these considerations in mind that the panel's recommendations were offered.

The PIDB report identifies 15 issues and makes 49 recommendations relating to the declassification of classified national security information. Among the recommendations are the following:

- Establishing by executive order or by statute a national declassification program under the supervision of the Archivist of the United States, with a new National Declassification Center (NDC), directed by a deputy Archivist for declassification policy and programs, to administer the program
- Requiring departments and agencies to consolidate all of their declassification activities in one office or to bring them under the control of a single office
- Ensuring, by presidential directive, that historically significant classified records are given priority at the 25-year review point, both in terms of what records are taken first and in terms of the quality of the review they receive
- Establishing and appointing, through the Archivist, a board composed of prominent historians, academicians, and former government officials to determine which events or activities of the federal government should be considered historically significant from a national security and foreign policy standpoint, for a particular year, and so advise the Archivist for purposes of setting priorities for declassification activities
- Establishing, through the Archivist, a single center within the Washington, D.C., metropolitan area, to house all future classified presidential records from the end of a presidential administration until their eventual declassification and physical transfer to a presidential library for public examination
- Directing agencies, by NDC guidelines or other appropriate executive branch issuance, to dedicate some specific percentage of their declassification review personnel to conducting reviews of classified records less than 25 years old that they know to be historically significant

- Charging the new NDC, through an executive order or other appropriate issuance, with prescribing uniform guidelines to govern the declassification of all executive departments and agencies
- Authorizing the NDC to conduct declassification reviews for other departments and agencies on a reimbursable basis
- Requiring that any withdrawal of records that were previously available to the public at the National Archives be approved by the Archivist
- Requiring that records identified as being of historical significance undergo a concurrent review for personal privacy or "controlled but unclassified" information at the same time as the review for declassification is conducted
- Developing, through the Archivist, a personnel plan, to be funded as part of NARA's annual budget, that would address the current archival processing backlog and otherwise enable the archives in the future to fully process all declassified records within five years of their declassification so that they may be available to the public
- Requiring, by amendment of the operative executive order, that all departments and agencies with significant classification activity establish historical advisory boards, composed of experts within and outside the agency
- Requiring, by appropriate executive branch issuance, that all departments and agencies with responsibilities in the national security area hire an appropriate number of historians, either to select classified records of historical significance for declassification review and publication or to write historical accounts based upon the department's or agency's classified holdings
- Establishing new arrangements to assure the preservation of the President's Daily Brief (PDB) as a presidential record under the Presidential Records Act, and allowing for the protection of the PDB under the terms of the Presidential Records Act
- Establishing formal procedures for the declassification review of classified congressional committee reports and hearing transcripts by the NDC[70]

On January 29, 2008, President Bush sent a memorandum to Cabinet officials and senior presidential assistants having responsibility for national security and homeland security policy soliciting their views on the recommendations in the PIDB report, to be submitted in writing no later than April 15.

Information Control Markings

Of related interest, the Bush administration reportedly is in the final stages of reducing the number of, and establishing better management arrangements for, markings used to identify and control various kinds of sensitive but otherwise unclassified information. The great variety of these markings and the lack of effective management regimes for them resulted in a situation that had been deplored by many analyses. A late 2004 information security report by the

JASON Program Office of the MITRE Corporation, for instance, proffered the following assessment:

> The status of sensitive information outside of the present classification system is murkier than ever. . . . "Sensitive but unclassified" data is increasingly defined by the eye of the beholder. Lacking in definition, it is correspondingly lacking in policies and procedures for protecting (or not protecting) it, and regarding how and by whom it is generated and used.[71]

A contemporaneous Heritage Foundation report appeared to agree with this appraisal, saying

> The process for classifying secret information in the federal government is disciplined and explicit. The same cannot be said for unclassified but security-related information for which there is no usable definition, no common understanding about how to control it, no agreement on what significance it has for U.S. national security, and no means for adjudicating concerns regarding appropriate levels of protection.[72]

Concerning the Sensitive But Unclassified (SBU) marking, a September 2004 report by the Federal Research Division of the Library of Congress commented that guidelines for its use were needed, and noted that "a uniform legal definition or set of procedures applicable to all Federal government agencies does not now exist." Indeed, the report indicated that SBU had been utilized in different contexts with little precision as to its scope or meaning, and, to add a bit of chaos to an already confusing situation, it is "often referred to as Sensitive Homeland Security Information."[73]

Unbeknown to these critics, however, the impetus for significantly reducing the variety of information control markings and better managing their use lay in provisions of the Intelligence Reform and Terrorism Prevention Act of 2004, which President Bush signed into law on December 17, 2004. It mandated a so-called Information Sharing Environment (ISE), an arrangement to facilitate, among federal, state, local, and tribal governments, as well as the private sector, the "sharing of terrorism information in a manner consistent with national security and with applicable legal standards relating to privacy and civil liberties."[74]

A December 16, 2005, presidential memorandum for the heads of executive departments and agencies, in support of ISE, explicitly noted, in one of its guidelines, the need to standardize procedures for sensitive but unclassified information, saying: "To promote and enhance the effective and efficient acquisition, access, retention, production, use, management, and sharing of Sensitive But Unclassified (SBU) information, including homeland security information, law enforcement information, and terrorism information, procedures and standards for designating, marking, and handling SBU information (collectively 'SBU procedures') must be standardized across the Federal Government."[75]

As part of the standardization effort, an interagency working group, led by the Department of Homeland Security and the Department of Justice, was formed and, according to May 10, 2006, congressional testimony by ISE Program Manager Thomas E. McNamara, completed an initial inventory of information control markings in March 2006. In his prepared statement, McNamara said:

Preliminary assessments indicate that there are no government-wide definitions, procedures, or training for designating information that may be SBU. Additionally, more than 60 different marking types are used across the Federal Government to identify SBU, including various designations within a single department. (It is important to note, seventeen of these markings are statutory.) Also, while different agencies may use the same marking to denote information that is to be handled as SBU, a chosen category of information is often defined differently from agency to agency, and agencies may impose different handling requirements. Some of these markings and handling procedures are not only inconsistent, but are contradictory.[76]

During the course of his testimony, McNamara reportedly indicated that some legislative action might be needed, possibly to adjust statutorily authorized markings or protections, or perhaps to prohibit the use of markings and designations not otherwise statutorily mandated.[77]

A few months later, it was revealed that the Department of Homeland Security and the Department of Justice were deadlocked over the information control markings to be commonly used to facilitate information sharing, a supporting management structure, and control over who gets information. As a consequence, a mid-June deadline set by the president to propose a new labeling system was missed.[78]

The ISE Implementation Plan, prepared by the ISE Program Manager and issued in November 2006, pointed out that "the growing and non-standardized inventory of SBU designations and markings is a serious impediment to information sharing among agencies, between levels of government, and, as appropriate, with the private sector. Elimination of this impediment," it continued, "is essential to ensure that the future ISE promotes and enhances the effective and efficient acquisition, access, retention, production, use, management, and sharing of unclassified information while also ensuring its appropriate and consistent safeguarding."[79] In accordance with the SBU procedures standardization guideline in the president's December 2005 memorandum, the secretary of homeland security and the attorney general, in coordination with the secretaries of state, defense, and energy, and the director of national intelligence, were to submit for presidential approval recommendations (1) "for government-wide policies and procedures to standardize SBU procedures" and (2) "for legislative, policy, regulatory, and administrative changes," as well as (3) an "assessment—by each department and agency participating in the SBU procedures review process—of the costs and budgetary considerations for all proposed changes to marking conventions, handling caveats, and other procedures pertaining to SBU information."[80]

In early February 2008 it was reported that the new SBU regime was ready for presidential approval and was being shared with some congressional staff in briefings. Information would be rated in three categories concerning "safeguards" as to how it should be stored, handled, and transmitted, and "dissemination" as to who is allowed to see it. The three categories, ranging from the lowest to the highest degree of protection, would be (1) "standard safeguards, standard dissemination," (2) "standard safeguards, specific dissemination," and (3) "enhanced safeguards, specific dissemination." At least four existing categories of SBU information will be grandfathered into the new system. These include the *Safeguards Information* of the Nuclear Regulatory Commission, *Sensitive Security Information* of the Transportation Security Administration, and *Pro-*

tected Critical Infrastructure Information and Chemical-Terrorism Vulnerability Information of the Department of Homeland Security.[81]

It is not clear how or by whom the implementation and use of these new arrangements will be monitored, or how infractions will be detected and punished. Similarly, the relationship between the three new information protection categories and the exemptions of the Freedom of Information Act is also uncertain due to the lack of more specific details concerning the new regime.

Other Developments

Efforts also were launched in the first session of the 110th Congress to revoke E.O. 13233 and return to the original intent of the Presidential Records Act concerning the public availability of the documentary materials of former presidents governed by that statute.[82] President Bush had issued E.O. 13233 on November 1, 2001.[83] While the statute authorized a former president to seek a court order to stop the disclosure of particular records by the Archivist as a violation of the former president's rights or privileges, the order effectively reversed this arrangement and prohibited the Archivist from releasing particular records unless and until both the incumbent and former presidents agreed to their disclosure, or until the Archivist is directed to disclose the records by a final court order resulting from a lawsuit brought by a person requesting the documentary materials. The order also vested a former vice president and a representative or group of representatives of a former president whose records are subject to the Presidential Records Act with authority to prohibit the Archivist from releasing particular records.

Opposition to the order was expressed by historians, political scientists, journalists, and lawyers, among others. A November 6, 2001, *Los Angeles Times* editorial, for example, indicated that the order "would nudge the nation's highest office back toward democracy's dark ages, when history effectively could be kept from the public." Three days later, the *Washington Post* editorially characterized the order's procedures as "a flawed approach on records." *USA Today,* in a November 12 editorial, regarded the order's arrangements as having a strong potential for "self-serving secrecy." In a November 15 editorial, the *New York Times* commented that the order "essentially ditches the law's presumption of public access in favor of a process that grants either an incumbent president or a former president the right to withhold the former president's papers from the public," and concluded that, if a remedy for the situation was to be realized, "Congress must pass a law doing so."[84]

Remedial legislation was introduced, amended, and favorably reported in the House in 2002, but did not receive a floor vote prior to the final adjournment of the 107th Congress.[85] The champion of the legislation, Rep. Steve Horn (R-Calif.), did not stand for re-election to the next Congress, and no successor legislation was subsequently introduced until the first session of the 110th Congress. On March 1, 2007, Rep. Henry Waxman (D-Calif.) introduced the Presidential Records Act Amendments (H.R. 1255), which would revoke E.O. 13233 and would allow the Archivist to reassume control of access to the records of recent former presidents. It was reported from the Committee on Oversight and Government Reform on March 8,[86] and the House approved it on March 14 under a suspension of the rules on a 333–93 vote.[87]

A companion bill (S. 886) was introduced by Sen. Jeff Bingaman (D-N.M.) on March 14, 2007, and was referred to the Committee on Homeland Security and Governmental Affairs, which reported the measure (no written report) without amendment on June 20, when it was placed on the Senate legislative calendar.[88]

Finally, there is the unresolved matter of what to do about the Bush administration's missing White House e-mail. A June 2007 majority staff report of the House Committee on Oversight and Government Reform indicates that committee investigators initially discovered that White House officials were using unofficial e-mail accounts during a 2006 probe of White House contacts with lobbyist Jack Abramoff. These unofficial accounts were those of the Republican National Committee (RNC). "Additional evidence that White House officials have used RNC e-mail accounts for official communications," said the report, "arose as part of two other investigations: (1) the investigation by the Senate and House Judiciary Committees into the firings of U.S. Attorneys and (2) the investigation of the Oversight Committee into White House political presentations to federal agencies." In March 2007 the House Oversight Committee asked the RNC and the Bush Cheney '04 campaign to preserve all records of e-mails sent to or from White House officials. About a week later, both entities were requested to provide e-mails "relating to political briefings provided to agency officials and the use of federal agencies and federal resources for partisan political purposes." When voluntary cooperation by the RNC did not result, the committee issued two subpoenas seeking "statistical information about White House officials' use of the accounts as well as the e-mails that had previously been requested."[89] This material revealed that 88 current and former White House Office officials held RNC e-mail accounts, including senior presidential adviser Karl Rove, Chief of Staff Andrew Card, and Counselor to the President Dan Bartlett, as well as all four individuals who served as the director of political affairs in the Bush White House. The Bush Cheney '04 campaign "provided only limited information" to the committee, but, from what was made available, it was determined that 11 White House officials held campaign e-mail accounts, including both Rove and Bartlett.[90] Among other concerns raised by this situation, the report noted, was the failure to retain e-mails generated from these accounts.

Whether intentionally or inadvertently, it appears that the RNC has destroyed a large volume of the e-mails of White House officials who used RNC e-mail accounts. The RNC has told the committee that it had a "document retention" policy under which e-mails that are more than 30 days old are deleted. In addition, the RNC has said that individual account holders had the ability to delete permanently e-mails less than 30 days old. As a result of these policies, potentially hundreds of thousands of White House e-mails have been destroyed, many of which may be presidential records (subject to the Presidential Records Act).

One indication of the scale of the loss of White House e-mail is the fact that the RNC has retained no e-mail messages whatsoever for 51 of the 88 White House officials with RNC e-mail accounts. It is possible that some of these individuals made minimal or no use of their accounts, but there is evidence that indicates that many of them used their accounts on a regular basis.[91]

For this phase of its investigation, the majority staff report offered the following conclusion:

> The Committee has obtained evidence of potentially extensive violations of the Presidential Records Act by senior White House officials. During President Bush's first term, momentous decisions were made, such as the decision to go to war in Iraq. Yet many e-mail communications during this period involving the President's most senior advisors, including Karl Rove, were destroyed by the RNC. These violations could be the most serious breach of the Presidential Records Act in the 30-year history of the law.[92]

Several months later, it was revealed that a 2005 study, produced by the Office of Administration within the Executive Office of the President (EOP), found that, for 473 days between 2003 and 2005, there were no archived e-mail messages for the office, some of its component agencies, and for the Office of the Vice President. While some EOP officials questioned the credibility of the study, it was disclosed that e-mail backup tapes were routinely recycled or erased and reused during the first three years of the Bush administration. Experts familiar with information technology indicated that, when tapes are repeatedly recycled, recovery of erased data becomes increasingly difficult and may be gone forever.[93] Shortly thereafter, it was reported that the Bush administration, immediately after assuming leadership, had scrapped a custom e-mail archiving system that the Clinton administration had adopted under a federal court order.[94] In early February a *Washington Post* editorial summed up the situation, saying: "With each passing week, the fate of e-mails generated by President Bush's staff grows more curious and troubling. While evidence has not emerged of a deliberate effort by the White House to destroy sensitive electronic messages, there's reason to be concerned about the potential loss of historical records."[95] Such loss has seemingly occurred in the face of laws enacted to prevent such a privation.

Notes

1. Joe Conason, *It Can Happen Here: Authoritarian Peril in the Age of Bush* (St. Martin's, 2007); John P. MacKenzie, *Absolute Power: How the Unitary Executive Theory Is Undermining the Constitution* (Century Foundation, 2008); Robert M. Pallitto and William G. Weaver, *Presidential Secrecy and the Law* (Johns Hopkins, 2007); Charlie Savage, *Takeover: The Return of the Imperial Presidency and the Subversion of American Democracy* (Little, Brown, 2007); Frederick A. O. Schwartz, Jr., and Aziz Z. Huq, *Unchecked and Unbalanced: Presidential Power in a Time of Terror* (New Press, 2007).

2. Savage, *Takeover: The Return of the Imperial Presidency and the Subversion of American Democracy,* p. 329.

3. 80 Stat. 250; codified in 1967, 81 Stat. 54; currently found at 5 U.S.C. 552.

4. 5 U.S.C. App.

5. 5 U.S.C. 552a.

6. 5 U.S.C. 552b.

7. Responding to a question at the American Society of Newspaper Editors convention, President Bush said, "I believe in open government. I've always believed in open government." U.S. White House Office, "President Addresses American Society of Newspaper Editors Convention," J. W. Marriott Hotel, Washington, D.C., April 14, 2005, available at http://www.whitehouse.gov/news/releases/2005/04/print/20050414-4.html.

8. See 50 U.S.C. 1801 et seq.

9. Eric Lichtblau and Scott Shane, "Agency First Acted on Its Own to Broaden Spying, Files Show," *New York Times,* Jan. 4, 2006, pp. A1, A13.

10. James Risen and Eric Lichtblau, "Spying Program Snared U.S. Calls," *New York Times,* Dec. 21, 2005, pp. A1, A23.

11. James Risen and Eric Lichtblau, "Bush Lets U.S. Spy on Callers Without Courts," *New York Times,* Dec. 16, 2005, pp. A1, A22.

12. U.S. White House Office, "Press Conference of the President," Washington, D.C., Dec. 19, 2005, available at http://www.whitehouse.gov/news/releases/2005/12/print/20051219-2.html.

13. Ibid.

14. U.S. White House Office, "President Bush Holds Press Conference: Press Conference by the President," Washington, D.C., March 13, 2002, available at http://www.whitehouse.gov/news/releases/2002/03/print/20020313-8html.

15. See Harold C. Relyea and L. Elaine Halchin, "Homeland Security and Information Management," *Bowker Annual Library and Book Trade Almanac,* 48th edition (Information Today, Inc., 2003), pp. 231–250.

16. See Harold C. Relyea, "Access to Federal Government Information: A Status Report," *Bowker Annual Library and Book Trade Almanac,* 51st edition (Information Today, Inc., 2006), pp. 267–290.

17. U.S. Department of Justice, Office of the Attorney General, "The Freedom of Information Act," Memorandum for the Heads of All Federal Departments and Agencies, Oct. 12, 2001, Washington, D.C.; available at http://www.usdoj.gov/04foia/011012.htm.

18. See U.S. Congress, House Committee on Government Operations [and] Senate Committee on the Judiciary, *Freedom of Information Act and Amendments of 1974 (P.L. 93-502), Source Book: Legislative History, Texts, and Other Documents,* joint committee print, 94th Cong., 1st sess. (GPO, 1975).

19. U.S. Congress, House Committee on Government Reform, *A Citizen's Guide on Using the Freedom of Information Act and the Privacy Act of 1974 to Request Government Records,* 107th Cong., 2nd sess., H. Rept. 107-371 (GPO, 2002), p. 3 (*emphasis added*).

20. Ralph Lindeman, "Agency Delays in FOIA Responses Increase, Even as Requests Decline, New Study Finds," *BNA Daily Report for Executives,* July 3, 2006, p. A-20; Coalition of Journalists for Open Government, *Frequent Filers: Businesses Make FOIA Their Business,* July 3, 2006, Arlington, Va., available at http://www.cjog.net/documents/Who_Uses_FOIA2.pdf.

21. See *Federal Register,* vol. 70, Dec. 19, 2005, pp. 75373–75377.

22. OpenTheGovernment.org, *FOIA's 40th Anniversary: Agencies Respond to the President's Call for Improved Disclosure of Information,* July 4, 2006, Washington, D.C., n.p.; available at http://www.OpenTheGovernment.org under "Reports, Testimony, Letters."

23. U.S. Government Accountability Office, *Freedom of Information Act: Processing Trends Show Importance of Improvement Plans,* GAO Report GAO-07-491T (Feb. 14, 2007), p. 4.

24. U.S. Congress, House Committee on Oversight and Government Reform, *Freedom of Information Act Amendments of 2007,* report to accompany H.R. 1309, 110th Cong., 1st sess., H. Rept. 110-45 (GPO, 2007).

25. *Congressional Record,* daily edition, vol. 153, March 14, 2007, pp. H2500–H2507.

26. U.S. Congress, Senate Committee on the Judiciary, *Open Government: Reinvigorating the Freedom of Information Act,* hearing, 110th Cong., 1st sess., March 14, 2007 (GPO, 2007).

27. U.S. Congress, Senate Committee on the Judiciary, *Open Government Act of 2007,* report to accompany S. 849, 110th Cong., 1st sess., S. Rept. 110-59 (GPO, 2007).

28. *Congressional Record,* daily edition, vol. 153, Aug. 3, 2007, pp. S10986–S10991.

29. Ibid., Dec. 6, 2007, pp. S14853–S14855.

30. Ibid., Dec. 14, 2007, pp. S15701–S15704.

31. The Office of Special Counsel is an independent agency within the executive branch that investigates allegations of certain activities prohibited by civil service laws, rules, or regulations and litigates before the Merit Systems Protection Board, another independent agency, which protects the integrity of the federal personnel merit systems and the rights of federal employees.

32. *Congressional Record,* daily edition, vol. 153, Dec. 18, 2007, pp. H16788–H16792.

33. P.L. 110-175; 121 Stat. 2524.

34. *Congressional Record,* daily edition, vol. 154, Jan. 23, 2008, pp. S201–S202; Dan Friedman, "Senators Say White House Plans to Eliminate Special FOIA Office," *CongressDaily,* Jan. 25, 2008, available at http://www.govexec.com/story_page_pf.cfm?articleid=39120&dcn= e_gvet.

35. U.S. Office of Management and Budget, *Budget of the United States Government, Fiscal Year 2009—Appendix* (GPO, 2008), p. 239.

36. 3 C.F.R., 1982 Comp., pp. 166–178; Richard C. Ehlke and Harold C. Relyea, "The Reagan Administration Order on Security Classification: A Critical Assessment," *Federal Bar News and Journal,* vol. 30, Feb. 1983, pp. 91–97.

37. 3 C.F.R., 2003 Comp., pp. 196–218.

38. Editorial, "The Dangerous Comfort of Secrecy," *New York Times,* July 12, 2005, p. A22.

39. Data from U.S. National Archives and Records Administration, Information Security Oversight Office, *Report to the President 2001* (Sept. 2002), p.16; U.S. National Archives and Records Administration, Information Security Oversight Office, *Report to the President 2002* (June 2003), pp. 14–15; U.S. National Archives and Records Administration, Information Security Oversight Office, *Report to the President 2003* (March 2004), pp. 20, 25; U.S. National Archives and Records Administration, Information Security Oversight Office, *Report to the President 2004* (March 2005), pp. 15, 17; U.S. National Archives and Records Administration, Information Security Oversight Office, *Report to the President 2005* (May 2006), pp. 13, 15; U.S. National Archives and Records Administration, Information Security Oversight Office, *Report to the President 2006* (May 2007), pp. 6, 22.

40. Data from U.S. National Archives and Records Administration, Information Security Oversight Office, *Report to the President 2001,* pp. 7–8; U.S. National Archives and Records Administration, Information Security Oversight Office, *Report to the President 2002,* p. 26; U.S. National Archives and Records Administration, Information Security Oversight Office, *Report to the President 2006,* pp. 29–30; U.S. National Archives and Records Administration, Information Security Oversight Office, *2003 Report on Cost Estimates for Security Classification Activities* (July 2004), pp. 2–3; U.S. National Archives and Records Administration, Information Security Oversight Office, *Report on Cost Estimates for Security Classification Activities for 2004* (May 2005), p. 3; U.S. National Archives and Records Administration, Information Security Oversight Office, *Report on Cost Estimates for Security Classification Activities for 2005* (2006), pp. 2, 5.

41. Data from U.S. National Archives and Records Administration, Information Security Oversight Office, *Report to the President 2001,* p. 5; U.S. National Archives and Records Administration, Information Security Oversight Office, *Report to the President 2002,* p. 9; U.S. National Archives and Records Administration, Information Security Oversight Office, *Report to the President 2003,* p. 9; U.S. National Archives and Records Administration, Information Security Oversight Office, *Report to the President 2004,* p. 7; U.S. National Archives and Records Administration, Information Security Oversight Office, *Report to the*

President 2005, p. 5; U.S. National Archives and Records Administration, Information Security Oversight Office, *Report to the President 2006,* p. 6.

42. U.S. National Archives and Records Administration, Information Security Oversight Office, *Report to the President 2001,* p. 12.

43. Personal communication to the author by J. William Leonard, June 2007.

44. While E.O. 12958 defined "agency" in terms of any "Executive agency" as defined in 5 U.S.C. 105 and "any other entity within the executive branch that comes into the possession of classified information," E.O. 13292 expanded the definition of agency to include any "Military department" as defined in 5 U.S.C. 102. The "entity" reference was the same in both orders.

45. U.S. National Archives and Records Administration, Information Security Oversight Office, *Report to the President 2003,* p. 12; U.S. National Archives and Records Administration, Information Security Oversight Office, *Report to the President 2004,* p. 11; U.S. National Archives and Records Administration, Information Security Oversight Office, *Report to the President 2005,* p. 9; U.S. National Archives and Records Administration, Information Security Oversight Office, *Report to the President 2006,* p. 18.

46. Peter Baker, "Cheney Defiant on Classified Material," *Washington Post,* June 22, 2007, pp. A1, A4; Scott Shane, "Agency Is Target in Cheney Fight on Secret Data," *New York Times,* June 22, 2007, pp. A1, A16.

47. Michael Abramowitz, "Cheney Aide Explains Stance on Classified Material," *Washington Post,* June 27, 2007, p. A5; the Office of the Vice President, formally recognized for the first time in the pages of the *United States Government Organization Manual 1972/73,* appeared at the end of the section profiling units of the Executive Office of the President, but has no organic charter, and appears to rest on a 1978 statutory provision (92 Stat. 2446, 3 U.S.C. 106) authorizing staff for the vice president in his executive capacity of assisting the president.

48. Jim Rutenberg, "White House Drops Vice President's Dual-Role Argument as Moot," *New York Times,* June 28, 2007, p. A15.

49. U.S. National Archives and Records Administration, Public Interest Declassification Board, *Improving Declassification: A Report to the President from the Public Interest Declassification Board* (Dec. 2007). Available at http://www.archives.gov/declassification/pidb/improving-declassification.pdf.

50. See U.S. Commission on Protecting and Reducing Government Secrecy, *Secrecy: Report of the Commission on Protecting and Reducing Government Secrecy* (GPO, 1997).

51. 114 Stat. 2856.

52. U.S. Congress, Senate Select Committee on Intelligence and House Permanent Select Committee on Intelligence, *Joint Inquiry into Intelligence Community Activities Before and After the Terrorist Attacks of September 11, 2001,* 107th Cong., 2nd sess., S. Rept. 107-351, H. Rept. 107-792 (GPO, 2002).

53. Editorial, "Credible Classifications," *Washington Post,* July 13, 2004, p. A14.

54. U.S. Congress, Senate Select Committee on Intelligence, *Report on the U.S. Intelligence Community's Prewar Intelligence Assessments on Iraq,* 108th Cong., 2nd sess., S. Rept. 108-301 (GPO, 2004).

55. Neil A. Lewis, "The Committee: C.I.A. Deleted Large Sections, Officials Say," *New York Times,* July 10, 2004, p. A9.

56. Editorial, "Credible Classifications," *Washington Post,* July 13, 2004, p. A14.

57. Ibid.

58. *Congressional Record,* daily edition, vol. 150, July 15, 2004, pp. S8234–S8237.

59. Ibid., Sept. 27, 2004, pp. S9726–S9728.

60. Ibid., pp. S9714–S9719.

61. Ibid., Sept. 29, 2004, pp. S9911–S9914.

62. Ibid., Oct. 6, 2004, p. S10543.

63. U.S. Congress, House, Committee of Conference, *Intelligence Reform and Terrorism Prevention Act of 2004,* a report to accompany S. 2845, 108th Cong., 2nd sess., H. Rept. 108-796 (GPO, 2004), p. 64.

64. 118 Stat. 3638.

65. See Christopher Lee, "Declassification Board: Named but Unfunded," *Washington Post,* May 2, 2005, p. A15; 119 Stat. 2680.

66. 121 Stat. 336.

67. U.S. National Archives and Records Administration, Public Interest Declassification Board, *Improving Declassification: A Report to the President from the Public Interest Declassification Board,* p. 3.

68. Ibid., p. 6.

69. Ibid.

70. Ibid., pp. 8–12.

71. MITRE Corporation, JASON Program Office, *Horizontal Integration: Broader Access Models for Realizing Information Dominance* (Dec. 2004), p. 5.

72. James Jay Carafano and David Heyman, "DHS 2.0: Rethinking the Department of Homeland Security," *Heritage Special Report SR-02* (Dec. 13, 2004), p. 20.

73. U.S. Library of Congress, Federal Research Division, *Laws and Regulations Governing the Protection of Sensitive But Unclassified Information,* by Alice R. Buchalter, John Gibbs, and Marieke Lewis (Sept. 2004), p. i.

74. 118 Stat. 3665.

75. U.S. White House Office, Office of the Press Secretary, *Memorandum for the Heads of Executive Departments and Agencies,* Subject: "Guidelines and Requirements in Support of the Information Sharing Environment (Dec. 16, 2005), p. 3, available at http://www.whitehouse.gov/news/releases/2005/12/print/20051216-10.html.

76. Thomas E. McNamara, Program Manager for the Information Sharing Environment, Statement for the Record, House Committee on Homeland Security, Subcommittee on Intelligence, Information Sharing, and Terrorism Risk Assessment, May 10, 2006, Washington, D.C., pp. 8–9.

77. Chris Strohm, "Congress Urged to Help Make More 'Sensitive' Information Public," *GovExec.com,* May 11, 2006, available at http://www.govexec.com/story_page.cfm?articleid=34062&printerfriendlyVers=1&.

78. Siobhan Gorman, "Turf War Hampers War on Terror," *Baltimore Sun,* July 13, 2006, p. 3A.

79. U.S. Office of the Director of National Intelligence, Program Manager, Information Sharing Environment, *Information Sharing Environment Implementation Plan* (Nov. 2006), p. 94.

80. Ibid., p. 95.

81. Shaun Waterman (UPI), "New Standards to Cover Restricted Data Types," *Washington Times,* Feb. 7, 2008, p. A6.

82. 44 U.S.C. 2201–2207.

83. 3 C.F.R., 2001 Comp., pp. 815–819.

84. U.S. Congress, House Committee on Government Reform, Subcommittee on Government Efficiency, Financial Management, and Intergovernmental Relations, *Hearings Regarding Executive Order 13233 and the Presidential Recordings Act,* hearings, 107th Cong., 1st and 2nd sess., Nov. 6, 2001; Apr. 11 and 24, 2002 (GPO, 2002), pp. 243–246.

85. U.S. Congress, House Committee on Government Reform, *Presidential Records Act Amendments of 2002,* report to accompany H.R. 4187, 107th Cong., 2nd sess., H. Rept. 107-790 (GPO, 2002).

86. U.S. Congress, House Committee on Oversight and Government Reform, *Presidential Records Act Amendments of 2007,* report to accompany H.R. 1255, 110th Cong., 1st sess., H. Rept. 110-44 (GPO, 2007).

87. *Congressional Record,* daily edition, vol. 153, Mar. 14, 2007, pp. H2496–H2500, H2508–H2509.

88. Ibid., pp. S3140–S3141.

89. U. S. House of Representatives, Committee on Oversight and Government Reform, Majority Staff, *Interim Report: Investigation of Possible Presidential Records Act Violations* (June 2007), p. 1.

90. Ibid., p. 2.

91. Ibid., pp. 4–5.

92. Ibid., p. 9.

93. Dan Eggen and Elizabeth Williamson, "White House Study Found 473 Days of E-Mail Gone," *Washington Post,* Jan. 18, 2008, pp. A1–A2.

94. Elizabeth Williamson and Dan Eggen, "White House Has No Comprehensive E-Mail Archive," *Washington Post,* Jan. 22, 2008, p. A3; also see U.S. General Accounting Office, *Electronic Records: Clinton Administration's Management of Executive Office of the President's E-Mail System,* GAO Report GAO-01-446 (April 2001).

95. Editorial, "Those Missing E-Mails," *Washington Post,* Feb. 11, 2008, p. A12.

Open Access Issues Continue to Lead Scholarly Publishing News

Nancy R. John

Associate Professor Emerita, University of Illinois at Chicago

Edward J. Valauskas

Graduate School of Library and Information Science, Dominican University
Chief Editor, *First Monday* (http://firstmonday.org)

Open access in the mainstream? In 2007 an increasing number of scholarly publishers became more "open"—that is, made more content openly available and opened up review and editing processes, as notions of "openness" became part of the policies of foundations, funding agencies, and governments worldwide. Hence in 2007 various players solidified and acted upon their strategic views of the future of scholarly publishing. For some, open access will play an increasingly important role.

Journals

The American Association for the Advancement of Science (AAAS) withdrew its journal *Science,* one of the premier scientific journals in the world, from participation in the scholarly journals archive JSTOR. AAAS left 1998–2002 issues in JSTOR for current JSTOR subscribers, thanks to a five-year moving wall for access. *Science* was the first journal to withdraw from participation in JSTOR since JSTOR's appearance in 1994. AAAS (in July 2007) noted that the departure was not precipitated by service issues with JSTOR, but was part of its strategic plan for *Science.* AAAS felt that "it is now time to assume the full responsibility for maintaining a complete electronic archive of its flagship publication." (AAAS, 2007)

The International Association of Scientific, Technical, and Medical (STM) Publishers also responded to the European Commission's announced plans for open access (see the section below on Government Actions) by issuing the Brussels Declaration on STM Publishing. The declaration, since adopted by the Association of American Publishers (AAP) and endorsed by a host of European STM publishers, asserts the key role that publishers play in assuring the quality of scientific research. Some publishers have routinely expressed concern that open access publishing undermines the peer review process. Publishers have suggested that government requirements for open access mean that some researchers have fewer options in publishing their work, restricting their freedom to publish wherever they would like.

In August 2007 AAP launched PRISM (Partnership for Research Integrity in Science and Medicine), an initiative "to bring together like-minded scholarly societies, publishers, researchers, and other professionals in an effort to safeguard the scientific and medical peer-review process and educate the public." Its Web site (http://www.prismcoalition.org) articulates "the PRISM Principles, an affirmation of publishers' contribution to science, research, and peer review, and an expression of support for continued private sector efforts to expand access to scientific information." A major activity for PRISM has been to argue against initiatives to promote or require publishing of scientific research in open access repositories.

Elsewhere in the publishing world, there was news from the emerging university e-prints sector and from self-publishers. Universities and their libraries continued to expand their in-house electronic publishing of open access journals, initiated in part by local scholarly communities. Thanks to the Public Knowledge Project's open source Open Journal Systems (OJS) software, any university, society, library, or other group or individual can become its own imprint for one or more online journals. In July 2007 OJS users, want-to-be users, and others interested in scholarly publishing gathered in Vancouver for the first Scholarly Publishing Conference (http://pkp.sfu.ca/ocs/pkp2007/index.php/pkp/1). As of August 2007 at least 1,200 journals on six continents were being published using the OJS software. Comparatively, as of the end of February 2008 the Directory of Open Access Journals (http://www.doaj.org) at Sweden's Lund University recorded 3,206 journals. As was evident in Vancouver, OJS is becoming an efficient and utilitarian tool, significantly helping scholars everywhere, but especially in developing countries. For those scholars, frustrated by barriers to the dissemination of their unique work, OJS will help develop new and diverse outlets for their important studies.

Within specific disciplines, 2007 witnessed shifting allegiances. The American Anthropological Association announced in September that Wiley-Blackwell would publish all of the association's 23 journals as well as hosting AnthroSource, the association's portal (Blackwell Publishing, 2007). How AnthroSource, and the association's journals, will evolve in this new environment is not clear. The original vision of AnthroSource—as "personalized workspaces where members can tailor the user interface, content, and services" (Nardi et al., 2004)—certainly will be different in its new Wiley-Blackwell home.

Desktop publishing has evolved, especially over the past few years, maturing into network publishing. Lulu.com (http://www.lulu.com) is an example of network publishing's "ability to grab hold of the long tail of user-generated content and provide an empowering outlet for creators of all types." Started by Red Hat founder Bob Young in 2003, Lulu.com provides advanced Web 2.0 tools for any user to take his or her own content and create, design, market, and sell that content—even register to secure an ISBN. Works are printed on demand with Lulu taking a commission, sending the remaining revenue to a specific author. A variety of offerings allow one, or Lulu, to undertake the marketing for one's work. By the end of 2007 Lulu had become the largest self-publisher community on the Internet.

Lulu.com is an example of the growing impact of Web 2.0 on scholars and their efforts to use new digital tools in exciting ways. Larry Sanger—whose involvement with Nupedia, Wikipedia, and Citizendium proved the utility of the Web and wikis—challenged the publishing community to encourage expert-led collaboration, albeit on a new and massive scale. Speaking at a meeting of the Society for Scholarly Publishing, Sanger (2007) noted that "experts together know the literature of their fields far better than any one of them individually."

Only time will tell if publishers are willing to take on massive collaboration led by experts on specialized topics.

Government Actions

In January 2007, while the National Science Foundation (NSF) enjoyed its largest budget increase in years, a group of network-savvy individuals met in Washington, D.C., to discuss the nation's "cyberinfrastructure." Cyberinfrastructure is the set of protocols and network architecture that supports widely distributed high-performance computing via the Internet for data- and computing-intensive collaborative research activities. Hence the cyberinfrastructure "offers a promise of informing and enabling innovation wherever it may occur—and in doing so, helping us better understand the processes, practices, and institutions of innovation. Since we look to innovation as a principal source of increased productivity and economic growth, NSF's initiative on cyberinfrastructure may prove as politically and strategically important as the development of the Internet . . ." (Kahin and Jackson, 2007). For publishers of all stripes and persuasions, a robust cyberinfrastructure literally makes digital scholarly publishing possible. As an example of the power of a mature cyberinfrastructure, Paul Avery (2007) of the University of Florida discussed the Open Science Grid, a consortium of more than 70 institutions supporting scientific research with 25,000 CPUs and four petabytes (4,000 terabytes) of storage. To imagine a digital publishing infrastructure on this scale, it would take resolution of a variety of legal—not technical—problems governing cooperation and access. Indeed, intellectual property (IP) issues relating to cyberinfrastructure were a large part of NSF's conference; solutions for these IP issues will not be easy or quick (from the conference, see, for example, Boettiger, 2007; Burk, 2007; and, Jackson et al., 2007).

The European Commission held a conference, "Scientific Publishing in the European Research Area: Access, Dissemination and Preservation in the Digital Age," in February 2007. Despite a petition ("Petition for guaranteed public access to publicly-funded research results," http://www.ec-petition.eu) circulated via the Web since January 2007 that gathered more than 15,000 signatures in the first few weeks of 2007, the European Commission did not endorse open access. It seems that the commission yielded to intensive pressure and lobbying from the European publishing industry. However, open access advocates were pleased that while the conference fell short of mandating open access, the costs of providing open access can now be part of research grants funded by the EU. But this failure to mandate open access didn't stop research councils across Europe from mandating open access to their funded research results six months after publication. In October a group of rectors from European universities met in Belgium to announce the formation of EurOpenScholarship, a strategic initiative to educate researchers in European universities about the opportunities afforded to them through open access and to build repositories in the universities to share open access scholarship.

Publishers reacted strongly to *Turn the Page: Making College Textbooks More Affordable* (May 2007), issued by the Advisory Committee on Financial Student Assistance (http://www.ed.gov/about/bdscomm/list/acsfa/edlite-index.

html), an independent committee providing information to Congress and the U.S. Department of Education. While AAP (2007) agreed with many of the ideas for using technology to reduce production costs, it strongly disagreed with a proposal to expand the used textbook market and another recommendation to expand e-reserves in libraries; AAP believes that an expanded used textbook marketplace will only increase the prices of textbooks, and that expanded e-reserves will violate copyright law. Certainly no one wants to see textbooks become even more expensive, with prices growing at twice the rate of inflation (U.S. Government Accountability Office, 2005). There will be no easy solution to this complex problem involving bookstores, faculty, students, publishers, and a thriving market in used books.

The end of 2007 saw a most peculiar quadrille in Washington as Congress and the president ultimately put into law the omnibus spending bill that contains wording to mandate open access to the published results of NIH-funded research within a year of their publication. The exact wording follows:

> The Director of the National Institutes of Health shall require that all investigators funded by the NIH submit or have submitted for them to the National Library of Medicine's PubMed Central an electronic version of their final, peer-reviewed manuscripts upon acceptance for publication to be made publicly available no later than 12 months after the official date of publication: Provided, That the NIH shall implement the public access policy in a manner consistent with copyright law (NIH 2008).

Between July and December—through various wording changes and compromises, a presidential veto that was not overridden, and the ever-approaching Christmas recess—open access advocates were on pins and needles. During the 32 months that NIH-funded research dissemination via open access had been encouraged but not mandatory, the number of articles submitted each month to PubMed Central had tripled from 400 articles in May 2005 to a high of 1,200 articles in June 2007 (Source: NIH, http://www.nihms.nih.gov/stats/aggregate. csv). The numbers are still disappointing; in 2008, thanks to mandatory submissions, we should see a significant increase.

As mentioned earlier, the Directory of Open Access Journals as of early this year listed more than 3,000 titles, an increase topping 25 percent from 2006. If anything, the rate of growth of open access scholarly journals seems to be accelerating. As of late February, one-third of these open access titles were searchable at the article level. How much of this increase in open access journals was instigated by governmental directives or the policies of foundations is anyone's guess.

Books

Though some maturing in the scholarly publishing of journals (with some expansion of openness) was to be expected, few were prepared for the amount of attention books—objects once predicted to go the way of the dinosaur and dodo—gained in 2007.

In recent years, scholarly books saw little publicity and generated little interest other than complaints about their invisibility and prices. Once-grand university presses, a source of revenue for their host institutions, had responded in a variety of ways to the challenge of forming sustainable business models: adjusting print runs and scaling back numbers of titles, going digital, and sticking it out in hopes that each would be "the last press standing." In July 2007 an important report took a look at monographs—books, those things that university presses are struggling to produce and market in a shrinking marketplace.

The report, *University Publishing in a Digital Age,* was authored by a group of individuals with stellar credentials in the field of scholarly publishing—in particular, of monographs—and is the result of interviews with not only university press directors and staff but also provosts, librarians, and technology experts. The report's issuer, the Ithaka Group, was founded in 2004 and is, in its own words (from its Web site), "an independent not-for-profit organization with a mission to accelerate the productive uses of information technologies for the benefit of higher education worldwide." Ithaka is led by former JSTOR President and leader Kevin Guthrie. Among its more visible projects is Portico, a permanent archive of electronic scholarly journals.

University Publishing in a Digital Age took a hard look at the status of the university press in the university. It portrays the large chasm that has been created through intentional neglect and marginalization of what the report argues should be a key undertaking of today's university—documenting and communicating knowledge for all time. But unlike other reports that take a grim view of today's situation, this report goes on to identify a variety of solutions that are well within the grasp of any university, and offers nearly a customizable strategic plan for any university to revitalize its efforts. The report recommends a plan, a team, and a willingness to collaborate beyond the university's border.

By the end of the year at least one group of presses had taken up the challenge to collaborate for a shared infrastructure (dare we call it a digital publishing cyberinfrastructure?). New York University Press, using funding from the Mellon Foundation, will collaborate with Fordham University Press, Rutgers University Press, Temple University Press, and the University of Virginia Press. The funding is earmarked to support creation of a joint infrastructure that may substantially reduce the costs of design and marketing and improve royalties to authors in the field of American literature. The production areas addressed by the grant represent more than half the costs of book production. While the sharing of design infrastructure may reduce the uniqueness of designs for each press, the university press directors argue that design funding had been so scaled back in recent years, due to the focus on bottom-line costs, that the new approach should, in fact, turn out to be a significant improvement in book aesthetics for their authors. (Note: Early in 2008, Mellon announced grants awarded for university press collaboration in other subject areas: Slavic studies, South Asian studies, ethnomusicology, and civil rights [AAUP, 2008].)

While several university libraries were starting up or ratcheting up their journal-publishing activities with OJS installations, the real news was the digitized book. The Google Book Search project continued to grow with the added participation of the 13 Committee on Institutional Cooperation (CIC) libraries and Columbia University, bringing the total to 28 libraries participating. The million-book mark was reached in 2007. But not all libraries have been supportive of this project. Initial unhappiness in 2004 was centered on Google's U.S.-centric approach and its exclusive membership. In 2007 a group of libraries in the Boston area, as well as the Smithsonian Institution, decided that the proprietary nature of Google's project was problematic for them, and opted to participate in the Open Content Alliance's (OCA's) efforts. It should be noted that many of Google's partners also participate in OCA, just not using the Google-scanned content. OCA content is focused on out-of-copyright materials only, so it can be made freely available on the Web by anyone. Google Book content is accessed through Google only, except for participants receiving digital copies of their owned items. Items still under copyright are available with permission from specific publishers or have restricted access while ongoing legal action determines the conditions under which Google and its partners can provide access.

While these initiatives appear to have given new life to academic book publishing and possibly book reading, at least in the near term, the folks at Amazon.com grabbed the e-book spotlight with their ten-ounce wonder dubbed Kindle. Kindle was announced in fall 2007 with great fanfare and a huge demand that led to 12-week delivery times, with back orders continuing into early 2008. Kindle's makers claim that it has a "revolutionary electronic-paper display [that] provides a sharp, high-resolution screen that looks and reads like real paper." Currently there are more than 100,000 books available for a typical price of $9.99. Reader reviews unanimously applaud the free book samples before you buy, and the very fast download speeds, but there are mixed comments on the physical layout of the controls and the lack of color.

Conclusion

The year started out slowly in the world of scholarly publishing, but the end of 2007 saw big gains for the open access movement, book publishers, and beleaguered university presses. We expect that 2008 will continue the momentum for open access scholarly publishing, diverse academic titles from Lulu.com and related sites, and more explicit governmental policies encouraging ready access to research results. With several presidential candidates calling for increased investment in research and technology (American Association for the Advancement of Science, 2008; Witze, 2008), funding will be available to strengthen cyberinfrastructure and to further aid digital distribution of scholarship. Indeed, more research will be available digitally; how will we be able to use it? That question may finally be addressed at different levels in 2008 and in the near future.

References

Advisory Committee on Student Financial Assistance (ACSFA), 2007. *Turn The Page: Making College Textbooks More Affordable,* at http://www.ed.gov/about/bdscomm/list/acsfa/turnthepage.pdf (viewed February 24, 2008).

American Association for the Advancement of Science (AAAS), 2007. "Science Announcement About JSTOR Partnership," (July 19), at http://www.sciencemag.org/marketing/jstor_partnership.dtl (viewed February 21, 2008).

American Association for the Advancement of Science (AAAS), 2008. "Science and Technology in the 2008 Presidential Election," at http://election2008. aaas.org/comparisons (viewed February 24, 2008).

American Association of Publishers, 2007. "AAP Reviews Proposed Solutions in ACSFA Textbook Report; Statement from Bruce Hildebrand, Executive Director for Higher Education," at http://www.publishers.org/main/Press Center/ACSFAStatement.htm (viewed February 21, 2008).

American Association of University Publishers, 2008. "University Presses Collaborate in Innovative New Publishing Projects: The Andrew W. Mellon Foundation Supports Collaborative Scholarly Publishing of First Books in Four Underserved Fields" (January 18), at http://aaupnet.org/news/press/ mellon12008.html (viewed February 21, 2008).

Paul Avery, 2007. "Open Science Grid: Building and Sustaining General Cyberinfrastructure Using a Collaborative Approach," First Monday, volume 12, number 6 (June), at http://journals.uic.edu/fm/article/view/1866/1749 (viewed February 24, 2008).

Blackwell Publishing, 2007. "Wiley-Blackwell and American Anthropological Association Announce Partnership," (September 19), at http://www. blackwellpublishing.com/press/pressitem.asp?ref=1435 (viewed February 24, 2008).

Sara Boettiger, 2007. "Issues in IP Management to Support Open Access in Collaborative Innovation Models," First Monday, volume 12, number 6 (June), at http://journals.uic.edu/fm/article/view/1869/1752 (viewed February 24, 2008).

Dan L. Burk, 2007. "Intellectual Property and Cyberinfrastructure," First Monday, volume 12, number 6 (June), at http://journals.uic.edu/fm/article/view/ 1870/1753 (viewed February 24, 2008).

Steven J. Jackson, Paul N. Edwards, Geoffrey C. Bowker, Cory P. Knobel, 2007. "Understanding Infrastructure: History, Heuristics and Cyberinfrastructure Policy," First Monday, volume 12, number 6 (June), at http://journals.uic. edu/fm/article/view/1904/1786 (viewed February 24, 2008).

Brian Kahin and Steven J. Jackson, 2007. "Preface [to special issue on cyberinfrastructure]," First Monday, volume 12, number 6 (June), at http://journals. uic.edu/fm/article/view/1865/1748 (viewed February 24, 2008).

Bonnie Nardi, Michael Adams, Melody Chu, Shiraz Khan, John Lai, and Elsy Lao, 2004. "AnthroSource: Designing a Portal for Anthropologists," First Monday, volume 9, number 10 (October), at http://journals.uic.edu/fm/ article/view/1181/1101 (viewed February 24, 2008).

NIH Public Access Policy Implements Division G, Title II, Section 218 of P.L. 110-161 (Consolidated Appropriations Act, 2008).

Larry Sanger, 2007. "What Strong Collaboration Means for Scholarly Publishing," keynote address at the annual meeting of the Society for Scholarly Publishing (June 7), at http://www.larrysanger.org/scholar_pub.html (viewed February 24, 2008).

U.S. Government Accountability Office, 2005. "College Textbooks: Enhanced Offerings Appear to Drive Recent Price Increases," *GAO-05-806,* at http://www.gao.gov/new.items/d05806.pdf (viewed February 24, 2008).

Alexandra Witze, 2008. "Scientists Urged to Plan for the Next U.S. President," *Nature,* volume 451, number 7181 (February 21), p. 875.

Building the World's Largest MLIS Program

Ken Haycock

San José State University's School of Library and Information Science has offered a Master of Library and Information Science (MLIS) degree in some form for more than 50 years. It is the only program accredited by the American Library Association (ALA) in the California State University system. It is one of the largest graduate programs in any discipline in the state, and is the world's largest accredited LIS program, with more than 2,200 graduate students.

The school is a recognized leader in making effective use of leading-edge technologies for distance learning. In 2007 *U.S. News and World Report* named it the No. 1 e-learning service provider in its discipline; by 2008 it was the largest e-learning program in the country in any discipline other than business and education. In 2008 the Association for Library and Information Science Education (ALISE) awarded its faculty innovation award to San José, pointing to a sustained record of adept, responsive, and pervasive adoption of new and innovative technologies that enhance student learning and support the needs of students throughout the entire lifespan of their relationship with the school. The school was nationally ranked by *U.S. News and World Report* for the first time in 2006 and received full and unconditional reaccreditation from ALA in 2007.

How did this happen? How does a smaller, less-known program develop itself as a leader in its field with a strategic orientation, technological prowess, and thousands of students from around the world? Several innovative approaches were introduced by faculty, laying the groundwork for sustained growth and development. These constitute a set of best practices for any program, in any discipline, in the 21st century.

Strategic Orientation

In 2005 the faculty recognized three major needs for the immediate future: a new director due to a retirement, a strategic plan, and a plan for reaccreditation of the MLIS program. Consequently, a director with expertise in planning and assessment, and the use of quality controls, was engaged. An external consultant worked with faculty, staff, students, and alumni to develop a profile of the school, including perceived strengths and weaknesses. A facilitated two-day process then led to a foundational plan; these short-term objectives resulted:

Engage in Strategic Planning

- Establish clear goals and objectives
- Focus on the future by revisiting the school's vision and mission

Ken Haycock is professor and director of the School of Library and Information Science at San José State University. He was previously director of the School of Library, Archival, and Information Studies at the University of British Columbia and is a past president of the Association for Library and Information Science Education and the recipient of numerous honors and awards for teaching, research, and service.

- Focus on innovation, especially in program development and delivery
- Focus on the school's profile and visibility
- Develop more effective and strategic communications

Define Roles

- Determine minimum expectations for all full-time faculty and particularly off-site faculty (the school has tenured faculty living in other states)
- Determine standards for research and scholarly productivity
- Revise standards for retention, tenure, and promotion
- Coordinate core required courses and program areas with lead faculty and part-time faculty
- Develop priorities for faculty renewal
- Implement a model of shared governance with broadly based and representative committees with clear responsibilities and accountability

Enhance Program Quality

- Review admissions standards and procedures
- Review student assessment procedures and outcomes
- Institute outcomes-based assessment; ensure core competencies for graduates
- Expand in related fields where there are natural intersections of programmatic strengths and priorities and a workable business plan
- Investigate a collaborative doctoral program

Develop Partnerships

- Build stronger relationships programmatically (joint programs with other units), academically (service to the university), professionally (leadership in associations; internships)
- Work more strategically and effectively with professional associations and alumni on recruitment

Invest Revenue for Return

- Address the disconnect between perceived quality and relatively low cost
- Develop improved and sustained development support from alumni and others
- Consider alternate forms of revenue through entrepreneurship
- Develop the role of faculty and others in planned fund raising
- Develop a strategy for increasing scholarships and awards

Ensure Assessment

- Establish fewer, clearer goals and objectives, known by all
- Align available resources with strategic goals and objectives

- Monitor and adjust the strategic plan on a continual and annual basis
- Demonstrate the impact and value of the graduate, the program, and the school
- Focus on outcomes
- Review the school's "culminating experience"

Essential pieces in this review included maintaining a culture of innovation, focusing on reaccreditation and its attendant issues, overall fund development, mentoring new faculty, integrating part-time faculty, and improving research productivity.

The result was a systematic, comprehensive, inclusive, and strategic planning process with a new vision, mission, and stated values.

Planning and Implementation

Strategic Planning

The school developed its plan in fall 2005. These guiding principles were defined:

- Our Vision for 2010: The School of Library and Information Science will be recognized as a leader in graduate education in library and information science, delivering innovative, high-quality programs across the state, the continent, and beyond.
- Our Shared Values (articulated with examples on the school's Web site, http://slisweb.sjsu.edu): Learning; student and faculty/staff success; excellence; integrity; diversity; community. The School of Library and Information Science is committed to the professions and disciplines it serves. In spite of distributed learning, centers and faculty, we are one team, one school.
- Our Mission: The school educates professionals and develops leaders who organize, manage, and enable the effective use of information and ideas in order to contribute to the well-being of our communities. (Note: The school is unique in its discipline in focusing on impact on community development.)

The resulting strategic plan had four specific strategic directions with measurable goals and objectives for each. These ranged from program development to operational reviews. Most importantly, the objectives were "smart"—specific, measurable, active, relevant, and timed—with responsibility assigned to the director's office or a representative committee. By having the deliverable tied to a completion date, the faculty agenda was driven by strategic deliberations.

Significantly, to grow student numbers, the school moved aggressively to establish a graduate program available fully online. This program, at 42 credits, became fully available in 2006.

Defining Roles

Clear role descriptions were developed for the director and associate director, graduate adviser, newly appointed course coordinators for required courses, and content cluster coordinators. Three new assistant directors were engaged for priority areas: distance learning, research and professional practice, and marketing and communications.

A new model of shared governance was introduced, with four broadly based committees with representation of full-time and part-time faculty, staff, students, and alumnae; the chairs of these committees sit on the director's School Leadership Team with presidents of alumnae and student associations.

Four new strategic directions were set with measurable objectives and assigned to the director and committees. Monthly faculty meetings were replaced in 2006 by quarterly two-day faculty retreats focusing on planning, quality controls, and assessment; administrative and operational issues were addressed through the director's blog and electronic discussion lists. Items come before the faculty through a deliberative committee process; a "consent agenda" is used to ensure that time is focused on issues requiring discussion and debate.

Clear and high expectations were set for faculty (all faculty attend the quarterly retreats). Standards for retention, tenure, and promotion were revised with greater attention to research and scholarly productivity. Standards and guidelines for peer review of faculty by specialization and in distance environments were developed and approved. Priorities for faculty renewal were defined and several new full-time lecturers as well as tenure-track faculty were added. The school offers a lower teaching load than the university standard due to the nature of the graduate program and research requirements. Faculty workload was further reviewed and restructured in 2006 to assure equity and research productivity. Each faculty member is provided with a graduate student assistant. Full- and part-time faculty also complete a required 24-hour faculty technology course before teaching on-line and attend a biennial faculty two-day institute (65 attending in 2007). No part-time faculty are retained if student opinions of teaching effectiveness fall below a minimum standard over three terms. Awards and recognition for faculty were introduced in 2006.

Enhancing Program Quality

With structures in place for improved decision making and strategic directions, the school had to ensure that its growth could not be construed as a reflection of lower standards. Admissions standards were raised beyond those of the university, and procedures were streamlined, eliminating steps that had no evidentiary base for program success.

Preference in hiring part-time faculty moved from "adjuncts" to true part-time faculty—selected, appointed, and evaluated by the same criteria as full-time faculty. The resulting successful candidates were more often individuals holding a doctorate and an academic appointment at another university. Many of these candidates indicated an interest in teaching for San José by distance due to an aggressive marketing program for specific areas and to the newly introduced required faculty technology workshop, outlining the range of options and opportunities for improved teaching and learning online.

Specifically, the school moved to create an e-learning community, with a learning management system (Blackboard, now migrating to Angel) for class management, course materials, links to Web sites, discussion forums, and library resources; Web conferencing (Elluminate) for real-time conversation, synchronous meetings, asynchronous recording, and break-out rooms for student small group work; and content management (Plone) for gathering content for a culminating e-portfolio. In addition, the school makes extensive use of blogs and wikis for disseminating information and consultation. In 2007 a virtual campus was built in Second Life and courses and classes offered in this immersive environment. In 2008 a new social networking program (SLISLife) is being introduced, allowing students to connect by areas of interest and geography as well as throughout their post-MLIS career. In order to enhance program success, a one-credit required course was added to the curriculum (making the degree 43 credits), to be completed before starting the regular program, focusing on information technology tools and techniques including the ability to access and use effectively the learning tools provided.

In 2007 the school joined WISE (Web-based Information Science Education), a consortium on distance education with high standards and rigorous review.

Course coordinators were assigned with release time for each required course. Research methods was added as a required course, but with several options from a survey course, to historical research, to market research, to evaluation of programs and services, with common learning objectives. Content cluster coordinators and program specialization advisers were named and assigned to a regular cycle of review for curriculum and programs.

Standards for grades were articulated and described in each syllabus. Student grade distribution is regularly collected and reported by course and instructor, and discussed by faculty.

The MLIS program objectives are now grounded in core competencies reflecting the theory, research, practice, values, and ethics of the discipline and the profession. At 43 credits, the program is among the longest in the country, with planned flexibility in course selection and four different delivery methods (onsite, distance, hybrid/blended, cohort). Three foundational courses (disciplinary foundations, management, information retrieval) are required at the beginning of the program, following the new required one-credit technology course, with an e-portfolio as the culminating experience to demonstrate program competencies; research methods was required beginning in 2007. Students can build specializations in several areas from family literacy to advanced technologies; program advisory committees of leading employers and professionals advise on specializations. Delivery methods are selected by course, not by program; for example, a student in San José can take classes on-site or by distance, a student in Canada may likewise take classes by distance or hybrid (and each does). Integrative learning is emphasized through extensive internships, planned and supervised, directed by a new assistant director for research and professional practice.

Regular student, recent graduate, and alumnae surveys inform annual review, revision, and development. The world's first (and still only) Executive MLIS program with international cohorts of senior managers not holding an MLIS degree continues to grow, with the fourth cohort beginning in 2008.

From the student perspective, it is important that class size is limited to 25, that there is a systematic and well-defined advising program (outlined in detail on the school's Web site), and that four active student associations provide presentations, tours, networking events, and special lectures, physically and virtually. Awards to outstanding graduating students were instituted in 2006. A director's forum is held synchronously and recorded for asynchronous access each term for consultation, dissemination of new information, and response to questions.

Weekly colloquia were introduced in 2007. Attendance averages 25 on-site with more than 120 viewings of the Webcast on average.

Priorities were set for expansion into allied areas with program strength; an extensive market research study was conducted in 2006 and a new degree, Master of Archives and Records Administration, will be introduced in 2008, the first in the nation to be delivered fully online.

A unique partnership with Queensland University of Technology in Brisbane, Australia, will enable San José to offer a custom-designed Ph.D. program in library and information science beginning this year, with specializations in archives and records administration, education for LIS, enterprise systems, information retrieval, information systems and technologies, information use (information literacy, human information behaviors), intelligent infrastructure, management and leadership, smart tools and services, and youth services. San José faculty will serve as associate supervisors and instructors. Students will complete all work in San José and by distance learning. Final examinations and assessment of dissertations will be completed by Queensland with an international independent panel of experts.

At the same time, the school has developed a proposal for a formal Center for Research, Innovation and Education in LIS with a director and full-time grant development officer. The doctoral program will be integrated with the center.

Developing Partnerships

In addition to the partnerships noted earlier, the school has provided support and mentoring to other graduate programs at San José launching Web-based delivery. Faculty have moved onto important university committees. Faculty have also been elected to positions of national prominence in academic and professional associations.

Greater attention and resources have been assigned to productive and supervised internships, through partnerships with potential employers, with a database of more than 250 possible placements in any one term. Students can search by preferred environment, location, and remuneration.

Program advisory committees of employers have been established for each of 15 program specializations.

A unique partnership with the university's Career Center has led to employ-ment advice, distance workshops on résumé writing and interviews, placement counseling, and access to hundreds of available positions.

In order to enhance student involvement in professional associations and to develop a bridge to the field, memberships in ALA and the state library associa-tions are provided to all entering students.

An international advisory council of leaders from government, industry, and the profession meets annually to review the school's progress, hear about new possibilities, and advise on priorities and approaches.

Investing Revenue for Return

The university supports innovation by enabling units to build on institutional strengths through "special session" programming and funding. Regular session students live in the local area, enroll in the program, pay tuition fees, and come with state support. Special session students, on the other hand, live outside the defined catchment area and pay fees that ensure sustainability and coverage of university overhead charges for a self-supporting program. Normally special ses-sion programs are new and unique. The school, however, has leveraged an exten-sion of its program to reach the world through the special session structure. Each is benefited by the other.

Regular session programming could not be as large without infrastructure support of special session monies, while special session programming could not be sustained without tenured faculty and program quality provided by institution-al expectations and frameworks. This unique blend of funding to enhance regular session programs and extend the reach through special session offerings has sup-ported remarkable growth.

Similarly, regular session programming provides support for campus facili-ties; in 2006 the school moved to new quarters with new offices and state-of-the-art labs; special session funds provide for learning and collaboration in virtual classrooms, with high impact and expensive software for synchronous audio advising and collaboration and social networking software. Both have access to high-quality library and database resources.

A quality program with state-of-the-art infrastructure requires resources for development, implementation, and maintenance. The school sought a significant student fee increase in 2006 and was successful in having it approved by a cam-pus fee advisory committee, including students, and the senior administration; a second fee increase was approved in 2008.

Better connections with students and alumni were developed by establishing a student association for consultation and deliberation and by supporting finan-cially the alumni association. Annual receptions were introduced at state and national conferences. The student and alumni association presidents also sit on the school leadership team.

A professional firm was engaged to develop a preliminary marketing plan and communication tools; brochures and bookmarks were designed, and adver-tisements were placed in professional journals across the continent. In 2006 the school redesigned its Web site, changing the focus from current students to identified target markets and prospective students, and "top of mind" for search engines. Daily traffic averaged 15,000 hits a day from 2001 to mid-2006, when it jumped to 25,000; it now exceeds 30,000. The school was granted the Public Relations Excellence Award by the California Library Association in 2006.

Priority target populations and locations for recruitment were identified. Aggressive print and electronic advertising was reinforced by information sessions given by the director across the United States and Canada and now in Australia. The response to these presentations has far exceeded expectations with, for example, more than 250 prospective students attending sessions in one week in Canada. The effect of these presentations has been easily measured through increased student enrollments from targeted areas.

New revenue streams were established through continuing education programs with several programs offered each week through a partnership with the Professional Education Network and through textbook sales with an online vendor.

More than 120 students each year receive tuition reimbursement from the California State Library through federal funds. In addition, the school's first five endowments were secured as a foundation for future scholarships and awards.

Ensuring Assessment

The school has taken a strategic but hard-line approach to matching resources with stated objectives. Financial resources are flowing to support more research productivity and less professional service.

The strategic plan is reviewed and revised annually, first by the governance committees, then with recommendations to the School Leadership Team and subsequently to the full faculty and advisory council.

In order to assure the abilities of graduates, the school's "culminating experience," required by the university, was changed to an e-portfolio addressing the 14 areas of competence identified as program goals.

In order to demonstrate impact and value, the school has developed a "balanced scorecard," addressing stakeholder perspectives, student progress, internal operations, organizational readiness for change and improvement, and financial oversight. Data is collected, analyzed, reported, and debated for possible changes and improvements. Benchmark programs have been identified for the school.

In order to ensure decisions based on evidence, the school instituted several approaches to outcomes-based assessment. First, core competencies were defined through a synthesis and consideration of competencies promulgated by several professional associations; students must demonstrate competence in each of areas, regardless of their area of specialization. Further, a research librarian was engaged to support faculty decision making by investigating areas of interest to the faculty as a whole and providing critical information before a faculty decision.

The school is also reviewed and accredited regularly through the program-planning review process for the university; through the regional accrediting body, the Western Association of Schools and Colleges; for its degree programs through its primary disciplinary association, the ALA Committee on Accreditation; and also through the National Council for the Accreditation of Teacher Education for the school credential program.

The Results

Planning—New directions and goals are set annually for the coming two years, with regular planning and review by governance committees and at quarterly faculty retreats. The school was specifically cited for its strategic planning process in the external review of the program in 2007.

Enrollment—Student numbers have increased dramatically, almost doubling to 2,200 students in four years, currently representing 40 states and 8 countries. Optimum student numbers have been reached to sustain infrastructure needs in terms of additional faculty, staff, and technology; increased student growth will ensure moving more California students into the tuition-bearing regular stream; limitations tend to be the low class size to which the school is committed and thus the need to recruit additional qualified faculty. Currently, more than 20 percent of the student body represent visible minorities and the school attracts more ALA Spectrum Scholars (the Spectrum program supports minority students) than any other school in the country. Contrary to perception reports, the smallest single preferred environment for San José students is school libraries; the two largest are public and academic libraries. Stanford University, for example, employs more than 40 San José graduates.

Curriculum—More than 200 course sections are offered each year, and more than 100 faculty are formally reviewed each year. More than 250 planned and supervised internships are undertaken each academic year.

Placement Services—As a result of the partnership with the Career Center, in the past six months alone, more than 500 SLIS students have registered and more than 100 have posted résumés; more than 300 jobs have been posted by employers recruiting SLIS students. There is a high success rate in placement of students in school, public, and university libraries as well as the for-profit (e.g., high-tech companies in Silicon Valley) and not-for-profit (e.g., Department of Homeland Security) corporate sectors.

Figure 1 / San José SLIS Faculty and Staff

Positions	Funded Through Regular Session	Funded Through Special Session	Total
Faculty			
Tenure-track Faculty FT*	16.0	0.0	16.0
Full-time Lecturers	0.0	7.0	7.0
Part-time Faculty FTE**	5.2	10.3	15.5
Total	21.2	17.3	38.5
Administrative and Technical Staff FTE			
Total	1.5	23.0	24.5
Total	22.7	40.3	63.0

* FT= Full-time

** FTE = full-time-equivalent

In Summary

San José offers the only ALA-accredited program in library and information science in the California state university system of 23 universities; it is the largest program in the world with unique offerings such as the Executive MLIS, a new Master of Archives and Records Administration, and a collaborative international Ph.D. program.

The program has achieved exceptional growth and recognition due to

- A deep understanding of its local context and opportunities
- A governance structure to develop and sustain a strategic orientation, clearly defined roles and responsibilities
- Strategic planning as a process, not an event, with accountability, resources, and consequences
- A focus on continual improvement through data collection and analysis and quality controls
- A process for curriculum review, development, and implementation
- Leveraged and formal partnerships taking advantage of mutual goals
- Identification of key target markets with aggressive and professional marketing
- Identifying and pursuing alternate revenue streams
- Vigorous assessment of outcomes

Through systematic and careful planning, the school blends revenue from regular session (tuition) and special session (fees) sources to build faculty and infrastructure for program quality overall. It attracted its first five endowments and established alternate revenue streams in 2006.

An aggressive strategic plan focusing on high expectations, quality controls, and innovation in programs and their delivery has been achieved through broadly based governance committees involving faculty, students, and alumnae. It is reviewed and renewed annually.

The school sets high standards for both entry (GPA) and exit (the e-portfolio). It takes a unique approach to part-time faculty with an international pool of recognized scholars as well as professional leaders, coordinated through full-time tenure-track faculty, trained in the use of technology and attending a biennial faculty institute on pedagogy in higher education. Class size is small and intensive training is provided for teaching on-line.

The school is on track to achieve its vision for 2010: to be recognized as a leader in graduate education in library and information science, delivering innovative, high-quality programs across the state, the continent, and beyond.

Developments in Copyright Law:
The Search for Balance Goes On

Sarah K. Wiant

Law Librarian and Professor of Law, Washington and Lee University

Controversy continues in the realm of copyright as stakeholders struggle to make copyright laws reflect the realities of the digital age.

Library Copyright Alliance

Among major players is the Library Copyright Alliance (LCA). The alliance was formed when the American Association of Law Libraries (AALL), the American Library Association (ALA), the Association of Research Libraries (ARL), the Medical Library Association (MLA), and the Special Libraries Association (SLA) joined together to represent more than 80,000 information professionals in libraries throughout the United States. These five associations had worked together for several years on varying issues of intellectual property, and the coalition is providing a common voice and strategy to respond to national and international copyright issues.

LCA is principally concerned that dramatic changes proposed in intellectual property laws, particularly to address the use of works in digital formats, enhance the ability of information specialists to meet the needs of their patrons through access, use and, in some cases, preservation. Principles prepared for discussions of the World Intellectual Property Organization (WIPO) addressing the significance of copyright exceptions for libraries and educational institutions were developed in December 2004 and endorsed by the coalition in January 2005. Four goals were set to establish important statements of principle:

- A robust and growing public domain to provide new opportunities for creativity, research, and scholarship
- Effective library programs and services as a means of advancing knowledge
- High levels of creativity and technological process resulting from individual research and study
- Harmonization of copyright[1]

ALA's Office for Information Technology Policy funded a pilot project to build expertise and broaden LCA's ability to be represented at the international level. Three new international copyright advocates will be trained to represent the coalition before WIPO, the World Summit on Information Society (WSIS), and the International Federation of Library Associations and Institutions (IFLA).

Section 108 Study Group

Libraries today want to supply digital copies in response to requests from users, rather than photocopies—the manner in which they responded historically. Section 108 of the Copyright Act, the "library exception," permits libraries and archives, if eligible, to reproduce and distribute no more than one copy under certain circumstances.

Interlibrary loan has changed over the years. Users now work from a variety of locations and seek access to digital information. The difficulty of preserving materials in paper or digital formats is aggravated by the extension of the term of protection. The digital world presents different expectations for users and creators. Publishers are concerned about the copies libraries claim are exempted under either Section 108 or Section 107, "fair use." They view digital copying as a potential market. Presuming some copying by libraries is legal, what restrictions should be placed on the practice? The ease with which multiple copies, equal in quality to the original, can be distributed downstream raises legitimate issues for publishers.

The Section 108 Study Group was convened in April 2005 under the sponsorship of the Library of Congress's National Digital Information Infrastructure and Preservation Program to examine issues relating to the changes facing libraries and publishers. The 19-member study group—which includes experts in copyright from various industries as well as libraries, archives, and museums—is charged with examining how the Section 108 exemptions and limitations may need to be amended in light of digital technology. The study group has focused on issues relating to "(1) eligibility for Section 108 exemptions; (2) amendments to the preservation and replacement exceptions in subsection 108(b) and (c), including amendments to the three copy limit, the subsection 108(c) triggers, the separate treatment of unpublished works, and off-site access restrictions; (3) proposal for a new exception to permit the creation of preservation-only/restricted access copies in limited circumstances; and, (4) proposal for a new exception to permit capture of websites and other online content."[2]

The library community believes that the current criteria in Section 108(a) granting exceptions to libraries and archives should be maintained. The current standard offers sufficient flexibility to allow libraries and archives to copy works for purposes other than for commercial advantage. Moreover, the community supports the extension of Section 108 to include museums and other cultural institutions that engage in important activities relating to the nation's scientific and cultural heritage. Because libraries devote significant resources and expertise to developing collections of electronic information and often that information is unstable and subject to risks of corruption and loss, libraries and archives believe that they should be able to preserve at-risk portions of the collection, both print and electronic. Currently, Section 108 is too limiting. Often by the time libraries are aware of damage to electronic information, it's too late to preserve it. Most creators and owners typically do not engage in long-term preservation, and if it were not for libraries, the resources would not be accessible to future generations.

In March 2006 the study group held roundtable discussions in Los Angeles and Washington, D.C., to discuss those four topics. Subsequent roundtables were scheduled for January 2007 to focus on three further issues: (1) whether the provisions of Section 108(d), (e), and (f) "for making and distributing copies for library and archive users should be amended to reflect reasonable changes in the way copies are made and used" (more particularly, the study group looked at whether single-copy restrictions should be replaced by a more flexible standard for use in subsections (e) and (d)); (2) "whether subsection 108(i) should be amended to expand subsections (d) and (e) to any non-text-based works or to text-based works that incorporate musical or audio-visual works"; and (3) "whether Section 108 should be amended to permit libraries and archives to make temporary and incidental copies of digital works to provide user access to those works."

Libraries and archives argue the social value of commercial and freely available Web sites for future generations. Limitations should not be placed on publicly available content. The default should allow libraries to capture and preserve those Web sites. Web sites that include copyrighted information should also be preserved, particularly once those resources become public-domain material. In order to assure use of those preserved Web sites, it is important to have access to the underlying software.

The study group expects to release the report of its work in 2008.

Collective Works

In 2001 the U.S. Supreme Court handed down *New York Times* v. *Tasini,*[3] which held that the revision privilege of publishers of collective works under Section 201(c) of the Copyright Act does not cover the republication of freelance writers' articles in an electronic database. *Tasini* established a new test for establishing whether a publication constitutes the privileged revision under Section 201(c). Since then, two federal circuits have addressed the issue as it relates to CD-ROM collections.

The U.S. Court of Appeals for the Second Circuit in *Faulkner* v. *Mindscape, Inc.*[4] concluded that a CD-ROM collection was analogous to a microfilm library of a periodical collection and that publishers had a right to produce the work under Section 201(c). The U.S. Court of Appeals for the 11th Circuit has revisited for the second time the issue of whether a CD-ROM collection including freelance photographers' copyrighted photographs originally published in print editions of the *National Geographic* was an infringing edition. The complete National Geographic package included individual back issues of the magazine, a computer program that facilitated storage and retrieval of content, and animated sequences of ten cover issues. The district court initially agreed with National Geographic that the CD-ROM constituted a privileged collective work protected under 17 U.S.C. Section 201(c). The 11th Circuit subsequently ruled that the use of the photographs in the CD-ROM version created an infringing work, not a privileged revision.[5] Soon after the district court on remand awarded judgment to the plaintiffs, the U.S. Supreme Court handed down *Tasini*. In June 2007 the 11th Circuit ruled again that a CD-ROM collection of the *National Geographic* magazine is a collective work that does not infringe a freelance photographer's copyright.[6] In August 2007 the court voted in favor of granting a rehearing *en banc* (by the full court) and vacated the previous opinion.[7] The critical difference from a copyright perspective is that in the National Geographic case a CD-ROM or a DVD, as opposed to machines previewing microfilm and microfiche, requires the interaction of software to accomplish a useful reproduction. Because this issue is of utmost importance to the information community, AALL, ALA, ARL, MLA, SLA, the National Association of State University and Land Grant Colleges, and the Society of American Archivists filed a friends-of-the-court brief representing institutions responsible for collecting and preserving materials.[8] The friends support the National Geographic Society's interpretation of Section 201(c) and view this CD-ROM as precisely the kind of revision that *Tasini* recognized and that Section 201(c) allows. The images reproduced in digital form on the CD-ROM are identical to the original works and are the same type that would be displayed in an analog microform collection that would be permissible.

The friends argued that a decision in favor of the plaintiffs in the National Geographic Society case could result in potentially "huge increases in costs of operation and maintenance."

Secondary Liability

In *Metro-Goldwyn-Mayer Studios, Inc.* v. *Grokster, Ltd.,* MGM and some 30 other companies sued file-sharing companies Grokster and StreamCast for distributing software designed to allow Internet users to locate and exchange files of sound recordings.[9] These software distributors are different from previous services such as Amister and its predecessor Napster because they do not have a centrally stored index. The Central District of California ruled under *Sony Corp.* v. *Universal City Studios, Inc.,* 464 U.S. 417, that the developers were not secondarily liable because the software in question was "capable of substantial noninfringing uses." The U.S. Court of Appeals for the Ninth Circuit affirmed a grant of summary judgment for the software developers, ruling that they did not have knowledge of impending infringement necessary to show contributory infringement. The U.S. Supreme Court found that the Ninth Circuit misapplied *Sony* to mean that when a product is capable of substantial lawful uses, a producer can never be held contributorily liable. In this case, there is ample evidence that Grokster did more than just distribute software. The software maker set out to capture users no longer served by Napster. When the defendants had actual knowledge (because users requested help in accessing unauthorized protected works), the developers made no attempt to curb possible infringing use. They made no attempt to incorporate filters intended to combat infringement and, finally, they benefited financially from advertising as a result of the high traffic to their site. The *Grokster* analysis focuses on the intent of the defendant to induce others to infringe.

The U.S. Court of Appeals for the Ninth Circuit vacated a preliminary injunction barring the search engine Google from displaying thumbnail versions of photographs found on adult-oriented Web sites. Perfect 10, Inc. operates and generates revenues from the sale of its magazine and subscriptions to its Web site, which features copyrighted photographs of nude models. Among Google's search engines is Google image search, which, in response to a text search string, returns reduced-size or "thumbnail" images. When the user clicks on the thumbnail, the computer pulls up a single integrated page, the top half of which consists of Google's copy of the thumbnail. The process used to incorporate content from a third party Web site is referred to as "inline linking." Google generates revenue through its AdSense program and through a licensing arrangement with Amazon.com that allows an inline link to Google's search result. In *Perfect 10 Inc. v. Amazon.com, Inc.,*[10] the court found that Perfect 10 was unlikely to overcome Google's fair use defense. The court found the nature of Google's search utility to be significantly transformative and to outweigh its superseding commercial use of thumbnail images. The appeals court agreed with the lower court that although Perfect 10 was likely to prevail in showing that Google directly infringed its display right, it is unlikely that the inline linking constitutes infringement. Moreover, the court agreed that because Google does not store copies of the full-size images, it did not directly infringe the display of the full-size images.

During summer 2007 a panel of the U.S. Court of Appeals for the Ninth Circuit returned to the issue of contributory or vicarious copyright infringement in *Perfect 10, Inc. v. Visa International Service Association.*[11] In this case, Perfect 10 argued that the credit card companies were infringing Perfect 10's rights because credit cards were used by costumers to buy infringing images online, typically by downloading images to mobile telephones. The court found that the credit card companies do not help locate and are not used to distribute infringing images and cannot be held liable for contributory or vicarious copyright infringement when their customers purchase infringing materials online. The holding was consistent with the *Amazon.com* court, saying that a search engine operator might be liable if it knew that the infringing images could be accessed through its service and if there had been a simple means of preventing such access. The court remanded the case after establishing that contributory liability attaches where a computer service operator "has actual knowledge that specific infringing material is available using its system" and can "take simple measures to prevent further damage" to the copyrighted works, but fails to do so.[12] Authorities argue that if an Internet service provider has noticed that an entire Web site is infringing, there ought to be responsibility for some sort of action. Thus the court established the simple measures test. The court found this to be a less burdensome standard than the "cyber-contributory standard of secondary liability" established by the *Grokster* court.

YouTube

For almost a decade, the Digital Millennium Copyright Act (DMCA) has allowed copyright holders to demand that their works be taken off line if there were unauthorized postings. A law professor posted on YouTube a snippet of the 2007 Super Bowl, specifically the copyright notice claiming that any use of the NFL copyrighted telecast for other than personal use was prohibited. She posted the video to demonstrate to her class how copyright holders exaggerate their rights. YouTube, upon receiving a take-down notice allowed under DMCA, removed the clip and warned the professor that repeated unauthorized postings would result in the deletion of her account.[13] This is just one of many suits brought by copyright holders for use of their materials by third parties posting on YouTube.

YouTube has been sued by Los Angeles News Service for allowing users to upload copyrighted works prior to Google's acquisition of YouTube. Some believe that Google bought a lawsuit; however, Google executives believe that they now have a larger voice in shaping legal precedence.[14]

Viacom sent shock waves across the Internet when it sued Google for $1 billion for disregarding copyright law by allowing more than 160,000 clips from Viacom's programs to be posted on YouTube. The issue is where liability lies when copyrighted works are posted on user-generated sites. Google argues that it is a neutral Internet service provider and is therefore protected by the exemptions in DMCA. Experts believe the parties will likely agree to a license.

With copyright owners' demands for DMCA take-down notices in this and hundreds of thousands of cases like it, holders must recognize legitimate free speech and fair use rights of creators who rely on a platform like YouTube.

In fall 2007 Google announced its long-awaited copyright filtering (video identification) system for YouTube. For users, this system presents a challenge because the filter cannot distinguish between an identical copy and a short excerpt used as part of a larger piece.

Google Book Project

In 2005 Google released details of Google Book Search, its historic effort to digitize the full text of the world's books and allow that text to be searched online.[15] A key attribute of Google Book Search's plan is to be comprehensive. Five of the world's largest libraries agreed to allow Google to digitize their collections: Harvard, Stanford, Oxford, and Michigan universities and the New York Public Library. In signing with Google, Michigan stipulated that each party was obligated to inform the other if either became aware of copyright infringement as a result of the agreement.

Publishing houses express concern that making these works available online without copyright permission would be illegal.[16] Google responded that it would provide full text of books that are no longer protected by copyright, but for those books that are protected by copyright and are out of print, only a brief excerpt would be available. Google argues that this use is a fair use.

In 2007 the California Digital Library of the University of California, with ten libraries and 34 million volumes, agreed to a six-year contract to permit Google to scan 2.5 million of its volumes.[17] Each university receives digital copies of the scanned works, but restrictions are placed on the use of the digital files. For example, California can offer the files as a service to its patrons, but it must implement procedures that prohibit those patrons from downloading portions of the files.

Internet Archive

Brewster Kahle, director and founder of Internet Archive, and Richard Prelinger built a nonprofit digital library that preserves films and offers free access to digital audiobooks, films, and Web sites. They intended to make available works that, although still protected by copyright, had no commercial value. They contended that the elimination of the notice requirement and automatic renewal prolonged copyright in works that would have been in the public domain because their owners would not have asserted or renewed copyright. The U.S. Court of Appeals for the Ninth Circuit in *Kahle* v. *Gonzales*[18] affirmed a lower court's dismissal, saying that the case too closely resembled the 2003 U.S. Supreme Court case *Eldred* v. *Ashcroft* that upheld the constitutionality of the Copyright Term Extension Act.[19]

Orphan Works

Content owners, publishers, and users all participated in the past year in the Copyright Office's investigation of problems raised by orphan works. The term orphan works refers to those works likely still protected by copyright but whose owners cannot be located after a reasonable search. In January 2006 the Copyright Office issued a report on orphan works.[20] Remarkably, very diverse organizations generally agree that a problem exists and, even more remarkably, agree on a solution. However, photographers and visual artists have been successful in their opposition to proposed orphan works legislation, which was stalled on Capitol Hill at this writing.

Stanford Copyright Renewal Database

In April 2007 Stanford University Libraries and Academic Information Resources (SULAIR), with a grant from the Hewlett Foundation, developed a copyright renewal database that has been nicknamed Copyright Determinator.[21] The database is intended to serve as a tool to determine whether a U.S. work published between 1923 and 1963 remains under copyright. (For U.S. works published from 1923 to 1963, renewal remains a concern; renewals are automatic for works published after January 1964.)

Fair Use Guidelines

The Association of American Publishers (AAP) reached agreements with several universities to establish fair use guidelines governing electronic reserves. Cornell was the first to agree that guidelines for printed materials should also apply to Web use,[22] and AAP has also entered into agreements with Hofstra, Marquette, and Syracuse. Under the guidelines, libraries and professors make portions of books and journals available online to students. The universities agreed to consider the four fair use factors set out in Section 107 of the Copyright Act and will not assume that the content on the Internet can be redistributed without the publisher's approval. Critics argued that the policies may be too vague to provide sufficient guidance to students and faculty in determining what they can lawfully use. The flexible doctrine of fair use can be interpreted differently by different courts even under the same circumstances. While protecting the financial stake of publishers, the copyright law does not quantify where fair use ends in allowing a limited use of material for educational purposes.

Copyright Clearance Center

In December 2007 the nonprofit Copyright Clearance Center (CCC)[23] announced the launch of Copyright Labs[24] as a testing ground for new services. Users and creators could interact by publicly testing new applications and products in an attempt to develop a steady stream of services and tools to reflect the ways in which users use content. A copyright permission utility (Copyright.com OpenSearch) aids licensing content found online. CCC also announced a third application, ACAP Validator, a tool that helps publishers to communicate access and usage permissions information to search engines and other automated digital content consumers.[25]

Music Industry

In the continuing effort to control rampant music downloading and file-sharing on college campuses, a number of bills have been introduced in both the House and Senate to require schools to develop plans for offering alternatives to illegal downloading, as well as to establish deterrents to prevent illegal activity. Higher education has expressed grave concerns about legislation that would include peer-to-peer provisions in higher education funding initiatives. The Recording Industry Association of America (RIAA) has continued an aggressive pursuit of college file-sharers with mixed results. Some federal courts—such as the U.S. District Court for New Mexico and the U.S. District Court for Oregon—have refused to grant subpoenas of student data, while the U.S. District Court for the District of Columbia granted a subpoena to record companies that sought student information.

In fall 2007 a jury in Minnesota was the first to award damages to record companies for copyright infringement. In *Virgin Records of America, Inc.* v. *Thomas,*[26] a single mother who made 1,700 unauthorized copies of copyright works available online was found liable for $222,000.

Conclusion

Settlements leave unresolved how people can use electronic versions of books or other materials whose owners cannot be identified (orphan works) and what is an acceptable use under fair use. H.R. 4279, the enhancements to the civil Intellectual Property Act of 2007, falls short of massive reform, but it is the beginning of a conversation concerning limits on secondary liability, protections against copyright abuse, fair and accessible licensing, and orphan works reform.

The Department of Justice immediately attacked the proposed legislation that would reorganize intellectual property enforcement structure, calling the proposal of a new "copyright czar" unnecessary and counterproductive. The department was also not pleased with the proposal for an intellectual property office inside the White House. Many are opposed to an amendment to Section 104 that would allow a copyright owner to collect statutory damages for each copyrighted work that is stolen. Opponents believe the provision could result in protracted lawsuits and unintended consequences, particularly when the copies at issue are music.

Copyright laws must reflect the realities of the digital age in setting a balance to allow users to enjoy content they acquire and artists and inventors new revenue without too many restrictions.

Copyright reform should allow users to make full use of lawfully acquired digital copies, which will drive demand for even more innovation. Most believe that artists and innovators, and other copyright holders, deserve to be compensated for their works. So the question is, how do we find the balance?

Notes

1. Library-Related Principles for the International Development Agenda of the World Intellectual Property Organization, http://www.librarycopyrightalliance.org/WIPO.htm.

2. 73 Fed. Reg. 7999 (Feb. 15, 2006).

3. 533 U.S. 483 (2nd Cir. 2001).

4. 409 F.3d 26 (2nd Cir. 2005).

5. *Greenberg* v. *National Geographic Society,* 244 F.3d 1267 (11th Cir. 2001).

6. *Greenberg* v. *National Geographic Society,* 488 F.3d 1331 (11th Cir. 2007).

7. 497 F.3d 1213 (11th Cir. 2007).

8. Brief for American Association of Law Libraries, et al. as amici curiae supporting defendants, *Greenberg* v. *National Geographic Society,* No. 15016964-JJ (11th Cir. Oct. 18, 2007), http://www.aallnet.org/aallwash/br10182007.pdf.

9. 543 U.S. 1032 (2004), vacated 545 U.S. 913 (2005).

10. 487 F.3d 701 (9th Cir. 2007).

11. 494 F.3d 788 (9th Cir. 2007).

12. Ibid.

13. Brock Read, "Brooklyn Law School Professor Is Told Her YouTube Video Infringed on Copyright," *Chronicle of Higher Education,* March 2, 2007, http://chronicle.com/weekly/v53/i26/26a03202.htm.

14. "A Brief Interview with EFF's Fred von Lohmann on YouTube, Copyright, Google, and More," http://battellemedia.com/archives/002973.php.

15. "Google's New Deals Promise to Realize a 60-Year-Old Vision," *Chronicle of Higher Education,* January 7, 2005, http://chronicle.com/weekly/v51/i18/18a03801.htm.

16. Jeffrey Toobin, "Google's Moon Shot: The Quest for the Universal Library," *New Yorker,* February 5, 2007.

17. "The Library as Search Engine," *Chronicle of Higher Education,* January 5, 2007, http://chronicle.com/weekly/v53/i18/18b02401.htm.

18. 474 F.3d 665 (9th Cir. 2007).

19. 537 U.S. (2003).

20. *Report on Orphan Works,* United States Copyright Office, http://www.copyright.gov/orphan.

21. "Database of Copyright Renewal Records Launched," Stanford News Service, April 2, 2007, http://news-service.stanford.edu/news/2007/april4/copy-040407.html.

22. James M. O'Neill, "Professors Get 'F' in Copyright Protection Knowledge," http://seattlepi.nwsource.com/business/292898_copyright20.html.

23. http://www.copyright.com.

24. http://www.copyrightlabs.com.

25. Michael LoPresti, "CCC Seeks a New Formula with the Launch of Copyright Labs," *NewsBreaks,* Information Today, Inc., December 17, 2007, http://newsbreaks.infotoday.com/nbReader.asp?ArticleId=40443.

26. No. 06-CV-1497, 2007 WL 2826645 (D.Minn. October 1, 2007).

Educational Fair Use Today

Jonathan Band

jband@policybandwidth.com

Three recent appellate decisions concerning fair use should give educators and librarians greater confidence and guidance for asserting this important privilege. In all three decisions, the courts permitted extensive copying and display in the commercial context because the uses involved repurposing and recontextualization. The reasoning of these opinions could have far-reaching implications in the educational environment.

Digital technology has dramatically increased the physical ability of educational institutions in general, and research libraries in particular, to make copyrighted materials available to faculty and students. When the reproduction, display, and distribution of materials occurs without the authorization of the copyright owners, the educational institutions rely on the exceptions contained in the Copyright Act, including fair use privilege provided by 17 U.S.C. 107. Section 107 specifically lists "teaching (including multiple copies for classroom use), scholarship, or research" as examples of the purposes that could justify use without the owner's permission. Moreover, the first fair use factor—the purpose and character of the use—explicitly contrasts "a commercial nature" with "nonprofit educational purposes."

Notwithstanding these multiple references to education, there is a remarkable paucity of judicial decisions considering fair use by educational institutions themselves, as opposed to third parties such as commercial copy centers. There are, to be sure, a wide variety of guidelines that have emerged from inter-sector negotiations or the internal deliberations of associations, but these guidelines do not have the force of law.

In the absence of recent decisions applying fair use in the educational context, a strong current of fair use pessimism has developed on many college campuses. This restrictive view of fair use has a number of sources. First, consistent with their short-term economic interest, copyright owners have consistently misstated the scope of the fair use privilege in a wide variety of forums. Second, certain academics have overstated the fragility of fair use in an effort to advance their theories of copyright law or their legislative proposals.[1] Third, some of the fair use guidelines mentioned above are three decades old, and thus do not reflect the expansion of fair use over time.

This paper will not offer a comprehensive analysis of the current state of fair use in the educational context.[2] Instead, it will discuss three recent fair use decisions by federal circuit courts. These decisions demonstrate that fair use pessimism, especially in the educational context, is ill founded. In all three cases,

Jonathan Band helps shape the laws governing intellectual property and the Internet through a combination of legislative and appellate advocacy. His clients include Internet companies, providers of information technology, universities, and library associations. He has written extensively on intellectual property and the Internet, including the book *Interfaces on Trial: Intellectual Property and Interoperability in the Global Software Industry* with Masanobu Katoh (Westview). He is an adjunct professor at the Georgetown University Law Center. This article was commissioned by the Association of Research Libraries and is used by permission.

the courts found commercial uses to be fair. In two of the three cases, the defendants copied several of the plaintiffs' works in their entirety, and only changed them by reducing them in size. The courts nonetheless found these uses to be transformative because the defendants repurposed and recontextualized the works. Additionally, in both these cases the courts gave little weight to the plaintiffs' loss of licensing revenue.

The first case discussed, *Blanch v. Koons,* is the most "traditional" fair use decision. Koons truly transformed Blanch's photograph by placing part of the image against a new background; Koons's purpose was to criticize the high fashion genre of Blanch's photograph; Koons only used a part of Blanch's photograph; and Koons's use had no impact on the market for Blanch's work. The other two cases, *Perfect 10 v. Amazon.com* and *Bill Graham Archives v. Dorling Kindersley,* reflect more expansive applications of Section 107.

Blanch v. Koons

Jeff Koons is a visual artist who specializes in "appropriations art"—that is, he incorporates images from popular media and advertising into his paintings and other artwork. In previous copyright infringement cases against him, courts have rejected his fair use defense. See, for example, *Rogers* v. *Koons,* 960 F.2d 301 (2d Cir.), cert. denied, 506 U.S. 934 (1992). This case concerns his painting "Niagara," commissioned by Deutsche Bank for display in the Deutsche Guggenheim Berlin art space. "Niagara" depicts four pairs of women's feet and lower legs dangling over images of various desserts, with a grassy field and Niagara Falls in the background. Koons derived one of the pairs of legs from "Silk Sandals," an advertisement for Gucci sandals created by fashion photographer Andrea Blanch and published in the magazine *Allure.* In the advertisement, the model's legs are resting on a man's lap in what appears to be a first class airline cabin. In an affidavit, Koons explained that by juxtaposing the women's legs against a backdrop of food and landscape, he intended to "comment on the ways in which some of our most basic appetites—for food, play, and sex—are mediated by popular images" (*Blanch* v. *Koons,* 467 F.3d 244, 247 [2d Cir. 2006]). By recontextualizing fragments of advertisements in this manner, he "tr[ies] to compel the viewer to break out of the conventional way of experiencing a particular appetite as mediated by mass media" (ibid.).

Blanch sued for copyright infringement, and the district court granted Koons summary judgment based on fair use. Blanch appealed to the Second Circuit, which affirmed on October 26, 2006. The Second Circuit repeated the Supreme Court's definition of transformative use in *Campbell* v. *Acuff-Rose Music,* 510 U.S. 569, 579 (1994): whether the use "merely supersedes the objects of the original creation, or instead adds something new, with a further purpose of different character, altering the first with new expression, meaning, or message." The court found that this test

almost perfectly describes Koons's adaptation of "Silk Sandals": the use of a fashion photograph created for publication in a glossy American 'lifestyles' magazine—with changes of its colors, the background against which it is portrayed, the medium, the size of the objects' pictures, the objects' details, and crucially, their entirely different purpose and meaning—as part of a massive painting commissioned for exhibition in a German art-gallery space (ibid. at 253).

The court underscored that "[t]he sharply different objectives that Koons had in using, and Blanch had in creating, 'Silk Sandals' confirms the transformative nature of the use" (ibid. at 252).

The court acknowledged that Koons made a substantial profit from the sale of "Niagara," but stated that when a new use is substantially transformative, "the significance of other factors, including commercialism, are of less significance" (ibid. at 254). Accordingly, the judges here "discount the secondary commercial nature of the use" (ibid).

The court also examined "whether Koons had a genuine creative rationale for borrowing Blanch's image, rather than using it merely to get attention or to avoid the drudgery in working up something fresh" (ibid. at 255). The court accepted Koons's uncontradicted testimony that he needed to use an existing fashion photograph:

> To me, the legs depicted in the *Allure* photograph are a fact in the world, something that everyone experiences constantly . . . By using a fragment of the *Allure* photograph in my painting, I thus comment upon the culture and attitude promoted and embodied in *Allure* magazine. By using an existing image, I also ensure a certain authenticity or veracity that enhances my commentary—it is the difference between quoting and paraphrasing—and ensure that the viewer will understand what I am referring to (ibid.)

The court considered the three other fair use factors relatively briefly. The court stated that "the second fair-use factor has limited weight in our analysis because Koons used Blanch's work in a transformative manner to comment on her image's social and aesthetic meaning rather than to exploit its creative virtues" (ibid. at 257). With respect to the third factor, the court found persuasive Koons's statement that "he copied only that portion of the image necessary to evoke 'a certain style of mass communication . . . ' " (ibid. at 258). Turning to the fourth factor, the court found that Blanch had never licensed the image subsequent to its appearance in *Allure,* had no plans to license or reuse the image, and had offered no evidence that Koons's use harmed her in any way.

Judge [Robert] Katzmann wrote a short concurring opinion in which he agreed with the court's ultimate conclusion of fair use, but disagreed with some of the court's sweeping language. In particular, Judge Katzmann felt that the commercial nature of a use should not be "discounted" where the use, while transformative, "is not one of the archetypal purposes specifically contemplated by Congress . . . " (ibid. at 262). Rather, in such cases the transformative quality of the use should simply be balanced against its commercial nature.

Perfect 10 v. Amazon.com

Perfect 10 published erotic photographs in a magazine and a Web site. It claimed that other Web sites copied and displayed its photographs without permission. In the course of its search engine operations, Google automatically scanned the photographs on the infringing Web sites, stored them in its search database, displayed low-resolution thumbnails of these infringing images in response to search queries, and provided links to the infringing sites. Additionally, Google provided the AdSense service. If a Web site was an AdSense partner, Google served ads to the Web site. Although AdSense and Google Search are distinct services, Google Search could lead a user to a Web site that was an AdSense partner. Perfect 10 alleged that some of the infringing sites to which Google linked were AdSense partners. A final fact: a company called Fonestarz licenses photos and makes them available for download on cell phones. Perfect 10 alleged that it had licensed its images to Fonestarz for download onto cell phones. It further alleged that cell phone users could download thumbnail Perfect 10 images from Google's site rather than from Fonestarz.

Perfect 10 sued Google both for displaying thumbnail images of Perfect 10 photographs in response to search queries and for linking to sites where infringing images were displayed. Perfect 10 filed a motion for preliminary injunction, which the district court granted (*Perfect 10* v. *Google,* 416 F. Supp 2d 828 (D. Cal. 2006), aff'd in part, rev'd in part, 487 F.3d 701 [9th Cir. 20070]). The district court's rulings on the linking to the infringing sites touched on issues other than fair use, and thus are not relevant to this discussion. In contrast, the district court's ruling on the display of the thumbnail images in the search results is directly relevant here. The district court distinguished *Kelly* v. *Arriba Soft Corporation,* 336 F.3d 811 (9th Cir. 2003), where the Ninth Circuit held that a search engine's display of thumbnail images was a fair use, and found that Google's display was not a fair use.

The district court identified two features that differentiated this case from *Kelly* v. *Arriba Soft*: AdSense and Fonestarz. In *Kelly,* Arriba Soft received no financial benefit from the display of the Kelly photograph. Here, by contrast, Google received a financial benefit from the display of the Perfect 10 thumbnails because the thumbnails led users to infringing sites from which Google profited via the AdSense program. The court concluded that this made Google's use "more commercial" than Arriba Soft's (*Perfect 10* at 847).

Moreover, the *Kelly* court found that Arriba Soft's display of thumbnails did not harm the market for Kelly's work, in part because there was no market for the licensing of thumbnail images of Western scenery, the subject of Kelly's photos. But the district court here found that there was an emerging market for thumbnail images of naked women. Fonestarz licenses photos and makes them available for download on cell phones, where they are the same size as the thumbnails Google displays. The district court found that it was possible that Google's display of the thumbnails would interfere with the success of the Fonestarz service because cell phone users could see the thumbnails through Google image search for free. Because of these factors, the district court concluded that Google was unlikely to prevail on its fair use defense.

On May 16, 2007, the U.S. Court of Appeals for the Ninth Circuit reversed the district court's rejection of Google's fair use defense (*Perfect 10* v. *Amazon. com,* 487 F.3d 701 [9th Cir. 2007]).[3] The Ninth Circuit rejected the district court's distinguishing of Kelly on the basis of the AdSense program and the cell phone downloads. The Ninth Circuit found that there was no evidence that the Google thumbnails superseded the Fonestarz cell phone downloads. Further, the court found no evidence that AdSense revenue derived from infringing sites was commercially significant. At the same time, the court held that Google's use of the thumbnails was "highly transformative" (*Amazon.com* at 721). In fact, the court went so far as to say that "a search engine may be more transformative than a parody," the quintessential fair use, "because a search engine provides an entirely new use for the original work, while a parody typically has the same entertainment purpose as the original work" (ibid.).

Accordingly, the Ninth Circuit "conclude[d] that the significantly transformative nature of Google's search engine, particularly in light of its public benefit, outweighs Google's superseding and commercial uses of the thumbnails in this case" (ibid. at 723). The Ninth Circuit stated that in reaching this conclusion, it was mindful that the Supreme Court had stressed "the importance of analyzing fair use flexibly in light of new circumstances[,] . . . especially during a period of rapid technological change" (ibid., quoting *Sony Corp.* v. *Universal City Studios, Inc.*, 464 U.S. 417, 431–432 (1984), quoting H.R. Rep. No. 94-1476, 65–66 (1976), *U.S. Code Cong. and Admin. News* 1976, p. 5680).

The Ninth Circuit made another important fair use holding. The district courts found that the cache copy made by a user's browser whenever he viewed a Web page is a fair use. The issue only arose because to prove secondary liability for Google, Perfect 10 needed to show that there was an underlying direct infringement by a third person. Among other possible direct infringements, Perfect 10 argued that users infringed its copyright in its images when they made temporary copies of these images in the random access memory (RAM) of their computers while viewing these sites that posted these images without authorization. The Ninth Circuit agreed with the district court that the RAM copies were a fair use. It stated:

> The copying function performed automatically by a user's computer to assist in accessing the Internet is a transformative use. Moreover . . . a cache copies no more than is necessary to assist the user in Internet use. It is designed to enhance an individual's computer use, not to supersede the copyright holders' exploitation of their works. Such automatic background copying has no more than a minimal effect on Perfect 10's rights, but a considerable public benefit (ibid at 726).

Bill Graham Archives v. Dorling Kindersley

Dorling Kindersley (DK) published a coffee table biography of the Grateful Dead with over 2,000 different images. Among these were seven posters whose copyright was owned by Bill Graham Archives (BGA). BGA sued for infringement, but the District Court found that DK's use was fair. The Second Circuit affirmed on May 9, 2006 (*Bill Graham Archives* v. *Dorling Kindersley*, 448 F.3d 605 [2d Cir. 2006]).

In its analysis of the first factor, the Second Circuit held that DK's inclusion of reduced images of the posters in a new work was transformative. The court noted that DK's

> purpose in using the copyrighted images at issue in its biography of the Grateful Dead is plainly different from the original purpose for which they were created. Originally, each of BGA's images fulfilled the dual purpose of artistic expression and promotion. [. . .] In contrast, DK

used each of BGA's images as historical artifacts to document and represent the actual occurrence of Grateful Dead concert events featured on [its] timeline (ibid. at 609).

The court found that "DK's image display enhances the reader's understanding of the biographical text" (ibid. at 609–610). Thus, the Second Circuit, like the Ninth Circuit in *Amazon.com*, focused on the repurposing of the original work, rather than on changes to the work itself.

Further strengthening the transformational nature of DK's use was "the manner in which DK displayed the images" (ibid. at 611). The court noted that DK reduced the size of the reproductions, and cited *Kelly* as authority for the transformational nature of reductions. The court stressed that DK's layout—combining the images with a timeline, textual material, and original graphical artwork— "ensures that the images at issue are employed only to enrich the presentation of the cultural history of the Grateful Dead, not to exploit copyrighted artwork for commercial gain" (ibid.). The court further noted that the images "constitute an inconsequential portion" of the book, suggesting that DK contributed significant original expression (ibid.).

With respect to the second fair use factor, the nature of the copyrighted work, the court acknowledged the creative nature of the artwork at issue. However, it found that in cases involving transformative uses, the second factor should be given "limited weight" (ibid. at 612). The Second Circuit ruled that the third factor, the amount and substantiality of the portion used in relation to the copyrighted work as a whole, did not weigh against fair use when "copying the entirety of a work is . . . necessary to make a fair use of the image" (ibid. at 613). Here, DK "displayed the minimal image size and quality necessary to ensure the reader's recognition of the images as historical artifacts of the Grateful Dead concert events" (ibid.).

BGA conceded that DK's use did not affect its primary market, the sale of poster images. BGA nonetheless argued that DK interfered with the market for licensing its images for use in books. The Second Circuit acknowledged that the impact of a use on potential licensing revenue is a proper subject for consideration in assessing the fourth fair use factor. The court hastened to add, however, that "were a court automatically to conclude in every case that potential licensing revenues were impermissibly impaired simply because the secondary use did not pay a fee for the right to engage in the use, the fair use factor would always favor the copyright holder" (ibid. at 614).

Instead, courts should look only at the impact on potential revenues for "traditional, reasonable, or likely to be developed markets" (ibid.). The Second Circuit held that a "transformative market" does not fall into one of these three categories. The court stated:

[W]e hold that DK's use of BGA's images is transformatively different from their original expressive purpose. In a case such as this, a copyright holder cannot prevent others from entering fair use markets merely by developing or licensing a market for parody, news reporting, educational, or other transformative uses of its own creative work. Copyright owners may not preempt exploitation of transformative markets. [. . .] Since DK's use of BGA's images falls within a transformative market, BGA does not suffer market harm due to the loss of license fees (ibid. at 615).

The Second Circuit took care to distinguish DK's use from the photocopying of scientific journal articles by Texaco's researchers in *Am. Geophysical Union v. Texaco, Inc.,* 60 F.3d 913 (2d Cir. 1994): "Here, unlike in Texaco, we hold that DK's use of BGA's images is transformatively different from their original expressive purpose" (448 F.3d at 615).

Significance of Decisions in the Educational Context

Fair use decisions are highly fact-specific. Nonetheless, courts rely on precedent when applying the fair use factors. Thus, these three recent circuit court opinions will guide lower courts as they weigh defendants' assertions of fair use in future copyright infringement cases. This means that these opinions should inform fair use analyses performed by educational institutions. The following principles can be derived from these opinions.

1   All three cases arose in commercial settings, yet the courts found fair use. This suggests that similar types of uses in a nonprofit educational context are *a fortiori* fair.

2   The transformative nature of the use increasingly appears to be the most important criterion, swallowing the other factors. However, the notion of the kind of use that a court will consider transformative is far broader than the term "transformative" suggests. While the term "transformative" implies that the work itself has been changed, i.e., the user has made what would be considered to some extent a derivative work, both *Amazon.com* and *BGA* make clear that repurposing a work or placing it in a new context may be sufficient to render a use transformative.

3   The amount and substantiality of the portion used has less relevance, particularly if the use is transformative. In both *Amazon.com* and *BGA,* the user used entire works. Indeed, in *Amazon.com,* Google allegedly used the entirety of thousands of images (albeit in compressed form).

4   The existence of a licensing market for a work does not defeat fair use, provided that the use is transformative. The *BGA* court gave little weight to the fact that BGA derived significant revenue from licensing the use of its images.

One cannot predict with any certainty how a court will apply these principles to the wide variety of uses made in the educational context. Nonetheless, these principles could reasonably be interpreted to support a more confident application of the fair use doctrine to certain uses in the educational environment. What follows is one possible analysis of the implications of these principles.

If repurposing a work renders its use transformative, then arguably an educational use of a work created for a different market also is transformative. In other words, an educational institution could reasonably take the position that an educational use of an entertainment product is transformative because the work is being repurposed. Under this view of fair use, when a teacher reproduces a poem, a sound recording, or a photograph so that his students can study the work, his use is transformative.

These three cases suggest that the transformative nature of the repurposing for educational use can be further enhanced if the work is recontextualized. That is, the more integrated a work is with other material, the stronger the claim of fair use. Tools like Blackboard permit an instructor to create an online anthology for a class, including copyrighted works, commentary, lecture notes, and student reactions. This recontextualization appears to provide a stronger fair use defense than would library-run e-reserves containing just the plain text of works.

The judicial decisions discussed above thus imply that teachers, scholars, educational institutions, and libraries can be more confident in their assertion of the fair use privilege when they repurpose and recontextualize works. The limitations of brevity, spontaneity, and cumulative effect contained in the 1976 Classroom Use Guidelines appear to have little relevance with respect to uses of this sort.

Of course, this reasoning can be taken too far. While it might be transformative for an English Literature professor to scan the full text of Joseph Heller's *Catch-22* onto the Web site for his 20th Century American Literature class, it still might not be a fair use. A court could well decide that the reproduction has too direct and negative an effect on the market for *Catch-22,* a novel still in print. In this transformative context, a court could draw a distinction between the effect on the market for copies already in existence and the market for a license to make a different kind of use. In the case of copies in existence, a court could decide that fairness dictates that the publisher have the ability to recoup its investment in producing the copies—a consideration not present in the case of a license for a different use.

In any event, these cases indicate that educators should take great care to insure that their repurposing and recontextualization cannot be misused. In both *Amazon.com* and *BGA,* the reduced size and low resolution of the images weighed in favor of fair use because they prevented non-transformative uses. In *Amazon.com*, for example, a thumbnail image would lose resolution if it were enlarged, thereby preventing it from "supersed[ing] the objects of the original creation." If the public could access an American Studies course Web site containing stories, photographs, and sound recordings, the public could make entertainment use of this content, notwithstanding the professor's educational objective in making the content available to her students. The professor could avoid this potential misuse by employing appropriate technological measures to permit access only to those who would make educational uses of the content— her students.[4]

Significantly, the repurposing argument provides less protection with respect to works that target the education market. Including a chapter of a statistics textbook in a statistics course Web site likely would not constitute repurposing. This does not mean that such a use necessarily is unfair; rather, the instructor would simply have to rely on more traditional fair use arguments.

At the same time, it is important to recognize that the education market contains many sub-markets; a court may view as repurposing the use in one sub-market of a work created for a different sub-market. Articles published in scholarly journals are directed at other scholars in the field, with the objective of advancing knowledge in that field. Because undergraduates are not the target audience of journal articles, inclusion of such articles in e-reserves or a course Web site might well be treated as a form of repurposing.

In between the extremes of textbooks and journal articles lie academic books. Many are aimed at scholars, some at students, and still others at both scholars and students. Accordingly, the repurposing nature of the inclusion of chapters from such books in e-reserves and course Web sites depends on the specific book. But even if the book is aimed to some extent at the student market, a course Web site could recontextualize the book.

Without doubt, many copyright owners will not agree with this analysis of the possible implications of the three decisions. Indeed, many rightsholders might not agree with the decisions themselves; trade associations representing the major content providers filed amicus briefs advocating positions ultimately rejected by the *Amazon.com* court.[5] Nonetheless, these decisions represent the current state of fair use jurisprudence, and they demonstrate strong judicial support for the doctrine.[6]

Conclusion

Three recent appellate decisions concerning fair use should give educators and librarians greater confidence and guidance for asserting this important privilege. All three courts found fair use notwithstanding the commercial context in which the use occurred. The defendants in two of the cases used entire works, and changed them only by compressing them. The courts nonetheless found these uses fair because the defendants repurposed and recontextualized the works.

The principles articulated in these opinions could reasonably be interpreted to support a more confident application of the fair use doctrine to certain uses in the educational environment. For example, educational uses of entertainment products could be viewed as constituting repurposing; as could the display to students of works targeted at scholars. These cases further suggest that educators could buttress their fair use claim by recontextualizing works on course Web sites through selection and arrangement and the addition of commentary, criticism, annotation, and student reactions. In short, these decisions should engender fair use optimism in the education milieu.

Notes

1. "It is commonplace in modern copyright scholarship to decry the demise of the fair use doctrine." Mark A. Lemley, "Should a Licensing Market Require Licensing?" 70 *Law and Contemporary Problems* 185 (2007).

2. See, e.g., Madelyn Wessel and Deborah Gerhardt, "Flexing Fair Use Muscles: Electronic Course Reserves, the Use of Art, Images and Thumbnails in Teaching and Learning, Fair Use for Scholars, and Finding the Public Domain Clock," presented at the National Association of College and University Attorneys, Nov. 7–9, 2007. I would like to thank Madelyn Wessel for her helpful comments on an earlier draft of this paper.

3. The case name is styled *Perfect 10* v. *Amazon.com* because an appeal in a related case involving Amazon was consolidated with Google's appeal. The Ninth Circuit made a variety of other copyright rulings not relevant to this discussion.

4. It should also be noted that the *Amazon.com* court considered transformative the high-resolution, full-sized cache copies made by users' browsers (487 F.3d at 726).

5. Amicus briefs supporting positions advocated by Perfect 10 were filed by the Motion Picture Association of America, the National Music Publishers' Association, the Recording Industry Association of America, the American Society of Media Photographers, the Picture Archive Council of America, the British Association of Picture Libraries and Agencies, Stock Artists Alliance, the Graphic Artists Guild, American Society of Picture Professionals, and National Press Photographers.

6. In September 2007, in a case concerning the constitutionality of the Uruguay Round Agreements Act, the Tenth Circuit made the following expansive statement about fair use:

[A]lthough Ralph Ellison's estate may retain the copyright to his classic novel *Invisible Man*, the fair use defense permits scholars and teachers to quote extensively from the book and even reproduce entire sections for the purpose of commenting on (say) the parallels between the narrator's literal and figurative vision. Because the purpose of the fair use defense is to afford considerable 'latitude for scholarship and comment,' the [Supreme] Court has described it as a "guarantee of breathing space within the confines of copyright" (*Golan* v. *Gonzales,* 501 F.3d 1170 [10th Cir. 2007] citations omitted). In June 2007 the Sixth Circuit in *Zomba Enterprises* v. *Panorama Records* (491 F.3d 574 [6th Cir. 2007]) rejected a frivolous fair use defense asserted by a company that recorded musical compositions without authorization onto karaoke CDs. The court affirmed the district court's finding of willful infringement and award of over $800,000 in statutory damages.

Federal Agency and
Federal Library Reports

Library of Congress

10 First St. S.E., Washington, DC 20540
202-707-5000, World Wide Web http://www.loc.gov

James H. Billington
Librarian of Congress

Founded in 1800, the Library of Congress is the nation's oldest federal cultural institution and the largest library in the world, with more than 138 million items in various languages, disciplines, and formats. As the world's largest repository of knowledge and creativity, the library is a symbol of democracy and the principles on which the United States was founded. The library serves Congress and the nation, both in its 20 reading rooms on Capitol Hill and through its award-winning Web site, http://www.loc.gov. More than 93 million visits and 614 million page-views were recorded on the Web site during 2007, and more than 1.4 million visited the library in person.

Highlights of the Year

- The library celebrated the 20-year tenure of Librarian of Congress James H. Billington, who was sworn in by President Ronald Reagan on September 14, 1987.
- The Law Library celebrated the 175th anniversary of its founding on July 14, 1832.
- The library's Preservation Directorate marked the 40th anniversary of its founding in 1967 following devastating floods in Florence, Italy, that brought national and international attention to the need for improved library preservation programs.
- The Center for the Book marked the 30th anniversary of its creation by former Librarian of Congress Daniel Boorstin in October 1977.
- On January 4 and 5, 2007, the library hosted a record number of congressional events as members of the 110th Congress took their oaths of office. This Congress includes the first woman Speaker of the House, Rep. Nancy Pelosi (D-Calif.), who swore in the first Muslim member of the House, Rep. Keith Ellison (D-Minn.). Rep. Ellison asked to take the cere-

Report compiled by Audrey Fischer, Public Affairs Specialist, Library of Congress.

monial oath on a two-volume copy of the Koran that belonged to Thomas Jefferson; the library provided the volumes, which reside in its Rare Book and Special Collections Division.

- On January 25 Librarian of Congress James H. Billington and Architect of the Capitol Alan M. Hantman commemorated the start of construction on Modules 3 and 4 of the library's book-storage facility at Fort Meade, Maryland. The groundbreaking ceremony marked the beginning of phase three of a comprehensive plan to build 13 modules on the 100-acre site located within the secure perimeters of the Army base northeast of Washington, D.C.

- On April 24—its 207th "birthday"—the library launched its first blog (http://www.loc.gov/blog).

- On May 23 singer/songwriter Paul Simon received the inaugural Gershwin Prize for Popular Song.

- On July 26 the library's Packard Campus for Audio-Visual Conservation in Culpeper, Virginia, opened to the public.

- In August the Librarian of Congress added labor folklorist Archie Green to the library's list of "Living Legends."

- The exhibition "American Treasures of the Library of Congress" closed August 18 after ten years on view. The closure was part of the process to create an interactive "Library of Congress Experience" in the Thomas Jefferson Building.

- On September 29 the library sponsored the seventh annual National Book Festival on the National Mall, once against hosted by First Lady Laura Bush.

- On October 1 the library implemented its strategic plan for fiscal years 2008–2013 (http://www.loc.gov/about/mission/StrategicPlan07-Full.pdf).

- In October the library presented a prototype for the World Digital Library at the 34th UNESCO General Conference in Paris.

- On December 1 the Working Group on the Future of Bibliographic Control issued its final report for comment.

- On December 17 the Librarian of Congress, members of the library's staff, and representatives of Walt Disney Pictures attended a Washington, D.C., screening of *National Treasure: The Book of Secrets,* sequel to the hit film *National Treasure.* The movie includes scenes filmed at the Library of Congress showing a search through the library's stacks for a 19th century "book of secrets."

Legislative Support to Congress

Serving Congress is the library's highest priority. During 2007 the library provided Congress with the most current, objective research and analysis relevant to the war in Iraq, terrorism and national security, nuclear nonproliferation, defense spending, trade agreements, higher education, immigration, global climate change, the State Children's Health Insurance Program, and other issues of national and international concern.

The library's Congressional Research Service responded to more than 822,000 research requests from members of Congress and committees during the year. The 11 percent decline in direct congressional research requests (down from 933,000 in 2006) can be attributed in part to improvements made to the CRS Web site and its other computer-based systems. These improvements made CRS products and resources more accessible. The Legislative Information System (LIS), developed solely for use by Congress and congressional staff members, continued to provide access to information on past and current legislation through all facets of the lawmaking process.

The Law Library—the world's largest, comprising 2.6 million items—provided comprehensive international, comparative, and foreign law research. During the year, Law Library staff wrote 634 legal research reports, special studies, and memoranda in response to congressional inquiries.

The Law Library kept Congress informed on matters pertaining to international law through the online publication of the *World Law Bulletin.* The Global Legal Information Network (GLIN) provided Congress with access to the laws of 32 member nations.

The Copyright Office provided policy advice and technical assistance to Congress on important copyright laws and such related issues as piracy of intellectual property, preservation of "orphan works," and music-licensing reform. The Register of Copyrights testified before Congress on matters pertaining to the library's budget; the need to amend Section 108 of the copyright law ("fair use" for libraries and archives) to address digital media; and digital music-licensing reform (under Section 115 of the copyright law).

The Congressional Relations Office (CRO) assisted members of Congress and their staff in making use of the library's collections, services, and facilities. CRO and other library offices worked with member and committee offices on current issues of legislative concern, such as the library's appropriations, the construction of a Capitol Visitor Center and passageway connecting the Capitol to the library, and the Veterans History Project. CRO helped to coordinate more than 125 congressional events held at the library during the year.

Security

With support from Congress, the library further developed its security program for staff, patrons, facilities, and collections. During the year the focus was on building an emergency preparedness program, improving security at the library's off-site facilities, and expanding staff security awareness. Work continued on installing a public address system in all three library buildings on Capitol Hill. In coordination with other Capitol Hill agencies, the library continued upgrading its emergency preparedness capabilities, perimeter security, entrance and exit screening procedures, and internal controls safeguarding the library's collections.

In April 2007 the library's Office of Security and Emergency Preparedness hired an emergency management program officer, who, with a staff of three emergency management specialists, oversees the library's emergency preparedness program. Emergency Preparedness staff conducted a comprehensive assessment at each of the library's eight facilities and developed a projects list for 2008–2013 that includes provisions for enhanced emergency communications systems, expanded drills and exercises for continuity of operations, and augmentation of shelter-in-place equipment and supplies for staff and visitors. The library continued to upgrade its emergency operations center through a contract awarded in September 2007 to install internal satellite telephone antennas and repeater stations in the Madison and Jefferson buildings. In collaboration with other federal agencies on Capitol Hill, the library continued to refine its continuity of operations plan for a pandemic health emergency.

With a theme of "Safeguarding the Collections: We Are the Key," the library launched a security-awareness poster campaign during National Library Week, April 15–21. The purpose of the campaign is to remind staff members of their role in safeguarding the library's collections for future generations. The hallmark of the campaign is a quarterly rollout of each of four posters underscoring the themes of protecting, handling, storing, and communicating about the collections.

Budget

During fiscal year (FY) 2007 the library, along with all other federal agencies, operated under a continuing resolution (Public Law 110-5) signed on February 15, 2007. The bill provided a total for FY 2007 of $600,417,000, including authority to spend $42,108,000 in offsetting receipts.

Development

During FY 2007 the library's fund-raising activities brought in a total of $13.4 million, made up of 794 gifts from 687 donors. Gifts from individuals, foundations, corporations, trusts, associations, councils, and societies represented a 52 percent increase in private sector gifts as compared with the previous year. Those gifts, including $1 million received through the library's Planned Giving Program, were made to 65 separate library funds. The library forged new partnerships with 296 first-time donors, who gave $3.6 million, or 27 percent, of the gifts received during the year. Six new gift and trust funds were established.

Private gifts supported a variety of new and continuing programs throughout the library, including exhibitions, acquisitions, symposia and other scholarly programs, and the seventh National Book Festival. Private donors gave more than $1.6 million to support the festival.

During FY 2007 the James Madison Council—the library's first private sector advisory group—continued to provide substantial support for a number of initiatives. Six new members joined the council during the year. Gifts from Madison Council members in FY 2007 totaled $6.1 million, bringing the council's total support since 1990 to $179 million. Most of the council's contributions in 2007 provided support for two major initiatives, the National Book Festival and the new Library of Congress Experience. Members also made gifts to support the general collections; retrospective acquisitions; the Phillips Society, a friends group in the Geography and Map Division; and travel for the curators of the Prints and Photographs Division.

The library received the largest private in-kind gift in its 207-year history—a value of more than $150 million—on July 26, 2007, when the Packard Humanities Institute, headed by David Woodley Packard, officially transferred the new Audio-Visual Conservation Center in Culpeper, Virginia, to the American people.

Collections

During 2007 the size of the library's collections grew to 138 million items, an increase of more than 3 million over the previous year. This figure included more than 32 million cataloged books and other print materials, 61 million manuscripts, 14.8 million microforms, 5.3 million maps, 5.5 million pieces of sheet music, 14 million visual materials (photographs, posters, moving images, prints, and drawings), 2.9 million audio materials, and more than 1 million items in miscellaneous formats.

Cataloging

During the year the Bibliographic Access Divisions and Serial Record Division cataloged a record total of 363,064 bibliographic volumes. Production of full- and core-level original cataloging totaled 212,342 bibliographic records. With the library serving as the secretariat for the international Program for Cooperative Cataloging, member institutions created 188,183 new name authorities and 10,464 new or updated subject and classification authorities. In addition, the library contributed 100,133 new name authorities and 9,206 new subject headings.

In November 2006 the library convened a Working Group on the Future of Bibliographic Control. Chaired by José-Marie Griffiths, dean of the School of Information and Library Science at the University of North Carolina at Chapel Hill, the group included representatives of the American Association of Law Libraries, the American Library Association, the Special Libraries Association, the Association of Research Libraries, the Program for Cooperative Cataloging, the Online Computer Library Center (OCLC), Google, Microsoft, and the Coalition for Networked Information. The group held public meetings in Washington, D.C., Chicago, and Mountain View, California, and issued a preliminary report in September. Comments were incorporated into a subsequent report issued on December 1 for additional public comment. The final report will be issued early in 2008.

The preliminary report recommended the following

- Increase the efficiency of bibliographic production for all libraries through cooperation and sharing of bibliographic records and through use of data produced in the overall supply chain
- Transfer effort into high-value activity; in particular, provide greater value for knowledge creation through leveraging access for unique materials held by libraries that are currently hidden and under-used

- Position technology by recognizing that the World Wide Web is libraries' technology platform as well as the appropriate platform for standards; recognize that library users are not only people but also applications that interact with library data
- Position the library community for the future by adding evaluative, qualitative, and quantitative analyses of resources; work to realize the potential provided by the Functional Requirements for Bibliographic Records framework
- Strengthen the library and information science profession through education and through development of metrics that will inform decision-making now and in the future

For more information, see http://www.loc.gov/bibliographic-future.

Important Acquisitions

The library receives millions of items each year from copyright deposits, federal agencies, and purchases, exchanges, and gifts. Significant acquisitions made possible by the James Madison Council during the year included ten panoramic views of Manhattan by photographer Richard Howe, rare drawings by Winold Reiss, and a limited edition of the Arthur Szyk Haggadah, a landmark of Jewish art and culture.

During the year the library also acquired the following significant items and collections:

- The *Speech of Thomas Jefferson, President of the United States, Delivered at His Installment, March 4, 1801* (Philadelphia: Mathew Carey, 1801), printed on silk satin
- The papers of Caspar Weinberger (1917–2006), former secretary of health, education, and welfare, and secretary of defense
- The founding papers of the National Endowment for Democracy, a private, nonprofit organization established in 1983
- The personal papers of Franklin Edward Kameny, a pioneering crusader for gay rights, covering the period 1961–1997
- The papers of Supreme Court Justice David Davis from 1840 through 1880
- The Tony Schwartz Collection of audio and video recordings, reflecting his work from 1947 through 1999
- More than 7,000 hours of live jazz and blues recordings spanning 15 years from WWOZ-FM in New Orleans

Reference Services

The Library of Congress provides reference services to the public in its 20 reading rooms and through its Web site. During FY 2007 library staff handled more than 682,672 reference requests that were received in person, on the telephone, and through written and electronic correspondence. Staff also responded to reference questions received from libraries around the globe through an online system known as QuestionPoint, and directly from patrons through Ask a Librarian at http://www.loc.gov/rr/askalib. More than 1.3 million items were circulated for use within the library.

Online Resources

Through its National Digital Library Program and digitization efforts by its divisions, the library has been adding high-quality digital content to its award-winning Web site, http://www.loc.gov. At year's end the site offered more than 22 million digital items.

The Web site provides access to the institution's unparalleled resources, such as its online catalog, selected collections in various formats, copyright and legislative information, exhibitions, and Webcasts of library events.

During the year the site's home page was redesigned and a new metasearch function was added to allow users to search across the various Web pages from a single search box. The public legislative information system known as Thomas (http://www.thomas.gov) and the Global Legal Information System known as GLIN (http://www.glin.gov) were both upgraded to improve access.

As a portal to the library's millions of online resources, the Wise Guide Web site (http://www.loc.gov/wiseguide) is updated monthly with articles containing links to the library's online resources.

Several new presentations were added to the American Memory Web site (http://memory.loc.gov), which comprises more than 135 American history collections.

Special presentations were dedicated to the various heritage months celebrating the achievements of African Americans, Hispanics, Jews, Asians, and women. These sites were produced in collaboration with other federal agencies in order to provide a single place from which to access these important historic materials.

Several new library exhibitions were added to the Web site at http://www.loc.gov/exhibits. They included "Illuminating the Word: The Saint John's Bible"; "Cartoon America"; "A Century of Creativity: The MacDowell Colony, 1907–2007"; "On the Cutting Edge: Contemporary Japanese Prints"; and "West Side Story: Birth of a Classic."

Joining the more than 4,400 individual recollections accessible on the Veterans History Project site at http://www.loc.gov/vets are new presentations added in 2007. These highlight the achievements of World War I veterans and Asian Pacific American veterans (including the highly decorated 442nd Regimental Combat Team, the "Go for Broke" outfit of Japanese Americans who fought during World War II).

The library's 207th anniversary on April 24 was marked by the launch of its first blog at http://www.loc.gov/blog. One of only a few official federal government blogs, it keeps readers informed about library initiatives and milestones and provides related links to online resources. The site invites comments from users and provides a forum for discussion.

The library continued to offer podcasts on its Web site at http://www.loc.gov/podcasts. These include interviews conducted with authors participating in the National Book Festival. Webcasts of selected programs held at the Library were also added to the Web site at http://www.loc.gov/today/cyberlc.

In 2007 the library began providing access to information about its programs and activities through RSS feeds (http://www.loc.gov/rss). RSS (Really Simple Syndication) is a technology that allows organizations to deliver news to a desktop computer or other Internet device. By subscribing to RSS feeds, users can easily stay up to date with areas of the library's site that are of interest to them.

Building on the success of RSS feeds, in September the library joined the growing number of federal agencies that participate in GovDelivery, an e-mail update service. By allowing subscribers to receive e-mail alerts about programs, activities, and initiatives, the service gives the library an on-demand public communication system.

World Digital Library

First proposed by the Librarian of Congress at the UNESCO General Conference in 2005, the World Digital Library (WDL) aims to make available on the Internet, free of charge and in multilingual format, significant primary materials from cultures around the world, including manuscripts, maps, rare books, musical scores, recordings, films, prints, photographs, architectural drawings, and other significant cultural materials.

A prototype WDL, which supports six languages, was built by library staff in a seven-month period and demonstrated at the 34th UNESCO General Conference in October 2007. The prototype draws upon the contributions of the Library of Congress and five partner institutions—the Bibliotheca Alexandrina of Alexandria, Egypt; the National Library of Brazil; the National Library and Archives of Egypt; the National Library of Russia; and the Russian State Library. The WDL multilateral partner approach builds on the library's long experience with bilateral digital conversion partnerships that are presented in the Global Gateway portion of the library's Web site.

On October 17, the Librarian of Congress and UNESCO Assistant Director for Communication and Information Abdul Waheed Khan signed an agreement pledging cooperative efforts to build a World Digital Library Web site.

Preservation

In 2007 the library's Preservation Directorate completed more than 20 million assessments, treatments, rehousings, and reformattings of books, paper, photographs, audiovisual, and other items. Through the coordinated efforts of the directorate's divisions and programs, more than 9 million items were conserved, mass deacidified, or reformatted.

The library took action to preserve its collections by

- Providing preservation care to more than 9.2 million items from its collection

- Surveying a total of 13,122,552 million rare and fragile special collections items so they could be stabilized by treatment or rehousings for access, digitization, exhibition, and relocation to off-site storage
- Deacidifying 293,648 books and 1,086,000 manuscript sheets as part of its Thirty Year (One Generation) Mass Deacidification Plan to stabilize more than 8.5 million general collection books and at least 30 million pages of manuscripts (since 1995 the library has extended the useful life of nearly 2 million books and more than 5 million sheets of manuscript materials from its collections, and in 2007 it completed the second year of a five-year contract for deacidification services that will save 1,250,000 books and more than 5 million sheets of original manuscript materials)
- Using a single-sheet treatment cylinder on site at the library to deacidify 4,000 pages per day of non-book, paper-based materials that were too valuable to be transported to the mass deacidification vendor plant near Pittsburgh
- Housing 428,665 items, including the preparation of 21,078 protective boxes
- Rehousing 150,660 photographs and 277,988 paper-based items
- Treating 18,579 items from 12 curatorial divisions, including 12,688 paper documents, 3,576 books, and 2,315 photographs
- Preservation microfilming of 4.1 million exposures (7.1 million pages)
- Working in partnership with other organizations to develop a digital preservation program to sort, acquire, describe, and preserve electronic materials

The library continued to play a leadership role in the preservation of materials in a variety of formats such as books, photographs, newspapers, films, and sound recordings. It also played an outreach role in the preservation of the nation's heritage through several oral history projects. Highlights appear below.

Books

The library continued to fill its book-storage modules at Fort Meade, Maryland. Construction of high-density storage modules 3 and 4, which began in October 2006, is scheduled for completion in December 2008. During the year 344,170 items were accessioned and transferred to the facility, bringing the total stored there to 2,341,222 items. As more and more items went into storage, the number of items requested daily from the facility also increased. For the more than 15,000 items requested, the retrieval rate was 100 percent.

With a $2 million grant from the Alfred P. Sloan Foundation, the library has embarked on a program to digitize thousands of public domain works. Announced on January 31, 2007, the project, "Digitizing American Imprints," will focus on at-risk "brittle books" from the library's general collections, U.S. genealogies, American history volumes, and six collections of rare books: the Benjamin Franklin Collection; selections from the Katherine Golden Bitting and the Elizabeth Robins Pennell gastronomy collections; a selection of first editions from the library's Rare Book and Special Collections Division; selections from the Confederate States of America Collection; the Henry Harrisse Collection of Columbiana; and selections from the Jean Hersholt Collection of Hans Christian Andersen materials.

Maps

In collaboration with the National Institute for Standards and Technology and the Alcoa Foundation, the Preservation Directorate and the Geography and Map Division completed the process of creating a permanent, oxygen-free housing for the 16th century Waldseemüller Map that depicts the name "America" for the first time. The encasement was delivered and the map was installed as part of a new exhibition, "Exploring the Early Americas: The Jay I. Kislak Collection," which opened December 13.

Newspapers

The library has a long history of preserving newspapers from around the world. With funding from the National Endowment for the Humanities (NEH), a 23-year project to preserve U.S. newspapers culminated in 2006 with the microfilming of nearly 72 million endangered newspaper pages.

Continuing its commitment to newspaper preservation, in 2005 NEH pledged $1.9 million to six institutions to develop an Internet-based, searchable database of U.S. newspapers now in the public domain. Two-year projects in California, Florida, Kentucky, New York, Utah, and Virginia each will digitize 100,000 or more pages of each state's most historically significant newspapers published between 1900 and 1910. The library pledged to make this material accessible on its Web site.

In March 2007 the library announced the launch of the Chronicling America Web site (http://www.loc.gov/chroniclingamerica) with nearly 227,000 pages from 26 newspaper titles published between 1900 and 1910, as well as approximately 138,000 bibliographic descriptions of American newspapers published from 1690 to the present. At year's end the site offered 413,205 newspaper pages, representing 49 newspapers. In June 2007 NEH awarded $2.6 million to three new state partners.

Audiovisual Materials

The library's Packard Campus for Audio-Visual Conservation in Culpeper, Virginia, opened in July. The 45-acre campus, which was built with private sector support from the Packard Humanities Institute (PHI), houses the library's recorded sound, videotape, safety film, and nitrate film collections. The site consolidates the activities of the library's Motion Picture, Broadcasting, and Recorded Sound Division (MBRS) in one location.

The MBRS Division holds approximately 6.2 million collection items, comprising 3 million sound recordings, 1.2 million moving-image items, and 2 million related documents (scripts, copyright records, photos, posters, and so forth). Of these, 5.7 million are destined for final storage in Culpeper. By the end of the fiscal year, nearly 5.2 million of these had been relocated to the 140,000-square-foot Collections Building from existing storage facilities in Washington, D.C.; Boyers, Pennsylvania; Elkwood, Virginia; and the Landover, Maryland, annex. The

500,000 items still to be moved comprise primarily the nitrate film in the library's motion picture preservation program at Dayton, Ohio, and additional moving-image items still stored at Boyers and Landover. An additional 500,000 collection items will remain in the Washington reading rooms for ongoing access there.

Films

The library continued its commitment to preserving the nation's motion picture heritage. The 25 films listed below were named to the National Film Registry in 2007, bringing the total to 475. The library works to ensure that the films listed on the registry are preserved either through the library's motion picture preservation program or through collaborative ventures with other archives, motion picture studios, and independent film makers.

Back to the Future (1985)

Bullitt (1968)

Close Encounters of the Third Kind (1977)

Dance, Girl, Dance (1940)

Dances with Wolves (1990)

Days of Heaven (1978)

Glimpse of the Garden (1957)

Grand Hotel (1932)

The House I Live In (1945)

In a Lonely Place (1950)

The Man Who Shot Liberty Valance (1962)

Mighty Like a Moose (1926)

The Naked City (1948)

Now, Voyager (1942)

Oklahoma! (1955)

Our Day (1938)

Peege (1972)

The Sex Life of the Polyp (1928)

The Strong Man (1926)

Three Little Pigs (1933)

Tol'able David (1921)

Tom, Tom the Piper's Son (1969–1971)

12 Angry Men (1957)

The Women (1939)

Wuthering Heights (1939)

Sound Recordings

The library's National Recording Preservation Board is conducting a study about the current state of recorded sound preservation and restoration in the United

States. The results of the study will be used to draft a comprehensive plan for a national audio preservation program, as directed by Congress in the National Recording Preservation Act of 2000.

Under the terms of the act, the Librarian of Congress is responsible for selecting recordings annually that are "culturally, historically, or aesthetically significant." In March 2007 the library announced the following additions to the National Recording Registry:

"Uncle Josh and the Insurance Agent," Cal Stewart (1904)

"Il Mio Tesoro" from "Don Giovanni," John McCormack (orchestra conducted by Walter Rogers) (1916)

National Defense Test, featuring General John J. Pershing and other Army generals speaking on a multi-city broadcast (1924)

"Black Bottom Stomp," Jelly Roll Morton's Red Hot Peppers (1926)

"Wildwood Flower," The Carter Family (1928)

"Pony Blues," Charley Patton (1929)

"You're the Top," Cole Porter (1934)

"The Osage Bank Robbery," an episode of "The Lone Ranger" (December 17, 1937)

Address to Congress by President Franklin D. Roosevelt on the day following the attack on Pearl Harbor (1941)

"Native Brazilian Music" recorded under the supervision of Leopold Stokowski (1942)

"Peace in the Valley," Red Foley and the Sunshine Boys (1951)

Chopin Polonaise, op. 40, no. 1 ("Polonaise militaire"), pianist Artur Rubinstein (1952)

"Blue Suede Shoes," Carl Perkins (1955)

Interviews with "northwoods" singer William "Billy" Bell, recorded by folklorist Edward D. Ives (1956)

"Howl," Allen Ginsberg reading his best-known poem (1959)

"The Button-Down Mind of Bob Newhart," comedy LP, Bob Newhart (1960)

"Be My Baby," The Ronettes (1963)

"We Shall Overcome," live recording by Pete Seeger at Carnegie Hall (1963)

"(I Can't Get No) Satisfaction," Rolling Stones (1965)

"A Change Is Gonna Come," Sam Cooke (1965)

"Velvet Underground and Nico," LP, Velvet Underground (1967)

"The Eighty-Six Years of Eubie Blake," LP, pianist and composer Eubie Blake (1969)

"Burnin'," LP, The Wailers (1973)

"Live in Japan," LP, Sarah Vaughan (1973)

"Graceland," LP, Paul Simon (1986)

In September 2007 the library entered into a partnership with WWOZ-FM in New Orleans and the GRAMMY Foundation to preserve legendary musical recordings. The contribution of more than 7,000 hours of live jazz and blues recordings spanning 15 years, which came after Hurricane Katrina's floodwaters nearly destroyed the station's primary tape storage facility, will ensure the safety of the station's collection of historic recordings. In support of this gift, the foundation has awarded $45,000 in grants to WWOZ to support the preservation of the collection.

Oral History

The library's American Folklife Center continued its mandate to "preserve and present American folklife" through a number of outreach and oral history programs such as the Veterans History Project (VHP) and StoryCorps.

VHP was established by Congress in 2000 to record and preserve first-person accounts of armed services personnel who served during wartime. During 2007 VHP staff continued to gather veterans' stories and make them accessible on the project's Web site at http://www.loc.gov/folklife/vets. In its seventh year, the collection grew to more than 55,000 individual audio- and videotaped submissions containing interviews, correspondence, diaries, memoirs, photos, scrapbooks, films, maps, and other artifacts. At year's end, 4,400 items had been digitized and more than 45,000 items were accessible through a searchable database.

The StoryCorps project was conceived by David Isay of Sound Portraits Productions, who was inspired by the library's collection of oral history recordings made by the Works Progress Administration (WPA) during the late 1930s and early 1940s. Like the WPA recordings, the interviews being collected by StoryCorps will be housed in the American Folklife Center. At year's end, the StoryCorps archive included more than 9,000 stories.

Digital Preservation

In December 2000 Congress asked the library to lead a collaborative project to develop a national strategy for preserving digital content for future generations. Through the project, known as the National Digital Information Infrastructure and Preservation Program (NDIIPP), the library is working with 100 partners from universities, libraries, archives, federal agencies, and the private sector to preserve items that are "born digital." Its Web site is at http://www.digitalpreservation.gov.

Preserving Creative America

In August 2007 the library awarded $2.15 million to eight private partners for the preservation of creative works in digital format. These partners are the Academy of Motion Picture Arts and Sciences, the American Society of Media Photographers, ARTstor, BMS/Chace, the Stock Artists Alliance, Universal Press Syndicate, the UCLA Film and Television Archive, and the University of Illinois at Urbana-Champaign.

The idea for the project began in April 2006 when the library's digital preservation partners met in Los Angeles with more than 50 private sector producers of digital content to assess their interest in, and plans for, the long-term preservation of creative works. The meeting resulted in the launch of the Preserving Creative America Project to target preservation issues across a broad range of creative works, including digital photographs, cartoons, motion pictures, sound recordings, and even video games.

State Records

States face formidable challenges in caring for digital records with long-term legal and historical value. In 2007 a total of 21 states, working in four multi-state consortiums, joined the Library of Congress in an initiative to catalyze collaborative efforts to preserve important state government information in digital form. The projects will collect several significant categories of digital information such as geospatial data, legislative records, court case files, Web-based publications, and executive agency records. Each project will also work to share tools, services, and best practices to help every state make progress in managing its digital heritage.

Web Capture

Since 2000 the library's Web Capture Team has preserved Internet content pertaining to a variety of specific topics. This multidisciplinary team of library staff representing cataloging, legal, public, and technology services has been studying and implementing methods to evaluate, select, collect, catalog, preserve, and provide access to these materials for future generations of researchers. In 2007 the team developed thematic Web archives on such topics as the 2008 elections, the war in Iraq, and law-related blogs. Since the project's inception, the team has archived 18 terabytes of content (approximately 1.5 billion documents) from the Web. These are accessible at http://www.loc.gov/webcapture.

Copyright

During the year the library's Copyright Office received 541,212 new claims to copyright, covering more than 1 million works. It registered 526,378 claims and recorded 11,534 documents covering more than 500,000 titles. The copyright public record, available for searching online, grew with the cataloging of 574,000 registrations and the indexing of thousands of parties and titles of works contained in documents recorded.

The Americana collections of the Library of Congress have been created largely through the copyright system. The Copyright Office annually transfers to the library about 1 million deposit copies in all formats. In 2007 the Copyright Office forwarded 1,077,152 copies of works with a net worth of approximately $45 million to the library; approximately half of these items were received from publishers under the mandatory deposit provisions of the copyright law.

During the year the Copyright Office completed the renovation of its facilities and implemented its re-engineered core business processes. The result was a new organizational structure and a new technology infrastructure to increase the efficiency of its public services. The Architect of the Capitol renovated the Copyright Office spaces in the Library's James Madison Building, allowing staff and contractors to move back to the newly renovated offices from temporary space in Arlington, Virginia, and other sites in the Capitol Hill complex. The Copyright Office also opened the Copyright Public Records Reading Room, which consolidates all copyright records for public access.

With its new technology infrastructure in place, the Copyright Office moved forward on the implementation of the electronic registration system (eCO) to facilitate registration and deposit through the Internet (including works that are "born digital"). During the year the office started alpha testing by inviting a small number of applicants to begin submitting their claims using the new eCO service. Following successful alpha testing, the office began beta testing by extending the invitation to more applicants through the copyright Web site. By the end of September 2007 more than 1,000 applicants had established eCO accounts and several hundred had submitted electronic claims.

The Copyright Royalty and Distribution Reform Act of 2004 (Public Law 108-419) replaced the Copyright Arbitration Royalty Panels with an entity comprising three Copyright Royalty Judges and their staff; the judges were sworn to office in January 2006. In their second year of operation, the judges set rates and terms for various statutory licenses and distributed royalty fees collected by the Copyright Office. The total distributions made in fiscal 2007 were more than $279,930,900, an increase of more than $88,887,750 over FY 2006.

National Library Service for the Blind and Physically Handicapped

Established in 1931 when President Herbert Hoover signed the Pratt-Smoot Act into law, the National Library Service for the Blind and Physically Handicapped (NLS) circulates more than 24 million copies of braille and recorded books and magazines to approximately 500,000 readers through a network of 131 cooperating libraries. NLS also provides a free service known as the 102 Talking-Book Club to 3,672 patrons who are 100 years of age or older. Eleven network libraries inducted 136 members in 2007.

During 2007 NLS continued to plan and prepare for a major upgrade to the next generation of audio technology—digital talking-books (DTBs). The project calls for the incremental phasing in of DTB playback machines and media in 2008 and the gradual elimination of analog cassettes and equipment. In April 2007 NLS authorized its national network of libraries to remove 8 ⅓ rpm recorded-disc books from their collections. Their discontinuation signifies another milestone in the conversion to digital books. During the year NLS approved the designs for the digital talking-book machine, cartridge, and cartridge container. NLS sought proposals to produce the cartridge container and player.

In late 2006 NLS launched a pilot project to make audiobooks available as downloadable files over the Internet. The project, which provided 100 users with 1,200 book titles and 35 magazine issues, was expanded in January 2007 to include more than 2,000 participants who downloaded 1,600 books and nearly 300 magazine issues. At year's end, the system offered 5,000 digital audio titles.

The Internet-based Web-braille service continued to provide access to braille books, magazines, and music scores online at http://www.loc.gov/nls/braille. The system provides access to braille material to more than 4,000 users with special braille keyboards and screens. To respond to patron demand, the braille version of *Harry Potter and the Deathly Hallows* by J. K. Rowling was made available on the Web-braille site within a week of its print publication.

John W. Kluge Center

The John W. Kluge Center was established in 2000 with a gift of $60 million from John W. Kluge, Metromedia president and founding chairman of the James Madison Council, the library's private sector advisory group. Located within the library's Office of Scholarly Programs, the center's goal is to bring the world's best thinkers to the Library of Congress, where they can use the institution's unparalleled resources and interact with public policymakers in Washington. The center also administers the Kluge Prize, which rewards lifetime achievement in the study of humanity for disciplines not recognized by Nobel prizes.

During 2007 the Kluge Center continued to draw outstanding senior scholars and postdoctoral fellows. Through their work, scholars, researchers, literary enthusiasts, and the general public deepened their understanding of the cultural, historical, philosophical, scientific, and creative dimensions of human experience.

The Kluge Center sponsored symposia, lectures, book talks, and conferences, as well as a series of talks by fellows and scholars on their particular areas of research. In February 2007 Václav Havel, former president of the Czech Republic who then held the Chair of Modern Culture at the Kluge Center, and eight dissidents from around the world participated in a discussion titled "Dissidents and Freedom." In conjunction with this event, Havel received awards from both the National Endowment for Democracy and the National Democratic Institute for International Affairs.

Also in February, former Secretary of State James L. Baker delivered the fifth Kissinger Lecture on Foreign Policy and International Relations before a capacity crowd that included former Secretary of State Henry A. Kissinger, in whose honor the lecture is named; Deputy Secretary of State John D. Negroponte; and several U.S. senators and representatives. Baker, who served as co-chairman of the bipartisan Iraq Study Group, prescribed ten guidelines for effective U.S. foreign policy, among them flexibility, communicating with the country's enemies, and changing course if necessary.

For more information about the Kluge Center, visit http://www.loc.gov/kluge.

Publications

The Publishing Office produced more than 40 books, calendars, and other products describing the library's collections in 2007, many in cooperation with trade publishers.

Major works published in 2007 that featured the collections in various formats included *The Library of Congress World War II Companion; Cartographia;*

Slave Narratives from the Federal Writers' Project, 1936–1938; Silent Movies: The Birth of Film and the Triumph of Movie Culture; Aeronautical and Astronautical Resources of the Library of Congress: A Comprehensive Guide; and *The Jay I. Kislak Collection at the Library of Congress.*

In collaboration with Pomegranate Communications, the library released an additional four titles in the series Women Who Dare. These included volumes on cultural anthropologist Margaret Mead, contralto Marian Anderson, women explorers, and women reformers.

Two titles were added to the Norton/Library of Congress Visual Sourcebook in Architecture, Design and Engineering series: *Bridges* and *Lighthouses.*

Exhibitions

Library exhibitions in 2007 ranged from Japanese prints to pre-Columbian artifacts.

"On the Cutting Edge: Contemporary Japanese Prints" (March 29–June 30) was an exceptional cross-cultural exchange and marked the 50th anniversary of the College Women's Association of Japan Print Show. A total of 212 contemporary prints, donated by the artists themselves and by two dealers, add new depth to the library's exceptional collection of Japanese prints.

"American Treasures of the Library of Congress," which closed on August 18 after a decade on view, featured two final presentations. "A Century of Creativity: The MacDowell Colony, 1907–2007" commemorated the centennial of the artists' colony, and "Shakespeare in America" was on display in conjunction with a citywide Shakespeare celebration held January through July.

On view September 2007 through March 2008 in the foyer of the Performing Arts Reading Room was "West Side Story: Birth of a Classic," marking the 50th anniversary of the Broadway debut of Leonard Bernstein's musical interpretation of "Romeo and Juliet."

"Exploring the Early Americas: The Jay I. Kislak Collection" opened on December 13 and will remain on view indefinitely. The exhibition features selections from the more than 3,000 rare maps, documents, paintings, prints, and artifacts that make up the library's Kislak Collection. The exhibit also features high-tech touch screens that allow visitors to interact virtually with artifacts.

Special Events

During the year the library presented more than 450 special events, such as poetry and literary programs, concerts, lectures, and symposia, many of which were broadcast live or archived on the library's Web site. For a list of upcoming events, visit http://www.loc.gov/loc/events.

Since its inception in 2001, the library's National Book Festival has become a well-received annual event. The 2007 festival was held on September 29 on the National Mall. Hosted once again by First Lady Laura Bush, with support from Target and other private donors, the festival drew more than 120,000 people. The free event featured 70 award-winning authors, illustrators, and poets. As part of the book festival's theme, "Lifelong Literacy," the library and the Ad Council announced a new campaign to encourage children in grades four to six to "explore new worlds" through reading. The message is conveyed through a series of public service announcements on television, radio, in print, and on the Internet. The campaign includes a new presentation on the Library's Web site at http://www.loc.gov/literacy.

The Library's Poetry and Literature Center sponsored a number of programs featuring new and renowned poets reading from their works. On May 10, U.S. Poet Laureate Donald Hall and British Poet Laureate Andrew Motion gave a joint reading at the library. In August Charles Simic was appointed the library's 15th Poet Laureate Consultant in Poetry. Prior to opening the library's 2007–2008 literary season on October 18, Simic appeared at the National Book Festival along with Jack Prelutsky, named the nation's first Children's Poet Laureate by the Poetry Foundation.

Poet W. S. Merwin received the 2006 Rebekah Johnson Bobbitt National Prize for Poetry and read selections of his work at the library on October 31. The prize, the ninth to be given, was awarded to Merwin for his book *Present Company* (Copper Canyon).

The library sponsored numerous book talks, many offered as part of the Center for the Book's "Books and Beyond" lecture series, which focuses on the importance of books and reading.

Concerts

Since its establishment in 1925 by Elizabeth Sprague Coolidge, the "Concerts from the Library of Congress" series has offered more than 2,000 concerts in the library's Coolidge Auditorium. Among the concerts offered in the 2006–2007 season were some that complemented other library programs. In conjunction with the library's exhibition marking the centennial of the famed artists' colony, a concert featured "Women Composers of the MacDowell Colony." A musical tribute to the Pete Seeger family was held as part of a larger symposium honoring the Seegers. A number of concerts featuring Irish composers and their music were planned in conjunction with "Rediscover Northern Ireland," a series of cultural events.

The American Folklife Center continued to sponsor its outdoor concert series titled "Homegrown: The Music of America" (April–December) with diverse musical traditions including blues and gospel and other cultural expressions such as Native American storytelling.

Symposia and Lectures

In addition to sponsoring symposia honoring the Seeger family and the culture of Northern Ireland, the American Folklife Center presented a program on labor folklorist Archie Green, who was honored at the event with the library's Living Legend medal.

The library sponsored a number of programs and lectures delivered in conjunction with various heritage month celebrations. Keynote speakers throughout the year included Congresswoman Juanita Millender-McDonald (D-Calif.), who delivered the African American Heritage Month keynote address in February, not long before her death on April 22. Rep. Debbie Wasserman Schultz (D-Fla.), chair of the House Committee on Appropriations, delivered the Women's History Month keynote address in March. Sen. Daniel Inouye (D-Hawaii) delivered the Asian Pacific American Heritage Month address in May, Rep. Tom Cole (R-Okla.) the Native American Heritage Month keynote speech in September, and Rep. Xavier Beccera (D-Calif.) the Hispanic Heritage Month keynote address in October.

Outreach

The library continued to share its treasures both nationally and internationally on its Web site, through its Learning Page for teachers, and through traveling exhibitions and other programs. The Center for the Book in the Library of Congress, with its network of affiliates in all 50 states and more than 80 organizational partners, promoted books, reading, libraries, and literacy. [See the following article, "Center for the Book"—*Ed.*]

Additional Sources of Information

Library of Congress telephone numbers for public information:

Main switchboard (with menu)	202-707-5000
Reading room hours and locations	202-707-6400
General reference	202-707-3399
	TTY 202-707-4210
Visitor information	202-707-8000
	TTY 202-707-6200
Exhibition hours	202-707-4604
Reference assistance	202-707-6500
Copyright information	202-707-3000
Copyright hotline (to order forms)	202-707-9100
Sales shop (credit card orders)	888-682-3557

Center for the Book

Library of Congress, Washington, DC 20540
World Wide Web http://www.loc.gov/cfbook

John Y. Cole
Director

With its network of affiliated centers in 50 states and the District of Columbia and more than 80 organizations serving as its national reading promotion partners, the Center for the Book is one of the Library of Congress's most dynamic and visible educational outreach programs. Created in 1977 by Public Law 95-129, it uses the resources and prestige of the Library of Congress to stimulate public interest in books, reading, and literacy and to promote public understanding of the role of the library in preserving and advancing the nation's cultural heritage. The center encourages the study of books, reading, and the printed word, at the state and local level, nationally, and internationally.

The Center for the Book is a successful public-private partnership. The Library of Congress supports its four full-time positions, but all of its activities must be funded through tax-deductible contributions from individuals, corporations, and foundations or by transfers of funds from other government agencies.

Highlights of 2007

- Development, in partnership with the Children's Book Council, of the new post of National Ambassador for Young People's Literature. On Jan. 3, 2008, Librarian of Congress James H. Billington named children's book author Jon Scieszka as the first National Ambassador
- A major contribution to the success of the 2007 National Book Festival, held on the National Mall on September 29
- Participation in BibliObraz 2007, an international book festival held in Moscow October 9–11 and hosted by Ludmila Putin, the wife of the Russian president
- Cosponsorship of the publication of the book *Agent of Change: Print Culture Studies After Elizabeth L. Eisenstein* (University of Massachusetts Press)

Themes and Campaigns

Since its national Year of the Reader campaign in 1987, the Center for the Book has developed and publicized national themes that stimulate interest in reading and literacy projects that benefit all age groups. In 2007 the center's 1992 theme "Explore New Worlds—READ!" was reshaped and expanded in scope and content for use by the library's Lifelong Literacy initiative, a national public service advertising campaign that encourages young people to become readers (see http://www.loc.gov/literacy).

State Centers for the Book

The center's state partnership affiliation program began in 1984 when the Florida Center for the Book, hosted by the Broward County Library, was approved as the first state center. Today there are affiliated centers in all 50 states and the District of Columbia. Most of them are hosted by state libraries, large public library systems, state humanities councils, or universities. Each works with the national center to promote books, reading, and libraries, as well as the state's own literary and intellectual heritage. Each also develops and funds its own operation and projects, making use of Library of Congress themes and assistance as appropriate. State centers must apply every three years to renew their affiliate status.

On May 1 and 2, 2007, state center representatives participated in their annual "idea exchange" at the Library of Congress. The sessions featured lively discussions about current Center for the Book reading promotion projects such as "Letters About Literature," "River of Words," and "One Book" community reading and discussion programs. Looking ahead, state center coordinators concerned themselves with the center's participation in the Library of Congress's Lifelong Literacy initiative, and their potential involvement in two other projects: the Pavilion of the States in the next National Book Festival and the forthcoming National Ambassador for Young People's Literature program. Special guest Maria Vedenyapina, director of the Pushkin Library Foundation in Moscow (the center's reading promotion partner in Russia), described the system of more than 30 Russian "reading centers" inspired by the Center for the Book. She also discussed the new Russian-English reading promotion handbook, *Building Nations of Readers: Experience, Ideas, Examples,* edited by John Y. Cole and Valeria Stelmakh.

The 2007 Boorstin Awards, named for former Librarian of Congress Daniel J. Boorstin, who established the Center for the Book in 1977, were presented to five state centers for their innovative reading promotion projects. Each included a $1,000 stipend. The winners were

- California, for its new "Book Clubs in a Box" and "Mysterious California" programs and its concise new slogan and focus, "We help librarians and teachers get California reading"
- Georgia, for its success as a cofounder and sponsor of the new *Atlanta Journal-Constitution* Decatur Book Festival and its "All Georgia Reads" projects
- Illinois, for three projects that honor Illinois authors: the Illinois Emerging Writers Competition, the Illinois Authors Directory, and the Illinois Literary Heritage Award
- Louisiana, for its work in planning a successful 2006 Louisiana Book Festival after the 2005 festival was canceled because of Hurricanes Katrina and Rita, and for its creative support of Louisiana public libraries during the hurricane recovery efforts
- Maine, for its innovative and wide-ranging community reading and education programs, particularly Community Reading Seminars; New Books, New Readers; Stories for Life; Born to Read; and Teachers for a New Century

Reading Promotion Partners

More than 80 civic, educational, and governmental organizations are "reading promotion partners" of the Center for the Book, working with it to promote books, reading, literacy, and libraries in ways that are compatible with their own organizational goals. In addition, the center is part of several reading, education, and literacy promotion networks sponsored both by governmental agencies and nonprofit organizations, including the Federal Interagency Committee on Education and the National Coalition on Literacy.

In March 2007 more than 40 of the center's organizational reading promotion partners gathered at the Library of Congress to display project materials, share ideas, and report on their reading and literacy promotion programs. New organizational partners during 2007 included Jumpstart, the National Humanities Alliance, the National Literary Society of the Deaf, and the Smithsonian Institution's Latino Center. During the year the center cohosted reading promotion events at the Library of Congress with several of its partners, including the American Library Association, Mystery Writers of America, and the National Newspaper Association Foundation.

The development during the year of the post of National Ambassador for Young People's Literature was a partnership project with the Children's Book Council. The inaugural ambassador, announced in January 2008 by Librarian of Congress James H. Billington, is award-winning children's book author Jon Scieszka, who will spend two years speaking and traveling on behalf of young people's books, reaching out in particular to children who are considered reluctant readers.

Events and Projects

For the seventh year, in 2007 the Center for the Book played a key role in the National Book Festival, which is organized and sponsored by the Library of Congress and was hosted by First Lady Laura Bush. The center develops, coordinates, and oversees arrangements for the presentations by the festival's authors, illustrators, and poets and manages the festival's Pavilion of the States. Held on the National Mall on September 29, the festival attracted a crowd of more than 120,000 book-lovers. Seventy popular authors, illustrators, and poets made presentations and signed books. The Pavilion of the States featured reading, literacy, and library promotion programs from all 50 states, the District of Columbia, American Samoa, Guam, Puerto Rico, and the U.S. Virgin Islands.

"Letters About Literature," a national reading and writing promotion program for children and young adults, attracted more than 56,000 entries in 2007. Each student wrote a letter to a favorite author, explaining why that writer's book helped shape the student's life. In 2007, as in past years, six national winners were selected from among the state winners and Target, the program's national sponsor, brought them and their parents to Washington, D.C., for the National Book Festival. The winners read their letters in a program in the Teens and Children pavilion.

During the year the center hosted 21 book talks at the Library of Congress, many of them in its "Books and Beyond" author series. Each featured the author of a newly published book that was based on the library's collections or related to a specific Library of Congress program. Speakers included Arnold Rampersad, biographer of novelist Ralph Ellison, and mystery writer Sara Paretsky. All of the talks can be seen as Webcasts on the center's Web site.

Outreach and Publications

The Library of Congress issued 30 press releases about Center for the Book activities in 2007, and a "News from the Center for the Book" feature by Center for the Book Director John Y. Cole appeared in ten issues of the monthly *Library of Congress Information Bulletin.* An associate member of the Standing Committee on Reading of the International Federation of Library Associations and Institutions (IFLA), Cole edits the IFLA *Section on Reading Newsletter,* which is produced and distributed twice a year by the Center for the Book.

Cole and Catherine Gourley, "Letters About Literature" coordinator, were members of the ten-person U.S. delegation (headed by the Librarian of Congress) to BibliObraz 2007, the third international book festival hosted by Ludmila Putin, wife of Russian President Vladimir Putin. Like its predecessors in 2003 and 2005, the Russian festival emphasized young readers and reading promotion activities in schools. Center for the Book presentations focused on the center's cooperation with Russian reading centers and its projects aimed at young readers, particularly "Letters About Literature."

Renowned book history scholar Elizabeth L. Eisenstein was a member of the Center for the Book's first advisory board and its first scholar-in-residence. With the University of Massachusetts Press, in 2007 the center published *Agent of Change: Print Culture Studies After Elizabeth L. Eisenstein,* a book of 20 essays in Eisenstein's honor. This volume and a subsequent symposium at the Library of Congress celebrated the publication and continuing influence of Eisenstein's *The Printing Press as an Agent of Change: Communications and the Cultural Trans-formations in Early–Modern Europe* (1979).

National Agricultural Library

U.S. Department of Agriculture, NAL Bldg.,
10301 Baltimore Ave., Beltsville, MD 20705-2351
E-mail agref@nal.usda.gov
World Wide Web http://www.nal.usda.gov

Len Carey
Public Affairs Officer

The U.S. Department of Agriculture's National Agricultural Library (NAL) is the world's largest and most accessible agricultural research library, offering service directly to the public and via its Web site, http://www.nal.usda.gov. The library was created with the U.S. Department of Agriculture (USDA) in 1862 and established as a national library by Congress (7 USCS § 3125a) as the primary agricultural information resource of the United States.

Congress assigned to the library the responsibilities to

- Acquire, preserve, and manage information resources relating to agriculture and allied sciences
- Organize agricultural information products and services and provide them within the United States and internationally
- Plan, coordinate, and evaluate information and library needs relating to agricultural research and education
- Cooperate with and coordinate efforts toward development of a comprehensive agricultural library and information network
- Coordinate the development of specialized subject information services among the agricultural and library information communities

NAL is the only library in the United States with the mandate to carry out these national and international responsibilities for the agricultural community. The library's vision is "advancing access to global information for agriculture."

The library is located in Beltsville, Maryland, near Washington, D.C., on the grounds of USDA's Henry A. Wallace Beltsville Agricultural Research Center. Its 15-story Abraham Lincoln Building is named in honor of the president who created the Department of Agriculture and signed many of the major U.S. laws affecting agriculture.

NAL employs about 165 librarians, information specialists, computer specialists, administrators, and clerical personnel, supplemented by about 80 contract staff, as well as volunteers and cooperators from NAL partnering organizations.

The library's expert staff, leadership in delivering information services, collaborations with other U.S. and international agricultural research and information organizations, extensive collection of agricultural information, AGRICOLA bibliographic database of citations to the agricultural literature, and advanced information technology infrastructure contribute to NAL's reputation as one of the world's foremost agricultural libraries.

The Collection

The NAL collection dates to the congressionally approved 1839 purchase of books for the Agricultural Division of the Patent Office, predating the 1862 establishment of USDA itself. Today, NAL provides access to billions of pages of agricultural information—an immense collection of scientific literature, books and journals, audiovisuals, reports, theses, software, laser discs, artifacts, and images in agriculture—and to a widening array of digital media, as well as databases and other information resources germane to the broad reach of agriculture-related sciences.

The library's collection contains nearly 3.6 million items dating from the 16th century to the present, including the most complete repository of U.S. Department of Agriculture publications and the most extensive set of materials anywhere on the history of agriculture in the United States. The collection covers all aspects of agriculture and related sciences and is a comprehensive resource for agricultural scientists, policy makers, regulators, and scholars.

Networks of Cooperation

The NAL collection and information resources are supplemented by networks of cooperation with other institutions, including arrangements with agricultural libraries at U.S. land-grant universities, other U.S. national libraries, agricultural libraries in other countries, and libraries of the United Nations and other international organizations.

The library serves as secretariat for the Agriculture Network Information Center (AgNIC) Alliance, a voluntary, collaborative partnership that hosts a distributed network of discipline-specific agricultural information Web sites (http://www.agnic.org). In 2007 the combined AgNIC partner Web statistics totaled more than 170 million Web hits.

AgNIC provides access to high-quality agricultural information selected by AgNIC partners, including land-grant universities, NAL, and other institutions globally. AgNIC welcomed one new institution during 2007—the University of Vermont will provide subject matter on maple syrup. AgNIC's 58 member institutions offer 56 subject-specific sites. During the year, partners adopted a new Strategic Plan, a new logo and Web site banner, launched two new features— "AgOAI" and a news aggregator—and continued to build full-text content through a variety of projects. The AgOAI feature uses the Open Archives Initiative protocols to harvest metadata for full-text resources from targeted institutional repositories and collections for a single point of access. The news aggregator pulls news from more than 20 reliable news sources into a central news site. Strategic goals include those to broaden and strengthen AgNIC, improve content and services, and explore and develop appropriate applications and technologies.

During 2007 NAL and AgNIC cooperated with the National Library of Medicine and with the American Veterinary Medical Association to develop a Web portal for veterinary medicine practitioners (http://vetmedinfo.org) in clinical settings. The Web portal brings needed information to such clinical practitioners, who may otherwise have only limited access to information resources and library services or who may be unaware of the resources and services available to them.

As the U.S. node of an international agricultural information system, the library also serves as a gateway to U.S. agricultural libraries and resources. NAL cooperates with other libraries and information centers and consortia via several reciprocal agreements. It is part of the Agricultural Libraries Network (AGLINET), a voluntary network of agricultural libraries around the world with strong regional/country coverage and other comprehensive or very specialized subject resource collections, and of the United Nations information system.

During 2007 NAL partnered with the Animal Science Education Consortium—15 colleges and universities in the northeast and mid-Atlantic states—to create an online Animal Science Image Gallery, funded through a USDA Higher Education Challenge Grant. The gallery contains more than 2,000 clinical veterinary medicine images, animations, and videos available for classroom use. The library will host the gallery in perpetuity. Gallery editors, reviewers, and submitters come from the membership of the American Society of Animal Science (ASAS), the American Dairy Science Association, the Poultry Science Association, the Equine Science Society, the American Society for Nutrition, the Society for the Study of Reproduction, and the American College of Theriogenologists.

Building the NAL Collection

NAL annually acquires approximately 13,000 serial titles, including purchase with archival display rights of 1,000 electronic journals in agriculture and related sciences. The library has primary responsibility for collecting and retaining all publications of USDA and its agencies, and is the only U.S. national library with a legislated mandate to collect comprehensively in the following disciplines: animal sciences, plant sciences, agricultural economics and statistics, agricultural products, agricultural chemistry and engineering, agronomy and soil conservation, forestry and forest products, rural sociology and rural life, food sciences, and nutrition. In addition to these core subjects, the NAL collection contains extensive materials in such related subjects as biology, natural history, wildlife ecology, pollution, genetics, natural resources, meteorology, and fisheries.

Since the mid-1800s NAL has carried out a strong global program to acquire publications through international exchange. The types of publications received on exchange are often difficult to acquire through established subscription vendors, and constitute a valuable body of "gray literature" that is not widely available in other U.S. libraries. Currently, NAL initiates and coordinates these exchanges with more than 5,000 partners from 106 countries, accounting for about 70 percent of all periodicals currently received.

In general, NAL's acquisition program and collection development policy are based upon its responsibility to provide service to the staff of the Department of Agriculture, U.S. land-grant universities, and the general public in all subjects pertaining to agriculture. The NAL Collection Development Policy (http://www. nal.usda.gov/about/policy/coll_dev_toc.shtml) outlines the scope of subjects collected and the degree of coverage for each subject. This policy is regularly revised to include emerging subject areas and incorporate guidelines for collecting new formats, especially digital formats. NAL collection policies reflect and differentiate the collecting responsibilities of the National Library of Medicine and the Library of Congress. The three national libraries have developed cooperative collection development policy statements for the following subject areas: biotechnology, human nutrition and food, and veterinary sciences.

National Digital Library for Agriculture

Since the mid-1990s NAL has continually revised its collection development strategies to emphasize electronic formats and World Wide Web resources. This has been accompanied by expansion of the amount of agricultural information collected and distributed in electronic formats, as the library makes a transition toward a future National Digital Library for Agriculture.

In January 2007 NAL released a design concept Web site for the digital library and invited public comment. Comments received discussed federated search of NAL collections, the e-Answer service of the American Distance Education Coalition (ADEC), Library of Congress Web sites, the Food and Agriculture Organization of the United Nations (FAO) document repository, the Germplasm Resources Information Network (GRIN) database, and Science.gov.

Special Collections

The NAL special collections program emphasizes access to and preservation of rare and unique materials documenting the history of agriculture and related sciences. Items in the library's special collections include rare books, manuscripts, nursery and seed trade catalogs, posters and photographs, and other rare or unique materials documenting agricultural subjects. Materials date from the 1500s to the late 1900s and include many international sources.

Detailed information about NAL special collections is available on the NAL Web site (http://www.nal.usda.gov/speccoll).

NAL special collections of note include the following:

- The U.S. Department of Agriculture History Collection (http://www.nal. usda.gov/speccoll/collect/history.html), assembled over 80 years by USDA historians, includes letters, memoranda, reports, and papers of USDA officials, as well as photographs, oral histories, and clippings covering the activities of the department from its founding through the early 1990s. A guide to this collection is viewable via the NAL Web site.
- The U.S. Department of Agriculture Pomological Watercolor Collection (http://www.nal.usda.gov/speccoll/collect/pomology.html) includes more than 7,000 expertly detailed, botanically accurate watercolor illustrations of fruits and nuts representing newly introduced varieties, healthy and diseased fruits, and depictions of various stages of development. Created between 1880 and 1915, the watercolor illustrations served as official documentation of the work of the Office of the Pomologist and were used

for creation of chromolithographs in publications distributed widely by the department. Although created for scientific accuracy, the works in this collection are artistic treasures in their own right.

- The Henry G. Gilbert Nursery and Seed Trade Catalog Collection (http://www.nal.usda.gov/speccoll/collect/nursery.html) is a rich collection of historic catalogs of the nursery and seed trade. Started in 1904 by USDA economic botanist Percy L. Ricker, the collection is used by researchers to document the introduction of plants to the United States, study economic trends, and illustrate early developments in American landscape design. The earliest catalogs document the trade to the mid-1700s. NAL continues to collect nursery and seed catalogs.
- The Rare Book Collection (http://www.nal.usda.gov/speccoll/collect/rarebook.html) highlights agriculture's printed historical record and covers a wide variety of subjects. The collection, international in scope, documents early agricultural practices in Britain and Europe as well as the Americas. In 2007 records of 52 items in the NAL Rare Book Collection were added to AGRICOLA (AGRICultural On-Line Access). NAL holdings of Carl Linnaeus, "father of taxonomy," include more than 300 books by or about Linnaeus, among them a rare first edition of his 1735 work *Systema Naturae.*
- NAL offers access to more than 300 manuscript collections (http://www.nal.usda.gov/speccoll/collectionsguide/mssindextemp.shtml) documenting the story of American agriculture and its influence on the world.

In recent years, the library has enhanced access to its special collections by putting digitized images on its Web site. NAL provides in-house research and reference services for its special collections, and offers fee-based duplication services. Detailed indexes to the content of many manuscript collections are available in print as well as on the Web. AGRICOLA—NAL's catalog and index to its collections—includes bibliographic entries for special collection items, manuscripts, and rare books.

In 2007 NAL installed newly acquired shelving in its fifth-floor special collections area to house special collections in secure and environmentally appropriate conditions.

Preservation

NAL is committed to the preservation of its print collections, and has greatly improved its environmental quality to extend the longevity of all materials in the collection. The long-term strategy is to ensure that the growing body of agricultural information is systematically identified, prioritized, preserved, and archived.

The library's digitizing program has digitized a growing collection of USDA publications, including the *Home and Garden Bulletin,* the *Agriculture Information Bulletin,* the *Agricultural Economic Report,* and the *Yearbook of the United States Department of Agriculture.* Other historical USDA publications include the *Report of the Commissioner of Agriculture,* published from 1862 to 1888, continued by the *Report of the Secretary of Agriculture,* published from 1889 to 1893. *Century of Service: The First 100 Years of the United States Department of Agriculture,* published in 1963, explores the history of the department from its establishment in 1862 through the Kennedy administration. NAL also has begun digitizing the popular Agriculture Handbook series, providing online access to these and other full-text publications via the NAL digital repository, known as AgSpace.

AgSpace

AgSpace, the library's digital repository, is a combination of several efforts within NAL under various stages of development and implementation. Among them are the following:

- The library has undertaken several projects to digitize, store, and provide online access to historic print documents. The majority of the nearly 300,000 pages currently available online are USDA documents. The full text of these materials and more information about these digitization projects can be found at http://naldr.nal.usda.gov.
- NAL is developing procedures to collect, store, and make publicly available the current research publications of USDA scientists and employees. As of the close of 2007, more than 7,000 articles had been added to the repository. AgSpace does not yet hold all appropriate research publications, but NAL is working to acquire them. Eventually, AgSpace will be the primary source and first resort to identify and use all USDA publications, research and otherwise.

Long-range plans include collecting, maintaining, and providing access to a broad range of agricultural information in a wide variety of digital formats.

The end result will be a perpetual, reliable, publicly accessible repository of digital documents, datasets, images, audiovisual files, and so forth related to agriculture.

AGRICOLA

AGRICOLA is the catalog and index to NAL collections, as well as a primary public source offering worldwide access to agricultural information. AGRICOLA is searchable on the Web (http://agricola.nal.usda.gov), but may also be accessed on a fee basis through several commercial vendors, both online and on CD-ROM. Users may also subscribe to the AGRICOLA file on a fee basis from the National Technical Information Service, part of the U.S. Department of Commerce.

The AGRICOLA database covers materials in all formats, including printed works from the 15th century onward. The records describe publications and resources encompassing all aspects of agriculture and allied disciplines. Thousands of AGRICOLA records contain links to networked Web resources.

The AGRICOLA database is organized into two components, updated with newly cataloged and indexed materials, searchable separately or together:

- NAL Public Access Catalog, containing citations to books, audiovisual materials, serial titles, and other materials in the NAL collection. AGRICOLA also contains some bibliographic records for items cataloged by other libraries but not held in the NAL collection
- NAL Article Citation Database, which includes citations to serial articles, book chapters, reports, and reprints

In 2007 NAL implemented a rescoped AGRICOLA Index to offer more links to full-text articles and avoid duplication with other abstracting and indexing services. To be considered for indexing in AGRICOLA, publications must meet at least one of the following criteria:

- Be a U.S. Department of Agriculture publication, or contain articles or chapters authored by USDA personnel
- Support NAL Information Centers
- Contain articles or chapters on core agricultural topics, written in English
- Not be indexed by any other abstracting and indexing service

The 2007 list of publications indexed in AGRICOLA can be found at http://riley.nal.usda.gov/nal_display/index.php?info_center=8&tax_level=2&tax_subject=157&topic_id=2010. The rescoped AGRICOLA index will continue to serve as the search tool to access NAL collections.

Information Management and Information Technology

Over the past quarter century, NAL has applied information technology to support managing and providing access to a diverse array of agricultural information. Technological developments spearheaded by the library date back to the 1940s and 1950s, when NAL Director Ralph Shaw invented "electronic machines" such as the photo charger, rapid selector, and photo clerk. NAL has made numerous technological improvements since.

NAL has fully implemented the Voyager integrated library management system (produced by Endeavor Information Systems, now known as the Ex Libris Group). The system supports ordering, receiving, and invoice processing for purchases; creating and maintaining indexing and cataloging records for AGRICOLA; circulation and Online Public Access Catalog. The Voyager system has also been integrated with the Relais (Relais International, Inc.) system for supporting NAL interlibrary loan and document delivery services.

NAL Agricultural Thesaurus

NAL is known for its expertise in developing and using a thesaurus, or controlled vocabulary, a critical component of effective electronic information systems. The NAL Agricultural Thesaurus (NALT) (http://agclass.nal.usda.gov/agt/agt.shtml)

is a hierarchical vocabulary of agricultural and biological terms. Updated annually, NALT broadly defines the subject scope of agriculture, organized according to 17 subject categories and with 2,418 definitions. Biological nomenclature comprises most terms in the thesaurus, although it also includes terminology in the supporting biological, physical, and social sciences. Suggestions for new terms or definitions can be sent by e-mail to thes@nal.usda.gov.

Originally prepared to meet the needs of Agricultural Research Service (ARS) scientists, the NAL Agricultural Thesaurus is now extensively used to aid retrieval in agricultural information systems within USDA and elsewhere. NALT is the indexing vocabulary for NAL's bibliographic database of 3.75 million article citations to agricultural resources included in the AGRICOLA database.

NAL released the sixth edition of NALT in January 2007, adding about 400 new definitions for a total of 68,564 terms. Terminology associated with geospatial technology, agricultural economics, tropical trees, and fire science was expanded in this latest edition. The taxonomic classification of fish was reviewed and updated according to nomenclature approved by the American Fisheries Society.

The NAL Glossary is a collection of definitions of agricultural terms developed in conjunction with the creation of the NAL Agricultural Thesaurus. The 2007 edition contains more than 2,400 terms ranging across agriculture and its many ancillary subjects, most composed by the NAL Thesaurus staff.

NALT-Espanol

In May 2007 NAL published Spanish-language versions of the NAL Agricultural Thesaurus and NAL Glossary in order to support increased access to agricultural information throughout the United States and the world.

This first Spanish-language edition of NALT has more than 15,700 translated concepts and contains definitions for more than 2,400 concepts in both English and Spanish, which are also published in a separate interface as the Glossary of Agricultural Terms. Both language versions of these publications can be accessed through the NAL Services Web page (http://www.nal.usda.gov/services).

Publishing a Spanish-language edition of NALT makes it a valuable bilingual reference tool benefiting both Spanish- and English-speakers. Organizations using NALT terms can easily add a Spanish-language capability to their agricultural information applications.

Of the world's estimated 480 million Spanish-speaking people, about 87 percent live in the Western Hemisphere. Spanish is the second most widely spoken language in the United States and is the most rapidly growing language used in U.S. agriculture. Future Spanish-language editions of NALT will change in response to recommendations from the Spanish-speaking agricultural community and NAL cooperators.

Translation of NALT into Spanish was accomplished by NAL with the American Distance Education Consortium (ADEC). ADEC is a nonprofit international distance education consortium of approximately 65 state universities and land-grant colleges that promotes the creation and provision of high-quality, economical distance education programs and services to diverse audiences.

Library Services

NAL serves the agricultural information needs of customers through traditional library reference, document delivery, and information center services. The main reading room in the library's Beltsville facility has a walk-up service desk, an extensive reference collection, a current periodicals collection, an electronic services center, and a selection of full-text scientific journals. NAL also operates a walk-in reference and electronic services center at USDA headquarters in downtown Washington, D.C. Services at both facilities are available 8:30 to 4:30 Monday through Friday, except federal holidays.

The library makes many of its information resources available to customers worldwide via the NAL Web site (http://www.nal.usda.gov). In 2007 the library delivered nearly 90 million direct customer services throughout the world via its Web site and other Internet-based services.

Information Centers

Operating within NAL's overall program structure, the library's national information centers are reliable sources of science-based information in key areas of U.S. agriculture. By collaborating with other organizations throughout government, the centers provide timely, accurate, comprehensive, and in-depth coverage in their specialized subject areas. Staffs of these information centers make specialized information available through the NAL Web site and help library users find answers to specific questions and undertake extensive research programs.

Each NAL information center has its own Web site and is a partner in the Agriculture Network Information Center (AgNIC). Presently, NAL has eight information centers:

- The Alternative Farming Systems Information Center (AFSIC) (http://afsic.nal.usda.gov) specializes in farming methods that maintain the health and productivity of the entire farming enterprise, including the natural resource base.
- The Animal Welfare Information Center (AWIC) (http://awic.nal.usda.gov) provides scientific information and referrals to help ensure the proper care and treatment of animals used in biomedical research, in teaching, in exhibition, and by animal dealers.
- The Food and Nutrition Information Center (FNIC) (http://fnic.nal.usda.gov) helps consumers, educators, health professionals, the media, researchers, and others locate scientific information relating to food and human nutrition. FNIC maintains a staff of expert information specialists with training in food science and human nutrition. In 2007 it helped launch a NutritionTalk listserv to support the food distribution program on Indian reservations
- The Food Safety Information Center (FSIC) (http://foodsafety.nal.usda.gov) provides links to intergovernmental information resources about food safety, links to nongovernmental food safety research resources, and

information on the risk of food-borne illness and about safe food handling and preparation. During 2007 FSIC added RSS feeds and video to its avian influenza and food safety news sites.

- The National Invasive Species Information Center (NISIC) (http://www. invasivespeciesinfo.gov) is a gateway to invasive species information, covering federal, state, local, and international sources.
- The Rural Information Center (http://ric.nal.usda.gov) provides information and referral services on community economic development, small business development, healthcare access and financing, housing, environment, quality of life, community leadership, and education to organizations and individuals working to maintain the vitality of the nation's communities.
- The Technology Transfer Information Center (http://ttic.nal.usda.gov) works to "get results of research into the hands of those individuals and organizations that can put it into practical use." The center helps individuals and organizations locate information and promote new products and processes.
- The Water Quality Information Center (WQIC) (http://www.nal.usda.gov/wqic) collects, organizes, and communicates the scientific findings, educational methodologies, and public policy issues relating to water resources and agriculture.

In light of intense agricultural interest in biofuels throughout 2007, NAL proposed establishment of a National Agricultural Biofuels Information Center and discussed the concept with USDA leaders. To encourage development of the proposal, NAL staff presented to the American Chemical Society on the subject of "Biofuels: From an Information Perspective."

Web-Based Products and Services

NAL continues to emphasize the expansion of its presence on the World Wide Web to provide access to information for its global clientele on an every-hour-of-every-day basis.

In 2007 the NAL Web site

- Received an average of more than 7 million hits each month from people seeking agricultural information; NAL anticipates that Web site usage will increase in response to the site's user-friendly design, enhanced searching capabilities, and continual improvement in content
- Supported 2007 Farm Bill deliberations with a Web spotlight featuring Farm Bill information resources and relevant links
- Incorporated Distributed eXplorIT into its entire Web site to facilitate comprehensive unified search
- Achieved an American Customer Services Index (ACSI) score of 71 points, an improvement of 5 points from the 2006 level

In September NAL launched an internal Intranet site to help staff access a wide range of administrative and operational tools and information.

In early October the library began its first blog, "InfoFarm: The NAL Blog" (http://weblogs.nal.usda.gov/infofarm), becoming (at the time) the 16th active blog within the federal government. The purpose of InfoFarm is to give NAL a personal "human" voice, give NAL customers a fresh glimpse into what NAL does, and give NAL a chance to converse with its customers. The Special Libraries Association wrote: "InfoFarm is written in an engaging style with lots of links to great Web sites and is certain to interest anyone who eats food. Thanks, NAL!"

Nutrition.gov

In collaboration with other USDA agencies, NAL operates the popular Nutrition.gov (http://www.nutrition.gov) Web site to provide vetted, science-based nutrition information for the general consumer and highlight the latest in nutrition news and tools from across government agencies. A team of dietitians and nutrition information specialists at NAL's Food and Nutrition Information Center maintain Nutrition.gov and provide reference services to answer customer questions on food and nutrition issues.

The site is an important tool for developing food- and exercise-based strategies for weight management, and for disseminating the work of multiple federal agencies in a national obesity-prevention effort.

Nutrition.gov includes databases, recipes, interactive tools, and specialized information for infants and children, adult men and women, and seniors. The site links to information on the USDA food pyramid, dietary guidelines, dietary supplements, fitness, and food safety. It provides a comprehensive source of information on nutrition and dietary guidance from multiple federal agencies.

In 2007 Nutrition.gov averaged more than 350,000 hits a month and was ranked No. 1 by the search engine Google as a source of information on human nutrition. In order of popularity, the top three subjects of information-seekers were "Smart Nutrition 101," weight management, and food composition.

DigiTop

DigiTop, the USDA's Digital Desktop Library, provides online access to thousands of journals in full text, 13 citation databases, hundreds of newspapers from around the world, significant additional digital reference resources, and an array of personalized services. DigiTop is available to the entire USDA work force worldwide—more than 110,000 people—24 hours a day. NAL staff provides continuous user education and training for DigiTop users.

With more than 900,000 articles downloaded from DigiTop in 2007, the monetized value of viewed content is yielding significant return on government's investment, generates unprecedented cost efficiencies, and demonstrates a high value of the program to USDA users.

Document Delivery Services

NAL's document delivery operation responds to requests received from around the world for agricultural information materials. For USDA employees, NAL acquires needed information materials that are not otherwise available from NAL collections.

NAL uses the Relais Enterprise document request system, integrated with its Voyager integrated library system, to support document delivery. This means NAL customers can both request and receive materials electronically and check on the status of their requests via the World Wide Web. NAL no longer accepts document requests submitted via e-mail, ARIEL (Agricultural Research Information Express Loan), fax, or mail. Documents must be requested from NAL via the Web, using AGRICOLA or blank request forms. NAL also accepts requests via OCLC (NAL's symbol is AGL) and DOCLINE (NAL's libid is MDUNAL).

To deliver documents, NAL uses an array of methods as requested by its customers. Library staff, contractors, and cooperators work together to fill document delivery and interlibrary loan requests and deliver them to customers via the Internet through ARIEL, fax, mail, courier, and other means.

National Library of Medicine

8600 Rockville Pike, Bethesda, MD 20894
301-496-6308, 888-346-3656, fax 301-496-4450, e-mail publicinfo@nlm.nih.gov
World Wide Web http://www.nlm.nih.gov

Kathleen Cravedi, Director
Melanie Modlin, Public Affairs Specialist
Office of Communications and Public Liaison

The National Library of Medicine (NLM), in Bethesda, Maryland, is a part of the National Institutes of Health (NIH), U.S. Department of Health and Human Services (HHS). Since its founding in 1836 NLM has played a pivotal role in translating biomedical research into practice. It is the world's largest biomedical library and the developer of electronic information services that deliver trillions of bytes of data to millions of users every day. Scientists, health professionals, and the public in the United States and around the globe search the library's online information resources more than 1 billion times each year.

In today's increasingly digital world, NLM carries out its mission of enabling biomedical research, supporting health care and public health, and promoting healthy behavior by

- Acquiring, organizing, and preserving the world's scholarly biomedical literature
- Providing access to biomedical and health information in partnership with the 5,800-member National Network of Libraries of Medicine (NN/LM)
- Serving, via its National Center for Biotechnology Information (NCBI), as a leading global resource for building, curating, and providing sophisticated access to molecular biology and genomic information, including that of the Human Genome Project and NIH Roadmap
- Creating high-quality information services relevant to toxicology and environmental health, health services research, and public health
- Conducting research and development on biomedical communications systems, methods, technologies, and networks and information dissemination and utilization among health professionals, patients, and the general public
- Funding advanced biomedical informatics research and serving as the primary supporter of pre- and post-doctoral research training in biomedical informatics at 20 U.S. universities

The library is open to all and has many services and resources—for scientists, health professionals, historians, and the general public. NLM has nearly 9.2 million books, journals, manuscripts, audiovisuals, and other forms of medical information on its shelves, making it the largest health science library in the world. Patrons can also have access to a vast collection of books, manuscripts, and art relating to the history of the health sciences. Used not only by scholars, these materials are frequently integrated into exhibitions and displays for visitors. Traveling versions of NLM exhibitions attract crowds across the country.

NLM continues to focus on the goals of its 2006–2016 long-range plan, including key activities in support of interoperable electronic health records, more effective disaster and emergency response, development of a robust knowledge base for personalized health care, and more.

Scientific Information Services

The most frequently consulted online scientific medical resource in the world is MEDLINE/PubMed, a publicly available database of references and abstracts for medical journal articles from 1949 to the present. Increasingly, as resources permit, older materials are being added. Topics such as tuberculosis (with its relevance to AIDS), smallpox (with its relevance to bioterrorism), and influenza (with its relevance to the current avian flu and a possible pandemic human flu) are all examples of how research conducted in the past might shed light on the present.

In 2007 PubMed celebrated its tenth anniversary and added its 17 millionth citation. In addition, links to full-text journals increased from 5,156 in July 2006 to 5,880 in July 2007. (Where links to electronic full text are not available, the user can use PubMed to place an online order for an article directly from a library in the National Network of Libraries of Medicine.)

Another important part of NLM's vast online holdings is PubMed Central (PMC), a Web-based repository of biomedical journal literature providing free, unrestricted access to the full-text of articles. PubMed Central reached the milestone of 1 million articles in June 2007. Web-based usage of PubMed and PubMed Central rose in 2007 by 14 percent worldwide.

The National Center for Biotechnology Information (NCBI) is the source of GenBank, the genetic sequence databank that contains all publicly available DNA sequences. The NCBI produces GenBank from thousands of sequence records submitted directly by researchers and institutions prior to publication. Records submitted to NCBI's international collaborators in Britain and Japan are shared through an automated system of daily updates, using standards developed under NLM's leadership. NCBI is responsible for all phases of GenBank production, support, and distribution, including timely and accurate processing of sequence records and biological review of both new sequence entries and updates to existing entries. Integrated retrieval tools allow seamless searching of the sequence data housed in GenBank and other related resources, including related literature and curated reference gene and genome databases. These resources are essential tools in the analysis of gene function, the identification of disease genes, and the development of new hypotheses about potential therapies.

NCBI collaborates with other NIH institutes to develop special resources and interfaces to support high-priority research initiatives. For example, the Influenza Virus Resource, developed in conjunction with the National Institute of Allergy and Infectious Disease, links researchers working on vaccines to genomic data about the influenza virus. As the data accumulate (about 20,000 new influenza virus sequences were entered into the Influenza Sequence Database in 2007) and the analyses progress, the discoveries made will ultimately lead to better prediction of large-scale outbreaks, more effective vaccine design, and the saving of many human lives.

NCBI also has a prominent role in the important new Genome-Wide Association Studies (GWAS) project, an area that figured prominently in the deliberations of NLM's long-range planners as they discussed the promise of new research correlating genotype, phenotype, and environmental data. GWAS is a major NIH-wide initiative directed at understanding the genetic factors underlying human disease. GWAS involves linking up genotype data with phenotype information in order to identify the genetic factors that influence health, disease, and response to treatment. NCBI is building the databases that will incorporate the clinical and genetic data, link them to the molecular and bibliographic resources at NCBI, and, for the first time, make these data available to the scientific and clinical research community.

In 2007 NCBI significantly expanded its breadth of public resources by developing the database of genotypes and phenotypes, or dbGaP. This database archives and distributes data from genome-wide association studies, medical resequencing, molecular diagnostic arrays, and associations between genotypes and phenotypes. DbGaP and related NCBI databases are important elements in providing a powerful discovery system in which users will be able to glean information from many areas of genetics from a single online search.

It has been 14 years since the Visible Human Male and Visible Human Female datasets were released by NLM's Lister Hill Center. They provide detailed image data sets that serve as a common reference for the study of human anatomy, for testing medical algorithms, and as a model for image libraries that can be accessed through networks. The data sets (some 50 gigabytes in all) are being applied in a wide range of projects by nearly 2,500 licensees in 49 countries. The Visible Human Project has been featured in almost 1,000 newspaper articles, magazines, and radio and television programs worldwide. The Insight Toolkit (ITK), an R&D initiative under the Visible Human Project, makes available a variety of open-source image processing algorithms for computing segmentation and registration of high dimensional medical data. This toolkit continues to have an impact on the medical imaging research community.

Information Services for the Public

The library has extensive information resources to serve the general public—from elementary school children to seniors. NLM's main portal for consumer health information is MedlinePlus, available in English and Spanish (MedlinePlus en Español). Much of this material is based on research done or sponsored by the NIH Institutes, and there are thousands of links to reliable health information that has been reviewed by medical librarians for suitability. MedlinePlus usage has climbed steadily since its introduction in 1998; during 2007 use by the public soared by almost 25 percent over the 2006 level. The site currently sees almost 80 million page views each month. MedlinePlus en Español accounts for about one-third of that total.

Hispanic television star Don Francisco, host of the weekly variety show "Sabado Gigante" ("Giant Saturday"), has teamed with NLM to increase awareness of the Spanish-language version of MedlinePlus. His radio and television public service announcements have expanded the Web site's reach to the growing numbers of Spanish speakers in the United States and throughout Latin America.

MedlinePlus has 750 "health topics." Each topic points the user to reliable information on all aspects of a disease or health condition, clinical trials, complementary and alternative medicine, prevention, management, therapies, current research, and the latest news from the print media. In addition to the health topics, there are medical dictionaries, a medical encyclopedia, directories of hospitals and providers, and links to the scientific literature. There is also a series of surgical videos that show actual operations of common surgical procedures. The MedlinePlus service known as Go Local links users to medical and social services in their community that are related to their interest. With four new sites added in 2007, Go Local now reaches 35 percent of the U.S. population.

One aspect of MedlinePlus relates especially to the long-range goal of providing information services that specifically promote health literacy and reduce health disparities. This is the popular section of MedlinePlus called Interactive Health Tutorials, where the user will find 165 interactive programs featuring color images and sound that explain medical tests, procedures, and conditions in easy-to-read language. Users can also listen as the script of the tutorial is read to them.

ClinicalTrials.gov provides the public with comprehensive information about all types of clinical research studies, both interventional and observational. The site has more than 43,000 protocol records sponsored by the U.S. government, the pharmaceutical industry, and academic and international organizations from all 50 states and in more than 140 countries. Some 44 percent of the trials listed are open to recruitment and the rest are closed to recruitment or completed. ClinicalTrials.gov receives more than 19 million page views a month and hosts approximately 29,000 visitors daily. Data are submitted by more than 3,400 study sponsors through a Web-based Protocol Registration System, which allows providers to maintain and validate information about their trials.

ClinicalTrials.gov also gives links to pages in Genetics Home Reference, NLM's Web site for consumer-friendly health information on genetic conditions. This information resource bridges consumer health information and scientific bioinformatics data, and it links to many existing resources, both at NLM and at other reliable sites. Genetics Home Reference, like ClinicalTrials.gov, is the work of information experts at NLM's Lister Hill Center. Created for the general public, particularly individuals with genetic conditions and their families, the site currently includes summaries for more than 230 genetic conditions, more than 395 genes, and all the human chromosomes. There is also a downloadable *Help Me Understand Genetics* handbook. Usage of Genetics Home Reference increased by more than 60 percent in the past year. The site is recognized as an important health resource.

NLM felt that doctors in the computer age would like to "prescribe" MedlinePlus for their patients as a source of information about health and wellness. Supplying physicians with special prescription pads and information kits, NLM began the Information Rx program (known formally as the Physician Information Prescription Project) in 2003 with the American College of Physicians. In 2007 more than 12,000 members of the American Osteopathic Association joined this outreach effort, which already included hospital library members of the Medical Library Association and disease-focused organizations such as the Fisher Center for Alzheimer's Disease Research, an arm of Rockefeller University. (Genetics Home Reference conducts its own Information Rx program, working with the American Academy of Pediatrics, the American Academy of Family Physicians, the American College of Obstetricians and Gynecologists, and the American College of Medical Genetics. Physicians in these organizations are encouraged to point patients to the online resources available at that NLM site.)

Another information resource for the public is NIHSeniorHealth.gov, which is maintained by the library in collaboration with the National Institute on Aging and other NIH institutes. At present there are 34 topics of interest to seniors, including Alzheimer's disease, macular degeneration, and stroke. NIHSenior Health.gov contains information in a format that is especially usable by seniors (large type, for example), and it also has a "talking" function that allows users to listen as the text is read to them.

There are also information services for the public on toxicology, environmental health, and HIV/AIDS. The Household Products Database, for example, provides easy-to-understand data in consumer-friendly language on the potential health effects of more than 2,000 ingredients contained in more than 7,000 common household products. The Household Products Database has proved to be popular with the news media, and there have been a number of newspaper and magazine articles about it. Another consumer health site is the colorful Tox Town, which looks at an ordinary town and points out many harmful substances and environmental hazards that might exist there. Users can click on a town location, like a school, office, factory, or park and find information about the toxic chemicals that may be encountered there. Other versions are available for a port, a big city, a farm, and the U.S.-Mexico border area. The division has also created a series of information portals targeted at special populations, including Native Americans, Asian Americans, and those living in the Arctic.

The newest Web site from Specialized Information Services is ToxMystery, an interactive Web site for children between ages 7 and 10. ToxMystery provides an animated, game-like interface that prompts children to find potential chemical hazards in a home, and then rewards them with "fun and interesting" sound effects when they successfully complete the task. Focus groups and feedback from the targeted user community have indicated that this innovative Web site provides children with an entertaining and educational experience. In 2007 NLM released the Spanish-language version of this lively interface.

National Network of Libraries of Medicine

NLM's key partner in making information available is the National Network of Libraries of Medicine. The network, begun in the 1960s, today consists of 5,700 member institutions, including eight Regional Medical Libraries that receive NLM support, 125 resource libraries connected to medical schools, and more than 5,000 libraries located primarily in hospitals and clinics.

This network is of great value in helping NLM to reach out to the wider community. Member libraries hold workshops and provide backup services for public libraries and other community organizations, demonstrate NLM databases to the public, and exhibit at meetings and conventions on behalf of NLM, providing the personal element that can be so important in connecting people to high-quality information. As part of the new contracts, the Regional Medical Libraries will be working collaboratively to define an effective national emergency preparedness plan. The experiences and lessons learned from Hurricane Katrina in 2005 will be critical elements in shaping the plan.

Administration

The director of the library, Donald A. B. Lindberg, M.D., is guided in matters of policy by a Board of Regents consisting of 10 appointed and 11 ex officio members.

Table 1 / Selected NLM Statistics*

Library Operation	Volume
Collection (book and nonbook)	11,479,000
Items cataloged	23,000
Serial titles received	20,000
Articles indexed for MEDLINE	608,000
Circulation requests processed	443,000
For interlibrary loan	247,000
For on-site users	196,000
Computerized searches (MEDLINE/PubMed)	845,000,000
Budget authority	$320,962,000
Staff	676

*For the year ending September 30, 2007

United States Government Printing Office

732 North Capitol St. N.W., Washington, DC 20401
202-512-1957, e-mail public-relations@gpo.gov
World Wide Web http://www.gpo.gov

Gary Somerset
Media and Public Relations Manager

The U.S. Government Printing Office (GPO) is the federal government's primary centralized resource for gathering, cataloging, producing, providing, and preserving published information in all its forms. Since its inception, GPO has offered Congress, the courts, and government agencies a set of centralized services, enabling them to produce printed documents easily and cost-effectively according to a uniform set of federal government specifications. In addition, GPO has offered these publications for sale to the public and made them widely available at no cost through the Federal Depository Library Program (FDLP).

Today GPO is at the epicenter of technological change as it embraces its historic mission while looking to the digital future.

GPO is part of the legislative branch of the federal government and operates under the authority of the public printing and documents chapters of Title 44 of the U.S. Code. In addition to Congress, all three branches of the federal government rely on GPO's services. Congressional documents, Supreme Court decisions, federal regulations and reports, IRS tax forms, and U.S. passports are all produced by or through GPO.

GPO's headquarters, which includes a bookstore, is located in Washington, D.C. Nationwide, GPO maintains 16 field locations and a major distribution facility in Pueblo, Colorado.

GPO's information-dissemination activities include FDLP, which disseminates information products from all three branches of the government to more than 1,250 libraries nationwide; GPO Access, which provides online access to titles on GPO servers as well as links to titles on other federal Web sites; and a Publications Sales Program that sells government publications to the public. Together, these activities disseminate one of the world's largest volumes of published information. This report focuses on GPO's role as the disseminator of government information in print and electronic formats.

Federal Digital System

GPO's Federal Digital System (FDsys) will manage, preserve, provide version control and access to, and disseminate authentic U.S. government information. FDsys will include all known federal government documents within the scope of GPO's FDLP and other information-dissemination programs. The system design is based on the Reference Model for an Open Archival Information System (OAIS) (ISO 14721:2003).

FDsys will allow federal content creators to submit content to be preserved, authenticated, managed, and delivered upon request. Content entered into the system will be cataloged according to GPO metadata and document-creation standards. This content will be available for Web searching, Internet viewing, downloading and printing, and as document masters for conventional and on-demand printing or other dissemination methods. Content may include text and associated graphics, including print, digital, video, audio, and other forms that may emerge.

FDsys capabilities will be deployed in a series of releases. An internal release of FDsys as a proof-of-concept to test core functionality was completed in September 2007. It supports FDsys formal and informal beta testing. This was released to limited internal and external audiences to ensure that the foundation for FDsys is operating as expected. The first public release of FDsys is expected to roll out in late 2008.

For a comprehensive discussion of system capabilities by release, see the FDsys documentation at http://www.gpo.gov/projects/fdsys_documents.htm.

Web Discovery and Harvesting

Harvesting technologies are used to discover and capture official U.S. government publications not cataloged by GPO but within the scope of its FDLP and Cataloging and Indexing Program. GPO defines harvested content as individual publications residing on publicly accessible federal agency Web sites and within the scope of its dissemination programs; these publications are archived digitally.

GPO currently acquires online publications primarily through manual and semi-manual harvesting of individual publications. GPO has begun testing technologies to harvest numerous online publications through automated tools that identify and assess them.

During 2006 GPO conducted a six-month pilot project to harvest online Environmental Protection Agency (EPA) publications automatically. This was a collaborative project implemented by GPO, EPA, and two vendors. The goal was to learn about available methodologies and technologies for automated Web discovery, assessment, and harvesting of U.S. government publications within the scope of GPO's information-dissemination programs. GPO will use the lessons learned from this project to continue the development of automated publication-harvesting tools and methodologies in preparation for full implementation along with FDsys.

GPO staff processed a sample of 300 publications harvested during the pilot project. The purpose was to determine workflow and staffing implications as well as to estimate the amount of time that would be required to process all of the publications acquired during the project.

GPO also tested two methods of making accessible those publications within the scope of FDLP. The majority of publications in the sample (200) are accessible through cataloging records in the Catalog of U.S. Government Publications (CGP). A smaller portion of the sample (approximately 100) is posted to GPO Access, using a browse table. These publications are not cataloged in CGP.

GPO has completed a study of the feasibility of classifying and cataloging the monographs and serials acquired through the automated Web harvesting pilot and is now beginning to process the remaining in-scope monographs and serials acquired during the pilot.

Authentication

As more government information becomes available electronically, data integrity and non-repudiation of information become more critical. In furthering its mission to provide permanent public access to authentic U.S. government publications, GPO is working to afford users further assurance that files electronically disseminated through GPO Access remain unchanged after GPO authenticates them, and to provide security for and safeguard federal government publications within the scope of FDLP.

In May 2007 GPO launched its beta release of authenticated Public and Private Laws, in pdf format, for the 110th Congress. Public and private laws within this application contain digitally signed and certified pdf files that feature GPO's Seal of Authenticity. These files have been signed digitally and certified using Public Key Infrastructure (PKI) technology. GPO is using PKI and Digital Signature technologies to verify the authenticity of the electronic U.S. government documents that it disseminates through FDLP. The Seal of Authenticity notifies users that a document has not been altered since it was authenticated and disseminated by GPO.

GPO also has awarded a contract for the development of an Automated pdf Signing (APS) system for the application of digital signatures on pdf files. This will enable application of digital signatures in a more timely, efficient, and cost-effective manner than can be achieved manually. The same procurement includes a validation mechanism that will enable users to view easily the authentication information for digitally signed pdf documents. GPO staff has been working with the contractors to develop this tool. Development of the APS system is nearly complete, and GPO staff will begin its implementation into the GPO Access workflow upon its deployment.

Online Training

GPO has begun to provide Web-based training sessions on subjects pertaining to FDLP, using Online Programming for All Libraries (OPAL). GPO has conducted online training sessions on some of its new initiatives, and these sessions have been collected and archived. GPO staff also is developing guidelines and evaluation criteria to allow the library community to present training sessions via OPAL. An archive of GPO OPAL presentations can be viewed at http://www.opal-online.org/archiveGPO.htm.

Handles

In early 1999 GPO initiated the use of Persistent Uniform Resource Locators (PURLs) to provide a persistent URL for cataloging records of depository items available online. A review of existing technologies available at the time pointed to OCLC's PURLs as the most appropriate software available to provide this service.

In the intervening years, problems have emerged in the use of PURLs, including, but not limited to, scalability issues intrinsic to the PURL software.

This software was developed with the expectation that it would be used for local products, and that far fewer PURLs would be needed than actually has been the case. In addition, security concerns associated with the technology suggested the need for migration from PURLs.

A review of existing persistent identifiers led GPO to select the Corporation for National Research Initiatives (CNRI) Handle System as the technology for the persistent identification solution. The open source nature of the CNRI Handle System software means it will be easier to make any special modifications GPO might require; and CNRI also actively upgrades its software as needs arise. The transition from PURLs to handles will be a gradual one, involving a series of tests. Ultimately, the plan includes not only the implementation of new procedures for handles, but also the migration of current PURLs.

Integrated Library System

The overall goal of the implementation of GPO's Integrated Library System (ILS) is the provision of access to bibliographic records of federal government publications, many containing links to the electronic version of the publication, by depositories and the public, as well as the use of the system's power and capabilities to provide needed services. The goal is also to streamline workflow and internal activities in support of FDLP, and to reduce use of and dependency on legacy systems.

The enhanced online *Catalog of Government Publications* (*CGP*) is an index of public documents from all three branches of the federal government, currently covering 1976 forward. In the online information environment, the new *CGP* is essential to GPO's core mission of ensuring that the public has access to federal government information. *CGP* continues to move forward in providing public access to government publications. From its launch in March 2006 through November 2007, more than 34,300,000 requests were made of *CGP,* for an average of 54,000 per day. The enhanced *CGP* is a component of a modernization plan to replace older legacy systems with GPO's state-of-the-art ILS. *CGP* can be found at http://catalog.gpo.gov.

Future enhancements to GPO's ILS include

- Enabling Z39.50 access, which allows libraries and the public to access and extract bibliographic records from *CGP*
- Upgrading the ILS Aleph software to version 18
- Implementing the MetaLib federated searching product (multi-database searching capability) available from *CGP*

Automated Metadata Extraction Project

GPO is working on an initiative to create cataloging records for publications identified from the Web-harvesting pilot project and other publications in its Library Technical Information Services workflow by using automated metadata extraction software tools and processes developed by the Defense Technical

Information Center (DTIC) in collaboration with Old Dominion University (ODU) in Norfolk, Virginia.

GPO has completed initial project and timeline planning and delivered 500 documents to ODU for analysis. Upon completion of the extensive analysis phase, GPO can then determine the ultimate feasibility of software developed through this project being used in its library services operations.

Federal Depository Library Handbook

In December 2007 GPO released the *Federal Depository Library Handbook*, a living policy document written by and for the FDLP community. This publication supersedes *Instructions to Depository Libraries* and the *Federal Depository Library Manual* (including its four supplements).

Within the handbook are best practices, tips, and links to additional information of interest to depository coordinators. The handbook includes 15 chapters and five appendices. Each includes requirements and performance examples, with an emphasis on the electronic FDLP.

The handbook is being developed in two phases. Phase 1 is complete, with the consolidation of the *Instructions* and *Manual* into one online publication. GPO is now beginning Phase 2, which will update the publication further, develop needed policies, and revise any policies that require it. GPO's work on the handbook is ongoing, using teams from the community, in-house GPO staff, the Depository Library Council, professional library associations, and others. To access the handbook, visit http://www.fdlp.gov/handbook/index.html.

FDLP Partnerships

GPO currently has 15 partnerships with federal depository libraries and federal agencies, and is working to increase the number of its partnerships to guarantee permanent public access to digitized government content and material contained within databases.

During fiscal year (FY) 2007 GPO entered into a partnership with the U.S. Commission on Civil Rights and the University of Maryland's Thurgood Marshall Law Library for Historic Publications of the U.S. Commission on Civil Rights. Also in FY 2007, GPO entered a partnership with Southern Methodist University for Historic Publications from World War II.

Distribution and Other Statistics

During FY 2007 GPO distributed a total of 4,509,718 tangible copies of 8,837 titles (this includes print, microfiche, CDs, and DVDs). U.S. Geological Survey (USGS) map distribution during FY 2007 included 585 titles and 151,065 copies, a jump from 72,018 copies in FY 2006.

For FY 2007, 17,177 bibliographic records were created, up from 11,414 in FY 2006. A total of 11,909 PURLs were created, of which 7,144 are links to publications on agency Web sites, up from 11,083 PURLs created in FY 2006 and 6,619 being linked to publications on agency Web sites.

For FY 2007, 94 percent of the depository titles distributed were available online, and only 6 percent were tangible-only with no electronic equivalent. About 22 percent of the titles distributed were available online and in one or more tangible formats.

GPO Access

Under the mandate of Public Law 103-40, GPO is required to maintain an electronic directory of federal electronic information, provide a system of online access to the *Congressional Record,* the *Federal Register,* and other appropriate publications, and operate an electronic storage facility for federal electronic information. GPO's response to this mandate was the launch of GPO Access in 1994. GPO Access began with three databases; today it allows worldwide access to almost 4,000 databases and more than 80 applications. GPO also has a firm commitment to permanent public access. Once federal information has been placed on GPO Access, this information will be archived there indefinitely.

Since its inception, GPO Access has experienced a continuous and steady usage increase. There were approximately 450,288,176 GPO Access retrievals in FY 2007.

With more than 283,000 available titles, GPO Access contains a wide variety of applications, ranging from congressional and legislative information to federal regulations and presidential materials. GPO also hosts 19 federal Web sites, including that of the United States Supreme Court, as well as a reference suite of services for finding federal government information.

Ben's Guide

Ben's Guide to U.S. Government (http://bensguide.gpo.gov), the educational component of GPO Access, strives to introduce and explain for school-age audiences the workings of all three branches of the federal government. Through the use of primary source materials, grade-appropriate explanations, and an educational and stimulating site design, Ben's Guide not only increases the access to and knowledge of the federal government, but makes learning fun.

The site is broken down into four grade levels (K–2, 3–5, 6–8, and 9–12) and also provides an area for parents and educators. The material in each of these sections is tailored specifically for its intended audience. Ben's Guide includes information such as historical documents, the legislative and regulatory processes, elections, and citizenship. The site also features learning activities and a list of federal Web sites designed for students, parents, and educators.

New and on the Horizon
FDLP Desktop

In May 2007 GPO unveiled a beta redesign of FDLP Desktop. The redesign's goal is to balance the mission of FDLP with the latest Web tools to enhance users' interaction with GPO and their colleagues.

The redesigned FDLP Desktop provides a complete site search, new and improved forms, and options that allow users to create individual profiles.

Another feature of the new Desktop is FDLP Express, which allows registered members of the FDLP Desktop to sign up and receive e-mail alerts based on various categories.

Additionally, users will have access to new features:

- Individual user profiles
- Self-moderated "Needs and Offers"
- Online ordering of GPO promotional materials with order tracking
- Private messaging
- Moderated online chats
- Discussion forums

The new FDLP Desktop is available at http://www.fdlp.gov.

Bound Congressional Record

The 2001 bound *Congressional Record* was made available on GPO Access in December 2007 at http://www.gpoaccess.gov/crecordbound/index.html.

The online version is fully searchable and browseable, making it a comprehensive guide to the contents and an enhanced aid in tracking legislation. The daily edition of the *Congressional Record* has been available on GPO Access since 1994. Because the page numbers and indices in the daily and bound *Congressional Record* are not the same, the addition of the online bound *Record* to GPO Access provides users with "one-stop shopping" when researching the work of Congress.

The *Congressional Record* is the official record of the proceedings and debates of the United States Congress, published daily when Congress is in session. At the end of each session, all of the daily editions are collected, re-paginated, and reindexed into a permanent, bound edition. The permanent edition is made up of one volume per session of Congress, with each volume containing multiple parts.

Statutes at Large

The *United States Statutes at Large* (Vol. 118, 108th Congress, Second Session) was made available online in February 2007 at http://www.gpoaccess.gov/statutes/index.html. The *Statutes at Large* is the permanent collection of all laws and resolutions enacted during each session of Congress. Every public and private law passed by Congress is published in the *Statutes at Large* in the order of the date it was enacted into law. The laws are arranged by public law number and are cited by volume and page number. Also included are concurrent resolutions, proclamations by the president, proposed and ratified amendments to the Constitution, and reorganization plans.

Public Papers of the Presidents of the United States

The *Public Papers of the Presidents of the United States: George W. Bush,* Books I and II–2003 and Book I–2004 were made available in 2007 at http://www. gpoaccess.gov/pubpapers/gwbush.html. Each *Public Papers* volume contains the papers and speeches of the president that were issued by the Office of the Press Secretary during the specified time period. The material is presented in chronological order, and the dates shown in the headings are the dates of the documents or events.

Guide to House and Senate Members

GPO Access now contains an online Guide to the House and Senate Members of the 110th Congress at http://www.memberguide.gpoaccess.gov. This resource is intended to be a single point of access for Member information from several different official sources and provides

- Access to data concerning House and Senate Members from various publications including the *Congressional Pictorial Directory, Congressional Biographical Directory,* and, in the near future, the *Congressional Directory*
- Search and retrieval capability for individual members by name, district, hometown, or groups of members by state, party affiliation, or number of terms
- Links to an individual member's corresponding information in the *Biographical Directory* maintained by the House and Senate

Conference Reports

To comply with an amendment to the Standing Rules of the Senate, GPO has updated the Conference Reports Web page on GPO Access at http://www. conferencereport.gpoaccess.gov. A conference report is an agreement on legislation that is negotiated between the House and Senate via conference committees. It is printed and submitted to each chamber for its consideration.

Normally, conference reports are printed and made available online in the *Congressional Record* the day after they have been filed. When GPO is unable to print a conference report the next day, GPO will scan the manuscript and post a searchable pdf of the manuscript on this Web page. Otherwise, links to the conference reports as they appear in the *Congressional Record* will be posted on the Web page. Links to each conference report will be date- and time-stamped to establish when the conference report was first made available to the public online. If a conference report is scanned as manuscript, that version will be superseded when the conference report is made available in the *Congressional Record.* Links to a conference report in the *Congressional Record* will be superseded when the conference report is made available in the congressional reports database.

Upcoming Releases

GPO plans to release the 2005 *United States Statutes at Large* (Volume 119, 109th Congress, First Session) by winter 2008.

Selling Government Publications

GPO's Sales Program currently offers approximately 5,500 individual government titles on a broad array of subjects. They are sold principally via the Internet, e-mail, telephone, fax, and mail. The program operates on a cost-recovery basis. Publications for sale include books, forms, posters, pamphlets, microfiche, CD-ROMs, computer diskettes, and magnetic tapes. Subscription services for both dated periodicals and basic-and-supplement services (involving an initial volume and supplemental issues) also are offered.

GPO's U.S. Government Online Bookstore is the public's prime source of information on its sales inventory. The Online Bookstore includes a searchable database of all in-print publications, as well as an extensive archive of recently out of print titles. It also includes a broad spectrum of special publication collections featuring new and popular titles and key product lines. GPO uses Pay.gov, a secure governmentwide financial management transaction portal available around the clock seven days a week for timely and efficient processing of online orders. The Online Bookstore also provides the option of expedited shipping via USPS Priority and Express Mail, new and improved shopping cart and order confirmation e-mails, and expanded ordering options for international customers.

Express service, which includes priority handling and expedited delivery, is available for orders placed by telephone for domestic delivery. Orders placed before noon eastern time for in-stock publications and single-copy subscriptions will be delivered within two working days. The telephone order desk can be reached toll-free at 866-512-1800 (or 202-512-1800 within the Washington, D.C., area).

Consumer-oriented publications also are either sold or distributed at no charge through the Federal Citizen Information Center, in Pueblo, Colorado, which GPO operates on behalf of the General Services Administration.

Members of the public can register free of charge to receive e-mail updates when new publications become available for sale through GPO's New Titles by Topic E-mail Alert Service. This service can be accessed at http://bookstore.gpo.gov/help/searching.jsp#email.

Standing Order Service is available to ensure automatic receipt of many of GPO's most popular recurring and series publications. Standing-order customers receive each new edition automatically as soon as it is published. This service can be set up using a MasterCard, American Express, or Discover credit card, or a Superintendent of Documents Deposit Account. For more information on how to set up a standing order for recurring or series publications, e-mail Contact Center@gpo.gov or call 866-512-1800.

The GPO sales program has begun using print-on-demand technology to increase the long-term availability of publications and is testing the capabilities of a number of vendors. Sales also has brought its bibliographic practices more in line with those of the commercial publishing sector by using ONIX (Online Information Exchange), the publishing industry's standard electronic format for sharing product data with wholesale and retail booksellers, other publishers, and anyone else involved in the sale of books. ONIX enables GPO to have government publications listed, promoted, and sold by commercial book dealers worldwide. GPO sales titles are listed on Amazon.com, Barnesandnoble.com, and other online commercial bookselling sites.

National Technical Information Service

U.S. Department of Commerce, Springfield, VA 22161
800-553-NTIS (6847) or 703-605-6000
World Wide Web http://www.ntis.gov

Linda Davis
Marketing Communications

The National Technical Information Service (NTIS) serves as the nation's largest central source and primary disseminator of scientific, technical, engineering, and business information produced or sponsored by U.S. and international government sources. NTIS is a federal agency within the U.S. Department of Commerce.

Since 1945 the NTIS mission has been to operate a central U.S. government access point for scientific and technical information useful to American industry and government. NTIS maintains a permanent archive of this declassified information for researchers, businesses, and the public to access quickly and easily. Release of the information is intended to promote U.S. economic growth and development and to increase U.S. competitiveness in the world market.

The NTIS collection of more than 2 million titles contains products available in various formats. Such information includes reports describing research conducted or sponsored by federal agencies and their contractors, statistical and business information, U.S. military publications, multimedia training programs, computer software and electronic databases developed by federal agencies, and technical reports prepared by research organizations worldwide. NTIS maintains a permanent repository of its information products.

More than 200 U.S. government agencies contribute to the NTIS collection, including the National Aeronautics and Space Administration; Environmental Protection Agency; the departments of Agriculture, Commerce, Defense, Energy, Health and Human Services, Interior, Labor, Treasury, Veterans Affairs, Housing and Urban Development, Education, and Transportation; and numerous other agencies. International contributors include Canada, Japan, Britain, and several European countries.

NTIS on The Web

NTIS offers Web-based access to the latest government scientific and technical research information products. Visitors to http://www.ntis.gov can search the entire collection dating back to 1964 free of charge. NTIS also provides downloading capability for many technical reports, and purchase of the publications on CD as well as paper copies.

NTIS Database

The NTIS Database (listings of information products acquired by NTIS since 1964) offers unparalleled bibliographic coverage of U.S. government and worldwide government-sponsored research. Its contents represent hundreds of billions of research dollars and cover a range of important topics including agriculture, biotechnology, business, communication, energy, engineering, the environment, health and safety, medicine, research and development, science, space, technology, and transportation.

Most records include abstracts. Database summaries describe technical reports, datafiles, multimedia/training programs, and software. These titles are often unique to NTIS and generally are difficult to locate from any other source. The complete NTIS Database provides instant access to more than 2 million records.

Free 30-day trials of the NTIS Database are available through the GOV. Research_Center (http://grc.ntis.gov). The NTIS Database can be leased directly from NTIS and can also be accessed through several commercial services. For an updated list of organizations offering NTIS Database products, see http://www. ntis.gov/products/commercial.aspx.

To lease the NTIS Database directly from NTIS, contact the NTIS Subscriptions Department at 800-363-2068 or 703-605-6060. For more information, see http://www.ntis.gov/products/ntisdb.aspx.

Other Databases Available from NTIS

NTIS offers several valuable research-oriented database products. To find out more about accessing the databases, visit http://www.ntis.gov/products/types/databases/data.asp.

FEDRIP

The Federal Research in Progress Database (FEDRIP) provides access to information about ongoing federally funded projects in the fields of the physical sciences, engineering, and life sciences. The ongoing research announced in FEDRIP is an important component of the technology transfer process in the United States; FEDRIP's uniqueness lies in its structure as a nonbibliographic information source of research in progress. Project descriptions generally include project title, keywords, start date, estimated completion date, principal investigator, performing and sponsoring organizations, summary, and progress report. Record content varies depending on the source agency.

There are many reasons to search FEDRIP. Among these are to avoid research duplication, locate sources of support, identify leads in the literature, stimulate ideas for planning, identify gaps in areas of investigation, and locate individuals with expertise. To access an updated list of organizations offering FEDRIP Database products, see http://www.ntis.gov/products/fedrip.aspx.

AGRICOLA

As one of the most comprehensive sources of U.S. agricultural and life sciences information, the Agricultural Online Access Database (AGRICOLA) contains bibliographic records for documents acquired by the National Agricultural Library (NAL) of the U.S. Department of Agriculture. The complete database dates from 1970 and contains more than 4 million citations to journal articles, monographs, theses, patents, software, audiovisual materials, and technical reports relating to agriculture. AGRICOLA serves as the document locator and bibliographic control system for the NAL collection. The extensive file provides comprehensive coverage of newly acquired worldwide publications in agriculture and related fields. AGRICOLA covers the field of agriculture in the broadest sense. Subjects include Agricultural Economics, Agricultural Education, Agricultural Products, Animal Science, Aquaculture, Biotechnology, Botany, Cytology, Energy, Engineering, Feed Science, Fertilizers, Fibers and Textiles, Food and Nutrition, Forestry, Horticulture, Human Ecology, Human Nutrition, Hydrology, Hydroponics, Microbiology, Natural Resources, Pesticides, Physiology, Plant and Animal, Plant Sciences, Public Health, Rural Sociology, Soil Sciences, Veterinary Medicine, and Water Quality. To access an updated list of organizations offering AGRICOLA Database products, see http://www.ntis.gov/products/agricola.aspx.

AGRIS

The International Information System for the Agricultural Science and Technology (AGRIS) Database is a cooperative system for collecting and disseminating information on the world's agricultural literature in which more than 100 national and multinational centers take part. References to citations for U.S. publications given coverage in the AGRICOLA Database are not included in AGRIS. A large number of citations in AGRIS are not found in any other database. References to nonconventional literature (documents not commercially available) contain a note explaining where a copy may be obtained. AGRIS can be used to find citations to agricultural information from around the world. Much of this information includes government documents, technical reports, and nonconventional literature that have their source in both developed and developing countries and that can be found nowhere else. To access an updated list of organizations offering AGRIS Database products, see http://www.ntis.gov/products/agris.aspx.

Energy Science and Technology

The Energy Science and Technology Database (EDB) is a multidisciplinary file containing worldwide references to basic and applied scientific and technical research literature. The information is collected for use by government managers, researchers at national laboratories, and other research efforts sponsored by the U.S. Department of Energy, and the results of this research are transferred to the public. Abstracts are included for records from 1976 to the present. EDB also contains the Nuclear Science Abstracts, a comprehensive abstract and index collection to the international nuclear science and technology literature for the period 1948–1976. Included are scientific and technical reports of the U.S. Atomic Energy Commission, U.S. Energy Research and Development Administration and its contractors, other agencies, universities, and industrial and research organizations. Approximately 25 percent of the records in the file contain abstracts. Nuclear Science Abstracts contains more than 900,000 bibliographic records. The entire EDB contains more than 3 million bibliographic records. To access an updated list of organizations offering EDB products, see http://www.ntis.gov/products/engsci.aspx.

Specialized Online Subscriptions

Those wishing to expand their access to subject-specific resources through use of the Internet are likely to benefit from the NTIS online options highlighted below. Online subscriptions offer quick, convenient online access to the most current information available.

Government Research Center

The GOV.Research_Center (GRC) is a collection of well-known government-sponsored research databases available on the World Wide Web via an online subscription service. Customers can subscribe to a single GRC Database product or to several databases. The following databases made available at the GOV. Research_Center by NTIS and the National Information Services Corporation (NISC) are searchable at the site utilizing NISC's Biblioline search engine: the NTIS Database, FEDRIP, NIOSHTIC, EDB, Nuclear Science Abstracts Database, AgroBase, AGRICOLA, and RTECS.

NTIS and NISC are constantly improving the content and features of GRC. Online ordering allows ordering of documents directly from the NTIS Database by using a credit card or NTIS deposit account; cross-database searching allows use of a single search query across all databases within a subscription plan. Limited day-pass access to the NTIS Database is available for a nominal fee.

For more information, visit the GOV.Research_Center at http://grc.ntis.gov.

World News Connection

World News Connection (WNC) is an NTIS online news service accessible only via the World Wide Web. WNC makes available English-language translations of time-sensitive news and information from thousands of non-U.S. media. Particularly effective in its coverage of local media, WNC provides the power to identify what is happening in a specific country or region. The information is obtained from speeches, television and radio broadcasts, newspaper articles, periodicals, and books. The subject matter focuses on socioeconomic, political, scientific, technical, and environmental issues and events.

The information in WNC is provided to NTIS by the Foreign Broadcast Information Service (FBIS), a U.S. government agency. For more than 60 years, analysts from FBIS's domestic and overseas bureaus have monitored timely and pertinent open source material, including gray literature. Uniquely, WNC allows subscribers to take advantage of the intelligence-gathering experience of FBIS.

WNC is updated every government business day. Generally, new information is available within 24 to 72 hours of the time of original publication or broadcast.

Subscribers can conduct unlimited interactive searches and have the ability to set up automated searches known as profiles. When a profile is created, a search is run against WNC's latest news feed to identify articles relevant to a subscriber's topic of interest. The results are automatically sent to the subscriber's e-mail address.

Access to WNC is available through Dialog Corporation. To use the service, complete the WNC form at http://www.dialog.com/contacts/forms/wnc.shtml.

U.S. Export Administration Regulations

U.S. Export Administration Regulations (EAR) provides the latest rules controlling the export of U.S. dual-use commodities, technology, and software. Step by step, EAR explains when an export license is necessary and when it is not, how to obtain an export license, policy changes as they are issued, new restrictions on exports to certain countries and of certain types of items, and where to obtain further help.

This information is now available through NTIS in looseleaf form, on CD-ROM, and online. An e-mail update notification service is also available.

For more information, see http://bxa.fedworld.gov.

Special Subscription Services

NTIS Alerts

More than 1,000 new titles are added to the NTIS collection every week. NTIS Alerts were developed in response to requests from customers to search and tap into this newly obtained information. NTIS prepares a list of search criteria that is run against all new studies and research and development reports in 16 subject areas. An NTIS Alert provides a twice-monthly information briefing service covering a wide range of technology topics.

An NTIS Alert provides numerous benefits: efficient, economical, and timely access to the latest U.S. government technical studies; concise, easy-to-read summaries; information not readily available from any other source; contributions from more than 100 countries; and subheadings within each issue designed to identify essential information quickly.

For more information, call the NTIS Subscriptions Department at 703-605-6060 or see http://www.ntis.gov/products/alerts.aspx.

SRIM

Selected Research in Microfiche (SRIM) is an inexpensive, tailored information service that delivers full-text microfiche copies of technical reports based on a customer's needs. Customers choose between Standard SRIM Service (selecting one or more of the 320 existing subject areas) or Custom SRIM Service, which creates a new subject area to meet their particular needs. Custom SRIM Service requires a one-time fee to cover the cost of strategy development and computer programming to set up a profile. Except for this fee, the cost of Custom SRIM is the same as the Standard SRIM. Through this ongoing subscription service, customers receive microfiche copies of new reports pertaining to their field(s) of interest, as NTIS obtains the reports.

For more information, see http://www.ntis.gov/products/srim.aspx. To place an order, call 800-363-2068 or 703-605-6060.

The SRIM service is also available in CD-ROM format—Science and Technology on CD. Documents are digitized and stored in pdf format that can easily be viewed using free Adobe Acrobat Reader software. With Science and Technology on CD, NTIS can provide more publications—those that cannot be rendered on microfiche, such as colorized illustrations or oversized formats.

For more information, see http://www.ntis.gov/products/STonCD.aspx. To place an order, call 800-363-2068 or 703-605-6060.

NTIS Customer Service

NTIS's automated systems keep it at the forefront when it comes to customer service. Shopping online at NTIS is safe and secure; its secure socket layer (SSL) software is among the best available today.

Electronic document storage is fully integrated with NTIS's order-taking process, allowing it to provide rapid reproduction for the most recent additions to the NTIS document collection. Most orders for shipment are filled and delivered anywhere in the United States in five to seven business days. Rush service is available for an additional fee.

Key NTIS Contacts for Ordering

Order by Phone

Sales Desk   800-553-6847 or 703-605-6000
8:30 A.M.–5:00 P.M. Eastern time, Monday–Friday

Subscriptions   800-363-2068 or 703-605-6060
8:30 A.M.–5:00 P.M. Eastern time, Monday–Friday

TDD (hearing impaired only)   703-487-4639
8:30 A.M.–5:00 P.M. Eastern time, Monday–Friday

Order by Fax

24 hours a day, seven days a week   703-605-6900

To verify receipt of fax, call 703-605-6090, 7:00 A.M.–5:00 P.M. Eastern time, Monday–Friday

Order by Mail

National Technical Information Service
5285 Port Royal Road
Springfield, VA 22161

RUSH Service (available for an additional fee)   800-553-6847 or 703-605-6000
Note: If requesting RUSH Service, please do not mail your order

Order Via World Wide Web

Direct and secure online ordering   http://www.ntis.gov

Order Via E-Mail

24 hours a day   orders@ntis.gov

For Internet security, customers placing an order by e-mail can register their credit card in advance. To do so, call 703-605-6070 between 7:00 A.M. and 5:00 P.M. Eastern time, Monday through Friday.

National Archives and Records Administration

8601 Adelphi Road, College Park, MD 20740
301-837-2000, World Wide Web http://www.archives.gov

Susan M. Ashtianie
Director, Policy and Planning Staff

The National Archives and Records Administration (NARA), an independent federal agency, is the nation's record keeper. NARA safeguards and preserves the records of the federal government so that the people can discover, use, and learn from this documentary heritage. NARA ensures continuing access to the essential documentation of the rights of U.S. citizens and the actions of their government.

NARA is singular among the world's archives as a unified federal institution that accessions and preserves materials from all three branches of government. It carries out its mission through a national network of archives and records services facilities stretching from Washington, D.C., to the West Coast, including presidential libraries documenting administrations back to President Herbert Hoover. NARA assists federal agencies in documenting their activities, administering records management programs, scheduling records, and retiring noncurrent records to federal records centers. The agency also assists the National Historical Publications and Records Commission in its grant program for state and local records and edited publications of the papers of prominent Americans; publishes the laws, regulations, presidential documents, and other official notices of the federal government through the *Federal Register*; and oversees classification and declassification policy in the federal government through the Information Security Oversight Office. NARA constituents include the federal government, educators and their students at all levels, a history-minded public, the media, the archival community, and a broad spectrum of professional associations and researchers in such fields as history, political science, law, library and information services, and genealogy.

The size and breadth of NARA's holdings are staggering. Together, NARA's facilities hold almost 29 million cubic feet (equivalent to more than 87 billion pieces of paper) of original textual and nontextual materials from the executive, legislative, and judicial branches of the federal government.

Its multimedia collections include close to 117,000 motion picture films; more than 8 million maps, charts, and architectural drawings; more than 250,000 sound and video recordings; more than 27 million aerial photographs; more than 14 million still pictures and posters; and more than 4.7 billion electronic records.

Strategic Directions

NARA's strategic priorities are laid out in *Preserving the Past to Protect the Future: The Strategic Plan of the National Archives and Records Administration*

2006–2016. Success for the agency as envisioned in the plan centers on six strategic goals:

- As the nation's record keeper, NARA will ensure the continuity and effective operation of federal programs by expanding its leadership and services in managing the government's records.
- NARA will preserve and process records to ensure access by the public as soon as legally possible.
- NARA will address the challenges of electronic records in government to ensure success in fulfilling NARA's mission in the digital era.
- NARA will provide prompt, easy, and secure access to its holdings anywhere, anytime.
- NARA will increase access to its records in ways that further civic literacy in the United States through museums, public outreach, and education programs.
- NARA will be equipped to meet the changing needs of its customers.

The plan lays out strategies for reaching these goals, sets milestone targets for accomplishments through 2016, and identifies measurements for gauging progress. The targets and measurements are further delineated in NARA's annual performance plans.

The strategic plan and annual performance plans, as well as performance and accountability reports, are available on the NARA Web site at http://www. archives.gov/about/plans-reports or by calling 301-837-1850.

Records and Access

Internet

NARA's Web site, http://www.archives.gov, provides the most widely available means of electronic access to information about the agency and its services. Feedback from visitors to the Web site as well as visitors to the National Archives Building in Washington, D.C., led to portals designed to support the particular needs of genealogists, veterans and their families, educators and students, researchers, the general public, records managers, journalists, information security specialists, members of Congress, and federal employees.

The site includes directions on how to contact NARA and do research at its facilities; descriptions of its holdings in an online catalog at http://www.archives. gov/research/arc; direct access to certain archival electronic records at http:// www.archives.gov/aad; digital copies of selected archival documents; an Internet Web form, at http://www.archives.gov/contact/inquire-form.html, for customer questions, reference requests, comments, and complaints; electronic versions of *Federal Register* publications; online exhibits; classroom resources for students and teachers; and online tools, such as the Web-based, interactive inquiry program at http://www.archives.gov/veterans/evetrecs that allows veterans and the next-of-kin of deceased veterans to complete and print, for mail-in submission, requests for their service records.

Copies of military pension records from the American Revolution through World War I, census pages, land files, court records, and microfilm publications can be ordered online as well as books, apparel, and accessories at http://www.archives.gov/order. Researchers can also submit reference questions about various research topics online.

Visitors to NARA's Web site can now obtain Really Simple Syndication (RSS) feeds of the "Document for Today" feature, NARA news, and press releases. In 2008 NARA's online National Archives Experience will launch a new interactive digital vault featuring more than 1,200 records including documents, photographs, videos, and audio files. The interactive digital vault allows visitors to create their own exhibit experience.

In cooperation with several federal agencies, NARA also has established a Web portal, http://www.regulations.gov/search/index.jsp, providing access to federal rules and instructions for submitting comments on federal regulatory actions.

Archival Research Catalog

As a result of NARA's Archival Research Catalog (ARC), anyone with a computer connected to the Internet can search descriptions of NARA's nationwide holdings and view digital copies of some of its most popular documents. A significant piece of the electronic access strategy outlined in NARA's strategic plan, this online catalog of all NARA holdings nationwide allows the public to search for information about NARA's vast holdings, including those in the regional archives and presidential libraries, in a single online data system. Because of the vast extent of NARA holdings, it will take several years to fully populate ARC. The catalog already contains more than 1.5 million descriptions of archival holdings, representing more than 55 percent of NARA's vast and growing collection, and more than 126,000 digital copies of high-interest documents. The documents available online include many of the holdings highlighted in the Public Vaults, NARA's permanent interactive exhibition. The catalog is available at http://www.archives.gov/research/arc.

Electronic Records Archives

NARA's Electronic Records Archives (ERA) is its strategic initiative to preserve and provide long-term access to uniquely valuable electronic records of the federal government, and to transition governmentwide management of the lifecycle of all records into the realm of e-government. ERA will be a comprehensive, systematic, and dynamic means of preserving virtually any kind of electronic record, free from dependence on any specific hardware or software, and will support NARA's mission by making it easy for the public and government officials to discover, use, and trust the records of the government, and to make it easy for the National Archives to deliver those records in formats people can use.

NARA's needs are multidimensional: it has to help all other agencies manage the records they need for current business; it has to provide access to all types of records in the National Archives, presidential libraries, and federal records centers to anyone interested in them; in doing so, it has to ensure that legal restrictions—in its case, virtually any restrictions on any type of government information—on access are met; and it has to find a way to preserve and provide sustained access to an ever larger and ever more complex body of electronic records in a way that ensures the authenticity of the records while taking advantage of continuing improvements in technologies for search, access, and delivery of digital information.

The development of the ERA system passed a significant milestone with the delivery of three software "pilots" from the developer, Lockheed Martin Corporation. The first software pilot supports creating and processing records schedules and requests for transfer of records; the second added system functions for transferring electronic records; and the third provides tools for automated inspection of electronic records.

Government testing of the first pilot was performed by engineers and other technical subject matter experts within the National Archives. Testing of the next two phases was expanded to include officials from other federal agencies and from members of the Advisory Committee on ERA. NARA expects to complete product and operational testing and put the system into operation by the end of June 2008.

NARA's main objective in developing the ERA system is to create a robust, high-quality system that meets the federal government's records management and archival needs, and to create a system that will be easy to use. Ensuring that ERA will help NARA meet its business needs as well as the needs of its stakeholders is not an easy task.

The National Archives Experience

In September 2003 NARA reopened the Rotunda for the Charters of Freedom at the National Archives Building in Washington, D.C., after a two-year renovation project. Returned to display were the Declaration of Independence, the Constitution, and the Bill of Rights, known collectively as the Charters of Freedom, which had received conservation treatment and were placed in new state-of-the-art encasements. For the first time, all four pages of the Constitution are on permanent display, and all the documents are now easier to view by young visitors and those using wheelchairs. The reopening of the Rotunda launched the National Archives Experience—a set of interconnected resources, made possible by a public-private partnership between NARA and the Foundation for the National Archives, that provide a variety of ways of exploring the power and importance of the nation's records.

The National Archives Experience continued to expand in 2004 with the opening of the William G. McGowan Theater, the unveiling of the Public Vaults, and the inauguration of the Lawrence F. O'Brien Gallery. The 290-seat McGowan Theater is a state-of-the-art showplace for NARA's extensive audiovisual holdings and serves as a forum for lectures and discussion. It also is home to the new Charles Guggenheim Center for the Documentary Film. The Public Vaults is a 9,000-square-foot permanent exhibition that conveys the feeling of going beyond the walls of the Rotunda and into the stacks and vaults of the working archives. Dozens of individual exhibits, many of them interactive, reveal the breadth and variety of NARA's holdings. Complementing the Public Vaults, the O'Brien Gallery hosts a changing array of topical exhibits based on National Archives records. In spring 2006 NARA opened the first phase of the Boeing Learning Center, the ReSource Room, which is an access point for teachers and parents to explore documents found in the exhibits and to use the records as teaching tools. In spring 2007 NARA opened the second phase of the Boeing Learning Center, its Constitution-in-Action Learning Lab, designed to provide an intense field trip adventure for middle and high school students that links to curriculum in the classroom.

A set of Web pages now makes the entire National Archives Experience available online. An illustrated history of the Charters of Freedom can be found, as well as information on educational programs, special events, and exhibits currently at the National Archives. For more information, see the National Archives Experience at http://www.archives.gov/national-archives-experience.

National Archives Building Research Center

At NARA's Robert M. Warner Research Center, researchers can consult with staff experts on records in the National Archives Building and submit requests to examine original documents. The center houses approximately 275,000 rolls of microfilmed records, documenting military service prior to the First World War, immigration into the United States, the federal census, Congress, federal courts in the District of Columbia, the Bureau of Indian Affairs, and the Freedmen's Bureau. The center also contains an ever-expanding system of reference reports, helping researchers conduct research in federal documents.

Archives Library Information Center

The Archives Library Information Center (ALIC) provides access to information on American history and government, archival administration, information management, and government documents. ALIC is physically located in two traditional libraries in the National Archives facilities in Washington and in College Park, Maryland. Customers also can visit ALIC on the Internet at http://www.archives.gov/research/alic, which offers "Reference at Your Desk" Internet links, staff-compiled bibliographies and publications, an online library catalog, and more. ALIC can be reached by phone at 202-357-5018 in Washington and 301-837-3415 in College Park.

Government Documents

Federal government publications are generally available to researchers at many of the 1,250 congressionally designated federal depository libraries throughout the United States. A record set of these publications also is part of NARA's archival holdings. Publications of the U.S. Government (Record Group 287) is a collection of selected publications of federal government agencies, arranged by the classification system (SuDoc System) devised by the Office of the Superintendent of Documents, Government Printing Office (GPO). The core of the collection is a library established in 1895 by GPO's Public Documents Division. By 1972, when NARA acquired the library, it included official publications dating from the early years of the federal government and selected publications produced for and by federal government agencies. Since 1972 the 25,000-cubic-foot collection has been augmented periodically with accessions of federal government publications selected by the Office of the Superintendent of Documents as a byproduct of its cataloging activity. As with the federal depository library collections, the holdings in NARA's Record Group 287 comprise only a portion of all federal government publications.

NARA Publications

NARA publishes guides and indexes to various portions of its archival holdings; catalogs of microfilmed records; informational leaflets and brochures; general interest books about NARA and its holdings that will appeal to anyone with an interest in U.S. history; more-specialized publications that will be useful to scholars, archivists, records managers, historians, researchers, and educators; facsimiles of certain documents; and *Prologue,* a scholarly journal published quarterly. Some publications are also available on NARA's Web site at http://www.archives.gov/publications/online.html. Many are available from NARA's Customer Service Center in College Park by phoning 800-234-8861 or 866-272-6272 or faxing 301-837-0483. The NARA Web site's publications home page, http://www.archives.gov/publications, provides detailed information about available publications and ordering.

Federal Register

The *Federal Register* is a daily gazette containing presidential documents, new and amended federal regulations, and public notices from executive agencies. The *Federal Register* is published by the Office of the Federal Register and printed and distributed by GPO. The two agencies collaborate in the same way to produce the annual revisions of the *Code of Federal Regulations (CFR).* Free access to the full text of the electronic version of the *Federal Register* and *CFR* is available through the GPO Access service, on the Internet at http://www.gpoaccess.gov. Access to rules published in the *Federal Register* and open for public comment, and a portal for submitting comments are also provided through the multiagency Web site http://www.regulations.gov. The full texts of other Federal Register publications are available through GPO Access, including the *Weekly Compilation of Presidential Documents, Public Papers of the President,* slip laws, *United States Statutes at Large,* and the *United States Government Manual.* All of these publications also are maintained at all federal depository libraries. The *Electronic Code of Federal Regulations (eCFR)* is an unofficial, currently updated online publication also available through the GPO Access service. Public Law Electronic Notification Service is a free subscription e-mail service that delivers notification of recently enacted public laws. The Federal Register Table of Contents Service is a free e-mail service available for delivery of the daily table of contents from the *Federal Register* with direct links to documents. The Office of the Federal Register also publishes information about its ministerial responsibilities associated with the operation of the Electoral College and ratification of constitutional amendments, and provides access to related records. Publication information concerning laws, regulations, and presidential documents and services is available from the Office of the Federal Register (telephone 202-741-6000). Information about, and additional finding aids, for Federal Register publications, the Electoral College, and constitutional amendments can also be found at http://www.archives.gov/federal-register. Publications can be ordered from GPO by writing to New Orders, Superintendent of Documents, P.O. Box 371954, Pittsburgh, PA 15250-7954.

Customer Service

Few records repositories serve as many customers as NARA. In fiscal year 2007 there were more than 138,000 research visits to NARA facilities nationwide, including archives, presidential libraries, and federal records centers. At the same time, more than 1.2 million customers requested information in writing. NARA also served the executive agencies of the federal government, the courts, and Congress by providing records storage, reference service, training, advice, and guidance on many issues relating to records management. Federal records centers replied to more than 10 million requests for information and records, including more than 1.1 million requests for information regarding military and civilian service records provided by the National Personnel Records Center in St. Louis. NARA also makes informative public programs available to more than 12,000 people at its various facilities. More than a million visited the National Archives Experience in Washington, and exhibits in the presidential library museums were visited by more than 2 million.

NARA knows it must understand who its customers are and what they need to ensure they can discover, use, and learn from their documentary heritage in the National Archives. Customers are surveyed regularly to help NARA align its standards of performance with their expectations. By repeating surveys at frequent, systematic intervals, changes in NARA's performance are measured and appropriate management actions are taken to ensure that service levels reflect an appropriate balance between customer needs and NARA resources. NARA also maintains an Internet form (http://www.archives.gov/contact/inquire-form.html) to facilitate continuous feedback from customers about what is most important to them and what NARA might do better to meet their needs.

Grants

The National Historical Publications and Records Commission (NHPRC) is the grant-making affiliate of NARA. The Archivist of the United States chairs the commission and makes grants on its recommendation. The commission's 14 other members represent the president of the United States (two appointees), the U.S. Supreme Court, the U.S. Senate and House of Representatives, the U.S. Departments of State and Defense, the Librarian of Congress, the American Association for State and Local History, the American Historical Association, the Association for Documentary Editing, the National Association of Government Archives and Records Administrators, the Organization of American Historians, and the Society of American Archivists.

NHPRC carries out a statutory mission to ensure understanding of the nation's past by promoting nationwide the identification, preservation, and dissemination of essential historical documentation. The commission supports the creation and publication of documentary editions and basic and applied research in the management and preservation of authentic electronic records, and it works in partnership with a national network of state historical records advisory boards to develop a national archival infrastructure. NHPRC grants help state and local governments, and archives, universities, historical societies, professional organizations, and other nonprofit organizations to establish or strengthen archival programs, improve training and techniques, preserve and process records collections, and provide access to them through finding aids and documentary editions of the papers of significant historical figures and movements in U.S. history. For more information about the commission, see http://www.archives.gov/nhprc.

Administration

NARA employs approximately 3,050 people, of whom about 2,400 are full-time permanent staff members. NARA's budget appropriation for fiscal year 2008 is $411.1 million.

Federal Library and Information Center Committee

101 Independence Ave. S.E., Room 217, Washington, DC 20540-4935
202-707-4800, fax 202-707-4818, e-mail flicc@loc.gov

Roberta I. Shaffer
Executive Director

Highlights of the Year

During fiscal year (FY) 2007, the Federal Library and Information Center Committee (FLICC) continued its mission to foster excellence in federal library and information services through interagency cooperation and to provide guidance and direction for FEDLINK, the Federal Library and Information Network.

FLICC membership quarterly meetings focused on a variety of broad federal information issues including strategic planning for federal information organizations and libraries.

FLICC working groups completed an ambitious agenda in FY 2007. Notably, the Competitive Sourcing Working Group completed an analysis of the history and current practices of federal competitive sourcing of federal libraries; the Education Working Group presented a variety of seminars and workshops, including a week-long program for federal library technicians, and a variety of other workshops, seminars, and institutes on cataloging, pay banding, creating wikis for federal libraries, competencies, digital futures, and other information science policy issues; and the Content Management Working Group sponsored an update on digital preservation and workshops on Web standards, information architecture, taxonomy, and librarians as members of the agency management team.

The FLICC Awards Working Group announced the winners of the Federal Library/Information Center of the Year, Federal Librarian of the Year, and Federal Library Technician of the Year.

FLICC added a new All About FEDLINK video series of four segments: *An Introduction to FLICC/FEDLINK, The Benefits of FEDLINK, FEDLINK Membership,* and *FEDLINK's Products and Services.* In addition to these basic program marketing videos, FLICC also posted the video *Careers in Federal Libraries,* an information session about federal job opportunities presented by a cadre of highly successful federal librarians.

FLICC also continued its collaboration with the general counsel of the Library of Congress on a series of meetings between federal agency legal counsels and agency librarians. Now in their ninth year, these forums grew out of the recognition that federal attorneys and librarians share many of the same concerns regarding issues relating to copyright law, privacy law, the Freedom of Information Act, and other laws in the electronic age, with regard both to using information within an agency and to publishing the agency's own information. These meetings have enhanced the relationship between agency attorneys and librarians and have helped them develop contacts with their counterparts at other agencies.

The 2007 series featured discussions on legal issues relating to electronically stored information, copyright issues, and best practices for federal agency Web sites.

FLICC's cooperative network, FEDLINK, continued to enhance its fiscal operations while providing its members with $68.8 million in transfer-pay services, $8.1 million in direct-pay services, and an estimated $41.6 million in Direct Express services, saving federal agencies more than $15.4 million in vendor volume discounts and approximately $17.4 million more in cost avoidance.

To meet the requirements of the Fiscal Operations Improvement Act of 2000 (P.L. 106-481), which created new statutory authority for FEDLINK's fee-based activities, FEDLINK governing bodies and staff members developed the second year of its rolling five-year business plan from FY 2006. In winter 2007 FEDLINK released, via the Internet, its annual survey directed at FLICC/FEDLINK leadership and members. Budgeting efforts projected both costs and revenue, looking at private sector and historic costs with adjustments calculated based on vendor and Government Accountability Office (GAO) predictions. Throughout June and July, FLICC/FEDLINK staff began work in earnest on the 2008–2012 Business Plan. With data compiled from this effort and programmatic planning assistance from FLICC's governing bodies, staff members applied these items to Library of Congress strategic planning and management reports for FY 2008.

During FY 2007 FEDLINK continued to give federal agencies cost-effective access to an array of automated information retrieval services for online research, cataloging, and resource sharing. FEDLINK members also procured print serials, electronic journals, books and other publications, and document delivery and preservation services via Library of Congress/FEDLINK contracts with more than 130 major vendors. The program obtained further discounts for customers through consortia and enterprise-wide licenses for journals, aggregated information retrieval services, and electronic books. FEDLINK awarded six new contracts for electronic retrieval services and competed requirements for serials subscription services for six agencies under contracts with seven serial subscription agents. FEDLINK staff consulted with six agencies to use the new preservation contracts to digitize and conserve special collections and create related metadata.

FY 2007 also saw innovative education initiatives, including workshops and seminars on cataloging, taxonomy, preservation and disaster planning, project management, copyright, digital content management, Web 2.0, and career development. Staff members sponsored 30 seminars and workshops for 1,147 participants, 25 on-site training classes for 198 students, and 3 off-site programs for 60 participants.

Staff members also served as principal speakers and leaders at a variety of national information community and professional association committees and conferences including the American Library Association (ALA) and its Federal and Armed Forces Libraries Round Table (FAFLRT), the Special Libraries Association (SLA), CENDI (the interagency working group of senior scientific and technical information managers), ARMA International, the North American Serials Interest Group (NASIG), the American Society for Information Science and Technology (ASIS&T), Army libraries, and the Military Librarians Workshop.

They also represented federal libraries' needs at national discussions focused on disaster recovery and preservation best practices and at such regional events as the GAO Expo.

FEDLINK also negotiated discounted rates for several national conferences, including Information Today, Inc.'s 2007 Computers in Libraries and WebSearch University conferences. More than 300 attendees registered through FEDLINK to attend Computers in Libraries 2007, saving the federal government approximately $70,000. FEDLINK also offered discount registrations for the Joint Spring Workshop and the Special Libraries Association conference.

FEDLINK Member Services, with the support of Library of Congress Information Technology Services (ITS), completed the release of the amendments module for the online interagency agreement (IAG) Customer Registration System. The amendments feature represents the last stage in automation of the requests for establishing and modifying customer agency agreements. It also allows customers and vendors to update their point of contact information and to review data online they have provided to FEDLINK within the parameters of the ITS security guidelines.

The FEDLINK program began undertaking initiatives to upgrade and restructure its customer-support systems to meet the objectives of the business plan and provide customers a more secure and user-friendly environment to acquire FEDLINK services. FEDLINK is collaborating with ITS to create the FEDLINK Customer Financial System (FCFS), which will significantly enhance the ability of vendors and member agencies to buy and sell library services online once it becomes fully operational.

FEDLINK's continuing financial management efforts also ensured that FEDLINK successfully passed the library's financial audit of FY 2006 transactions.

Quarterly Membership Meetings

Beyond regular FLICC Working Group updates and reports from FLICC/FEDLINK staff members, each FLICC quarterly meeting included a special meeting focus on a variety of broad federal information issues, including strategic planning for federal information organizations and libraries with a showcase from the Library of Congress, Government Printing Office, and the National Library of Medicine; the Library of Congress preservation strategy and disaster planning initiatives; skill sets and services for future federal librarians; and a variety of special reports on the National Agricultural Library, the National Aeronautics and Space Administration (NASA) Goddard Library, the Online Computer Library Center (OCLC), and a number of library association efforts.

Executive Board

The FLICC Executive Board focused its efforts on a number of initiatives relating to the FLICC/FEDLINK Business Plan, the future of the Environmental Protection Agency and NASA libraries and other agency libraries, the Department of Defense policy on advanced funding, a federal library census, the Library of Congress national preservation strategy, and disaster planning.

FLICC Working Groups

Awards

To honor the innovative ways in which federal libraries, librarians, and library technicians fulfill the information demands of government, business, research, scholarly communities, and the public, the FLICC Awards Working Group administered a series of national awards for federal librarianship.

The Federal Library/Information Center of the Year award, Large Library/ Information Center Category (for libraries with a staff of 11 or more federal and/or contract employees) went to the Camp S. D. Butler Library System, Marine Corps Community Services, Okinawa, Japan. The library was recognized for superior effort in enhancing the quality of life for more than 50,000 U.S. servicemen and servicewomen in Japan. In FY 2006 the library system supported 550,000 patron visits, increasing customer use by 14 percent and receiving a customer satisfaction rating above 98 percent. Evidence of the system's energy, enthusiasm, and success was shown in streamlined efforts in economical and efficient acquisitions, cataloging and processing of materials, the ability to offer nearly 500 individual programs for service members and their families, and dedication to maintaining eight libraries, three reading rooms, and a technical services facility.

The award in the Small Library/Information Center Category (for facilities with a staff of 10 or fewer federal and/or contract employees) went to the George C. Marshall European Center for Security Studies Library, Garmisch-Partenkirchen, Germany. The library was recognized for effectiveness, versatility, and dedication to the customer. The library embarked on a series of planning, marketing, training, outreach, and service enhancement initiatives in 2006. By realigning duties, introducing efficiencies, and making judicious use of staff language skills, the library developed and achieved nearly 60 percent of a multiyear strategic plan, expanded a multilingual Web site, hosted 120 facility tours, and completed more than 50 briefings to visiting members of the German parliament and U.S. defense leadership. The library also expanded and enhanced its collection, reference, and cataloging functions at an exacting pace. This led to an increase in e-book collections and database and online services, the creation of bibliographies on terrorism and knowledge portals, and the development of a value-added online catalog.

The award for Federal Librarian of the Year went to Carla Pomager, systems/acquisition librarian for the Army General Library Program within Community Recreation, Family and Morale, Welfare and Recreation Command, U.S. Army, Alexandria, Virginia. Pomager was honored for her role in creating the General Library Information System (GLIS), which provides information services to deployed servicemen and servicewomen as if they were visiting their home base library. Pomager led the effort to create the "My Library Page" on the Army Knowledge Online Web site, which saw nearly 120,000 hits in just three months.

Sabrina D. Honda, a library technician at Hurlburt (Florida) Field Library, was named Federal Library Technician of the Year. Known for her innovative programs, Honda implemented 120 events that attracted more than 3,000 participants. She also coordinated the logistics for the library's renovation and led the team responsible for relocating more than 35,000 volumes.

Budget and Finance

The Budget and Finance Working Group developed the FY 2008 FEDLINK budget and fee structure in the spring quarter. The group produced an online budget questionnaire for FEDLINK members and used the results to verify assumptions for the FY 2008 budget. The final budget for FY 2008 kept membership fees for transfer-pay customers at FY 2007 levels: 7.75 percent on accounts up to $300,000 and 7 percent on amounts exceeding $300,000. Direct-pay fees also remained at FY 2007 levels, as did Direct Express fees of 0.75 percent for all participating commercial online information services vendors. Library officials approved the budget in August 2007.

Consortia and InterAgency Cooperative Activities

During summer 2007 FLICC established the Consortia and InterAgency Cooperative Activities (CIC) Working Group. CIC serves as a steering committee to help identify opportunities for establishing more consortia under the FEDLINK program; to help define best practices and the necessary parameters for successful federal consortia; to serve as adviser to FLICC/FEDLINK program managers and contracting officers when they are negotiating specific consortia terms and conditions; and to serve as adviser to FLICC/FEDLINK program managers concerning communications to members and vendors about existing and potential consortia. The working group reviewed existing consortia to help explore what value FEDLINK could add to efforts to expand or maintain federal consortial arrangements. Members established contact with several vendor management teams to encourage the establishment of FEDLINK group contracts and group purchases of selected services.

Education

During FY 2007 the Education Working Group, in concert with other FLICC working groups, sponsored a total of 30 seminars, workshops, and lunchtime discussions for 1,147 members of the federal library and information center community. These programs focused on cataloging, taxonomy, preservation and disaster planning, project management, copyright, digital content management, Web 2.0, and career development.

Human Resources

The Human Resources Working Group developed draft guidelines of competencies for federal librarians for the U.S. Office of Personnel Management (OPM). The working group also met with representatives of OPM to understand better and comply with federal personnel initiatives.

Libraries and Emerging Technologies

The Libraries and Emerging Technologies working group broadened its focus to better address changing technologies in information services. It developed a federal track of sessions for the Computers in Libraries conference and helped

Figure 1 / FLICC Education Events and Attendees

Event	Attendees
U.S. Copyright Issues Online	10
Great Escape/U.S. Naval Observatory Library	20
Digital Content Management: Compliance in the Digital Age	5
Managing Copyright Issues Online (online course)	8
FEDLINK Fall Membership Meeting and Vendor Forum	82
FEDLINK Fall OCLC Users Group Meeting	38
Great Escape/National Gallery of Art Library	30
Planning Your Library's Physical Space to Maximize Position	46
Identifying and Analyzing Extremist Groups' Digital Artifacts	23
Great Escapes/National Library of Medicine	35
Proving Ground for Information Architecture and Taxonomy	36
Soaring to Excellence/Best New Technologies	32
Library Project Management	39
Great Escape/Institute for Defense Analysis	15
Soaring to Excellence/Next Generation Librarianship	32
Using the GPO Contract for Library Binding	33
Web Conferencing for Libraries	28
Joint Spring Workshop/Envisioning the Future	148
Disaster Planning for Libraries	20
Great Escapes/Pentagon Library	22
Soaring to Excellence/The Best from the Web	32
Spring OCLC Users Meeting	43
Everything You Should Know About Starting a Privacy Program	18
Spring FEDLINK Membership Meeting	56
User Generated Content and Traditional Publishing	36
ALA Annual Conference: "Ever Thought of Working as a FED?"	150
Great Escapes/Census Bureau Library	40
Demystifying Mold	30
Integrated Pest Management	15
Managing and Preserving Digital Materials	25
Total attendance	1,147

ALA's Federal and Armed Forces Libraries Round Table develop a conference session on open access.

Nominating

The Nominating Working Group oversaw the 2007 election process for FLICC rotating members, FLICC Executive Board members, and the FEDLINK Advisory Council. Librarians representing a variety of federal agencies agreed to place their names in nomination for these positions.

Policy and Advocacy

The Policy and Advocacy Working Group established an advisory group to provide recommendations for the planning and modernization of the Environmental Protection Agency (EPA) library (at EPA's request) and formed a marketing subgroup. The subgroup planned a template/guidelines for federal libraries to communicate with their customers and for marketing purposes, and produced a marketing and advocacy resource bibliography.

Preservation and Binding

The Preservation and Binding Working Group continued its oversight of FEDLINK's preservation basic ordering agreements (BOAs) with preservation services vendors and use of the U.S. Government Printing Office (GPO) binding contract. It also planned and cosponsored, with the Education Working Group, several preservation workshops for the Library of Congress and other federal libraries.

Executive Director's Office

FLICC staff participated in the library-wide supervisory focus group and development of mandatory supervisory courses. Staff members also participated in the overall Library of Congress strategic planning process.

A number of staff volunteered for a variety of strategic planning working groups. Staff members contributed their expertise to determine the types of works to be acquired for the library's collections, including international acquisitions, with input from federal agencies, the scholarly community, and university libraries. Other strategic planning groups involving FLICC staff looked into federal government document digitization and access, reference and loan copy services, and national and international disaster response efforts, and offered disaster-recovery training for library professionals, a Knowledge Navigators program to prepare librarians for service in the digital era, and approaches to strengthen communication with FLICC users and monitor satisfaction with its services. Staff also participated in the annual Blacks in Government (BIG) conference and were active within the library's BIG chapter.

Publications and Education Office

In FY 2007 FLICC continued its publication program as a digital communication provider and used the FEDLIB listserv to communicate advocacy and program information to more than 3,000 electronic subscribers.

The office revised mission-critical materials and developed targeted resources to support the FEDLINK program, including revisions to the 2007–2011 Business Plan and three FEDLINK Information Alerts. It also produced the minutes of the four FY 2007 FLICC Quarterly Meetings and six FLICC Executive Board meetings, and all FLICC Education Program promotional and support materials, including the FLICC Forum announcement, forum attendee and speaker badges, press advisories, speeches and speaker remarks, and forum collateral materials. Thirty-two meeting announcements were produced to promote FLICC education programs, FEDLINK membership and OCLC users' meetings, brown-bag discussion series, and education institutes, along with badges, programs, certificates of completion, and other supporting materials. Staff members also contributed to strategic planning working groups and created program management documentation for management reports and other support materials.

FLICC and FEDLINK staff members continued to manage, support, and update the FLICC/FEDLINK Web site, which consists of more than 3,000 pages of content, video, and resource links. Special Web projects this year included redesigning electronic meeting announcements, information alerts, continuing to update the HTML code on all new and revised Web pages to meet both the library's and the World Wide Web Consortium's HTML code validation and access requirements, and working closely with the library's Office of Strategic Initiatives to lay the groundwork for a complete site redesign to meet Library of Congress branding initiatives. Staff also joined the Federal Consortium on Second Life as part of ongoing efforts to monitor the development of Web 2.0 emerging technologies.

In collaboration with FEDLINK Network Operations staff members, FLICC Publications staff continued to offer resources for the FEDLINK members/ vendors forums, OCLC Usage Analysis Reports, pricing data, and many other new documents, including the FY 2007 budget questionnaire and ballot, the FLICC/FEDLINK customer survey in support of the business plan, and the development of the Policy Working Group's marketing and advocacy survey, in addition to a variety of training resources.

During FY 2007 publications staff members continued to support the Member Services Unit and their Online Registration/Online Interagency Agreement (IAG) system. As part of the inaugural of the Online Amendments module, staff redesigned and updated the Online Registration site to achieve its seamless fiscal year transitions.

In conjunction with the working groups, FLICC offered a total of 30 seminars, workshops, and lunchtime discussions to 1,147 members of the federal library and information center community. Institutes and workshops looked at cataloging, taxonomy, preservation and disaster planning, project management, copyright, digital content management, Web 2.0, and career development. FLICC also collaborated with OCLC CAPCON on educational events by co-promoting programs and opening events to each other's members when registrations were available.

FLICC demonstrated its ongoing commitment to library technicians' continuing education by hosting a popular teleconference series, "Soaring to . . . Excellence," produced by the College of DuPage. Federal and academic librarians also joined FLICC professionals to discuss various areas of librarianship, including taxonomies, acquisitions, cataloging, copyright laws, reference, and automation. The ongoing FLICC Great Escapes series returned in FY 2007 with library tours at the U.S. Naval Observatory, the Pentagon, and the Census Bureau.

FLICC also provided organizational, promotional, and logistical support for FEDLINK meetings and events including the FEDLINK Fall and Spring Membership Meetings, two FEDLINK OCLC Users Group meetings, and 49 vendor presentations with 345 customers attending.

FEDLINK

In FY 2007 FEDLINK, the Federal Library and Information Network, continued to give federal agencies cost-effective access to an array of automated information-retrieval services for online research, cataloging, and interlibrary loan. FEDLINK members also procured print serials, electronic journals, books and other publications, document delivery, and preservation services via Library of Congress/FEDLINK contracts with approximately 130 major vendors. The program obtained further discounts for customers through consortia and enterprise-wide licenses for journals, aggregated information retrieval services, and electronic books.

Specifically, FEDLINK awarded six new contracts for electronic retrieval services and competed requirements for serials subscription services for six agencies under contracts with seven serial subscription agents. FEDLINK staff assisted six agencies in using the preservation contracts to digitize and conserve special collections and to create related metadata.

FEDLINK staff highlighted services at national library conferences including those held by ALA, SLA, CENDI, and others as well as such regional events as the Government Accountability Office Expo. During ALA's Annual Conference in Washington, D.C., FLICC joined with the Library of Congress in welcoming attendees and cosponsored a session on careers in federal libraries that drew more than 300 participants from library schools across the country using Web conferencing technologies.

At the North American Serials Interest Group (NASIG), FEDLINK staff represented federal libraries' needs in a discussion about increasing NASIG's relevancy to nonacademic libraries. They also represented federal libraries' needs at national discussions focused on disaster recovery and preservation best practices.

The FEDLINK Advisory Council met six times during the fiscal year. In addition to its general oversight activities, the council advised FEDLINK managers on priorities for the 2008–2012 five-year business plan, provided valuable insight into trends in the information industry, and supported adoption of the proposed FY 2008 budget.

When the Department of Defense issued a directive prohibiting prepayment for services procured from other agencies, FLICC worked with library leaders and general counsels in the Army, Navy, and Air Force to establish that the directive did not apply to the FEDLINK program.

FEDLINK's liaison to the FLICC Preservation and Binding Working Group has also worked with the Library of Congress Preservation Directorate, and has been answering preservation-related inquiries received from the public through the Library of Congress "Ask a Librarian" service.

To expand its customer service communications, FLICC investigated options for Web conferencing, resulting in a test of the Ohio Private Academic Libraries (OPAL) system and a subsequent pilot project with "Elluminate Live!" to improve remote access to FLICC/FEDLINK programs and workshops, vendor demonstrations, and working group and oversight committee meetings. FEDLINK also began a new monthly electronic newsletter to communicate training opportunities and items of interest relating to contracts and program activities.

FEDLINK/OCLC Network Activity

Both FEDLINK OCLC Users Group meetings, held in November and May, provided in-depth presentations on OCLC's expanded Web services with improved interfaces for cataloging, interlibrary loan, reference databases, and full text in FirstSearch and NetLibrary, and with QuestionPoint, the Library of Congress-OCLC cooperative digital reference system. FEDLINK collaborated with CAPCON to sponsored joint QuestionPoint Users Group meetings to help libraries share information about implementation and user-training issues and to provide updates on new functionality. FEDLINK staff members supplemented OCLC meetings with postings on electronic lists, extensive telephone consultations, and e-mail.

Eleanor Frierson, deputy director of the National Agricultural Library, and Suzanne Ryder, associate librarian at the Naval Research Laboratory Library, represented FEDLINK on the OCLC Members Council, adding a federal perspective to the larger issues in librarianship and information science and contributing to plans that meet the cooperative needs of libraries and similar institutions.

Training Program

The 2007 FEDLINK training program included 25 on-site training classes for 198 students and 3 offsite programs for 60 recipients. These included presentations at the U.S. Army-Europe Headquarters in Germany on creating a business plan, the OCLC Collection Analysis tool, and a FLICC/FEDLINK update.

During 2007 FEDLINK allowed members to use their FEDLINK training accounts to pay for conference attendance and brokered member attendance rates at both the Joint Spring Workshop and the SLA Annual Conference. Forty-five FEDLINK members registered through FEDLINK for the Joint Spring Workshop, saving $1,100, and nine attendees registered for SLA through FEDLINK. FEDLINK also negotiated discounted rates for several national conferences, including Information Today, Inc.'s Computers in Libraries 2007 and WebSearch University conferences.

FEDLINK Fiscal Operations

FEDLINK, continued to enhance its fiscal operations while providing its members with $68.8 million in transfer-pay services, $8.1 million in direct-pay services, and an estimated $41.6 million in Direct Express services, saving federal agencies more than $15.4 million in vendor volume discounts and approximately $17.4 million more in cost avoidance.

FLICC's governing bodies and FEDLINK staff members revisited the five-year business plan to support requirements of the Fiscal Operations Improvement Act of 2000 (P.L. 106-481) that created revolving fund statutory authority for FEDLINK's fee-based activities. The focus of the review was to assess performance in FY 2007 and update strategic initiatives and financial objectives for FY 2008 through FY 2012.

Staff members supported business plan goals for improving processes and expanding the market for product and services through several initiatives, including giving approval for customer credit card purchases under $100,000; establishing guidelines for vendor electronic invoicing; streamlining the invoicing and payment process, and establishing partnership agreements with ITS to develop and upgrade critical components of the FEDLINK subsidiary financial system.

FEDLINK Vendor Services

Total FEDLINK vendor service dollars for FY 2007 comprised $68.8 million for transfer-pay customers, $8.1 million for direct-pay customers and $41.6 million of estimated vendor billings to Direct Express customers. Database retrieval services, available only through the transfer-pay and Direct Express options, represented $28.9 million and $41.6 million, respectively. Within this service category, online services comprised the largest procurement for transfer-pay and Direct Express customers, representing $26.0 million and $41.6 million, respectively. Publication acquisition services, available only through the transfer-pay and standard direct-pay options, represented $31.1 million and $8.1 million, respectively. Within this service category, serials subscription services comprised the largest procurement for transfer-pay and direct-pay customers, representing $20.5 million and $8.0 million, respectively. Library support and other miscellaneous services, available only through the transfer-pay option, represented $8.7 million. Within this service category, bibliographic utilities constituted the largest procurement area, representing $4.8 million.

Accounts Receivable and Member Services

FEDLINK processed FY 2007 registrations from federal libraries, information centers, and other federal offices for a total of 452 signed interagency agreement (IAGs). In addition, FEDLINK processed 1,904 IAG amendments (912 for current-year and 992 for prior-year adjustments) for agencies that added, adjusted, or ended service funding. These IAGs and IAG amendments represented 6,920 individual service requests to begin, move, convert, or cancel service from FEDLINK vendors. For FY 2007 alone, FEDLINK processed $68.8 million in service dollars for 2,131 transfer-pay accounts and $8.1 million in service dollars for 16 direct-pay accounts.

Transfer-Pay Accounts Payable Services

For transfer-pay users, FEDLINK processed 51,742 invoices for payment during FY 2007 for both current-year and prior-year orders. Staff members efficiently processed vendor invoices and earned $25,348 in discounts in excess of interest payment penalties levied for the late payment of invoices to FEDLINK vendors. FEDLINK rejected 2,943 invoices for the following reasons: insufficient customer funds (59 percent); duplicate vendor invoices (27 percent); no authority (i.e., IAG and/or delivery order) (3 percent); or unidentified customer/other (11 percent). FEDLINK continued to maintain open accounts for three prior years to pay publications service invoices ("bill laters" and "back orders") for members using books and serials services. Staff issued 73,978 statements to members (20,151 for the current year and 53,827 for prior years) and continued to generate current fiscal year statements for electronic information retrieval service accounts on the 30th or the last working day of each month, and publications and acquisitions account statements on the 15th of each month. FEDLINK issued final FY 2002 statements in support of closing obligations for expired FY 2002 appropriations and quarterly statements for prior fiscal years while supporting the reconciliation of FY 2002–2007 FEDLINK vendor services accounts. FEDLINK issued the final call for FY 2002 and 2003 invoices to vendors March 2006 and 2007, respectively.

Direct Express Services

The Direct Express Program now includes nearly 70 vendors offering database retrieval services. The program is set up to give customers procurement and payment options in which the vendors pay a quarterly service fee to FEDLINK based on customer billings for usage. The advantage for the customers and the vendors is the elimination of the process steps for setting up an IAG for the direct purchase of online services citing FEDLINK contract terms and conditions. The Direct Express program generated 78 percent of the fee revenue initially anticipated in the budget and the forecast for FY 2007.

Budget and Revenue

During FY 2007 FEDLINK fee revenue from signed IAGs was approximately 6.8 percent, or $331,336 above FY 2006 levels and 8 percent, or $387,726, more than the FY 2007 budget. The FEDLINK fee revenue is expected to exceed program FY 2007 expenditure obligations by $544,237.

Financial Systems

The FEDLINK program began several initiatives to upgrade and restructure its customer support systems to meet the objectives of the business plan and give customers a more secure and user-friendly environment to acquire FEDLINK services. FEDLINK is partnering with the Library of Congress Information Technology Services (ITS) to create the FEDLINK Customer Financial System (FCFS), which will significantly enhance the ability of vendors and member agencies to buy and sell library services online. FCFS will replace the program's On-line IAG Customer Registration System, which will continue to operate during the changeover.

Financial Management, Reporting, and Control

FEDLINK successfully passed the Library of Congress financial audit of FY 2006 transactions and completed vulnerability assessments of program financial risks for library services. Support for these audits includes financial systems briefings, documented review and analysis of financial system, testing and verification of account balances in the central and subsidiary financial system, financial statement preparation support, security briefings and reviews, and research and documented responses to follow-up audit questions and findings.

National Center for Education Statistics
Library Statistics Program

U.S. Department of Education, Institute of Education Sciences
Elementary/Secondary and Libraries Studies Division
1990 K St. N.W., Washington, DC 20006

Adrienne Chute and Barbara Holton

In an effort to collect and disseminate more-complete statistical information about libraries, the National Center for Education Statistics (NCES) initiated a formal library statistics program in 1989 that included surveys on academic libraries, school library media centers, public libraries, and state libraries.*

At the end of December 2007 the Public Libraries Survey and the State Library Agencies Survey were officially transferred from NCES to the Institute of Museum and Library Services' (IMLS's) Office of Library Programs. NCES, IMLS, and the U.S. Bureau of the Census have worked cooperatively to make this a smooth transition. The Academic Libraries Survey and the School Library Media Centers Survey continue to be administered and funded by NCES, under the leadership of Tai Phan, program director, Library Statistics Program. [For detailed information on the surveys now being handled by IMLS, see "Institute of Museum and Library Services Library Programs" in Part 2—*Ed.*]

The library surveys conducted by NCES are designed to provide comprehensive, nationwide data on the status of libraries. Federal, state, and local officials, professional associations, and local practitioners use these surveys for planning, evaluating, and making policy. These data are also available to researchers and educators.

The NCES Library Statistics Program's Web site is at http://nces.ed.gov/surveys/libraries. The site provides links to data search tools, data files, survey definitions, and survey designs for each survey. The two surveys are described in this article.

Academic Libraries Survey

The Academic Libraries Survey (ALS) provides descriptive statistics from approximately 3,700 academic libraries in the 50 states, the District of Columbia, and the outlying areas of the United States. NCES surveyed academic libraries on a three-year cycle between 1966 and 1988. From 1988 to 1998, ALS was a component of the Integrated Postsecondary Education Data System (IPEDS) and was on a two-year cycle. Beginning with fiscal year 2000, the Academic Libraries Survey is no longer a component of IPEDS, but remains on a two-year cycle. IPEDS and ALS data can still be linked by the identification codes of the postsecondary education institutions. In aggregate, these data provide an overview of the status of academic libraries nationally and by state. ALS collects data on libraries in the entire universe of degree-granting postsecondary institutions, using a Web-based data collection system.

*The authorization for NCES to collect library statistics is included in the Education Sciences Reform Act of 2002 (P.L. 107-279) under Title I, Part C.)

ALS has an established working group made up of representatives from the academic library community. Its mission is to improve data quality and the timeliness of data collection, processing, and release. NCES also works cooperatively with the American Library Association, the Association of Research Libraries, the Association of College and Research Libraries, and academic libraries in the collection of ALS data.

The survey collects data on total library operating expenditures, full-time-equivalent library staff, service outlets, collection size, number of documents digitized by library staff, circulation, interlibrary loans, public service hours, library visits, reference transactions, consortia services, number of presentations, attendance at presentations, and online services. Academic libraries are also asked whether they offer library reference services by e-mail and technology for patrons with disabilities.

A First Look report, *Academic Libraries, 2004* (NCES 2007-301), was released on the NCES Web site in November 2006, as was the final data file and documentation for the 2004 ALS. NCES has developed a Web-based peer analysis tool, the Compare Academic Libraries Tool, for ALS.

More information on academic library statistics can be obtained from Barbara Holton, Elementary/Secondary and Libraries Studies Division, National Center for Education Statistics, Room 9030, 1990 K St. N.W., Washington, DC 20006 (telephone 202-219-7095, e-mail barbara.holton@ed.gov).

School Library Media Centers

National surveys of school library media centers in elementary and secondary schools in the United States were conducted in 1958, 1962, 1974, 1978, 1986, 1993–1994, 1999–2000, and 2003–2004. Data collection for the 2007–2008 survey began during fall 2007 and continued through spring 2008.

NCES, with the assistance of the U.S. Bureau of the Census, conducts the School Library Media Centers Survey as part of the Schools and Staffing Survey (SASS). SASS is the nation's largest sample survey of teachers, schools, and principals in U.S. K–12 public and private schools. Data from the school library media center questionnaire provide a national picture of school library staffing, collections, expenditures, technology, and services. Results from the 2003–2004 survey can be found in *Characteristics of Schools, Districts, Teachers, Principals, and School Libraries in the United States: 2003–2004 Schools and Staffing Survey* (NCES 2006-313).

NCES also published a historical report about school libraries entitled *Fifty Years of Supporting Children's Learning: A History of Public School Libraries and Federal Legislation from 1953–2000*. Drawn from more than 50 sources, this report presents descriptive data about public school libraries since 1953. Along with key characteristics of school libraries, the report also presents national and regional standards, and federal legislation affecting school library media centers. Data from sample surveys are presented at the national, regional, and school levels, and by state.

NCES has included some library-oriented questions on the parent and the teacher instruments of their new Early Childhood Longitudinal Study (ECLS).

For additional information, visit http://nces.ed.gov/ecls. Library items also appear in National Household Education Survey (NHES) instruments. For more information about that survey, visit http://nces.ed.gov/nhes.

NCES also included a questionnaire about high school library media centers in the Education Longitudinal Study of 2002 (ELS: 2002). This survey collected data from tenth graders about their schools, their school library media centers, their communities, and their home life. The report *School Library Media Centers: Selected Results from the Education Longitudinal Study of 2002* (ELS: 2002) (NCES 2005-302) is available on the NCES Web site and can be ordered through EDPubs. For additional information about this survey, visit http://nces.ed.gov/surveys/els2002.

More information on school library media center statistics may be obtained from Barbara Holton, Elementary/Secondary and Libraries Studies Division, National Center for Education Statistics, Room 9030, 1990 K St., N.W., Washington, DC 20006 (telephone 202-219-7095, e-mail barbara.holton@ed.gov).

How to Obtain Printed and Electronic Products

NCES currently publishes First Look reports, which consist of a short collection of tables presenting state and national totals, a survey description, and data highlights. NCES also publishes separate, more in-depth studies analyzing these data.

Internet Access

Many NCES publications (including out-of-print publications) and edited raw data files from the library surveys are available for viewing or downloading free of charge through the Electronic Catalog on the NCES Web site at http://nces.ed.gov/pubsearch.

Ordering Printed Products

Many NCES publications are also available in printed format. To order one free copy of recent NCES reports, contact the Education Publications Center (ED Pubs) at http://www.edpubs.org, by e-mail at edpubs@inet.ed.gov, by toll-free telephone at 877-433-7827 (TTY/TDD 877-576-7734), by fax at 301-470-1244, or by mail at ED Pubs, P.O. Box 1398, Jessup, MD 20794-1398.

Many publications are available through the Educational Resources Information Center (ERIC) system. For further information on services and products, visit the http://www.eric.ed.gov. [For more information on the products available from ERIC, see "Educational Resources Information Center" later in Part 1—*Ed.*]

Out-of-print publications and data files may be available through the NCES Electronic Catalog on the NCES Web site at http://nces.ed.gov/pubsearch or from the 1,400 Federal Depository Libraries throughout the United States at http://catalog.gpo.gov/fdlpdir/FDLPdir.jsp. Use the NCES publication number included in the citations for publications and data files to quickly locate items in the NCES Electronic Catalog. Use the GPO number to locate items in a federal depository library.

National Commission on Libraries and Information Science

1800 M St. N.W., Suite 350, Washington, DC 20036-5841
World Wide Web http://www.nclis.gov

C. Beth Fitzsimmons
Chairman

The law that created the U.S. National Commission on Libraries and Information Science (NCLIS)—Public Law 91-345 (20 U.S.C. 1501 *et seq.*), signed July 20, 1970—states that "library and information services adequate to meet the needs of the people of the United States are essential to achieve national goals." It is the responsibility of the commission to develop and recommend plans that enable adequate library and information services.

In meeting this responsibility, the commission seeks to identify the needs of the American people for library and information services and to translate those needs into recommendations for national policy. The commission is expected to advise the president, Congress, state and local governments, and others with its recommendations. To arrive at those recommendations, the commission has undertaken many important initiatives during its 37 years, thus meeting its statutory mandate.

NCLIS also plays a role in studying and publishing statistics relating to library and information services delivery. In this work, it has partnered for 23 years with the National Center for Educational Statistics (NCES) to develop and implement the Library Statistics Program, serving as liaison to the library community, organizing meetings and training workshops, supporting in-state training and technical assistance, monitoring trends, and advising NCES on policy matters. As a result, the Library Statistics Program has led to the development of standards for library statistics, as well as the accurate and timely collection of relevant statistics to assist in policy development and implementation at the federal, state, and local levels.

NCLIS was established as a permanent, independent agency of the United States government. Its members include the Librarian of Congress, the director of the Institute of Museum and Library Services (IMLS), and 14 commissioners appointed by the president and confirmed by the Senate for terms not to exceed five years (although the law was later amended to require appointees to continue in service until a replacement commissioner has been appointed). The establishing legislation for NCLIS required that five of the appointees be librarians or information specialists, and that at least one commissioner be "knowledgeable with respect to the technological aspects of library and information services and sciences." Another commissioner must be "knowledgeable with respect to the library and information service and science needs of the elderly."

The members of NCLIS are Beth Fitzsimmons, chairman; Bridget L. Lamont, vice chairman; José A. Aponte; Sandra F. Ashworth; Edward L. Bertorelli; Librarian of Congress James H. Billington (ex officio); Jan Cellucci; Carol L. Diehl; Allison Druin; Colleen E. Huebner; Stephen M. Kennedy; Mary H. Perdue; IMLS Director Anne-Imelda Radice (ex officio); S. Diane Rivers; and

Herman L. Totten. At the call of the chairman, the commission had one meeting during 2007, June 4–5 in Washington, D.C.

NCLIS As a Federal Agency

As an independent agency of the executive branch of the federal government, NCLIS presents its budget request to the president, who, through the Office of Management and Budget (OMB), then sends to Congress an appropriations funding request to support the commission's work for the coming fiscal year. Since 2001 the commission's annual appropriation has been $1,000,000.

In addition to the commissioners, who for employment purposes are considered "special government employees" (SGEs), NCLIS staff is made up of the executive director, the director of operations, the director of statistics and surveys, a management analyst (operations), and a special assistant for technology. Consultants and temporary support staff are engaged to provide additional specialized services. The position of executive director has been vacant since June 2006, with NCLIS Chairman Fitzsimmons assuming many of those responsibilities as the commission's future status was determined. That status has been unstable since February 2006 when OMB proposed the consolidation of NCLIS into IMLS, with the consolidation to be completed by fiscal year (FY) 2008—that is, by October 1, 2007. The administration also proposed the merger of NCES programs for public and state library surveys into IMLS, using the rationale that merging the survey programs into IMLS would consolidate grant making (the primary function of IMLS) with data collection.

The proposed consolidation was described in an implementation plan put forward by IMLS (http://www.imls.gov/pdf/consolidationplan_draft.pdf). In August 2006 the NCLIS commissioners agreed to oppose the plan and determined to work with legislative leaders and the library and information science community to seek to continue its authorization as an independent advisory agency. These activities were not successful. In 2007, as NCLIS sought appropriations to continue its work, it was made clear that the agency's minimal annual funding had been intended only to be used to keep its doors open. The commissioners had expected to implement NCLIS's statutory mandate.

With the election of November 2006, the proposed consolidation seemed less urgent. Unaware that they had been appointed to close the agency, the commissioners continued to engage in initiatives in support of their legislated and statutory mandate, as described below. However, as the end of FY 2007 approached, the commissioners recognized that the work of NCLIS as a federal agency was no longer required. The commissioners and staff then focused their efforts on closing the agency. Funding has been provided for the closure, and the commission expected to vacate its offices by March 31, 2008.

Policy

In light of the impending closure, the commissioners made a decision during 2007 to authorize a study to identify a future research agenda for the commission or, if required, for its successor organization, and particularly for significant issues that need to be addressed in the near term, over the next 12 to 18 months. Information was sought from opinion leaders in the library and information science community; leaders in information policy and publishing; academics; school, state, and public librarians; librarians in the national libraries and other government experts in areas of information; faculty in graduate schools of library and information science; employees in trade and professional associations; foundations; experts in intellectual property; and experts in digital libraries.

The goal of the study was to produce a mosaic-like document demonstrating the interests and information needs of the American people, building on the fundamental statement of why NCLIS was created originally, and, through that, approaching a national information agenda for the public and for those who deliver services to the various segments of the public.

Initiatives

In organizing and implementing its activities during 2007, NCLIS has been guided by its strategic plan of April 2004. In the plan, the commission established three goals for its work:

- To appraise library and information services provided for the American people
- To strengthen the relevance of libraries and information science in the lives of the American people
- To promote research and development for extending and improving library and information services for the American people

To achieve these goals, NCLIS identified the following strategic initiatives for its work, and each initiative resulted in specific policy advice or comment delivered to the president and to Congress as required by law:

1 Health communication and the role of libraries in distributing consumer health information and in promoting healthy lifestyles (http://www.nclis. gov/activities/librariesandhealth.html).

2 Digitized information and the role of libraries in the development and implementation of large-scale digitization programs (http://www.nclis. gov/digitization/digitization.html). In 2007 the commission continued to study the subject, and at its June 2007 meeting it was addressed by Paul Courant, university librarian and dean of university libraries at the University of Michigan. A specialist in the study of the economics of universities, the economics of libraries and archives, and the changes in the system of scholarly communication that derive from new information technologies, Courant has written that ideas must be made public to qualify as ideas, just as art must take physical form in order to qualify as art. Noting that "literally and metaphorically, universities are built around their libraries," Courant told the commissioners that libraries "hold, catalog, and curate expensive material that not everyone can afford to have, and they make it available to everyone." He declared that "This funda-

mental requirement of an effective infrastructure for scholarship is that it puts ideas into the library, and lets others get them out again, reliably, the same ones every time." In his presentation, Courant linked his remarks about scholarly resources and their connection with the University of Michigan's master digitization project, framing his presentation around the structure of the symposium on large-scale digitization held in Ann Arbor in March 2006 (jointly sponsored by the University of Michigan and NCLIS).

3 Adequacies and deficiencies of current library and information resources and services (http://www.nclis.gov/survey.htm). NCLIS continued its discussions about the desirability of an assessment tool for the nation's libraries. Unfortunately, work was limited as reductions were required in the commission's Statistics and Surveys program.

4 The relationship between school libraries and educational achievement (http://www.nclis.gov/info/schoollibraryactivities.html). The commission continued its efforts in this matter and in July 2007 distributed a press release on the subject. "From our perspective," Fitzsimmons said in the press release, "a critical part of the comprehensive and renewed strategy to ensure that students learn to read and are effective users of information and ideas is the requirement that every school have a school library and that school libraries be staffed by highly qualified, state-certified school library media specialists."

5 Adult and family literacy. In 2007 Commissioners Totten and Druin reviewed the literacy work being done at the Illinois State Library. They noted the exemplary commitment of the library and its partnering abilities, with program funding not only from the state of Illinois but through collaborative and partnering arrangements with almost every organization in America focusing on literacy. They recommended that identifying funding agencies for conducting further targeted research in this subject is a major concern. In a related matter, NCLIS in 2007 served a second time as cosponsor for the Chicago Public Schools' Battle of the Books program (the only large urban program sponsoring a Battle of the Books activity). At the commission's June 2007 meeting, Carol Josefowicz, who has been actively involved in the program, spoke to NCLIS and related the work to the commission's interest in linking school libraries and educational achievement. Josefowicz described the details of the program and the role of volunteers and encouraged further work in this area.

6 Library and information services for the aging (http://www.nclis.gov/info/nationalinfo.html#elderly). NCLIS continued its discussions on this important subject, monitoring situations in which libraries are able to provide needed services for seniors.

7 Emergency preparedness and the role of libraries as community distribution centers for emergency preparedness and disaster-response information. During 2007 NCLIS continued its dialogue with state officials in New Hampshire, with the goal of establishing a pilot program for emer-

gency response in disaster conditions and utilizing the library network to help inform the public.

Additionally, in keeping with the commission's charge as described in the enabling legislation, other subjects relating to policy development with respect to libraries and information science require attention and ongoing review. Among these, the following were given consideration in 2007:

Internet neutrality—NCLIS continued its work relating to Internet neutrality, and in October 2007 it distributed a press release (http://www.nclis.gov/news/pressrelease/pr2007/nclisnewsrelease-internettaxban2007-04.pdf) urging Congress to make permanent a moratorium on Internet access taxes. In the press release Chairman Fitzsimmons noted the unfairness of taxing citizens for Internet access in order to fill out tax forms and Medicare forms required by the government. "If the government is increasingly requiring citizens to use the Internet, then federal, state, or local taxes on its use should be prohibited," she said.

Access to information in federal libraries—In February 2007 the commission published a statement recognizing its earlier study with respect to this issue (*A Comprehensive Assessment of Public Information Dissemination, 2001*). NCLIS distributed a press release (http://www.nclis.gov/news/pressrelease/pr2007/nclisnewsrelease-libraryclose2007-02.pdf) describing a presentation of NCLIS Vice Chairman Lamont to the commission in which she acknowledged the debt of the library and information science community and the general public to the earlier commission study. NCLIS then restated its earlier position on the matter and recommended to the president and Congress that the study be revisited. In the original study, the commission took a very strong position on the role of the federal government in assuring access to federal government information. In other work in this area, NCLIS continued to study the concept of open access and the relationship between open access and public access policies. As the call for public access seems to be an issue growing in scope and intensity, not only in the United States but globally, NCLIS met with Heather Joseph, executive director of the Scholarly Publishing and Academic Resources Coalition (SPARC); Eric Slater, manager of the Copyright Office at the American Chemical Society, Obligations Division; and Glenn Ruskin, director of the Office of Legislative Affairs of the American Chemical Society, to discuss this issue.

Statistics and Surveys

In March 2007 the NCLIS position of director, statistics and surveys, became vacant, affecting the agency's ability to fulfill its commitment to the NCLIS/NCES interagency agreement. As a result, the agreement was renegotiated to reflect task areas NCLIS would no longer be capable of performing, with an NCES/NCLIS memorandum of understanding signed by both parties in April. However, under terms of the new NCES/NCLIS interagency agreement, the agency has been able to support the State Library Programs Survey in Federal-State Cooperative System meetings.

Additionally, in 2007 the commission continued to manage two related studies that were completed at the end of the fiscal year:

* "The Search for Cause-and-Effect Relationships Between Student Achievement and Factors Relating to the Libraries to Which the Students Have Access" (Kathleen Kennedy), to investigate possible cause-and-effect relationships between student achievement and factors relating to the schools and the libraries to which the students have access
* "Library Service Area Demographic and Statistical Display System" (Christine Koontz), to define and design an interactive information dashboard that provides administrators of public libraries with the library's current demographic data from the U.S. Census projected on maps with overlays of that library's statistical data and current Federal-State Cooperative System data; the project focuses on defining the data elements that are most needed by the users, administrators, and public libraries, and the functions desired and required by those users

Conclusion

A review of the commission's service to the American people makes it clear that NCLIS has played a significant role in addressing the nation's library and information science needs. By its second year of operation, NCLIS had put forward a draft of a new national program of library and information services, culminating in the 1975 publication of *Toward a National Program for Library and Information Services: Goals for Action.* A second major publication, following soon after, was *Library and Information Service Needs of the Nation,* a seminal document in the development of this critical societal element.

Other highlights of the commission's work have been

* Influencing authorization legislation for a White House Conference on Library and Information Services
* Studying the role of Library of Congress in the national network
* Surveying the impact of federal funding programs on public libraries
* Compiling an inventory of national library needs
* Examining the volume and characteristics of library photocopying
* Surveying the role of school libraries in a national network
* Examining continuing library and information science education
* Sponsoring research in the coordination of bibliographic control
* Organizing the first White House Conference on Libraries and Information Services, resulting in the development of task forces to examine such issues as community information and referral services, library and information services for cultural minorities, and the role of the special library in nationwide networks and cooperative programs
* Studying the adequacy of library and information services to the Native American population

- Reacting to the Office of Technology Assessment's report *Informing the Nation: Federal Information Dissemination in an Electronic Age*
- Establishing recognition awards, honoring initiatives taken by individuals (not librarians) and organizations (not library-related) to promote and improve library and information services
- Organizing a second White House Conference, with the three conference themes of library and information services for literacy, democracy, and productivity
- Developing and adopting the Principles of Public Information
- Organizing and collecting the first public library data from all states, based on standard data elements and definitions
- Investigating public libraries and the Internet, resulting in the publication of *Internet Costs and Cost Models for Public Libraries* and *The 1996 National Survey of Public Libraries and the Internet*
- Publishing *Assessment of Standards for the Creation, Dissemination, and Permanent Accessibility of Electronic Government Information Products*
- Advising the IMLS director on policies and financial assistance for library services
- Providing information relating to a variety of proposals for federally mandated use of Internet filtering software for schools and libraries
- Organizing discussions with stakeholders about the Department of Commerce's intention to close down the National Technical Information Service (NTIS) and the future of NTIS
- Continuing participation (since 1985) with the Department of State to coordinate the library and information aspect of the International Contributions for Scientific, Educational, and Cultural Activities (ICSECA) program
- Partnering with NCES (since 1987) in implementing a formal collaborative activity for library statistics
- Responding to an invitation from Congress to refute an OMB proposal to eliminate the commission
- Organizing and developing the research studies that culminated in the publication of *A Comprehensive Assessment of Public Information Dissemination*
- Organizing the Sister Libraries Program White House Millennium Project, created to provide a framework for the international sharing of mutual interests between libraries
- Sponsoring the production of "Trust and Terror," an audiovisual briefing on the role libraries can take to provide needed information to the public in the immediate aftermath of a manmade or natural disaster
- Organizing and conducting, with UNESCO and the National Forum on Information Literacy, the Information Literacy Meeting of Experts in Prague in September 2003, resulting in the publication of *The Prague Declaration: Towards an Information Literate Society*

- Providing a delegation to the 2003 World Summit on the Information Society in November 2003 in Geneva
- In 2005 and 2006, identifying and recognizing libraries that excel in meeting the consumer health information needs of American citizens and publishing *Libraries and Health Communication: Model Programs in Health Information Provided by Libraries Throughout the Nation*
- Commissioning, in collaboration with UNESCO and the U.S. Department of State, the study of information dissemination in sub-Saharan Africa with respect to HIV/AIDS and publishing in September 2005 *The Role of Libraries in HIV/AIDS Information Dissemination in Sub-Saharan Africa*
- Studying the library needs of the elderly and publishing *Recommendations to the American Library Association's Library Service to an Aging Population Committee for the White House Conference on Aging,* December 2005
- Cohosting, with the University of Michigan, "Scholarship and Libraries in Transition: A Dialogue About the Impacts of Mass Digitization Projects," a symposium held in March 2006 in Ann Arbor, Michigan, and publishing *Mass Digitization: Implications for Information Policy*

This was work on a grand scale, and no other government agency, professional association, trade association, research and development organization, academic institution, or philanthropic organization was given the statutory responsibility that was given to NCLIS in July 1970. To provide policy advice to the president and Congress with respect to libraries and information science was a great responsibility, and for nearly four decades the commission has embraced this responsibility with much enthusiasm and prodigious effort. Other organizations and individuals did, of course, become involved in these matters, for NCLIS had made it clear from the beginning that such partnerships and collaborations were required if the commission was to succeed in its mission. Over time, these organizations thoughtfully and sincerely informed the commission's work, and for this support, enthusiasm, and cooperation, the commissioners are grateful.

Defense Technical Information Center

Fort Belvoir, VA 22060
703-767-8217, World Wide Web http://www.dtic.mil

Sandy Schwalb
Public Affairs Officer

The Defense Technical Information Center (DTIC) has served the information needs of the defense community for more than 60 years. DTIC is the central facility for the collection, storage, retrieval, and dissemination of scientific and technical information for the Department of Defense (DOD). DTIC is a DOD "field activity," which is an organization whose work reaches across all segments of DOD. In the office of the Under Secretary of Defense (Acquisition, Technology, and Logistics), DTIC reports to the Director, Defense Research and Engineering (DDR&E), and

- Provides controlled access to DOD information
- Is a vital link in the transfer of information among the defense-related government and civilian research and development communities
- Is a primary provider of Web services for organizations within DOD

DTIC is located in the Andrew T. McNamara Headquarters Complex Building at Fort Belvoir, Virginia, and has four regional offices, whose addresses appear at the end of this article.

Research and Engineering Portal

DTIC's No. 1 priority is the Research and Engineering (R&E) Portal launched by DTIC and DDR&E in 2005. A working research tool, the portal (https://rdte.osd.mil) provides free access to current and historical research and engineering information, including DTIC technical data resources. This single-sign-on, password-protected site is available to DOD and federal government employees and contractors.

Portal users are at all organizational levels from Pentagon managers, planners, and policymakers to bench-level researchers at DOD research installations. The R&E portal offers a greatly expanded search capability, with customized views of results. Access is controlled by the DTIC registration process. For more registration information, see https://register.dtic.mil/DTIC.

New Strategic Plan

In 2007 DTIC released a new strategic plan. This five-year plan has a noticeably different look and feel from previous ones and is a more appropriate document now that DTIC is a DOD field activity. The plan highlights linkages from it to the President's Management Agenda as well as to organizations to which DTIC reports at the Pentagon. In his introduction to the plan, DTIC Administrator R.

Paul Ryan said, "This strategic plan serves as DTIC's road map to the future and guides us in establishing the annual goals we need to meet along the way."

Combatant Commanders Workshop

DTIC, in conjunction with the Under Secretary of Defense for Acquisitions, Technology, and Logistics, hosted the 2007 Combatant Commanders Workshop, "Rapid Technical Support for the Warfighter," in Suffolk, Virginia, October 29–30. This first Combatant Commanders meeting brought together DDR&E and DTIC personnel, military, contractors, and Information Analysis Centers (IAC) managers. The objectives of the workshop were to position DTIC as an agent of information excellence within DOD, educate key stakeholders, and provide an opportunity for networking and fostering relationships. DTIC was able to showcase its information tools: the R&E Portal, the Scientific and Technical Information Network (STINET) databases, and IAC services.

The keynote address was presented by Lt. Gen. Michael A. Vane, director of the Army Capabilities Integration Center (ARCIC), who provided an overview of his organization and how it supports the military in the field.

DTIC Administrator Ryan and other DTIC personnel explained DTIC's evolution from paper products to real-time online services. There were presentations from managers of the IAC program, who explained their specific research areas and services to nearly 100 attendees.

Enhanced Search Capability

DTIC's search page promotes its key mission—to provide effective access to information relevant to DOD and provide access to more than 13 million Web pages and documents across DOD. In order to ensure that its home page is more in line with what people are used to seeing on other search engines, DTIC's Web site (http://www.dtic.mil) offers users the option of conducting a simple search in three separate resources:

- DTIC Science and Technology (S&T)—Publicly available information from the DTIC Technical Reports collection with an advanced search capability
- DOD-Wide Science and Technology—S&T-related sites throughout DOD, with the ability to narrow the search to specific organizations
- All DOD Web Sites—Public defense information throughout the department or by agencies, unified commands, military services, or other DOD components

Security of Information

While there is much publicly accessible material in the DTIC collection (in fact, almost one-half of DOD's technical reports are publicly available the day they are published), some information is restricted by security classifications. DOD's scientific and technical information is always categorized (or "marked," which is the term used in the defense community) by the office that originates the document. This marking determines how, and to whom, the information can be disseminated.

Some information is marked to protect national security. DTIC's databases contain such classified information, which may be marked "confidential" or "secret."

DTIC's databases also contain information that, although not classified, is still sensitive for various reasons. These documents are marked to show why the information is sensitive and with whom the document can be shared. Such documents are considered "unclassified, limited." Information in DTIC's databases that is neither classified nor limited can be released to the public and is referred to as "unclassified, unlimited."

The information in DTIC's collection is 42 percent "unclassified, unlimited," 51 percent "unclassified, limited," and 7 percent "classified."

Resources

DTIC's holdings include technical reports on completed research; research summaries of planned, ongoing, and completed work; independent research and development summaries; defense technology transfer agreements; DOD planning documents; DOD directives and instructions; conference proceedings; security classification guides; command histories; and special collections that date back to World War II.

DOD-funded researchers are required to search DTIC's collections to ensure that they do not "reinvent the wheel" and undertake unnecessary or redundant research.

The scope of DTIC's collection includes areas normally associated with defense research. DOD's interests are widespread, however; examples of the types of information found in DTIC include agriculture; atmospheric sciences; behavioral and social sciences; human factors engineering; information warfare; mathematic and computer sciences; nuclear science and technology; propulsion, engines, and fuels; radiation studies; and virtual reality.

Registering for Services

DTIC offers its information services to a diverse population of the defense community. Because of the nature of the information that DTIC handles, users must prequalify for services. In December 2007 DTIC had nearly 16,000 registered users. DTIC's varied customers include engineers; scientists; program managers; policy analysts; planners; and information specialists working for DOD, other U.S. government agencies, and their contractors. DTIC's customers can be found in academia, the intelligence community, foreign governments (e.g., under negotiated agreements with Australia, Britain, Canada, France, Germany, the Netherlands, and the Republic of Korea), and also include military school students and the public.

Everyone can search DTIC's publicly accessible collections and display or download such information. Below are descriptions of the various DTIC databases. Unless otherwise noted, the databases are available to the public.

Registered users can order documents directly from DTIC. Individuals who are not eligible to register with DTIC can order "unclassified, unlimited" documents by contacting the National Technical Information Service (NTIS) at 800-553-6847 or by visiting http://www.ntis.gov.

DTIC's Primary Collections

The Technical Reports (TR) database contains more than 2 million reports in print, nonprint (CDs, DVDs, software, data files, databases, and video recordings), and electronic formats, conveying the results of defense-sponsored research, development, test, and evaluation efforts. It includes journal articles, DOD-sponsored patent applications, studies, analyses, open source literature from other countries, conference proceedings, and theses. Between 25,000 and 30,000 new documents are added each year.

The Research Summaries (RS) database contains descriptions of DOD research that provide information on technical content, responsible individuals and organizations, principal investigators, and funding sources at the work-unit level. Available only to certain registered users, this collection is controlled by individual access restrictions. The collection consists of approximately 309,000 active and inactive summaries from 1965 to the present.

The Independent Research and Development (IR&D) database contains more than 172,000 descriptions (dating back to the mid-1970s) of research and development projects initiated and conducted by defense contractors independent of DOD control and without direct DOD funding. On average, nearly $3 billion worth of IR&D projects are submitted to DTIC each year. The database includes basic and applied research, technology development efforts, and systems and concept formulation studies. Defense contractors and potential contractors are encouraged to submit project descriptions to the IR&D database. Accessible only to U.S. government organizations, the proprietary IR&D information is used to identify contractors with expertise in areas of interest to DOD and to avoid DOD duplication of industry research and development.

STINET Services

DTIC's STINET is among DOD's largest repositories of scientific and technical information currently available. There are three versions of the database.

Public STINET, available to the general public free of charge, provides access to citations of "unclassified, unlimited" reports that describe the progress or results of research efforts and other scientific and technical information held by DTIC. Many of these documents are available in full text and can be downloaded.

Private STINET is a password-protected, value-added service for individuals who have registered with DTIC. Other information available through Private STINET includes

- Free online limited distribution documents as well as all "unclassified, unlimited" documents in DTIC's Technical Reports database
- The Research Summaries database
- Free access to two international database services, Canada Institute for Scientific and Technical Information's CISTI Source and the British Library Document Supply Centre's Inside Web
- Information from the Interagency Gray Literature Working Group
- ProQuest Research Library Complete, an index to journal articles
- DTIC's Scheduled Search Service, which is available free of charge and provides the latest information in particular subject areas of interest

Two services are available in both Public and Private STINET. STINET MultiSearch (http://multisearch.dtic.mil) is a portal to the "deep Web" for government scientific and technical information, which searches content below the "surface" Web for information not accessible through commercial and government search engines. Technical Reports Automated Information List (TRAIL) (http://www.dtic.mil/trail) is a free electronic mailing list that automatically distributes citations to "unclassified, unlimited" technical reports recently added to the DTIC Technical Reports database.

Classified STINET is located on the Secret Internet Protocol Router Network (SIPRNET). This database contains the complete DTIC collection, including "unclassified, limited" reports and "classified" citations. In order to use this service a user must be able to access the SIPRNET and must register with DTIC. Some of the information available in Classified STINET includes the DOD Index of Specifications and Standards (DODISS) database, the Militarily Critical Technologies List, and the DOD Index of Security Classification Guides.

Information Sources

DTIC information is derived from many sources—DOD organizations (civilian and military) and DOD contractors; U.S. government organizations and their contractors; nonprofit organizations working on DOD scientific, research, and engineering activities; academia; and foreign governments. DTIC accepts a wide array of information in print and nonprint forms (such as computer diskettes, videotapes, and CD-ROMs), as well as via the Internet. DTIC gets information from the defense community, for the defense community, about defense and beyond. Having a full range of science and technology and research and development information within the DTIC collection ensures that technological innovations are linked to defense development and acquisition efforts. New research projects can begin with the highest level of information available. This, in turn, maximizes the use of DOD project dollars.

In fiscal year 2007 (ending September 30, 2007), DTIC processed 13 percent more electronic documents than in the previous fiscal year. There was also an 11 percent increase in materials that went into the Technical Reports.

Training Opportunities

Free training is available to DTIC registered users at DTIC headquarters and at its four regional offices, listed below. Training can be arranged off site if the instructor's travel costs are borne by the host organization or user. Customized courses can also be provided.

A three-day, hands-on class, "Searching DTIC Databases," covers methods of searching and retrieving scientific, research, and engineering information in the DTIC collection. The course provides additional information about a variety of defense-related resources and services.

DTIC offers a three-day course designed to acquaint Scientific and Technical Information (STINFO) managers and other interested personnel with the requirements of the DOD Scientific and Technical Information Program. Marking documents and contract reporting requirements are covered. A one-day STINFO manager overview covers the highlights. A customized class that examines the rationale and mechanics of marking technical documents is available by arrangement with the instructor.

For additional training information, visit http://www.dtic.mil, click on DTIC A-Z, and select Training.

Web Hosting Expertise

A pioneer in Internet use for information dissemination, DTIC has designed and hosted more than 150 Web sites sponsored by components of the Office of the Secretary of Defense, military service headquarters organizations, and several defense agencies.

DTIC also supports many DOD components in developing tools and processes that enhance the storage, retrieval, and use of information. An effective support program has been created for senior-level planners and other users of information resources. This shared infrastructure allows many organizations to obtain technologies and resources that no single organization could afford on its own.

In 2007 the completely revised Web site for the Office of the Secretary of Defense (OSD)/Joint Staff Freedom of Information Act (FOIA) Requester Service Center and the new Privacy Office site were released. The requester service "supports all actions related to the Freedom of Information Act requests submitted by the public for access to records under the control of the Offices of the Secretary of Defense and the Joint Staff."

The OSD/Joint Staff Privacy Office was created in May 2007. Its new site offers a Web-based means to "provide guidance and direction to members of the Office of the Secretary of Defense and the Joint Staff as it relates to the Privacy Act of 1974."

The OSD/Joint Staff FOIA Requester Service Center site is at http://www. dod.mil/pubs/foi and the new OSD/Joint Staff Privacy Office site is at http://www.dod.mil/pubs/foi/privacy.

Information Analysis Centers

Another facet of DTIC administrative activities is the management and funding of contractor-operated joint service-oriented Information Analysis Centers (IACs), which are research organizations. Chartered by DOD, IACs identify, analyze, and use scientific and technical information in specific technology areas. They also develop information and analysis products for the defense science and engineering communities. IACs are staffed by experienced technical area scientists, engineers, and information specialists who help users locate and analyze scientific and technical information in specific subject areas. They improve productivity in the defense research, development, and acquisition communities. For more information, visit http://iac.dtic.mil.

In 2007 the Chemical and Biological Defense Information Analysis Center (CBIAC) was officially redesignated the Chemical, Biological, Radiological, and Nuclear Defense Information Analysis Center (CBRNIAC). This new designation was seen as a more accurate reflection of the IAC's technical scope and the products and services provided to the chemical, biological, radiological, and nuclear defense and homeland security communities. Also in 2007 the Modeling and Simulation IAC was added to the roster of DTIC-managed IACs.

As of January 2008 the DTIC-managed IACs, in addition to CBRNIAC, were AMMTIAC (Advanced Materials, Manufacturing, and Testing); CPIAC (Chemical Propulsion); DACS (Data and Analysis Center for Software); IATAC (Information Assurance Technology Analysis Center); MSIAC (Modeling and Simulation); RIAC (Reliability); SENSIAC (Sensors); SURVIAC (Survivability); and WSTIAC (Weapons Systems Technology).

Many of the products and services produced by IACs are free of charge and include announcements of reports relevant to the particular IAC's field of interest, authoritative bibliographic search reports, the latest scientific and engineering information on specific technical subjects, consultation with or referral to world-recognized technical experts, and status of current technologies. The Total Electronic Migration System (TEMS), a gateway to the IAC collection, is available online. TEMS provides DTIC registered users the ability to perform full-text searches and retrieve mission-critical information. See http://ammtiac. alionscience.com/pdf/AQV1N2_ART02.pdf for more information.

QuestionPoint

DTIC is a participating member of QuestionPoint, a virtual reference service developed jointly by the Library of Congress and the Online Computer Library Center (OCLC) and supported by cooperating institutions worldwide. This digital, collaborative reference service allows libraries and information centers to expand reference services with shared resources and subject specialists around the world. DTIC is part of the Global Reference Network, a worldwide group of libraries and institutions committed to digital reference, and the Defense Digital Library Research Service (DDLRS), an around-the-clock electronic reference assistance for DOD libraries.

Annual Conference

DTIC's 2007 Annual Conference, "Defense Information for All," was held March 26–28 at the Hilton Alexandria Old Town in Alexandria, Virginia. Attendees included scientists, engineers, and professionals in technology research and development, information science, and acquisition from DOD, federal, and contractor communities. Government and commercial exhibitors demonstrated their latest information services and technologies. The more than 280 registrants included representatives from the Navy, Air Force, Army, DOD agencies, the contractor community, and academic institutions.

Speakers included representatives from the offices of the DOD Chief Information Officer and the Director of National Intelligence as well as from the Defense Advanced Research Projects Agency. The luncheon speaker provided a history and overview of the National Museum of the Marine Corps in Quantico, Virginia, which opened in November 2006.

The conference was followed by a meeting of the DOD Interlaboratory Committee on Editing and Publishing (ILCEP), providing an opportunity to exchange information on the editing and publishing efforts of members, share experiences and techniques, and develop solutions to common problems that DOD activities face in editing and publishing scientific and technical information. The ILCEP focus on production issues complemented the 2007 DTIC conference, which examined access and dissemination concerns. For more information, see http://www.cotf.navy.mil/ilcep/index.html.

A guest at the conference was the son of the late Col. Howard M. McCoy, who headed the immediate post-World War II collection of documents that provided the foundation of what became DTIC.

DTIC's 2008 Annual Conference was scheduled to be held in April, again in Alexandria, with the theme "Protecting While Sharing Defense Information." Topics were to include "Web 2.0 Initiatives and Collaboration in the Federal Government," "Export Control," "Homeland Security Research from A to Z," "DOD Lean Six Sigma Activities," "Journal Articles: Managing Preprints, Reprints and Copyright," and "International Cooperation and Collaboration."

DTIC Exposure

DTIC Administrator Ryan was interviewed in August 2007 for the radio program "IBM Business of Government Hour." The hour-long question-and-answer session covered a wide range of topics including a review of DTIC's more than 60 years of serving the defense community, background and current status of the Research and Engineering Portal, and how DTIC helps in time of war. The weekly program airs on Saturday mornings in the Washington, D.C., area.

Ryan and other DTIC staff participated in a "Careers in Federal Libraries" seminar held at the Library of Congress during the June 2007 American Library Association (ALA) Annual Conference in Washington, D.C. Ryan spoke about the mission of DTIC and the many roles that librarians and technical information specialists play in the agency. The session included 12 federal employees, both experienced and new, discussing the diverse job opportunities available to librarians in the federal government. Hundreds of individuals unable to attend the conference actively participated in the program via the Internet.

Commendation for STINET

Choice, an ALA publication, is designed to guide academic librarians in the selection of high-quality material for their collections. A review of DTIC's Public STINET appeared in the publication's January 2007 issue and praised Public STINET's content as a "well-designed, easily searchable site," calling the technical reports collection "the gem of this site."

Open Archives Initiative

The Open Archives Initiative (OAI) is an international effort focused on furthering the interoperability of digital libraries, and its objective is to develop a framework to make it easier to find content stored in distributed archives. Much authoritative information has resided on the "deep Web," composed of content-rich databases from universities, libraries, associations, businesses, and government agencies, including DTIC. In 2005 DTIC launched its OAI effort to disseminate the publicly accessible DOD science research contents with OAI partners such as DOD libraries, OCLC, universities, and commercial search engines including Google, Yahoo!, and MSN.com.

DTIC disseminates the metadata in multiple formats such as COSATI, MARC, DC (Dublin Core), and HTML with links to digital content using Handles (DTIC's persistent identification system). OCLC has also become part of this digital network through WorldCat. Since OAI went live in 2005, DTIC has disseminated citations for more than 700,000 documents.

This is another way to make sure DTIC's customers find more relevant data when they search. If one is looking for something defense-related using a typical Internet search engine, the record from DTIC will show up. This will ensure that the material in DTIC's collection is linked back to DTIC and not to a commercial Web site.

Outreach

DTIC customers can host, at their location, a briefing or demonstration of DTIC's products and services tailored to their schedule and information needs. For more information, email training@dtic.mil.

Tours and briefings are available at DTIC's headquarters. Most visitors do not need a security clearance to attend; however, special arrangements are needed for foreign nationals and employees of foreign governments. For more information, visit http://www.dtic.mil, click on DTIC A-Z, and select Tours and Briefings.

In 2007 DTIC hosted a number of librarians and researchers from the Republic of Korea, Spain, and Italy.

DTIC Review

DTIC Review, published on CD-ROM, provides the full text of selected technical reports and a bibliography of other references of interest in a single publication. Each volume provides a sampling of documents from the DTIC collection on a specific topic of current interest. Titles in 2007 were "Advanced Ceramics," "Biometric Security," "Advanced Energetic Materials," and "Shifting Paradigms and Disruptive Technology." The January 2008 edition's topic was "Human, Social, Cultural and Behavior Modeling." For more information, visit http://www.dtic.mil/dtic/prodsrvc/review/index.html.

Cooperation and Collaboration

DTIC works with the information and library communities through many partnerships and affiliations. The following are among them:

- CENDI, an interagency working group of senior scientific and technical information managers from a number of U.S. federal agencies including the departments of Commerce, Energy, Interior, and Defense; the National Aeronautics and Space Administration; the Government Printing Office; and the Library of Congress (DTIC Administrator Ryan serves as CENDI's 2006–2008 chair)
- Science.gov, a collaboration of scientific and technical organizations in the federal government, a free gateway to more than 1,700 government information resources about science, including technical reports, journal citations, databases, federal Web sites, and fact sheets
- US CODATA (Committee on Data for Science and Technology), whose goal is to improve the compilation, evaluation, storage, and retrieval of data of importance to science and technology
- NFAIS, the National Federation of Advanced Information Services (DTIC was a charter member of this organization, founded in 1958)
- FLICC, the Federal Library and Information Center Committee
- ASIDIC, the Association of Information and Dissemination Centers
- NISO, the National Information Standards Organization
- SLA, the Special Libraries Association

A number of DTIC staff members had leadership roles in planning the Military Librarians Workshop held in December 2007. DTIC librarians and information specialists were involved in conducting the workshop's executive board and business meetings, registering all attendees for the workshop, presenting the annual DTIC Update, creating and providing the workshop's Web services, and hosting an exhibit table providing DTIC customers and prospective customers with consultation and information on new and traditional DTIC products and services. The event is sponsored annually by the Military Librarians Division of SLA.

DTIC Regional Offices

Midwestern Regional Office
Wright-Patterson Air Force Base, Ohio
Tel. 937-255-7905, fax 937-986-7002
E-mail dayton@dtic.mil

Northeastern Regional Office
Hanscom Air Force Base
Bedford, Massachusetts
Tel. 781-377-2413, fax 781-377-5627
E-mail boston@dtic.mil

Southwestern Regional Office
Kirtland Air Force Base, New Mexico
Tel. 505-846-6797, fax 505-846-6799
E-mail albuq@dtic.mil

Western Regional Office
El Segundo, California
Tel. 310-653-2483, fax 310-353-2159
E-mail losangel@dtic.mil

Note: DTIC and STINET are registered service marks of the Defense Technical Information Center.

National Library of Education

Knowledge Utilization Division
National Center for Education Evaluation and Regional Assistance
Institute of Education Sciences, U.S. Department of Education
400 Maryland Ave. S.W., Washington, DC 20202
World Wide Web http://ies.ed.gov/ncee/projects/nat_ed_library.asp

Christina Dunn
Director, National Library of Education
202-219-1012, e-mail christina.dunn@ed.gov

The U.S. Department of Education's National Library of Education (NLE) has served the information needs of the education community since its creation in 1994. As part of the department's Institute of Education Sciences (IES), National Center for Education Evaluation and Regional Assistance, Knowledge Utilization Division, it serves as the center for the collection, preservation, discovery, and retrieval of education information, especially information produced by and for the agency. It delivers information to millions of users annually, supporting the agency's mission of promoting student achievement and preparation for global competitiveness by fostering educational excellence and ensuring equal access, as well as the IES mission of providing rigorous evidence on which to ground education practice and policy.

NLE was originally created under Public Law 103-227, the Educational Research, Development, Dissemination, and Improvement Act of 1994 and reauthorized under Public Law 107-279, the Education Sciences Reform Act of 2002. Headed by a director qualified in library science and assisted by six federal staff, including the Education Resources Information Center (ERIC) director, NLE is responsible for

- Collecting and archiving information, including products and publications developed through, or supported by, the Institute of Education Sciences; and other relevant and useful education-related research, statistics, and evaluation materials and other information, projects, and publications that are consistent with scientifically valid research or the priorities and mission of the institute, and developed by the department, other federal agencies, or entities
- Providing a central location within the federal government for information about education
- Providing comprehensive reference services on matters relating to education to employees of the U.S. Department of Education and its contractors and grantees, other federal employees, and members of the public
- Promoting greater cooperation and resource sharing among providers and repositories of education information in the United States

These responsibilities are met through two programs: the Education Resources Information Center, better known as ERIC, and the Education (ED) Reference Center. As ERIC is the primary program of NLE, it is covered in the following separate article. This article gives a brief overview of NLE, but focuses mostly on the ED Reference Center, which has responsibility for providing comprehensive reference services.

ED Reference Center

The ED Reference Center operates with a staff of 13—five federal staff and eight contract librarians. Technical and public services once operated as a single unit; however, this year it became necessary to separate these services into two units— Technical Services and Serials Management, and Reference and Document Delivery Services. While this change resulted in a loss of some flexibility, in light of the growing number of users and programs it supports, the center is better able to respond to user needs, institutional initiatives, and changing technologies. Although the main library is housed in the department's headquarters building, with satellites serving the Office of Vocational and Adult Education and the Institute of Education Sciences, most of the center's services are desktop-accessible to the agency's 5,000 staff. The center also connects to the What Works Clearinghouse, Regional Education Laboratories, and ERIC via e-mail and/or intranet. Currently it provides document delivery, as well as reference and citation analysis support to these initiatives, as well as to the National Center for Education Statistics and the National Institute on Disability and Rehabilitation Research. In fiscal year 2007 the center's budget was $1.5 million.

The center collects and archives information on education issues, research, statistics, and policy, with a special emphasis on providing historical and current collections of Department of Education documents, journals supporting the ERIC database, research reports supporting the What Works Clearinghouse, and resources supporting current and historical federal education legislation.

During 2007 the reference center continued existing initiatives, including improving information and document delivery services to agency staff through the redesign and upgrade of its portal and catalog on the department's intranet; and strengthening its position as a provider of resources to department initiatives and other libraries by adding new journal titles and research reports to its collection. New initiatives started in 2007 include improving communication and services to agency contractors by expanding virtual reference services and promoting digital archiving as a solution for organizing documents that support special agency initiatives. One initiative started in 2006 has not been realized; the center's catalog has not yet been made available on the agency's Web site, but efforts are under way for implementation in 2008.

An underlying factor in achieving these initiatives is better marketing of services and collections. During 2006 and 2007 the center has placed more emphasis on marketing, and it appears that its efforts are beginning to pay off. Use of the center has increased substantially during this period and requests for new services are up by almost 27 percent over two years ago. As part of this effort, the center has improved its collection and analysis of performance metrics, with findings on usability and user satisfaction driving changes in procedures, collection development, and user services, as well as the overall marketing initiative.

Customers

While its primary customers include department staff and contractors, the reference center also serves the general public, agency grantees, other federal agencies, and other libraries. Overall use grew from around 15,000 requests in 2006 to more than 18,000 in 2007, with most growth continuing to occur in document delivery and interlibrary loan services. While most information requests came from the general public, almost 70 percent of reference staff time is devoted to addressing the information needs of department staff and contractors, representing a 20 percent increase over 2006. This group generated around 5,700 requests or 32 percent of all requests in 2007, with the agency's research offices, including the Institute of Education Sciences, being the largest users. The general public generated approximately 7,900 requests, or 44 percent, with most of these being reference requests. The remaining 4,320 requests, or 24 percent, came from other libraries (22 percent) and other government agencies (2 percent).

During 2007 the number of reference questions increased to more than 9,000, up from about 8,000 in 2006, with approximately 70 percent of these requests coming from the general public. About 26.6 percent of these were referrals generated by the department's EDPubs service, its 1-800-USA-LEARN service, the Regional Education Laboratories Virtual Reference Desk, the ERIC Help Desk, and the Library of Congress Virtual Reference Desk.

More than 67 percent of the general public contacting the reference center in 2007 were K–12 educators, students in institutions of higher education, and researchers; 31 percent were parents; and about 2 percent were unknown. As in 2006, the majority of these customers continued to access the reference center by telephone (60 percent) or e-mail (38 percent); less than 2 percent actually visited the reference center or its satellites. Fewer visitors to the center may be the result of improved desktop access to resources. During 2007 agency staff use of the center's desktop information services almost doubled, with downloads of journal articles being the most popular activity and database searching running a close second.

Collections

The reference center's collection focuses on education issues, with an emphasis on research and policy, and on related topics including law, public policy, economics, urban affairs, sociology, history, philosophy, psychology, cognitive development, and library and information science. In 2007 the center added almost 1,000 monographs on education research, plus about 1,700 titles in other areas of interest. In addition, it currently subscribes to more than 850 English-language electronic and print journals, including most of the journals indexed by ERIC and other major education and psychology databases. Almost 68 percent of current subscriptions provide journals in electronic format, which is the preferred medium because of the facility's limited storage capacity and customer demand for desktop accessibility to journal articles.

The center maintains special collections of documents associated with its parent agency, having a complete collection of ERIC microfiche; research reports supporting the work of the What Works Clearinghouse and special panels; and current and historical publications of or related to the agency, including a special collection of federal education legislation. Other historical collections include documents and archives of the former National Institute of Education and the former U.S. Office of Education, including reports, studies, manuals, statistical publications, speeches, and policy papers. Together, these collections represent a resource covering the history of the U.S. Department of Education and its predecessor agencies. Currently the center is identifying resources from these special collections as candidates for digitization. The reference center also serves as a federal depository library under the Government Printing Office program.

The collection will be enhanced by ERIC's microfiche digitization initiative, which is scheduled to be completed in 2009. About 340,000 full-text microfiche documents indexed from 1966 to 1992 are being digitized. While ERIC will make available online only those documents for which copyright clearance is received, the entire digitized collection will reside at the center and will be available for interlibrary loan, with the center responsible for managing copyright permissions.

Services

The reference center's major role is to provide reference and other information services, including legislative reference and statistical information services, to the education community at large, as well as to provide document delivery services to department staff and contractors and interlibrary loan services to other libraries and federal agencies. As stated earlier, services to agency staff and contractors continued to grow, with 2007 demonstrating the greatest increase to date. While the information needs of this community are predictable; the information needs of the public vary widely. Of the more than 6,000 questions from the public to which the center responded, most pertained to such education-related issues as No Child Left Behind Act requirements, agency programs, student achievement and assessment, teacher quality, and national statistics. Other popular topics included agency policy and budget, federal funding to states and local school districts, current education issues covered in the news, and teacher certification requirements.

The center serves other libraries by lending books and other materials from its collection. During the past year it made available about 2,600 items, mostly research reports and agency documents, in response to about 2,200 requests from institutions of higher education, federal and state agencies, and other libraries. This continues a trend in interlibrary loan, with the number of items lent to other institutions growing steadily over the past several years. Growth is probably attributable to a stronger collection of current education research reports (including those from other English-speaking countries), and government documents, especially historical documents from the department. Agency staff conducted about 26,400 searches of the center's databases, and the center delivered more than 5,800 journal articles and documents to these customers. Of this number, about 8.5 percent were borrowed from other libraries, almost 40 percent came from document delivery services, 9 percent were purchased from book vendors, and the remainder (about 43.5 percent) came from the center's own collection. In addition, a large number of electronic-journal articles were directly downloaded by users.

The ED Reference Center can be reached by e-mail at library@ed.gov or by telephone at 800-424-1616 (toll-free), 202-205-5015 or 202-205-5019 (reference desk), 202-205-7561 (TTY), or 202-401-0547 (fax). Located in the U.S. Department of Education's headquarters building at 400 Maryland Ave. S.W., Washington, D.C., it is open from 9:00 A.M. to 5:00 P.M. weekdays, except federal holidays.

Education Resources Information Center

National Library of Education
National Center for Education Evaluation and Regional Assistance
Institute of Education Sciences, U.S. Department of Education
400 Maryland Ave. S.W., Washington, DC 20202
World Wide Web http://www.eric.ed.gov

Luna Levinson
Director, ERIC Program
202-208-2321, e-mail Luna.Levinson@ed.gov

As the world's largest digital education library, the Education Resources Information Center (ERIC) provides public access to education research and information through a database of more than 1.2 million bibliographic records from 1966 to the present as well as links to publishers' Web sites and full-text documents when feasible.

ERIC was started in 1966 to collect, catalog, and provide centralized access to federally funded research and related education documents. The vast collection of education-related material was built by a decentralized network of 16 ERIC clearinghouses with specific collection scopes. Modernization of ERIC began in 2003, following the enactment of the Education Sciences Reform Act of 2002 (Sec. 172 [a] 3 of Public Law 107-279). In the past, legislation had required the continuation of the clearinghouse structure, procedures, and products, but the new legislation envisioned the ERIC topics as part of the totality of enhanced dissemination to be conducted by the Institute of Education Sciences (IES). The Department of Education issued a new statement of work for ERIC in 2003 and awarded a single contract for the operation of ERIC to Computer Sciences Corporation (CSC) in March 2004.

ERIC Mission

The ERIC mission is to provide a comprehensive, easy-to-use, searchable, Internet-based bibliographic and full-text database of education research and information for educators, researchers, and the general public. Specific terms of the ERIC mission include

- *Comprehensive,* consisting of journal articles and non-journal materials, including materials not published by commercial publishers, that are directly related to education
- *Easy-to-use and searchable,* allowing database users to find the information they need quickly and efficiently
- *Electronic,* making ERIC operations accessible to the maximum extent feasible and linking to publishers and commercial sources of journal articles
- *Bibliographic and full-text,* with bibliographic records conveying the information users need in a simple and straightforward manner, and whenever possible including full-text journal articles and non-journal materials free of charge

Following this mission, the overarching goal of ERIC is to increase the availability and quality of research and information for ERIC users.

Increased Access to Education Materials

In September 2004 ERIC launched a Web site at http://www.eric.ed.gov providing accessibility to all the database bibliographic records, and a month later added 107,000 full-text non-journal documents (issued 1993–2004) that previously had been sold through the ERIC Document Reproduction Service (EDRS). One of the most significant developments in increasing public access to ERIC resources is the elimination of fee subscriptions for libraries, organizations, and individuals.

Since opening the new Web site, ERIC has added 84,700 bibliographic records covering materials from 2004 to the present. As of December 2007 there were more than 182,000 full-text documents available in ERIC.

Searches of the ERIC database have grown dramatically during the modernization phase. In 2007 there were more than 98 million searches of ERIC; in 2006, about 62 million searches; and in 2005, roughly 52 million searches. While complete utilization data was not captured prior to 2005, an estimated 7 million searches were reported from three Web sites in 2001. The ERIC database is available through the following commercial services: Cambridge Scientific Abstracts, EBSCO, Google and Google Scholar, MSN, OCLC FirstSearch, OVID, ProQuest, SilverPlatter, Thomson Dialog, and Yahoo!

ERIC is also available through statewide networks in Ohio, Texas, Kentucky, and North Carolina. New content is added to the ERIC database every week, and commercial vendors receive updates to the database monthly.

Web Site Enhancements

Recent enhancements to ERIC focus on increased functionality of the Web site. Searchers can mark records for placement in a temporary workspace called My Clipboard, which permits users to print, e-mail, or export records, or save them to a My ERIC account. Additional Web site improvements include search term highlighting so that users see where and how frequently their search terms occur in the results set; a new metadata field indicating peer-reviewed articles for records acquired 2004 to the present; and quicker loading of search results. Users can also easily submit electronic files of their full-text papers and accompanying bibliographic data to ERIC for consideration using the online submission system.

While the ERIC database has traditionally used narrative abstracts to describe full-text documents, database contributors now have the option of writing structured abstracts for their research papers and conference presentations. Structured abstracts present important details about research studies and their outcomes under predefined headings or elements such as research design types and study samples. A Web site video featuring Institute of Education Sciences Commissioner Phoebe Cottingham explains why the structured abstracts initiative is a key advancement for the entire ERIC audience.

To facilitate electronic access to archived materials, ERIC launched a microfiche digitization project in 2006. Approximately 340,000 full-text documents, indexed 1966–1992, will be converted from microfiche to digital image files. ERIC plans to undertake a major effort to locate document copyright holders to seek permission to provide online access in ERIC. Communication about the digitization initiative includes Web site announcements and conference presentations. As copyright permission is received, full-text documents are added monthly to the ERIC database. More than 64,000 documents were added by December 2007. The project is scheduled for completion in March 2009, and the entire digital archive will reside in the National Library of Education.

Connections to Researchers and Educators

An explicit provision of the 2004 ERIC contract is the creation of an ERIC steering committee and a content experts group. The idea behind this provision is to connect to the field of researchers and educators so that ERIC avoids technical obsolescence and continues to grow as a highly valued education resource for its audiences.

The steering committee provides recommendations to the ERIC contractor, CSC, on implementing the ERIC mission. The steering committee members have expertise in education research methodology and in the major technical aspects of an online database, database search engine, and Web site. The members also have complementary strengths so that they can address separate issues such as database and Web site building and usability, metadata and indexing, and archiving and migration of files.

Priorities for steering committee discussions and research in 2007 included peer review identification and discovery, widespread record updates to the ERIC collection, and ERIC's Open URL project. In 2004–2006, the steering committee provided advice on the ERIC standards and criteria for selecting journals and non-journal materials for the database and general outreach and dissemination guidelines as well as additional products and services. Recommendations for new projects have contributed to the structured abstracts initiative and the Web-crawler technology to augment source selection.

Content experts provide recommendations to help the ERIC curators ensure that the database reflects a high level of expertise in each of the 16 ERIC topics as well as other content areas required by the authorizing legislation. Content experts provide input on the journals indexed in ERIC and the sources and types of non-journal materials that are directly related to education and based on the approved standards and criteria for inclusion in the ERIC database. Examples of information sources include education membership associations, research organizations, conferences, groups organized around specific education issues, and other organizations that have contributed to the ERIC database.

The ERIC Collection

In addition to being the largest education library, ERIC is one of the few collections to index non-journal materials as well as journal literature. The largest share of the collection (about 58 percent) consists of citations to journal articles, and a smaller portion (about 42 percent) consists of non-journal materials, according to a 2001 estimate. The non-journal materials, frequently called gray literature, are not produced by commercial publishers and are not easy to find. In ERIC, the gray literature consists of research synthesis, dissertations, conference proceedings, and selected papers such as keynote speeches, technical reports, policy papers, literature reviews, bibliographies, congressional hearings and reports, reports on federal and state standards, testing and regulations, U.S. Department of Education contractor reports (such as the What Works Clearinghouse and the National Center for Education Statistics), and working papers for established research and policy organizations.

To support consistency and reliability in content coverage, most education journals are indexed comprehensively so that all articles in each issue are included. This was not always the policy in ERIC. In 2006 ERIC indexed roughly 570 journals comprehensively, whereas in 2003 it covered only 350 journals comprehensively; this represents more than a 60 percent increase in comprehensively covered journals. A small number of journals, 31, were indexed selectively in ERIC in 2006; about 650 journals were indexed selectively in 2003. Articles from selectively covered journals are acquired by ERIC curators, subject specialists who determine individual documents for the ERIC database according to the ERIC selection policy.

The broad selection standard provides that all materials added to the ERIC database are directly related to the field of education. The collection scope includes early childhood education through higher education, vocational education, and special education; it includes teacher education, education administration, assessment and evaluation, counseling, information technology, and the academic areas of reading, mathematics, science, environmental education, languages, and social studies. In addition, the collection also includes resources addressing one of the three objectives identified in Section 172 of the Education Sciences Reform Act—closing the achievement gap, encouraging educational practices that improve academic achievement, and conducting education research.

Following that standard, there are three sets of specific criteria providing guidance for document selection. The quality criteria consist of five basic factors: completeness, integrity, objectivity, substantive merit, and utility/importance. Selection is further determined by sponsorship criteria, and preference for inclusion in ERIC is given to those resources with identified sponsorship (for example, professional societies and government agencies). Detailed editorial criteria also provide factors for consideration, especially with regard to journals considered for comprehensive indexing.

All submissions considered for selection must be in digital format and are accompanied by author permission for dissemination. For individual document submissions, authors (copyright holders) register through the ERIC Web site feature My ERIC; follow the steps to enter bibliographic information, abstract, and document file; and submit the electronic document release form authorizing ERIC to disseminate the materials. Journal publishers, associations, and other entities with multiple documents also submit electronic content following guidance and instructions consistent with provider agreements from ERIC.

The complete list of journals indexed in ERIC, including the years of coverage and the number of articles indexed, is a new tool on the ERIC Web site enabling users to identify more easily specific journal literature. Another convenience for users, designed to streamline the process of obtaining full text, is the Find in a Library feature, which leverages the Open URL Gateway and WorldCat to provide a link from ERIC records to electronic and print resources available in libraries. For all journals currently indexed in ERIC, there are links to publishers' Web sites if users choose to purchase full-text articles.

Refinements to ERIC's technical architecture continue to improve system functionality and user satisfaction. Usability tests with participant groups including librarians, researchers, and students provide input on issues such as online submission, the help section, and an extensive range of search operations. With all database enhancements, the development process contributes to increasing accessibility, efficiency, and quality.

National Association and Organization Reports

American Library Association

50 E. Huron St., Chicago, IL 60611
800-545-2433
World Wide Web http://www.ala.org

Loriene Roy
President

The oldest, largest, and most influential library association in the world, the American Library Association (ALA) was founded in 1876 in Philadelphia and later chartered in the Commonwealth of Massachusetts. ALA's membership of about 65,000 includes not only librarians but also library trustees, publishers, and other interested people from every U.S. state and many nations. The association serves public, state, school, and academic libraries, plus special libraries for people working in government, commerce and industry, the arts, and the armed services as well as in hospitals, prisons, and other institutions.

ALA's mission is "to provide leadership for the development, promotion, and improvement of library and information services and the profession of librarianship in order to enhance learning and ensure access to information for all."

ALA is governed by an elected council—its policy-making body—and an executive board, which acts for the council in the administration of established policies and programs and manages the affairs of the association. Day-to-day operations are delegated to the association's executive director and implemented by staff through a structure of programmatic offices and support units. ALA also has 37 standing committees, designated as committees of the association or of its council.

ALA is home to 11 membership divisions, each focused on a type of library, library function, or area of special interest. They are the American Association of School Librarians (AASL), the Association for Library Collections and Technical Services (ALCTS), the Association for Library Service to Children (ALSC), the Association for Library Trustees and Advocates (ALTA), the Association of College and Research Libraries (ACRL), the Association of Specialized and Cooperative Library Agencies (ASCLA), the Library Administration and Management Association (LAMA), the Library and Information Technology Association (LITA), the Public Library Association (PLA), the Reference and User Services Association (RUSA), and the Young Adult Library Services Association (YALSA).

ALA also hosts 17 roundtables for members who share interests that do not fall within the scope of the divisions. A network of affiliates, chapters, and other organizations enables the association to reach a broad audience.

Key action areas include diversity, equitable access to information and library services, education and lifelong learning, intellectual freedom, advocacy for libraries and the profession, literacy, and organizational excellence.

ALA offices are units of the association that address broad interests and issues of concern to its members; they track issues and provide information, services, and products for members and the general public. Current ALA offices are the Chapter Relations Office, the Development Office, the Governance Office, the International Relations Office, the Office for Accreditation, the Office for Diversity, the Office for Government Relations, the Office for Human Resource Development and Recruitment, the Office for Information Technology Policy, the Office for Intellectual Freedom, the Office for Library Advocacy, the Office for Literacy and Outreach Services, the Office for Research and Statistics, the Public Information Office, the Public Programs Office, and the Washington (D.C.) Office.

ALA headquarters is in Chicago; the Office for Government Relations and Office for Information Technology Policy are housed in ALA's Washington Office. ALA also has an editorial office for *Choice,* a review journal for academic libraries, in Middletown, Connecticut.

ALA is a 501(c)(3) charitable and educational organization.

Literacy, Workplace Wellness, Education

During her presidential year, 2007–2008 ALA President Loriene Roy focused her activities on literacy, with an emphasis on reading initiatives; workplace wellness, and support for library and information science (LIS) education.

ALA's first American Indian president, Roy is a member of the Anishinabe (Ojibwe) people, whom she described at her inaugural banquet as "dreamers and predictors. Dreamers are acknowledged and young people are encouraged to find their dreams and their guardians," she said. "Let us examine the dream we want to build."

Roy, a professor in the School of Information at the University of Texas at Austin, vowed that her Circle of Literacy initiative would serve as "an opportunity to celebrate reading, especially reading and culture as it is experienced among indigenous peoples in the United States and around the world." In conjunction with National Library Week 2008, she planned to host a celebratory week involving as many as 100 schools from around the world that serve indigenous children. The literacy initiative also aimed to promote indigenous writers and publishers and to explore literacy among new immigrants and people who are incarcerated.

Other agenda items included planning a wellness fair and other events for the 2008 Annual Conference, developing a national database of field work options for LIS students, initiating a national oral history project for retired or retiring librarians, and examining the feasibility of a national library camp for youth.

Highlights of the Year

EPA Libraries Ordered to Reopen

ALA, librarians, and the public won a victory in June 2007 when Congress ordered the Environmental Protection Agency (EPA) to restore its library network, threatened by a $2 million cut proposed by EPA itself and included in President George W. Bush's budget proposals for fiscal year (FY) 2007. The cut reduced the 35-year-old EPA library network's budget by 80 percent and forced closure of several regional EPA libraries. ALA's Washington Office worked with Congress and EPA to stem the tide of information loss from what 2006–2007 ALA President Leslie Burger, in testimony before the Senate, called "a virtual National Library on the Environment." In the FY 2008 Interior Appropriations bill, the Senate Appropriations Committee ordered EPA to reopen the closed libraries.

Monitoring the Use of National Security Letters

ALA continued its active role in the debate over the use of National Security Letters (NSLs), administrative subpoenas issued with no judicial oversight under provisions of the USAPatriot Act of 2001. In June 2007 ALA Council urged ALA members, state chapters, and all library advocates to ask Congress to restore civil liberties and correct the abuse and misuse of NSLs, and the Campaign for Reader Privacy, whose members include ALA, praised the National Security Letter Reform Act of 2007, introduced by Sen. Russ Feingold (D.-Wis.) and others. That bill responds to a report by the Department of Justice inspector general that documented misuse of NSLs and to two federal court decisions that struck down the NSL provisions of the USAPatriot Act as unconstitutional. A similar bill was introduced in the House in July.

American Libraries' Centennial Suite of Publications

American Libraries, ALA's flagship news and feature magazine and chief perquisite of membership in the association, marked its centennial year both by celebrating the past (more than 29 million copies published since 1907) and by starting new projects that will carry it to its next centennial. In January *American Libraries* debuted its new print design, followed by integrated redesigns of *AL Direct* (the weekly e-newsletter) and *AL Online.* New content and organization reflect the greater emphasis on technology requested by respondents to a 2006 reader survey, and a second blog, "CentenniAL," was added.

In June 2007 the staff launched "AL Focus," the video and podcasting component of *AL Online.* Editors initiated videocast coverage at the Association of College and Research Libraries conference and continued this at ALA's Annual Conference. Centennial celebrations culminated at the Annual Conference with sponsored programs (including an appearance by actress and author Julie Andrews before an overflow crowd; a highly praised vendor forum led by Andrew Pace, head of information technology at North Carolina State University, in the exhibit hall; and "Next Generation Libraries: The 2.0 Phenomenon"), cake events complete with tattoos and T-shirts, and distribution of the June/July commemorative print issue.

ALA Unit Joins Forces with 'Friends' Group

Under an agreement reached in September, Friends of Libraries USA (FOLUSA) is providing executive management for ALTA through August 31, 2008, with the expectation that FOLUSA and ALTA will seek to combine into an expanded division of ALA on that date. Don Roalkvam, 2007–2008 ALTA president, noted that an expanded array of products and services would help the enlarged division "move our combined vision of library advocacy forward with new membership and resources."

AASL Toolkit Targets '65 Percent Solution'

AASL's Task Force on Instructional Classification developed a toolkit that addresses the issue of the categorization of school library media specialists as "non-instructional." The toolkit is designed to help school library media specialists explain their role as educators within their schools and districts and to provide talking points for opposing "65 percent solution" legislation, which threatens funding for school library media services on the state level. The "65 percent solution" was originated in 2005 by First Class Education, which began a campaign to mandate that 65 percent of every school district budget in the nation be spent on classroom instruction and opposed rewriting the 30-year-old National Center for Education Statistics definition of classroom instruction to include librarians, who are grouped with food, transportation, and other non-instructional staff.

New Office for Library Advocacy

ALA formed an Office for Library Advocacy (OLA) to support the efforts of advocates seeking to improve libraries of all types by developing resources, a peer-to-peer advocacy network, and training for advocates at the local, state, and national levels. To better integrate these efforts into the overall advocacy planning and strategies of the association, OLA works closely with the Public Information Office, the Chapter Relations Office, the Office for Government Relations, and other ALA units involved in advocacy on behalf of particular types of libraries or particular issues. OLA also works to cultivate future leadership in order to sustain the advocacy efforts of the association.

National Library Legislative Day

Approximately 425 librarians, friends of libraries, trustees, and patrons from 47 states went to Washington, D.C., May 1–2, 2007, for National Library Legislative Day. Participants spoke with their representatives in Congress about the needs of libraries in the areas of funding, telecommunications, copyright, privacy, and government information. In addition, several individuals and state organizations participated in Virtual Library Legislative Day by phoning, faxing letters, and e-mailing members of Congress. FOLUSA presented an award to Sen. Susan Collins (R-Maine) for her work in support of libraries. The day's theme was "Check Out the Future."

Banned Books Week 2007

Banned Books Week marked its 26th anniversary September 29–October 6 with the theme "Ahoy! Treasure Your Freedom to Read and Get Hooked on a Banned Book." Readings, exhibits, and programs nationwide highlighted this annual celebration of the freedom to read, which gives librarians, teachers, booksellers, and others an opportunity to raise awareness in their communities about the importance of free speech and free expression. Among the year's activities were a kickoff Read-Out! event in Chicago September 29, with authors reading from their banned books, as well as interactive Internet experiences on the social networking Web sites Second Life, Teen Second Life, MySpace, and Facebook.

Teen Read Week

Celebrating its tenth anniversary October 14–20, Teen Read Week 2007 urged teens to "laugh out loud" at their libraries—and participate in a range of activities centered around the theme "LOL @ your library." Thousands of librarians and educators participated, and more than 6,000 online votes were cast for the Teens' Top Ten list of most popular young adult books. The theme for Teen Read Week 2008, to be held October 12–18, will be "Books with Bite @ your library."

Record Number of Spectrum Scholars

Also marking its tenth anniversary, the Spectrum Scholarship Program—a national diversity and recruitment effort that unifies the profession's diversity recruitment and retention efforts at all levels—awarded 80 scholarships in 2006–2007, the largest cohort to date. The substantial increase in available scholarships was due both to the generosity of individuals and organizations and to a substantial grant from the Institute for Museum and Library Services (IMLS). Scholarships for 2007 were awarded in honor of Leo Albert, Louise Giles, and Howard M. and Gladys B. Teeple. Ten of the 2007 Spectrum Scholarships were funded by proceeds from the ALA/ProQuest Scholarship Bash, which is held each year at the Annual Conference.

   In June ALA and the University of Pittsburgh School of Information Sciences announced the first six recipients of the Spectrum Doctoral Fellowship, for which IMLS is providing nearly $1 million. IMLS has also awarded the Office for Diversity $872,920 to double the number of annual Spectrum Scholarship awards for the next three years and to expand Spectrum's reach and leverage its impact by providing support to other diversity recruitment initiatives and LIS institutions.

Three Divisions Turn 50

ALCTS, LAMA, and YALSA all celebrated 50 years of service in 2006–2007. ALCTS marked the occasion with a commemorative publication, three 50th anniversary presidential citations, and a special 50th anniversary Ross Atkinson Lifetime Achievement Award; the division also inaugurated a fund-raising campaign, "50for50." LAMA launched a campaign to raise $50,000 for its endowment fund. YALSA created a logo for its anniversary year; special events included a party at the Annual Conference, at which YALSA also hosted a day of readings at the Public Programs Office's Authors' Stage.

Assessing the Future of Academic Libraries

In February 2007 ACRL published "Changing Roles of Academic and Research Libraries," an essay on technology and change in academic libraries that resulted from a November 2006 summit held in Chicago. Attended by 30 library leaders, the unscripted roundtable discussion imagined an alternative future for academic libraries; the resulting paper asks key questions and suggests answers that should expand the national discussion of how academic libraries can best serve their institutions and the nation at large.

Spanish Translation of 'KIDS @ your library'

ALSC offered a major enhancement to the "KIDS! @ your library" public-awareness campaign with the translation of toolkit components into Spanish, including the logo and tag line "So Much to See. So Much to Do @ your library" ("Tanto que Ver. Tanto que Hacer en tu biblioteca"), print public service announcements in a variety of sizes, and a "Top Ten List of Things to Do at your library." ALSC also worked with HarperCollins Children's Books to promote National "Drop Everything and Read (DEAR) Day," an initiative that encouraged families to put aside all distractions and take at least 30 minutes to enjoy books together.

Service to Special Populations

ASCLA has published *Guidelines for Library Services for People with Mental Illnesses,* designed to help librarians establish detailed crisis-management procedures and to provide the background librarians need to avert crises and arrive at successful library experiences for people with mental illnesses.

New List of Best Titles for Adults

RUSA's Collection Development and Evaluation Section has added to its nationally recognized book award programs with the Reading List, a juried list of the best titles published in eight genre areas for adults—fantasy, historical fiction, horror, mystery, romance, science fiction, women's fiction, and "adrenaline titles," which collectively encompass suspense, thrillers, and action adventure works. Lists will be juried yearly and the winning titles announced at each ALA Midwinter Meeting.

Public Library Funding and Technology Access Study

The 2007 Public Library Funding and Technology Access Study showed that 99.1 percent of U.S. public libraries now offer free public access to the Internet; 73 percent of libraries reported they were the only source of free public access to computers and the Internet in their communities. On the down side, many library buildings are ill-equipped to accommodate the space and infrastructure for more than a few computer workstations, and the study revealed that the need for more bandwidth was another consistent capacity concern. The study, conducted by ALA and the Information Use Management and Policy Institute at Florida State University, was funded by ALA and the Bill and Melinda Gates Foundation.

Public Library Data Reports Move Online

PLA has launched an online version of its *Public Library Data Service Statistical Report,* which is designed to provide timely, library-specific data that illuminate and support a wide variety of management decisions. The online service allows subscribers to view 2007 Public Library Data Service (PLDS) tables, including summary and comparison tables; access 2006 and 2007 summary tables in interactive charts; and create customized PLDS datasets that can be saved and exported into Excel/CSV file formats.

New Events for Young Adult Readers

YALSA established several new national events. Teen Tech Week, held the first week of March each year, encourages teens to explore the nonprint resources available at their libraries, including DVDs, databases, audiobooks, and electronic games. Support Teen Literature Day aims to help raise awareness about teen literature and will serve as the launch for each year's Teen Read Week. Support Teen Literature Day was held in conjunction with National Library Week, April 15–21, the theme of which was "Come Together @ your library." The Wrestle-Mania Reading Challenge, expanded from a pilot program in Chicago, extended Teen Read Week beyond the third week of October. Almost 500 high school libraries participated in the first year of the challenge.

Campaign for America's Libraries

Continuing PLA's "Smartest Card" campaign, ALA promoted new radio public service announcements from actor-comedian George Lopez, and more than 80 Spanish-language news sources talked about Lopez's five favorite things about his library card.

Grammy-nominated children's singer-storyteller Bill Harley took to the stage to promote ALSC's "KIDS! @ your library" campaign at Boston Public Library. To help libraries get the word out about the campaign—a national effort to raise awareness of all the free library resources available for children and families—Harley created an original song that includes the "So Much to See. So Much to Do @ your library" refrain. The song was made available in the online "KIDS! @ your library" toolkit. ALSC also launched a Web page of resources for families that includes a list of award-winning children's books, kid-friendly Web sites, downloadable games and activities, and resources for parents to help support reading at home.

Campaign for the World's Libraries

South Africa and Trinidad and Tobago joined the Campaign for the World's Libraries at the conference of the International Federation of Library Associations and Institutions (IFLA) in Durban, South Africa, in August. ALA and IFLA developed the Campaign for the World's Libraries to showcase the unique and vital roles played by public, school, academic, and special libraries worldwide. Thirty-three countries have joined the campaign, and the "@ your library" brand has been translated into each country's language.

Programs and Partners

Campaign Partnerships

As the Campaign for America's Libraries newest Founding Partner, Dollar General, a Fortune 500 discount retailer, came on board to develop the "American Dream Starts @ your library," a two-year program focusing on adult literacy services. Through the program, which is administered by the Office for Literacy and Outreach Services, libraries will receive grants to expand their literacy collections, services, and programs for adult immigrants and English-language learners and to provide examples of best practices to inspire and inform other libraries. In year two ALA will develop an "American Dream Starts @ your library" training module focusing on assessing and expanding libraries' literacy and English-as-a-second-language programs, services, and resources.

Continuing a six-year partnership with the Campaign for America's Libraries, *Woman's Day* magazine featured the four winners of the "How the library changed my life" initiative in its March 2007 issue. The magazine received almost 2,000 essays in response to its call for entries, including stories about a mother who turned to the library during a bout of postpartum depression and an Indonesian immigrant who used books from her childhood public library to learn English. The magazine also announced its next initiative, asking readers to submit stories of how they used the library to start businesses. Four of the submissions were featured the March 2008 issue of *Woman's Day*.

The second season of the "Step Up to the Plate @ your library" program, developed by ALA and the National Baseball Hall of Fame and Museum, kicked off in April in Peoria, Illinois, with Hall of Famers and former baseball rivals Ryne Sandberg and Ozzie Smith serving as program spokespeople. Both appeared on the field with the Peoria Chiefs, the minor league team Sandberg now manages. Year two encouraged children and young adults to visit their library, check out a baseball book, and write about how their favorite character inspired them. The grand prize was a trip to the National Baseball Hall of Fame in Cooperstown, New York.

The Campaign for America's Libraries has begun planning for a first-ever national advertising campaign exclusively designed for—and targeting the specific needs of—Latino/Hispanic communities. Working with the Metropolitan Group, a national strategic communications firm that specializes in work with libraries and socially responsible businesses, ALA will target Spanish-speaking populations in the top 20 media markets through radio, outdoor, and transit advertising. Corporate partners will underwrite the cost of producing and placing the advertising. ALA will also partner with libraries in the 20 markets to provide a local base for the campaign.

RUSA continued to take a leadership role in investor education programming with "Smart Investing @ your library," a program funded by the FINRA

Investor Education Foundation. The program aims to help public libraries provide effective, unbiased investor education. During the two-year pilot, a select group of libraries will compete for up to 12 grants ranging from $5,000 to $100,000. The grants will encourage innovation by helping libraries serve patrons not only at the libraries but also online and in a variety of community settings. The program will also provide objective investor education materials to the participating libraries, as well as professional development for librarians.

Exhibitions on the Road

The Public Programs Office toured three exhibitions nationwide in 2007: "Changing the Face of Medicine: Celebrating America's Women Physicians," "Alexander Hamilton: The Man Who Made Modern America," and "Forever Free: Abraham Lincoln's Journey to Emancipation." The office also announced two new traveling exhibitions that will tour public and academic libraries through 2011. "Lewis and Clark and the Indian Country," which is based on the Newberry Library's major exhibition of the same title, will visit 23 libraries, while 40 libraries will host "Benjamin Franklin: In Search of a Better World," which is based on a major exhibition of the same title shown at the National Constitution Center in Philadelphia. The Lewis and Clark exhibition received major funding from the National Endowment for the Humanities (NEH) and additional support from the University of Illinois at Urbana-Champaign. NEH also provided major funding for the Benjamin Franklin exhibition, which is presented by ALA in collaboration with the Benjamin Franklin Tercentenary in Philadelphia.

We the People Initiatives

NEH and ALA partnered to present the fourth We the People Bookshelf, providing sets of 15 classic children's books on the theme "Pursuit of Happiness" to 2,000 public and school libraries in all 50 states. Library programs were to take place nationally through May 2008. We the People Bookshelf aims to encourage young people to read and understand great literature while exploring themes in American history.

NEH also partnered with the Public Programs Office to offer a pilot grant initiative to schools and school libraries. Also part of NEH's We the People program, "Picturing America" offers grants of a collection of large-scale laminated reproductions of American art, as well as educational resources on American art and history. In May 2007 more than 1,500 schools and school libraries were selected to receive the collections.

El Día de los Niños/El Día de los Libros

El Día de los Niños/El Día de los Libros (Children's Day/Book Day), celebrated April 30, was an unprecedented success in 2007, as its first official national sponsor, the retailer Target, enabled the program to offer $40,000 in mini-grants, signage, and giveaway materials to eight "Super-Site" libraries around the country, plus giveaway materials to 80 percent of the 460-plus libraries that registered their Día events on the ALSC Web site.

Conferences and Workshops

2007 Annual Conference

In what was the largest conference in the history of the association, some 28,635 librarians, exhibitors, and library supporters attended ALA's 2007 Annual Conference in Washington, D.C., June 21–27.

Former U.S. Senator Bill Bradley, keynote speaker at the opening general session, stressed that activism is needed to ensure a healthy future for America. "We need collective caring and individual action," he stated.

Robert F. Kennedy, Jr. joined Leslie Burger at her ALA President's Program for a discussion of the important role that natural surroundings play in our work, our health, and our identity as Americans. By taking steps to ensure that our libraries follow sound environmental policies and procedures, Kennedy said, we can contribute to the transformation of our communities, our nation, and our planet, enabling future generations to live in an environment that is safe, clean, and beautiful.

Nearly 1,300 people—a record number—attended the Newbery/Caldecott/Wilder awards banquet to celebrate winners Susan Patron for the Newbery Medal-winning *The Higher Power of Lucky,* David Wiesner for the Caldecott Medal-winning *Flotsam,* and a video in tribute to the Wilder Medal winner, the late James Marshall.

As part of Library Day on the Hill, some 2,000 librarians and library supporters visited members of Congress June 26 to call attention to the value of today's libraries and the issues the library community is facing—with threats to funding high on the list.

Actress and author Julie Andrews was the special guest at a program celebrating the centennial of *American Libraries* magazine. She later held a press conference at the Martin Luther King, Jr. Library, where she spoke about the value of America's libraries and announced she would serve as the spokesperson and honorary chair for National Library Week 2008.

The Public Programs Office and YALSA presented the 13th annual "LIVE! @ your library" Reading Stage, which drew crowds for readings by Sherman Alexie, Donna Leon, Lois Lowry, Nick Hornby, Dinaw Mengestu, and other authors and poets. In celebration of YALSA's 50th anniversary, an entire afternoon was devoted to readings by young adult authors.

Some 225 people attended the 2007 Empowerment Conference—called "Mama Said There'd Be Days Like This (But I Didn't Believe Her)"—held June 23–24 for library support staff and sponsored by the Office for Human Resource Development and Recruitment. Programs addressed topics such as career paths/transitions, e-learning, wellness, safety and security, and diversity.

In other offerings, the Public Programs Office began a year-long 25th-anniversary celebration of its "Let's Talk About It" discussion series with a reception and a conference program focused on new themes and resources; *Booklist*'s "Books for Youth Forum" commemorated the 50th anniversary of YALSA by hosting a Printz reunion, including the winner of the first Michael L. Printz Award and the Honor Book authors who shared the podium at the Printz forum in 2000; and PLA's President's Program featured Armistead Maupin, author of *Tales of the City, More Tales of the City, Further Tales of the City,* and *Michael Tolliver Lives.*

2008 Midwinter Meeting

More than 13,600 librarians and library supporters attended the 2008 Midwinter Meeting January 11–16 in Philadelphia.

Retired pro basketball star Kareem Abdul-Jabbar delivered a heartfelt address, telling a packed house, "I am not standing here as a basketball player but as a historian and book lover, all because of a library and librarians like you." Discovering the New York Public Library's Schomburg Center while researching the Harlem Renaissance, he said, was a revelation that turned his life around.

Another highlight was the annual announcement of the 2008 Newbery and Caldecott medals, as well as other youth media awards. Brian Selznick won the Caldecott Medal for *The Invention of Hugo Cabret,* a 500-plus-page category-buster that the author has called "not exactly a novel, not quite a picture book, not really a graphic novel or a flip book or a movie, but a combination of all these things." Laura Amy Schlitz won the Newbery Medal for *Good Masters! Sweet Ladies! Voices from a Medieval Village.* A collection of theatrical mono-logues, it was originally written as a performance piece for fifth-grade students studying the Middle Ages.

Conference participants benefited from some 800 meetings, many of them planning sessions for the 2008 Annual Conference in Anaheim, California. Some 500 technology vendors and publishers filled the exhibition hall in the Pennsyl-vania Convention Center, enabling attendees to examine firsthand a wide variety of information-industry products.

Speakers and discussion forums added variety to the association's annual business meeting, foremost among them an appearance by FBI whistleblower Bassem Youssef at the Washington Office session. Despite a warning from his superiors, Special Agent Youssef appeared at the meeting with his attorney, cau-tiously explaining his dilemma and answering questions from the audience about problems with the FBI's counterterrorism program.

Jazz violinist Regina Carter helped conferees take a format break with a con-cert at the ninth annual Arthur Curley Memorial Lecture. And Pulitzer Prize-win-ning journalist Anthony Lewis spoke candidly about his career and key Supreme Court decisions on the First Amendment with Chris Finan, president of the American Booksellers Foundation for Free Expression, in a fund-raising session sponsored by the Freedom to Read Foundation.

ACRL National Conference

ACRL held its 13th National Conference March 29–April 1 in Baltimore, offer-ing more than 250 programs on the theme "Sailing Into the Future—Charting Our Destiny." Programs included a full range of papers, panels, poster sessions, workshops, forums, Cyber Zed Shed presentations on emerging technologies, and roundtable discussions. Key areas of discussion included interactive gaming, the future of reference and online searching, open access to research, and federated searching. The flavor and discussions of the conference were also represented online by a group of more than 20 official conference bloggers.

PLA Spring Symposium

More than 700 public librarians gathered March 1–3 for PLA's 2007 Spring Symposium, held in San José, California. The opening general session featured a keynote address by Mary Baykan, who serves as director of the Washington County (Maryland) Free Library, executive director of the Western Maryland Public Library, and legislative officer of the Maryland Library Association. Six one-day workshops included continuing education programming, sold-out tours of San José's public libraries, and a luncheon with bestselling author Po Bronson.

LITA National Forum

With the theme "Technology with Altitude," LITA's 2007 National Forum was held October 4–7 in Denver. Keynote speakers included Jeffrey Kiehl of the National Center for Atmospheric Research; David King of the Topeka and Shawnee County (Kansas) Public Library; and Jeremy Frumkin, Gray Chair for Innovative Library Services at Oregon State University. Thirty-six concurrent sessions were held, along with a vendor showcase and poster sessions. Preconference workshops included "The-Library-Knowledge-Kills," a live-action experiment in alternative reality game design; and "Library-wide IT Proficiency."

Publishing

ALA Editions Offers 24 New Titles

ALA Editions published 24 new titles in 2007, offering ways for library professionals to maximize expertise in areas as diverse as preschool activities, gaming, designing and managing facilities, analyzing library collection use, and readers' advisory. Among the top new releases were *Out Front with Stephen Abram* by Judith A. Siess and Jonathan Lorig, *Gamers . . . in the Library?!* by Eli Neiburger, and *The Readers' Advisory Guide to Nonfiction* by Neal Wyatt. In addition, *Serving Teens Through Readers' Advisory* by Heather Booth was selected for the Voice of Youth Advocates "Five-Foot Bookshelf"—books deemed essential for professionals who serve teens.

Popular Products from ALA Graphics

ALA Graphics' READ CDs, which allow users to create their own posters and bookmarks, were among its star products of 2007. Sharing stories of how libraries, schools, and local governments have used the posters in their communities formed the basis of a campaign that included direct mail and e-mail, an online tutorial accessible through the ALA Store, and the creation of a Flickr pool where people can submit the posters they make.

New Celebrity READ posters included Dakota Fanning, Ewan McGregor, Sasha Cohen, Hilary Swank, William H. Macy, Cesar Millan, Corbin Bleu, and James Patterson. Child- and young adult-themed posters included Cantarella, from a Japanese manga series; original art from Patrick McDonnell of "Mutts" comic strip fame; X-Men, in partnership with Marvel Comics; Raymond Briggs's wintertime classic *The Snowman;* and original art from Karen Katz based on her book *Can You Say Peace?*

Expanding on the READ series, the LISTEN poster series—in which stars showcase their favorite CD or audiobook—was launched with Cedric the Entertainer, closely followed by Los Lonely Boys. Another new line of posters celebrated the ALA youth media awards.

ALA TechSource Continues to Innovate

ALA TechSource, publisher of *Library Technology Reports (LTR,) Smart Libraries Newsletter,* and the TechSource Web site, continued to garner attention for innovation as well as high traffic for its blog (running as much as 160,000 visits some months, and close to 1,000,000 total for the year). High-profile library bloggers offering expert perspectives on the latest issues in 2007 included Michelle Boule, Tom Peters, Karen G. Schneider, and Michael Stephens.

Interactive gaming on the exhibit floor at ALA conferences helped highlight the related *LTR* issue "Gaming and Libraries." The popular theme eventually became the focus for the first-ever ALA TechSource symposium, "Gaming, Learning, and Libraries," held in July in Chicago.

Booklist Publishes More Than 8,000 Reviews

Booklist spent its 103rd year again assisting, supporting, and entertaining collection developers and readers' advisers with nearly 8,000 recommended-only reviews and with features on a variety of topics. In addition to the regular publication schedule of *Booklist* and *Book Links* print magazines, *Booklist Online* added content and features, and statistics showed a dramatic increase in *Booklist Online* usage, with more than 1.2 million visits. Four regional OCLC and other sales groups came under contract to sell *Booklist Online* subscriptions in various regions of the country. A partnership with the Downers Grove (Illinois) Public Library led to a free, interactive, expert-moderated book club with forums for readers to get and share information and ideas.

PLA Adds Titles to 'Results' Series

Building on its "Results" model, PLA has published *Managing Facilities for Results: Optimizing Space for Services* by Cheryl Bryan, and *Human Resources for Results: The Right Person for the Right Job* by Jeanne Goodrich and Paula M. Singer. Other PLA releases included *Libraries Prosper with Passion, Purpose, and Persuasion: A PLA Toolkit for Success*; a new monograph, *Field Guide to Emergency Response;* and its first-ever digital download, *The Public Library Service Responses,* a revision of the original 13 service responses as defined in the 1997 publication *Planning for Results: A Public Library Transformation Process.*

ACRL Publications

ACRL has published *Global Evolution: A Chronological Annotated Bibliography of International Students in U.S. Academic Libraries* by Kaetrena D. Davis (made available as a free, open access download in addition to the print version), and *Sailing Into the Future: Charting Our Destiny* (Proceedings of the 2007 ACRL National Conference). Standards and guidelines published during the past year include "Research Competency Guidelines for Literatures in English" and "Guidelines for Instruction Programs in Academic Libraries."

RUSA Journal Redesigned

RUSA redesigned its print journal, *Reference & User Services Quarterly* (*RUSQ*), and launched the *RUSQ Online Companion* Web site. Guided by the philosophy of the open access movement, the online companion is open to all users, provides full text of articles, and runs on blog software so readers can communicate with authors.

Leadership

Loriene Roy, professor in the School of Information at the University of Texas at Austin, was inaugurated as ALA's 2007–2008 president at the 2007 Annual Conference in Washington, D.C.

ALA's first American Indian president, Roy is Anishinabe (Ojibwe), enrolled on the White Earth Reservation and a member of the Minnesota Chippewa Tribe. She was once an allied health worker who served as an x-ray technician, and she says her experience in that field led to an understanding that wellness affects both individuals and whole families, including workplace families.

James Rettig, university librarian at the University of Richmond in Virginia, was elected ALA president-elect in the 2007 election. He will be inaugurated as ALA president at the 2008 Annual Conference in Anaheim. Rettig vowed to work on behalf of library workers and all types of libraries, as well as to continue discussions about creating new opportunities for participation in ALA.

Rodney M. Hersberger, dean of the University Library at California State University–Bakersfield, was elected to a three-year term as ALA treasurer. He will serve through the 2010 ALA Annual Conference.

The ALA Council elected three new ALA Executive Board members in a vote taken at the 2008 Midwinter Meeting. They are Joseph Eagan, manager of the Olney (Maryland) Library, Montgomery County Public Libraries; Em Claire Knowles, assistant dean, Graduate School of Library and Information Science, Simmons College, Boston; and Diane R. Chen, library information specialist, Hickman Elementary School, Nashville. Each will serve a three-year term that will begin at the 2008 ALA Annual Conference.

Grants and Contributions

Gates Foundation Grant for Advocacy Training

The Bill and Melinda Gates Foundation awarded PLA a $7.7 million grant in June 2007 to develop and provide an advocacy training program for public librarians. The Sustaining Libraries Symposium aims to teach librarians how to seek funding, create partnerships, and build alliances with local decision-makers, and will support libraries that are eligible to receive Gates Foundation Opportunity Online hardware grants, which require matching local dollars, and will also be available to non-grantees on a limited basis.

Cultural Communities Fund

ALA raised more than $230,000 in 2007 for the Cultural Communities Fund, an endowment established to support diverse and excellent cultural programming in all types of libraries. These funds will be matched under terms of a $350,000 challenge grant from NEH. The fund has received more than $1 million in contributions from individuals and other organizations, including the H. W. Wilson Foundation, Sara Jaffarian, NEH, PLA, the Wallace Foundation, Nextbook, Random House, ACRL, Barnes and Noble, RUSA, and Severn House Publishers.

IMLS Award for Certification Program

IMLS has awarded ALA, in partnership with the Western Council of State Libraries (WCSL), $407,111 to develop the Library Support Staff Certification Program. ALA and WCSL will develop a national voluntary certification program for support staff in public and academic libraries. The three-year project will result in a set of core competencies, an assessment methodology, and policies and procedures.

Major Grant for Online Resource Center

The Public Programs Office received a $358,000 grant from IMLS to fund development of an Online Resource Center (ORC) for Library Cultural Programming. ORC will serve as a Web-based professional development space to help librarians find authoritative resources for cultural programming, train librarians in cultural programming techniques, and involve library schools in examining the need for courses in cultural programming. Through the new ORC, Public Programs will make available an array of online cultural programming information and training tools, provide access to "turnkey" cultural programs developed by organizations and funding agencies that have already been successful on a national level, provide professional development tools by converting printed training materials to digital format, and offer free real-time online training sessions that are pedagogically sound.

YALSA Wins World Book-ALA Goal Award

YALSA was named the recipient of the 2007 World Book-ALA Goal Award, with a grant totaling $10,000 to improve teen library services in Arkansas, Louisiana, and Mississippi. YALSA trainers provided two workshops—"A Beginner's Guide to Teens in Libraries" and "Power Up with Print"—in each state and gave free Teen Read Week resource kits to library workers, including tips on collection development, programming, and marketing library services to teens. The grant funded increased professional development in the targeted states to boost teen library use and ultimately teen reading and literacy.

Major Awards and Honors

Honorary Members

David Cohen, Alice L. Hagemeyer, Anita R. Schiller, and Alphonse F. Trezza were chosen as the 2007 ALA Honorary Members, the highest award bestowed by the association in recognition of outstanding contributions of lasting importance to libraries and librarianship.

Cohen, professor emeritus at the Graduate School of Library and Information Studies at Queens College, City University of New York, was chosen for his contributions to multicultural librarianship and intellectual freedom in a career stretching over seven decades.

Hagemeyer, the first librarian for the deaf community at the District of Columbia Public Library, was nominated for her passionate, lifelong interest in promoting information about the language, culture, and achievements of deaf individuals.

Schiller, librarian emerita at the University of California at San Diego, was nominated for her groundbreaking efforts to enhance the status of women in librarianship through her accomplishments as a researcher, writer, speaker, and mentor.

Trezza, professor emeritus at Florida State University School of Library and Information Studies, was chosen for his accomplishments in fostering resource sharing between libraries and the development of cooperative library systems, and in library education, library association management, and library management and leadership at the state and national levels.

James Madison Award

ALA presented the 2007 James Madison Award to Paul K. McMasters, who established and directed the Freedom Forum's First Amendment Center and in 1995 was named the organization's First Amendment Ombudsman. McMasters was given the award for his tireless work toward openness in government and was noted for his leadership efforts in celebration of Freedom of Information Day and his creation of the National Freedom of Information Act Hall of Fame. The Madison Award, named for the nation's fifth president, was established in 1986.

Association of American Publishers

71 Fifth Ave., New York, NY 10010
212-255-0200, fax 212-255-7007

50 F St. N.W., Washington, DC 20001
202-347-3375, fax 202-347-3690

World Wide Web http://www.publishers.org

Judith Platt
Director, Communications/Public Affairs

The Association of American Publishers (AAP) is the national trade association of the U.S. book publishing industry. The association was created in 1970 through the merger of the American Book Publishers Council, a trade publishing group, and the American Educational Publishers Institute, an organization of textbook publishers. AAP's more than 300 corporate members include most of the major commercial book publishers in the United States as well as smaller and medium-sized houses, not-for-profit publishers, university presses, and scholarly societies.

AAP members publish hardcover and paperback books in every field including general fiction and nonfiction; poetry; children's books; textbooks; Bibles and other religious works; reference works; scientific, medical, technical, professional, and scholarly books and journals; computer software; and a range of electronic products and services.

AAP also works closely with some 2,000 smaller regional publishers through formal affiliations with the Publishers Association of the West, the Publishers Association of the South, the Florida Publishers Association, the Small Publishers Association of North America, and the Evangelical Christian Publishers Association.

AAP policy is set by a board of directors, elected by the membership for four-year terms, under a chair who serves for two years. There is an executive committee composed of the chair, vice chair, secretary, and treasurer and a minimum of two at-large members. Management of the association, within the guidelines set by the board, is the responsibility of AAP President and CEO Pat Schroeder.

AAP maintains two offices, in New York and Washington, D.C.

Highlights of 2007

Among the highlights of the year in publishing:

- AAP's 2007 Honors went to ABC Television's *The View* for its outstanding work in promoting American books and authors.
- The Miriam Bass Independent Publishing Award went to Dennis Loy Johnson and Valerie Merians, co-publishers of Melville House.
- Richard Sarnoff, executive vice president of Random House, was elected to a two-year term as AAP chairman.

- The R. R. Hawkins Award for the outstanding professional, scholarly, or reference work went to Harvard University Press for *Evolutionary Dynamics* by Martin Novak.
- Book sales in 2006 totaled $24.2 billion, according to figures released by AAP in May.
- AAP's Young to Publishing Group celebrated the sixth anniversary of its founding.
- Get Caught Reading entered its ninth year with a list of new celebrities, and on Capitol Hill 47 members of Congress were photographed reading their favorite books.
- AAP joined a nationwide campaign to protest cutbacks in book coverage at newspapers across the country.
- The International Freedom to Publish Committee's Jeri Laber Award was given to the entire beleaguered publishing community in Iran for its ongoing commitment to freedom of expression under extreme duress.
- AAP Professional and Scholarly Publishing Division medical publishers worked with the Iraqi cultural attaché to get desperately needed textbooks to Iraqi medical schools.
- AAP School Division held a 2008 "summit" focusing on math and science education.
- AAP Professional and Scholarly Publishing Division and coplaintiffs announced the successful resolution of their lawsuit against the U.S. Treasury's Office of Foreign Assets Control.

Government Affairs

AAP's Washington office is the industry's front line on matters of federal legislation and government policy. The office keeps AAP members informed about developments on Capitol Hill and in the executive branch to enable them to develop consensus positions on national policy issues. AAP's government affairs professionals serve as the industry's voice in advocating the views and concerns of U.S. publishers on questions of national policy.

A separate report details legislation and regulatory actions affecting book publishers in 2007. [See "Legislation and Regulations Affecting Publishing in 2007" in Part 2—*Ed.*].

Communications/Public Affairs

AAP's Communications and Public Affairs program informs the trade press and other media, the AAP membership, and the general public about the association's work and serves as the industry's voice on publishing issues. Through the program's regular publications, press releases and advisories, op-ed pieces, and other means, AAP disseminates the publishing industry's views and provides up-to-the-minute information on subjects of concern to its members. The program has primary responsibility for the AAP Web site.

AAP's public affairs activities include outreach and cooperative programs with such organizations as the Center for the Book in the Library of Congress, the Arts Advocacy Alliance (supporting the National Endowment for the Arts and other federal arts programs), PEN American Center and its International Freedom to Write program, a host of literacy and reading promotion efforts including the early childhood literacy initiative, Reach Out and Read.

In addition to the *AAP Monthly Report,* the association's regular newsletter, the communications program publishes a weekly electronic news bulletin for AAP members, *The Insider.*

BookExpo America

AAP is a cosponsor of BookExpo America (BEA), the premiere English-language book event. BookExpo 2007 was held in New York June 1–3.

AAP's Publishing Latino Voices for America task force hosted a series of industry discussions at BEA, launching the 2007 celebration of Latino Books Month.

Get Caught Reading

AAP continued to promote literacy and the joy of reading through its Get Caught Reading/¡Ajá, leyendo! campaign. New Get Caught Reading celebrities in 2007 included tennis star Nicole Vaidisova, Dylan and Cole Sprouse of the Disney Channel's "Suite Life," Emma Roberts as Nancy Drew, and "First Daughter" Jenna Bush.

In 2007 a subcommittee was created to extend the campaign to audio books, highlighting their educational and entertainment value. Although the Get Caught Listening program is still in development, a number of authors and performers including hip hop artist LL Cool J, thriller writer Lisa Scottoline, author and memoirist Frank McCourt, actress Valerie Bertinelli, and Dr. Seuss's "Horton" have agreed to record campaign voiceovers or provide photographs showing them "caught listening" to audio books.

On May 2, 2007, AAP hosted another of its popular Get Caught Reading photo shoots on Capitol Hill to capture members of Congress reading their favorite books. A total of 47 members of the House and Senate from both sides of the aisle turned out to have their pictures taken. Once again, a C-SPAN camera crew was on hand to talk with members about the importance of books and reading in their lives and ran the interviews on "BookTV." Get Caught Reading exhibits in 2007 were part of BookExpo, the Harlem Book Fair, and Brooklyn Book Fair.

Thousands of booksellers, educators, and librarians continued to use the Get Caught Reading Web site (http://www.getcaughtreading.org) as a resource to initiate Get Caught Reading campaigns in their communities and to order artwork. AAP continued its reading promotion partnership with the American Booksellers Association.

Copyright

The AAP Copyright Committee coordinates efforts to protect and strengthen intellectual property rights and to enhance public awareness of the importance of copyright as an incentive to creativity. The committee monitors intellectual property legislation in the United States and abroad and serves as an advisory body to the AAP Board of Directors in formulating policy on legislation and compliance activities, including litigation.

The committee also coordinates AAP's efforts to promote understanding and compliance with U.S. copyright law on college and university campuses. Carol Richman (Sage Publications) chaired the committee in 2007.

Among its activities in 2007, the committee continued to monitor copyright issues relating to the Google Book Search Program, including the lawsuit filed in federal court in fall 2005 by five major AAP members (McGraw-Hill, Pearson Education, Penguin Group USA, Simon & Schuster, and John Wiley & Sons) asserting that the mass digitization without permission of books obtained from Google's library partners, being carried out in the Google Library Project, represents massive copyright infringement. The case is proceeding more slowly than anticipated, as the discovery phase of the litigation has been repeatedly extended by the court, with the approval of all parties, to accommodate electronic and other document production issues. The committee monitored a number of important court decisions in cases against Google, along with domestic and foreign news coverage of Google's views and business transactions that may have an impact on the publishers' pending litigation. The majority of these developments are seen as helpful to the publishers' position.

The committee also continued to closely monitor issues arising from the use of copyrighted works in digital formats on college campuses, including library e-reserves. Following the agreement reached between AAP and Cornell University in 2006 on substantive guidelines for the use of electronic course content, the committee turned its attention to identifying other schools to be contacted regarding copyright problems in policies and practices governing the use of electronic course content. Following months of active negotiations, agreements regarding electronic course content use guidelines were reached with Hofstra, Syracuse, and Marquette. Announcement of the agreements was delayed until January 2008 to accommodate implementation at one of the universities. AAP is pursuing discussions with other schools.

In July AAP joined an amicus (friend of the court) brief to the Second Circuit Court of Appeals in *Cartoon Network* v. *CSC Holdings,* supporting the district court's finding of copyright infringement liability against Cablevision in connection with a new digital video recording being offered by the cable provider to its customers. In addressing the issue of whether direct infringement of the reproduction right occurs when a party sets up a separate system that is designed to create and transmit copies automatically at the request of users, the district court cited both the Kinko's and MDS decisions as relevant precedent.

The committee approved AAP's participation in an amicus brief in *Davis* v. *Blige,* asking the Second Circuit Court of Appeals to reconsider a ruling by a three-judge panel allowing a copyright infringement action to go forward despite a retroactive transfer of copyright by the plaintiff's co-author to one of the defendants. AAP supported the defendants' request for a rehearing in light of the panel's departure from judicial precedents that have accepted the effectiveness of such retroactive grants of permission in cases involving co-authors and co-owners of copyright.

In December the committee approved AAP participation in another amicus brief, asking the Tenth Circuit to rehear a troubling panel decision in *Golan* v. *Mukasey.* The panel ruled that an amendment to the Copyright Act under the Uruguay Round Agreements Act (URAA) that restored copyright for certain foreign works in the United States, consistent with the requirements of an international copyright treaty, might impinge upon constitutionally protected expression in the use of such works, and thus should be subject to judicial review under established First Amendment standards.

There was no action in 2007 on the issue of "orphan works" (works whose copyright owners cannot be identified or located by third parties seeking permission to use them), in contrast to 2006 when orphan works were the focus of a House hearing that led to the introduction and subcommittee approval of proposed amendments to the Copyright Act. With patent reform dominating the intellectual property agenda in both the House and Senate, the reintroduction of "orphan works" legislation was repeatedly postponed by congressional committees. It was expected to be picked up again early in 2008.

AAP's Rights and Permissions Advisory Committee (RPAC), which operates under the aegis of the Copyright Committee, sponsors educational programs for rights-and-permissions professionals. Chaired by Bonnie Beacher (McGraw-Hill), RPAC sponsored a half-day seminar on rights issues and new publishing technologies, at which publishing executives discussed ways in which their companies are using new technologies to create new products and delivery methods and rights professionals offered advice on avoiding pitfalls and taking advantage of new publishing technologies. In May 2007 RPAC hosted its Spring Conference in New York, attracting rights-and-permissions professionals from around the country and covering such topics as advances in photo licensing, Section 108 of the Copyright Act, accessibility, and legislative interference with textbook content. RPAC maintains the AAP Imprints List (http://www.publishers.org/main/Membership/member_03.htm), which provides contact information and information on various imprints for those seeking permission. RPAC members also revised and updated the *Copyright Primer,* which is scheduled for release in 2008.

The Copyright Education Committee (CEC), which also operates under the direction of the Copyright Committee and is chaired by Diann Korta (Pearson), worked on AAP's FAQs on e-reserves and other revisions for the seventh edition of the *Questions and Answers on Copyright for the Campus Community,* which was published in 2007. CEC has also been in contact with the Copyright Clearance Center to discuss joint copyright education and compliance activities on university campuses.

Digital Issues

AAP's Digital Issues Working Group, a forum for publishers to share information and learn about business opportunities and strategies in the digital world, held a series of meetings featuring guest speakers on a range of subjects in 2007. Maja Thomas (Hachette Book Group USA), and Matt Shatz (Random House) served as co-chairs.

Meeting topics included the digital audiobook market; sharing of book information on social networking sites; author marketing and interaction with readers online; distance education for K–12 and postsecondary students; and whether publishers should consider distributing e-books, digital audiobooks, and other digital products without technical security measures (i.e., "DRM-free").

The Working Group sponsored a panel discussion at BookExpo America titled "Digital Book Search Intermediaries: New Roles and Channels for Publishers." The focus was publisher-owned portals of digitized versions of their books and their value to authors, publishers, and consumers of content. Speakers included Matt Shatz (Random House), Carolyn Pittis (HarperCollins), Brian Napack (Holtzbrinck), and Kent Freeman (Ingram Digital Ventures), and the event was moderated by Mike Shatzkin (Idea Logical Company).

Diversity/Recruit and Retain

AAP's Diversity/Recruit and Retain Committee (DRRC) continued to fulfill its mandate to attract a talented and diverse work force to book publishing with its "Book Yourself a Career" campaign. The committee was chaired in 2007 by Bridget Marmion (Houghton Mifflin). College Outreach chair was Francine Rosado-Cruz (Penguin/Pearson.)

AAP is participating in Google Adwords to promote the campaign's Web site, http://www.bookjobs.com, which currently boasts traffic of more than 30,000 per quarter, with heightened traffic during semester breaks and at graduations. Planned projects include an updated *Voices of Diversity* video, to be shown at college fairs, featuring interviews with industry professionals from diverse backgrounds.

Among the committee's initiatives was development and implementation of a substantive "Introduction to Publishing Course," the only course designed to provide young professionals with an understanding of the many facets of the industry, including the editorial, marketing, sales, and publicity functions. The 2007 course "Advance Your Titles; Advance Your Career" was given in November with more than 150 in attendance and featured industry veterans who spoke about managing daily responsibilities while navigating upward in a publishing career. Sessions illustrated how editors work with authors and agents, how to leverage publicity in the blogosphere and traditional broadcast outlets (with speakers from "Good Morning America" and NBC News), how to manage a publishing career while moonlighting as a writer, and how retailers work with publishers. The keynote session featured *Reservation Road* author Jonathan Burnham Schwartz, interviewed by Random House Films head Edward Volini, on the process of bringing a book to the screen.

In pursuit of publishing industry work force diversity, AAP continued its college outreach, focusing on five key schools with diverse student populations in the greater New York area: City College of New York, City University of New York, Baruch College, Queens College, and Medgar Evers College. Participating in career fairs and informational sessions, AAP outreach efforts emphasized the viability of publishing as a career choice. AAP also visited Pace University in New York and several other schools including Hobart College, William Smith College, and Rutgers University. In 2007 AAP also participated in the National Association of College Recruiters annual meeting, exhibiting at its event in New York at the end of May and reaching out to hundreds of professionals who oversee career center programs on campuses across the country. The bookjobs.com Web site is the cornerstone of the program, illustrating the benefits of pursuing a career in publishing and providing guidance on how to enter the field.

Young to Publishing Group

The Young to Publishing Group (YPG), a subcommittee of DRRC, boasts membership of more than 1,000 young professionals who have been in the publishing industry from one to five years. In February 2007 YPG celebrated the sixth anniversary of its founding. Each month YPG hosts brown-bag lunches featuring speakers from the top of their fields in publishing, ranging from bloggers at the pop culture Web site Gawker to editors and publishers from a broad array of trade publishing houses. YPG also hosts evening networking events, and in 2007 launched a Web site for young publishing professionals at http://www.youngtopublishinggroup.blogspot.com. In 2008 the group plans to launch a volunteer services program for young professionals willing to donate time and effort to a worthy cause.

Freedom to Read

The mandate of the AAP Freedom to Read Committee is to protect the free marketplace of ideas for American publishers. The committee serves as the publishing industry's early warning system on such issues as libel, privacy, school and library censorship, journalists' privilege, Internet censorship, government regulation of protected speech, and third-party liability for protected speech. The committee coordinates AAP participation in First Amendment court cases, sponsors educational programs, plays an active role in the Media Coalition (a trade association of business-oriented groups concerned with censorship issues), and works with groups within and beyond the book community to advance common interests in the area of intellectual freedom. Nancy Miller (Random House) chaired the committee for the first half of 2007, with Elisabeth Sifton (Farrar, Straus & Giroux) assuming the chair in October.

Campaign for Reader Privacy

The restoration of reader privacy safeguards affected by the USAPatriot Act remained a top priority for AAP and its sister organizations in the Campaign for Reader Privacy in 2007.

Changes in Congress resulting from the November 2006 elections and a call by the new chairman of the Senate Judiciary Committee, Sen. Patrick Leahy (D-Vt.), for legislation to restore civil liberties, re-energized the campaign and in early 2007 representatives of its four sponsors (AAP, the American Library

Association, the American Booksellers Association, and PEN American Center) met with a member of Sen. Leahy's Judiciary Committee staff to lay out concerns. The meeting was well timed, coming just days after the release of a report by the Justice Department's inspector general documenting widespread abuse by the FBI of the National Security Letter (NSL) provision of the USAPatriot Act.

Reader privacy concerns were brought before Congress on April 11 when one of the four "John Doe" librarians from Connecticut who had successfully challenged an FBI NSL told the Senate Judiciary Committee that "Because of the gag order, you, our senators and elected representatives, and the American public are denied access to the stories and information about these abuses." As a direct result of these revelations, bipartisan bills were introduced in the Senate and the House intended to curb NSL abuses.

On September 6, 2007, in a challenge brought by the American Civil Liberties Union and a "John Doe" Internet service provider and supported by an amicus brief filed by AAP and others, U.S. District Court Judge Victor Marrero held the entire NSL statute in the reauthorized USAPatriot Act to be unconstitutional, ruling that the gag order and the standard of judicial review mandated by the amended statute violated both the First Amendment and the constitutional separation of powers. Judge Marrero enjoined the FBI from issuing any NSLs, but, in deference to the government's national security claims, stayed enforcement of his ruling pending appeal. The case was before the Second Circuit at year's end, and AAP was preparing to join another amicus brief in support of the challenge.

In the Courts

The Freedom to Read Committee coordinated AAP participation in a number of significant First Amendment cases in 2007. The following were among them:

COPA Redux—Nearly nine years after its passage, the Child Online Protection Act (COPA), which sought to impose criminal and civil penalties for any "harmful-to-minors" communication via the World Wide Web "for commercial purposes," was struck down for a second time by the same federal judge who issued a preliminary injunction barring its enforcement in 1999. The Supreme Court had upheld the injunction in 2004, but sent the case back for a new trial. AAP took the lead on two separate amicus briefs, arguing that COPA placed an unconstitutional burden on protected speech between adults, and that filtering technology administered by parents provided a more effective, less intrusive way of protecting minors than criminalizing Internet speech. When this report was prepared, the case was again on appeal to the Third Circuit. On October 29 AAP joined with the Center for Democracy and Technology and a number of Media Coalition members in filing an amicus brief urging the federal appeals court to declare COPA unconstitutional.

Libel Tourism and the Ehrenfeld Case—In October AAP joined a broad coalition of media groups, including Amazon.com and the Reporters Committee for Freedom of the Press, in asking the New York Court of Appeals to allow American author Rachel Ehrenfeld to proceed with efforts to have a British libel judgment against her declared unenforceable in the United States. A default judgment—involving substantial monetary damages, a declaration of falsity against her book *Funding Evil: How Terrorism Is Financed—And How to Stop It,* a demand for a public apology, and the destruction of copies of the book—was entered against Ehrenfeld after she refused to participate in a libel suit brought in London by Saudi billionaire Khalid bin Mahfouz. Neither bin Mahfouz nor Ehrenfeld resides in Britain, the book was never published there, and the case is seen as a classic example of "libel tourism," in which individuals exploit plaintiff-friendly foreign libel laws in an effort to intimidate U.S. authors and publishers and circumvent the constitutional protections afforded libel defendants in this country.

In April 2006 a federal judge dismissed Ehrenfeld's motion, saying the court lacked personal jurisdiction over bin Mahfouz. New York courts are able to exercise personal jurisdiction over non-residents under the state's "long-arm statute" if a non-resident has transacted business within the state, but the federal district court found that bin Mahfouz's actions in New York, which were taken in connection with his British libel suit, did not qualify as "transacting business." The Second Circuit Court of Appeals then found that this question had not been addressed by New York courts and, recognizing the important First Amendment issues involved, asked the state's highest appellate court for a ruling on the question of whether bin Mahfouz's actions constituted "transacting business" in New York, thus permitting Ehrenfeld's legal action to proceed.

In late December the New York Court of Appeals found that the actions did not meet the statutory standard of a "sustained and substantial transaction of business in New York." AAP issued a statement expressing disappointment and vowing to continue the fight against libel tourism. By the end of the year there were indications of interest on the part of members of the New York State legislature to clarify the statutory authority in a way that might help to safeguard New York authors and publishers from attacks by libel tourists.

Plame v. McConnell—In spring 2007 former CIA operative Valerie Plame Wilson and her publisher, Simon & Schuster, asked a federal court in New York to rule that the government was imposing an unlawful prior restraint in demanding the removal of all references to the dates of her CIA employment prior to 2002 from her memoir, which was slated for publication in the fall. The government's redactions were made despite the fact that Wilson had received an unclassified letter from a CIA benefits official clearly spelling out the dates of her employment and that this letter was introduced at House hearings, was published in the *Congressional Record,* and is widely available on the Internet. The government filed a cross-motion for summary judgment, and in August the court granted the government's motion, finding that the information had been properly classified by the CIA, had never been declassified, and was not "officially acknowledged" by the agency. Wilson's book, *Fair Game: My Life as a Spy, My Betrayal by the White House,* was published in October with the redactions clearly shown, accompanied by a note from the publisher explaining what had been done and why. The book also contained an afterword by journalist Laura Rozen providing the historical context that Wilson was unable to include herself. The case is on appeal to the Second Circuit and at year's end AAP was organizing an amicus effort to support Wilson and her publisher.

Red Hat Club Libel-in-Fiction Suit—In late July AAP filed a brief asking the Georgia State Court of Appeals to dismiss a defamation suit against St. Martin's Press and one of its authors, Haywood Smith, by a woman claiming to be the model for a character in Smith's novel *The Red Hat Club*. The plaintiff claimed the novel's depiction of the character's drinking and sexual escapades defamed her and a Georgia trial court found there to be factual issues to be determined at trial and refused to dismiss the case. Pointing out that many fictional characters are "based on" real people an author has known, the AAP brief argued that the plaintiff needed to show that a reasonable reader would believe she and the fictional character were one and the same and confuse the actions of the fictional character with those of the plaintiff. The brief pointed out that the lower court's failure to dismiss the case in the absence of such a showing exerted a profound chilling effect on the free speech rights of the author and publisher.

Trump v. O'Brien—AAP was one of 19 media organizations that filed an amicus brief in the New Jersey state appeals court opposing an order to compel author Timothy O'Brien to turn over research material and identify confidential sources for his book *TrumpNation: The Art of Being The Donald*. O'Brien and his publisher, Warner Business Books, were sued for defamation by entrepreneur Donald Trump, who claimed injury to his business reputation from the book's estimation of his net worth as somewhere between $150 and $250 million rather than the billions he claims it to be. The trial judge's order was particularly disturbing because he concluded that O'Brien's confidential sources were not entitled to any state shield law protection since the book was "entertainment" not "news," notwithstanding the fact that O'Brien is a financial reporter for the *New York Times* who has covered Trump's business dealings for years. The amicus brief argued that by basing its decision on the book's "sardonic and sometimes sarcastic tone," the trial court's reasoning posed a serious danger to the news media's ability to report or comment on matters of public interest. "It erroneously holds that the style or tone of a work controls the amount of protection it receives, and it requires judges to make subjective decisions about style in deciding how much protection a work should receive. The law has long been clear that such decisions must by made by authors, journalists, editors, and publishers, and not any governmental entity, including the courts."

Hatfill v. New York Times—AAP welcomed the action of federal district judge Claude M. Hilton in throwing out—for the second time—a defamation suit against the *New York Times* brought by former Army biological weapons expert Stephen Hatfill over a series of columns by Nicholas Kristof about the FBI's investigation into the 2001 anthrax killings. The judge announced his intention to dismiss the suit in January 2007, canceling the trial due to begin at the end of the month. Earlier, AAP had joined an amicus brief asking the U.S. Supreme Court to overturn the federal appellate court ruling that sent the case back for trial. In his opinion, Judge Hilton ruled that Hatfill was both a "public official" and a "public figure," which would require him to show that Kristof and the *Times* acted with "actual malice," a very high burden of proof.

Harvest House Libel Case—As its term drew to a close in June 2007, the Supreme Court refused to review a ruling by the Texas Court of Appeals dismissing a libel suit against Harvest House Publishers brought by a group called The Local Church. The Supreme Court's refusal to hear the case effectively ended a six-year legal assault by The Local Church, which claimed that its inclusion in *The Encyclopedia of Cults and New Religions,* published by Harvest House, was defamatory because of general comments regarding cults in the book's introduction and appendix. AAP had taken the lead in providing amicus support for Harvest House, citing The Local Church's long history of using libel litigation to silence criticism.

Vegan-Sponsored Publicity Campaign—AAP took the lead on an amicus brief filed in April 2007 in *Gorran* v. *Atkins* in the U.S. Court of Appeals for the Second Circuit. The brief urges the court to reject arguments by a disgruntled former Atkins dieter that the bestselling book *Dr. Atkins New Diet Revolution,* as well as portions of the Atkins Web site, are "commercial speech" because they promote the sale of Atkins-branded products, and thus are unprotected by the First Amendment and subject to state unfair-competition laws. The amicus brief calls the litigation "a vegan-sponsored anti-Atkins publicity campaign in the guise of a lawsuit that is profoundly hostile to core First Amendment values."

A Publisher's Right to Shield His Subscriber List—In February 2007 AAP joined in filing an amicus brief to the Maryland Court of Appeals in *Forensic Advisors* v. *Matrixx Initiatives,* supporting a publisher's right to protect the confidentiality of his subscriber list, which was being sought by a pharmaceutical company to learn the identities of "John Doe" defendants in an Internet defamation suit in another state. The brief argued that Maryland's shield law bars disclosure of the publisher's sources and information collected in the course of reporting, and that First Amendment protections of the right to speak and to receive information anonymously protect the publisher's subscriber list. The brief argued that in civil litigation, before intruding upon the First Amendment right to anonymous speech, the court should require a showing that the information is central to the claim and unavailable from other sources, and then proceed to consider whether the need for disclosure outweighs the First Amendment harm. The case was subsequently mooted without the need for disclosure by the publisher when the pharmaceutical company dismissed its out-of-state lawsuit.

Book Banning and Censorship

Battles continued in school libraries and classrooms across the country as students, teachers, librarians, and others fought for the right of students to read a wide variety of books of their own choosing.

In February 2007 AAP joined in sending a letter to the local board of education in Howell, Michigan, opposing the efforts of a local group called Livingston Organization for Values in Education (LOVE), to remove Toni Morrison's *The Bluest Eye* and Richard Wright's *Black Boy* from the 11th grade English curriculum because of sexual content and profanity. When the Howell board of education voted to retain the books, one of LOVE's members filed an obscenity complaint with the U.S. Attorney for the Eastern District of Michigan. In a surprising move, the U.S. Attorney referred the matter to the local FBI field office and to Michigan's attorney general. The investigation was dropped, but the incident highlighted a disturbing new edge to these challenges: censors who characterize targeted books as "harmful-to-minors" or "obscene," threatening educators with criminal charges.

In April 2007 AAP joined in sending a letter protesting the removal of Robert Cormier's highly acclaimed novel *The Chocolate War* from a ninth grade social studies curriculum in Harford County, Maryland. The removal came in response to complaints from some parents about language and references to homosexuality. The letter pointed out that "the practical effect of acceding to any request to censor materials will be to invite others to demand changes in the curriculum to reflect their beliefs and to leave school officials vulnerable to multiple, possibly conflicting, demands." In December the school superintendent reversed the earlier decision to ban the book, giving teachers the option of using *The Chocolate War* as required reading in a unit on school bullying if permission was obtained from the parents of all students in a class.

In the wake of a book-banning controversy in West Virginia involving two of author Pat Conroy's most popular works, AAP joined in sending a letter that was published in the *Charleston Gazette* on December 13, calling a proposed rating system for books used in an honors English class unwise and unworkable. The controversy arose when several parents in Kanawha County raised objections to the use of *The Prince of Tides* and *Beach Music* in a 12th grade advanced placement English class. Use of the books was suspended at one county high school, prompting outraged students to form an anticensorship coalition and threaten the Kanawha County Board of Education with a lawsuit. The author himself got into the fray after being contacted by a student. Conroy wrote a scathing letter that said, in part, "Because you banned my books, every kid in that county will read them, every single one of them. Because book banners are invariably idiots, they don't know how the world works—but writers and English teachers do."

Educational Programs

At its Open Forum, held each spring to bring current members together with alumni and guests for a wide-ranging discussion of First Amendment issues, the Freedom to Read Committee hosted playwright and activist Eve Ensler in a lively dialogue on censorship and the culture wars. Ensler is the author of the play "The Vagina Monologues," which the *New York Times* called "the most important piece of political theater of the past decade." Among other topics, the wide-ranging discussion looked at the absurd lengths to which censors go to "protect" young people from material dealing with sex and their own bodies.

The committee also joined in sponsoring a program at the Annual Conference of the American Library Association held in Washington, D.C., in late June 2007. The symposium featured Judge Richard Posner of the U.S. Court of Appeals for the Seventh Circuit and Chicago University Law Professor and best-selling author Geoffrey Stone in a dialogue on whether the Constitution should be "bent" in times of war and other crises.

Higher Education

AAP's Higher Education group serves the needs and interests of AAP members who publish for the postsecondary education market. John Isley (Pearson Education) chaired the committee in 2007.

In 2007 AAP continued to work at the federal and state levels with legislators and policymakers, bookstores, and students to address concerns about the price of college course materials. AAP worked to head off or defeat misguided legislative initiatives that would limit the ability of textbook publishers to develop the best materials for faculty and students, restricting the sale of course materials and the release of new editions, and mandating methods for disclosing pricing and product information.

AAP monitored legislative activity in 32 states and was able to see amended or defeated more than 80 legislative proposals that would have adversely affected college textbook publishers and impaired the education of postsecondary students. Amended bills were passed and signed into law in ten states: Arkansas, California, Maryland, Minnesota, New York, Oklahoma, Oregon, Tennessee, Texas, and Washington.

The Public Interest Research Group (PIRG) continued to target publishers with a disinformation campaign, enlisting the assistance of state student associations and ratcheting up pressure at the federal level. In February 2007 Massachusetts PIRG released a study entitled "Exposing the Textbook Industry: How Publishers' Pricing Tactics Drive Up the Cost of College Textbooks," claiming that "publishers withhold price and product information from faculty members" while ignoring the vast quantity of such information readily available online, specifically via publishers' Web sites and online catalogs.

With the Higher Education Act due for reauthorization, debate over textbook issues in Congress gained momentum. In August the Advisory Committee on Student Financial Assistance released its year-long study, carried out at the request of Congress, on the cost of textbooks and its impact on students. The report concluded that federal legislation would serve to inhibit innovation and could increase prices, that voluntary efforts to reduce costs are already under way, and that the factors affecting textbook affordability are complex and the active engagement of all interested parties will be required to seek solutions. The report also called for a move toward digital materials, a move that publishers support.

In strengthening its public outreach, AAP worked with the National Association of College Admissions Counselors (NACAC) and the American School Counselor Association (ASCA) to increase understanding of the value of course materials and the need for budgeting for college textbook expenses. Both organizations focus on helping high school students and their parents prepare for the transition into college. AAP's information was posted on the online resource centers of both organizations, used in the November/December issue of *ASCA School Counselor* magazine, and posted to NACAC's *Steps to College* newsletter Web site.

In September 2007 AAP launched http://www.textbooks360.org, an interactive exploration of current learning technologies. This online tool enables students, parents, instructors, administrators, and legislators to explore modern course materials, to gain an understanding that they are complete learning systems integrating innovative features and formats into the traditional textbook, and tailoring the educational experience to meet faculty requests and student needs.

The past year reflected continuing focus on the issue of "accessibility"—providing print-disabled postsecondary students with better, faster access to their educational materials. "Accessibility" legislation was introduced in several states and AAP's Critical Issues Task Force expanded the work of the Alternative Formats Solutions Initiative, a national effort to identify ways to provide print-disabled postsecondary students with specially formatted course materials on a timely basis.

Higher Education Critical Issues Task Force

Members of the Higher Education Critical Issues Task Force (CITF) represent publishers of textbooks and other instructional materials for the postsecondary education market in the United States. CITF works exclusively on issues involving the provision of accessible instructional materials to students with disabilities in postsecondary education.

Various federal and state laws mandate that colleges and universities provide disabled students with equal and effective access to instructional materials. Educational institutions sometimes provide services such as human readers; an alternative is to make the materials available in specialized formats (such as braille, audio, or digital text). Some states have passed additional legislation—known as "e-text" laws—mandating that when instructional materials are adopted for use in a course in which a disabled student is enrolled, the publisher will deliver the course material to the college in an electronic format that can either be used directly or converted into another specialized format for use by the student with a print disability. Most publishers already voluntarily provide e-text to campuses in states without such legislation.

CITF's efforts in 2007 included:

- Responding to legislative proposals in Maryland, Oregon, Texas, and Wisconsin
- Providing input to shape the accessibility provisions in draft legislation to amend the Higher Education Act reauthorization—the bill provides for the creation of a national commission to study accessibility and authorizes the awarding of grants for model accessibility demonstration projects
- Introducing standardized forms and guidelines for college campus disability-services-for-students (DSS) professionals to use when requesting electronic formats from publishers
- Increasing the amount of publisher data on the Publisher Look-Up Service (http://www.publisherlookup.org), a site created by AAP to help DSS offices find the right contacts at publishing houses from whom to request electronic files or permissions to reproduce instructional materials in electronic form
- Investigating the possibility of developing a national portal to further help campuses around the country provide accessible materials to their print-disabled populations more quickly and effectively

International Copyright Protection

AAP's International Copyright Protection Committee works to combat international copyright piracy, increase fair access to foreign markets, and strengthen foreign intellectual property law regimes. The program continued to expand its reach in 2007, pioneering substantive new projects in its most active markets and strengthening ties with government authorities charged with intellectual property rights protection. Deborah Wiley (John Wiley & Sons) chaired the committee in 2007.

In bolstering its overseas antipiracy campaigns, AAP continued to work closely with local representatives of member publishers and with government authorities (U.S. and foreign) and to strengthen ties with local publishing groups. These efforts produced a number of raids on pirate operations, along with educational campaigns and new policy initiatives. AAP and member publishers are pursuing legal action stemming from the raids. AAP also worked to shape policy to benefit American publishers in a number of global markets, including Japan, Russia, Vietnam, Brazil, and Chile.

The People's Republic of China was the primary focus of AAP's intellectual property and market access efforts in 2007, and the copyright program in particular realized significant progress. Working with colleagues in Britain's Publishers Association (PA), AAP intensified engagement with the Chinese government on copyright issues in two key areas: the systematic copying of textbooks on China's university campuses, and Internet piracy. As a result, Chinese authorities at the national and regional level investigated and sanctioned four universities for unauthorized reproduction of books. Each of these universities, located in Wuhan (Hubei Province), Chengdu (Sichuan Province) and Xi'an (Shaan'xi Province), were issued administrative penalties and ordered to stop infringing activity. Authorities also demanded the destruction of stock seized in the raids, in most cases amounting to thousands of copies.

In late 2006 the Chinese National Copyright Administration and the General Administration of Press and Publication joined forces with the Ministry of Education in issuing a series of warnings alerting regional and local bureaus and universities throughout the country to the crackdown on illegal copying. The notices, issued in August, September, and November 2006, ordered universities to cease unauthorized activities and implement measures to ensure the use of legal materials by students and faculty. AAP and PA spent considerable time and effort during 2007 pressing authorities on the implementation of these notices.

Internet piracy in China continued to grow in 2007, prompting AAP and PA to intensify focus on the problem. Having signed a memorandum of understanding with Chinese copyright authorities in late 2006 outlining specific means of cooperation on Internet enforcement, AAP and PA pressed Chinese authorities to act against a particularly notorious site offering an extensive selection of medical journals for download in competition with AAP's professional and scholarly publishers. National and local authorities in China are investigating the site's operators in an ongoing effort.

AAP and PA continued to strengthen ties with the Publishers Association of China, meeting with the association regularly in Beijing. Chinese publishers suffer from high rates of piracy of their own products, and AAP and PA continue to seek ways to join forces.

AAP also seeks alliances with other U.S. industries affected by piracy in China, and in 2007—supported by a number of other industry groups facing piracy and market access barriers—AAP worked closely with U.S. government authorities in the initiation of two dispute resolution cases in the World Trade Organization (WTO), challenging Chinese practices that are noncompliant with WTO obligations. One case focuses on gaps in intellectual property protection that contravene China's obligations under the Agreement on Trade Related Aspects of Intellectual Property Rights; the other focuses on specific market access barriers that violate WTO provisions and other commitments made upon China's accession to WTO in 2001. Both cases were launched through formal requests by the U.S. government for WTO consultations in April 2007 and were pending before WTO at year's end.

The year saw months of negotiations between the government of South Korea and the United States in pursuit of a free trade agreement between the two countries. AAP worked closely and successfully with the U.S. government during the negotiations to ensure that specific language addressing book piracy was included in the final agreement. The language focuses on efforts by the Korean Ministry of Education and individual universities to stamp out on-campus reproduction and use of infringing materials. In addition, raids in March and September continued to target large-scale pirate operations and numerous photocopy shops found near university campuses. Prosecutions stemming from those raids are pending.

In Thailand, AAP pursued its ongoing investigation of a sophisticated syndicate suspected of mass production of high-quality pirated books designed for the export market. AAP has also worked with the Thai government, especially its Department of Intellectual Property, on such issues as fair use, educational campaigns, and copyright law reform.

In Taiwan, AAP continued its work through the Taiwan Book Publishers Association (TBPA), an alliance between AAP member companies and Taiwanese publishers. Joining with local police under the supervision of Taiwan's Ministry of Justice in the spring and fall to coincide with the start of the university terms, TBPA raided pirate operations. AAP and TBPA also worked closely with the Taiwan Intellectual Property Office on a number of educational and policy initiatives, and significantly increased its involvement with the Ministry of Education regarding its involvement in curbing on-campus infringement. Over the past year, a government-industry task force was created and the Ministry of Education developed an action plan to combat on-campus infringement—an effort that AAP hopes can become a model in the region.

AAP's primary focus for 2007 in Hong Kong was the ongoing legislative process affecting foreign and local publishers and covering such issues as the scope of criminal liability for infringement of books and journals, exemptions from liability, and the application of copyright in the digital environment. AAP continued to cooperate on enforcement activities with the Hong Kong Customs and Excise Department, with a sharpened focus on ferreting out underground copy facilities. Efforts in 2007 resulted in citywide raids and impressive seizures timed to coincide with the start of the university sessions.

AAP continued to seek prosecutorial and judicial reform in the Philippines, working to raise awareness of the negative effects of the system's weaknesses on legitimate publishers and other intellectual property owners seeking to do business there. AAP also worked closely with authorities, including the Intellectual Property Office of the Philippines and the National Book Development Board, to ensure that publishers' voices were being heard with respect to policy development procedures within the two organizations on such subjects as fair use in an educational context and collective licensing for printed materials.

In Malaysia, enforcement actions continued with the cooperation of the Ministry of Domestic Trade and Consumer Affairs, resulting in several raids between January and August. Activity centered around universities in cities including Cyberjaya, Penang, Bandar Sungai Long, Seri Kembangan, and Melaka. The raids yielded more than 1,500 infringing copies and resulted in seizure of dozens of copy machines. AAP also continued educational efforts in Malaysia targeting university administrations, students, and copy shops.

In Japan, AAP participated in an end-of-the-year effort to raise and publicize concerns over a proposed limitation of Japanese copyright law that would have a serious adverse effect on scientific publishers. The effort was mobilized largely by the Japan Medical Publishers Association, in cooperation with other groups based in Japan, along with several international publishing associations. AAP worked closely with U.S. government officials to place the issue on agendas for government-to-government dialogue.

Until efforts were slowed by political turmoil in Pakistan, AAP worked with U.S. government officials in moving toward a dialogue with that country on intellectual property issues. In India, with the full support of Britain's Publishers Association, AAP continued to push for official action to discourage use of infringing academic materials on university campuses.

AAP and its member companies were active in education, policymaking, and related initiatives in Brazil, Russia, Vietnam, Chile, Indonesia, Canada, and elsewhere. In February 2007 AAP, as a member of the International Intellectual Property Alliance, submitted specific recommendations regarding intellectual property protection in various foreign countries to the U.S. Trade Representative (USTR) as part of USTR's annual Special 301 review of intellectual property problems worldwide. AAP members estimated annual losses of nearly $600 million as a result of copyright piracy and related intellectual property theft.

International Freedom to Publish

AAP's International Freedom to Publish (IFTP) Committee defends and promotes freedom of written communication worldwide. The committee monitors human rights issues and provides moral support and practical assistance to publishers and authors outside the United States who are denied basic freedoms. The committee carries on its work in close cooperation with other human rights groups, including the International Publishers Association's Freedom to Publish Committee, Human Rights Watch, and PEN American Center, and maintains its own Web site at http://www.iftpc.org. Hal Fessenden (Viking Penguin) served as committee chairman in 2007.

In 2003 the committee established the Jeri Laber International Freedom to Publish Award, to be given annually to a book publisher outside the United States who has demonstrated courage in the face of political persecution. The award, which carries a cash prize, is named in honor of human rights activist Jeri Laber, one of the committee's founding members, who continues to direct its work as an AAP consultant. The award has been given to publishers in Iran, Turkey, Indonesia, and Egypt.

The committee's candidate for the 2007 Jeri Laber Award, a prominent independent book publisher in Iran, declined the honor for fear of government reprisal, saying that "The business of publishing books is confronted with very dire and troubling conditions in our country. Independent publishers, including our publishing house, are under immense pressure and censorship. Accepting a prize would certainly double these pressures. I am very sad to say that I no longer have the stamina to bear more pressure or to engage in further confrontations."

Given this response, the committee decided to honor instead the entire beleaguered publishing community in Iran for its ongoing commitment to freedom of expression under extreme duress. The award was announced in April 2007 at the PEN Gala in New York City. Because it is not advisable to send U.S. funds into Iran, the 2007 Jeri Laber Award is being used in the United States to help Iranian publishers traveling here.

In December 2004, in an effort to encourage and increase the diversity of literary works being published in the United States, the committee offered U.S. publishers a unique opportunity to bring the works of three gifted Iranian authors to a U.S. audience. In consultation with a distinguished group of scholars and writers in the United States and Iran, IFTP commissioned partial translations and a precis of several Iranian literary works, and secured funding that enabled it to provide $10,000 to each U.S. publisher contracting for English-language rights. The money was used to assist in additional translation costs and for promotion and publicity. The project was completed in late 2005. *Strange Times, My Dear: The PEN Anthology of Contemporary Iranian Literature* was published by Arcade Publishing in 2005; Shahrnush Parsipur's *Tooba and the Meaning of Night* was published in March 2006 by Feminist Press; and Mahmoud Dowlatabadi's *The Empty House of Solouch* was published by Melville House in 2007.

The committee continues to monitor events in Iran and the situation of writers and publishers there. It has expressed its deep concern over "Procedural Guidelines for Publication" issued by the Iranian Ministry of Culture and Islamic Guidance. Intended to eliminate "unhealthy products," the guidelines require a permit from the ministry for the distribution of all books.

IFTP members undertake missions to meet with writers, publishers, human rights activists, and others in areas where freedom of expression is seriously threatened. In 2007 the committee began making plans to visit Cambodia. Hal Fessenden, Wendy Wolf, and Larry Siems of PEN were to make the visit in early 2008 with a full agenda including visits to publishers and bookstores. Fessenden and Wolf were to conduct a master class in publishing, Siems to discuss the possibility of setting up a PEN chapter in Cambodia.

In January 2007 AAP President Schroeder and Fessenden, on behalf of the committee, sent letters to four Turkish officials protesting the assassination of the Armenian publisher and editor Hrant Dink and demanding a full investigation into the circumstances surrounding the event. Ragip Zarakolu, a Turkish publisher often subjected to legal trials in Turkey, visited the committee to discuss the

Dink assassination and the response to it in Turkey. The committee subsequently nominated Dink for the posthumous receipt of the Robert F. Kennedy Award and (along with Anna Politkovskaya, the murdered Russian journalist) the International Publishers Association Freedom Award.

The committee continues to monitor events in Turkey, including the ongoing harassment and persecution of writers, publishers, and journalists through the continued indiscriminate application of Article 301 of the Turkish penal code, which makes it a crime to "insult Turkishness."

During 2007 the committee hosted a number of speakers on various topics and from different parts of the world. In April the committee hosted three Iranian writers—Shahriyar Mandanipur, Moniru Ravanipur, and Goli Taraghi—and the Iranian publisher Babak Takhti. They participated in an off-the-record symposium on the situation of writers and publishers in Iran.

Ahmed Rashid, journalist and author of *Taliban: Militant Islam, Oil, and Fundamentalism in Central Asia* and the forthcoming book *Failing States* spoke about Pakistan and Afghanistan at the committee's December meeting.

Chris Deckerd, formerly of the *Cambodia Daily* and currently with Voice of America, discussed the current situation in Cambodia and also offered his assistance in arrangements for the committee's forthcoming trip to Cambodia.

The committee also hosted several speakers from Human Rights Watch and the Committee to Protect Journalists.

International Sales Committee

The International Sales Committee represents a broad cross-section of the AAP membership with interests in overseas markets, focusing on issues relating to the export of mass market paperbacks and publishers' rights to sell English-language titles in select English-language markets. Composed of export sales directors from AAP member houses and chaired in 2007 by Dan Vidra (Simon & Schuster), the group's major concerns are piracy, export online, distribution, and currency issues associated with British-U.S. territorial exclusives as well as other issues relating to export sales to and from the United States, overseas schools, hotels, bookstores, and airports. The committee hosted speakers during its committee meetings at events including Pubnet and the Frankfurt Book Fair, and attended a presentation on the British-U.S. territorial issues at the London Book Fair. The group continues to host the international sales meeting room at BookExpo America each year, and shares success stories from the international sales field. The committee is also exploring the viability of hosting various networking forums with industry media.

Professional/Scholarly Publishing

AAP's Professional/Scholarly Publishing Division (PSP) is composed of association members who publish books, journals, looseleaf, and electronic products in technology, science, medicine, business, law, humanities, the behavioral sciences, and scholarly reference. Professional societies and university presses play an important role in the division. Brian Crawford (American Chemical Society) chaired the PSP Executive Council in 2007.

The 2007 PSP Annual Conference, "Global Publishing: Emerging Markets, New Models," was held in Washington, D.C., in February. Prior to the opening of the meeting, the PSP Electronic Information Committee sponsored a preconference seminar on "Publishing 2.0: Flourishing in the Era of Digital Natives," and the PSP American Medical Publishers Committee, in conjunction with the National Library of Medicine, sponsored a preconference session on "Interactive Media: Implications for Content and Preservation."

The division sponsors a prestigious awards program, open only to AAP/PSP members, to acknowledge outstanding achievements in professional, scholarly, and reference publishing. In 2007 the R. R. Hawkins Award for the outstanding professional/scholarly work of the year went to *Evolutionary Dynamics: Exploring the Equations of Life* by Martin A. Nowak, published by Harvard University Press. In addition, book awards were presented in more than 30 subject categories, in design and production, and in journal and electronic publishing. The PSP awards program donated more than 250 books to the Charles Evans Inniss Memorial Library, a part of Medgar Evers College in Brooklyn, New York. Each year PSP donates scholarly works that have competed for PSP awards on the basis of their contribution to research, innovation, and excellence.

On October 1, PSP joined co-plaintiffs in announcing the successful resolution of a lawsuit against the U.S. Treasury Department's Office of Foreign Assets Control (OFAC). Revised regulations issued by OFAC (which enforces trade embargoes against "enemy" nations) no longer require specific license applications for government permission to engage in basic publishing activities with countries under U.S. trade embargo. The lawsuit was filed in September 2004 by AAP/PSP, the Association of American University Presses, PEN American Center, and Arcade Publishing, an independent publishing house, in response to the Treasury Department's continued attempts to exert control over publishing activities involving information and literature from countries under U.S. trade embargoes. The regulations, which required publishers and authors to seek a license from the government to perform routine activities necessary to publish foreign works, including paying advances, doing substantive editing, or marketing works from Cuba, Iran, and Sudan, were seen as a violation of the First Amendment and of specific laws passed by Congress that exempt "information and informational materials" from trade embargoes. The lawsuit cited more than a dozen works that were jeopardized by the regulations, ranging from an article by Iranian scientists on identifying earthquake hazards, to an encyclopedia of Cuban music, and the PEN Anthology of Contemporary Iranian Literature.

PSP cosponsored a demonstration of patientINFORM on Capitol Hill as part of the launch of the Congressional Internet Caucus "State of the Net" event. In line with their commitment to make research information available to patients and caregivers, medical publishers joined with the American Diabetes Association, the American Cancer Society, the American Heart Association, the National Organization for Rare Disorders, and other leading organizations to create patientINFORM, a free service offering easy and comprehensible access to some of the most up-to-date diagnostic and treatment research available.

The PSP Division joined with 45 international publishers and publishing organizations in signing on to ten principles (see "The Brussels Declaration," http://www.stm-assoc.org/brussels-declaration) issued by the International Scientific, Technical, and Medical (STM) Association in response to the European Commission's "Communication on Scientific Communication in the Digital Age." Neither pro- nor anti-open access, the declaration of principles emphasizes the strength, breadth, and unity of the scientific, technical, and medical publishing community, how it conducts business, and how its activities benefit science and society, and seeks to respond to intervention by governments worldwide that would force unfunded mandates on the publishing community.

The PSP American Medical Publishers Committee worked with Iraq's cultural attaché in Washington to get medical books to 20 Iraqi medical schools whose students and house staff were in desperate need of current medical information. With the help of Doody Publishing, they identified a core list of 209 titles and worked with the Brother's Brother Foundation to facilitate collection and shipment of the materials.

To enable prospective users to identify, locate, and contact PSP member copyright holders, PSP compiled an imprints list of member companies with a point of contact and other information. The list is intended to facilitate the process of seeking permissions, obtaining general information, and locating personnel, and is available on the PSP Web site at http://www.pspcentral.org.

Among the division's educational activities in 2007

- The PSP American Medical Publishers Committee sponsored a seminar, "Medical Informatics: Opportunities and Challenges for Publishers," clarifying for the medical publishing community what the domain of medical informatics is, and how it is, or may be, relevant for publishers and content owners.

- The PSP Books Committee sponsored two one-day seminars, "Basics of Books Boot Camp," an entry-level overview of professional and scholarly book publishing, one in New York and one in California, as well as a one-day seminar for mid-level book publishers, "Finance for Non-Financial Professionals."

- The PSP Journals Committee sponsored its tenth biennial "Journals Boot Camp," an intensive four-day course on journals publishing.

- The PSP Public Issues Task Force has developed and maintains a PSP Issues Glossary, an online reference and research tool for PSP members. This glossary is available through a new link on the home page of the PSP Web site.

- The PSP Executive Council directs an ongoing campaign to improve relationships between the PSP communities and user and scholar communities. The campaign explains the role that PSP members play and the value they add to the dissemination of scholarly information.

On other government fronts, PSP has been actively representing publisher interests in dealing with government Web sites that want to republish, modify, and deliver—free of charge—articles that are based in part on government-funded research.

In other countries, PSP has cooperated with international publishing associations to find the right balance between fair use of intellectual property and rights holders' needs to realize a fair return for their works. The division has worked with the British Publishers Association and the International Association of Scientific, Technical, and Medical Publishers to produce ongoing international annual journals statistics surveys.

Resources for the Book Publishing Industry

Compensation Reports

AAP publishes a variety of resources for the book publishing industry, including the *Survey of Compensation and Personnel Practices in the Publishing Industry,* widely regarded as the most comprehensive and reliable source of data in this area. AAP's Compensation Committee, composed of senior compensation and human resources professionals, met throughout the year to create job descriptions and manage the survey process.

Total Compensation Solutions, which produces the report for AAP, presented highlights of the 2007 report at AAP's "Human Resources Seminar: Compensation and Human Resources Practices in the Book-Publishing Industry" in November. The impact and cost structures of health benefits was addressed in a keynote presented by Buck Consultants.

AAP also tracks holiday benefits of the publishing community and shares the data with a compensation committee composed of publishing industry professionals who independently oversee the holiday and vacation compensation for their respective houses.

Annual Statistics

AAP publishes industry statistics for all segments of book publishing, on a monthly and annual basis. Committees in the areas of consumer, trade, higher education, and professional publishing met throughout 2007 to revise the program and develop a seamless system for the distribution of electronic monthly reports. More than 80 publishers participate in AAP's monthly statistical reports, the only resource in publishing that aggregates revenue and compiles raw data on market size on a month-to-month basis, and provides year-to-date growth, based on participation by a cross section of the industry.

In 2007 AAP commissioned a third-party contractor to write front material for "Estimated Net Industry Sales of 2006" to provide information and support for the press and the investment community. AAP is also working in concert with the Book Industry Study Group to streamline the industrywide collection and communication of statistics.

School Division

During the year the AAP School Division continued to serve as the national voice of the U.S. pre-K–12 school publishing industry. Throughout the year, the division worked to ensure access to instructional materials, to increase funding for all types of instructional materials, and to foster a fair, competitive, and robust market for all education publishers. Once again, the division succeeded in its core mission of protecting more than $8 billion in state and federal funding for instructional materials. Buzz Ellis (McGraw-Hill Education) chaired the School Division Executive Committee in 2007.

Industry Highlights

In 2007 the pre-K–12 publishing market achieved a 2.7 percent overall increase in sales over the previous year. The year was also marked by ongoing merger and acquisition activity, notably Houghton Mifflin's acquisition of the Harcourt Education, Harcourt Trade, and Greenwood-Heinemann divisions from Reed Elsevier.

Public Policy

Under the direction and coordination of the School Division, school publishers achieved significant public policy victories in 2007, resulting in increased levels of funding for instructional materials and improvements in the regulatory environment.

- In Florida, in the face of a number of adverse legislative and funding factors, AAP succeeded in increasing funding for instructional materials by $5.27 million (2 percent) to a level of $272 million. This increase marks the tenth time in 12 years that AAP has been able to achieve full funding for the "IM categorical." In addition, AAP was able to achieve a 2 percent increase ($2.23 million) in the Just Read program.

- In Texas, school publishers faced a variety of challenges in the 80th legislative session in Austin. However, by the end of the session, AAP and the school publishing industry had prevailed, with the legislature agreeing to full funding of $498 million for el-hi mathematics materials. The legislature also agreed to maintain the current constitutionally protected system for funding textbooks, and approved legislation lifting a moratorium on future adoptions of instructional materials. AAP also worked successfully to ensure that "Proclamation 2010" for English, Language Arts, and Reading remains on track.

- In California, the School Division supported legislative efforts to reauthorize and extend the instructional materials program. The final budget provided $545.9 million in support of instructional materials. In addition, AAP worked extensively to respond to the State Board of Education's draft regulations for instructional materials adoptions.

- In New York, thanks in part to AAP efforts, textbook formula aid received a $0.95 million boost to $43.25 million and the aid was preserved as a discrete categorical fund despite proposals to open the fund to other items.

- At the federal level, AAP developed extensive recommendations and legislative language for reauthorization of the No Child Left Behind Act (NCLB) and sponsored a successful "Capitol Hill Day" in March in which School Division members visited with members of Congress and their staff. Efforts to support NCLB will continue in 2008 as the Senate takes up reauthorization. AAP also worked to implement the National Instructional Materials Accessibility Standard (NIMAS). Thanks to AAP's direct interventions with the U.S. Department of Education, current NIMAS implementation efforts align more closely with the federal statute.

Public Relations and Outreach

The School Division continued to enhance and extend its public relations initiatives to members, nonmembers, and key participants in the education policy arena.

- Re-branding—As part of AAP's efforts to re-brand the School Division, the School Division Website (http://www.aapschool.org) was redesigned and new outreach materials developed.
- New Web sites—The School Division unveiled http://www.californiak12 books.org, designed to communicate the important role that instructional materials play in California classrooms. The Test Committee unveiled http://www.testingfacts.org as part of its national public relations effort to educate parents and teachers about the importance of education assessment in today's classrooms.
- *School Division Weekly*—The division continued distribution of a weekly electronic newsletter to AAP members, providing public policy updates, education reports, and AAP activities.
- Conferences and meetings—AAP held a successful Summit on Mathematics and Science that addressed many emerging issues relating to new standards and instructional strategies.
- New awards program—In recognition of members who have made extensive contributions to AAP and the school publishing industry, the School Division expanded its awards program. In addition to the McNulty Award, the division has added two new award categories: Meritorious Achievement in Educational Publishing and Distinguished Service Awards.
- Educational Publishing Inter-Industry Council (EPIC)—The School Division partnered with the Association of Educational Publishers (AEP) and the Software and Information Industry Association (SIIA) to sponsor "What You Really Need to Succeed in Educational Publishing." The one-day professional development seminar in Chicago attracted more than 50 people. AAP will continue to work with AEP and SIIA on this important effort to attract and prepare individuals for careers in school publishing.

Smaller and Independent Publishers

AAP's Smaller and Independent Publishing Committee (SIP) was created in 1998 to serve the special needs and interests of this segment of the AAP membership. Gene Gollogley (Booklight) continued as committee chair in 2007.

In an effort to reach out to smaller and independent publishers on the West Coast, and in light of the thousands of publishers who participate in BookExpo

America (BEA) each year, SIP decided to move its 2008 annual meeting to Los Angeles to coincide with BEA. The program is entitled: "How to Navigate the Life Cycles of a Publishing House." The event also featured presentation of the annual Miriam Bass Award for Creativity in Independent Publishing.

AAP's ninth annual Meeting for Smaller and Independent Publishers, held in March 2007 at New York University's Kimmel Center, drew more than 100 independent publishers. The meeting explored seven approaches for making small and independent publishing houses more successful. The event opened with presentation of the Miriam Bass Award for Creativity in Independent Publishing to Dennis Loy Johnson and Valerie Merians, co-publishers of Hoboken (New Jersey)-based Melville House Publishing. Johnson paid tribute to all of the independent voices in publishing, saying, "Let me tell you, there are a lot of publishers out there right now who deserve an award for creativity by simply staying alive." The award is cosponsored by AAP, Rowman & Littlefield Publishing Group, and National Book Network (NBN) and carries a $5,000 cash prize, fully funded by Rowman & Littlefield and NBN.

At an event at the New York Public Library on December 14 sponsored by SIP, some 100 collection development librarians from the New York Public Library system got a sneak preview of new titles from five of the nation's premier independent presses. Featured speakers included Johnny Temple (Akashic), Scott Watrous (Globe Pequot), Dennis Loy Johnson (Melville House), Richard Nash (Soft Skull), and Michael Rockliff (Workman).

Trade Publishing

AAP's Trade Publishing Group comprises publishers of fiction, general nonfiction, poetry, children's literature, religious, and reference publications, in hardcover, paperback, and electronic formats. Robert Miller (Hyperion) chaired the Trade Executive Committee in 2007.

During 2007 the group's executive committee continued to explore ways to support book reviewers in their campaign to stem cutbacks in book-review pages at newspapers throughout the country, and to provide forums for sharing the launch of new titles with reviewers. In March 2007 the group hosted a breakfast following the National Book Critics Circle (NBCC) Awards, providing an opportunity for editors to meet with book reviewers in an informal setting, and sponsored a cocktail reception in September attended by more than 150 publishers and reviewers.

In cooperation with NBCC, the Trade Group hosted a breakfast meeting that brought leading editors and publishers together with NBCC members to discuss efforts to save book reviews. The National Endowment for the Arts and *Bookforum* magazine also participated. AAP subsequently worked with the National Newspaper Association (NNA) to explore cooperative educational seminars at the NNA Annual Meeting and to look at book-buyer demographics in an effort to gauge the value of book advertising throughout select newspapers in key media markets. The Trade Executive Committee is exploring a possible fall 2008 networking event, either live or online, as a vehicle for sharing editors' top picks with key book media.

The Trade Group is responsible for identifying and selecting candidates for the AAP Honors award, which is given to individuals and institutions outside the publishing industry for outstanding work in promoting U.S. books and authors, and is presented each year at the AAP Annual Meeting. The award was presented in March 2007 to the ABC television show "The View." In December 2007 AAP announced the selection of the 2008 honoree, the National Book Critics Circle.

Publishing Latino Voices of America

AAP works to increase awareness of Latino books through its Publishing Latino Voices for America (PLVA) Task Force. A number of new programs were implemented in 2007, including a partnership with "Las Comadres," a network of more than 7,000 Latinas in 60 cities nationwide. The PLVA program with Las Comadres featured monthly author teleconferences that attracted more than 100 Las Comadres members each month. The partnership is developing a new "Las Comadres and Friends" book club that will feature live author programming for Las Comadres members at select Borders stores across the country.

PLVA, working with the Association of Library Services to Children (ALSC), is developing new ideas to mark the observance of Día de los Niños/Día de los Libros (http://www.ala.org/dia). Held each year held on April 30, it is a celebration of the written word for children of all cultural backgrounds. PLVA and ALSC are working together on a list of recommended children's titles that will be posted on the Web site of ¡Ajá, leyendo!, AAP's "Get Caught Reading" Spanish component, at http://www.getcaughtreading.org.

PLVA hosted a series of sessions on the Spanish-language and Latin American market, examining ways in which smaller and independent publishers can leverage the Spanish-language market by publishing select titles, and how libraries and bookstores can create Spanish-language components. An author event was also featured.

PLVA meets on a regular basis at AAP, hosting speakers from various parts of the Latino publishing community including Spanish-language library collection development professionals and media such as *Tinta Fresca*, a Web site featuring reviews of Spanish-language titles.

Adopt-A-School

AAP continued to match authors with schools throughout New York City's five boroughs as part of its Adopt-A-School program with the New York City Department of Education. Some 25 schools have been matched each year since the program's launch in 2004, bringing the joy of books and reading to urban area children of all ages from pre-kindergarten through high school. AAP presented the program at a reception for school representatives at AAP's New York office in May 2007 and matched several elementary, middle, and high schools with publishers for author visits during Children's Book Week in November.

Trade Libraries Committee

AAP's Trade Libraries Committee, chaired by Talia Ross (Macmillan), comprises representatives of major book publishing houses in partnership with organizations including ALA, Friends of Libraries U.S.A (FOLUSA), and *Library Journal*. The committee's mandate is to expand networking and education with public libraries across the country at trade events such as the Public Library Association Conference and BookExpo America. In 2007 the committee inaugurated an author dinner at BookExpo America exclusively for librarians; this proved so successful that it is now being planned as an annual event for more than 250 librarians. The 2007 author dinner featured Elizabeth Gilbert, Dorothea Benton Frank, Marisha Pessl, Ann Patchett, Valerie Martin, and Amy Bloom. The committee also hosted a forum on publishers' top picks exclusively for New York Public Library collection development staff, and hosted a similar event at the New York Library Association's Annual Conference.

2007 Annual Meeting

Honors for 'The View'

ABC's award-winning talk show "The View" was chosen to receive the 2007 AAP Honors award for its work in promoting American books and authors, and was presented with the award on March 6 at the AAP Annual Meeting.

"The View" is broadcast live Monday through Friday and features a team of four women discussing contemporary events. In the ten years it has been on the air, "The View" has featured authors covering a broad range of subjects including politics, finance, autobiography, and fashion.

The show's executive producer, Bill Geddie, and Sue Solomon, the talent producer, along with two of the show's hosts, Joy Behar and Elisabeth Hasselbeck, were on hand to accept the award, which comes with a $5,000 donation to a charity of the winners' choosing. "The View" designated First Book, an international nonprofit organization that provides children from low-income families with new books, often the first books they have ever owned.

The AAP Honors were inaugurated in 1997 to acknowledge the contributions of individuals and organizations outside the book industry who have helped focus public attention on American books and their importance in society. Previous winners have included C-SPAN's Brian Lamb, country music star Dolly Parton (who created the "Imagination Library" literacy program), and Oprah Winfrey.

Meeting Highlights

Digital was the name of the game as some 250 attendees crowded the ballroom at the Yale Club to hear a roster of speakers explore the ways in which traditional media is being redefined and reconfigured by the digital landscape, from changing business models, to content access and delivery, intellectual property rights management, and market strategies.

Time, Inc. CEO Ann Moore emphasized the strategic importance of getting her company's strongest brands onto digital platforms. She stressed the huge power of collaboration, with traditional media bringing the "great, trusted editing skills" to online news and information. She admitted, however, that Time, Inc. will try to keep its print readers, who generate about $118 in annual revenue compared with $5 for online users, as long as possible.

Quoting the late Charles Clark's observation that "the answer to the machine is the machine," Mark Bide of Rightscom Ltd. described the work of Automated Content Access Protocol (ACAP) to develop a standard system that will allow publishers to express digital content access and usage policies in a language that search engines can be programmed to recognize. AAP subsequently announced that it had joined ACAP.

In a spirited dialogue with Richard Sarnoff of Random House, Adobe CEO Bruce Chizen highlighted the growing demand for free Web content accessed through mobile devices, and the scramble to upgrade wireless technology in the United States, which he said is far behind that of Japan and Europe. Adobe innovations—including new desktop software—will make it easy for publishers to take their content and repurpose it, but he cautioned publishers to remain focused on the fact that their true strength lies in producing quality content; "Somebody needs to filter out all the garbage out there." Addressing the serious threat of digital piracy, Chizen said that Adobe and other members of the Business Software Alliance lose one-third of their revenue annually to piracy and those losses represent more than the total losses of AAP, Recording Industry Association of America, and Motion Picture Association of America members combined. Fighting back, he said, will require new initiatives in education, digital rights management, and enforcement, and a willingness to "continue to prosecute and to publicize those prosecutions."

Tina Sharkey, CEO of BabyCenter, LLC, stressed the importance for "GenY" of social media connecting people with one another. While previous generations "went online" GenY "lives online," a critical difference. These sites, while not creating content themselves are powerful "buzz" generators, and Sharkey emphasized the importance of getting users to "act passionately on your behalf," and to harness the power of bloggers.

In a speech that generated a good deal of media interest even before the meeting began, Microsoft's Associate General Counsel Tom Rubin hammered Google for "making money on the backs of others" in its online book search project, and contrasted its approach with Microsoft's, which he maintains grows out of a "common understanding of the creative process." Stressing the need to advance technology in ways that respect copyright, Rubin spoke of the need for collaborative efforts to address a host of issues, including a process or safety net to deal with the problem of "orphan works."

FY 2007–2008 Budget Approved

The membership approved an operating budget of $9 million for fiscal year 2007–2008, with $5.2 million allocated to core activities; $1.1 million to Higher Education, and $2.7 million to the two divisions ($1.5 million for School Division and $1.2 million for PSP). A shortfall of $700,000 will be drawn from cash reserves.

American Booksellers Association

200 White Plains Rd., Tarrytown, NY 10591
914-591-2665
World Wide Web http://www.BookWeb.org

Jill Perlstein
Director, Member Services

Founded in 1900, the American Booksellers Association (ABA) is a not-for-profit trade organization devoted to meeting the needs of its core members—independently owned bookstores with storefront locations—by providing advocacy, opportunities for peer interaction, education, support services, and new business models. ABA actively supports free speech, literacy, and programs that encourage reading. The association also hosts the annual ABA Convention in conjunction with the BookExpo America (BEA) conference and trade show.

2007 Highlights

In the face of fierce competition from other media and bookselling outlets, rising rents, increases in costs, and a variety of daily challenges, independent bookstores continue to open in communities throughout the United States. ABA membership remains strong as booksellers look to their association for education, products and services, advocacy, and networking opportunities.

Although ABA provides programs and services to a variety of industry professionals, its primary focus is on its core members. These businesspeople, operating according to sound business principles, thrive through innovation. Independent booksellers are a vibrant, profitable, and growing force in a diverse marketplace and are recognized as influential and vital links between authors, readers, publishers, and the community.

Key components of the association's strategic plan, "Independent Bookselling: Competing in a Changing World" (as adopted July 13, 2002), with implementation examples, follow:

Goal I—Provide independent professional booksellers with access to the education, information, and business services they need to succeed in a changing world.

In early February 2007 ABA held its second annual Winter Institute in Portland, Oregon. At the sold-out event attended by more than 500 booksellers, ABA conducted 22 education sessions over an intense two-day period. Opportunities to network with authors and publishers were made possible through sponsorships. ABA and publishers provided scholarships to a number of booksellers who otherwise might not have had the means to attend. The Winter Institute is free to ABA bookstore members and was repeated in early 2008 in Louisville, Kentucky. Member booksellers need only to pay for transportation and accommodation.

Senior ABA staff and board members toured the country in February, March, and April 2007 to hold Bookseller Forums in conjunction with regional bookseller association events. This was the tenth anniversary of the forums, which have no agenda and are designed to allow booksellers to have direct conversations with association staff and board members. In keeping with the No. 1 goal of the strategic plan, education sessions were presented at each of 11 forums in 10 states.

ABA once again held its annual convention in conjunction with BEA. ABA offered a full day of educational programming highlighted by a variety of peer-to-peer and interactive opportunities. New York's Jacob K. Javits Convention Center hosted more than 37,000 book industry professionals and "Hotel ABA" in Brooklyn was a sold-out success. (Hotel ABA is the exclusive bookseller-only hotel where members receive group-rate rooms as well as other benefits, including publisher-sponsored receptions, welcome bags, shuttle buses, and more.) A "Welcome to Brooklyn" pre-BEA event included a series of walking tours led by local authors and concluded with an author reception at Brooklyn Borough Hall. An address by Pulitzer Prize-winning author, historian, and former Brooklynite David McCullough was a highlight of the opening event.

Year five of ABACUS, the financial benchmark study by and for independent booksellers, was completed and provided participants with information essential to improving their store's bottom line. Based on findings from the study and input from booksellers, ABA offered a variety of programs at Hotel ABA, including "Expanding Your Bookstore: Why, When, and How," "What to Do When the Competition Comes to Town: A Case Study," and "Building and Rewarding Customer Loyalty." Other sessions included "Staff Development: An Overview," "Handselling: Customer Service with Results," "Improve Efficiency to Achieve Success," "Participating in the Digital Revolution: Low and High Altitude," "Book Clubs: A Panel," and "Getting More Out of Your Children's Section: Managing Selection, Service, and Store Environment for Category Growth." ABA worked with outside sources to offer "Adapting to Change," presented by Cathleen Black, president of the Hearst Magazine Group and author of *Basic Black: Make Passion Your Strategy and Other Lessons for Work and Life,* and "Social Entrepreneurs: Changing the World," moderated by Brian Lamb, founder and chairman of C-Span and author of the Booknotes books series. The panel featured George Soros, chairman of the Open Society Institute and author of *The Age of Fallibility: Consequences of the War on Terror;* Wendy Kopp, founder and chairperson of Teach for America and author of *One Day, All Children . . . : The Unlikely Triumph of Teach for America and What I Learned Along the Way;* James D. Wolfensohn, former president of the World Bank and author of *A Global Life: My Journey Among Rich and Poor, from Wall Street to the World Bank;* Mohammud Yunus, winner of the Nobel Peace Prize and author of *Banker to the Poor: Micro-Lending and the Battle Against World Poverty;* and Teresa Heinz Kerry, co-author with husband U.S. Sen. John Kerry of *This Moment on Earth: Today's New Environmentalists and Their Vision for the Future.*

In conjunction with Paz & Associates, ABA sponsored a bookseller's school aimed at prospective and new booksellers at BookExpo America in addition to offering schools and sessions at other times during the year.

ABA continues to host educational programs at regional trade shows. Staff presented educational sessions and spotlighted the redesigned ABA trade Web site, BookWeb.org, which now includes a wiki, a blog, and improved navigation and search tools. The wiki is a growing reference work created by and for independent booksellers. It includes such topics as "Improving Efficiency to Achieve Success," "Implementing a Public Relations Plan—How to Be the Story," "Starting Inventory for Science Fiction and Fantasy," the advantages of hosting special events, and the benefits of sponsoring one-book reading programs.

The association's *Bookselling This Week (BTW)* offers news dispatches e-mailed to more than 13,000 subscribers every Thursday. *BTW* features ABA and industry news, in-depth features, the latest developments in the Book Sense marketing program, and the Book Sense Bestsellers and Picks lists. Industry professionals also have access to *BTW* via http://news.bookweb.org, and readers have the ability to create their own easy-to-print editions of the newsletter. BTW Flashes alert readers to important developments on a variety of subjects.

The *ABA Book Buyer's Handbook,* available online as an exclusive benefit to ABA members, is a source for publishers' discount schedules, returns policies, trade terms, and more, including links to publishers' Web sites and e-mail addresses. Fully searchable and continually updated, it also includes the latest information on publishers' special offers.

Goal II—Serve as the voice of professional independent booksellers and advocate on their behalf on such issues as free expression, trade practices, literacy, and community activism.

On November 29 and 30, several independent trade organizations, including ABA, met for an Independent Trades Summit in Washington, D.C. The gathering provided the associations with an opportunity to discuss common goals and challenges specific to independent retailers and businesses. Industries represented at the summit included ABA, American Specialty Toy Retailing Association, the Gift and Home Trade Association, the Coalition of Independent Music Stores, the Independent Florist Association, the Independent Office Products and Furniture Dealers Association, the North American Retail Dealers Association, and the National Bicycle Dealers Association. On December 13 the seven independent trade groups joined together to call for the equitable collection of sales tax on online purchases. Letters were sent to the governors of the 45 states that collect sales tax, urging that they require out-of-state online businesses to comply with individual states' sales tax laws.

With its partners in the Campaign for Reader Privacy, the association continued to play a leading role in the fight to restore safeguards for the privacy of bookstore and library records that were affected by the USAPatriot Act. (See American Booksellers Foundation for Free Expression below.)

ABA continued its work with the Book Industry Study Group (BISG) to disseminate information about the 13-digit ISBN transition, which went into effect on January 1, 2007. ABA monitored transition issues and facilitated ISBN-13 roundtables at BEA. ABA continues to sit on the board of BISG to represent the concerns of independent booksellers who face industry standardization and global influences.

Ongoing industry initiatives include working with publishers to improve packing and shipping practices, continuing the fight for sales tax equity, and facilitating meetings with booksellers and publishers. The association provided information to booksellers about the Small Employers Health Benefits Program Act of 2006 (S. 2510) and the Small Business Health Fairness Act (S. 406).

ABA continued to work closely and build relationships with the Institute for Local Self-Reliance, the American Independent Business Alliance, the Business Alliance for Local Living Economies, and Civic Economics to disseminate information about the importance of locally based independent businesses and how booksellers can form local business alliances. Additional studies measuring the greater economic impact of locally owned businesses were conducted, and general ads promoting the value of shopping locally were created and published in a number of ABA Book Sense Picks lists.

In addition, the association supported the following industry-wide observances: the Academy of American Poets' National Poetry Month, Banned Books Week, the American Library Association's Teen Read Week, the Association of American Publishers' (AAP's) Get Caught Reading campaign, AAP's Latino Book Month, the Children's Book Council's National Children's Book Week, the Lambda Literary Awards, the National Book Awards, the Quills Awards, and the Small Press Center's Small Press Month.

In support of future industry leaders, ABA continued its work with the Emerging Leaders Project, which had its inception at the 2006 ABA Winter Institute. The project recognizes the need to deliberately retain, develop, and support the industry's future leaders. The group of young booksellers networked and discussed topics of interest throughout the year.

Goal III—Promote the value of independent booksellers as a group through Book Sense and other cooperative activities.

Book Sense ("Independent Bookstores for Independent Minds") is ABA's national branding and marketing program for independent bookstores. The program has maintained its popularity, with many stores joining ABA to take advantage of the Book Sense marketing program. More than 1,150 bookstores throughout the United States display the Book Sense logo and benefit from the selling power of the Book Sense Picks and the Book Sense Bestsellers lists.

The main components of the Book Sense program are

- Book Sense Picks—Consumer-focused lists featuring titles recommended by independent booksellers. The program includes a monthly list of recommended books, quarterly children's lists, an annual reading group, paperback and highlights lists, and a number of top-ten lists.
- Book Sense Bestseller List—A timely bestseller list compiled from nearly 500 reporting stores each week. Regional and Extended lists are created each week, specialty-category lists biweekly.
- Book Sense Book of the Year Awards for adult fiction, nonfiction, children's illustrated, and children's literature—These honors are announced at ABA's annual Celebration of Bookselling at BEA; the list of winners and honor books can be found on ABA's Web site at http://news. bookweb.org/news/5160.html.
- Book Sense Gift Card Program—A program through which consumers can purchase and redeem gift cards at more than 380 locations in 48 states

and on a number of bookstores' Web sites. Book Sense Gift Cards never expire and carry no inactivity fees or other hidden fees.

- BookSense.com—This e-commerce Web site allows participating stores to market their bookstores and offer a secure shopping environment. BookSense.com hosts more than 240 independent bookstores' Web sites. Enhancements include smarter title searches, improved location directories for consumers, co-op programs, inventory uploads, and other tools that help booksellers to create Web sites that reflect their store's personality. BookSense.com has more than 2,000 affiliates and offers consumers a choice for online shopping. Consumers can purchase e-books, browse sample pages, sign up for bookstore newsletters, and enjoy an online shopping experience while supporting local businesses.

The Book Sense Marketing Program provides its publisher partners with effective marketing tools, including Advance Access, a biweekly and monthly e-mail offering advance reader copies (ARCs) and other marketing and promotional materials.

Throughout the year Book Sense works with publisher partners to create in-store promotions for specific books and movies with book tie-ins. The "Independent Muggles for Harry Potter Sweepstakes" drew 28,500 customer entries at close to 300 ABA member stores. The grand prize was a trip for four to London.

In mid-2007 ABA began investigating how to rebrand Book Sense. The evaluation is continuing, and news of a new initiative will be announced in mid-2008.

Goal IV—Foster development of new and enhanced business models, systems, and services.

ABA continued in 2007 to offer business management services to its members. These include AAA Label, a source for low-tack book stickers; Above the Treeline, an innovative online software product designed to help bookstores improve finances by optimizing inventory selection; special access to Atlas Paper Company, a source for paper and plastic bags and wrapping paper; competitive rates for credit and debit card processing through Bank of America; access to computer hardware at reduced prices through CDW Computer Centers; check risk management, electronic check conversion, check collections, and check cashing services through Certegy Check Services, a Fidelity National Information Services Company; Constant Contact, which provides a Web-based e-mail marketing service to create, mail, and manage e-mail newsletter campaigns; casualty and property insurance for booksellers and liability insurance for publishers through LIBRIS; and PartnerShip, providing small- and large-package shipping services via FedEx Ground, FedEx Express, FedEx Kinko's, and Yellow Freight.

Looking to the Future

In November ABA President Russ Lawrence of Chapter One Book Store in Hamilton, Montana, announced in *Bookselling This Week* the creation of organizational ends statements, expressing the ABA board's long-term goals. Ends statements are an expression of what good ABA does, for whom, and at what cost or priority to the organization. The top-level ends statement that ABA adopted states that "ABA member bookstores will be professionally operated and profitable, and income derived from regular members' fees will be equal to, or less than, those of comparable trade associations." ABA CEO Avin Mark Domnitz will be responsible for creating an annual strategic plan for the staff to follow in achieving those ends. This organizational change allows the ABA board to react more swiftly to shifts in membership priorities and other situations, thus positioning ABA to continue to lead in the bookselling industry.

American Booksellers Foundation for Free Expression

In 2007 the American Booksellers Foundation for Free Expression (ABFFE) joined the National Coalition Against Censorship (NCAC) in launching the Kids' Right to Read Project to oppose efforts to remove books from public school classrooms and libraries. There are hundreds of challenges to books in America's schools every year, and booksellers frequently take the lead in opposing book censorship by organizing events or petition drives in their stores, by writing letters to local school boards, and by speaking with journalists. In-store events and displays often generate a forum for discussion of a controversial issue. ABFFE provides advice and assistance to booksellers and others opposing book-banning, education materials to promote awareness about the right to read, and support for local activism on free speech issues. During the first year of the Kids' Right to Read Project, ABFFE fought efforts to ban more than 30 books in 19 states and prevailed in nearly all of the cases.

ABFFE is a leader in the fight to protect reader privacy. In 2007 it continued its work of the previous six years to educate the book community and the public about the importance of re-establishing the safeguards for reader privacy affected by the USAPatriot Act. In April 2007 ABFFE hailed the congressional testimony of a Connecticut librarian who successfully challenged a National Security Letter (NSL) issued by the FBI. George Christian testified about the fight that he and three other librarians waged against the NSL, which they received in 2005, that demanded the Internet records of library patrons. In June ABFFE urged the repeal of a Madison, Wisconsin, ordinance that required bookstores that purchase used textbooks to give police the names of the sellers and the titles purchased. In late September ABFFE and the Campaign for Reader Privacy welcomed the introduction of the National Security Letter Reform Act of 2007 (S. 2088) by Sen. Russ Feingold (D-Wis.). The bill limits the government's power to use the USAPatriot Act to secretly examine a person's library or bookstore records unless it can show that the person is a suspected spy or terrorist or in contact with such a person. ABFFE officially endorsed the legislation.

ABFFE submitted two amicus (friend-of-the-court) briefs to the U.S. Supreme Court in 2007. In September it joined AAP, the Freedom to Read Foundation, and other book industry groups in warning of the potential chilling effect of the PROTECT Act of 2003. The brief in *U.S.* v. *Williams* urged the court to uphold a lower court decision that struck down a provision of the law that bans advertisements that falsely present as child pornography books, magazines, and other works protected by the First Amendment. The brief argues that producers, distributors, and retailers must be free to advertise First Amendment-protected books and other works without the fear that they will be charged with a crime. In February ABFFE and NCAC submitted an amicus brief in *Morse* v. *Frederick,* arguing that it was wrong to punish a high school student for displaying a banner reading "Bong Hits 4 Jesus." Free speech advocates were disappointed in June when the court upheld the right of school officials to punish the student because they believed his banner advocated the use of illegal drugs. However, the decision was narrow, applying only to advocacy of illegal drug use (and presumably other illegal activities) in school or at a school-sponsored event.

ABFFE continues to fight the Miami (Florida) school board's effort to ban a children's picture book, *Vamos a Cuba.* In June a school board attorney told the 11th Circuit Court of Appeals that the board was entitled to ban the book from school libraries because it contained "inaccuracies." The board is appealing a lower court decision that ordered it to keep the book in the libraries. ABFFE has filed two amicus briefs supporting the American Civil Liberties Union's challenge to the ban.

In June ABFFE and other free-expression groups celebrated a decision by the U.S. Court of Appeals for the Second Circuit that rejected the Federal Communications Commission's (FCC's) rule banning "fleeting expletives" that occur occasionally on broadcast television. In 2006 ABFFE had joined a coalition in filing an amicus brief arguing that new standards adopted by the commission to censor "indecency" on the airwaves are overly vague and unconstitutional. FCC has appealed the decision to the Supreme Court.

ABFFE was founded by ABA in 1990. Its address is 275 Seventh Ave., Suite 1504, New York, NY 10001 (telephone 212-587-4025, World Wide Web http://www.abffe.org). Its president is Chris Finan.

Association of Research Libraries

21 Dupont Circle N.W., Washington, DC 20036
202-296-2296, e-mail arlhq@arl.org
World Wide Web http://www.arl.org

Duane E. Webster
Executive Director

The Association of Research Libraries (ARL) represents 123 principal research libraries serving major research institutions in the United States and Canada. ARL influences the changing environment of scholarly communication and the public policies that affect research libraries and the diverse communities they serve. ARL pursues this mission by advancing the goals of its member research libraries, providing leadership in public and information policy to the scholarly and higher education communities, fostering the exchange of ideas and expertise, and shaping a future environment that leverages its interests with those of allied organizations.

In November 2004 the ARL Board of Directors approved a new Strategic Plan for 2005–2009 that focused ARL's mission and programs along three strategic directions: scholarly communication; public policies affecting research libraries; and the library's role in the transformation of research, teaching, and learning. In 2007 the strategic direction steering committees, task forces, and working groups continued the implementation of the strategic plan's goals. Following are highlights of the association's activities.

Strategic Direction I

Scholarly Communication

ARL will be a leader in the development of effective, extensible, sustainable, and economically viable models of scholarly communication that provide barrier-free access to quality information in support of teaching, learning, research, and service to the community.

This strategic direction supports "new and enhanced models of scholarly communication that promote wide availability and enduring access." The roles of the university and library in publishing scholarship and research are shifting rapidly in the 21st century as new technologies and new needs emerge. A special issue of *ARL: A Bimonthly Report* (no. 252/253, July/August 2007) focused on the state of university publishing and the evolving role of research libraries in the delivery of publishing services. The report *University Publishing in a Digital Age* by Ithaka, an independent not-for-profit organization with a mission to accelerate the productive uses of information technologies for the benefit of higher education worldwide, provided the focus for two articles examining the university's role in publishing research: a summary of the Ithaka report by its original authors and an assessment by David Shulenburger of the report's suggestion that research institutions should have "publishing strategies." These are complemented by three articles characterizing new publishing initiatives involving libraries: the joint project of the California Digital Library and the University of California Press; the publishing services developed at the University of Illinois at Chicago; and the Canadian collaborative project Synergies, a national multi-institutional project to create a publishing infrastructure to support society publishing in the humanities and social sciences as well as other scholarly publishing. Together the articles provide a set of perspectives on key shifts in the university's role in scholarly publishing. See http://www.arl.org/resources/pubs/br/br252-253.shtml.

Within a landscape of new and emerging publishing models with libraries developing new roles in the production of scholarly works, ARL and its member libraries continue to see the need to build on a distinguished history of activities fostering and promoting preservation activities to ensure enduring access to scholarly works. As their collections expand to incorporate digital materials, and with enormous collections of works in paper and other media, research libraries face a growing set of challenges. The ARL statement "Research Libraries' Enduring Responsibility for Preservation" articulated the need for the community to intensify its attention to preservation concerns. As the statement notes, "Each research library has a core of preservation responsibilities, some that can be met only locally, but others that increasingly should or can only be met through cooperative strategies." The statement reflects a series of recommendations generated by ARL's Task Force on the Future of Preservation in ARL Libraries. The task force's report was based on a meeting of preservation librarians and leaders of libraries, library organizations, and funders hosted by ARL at the University of North Carolina at Chapel Hill. See http://www.arl.org/bm~doc/preservation_responsibility_24july07.pdf. For a summary of the task force's report and recommendations see http://www.arl.org/bm~doc/arlbr251preserv.pdf.

Another issue in the evolving publishing environment is the ongoing transition of print publications to fully electronic form. ARL commissioned an analysis, "The E-Only Tipping Point for Journals: What's Ahead in the Print to Electronic Transition Zone," to explore the current world of dual-format publishing from the standpoint of both librarians and publishers. The report provides an assessment of the current transition state, drivers, and barriers to change and offers an outlook for the near term along with recommendations that identify areas where focused attention offers the greatest potential to accelerate the change process. See http://www.arl.org/bm~doc/Electronic_Transition.pdf.

One of the many concerns affecting journals' format transition is long-term preservation. To encourage the development of a more robust archiving environment for scholarly journals, ARL endorsed the recommendations made in the report "E-Journal Archiving Metes and Bounds: A Survey of the Landscape," published in 2006 by the Council on Library and Information Resources (CLIR). ARL urged its member libraries to support and participate in trustworthy and effective e-journal archiving initiatives as recommended in the report, and to press publishers of e-journals to participate in and support trustworthy and effective archiving of their titles. See http://www.arl.org/news/pr/arlendorsesclirrpt.shtml.

This strategic direction also focuses on "the development of library professionals who have the expertise and knowledge to contribute to enhanced and transformed systems of scholarly communication." To this end, ARL and the Association of College and Research Libraries (ACRL), a division of the American Library Association (ALA), jointly manage the Institute on Scholarly Communication. In July the third face-to-face institute was offered in Washington, D.C., bringing teams from a range of academic libraries together to work on developing customized plans for their campus outreach programs. ARL and ACRL also launched a program that offers consortia the opportunity to partner in offering the institute's face-to-face event. The Consortium of Academic and Research Libraries in Illinois (CARLI) hosted the first regional institute in December in Chicago; another regional institute is planned for 2008. The institute also offers a growing range of resources to support libraries in developing scholarly communication programs. Popular tools created for the institute are publicly available for use under a Creative Commons share-alike license through the Web page Freely Available Institute Resources (FAIR). See http://www.arl. org/sc/institute/instres.shtml.

ACRL and ARL, through the Institute on Scholarly Communication and along with ARL's sister organization the Scholarly Publishing and Academic Resources Coalition (SPARC), offered four joint Webcasts on author rights. The presenters discussed ways authors can amend publisher copyright transfer agreements to keep key rights to journal articles and provided librarians with the basic information needed to educate faculty about the consequences and options before they transfer ownership of their intellectual output. An archived version of the final Webcast, "Understanding Author Rights," continues to be freely available to the broader community with a free LearningTimes account available at http://www.learningtimes.net/acrl_arrarchive.html. The "Author Rights Resources" handout from the Webcast is also freely available. See http://www.arl.org/bm~doc/ARresources.pdf.

The Office of Scholarly Communication independently offers additional resources for learning about scholarly communication resources. A newly created Web page, "Authors and Their Rights," brings together a range of resources—many developed by ARL member libraries—that support author management of copyrights. The page offers general strategies, a range of examples of resources from research libraries, policy statements supporting rights retention, example addenda, and informational resources. See http://www.arl.org/sc/copyright/author-rights-resources.shtml.

The Office of Scholarly Communication also created a set of six brown-bag lunch discussion guides to facilitate informal conversations among library staff on key scholarly communication issues. Such discussions allow staff to deepen their knowledge of key topics, learn from one another, and track changing perspectives. Guides are available on starting discussions of scholarly communication, talking with faculty, access to publicly funded research, author rights, scholarly society roles, and peer review. Each guide offers pre-work and discussion questions for a meeting, along with resources that provide further background for the discussion leader of an hour-long session. The guides can serve as a starting point for a single discussion or for a series of six conversations. See http://www.arl.org/sc/brownbag.

The licensing process is an important part of the creation and management of electronic resources. Until recently libraries mainly licensed resources from publishers, but the advent of mass digitization capabilities has initiated a wave of negotiations between libraries and extra-institutional partners to allow large segments of library collections to be scanned. The *ARL: A Bimonthly Report* no. 250

(February 2007) article, "In Google's Broad Wake: Taking Responsibility for Shaping the Global Digital Library," identified seven core library interests in evaluating digitization partnerships. The author urges libraries to reject the notion that recent mass digitization contracts have established the norms for future agreements and to "make full use of whatever leverage they have to ensure the global digital library is open and dynamic." As stewards of their collections, librarians should consider carefully issues of exclusivity, uses of the digital files, respect for the public domain and copyright, preservation, use of standards, the quid pro quo, and transparency. A checklist accompanying the article suggests some of the questions negotiators should ask themselves as they define their objectives in entering into an agreement. See http://www.arl.org/resources/pubs/br/br250.shtml.

With the continuing proliferation of scholarly resources in electronic formats, the practice of negotiating license agreements for electronic resources can become a burdensome exercise for both libraries and publishers. ARL, the Association of Learned and Professional Society Publishers (ALPSP), SPARC, and the Society for Scholarly Publishing (SSP) agreed that finding an alternative to license agreements was an important issue that librarians and publishers should work together to address. The National Information Standards Organization (NISO) was identified as a trusted third party to develop a best-practice statement and provide a mechanism for adoption within the library and publishing communities. The Simplified Electronic Resource Understanding (SERU) Working Group was formed to work with NISO to develop the best-practice statement. They released a draft document, "The SERU Approach to E-Resource Subscriptions: Framework for Development and Use of SERU," that presented a shared set of understandings to which publishers and libraries can point when negotiating the sale of electronic content. NISO then sponsored the pilot use of the framework in 2007. The article, "SERU (Shared Electronic Resource Understanding): Opening Up New Possibilities for Electronic Resource Transactions," which appears in the November issue of *D-Lib Magazine,* provides context for the SERU project and details the shared understanding approach. See http://www.dlib.org/dlib/november07/hahn/11hahn.html.

Strategic Direction II

Public Policies Affecting Research Libraries

ARL will influence information and other public policies, both nationally and internationally, that govern the way information is managed and made available.

Part of the scope of this strategic direction is "influencing laws, public policies, regulations, and judicial decisions that are key to research libraries and their users." In 2007 ARL engaged in a variety of efforts to promote fair use in the digital environment, support public access to federally funded research, and protect the openness of the Internet.

The Library Copyright Alliance (LCA), of which ARL is a member, supported the introduction of the Freedom and Innovation Revitalizing U.S. Entrepreneurship (FAIR USE) Act of 2007 (H.R. 1201) that seeks to ensure that fair use is robust and effective in the digital, networked environment. The legislation would make permanent six exemptions approved by the Librarian of Congress stemming from the Digital Millennium Copyright Act (DMCA) anticircumvention rulemaking—for example, the ability to circumvent digital locks to use AV works from an educational library or a university media studies department in the classroom. There are six additional provisions in the legislation of interest to the library and education communities, including one that would permit a library or archive to circumvent technological protection measures to preserve a copy of a work or replace a copy that is damaged, deteriorated, lost, or stolen. While technology companies are the most likely beneficiaries of this new provision, it will also reduce the potential exposure of libraries and universities to claims for excessive damages for the infringing conduct of users of their services. See http://www.arl.org/news/pr/lca_fair_use_feb07.shtml.

LCA also supported the Computer and Communications Industry Association (CCIA) complaint filed before the Federal Trade Commission (FTC) in August concerning misrepresentation of consumer rights regarding the legitimate use of copyrighted works. The complaint called for investigation by FTC and the immediate end to deceptive practices by certain publishers and motion picture distributors. The complaint noted that these "corporations have engaged, and continue to engage in, a nationwide pattern of unfair and deceptive trade practices by misrepresenting consumer rights under copyright law, and in some cases threatening criminal and civil penalties against consumers who choose to exercise statutorily or constitutionally guaranteed rights. These false representations violate the letter and spirit of the FTC Act's prohibition against unfair or deceptive acts or practices in or affecting commerce." CCIA demanded an end to these deceptive practices and asked that FTC order the offenders to cease misrepresenting copyright law, correct prior misrepresentations, and develop a plan for preventing future misrepresentations of consumer rights. See http://www.arl.org/pp.

In December ARL released a white paper, *Educational Fair Use Today,* that discusses three recent appellate decisions concerning fair use that should give educators and librarians greater confidence and guidance for asserting this important privilege. The paper summarizes three cases—*Blanch* v. *Koons, Perfect 10* v. *Amazon.com,* and *Bill Graham Archives* v. *Dorling Kindersley*—and analyzes the significance of the appellate decisions in the educational context. In all three decisions the courts permitted extensive copying and display in the commercial context because the uses involved repurposing and recontextualization. The reasoning of these opinions could have far-reaching implications in the educational environment. [The report is published in its entirety earlier in Part 1—*Ed.*]

After a year-long process of securing input from ARL members, campus legal counsel, and copyright experts, ARL launched a copyright education initiative trademarked Know Your Copy Rights. The initiative's inaugural product was the brochure *Know Your Copy Rights—What You CAN Do,* which gives faculty and teaching assistants in higher education a concise guide to when and how they can legally use copyrighted works in their teaching, often without requesting permission or paying fees. The brochure accentuates the positive by telling faculty what can be done under the law. With encouragement from the National Association of College and University Attorneys, ARL sent a letter to legal counsel in ARL university member institutions urging their support for local Know Your Copy Rights initiatives. The letter urged counsel to work with their libraries and other campus leadership to reframe campus discussion of copyright by providing a positive message focused on uses and users in higher education, a message free of the biases often reflected in materials made available by commercial interests. See http://www.knowyourcopyrights.org.

In the February 15, 2006, *Federal Register,* the Section 108 Study Group requested feedback on its initial areas of study: access to digital copies and two new exceptions—preservation-only copies and Web site preservation. ARL and ALA were represented at a March 2006 roundtable sponsored by the study group and convened a workshop in June to consider and receive additional input from members of the library and archival communities regarding the deliberations of the study group. In January 2007 the Section 108 Study Group and the U.S. Copyright Office conducted a second roundtable to explore possible revisions to Section 108 of the Copyright Act. This roundtable focused on copies for users, such as interlibrary loan (ILL). In anticipation of the second roundtable, ARL and ALA convened a meeting to consider the questions raised by the study group and to provide input to the second roundtable. Position papers and other resources relating to the Section 108 Study Group can be found at http://www. arl.org/pp/ppcopyright/sec108. ARL also released a white paper that analyzed trends in ILL activity in U.S. academic and research libraries over the past two decades. The paper provides a description of current ILL practices for borrowing requests, most of which are placed via the OCLC WorldCat Resource Sharing system. See http://www.arl.org/bm~doc/ARL_white_paper_ILL_june07.pdf.

Enhancing access to federally funded research is a priority for the library community as such initiatives improve access by the public, provide for effective archiving strategies for these resources, and ensure accountability of the federal investment. With strong bipartisan support, in July the U.S. House of Representatives passed the fiscal year (FY) 2008 Labor, Health and Human Services, and Education and Related Agencies Appropriations Act (H.R. 3043), which included language requiring grantees of the National Institutes of Health (NIH) to deposit the final, electronic, peer-reviewed manuscripts of NIH-funded research articles in NIH's online archive within 12 months of publication. A comparable bill in the Senate (S. 1710), including the same provision, was passed in October. In December President Bush signed into law the Consolidated Appropriations Act of 2007 (H.R. 2764), which includes a provision directing NIH to change its existing Public Access Policy, implemented as a voluntary measure in 2005, so that participation is required for agency-funded investigators. Researchers will now be required to deposit electronic copies of their peer-reviewed manuscripts into the National Library of Medicine's online archive, PubMed Central. Full texts of the articles will be publicly available and searchable online in PubMed Central no later than 12 months after publication in a journal. ARL, SPARC, and the Alliance for Taxpayer Access (ATA) urged members to support this legislation. Facilitating this kind of broad and often unexpected use of research will have direct, positive results on discovery and innovation.

The Foreign Intelligence Surveillance Act (FISA), enacted in 1978, provides some checks and balances on electronic surveillance by law enforcement for the purposes of national security. In July Congress passed the Protect America Act of 2007, which made far-reaching changes to FISA and greatly expanded the authorities and powers of the Executive Branch. ARL joined in letters to House and Senate leadership requesting that Congress conduct public hearings on the legislation. President Bush signed the new legislation into law in August. Congress then focused on updating the temporary legislation that is set to expire early in 2008. In November the House passed the RESTORE Act of 2007 that provides for court oversight of communications between foreign and domestic surveillance targets and does not include retroactive immunity for telecommunications companies that aided the administration in conducting warrantless surveillance. Two bills were under consideration in the Senate at the time this report was prepared. Whereas the Senate Select Committee on Intelligence approved legislation that is very similar to the expansive August 2007 law, the Senate Committee on the Judiciary approved a bill that is narrower in scope and does not include retroactive immunity for telecommunications companies. ARL and ALA have raised privacy issues as a key concern requiring a change to the law and are advocating that there should be judicial review by the FISA Court if law enforcement demands library records or communications.

The Communications Assistance Law Enforcement Act (CALEA), passed by Congress in 1994, addresses the concerns of the law enforcement community regarding the use of wiretaps in digital telephone networks; the law specifically provided law enforcement with additional powers to enhance government surveillance capabilities. In 2007 ARL joined commercial and not-for-profit organizations in a Center for Democracy and Technology (CDT) filing before the Federal Communications Commission (FCC) regarding a rulemaking to establish CALEA technical requirements and standards. FCC was considering what action to take on a petition by the Department of Justice (DOJ) to declare deficient CALEA standards for broadband Internet access surveillance. CALEA allows industry to set the technical standards for how wiretaps will be done. If DOJ or other agencies do not believe that the standards meet the law, they can petition FCC to change them. In this case, DOJ asked that FCC require access providers to build a capability to examine every packet sent by a user during a session regardless of who provides the application. In addition, DOJ called for access providers to store the intercepted information at their own expense for later retrieval by DOJ. Finally, in an issue of great importance to the privacy community and wireless carriers, DOJ wanted to undo prior court decisions and FCC rules to require wireless carriers to report the location of a mobile device whether a call is in progress or not—in other words, to use the system to provide detailed tracking of the user's movements. Because libraries are exempt from CALEA, these technical standard issues do not directly affect them but, in the event that libraries are covered in the future, these are the capabilities that would burden libraries if they provide broadband Internet access directly. See http://www.arl.org/pp/pscl/calea/index.shtml.

Strategic Direction III

The Library's Role in Research, Teaching, and Learning

ARL will promote and facilitate new and expanding roles for ARL libraries to engage in the transformations affecting research and undergraduate and graduate education.

In January 2007 the Steering Committee for Research, Teaching, and Learning (RTL) reviewed and supported the recommendations of the Task Force on Enhanced Environments for Teaching and Learning. The recommendations include undertaking a broad environmental scan of member activities in support of teaching and learning; securing professional assistance in defining an advocacy campaign that addresses the roles research libraries play in the teaching and learning enterprise; strengthening partnerships that leverage common interests, particularly with the EDUCAUSE Learning Initiative and the Coalition for Networked Information (CNI); enabling professional development opportunities for library staff; and identifying best practices for library facilities. These actions were incorporated into the RTL Program Plan for 2007, which was endorsed by the ARL Board in February.

The first Program Director for Research, Teaching, and Learning was hired and began work in May. In addition, a Visiting Program Officer (VPO) was named to focus on library support for research and e-science.

In October ARL and CNI hosted a Fall Forum on "Enhancing Graduate Education: A Fresh Look at Library Engagement." Keynote speakers reviewed emerging trends in master's and Ph.D. programs in American graduate schools, followed by a panel summary of case studies of graduate student research behaviors conducted by three ARL libraries. The forum's 125 attendees were audience to an interview with Ph.D. students over lunch, followed by break-out sessions in which participants brainstormed opportunities for engaging graduate students around their research practices, processes for discovery and access to information, and spaces for convening communities of scholars. Proceedings of the forum are available at http://www.arl.org/resources/pubs/fallforumproceedings/forum07proceedings.shtml. A summary report on the forum also appears in *ARL: A Bimonthly Report* no. 256 (February 2008). See http://www.arl.org/bm~doc/arl-br-256-grad.pdf.

The Joint Task Force on Library Support for E-Science released its final report, *Agenda for Developing E-Science in Research Libraries*. The report states, "E-science has the potential to be transformational within research libraries by impacting their operations, functions, and possibly even their mission. . . . The [task force] focused its attention on the implications of trends in e-science for research libraries, exploring the dimensions that impact collections, services, research infrastructure, and professional development." The task force concluded that "ARL's engagement in the issues of e-science is best focused on educational and policy roles, while partnering with other relevant organizations to contribute in strategic areas of technology development and new genres of publication. These types of strategic collaborations will also provide opportunities to re-envision the research library's role and contribution as 21st century science takes shape." With the support of ARL's three strategic direction steering committees, the recommendations in the report were to be incorporated into the annual program planning for the association to be undertaken by the ARL Board of Directors in February 2008. See http://www.arl.org/rtl/escience/eresource.shtml.

"Changing Global Book Collection Patterns in ARL Libraries," a report analyzing ARL member library cataloging records in the OCLC WorldCat database, presents evidence of changing patterns of collecting books with foreign imprints.

This analysis of book records and holdings in WorldCat finds that the overlap of global book collections among ARL libraries is not as extensive as was expected. See http://www.arl.org/resources/pubs/grn_global_book.shtml.

Diversity Initiatives and Work Force Issues

ARL's Diversity Initiatives encapsulate a suite of efforts implemented across ARL's strategic directions that aid the association with defining and addressing diversity issues in ARL libraries while supporting activities that encourage broad participation in the library field. ARL Diversity Initiatives seek to encourage exploration of the rich gifts and talents that diverse individuals bring to the library. ARL staff work closely with a broad range of libraries, graduate library education programs, and other library associations to promote awareness of career opportunities in research libraries and support the academic success of students from groups currently underrepresented in the profession.

Diversity Initiatives joined the social networking scene by creating a group for ARL librarians on the Web site Facebook. The group provides an online networking community for ARL librarians and a recruiting opportunity for undergraduates who are heavily involved in social networks. ARL is also promoting the Initiative to Recruit a Diverse Work Force via Facebook's flyer program by posting 175,000 ads that read "$10,000 for Graduate School." The flyer includes information about the initiative and a photo of the current class of Diversity Scholars. The campaign targets the following historically black colleges and universities: Howard University, Florida A&M University, Morehouse College, Lincoln University of Missouri, North Carolina A&T University, Hampton University, Prairie View A&M University, and University of Maryland Eastern Shore. See http://www.facebook.com/p.php?i=682700187&k=c2896239d6.

In 2007 the ARL Career Resources Web site, which provides job hunters with an easy-to-use resource for finding positions in ARL libraries, was redesigned. This service assists ARL member institutions with attracting a qualified, talented, and diverse applicant pool. The new interface is easier to use for both the recruiter and the job seeker. The Career Resources Online Service is located at http://careers.arl.org.

ARL supports residency programs and their vital role in the recruitment and training of new professionals by collecting and providing access to information on a broad range of career opportunities for future and new professionals. ARL is particularly interested in attracting new and transitioning professionals to careers in research libraries. In 2007 the Research Library Residency Programs Database—a free, Web-based registry for descriptions of residency programs and internships in academic and research libraries and in library and information science education programs—was redesigned to improve searching. ARL member institutions are encouraged to post their residency listings in the database, which is located at http://residencies.arl.org.

Funded by the Institute of Museum and Library Services (IMLS) and ARL member libraries, the Initiative to Recruit a Diverse Work Force (IRDW) offers a stipend of up to $10,000 over two years, a mentoring relationship with an experienced librarian, and a leadership training curriculum for MLS students from underrepresented groups who are interested in careers in research libraries. This multi-year initiative reflects the commitment of ARL members to create a diverse academic and research library community that will better meet the new challenges of global competition and changing demographics. In 2006 the program was awarded a three-year grant through the IMLS Laura Bush 21st Century Librarian Program. These additional funds from IMLS allow ARL to address the growing need for specialized librarians to help users who create and need access to digital resources and scientific data. The primary goal of the project is to educate, develop, and hire new librarians from underrepresented racial and ethnic groups, especially those with a background in applied and natural sciences and information technology. The ARL Diversity Initiatives Working Group selected 24 MLS students from underrepresented groups to participate in the 2007–2009 Initiative to Recruit a Diverse Work Force. For more information, see http://www. arl.org/diversity/init/index.shtml.

ARL Diversity Initiatives hosted the third annual Leadership Symposium in conjunction with the ALA Midwinter Meeting in Seattle in January 2007. The symposium targeted all MLS graduate students who have an interest in research libraries and fellows who are a part of the ARL Initiative to Recruit a Diverse Work Force and the ARL Academy. The symposium provided an introduction to issues and trends in research libraries.

The Leadership and Career Development Program (LCDP) is an 18-month program to prepare mid-career librarians from underrepresented racial and ethnic groups to take on increasingly demanding leadership roles in ARL libraries. The program addresses the needs of research libraries to develop a more diverse professional work force that can contribute to library success in serving increasingly diverse scholarly and learning communities. The goal of the newly redesigned LCDP is twofold: to provide meaningful exposure to and experience with the strategic issues that are shaping the future of research libraries, and to prepare professionals of color for increasingly demanding leadership roles in ARL libraries. For more information see http://www.arl.org/diversity/lcdp/index.shtml.

The second offering of the ARL Research Library Leadership Fellows (RLLF) Program was designed and sponsored by six ARL member libraries: University of California–Berkeley and the California Digital Library, Harvard University, University of Minnesota, North Carolina State University, Pennsylvania State University, and the University of Toronto. Created in response to increasing demands for succession planning for research libraries, this executive leadership program offers a new approach to preparing the next generation of deans and directors. Library directors are seeking a new cohort of well-trained and sophisticated candidates who possess the unique skills to succeed in premier leadership positions in large, complex institutions. The 2007–2008 RLLF applicant pool was highly competitive and the selection committee, composed of the ARL directors sponsoring the program, chose 23 fellows representing a broad array of backgrounds and experiences from multiple ARL institutions. See http://www.arl.org/leadership/rllf.

In a *Chronicle of Higher Education* article, Stanley Wilder, associate dean of River Campus libraries at the University of Rochester, used 2005 demographic data from ARL to analyze the state of research librarianship for those under age 35. Wilder found that 39 percent of library professionals under 35 work in nontraditional jobs—such as information technology and systems, human resources, and fund development—compared with 21 percent of those 35 and older. He noted that, on average, nontraditional professional positions also pay more than traditional jobs. Wilder observed that young professionals in ARL libraries are also "nontraditional" in that, as a group, they are somewhat more diverse than their older colleagues; in 2005 18 percent of ARL professionals under 35 were minorities, compared with 12 percent of their 35-and-over colleagues. See Stanley J. Wilder, "The New Library Professional: What Does the Growing Generation Gap Among Their Employees Mean for Academic Research Libraries and for the Profession?" (*Chronicle of Higher Education* 53, no. 25, February 23, 2007).

In an analysis of the same data for ARL, Wilder posits that U.S. ARL member libraries are likely to experience a professional "youth movement" in the next few years, much as their Canadian peers—whose professional employees appear to be five years ahead of U.S. ARL libraries on the age curve—have experienced recently. Canadian ARL libraries are already experiencing rapidly growing percentages of younger professionals joining their ranks as older professionals retire; the percentage of the Canadian ARL population under the age of 35 nearly doubled between 2000 and 2005. They are seeing the same kind of growth in new hires and new professionals, indicating that Canadian administrators do appear to be filling vacancies created by retirement. Wilder suggests that U.S. ARL libraries may see a similar doubling of new hires and new professionals in 2010, since there is a "healthy supply of library professionals" upon which to draw. This bodes well for "a smooth transition to a younger population, with new skill sets to address changing needs." See Stanley J. Wilder, "The ARL Youth Movement: Reshaping the ARL Work Force," *ARL: A Bimonthly Report* no. 254, October 2007 (http://www.arl.org/bm~doc/arl-br-254-youth.pdf).

Research, Statistics, and Measurement

ARL's Research, Statistics, and Measurement enabling capability encompasses the Statistics and Measurement Program to identify quantitative and qualitative metrics and assessment tools needed to support all three strategic objectives. The Statistics and Measurement Program seeks to describe and measure the performance of research libraries and their contributions to teaching, research, scholarship, and community service. The program also includes the New Measures Initiative, a series of projects and services to develop new approaches for describing and evaluating library service effectiveness, diversity, and leadership. More information is available at http://www.arl.org/stats.

Through a variety of New Measures Initiatives, ARL continues to develop new assessment methods for understanding changes in user behavior. The Task Force on New Ways of Measuring Collections was charged to propose changes in how ARL should be measuring research library collections. In response to the recommendation from the task force, the ARL Statistics and Assessment Committee and the Board of Directors developed an implementation plan that included: development of an expenditures-focused index starting with 2005–2006 data; revision of definitions in ARL statistics of collection-related data categories; collection of qualitative data to develop a profile of member libraries; and development of a services-based index that combines the three factors of collections, services, and collaborative relationships. See http://www.arl.org/bm~doc/arl-br-256-stats.pdf.

In 2007 ARL introduced the Expenditures-Focused Index, a summary measure of relative size among the association's university library members. The new index is composed of four variables that are part of the historical data elements in which ARL university library members most resemble one another: total library expenditures, salaries and wages of professional staff, total library materials expenditures, and total professional and support staff. This index does not attempt to measure a library's services, quality of collections, or success in meeting the needs of users. The Expenditures-Focused Index for 2005–2006 is available at http://www.arl.org/stats/index.

In 2007 Canadian academic libraries and some nonacademic libraries formed a consortium, LibQUAL Canada, to participate in the LibQUAL+ survey on behalf of the Canadian Association of Research Libraries (CARL). This brought a dynamic group of libraries to the LibQUAL+ roster, many of which are running bilingual surveys in American English and Canadian French. The 2007 LibQUAL+ Session I closed in May and collected more than 152,000 responses from 218 institutions. International institutions accounted for 40 percent of all registrants and collected 47 percent of the total responses. Of the international participants, Canada had the largest number of participating institutions (63) and collected more than 50,000 responses. The 2007 LibQUAL+ survey cycle closed in December. Hong Kong Polytechnic University received a record number of completed surveys (more than 5,700) implementing the Chinese (Traditional) version of the survey.

ARL offered a workshop on Performance Measurement in Academic Libraries in conjunction with the Fourth International Evidence-Based Library and Information Practice Conference (EBLIP4) in North Carolina in May. Participants learned about ARL's New Measures Initiatives and how they have led to the establishment of the StatsQUAL service, which includes assessment protocols like LibQUAL+, DigiQUAL, and MINES (Measuring the Impact of Networked Electronic Services) for Libraries. The workshop presenters shared lessons learned from ARL's Effective, Sustainable, and Practical Assessment service. Based on these discussions, participants explored how they can start thinking about assessment at their own institutions.

ClimateQUAL is the newest tool in the StatsQUAL family, developed in partnership with the University of Maryland and supported by the ARL Statistics and Measurement Program. In 2007 a group of five ARL libraries completed a successful Phase I pilot implementing the organizational culture and diversity assessment survey that provides information on climate for justice, service, and other dimensions critical for the delivery of excellent service. The project moves into Phase II with a group of ten libraries further testing and improving the application of the survey during spring and summer 2008. Operations will be collaboratively managed for the University of Maryland in Phase III—late fall of 2009 and beyond. For more information, see http://www.lib.umd.edu/ocda.

The Statistics and Measurement Program produces a series of annual publications that describe salary compensation and collection, staffing, expenditure, and service trends for research libraries. The series includes the *ARL Annual*

Salary Survey, ARL Statistics, ARL Academic Law Library Statistics, ARL Academic Health Sciences Library Statistics, and *ARL Preservation Statistics.* The ARL Interactive Statistics, hosted at the Geostat Center of the University of Virginia, continues to be one of the most popular ways of accessing the annual data collected by ARL. The ranked lists allow users to pick from more than 30 variables for data reports. This site is at http://fisher.lib.virginia.edu/arl/index.html.

The Library Assessment Conference: Building Effective, Sustainable, Practical Assessment was held in Charlottesville, Virginia, in September 2006. The first Library Assessment Conference offered in North America brought together more than 200 participants from 36 states and 6 countries outside North America. The attendees—representing 109 libraries, associations, library systems, and vendors—participated in more than 40 paper and panel sessions. The conference featured 20 poster presentations and three plenary sessions on the topics of Library Performance Measures That Matter, Changing User Needs and Perceptions, and Organizational Diversity and Climate Assessment. ARL published the proceedings of the conference in 2007. See http://libraryassessment.org/archive.

ARL also published a collection of papers presented at the Library Assessment Conference in Thessaloniki, Greece, in 2005. The collected papers describe the activities of the program, the implications of British and U.S. collaborations in assessment, the development and use of LibQUAL+ and the work in MINES for Libraries.

The SPEC survey program gathers information on current research library operating practices and policies and publishes the SPEC Kit series as guides for libraries as they face ever-changing management issues. Six SPEC Kits were published in 2007: *SPEC Kit 298 Metadata, SPEC Kit 299 Scholarly Communication Education Initiatives, SPEC Kit 300 Open Access Resources, SPEC Kit 301 Liaison Services, SPEC Kit 302 Managing Public Computing,* and *SPEC Kit 303 Library Assessment.* See http://www.arl.org/resources/pubs/spec/complete.shtml.

Communications and Alliances

The Communications and Alliances enabling capability is engaged in many activities that support ARL's strategic directions. These include acquainting ARL members with current, important developments of interest to research libraries; influencing policy and decision makers within the higher education, research, and scholarly communities; educating academic communities about issues relating to scholarly communication and research libraries; and providing the library community with information about activities in which research libraries are engaged. Using print and electronic media as well as direct outreach, the communications capability disseminates information about ARL to the higher education and scholarly communities, as well as to ARL member institutions, and publishes a full range of timely, accurate, and informative resources to assist library and higher education communities in their efforts to improve the delivery of scholarly communication. ARL makes many of its titles available electronically via the World Wide Web; some are available in excerpted form for preview before purchase and others are available in their entirety. See http://www.arl.org/resources/

pubs. News about ARL activities and publications is available through the ARL-ANNOUNCE list, distributed widely to the library and higher education communities. To subscribe, visit http://www.arl.org/resources/emaillists.

ARL has launched a newly designed Web site. The updated, streamlined design was developed to improve navigation within the site. New features of the site include a consistent navigation bar across the top of each page, "breadcrumbs" to help the user track their location in the site, highlights of the most visited resources on the site, a conveniently located search box in the top right corner of every page, a cleaner site map, and RSS news feeds that enable the user to subscribe to some or all of the site's new postings. As on the old site, a "members only" section provides a selected set of resources for directors of ARL libraries or their designated staff.

Governance and Membership Meetings

A total of 106 ARL member representatives attended the 150th Membership Meeting of ARL May 23–25, 2007, in St. Louis. ARL President Sherrie Schmidt (Arizona State University) introduced the program sessions on "Libraries and the Research Process: Exploring How to Demonstrate Returns on Investment." The program was complemented with briefings and informal discussions led by ARL directors and others. The business meeting featured updates from the board and key committees, including a report on implementation plans for new ways for ARL to measure collections and the introduction of a new expenditures-focused index. Speakers' presentations are on the ARL Web site at http://www.arl.org/resources/pubs/mmproceedings/150mmproceedings.shtml.

The 151st ARL Membership Meeting was held October 10–11 in Washington, D.C. In addition to 120 member library representatives, 48 former member representatives, 11 ARL Research Library Leadership Fellows, and other special guests attended the meeting to celebrate the 75th anniversary of the association's founding. Hunter R. Rawlings III, president emeritus and professor of classics at Cornell University, delivered a keynote address on "authority" as that term applies to information, knowledge, and democracy. Other program sessions focused on initiatives to enable e-scholarship, in particular those being led by the Council on Library and Information Resources; the future of university publishing, or as Dave Shulenburger of the National Association of State Universities and Land-Grant Colleges proposed, the future of each university's "research distribution" strategy; and open access, specifically, how a cell biologist and his society, the American Society for Cell Biology, have responded to open access. The meeting also featured a gala evening at the Library of Congress with toasts to ARL's 75 years and the 20-year leadership of Duane Webster as ARL executive director. Speakers' slides are on the ARL Web site at http://www.arl.org/resources/pubs/mmproceedings/151mm-proceedings.shtml.

In commemoration of ARL's 75th anniversary, the association published a book and Web site profiling selected rare and special collections in major research libraries of North America, *Celebrating Research: Rare and Special Collections from the Membership of the Association of Research Libraries.* The compendium includes 118 collection profiles, each from a different ARL member library. Each profile is illustrated with color photographs and tells a story of a single collection, recounting how the resources were acquired and developed. The compilation is rich with examples of how research libraries are engaging various communities to deliver library services and encourage the use of such distinctive collections. Also included are an introductory essay by British rare book expert Nicolas Barker and an appendix that provides a broad description of each library's special collection holdings and pertinent contact information. The book contains a detailed index; the Web site provides a search engine. See http://www.celebratingresearch.org.

On October 11, Marianne Gaunt (Rutgers) began her term as ARL president. The board elected Tom Leonard (California–Berkeley) as vice president/president-elect and the membership elected three new board members—Winston Tabb (Johns Hopkins), Karin Trainer (Princeton), and Paul Wiens (Queen's).

SPARC—The Scholarly Publishing and Academic Resources Coalition

Executive Director, Heather Joseph
21 Dupont Circle, Ste. 800, Washington, DC 20036
202-296-2296, fax 202-872-0884, e-mail sparc@arl.org
World Wide Web http://www.arl.org/sparc

SPARC—the Scholarly Publishing and Academic Resources Coalition, launched in 1997 as an initiative of the Association of Research Libraries (ARL), is an alliance of academic and research libraries working to correct imbalances in the scholarly publishing system. These imbalances have driven the cost of scholarly journals (especially in science, technology, and medicine) to insupportably high levels, and have critically diminished the scholarly community's ability to access, share, and use information. At the core of SPARC's mission is the belief that these imbalances inhibit the advancement of scholarship and are at odds with fundamental needs of scholars and the academic enterprise.

Mission

SPARC is a catalyst for action. Its pragmatic agenda focuses on collaborating with other stakeholders to stimulate the emergence of new communication models that expand dissemination of scholarly research, reduce financial pressures on libraries, and leverage the networked digital environment to advance the conduct of scholarship.

Strategy

SPARC's strategy is focused on reducing barriers to the access, sharing, and use of scholarship and, in particular, scientific research. SPARC's highest priority is advancing the understanding and implementation of open access to research results. While much of SPARC's focus to date has been on primary journal literature, its strategy reflects an increasing focus on digital data of all kinds.

SPARC's role in stimulating change centers on three key program areas:

- Educating stakeholders about the problems facing scholarly communication and the opportunities for change
- Advocating policy changes that advance the potential of technology to advance scholarly communication and that explicitly recognize that dissemination is an essential, inseparable component of the research process
- Incubating real-world demonstrations of business and publishing models that advance changes benefiting scholarship and academe

It is critical to SPARC's ultimate success that programs continue to be vigorously pursued in all three program areas.

Developments in 2007

SPARC's 2007 actions were designed to advance the viability and acceptance of a more open system of scholarship, with a primary focus on open access models for both publishing and archiving the results of scholarly research. In particular, as interest in public access to the results of federally funded research continued to accelerate, SPARC worked to deploy a focused and disciplined advocacy strategy while remaining sufficiently agile to capitalize on emerging market opportunities that aligned with its objectives. Reviewed below are the year's key program activities and outcomes.

Advocacy and Public Policy

SPARC's highly visible public policy initiative to advance public access to the results of federally funded research was expanded to further raise the profile of open access in the United States and internationally.

In partnership with its allies in the Open Access Working Group, the Alliance for Taxpayer Access, and beyond, SPARC and its members advocated for the United States' first policy for public access to federally funded research to become law. On December 26, 2007, President George W. Bush signed into law the Consolidated Appropriations Act of 2008 (H.R. 2764), including a provision directing the National Institutes of Health (NIH) to provide the public with open online access to findings from its funded research. Effective April 7, 2008, NIH-funded researchers will be required to deposit a copy of final, peer-reviewed manuscripts into PubMed Central, NIH's digital archive of biomedical and life sciences journal literature, so that they can be made publicly available no later than 12 months after publication in a journal.

SPARC was equally active in pressing for the implementation of public access policies and mandates in Canada, submitting comments to the Canadian Institutes for Health Research; in Australia, submitting comments to the Productivity Commission; in Britain, which has now implemented policies for six of nine research councils; and to the European Commission, to which SPARC Europe presented a petition for public access representing 26,000 signatures from the academic community.

Student Campaign

SPARC launched a robust program to partner with student groups and educate the next generation of academics on issues relating to scholarly communication.

Working partnerships have been established with such student organizations as Universities Allied for Essential Medicines, the American Medical Student Association, and Students for Free Culture. SPARC created a Web site and other promotional materials dedicated to student education and advocacy of open access/public access, profiled five student leaders for the SPARC Innovator series, and planned a full program for the 2008 Midwinter Meeting of the American Library Association (ALA). With the Association of College and Research Libraries (ACRL), a division of ALA, SPARC held a joint forum centered on student engagement opportunities.

SPARC conceived, created, and ran the "MindMashup 2007" contest, calling on students to create short, YouTube-style videos on the power of sharing information. This inaugural contest was designed to help students articulate the characteristics they value about the open Web and electronic communication. The winner, announced at the SPARC/ACRL Forum at the 2008 ALA Midwinter Meeting, at which the video was screened, was Habib Yazdi of the University of North Carolina at Chapel Hill for his entry, "Share."

Institutional Repositories

SPARC continued to maintain and expand its content-rich resource on institutional repositories (http://www.arl.org/sparc/repositories).

Along with Microsoft, Sun Microsystems, the University of Texas, Texas A&M, and Texas Tech, SPARC cosponsored "Open Repositories 2007," a meeting focusing on the emerging roles that institutional repositories are playing in the scholarly world.

SPARC began the planning process for the second SPARC Institutional Repositories Meeting, to be held in Baltimore in November 2008. A full program and planning committee is in place.

As the discussion surrounding institutional repositories evolves from issues relating to their establishment and launch to issues central to identifying and adding content, SPARC has worked to advance the understanding of the role played by data, and policies surrounding access to data, in scholarly communications. Notably, SPARC has collaborated with Peter Murray-Rust to foster ongoing interest and discussion on issues surrounding data in its online Open Data discussion list (http://www.arl.org/sparc/opendata).

Finding Common Cause with Not-for-Profit Publishers

SPARC worked to identify and participate in programs that specifically highlight areas of common concern to the library and not-for-profit publishing communities, and to determine where collaborative action can be beneficial.

The coalition actively supported a new effort backed by the National Information Standards Organization (NISO) on creating alternatives to licenses. The effort is designed to develop a set of mutually agreed-upon best practices that can be substituted for time- and resource-consuming license agreements. SPARC serves on the working group for this venture, and will continue to provide ongoing promotional and administrative support.

SPARC continued to support collaboration with the nonprofit publishing community by announcing a new partnership with the University of Minnesota's AgEcon Search (http://AgEconSearch.umn.edu), an open digital repository that delivers current and archival working papers, journal articles, and conference papers that focus on agricultural economics and such subdisciplines as agribusiness, food supply, natural resource economics, environmental economics, policy issues, agricultural trade, and economic development. The project is a collaboration of the University of Minnesota Libraries, the university's Department of Applied Economics, and the American Agricultural Economics Association.

Author Addendum and Author Rights Campaign

To support its recently launched Author Rights campaign, SPARC worked in partnership with Science Commons to launch a tool for authors to complete an addendum online (the Scholar's Copyright Addendum Engine), and, with the Canadian Association of Research Libraries, worked on the introduction of a Canadian version of the SPARC Author Addendum and brochure. In addition, SPARC is working with Science Commons to collect and communicate data on the use of the addendum and to actively solicit responses to the addenda from authors and publishers.

SPARC's Author Rights educational program continued to increase awareness, and the coalition deployed a variety of publicity activities to promote widespread adoption and use of the author addendum. SPARC cohosted three Webcasts with ARL and ACRL, and SPARC staff participated in several campus presentations on the topic.

International Activity

Because change in scholarly communications is needed on a system-wide, global scale, SPARC continued to amplify its impact by working in collaboration with global allies such as SPARC Europe, the Canadian Association of Research Libraries, and various national and regional university library associations.

In partnership with the Japan Association of National and University Libraries and the Tokyo-based National Institute of Informatics, SPARC celebrated the launch of SPARC Japan in December 2006. In 2007 a full range of promotional activities were deployed in support of this launch.

To raise the profile of libraries as a key stakeholder in policy decisions that affect the communication of research results, SPARC successfully reapplied for observer status to the World Intellectual Property Organization.

Antitrust Issues in Journal Publishing

SPARC continued to participate in the Information Access Alliance (IAA), a group of library organizations working to highlight the budgetary impact of the rapid escalation of the price of information, particularly of journals in science, technology, and medicine. SPARC supported activities of IAA designed to seek new solutions to the problems associated with publishers' bundling practices, and helped to support the work of economists and antitrust scholars interested in looking at an area where unrestrained concentration is rapidly developing.

SPARC Innovator Series

Following the successful launch of the SPARC Innovator Series, a new program highlighting the efforts of key individuals and institutions in successfully promoting positive change in the scholarly communications arena, the coalition identified and profiled two additional key contributors in 2007:

- Melissa Hagemann, program officer for open access at the Open Society Institute, whose role in supporting the open access movement during the past five years has helped set into motion a series of events to affect scholarship around the globe

• Ted and Carl Bergstrom, professors in economics and theoretical and evolutionary biology, respectively, and leading contributors to such scholarly communications reform issues as journal pricing and alternatives to impact factors

Publisher Partnership Programs

SPARC supports, demonstrates, and promotes useful examples of open access or selected other innovative publishing initiatives via its Alternative, Leading Edge, and Scientific Communities publishing partnership programs. In 2007 the coalition began work on redefining its Leading Edge and Alternative programs to begin to highlight alternative forms of widely available scholarship, such as researcher-driven subject-specific blogs and wikis.

With the International Coalition of Library Consortia and the Southeastern Library Network, SPARC supported efforts by the Stanford Encyclopedia of Philosophy to build an endowment sufficient to sustain perpetual open access publication. That publication is now nearly 80 percent toward achieving its goal of self-sustainability.

Via promotional and other activity (including service on advisory boards), SPARC continued to aid both BioOne (http://www.bioone.org) and Cornell University's Project Euclid (http://projecteuclid.org) in evolving sound, sustainable business practices needed to become leading platforms for digital dissemination of independent journals.

Campus Education

SPARC encourages and aids libraries' grassroots advocacy efforts, cosponsoring the newly revamped Create Change program and Web site (http://www.createchange.org) and collaborating with ACRL and other organizations to engage beyond the SPARC membership. Other SPARC activities support institutionally based scholarly communication programs directed at faculty and administrators in higher education.

As part of an ongoing campaign to extend the usefulness of SPARC forums and other programs, podcasts and written summaries of SPARC/ACRL forums are now available via the SPARC podcast series. In 2007 SPARC continued to refine and expand SPARC's communications program with the launch of a new Web site, the introduction of SPARC podcasts, the redesign of SPARC enews (http://www.arl.org/sparc/publications/enews), and by continuing to work with the mainstream press to keep the global momentum for change in the media spotlight.

Continuing to work in full partnership with ACRL, SPARC held the 15th SPARC-ACRL Forum on Emerging Issues in Communication, hosting executives from the three largest open access publishers for a conversation on the challenges of sustainability. Additionally, a comparative document of the business models of the "big three" open access publishers—PLoS, BMC and Hindawi—was made available via the SPARC Web site.

Business Consulting Services

SPARC provides ongoing consulting support to the library and publishing communities. SPARC-subsidized advisory services were made available to more than a dozen organizations and alternative publishing ventures in 2007. Because demand for this service continues to be strong, SPARC added Greg Tanabaum, former executive director of Berkeley Electronic Press (BePress), to its slate of expert consultants.

Governance

SPARC is guided by a Steering Committee, which is currently led by Ray English, Oberlin College. Other members are Larry Alford (Temple University), Sherrie Bergman (Bowdoin College), David Carlson (Southern Illinois University at Carbondale), Faye Chadwell (Oregon State), Diane Graves (Trinity University), Thomas Hickerson (University of Calgary), Paula Kaufman (University of Illinois at Urbana-Champaign), John Ober (California Digital Library), Sarah Pritchard (Northwestern University), Bas Savenije (Utrecht University), and Vicki Williamson (University of Saskatchewan).

Council on Library and Information Resources

1755 Massachusetts Ave. N.W., Suite 500, Washington, DC 20036-2124
202-939-4754; fax 202-939-4765
World Wide Web http://www.clir.org

Kathlin Smith
Director of Communications

The Council on Library and Information Resources (CLIR) is an independent, nonprofit organization that works at the intersection of libraries, scholarship, and technology. CLIR helps organize, structure, and sustain the collaborative effort needed to realize a new digital environment for research, teaching, and learning.

CLIR is supported by fees from sponsoring institutions, grants from public and private foundations, contracts with federal agencies, and donations from individuals. CLIR's board establishes policy, oversees the investment of funds, sets goals, and approves strategies for their achievement. In November 2007 the board appointed Lizabeth Wilson, dean of university libraries at the University of Washington, as its newest member.

There were significant changes to the CLIR staff in 2007. In March Charles Henry began his tenure as president. Henry was formerly vice provost and university librarian at Rice University. In May Amy Friedlander, former senior program manager at Shinkuro, Inc., joined the staff as director of programs. In July CLIR appointed Michael Keller of Stanford University as CLIR senior presidential fellow. Keller is university librarian, director of academic information resources, founder and publisher of HighWire Press, and publisher of the Stanford University Press. In November Elliott Shore, chief information officer at Bryn Mawr College, was named CLIR distinguished fellow for leadership programs.

In March 2007 CLIR announced a new three-year agenda, supported by a significant grant from the Andrew W. Mellon Foundation. The agenda, influenced by a series of meetings and discussions throughout 2006, deepens CLIR's traditional work in scholarly communications, preservation, leadership, and the emerging library, while also strengthening their interconnections. It integrates CLIR's work more tightly with efforts to develop a cyberinfrastructure that will promote, sustain, and advance research and teaching in the humanities and social sciences. The agenda is available at http://www.clir.org/activities/agenda.htm.

Since early 2007 CLIR staff has been laying the foundation for new partnerships with foundations and other organizations that will play key roles in cyberinfrastructure development.

Developments in 2007

Preservation in the Age of Large-Scale Digitization

The digitization of millions of books under programs such as Google Book Search and MSN Book Search is dramatically expanding the ability to search and find information. For scholars, it is the unparalleled scale of these undertakings that holds such promise. That very scale, however, has given rise to concerns about the quality and long-term accessibility of digitized material.

In May 2007 CLIR commissioned Oya Rieger, interim assistant university librarian for digital library and information technologies at Cornell University Library, to examine large-scale digital initiatives and to identify issues that will influence the availability and usability, over time, of the digital books that these projects create. The report was circulated for comment in fall 2007, and Rieger presented her findings at the Digital Library Federation Fall Forum. The final report was to be published in early 2008.

Review of Literature on Mass Digitization and Institutional Repositories

In July CLIR commissioned postdoctoral fellow Dawn Schmitz to write a report that relates user studies to literature on the planning of cyberinfrastructure initiatives, focusing on mass digitization and institutional repositories. In synthesizing the literature from these two areas, Schmitz is focusing on the extent to which user needs and behaviors are taken into account in the planning of a cyberinfrastructure that will serve scholars by considering changing methodologies, pedagogies, and research behaviors across disciplines. The report was to be issued in early 2008.

Blue Ribbon Task Force on Sustainable Digital Preservation

In June 2007 CLIR was invited to become a contributing partner in a National Science Foundation (NSF) Blue Ribbon Task Force on Sustainable Digital Preservation and Access that will conduct a two-year study on the economics of sustainable digital preservation. The task force is charged with developing recommendations for promoting the economic sustainability of digital information for the academic, public, and private sectors. The task force also plans to produce a series of articles about the challenges and opportunities of digital information preservation for both the scholarly community and the public. CLIR Director of Programs Amy Friedlander, a member of the task force's executive team, will write the first-year report, anticipated for release by early 2009.

In addition to NSF, sponsors of the task force include the Andrew W. Mellon Foundation, the Joint Information Systems Committee, and the Library of Congress.

Scholarly Communications Institute

CLIR cosponsors, with the University of Virginia and American Council of Learned Societies (ACLS), the Scholarly Communications Institute (SCI). This institute began in 2003 with funding from the Andrew W. Mellon Foundation. Its aim is to provide an opportunity for librarians, advanced technologists, higher education administrators, and scholars and leaders in scholarly disciplines and societies to design, test, and implement strategies to advance humanities scholarship and its dissemination in the context of the digital revolution.

In July the University of Virginia hosted SCI 5, which focused on visual studies. Visual media—motion pictures, photography, video, 3-D images, simulations, and new media artworks—are having profound effects on scholarship. SCI 5 brought together scholars from the humanities and sciences, including both theorists and practitioners. The meeting focused primarily on "visual scholars," those who use visual resources in all facets of scholarly communication. A small number of individuals with expertise in libraries, advanced technologies, publishing, museums, and other relevant arenas joined these scholars. Plenary and small-group discussions focused on the following aspects of visual communication and its impact and implications for scholarship: research and discovery, analysis, presentation, dissemination, and persistent access.

Survey of Digital Humanities Centers in the United States

In May 2007 CLIR commissioned information management consultant Diane Zorich to survey selected digital humanities centers. The survey will investigate the scope of these centers and their financing, organizational structure, products, services, and sustainability.

The survey is being conducted in two major phases. In the initial phase, Zorich identified the organizations to be surveyed and topics to be covered, and designed the survey methodology and survey instrument. In the second phase, which began in September, she is collecting and analyzing data. Her final report was to be submitted in May 2008. Study findings will be used to inform the 2008 SCI, which will be devoted to assessing the needs, priorities, and challenges of national digital humanities centers. The report will also inform the national debate over the structure and function of these centers, as called for in *Our Cultural Commonwealth,* a report issued in 2007 by ACLS.

In conjunction with the survey, CLIR has also commissioned a project to evaluate Web-based tools offered by the digital humanities centers under investigation. The evaluation focuses on such factors as the usability of these tools, how well their purpose is conveyed, the extent of their documentation, ease of downloading, portability to multiple platforms, and the availability of operational specifications.

Faculty Research Behavior Workshops

As part of a larger effort to improve library and information services, in 2007 CLIR offered, for the first time, workshops on ethnographic techniques for gathering information about the faculty research process. Three such workshops were held. Led by University of Rochester anthropologist Nancy Foster, workshop participants learned skills for observing faculty behavior, interviewed faculty members, and analyzed the results of those interviews. At the end of the workshop, they planned how they would apply their new skills at their home institutions.

Liberal arts colleges with merged library instruction and information technology (IT) units were invited to send a staff member to one of the workshops. The first workshop was held at Wesleyan University in February, the second at Kenyon College in April, and the third at Cornell University in November. CLIR will continue to offer the workshops at academic institutions across the country in 2008.

National Digital Information Infrastructure Preservation Program

CLIR continued in 2007 to work in partnership with the Library of Congress's National Digital Information Infrastructure Preservation Program. As part of this collaborative effort, CLIR provided editorial support for the final report of the working group on revisions to Section 108 of the Copyright Act. CLIR staff also provided support to the Motion Picture, Broadcast, and Recorded Sound Division, commissioning Columbia University legal scholar June Besek to write a report on copyright issues relating to the preservation of and access to unpublished audio recordings.

Frye Leadership Institute

The purpose of the Frye Leadership Institute is to develop leaders who can guide and transform academic information services for higher education. The institute, which CLIR sponsors with EDUCAUSE and Emory University, is in its eighth year. It has trained more than 350 librarians, faculty members, and IT experts.

The 2007 institute was held June 3–14 at the Emory Conference Center in Atlanta. The 46 participants came from research universities, master's degree institutions, liberal arts colleges, and community colleges. Five participants came from universities abroad. Susan Perry, former CLIR interim president, and EDUCAUSE President Brian Hawkins served as deans.

The Frye Institute is supported with funds from the Robert W. Woodruff Foundation.

Chief Information Officers

CLIR facilitates a semiannual forum that enables chief information officers (CIOs) of merged library and computing units in liberal arts colleges to discuss issues affecting teaching and learning on their campuses. The 35 participants use their twice-yearly meetings and a listserv to share information on such topics as recent changes in merged organizations, policies governing content and archiving practices of college Web sites, handling of copyright-infringement notices, and creating job descriptions.

In 2005 the group developed a Web-based survey designed to measure how students, faculty, and staff use and evaluate the services and resources of merged library and computing units. Members can use the survey instrument to gauge their effectiveness. They continue to analyze the results and to share their findings.

In 2007 the CIOs started the Work Exchange Database, a resource for IT and library managers that provides midlevel career-development opportunities for staff. The database enables institutions to offer and seek expertise and exchange staff.

Academic Librarians Advisory Committee

CLIR formed the Academic Librarians Advisory Committee to provide guidance on issues of relevance to libraries at colleges and small and midsize universities. Members, who represent both public and private institutions, met twice during 2007 to discuss professional development for library directors, how to work with consultants on library space planning, off-site storage, and information literacy assessments, such as the National Survey of Student Engagement and what the results of such assessments mean for libraries. Connie Vinita Dowell, dean of libraries and information access at San Diego State University, chairs the group.

Awards

Mellon Fellowships for Dissertation Research in Original Sources

The Mellon Dissertation Fellowship program supports original-source doctoral research in libraries and archives, without regard to the location or format of those sources. Established in 2001 and administered by CLIR, the program awards 10 to 15 annual fellowships of up to $20,000 each. In 2007, 13 fellows were selected from more than 360 candidates. The fellows proposed work in a wide range of repositories and their topics of study were broad in scope. In May the fellows convened at the Library of Congress for a one-day workshop on research in archives and special collections.

Postdoctoral Fellowships in Scholarly Information Resources

In May 2007 five individuals were awarded CLIR Postdoctoral Fellowships in Scholarly Information Resources for 2007–2008. The fellows, each of whom recently received a Ph.D. in the humanities, are spending the year at an academic research library, where they are gaining hands-on experience relating to the issues facing scholars at research libraries. Six fellows from 2006–2007 continued in the program for a second year, bringing the total number of CLIR fellows to 11 for 2007–2008.

CLIR created this program in response to changes in scholarly communication and a growing need to develop linkages between disciplinary scholarship, libraries, archives, and evolving digital tools. Fellows reside at their host institutions and undertake such projects as developing writing and research guides for students, designing and implementing metadata standards for faculty using digital visual resources, improving library sites and portals to reflect undergraduate-user patterns, and advising on and contributing to inventories of digital projects in area collections.

Elliott Shore, Bryn Mawr College library director and chief information officer, is lead instructor of the fellowship program. In summer 2007 he led an orientation seminar that all fellows attended before starting their assignments. He advised the fellows throughout the year on work in progress and organized virtual seminars with leading figures in librarianship, the humanities, and related areas.

Sponsoring postdoctoral fellowships in 2008 are Johns Hopkins University, Princeton University, the University of California at Los Angeles, and the University of North Carolina at Greensboro.

Rovelstad Scholarship in International Librarianship

Lorraine Alison Dong, a master's degree candidate in the School of Information at the University of Texas at Austin, was selected for the Rovelstad Scholarship in International Librarianship, which enabled her to attend the World Library and Information Congress of the International Federation of Library Associations and Institutions (IFLA) in South Africa. She is studying preservation administration while working toward a graduate portfolio in nonprofit studies at the Lyndon B. Johnson School of Public Affairs' RGK Center for Philanthropy and Community Service.

A. R. Zipf Fellowship in Information Management

Alvin K. Cheung, a doctoral student in computer science at the Massachusetts Institute of Technology, was named the recipient of the 2007 A. R. Zipf Fellowship in Information Management. Cheung's research focuses on the collection and processing of contextual information called ContextDB. "While many types of contextual information are readily accessible from the operating system or networking layer, in current systems they are rarely collected," says Cheung. "In ContextDB, I propose to capture this low-level contextual information and allow users to retrieve documents by running context-based queries, perhaps in concert with traditional structured or keyword queries." He holds bachelor's degrees in electrical engineering and music and a master's degree in electrical engineering from Stanford University.

Named in honor of A. R. Zipf, a pioneer in information management systems, the fellowship is awarded annually to a student who is enrolled in graduate school, is in the early stages of study, and shows exceptional promise for leadership and technical achievement in information management.

Publications

Library Workflow Redesign: Six Case Studies

The proliferation of electronic information and tools has changed the way in which readers and researchers do their work. It has also changed the way in which library staff members provide materials and services. While technology now makes it possible to deliver more content and services, libraries are often expected to do so with little or no increase in funding, or even with reduced budgets.

Beginning in 2002, with support from the Andrew W. Mellon Foundation, CLIR offered workflow redesign support to teams from six liberal arts colleges that are part of consortia. One outcome of that work was the publication of *Library Workflow Redesign: Six Case Studies*. Edited by Marilyn Mitchell and published in January 2007, the report describes in detail the workflow redesign projects undertaken by the six libraries and includes a series of recommendations summarizing lessons learned.

Census of Institutional Repositories

Published in February 2007, *Census of Institutional Repositories in the United States* is the product of an extensive survey conducted in 2006 by Karen Markey, Soo Young Rieh, and Beth Yakel at the University of Michigan. The authors investigated the development of institutional repositories in colleges and universities with the aim of identifying models and best practices in the administration, technical infrastructure, and access policies of repository collections.

The census was a first step in the larger MIRACLE (Making Institutional Repositories in a Collaborative Learning Environment) project, whose aim is to identify specific factors contributing to the success of institutional repositories and effective ways of accessing and using repositories.

Whole Digital Library Handbook

In February 2007 American Library Association Publishing released *The Whole Digital Library Handbook,* edited by Diane Kresh under commission from CLIR. The handbook is a comprehensive guide for anyone who manages, works in, or uses digital collections. It contains facts, tips, and miscellanea on the current state of digital collections and on where the field is headed.

In 2007 CLIR also published its *Annual Report 2006–2007* and the bimonthly newsletter *CLIR Issues,* nos. 55–60.

Digital Library Federation

1755 Massachusetts Ave. N.W., Suite 500, Washington, DC 20036-2124
202-939-4761, fax 202-939-4765
World Wide Web http://www.diglib.org

Barrie Howard
Program Manager

The Digital Library Federation (DLF) is an international consortium of research libraries and related agencies that are pioneering the use of electronic-information technologies to extend library collections and services. DLF provides leadership to libraries by identifying standards and best practices for building and providing access to digital collections, coordinating innovative research and development, and incubating products and services that libraries need but cannot develop individually.

DLF operates as a tax-exempt, nonprofit corporation through a small, professional staff and is governed by a board of trustees on which each member institution is represented. Drawing from its members and others in the scholarly, library, and computing communities, DLF brings together teams of experts to identify issues and lead initiatives and special projects toward shared solutions.

In 2007 DLF welcomed three new domestic members, the Inter-university Consortium for Political and Social Research, the University of California–Los Angeles, and the National Library of Medicine, increasing organizational capacity to 42 members.

Organizational Leadership

Peter Brantley became DLF executive director in February 2007. Brantley was previously director of strategic technology for academic information systems in the University of California's (UC's) Office of the President. He has 20 years' experience in systems development and management, including academic computing services at UC–Berkeley and academic information systems management and digital library development at UC–San Francisco and New York University.

Programmatic Activities

DLF pools achievement, effort, resources, and talent from its individual members for the advancement of the whole, and provides the following services:

- Coordination, facilitation, and support for collaborative research, standards development, and project start-ups
- Semiannual conferences for guiding the organization, reporting on new projects and updates, and sharing experiences in developing and managing electronic resources

- E-mail lists for exchanging information about developments within the membership and the broader digital library community and stimulating discussion
- A publicly accessible Web site for disseminating information about ongoing DLF activities, news, resources, and the organization itself
- Online and print publications, including conference proceedings, surveys, technical reports and specifications, white papers, and other digital library information resources

DLF Forums

DLF's semiannual conferences (forums) continue to catalyze initiatives, providing a platform for project progress reports, research paper presentations, proof-of-concept demonstrations, panel and roundtable discussions, and an opportunity for networking with colleagues to share information, create or renew cross-institutional collaboration, and recruit initiative participants. Forums are typically scheduled in April and November. The most recent forums took place in Pasadena and Philadelphia.

DLF continues to support a forum-related program providing travel awards to rising stars of the digital library community. The DLF Forum Fellowships for Librarians New to the Profession support a small group of professionals and enable travel to conferences at which they can learn more about the library profession, see the results of digital projects from other institutions, and meet leaders in the profession. The success of the fellows program has resulted in many of the award winners returning to forums as presenters, participating in initiatives as key collaborators, or serving on the DLF Program Committee, which is responsible for some of the planning of future forums and for peer review and selection of content for each forum program.

DLF Aquifer

DLF Aquifer models and develops network-based, scalable solutions to make a growing body of digital-library content easy to find and use across institutional boundaries.

In 2007 DLF received momentum for the Aquifer initiative through an $816,000 grant from the Andrew W. Mellon Foundation for a two-year project, DLF Aquifer Development for Interoperability Across Scholarly Repositories: American Social History Online. Deliverables include implementation schemas, data models, and technologies that enable scholars to use digital collections as one in a variety of local environments.

Approaching the end of its first year, DLF's American Social History Online project boasts a Web site (http://www.dlfaquifer.org) designed for easy discovery of previously unknown digital library collections, as well as easy retrieval of known items. Using Zotero, a free, easy-to-use Firefox extension, scholars can gather and use online resources, as well as annotate and share them.

To support the use of images, the American Social History Online Web site has integrated the Collectus and ImageViewer tools developed at the University of Virginia. These tools not only support saving and organizing items from image collections, but also enable slide-show creation so that images can be easily repurposed for classroom instruction.

American Social History Online has been developed using open source software and is currently available without fees or restrictions. The project team continues to add collections and is interested in adding data sets. The team is also developing integrations with the Sakai open source course management system and a federated search solution that will combine search results with commercially available content.

ERMI 2

Following the success of the Electronic Resources Management Initiative (ERMI) launched in 2002, DLF has continued to foster rapid development of systems for managing electronic resources by providing a template for the detailed description of e-resource management problems and functional requirements and by promoting data standards. During the first phase of the initiative, the ERMI Steering Group realized that the environment, technologies, and business models relating to e-resources would continue to be highly dynamic. As a result, the work of the initiative would require ongoing review, assessment, and modification.

A second phase (ERMI 2), focuses on further refinement of data standards—especially those having to do with how license terms are summarized and interpreted and how usage data is transmitted and received—and made great progress over the last year through four sub-projects:

- Drafting of the *White Paper on Interoperability Between Acquisitions Modules of Integrated Library Systems and Electronic Resource Management Systems,* which is a brief analysis of four case studies investigating the interoperability between the acquisitions modules of integrated library systems (ILSs) and electronic resource management systems (ERMs)
- Curriculum development and outcomes-based evaluation of professional training in license term mapping to ERM systems delivered through a series of workshops sponsored by DLF and the Association of Research Libraries
- Affirmation of the ANSI/NISO Z39.39—2007 Standardized Usage Statistics Harvesting Initiative (SUSHI) Protocol, which defines an automated request and response model for the harvesting of e-resource usage data utilizing a Web services framework that can replace user-mediated collections of usage data reports, available at http://www.niso.org/standards/standard_detail.cfm?std_id=817
- Collaboration with the international standards group EDItEUR to create a specification for license term mapping to enable an ERMI subset to be extracted from another standard, ONIX for Licensing Terms

Integrated Library Systems

In summer 2007 DLF convened the ILS-DI Task Force for examining integrated library systems (ILSs) and their discovery systems, and exploring the development of a lightweight application programming interface (API) or computational framework that would permit the abstraction of the discovery layer away from an ILS, which often includes discovery via the Online Public Access Catalog (OPAC), in addition to cataloging, acquisition, and circulation functions.

The public interface provided by a typical ILS cannot meet the demands of users in a world where the availability and sophistication of digital resources and Web applications has increased significantly. Poor design and limited functionality challenge the capacity of any one software package to deliver a range of functionality required of today's library users. At the same time, the bibliographic data and services that an ILS manages are crucial for the effective use of libraries. Current trends imply that the ILS needs to become an underlying platform that supports appropriate plug-and-play interfaces for discovery applications rather than a one-size-fits-all solution.

In six months, the DLF ILS-DI Task Force has worked collaboratively using a wiki, available at http://project.library.upenn.edu/confluence/display/ilsapi/home, to draft a set of technical recommendations for integrating the ILS with external discovery applications, including

- A survey summary articulating the needs of and discovery applications implemented by DLF member libraries and others
- A summary of abstract functions that discovery applications should be able to invoke from ILSs and data that supports discovery applications, as well as outgoing services ILS software provides to other applications
- Recommendations for concrete bindings of the above-mentioned functions, i.e., specific protocols, APIs, data standards, and so forth, that could be used with existing and future ILSs
- Practical recommendations to encourage libraries, ILS developers, and discovery application developers to expeditiously integrate discovery systems with ILSs and other sources of bibliographic data

METS

DLF continued support for the Metadata Encoding and Transmission Standard (METS), an XML schema for encoding descriptive, administrative, and structural metadata for digital resources maintained by the Library of Congress, through the work of the METS Editorial Board.

In 2007 a subset of the METS Editorial Board completed preparation of technical documentation for the METS schema that is targeted both to the METS developer and to metadata consultants and technical managers for METS implementations. The *METS Metadata Encoding Transmission Standard: Primer and Reference Manual* is available online from the METS Web site (http://www.loc.gov/standards/mets) and provides a comprehensive guide to working with METS for a wide audience from novice implementers to experienced developers. The publication includes background information about the schema, a step-by-step tutorial for creating a METS document, a review of the anatomy of the schema, and discussion of extending the use of METS through integration with external schema and profiles. DLF will publish a print version of the *METS Primer* in 2008.

Moving-Image Collections

With support from the Andrew W. Mellon Foundation, DLF completed an environmental scan of traditional moving-image archives and of major public and university libraries, museums, and other cultural institutions such as U.S. public television broadcasters with significant film and video collections. The goal of the project is to summarize which moving-image collections are potentially available for digitization, with an emphasis on open access to increase the volume of online content for teaching and learning. A final report will be released in 2008.

The primary goal of the survey was to identify the size, scope, material condition, and metadata coverage of moving-image collections held by U.S. cultural institutions. The final report will include a brief enumeration of technical, logistical, organizational, and legal impediments that affect the suitability of these collections for digitization, and an analysis of other surveys and inventories conducted in recent years that informed and provided context for the project.

In addition to providing information about moving-image collections, DLF hopes to generate support for creating a "bill of rights" for stewards of moving-image collections, asserting the value and significance of providing access to moving-image collections as a public good. Currently, many moving-image collections are hidden from public view in dark storage, providing some level of preservation while sidestepping the objectives of access policies embodied in the missions of many cultural institutions. Providing exposure and access to moving-image collections has great potential for increasing the visibility of an institution, driving preservation programs, increasing the effectiveness of mission-critical services, and supporting teaching and learning.

Virtual Worlds

The DLF Second Life initiative was launched in spring 2007 to explore the issues and opportunities presented by virtual worlds in the context of digital libraries and their roles in scholarship and publishing. Since virtual environments present a new model for information creation and interaction through the simulation of three-dimensional space, DLF built an island in Second Life (Entropia) to investigate the potential use of virtual environments for and by digital libraries. In a platform originally predicated on a gaming environment that has since grown organically, Second Life's underlying information design and infrastructure has not yet evolved to robustly support functions such as search or preservation.

Some digital libraries have begun to experiment in the space, but serious exploration by a large number of libraries has yet to occur. Most of the current presentations and uses of information in Second Life mimic present digital library activities. Richer experiences in virtual worlds are likely possible through further exploration. Similarly, digital library building and development opportunities in a virtual world are markedly different, and more expansive, from in the real world, and must also be further explored.

In addition to the construction of Entropia as a "collaboratory," DLF has convened a small working group to lead the initiative and set into motion an agenda of three main objectives:

- To establish a social framework within Second Life that will foster engagement by DLF-member library staff with each other, their faculty and students, other Second Life libraries and associated avatars, and the Second Life community as a whole
- To conduct experimentation on the form, substance, processes, and social order of digital scholarship by leveraging the inherent properties of a virtual world to create new tools and environments rapidly and at low cost
- To apply established library and information science standards and best practices in a serious analysis of Second Life as a living, evolving information environment

Association for Library and Information Science Education

ALISE Headquarters, 65 E. Wacker Place, Suite 1900, Chicago, IL 60601-7246
312-795-0996, fax 312-419-8950, e-mail contact@alise.org
World Wide Web http://www.alise.org

Connie Van Fleet
President 2007–2008

The Association for Library and Information Science Education (ALISE) is an independent, nonprofit professional association whose mission is to promote excellence in research, teaching, and service for library and information science (LIS) education through leadership, collaboration, advocacy, and dissemination of research. Its enduring purpose is to promote research that informs the scholarship of teaching and learning for library and information science, enabling members to integrate research into teaching and learning. The association provides a forum in which to share ideas, discuss issues, address challenges, and shape the future of education for library and information science.

ALISE's history reflects the evolving nature of library and information science education and an increasingly expansive approach. The Association of American Library Schools was founded in 1915, the outcome of a vote by the Round Table of Library School Instructors, to establish a permanent organization independent of the American Library Association (ALA). In 1970, recognizing that concerns about LIS education transcended those of the accredited programs, membership was extended to full-time faculty and administrators in all graduate programs in library science and cognate fields. A 1975 bylaws revision opened membership to "any individual with an interest in the objectives of the association." In 1983 the Association of American Library Schools became the Association for Library and Information Science Education, changing its name to better reflect the scope of the discipline and its membership.

ALISE is an independent association that provides a forum for those individuals and associations who are stakeholders in education for library and information science education. It is a designated affiliate organization of ALA, and continues to enjoy close ties with ALA while it has expanded collaborative activities with other organizations that share common interests. ALISE's mission, goals, and membership reflect its inclusive approach to the discipline and related professions.

Membership

The organization's membership has shown steady growth, from about 350 members in 2003 to 625 in 2007. ALISE is primarily a North American organization, with the majority of its membership drawn from the United States and Canada, although provision is made for international members. There are four categories of membership: personal members, institutional members, international affiliate institutional members, and associate institutional members. Personal membership is open to any individual who has an interest in the objectives of the association.

Although the majority of personal members are full-time instructors, doctoral students are an active group and efforts are being made to reach out to library and information science professionals. In 2007 the ALISE board submitted a grant proposal to the Institute for Museum and Library Services (IMLS), "Enhancing Instructional Quality: Preparing Adjunct and Part-Time Teachers," to more fully prepare and integrate adjunct and part-time faculty into the academic process. Developed in recognition of the growing role and impact of these individuals, the grant would support attendance at the 2009 ALISE conference and a series of online tutorials.

Institutional membership is extended to any school that offers a degree in library and information science or a cognate field and is accredited by the appropriate authority. The majority of institutional members are programs accredited by the ALA Committee on Accreditation. Only institutional representatives are permitted to vote on matters of policy that commit the individual member schools to any definite action. The Council of Deans, Directors, and Program Chairs, which consists of the chief executive officer of each individual institutional member school or program, meets annually at the ALISE Conference to discuss issues and plan professional development activities for its members. International affiliate institutional member status may be granted to any school outside the United States or Canada that offers a program to educate participants for the practice of library and information science at the professional level as defined or accepted in the country in which the school is located. Associate institutional member status is granted to libraries and organizations other than schools of library and information science. Dues from institutional and personal members are the single largest source of operating funds for the association.

The association's structure is designed to encourage effective use of ALISE's resources and promote wide participation by its members. The business of the association is carried out by a board of directors elected by the membership. The board establishes policy, sets goals and strategic directions, and provides oversight for association management. It consists of a president, vice president/president-elect, past president, secretary-treasurer, and three directors elected on a rotating basis. The executive director is an ex officio member of the board. All elected board members serve three year terms. The 2007 officers were Connie Van Fleet (University of Oklahoma), president; Michèle Cloonan (Simmons College), vice president/president-elect; John Budd (University of Missouri), past president; and Lisa Given (University of Alberta), secretary-treasurer. Directors were Julie Hersberger (University of North Carolina–Greensboro), director for special interest groups; Heidi Julien (University of Alberta), director for external relations; and Melissa Gross (Florida State University), director for membership services. The executive director is Kathleen Combs. In 2007 membership elected a new president, Linda C. Smith (University of Illinois at Urbana-Champaign) and director for special interest groups, Susan Roman (Dominican University).

Standing and special committees attend to general and specific areas of association concern. Standing committees that report directly to the board include the

Budget and Finance, Governance, Nominating, Recruitment, and Tellers committees and the Membership Advisory Board. Development and Advancement is a subcommittee of Budget and Finance. Other standing committees are grouped and report through an appropriate coordinating committee: the Awards and Honors Coordinating Committee, which organizes and facilitates the work of committees that recognize service, teaching, and professional contribution; the Conference Program Planning Coordinating Committee, which organizes and facilitates work of all committees involved in conference program planning; the Publications Coordinating Committee, which attends to fiscal and operational matters relative to the association's publications program and facilitates the work of the publications advisory boards; and the Research Coordinating Committee, which organizes and facilitates the work of the research awards committees. Each coordinating committee has a designated board liaison. Incoming committee chairs are appointed by the vice president/president-elect; committee members are appointed by their respective chairs. Each committee is given an ongoing term of reference to guide its work, as well as specific charges for the year. In addition, the president may appoint ad hoc committees or task forces to pursue special projects. In 2007 a task force to develop a code of ethics for library and information science educators was created, with a charge to present a recommendation at the 2009 annual conference.

Special Interest Groups

Special interest groups (SIGs) are a means for individuals to become involved in a relatively small group of people with similar research or teaching interests. Their primary purpose is to provide a forum for ALISE members to share ideas, plans, news, and opinions relating to a particular area of interest. The groups are distinct from the usual committee structure in that participation is voluntary rather than appointive, and no charges are assigned. The SIG structure is fairly fluid and SIGs are created and dissolved depending on participation and interest. SIGs have been clustered for organizational purposes by overall topic area. The Roles and Responsibilities Cluster includes the Assistant/Associate Deans and Directors, Doctoral Students, New Faculty, and Part–time and Adjunct Faculty SIGs; the Teaching and Learning Cluster includes the Continuing Education, Curriculum, Distance Education, and Teaching Methods SIGs. The largest number of SIGs are grouped in the Topics and Courses Cluster, which includes Archival/Records Management Education; Gender Issues; Historical Perspectives; Information Ethics; Information Policy; International Library Education; Multicultural, Ethnic, and Humanistic Concerns; Preservation Education; Research; Technical Services Education; and Youth Services.

School representatives serve as a direct link between membership and the board of directors. Each member school/program designates a faculty member who is a current member of ALISE to act as the ALISE liaison. These representatives disseminate information from ALISE and encourage individual membership. They communicate priorities, ideas, information, and concerns from members to the board through the director for membership services.

ALISE works toward its mission of promoting excellence in research, teaching, and service for library and information science education through three primary venues: an ongoing publications program, an annual conference, and a grants and awards program. There are four primary components of the ALISE publications program, including a scholarly journal, a membership directory, a statistical report, and a Web site. The *Journal of Education for Library and Information Science,* a quarterly peer-reviewed journal, presents refereed articles and research, as well as columns, relating to library and information science education. ALISE members Cheryl Knott Malone and Anita Sandaram Coleman of the University of Arizona serve as co-editors. Published annually, the *ALISE Directory of Library and Information Science Programs and Faculty in the United States and Canada* is a print volume that combines the ALISE membership directory and a directory of LIS programs and faculty in the United States and Canada. An online membership database, implemented in 2007, now complements the print version. Both versions include contact information, as well as an indication of each member's areas of teaching and research interests. The *ALISE Library and Information Science Education Statistical Report,* published in cooperation with ALA's Committee on Accreditation, is an annual compilation of statistical data on curriculum, faculty, students, income and expenditures, and continuing professional education. In 2007 long-time editor Jerry Saye retired from the publication. The association implemented a plan to bring the print series up to date (through 2007) and conducted a needs analysis to enhance the process of data collection and the utility of the final product. A primary communication mechanism with membership, the ALISE Web site was redesigned to provide improved access and expanded content. The association's vision, mission, and enduring purpose and strategic directions are posted on the Web site. Conference information, including abstracts of papers and posters, is available online. The electronic *ALISE News* was revived and two issues were posted to the site in 2007. A members-only segment of the Web site was developed with the intent of expediting the work of the association and was used in 2007 to test the process for soliciting feedback on position papers prior to a vote of membership.

Annual Conference

The major activity of the association, in addition to its publications program, is its Annual Conference, currently held immediately prior to the ALA Midwinter Meeting in January. The conference serves scholarly, career development, and social purposes. Attendance continues to grow, with registration reaching 444 in 2007. The 2007 ALISE Annual Conference, held in Seattle January 8–11, was organized by program co-chairs Melissa Gross (Florida State University) and Michele Besant (University of Wisconsin–Madison) and offered a rich mixture of activities relating to the theme of then-ALISE President John Budd, "Habits of Mind and Practice: Preparing Reflective Practitioners." William M. Sullivan, senior scholar at the Carnegie Foundation for the Advancement of Teaching, opened the conference with his keynote address, "The Civic Life of Information: Teaching Professionalism for the Knowledge Age," and led a plenary session,

"Reflecting on LIS and William Sullivan's Three Apprenticeships in Professional Education."

Twenty-six peer-reviewed papers, representing a 38 percent acceptance rate, were presented at the 2007 conference, along with 14 juried panels (a 71 percent acceptance rate), and 8 SIG-sponsored programs. A half-day preconference workshop, "Best Practices for Online Pedagogy: Preparing WISE Scholars," focused on distance education. Two poster sessions offered a vehicle for discussing work on a one-to-one basis. The annual Doctoral Student Research Poster Reception offers doctoral students an opportunity to share information about their research projects with the LIS community. The ALISE/Jean Tague Sutcliffe Doctoral Research Poster Award—which is supported by Western Ontario University in honor of the late dean of the university's School of Library and Information Science (now the faculty of Information and Media Studies) and consists of a certificate, a one-year membership in ALISE, and a $250 monetary prize—is awarded for the best poster. Posters are judged on the significance of the research topic to the LIS field, the appropriateness of research design and methodology, and a concise description of the results, as well as on the organization, clarity, and aesthetics of the poster. The recipient of the 2007 Sutcliffe Award was Rachel A. Fleming-May (University of Alabama) for "Use: The Discursive Construction of a Concept and a Typology of its Application in the Literature of Library and Information Science." The second annual Works-in-Progress Poster Session encouraged faculty, students, and practicing professionals to share work in its formative stage. Practical restraints required limiting each of these events to 60 presenters, although in the past as many as 90 posters have been included in the doctoral student competition. SIG meetings and a Birds-of-a-Feather event offered opportunities for informal discussion among those who shared an interest in a common research or teaching area.

The conference also offers opportunities for career development. The association's placement service enjoys a high level of activity. ALISE staff collect applicant résumés and distribute them to schools prior to the conference, book interview space, and provide communication support at the conference. The ALISE conference remains the major opportunity for many schools to meet and conduct preliminary interviews with prospective faculty members. In another career development opportunity, doctoral students and junior faculty are able to take advantage of one-on-one interaction with senior faculty who critique their résumés and portfolios.

Each year the association encourages early involvement in professional activities with the Doctoral Students to ALISE Award. The student, who is selected on the basis of a short essay and the recommendation of his or her program head, receives a complimentary conference registration and a $500 stipend (sponsored by Libraries Unlimited), to defray conference expenses. The 2007 recipients were Maria Soudan (University of Michigan) and Rachel Fleming-May. The ALISE University of Washington Information School Youth Services Graduate Student Travel Award, a $750 annual award to support the costs associated with travel to and participation in the ALISE annual conference, was established in 2007. The first award will be given in 2009 to one student currently enrolled in an LIS graduate program, including both doctoral and master's studies, with a concentration in youth services. Expanded career development opportunities for educators at every level will be available at future conferences.

The ALISE Academy was created in 2007 to offer professional development workshops relevant to members at various stages throughout their careers, thus realizing part of a plan to develop sustained interest by delivering relevant, high-value services. The first offerings will be available at the 2009 annual conference in Denver.

ALISE supports research and scholarship through a thriving grants and awards program that recognizes excellence and fosters research in diverse subject areas within library and information science. The 2007 recipients of ALISE research grants were Eileen Abels and Denise Agosto (Drexel University) and Lorri Mon (Florida State University), who received the 2007 ALISE Research Grant ($5,000) to support "Remote Reference in Practice and the Classroom" and Charles Hildreth and Selena Aytac (Long Island University) who received the ALISE/Bohdan S. Wynar Research Paper Competition Award ($2,500) for "Recent Library Practitioner Research: A Methodological Analysis and Critique." Two proposals received the 2007 OCLC/ALISE Library and Information Science Research Grant ($15,000): "Investigating the User Needs and Preferences for a Specialized Environmental Library" by M. Asim Qayyum, Carlos Suarez, Balseiro Rio Piedras, and Tania Garcia-Ramos (University of Puerto Rico) and "Self–Views of Information Seeking Skills: Undergraduates' Understanding of What It Means to Be Information Literate" by Melissa Gross and Don Latham (Florida State University). Kate Williams (Dominican University) received the ALISE/Eugene Garfield Doctoral Dissertation Award ($500, conference registration, and one-year membership in ALISE) for "Social Networks, Social Capital, and the Use of Information and Communications Technology in Socially Excluded Communities: A Study of Community Groups in Manchester, England," which she completed at the University of Michigan.

Professional Awards

ALISE honors individuals who have made significant contributions to the profession and the organization through teaching, service, and scholarship. The Service to ALISE Award, which recognizes an ALISE member who has provided regular and sustained service to the association and whose participation in activities has enhanced its reputation and strength, was presented to Toni Carbo (University of Pittsburgh). The ALISE Teaching Excellence Award, which recognizes an ALISE member who has provided sustained excellence in teaching library and information science, including using effective and innovative teaching methods, making ongoing contributions to curriculum design, and mentoring students, alumni, and/or practicing professionals outside the classroom, was presented in 2007 to Dania Bilal (University of Tennessee) and Betsy Hearne (University of Illinois at Urbana-Champaign). The ALISE Professional Contribution to Library and Information Science Education Award was granted to Brooke E. Sheldon (San José State University) in recognition of contributions that enhance the status of library and information science education and demonstrate leadership in addressing issues relating to the profession. The ALISE Norman Horrocks

Leadership Award, consisting of a plaque and monetary prize of $500, was created in 2007 to recognize a member who has belonged to the association for fewer than seven years and has demonstrated outstanding leadership qualities in professional ALISE activities. This award, which will first be presented in 2009, carries the name of Norman Horrocks, whose long and productive service to the association and the profession serves as a model for a new generation of library and information science educators.

'Planning for Tomorrow'

ALISE is building on its rich traditions and a solid foundation. The work of the association is guided by the ALISE mission and priorities outlined in "Planning for Tomorrow: Strategic Directions 2007–2010," approved by the board in April 2007 and available on the association's Web site. An effective administrative and fiscal infrastructure, a necessary precondition to accomplishing strategic goals, is in place. The organization is in sound fiscal shape and has created an operating reserve as well as an endowment fund that will fully support its grants and awards program. Initiatives are in place to enhance existing services, create new services, and engage new members. Members continue to work diligently and creatively in support of ALISE's ambitious mission to foster excellence in research, teaching, and service for library and information science education.

Friends of Libraries U.S.A.

1420 Walnut St., Suite 450, Philadelphia, PA 19102
800-936-5872, e-mail friends@folusa.org
World Wide Web http://www.folusa.org

Sally Gardner Reed
Executive Director

Friends of Libraries U.S.A. (FOLUSA) is a national nonprofit organization providing networking opportunities, education, and consultation to local friends-of-the-library groups, library trustees, library foundation members, and librarians across the United States. Friends groups and foundations raise money and, along with trustees, raise awareness and political support for their libraries. More than 3,000 friends groups, libraries, trustees, foundations, and individuals are members of FOLUSA, representing hundreds of thousands of library supporters.

Established in 1979 as a committee of the Library Administration and Management Association of the American Library Association (ALA), FOLUSA is a national leader in library advocacy and support. Its mission is to motivate and support local friends groups in their efforts to preserve and strengthen libraries and to create awareness and appreciation for library services by

- Assisting in developing all library support groups in order to generate local, state, and national support
- Providing guidance, education, and consulting services to friends, trustees, foundations, and libraries
- Promoting the development of strong library-advocacy programs
- Providing expert information for friends groups and librarians via toolkits, workshops, and the publication of book and Web-based resources
- Promoting early childhood literacy in partnership with friends groups
- Promoting appreciation of the nation's literary heritage

Governance

FOLUSA is governed by a 25- to 30-member board of directors. Board members come from all avenues of the library world: friends group members, librarians, leaders of library corporations, publishers, and library supporters.

In June 2007 FOLUSA inaugurated as its president John Carson, national accounts manager for Brodart. The vice president/president-elect is Peggy Barber, Library Communications Strategies; the secretary is Robin Hoklotubbe, friends and volunteers services coordinator, San Bernardino County (California) Library; and the treasurer is Laura Salmon, LexisNexis Corporation.

Advocacy and Public Awareness

FOLUSA engages in efforts to raise the political profile of libraries and to help friends groups and other supporters of libraries use the power of their voices to ensure that libraries are supported. FOLUSA is an affiliate of ALA and works closely with ALA's Washington Office and Public Information Office to create programs that engage friends groups and library supporters in library-promotion activities.

In 2003 FOLUSA organized a "virtual march on Washington" to coincide with ALA's National Library Legislation Day, and this effort has become an annual event. It helps friends of libraries contact their legislative representatives via telephone, Internet, or fax to reinforce the messages that librarians are delivering in person on Capitol Hill that day.

Also on National Library Legislation Day, FOLUSA presents its public service award to a member of Congress who has done the most to support libraries during the previous year. In 2007 the award went to U.S. Senator Susan Collins (R-Maine). In 2005 FOLUSA partnered with ALA to present the first Advocacy Institute preconference at ALA's Midwinter Meeting in Boston, and the institute continues to be held on a semiannual basis in conjunction with ALA's Annual Conference and Midwinter Meeting. The Advocacy Institute focuses on training friends, librarians, and trustees to work together to develop successful local-level advocacy campaigns in the community or on campus.

FOLUSA traveled to more than a dozen state and regional library gatherings during the year to work with friends and librarians in creating effective public awareness and advocacy efforts.

Networking Opportunities

Friends groups and trustees typically work in isolation from one another. To help them exchange advice and counsel and to provide a forum for best practices, FOLUSA hosts a listserv at http://www.folusa.org/sharing/listserv.php. Approximately 500 friends members and librarians subscribe to and participate in the listserv.

NewsUpdate, FOLUSA's bimonthly newsletter, is another vehicle for the sharing of ideas and best practices. The newsletter, which has more than 3,500 subscriptions, includes articles and information of interest to friends groups as well as good ideas from groups across the country. Many of these ideas are archived on FOLUSA's Web site.

Publications and Resources

In addition to *NewsUpdate*, FOLUSA publishes occasional resources and online toolkits to help friends groups increase their effectiveness.

Toolkits are available free of charge to FOLUSA members via the Friends Zone page of the organization's Web site. They currently include *Starting a New Friends Group or Revitalizing the Group You Have; School Media Center Friends*

Groups: A Prescription for Success; Friends and Libraries: Working Effectively Together; and *Incorporating and Tax Exempting Procedures for Friends.*

Additional resources available to members of FOLUSA include scripts for radio public service announcements promoting libraries; an organizational chart showing the roles of the players in the library world (librarians, trustees, and friends); "Notable Quotables" (quotes about libraries, books, and reading for use in friends groups' newsletters, Web sites, and other promotions); more than 20 fact sheets on organizational effectiveness and other issues of concern to friends; information about special discount offers for members; and information about FOLUSA award opportunities.

Other publications available to friends and librarians (members get discounted prices) include *101+ Great Ideas for Libraries and Friends, Making Our Voices Heard: Citizens Speak Out for Libraries,* and *Getting Grants in Your Community.*

Programs

FOLUSA presents a variety of literary programs during ALA's Midwinter Meeting and Annual Conference. Working with publisher sponsors, FOLUSA highlights bestselling authors at its semiannual Author Tea. At annual conferences, additional programs feature first-time published writers in a variety of genres.

At the 2007 ALA Midwinter Meeting, writers taking part in the Author Tea were Frank Delaney, Eileen Goudge, Joyce Carol Oates, Susan Vreeland, and Markus Zusak.

Literary Landmarks

In support of its goal to promote appreciation for America's literary heritage, FOLUSA's Literary Landmarks program marks, with foundry-crafted plaques, locations connected to important writers. Begun in 1987, the program has designated 90 landmarks honoring such authors as Willa Cather, Jack London, Theodore Roethke, Zora Neale Hurston, Carl Sandburg, and W. E. B. Dubois.

The following Literary Landmark designations were made in 2007:

- Kate Chopin House, Kirkwood, Missouri, dedicated April 22
- Frederick Douglass National Historic Site, Washington, D.C., dedicated June 24
- William Rogers Memorial Museum, Claremore, Oklahoma, dedicated October 26

Books for Babies

Books for Babies is FOLUSA's national literacy program that acquaints parents of newborns with the important role they play in the development of their children. Parents are given a Books for Babies kit containing a book, baby's first library card, and brochures with reading tips for parents and caregivers. Kits are available in English and Spanish.

Library friends groups and women's clubs are among the organizations that purchase Books for Babies packets, often supplementing them with information about local resources, such as library locations and contact information, as well as details about lap-sit and preschool story hours.

Books for Babies is designed to encourage parents to engage in developmentally appropriate literacy activities with their babies. Reading aloud to babies is an ideal form of stimulation because it engages visual, auditory, interactive, and attention processes in a pleasurable context. Research shows that babies who are read to and engaged in verbal interaction show superior language and math skills.

In 2007, with a $10,000 grant from Nordstrom, FOLUSA launched a new Web site (http://www.babieslovebooks.org) to help parents learn the value of reading to their children at the earliest ages. The site provides tips on how to read aloud, age-appropriate book suggestions, and links to research showing the importance of reading to babies.

The program is believed to have benefited approximately 100,000 babies since its launch in 1992.

Awards

FOLUSA presents several awards to friends groups each year.

Baker & Taylor Awards

In 2007 Baker & Taylor sponsored three awards to friends groups that distinguished themselves in their support of their libraries. Each of these awards presents $2,000 to the winning friends group, as well as a plaque commemorating its accomplishments. The 2007 winners were (small library) Friends of the Mineola (Texas) Memorial Library; (large library) Friends of the Leesburg (Florida) Public Library and Friends of the Minneapolis (Minnesota) Public Library (tie).

The 2007 awards were presented at the ALA Annual Conference in Washington, D.C., in June.

Best Friends Award

In 2005 FOLUSA launched the Best Friends Award, which recognizes friends groups for print and electronic materials that promote the group and its special programs and projects. The awards do not evaluate the type or scope of the group's programs, only the printed and electronic materials. The winners are recognized in *NewsUpdate* and on the FOLUSA Web site. Winners also receive a certificate of recognition from FOLUSA and are given a press release to help them promote their recognition locally. Winning entries are posted in the Friends Zone, a members-only section of the FOLUSA Web site, for groups around the country to view. The program's 2006 awards were: (print newsletters and planned giving brochures) (small library) Friends of Huntingdon Valley (Pennsylvania) Library, (large library) Friends of the Minneapolis (Minnesota) Public Library; (membership brochures) (small library) Friends of the Huntington

(Indiana) Library, (medium library) Friends of the South Pasadena (California) Public Library, (large library) Friends of the Northside ISD Libraries in Texas; (book sales) (large library) Friends of the Library, Gainesville, Florida; (special project publicity) (medium library) Friends of Berks County (Pennsylvania) Public Libraries; (program publicity) (small library) Friends of the Roswell (Georgia) Library, (medium library) Friends of the Pasco County (Florida) Library System, (large library) Friends of the Minneapolis (Minnesota) Public Library; (advocacy materials) (medium library) Friends of the Leesburg (Florida) Library, (large library) Franklin Community (California) Library Friends.

New National Spokesperson

In 2007 comedian Paula Poundstone became the national spokesperson for FOLUSA and will work with local friends groups in every town and city in which she performs to help them raise their profile and extra funding. A national publicity campaign will be launched in 2008 will be called "If you haven't visited your library lately, you're overdue!"

FOLUSA's Funding

As a nonprofit organization, FOLUSA receives its funding through three basic revenue streams: corporate sponsorship, membership dues, and the sale of products and services that further its mission. A list of corporate sponsors, as well as membership and sponsorship opportunities, is available at http://www.folusa.org.

Looking to the Future

In 2007 FOLUSA entered into discussions with the leadership of the Association of Library Trustees and Advocates (ALTA), a division of ALA, to determine whether an ALA Division of Friends and Trustees, combining FOLUSA and ALTA, would increase the power of library supporters in advocating for libraries. A decision was expected in 2008.

International Reports

International Federation of Library Associations and Institutions

P.O. Box 95312, 2509 CH The Hague, Netherlands
Tel. 31-70-314-0884, fax 31-70-383-4827, e-mail ifla@ifla.org
World Wide Web http://www.ifla.org

Beacher Wiggins

Director for Acquisitions and Bibliographic Access, Library of Congress
Library of Congress Representative to the Standing Committee of the
IFLA Section on Bibliography

The International Federation of Library Associations and Institutions (IFLA) is the preeminent international organization representing librarians, other information professionals, and library users. During 2007 IFLA protected the world's cultural and documentary heritage from the ravages of war and natural disaster; broadened participation in its activities by countries with developing economies; expanded the theory and practice of bibliographic control; and promoted equitable access to information without regard to barriers of poverty, handicap, and geographical isolation. Throughout the year IFLA promoted an understanding of libraries as cultural heritage resources that are the patrimony of every nation.

World Library and Information Congress

The World Library and Information Congress and 73rd IFLA General Conference and Council attracted 3,100 participants from 116 countries to Durban, South Africa, August 19–23, 2007. IFLA President Alex Byrne's opening speech tied the congress theme, "Libraries for the Future: Progress, Development, and Partnerships," to the quest for justice, truth, and reconciliation in South Africa and elsewhere. The congress was hosted by the Library and Information Association of South Africa, which celebrated its tenth anniversary at the same time. Noting that Australian librarians had raised funds to permit 16 librarians from African countries to attend the Durban congress, Byrne challenged North American libraries to a similar effort to support the attendance of Latin American colleagues at the 2008 congress to be held in Quebec City, Canada.

The governing board announced the formation of three IFLA Language Centers, at the Bibliotheca Alexandrina, Alexandria, Egypt; l'Universite Cheikh Anta Diop, Dakar, Senegal; and the Russian State Library, Moscow. These centers will promote the work of the federation in regions that use Arabic, French, and Russian as everyday languages.

Seventeen satellite meetings permitted intensive focus on special topics. These included "Information Technology and Research in African University Libraries" (held at the University of KwaZulu-Natal in Durban, cosponsored with Makerere University, Uganda); "Library Frontiers: Disasters, Emergency Preparedness, and Emerging Diseases" (held in Durban); "Innovative Multicultural Library Services for All" (held in Pretoria, South Africa, cosponsored by CSX Customer Services); "Best Practices/Lessons Learned" in library management, cosponsored by SirsiDynix (held at the University of KwaZulu-Natal); "Electronic Resource Management Systems" (held in Cape Town, South Africa, cosponsored by the University of the Western Cape); and the "Seventh Northumbria International Conference on Performance Measurements in Libraries and Information Services" (held in Cape Town and cosponsored by the universities of Cape Town, Stellenbosch, and Northumbria).

At the Durban congress, the Bill and Melinda Gates Foundation announced that its Global Libraries initiative would donate $1 million to IFLA. This gift would enable IFLA to promote libraries throughout the world, particularly by providing public access to libraries and the Internet via libraries.

Conference of Directors of National Libraries

The Conference of Directors of National Libraries (CDNL) is an independent association that meets in conjunction with the IFLA Conference to promote cooperation on matters of common interest to national libraries around the world. CDNL's president is Penny Carnaby, chief executive of the National Library of New Zealand, which hosts the CDNL Secretariat through 2009.

Follow-Up to World Summit

The second World Summit on the Information Society (WSIS) was held in Tunis, Tunisia, November 16–18, 2005. The conference is sponsored by the International Telecommunications Union, a United Nations organization separate from UNESCO, and IFLA was concerned that without substantial input from the library community, the summit would address only a technical and corporate agenda. To ensure a strong advocacy role for libraries at WSIS, IFLA Presidents Kay Raseroka (2003–2005) and Alex Byrne (2005–2007) led in drafting IFLA's "Alexandria Manifesto on Libraries, the Information Society in Action." IFLA's advocacy ensured that the concluding document of WSIS, the "Tunis Agenda for the Information Society," recognized the role of libraries in providing equitable access to information and knowledge for all people and called on governments to support libraries in this role.

IFLA leadership has worked to ensure a continued role for libraries in WSIS follow-up meetings and projects since 2005. IFLA was appointed moderator of the "Libraries and Archives" subtheme of WSIS action line C3, "Access to information and knowledge," and of the "Heritage" sub-theme of action line C8, "Cultural diversity." An IFLA representative was also active in meetings of the

WSIS-derived Global Alliance for ICT (Information and Communication Technologies) and Development and the United Nations Commission for Science and Technology for Development. However, IFLA was still endeavoring to obtain full consultative status in the United Nations Economic and Social Council and to be represented in WSIS action line C-7, "e-science." The IFLA Governing Board considered whether to make support for WSIS an IFLA core activity in 2007, but decided instead to establish an IFLA presidential committee on WSIS.

Response to War and Natural Disaster

In 1996 IFLA was a founding member of the International Committee of the Blue Shield (ICBS) to protect cultural property in the event of natural and human disasters. Its current partners in ICBS are the International Council on Archives, the International Council on Monuments and Sites, the International Council of Museums, and the Coordinating Council of Audiovisual Archives Associations. In 2007 ICBS continued its concern for the preservation of cultural heritage in the ongoing war in Iraq and for the consequences of natural disasters such as the massive earthquake in Bam, Iran, in 2003, the Asian tsunami of December 2004, and Hurricane Katrina in August 2005. The IFLA North American regional center for preservation and conservation, hosted at the Library of Congress, continued to develop a network of colleague institutions to provide a safety net for library collections during emergencies. Rescue work for Sri Lankan and other South Asian libraries in the wake of the tsunami will continue for years to come.

Bibliographic Control

IFLA has worked steadily over the decades to improve bibliographic control, through practical workshops, support of the International Standard Bibliographic Description, and research that seeks to establish basic principles of bibliographic control and to identify areas where cataloging practice in different cultures can be harmonized to make library catalogs less expensive to produce and easier for patrons to use.

In 2003 the IFLA Governing Board joined with six national libraries—the British Library, the Deutsche Nationalbibliothek, the Library of Congress, the National Library of Australia, the Biblioteca Nacional de Portugal, and the Koninklijke Bibliotheek (Netherlands)—and the Conference of Directors of National Libraries (CDNL) to form the IFLA-CDNL Alliance for Bibliographic Standards (ICABS), now an IFLA core activity. In addition to general issues of related bibliographic control, ICABS works to advance the understanding of issues relating to long-term archiving of electronic resources. The ICABS program in Durban focused on libraries and "Web 2.0," collaborative Internet content often created by end users.

Closely related to ICABS is the separate IFLA UNIMARC Core Activity (UCA), which maintains, develops, documents, and promotes the four UNIMARC formats for bibliographic, authority, classification, and holdings data. Since 2003, when it succeeded IFLA's former Universal Bibliographic Control and International MARC program, UCA has been hosted by the National Library of Portugal. Under UCA, the Permanent UNIMARC Committee, currently chaired by Alan Hopkinson of Middlesex University Learning Resources in Britain, maintains the formats and also advises ICABS on matters relating to UNIMARC. In 2007 the third edition of the UNIMARC Bibliographic Format was prepared, work began on a third edition of the UNIMARC Authorities Format, and the updated UNIMARC Bibliographic Concise Format was published on the World Wide Web.

The IFLA Bibliography Section's Working Group on Electronic National Bibliographies completed guidelines for new bibliographies, to be issued for worldwide review during 2008.

The International Meeting of Experts on an International Cataloging Code (IME ICC) gatherings were a series of five regional invitational conferences planned by the IFLA Cataloguing Section to explore similarities and differences in current national and regional cataloging rules, in an attempt to clarify where variations for languages and cultural differences may be needed. The first meeting was held in Frankfurt, Germany, in 2003 for experts from Europe and North America; the second took place in Buenos Aires, Argentina, in conjunction with the 2004 World Library and Information Conference/IFLA General Conference. The third was held in Cairo, Egypt, December 12–14, 2005. The fourth and fifth regional conferences took place in Seoul, South Korea, and in Pretoria, South Africa, in conjunction with the 2006 and 2007 World Library and Information Conference/IFLA General Conferences. The IME ICC goal is to increase the ability to share cataloging information worldwide by promoting standards for the content of bibliographic and authority records used in library catalogs. A final draft statement of principles for an international cataloging code was to be issued for worldwide review early in 2008.

Copyright

With the International Publishers' Association (IPA), IFLA formed a joint steering group to consider how so-called orphan works—works under copyright but whose rights owners cannot be identified or located—may be used. In June 2007 IFLA and IPA announced agreement on five principles for use of orphan works: a reasonably diligent search for the copyright owner must be undertaken; attribution to the copyright owner is required; if the owner appears in the future, remuneration or restitution must be offered; any injunctive relief, however, should take into account the investment made in good faith by the user of the orphan work; and use of an orphan work is non-exclusive. Work would continue in 2008, with particular attention to inclusion of orphan works in mass digitization projects.

IFLA and IPA also worked in 2007 on issues of collective licensing and of VAT (value added tax) as applied to copyright.

Digital Libraries

The IFLA-World Digital Library Working Group on Digital Library Guidelines began work in May 2007 and expected to issue recommendations and guidelines for content selection, metadata, technology, service, and organization of digital libraries by mid-2008. The working group is a contribution to the development of the World Digital Library, a digital repository of world culture cosponsored by UNESCO, the Library of Congress, national libraries in other countries, and IFLA.

In a separate action, the IFLA Governing Board approved a Digital Library Manifesto, drafted by incoming IFLA President Claudia Lux, for eventual submission to UNESCO. The manifesto stresses the importance of public access to the Internet and the critical role of libraries in bridging the "digital divide" between those who can afford commercial Internet access and those who cannot.

Grants and Awards

The federation continues to collaborate with corporate partners and national libraries to maintain programs and opportunities that would otherwise not be possible, especially for librarians and libraries in developing countries. IFLA/Online Computer Library Center (OCLC) Early Career Development Fellowships bring library and information science professionals from countries with developing economies who are in the early stages of their careers to OCLC headquarters in Ohio for four weeks of intensive experience in librarianship. Beginning in 2007 the fellows also spend a week at the OCLC PICA campus in Leiden, Netherlands. In 2007 the fellows were from Brazil, Ghana, Jamaica, the Philippines, and Serbia. Announced in Durban in 2007, the five fellows for 2008 will be from India, Morocco, Nepal, South Africa, and Uganda. The American Theological Library Association is the third sponsor of the program, and one of the fellows must be a theological librarian. Since its inception in 2001, the program has supported 38 librarians from 26 developing countries.

The Guust van Wesemael Literacy Prize of 3,000 euros is awarded biennially to a school or public library in a country with a developing economy. The recipient in 2007 was the National Book Trust of Uganda. The Harry Campbell Conference Attendance Grant supports travel to the IFLA Conference from a developing country that has not had conference participants in recent years. The Dr. Shawky Salem Conference Grant supports conference attendance from an Arab country.

The Frederic Thorpe Award was established in 2003, administered by the IFLA Libraries for the Blind Section and the Ulverscroft Foundation of Leicester, England, which Thorpe founded to support the visually impaired. The Ulverscroft Foundation renewed the program as the Ulverscroft/IFLA Best Practice Awards (Frederic Thorpe Awards) in 2006. The deadline for applications for the 2007 individual and organizational awards was November 30, 2007, with awards to be announced in February 2008 [See "Library Scholarship and Award Recipients, 2007" in Part 3—Ed.].

The Bill and Melinda Gates Foundation Access to Learning Award in 2007 was presented to the library system of Northern Territory, Australia, for its Libraries and Knowledge Centers program, which serves 60,000 indigenous Australians, and its Our Story digital archive of indigenous culture. This annual award, managed by the Council on Library and Information Resources, presents up to $1 million to libraries, library agencies, or comparable organizations outside the United States that have been innovative in providing free public access to information.

The IFLA International Marketing Award includes a stipend and travel to the annual IFLA Conference. The first-place winner in 2007 was Olga Einasto of Tartu University Library, Estonia, for "The Night Library and the Mom-Student Library Project," a marketing campaign to attract diverse students to the university library during exam week. In 2002, 2003, and 2004, IFLA and 3M Library Systems cosponsored the marketing awards. After a hiatus in 2005, IFLA cosponsored the awards with SirsiDynix in 2006 and 2007.

Membership and Finances

IFLA has approximately 1,600 members in 150 countries. Initially established at a conference in Edinburgh in 1927, it has been registered in the Netherlands since 1971 and has headquarters facilities at the Koninklijke Bibliotheek (Royal Library) in The Hague. Although IFLA did not hold a General Conference outside Europe and North America until 1980, there has since been steadily increasing participation from Asia, Africa, South America, and Australia. The federation now maintains regional offices for Africa (in Pretoria); Asia and Oceania (in Singapore); and Latin America and the Caribbean (in Brazil). The organization has seven official working languages—Arabic, Chinese, English, French, German, Russian and Spanish—and offers a range of membership categories: international library associations, national library associations, other associations (generally regional or special library associations), institutions, institutional subunits, one-person libraries, school libraries, personal affiliates, and student affiliates. Association and institution members have voting rights in the IFLA General Council and may nominate candidates for IFLA offices; personal affiliates have no voting rights, but may run for any office. Except for personal and student affiliates, membership fees are keyed to the UNESCO Scale of Assessment and the United Nations List of Least Developed Countries, to encourage participation regardless of economic circumstances. The IFLA Core Activity Fund is supported by national libraries worldwide. In 2007 about 95 percent of contributions to this fund came from the national libraries of Japan, France, the United States, Australia, the Netherlands, Germany, Canada, Finland, Singapore, and Britain.

In addition, more than two dozen corporations in the information industry have formed a working relationship with IFLA as corporate partners, providing financial and in-kind support. Corporate partners in 2007, in addition to many firms in the United States and Europe, included the Beijing Security Electronics Engineering Co. of China and Sileon.Info of Bogota, Colombia. In 2005 the IFLA Governing Board established the IFLA Fund, through which individuals and corporations can donate support for new initiatives, disaster relief, or the federation's operating budget. This was followed in 2007 by the establishment of the IFLA Foundation (Stichting IFLA). UNESCO has given IFLA formal associate relations status, the highest level of relationship UNESCO accords nongovernmental organizations.

Personnel, Structure, and Governance

The secretary general of IFLA is Peter Johan Lor. Sjoerd M. J. Koopman is coordinator of professional activities, an IFLA headquarters position. The editor of the quarterly *IFLA Journal* is J. Stephen Parker.

The current President of IFLA is Claudia Lux, director general, Zentral- und Landesbibliothek Berlin, Germany. She began her two-year presidential term at the close of the Durban congress, with "Libraries on the Agenda" as the theme of her presidency. She planned to host three international conferences on free access to information during her two-year term. The first took place in Berlin, January 18–19, 2007.

Alex Byrne, university librarian of the University of Technology, Sydney, Australia, was president from August 2005 until August 2007. The current president-elect is Ellen R. Tise, senior director for library and information services, University of Stellenbosch, South Africa. She will assume the presidency in 2009. The current treasurer is Gunnar Sahlin, National Librarian of Sweden.

Under revised statutes that took effect in 2001, IFLA's former Executive Board and Professional Board were combined in a new Governing Board. The 21-member board (plus the secretary general, ex officio) is responsible for the federation's general policies, management and finance, and external communications. The current members, in addition to Lux, Tise, Sahlin, and Lor, are Helena Asamoah-Hassan (Ghana), Barbara J. Ford (United States), Bob McKee (Britain), Danielle Mincio (Switzerland), Pascal Sanz (France), Réjean Savard (Canada), Barbara Schleihagen (Germany), Joaquin Selgas Gutierrez (Spain), and Zhang Xiaolin (China), plus the chair and eight members of the Professional Committee, named below. In addition, Jesus Lau, Universidad Veracruzana, Mexico, and Sinikka Sipila, Finnish Library Association, were co-opted to the Governing Board in 2007.

The Governing Board delegates responsibility for overseeing the direction of IFLA between board meetings, within the policies established by the board, to the IFLA Executive Committee, which includes the president, president-elect, treasurer, chair of the Professional Committee, two members of the Governing Board (elected every two years by members of the board from among its elected members), and IFLA's secretary general, ex officio. The current elected Governing Board members of the Executive Committee are McKee and Savard.

The IFLA Professional Committee monitors the planning and programming of professional activities carried out by IFLA's two types of bodies: professional groups—8 divisions, 47 sections, and discussion groups—and core activities (formerly called core programs). The Professional Committee is composed of one elected officer from each division, plus a chair elected by the incoming members; the president and the coordinator of professional activities; and two elected members of the Governing Board, currently Sanz and Zhang. Nancy E. Gwinn, director, Smithsonian Institution Libraries, chairs the Professional Committee. To ensure an arena within IFLA for discussion of new social, professional, and cultural issues, discussion groups are formed within divisions or sections, generally for a two-year period, with the approval of the Professional Committee. Discussion groups often evolve into permanent separate sections if the Professional Committee agrees that there is sufficient interest to warrant support from IFLA. There currently are discussion groups for Access to Information Network/Africa; Agricultural Libraries; E-Learning; Libraries and Web 2.0; Library and Information Science Education in Developing Countries; New Professionals; and Women, Information, and Libraries.

The eight divisions of IFLA and their representatives on the Professional Committee are I: General Research Libraries (Ingrid Parent, Canada); II: Special Libraries (Steve Witt, United States); III: Libraries Serving the General Public (Torny Kjekstad, Norway); IV: Bibliographic Control (Patrice Landry, Switzerland); V: Collections and Services (Lynn F. Sipe, United States); VI: Management and Technology (Trine Kolderup Flaten, Norway); VII: Education and Research (Anna Maria Tammaro, Italy); and VIII: Regional Activities (Premila Gamage, Sri Lanka). Each division has such interest sections as Statistics and Evaluation, Library Theory and Research, and Management and Marketing; other sections focus on particular types of libraries or parts of the world.

The six core activities are Action for Development Through Libraries (ALP, formerly Advancement of Librarianship); Preservation and Conservation (PAC); IFLA-CDNL Alliance for Bibliographic Standards (ICABS); IFLA UNIMARC Core Activity, which maintains and develops the Universal MARC Format, UNIMARC; Free Access to Information and Freedom of Expression (FAIFE); and Copyright and Other Legal Matters (CLM). Two other longstanding IFLA projects are now considered core activities: the IFLA World Wide Web site IFLANET and the IFLA Voucher Scheme, which replaced the IFLA Office for International Lending. The Voucher Scheme enables libraries to pay for international interlibrary loan requests using vouchers purchased from IFLA rather than actual currency or credit accounts. By eliminating bank charges and invoices for each transaction, the voucher scheme reduces the administrative costs of international library loans and allows libraries to plan budgets with less regard to short-term fluctuations in the value of different national currencies. The Voucher Scheme has also encouraged participating libraries to voluntarily standardize their charges for loans at the rate of 1 voucher for up to 15 pages.

IFLA's Three Pillars: Society, Members, and Profession

In December 2004 the Governing Board of IFLA endorsed a new operational model for IFLA based on the three pillars of society, membership, and professional matters. A review of IFLA's core activities, conducted in 2003 and 2004, showed that all of the federation's core functions related to three strategic factors: the societal contexts in which libraries and information services operate; the membership of the federation; and the library profession.

Although the three pillars and the infrastructure of IFLA are interdependent, they can be roughly analyzed as follows: The Society Pillar focuses on the role and impact of libraries and information services in society. Activities supported by the Society Pillar include FAIFE, CLM, Blue Shield, IFLA's presence at the World Summit on the Information Society, and a new advocacy office to be established at IFLA headquarters—all activities that preserve memory, feed development, enable education and research, and support international understanding and community well-being. The Profession Pillar focuses on IFLA's role as the global voice for libraries and information services through the work of its sections and divisions and its core activities ALP, ICABS, PAC, and UNIMARC. The Members Pillar includes IFLA's member services, conferences, and publications. The federation recognized a need to make IFLA more attractive to members around the world, and initiated the Global Library Association Development program (GLAD) to encourage membership from countries with developing economies.

IFLA's operational infrastructure, consisting of IFLA Headquarters, the IFLANET Web site, and the IFLA governance structure, supports and receives strategic direction from the three pillars. The three pillars enable IFLA to promote its four core values: freedom of access to information and expression, as stated in Article 19 of the Universal Declaration of Human Rights; the belief that such access must be universal and equitable access to support human well-being; delivery of high-quality library and information services in support of that access; and the commitment to enabling all members of IFLA to participate without regard to citizenship, disability, ethnic origin, gender, geographical location, political philosophy, race, or religion.

Canadian Library Association

328 Frank St., Ottawa, ON K2P 0X8
613-232-9625, fax 613-563-9895, e-mail info@cla.ca
World Wide Web http://www.cla.ca

Don Butcher
Executive Director

The Canadian Library Association/Association Canadienne des Bibliothèques (CLA) is Canada's major national professional and sector association for the library and information community. It is predominately English-language, with selected activities also in French. Its mission: "CLA is my advocate and public voice, educator and network. We build the Canadian library and information community and advance its information professionals."

Founded in 1946, CLA is a federally incorporated not-for-profit organization. It is governed by a 12-person Executive Council, which is advised by 14 standing committees and as-needed task forces.

Membership is composed both of individuals (librarians and other information professionals, library board trustees) and of institutions (predominantly libraries, but also encompassing suppliers to the library and information community).

Much of CLA's work is done through its five divisions:

- Canadian Association of College and University Libraries (CACUL), including the Community and Technical College Libraries (CTCL) section
- The Canadian Association of Public Libraries (CAPL), including the Canadian Association of Childrens' Librarians (CACL) section
- Canadian Library Trustees Association (CLTA)
- Canadian Association for School Libraries (CASL)
- Canadian Association of Special Libraries and Information Services (CASLIS), which has geographic chapters in Calgary, Edmonton, Manitoba, Ottawa, Toronto, and Atlantic Canada

In 2007 each of the six English-language library and information science (LIS) university-level schools in Canada had a CLA student chapter, and there is a student chapter at a library technician program.

To facilitate sharing of information in specific areas of interest, CLA has 23 interest groups on topics as diverse as Access to Government Information, Action for Literacy, Library and Information Needs of Native People, New Librarians and Information Professionals, and Rural and Remote Libraries.

Governance

In May 2007 CLA inaugurated as its president Alvin M. Schrader, professor at the University of Alberta's School of Library and Information Studies. He succeeded Linda Cook, director of Edmonton Public Library in Alberta, who had served as president since June 2006.

Serving as officers for 2007–2008 in addition to Schrader are Vice President Ken Roberts, Treasurer Theresa Tomchyshyn, and CLA Executive Director Don Butcher.

Major Activities

CLA's 2004–2007 Strategic Plan called for CLA to lead in national advocacy and professional development, and major activities focused on those two themes, with other important activities receiving considerable effort.

Advocacy and Public Awareness

CLA continued its leadership as the national voice for the Canadian library and information community, and in 2007 achieved tangible movement on some of its major advocacy files.

In June 2007, after lobbying by CLA and others, the federal government resurrected the Community Access Program, which provides funding for public libraries and other not-for-profit organizations to improve access to the Internet and help to overcome the "digital divide."

In October the federal government released long-promised development funds for the provision of equitable library service for the print-disabled through a nationwide network of public libraries. This is a significant step forward, and CLA has created a Task Force to work with Library and Archives Canada on its Initiative for Equitable Library Access.

Also in October, Canada Post announced a one-year renewal of the Library Book Rate, a special rate for the interlibrary loan of books, with no increase. Partnering with Canada Post, CLA created the database of libraries eligible to use the special rate, and provides access to a Canada Post shipping tool of benefit to smaller public, school, academic, and qualifying special libraries. The project is allowing Canada Post to gather usage data to be able to work with the federal government for the rate's long-term sustainability. A private member's bill (C-458) in the House of Commons introduced by Member of Parliament Merv Tweed asks the government to put the rate in legislation and to expand the scope of library materials eligible for the rate. CLA has been encouraging other members of Parliament to support the legislation.

Copyright legislation was again delayed in 2007, allowing CLA to continue and expand its lobbying efforts. In February 2007 the chair of CLA's Copyright Committee met with a number of members of Parliament, including the then-Minister of Canadian Heritage, on the copyright file. In December a media event led to the library community's position being reported on by major national print, broadcast, and Internet media. The library community is seen as a strong defender of users' rights.

A major CLA public relations program conducted in 2006 received multiple honors in 2007. In fall 2006, to increase awareness of the importance of reading for children, CLA and the Canadian Space Agency held national essay and question-and-answer contests for school-age children that were tied into the flight of Canadian astronaut Steve MacLean aboard the Space Shuttle *Atlantis*. The contests concluded with an event featuring the entire crew of STS-115 (the *Atlantis* mission) and hundreds of thrilled children. The project tied for the award for the top public relations program given out by the Canadian Society of Association Executives, received a silver (no gold was awarded) in the Summit International public relations awards, and earned an honorable mention in the Not-for-Profit PR Awards.

CLA again spearheaded Canadian Library Month/Le Mois Canadien des Bibliothèques, partnering with provincial, regional, and territorial library associations and governments. Under the theme "The World at Your Fingertips," this bilingual collection of events helped raise awareness of all types of libraries—public, academic, school, special—and their roles in disseminating digital as well as print information. This activity has shown tremendous growth in the past four years due to the work of all the partners.

Participation continued in other library and literacy projects, such as Freedom to Read Week; National Literacy Action Day; the Mathieu da Costa Challenge, African Heritage Month event; and a survey of challenged library materials.

New Position Statements

Being the voice of the Canadian library and information community involves CLA in setting out formal positions on issues of importance to that community. The association adopted two new position statements in 2007, on the deliberate destruction of libraries (prompted by recent incidents within Canada and elsewhere) and on equitable compensation for library workers (CLA endorses efforts to ensure that library workers are financially compensated at a level equitable to others with similar levels of education, responsibilities, and working conditions).

Continuing Professional Development

Members' stated interest in continuing professional development increases the importance of CLA's Annual Conference, held in May 2007 in St. John's, Newfoundland and Labrador, in partnership with the Atlantic Provinces and the Newfoundland and Labrador library associations. It was CLA's first annual conference in St. John's in 39 years. While, as expected, delegate and exhibitor attendance was lower, financial results exceeded expectations.

International Activities

CLA maintained its international activities in 2007 through active participation in the International Federation of Library Associations and Institutions (IFLA). CLA's work with l'Assocation pour l'Avancement des Sciences et des Techniques de la Documentation (ASTED), as that organization prepares to host IFLA's World Library and Information Congress in Quebec City this year, expanded greatly in 2007.

CLA and ASTED created a new organization, Bibliomondialis, to strengthen opportunities in international librarianship. Bibliomondialis has as its first project fund raising and awarding bursaries for delegates from developing countries to the IFLA congress. In future years, the emphasis will be on assisting Canadian librarians and information professionals to gain international experience.

Communications

As information professionals, Canadian librarians depend on timely and attractive publications and resources from their professional association; and those outside the community look to the major national associations as a significant source of information.

CLA's Web site (http://www.cla.ca) underwent a major rebuild in 2007, resulting in the launching of a totally new site, on schedule and under budget, on November 1, 2007. The new Web site and its simpler navigation have drawn positive feedback from users. A special feature is a "news crawl" with items from libraries around the world.

CLA's bimonthly publication *Feliciter* continued to explore core themes in the library community: research and evidence-based librarianship, new professionals, marketing, and technical services.

The *CLA Digest* is a biweekly newsletter for members, with links to more in-depth news.

Awards and Honors

CLA recognized individuals from the library and information community with awards and honors in 2007.

CLA's most significant award is for Outstanding Service to Librarianship. It is presented only when there is a candidate worthy to receive it. In 2007 CLA presented the award to Larry Moore, a 40-year member of the library and information community, including 24 years as executive director of the Ontario Library Association.

The CLA/Ken Haycock Award—established in honor of educator, administrator, advocate, and former CLA president Ken Haycock—honors an individual for demonstrating exceptional success in enhancing the public recognition and appreciation of librarianship. The 2007 recipient was Christiane Charette of Montreal.

The CLA Award for the Advancement of Intellectual Freedom was presented to Canadian Journalists for Free Expression, a Toronto-based organization that advocates for freedom of expression and manages the world's only freedom-of-expression network.

The CLA/Information Today Award for Innovative Technology was presented to the University of Lethbridge (Alberta) Library for the development of an internal staff resource called SourceWeb.

The CLA/3M Canada Award for Achievement in Technical Services was presented to the Kingston (Ontario) Public Library for its project "RFP Application Mashup."

The CLA 24th annual Student Article contest was won by Melissa Poremba for her article "Resources You Can Count On @ your library."

Conclusion

CLA enjoyed demonstrable success in 2007 in the areas of advocacy and professional development, which members identified as priorities. Through achieving
tangible success with government on some key files, continued progress in
increasing public awareness of the role and importance of libraries and literacy,
and taking public positions on critical issues in the library and information community, CLA more than fulfilled its mission during the year.

Library and Archives Canada

395 Wellington St., Ottawa, ON K1A 0N4
866-578-7777, fax 613-995-6274
World Wide Web http://www.collectionscanada.gc.ca

Ian E. Wilson
Librarian and Archivist of Canada

The Canadian cultural critic Northrop Frye once remarked that because Canada has no revolutionary tradition, its people have developed a tendency to move continuously rather than discontinuously through time. According to Frye, this characteristic, coupled with Canadians' natural inclination to itemize and catalog everything, has made the nation peculiarly well adapted to preserving its heritage. Frye also suggested that Canadians believe all coherent action and moral integrity depend on the continuity of past, present, and future.[1]

Library and Archives Canada (LAC) was created to harness this continuity in the form of a single organization. While LAC is still very much a work in progress, the power and potential of the information it holds, its ability to bridge the distances between past and present, between memory and fact, and between space and time, remain the same.

This article will describe some of LAC's achievements since 2004, when it was Canada's newest knowledge organization (succeeding the former National Archives, dating back to 1872, and the National Library of Canada, established in 1953), as well as the challenges it faces and its aspirations for the future.

Experiencing LAC Online

One of LAC's most popular features is the search-all single window that provides online integrated access to the library's collection. The pilot for this feature won the 2006 silver medal of distinction from the Government Technology Exhibition Conference (GTEC), and LAC is proud of the work that has gone and continues to go into it, particularly the merger of multiple databases.

This initiative is successful because it responds to the way Canadians seek and use information. According to a recent survey by EKOS Research Associates, 88 percent of Canadians surveyed said they want to access LAC's information via the Internet; LAC's clients expect information instantly, on the Web, and want it to be easily accessible.

LAC has created a massive online presence in three short years, and with a million visits per month, its Web site is one of the busiest in government. Between 2004 and 2006 the site registered a 276 percent increase in page views and a 281 percent increase in digital media downloaded by visitors. The LAC site is No. 1 when ranked with those of similar Canadian cultural organizations.

Government of Canada Web Archive

In November 2007 LAC launched the Government of Canada Web Archive (http://www.collectionscanada.gc.ca/webarchives/index-e.html), and the most recent harvest of federal government Web sites resulted in a collection of more than 55 million digital objects. Snapshots of entire Web sites of federal departments are now available.

This collection will continue to grow both in size and content. LAC has already archived political Web sites, a few blogs, and the Quebec version of YouTube. Archived treasures include "Moving Forward on Climate Change: A Plan for Honouring Our Kyoto Commitment" and "Protecting Canadians/ Rebuilding Afghanistan," which includes videos of services for slain military personnel and information on troop numbers and deployments.

Five Key Choices

The Web environment is particularly important because it allows LAC to respond to a constantly evolving landscape and to deliver on the five key choices it has made for the future:

- To go digital, taking advantage of every opportunity to use technology to make the nation's heritage available to Canadians
- To go national, becoming more relevant to Canadians wherever they live
- To continue LAC's focus on record-keeping in the Government of Canada by offering expert advice and sharing the best practices of accountable government
- To work with LAC's partners to find new ways to share the library's resources, deliver its services, and act on its mandate
- To heighten consultation with the Canadian people so that LAC's programs and services truly meet their needs

As a national institution, LAC holds the collective imagination of an entire nation, but it has realized that it cannot do everything itself. It is very important that LAC reinforce its role as public steward of the nation's intellectual heritage, raise its voice in government, engage its partners and clients, and act as a catalyst in the development of a comprehensive national approach. The challenge is to do this while maintaining a balance between making the best use of new technology and continuing to provide the traditional services LAC clients have come to expect.

The Canada Project

Much of Canada's cultural heritage today is "born digital," originating in a digital format rather than in the form of paper and ink. The modern generation believes that everything is available on the Web, yet there is a major gap between what is available digitally and what is available in publication. Millions of print volumes sit in archives, libraries, and storage facilities across the country, unused and difficult to access.

Through the Canada Project, LAC plans to position Canada as a leader in the digital world by preserving the nation's documentary heritage and making it easily available online, in both English and French—a task yet to be successfully achieved by any nation. By filling the digital gap, the Canada Project will build a virtual knowledge hub for Canadians about Canada. And it will do so collectively, as a public, private, and academic partnership. Ultimately the project will include materials as varied as books, newspapers, serials, music, films, maps, and broadcasts, creating a springboard for dialogue and discussion about Canada—where we have been, where we are headed.

The Canada Project has the potential to make a fundamental contribution to Canadian history. It will cross disciplines, unite organizations, and connect ideas. Sitting at the intersection of cultural heritage, technological innovation, scholarly research, and commercialization, it provides a good example of how the Internet has changed the way we communicate and distribute information.

Digital information is created everywhere, stored everywhere, and consumed everywhere. LAC realized that it needed to look at the challenges strategically and collectively, as a nation. It started a dialogue in 2005, talking to more than 200 stakeholder organizations. LAC went to publishing and media producers, to creators and rights bodies, to academics and provincial and federal officials, and to memory institutions.

As a result, LAC now has a plan for action. The shift to the digital realm is the most significant change to information production and dissemination since the advent of the printing press in the 15th century. The Canadian Digital Information Strategy, led by LAC, is designed to ensure that vital digital information assets are created, managed, and preserved well into the future by strengthening content, ensuring preservation, and maximizing access.

LAC has also carried out massive digitization projects, including the 1911 census records and ships' passenger lists, which are popular genealogical resources. Through major digitization projects at LAC, including Cabinet Conclusions, LAC has now digitized more than 3 million images from its collection. And through a new partnership with the British Library, the Library of Congress, and the National Library of Australia, LAC will implement a standard for resource description and access designed specifically for the digital environment.

Working Smart, Working Together

Innovative partnerships are an important part of the picture. Working with the Canadian Broadcasting Corporation (CBC), LAC's Canadian Genealogy Centre provided the resources and expertise for "Who Do You Think You Are?"—a weekly television series that features the family histories of well-known Canadians. The night the first episode was broadcast, more than 92,000 Internet searches were made via Ancestors Search (http://search-recherche.collections canada.ca/ancestors/search.jsp?Language=eng) between 7 P.M. and midnight. Eighteen new genealogical databases were added in anticipation of the heavy demand.

In cooperation with the Bibliothèque et Archives Nationales de Québec, LAC is copublishing a book-length collection of articles on innovations in libraries. Featuring in-depth profiles of outstanding and innovative programs, projects, and approaches in libraries throughout Canada, the publication's release will coincide with the World Library and Information Congress of the International Federation of Library Associations and Institutions (IFLA) in Quebec City in August 2008.

In the past two years the outreach and exhibition program of the Portrait Gallery of Canada has introduced thousands of visitors abroad to Canadian art and culture. LAC exhibited the works of renowned photographer Yousef Karsh in Paris and sent the 18th-century oil paintings known collectively as the "Four Indian Kings"—considered to be the earliest surviving full-length oil portraits of North American aboriginal people painted from life—to the National Portrait Gallery in London. The gallery recently partnered with the Art Gallery of Ontario to create a three-way Web on-site exhibition, and this fall LAC will launch community portraits via "Québec de Nos Jours."

Open Government

The Canadian government is committed to providing open, transparent, and accountable government. As the continuing memory of the Government of Canada and the main source of federal government records, LAC has a key leadership role to play in this area. It also has one of the busiest access-to-information divisions in government. One valuable contribution LAC has made in this area is the launch of the Public Opinion Research Reports site (http://www.porr-rrop.gc.ca/index-e.html), which makes it easy to access research undertaken on behalf of the government through a single access point. Thousands of records from crown corporations and their wholly owned subsidiaries will now also be available for public review through LAC as part of the Federal Accountability Act.

The LAC Forum on Democracy (http://www.collectionscanada.gc.ca/democracy/index-e.html) is another innovation of note, combining public programming events such as conferences and public lectures with Web-based information. The first public event, held in partnership with the University of Ottawa Graduate School of Public and International Affairs in November 2007, brought together top political journalists in a panel discussion on the recently published memoirs of former Prime Ministers Brian Mulroney and Jean Chrétien.

Acquisitions, Exhibitions, and Repatriations

Library and Archives Canada is framed by the vision of one national collection that truly reflects the diversity of Canadian experience. This is achieved partly through acquisitions and donations, some highlights of which follow.

- Through the efforts of the Friends of LAC, the library acquired a collection of 90 rare 78-rpm recordings manufactured by the Berliner Company of Montreal, making a notable addition to its music section.

- The Portrait Gallery of Canada recently acquired an album of 31 black-and-white photographs by Albert Chesterfield. These portraits of Inuit and Cree are not available in any other Canadian collection.
- In February 2007 Stanley Grizzle, the first African Canadian officer in the Ontario Ministry of Labour and the first African Canadian judge of the Canadian Court of Citizenship, donated his personal papers to LAC.
- LAC also had a special success story with the repatriation of an Australian playbill. One of LAC's rare-book librarians made a noteworthy discovery when she traced the history of what is now known as Australia's oldest printed document. Prime Minister Stephen Harper returned the playbill to the Australian people, demonstrating LAC's commitment to international cooperation and respect for historical treasures.

Other major acquisitions included the papers, photographs, and electronic records of former Prime Minister Chrétien; the R. Murray Schafer fonds, which include autographed manuscripts of 17 of his works; the rich correspondence between Québécoise author Marie-Claire Blais and fellow writers Anne Hébert and Réjean Ducharme; and the historical records of the International Joint Commission of Canada and the United States of America between 1912 and 1989.

Increasing Access

While much of the work undertaken by LAC is aimed at providing easier access to information, there are some initiatives that demonstrate this goal in a particularly tangible way. For example, in the spirit of making more information available to more Canadians in more formats, LAC established the Initiative for Equitable Library Access in 2007, a three-year project that will open a window of knowledge and learning to millions of Canadians with print disabilities.

Work is also well under way toward permitting online ordering, which will make it easier for inquirers to get the information they need. Through the support of the Treasury Board of Canada, LAC will also inaugurate a number of pilot projects designed to standardize record keeping across the Government of Canada.

LAC also opened some of its vaults in 2007. The Portrait Gallery had a sold-out program with its tours of some of LAC's art collection, currently being housed in the Library and Archives Canada Preservation Centre. In the tenth anniversary year of the Preservation Centre, visitors had the chance to view portraits of the first woman to receive an honorary doctorate in Canada, a battling British admiral of the 17th century who argued with the king to make Newfoundland a colony, and the only Beothuk (aboriginal Newfoundlander) to be painted from life.

Exhibitions Program

LAC continued to create online and on-site exhibitions to showcase its collections, including "Spirit and Intent," featuring treaty documents and such artifacts as wampum beads, a display illustrating why Canadians have been called "a treaty people" and emphasizing the point that treaties are living documents that respect the traditions of the past.

Early this year, LAC mounted an exhibition telling the stories of people of Grosse-Île, Quebec, from 1832 to 1937 through documents, journals, letters, photographs, and maps.

Moving Ahead

The year 2007 also boasted the release of a new corporate LAC publication. *Moving Ahead* is an 88-page review of LAC's achievements over its first three years, illustrated with photographs of some of its collections and profiles of some of the human stories behind the programs and the impact that LAC has had on individual lives. Copies of *Moving Ahead* can be ordered by e-mail at publications @lac-bac.gc.ca.

Conclusion

William Blake wrote of seeing a world "in a grain of sand,"[2] and in a sense this is what LAC does as the guardian of a nation's inheritance. From something small, like a page from a diary or a well-preserved 78-rpm recording, we can spin a world of stories, re-create a period in our history, and capture a moment in time forever.

The power of information in the 21st century is enormous, and libraries and archives across the world have the responsibility of harnessing that information and making it available. LAC in the future is likely to provide complete access to the nation's cultural inheritance. It will be a dynamic and digitized source of ideas and debate, connected to networks via the Internet and powered by an increasing number of partnerships, and will continue to provide seamless service delivery with other libraries and archives.

Notes

1. Northrop Frye, *Divisions on a Ground: Essays in Canadian Culture* (Anansi Press, 1982). Frye's 1975 address to the Royal Society of Canada.

2. William Blake, "Auguries of Innocence," *The Oxford Book of English Mystical Verse* (1917).

Canadian Libraries in 2007:
Copyright, Digital Divide, Access Among Top Issues

Karen G. Adams

Director of Library Services and Information Resources
University of Alberta Libraries

Canada's minority Conservative national government continued through 2007, based in part on the high probability that an election would simply have returned a relatively similar mix of members of parliament without achieving a majority for any one party. The March budget added C$39 billion to funding for the provinces and territories, with a view to improving provision of those services under provincial and territorial jurisdiction: roads, bridges, public transit, education, universities, health care, clean rivers, and job training.[1] This was followed by an October economic statement that promised to reduce the goods and services tax (GST) by 1 percent to 5 percent, effective January 1, 2008.[2] This sense of economic good news for the nation was triggered in part by the Canadian dollar achieving parity with the U.S. dollar in late September.[3] However, this situation posed a challenge for Canadian booksellers, because Canadian cover prices are generally higher than U.S. cover prices, and consumers expected that the parity of the dollars should make Canadian books cost only as much as the U.S. price.[4]

Canada's gross domestic product (GDP) rose by 2.7 percent from November 2006 to November 2007, with the greatest gain being in wholesale trade and the only losses being in agriculture, forestry, fishing, hunting, mining and oil and gas extraction, and nondurables manufacturing.[5]

In keeping with the previous year's trend, provincial government funding for public libraries saw small increases or no change to unconditional operating grants, with increases generally tied to specific projects in support of the individual province's agenda. The Ontario government reflected this trend, with C$5 million awarded to rural, remote, and aboriginal libraries for literacy programs,[6] an increase in the Library Strategic Development Fund to bring it to C$599,000 in support of new technologies,[7] and C$2.3million awarded to five libraries for construction and renovation.[8] Following a spring election, the Manitoba government awarded C$1million for construction of two rural libraries, new funding to support technology in Winnipeg Public Library's 20 branches, the establishment of a permanent Rural and Northern Technology Fund to extend the one-time program established the previous year, and new libraries for six additional First Nations (aboriginal) libraries.[9] The British Columbia government also supported library service in remote areas by funding the establishment of the North Central Library Federation (C$88,000) and the North East Library Federation (C$47,000).[10] British Columbia also awarded C$4.25 million to support two province-wide programs: the OneCard program, which enables cardholders to borrow a book at any library in the province and return it to their local library, and the AskAway Web-supported reference service.[11]

National and International Information Policy

Copyright

The year 2007 was one of copyright rumors. January began with speculation that a bill was nearly ready, but that the two ministers responsible (Industry and Canadian Heritage) were still unable to agree on the final wording.[12] In March two U.S. Senators, Diane Feinstein (D-Calif.) and John Cornyn (R-Texas), wrote to the prime minister and selected ministers asking the government to crack down on piracy of audio and video materials, especially the recording of movies before they have been released to video, with the argument based on the senators' belief that since the United States introduced tougher rules, piracy had moved to Canada. Canada's Copyright Act permits the copying of movies in theaters for personal use.[13] By March speculation had moved the bill to the prime minister's office, as the U.S. ambassador to Canada had publicly given his views on Canada's contribution to piracy of American music and movies.[14] Then the U.S. studio Warner Bros. Pictures added its voice by canceling promotional previews of its new releases in Canada and calling on the Canadian government to strengthen antipiracy legislation.[15]

In May the Department of Canadian Heritage issued its 2006–2007 Performance Report, which included its list of priorities, one of which was revising the Copyright Act to address issues relating to technology and the Internet.[16] At the end of May, California Governor Arnold Schwarzenegger visited Canada, with the government giving notice to the House of Commons of its plan to table a bill on video piracy just after the prime minister and the governor met.[17] The bill was introduced in June with the intention of making recording a movie without the consent of the theater manager a criminal offence, but parliament prorogued before the legislative process for the bill was completed.[18]

While the American entertainment industry sought to influence legislative reform of copyright, it also took direct action by working with major Canadian Internet service providers (ISPs) Rogers, Bell, and Telus. In February 2007 these ISPs agreed to distribute e-mails from industry companies to their customers reminding them that, in the view of industry, all downloading is copyright infringement.[19]

August brought a cabinet shuffle that changed the ministers of both industry and Canadian heritage, and fueled further speculation about the fate of copyright reform.[20] Copyright returned to the news in November when a spokesperson from Industry Canada confirmed the government's intention to introduce new copyright legislation, as promised in the fall speech from the throne.[21] In late November the Royal Canadian Mounted Police indicated that the priorities for their work on intellectual property crimes would be health and safety risks, links to organized crime, or large shipments, suggesting that downloading for personal use would be well outside their immediate activities.[22]

November and December saw continued media coverage of the copyright reform issue, with some expressing fear of a bill replicating the U.S. Digital Millennium Copyright Act (DMCA), and some continuing to cite concerns about piracy and music downloading. Library and education groups reinforced their positions to the ministers involved, and on December 10 the parliamentary notice paper introduced "An Act to Amend the Copyright Act."[23] When Industry Minister Jim Prentice held his pre-Christmas open house in Calgary, he was met by a group of protesters who feared a DMCA-style bill,[24] and some 20,000 Canadians joined a group on the social networking Web site Facebook supporting fair copyright reform. By the end of the week, the government announced the bill would not be introduced before the House recessed for Christmas.[25] The House resumed sitting in late January 2008, with the upcoming federal budget the focus of attention for the government during February.

Access Copyright, Canada's copyright licensing agency, allowed the automatic renewal of its license for three more years with universities, colleges, and community colleges at the same per-student tariff as for the previous three years. The question of similar tariffs for K–12 educational institutions with Access Copyright licenses remained a decision under advisement at Copyright Board Canada, with a decision expected in early 2008.[26] In November Access Copyright launched a lawsuit seeking C$10 million in damages from Staples/The Business Depot for copyright infringement in its commercial photocopying service.[27]

Early in 2008 the Federal Court of Appeal rejected the "iPod tax" of C$75 proposed by the Copyright Board of Canada in response to a request for such a levy from the Canadian Private Copyright Collective (CPCC), based on the premise that the iPod is a device and not a medium. CPCC collects levies on blank audio recording media and redistributes them to copyright holders.[28] CPCC had applied to have iPods classified as a recording medium. The Canadian Recording Industry Association (CRIA) objected to the proposed levy on iPods because the payment could have been perceived as legitimizing the downloading of music from the Internet onto iPods, as is currently the case in Canada with CDs and tapes.[29] CPCC was successful in its application to the copyright board to institute a new tax on downloading legally digital MP3 music files, adding 3 cents to the per-song cost.[30] However, the levy on other blank recording media remained unchanged for 2008 and 2009, at least until a new hearing takes place.[31] Notwithstanding the music industry's views of the damage done to its own profitability by downloading, Statistics Canada released a study indicating that recording industry profits were at 7 percent in 2005, up from 0.1 percent in 2003.[32]

Industry Canada studied the impact of music downloading on the purchase of music and found a strong positive relationship between peer-to-peer (P2P) file sharing and CD purchasing, while concluding that the net effect of P2P file sharing overall on CD purchasing was neither positive nor negative.[33]

Access to Information

Following the October 2006 announcement by the minister of natural resources (NRCan) that the Canada Map Office would remain open and topographic maps would continue to be printed, on April 1, 2007, NRCan released Canadian topographic maps, data, and satellite imagery on the Internet without restriction on their use or access. The move was intended to encourage research, environmental reviews, business initiatives, tourism, and industry. This improved access had long been advocated by the Canadian Association of Research Libraries (CARL), the Association of Canadian Map Libraries and Archives, and many other public interest groups.[34]

On January 1, 2007, the federal government extended legal deposit to online maps and publications. Library and Archives Canada provided two options for online documents—restricted and open access—and encouraged publishers to choose open access.[35] At the provincial level, new legislation from the Manitoba government established the Legislative Library as the official site for deposit of Manitoba government publications, including electronic formats.[36]

In September the Canadian Institutes of Health Research (CIHR) unveiled its new policy promoting public access to the results of research it has funded. The policy required CIHR researchers to ensure that their original research articles become freely available online within six months of publication.[37] CARL and the Canadian Library Association (CLA) both responded positively to the announcement.

CLA also took a position on open access and approved a policy providing for full and immediate open access for all CLA publications with the exception of its publication *Feliciter* and monographs. The embargo period for *Feliciter* was one issue (*Feliciter* is published six times a year), with monographs being considered for open access publishing on a case-by-case basis.

CLA actively encouraged its members to self-archive in institutional and/or disciplinary repositories.[38]

Following the 2006 firings of the editor and deputy editor of the *Canadian Medical Association Journal*, a number of members of the publication's editorial board resigned. They launched a new open access journal, *Open Medicine*, in 2007, without corporate or medical association ownership.[39]

Digital Divide

Ipsos Reid released a study, "Older Canadians and the Internet," which found that older Canadians were significantly behind other age groups in use of online resources. Only 61 percent of Canadians over the age of 55 had access to the Internet, compared with 88 percent of adults aged 18 to 54. Another finding: older adults were more likely to participate in online courses, managing investments, and earning degrees and diplomas than younger users.[40] In another study of technology skills, Ipsos Reid found that only 1 in 3 (32 percent) of Canadians felt that they were expert or very skilled at using the Internet, a small increase since 2001 when the figure was 27 percent. The two most frequently used sources of information for keeping up with technology news were family and friends (25 percent) and newspaper articles (23 percent).[41]

The federal government announced another year of funding for its Community Access Program (CAP), which seeks to provide Canadians with affordable public access to the Internet through public libraries and other community organizations, and with the skills they need to use the Internet. Funding was extended for the 2007–2008 fiscal year, with priority given to CAP sites that provide support for public access, have demonstrated success in reaching Canadians who face the digital divide, support other service delivery objectives of the federal government, and support access for people with disabilities.[42]

Censorship

After review by a board-established Challenged Materials Committee, the Dufferin Peel (Ontario) Catholic School Board decided not to ban David Guterson's *Snow Falling on Cedars* following a parental complaint about crude language in the novel.[43]

In Saskatchewan, a school library in Kindersley banned Nikki Tate's *Trouble on Tarragon Island* following a complaint that the novel contained the word *bazoongas,* a slang term for breasts.[44]

Concerns about Philip Pullman's *The Golden Compass* led to the book being pulled from the Peterborough (Ontario) Catholic School. At the same time, the Peterborough Public Library reported brisk circulation for the title.[45] The Halton District (Ontario) School Board also banned the title, as well as the companion titles in Pullman's trilogy.[46] In Alberta, the Calgary Catholic School Board also removed *The Golden Compass.*[47]

In November the London (Ontario) Public Library Board voted to continue filtering sexually explicit content on the majority of its public access Internet workstations. Unfiltered access will still be available at all of the library's 16 locations, with a minimum of 1 unfiltered workstation in all communities. The decision marked the end of a five-month test project that began in June.[48]

Reports

Hill Strategies released its analysis of the Statistics Canada survey of household spending during 2005, "Consumer Spending on Culture in Canada, the Provinces and 15 Metropolitan Areas." Reading materials ranked second at C$4.8 billion, or 19 percent of total cultural spending, well behind the C$13 billion (52 percent) spent on home entertainment equipment and services. The figure for reading materials had increased by 26 percent since 1997, a greater increase than inflation, but less than the overall increase in cultural spending of 48 percent.[49]

Statistics Canada published its service bulletin, *Periodical Publishing: Data Tables 2005,* which documented an overall decline in the profit margins of Canadian periodicals publishers, from 13 percent in 2004 to 8.7 percent in 2005. Publishers in British Columbia enjoyed the highest margins in 2005 at 10.7 percent; Atlantic Canada had the lowest, at 3.8 percent.[50]

Events

In September Library and Archives Canada (LAC) presented the National Library of Australia with a theater playbill from 1796, the earliest surviving document printed in Australia. It was found at LAC, in a scrapbook of mainly Canadian ephemera.[51]

The Winnipeg-based Hudson's Bay Archives (1670 to 1920) were included in the United Nations Educational, Scientific and Cultural Organization's (UNESCO's) Memory of the World Registry. The archives are the record of the Hudson's Bay Company from its beginnings, through the development of the fur trade and North American settlement, to the business environment of the 20th century.[52]

The University of Manitoba Libraries acquired the only extant copy of a public notice dated December 6, 1868, asking for financial help for 435 families in the Red River settlement, where the crops, buffalo hunt, and fisheries had all failed.[53]

In Alberta, Red Crow College Library became the first First Nations institution to join the Alberta Library. The library has been the vehicle for delivering the Lois Hole Campus Alberta Digital Library to all postsecondary institutions in the province, with some 4.5 million licensed items.[54]

Three Canadian libraries were seriously affected by fires. In March Springhill (Nova Scotia) Public Library closed to deal with smoke- and water-damaged books as the result of a fire that started in the basement.[55] The contents of the library at Victoria School of Performing and Visual Arts in Edmonton were destroyed in April by a fire that was deliberately set; a suspect was charged with arson.[56] In September Saint John (New Brunswick) Free Public Library had a fire set by two 12-year-old boys using the book return slot.[57]

The Labrador City (Newfoundland and Labrador) Public Library was closed as the result of broken pipes under the building,[58] and a Saskatchewan January blizzard caused Saskatoon Public Library to close for two full days.[59]

The British Columbia Legislature Library closed in spring 2007 for an indefinite period so that the building can undergo a seismic upgrade. The collections were relocated, and were not expected to return after completion of the upgrade because the space will be converted to offices for members of the legislative assembly.[60]

Library and Archives Canada (LAC) reduced its public service hours in September, leading to a petition signed by more than 500 graduate students whose productivity was affected.[61] The Canadian Historical Association, the Canadian Library Association, and Canadian authors also wrote the National Librarian and Archivist to protest the change. LAC announced restoration of the hours in November.[62]

Toronto Public Library Board voted in July to save C$1.2 million by closing 16 branches on Sundays and by purchasing fewer items for its collection.[63] A local union filed a grievance because of the proposed loss of wages and benefits, and the arbitrator's ruling supported the grievance.[64] In October the board voted to restore Sunday hours.[65]

The year saw a number of labor strikes in Canadian libraries. The Universities of Saskatchewan and Regina saw 30 days of job action by support staff in November and December.[66] Vancouver Public Library unionized staff were on strike from late July to October over pay equity issues with other city workers,[67] and job action reduced services at eight branches of the Greater Victoria (British Columbia) Public Library in October, also over pay equity issues.[68]

Initiatives

In November LAC launched its Web archive. LAC has been harvesting the Web domain of the federal government since 2005 on a semiannual basis, and this was a first step in a broader strategy with respect to Canadian Web sites.[69]

In October the federal government announced C$3 million over three years for LAC to develop an implementation strategy to improve access to information for those who cannot read traditional print, with emphasis on using public libraries for production and dissemination.[70]

The Canadian National Institute for the Blind (CNIB) closed its books-on-cassette service in March and moved to the digital library model, including electronic books, DAISY talking books, streamed audio via the Internet, and newspapers online and by telephone.[71]

After much discussion in 2007, early in 2008 the board of the Canadian Association of Research Libraries voted to merge Canadiana.org and Alouette-Canada into a single organization, Canadiana.org. The two organizations both supported national digitization projects.[72] AlouetteCanada had served as the vehicle for developing a metadata toolkit project using Canadian Heritage funding. The merger followed the dissolution of the Canadian Initiative on Digital Libraries (CIDL) in March 2007.

The Bibliothèque et Archives Nationales du Québec (BAnQ) announced in December that it had signed an agreement with Publicité Sauvage, an ad agency specializing in commercial posters. BAnQ will receive, display, and preserve two copies of each poster created.[73]

Nunavut Public Library Services launched its Online Book Club, which delivers books electronically. Each Monday through Friday the library e-mails subscribers a portion of a book that takes about three to five minutes to read.[74]

Toronto Public Library (TPL) announced a partnership designed to improve access to the city's arts and cultural institutions. Those holding a TPL card are able to borrow a "museum and arts pass" from the library. The pass enables a family of two adults and five children to visit one of five significant Toronto-area museums.[75] Ottawa Public Library offered a similar service to its community.[76]

The University of Prince Edward Island launched its Virtual Research Environment (VRE), providing support for the full range of activities in the knowledge-creation life cycle. More than 20 research groups were taking advantage of the VRE system.[77]

The University of British Columbia Library launched its Library Vault digital collection. The site provides access to rare books, manuscripts, fine art, maps, and archival material that is stored in climate-controlled environments across the campus.[78]

Sources

1. http://www.fin.gc.ca/news07/07-022e.html.

2. http://www.budget.gc.ca/2007/index_e.html.

3. http://www.cbc.ca/news/background/economy/loonie.html.

4. http://www.publishers.ca/pricing-statement.htm.

5. http://www.statcan.ca/Daily/English/080131/d080131a.htm.

6. http://www.culture.gov.on.ca/english/about/n270407.htm.

7. http://www.culture.gov.on.ca/english/about/n160807.htm.

8. http://www.culture.gov.on.ca/english/about/n020207_3.htm.

9. http://www.mb.ndp.ca/index.php?q=newsArticle&ArticlePageID=110.

10. http://www2.news.gov.bc.ca/news_releases_2005-2009/2007EDU0136-001247.htm.

11. http://www2.news.gov.bc.ca/news_releases_2005-2009/2007EDU0009-000064.htm.

12. http://www.slyck.com/story1380_Rumours_Circulate_Canadian_Copyright_Reform_ Imminent.

13. http://www.cbc.ca/arts/story/2007/03/07/senators-piracy.html?ref=rss.

14. http://www.counterfeitlawblog.com/archives/canada-us-ambassador-urges-canada-to-strengthen-copyright-laws-to-stem-piracy.html.

15. http://www.cbc.ca/arts/film/story/2007/05/08/warner-preview-cancel.html.

16. http://www.tbs-sct.gc.ca/dpr-rmr/2006-2007/inst/pch/pch01-eng.asp.

17. http://www.theglobeandmail.com/servlet/ArticleNews/freeheadlines/LAC/20070531/PIRACY31/national/National.

18. http://www.pch.gc.ca/pc-ch/news-comm/CBO070615_e.htm.

19. http://www.cbc.ca/consumer/story/2007/02/14/software-warnings.html.

20. http://www.canada.com/components/print.aspx?id=971573e1-1357-4015-872d-67ebd326771e.

21. http://www.cbc.ca/arts/music/story/2007/11/19/copyright-law.html?ref=rss.

22. http://www.rcmp-grc.gc.ca/fio/ipo_guide_e.htm#policy.

23. http://www2.parl.gc.ca/HousePublications/Publication.aspx?Language=E&Mode=1&Parl=39&Ses=2&DocId=3187201&File=4.

24. http://www.cbc.ca/technology/story/2007/12/10/tech-copyright.html.

25. http://www.cbc.ca/canada/story/2007/12/13/tech-copyright-delay.html.

26. http://www.cb-cda.gc.ca/new-e.html.

27. http://www.cnw.ca/fr/releases/archive/November2007/15/c8764.html.

28. http://www.nationalpost.com/story-printer.html?id=235987.

29. http://arstechnica.com/news.ars/post/20070917-cria-about-face-on-ipod-levies-tied-to-concerns-over-legitimizing-downloads.html.

30. http://www.financialpost.com/story.html?id=9cdcf5b0-f2e2-48c3-b286-832236ccccf7&k=76096.

31. http://www.cb-cda.gc.ca/decisions/c20071218-b.pdf.

32. http://www.statcan.ca/english/freepub/87F0008XIE/2006001/part2.htm.

33. http://www.ic.gc.ca/epic/site/ippd-dppi.nsf/en/h_ip01456e.html.

34. http://www.nrcan-rncan.gc.ca/media/newsreleases/2007/200728_e.htm.

35. http://www.collectionscanada.ca/electroniccollection/003008-1000-e.html.

36. http://www.gov.mb.ca/chc/press/top/2007/12/2007-12-03-140500-2715.html.

37. http://www.cihr-irsc.gc.ca/e/34851.html.

38. http://cla.informz.net/cla/archives/archive_155065.html.

39. http://www.openmedicine.ca.

40. http://www.ipsos-na.com/news/pressrelease.cfm?id=3365.

41. http://www.ipsos-na.com/news/pressrelease.cfm?id=3405.

42. http://ic.gc.ca/cmb/welcomeic.nsf/261ce500dfcd7259852564820068dc6d/85256a5d006b9720852572f2005128b5!OpenDocument.

43. http://www.mississauga.com/mi/news/story/3870885p-4478062c.html.

44. Chamberlain, Adrian, "They Don't Allow 'Bazoongas' in Kindersley," *Edmonton Journal,* July 6, 2007, p. A5.

45. http://www.thepeterboroughexaminer.com/PrintArticle.aspx?e=789164.

46. http://www.cbc.ca/arts/books/story/2007/12/20/pullman-compass-ban.html?ref=rss.

47. http://www.theglobeandmail.com/servlet/story/RTGAM.20071205.wgoldcompass1205/BNStory/National.

48. http://www.londonpubliclibrary.ca/node/353.

49. http://www.hillstrategies.com/resources_details.php?resUID=1000215.

50. http://www.statcan.ca/english/freepub/87F0005XIE/87F0005XIE2006001.pdf.

51. http://www.nla.gov.au/pressrel/canada.html.

52. http://news.gov.mb.ca/news/index.html?archive=2007-06-01&item=1838.

53. "Settlers Pleaded for Aid to Survive Manitoba Winter," *Edmonton Journal,* July 7, 2007, p. A7.

54. http://www.thealbertalibrary.ab.ca/files/Red-Crow-release_1107.doc.

55. http://thechronicleherald.ca/Search/565644.html.

56. http://www.canada.com/edmontonjournal/news/story.html?id=96068195-924f-4017-bd6f-2569fe37ad5c&k=19250.

57. http://www.cbc.ca/canada/new-brunswick/story/2007/09/19/nb-libraryfire.html.

58. http://www.cbc.ca/canada/newfoundland-labrador/story/2007/03/30/plumbing-library.html.

59. http://www.saskatoonlibrary.ca/pdf/Blizzardshutsdownlibraries.pdf.

60. http://www.canada.com/victoriatimescolonist/news/story.html?id=375548cd-cb33-49d2-8acf-9749308d9bbb&k=64944.

61. http://petitiononline.com/history8/petition.html.

62. http://www.collectionscanada.gc.ca/whats-new/013-316-e.html.

63. http://www.thestar.com/printArticle/239972.

64. http://www.torontopubliclibrary.ca/new_arc_07oct15_sun.jsp.

65. http://www.theglobeandmail.com/servlet/story/RTGAM.20071016.wcouncil16/BNStory/National.

66. http://www.canada.com/reginaleaderpost/news/story.html?id=cc711e2a-2ade-42b9-bb7e-c407c637c9cd.

67. http://www.cbc.ca/canada/british-columbia/story/2007/10/22/bc-librariesopening.html.

68. http://www.canada.com/victoriatimescolonist/news/story.html?id=da276010-a2b6-4499-a887-ee84757f1749&k=14803.

69. http://www.collectionscanada.ca/webarchives/index-e.html.

70. http://cla.ca/AM/Template.cfm?Section=Home&CONTENTID=3968&TEMPLATE=/CM/ContentDisplay.cfm.

71. http://www.cnib.ca/en/services/library/about/digital-transformation/Default.aspx.

72. "AlouetteCanada Merger with Canadiana.org Under Discussion," *Canadiana.org Bulletin,* December 2007, p.1.

73. http://communiques.gouv.qc.ca/gouvqc/communiques/ME/Decembre2007/03/c6613.html.

74. http://www.publiclibraries.nu.ca/bookclub.html.

75. http://www.newswire.ca/en/releases/archive/June2007/27/c9555.html.

76. http://www.biblioottawalibrary.ca/explore/about/partners_e.html#museum.

77. http://www.upei.ca/library/OffTheShelf-September2007.pdf.

78. http://www.publicaffairs.ubc.ca/ubcreports/2007/07dec06/vault.html.

Special Libraries Association

331 South Patrick St., Alexandria, VA 22314
703-647-4900, fax 703-647-4901, e-mail sla@sla.org
World Wide Web http://www.sla.org

Janice R. Lachance
Chief Executive Officer

Founded in 1909 and headquartered in Alexandria, Virginia, the Special Libraries Association (SLA) is the premier global organization for innovative information professionals and their strategic partners. As an international professional association, SLA represents thousands of information experts in 83 countries who collect, analyze, evaluate, package, and disseminate information to facilitate strategic decision making.

SLA members work in various settings including Fortune 500 companies, consulting firms, government agencies, not-for-profit organizations, technical and academic institutions, museums, law firms, and medical facilities. SLA promotes and strengthens its members through learning, advocacy, and networking initiatives.

SLA's Core Values

Leadership—Strengthening members' roles as information leaders in their organizations and communities, including shaping information policy and the ethical use and gathering of information

Service—Responding to clients' needs, adding qualitative and quantitative value to information services and products

Innovation and continuous learning—Embracing innovative solutions for the enhancement of services and intellectual advancement within the profession

Results and accountability—Delivering measurable results in the information economy and members' organizations; the association and its members are expected to operate with the highest level of ethics and honesty

Collaboration and partnering—Providing opportunities to meet, communicate, collaborate, and partner within the information industry and the business community

Chapters, Divisions, and Caucuses

SLA chapters provide a network of information professionals across local communities and regions; SLA divisions link members with information professionals within specific areas of expertise. SLA membership includes participation in one chapter and one division. For a nominal fee, members can join additional chapters, divisions, and caucuses (a caucus is an informal network focusing on a discipline or interest not covered in other divisions).

SLA has 58 regional chapters in the United States, Canada, Europe, Asia, and the Middle East; 25 divisions representing a variety of industries; and 11 special-interest caucuses.

The association is governed by a board of directors elected by the membership. As representatives of that membership, the directors are the primary force pressing the association to the realization of its opportunities for service and the fulfillment of its obligations to the membership, to the association as a single entity, and to the library and information services profession. The board and the association both operate on a calendar year, with newly elected officers, as well as chapter and division leaders, taking office in January.

Programs and Services

Click University

SLA's Click University, launched in 2005, is the first and only online learning community focusing on continuing professional education for librarians and information professionals. Click U is primarily designed to provide SLA members with state-of-the-art learning opportunities in partnership with information industry experts. Courses on software and technology, management, communications, and leadership are designed to enhance the skills acquired through traditional library education.

Click University provides certificate programs for information professionals looking to take the next step into a new career and utilize their traditional information skills in fields such as competitive intelligence, knowledge management, and copyright management.

Click U is constantly adding programs and courses for SLA members. Courses are available on topics ranging from public speaking to copyright law. Many courses involve a small fee to members, but SLA is also committed to providing many options free of charge. A sampling of the programs available free to members:

- Gary Price's Research Tool Box, which defines the latest tools, trends, resources, and tricks available on the Internet
- Course of the Month, which offers the opportunity to take part in a new Click University experience
- Leadership and Management Library from ebrary, a complimentary collection of resources for SLA members only, containing more than 900 titles

SLA also offers in-person training and continuing education at its Annual Conference and INFO-EXPO. SLA workshops (half day) and learning forums (full day) are designed to educate and inspire participants to make an impact in their organizations.

Advocacy

SLA serves the profession by advocating publicly on its value and its values. Whether by communicating with executives and hiring professionals about the important role that information professionals play in the workplace or by sharing the views and opinions of the membership with government officials worldwide, SLA exists to represent the profession and perpetuate its existence.

Public Policy Program

Government bodies and related international organizations play a critical role in establishing the legal and social framework within which SLA members conduct information services. Because of the importance of governments and international organizations to its membership, SLA maintains an active public policy program. SLA staff and the SLA Public Policy Advisory Council monitor and proactively work to shape legislation and regulatory proposals that affect SLA's membership.

SLA supports government policies that

- Strike a fair and equitable balance among the rights and interests of all parties in the creation, distribution, and use of information and other intellectual property
- Strengthen the library and information management operations of government agencies
- Promote access to government public information through the application of modern technologies and sound information management practices
- Encourage the development and application of new information and communications technologies to improve library services, information services, and information management
- Protect individual intellectual freedom and the confidentiality of library records, safeguard freedom of expression, and oppose government censorship
- Foster international exchange of information

With regard to the actions of government bodies and related international organizations in the policy areas listed above, the association will

- Monitor executive, legislative, and judicial actions and initiatives at the national and international level, and, to the extent practical, at the subnational level
- Educate key decision-makers on the concerns of SLA's membership
- Provide timely updates to the membership on critical issues and actions
- Encourage members to influence actions by expressing their opinions
- Develop cooperative relationships with like-minded organizations so as to expand SLA's visibility and impact

Legislative Action Center

A Legislative Action Center tool on the SLA Web site allows members to monitor legislation and activities at the U.S. federal level. The Legislative Action Center provides automated and electronic outreach to elected officials in an effort to shape legislation and regulatory proposals that affect SLA's membership.

Employment and Career Services

The association provides members with the robust and constantly changing online SLA Career Center. The center offers a variety of services to meet the needs of members including career coaching, articles and resources, and career disruption assistance mentoring. Additionally, the center includes a job bank that serves the needs of employers and of SLA members looking for employment.

SLA Career Connection combines the power of the Web with the power of the face-to-face meeting. By participating online in SLA Career Connection, job seekers and employers are able to connect regarding job opportunities and meet face-to-face at the next SLA Annual Conference.

Information Center

The SLA Information Center provides access to resources created to assist members in their day-to-day tasks and management decisions and in their roles as SLA leaders. Among the Information Center's most successful and popular resources are

- Information Portals—links to articles, Web sites, books, and other resources on more than 40 topics
- News Connections—the latest industry news items, summarized by topic
- Recent reports on information industry issues
- Research and surveys to help with benchmarking and strategic planning
- SLA Podcast Center, containing audio files from SLA Career Center experts as well as tips from the pages of the SLA magazine *Information Outlook*
- SLA Leadership Center, which facilitates the leadership experience by guiding members through the resources created on best practices, training, guidelines, and responsibilities and offers links to resources relevant to the operation and management of special libraries

Professional and Student Networks

SLA's student groups are located throughout the world and are affiliated with accredited graduate schools of library and information science. Through membership in SLA, students gain valuable professional experience and make important industry contacts.

Publications

SLA's monthly magazine *Information Outlook* provides news, features, and evaluation of trends in information management. The association also provides members with *SLA Connections* e-newsletters, which cover information industry breaking news, association news, and updates on Click University.

SLA Honors and Awards Program

The SLA Awards and Honors Program was created in 1948 to honor exceptional individuals, achievements, and contributions to the association and the information profession. Each year, SLA seeks out and recognizes the best and brightest stars in the information profession from across the globe. The purpose of the program is to bring attention to the important work of special librarians and information professionals within the corporate and academic setting. The association offers 12 such awards annually. In addition, SLA awards $30,000 each year to at least five students who have demonstrated their ability and desire to contribute to the special librarian and information management field. SLA's Scholarship Program consists of awards for graduate study leading to a master's degree, graduate study leading to a Ph.D., and for post-M.L.S. study. The association also offers grants for research projects for the advancement of library sciences; the support of programs developed by SLA chapters, divisions, or committees; and the support of the association's expanding international agenda. Additionally, grants, scholarships, and stipends are offered by many of SLA's chapters and divisions. [For a list of the winners of SLA's awards and grants, see Library Scholarship and Award Recipients, 2007 in Part 3—*Ed.*]

SLA Events and Conferences

SLA Annual Conference and INFO-EXPO

SLA's Annual Conference brings together thousands of information professionals from around the world and provides a forum for discussion of issues shaping the information industry. The conference offers more than 400 events, programs, panel discussions, and seminars, and includes an exhibit hall that in 2007 featured more than 400 companies.

Exhibition and attendance figures for the 2007 SLA Annual Conference and INFO-EXPO held in Denver June 3–6 exceeded expectations. Every chapter, worldwide, was represented. Final attendance figures for SLA 2007 totaled 5,047 individuals representing 41 nations.

The opening session culminated with a keynote address by former U.S. Vice President Al Gore, who urged his audience to become involved in helping countries around the world in navigating matters of information access.

The 2008 Annual Conference and INFO-EXPO was set for June 15–18 in Seattle with the theme Breaking Rules, Building Bridges.

SLA Leadership Summit

The annual SLA Leadership Summit is held in January at the beginning of the association year. SLA members come together with hundreds of leaders of the association, its chapters, divisions, sections, caucuses, and committees. Attendees learn skills to prepare for the year of leadership ahead, and participants are offered an introduction to new technologies, new concepts for the future of SLA, leadership training, and networking opportunities.

Part 2
Legislation, Funding, and Grants

Legislation

Legislation and Regulations Affecting Libraries in 2007

Emily Sheketoff
Executive Director, Washington Office, American Library Association

Appropriations

Congress passed a fiscal year (FY) 2008 Labor, Health and Human Services, Education and Related Agencies appropriations (Labor-HHS) bill in 2007. Despite the extremely tight budget environment, in which many programs were cut significantly or eliminated altogether, the conference report funded the Institute of Museum and Library Services (IMLS) at $277,131,000, an increase of $29,926,000. The Library Services and Technology Act (LSTA) was funded at $224,066,000, with $171,500,000 for the State Grant program.

Unfortunately, President George W. Bush vetoed the bill and the House was unable to override the veto. Congress combined the 11 remaining appropriations bills into an omnibus bill and, to avoid another veto, lowered the funding levels for many programs. The bill also included a 1.74 percent across-the-board cut.

The conference agreement also includes language that gives IMLS the authority and resources to carry out the mission of the National Commission on Libraries and Information Science (NCLIS) and includes $400,000 for NCLIS's closeout activities. [For a report on NCLIS's final year, see "National Commission on Libraries and Information Science" in Part 1—*Ed.*] Language in the bill also calls for the National Center for Education Statistics (NCES) survey on libraries to be moved from the Department of Education to IMLS. The president signed the omnibus appropriations bill in December.

School Libraries

A major part of the American Library Association's (ALA's) school libraries effort involves the Strengthening Kids' Interest in Learning and Libraries (SKILLs) Act, part of No Child Left Behind (NCLB).

The SKILLs Act (H.R. 2864, S. 1699) requires school districts, to the extent feasible, to ensure that every school within the district employs at least one state-certified school library media specialist in each school library. In addition, the SKILLs Act broadens the focus of training, professional development, and recruitment activities to include school library media specialists, and ensures that

Table 1 / Funding for Federal Library and Related Programs, FY 2008
(amounts in thousands)

Funding for Selected Programs	FY 2007	FY 2008
Institute of Museum and Library Services	$210,597	$263,508
Grants to State Library Agencies	163,746	160,855
National Commission on Libraries and Information Science (NCLIS)	983	400
GPO—Office of Superintendent of Documents	33,000	35,000
Library of Congress	508,000	562,000
Talking Book Program	0	12,500
National Archives	341,000	411,000
Department of Education		
Title I, Grants to Local Education Agencies (ESEA I-A)	12,713,125	13,898,875
Even Start (ESEA I-B-3)	111,584	66,545
Reading First State Grants (ESEA I-B-1)	1,018,692	393,012
Early Reading First (ESEA I-B-2)	103,118	112,549
Striving Readers Initiative	31,596	35,371
Improving Literacy Through School Libraries (ESEA I-B-4)	19,486	19,145
Education Technology (ESEA II-D-1 &2)	273,062	267,494
21st Century Community Learning Centers (ESEA IV-B)	981,180	1,081,166
Innovative Education Program Strategies (ESEA V-Part A)	99,183	0
Inexpensive Book Distribution (RIF) (ESEA V-D, 5)	25,043	23,831
Special Education (IDEA) State Grants	10,491,941	10,947,511
Adult Education and Literacy State Grants	564,074	554,122
Adult Education National Leadership	9,096	9,878
Institute of Education Sciences		
Educational Research	162,535	159,696
Educational Statistics	89,952	88,494
Educational Assessment	93,117	104,063
Other Agencies & Programs		
Head Start (HHS)	6,789,000	6,900,000
National Endowment for the Arts	124,000	145,000
National Endowment for the Humanities	139,000	145,000

funds will serve elementary, middle, and high school students. Finally, it requires books and materials to be appropriate for and engage the interest of students in all grade levels and students with special learning needs, including English-language learners.

Multiple studies have affirmed that there is a clear link between school library media programs that are staffed by a school library media specialist and student academic achievement. Across the United States, research has shown that students in schools with good school libraries learn more, get better grades, and score higher on standardized tests than their peers in schools without libraries. Because NCLB does not highlight the direct correlation between school library media specialists and increased student academic achievement, library resource budgets are increasingly being used to mitigate the effects of budgetary constraints.

Head Start

In a major victory for libraries and the cause of literacy, the president signed into law the Improving Head Start Act. Head Start is a comprehensive child-development program with the aim of increasing the school readiness of young children of low-income families.

With members of the Association for Library Service to Children, a division of ALA, ALA advocated for language to be included in the bill that provides opportunities for libraries to play a greater role in Head Start programs. That language was included in the final bill. By recognizing the important role that public libraries play in improving literacy and school readiness in the Head Start reauthorization bill, libraries across the country can continue to develop innovative programs to provide young children with the tools they need to succeed in school and life.

Higher Education

For more than a year, ALA has been working with U.S. Sen. Jack Reed (D-R.I.) and U.S. Rep. Xavier Becerra (D-Calif.) on student loan forgiveness for librarians. In April 2007 the Librarian Incentive to Boost Recruitment and Retention in Areas of Need (LIBRARIAN) Act of 2007 was introduced in both the Senate and the House. It would apply to full-time librarians with MLS degrees who have worked in low-income areas for the last five years.

This was one of several bills dealing with federal student loan forgiveness emerging during the year. Another from which librarians benefit is the College Cost Reduction Act of 2007. In September House and Senate conferees reached an agreement on this bill. The legislation creates a new student loan forgiveness plan through the Direct Loan program for public service employees. Qualifying areas of employment include librarians. The president signed the bill. Under the program, the Secretary of Education shall forgive the remaining loan balance for a borrower who has been employed in a public sector job and making payments on such loans for a period of 10 years (which need not be consecutive). Such borrowers shall be eligible to have one-tenth of the remaining loan balance forgiven for each of the 10 years in which the borrowers have made payments.

As this report was being prepared, Congress was reauthorizing the Higher Education Act. The Senate version included Perkins loan forgiveness for public or school librarians who serve in an area of high need (areas that receive Title I funding). A percentage of the loan was to be forgiven each year over a period of five years. This bill adopts language and criteria used in the LIBRARIAN Act.

The latest bill was introduced by House Education and Labor Committee Chairman George Miller (D-Calif.). It includes a program designed to encourage students to enter vital public service jobs by authorizing up to $2,000 a year for five years in loan forgiveness for public service employees, including librarians who work in a public library or a high-need school.

Copyright

Legislation

In 2007 several hearings were held regarding piracy and filtering technology, copyright education, and the role of higher education in policing institutional networks. Even though data indicates that the bulk of piracy occurs overseas, Congress continued to focus on the individual consumer of protected content with a special scrutiny of college students.

The Freedom and Innovation Revitalizing U.S. Entrepreneurship (FAIR USE) Act of 2007 stalled in the House Judiciary Committee. This bill would amend the Digital Millennium Copyright Act (DMCA) by codifying the Library of Congress exceptions for circumvention of technological measures identified in Section 1201 rulemakings and requiring rights holders to label works that contain technological controls. Rights holders vehemently opposed versions of this bill, introduced in each of the last three congressional sessions by Rep. Rick Boucher (D-Va.).

A number of bills aimed at boosting copyright enforcement were introduced in both the House and the Senate. The Prioritizing Resources and Organization for Intellectual Property (PRO-IP) Act of 2007, about which ALA signed on to a letter of opposition, seemed to lose traction. Its purpose was to create a new United States Intellectual Property Enforcement Representative, appointed by the president, a new Intellectual Property Enforcement Division in the Department of Justice, and additional intellectual property attachés assigned to U.S. embassies, all paid for with U.S. tax dollars. In addition, the bill would ratchet up statutory damages for infringement of compilations, such as a CD with 12 songs, by increasing statutory damages tenfold in some cases. Critics said the bill would not curtail piracy originating overseas because only 1 percent of imported cargo is examined upon entry into the United States. The bill would also ease the requirements of copyright registration in order for rights holders to bring infringement proceedings prior to registering their works (currently a requirement for statutory damage awards). Further, ALA argued that the PRO-IP bill would likely chill innovation and fair use.

There was no congressional action on "orphan works" legislation in the latter half of 2007. Orphan works are those for which a copyright holder cannot be identified or contacted. Legislation would practically eliminate any risk associated with using protected works when a "reasonable search" fails to identify the rights holder.

Section 108 Study

The Library of Congress Study Group on Section 108 of the Copyright Act—which provides limited exceptions for libraries and archives—did not complete its report on proposed changes to the section to account for the digital environment. The Library of Congress and the Copyright Office initiated the study in April 2005 by appointing a Study Group representing both rights holders and users of protected works. During that time, ALA's Washington Office prepared two reports with comments (http://www.ala.org/ala/washoff/woissues/copyrightb/section108/Section108.cfm) for the Study Group and participated in two public roundtables. Unfortunately, at this writing, the number of library representatives in the group had decreased; ALA's representative had moved overseas, and a noted member of the group, copyright scholar and law librarian Robert L. Oakley, died in late September.

International Copyright

At the September 2007 meeting of the General Assembly of the World Intellectual Property Organization (WIPO), the delegates voted to continue work on a "development agenda" that would bring developing nations into an intellectual property legal framework, and on traditional knowledge and cultural expression, which would consider intellectual property protection for traditional knowledge such as folklore. These activities will have a profound effect on world trade and access to information as well as the United States' own copyright and patent laws.

ALA's Office for Information Technology Policy (OITP) worked with the Library Copyright Alliance—a coalition of five library associations cooperating to address copyright issues that affect libraries and their patrons—to further international copyright advocacy for libraries through its International Copyright Advocate program. Three advocates were named to the program, which was established in 2007. The International Copyright Advocate initiative was established to broaden library representation at international copyright meetings, at which copyright activities have intensified. In addition to ALA, the alliance involves the American Association of Law Libraries, the Association of Research Libraries, the Medical Library Association, and the Special Libraries Association.

Complaint on Misleading Copyright Notices

In fall 2007 OITP collected data in support of the Computer and Communications Industry Association (CCIA) complaint to the Federal Trade Commission (FTC) regarding false and misleading copyright warnings provided by publishers and motion picture distributors. A misleading copyright notice is a copyright statement that overstates the authority of copyright holders and their legal control over use of protected works. An example is "for home use only," which is consistently used by the motion picture industry at the beginning of a video or DVD whether the DVD is rented or owned. "Home-use-only" videos can be used in the face-to-face classroom (17 U.S.C. §110(1)), and, to a lesser extent, in the distance-education classroom (§110(2)) because of exemptions provided to nonprofit educational institutions. Another example of a misleading copyright notice is "all rights reserved" printed on the verso of a book of public domain materials. False copyright warnings confuse library patrons and can lead to schools and colleges mistakenly purchasing additional rights to use a work that are not required by law.

Telecommunications and the Internet

Education v. Filtering—Interactive Web Sites

A major shift in the approach to children's Internet safety issues was welcomed in new bills. Some of the same proponents of blocking and filtering at the beginning of the first session of the 110th Congress later shifted their support to an "education" approach to Internet safety. Fall 2007 saw clear recognition by some members of Congress that Internet education surpasses mandated blocking and filtering requirements. ALA's Office of Government Relations (OGR) monitored these bills closely, including the follow proposals:

- A bill "to Direct the Attorney General to Provide Grants for Internet Safety Education Programs" (H.R. 3577), sponsored by Rep. Linda Sanchez (D-Calif.)
- The "Safeguarding America's Families by Enhancing and Reorganizing New and Efficient Technology Act of 2007" (H.R. 3461) bill introduced by Rep. Melissa Bean (D-Ill.) that would establish a public-awareness campaign on Internet safety; it includes in program activities a national outreach and education campaign, and information access and exchange
- The "Safer Net Act" (H.R. 1008), also sponsored by Bean, that would "improve public awareness in the United States regarding safe use of the Internet through the establishment of an Office of Internet Safety and Public Awareness within the Federal Trade Commission"
- The "Protecting Children in the 21st Century Act" (S. 1965), sponsored by Sen. Ted Stevens (R-Alaska), the stated purpose of which is "To protect children from cybercrimes, including crimes by online predators, to enhance efforts to identify and eliminate child pornography, and to help parents shield their children from material that is inappropriate for minors" (there is a companion bill in the house)
- The e-KIDS Act of 2007 (H.R. 3871), a bill introduced by Rep. Brad Ellsworth (D-Ind.) that would require certain schools having computers with Internet access that receive services at discounted rates (the so-called E-rate) to certify that they are educating children about appropriate online behavior

Report on Public Library Connectivity

OITP completed a study that provides findings and recommendations on improving broadband connectivity in public libraries. The study team of Rick Weingarten and Mark Bard, with consultants Nancy Bolt and John Windhausen, and Lynne Bradley of ALA's OGR, identified a number of difficult challenges.

These include the varying needs across states, the need for training and support, the lack of understanding of why public libraries need broadband, and the need for planning. Collaboration and aggregation among public libraries and multiple funding models can help to mitigate some of these challenges. Regional library cooperatives will almost certainly be a key part of this solution, as a 2007 meeting of cooperatives in Denver indicated. The report is available at http://www.ala.org/ala/washoff/oitp/papersa/public_version_final.pdf. This study was supported by a grant from the Bill and Melinda Gates Foundation.

Broadband

While there was much discussion and some oversight hearings about broadband deployment at the Federal Communications Commission (FCC), in Congress, and elsewhere, there was little real action in terms of legislation or regulation. ALA held various discussions about libraries' needs for "big broadband" with Capitol Hill offices, potential allies, and others, especially as the results of the OITP connectivity study became available. The promotion of broadband deployment and ensuring that libraries have ubiquitous and affordable connectivity to advanced services remains an ongoing high priority for ALA.

Universal Service and the E-Rate

Key stakeholders, such as Verizon and AT&T, became publicly rather silent about Universal Service Fund (USF) reform during the first session of the 110th Congress. While parts of the industry claimed to want to stabilize USF, on the whole it appeared that opening the USF debate threatened them more than the gains they might make—not an unusual dynamic given the pace of telecommunications reform in general.

However, it also meant that these stakeholders did not support a permanent exemption for FCC from compliance with the Anti-Deficiency Act (ADA), which sets government accounting rules relating to cash flow. ALA supported a permanent exemption so that E-rate and other USF programs would not be frozen because of the requirements of ADA. However, Congress did pass another one-year exemption by tacking the provision onto the omnibus appropriations package.

ALA proposed a major simplification of the E-rate application and disbursement process to FCC in October 2005. During 2007 ALA continued to meet with stakeholders and decision-makers to explain the proposal and seek its approval. There were several meetings at FCC and with the K–12 E-rate community, as well as with a large group of service providers. It was hoped that FCC would issue a rule on simplification in 2008.

Digital Television Transition

On February 19, 2009, free over-the-air analog television broadcasting as we know it will end as the United States transitions to an all-digital signal. The impact of this change may be immense, as millions of Americans may need to purchase a digital converter box to receive the new signal. Responsibility for the digital television (DTV) transition, the coupon program that will provide discounts on the converter boxes, and the education program is shared by FCC and the National Telecommunications and Information Administration (NTIA). A wide range of commercial and public interest groups, including ALA, are involved in working toward a smooth transition process.

ALA continued to work with the DTV Transition Coalition, an ad hoc group of broadcasters, manufacturers, and public interest organizations that is preparing for the transition. It has also been in contact with NTIA and FCC.

The week of December 1–7 was FCC and ALA's DTV Awareness Week, with libraries across the country cohosting DTV community education events.

Additionally, ALA continues work with public broadcasting, NTIA, and other organizations on education initiatives.

Network Neutrality

The concept of net neutrality—the non-discrimination of content on the Internet—became a focus of telecommunications policy discussions two years ago. Since that time, the issue has been discussed more in concept than as reality, with some stakeholders arguing that net neutrality is a non-issue. Toward the end of 2007 at least two high-profile cases demonstrated the problems of failing to have a national network neutrality policy in place.

ALA closely followed the November 2007 petition to FCC by a coalition of groups led by Free Press, which argued that Comcast's practice of degrading certain Internet applications—namely, peer-to-peer traffic—violated FCC's 2005 Internet Policy Statement. The FCC statement emphasizes that consumers are entitled to access to all Internet content. The Free Press group argued that Comcast's claim that it was merely engaging in "reasonable network management," a clause outlined in a footnote to the Internet Policy Statement, was not sufficient.

In response, FCC released two public notices seeking comment on the situation. The first announced that FCC was considering making a declaratory ruling on whether the practice of degrading peer-to-peer traffic violates the Internet Policy Statement, and the second that FCC would like to clarify the meaning of the phrase "reasonable network management." ALA expected to file in these proceedings during 2008. More information is available at both http://www.fcc.gov and http://www.freepress.net.

Also in 2007, NARAL Pro-Choice America, an abortion rights group, tried to offer its members a new way to keep in touch with the organization: text messaging. However, Verizon turned down the group's request for a five-digit "short code," which members would use to get updates, seemingly violating one of the principles of net neutrality—that Internet providers not favor or block any content. Verizon claimed that its system was closed to groups whose content "may be seen as controversial or unsavory to any of our users." Verizon later reversed this decision.

FCC also put out a public notice on this issue, seeking comment to "clarify the regulatory status of text messaging services, including short-code based services sent from and received by mobile phones . . ." ALA will file in this proceeding as well.

ALA remained active during 2007 in various telecommunications coalitions, including the Education and Library Networks Coalition (EdLiNC), focusing primarily on E-rate issues, the Alliance for Public Technology, and the Open Internet Coalition.

Government Information

Open Government Legislation

Key legislation in 2007 brought positive developments for Freedom of Information Act (FOIA) issues. The Freedom of Information Act Amendments of 2007

(H.R. 1309) and the OPEN Government Act of 2007 (S. 849) included reforms to reduce FOIA backlogs and delays in responding to requests, provide incentives for agency compliance, and in general strengthen FOIA. (H.R. 1309 passed in March 2007 by a vote of 308–117, and S. 849 passed in the Senate by unanimous consent in August.)

ALA's OGR worked with a coalition of open government groups to move legislation that would improve the FOIA bills, the Presidential Records Act, and whistleblower protections. Activities included strategy meetings, meetings with congressional staff, group letters, and press coverage. At the time this report was prepared, all of these bills had passed the House and were either stalled in the Senate or in preconference discussions.

E-Government

OGR participated in various meetings and discussions with staff in the Senate's Homeland Security and Governmental Affairs Committee to generate awareness of and support for library e-government efforts and to develop legislation that reflects the reality that public libraries are the primary access points for e-government services. In addition to submitting a statement for the record, ALA proposed questions for committee Chairman Joseph Lieberman (ID-Conn.) to ask during a hearing on e-government in December 2007. The focus of the hearing was e-government and Web 2.0.

The committee proposed the possibility of a capitol briefing on e-government and libraries. ALA prepared documentation on e-government and began preplanning for an e-government initiative within ALA. The gathering and analysis of information relating to e-government is ongoing in order to identify the resources that would be most helpful to local libraries as they manage these new demands.

Examples of such resources include the following:

- The Internal Revenue Service announced new requirements for small tax-exempt organizations. Groups that normally would register once for tax-exempt status now have to file an electronic registration every three years.
- ALA renewed its commitment to seek legislation that reflects the reality that public libraries are the primary providers for e-government services. Financial support will be required to provide training, technology (including broadband services), and the necessary resources to provide government services that are reliable, trusted, expert, and available to citizens in their communities. In their expanding role as front-line service providers during emergencies and natural disasters, support and more coordination with federal, state, and local agencies is also necessary.

Open Access to Publicly Funded Research

The ALA Office of Government Relations actively worked in the area of open access to publicly funded research, especially with the Alliance for Taxpayer Access (ATA), a coalition of more than 60 library, nonprofit, and patient-advocacy groups. Through ATA, ALA focused on various aspects of improving open access:

One affected area is the National Institutes of Health (NIH) Public Access Policy. Under a mandatory policy, included in the fiscal year (FY) 2008 omnibus appropriations bill signed by President Bush, NIH-funded researchers are now required to deposit copies of eligible manuscripts into the National Library of Medicine's online database, PubMed Central. Articles will be made publicly available no later than 12 months after publication in a peer-reviewed journal.

Federal Libraries

ALA activities in the area of federal libraries focused on addressing specific threats to libraries' continued existence or closings as well as on developing larger strategies to advocate for federal libraries. In meetings with other library associations, the consensus evolved that a more proactive and top-down approach would be beneficial in addressing federal library issues. Often it seemed that leadership in federal agencies did not seem to be aware of the responsibilities and regulations they must follow in providing access to the public. ALA will continue to include in its strategies the building of relationships with federal agency chief information officers and appropriate congressional committees.

Environmental Protection Agency

In late December the Environmental Protection Agency (EPA) was ordered under the FY 2008 omnibus appropriations bill signed by President Bush to reopen many of its libraries that had been closed over the course of the previous year. EPA was required to "restore the network of EPA libraries recently closed or consolidated by the Administration . . ." and report on its plans to "restore publicly available libraries to provide environmental information and data to each EPA region . . ."

In 2006 EPA had closed its headquarters library in Washington, D.C., to walk-in patrons. EPA also closed several regional libraries, the toxics and pesticides library, and the Fort Meade Environmental Science Center Library. Reestablishment of these library services will be a major project for 2008.

Privacy and Surveillance

ALA continued its firm opposition to the use of National Security Letters (NSLs) to obtain library records without some level of court review. At its 2007 Annual Conference, ALA adopted a resolution calling for Congress to reform laws governing the government's use of NSLs.

Working with the American Civil Liberties Union, the Center for Democracy and Technology, and others, ALA urged reforms of NSL procedures. The Protect America Act (S. 2557) had passed quickly just as Congress was starting its summer recess with a February 1, 2008, sunset. In the autumn, when the Protect America Act debate restarted, ALA targeted the RESTORE Act (H.R. 3773) in the House and the FISA reform legislation in the Senate (S. 2088).

Although it was often expected that these latter pieces of legislation would pass before the end of the year, discussion bogged down in Congress and the debate moved to 2008. By the end of 2007, ALA supported the Senate Judiciary Committee version of FISA reform over the Intelligence Committee version of S. 2088. Efforts by ALA to get additional safeguards, so that there would be more individualized suspicion in order for law enforcement to get a warrant for library records, did not prevail.

Legislation and Regulations Affecting Publishing in 2007

Allan Adler
Vice President, Legal and Governmental Affairs

Emilia Varga-West
Executive Assistant for Government Relations and International Enforcement

Association of American Publishers
50 F St. N.W., Fourth Floor, Washington, DC 20001
202-347-3375, fax 202-347-3690
E-mail adler@publishers.org, ewest@publishers.org

The First Session of the 110th Congress was marked by partisan politics as Democrats in control of Congress for the first time in a dozen years generated even greater disagreements with the Republican administration. Consequently, inter-party disputes continued over the Bush administration's Iraq war policies and there were a succession of stalemates between the House and Senate over the congressional appropriations process. While most copyright initiatives were put on the legislative back burner, a variety of legislative activities of interest to publishers continued to percolate.

This is a review of the significant legislative activities dealt with by the Association of American Publishers' (AAP's) Washington office over the past year, focusing on legislative actions that affect book- and journal-publishing interests, primarily concerning (1) intellectual property protection, (2) freedom of expression, (3) "e-commerce" taxes, and (4) educational issues.

A summary, text, and status report for each piece of referenced legislation, whether enacted or not, can be found online in the Congressional Legislative Reference Service of the Library of Congress at http://thomas.loc.gov/home/multicongress/multicongress.html. Look under either "Bill Summary" or "Bill Text," click on the icon labeled "110th Congress," and follow the instructions from there.

Intellectual Property Issues

Consolidated Appropriations Act of 2008

(H.R. 2764; Public Law 110-161; December 26, 2007)

America COMPETES Act

(H.R. 2272; Public Law 110-69; August 9, 2007)
Although efforts to advance major patent reform legislation dominated the intellectual property agenda of Congress during the First Session of the 110th Congress, several pieces of copyright and copyright-related legislation required attention.

Concerns that scientific journal publishers have voiced about the National Institutes of Health (NIH) Enhanced Public Access Policy since it was proposed in 2004 moved to a heightened stage early in 2007 with the appearance of a legislative proposal to make the voluntary manuscript submission aspect of the policy mandatory.

Under the voluntary NIH policy, which was implemented in May 2005, NIH-funded researchers who wrote articles for publication in scientific journals were "requested" to submit an electronic version of their final, peer-reviewed manuscripts to NIH immediately upon acceptance by a journal for publication, so that the agency could make them freely available to the international online world through its PubMed Central Web site no more than 12 months after the date of journal publication.

Claiming that a compliance rate of only about 4 percent by NIH-funded researchers justified changing its submission policy from voluntary to mandatory, NIH began lobbying for such a change in 2006 and managed to convince both the House and Senate Appropriations Committees to include obliging statutory language in their respective versions of the Departments of Labor, Health and Human Services, Education, and Related Agencies Appropriations Act, 2008 (H.R. 3043; S. 1710).

Procedurally, journal publishers decried this attempt to enact the change in policy through a "rider" on appropriations legislation, without hearings or studies to assess its merits and without scrutiny from the congressional committees that have expertise and legislative jurisdiction regarding laws governing federal scientific research programs and intellectual property rights.

On substance, they responded that changing from a voluntary to mandatory submission policy was premature, in that NIH had begun seeking the change barely a year after implementing the voluntary policy and without giving publishers an opportunity to work with the agency to raise the compliance rate. They also argued that such a change would be inconsistent with policies embodied in U.S. copyright law, insofar as it would eliminate the concept of permission for NIH's use of the copyrighted work, and effectively allow the agency to take important publisher property interests without compensation, including the value added to the article by the publishers' investments in the peer review process and other quality-assurance aspects of journal publication.

Journal publishers also argued that a mandatory policy would undermine publishers' ability to exercise their copyrights in the published articles, which is the means by which they support their investments in such value-adding operations. Journals published in the United States have strong markets abroad, and AAP believes that a government policy requiring these works to be made freely available for international distribution is inherently incompatible with the maintenance of global markets for these highly successful U.S. exports. Smaller and nonprofit scientific societies and their scholarly missions would be particularly at risk as their journal subscribers around the world turn to NIH for free access to the same content for which they would otherwise pay.

AAP, working with its Professional/Scholarly Publishing (PSP) members and the Washington D.C. Principles for Free Access to Science Coalition (representing more than 75 of the nation's leading nonprofit medical and scientific societies and publishers), lobbied vigorously against the proposed mandatory policy throughout the year, meeting with House and Senate legislators and staff on committees with appropriations and authorizing jurisdiction over NIH, or committees with jurisdiction over copyright law and trade policies. In addition, meetings were held with key Bush administration officials at the Office of the United States Trade Representative, the Office of Management and Budget, and the Department of Health and Human Services. Although these lobbying efforts produced bipartisan letters from House Judiciary Committee leaders to the House Rules Committee, demanding removal of the NIH provision from the House bill, the Appropriations Committee's prior insulating action in adding a proviso that required NIH to "implement the public access policy in a manner consistent with copyright law" blunted objections from the Judiciary Committee and allowed the House to pass the bill with the NIH provision intact. When action moved to the Senate, publishers' lobbying efforts resulted in language in the Senate Appropriations Committee report directing NIH "to seek and carefully take into account the advice of journal publishers on the implementation of this policy," as well as in a floor colloquy among several senior senators that raised several of the publishers' concerns regarding the proposed change to a mandatory policy. Unfortunately, Senate passage nevertheless ensued with the NIH provision intact.

After Congress passed the conference report that reconciled the differing House- and Senate-passed appropriations bills, President Bush quickly vetoed this legislation, based on a Statement of Administration Policy that, among other things, criticized the NIH provision. Congress was unable to override the president's veto, but that did not mark the end of the NIH policy provision, as year-end budgetary pressures led Congress to wrap all of the pending appropriations measures—including a reduced-funding version of the Labor, Health and Human Services legislation—into the omnibus Consolidated Appropriations Act of 2008 (H.R. 2764; P.L. 110-161), which was signed into law in December. The mandatory NIH policy was enacted as Section 218 of Division G, Title II of that act.

One of the frustrating ironies of the lobbying efforts against the NIH mandatory policy was the inability to get legislators to focus on the fact that last August, even as the proposed NIH policy was under legislative consideration, Congress took a very different approach to ensuring public access to the results of government-funded scientific research when it reauthorized activities of the National Science Foundation in the America COMPETES Act. Instead of mandating free public access to articles published by private sector journals, Congress instructed the National Science Foundation (NSF) "to provide the public *a readily accessible summary of the outcomes of NSF-sponsored projects,"* along with "*citations to journal publications* in which funded researchers have published articles regarding such research" (emphasis added). With the House Science Committee acting through the regular legislative process, Congress thus not only avoided controversies over intellectual property interests in science publishing, but also recognized the value of publication in peer-reviewed science journals and the increasing availability of journal articles from a variety of sources.

Following the enactment of the NIH mandatory policy directive, AAP has petitioned the Department of Health and Human Services to conduct a public notice-and-comment rulemaking prior to implementing the new policy. AAP will continue to pursue publisher interests in the implementation process, and will work to ensure that similar submission mandates for other agencies do not come into effect.

Copyright

During the past three years, AAP, along with other representatives of copyright-based industries, periodically engaged in ongoing discussions with the U.S. Department of Justice and key staff from the House and Senate Judiciary Committees regarding the development of a package of legislative proposals that would enhance civil and criminal enforcement capabilities for copyright owners and provide restructuring and additional resources for interagency efforts within the executive branch to address piracy and counterfeiting of copyrighted works in the international arena. Although AAP did not pursue any specific requests in this process, it was supported by other industry representatives in voicing its concerns about opening the Digital Millennium Copyright Act (DMCA) to possible amendment, as well as the possibility that certain controversial proposed amendments (including, for example, one that would make it a felony to "attempt to infringe") might be viewed as overreaching by copyright interests.

Not surprisingly, these discussions eventually resulted in the introduction in 2007 of two different packages of proposed legislation concerning copyright enforcement. In the Senate, the chairman and ranking member of the Judiciary Committee introduced the Intellectual Property Enforcement Act of 2007 (S. 2317), and in the House, the bipartisan leadership of the House Judiciary Committee and its Intellectual Property subcommittee introduced and quickly held a hearing on the Prioritizing Resources and Organization for Intellectual Property (PRO IP) Act of 2007 (H.R. 4279).

Both bills contain a variety of measures to enhance civil and criminal copyright enforcement in specific ways, while also proposing to revamp the organizational structure and resources available within the federal executive branch for interagency coordination of intellectual property enforcement efforts in the international arena.

One notable provision that is common to both packages is a proposal to amend Section 411 of the Copyright Act, which currently says that "no action for infringement" of any U.S. work can be instituted until registration of the copyright claim has been made. The proposed amendment would revise this provision to clarify that a failure to register affects only the ability to bring civil actions for infringement, not criminal actions. Both packages also contain proposed amendments intended to harmonize current civil and criminal asset forfeiture provisions as they apply across a variety of intellectual property laws. The civil forfeiture provisions in the House bill were criticized by witnesses at the House hearing as creating penalties that would be disproportionate to the offenses involved, and would apply not only to infringing goods but to computers, cars, houses, and arguably any other real or personal property under the proposed language embracing "any property used, or intended to be used, to commit or substantially facilitate the commission of an offense."

Despite earlier discussions, the Senate bill contains proposed amendments to the DMCA that focus on "harmonizing" the definitions of "trafficking" and "private gain" in that act with other criminal statutes that use those terms. It also contains a controversial provision, derived from earlier legislative proposals that would allow the U.S. attorney general to bring civil copyright-enforcement actions in lieu of criminal actions in circumstances where the infringing conduct would also qualify as a criminal offense. Critics have derided this provision as an unnecessary and unjustifiable effort to effectively turn the Justice Department into a private law firm for copyright owners; however, supporters of the provision claim it would ensure that the Justice Department could act against criminal infringers even in cases where criminal actions would be difficult to bring.

Although the House bill does not contain proposed amendments to DMCA, it has generated further controversy around a proposal to change the existing rule on statutory damages that treats all parts of a compilation or derivative work as one work for purposes of such awards. The provision in the House bill would give federal courts discretion to make multiple awards of statutory damages in such cases, where the constituent parts of a compilation, or a derivative work and any previous existing work on which it is based, can be considered "distinct works having independent economic value." Critics claim that current law has functioned well, and that the proposed change in law would result in awards of statutory damages that are greatly disproportionate to the harm suffered by the copyright owner. Although publishers routinely publish derivative works, as well as anthologies and other types of compilations, they have not called for a change in current law and have concerns regarding how such a change might impact them as users of third-party works who might be sued for infringement in such cases.

Given the tighter and shorter election-year calendar that confronts the 110th Congress, it is likely that the proponents of these measures will have to work quickly to fashion a single "package" of copyright legislation if enactment this year is a serious goal. Such a "package" might also include provisions from one or more of the stand-alone copyright measures that are currently pending in Congress, or are shortly expected to be introduced. In the former category would be such bills as the proposed Freedom and Innovation Revitalizing U.S. Entrepreneurship (FAIR USE) Act of 2007 (H.R. 1201), the proposed Performance Rights Act (H.R. 4789/S. 2500), the proposed PERFORM Act (S. 256), and various measures proposed to nullify or delay implementation of copyright royalty rates recently determined to apply to Internet "Webcasting" of sound recordings. In the latter category, one might expect to see the introduction of an "orphan works" bill that would pick up the development of that legislation where it was left by the previous Congress after a bill approved by the House Intellectual Property Subcommittee in May 2006 expired upon adjournment later that year without further advancement.

AAP has been supportive of enacting "orphan works" legislation, and can be expected to be deeply involved in Second Session efforts to revive the issue. With the exception of the proposed FAIR USE Act of 2007 (H.R. 1201), advanced by Rep. Dick Boucher (D-Va.)—which AAP opposes and has previously opposed in earlier versions—the other pending copyright bills are either unrelated to the interests of book and journal publishers or, as in the case of the pending House and Senate "package" bills, find AAP taking a wait-and-see approach to proposed amendments that publishers may consider useful or otherwise acceptable. However, AAP has not actively advocated.

Freedom of Expression Issues

Bills to Enhance National Security and to Protect Civil Liberties

Since the enactment of the USAPatriot Act little more than a month after the terrorist attacks of September 11, 2001, AAP has supported legislative proposals to cut back on the broadened "national security letter" (NSL) authority that was given to the Federal Bureau of Investigation (FBI) under that legislation. Despite denials of abusive use by the FBI, congressional hearings and reports from the Justice Department have revealed highly dubious uses of the FBI's sweeping administrative power to demand from any entity or organization records relating to identified individuals, without probable cause or judicial review but subject to a "gag order" prohibiting the recipient from disclosing the existence of the letter. For example, in August 2005 it was disclosed that the FBI used an NSL to demand records from the Library Connection, a consortium of 26 Connecticut libraries, including records concerning borrowed reading materials and Internet usage. Although the ensuing controversy eventually resulted in the FBI's abandonment of its demand, it took action by two federal courts to lift the gag order that prevented the libraries from publicly discussing receipt of the NSL.

Although federal courts have held the NSL provisions of the USAPatriot Act to violate both the First Amendment and the constitutional doctrine of separation of powers among the three branches of the federal government, both before and after Congress amended the provisions as part of its reauthorization of the act in March 2006, opponents of this abusive authority continue to focus on legislation to curb abusive use of NSLs in light of those aspects of the 2006 amendments that added specific penalties for noncompliance or disclosure.

AAP continues to support the proposed National Security Letters Reform Act (H.R. 3189), which was introduced by Rep. Jerry Nadler (D-N.Y.) in July 2007, as well as the bill's Senate counterpart, the NSL Reform Act (S. 2088), which was introduced two months later. Both bills would limit the use of NSLs to criminal investigations where the records sought concern suspected spies, foreign powers, or individuals suspected of related criminal activity. Unfortunately, as of this writing neither measure had been the subject of legislative action since its introduction.

Bills to Provide Confidential Source Protection for Journalists

As in the previous Congress, highly publicized investigations and court actions in which journalists were subject to demands to reveal the identities of their confidential news sources sparked continued debate over whether federal law should provide a "confidential source" privilege for journalists. Although unprecedented progress was made in 2007, when the House passed the Free Flow of Information Act (H.R. 2102) and the Senate Judiciary Committee approved a different version of identically titled legislation (S. 2035), continued opposition to federal "shield law" legislation from the Bush administration and the inability of advocates to reach consensus on a single version may ultimately prevent enactment in this Congress.

The chief disputes over the terms of the legislation concern the scope of the privilege, the nature of permitted exceptions, and the question of who would be entitled to claim protection under the privilege. Starting from the premise that journalists should have some protection from being compelled by a federal entity to produce documents, provide testimony, and identify confidential sources in connection with any "matter arising under federal law," the House-passed bill would exempt a "covered person" from having to comply with a subpoena requiring documents or testimony, unless a court, after affording such "covered person" notice and an opportunity to be heard, determines that all reasonable alternative sources for the information sought have been exhausted; that there is a reasonable belief that a crime occurred and the information sought is critical to the resulting investigation, prosecution, or defense; or, that the information sought is critical to the successful completion of a non-criminal proceeding that is based on information provided by a third party. Where the testimony or documents sought "could reveal the identity of a source of information or include any information that could reasonably be expected to lead to the discovery of the identity of such a source," the privilege would attach unless disclosure of the identity of such source is "necessary" to (1) prevent or identify the perpetrator of an act of terrorism or significant and specified harm to national security; (2) prevent imminent death or significant bodily harm; or (3) identify someone who has disclosed a trade secret, individually identifiable health information, or nonpublic personal information about any consumer, in violation of federal law; or (4) is "essential" to identify, as part of a criminal investigation or prosecution, a person with authorized access to classified national security information who disclosed such information without authorization; and the court also determines that "the public interest in compelling disclosure of the information or document involved outweighs the public interest in gathering or disseminating news or information." The bill further provides an exception for "criminal or tortious conduct," generally excluding an otherwise "covered person" from asserting the privilege if the information sought was obtained by such person through "eyewitness observation" of alleged criminal conduct or as the result of the commission of alleged criminal or tortious conduct by such person.

With the exclusion of certain persons designated as a "foreign power" or "agent of a foreign power," or persons affiliated with organizations or entities designated as terrorists or terrorist organizations, the House-passed bill defines a "covered person" as one who "regularly gathers, prepares, collects, photographs, records, writes, edits, reports, or publishes news or information that concerns local, national, or international events or other matters of public interest for dissemination to the public for a substantial portion of the person's livelihood or for substantial financial gain and includes a supervisor, employer, parent, subsidiary, or affiliate of" such person. It defines "journalism" as "the gathering, preparing, collecting, photographing, recording, writing, editing, reporting, or publishing of news or information that concerns local, national, or international events or other matters of public interest for dissemination to the public."

In determining who should be eligible to claim the protection of the privilege provided by the bill, legislators argued over whether the coverage of bloggers would unreasonably extend the privilege to any person with Internet access. The requirement that a "covered person" must engage in the described activities "for a substantial portion of the person's livelihood or for substantial financial gain" reflect the majority desire to restrict, if not entirely eliminate, the ability of bloggers to claim the bill's protections. Unfortunately, this qualification may also exclude freelancers and many other types of writers and authors who cannot meet its terms. The bill approved by the Senate Judiciary Committee (S. 2035), which generally tracks the House-passed bill in most respects, contains the same definition of "covered person" but without this qualifying language.

Prior to the introduction of H.R. 2102, AAP expressed concerns that explicit reference to authors and publishers of books should be included in the bill to ensure that they would be able to assert the privilege against compelled disclosure. Similar expressions of concern that use of the term *journalist* to define parties eligible to claim the privilege had resulted in the addition of specific references to "book" authors and publishers in proposed "shield law" legislation in the previous Congress. However, with respect to H.R. 2102, the news media advocates who are viewed as the primary constituency for this legislation resisted such specificity, preferring the broader, less specific reference to *journalism* as a way of blurring the controversy over blogger coverage. AAP was successful in insisting that the definition of *journalism* should include "news or information that concerns local, national, or international events or other matters of public interest for dissemination to the public," and should not be limited to "current" or "contemporary" events, so that books—which may concern matters of historical interest and take more time to produce than "hot news"—would not be excluded from a broad reading of the definition.

AAP will continue to advocate enactment of a federal *shield law* this year, and will continue to press for assurance that authors and publishers of books are acknowledged to be "covered persons" eligible to assert the privilege against compelled disclosure.

Bills to Improve Public Access to Federal Agency Records

OPEN Government Act of 2007
(S. 2488; Public Law 110-175; December 31, 2007)

With the Bush administration continuing to polish its reputation as being among the most secretive in the history of the United States, congressional efforts to improve public access to federal records and promote accountability and openness in the executive branch continued during the First Session of the 110th Congress through the introduction of a variety of House and Senate bills. While most of this proposed legislation received little or no further legislative attention after its introduction, two measures that sought to improve existing federal records legislation managed to advance through the legislative process.

The OPEN Government Act (S. 2488; P.L. No. 110-175) was enacted as a result of legislative activity in both houses. Such bills as the proposed Freedom of Information Act Amendments (H.R. 1309) and the proposed OPEN Government Act (H.R. 1326) originated in the House but played important roles as stepping stones to enactment of the similar Senate bill. The bipartisan team of Senate Judiciary Committee Chair Patrick Leahy (D-Vt.) and committee member John Cornyn (R-Texas) led the way toward enactment with the reintroduction of legislation that they had proposed but were unable to advance in the previous Congress. The initial version of the proposed OPEN Government Act (S. 849) passed through the Senate just before the August recess in 2007, but then stalled for several months in the House Oversight and Government Reform Committee. Negotiations with the House committee leadership resulted in Sen. Leahy's introduction of a slightly revised measure (S. 2427) that was then further amended to address additional concerns of the House and the Bush administration. The final version of this legislation (S. 2488) was immediately passed by both houses and signed into law by President Bush less than a week after its introduction in December.

As enacted, the OPEN Government Act was primarily intended to ease agency compliance and reduce excessive delays in agency response to requests for agency records under the Freedom of Information Act (FOIA). Specifically, it ensures that any member of the news media, including freelance journalists, bloggers, and anyone writing for free magazines—even without a prior history of publication—may be eligible for a waiver of search and copying fees. In addition, it requires an agency to refund FOIA search fees if it does not fulfill the related request within the 20-day statutory time period. In response to the problem of growing FOIA litigation costs, the legislation creates an Office of Government Information Services within the National Archives, with the responsibility to mediate agency-level FOIA disputes in order to resolve them without litigation. Finally, in order to help the public and the news media monitor the status of their FOIA requests, the act creates a tracking system and establishes a hotline service for all federal agencies via which requesters may make inquiries either by telephone or the Internet.

Meanwhile, the Presidential Records Act Amendments of 2007 (H.R. 1255), which was introduced in March 2007 by Rep. Henry Waxman (D-Calif.), chair of the House Oversight and Government Reform Committee, was a response to a restrictive executive order issued by President Bush in 2001 that created unjustified new obstacles to public access to presidential records widely viewed as inconsistent with the letter and spirit of the Presidential Records Act of 1974.

The Presidential Records Act, enacted by Congress after the Watergate scandal raised questions about the wisdom of letting a former president have custodial authority over presidential records, established that such records belong to the American people, not to the president. It gave the Archivist of the United States custody of the records of a former president, with the "affirmative duty to make such records available to the public as rapidly and completely as possible . . . " Under its provisions, a president may restrict access to records for up to 12 years, after which records are to be released in accordance with the Freedom of Information Act, excluding application of FOIA's "deliberative process" exemption. The Presidential Records Act recognizes presidential authority to assert executive privilege, maintaining the status quo with respect to whatever constitutionally based privilege may be available to an incumbent or former president.

The 1974 act was first applied to the records of former President Ronald Reagan, pursuant to the terms of an executive order he had issued to establish a process for dealing with potential executive privilege claims over records covered by the act. The executive order required the Archivist of the United States to give incumbent and former presidents 30 calendar days' advance notice before releasing presidential records. It authorized the archivist to release the records at the end of that period unless the incumbent or former president claimed executive privilege, or unless the incumbent president instructed the archivist to extend the period indefinitely. If the incumbent president decided to invoke executive privilege, the archivist would withhold the records unless directed to release them by a final court order. If the incumbent president decided not to support a former president's claim of privilege, the archivist would decide whether or not to honor the claim.

In November 2001 President Bush issued another executive order that overturned the Reagan executive order and gives current and former presidents and vice presidents broad authority to withhold presidential records or to delay their release indefinitely. In addition, it requires the archivist to honor executive privilege claims made by either incumbent or former presidents; even if the incumbent disagrees with the former president's claim, the archivist must honor the claim and withhold the records.

Unlike the Reagan executive order, which stated that records were to be released on a schedule unless some other action occurred, the Bush executive order states that records will be released only after actions by former and current presidents have occurred. Therefore, if either the current or former president does not respond to the archivist, the records would not be released. Moreover, under the Bush executive order, designees of the former president may assert privilege claims after the death of the president, in effect making the right to assert executive privilege an asset of the former president's estate. The executive order also authorizes former vice presidents to assert executive privilege claims over their records.

H.R. 1255 would create a set of guidelines regarding the process of publicly disclosing any presidential records for the first time. The bill requires that both the incumbent and the former president during whose term the documents were created should be notified of such action, and grants them the right to file privilege claims to hold the records for a specified time, if necessary, to review the files. However, without any time extension request, the records would become publicly available within 20 days of providing initial notice to the incumbent and former presidents.

Despite unsurprising opposition from the Bush administration, H.R. 1255 passed the House in March 2007 and was approved by the Senate Committee on Homeland Security and Governmental Affairs without amendment just three months later. Unfortunately, since that time, the bill has been the subject of successive "holds" in the Senate, first by Sen. Jim Bunning (R-Ky.) and then by Sen. Tom Coburn (R-Okla.), which have kept it from being considered by the full Senate. Although there may be hope that the Senate will consider the bill before adjournment, it is likely that passage will result in a presidential veto.

The rest of the "freedom of information" bills introduced during the First Session of the 110th Congress have not yet received any consideration by the committees of jurisdiction. The Faster FOIA Act (H.R. 541), proposed by Rep. Brad Sherman (D-Calif.), would establish a Commission on Freedom of Information Act Processing Delays to conduct a study concerning methods to reduce delays in processing FOIA requests submitted to federal agencies. Subsequent to the introduction of that bill, Rep. Dennis Cardoza (D-Calif.) proposed further amendments to improve transparency of government operations in the Freedom of Information Improvement Act (H.R. 1775). That bill would bar treating federal contracts as privileged confidential business information or trade secrets under

FOIA, and would require federal agencies to provide access to federal contract records pursuant to FOIA requests except for specific information demonstrated to be proprietary to private persons.

Education Issues

College Cost Reduction and Access Act of 2007

(H.R. 2669; Public Law 110-84; September 27, 2007)

Improving Head Start for School Readiness Act of 2007

(H.R. 1429; Public Law 110-134; December 12, 2007)

During the past five years, at the beginning of each academic semester, there has been a steady drumbeat in the news media complaining about the prices students must pay for college textbooks and the perceived reasons for the claim that prices are unjustifiably high. These complaints have continued despite a 2005 study by the U.S. Government Accountability Office, which concluded that textbook prices have been largely driven by publishers' investments in additional instructional materials and new technologies in response to faculty needs and to enhance student success. Similarly, efforts to enact federal legislation addressing the cost of college textbooks have continued, despite a subsequent study published in May of last year by the Advisory Committee on Student Financial Assistance, a congressionally chartered federal advisory committee, which recommended against enactment of federal legislation that would compel stakeholders to take specific actions, impose price controls, or condition federal funding eligibility on particular actions by colleges with respect to textbook pricing.

An opportunity for proposed federal legislation on college textbooks loomed with the need for Congress to reauthorize the Higher Education Act of 1965 (HEA), which was last formally reauthorized in 1998 and, since 2004, has been maintained in effect only by a long series of temporary extensions that did not make substantive changes to the act. Having already separately addressed reauthorization of those parts of HEA that concern student loans and grants by enacting the College Cost Reduction and Access Act (H.R. 2669; P.L. No. 110-84) in September, key House and Senate committees were now preparing separate legislation to reauthorize the substantive programs and policies of HEA.

Taking up that challenge, Sen. Richard Durbin (D-Ill.) and Rep. Julia Carson (D-Ind.) introduced identical measures that would establish federal policy with respect to the issue of college textbook affordability. Among other requirements, Sen. Durbin's proposed College Textbook Affordability Act (S. 945) and Rep. Carson's proposed College Textbook Affordability and Transparency Act (H.R. 3512) would have required publishers informing teachers about available textbooks or supplements to include written information concerning: (1) the price the publisher would charge the bookstore associated with such institution for such items; (2) the full history of revisions for such items; and (3) whether such items are available in other formats, including paperback and unbound, and the price the publisher would charge the bookstore for items in those formats. The bills also would have required any publisher that sells a textbook and any accompanying supplement as a single bundled item to also sell them as separately priced and unbundled items.

Working with the sponsors of the legislation, as well as with the leadership and staff of the House Education and Labor Committee, AAP was able to negotiate a number of changes in these proposed requirements before they were included in the College Opportunity and Affordability Act (H.R. 4137), the primary House vehicle for reauthorizing the substantive programs and policies of HEA. The revised language would allow publishers to provide faculty with a list of substantial content revisions, rather than a full list of all changes, as originally proposed; provide an exemption from the requirement to "unbundle" packages that include third-party materials that cannot be sold separately; and add flexibility for publishers providing information on custom textbooks.

When the House Education and Labor Committee took up H.R. 4137 in November, AAP had to fight for improvements in the two proposed provisions affecting college textbook publishers, which sought to (1) expand transparency in textbook marketing and (2) make alternative formats of print course materials more readily available to students with print disabilities.

On textbook transparency, AAP would obtain new language to enable the use of alternative means of communication between publishers and faculty, such as through e-mail or Web sites, to avoid unnecessary additional burdens and cost increases as a result of forcing publishers to provide price and product information "in writing" on paper.

On the accessibility issues, however, AAP first had to convince Rep. Raul Grijalva (D-Ariz.) not to offer an amendment proposed by the National Federation of the Blind that would have basically extended the requirements of the IDEA Amendments of 2004 to higher education. AAP spent a great deal of time explaining to Rep. Grijalva and his staff, along with committee staff, why the 2004 legislation, which AAP had worked to craft and enact, was designed for elementary and secondary education students and would not work on the higher education level. The alternative provisions that resulted from these negotiations were added to H.R. 4137 and consequently approved by the House committee in mid-November, providing for establishment of a two-year federal commission to study the accessibility issue and a three-year grant program for model demonstration projects. Hopefully, this compromise will give AAP breathing room to continue developing an industry-based proposal for addressing the needs of college students with print disabilities, while also giving AAP the ability to argue that enactment of legislation in this area by individual states is neither necessary nor appropriate in light of the federal legislation.

Although AAP took no position on them, it is worth noting a set of provisions in H.R. 4137, as reported by committee, that were advocated by the motion picture and music industries in an effort to address the problem of illegal peer-to-peer file-sharing by college students of unauthorized copies of motion pictures and recorded music through campus Internet networks. Typically, efforts to address these problems have focused on proposed amendments to the federal Copyright Act, which means legislation within the jurisdiction of the Judiciary committees. However—in an effort that bears watching by AAP regarding its own members' issues with "electronic reserves" and other unauthorized uses of copyrighted works in the form of electronic course content—these copyright-based industries have taken their efforts to the committees with jurisdiction over key legislation affecting the institutions of higher education that they need to enlist in their efforts to combat these kinds of activities on campus.

Under the heading of "Campus-Based Digital Theft Prevention," provisions in H.R. 4137 would direct institutions that receive funds under Title IV of HEA to annually inform students about copyright law and campus policies on peer-to-peer copyright infringement; report on institutional policies and actions to prevent, detect, and punish peer-to-peer infringements by students; and, "to the extent practicable," develop plans to offer alternatives and explore technology-based deterrents to illegal downloading and peer-to-peer distribution of intellectual property.

Not surprisingly, the higher education community is vigorously opposing these provisions as draconian threats against continued funding eligibility, although it is unclear how significant they would be in practice if enacted. The report of the House Education and Labor Committee, in approving these provisions, attempted to clear up some "misperceptions" about them by noting that "no financial aid shall be taken away from colleges and students who engage in illegal file sharing" and that "the bill does not mandate the use of any particular alternative plan by colleges . . ."

AAP will continue to work with key House members and staff to secure additional improvements in the textbook-related provisions of H.R. 4137 when the bill is scheduled for consideration by the full House. Given Senate passage last July of its own version of this legislation, the proposed Higher Education Amendments (S. 1642), without any provisions concerning college textbooks or accessibility, an expected House-Senate conference to agree on a final version of HEA reauthorizing legislation may give AAP an additional opportunity to deal with any problems that might remain in the House-passed version of H.R. 4137.

Head Start

Another major educational reauthorization effort successfully achieved during the First Session of the 110th Congress was the reauthorization of the Head Start program, which has been a cornerstone federal education "safety net" program that ensures that poor children are provided with education, nutrition, and health services before kindergarten.

Two bipartisan measures to improve and reauthorize Head Start were introduced early last year. The Improving Head Start Act of 2007 (H.R. 1429), which was passed by the House in May 2007, had a number of features that were recognized by AAP as important to educational and test publishers and literacy improvement. These included funding to give as many as 10,000 more children access to the program in 2008; provisions for research-based practices to support the growth of children's pre-literacy and vocabulary skills; a prohibition on further use of the National Reporting System, a testing system that had been criticized by child development experts, including AAP members; and new requirements for teacher qualifications. In June 2007 action moved to the Senate, where the Head Start for School Readiness Act of 2007 (S. 556) was passed, with additional provisions for establishing an Early Care and Education Council in each state to develop a coordinated and comprehensive system of early childhood education and development; aligning standards and services with state early learning standards; and supporting National Academy of Sciences review of child outcomes and assessments.

After differences between the two versions of the legislation were resolved in conference, the Improving Head Start for School Readiness Act of 2007 (H.R. 1429; P.L. 110-134) was passed by Congress and signed into law in December.

No Child Left Behind

The other major daunting task remaining on the education agenda of the 110th Congress is reauthorization of the No Child Left Behind (NCLB) Act, which was enacted in 2002 as a successor to the Elementary and Secondary Education Act and has been considered the major domestic legislative achievement of the Bush administration.

Although enacted with strong bipartisan support, this federal law has increasingly become the subject of controversy regarding its effectiveness and the repeated refusal of the Bush administration to fully fund requirements the NCLB Act imposes on state and local educational agencies. As NCLB approached its five-year reauthorization deadline in March 2007, the debate over the act's merits breached partisan lines, prompting introduction of the Academic Partnerships Lead Us to Success (A PLUS) Act (H.R. 1539) by 64 Republican members of Congress who assert that the NCLB Act has improperly interfered in state and local decision making on education and has produced a number of other negative impacts.

AAP's School Division developed a position paper on the extension of NCLB, which was distributed to members of Congress. The instructional programs, services, and assessments developed by AAP members play a critical role in NCLB programs; therefore, AAP expressed its strong support for the reauthorization of the act. Specifically, in order to help all students attain academic proficiency and to close achievement gaps, publishers recommended (1) access to up-to-date instructional materials in the classroom and at home; (2) authorization and expansion of reading programs for adolescents, such as the Striving Readers Program; (3) access to a selection of instructional materials, and assurance that programs implemented under the Reading First program should continue to meet rigorous and scientifically based criteria; (4) continuation of funding to expand math and science programs; (5) strengthened and expanded annual assessment systems for improved teaching and learning; (6) leveraging technology; and (7) improving teacher quality through training to effectively use and integrate instructional materials, assessments, and data.

Despite much activity surrounding NCLB reauthorization, the process ground to a halt in November, and congressional leaders announced that they expected no further action before the end of the First Session. While both the House and Senate education committees have distributed discussion drafts of the reauthorization bill, neither committee has been able to formally introduce legislation. In the House, reauthorization efforts halted due to a protracted fight over performance-pay measures for teachers. Meanwhile, the two top lawmakers on the Senate Education Committee—Sen. Edward Kennedy (D-Mass, chairman) and Sen. Mike Enzi (R-Wyo., ranking minority member) did not believe that the committee would consider NCLB until early 2008.

Since NCLB reauthorization did not occur during the First Session, the current law has been temporarily extended to remain in effect as Congress considers making a final thrust at reauthorization in 2008, or until a new president and a new Congress can address it in 2009.

Internet Tax Issues

Internet Tax Freedom Act Amendments Act of 2007

(H.R. 3678; Public Law 110-108; October 31, 2007)
Another area where Congress moved quickly in 2007 to renew an expiring federal law concerned Internet taxation.

The Internet Tax Freedom Act of 1998 (ITFA) created a moratorium on multiple and discriminatory taxes and Internet access taxes for three years. ITFA expired in 2001 but was extended by Congress until November 1, 2003. Advocates of a permanent moratorium sought to permanently prohibit taxes on Internet access and multiple and discriminatory taxes on electronic commerce, while phasing out the "grandfather clause" that permitted some state and local governments to continue to collect certain Internet access taxes. It also proposed to change the definition of "Internet access" to cover high-speed DSL, cable modem, wireless, satellite, and dial-up services to ensure that they are covered by the prohibition and exempt from state and local taxation.

However, opponents of that approach argued that such legislation would constitute an unfunded federal mandate to state and local governments, costing these deficit-ridden governments billions of dollars in desperately needed tax revenues. They also claimed that the bill, by altering the definition of "Internet access" to include services that were already being taxed, could further result in a substantial loss of revenue to already struggling states. State and local governments also raised a concern that Internet access providers could begin to "bundle" products and refer to the packages as providing "Internet access" in order to avoid being taxed.

The enacted compromise Internet Tax Nondiscrimination Act of 2004 (S. 150; P.L. 108-435) changed the definition of access service to exclude telecommunications services, except to the extent these are used by an Internet access provider to provide access. It also changed the definition of "tax on Internet access" to include any tax on Internet access regardless of whether it is imposed on a provider or purchaser of such service and regardless of the terminology used to describe the tax. The legislation extended the ban on state taxation of Internet access and on multiple or discriminatory taxes on electronic commerce until November 1, 2007, while "grandfathering" until that date the Internet access taxing authority of states that had such a tax prior to the enactment of IFTA in 1998.

During the 109th Congress, a number of Internet tax measures were introduced to build upon the ground plowed by the 2004 act, but none were enacted.

Early in the First Session of the 110th Congress, the Permanent Internet Tax Freedom Act of 2007 (S. 156; H.R. 743) was introduced in the House and Senate in anticipation of the expiration of the 2004 act in November 2007. This legislation would have permanently prohibited state and local taxation of Internet access and discriminatory or multiple taxes on electronic commerce, but it made no progress in either body despite bipartisan sponsorship.

Several other bills were subsequently introduced, with a less ambitious goal of merely extending the moratorium for another four years, e.g., the proposed ITFA Extension Act of 2007 (S. 1453), but these also received little attention.

In September, as the clock ticked toward expiration of ITFA, the chair of the House Judiciary Committee, Rep. John Conyers (D-Mich.), introduced the ITFA Amendments Act of 2007 (H.R. 3678). A week later, Sen. John Sununu (R-N.H.) reintroduced the language of S. 156 in the Permanent Internet Tax Freedom Act of 2007 (S. 2128). During the following three weeks, H.R. 3678 moved quickly through the House and was received in the Senate, where Sen. Sununu amended the bill during Senate floor passage. Shortly thereafter, the Senate-amended version was approved in the House and signed into law by President Bush just one day before ITFA was slated to expire.

As enacted, the ITF Act Amendments of 2007 extended until November 1, 2014, the existing moratorium on state and local taxation of Internet access and electronic commerce, as well as the "grandfathered" exemptions from that moratorium for states with previously enacted Internet tax laws. In a complicated set of provisions, it expanded the definition of "Internet access" to include related communication services, such as e-mails and instant messaging, and redefined "telecommunications" to include unregulated non-utility services, such as cable service. The new law also repealed an earlier exception from the moratorium for taxing "Voice over Internet Protocol" (Internet VoIP telephony).

As with previous enactments on these matters, AAP took no position on this legislation, recognizing that online businesses and bricks-and-mortar enterprises hold different views on the various issues involved. However, with the expectation that advocates of a permanent moratorium will continue to seek one, and that their efforts could implicate broader issues regarding the collection of sales tax for out-of-state purchases, AAP will continue to monitor Internet tax issues as they arise in the legislative context and inform its members if their interests are likely to be affected.

Funding Programs and Grant-Making Agencies

National Endowment for the Humanities

1100 Pennsylvania Ave. N.W., Washington, DC 20506
202-606-8400, 1-800-634-1121
TDD (hearing impaired) 202-606-8282 or 866-372-2930 (toll free)
E-mail Info@NEH.gov, World Wide Web http://www.neh.gov

Bruce Cole
Chairman

The National Endowment for the Humanities (NEH) is an independent federal agency created in 1965. It is the largest funder of humanities programs in the United States.

Because democracy demands wisdom, NEH serves and strengthens the republic by promoting excellence in the humanities and conveying the lessons of history to all Americans. It accomplishes this mission by providing grants for high-quality humanities projects in five funding areas: education, preservation and access, public programs, research, and challenge grants.

NEH grants typically go to cultural institutions, such as museums, archives, libraries, colleges, universities, public television and radio stations, and to individual scholars. The grants

- Strengthen teaching and learning in the humanities in schools and colleges
- Preserve and provide access to cultural and educational resources
- Provide opportunities for lifelong learning
- Facilitate research and original scholarship
- Strengthen the institutional base of the humanities

Over the past 40 years, NEH has reached millions of Americans with projects and programs that preserve and study the nation's culture and history while providing a foundation for the future.

The endowment's mission is to enrich American cultural life by promoting the study of the humanities. According to the National Foundation on the Arts and the Humanities Act of 1965, "The term 'humanities' includes, but is not limited to, the study of the following: language, both modern and classical; linguistics; literature; history; jurisprudence; philosophy; archaeology; comparative religion; ethics; the history, criticism, and theory of the arts; those aspects of social sciences which have humanistic content and employ humanistic methods; and the study and application of the humanities to the human environment with particular attention to reflecting our diverse heritage, traditions, and history and to the relevance of the humanities to the current conditions of national life."

The act provided for the establishment of the National Foundation on the Arts and the Humanities in order to promote progress and scholarship in the humanities and the arts in the United States. The act included the following findings:

- The arts and the humanities belong to all the people of the United States.
- The encouragement and support of national progress and scholarship in the humanities and the arts, while primarily matters for private and local initiative, are also appropriate matters of concern to the federal government.
- An advanced civilization must not limit its efforts to science and technology alone, but must give full value and support to the other great branches of scholarly and cultural activity in order to achieve a better understanding of the past, a better analysis of the present, and a better view of the future.
- Democracy demands wisdom and vision in its citizens. It must therefore foster and support a form of education, and access to the arts and the humanities, designed to make people of all backgrounds and locations masters of technology and not its unthinking servants.
- It is necessary and appropriate for the federal government to complement, assist, and add to programs for the advancement of the humanities and the arts by local, state, regional, and private agencies and their organizations. In doing so, the government must be sensitive to the nature of public sponsorship. Public funding of the arts and humanities is subject to the conditions that traditionally govern the use of public money. Such funding should contribute to public support and confidence in the use of taxpayer funds. Public funds provided by the federal government ultimately must serve public purposes the Congress defines.
- The arts and the humanities reflect the high place accorded by the American people to the nation's rich culture and history and to the fostering of mutual respect for the diverse beliefs and values of all persons and groups.

What NEH Grants Accomplish

Since its founding in 1965, NEH has awarded more than 65,000 grants.

Interpretive Exhibitions

Interpretive exhibitions provide opportunities for lifelong learning in the humanities for millions of Americans. Since 1967 NEH has awarded more than $240 million in grants for interpretive exhibitions, catalogs, and public programs, which are among the most highly visible activities the endowment supports. During 2008 a total of 31 traveling exhibitions and 123 long-term exhibitions funded with NEH support will appear in 44 states and the District of Columbia.

Renewing Teaching

Over the years more than 70,000 high school and college teachers have deepened their knowledge of the humanities through intensive summer study supported by NEH; tens of thousands of students benefit from these better-educated teachers every year.

Reading and Discussion Programs

Since 1982 the endowment has supported reading and discussion programs in the nation's libraries, bringing people together to discuss works of literature and history. Scholars in the humanities provide thematic direction for the discussion programs. Using selected texts and themes such as "Work," "Family," "Diversity," and "Not for Children Only," these programs have attracted more than 1 million people to read and talk about what they've read.

Preserving the Nation's Heritage

NEH has launched an innovative program, the National Digital Newspaper Program, which is supporting projects to convert microfilm of historically important U.S. newspapers into fully searchable digital files and to mount these files on the Internet. Developed in partnership with the Library of Congress, this complex, long-term project ultimately will make more than 30 million pages of newspapers accessible online.

Stimulating Private Support

More than $1.5 billion in humanities support has been generated by the NEH Challenge Grants program, which requires most grant recipients to raise $3 or $4 in nonfederal funds for every dollar they receive.

Presidential Papers

Ten presidential papers projects are underwritten by NEH, covering presidents from Washington to Eisenhower. Matching grants for the ten projects have leveraged $7 million in nonfederal contributions.

New Scholarship

NEH grants enable scholars to do in-depth study. Jack Rakove explored the making of the Constitution in his *Original Meanings* and James McPherson chronicled the Civil War in his *Battle Cry of Freedom*. Both won the Pulitzer Prize, as have 13 other recipients of NEH grants.

History on Screen

In 2007 two NEH-supported documentary films on World War II premiered to critical acclaim—*The Rape of Europa* and the Ken Burns series *The War. The Rape of Europa* tells the story of the systematic theft, deliberate destruction, and in other cases the miraculous survival of Europe's art treasures during the Third Reich and the war; the seven-episode series *The War* details the experiences of

American soldiers and their families through eyewitness testimony. Since 1967 the endowment has awarded more than $260 million to support the production of films for broad public distribution, including the Emmy Award-winning series *The Civil War,* the Oscar-nominated films *Brooklyn Bridge, The Restless Conscience,* and *Freedom on My Mind,* and film biographies of John and Abigail Adams, Eugene O'Neill, and Ernest Hemingway.

Library of America

Millions of books have been sold as part of the Library of America series, a collection of the riches of the nation's literature. Begun with NEH seed money, the more than 170 published volumes include the writings of Henry Adams, Edith Wharton, William James, Eudora Welty, W. E. B. DuBois, and many others.

The Library of America also received a $150,000 grant for the publication of *American Poetry: The Seventeenth and Eighteenth Centuries* (two volumes) and an expanded volume of selected works by Captain John Smith—a key figure in the establishment of the first permanent English settlement in North America, at Jamestown, Virginia—and other early exploration narratives.

Science and the Humanities

The scientific past is being preserved with NEH-supported editions of the letters of Charles Darwin, the works of Albert Einstein, and the 14-volume papers of Thomas A. Edison. Additionally, NEH and the National Science Foundation (NSF) have joined forces in Documenting Endangered Languages (DEL), a multiyear effort to preserve records of key languages before they become extinct.

Learning Under the Tent

Across the country, state humanities councils bring a 21st-century version of Chautauqua to the public, embracing populations of entire towns, cities, even regions. Scholars portray such significant figures as Meriwether Lewis, Sojourner Truth, Willa Cather, Teddy Roosevelt, and Sacagawea, first speaking as the historic character and later giving audiences opportunities to ask questions. The give-and-take between the scholar/performer and the audiences provides an entertaining, energetic, and thought-provoking exchange about experiences and attitudes in the present and the past.

Special Initiatives

We the People

We the People is a program launched by NEH to encourage the teaching, study, and understanding of American history and culture. Under this program, the endowment invites scholars, teachers, filmmakers, curators, librarians, and others to submit grant applications for projects that explore significant events and themes in the nation's history and culture and advance knowledge of the principles that define the United States. Since its inception in 2002, We the People has provided support to more than 1,350 projects.

Proposals responding to the initiative can take the form of

- New scholarship
- Projects to preserve and provide access to documents and artifacts significant to the national heritage
- Professional development programs for teachers and educators at every level, from kindergarten through college
- Public programs in libraries, museums, and historical societies, including exhibitions, film, radio, and Internet-based programs

NEH will accept We the People proposals in all programs and at all deadlines. Proposals are expected to meet the guidelines of the program that best fits the character of the project. A list of programs and deadlines is available on NEH's Web site, http://www.neh.gov.

Proposals will be evaluated through the endowment's established review process and will not receive special consideration. The NEH chairman reserves the right to determine which grants will be designated as We the People projects.

The main components of We the People are

- A call for applications to NEH for projects designed to explore significant events and themes in the nation's history
- Landmarks of American History and Culture workshops for K–12 teachers and community college faculty at important historic sites
- Interpreting America's Historic Places grants to enhance opportunities for local residents and the traveling public to learn more about American history and culture
- The National Digital Newspaper Program, which supports projects to digitize historically important U.S. newspapers and to make these files available on the Internet
- Picturing America, a program to provide schools and teachers with high-quality poster reproductions of some of America's greatest art, along with materials that help educators incorporate these art works into their teaching of history, literature, art history, and architecture
- The We the People Bookshelf, a set of classic books for young readers on significant American themes, to be awarded to schools and libraries for use in local programs

Picturing America

In February 2008 NEH launched Picturing America, an initiative designed to promote the teaching, study, and understanding of American history and culture in K–12 schools and public libraries. Part of the We the People program, Picturing America is a free resource that provides an innovative way for citizens of all ages to explore the history and character of America through some of the nation's greatest works of art, including Emanuel Leutze's "Washington Crossing the Delaware" and Norman Rockwell's "Freedom of Speech."

Picturing America features 40 high-quality reproductions (24 by 36 inches) of American art, an illustrated resource book, and a comprehensive Web site, http://picturingamerica.neh.gov, with additional information about the artwork, artists, and more.

Digital Humanities

Launched as an initiative in 2006, the endowment's digital humanities efforts support projects that utilize or study the impact of digital technology. NEH is interested in fostering the growth of digital humanities and lending support to a wide variety of projects, including those that deploy digital technologies and methods to enhance understanding of a topic or issue; those that study the impact of digital technology on the humanities; and those that digitize important materials, thereby increasing the public's ability to search and access humanities information. The endowment has numerous programs that are actively funding digital scholarship, including humanities collections and resources, institutes for advanced technology in the digital humanities, fellowships at digital humanities centers, digital humanities start-up grants, and many others. The endowment is also actively working with other funding partners, both domestically and abroad, in order to better coordinate spending on digital infrastructure for the humanities.

EDSITEment

NEH's EDSITEment Web site, http://www.edsitement.neh.gov, assembles the best humanities resources on the Web, drawing more than 400,000 visitors a month. Incorporating these Internet resources, particularly primary documents, from more than 200 peer-reviewed Web sites, EDSITEment features more than 400 online lesson plans in all areas of the humanities. Teachers use EDSITEment's digital resources to enhance their teaching and to engage their students through interactive technology tools that hone critical-thinking skills.

Federal-State Partnership

The Office of Federal-State Partnership links the endowment with a nationwide network of 56 humanities councils, which are located in each state, the District of Columbia, Puerto Rico, the U.S. Virgin Islands, the Northern Mariana Islands, American Samoa, and Guam. Each humanities council funds humanities programs in its own jurisdiction.

Directory of State Humanities Councils

Alabama

Alabama Humanities Foundation
1100 Ireland Way, Suite 101
Birmingham, AL 35205-7001
205-558-3980, fax 205-558-3981
http://www.ahf.net

Alaska

Alaska Humanities Forum
421 W. First Ave., Suite 300
Anchorage, AK 99501
907-272-5341, fax 907-272-3979
http://www.akhf.org

Arizona

Arizona Humanities Council
Ellis-Shackelford House
1242 N. Central Ave.
Phoenix, AZ 85004-1887
602-257-0335, fax 602-257-0392
http://www.azhumanities.org

Arkansas

Arkansas Humanities Council
10800 Financial Centre Pkwy., Suite 465
Little Rock, AR 72211
501-221-0091, fax 501-221-9860
http://www.arkhums.org

California

California Council for the Humanities
312 Sutter St., Suite 601
San Francisco, CA 94108
415-391-1474, fax 415-391-1312
http://www.calhum.org

Colorado

Colorado Humanities
1490 Lafayette St., Suite 101
Denver, CO 80218
303-894-7951, fax 303-864-9361
http://www.ceh.org

Connecticut

Connecticut Humanities Council
955 S. Main St., Suite E
Middletown, CT 06457
860-685-2260, fax 860-704-0429
http://www.ctculture.org

Delaware

Delaware Humanities Forum
100 W. 10 St., Suite 1009
Wilmington, DE 19801
302-657-0650, fax 302-657-0655
http://www.dhf.org

District of Columbia

Humanities Council of Washington, D.C.
925 U St. N.W.
Washington, DC 20001

202-387-8393, fax 202-387-8149
http://wdchumanities.org

Florida

Florida Humanities Council
599 2nd St. S.
St. Petersburg, FL 33701-5005
727-873-2000, fax 727-873-2014
http://www.flahum.org

Georgia

Georgia Humanities Council
50 Hurt Plaza S.E., Suite 595
Atlanta, GA 30303-2915
404-523-6220, fax 404-523-5702
http://www.georgiahumanities.org

Hawaii

Hawaii Council for the Humanities
First Hawaiian Bank Bldg.
3599 Waialae Ave., Room 23
Honolulu, HI 96816
808-732-5402, fax 808-732-5402
http://www.hihumanities.org

Idaho

Idaho Humanities Council
217 W. State St.
Boise, ID 83702
208-345-5346, fax 208-345-5347
http://www.idahohumanities.org

Illinois

Illinois Humanities Council
17 N. State St., No. 1400
Chicago, IL 60602-3296
312-422-5580, fax 312-422-5588
http://www.prairie.org

Indiana

Indiana Humanities Council
1500 N. Delaware St.
Indianapolis, IN 46202
317-638-1500, fax 317-634-9503
http://www.ihc4u.org

Iowa

Humanities Iowa
100 Oakdale Campus N310 OH
University of Iowa
Iowa City, IA 52242-5000
319-335-4153, fax 319-335-4154
http://www.humanitiesiowa.org

Kansas

Kansas Humanities Council
112 S.W. Sixth Ave., Suite 210
Topeka, KS 66603
785-357-0359, fax 785-357-1723
http://www.kansashumanities.org

Kentucky

Kentucky Humanities Council
206 E. Maxwell St.
Lexington, KY 40508
859-257-5932, fax 859-257-5933
http://www.kyhumanities.org

Louisiana

Louisiana Endowment for the Humanities
938 Lafayette St., Suite 300
New Orleans, LA 70113-1027
504-523-4352, fax 504-529-2358
http://www.leh.org

Maine

Maine Humanities Council
674 Brighton Ave.
Portland, ME 04102-1012
207-773-5051, fax 207-773-2416
http://www.mainehumanities.org

Maryland

Maryland Humanities Council
108 W. Centre St.
Baltimore, MD 21201-4565
410-685-0095, fax 410-685-0795
http://www.mdhc.org

Massachusetts

Massachusetts Foundation for the Humanities
66 Bridge St.
Northampton, MA 01060

413-584-8440, fax 413-584-8454
http://www.mfh.org

Michigan

Michigan Humanities Council
119 Pere Marquette Drive, Suite 3B
Lansing, MI 48912-1270
517-372-7770, fax 517-372-0027
http://michiganhumanities.org

Minnesota

Minnesota Humanities Commission
987 E. Ivy Ave.
St. Paul, MN 55106-2046
651-774-0105, fax 651-774-0205
http://www.minnesotahumanities.org

Mississippi

Mississippi Humanities Council
3825 Ridgewood Rd., Room 311
Jackson, MS 39211
601-432-6752, fax 601-432-6750
http://www.mshumanities.org

Missouri

Missouri Humanities Council
543 Hanley Industrial Court, Suite 201
St. Louis, MO 63144-1905
314-781-9660, fax 314-781-9681
http://www.mohumanities.org

Montana

Montana Committee for the Humanities
311 Brantly Hall
University of Montana
Missoula, MT 59812-8214
406-243-6022, fax 406-243-4836
http://www.humanities-mt.org

Nebraska

Nebraska Humanities Council
Lincoln Center Bldg., Suite 500
215 Centennial Mall South
Lincoln, NE 68508
402-474-2131, fax 402-474-4852
http://www.nebraskahumanties.org

Nevada

Nevada Humanities
1034 N. Sierra St.
Reno, NV 89507
775-784-6587, fax 775-784-6527
http://www.nevadahumanities.org

New Hampshire

New Hampshire Humanities Council
19 Pillsbury St.
Concord, NH 03302-2228
603-224-4071, fax 603-224-4072
http://www.nhhc.org

New Jersey

New Jersey Council for the Humanities
28 W. State St.
Trenton, NJ 08608
609-695-4838, fax 609-695-4929
http://www.njch.org

New Mexico

New Mexico Humanities Council
1 University of New Mexico
Albuquerque, NM 87131-0001
505-277-3705, fax 505-277-6056
http://www.nmhum.org

New York

New York Council for the Humanities
150 Broadway, Suite 1700
New York, NY 10038
212-233-1131, fax 212-233-4607
http://www.nyhumanities.org

North Carolina

North Carolina Humanities Council
200 S. Elm St., Suite 403
Greensboro, NC 27401
336-334-5325, fax 336-334-5052
http://www.nchumanities.org

North Dakota

North Dakota Humanities Council
418 E. Broadway, Suite 8
P.O. Box 2191
Bismarck, ND 58502

701-255-3360, fax 701-223-8724
http://www.nd-humanities.org

Ohio

Ohio Humanities Council
471 E. Broad St., Suite 1620
Columbus, OH 43215-3857
614-461-7802, fax 614-461-4651
http://www.ohiohumanities.org

Oklahoma

Oklahoma Humanities Council
Festival Plaza
428 W. California, Suite 270
Oklahoma City, OK 73102
405-235-0280, fax 405-235-0289
http://www.okhumanitiescouncil.org

Oregon

Oregon Council for the Humanities
812 S.W. Washington St., Suite 225
Portland, OR 97205
503-241-0543, fax 503-241-0024
http://www.oregonhum.org

Pennsylvania

Pennsylvania Humanities Council
325 Chestnut St., Suite 715
Philadelphia, PA 19106-2607
215-925-1005, fax 215-925-3054
http://www.pahumanities.org

Rhode Island

Rhode Island Council for the Humanities
385 Westminster St., Suite 2
Providence, RI 02903
401-273-2250, fax 401-454-4872
http://www.rihumanities.org

South Carolina

Humanities Council of South Carolina
2711 Middleburg Drive, Suite 308
P.O. Box 5287
Columbia, SC 29254
803-771-2477, fax 803-771-2487
http://www.schumanities.org

South Dakota

South Dakota Humanities Council
1215 Trail Ridge Road, Suite A
Brookings, SD 57006
605-688-6113, fax 605-688-4531
http://web.sdstate.edu/humanities

Tennessee

Humanities Tennessee
306 Gay St., Suite 306
Nashville, TN 37201
615-770-0006, fax 615-770-0007
http://www.humanitiestennessee.org

Texas

Humanities Texas
1410 Rio Grande St.
Austin, TX 78701
512-440-1991, fax 512-440-0115
http://www.humanitiestexas.org

Utah

Utah Humanities Council
202 W. 300 North
Salt Lake City, UT 84103-1108
801-359-9670, fax 801-531-7869
http://www.utahhumanities.org

Vermont

Vermont Humanities Council
11 Loomis St.
Montpelier, VT 05602
802-262-2626, fax 802-262-2620
http://www.vermonthumanities.org

Virginia

Virginia Foundation for the Humanities and
    Public Policy
145 Ednam Dr.
Charlottesville, VA 22903-4629
434-924-3296, fax 434-296-4714
http://www.virginia.edu/vfh

Washington

Humanities Washington
615 Second Ave., Suite 300
Seattle, WA 98104

206-682-1770, fax 206-682-4158
http://www.humanities.org

West Virginia

West Virginia Humanities Council
1310 Kanawha Blvd. E.
Charleston, WV 25301
304-346-8500, fax 304-346-8504
http://www.wvhumanities.org

Wisconsin

Wisconsin Humanities Council
222 S. Bedford St., Suite F
Madison, WI 53703-3688
608-262-0706, fax 608-263-7970
http://www.wisconsinhumanities.org

Wyoming

Wyoming Council for the Humanities
1315 E. Lewis St.
Laramie, WY 82072-3459
307-721-9243, fax 307-742-4914
http://uwadmnweb.uwyo.edu/humanities

American Samoa

Amerika Samoa Humanities Council
P.O. Box 5800
Pago Pago, AS 96799
684-633-4870, fax 684-633-4873
http://www.ashumanities.org

Guam

Guam Humanities Council
222 Chalan Santo Papa
Reflection Center, Suite 106
Hagatna, Guam 96910
671-472-4460, fax 671-472-4465
http://www.guamhumanitiescouncil.org

Northern Mariana Islands

Northern Mariana Islands Council for the
    Humanities
P.O. Box 506437
Saipan, MP 96950
670-235-4785, fax 670-235-4786
http://cnmi.humanities.org.mp

Puerto Rico

Fundación Puertorriqueña de las
Humanidades
109 San José St.
Box 9023920
San Juan, PR 00902-3920
787-721-2087, fax 787-721-2684
http://www.fprh.org

Virgin Islands

Virgin Islands Humanities Council
1826 Kongens Gade 5-6, Suite 2
St. Thomas, VI 00802
340-776-4044, fax 340-774-3972
http://www.vihumanities.org

NEH Overview

Division of Education

Through grants to educational institutions, fellowships to scholars and teachers, and the support of significant research, this division is designed to strengthen sustained, thoughtful study of the humanities at all levels of education.

Grants support curriculum and materials development efforts, faculty study programs among educational institutions, and conferences and networks of institutions. NEH is interested in projects that help teachers use electronic technologies to enhance students' understanding of humanities subjects.

Eligible applicants:	Public and private elementary and secondary schools, school systems, colleges and universities, nonprofit academic associations, and cultural institutions, such as libraries and museums
Application deadlines:	Grants for Teaching and Learning Resources and Curriculum Development, October 1, 2008; Humanities Initiatives for Faculty at Historically Black, Hispanic-Serving, and Tribal Colleges and Universities, January 15, 2009; Landmarks of American History and Culture: Workshops for School Teachers, March 15, 2008; Landmarks of American History and Culture: Workshops for Community College Faculty, March 15, 2008
Contact:	202-606-8500, e-mail education@neh.gov

Seminars and Institutes

Grants support summer seminars and national institutes in the humanities for college and school teachers. These faculty-development activities are conducted at colleges and universities across the country. Those wishing to participate in seminars submit their applications to the seminar director.

Eligibility:	Individuals and institutions of higher learning
Application deadlines:	Participants, March 1, 2008, for summer seminars and institutes in 2008; directors, March 1, 2008, for summer seminars and institutes in 2009
Contact:	202-606-8463, e-mail sem-inst@neh.gov

Division of Preservation and Access

Grants are made for projects that will create, preserve, and increase the availability of resources important for research, education, and public programming in the humanities.

Projects may encompass books, journals, newspapers, manuscript and archival materials, maps, still and moving images, sound recordings, and objects of material culture held by libraries, archives, museums, historical organizations, and other repositories.

Preservation and Access Projects

Support may be sought to preserve the intellectual content and aid bibliographic control of collections; to compile bibliographies, descriptive catalogs, and guides to cultural holdings; and to create dictionaries, encyclopedias, databases, and other types of research tools and reference works. Applications may also be submitted for education and training projects, regional preservation field service programs, and research and development projects that are intended to enhance institutional practice and the use of digital technology for preservation and access.

Proposals may combine preservation and access activities within a single project.

Eligible applicants:	Nonprofit institutions, cultural organizations, state agencies, and institutional consortia
Application deadlines:	March 18, May 15, July 1, July 15, September 15, and November 4, 2008
Contact:	202-606-8570, e-mail preservation@neh.gov

Division of Public Programs

Public humanities programs promote the experience of lifelong learning in American and world history, literature, comparative religion, philosophy, and other fields of the humanities. They offer new insights into familiar subjects and invite conversation about important humanities ideas and questions.

The Division of Public Programs supports a wide range of public humanities programs that reach large and diverse public audiences through a variety of program formats, including interpretive exhibitions, radio and television broadcasts, lectures, symposia, interpretive multimedia projects, printed materials, and reading and discussion programs.

Grants support the development and production of television, radio and digital media programs; the planning and implementation of museum exhibitions, the interpretation of historic sites, the production of related publications, multimedia components, and educational programs; the planning and implementation of reading and discussion programs, lectures, symposia, and interpretive exhibitions of books, manuscripts, and other library resources.

Eligible applicants:	Nonprofit institutions and organizations including public television and radio stations and state humanities councils

> *Application deadlines:* Planning, implementation, development, production: August 27, 2008, and January 21, 2009.
> *Contact:* 202-606-8269, e-mail publicpgms@neh.gov

Division of Research Programs

Through fellowships to individual scholars and grants to support complex, frequently collaborative, research, the Division of Research Programs contributes to the creation of knowledge in the humanities.

Fellowships and Stipends

Grants provide support for scholars to undertake full-time independent research and writing in the humanities. Grants are available for a maximum of one year and a minimum of two months of summer study.

> *Eligible applicants:* Individuals
> *Application deadlines:* Fellowships, May 1, 2008; Summer Stipends, October 1, 2008
> *Contact:* 202-606-8200, e-mail (fellowships) fellowships@neh.gov, (summer stipends) stipends@neh.gov

Research

Grants provide up to three years of support for collaborative research in the preparation of publication of editions, translations, and other important works in the humanities, and in the conduct of large or complex interpretive studies, including archaeology projects and humanities studies of science and technology. Grants also support research opportunities offered through independent research centers and international research organizations.

> *Eligible applicants:* Individuals, institutions of higher education, nonprofit professional associations, scholarly societies, and other nonprofit organizations
> *Application deadlines:* Collaborative Research, November 1, 2008; Fellowship Programs at Independent Research Institutions, September 1, 2008
> *Contact:* 202-606-8200, e-mail research@neh.gov

Office of Challenge Grants

Nonprofit institutions interested in developing new sources of long-term support for educational, scholarly, preservation, and public programs in the humanities may be assisted in these efforts by an NEH Challenge Grant. Grantees are required to raise $3 or $4 in nonfederal donations for every federal dollar offered. Both federal and nonfederal funds may be used to establish or increase institutional endowments and therefore guarantee long-term support for a variety of humanities needs. Funds also may be used for limited direct capital expenditures where such needs are compelling and clearly related to improvements in the humanities.

Eligible applicants: Nonprofit postsecondary, educational, research, or cultural institutions and organizations working within the humanities.

Application deadlines: Challenge Grants, May 1, 2008; *We the People* Challenge Grants, February 1, 2009

Contact: 202-606-8309, e-mail challenge@neh.gov

Institute of Museum and Library Services Library Programs

1800 M St. N.W., Ninth Floor, Washington, DC 20036-5802
202-653-4657, fax 202-653-4625
World Wide Web http://www.imls.gov

Anne-Imelda M. Radice
Director, IMLS

Mary L. Chute
Deputy Director for Libraries

Mission

The Institute of Museum and Library Services (IMLS) is the primary source of federal support for the nation's 122,000 libraries and 17,500 museums. The institute's mission is to create strong libraries and museums that connect people to information and ideas. The institute works at the national level and in coordination with state and local organizations to sustain heritage, culture, and knowledge; enhance learning and innovation; and support professional development.

Overview

Libraries and museums help create vibrant, energized learning communities. Our achievement as individuals and our success as a democratic society depend on learning continually, adapting to change readily, and evaluating information critically.

As stewards of cultural heritage, information, and ideas, museums and libraries traditionally have played a vital role in helping us experience, explore, discover, and make sense of the world. That role is now more essential than ever. Through building technological infrastructure and strengthening community relationships, libraries and museums can offer the public unprecedented access and expertise in transforming information overload into knowledge.

The role of IMLS is to provide leadership and funding for the nation's museums and libraries, resources these institutions need to fulfill their mission of becoming centers of learning for life crucial to achieving personal fulfillment, a productive work force, and an engaged citizenry.

Specifically, the Museum and Library Services Act authorizes the institute to support the following activities:

Library Services and Technology Act (LSTA)

- To promote improvements in library services in all types of libraries to better serve the people of the United States
- To facilitate access to resources and in all types of libraries for the purpose of cultivating an educated and informed citizenry
- To encourage resource sharing among all types of libraries for the purpose of achieving economical and efficient delivery of library services to the public

Museum Services Act

- To encourage and support museums in carrying out their public service role of connecting the whole society to cultural, artistic, historic, natural, and scientific understandings that constitute our heritage
- To encourage and support museums in carrying out their educational role as core providers of learning and in conjunction with schools, families, and communities
- To encourage leadership, innovation, and applications of the most current technologies and practices to enhance museum services
- To assist, encourage, and support museums in carrying out their stewardship responsibilities to achieve the highest standards in conservation and care of the cultural, historic, natural, and scientific heritage of the United States to benefit future generations
- To assist, encourage, and support museums in achieving the highest standards of management and service to the public, and to ease the financial burden borne by museums as a result of their increasing use by the public
- To support resource sharing and partnerships among museums, libraries, schools, and other community organizations

In fiscal year (FY) 2007 Congress appropriated $213,695,000 for the programs and administrative support authorized by LSTA. The Office of Library Services within IMLS, under the policy direction of the IMLS director and deputy director, administers LSTA programs. The office comprises the Division of State Programs, which administers the Grants to States program, and the Division of Discretionary Programs, which administers the National Leadership Grants program, the Laura Bush 21st Century Librarian program, the Native American Library Services program, and the Native Hawaiian Library Services program. IMLS also presents annual awards to libraries through the National Awards for Museum and Library Service program. Additionally, IMLS is one of the sponsoring organizations supporting the Coming Up Taller awards (in conjunction with the President's Committee on the Arts and the Humanities, the National Endowment for the Arts, and the National Endowment for the Humanities), the Big Read program (in partnership with the National Endowment for the Arts), and Save America's Treasures (in partnership with the National Park Service, the National Trust for Historic Preservation, Heritage Preservation, the National Endowment for the Arts, and the National Park Foundation).

Impact of Museum and Library Services

A general provision of the Museum and Library Services Act states that "the Director shall carry out and publish analyses of the impact of museum and library services. Such analyses

- Shall be conducted in ongoing consultation with state library administrative agencies; state, regional, and national library and museum organizations; and other relevant agencies and organizations

- Shall identify national needs for, and trends of, museum and library services provided with funds made available under subchapters II and III of this chapter
- Shall report on the impact and effectiveness of programs conducted with funds made available by the Institute in addressing such needs
- Shall identify, and disseminate information on, the best practices of such programs to the agencies and entities described"

Library Statistics

The president's budget request for FY 2008 included funds for IMLS to administer the Public Library Survey and the State Library Agency Survey, effective October 1, 2007. From its inception in 1989 though 2007, these two surveys were administered by the National Center for Education Statistics (NCES). In anticipation of congressional appropriation, NCES and IMLS have been working cooperatively to implement this policy. Current, accurate, and ongoing collection of library data is an essential foundation for quality library services. The institute is committed to the continued excellence of this program.

NCES continues to conduct the Academic Libraries Survey and the School Library Media Center Survey. [See "National Center for Education Statistics" in Part 1—*Ed.*]

On the Library Statistics section of the IMLS Web site (http://www.imls. gov/statistics), visitors can link to data search tools, the latest available data for each survey, other publications, data files, and survey definitions.

Public Libraries Survey

Descriptive statistics for more 9,000 public libraries are collected and disseminated annually through a voluntary census, the Public Libraries Survey. The survey is conducted through the Public Library Statistics Cooperative (PLSC, formerly FSCS). In FY 2008 IMLS will complete the 19th collection of this data (all previous collections were completed by NCES).

The Public Libraries Survey collects identifying information about public libraries and each of their service outlets, including street address, city, county, zip code, and telephone number. Additional identifying information is collected, including library Web address and library mailing address. The survey collects data on staffing; type of legal basis; type of geographic boundary; type of administrative structure; type of interlibrary relationship; type and number of public service outlets; operating revenue and expenditures; capital revenue and expenditures; size of collection (including number of electronic books and databases); current serial subscriptions (including electronic); and service measures such as number of reference transactions, interlibrary loans, circulation, public service hours, library visits, circulation of children's materials, number of children's programs, children's program attendance, total number of library programs, total attendance at library programs, number of Internet terminals used by the general public, and number of users of electronic resources per year.

This survey also collects several data items about outlets, including the location of an outlet relative to a metropolitan area, number of books-by-mail only outlets, number of bookmobiles by bookmobile outlet, and square footage of the outlet.

The 50 states and the District of Columbia participate in data collection. Beginning in 1993, four outlying areas—Guam, the Commonwealth of the Northern Mariana Islands, Puerto Rico, and the U.S. Virgin Islands—joined in the survey. The first release of Public Libraries Survey data occurs with the release of the updated Compare Public Libraries Tool on the Library Statistics section of the IMLS Web site (http://www.imls.gov/statistics). The data used in this Web tool are final, but do not include imputations for missing data (imputation is a statistical means for providing an estimate for each missing data item).

Final imputed data files that contain FY 2005 data on more than 9,000 responding libraries and identifying information about their outlets were made available in November 2007 on the Library Statistics section of the IMLS Web site The FY 2005 data were aggregated to state and national levels in a First Look report, *Public Libraries in the United States: Fiscal Year 2005*, and released in November 2007 on the Web site. Release of the FY 2006 data and a report are expected in the summer of 2008.

The Compare Public Libraries Tool and the Find Public Libraries Tool have been updated with FY 2005 data. FY 2006 data were expected to be available on these tools in spring 2008.

Beginning with the FY 2005 data collection cycle, descriptive data on public libraries are collected via a Web-based data collection application called WebPLUS. The resulting universe file has been a resource for use in drawing samples for special surveys on such topics as literacy, access for the disabled, and library construction. At the state level and in the outlying areas, data coordinators, appointed by each state or outlying area's chief officer of the state library agency, administer the Public Library Statistics Cooperative (PLSC). PLSC is a working network. State data coordinators collect the requested data from public libraries and submit these data to IMLS. IMLS aggregates the data to provide state and national totals. An annual training conference is provided for the state data coordinators, and a steering committee that represents them is active in the development of the Public Libraries Survey and its Web-based data collection. Technical assistance to states is provided by state data coordinators, by the Bureau of the Census, and by the National Commission on Libraries and Information Science (NCLIS). IMLS also works cooperatively with NCLIS, the Bureau of the Census, the Chief Officers of State Library Agencies (COSLA), the American Library Association (ALA), and the U.S. Department of Education's National Library of Education.

State Library Agencies Survey

The State Library Agencies Survey collects and disseminates information about the state library agencies in the 50 states and the District of Columbia. A state library agency (StLA) is the official unit of state government charged with statewide library development and the administration of federal funds under LSTA. StLAs' administrative and developmental responsibilities affect the operation of thousands of public, academic, school, and special libraries. StLAs provide important reference and information services to state government and sometimes also provide service to the general public. StLAs often administer state library and special operations such as state archives and libraries for the blind and physically handicapped and the state Center for the Book.

The State Library Agencies Survey began in 1994, and was administered by NCES until 2007. The FY 2005 StLA Survey collected data on the following areas: direct library services; adult literacy and family literacy; library development services; resources assigned to allied operations such as archive and records management; organizational and governance structure within which the agency operates; electronic networking; staffing; collections; and expenditures. These data are edited electronically, and before FY 1999, missing data were not imputed. Beginning with FY 1999 data, however, national totals included imputations for missing data. Another change is that beginning with FY 1999 data, the StLA became a Web-based data collection system. The most recent data available are for FY 2006. The survey database and report were released in November 2007.

National Medal for Museum and Library Service

The National Medal for Museum and Library Service (formerly the National Award) honors outstanding institutions that make significant and exceptional contributions to their communities. Selected institutions demonstrate extraordinary and innovative approaches to public service, exceeding the expected levels of community outreach and core programs generally associated with its services. The medal includes a prize of $10,000 to each recipient. The awards ceremony is held in Washington, D.C.

The winners of the 2007 National Medal for Museum and Library Service were:

- Birmingham (Alabama) Civil Rights Institute
- Brookfield Zoo of the Chicago Zoological Society
- Georgetown (South Carolina) County Library
- Kim Yerton Branch of the Humboldt County Library, Hoopa, California
- Memphis (Tennessee) Public Library and Information Center
- National Museum of Women in the Arts, Washington, D.C.
- Ocean County Library, Toms River, New Jersey
- Oregon Museum of Science and Industry, Portland
- The Newberry Library, Chicago
- Vermont Historical Society, Barre

State-Administered Programs

In FY 2007 approximately 80 percent of the annual federal appropriation under LSTA was distributed through the Grants to States program to the state library administrative agencies (SLAAs) according to a population-based formula. The formula consists of a minimum amount set by law plus a supplemental amount based on population. Population data were based on the information available from the Bureau of Census Web site on October 1, 2006. The 2003 reauthorization requires that base allotments of $340,000 to the states and $40,000 to the Pacific Territories be increased to $680,000 for the states and $60,000 for the Pacific Territories if IMLS is fully funded. The new base allotments will be phased in gradually as the total appropriation increases. For 2007 the adjusted base allotment to the states was $595,981; that for the Pacific Territories remained at $40,000.

For FY 2007 the Grants to States program total appropriation was $163,746,000 (see Table 1). State agencies may use the appropriation for statewide initiatives and services. They may also distribute the funds through competitive subgrants or cooperative agreements to public, academic, research, school, or special libraries. For-profit and federal libraries are not eligible applicants. LSTA State Grant funds have been used to meet the special needs of children, parents, teenagers, the unemployed, senior citizens, and the business community, as well as adult learners. Many libraries have partnered with community organizations to provide a variety of services and programs, including access to elec-

(text continues on page 362)

Table 1 / Library Services and Technology Act, State Allotment Table, FY 2007
Total Distributed to States: $163,746,000[1]

State	Federal Funds from IMLS (66%)[2]	State Matching Funds (34%)	Total Federal and State Funds
Alabama	$2,602,935	$1,340,906	$3,943,841
Alaska	888,213	457,564	1,345,778
Arizona	3,211,248	1,654,279	4,865,527
Arkansas	1,819,735	937,439	2,757,174
California	16,506,165	8,503,176	25,009,340
Colorado	2,650,214	1,365,262	4,015,475
Connecticut	2,141,681	1,103,290	3,244,971
Delaware	967,412	498,364	1,465,776
Florida	8,429,449	4,342,443	12,771,892
Georgia	4,590,936	2,365,028	6,955,964
Hawaii	1,157,492	596,284	1,753,775
Idaho	1,225,260	631,194	1,856,454
Illinois	6,216,116	3,202,242	9,418,358
Indiana	3,357,739	1,729,744	5,087,483
Iowa	1,902,157	979,899	2,882,055
Kansas	1,804,558	929,621	2,734,178
Kentucky	2,433,669	1,253,708	3,687,378
Louisiana	2,587,884	1,333,152	3,921,036
Maine	1,177,883	606,788	1,784,671
Maryland	3,062,016	1,577,402	4,639,419
Massachusetts	3,413,560	1,758,500	5,172,060
Michigan	5,052,531	2,602,819	7,655,350
Minnesota	2,856,123	1,471,336	4,327,459
Mississippi	1,882,233	969,635	2,851,869

Table 1 / Library Services and Technology Act, State Allotment Table, FY 2007 *(cont.)*

Missouri	3,150,050	1,622,753	4,772,803
Montana	1,007,986	519,266	1,527,252
Nebraska	1,370,433	705,981	2,076,414
Nevada	1,659,300	854,791	2,514,091
New Hampshire	1,172,791	604,165	1,776,955
New Jersey	4,434,773	2,284,580	6,719,353
New Mexico	1,455,113	744,452	2,189,565
New York	9,074,434	4,674,709	13,749,143
North Carolina	4,419,501	2,276,712	6,696,213
North Dakota	876,330	451,443	1,327,773
Ohio	5,643,980	2,907,505	8,551,484
Oklahoma	2,158,232	1,111,817	3,270,049
Oregon	2,199,259	1,132,952	3,332,211
Pennsylvania	6,034,092	3,108,472	9,142,564
Rhode Island	1,069,862	551,141	1,621,004
South Carolina	2,469,636	1,272,237	3,741,872
South Dakota	937,650	483,032	1,420,682
Tennessee	3,221,670	1,659,648	4,881,318
Texas	10,661,984	5,492,537	16,154,522
Utah	1,683,421	867,217	2,550,637
Vermont	870,331	448,352	1,318,683
Virginia	3,928,187	2,023,611	5,951,798
Washington	3,364,690	1,733,325	5,098,015
West Virginia	1,396,003	719,153	2,115,156
Wisconsin	3,033,754	1,562,843	4,596,597
Wyoming	820,240	422,548	1,242,788
District of Columbia	838,393	431,899	1,270,293
Puerto Rico	2,318,588	1,194,424	3,513,012
American Samoa	65,449	33,716	99,165
Northern Marianas	76,310	39,311	115,621
Guam	115,305	59,400	174,704
Virgin Islands	87,823	45,242	133,065
Pacific Territories[3]	203,225	104,692	307,917
Total	$163,746,000	$84,354,000	$248,100,000

1 The amount available to states is based on the balance remaining after enacted allocations have been subtracted from the total appropriation as follows:

LIBRARY ALLOCATION, FY 2007	$210,597,000
Laura Bush 21st Century Librarian Program	$23,760,000
National Leadership Grants	$12,375,000
Native American/Native Hawaiian	$3,638,000
Administration	$7,078,000
Total Distributed to States	$163,746,000

2 Calculation is based on minimum set in the law (P.L. 108-81) and reflects appropriations enacted by P.L. 109-149.
Population data are from the Bureau of Census (BOC) estimates. Data used in the state allotment table are the most current published population estimates available the first day of the fiscal year. Therefore, the population data used in the 2006 table are what was available on the BOC Web site http://www.census.gov/popest/states/tables/ on October 1, 2006.
Population data for American Samoa, Northern Marianas, Guam, Virgin Islands, Marshall Islands, Federated States of Micronesia, and Palau can be accessed at http://www.census.gov/cgi-bin/ipc/idbrank.pl. This table reflects what was available on October 1, 2006.

3 Aggregate allotments (including administrative costs) for Palau, Marshall Islands, and Federated States of Micronesia are awarded on a competitive basis to eligible applicants, and are administered by Pacific Resources for Education and Learning (PREL).

(continued from page 360)
tronic databases, computer instruction, homework centers, summer reading programs, digitization of special collections, access to e-books and adaptive technology, bookmobile service, and development of outreach programs to the underserved. The act limits the amount of funds available for administration at the state level to 4 percent and requires a 34 percent match from nonfederal state or local funds.

Grants to the Pacific Territories and the Freely Associated States (FAS) are funded under a Special Rule, 20 USCA 9131(b)(3), that authorizes a small competitive grants program in the Pacific and the U.S. Virgin Islands. There are seven eligible entities: Guam (GU), American Samoa (AS), and the Commonwealth of Northern Mariana Islands (CNMI), which together are the Pacific Territories (Insular Areas); the Federated States of Micronesia (FSM), the Republic of the Marshall Islands (RMI), and the Republic of Palau (PU), which together are the FAS; and the U.S. Virgin Islands (VI). The funds for this grant program are taken from the allotments for the FAS (FSM, RMI, and PU), but not from the allotments to the territories. The territories (GU, AS, CNMI, VI) receive their allotments through the regular program and, in addition, may apply for funds under this program. In FY 2007, $203,371 was available for the seven entities. This amount included a set-aside of 5 percent because Pacific Resources for Education and Learning (PREL), based in Hawaii, facilitated the competition. PREL received the set-aside amount to administer parts of the program. Therefore, the total amount awarded in FY 2007 was $193,202.

Priorities for funding programs and services that support the goals of LSTA are set by the individual SLAAs based on needs they identify in the statutorily required five-year plans that they submit to IMLS. In response to the Youth Initiative of First Lady Laura Bush, the Grants to States program developed the outcomes-based evaluation Task Force on Summer Reading Programs. This task force developed evaluation tools that 20 public libraries in 10 states tested during the summer 2006 reading programs. These tools will be revised and made available to the general public library community.

On a rotating basis, States program staff members conduct site visits to state libraries to provide technical support and to monitor the states' success in administering the program. This year, program officers visited the 19 state libraries of Alaska, Arkansas, Arizona, Delaware, Illinois, Indiana, Louisiana, Maryland, Michigan, Minnesota, Nebraska, New Hampshire, New Mexico, Oklahoma, Pennsylvania, Tennessee, Texas, Utah, and Virginia.

Discretionary Programs

IMLS began administering the discretionary programs of LSTA in 1998. In FY 2007, $40,684,000 was allocated for discretionary programs, including National Leadership Grants, the Laura Bush 21st Century Librarian Program, Native American Library Services, and Native Hawaiian Library Services.

The FY 2007 congressional appropriation for discretionary programs was:

- National Leadership Grants
  (including Collaborative Planning Grants) $12,375,000

- Laura Bush 21st Century Librarian Program $23,760,000
- Native American Library Services $3,118,300
- Native Hawaiian Library Services $519,700

National Leadership Grants Program

The National Leadership Grants program provides funding for innovative model programs to enhance the quality of library services nationwide. National Leadership Grants are competitive and intended to produce results useful for the broader library community.

In 2007 IMLS awarded 27 National Leadership Grants totaling $12,199,800. A total of 154 applications were received, requesting more than $54,000,000. Projects were funded in three categories: Building Digital Resources, Research and Demonstration, and Library and Museum Community Collaboration (see Table 2). In addition, IMLS created a new Collaborative Planning Grant within the National Leadership Grant program in 2007. This new category was designed to enable project teams from libraries, museums, and other partner organizations to work together on a collaborative project in any of the National Leadership Grant categories; partnerships with museums were not required for planning grants except within the Library and Museum Collaboration category.

Building Digital Resources

The Building Digital Resources category (maximum award $1 million) supports the creation, use, preservation, and presentation of significant digital resources as well as the development of tools to manage digital assets. IMLS supported projects that

- Digitized, preserved, and aggregated digital content from libraries and partner organizations, including museums and/or archives on a large-scale, statewide, or thematic basis
- Developed and disseminated new tools to improve management, preservation, presentation, and/or use of digital resources
- Increased community access to library and information resources through innovative approaches and/or improved practice

Research and Demonstration

The Research and Demonstration category (maximum award $1 million) supports research on issues of national concern and demonstrating new solutions to real-world problems. Funded projects

- Evaluated the impact of library or museum services
- Investigated how learning takes place and how use of library and information resources enhances learning
- Conducted research or demonstration projects to improve the quality, effectiveness, or efficiency of library management, programs, or services

(text continues on page 368)

Table 2 / National Leadership Grants, FY 2007

Building Digital Resources

Denver Public Library $778,509

The library—in partnership with the City of Denver, the Colorado Alliance of Research Libraries, Denver Historical Society, the University of Colorado at Denver Auraria Library, and the University of Denver Penrose Library—will inventory, catalog, and digitize historic documents of the city and county of Denver, linking them to existing information about buildings and neighborhoods and preserving the digital files in the Alliance Digital Repository. This project will create a model of local public-private collaboration to preserve and provide access to cultural and historical materials.

New England Law Library Consortium $364,150

The New England Law Library Consortium, Inc., will address a pervasive problem that libraries and researchers commonly face: connecting the library researcher to the relevant e-resources that the library has acquired. The "Universal Search Solution" project will take a different approach from federated searching by developing a "one box" search solution: an open source, dynamic, searchable index across library-defined e-resources, including each library's Online Public Access Catalog, subscription-based publications, and free Web resources.

Fondren Library, Rice University, Houston $979,578

The library, in partnership with the Maryland Institute for Technology in the Humanities at the University of Maryland, will develop an innovative approach to helping users search, browse, analyze, and share content from distributed online collections through its "Our Americas Archive Partnership" (OAAP). OAAP will incorporate Web 2.0 technologies to help users discover and use relevant source materials in languages other than English and will improve users' ability to find relevant materials using domain-specific vocabulary searches. Two online collections of materials in English and Spanish, the Early Americas Digital Archive, and a new digital archive of materials to be developed at Rice will provide an initial corpus for testing the tools.

Syracuse University $191,114

The university's Center for Natural Language Processing in the School of Information Studies, partnering with a team from the University Corporation for Atmospheric Research, will integrate three digital library tools and services to create a new hybrid computer-assisted cataloging system, the Metadata Assignment and Search Tool (MAST). MAST will enable libraries and museums to describe and disseminate their digital materials efficiently and link them to state-level educational standards, making these materials fully available in a digital library or searchable through Web services from their own Web sites.

Texas A&M University $403,737

Texas A&M, through the Texas Digital Library, a cooperative organization of institutions of higher learning in Texas, will develop and implement the Texas ETD Repository, a statewide system for managing the entire life cycle of electronic theses and dissertations (ETDs) from initial submission to final publication. By ensuring consistent standards and interoperability, the Texas ETD Repository will establish a federated statewide repository for long-term preservation.

University of California, Los Angeles $249,326

The University Library and UCLA's Department of Near Eastern Languages and Cultures will create the Cuneiform Digital Library Initiative: Second Generation (CDLI2). The project will migrate 450,000 legacy archival and access images and metadata from CDLI to UCLA's Digital Library Content System, standardizing and upgrading the metadata to improve discovery and enable content archival within the California Digital Library's Digital Preservation Repository. The project will add 7,000 digital artifacts with cuneiform inscriptions, including collections housed at the University of Chicago's Oriental Institute and in the Middle East, to be scanned by the Max Planck Institute and the French Institute of the Near East. This proj-

Table 2 / National Leadership Grants, FY 2007 *(cont.)*

ect will ensure the long-term preservation of text inscribed on endangered ancient cuneiform tablets.

J. Willard Marriott Library, University of Utah $353,237

The library—partnering with the National Park Service, the U.S. Geological Survey, the Utah Division of Wildlife Resources, and other partners, will build the Western Soundscape Archive, a comprehensive online resource of animal and environmental sounds of the western United States. Through freely available streaming audio files and downloadable podcasts, scientists, scholars, educators, students, and nature enthusiasts will be able to identify animals and hear ambient recordings of places that no longer exist or that have been altered. In addition to creating or repurposing existing digital natural sound recordings, the project team will interview scientists and generate stories for National Public Radio.

WGBH Educational Foundation $709,420

The WGBH Educational Foundation Media Library and Archives, in collaboration with the University of Massachusetts–Boston and the Columbia University Center for New Media Teaching and Learning, will create a digital library of material relating to the 1983 television series "Vietnam: A Television History." Scholars, academics, and the general public will access the original interview materials, stills, and most of the stock footage gathered for the series. Entire interviews will stream online and link to interactive transcripts, allowing users to explore an interview at any point. The project will be a model partnership among a public television station's moving image archive, university library staff, and a university digital media center.

William Paterson University $971,512

William Paterson University's NJVid project will create and test a statewide digital video repository and portal with tools and services, providing "lectures on demand," licensed commercial videos, and locally owned videos for use by members of the partner collaborative. Three major consortia representing most educational information organizations throughout New Jersey—VALE (Virtual Academic Library Environment); New Jersey Digital Highway, the statewide cultural heritage consortium; and NJEdge.Net, the statewide Internet2 networking consortium—will incorporate and extend their video resources and services in this strategic initiative. William Paterson University, Rutgers University, and eight other institutions—including universities, community colleges, a high school, a county public library system, and a museum—will serve as initial testers of this model integrated resource.

Research and Demonstration

Millar Library, Portland (Oregon) State University $910,064

The library will conduct a national demonstration and evaluation of the Learner Web, an Internet- and telephone-accessed tool that connects self-directed adults with basic literacy skill needs to learning-management systems supported by online and local community-based resources. With a consortium of libraries, community organizations, state agencies, and educational institutions in six states, the project will field test the Learner Web to determine what is needed to implement it in rural and city public libraries of varying sizes, creating the documentation and organizational capacity to implement the system nationally.

Purdue University $421,068

Investigators in the Distributed Data Curation Center in the libraries at Purdue University and the University of Illinois at Urbana-Champaign will address the question "Which researchers are willing to share data, when, with whom, and under what conditions?" The team will produce case studies of researcher data/metadata workflow, curation profiles describing policies for archiving and making available research data, a matrix to compare parameters across disciplines, system requirements for managing data in a repository, and recommendations for implementing results under diverse systems.

Table 2 / National Leadership Grants, FY 2007 *(cont.)*

Rochester Institute of Technology $314,215

Rochester's Image Permanence Institute will research the effects on digital prints in libraries and museums of housing and display materials and of handling. The project will also assess the risk of flood damage to these materials. Results will be freely accessible on a new Web site, the DP3 Project: Digital Print Preservation Portal.

Rutgers University $964,887

Researchers at the Rutgers School of Communication, Information, and Library Studies will investigate ways to improve the ability of people to find information they need in digital libraries. By examining the interaction of factors such as the searcher's location, individual characteristics, the nature of his or her task, and similar data, the team will create a "personalization assistant" that will help searchers use digital libraries more effectively.

University of Illinois at Urbana-Champaign $225,747

The university library will develop and test prototype library portals designed to enhance resource integration in academic libraries. The project will develop portal mechanisms that better integrate a library's multiple search and discovery tools and provide enhanced access to distributed primary and secondary information. Utilizing transaction log analysis, focus groups, and individual interviews, the research team will investigate the utility of search assistance techniques. The portal mechanisms developed in this project will be useful to the development of next-generation resource discovery and metasearch systems.

University of Illinois at Urbana-Champaign $975,903

In a cooperative agreement with IMLS, the university will investigate and implement a systematic approach to developing useful, meaningful, and usable digital collections. Building on the prior work of the IMLS Digital Collections and Content project, the researchers will explore how to use the relationships between collection-level and item-level metadata in federated digital repositories to preserve content and make the content more useful for scholars and the public.

University of North Texas $448,548

The university libraries will develop a model for an iterative user-centered design process in a rapid development framework that digital libraries can implement to improve the usability and effectiveness of their resources for targeted user groups. This project will focus on the information-seeking behavior and needs of genealogists.

Library and Museum Community Collaboration

Americans for Libraries Council $241,808

The council and its partners in New York, Connecticut, and Virginia will develop public programming among cultural institutions that engage intergenerational audiences in exploring the experience of aging in the United States from historical, cultural, and artistic perspectives. The project will occur in Norfolk, Virginia; Hartford, Connecticut; and Suffolk County, New York, which were selected for their relatively large numbers of active older residents. A report, "Designs for Change: Libraries and Museum Collaborations on Aging," will enable local libraries and museums to build a community of practice.

Children's Museum of Houston $946,396

The museum, in partnership with the Houston Public Library and others, will develop and make available nationally multilingual kits that will increase literacy and family learning through "CLiCK: City of Learners/Collection of Kits." The project builds on two earlier IMLS-funded National Leadership Grant collaborations, "Tot Spot," which studied learning in early childhood and provided information to caregivers, and "Para los Niños," which extended the project to Hispanic communities. The new project will engage two additional cities—Brooklyn, New York, and San José, California. Language kits including Vietnamese, Cantonese, and Spanish will be developed to meet the needs of audiences in each city.

Table 2 / National Leadership Grants, FY 2007 *(cont.)*

Fresno Art Museum $361,471

The Fresno (California) Art Museum, in partnership with the Fresno Public Library, will deliver arts programming to three majority Hispanic communities in Fresno County—Mendota, Orange Cove, and Tranquility. Together with the local school district and government entities, they will create bilingual lifelong learning experiences for children and adults and will serve as a model for other ethnically diverse agricultural communities.

Libraries of Eastern Oregon $363,576

The Libraries of Eastern Oregon consortium, in partnership with the Oregon Museum of Science and Industry and other partners, will deliver programs in science and art to 30 disadvantaged rural communities, including three Native American reservations. The public libraries will host onsite programs, interactive distance learning, and hands-on activities for lifelong learning and community enrichment. The Smithsonian American Art Museum and the Oregon Council for the Humanities will contribute programming in the arts.

Maine Historical Society $852,058

The historical society, in partnership with the Maine State Library, will coordinate local teams from 16 Maine communities—one from each county in the state—to develop a statewide Community Heritage Project that will create content-rich Web sites for the Maine Memory Network (see http://www.mainememory.net). Librarians, museum professionals, teachers, and students will work together to provide local history resources for broader user access.

Collaborative Planning Grants

Brown University Library $29,609

The library, partnering with the library and the museum of the Rhode Island School of Design, plans to develop new database architecture for silverware collections that are held by museums around the world. Based on the Gorham Manufacturing Company's catalog, the digital library will include archival drawings, sketches, and product descriptions that will enable users to identify their pieces and contribute to a union catalog of holdings.

College of New Jersey $24,417

The college will collaborate with the New Jersey Institute of Technology and William Paterson University to plan for the development of a shared, open source integrated library system to support shared library services and operations. The project team will develop a report that will be presented to the Virtual Academic Library Environment of New Jersey (VALE) as well as made available to other interested parties via a creative common license.

Council on Library and Information Resources $30,000

The Council on Library and Information Resources (CLIR) will plan a project to develop a cohort of humanities and social sciences scholars, drawn from and building on the graduates of the CLIR Postdoctoral Fellowship Program in Scholarly Information Resources. The scholars will work toward coordinating and linking together the new large-scale digital initiatives that are being developed across the country in line with the recommendations of the American Council of Learned Societies Commission on Cyberinfrastructure for the Humanities and Social Sciences.

New York Public Library $30,000

The library, with partnering institutions Brooklyn Public Library and Queens Borough Public Library, will plan a project to identify and evaluate the homework reference needs of students, educators, parents, and librarians for the purpose of designing an integrated homework help Web site that will effectively respond to young people's needs regarding new digital technologies.

University of California, Los Angeles $29,675

UCLA and Indiana University will explore the additional tools needed by institutions that wish to contribute data to the Sheet Music Consortium, a metadata harvesting service designed to

Table 2 / National Leadership Grants, FY 2007 *(cont.)*

provide searching capabilities for sheet music collections hosted by diverse institutions in a single interface. The partners will investigate the services that end users of the consortium value most highly as a basis for future improvement.

Wildlife Conservation Society $29,775

The society, in partnership with Poet's House, will build on an earlier IMLS-funded project that brought poetic expression to the Central Park Zoo by hiring a poet-in-residence who assisted with the development of zoo signage and contributed innovative language to visual resources to promote conservation. The planning project will extend this concept to five diverse communities across the country, tentatively New Orleans, Salt Lake City, Milwaukee, Little Rock, and Jacksonville. The planning project will engage libraries in each community with a local zoo and help them to develop partnerships that promote conservation and draw on local strengths and resources.

(continued from page 363)

through new or enhanced technology, new or substantially revised "promising practices," or collaborative initiatives

- Investigated ways to enhance the archiving, reservation, management, discovery, and use of digital assets and resources

Library and Museum Community Collaboration

The Library and Museum Community Collaboration category (maximum award $1 million) helps to create new opportunities for libraries and museums to engage with each other, and with other organizations as appropriate, to support the educational, economic, and social needs of their communities. In addition to libraries, archives, and museums, partners can include community organizations, public media, and other institutions and agencies that help libraries and museums to better serve their communities. A partnership of at least one eligible library entity and one eligible museum entity is required. Additional partners are encouraged where appropriate. Grant funds supported innovative collaborative projects, whether they were new partnerships or were building on an existing collaboration. Funded projects

- Addressed community civic and educational needs
- Increased the organizations' capacity to serve as effective venues and resources for learning
- Used technology in innovative ways to serve audiences more effectively

Collaborative Planning Grants

The new category of Collaborative Planning Grants (maximum award $30,000) was designed to enable project teams from libraries, museums, and other partnering organizations to work collaboratively in any of the National Leadership Grant categories. The guidelines required that at least one of the partners must be an eligible library entity or an eligible museum entity. Funded projects were expected to result in deliverable products such as plans, prototypes, or proofs of concept for dissemination to and evaluation by appropriate audiences.

Laura Bush 21st Century Librarian Program

The Laura Bush 21st Century Librarian Program (maximum award $1 million) was established in 2003 as the Librarians for the 21st Century program; the name was changed in 2006 in accordance with the provisions of IMLS's congressional appropriation. The program provides competitive funding to support projects to recruit and educate the next generation of librarians and library leaders, build institutional capacity in graduate schools of library and information science and develop faculty who will help in this endeavor, conduct needed research on the demographics and needs of the profession, and support programs of continuing education and training in library and information science for librarians and library staff.

In FY 2007 IMLS awarded 43 grants totaling $27,851,200 for the program (see Table 3). A total of 107 applications requesting $56,110,930 were received.

The 2007 priorities for Laura Bush 21st Century Librarian Program funding were:

Doctoral Programs

- To develop faculty to educate the next generation of library professionals. In particular, to increase the number of students enrolled in doctoral programs that will prepare faculty to teach master's students who will work in school, public, and academic libraries.
- To develop the next generation of library leaders. In particular, to increase the number of students enrolled in doctoral programs that will prepare them to assume positions as library managers and administrators.

Master's Programs

- To educate the next generation of librarians. In particular, to increase the number of students enrolled in nationally accredited graduate library programs preparing for careers of service in libraries.

Research

- *Early Career Development Program*—To support the early career development of new faculty members who are likely to become leaders in library and information science by supporting innovative research by untenured, tenure-track faculty.
- *Research*—To provide the library community with information needed to support successful recruitment and education of the next generation of librarians. In particular, through funded research, to establish baseline data on professional demographics and job availability, and to evaluate current programs in library education for their capacity to meet the identified needs; and to conduct research and establish ongoing research capacity in the field of library and information science, particularly the evaluation of library and information services, assessment of the value and use of public libraries and their services by the public, and assessment of the public value and use of the Internet.

Preprofessional Programs

- To recruit future librarians. In particular, to attract promising junior high, high school, or college students to consider careers in librarianship through statewide or regional pilot projects employing recruitment strategies that are cost-effective and measurable; and to introduce high school or college students to potential careers in library and information science by employing them to assist with library disaster recovery or service operation in areas that have suffered major disasters. Participation of at least one library, as the applicant or as an official partner, in a location certified by the Federal Emergency Management Agency as a major disaster area in 2005 or 2006, is required.

Programs to Build Institutional Capacity

- To develop or enhance curricula within graduate schools of library and information science. In particular, to develop or enhance courses or programs of study for library, museum, and archives professionals in the creation, management, preservation, presentation, and use of digital assets; to develop or enhance courses or programs of study relating to the development of critical-thinking skills, such as organization leadership and research methods; to broaden the library and information science curriculum by incorporating perspectives from other disciplines and fields of scholarship, such as public policy, ethics, American studies, urban planning, mass communication, and instructional design; and to develop projects or programs in data curation as training programs for graduate students in library and information science.

Continuing Education

- To develop or enhance programs of continuing education and training in library and information science for librarians and library staff
- To develop or enhance programs of continuing education and training for librarians and library staff to improve library services to specialized audiences such as at-risk youth, seniors, and those with ethnic, language, or other barriers to service
- To develop or enhance programs to promote collaboration between educators and librarians employed in education institutions
- To provide internships in conservation practice in libraries that have suffered disaster-related collections damage

(text continues on page 377)

Table 3 / Laura Bush 21st Century Librarian Program, FY 2007

Doctoral Programs

Drexel University College of Information Science and Technology $992,100

The college will prepare new faculty who will be trained in information systems and technologies, have the knowledge and skills to conduct research on digital libraries and related issues, and have the passion and expertise to educate the next generation of library professionals.

Syracuse University School of Information Studies $885,598

The program will develop faculty to educate the next generation of library professionals to work in academic, public, or school libraries. Preparation for university-level teaching will be integrated with targeted library research activities to help Ph.D. students successfully make the transition to becoming assistant professors in library science programs.

University of Illinois at Urbana-Champaign Graduate School of Library and Information Science $990,234

The school will enhance its doctoral program by building a stronger research community within the school for the study of information in society, including policy, economic, and historical dimensions. Project goals include enhancing the doctoral program curriculum; connecting the research community to the wider world of librarianship; and attracting and supporting thirteen diverse students, especially those from underrepresented groups, with a specific focus on recruiting doctoral students who will teach master's students capable of becoming future leaders in public, academic, and school libraries.

University of Texas at Austin School of Information $911,928

The school and the Kilgarlin Center for Preservation of the Cultural Record will support a cohort of five doctoral preservation fellowships. The primary goals of the project are to develop faculty leaders in preservation education and high-level administrators of major cultural repositories who are educated in preservation.

University of Washington Information School $731,965

A cohort of four students will be recruited from traditionally underrepresented groups for a doctoral fellowship program that will become a model for intensive mentoring in library and information science doctoral education. The goals of this project are to mount a vigorous recruitment effort to attract a highly competitive pool of students from traditionally underrepresented groups; to provide intensive faculty mentoring for those students; to provide intensive mentoring and engagement with library leaders in the Seattle area; and, based on these mentoring efforts, to create a model of intensively mentored doctoral education for library and information science.

Master's Programs

American Library Association $872,920

Building on the success of the Spectrum scholarship program, which provides scholarships for ethnically and racially underrepresented students attending graduate library and information science programs, the association will initiate "REACH 21: Preparing the Next Generation of Librarians for 21st Century Library Leadership." The project will foster the recruitment, matriculation, and early-career development of 150 minority students in master's level library and information science programs; provide mentoring and coaching of 60 additional students from underrepresented backgrounds; establish a year-long mentoring program that will leverage community and support networks and aid educational and early career retention; and create an outreach services component.

Catholic University of America School of Library and Information Science $412,660

The school will partner with District of Columbia public schools and the District of Columbia Library Association to create a project that will select, educate, mentor, and employ ten new school librarians.

Table 3 / Laura Bush 21st Century Librarian Program, FY 2007 *(cont.)*

Denver Public Library $988,518

Building on an earlier IMLS-funded project, the Denver Public Library will partner with REFORMA Colorado and the University of Denver to further develop and refine the Future LEADers of America scholarship program in order to increase community access to libraries. The project will provide full scholarships for 18 racially and linguistically diverse students to earn master's degrees in library science at the university.

East Central University $800,733

East Central—in partnership with Cameron University, Oklahoma Panhandle State University, Northwestern Oklahoma State University, and the Oklahoma State Regents for Higher Education—will develop the "Westward Expansion Project" to meet the work force needs of 156 rural school districts located in 30 counties in the western half of Oklahoma. Distance learning technology will be used to expand an existing library media specialist program into this area of Oklahoma, based on East Central University's existing distance-education model.

Emory University $773,336

The Emory libraries and their partners—the University of North Texas and the Atlanta University Center—will address the need for professional librarians with contemporary skill sets in northern Georgia. Currently, no ALA-accredited graduate library program exists in Georgia. The project will recruit, educate, and prepare an Atlanta-based cohort of 35 diverse graduate students for library careers with an emphasis on digital knowledge management.

Florida State University College of Information $559,872

The college will partner with Broward County Library, Miami-Dade Public Library, Southeast Florida Library Information Network, and the State Archives and Library of Florida to provide a master's scholarship program for the next generation of leaders and managers who will serve underserved populations in southeast Florida public libraries.

Free Library of Philadelphia Foundation $999,980

Building on a previous IMLS-funded project, the foundation will increase minority representation among professional librarians and the number of youth librarians throughout the library system. Grant funds will be used to recruit and support 25 internal candidates with bachelor's degrees from three different applicant pools: full-time paraprofessional staff, library interns, and part-time or seasonal outreach staff. Students will earn master's degrees in library and information science at the University of Pittsburgh.

Houston Independent School District $787,126

The district's Department of Library Services, in collaboration with the University of North Texas School of Library and Information Science, will recruit and educate teachers to become certified school librarians to address the need for certified librarians to serve an increasingly racially, ethnically, and culturally diverse student population.

Kent State University School of Library and Information Science $643,007

Kent State proposes to recruit and educate 18 youth services librarians with an emphasis on the use of museums. The selected students will receive scholarships to complete a master's degree in library and information science through a combination of distance education throughout the academic year and two four-week summer sessions on campus, with a focus on using new technologies and applications such as wikis, podcasts, and blogs.

Los Angeles Public Library $362,358

The library will meet the need for professional public librarians in the ethnically and culturally diverse city of Los Angeles by partnering with the University of California, Los Angeles, and San José State University School of Library and Information Science to promote the library as a potential employer.

Table 3 / Laura Bush 21st Century Librarian Program, FY 2007 (cont.)

Mansfield University of Pennsylvania School of Library and Information Technologies $997,388

The school will partner with Antioch University–Seattle and the Pennsylvania Department of Education to increase the number of school library media specialists across the nation by awarding 72 scholarships for master's degree programs to highly qualified teachers. The universities will also collaborate with the Tacoma (Washington) School District, training 60 principals in library advocacy and improving collaboration and leadership skills of school library media specialists.

Network of Illinois Learning Resources in Community Colleges $994,610

The network, along with ten partner libraries in community colleges in Illinois and Missouri, will build a diverse professional workforce that understands community-based library staffing and service strategies as well as the challenges of serving a nontraditional, diverse, commuter-based student population. The project will support the education of 20 students at the Graduate School of Library and Information Science at the University of Illinois at Urbana-Champaign. The school will collaborate with the university's College of Education to provide a varied curriculum. The partner libraries offer the students mentoring throughout the graduate program and for six months following graduation.

New York University Graduate School of Arts and Sciences $700,133

The graduate school, in collaboration with Long Island University's Palmer School of Library and Information Science, will address the need for academic librarians with scholarly training by recruiting and educating students in a dual master's degree program. Twenty students will receive scholarships and a reduction in the number of credits required to complete the two master's degrees—one in library and information science and the other in a subject area of the student's choice.

Sam Houston State University Department of Library Science $330,746

The department will partner with the Region One Education Service Center to provide 20 scholarships for students from the South Texas area to earn master's degrees in library science. Most of the recruits will be bilingual and/or of Hispanic heritage.

San José State University $943,336

The San José State University (SJSU) Library and its partners, the San José Public Library and the National Hispanic University, will recruit 15 people of color into SJSU's graduate program of library and information science, provide full scholarships and living stipends, train them to meet the needs of diverse communities, and prepare them to serve as leaders throughout their library careers.

St. John's University $988,419

St. John's—in partnership with the Queens Borough Public Library, the Office of School Libraries of the New York City Education Department, and the New York Hall of Science—will improve literacy and academic performance of youth in underserved metropolitan areas by recruiting and training 40 students for future employment in public libraries, school library media centers, and museums in the New York City metropolitan area.

Texas Woman's University School of Library and Information Studies $691,323

The school will offer an online degree program enabling library workers currently serving small and rural communities throughout Texas to obtain a library and information science master's degree. Thirty students will receive full tuition and stipends. Formal partners include the Texas State Library and Archives Commission and the Texas Library Association.

University of Iowa School of Library and Information Science $881,692

The school will recruit two cohorts of 20 students each into its master's degree program in library and information science. Formal partners include Iowa's Area Education Agencies,

Table 3 / Laura Bush 21st Century Librarian Program, FY 2007 *(cont.)*

the State Library of Iowa, and the Iowa Association of School Librarians, all of which will assist in the recruitment process.

University of Missouri–Columbia School of Information Science and Learning Technologies $766,610

In partnership with four Missouri libraries (University of Missouri–Columbia, University of Missouri–St. Louis, University of Missouri–Kansas City, and Missouri State University), the school will prepare students at the master's level for leadership and management careers in academic libraries by creating an academic library fellows program.

University of Texas at Austin $407,780

The University of Texas at Austin School of Information's Stepping Up program will provide a replicable model of community cooperation designed to recruit, retain, and foster the professional growth of current library support staff with an interest in earning a master's degree in library and information science. On admittance to the program, 11 current librarians from partner libraries will receive tuition, a small stipend, and a laptop computer, and be matched with mentors. In addition to increasing the number of professional librarians prepared for leadership positions, the project will facilitate a series of management workshops, developed jointly by faculty members and local library managers, to be offered to the library community.

Research

Early Career Development

Dominican University Graduate School of Library and Information Science $199,796

Kate Williams of the Dominican University Graduate School of Library and Information Science will use a social capital/social network model to research actual and potential information technology use in six disadvantaged communities across Chicago. The research will analyze how people and communities are already using computers and the Internet, and how their own lives and identities might be represented as part of the nation's cyberinfrastructure.

University of Arizona–Tucson $301,618

Patricia Montiel Overall of the University of Arizona, in partnership with Sunnyside Unified School District and Tucson Unified School District, will examine the effect of teacher/librarian collaboration on science information literacy of Latino students. Using qualitative and quantitative methodologies over three years, this study will look at teacher/librarian collaboration in the preparation of science instructional modules for third, fourth, and fifth graders in predominantly Latino elementary schools.

Old Dominion University $291,244

The university will conduct an exploratory study of the relationship between national board certification in library media and information science and student academic achievement. The project will provide a scientifically rigorous research framework and pilot that framework with a subset of the nation's library and information professionals.

University of North Carolina at Chapel Hill $566,385

The university will implement a career-tracking model for library and information science (LIS) graduates based on a previous IMLS-funded comprehensive study of career patterns of graduates of LIS programs in North Carolina. The goals for national implementation are to refine the career-tracking survey and methodology so that they are suitable for all LIS programs to use with their recent graduates; recruit as many LIS programs as possible to participate in a staged national launch of the career-tracking model; conduct surveys and provide access to results for the participating LIS programs; explore options for sustaining the national career-tracking model; and disseminate findings and publicize the availability of the model.

Table 3 / Laura Bush 21st Century Librarian Program, FY 2007 *(cont.)*

University of North Texas $70,144

The university will study the impact of implementing Web-based training in public libraries. The study will model practical yet theoretically based implementation practices and assessment measures of online training; inform library administrators of both implementation practices and measures of staff and organizational impacts of investment in staff e-training courses; and contribute to the library literature on establishing best practices in delivery of computer-mediated courses for continuing education and training in public libraries.

Preprofessional Programs

University of Illinois at Urbana-Champaign Graduate School of Library and Information Science $788,895

The school and the University of Illinois Extension's statewide 4-H network will partner to reach youth and youth leaders with engaging, educational activities to recruit underserved youth into library and information science. Five Illinois communities—Urbana-Champaign, Chicago, Danville, East St. Louis, and Rockford—with a high concentration of minority, low-income, and English-language-learner populations will pilot the program. Junior high and high school students will participate in a variety of activities designed to give them familiarity with a range of information science topics and a variety of library careers.

Programs to Build Institutional Capacity

College of St. Catherine $352,526

The college will develop an innovative library and information science curriculum that combines competence in librarianship/information science with the knowledge, attributes, skills, and capacities that will be essential for future successful professionals. These include an understanding of ethical principles as they apply to librarianship and information science, exposure to and practice with research methods, development of leadership and communications skills, and technological fluency. The new curriculum will incorporate interdisciplinary learning in leadership, research, communication, philosophy, ethics, education, and information technology.

Drexel University College of Information Science and Technology $613,478

The college—in collaboration with the University of Michigan, Florida State University, and the University of Pittsburgh—will transform the Internet Public Library (IPL) into a fully featured virtual learning laboratory for digital reference. IPL is a public service organization founded at the University of Michigan and hosted by Drexel University. Enhancements that will result from this grant include digital reference learning objects available to faculty in all ALA-accredited library and information science programs; a laboratory with access to new technologies used to offer digital reference service; and a collaborative learning community for faculty, students, and working librarians.

Indiana University School of Library and Information Science $343,420

The Indiana University School of Library and Information Science at Indianapolis is partnering with the Indiana Library Federation and Indiana State Library to develop the Career Transitions Executive Leadership Program (CTELP). CTELP is designed to build capacity for identifying, recruiting, educating, and mentoring the next generation of library managers and leaders.

Long Island University Palmer School of Library and Information Science $316,967

The school, in partnership with the City University of New York (CUNY), will place 30 specially trained interns in the special collections departments of CUNY over a three-year period to assist with digital projects to expand access to CUNY's historical, cultural, and aesthetic materials. The Palmer School will also expand its curriculum by at least one course to teach up-to-the-minute skills suited to CUNY's needs.

Table 3 / Laura Bush 21st Century Librarian Program, FY 2007 *(cont.)*

University of Illinois at Urbana-Champaign Graduate School of Library and Information Science $996,243

The school will expand and enhance its pilot Community Informatics Corps (CIC) master's program. Community informatics is the field of study and practice devoted to understanding how information processes and technologies help communities achieve their goals. The aim of CIC is to recruit and mentor a group of Latino, African American, and other students interested in the experiences of underserved groups in society who are eager for a career that gives them the opportunity to contribute to their communities.

Continuing Education

American Library Association $407,111

In partnership with the Western Council of State Librarians, ALA will develop a national voluntary certification program for support staff in rural or small-town public and academic libraries. The three-year project will result in a set of core competencies and policies and procedures and will provide alternative options for assessing current knowledge of the field and experience for nontraditionally trained library staff.

American Library Association $358,690

ALA's Public Programs Office will create and administer the Online Resource Center for Library Cultural Programming (ORC), a professional development Web site to help librarians find authoritative resources for cultural programming, and will train librarians in cultural programming techniques. ORC will organize and make accessible through links and online documents a wide array of national cultural program information and training tools, and provide access to successful turnkey programs developed by cultural organizations such as state humanities councils, thus extending the value of the original investment in the programs.

Indiana University School of Library and Information Science $362,490

The school will offer, enhance, and revise the instructor-mediated courseware Shaping Outcomes, developed and tested through a three-year collaborative agreement between IMLS and Indiana University Purdue University Indianapolis (IUPUI) Museum Studies program and the school of library and information science. The school will develop partnerships with organizations and agencies involved in librarian continuing education and evaluate the effectiveness of the Shaping Outcomes project in improving approaches to project planning, grant preparation, and successfully addressing the needs of library and museum professionals.

New York Public Library $329,750

The project Leadership Now! will develop an enhanced workforce of mid-level managers equipped with the skills and vision to enhance the library's role as a learning organization.

Pacific Resources for Education and Learning $652,127

The Leaders for Pacific Libraries project will provide specialized continuing education training to library staff in six jurisdictions of the U.S.-affiliated Pacific: American Samoa, the Commonwealth of the Northern Mariana Islands, the Federated States of Micronesia, Guam, the Republic of the Marshall Islands, and the Republic of Palau. The training, which will be provided through three workshops and a summer institute, will focus on digital library development, grant writing, and preservation.

Southeastern Library Network $866,284

Southeastern Library Network (SOLINET) will create staff capacity and strengthen staff skills in 16 public library systems in Louisiana and Mississippi that suffered severe damage and destruction from hurricanes Katrina and Rita in 2005. In partnership with the affected libraries, SOLINET will provide staff to run temporary library facilities in communities while permanent libraries are planned and rebuilt, and continuing education to build knowledgeable, skilled library staff to support these communities as they rebuild and recover. The two-year Staffing Gulf Coast Libraries Project will work in synergy with a multiyear project funded by the Bill and Melinda Gates Foundation. The Gates Foundation project supports recovery

Table 3 / Laura Bush 21st Century Librarian Program, FY 2007 *(cont.)*

of public libraries in Louisiana and Mississippi by providing and operating temporary library facilities where services are currently unavailable due to building loss, assisting libraries with planning for rebuilding, and replacing all lost public access computers.

Valley City State University $573,909

The university—in partnership with North Dakota Indian Education Association, North Dakota Education Association–Library Media Association, and the North Dakota Teacher Center—will develop and institutionalize Project Nexus, a graduate curriculum in library and information technologies. North Dakota has been without a master's-level library media degree program since the mid-1970s.

(continued from page 370)

Native American Library Services

The Native American Library Services program provides opportunities for improved library services to an important part of the nation's community of library users. The Native American Library Services program offers three types of support to serve the range of needs of Indian tribes and Alaska Native villages, the latter coming under the definition of eligible Indian tribes as recognized by the secretary of the interior.

In 2007 IMLS distributed $3,118,300 in grants for American Indian tribes and Alaska Native villages. The program offers three types of support:

- Basic library services grants, in the amount of $5,000, which support core library operations on a noncompetitive basis for all eligible Indian tribes and Alaska Native villages that apply for such support; IMLS awarded basic grants to 51 tribes in 13 states in 2007
- Basic library services grants with a supplemental education/assessment option of $1,000, totaling $6,000; IMLS awarded basic grants with the education/assessment option to 186 tribes in 26 states (the purpose of the education/assessment option is to provide funding for library staff to attend continuing education courses and/or training workshops onsite or offsite, for library staff to attend or give presentations at conferences relating to library services, and/or to hire a consultant for an onsite professional library assessment)
- Enhancement grants, which support new levels of library service for activities specifically identified under LSTA; of the 55 applications received, IMLS awarded 14 enhancement grants for a total of $1,753,300 (see Table 4)

Native Hawaiian Library Services

The Native Hawaiian Library Services program provides opportunities for improved library services through grants to nonprofit organizations that primarily serve and represent Native Hawaiians, as the term *Native Hawaiian* is defined in section 7207 of the Native Hawaiian Education Act (20 U.S.C. 7517). In 2007 one Native Hawaiian Library Services grant was awarded to Alu Like, Inc. of Honolulu in the amount of $519,700.

(text continues on page 379)

Table 4 / Native American Library Services Enhancement Grants, FY 2007

Arctic Slope Regional Corporation $119,886

On behalf of the corporation, Tuzzy Consortium Library of Ilisagvik College in Barrow, Alaska, will implement the Nunaaqqiq 2.0 Project (*Nunaaqqiq* in Iñupiaq is a village or community). The primary goals of the project are to build an online community exclusively for the people of the North Slope in which contributors will add information, pictures, and sounds to the body of local knowledge; to provide a forum for North Slope residents to discuss issues of community concern; and to provide enhanced information resources that meet the needs of the community.

Chilkat Indian Village $149,933

The Alaskan village library project will focus on supporting literacy for all ages, along with wellness and job skills training for Chilkat Tlingit community members. Literacy programs for students will include storytelling by community elders and an annual summer reading program. Adult educational programs will be on business management and tourism-related job skills as well as technology training in software programs and electronic databases.

Chilkoot Indian Association $149,970

Chilkoot Indian Association in Haines, Alaska, will continue its successful partnership with the Haines Borough Public Library and develop new partnerships in this multifaceted cultural connections program called Dreamcatchers. Project goals are to empower patrons to improve their lives through educational and artistic skill development; to partner with the school district to increase the understanding of native history, culture, and traditional lifestyle and support learning in culturally appropriate ways; and to increase the number of high-quality partnerships between tribes and other organizations.

Chippewa Cree Indians of Rocky Boy's Reservation $150,000

On behalf of the Chippewa Cree Indians of this Montana reservation, the Stone Child College academic/community library will enhance library services to the children, students, and adults of the reservation by increasing its library collection in all subject areas to meet community needs for educational and recreational reading. Additional computer workstations will provide increased access to the library's holdings and the Internet.

Hopi Tribe of Arizona $136,094

The tribe will provide library services to its 11 villages situated along a 90-mile stretch of highway transecting the reservation with the Hopi Public Tutuqayki Sikisve or "librarymobile."

Lac Courte Oreilles Band of Lake Superior Chippewa Indians $149,931

The Lac Courte Oreilles (LCO) Ojibwa Community College library, both an academic and a public library housed in a new 10,000-square-foot space at the college in Wisconsin, will improve library access and services to the community and to the college's four satellite outreach campuses. The library will become a full member of the Northwest Waters Library Service Merlin Consortium, which will provide access to the other 29 member libraries' collections in addition to LCO library materials.

Lower Elwha Tribal Community $72,467

The project in Washington State will contract with a part-time professional librarian to organize and expand the current collection and to train tribal members to be community librarians. The goal is to provide Lower Elwha tribal members and the public with ready access to a wide variety of educational and recreational library resources and to create a friendly, inviting atmosphere for all ages.

Organized Village of Kasaan $122,634

The village, on Prince of Wales Island in southeast Alaska, will transform its existing library into a community learning center that is accessible and welcoming to all ages with open and easy access to the world of Internet information. The village will hire a librarian to work with the community and to organize the current collection and to purchase new library materials, comfortable furnishings, and Internet-access computers.

Table 4 / Native American Library Services Enhancement Grants, FY 2007 *(cont.)*

Pascua Yaqui Tribe of Arizona　　　　　　　　　　　　　　　$141,700

The tribe will create a Community Library and Resource Center to enhance library services on the reservation, to support literacy and educational achievement, and to promote the preservation of Yaqui culture and heritage.

Pueblo of Pojoaque　　　　　　　　　　　　　　　　　　　$120,641

This New Mexico project, "Raising Readers Through Programs and Outreach," addresses specific needs identified through meetings, surveys, and interviews with community stakeholders to provide pre-literacy and reading incentive programs that will stimulate interest in reading and involve parents and caregivers in the learning process.

Sealaska Corporation　　　　　　　　　　　　　　　　　　$75,164

In conjunction with Sealaska Heritage Institute, Sealaska Corporation—an Alaska Native regional corporation representing more than 16,000 native shareholders—will undertake the Sealaska Electronic Cultural Research Access Project. The project will bridge the gap in access to library resources faced by their Alaska Native service population by creating an onsite facility to enable the public to effectively access Sealaska's specialized library holdings on Tlingit, Haida, and Tsimshian culture when visiting their headquarters in Juneau.

Spirit Lake Tribe　　　　　　　　　　　　　　　　　　　$145,222

The Valerie Merrick Memorial Library at Cankdeska Cikana Community College in Fort Totten, North Dakota, will expand existing library services to tribal members by increasing its outreach to young children and their families through improved collections for children and youth, storytimes for preschool children, programming to encourage regular library use and lifelong enjoyment of reading for young people, and parent-child reading partnerships through "family night" activities.

Spokane Tribe　　　　　　　　　　　　　　　　　　　　$144,658

On behalf of the Spokane Tribe of Wellpinit, Washington, the Circle of Knowledge Library at Spokane Tribal College, a combined academic and community library, will use this grant to hire new staff and expand library hours. This will result in increased evening and weekend access as well as the development of outreach services to two remote communities and the Spokane Agency correctional facility.

White Mountain Apache Tribe　　　　　　　　　　　　　　$75,000

The White Mountain Apache Tribal libraries in Whiteriver, McNary, and Cibecue in east-central Arizona, will enhance their collections and undertake programs that will enable them to address critical problems faced by a sizeable portion of the reservation's population. These include teen pregnancy, diabetes, obesity, drug and alcohol abuse, domestic violence, and related issues.

(continued from page 377)

Partnerships

National Endowment for the Arts—The Big Read

IMLS continued its partnership with the National Endowment for the Arts (NEA) to promote reading through the distribution of books to support community reading and discussion programs based on selected works of fiction. The IMLS contribution was made through the Laura Bush 21st Century Librarian Program.

IMLS/NEH Digital Partnership

IMLS entered into a partnership with the National Endowment for the Humanities (NEH) to promote development of the digital humanities through two grant programs administered by NEH: Digital Humanities Start-up Grants of up to $30,000 and IMLS/NEH Advancing Knowledge project grants of up to $350,000. IMLS funds were provided through the National Leadership Grants program. Three Advancing Knowledge grants were awarded in 2007:

- Historical Society of Pennsylvania for "PhilaPlace: A Neighborhood History and Culture Project," an interactive resource chronicling the history, culture, and architecture of Philadelphia's neighborhoods
- Tufts University for "Scalable Named Entity Identification in Classical Studies," which will construct a testing database of scholarly and cultural documents on the ancient world and build a digital reference tool to allow researchers to conduct context-based "smart searches"
- University of California, Berkeley, for "Content and Relationships: Ireland and Irish Studies," to develop a database of Irish studies materials and test three open source digital tools—Context Finder, Context Builder, and Context Provider—in collaboration with Queen's University, Belfast, Northern Ireland

Evaluation of IMLS Programs

IMLS encourages grant projects with strong evaluation components. In 2007 IMLS awarded a grant of $362,490 through the Laura Bush 21st Century Librarian Program to the Indiana University School of Library and Information Science to offer, enhance, and revise the online instructor-mediated courseware "Shaping Outcomes" (http://www.shapingoutcomes.org/course). The course was developed and tested through a three-year collaborative agreement between IMLS and Indiana University Purdue University Indianapolis's (IUPUI) Museum Studies program and School of Library and Information Science, awarded in 2005. The new project provides opportunities for all IMLS grantees and prospective applicants to improve their approaches to project planning, grant preparation, and measurement of results to successfully address the needs of audiences and users.

IMLS Conferences and Activities

WebWise

The eighth annual WebWise conference was held February 28–March 2, 2007, at the Hyatt Regency Hotel in Washington, D.C. The conference was cosponsored by Online Computer Library Center and the J. Paul Getty Trust, and its theme was "Stewardship in the Digital Age: Managing Museum and Library Collections for Preservation and Use." More than 400 participants, representing all types of museums and libraries nationwide, attended.

The theme of digital stewardship linked the 2007 conference directly to the IMLS Connecting to Collections initiative. Stewardship is a core responsibility of museums, libraries, and archives, yet the Heritage Health Index Report on the State of America's Collections, supported by IMLS funding and issued in late 2005, revealed the inadequate conditions under which many collections are held. Particularly for materials on unstable media, such as sound recordings and videotape, digitization has been found to be the best and perhaps only solution for ensuring preservation of the content. In other cases, digital surrogates preserve information on fragile media, including many photographic images, and provide valuable documentation if originals are lost due to destruction or theft. Digital technologies provide the only solution to preservation of born-digital formats and intangible forms of expression, and they can also be used to document, track, and manage collections more effectively. The WebWise conference explored the many ways that museums and libraries can use digital technologies to position themselves as stewards for the future of the collections in their care.

The proportional representation of participants by type was as follows: librarians, 39.7 percent; museum professionals, 21.8 percent; archivists, 12.3 percent; computer scientists, 5.0 percent; educators, 9.5 percent; others, 11.7 percent.

Nearly half the participants completed an online evaluation survey sent shortly after the conference. Responses were overwhelmingly positive. More than 97 percent said they would attend WebWise again, and 98.2 percent said they would recommend it to others. Fifty-six percent of attendees had not attended a previous WebWise conference.

Audio and PowerPoint presentations of the main conference are posted on the IMLS Web site at http://www.imls.gov/news/events/webwise07.shtm. Full text of many of the presentations—including the keynote speeches by Elizabeth Broun, director of the Smithsonian American Art Museum, and Deanna Marcum, associate librarian for library services at the Library of Congress—appeared in the July issue of the online journal *First Monday*. In addition, IMLS published a summary of the proceedings both electronically and in hard copy.

Framework of Guidance for Building Good Digital Collections

IMLS awarded a contract to the National Information Standards Organization (NISO) to revise the Framework of Guidance for Building Good Digital Collections, first created with IMLS support in 2000. The framework assists museum, library, and archival practitioners and educators by providing principles and current standards for the creation, management, and preservation of digital assets. The third edition updates the standards and other aspects of the framework and converts the framework to a wiki-style "living document" to support an active community of users. Contributors will be able to post commentary, case studies, and related information to help others to understand and use the framework. The framework is hosted on the NISO Web site at http://www.niso.org/framework/framework3.pdf.

The NISO committee, which functions as a governing body to maintain the core principles and standards, comprises Grace Agnew, Rutgers University; Murtha Baca, Getty Research Institute; Priscilla Caplan, Florida Center for Library

Automation (chair); Carl Fleischhauer, Library of Congress; Tony Gill, Center for Jewish History; Ingrid Hsieh-Yee, Catholic University of America School of Library and Information Science; Jill Koelling, Denver Museum of Nature and Science; and Christie Stephenson, American Museum of Natural History.

IMLS Web Site and Publications

IMLS maintains a Web site (http://www.imls.gov) that provides information on the various grant programs, the National Medal for Museum and Library Service, funded projects, application forms, and staff contacts. The Web site also highlights model projects developed by libraries and museums throughout the country and provides information about IMLS-sponsored conferences, publications, and studies. Through an electronic newsletter, *Primary Source,* IMLS provides timely information on grant deadlines and opportunities. Information on subscribing to the IMLS newsletter is available on the Web site.

The following recent publications are available at the IMLS Web site: the 2008 *Grant and Award Opportunities* brochure; proceedings from the WebWise 2007 Conference; *Museums and Libraries Engaging America's Youth: Final Report of a Study of IMLS Youth Programs, 1998–2003;* the 2007 National Medal for Museum and Library Service brochure; and guidelines for each of the grant programs.

Part 3
Library/Information Science Education, Placement, and Salaries

Employment Sources on the Internet

Catherine Barr
Contributing Editor

For the second year in a row *U.S. News & World Report* selected "librarian" as one of the best careers, based on strong outlook and high job satisfaction (http://www.usnews.com/features/business/best-careers/best-careers-2008.html; retrieved March 25, 2008). Special librarianship was again selected as the "smart specialty" and the fastest-growing job market in an "underrated" field. *Library Journal's* "Job Satisfaction" series included generally upbeat results from its 2007 survey ("Great Work, Genuine Problems," October 1, 2007, http://www.libraryjournal.com/article/CA6483878.html?q=great+work) with reports on academic libraries ("Take This Job and Love It," February 1, 2008, http://www.libraryjournal.com/article/CA6523442.html?q=take+this+job+and+love) and public libraries ("I ♥ Librarianship," March 1, 2008, http://www.libraryjournal.com/article/CA6533042.html?q=I+%3F+Librarianship).

The following is not a comprehensive list of the hundreds of job-related sites on the Internet of interest to librarians and information professionals. These are, however, the best starting places for a job search in this area. Many offer additional information that will be helpful to those considering a career in librarianship, including advice on conducting a successful search, writing résumés, preparing for interviews, and negotiating salaries.

Before spending a lot of time on any Web site, users should check that the site has been updated recently and that out-of-date job listings no longer appear. If a job seeker has a particular geographic location or specialized field in mind, he or she may find that the Directory of Organizations in Part 6 of this volume will provide a relevant Web address faster than a search of the Web.

Background Information

One particularly useful print resource, *The Information Professional's Guide to Career Development Online* (Information Today, Inc., 2002), has a companion Web site at http://www.lisjobs.com/careerdev. Both the print and the updated online versions present information on job hunting, networking, and online and continuing education. An article by the same authors—Rachel Singer Gordon and Sarah L. Nesbeitt—titled "Market Yourself Online!" appeared in the October/November 2001 issue of *Marketing Library Services*. The article presents practical advice on promoting yourself and your abilities on the Web; it is available at http://www.infotoday.com/mls/oct01/gordon&nesbeitt.htm.

The Bureau of Labor Statistics of the Department of Labor provides a thorough overview of the work of a librarian, necessary qualifications, and the job and salary outlook at http://stats.bls.gov/oco/ocos068.htm. Similar pages are available for archivists, curators, and museum technicians (http://stats.bls.gov/oco/ocos065.htm) and for library technicians (http://stats.bls.gov/oco/ocos113.htm). More-detailed employment and wage estimates can be found at http://stats.bls.gov/oes/current/oes254021.htm for librarians, at http://stats.bls.gov/oes/current/oes254011.htm for archivists, and at http://stats.bls.gov/oes/current/oes254031.htm for library technicians.

An excellent 2002 *American Libraries* feature article by Linda K. Wallace on the breadth of opportunities available to librarians and information professionals—"Places an MLS Can Take You"—is archived at http://www.ala.org/ala/hrdr/careersinlibraries/al_mls.pdf.

The American Library Association (ALA) provides a user-friendly overview of librarianship at LibraryCareer.org (http://www.ala.org/ala/hrdr/librarycareers site/ohtheplaces.cfm), and Info*Nation: Choose a Career in Libraries (http://www.cla.ca/infonation/welcome.htm) is an excellent Canadian site that describes the work of librarians, combining brief information on a variety of career options with statements by individual librarians about why they love their jobs. These two sites will be particularly useful for young people considering a possible career in librarianship.

Finally, How to Apply for a Library Job (http://www.liswiki.com/wiki/HOW TO:Apply_for_a_library_job) offers thoughtful and practical interview tips.

General Sites/Portals

American Library Association: http://www.ala.org/
Education and Careers   ala/education/educationcareers.htm
Maintained by ALA. A useful source of information on library careers, education and professional development, scholarships, and salaries.

ALA JobLIST   http://joblist.ala.org
Sponsored by ALA and the Association of College and Research Libraries. This site incorporates the former job sites of *American Libraries* magazine and *C&RL News*. Registration is free for jobseekers, who can post their résumés and search jobs by library type, date, state, institution name, salary range, and other parameters. Employers can choose from a menu of print and electronic posting combinations.

Employment Resources: http://slisweb.sjsu.edu/
Organizations and Associations   resources/employment.htm
Maintained by San José State University's School of Library and Information Science. Gives links to organizations that will be of interest to students at the university, including a number of California sites. A related page, Professional Associations in the Information Sciences (http://slisweb.sjsu.edu/resources/orgs.htm), is a comprehensive listing of associations in the United States and abroad. And excellent information on conducting job searches and professional development in general can be found at http://slisgroups.sjsu.edu/alumni/jobseekers/index.html.

Library Job Postings on the Internet   http://www.libraryjobpostings.org
Compiled by Sarah (Nesbeitt) Johnson of Booth Library, Eastern Illinois University, coauthor of *The Information Professional's Guide to Career Development Online* (Information Today, Inc., 2002); there is a link to the book's companion Web site on this site. Provides links to library employment sites in the United States and abroad, with access by location and by category of job.

LIScareer.com   http://www.liscareer.com
Maintained by Priscilla Shontz and Richard Murray, coeditors of *A Day in the Life: Career Options in Library and Information Science* (Libraries Unlimited, 2007). Subtitled The Library and Information Science Professional's Career Development Center, this helpful and up-to-date site provides no job listings but offers bibliographies of resources of interest in the areas of career planning, education, job hunting, experience, work/life balance, networking, mentoring, interpersonal skills, leadership, and publishing. This is an excellent place to begin research on library jobs.

Lisjobs.com—Jobs for Librarians and   http://www.lisjobs.com
Information Professionals
Maintained by Rachel Singer Gordon, author of books including *Information Tomorrow: Reflections on Technology and the Future of Public and Academic Libraries* (Information Today, Inc., 2007), *The NextGen Librarian's Survival Guide* (Information Today, Inc., 2006), and *The Accidental Library Manager* (Information Today, Inc., 2005), and coauthor of *The Information Professional's Guide to Career Development Online* (Information Today, Inc., 2001). A searchable database of job listings and guide to online job resources in the United States and abroad. The Job Postings section—which includes listings provided by Library Job Postings on the Internet (see above)—lists openings in reverse chronological order, making it easy to find the most recent. Job seekers can post résumés for a small fee. Also features an interesting professional development newsletter, *Info Career Trends* (http://lisjobs.com/career_trends), which is also available via RSS feed.

The Riley Guide: http://www.rileyguide.com
Employment Opportunities and Job Resources on the Internet
Compiled by Margaret F. Dikel, a private consultant and coauthor with Frances Roehm of *The Guide to Internet Job Searching* (McGraw-Hill, 2006). A general site rich in advice for the job seeker, from résumé writing and how to target a new employer to tips on networking and interviewing. Links to job sites are organized by type of opportunity; Information Delivery, Design, and Management is found under The Humanities, Social Sciences, and Personal Services.

Sites by Sector

Public Libraries

Public library openings can be found at all the general sites/portals listed above.

Public Librarian Recruitment   http://www.pla.org/ala/pla/projects/
publiclibrecruit/publiclibrarian.htm

The Public Library Association offers information on public librarianship—from educational requirements and salaries to testimonials from public librarians and the opportunity to participate in Job Shadow Day.

School Libraries

School library openings can be found at many of the sites listed above. Sites with interesting material for aspiring school librarians include those listed below. School library job seekers should read "Interviewing Teacher-Librarian Candidates" by Alice Yucht (*Teacher Librarian*, February 2004.)

AASL: Recruitment to School Librarianship   http://www.ala.org/ala/aasl/
aasleducation/recruitmentlib/aaslrecruitment.htm

The American Association of School Librarians hosts this site, which describes the role of school librarians, salary and job outlooks, and mentoring programs; provides testimonials from working library media specialists; and offers state-by-state information on licensure, scholarships, library education, job hunting, mentoring, and recruitment efforts.

General education sites usually include school library openings. Among sites with nationwide coverage is:

Education America   http://www.educationamerica.net

Library openings can be searched by geographic location.

Special and Academic Libraries

AALL Job Placement Hotline   http://www.aallnet.org/hotline/hotline.asp

Maintained by the American Association of Law Librarians.

ACRL: Career Opportunities from Across the Country

See ALA JobLIST above.

ALISE: Job Placement   http://www.alise.org

The Association for Library and Information Science Education posts jobs for deans, directors, program chairs, faculty, visiting and summer faculty, and support positions in the field of library and information science.

ASIS&T: Careers   http://www.asist.org/careers.html

Maintained by the American Society for Information Science and Technology.

Association of Research Libraries: http://www.arl.org/resources/
Career Resources   careers/index.shtml

In addition to listings of openings at ARL member institutions and at other organizations, there is information on ARL's Initiative to Recruit a Diverse Work Force plus a database of research library residency and internship programs and a link to ARL's annual salary survey.

Chronicle of Higher Education   http://chronicle.com/jobs

Access job openings from more than 1,350 institutions. Listings can be browsed, with geographical options, under the category "Library/information sciences" (found under "Professional fields") or searched by simple keyword such as "library." Articles and advice on job searching are also available.

EDUCAUSE Job Posting Service   http://www.educause.edu/jobpost
EDUCAUSE member organizations post positions "in the broad field of information technology in higher education."

HigherEdJobs.com   http://www.higheredjobs.com
Published by Internet Employment Linkage, Inc. Job openings from more than 1,675 institutions can be searched by location, job category, or keyword.

Major Orchestra Librarians' Association   http://www.mola-inc.org
A nice site for a field that might be overlooked. The Resources section includes an introduction to the work of an orchestra librarian.

Medical Library Association: http://www.mlanet.org/career/index.html
Career Development
The Medical Library Association offers much more than job listings here, with brochures on medical librarianship, a video, career tips, and a mentor program.

Music Library   http://www.musiclibraryassoc.org/
Association Job Openings   employmentanded/joblist/openings.shtml
Along with job postings, this site features an article titled "Music Librarianship— Is It for You?" and a listing of resources for the mid-career music librarian.

SLA Career Center   http://www.sla.org/content/jobs/index.cfm
In addition to salary information and searchable job listings that are available to all users, the Special Libraries Association provides around-the-clock job advice and mentoring to association members. A Career Articles and Resources page offers tips and tools, but is available only to members.

Government

Library of Congress   http://www.loc.gov/hr/employment
Current job openings, internships, fellowships, and volunteering.

National Archives and   http://www.archives.gov/careers
Records Administration
Employment opportunities, internships, and volunteering.

Library Support Staff

Library Support Staff Resource Center   http://www.ala.org/ala/hrdr/
librarysupportstaff/Library_Support_Staff_Resource_Center.htm
Maintained by ALA, this page includes information on the kinds of jobs available and the work environments, relevant events, certification requirements, financial assistance, advancement opportunities, and so forth.

Miscellaneous

REFORMA Employment   http://www.reforma.org/refoempl.htm
REFORMA (The National Association to Promote Library and Information Services to Latinos and the Spanish-Speaking) collects job postings from list-

servs and direct mailings. The page is updated weekly. Knowledge of Spanish is required for some jobs listed here.

Library Periodicals

American Libraries. See ALA JobList above.

Feliciter   http://www.cla.ca/careers/careeropp.htm
The Canadian Library Association lists openings here; some may have already appeared in the association's publication *Feliciter.*

Library Journal   http://jobs.libraryjournal.com
Easy access to online job listings.

School Library Journal   http://www.schoollibraryjournal.com
Click on the Jobs tab for access to a general list of job openings (jointly maintained with *Library Journal;* you must filter by Children's/Young Adult to access school positions.

Employment Agencies/Commercial Services

A number of employment agencies and commercial services in the United States and abroad specialize in library-related jobs. Among those that keep up-to-date listings on their Web sites are:

Advanced Information Management   http://www.aimusa.com
Specializes in librarians and support staff in a variety of types of libraries across the country.

ASLIB   http://www.aslib.co.uk/recruitment/index.htm
Lists jobs available in Britain.

Library Associates   http://www.libraryassociates.com/index.php4?page=jobs
An easy-to-use list of openings that can be sorted by state.

TPFL: The Information People: http://www.tfpl.com/permanent_recruitment/
Recruitment and Executive Search   candidates/pjobs.cfm
Specializes in jobs in the fields of knowledge management, library and information management, records management, and Web and content management. Jobs around the world are listed, with the majority in the United Kingdom.

Listservs

Many listservs allow members to post job openings on a casual basis.

jESSE   http://web.utk.edu/~gwhitney/jesse.html
This worldwide discussion group focuses on library and information science education; LIS faculty position announcements frequently appear here.

LIBJOBS   http://www.ifla.org/II/lists/libjobs.htm
Managed by the International Federation of Library Associations and Institutions (IFLA). Subscribers to this list receive posted job opportunities by e-mail.

NASIGWeb Job Listings   http://www.nasig.org/jobs/list.htm
This site collects serials-related job openings posted on the following listservs: ACQNET, AUTOCAT, COLLIB-L, INNOPAC, LIBJOBS, LITA-L, PACS-L, SERIALST, SLAJOB, STS-L, and ERIL-L.

PUBLIB   http://sunsite.berkeley.edu/PubLib
Public library job openings often appear on this list.

Blogs

The Blogging Libraries Wiki (http://www.blogwithoutalibrary.net/links/index. php?title=Welcome_to_the_Blogging_Libraries_Wiki) provides lists of library blogs in the following fields: Academic Libraries, Public Libraries, School Libraries, Special Libraries, Blogs for Internal Library Communication, Library Associations, and Library Director.

Beyond the Job   http://www.beyondthejob.org
Maintained by Sarah Johnson and Rachel Singer Gordon, this blog focuses on job-hunting advice and professional development.

Career Q&A with the Library   http://www.lisjobs.com/careerqa_blog
Career People
Formerly an advice column in the *Info Career Trends Newsletter,* this attractive and user-friendly blog is maintained by librarians Tiffany Allen and Susanne Markgren and is intended to "create an enlightening discussion forum of professional guidance and advice for librarians, library staff, and those thinking of entering the profession." Categories include job satisfaction, job seeking, and professional development.

LIScareers News   http://liscareer.blogspot.com
Posts alerts to new features on LIScareer.com.

Placements and Salaries:
What's an MLIS Worth?

Stephanie Maatta, Ph.D.

Assistant Professor, University of South Florida
School of Library and Information Science, Tampa

It was a banner year for women in 2006. Their average annual starting salary finally cracked through the $40,000 glass barrier, increasing to $40,566 for all women and with a substantial gain of 11.3 percent for women in the Southwest. There was small, but solid, growth in salaries overall. Reported annual starting salaries for new graduates increased approximately 2.2 percent overall, from $40,118 in 2005 to $41,014.

Another surprise was the substantial leap in graduates reporting jobs outside of the library and information science (LIS) professions (up 43.7 percent). The number of LIS graduates participating in the annual placements and salaries survey increased by 12 percent for 2006. A total of 1,992 graduates submitted responses (approximately 37 percent of the estimated total graduates). The percentage of graduates reporting employment of any type has remained steady at 90.8 percent (totaling 1,809). Of these graduates, 89.9 percent reported placements in some type of library agency, down slightly from 92.9 percent in 2005, while those reporting placements outside of library agencies increased by 37.4 percent, continuing a trend from previous years.

However, fissures appeared in the job outlook because of more graduates in nonprofessional jobs, a rising number of temporary positions, more graduates taking multiple part-time positions, and a longer average job search.

Entry-level 'Gap'?

Over the past several years there has been speculation that an entry-level gap exists—that there are more graduates than available entry-level jobs. This is a complex situation. Approximately 37 percent of the LIS graduate programs responding to the institutional questionnaire reported a rise in the number of available jobs, while 16 percent reported a decrease. None of the responding institutions reported difficulties in placing graduates. In fact, few LIS graduates commented that entry-level jobs were not available. Instead, the graduates' concerns reflected salary levels that were not competitive with other professions or the inability to find a job in their area that fit their interests and skills.

It may be useful to examine some of the other factors that impact job placement. For example, there are heavy concentrations of LIS schools in some regions of the United States—the Midwestern and Northeastern programs combined produce more than half of the graduates, providing dense pools of job applicants. For geographically bound graduates, this makes the job search more arduous since more candidates compete for the same positions. Another factor is the hiring process itself. Graduates frequently discuss taking civil service exams and undergoing background checks and security clearances that all add time and,

Adapted from *Library Journal*, October 15, 2007.
(text continues on page 398)

Table 1 / Status of 2006 Graduates in Library Professions*

	Number of Schools Reporting	Number of Graduates Responding	Permanent Professional	Temporary Professional	Non-professional	Total	Graduates Outside of Profession	Unemployed or Status Unreported
Northeast	13	580	346	46	72	464	56	60
Southeast	11	331	250	17	20	287	26	18
Midwest	11	566	368	46	43	457	46	63
Southwest	4	211	148	19	10	177	21	13
West	4	229	127	26	29	182	25	22
Canada	2	38	28	7	—	35	1	2
Total	45	1,992	1,285	163	180	1,628	181	183

* Table based on survey responses from schools and individual graduates. Figures will not necessarily be fully consistent with some of the other data reported. Tables do not always add up, individually or collectively, since both schools and individuals omitted data in some cases.

Table 2 / Placements and Full-Time Salaries of 2006 Graduates/Summary by Region*

Region	Number of Placements	Salaries			Low Salary		High Salary		Average Salary			Median Salary		
		Women	Men	Total	Women	Men	Women	Men	Women	Men	All	Women	Men	All
Northeast	359	259	72	331	$12,000	$11,000	$100,000	$110,000	$40,566	$44,044	$41,277	$40,000	$41,000	$40,000
Southeast	330	239	73	312	16,600	20,000	74,000	65,000	37,842	39,453	38,159	37,000	38,000	37,300
Midwest	336	187	61	248	15,000	20,000	80,000	85,000	38,638	44,593	38,465	38,500	41,000	38,500
Southwest	171	120	32	152	19,000	26,000	63,000	80,000	39,793	40,587	39,911	40,000	40,000	40,000
West	210	152	34	186	23,956	28,000	120,000	85,000	47,921	49,642	48,236	45,624	46,500	45,824
Canada/Intl.**	46	33	12	45	20,000	15,248	74,000	61,248	43,542	43,126	43,321	43,000	46,269	43,000
Combined	1,485	1,042	288	1,346	$12,000	$11,000	$120,000	$110,000	$40,566	$43,194	$41,040	$39,512	$41,000	$40,000

* This table represents only salaries reported as full-time. Some data were reported as aggregate without breakdown by gender or region. Comparison with other tables will show different numbers of placements.

** All international salaries converted to U.S. dollars based on conversion rates for August 21, 2007.

Table 3 / 2006 Total Graduates/Placements by School**

Schools	Graduates			Employed			Unemployed			Students		
	Women	Men	Total	Women	Men	Total	Women	Men	Total	Women	Men	Total
Alabama	68	17	85	9	1	10	2	1	3	—	—	—
Albany	71	31	102	17	6	24	—	—	—	1	—	1
British Columbia	52	16	68	19	2	21	—	—	—	—	1	1
Buffalo*	50	8	59	47	7	55	3	—	3	—	1	1
Catholic	66	17	83	18	5	23	1	—	1	1	—	—
Clarion	107	20	127	36	5	41	2	—	2	1	—	1
Dalhousie*	10	5	15	10	5	15	—	—	—	—	—	—
Dominican*	14	6	20	8	6	14	2	—	2	—	—	—
Drexel	99	25	124	20	5	25	—	—	—	—	—	—
Emporia*	18	1	19	18	1	19	—	—	—	—	—	—
Florida State	147	65	212	13	6	19	—	1	1	1	—	1
Hawaii	42	10	52	14	4	18	—	1	1	—	—	—
Illinois	132	47	179	61	19	80	6	1	7	1	—	1
Indiana	193	47	240	60	10	70	1	—	1	—	—	—
Iowa*	—	—	14	—	—	13	—	—	—	—	—	—
Kent State	235	54	289	55	17	72	2	—	2	—	—	—
Kentucky	93	20	113	25	8	33	1	1	2	1	—	1
Long Island	135	32	167	47	5	52	—	—	—	—	—	—
Louisiana State	58	6	64	20	1	22	—	—	—	—	—	—
Michigan*	37	24	64	33	24	58	—	—	—	4	—	6
Missouri–Columbia	79	20	99	5	—	5	—	—	—	—	—	—
N.C. Central	48	12	60	16	5	21	—	—	—	—	—	—

N.C. Chapel Hill*	22	5	27	19	4	23	2	—	2	—	—	—
N.C. Greensboro	49	24	73	34	16	50	2	—	2	—	—	—
North Texas	297	49	346	95	25	122	5	—	5	—	1	1
Oklahoma	36	8	44	11	3	14	—	—	—	—	—	—
Pittsburgh	189	140	329	42	10	52	1	—	1	—	—	—
Pratt*	1	—	1	—	—	—	1	—	1	—	—	—
Rhode Island	40	12	52	10	6	16	1	—	1	—	—	—
Rutgers	123	30	153	30	10	40	1	—	—	—	—	—
San José	327	110	437	130	27	157	9	1	10	1	1	1
Simmons*	170	33	205	134	25	160	36	8	45	—	—	—
South Carolina	192	26	218	19	4	23	—	—	—	—	—	—
South Florida	159	28	187	46	12	58	—	—	—	—	—	—
Southern Connecticut	115	17	132	31	5	36	2	1	3	—	—	—
St. John's*	8	2	10	8	2	10	—	—	—	—	—	—
Syracuse*	6	6	12	6	4	10	—	—	—	—	—	—
Tennessee*	23	7	30	21	7	28	2	—	2	—	—	—
Texas (Austin)	68	22	90	29	6	35	—	—	—	—	—	—
Texas Woman's	160	11	171	25	2	27	—	—	—	—	—	—
UCLA	57	21	78	8	2	10	—	—	—	—	—	—
Washington	75	32	107	16	5	21	—	2	2	—	—	—
Wayne State	171	41	212	78	17	97	4	—	4	—	2	2
Wisconsin (Madison)	60	17	77	48	13	61	3	—	3	1	1	2
Wisconsin (Milwaukee)	84	25	109	12	5	17	2	—	2	—	—	—
Total	4,186	1,149	5,355	1,423	361	1,807	90	16	107	12	6	18

* For schools that did not fill out the institutional survey, data were taken from graduate surveys, thus there is not full representation of their graduating classes. Unknown status: 2,681 women, 775 men, with a total of 3,456.

** Tables do not always add up, individually or collectively, since both schools and individuals omitted data in some cases. This table represents placements of any kind. Comparison with other tables will show different numbers of placements.

Table 4 / Placements by Type of Organization*

Schools	Public		Elementary and Secondary		College and University		Special		Government		Library and Co-op Network		Vendor		Other		Total		
	Women	Men	Women	Men	Women	Men	Women	Men	Women	Men	Women	Men	Women	Men	Women	Men	Women	Men	Total
Alabama	2	—	1	—	4	—	—	1	—	—	—	—	—	—	2	1	9	2	11
Albany	5	1	6	—	2	—	—	—	—	—	—	—	—	—	4	4	17	5	23
British Columbia	7	—	—	—	6	1	3	—	1	—	—	—	—	1	1	—	18	2	20
Buffalo	6	—	16	—	8	4	6	—	1	—	—	—	1	1	5	3	43	8	52
Catholic University	3	3	3	—	3	—	4	—	3	2	—	—	—	—	2	—	18	5	23
Clarion	15	—	7	1	7	—	1	—	—	—	1	—	—	—	3	1	34	4	38
Dalhousie	4	2	—	—	2	1	—	—	1	—	—	—	—	—	3	2	10	5	15
Dominican	7	—	2	—	—	2	—	—	—	—	—	—	—	—	3	3	12	5	17
Drexel	1	1	3	—	8	1	5	—	—	—	—	—	1	—	2	—	20	4	24
Emporia State	4	—	1	—	9	1	1	—	—	—	—	—	—	—	3	—	18	1	19
Florida State	5	4	1	—	4	—	—	—	1	—	—	1	—	1	2	1	13	6	19
Hawaii	6	1	3	—	1	3	—	—	—	—	—	—	—	—	2	—	12	4	16
Illinois	22	1	7	—	24	10	3	—	—	—	—	—	1	—	7	8	64	19	83
Indiana	26	2	5	—	21	2	1	1	2	—	—	—	—	—	5	5	60	10	70
Iowa	—	—	—	—	—	—	—	—	—	—	—	—	—	—	—	—	0	0	13
Kent State	32	10	7	1	5	1	3	1	—	—	—	—	1	—	7	4	55	17	72
Kentucky	6	4	2	1	10	2	2	1	1	—	—	—	—	—	4	—	25	8	33
Long Island	26	1	10	1	4	3	2	—	—	—	1	—	1	—	3	—	47	5	52
Louisiana State	4	—	5	—	6	1	4	—	—	—	—	—	—	—	1	—	20	1	22
Michigan	5	2	2	—	10	3	4	—	2	1	—	—	—	—	10	18	33	24	58
Missouri–Columbia	3	—	—	—	2	—	—	—	—	—	—	—	—	—	—	—	5	0	5

N.C. Central	3	1	6	1	2	1	1	—	1	—	—	—	1	—	3	2	16	5	21
N.C. Chapel Hill	6	1	1	—	6	—	1	—	3	—	—	—	—	—	2	3	19	4	23
N.C. Greensboro	9	2	14	4	8	4	—	1	—	1	—	—	—	—	3	3	34	15	49
North Texas	29	6	27	3	22	8	6	1	1	—	—	—	1	—	8	7	94	25	121
Oklahoma	1	1	3	—	1	—	1	—	1	—	—	—	—	—	4	2	11	3	14
Pittsburgh	14	—	9	2	10	4	4	1	1	—	—	—	1	—	2	3	41	10	51
Rhode Island	4	3	3	1	1	1	4	1	1	—	—	—	—	—	1	—	10	6	16
Rutgers	14	2	6	—	3	5	3	1	—	—	—	—	—	—	4	2	30	10	40
San José	59	6	8	3	24	6	11	3	1	—	1	—	1	—	22	6	126	24	150
Simmons	30	4	8	1	47	8	20	2	3	—	1	—	2	3	14	4	125	23	141
South Carolina	9	—	4	2	5	2	—	—	—	1	—	—	—	—	1	—	19	4	23
South Florida	21	4	8	3	13	2	—	—	—	—	—	—	—	—	3	2	45	11	56
Southern Conn.	8	3	10	—	3	1	1	1	1	—	—	—	—	—	6	—	30	4	34
St. John's	4	1	2	—	1	—	1	—	—	—	—	—	—	—	—	1	8	2	10
Syracuse	2	2	—	—	2	2	—	—	1	—	—	—	—	—	1	—	6	4	10
Tennessee	10	1	6	2	2	2	—	—	1	—	—	—	—	—	1	—	21	7	28
Texas (Austin)	8	—	3	—	4	4	2	—	—	1	—	—	—	—	6	2	28	6	34
Texas Woman's	9	1	7	—	3	3	—	1	—	—	—	—	—	—	1	1	25	2	27
UCLA	2	—	1	—	3	—	1	1	—	—	—	—	—	—	2	—	8	2	10
Washington	4	1	1	—	5	1	1	—	1	1	—	—	—	—	3	3	15	4	19
Wayne State	37	6	13	1	10	7	4	—	—	—	—	—	3	—	8	1	75	16	89
Wisc. (Madison)	17	2	5	1	15	6	5	2	—	—	—	—	—	—	3	—	46	11	57
Wisc. (Milwaukee)	4	1	1	—	5	3	2	1	1	—	—	—	1	—	1	—	14	5	19
Total	495	84	231	29	350	105	105	19	28	7	4	2	15	6	170	95	1,398	347	1,745

* This table represents only placements reported by type. Some individuals omitted placement or gender information, rendering some information unusable. Comparison with other tables will show different numbers of placements.

(continued from page 392)
perhaps, frustration to the job search. Employers also go through a lengthy process of contacting references and interviewing. There is no doubt that employers look for experience; it may behoove LIS programs to be more proactive in encouraging students to participate in fieldwork or internship activities and service learning projects and volunteer at library and information agencies.

Some Ups, Some Downs

Despite some good news, there were disturbing trends. An increasing number of graduates reported taking nonprofessional positions. While they make up less than 10 percent of the overall placements, nonprofessional positions increased by almost 37.5 percent between 2005 and 2006 after declining between 2003 and 2005. Nonprofessional positions most frequently included titles such as technical assistant, clerk, or customer service assistant, suggesting that LIS graduates are accepting jobs typically filled by support staff without graduate degrees in order to gain experience or simply to find a job—any job.

Serious salary decreases in the Southeast in 2006 reversed multiyear rises in the region. This may be attributable to the greater response rate from graduates in the Southeast. Placements in public libraries increased by 42 percent compared with 2005, and public libraries there offer the lowest pay—an average of $34,496 annually. It was quite the opposite in the Southwest, where public library placements increased by 53.3 percent and salaries were up 13.6 percent.

Jobs as school media specialists fell by 6.6 percent from 2005. Interestingly, the number who said they worked in school libraries remained steady. This suggests that graduates in school media centers may be redefining their job titles or accepting other types of jobs in school media centers. Average annual salaries for school library spots changed little, except in the Southeast and the West. In the Southeast, you'd be better off working in a school; despite overall salary drops there, school library salaries rose by 7.7 percent to $40,526. But in the West, average annual salaries for those jobs dropped 11.7 percent to $47,257.

On the up side, placements with public libraries, special libraries, and vendors experienced salary growth and more jobs. A rise in the number of placements (up about 24 percent) in public libraries across the United States and Canada was complemented by 6 percent salary growth (up by $2,268 to $37,875). Special libraries saw a healthy 6.1 percent increase above 2005 salaries, from $41,779 to $44,494, though the number of jobs remained steady. These findings continue trends for both of these types of libraries.

Work with vendors has seen steady growth since 2003. The average salary in that sector jumped from $38,273 in 2003 to $46,799 in 2006, with an approximate 28.5 percent growth in placements. Between 2005 and 2006, vendor salaries in the Northeast rose a whopping 19.5 percent, from $40,843 to $50,738. Vendor jobs vary and include cataloging and classification, reference/information services, and instruction.

More Compromises

Part-time placements decreased slightly, but, on the flip side, more graduates are cobbling together multiple part-time jobs to approximate a full-time salary (29.1 percent hold two or more part-time positions). Nearly half of part-time placements were in public libraries, followed by 22.6 percent in academic libraries. Reference work had the highest rate of part-time employment.

As seen last year, some graduates deliberately chose to delay the job search and seek part-time employment, whether to meet family demands or to go after additional certifications. Others chose to stay in current jobs while waiting for full-time professional positions to open up.

Just over 10 percent of respondents identified their jobs as temporary professional, up from 8.5 percent in 2005. Temporary status, of course, implies that employment is likely to end after a contractual period has expired; there is no guarantee that a position will remain in a budget. Many graduates said they continued their job search while in a temporary position. One reported that lack of experience hindered her attempts to find the right job, resulting in her moving through several temporary roles—two months here, three months there—until she felt she had what it took to land a permanent spot. Graduates also accepted unrelated temporary positions while searching for the "perfect" job.

Seamless for Some

The job search was relatively seamless for many graduates. Of the 1,809 who reported employment, approximately 36.9 percent remained with a current employer while getting their master's degree. For some this meant promotion upon graduation, with respondents noting salary hikes from the high $20,000s as a nonprofessional employee to the low $40,000s with a new professional title (LTA to Librarian I, for example). Additionally, of the 1,117 graduates who shared stories about their job search, 46 percent found employment before graduation, a jump from previous years (25.2 percent in 2005; 23 percent in 2004; 30 percent in 2003). Several said that they started their job search a semester or two before graduation, and many familiarized themselves with the potential job market before beginning to look.

The types of jobs graduates reported fluctuated in 2006. For example, spots in reference/information service had been slowly decreasing over the past couple of years; however, in 2006 the percentage of these positions came closer to 2004 levels (22.9 percent), with 21.1 percent of the full-time professional jobs in reference/information service. Positions in adult services decreased by 35 percent from 2005 (50 positions reported in 2005; 37 reported in 2006), while positions in youth services (teen librarians, young adult librarians) increased (80 positions reported in 2005 compared to 60 in 2004). This reflects a growing trend in many public libraries to serve the young adult population with dedicated staffing.

The biggest leap occurred in information technology, which saw a 57.8 percent rise (from 30 reported positions in 2005 to 71 in 2006). Along with the

Table 5 / Average Salary Index Starting Library Positions, 1990–2006

Year	Library Schools	Average Beginning Salary	Dollar Increase in Average Salary	Salary Index	BLS-CPI*
1990	38	$25,306	$725	143.03	130.7
1991	46	25,583	277	144.59	136.2
1992	41	26,666	1,083	150.71	140.5
1993	50	27,116	450	153.26	144.4
1994	43	28,086	970	158.74	148.4
1995	41	28,997	911	163.89	152.5
1996	44	29,480	483	166.62	159.1
1997	43	30,270	790	171.05	161.6
1998	47	31,915	1,645	180.38	164.3
1999	37	33,976	2,061	192.03	168.7
2000	37	34,871	895	197.26	175.1
2001	40	36,818	1,947	208.09	177.1
2002	30	37,456	638	211.70	179.9
2003	43	37,975	519	214.63	184.0
2004	46	39,079	1,104	220.87	188.9
2005	37	40,115	1,036	226.73	195.3
2006	45	41,014	899	231.81	201.6

* U.S. Department of Labor, Bureau of Labor Statistics, Consumer Price index, All Urban Consumers (CPI-U), U.S. city average, all items, 1982–1984=100. The average beginning professional salary for that period was $17,693.

increased number of positions, graduates reported an 8.8 percent increase in the average annual salaries for positions related to information technology, to $53,083. "Information technology" is a bit of a catch-all, but graduates reported exciting positions within the category, including information policy analysis, software engineering, and training specialist. While 57 percent of the information technology placements were in outside agencies, graduates found IT jobs in all types of libraries, including academic, public, special, and government facilities.

Looking to other types of jobs, acquisitions saw the best salary increase (up approximately 16.7 percent to $38,894), while circulation salaries experienced the worst drop (down 10.8 percent to $32,334). In fact, the broader areas of access services and technical services continue to raise concerns. Cataloging and circulation continue to be among the lowest paid of the professional and nonprofessional positions, falling well below the average starting salaries for all LIS graduates (at $35,976 and $32,334, respectively, approximately 20 percent less). As in previous survey analyses, location and professional/nonprofessional classification in these jobs do not seem to factor into salary, though it is beginning to appear that the type of organization may impact salaries for both. For example, salaries for catalogers in public libraries average $34,864, 5 percent below the average salary reported for all catalogers, and positions in circulation and interlibrary loan/document delivery follow suit.

Other positions that saw strong salary improvements include administration (up 12.27 percent to $43,303), which encompasses all levels from assistant department head to library director, and government documents (up from $33,600 to $38,743) at the state and federal levels.

Table 6 / Salaries of Reporting Professionals* by Area of Job Assignment*

Assignment	Number	Percent of Total	Low Salary	High Salary	Average Salary	Median Salary
Acquisitions	22	1.54%	$25,000	$62,000	$38,894	$39,150
Administration	80	5.61	11,000	120,000	43,303	40,000
Adult Services	37	2.60	22,000	62,000	37,080	36,000
Archives	46	3.23	23,956	50,000	35,212	35,000
Automation/Systems	7	0.49	36,000	50,000	42,990	42,000
Cataloging and Classification	84	5.89	15,000	52,000	35,976	36,000
Children's Services	99	6.95	24,000	60,000	38,037	37,560
Circulation	43	3.02	19,000	56,000	32,334	30,000
Collection Development	16	1.12	30,000	60,000	40,146	40,160
Database Management	17	1.19	25,480	68,000	43,646	44,000
Electronic or Digital Services	28	1.96	28,900	10,000	43,366	40,750
Government Documents	7	0.49	25,000	50,200	38,743	42,000
Indexing/Abstracting	3	0.21	38,000	43,000	40,000	39,000
Info Technology	71	4.98	24,000	110,000	53,083	50,000
Instruction	41	2.88	20,000	55,000	41,175	41,000
Interlibrary Loan/ Document Delivery	15	1.05	26,500	50,000	37,378	37,000
Knowledge Mgt.	17	1.19	26,000	100,000	55,500	55,000
Other	134	9.40	20,000	92,000	41,581	40,000
Reference/Info Services	301	21.12	22,000	70,000	40,292	39,000
School Library Media Specialist	212	14.88	21,000	85,000	42,542	42,000
Solo Librarian	44	3.09	18,000	74,000	41,850	39,550
Telecommunications	1	0.07	66,000	66,000	66,000	66,000
Usability/Usability Testing	17	1.19	24,000	84,000	61,059	62,500
Webmaster	1	0.07	58,000	58,000	58,000	58,000
Youth Services	80	5.61	15,000	60,000	37,199	36,246
Total	1,425	100.00	11,000	120,000	41,102	40,000

* This table represents only full-time placements reported by job assignment. Some individuals omitted placement information, rendering some information unusable. Comparison with other tables will show different numbers of placements.

Diversity in the Profession

The number of graduates reporting minority status continued to decline—from 12 percent in 2005 to 10.7 percent in 2006—this despite increased overall numbers of respondents and more graduates reporting race and ethnicity than in previous years. Salaries also took a step back. The 2006 minority graduates reported an average annual salary of $40,750, a 3.5 percent decrease from a high of $42,233 in 2005. In 2006 there was less than 1 percent difference between the salaries obtained by minority graduates and overall salaries—a reversal of past patterns when reported salaries for this group were an average of 6 percent higher. Increased placements in the Southeast (up by approximately 32.6 percent from 2005), where salaries are among the lowest, may be the culprit.

(text continues on page 406)

Table 7 / Comparison of Salaries by Type of Organization*

	Total Placements	Salaries		Low Salary		High Salary		Average Salary			Median Salary		
		Women	Men	Women	Men	Women	Men	Women	Men	All	Women	Men	All
Public Libraries													
Northeast	96	77	15	$22,880	$28,000	$51,000	$55,000	$37,484	$38,770	$37,675	$37,500	$38,000	$37,500
Southeast	102	76	21	16,600	27,000	53,000	46,000	34,881	35,418	34,946	35,000	35,000	35,000
Midwest	111	86	13	15,000	30,000	54,900	47,000	35,171	35,106	35,109	36,000	33,100	35,525
Southwest	42	30	10	20,000	28,000	63,000	49,000	38,270	37,900	38,178	38,100	40,000	38,600
West	79	59	9	30,000	31,000	63,000	62,000	44,665	46,056	44,849	43,000	45,000	44,500
Canada/International	12	10	2	28,000	28,268	65,960	37,691	43,902	32,980	42,802	42,968	32,980	40,377
All Public	446	368	70	15,000	27,000	65,960	62,000	37,825	37,731	37,875	37,500	37,521	37,500
School Libraries													
Northeast	78	67	6	12,000	37,000	62,000	45,000	42,177	40,387	42,137	42,000	40,000	42,000
Southeast	65	50	13	23,300	30,000	74,000	51,000	40,633	40,115	40,526	40,000	40,000	40,000
Midwest	39	32	2	21,000	45,000	67,000	85,000	43,745	65,000	44,825	45,000	65,000	45,000
Southwest	39	33	2	21,000	47,000	53,000	49,000	40,747	48,000	41,162	42,000	48,000	42,000
West	16	12	3	36,000	32,885	65,000	63,000	46,915	48,628	47,257	45,000	50,000	45,000
Canada/International	1	1	—	46,000		46,000		46,000		46,000	46,000	—	46,000
All School	245	214	26	12,000	30,000	74,000	85,000	42,089	43,681	42,420	42,000	41,260	42,000
College/University Libraries													
Northeast	82	51	24	24,000	15,000	57,000	78,000	38,221	41,374	39,062	38,000	41,000	38,580
Southeast	101	71	22	19,000	30,000	52,000	48,000	36,836	39,377	37,385	38,000	40,000	38,000
Midwest	98	64	18	24,000	25,000	55,243	56,899	38,345	39,412	37,855	39,752	38,273	39,000
Southwest	47	34	10	19,000	28,000	56,000	43,000	38,396	36,295	37,918	37,500	37,000	37,500
West	51	36	10	23,956	32,000	65,000	52,000	43,394	44,293	43,590	43,623	44,865	44,365
Canada/International	15	10	4	24,000	36,000	51,826	48,000	42,508	44,308	43,176	44,115	46,615	45,230
All Academic	403	297	90	18,000	15,000	65,000	78,000	38,664	40,519	38,956	39,000	40,500	39,000
Special Libraries													
Northeast	37	30	3	23,566	31,000	72,500	58,000	44,518	48,333	44,865	43,500	56,000	45,000
Southeast	17	14	3	30,000	20,000	52,000	55,000	40,107	36,667	39,500	39,750	33,000	39,500
Midwest	22	14	4	24,000	34,000	67,000	46,000	43,646	39,500	42,724	40,500	39,000	39,250
Southwest	12	8	1	33,000	26,000	57,000	26,000	41,938	26,000	40,167	42,000	26,000	42,000

West	18	15	2	25,000	28,000	120,000	42,500	53,651	35,250	51,486	56,000	35,250	52,000
Canada/International	5	4	1	37,691	15,248	74,000	15,248	57,201	15,248	48,811	58,557	15,248	47,114
All Special	112	86	14	23,566	15,248	120,000	58,000	45,606	37,482	44,494	42,000	36,250	42,000
Government Libraries													
Northeast	3	3	—	39,000	—	40,500	—	39,500	—	39,500	39,000	—	39,000
Southeast	17	12	4	30,000	30,600	62,400	59,000	44,509	39,900	43,747	44,500	35,000	44,000
Midwest	5	1	3	34,000	37,000	34,000	45,000	34,000	40,667	39,000	34,000	40,000	38,500
Southwest	3	3	—	24,000	—	44,000	—	36,417	—	36,417	41,250	—	41,250
West	3	3	—	26,000	—	52,000	—	39,000	—	39,000	39,000	—	39,000
Canada/International	4	4	—	20,000	—	56,000	—	38,832	—	38,832	39,664	—	39,664
All Government	35	25	7	20,000	30,600	62,400	59,000	41,024	40,229	41,127	41,250	39,000	40,500
Library Cooperatives/Networks													
Northeast	4	1	2	23,400	40,780	23,400	50,000	23,400	45,390	38,060	23,400	45,390	40,780
All Co-op./Networks	4	2	2	23,400	40,780	23,400	50,000	23,400	45,390	38,060	23,400	45,390	40,780
Vendors													
Northeast	12	8	4	33,000	37,000	80,000	66,000	50,483	51,250	50,738	45,500	51,000	45,500
Southeast	3	2	—	30,000	—	35,000	—	32,500	—	32,500	32,500	—	32,500
Midwest	2	2	—	42,000	—	42,603	—	42,302	—	42,302	42,302	—	42,302
Southwest	1	1	—	40,000	—	40,000	—	40,000	—	40,000	40,000	—	40,000
West	1	1	—	47,000	—	47,000	—	47,000	—	47,000	47,000	—	47,000
Canada/International	2	—	2	—	40,518	—	50,000	—	45,259	45,259	—	45,259	45,259
All Vendors	21	14	6	30,000	37,000	80,000	66,000	42,789	49,253	46,799	42,302	46,000	42,302
Other Organizations													
Northeast	45	21	17	24,500	32,000	100,000	110,000	43,645	53,088	47,870	42,000	46,000	43,911
Southeast	24	14	9	22,000	20,000	62,000	65,000	40,734	49,956	43,168	37,500	51,000	49,500
Midwest	59	22	21	20,000	20,000	80,000	85,000	43,632	54,494	48,620	42,300	52,000	45,000
Southwest	27	9	9	28,800	26,000	57,000	80,000	46,640	48,317	46,221	50,960	43,000	44,000
West	42	26	10	33,000	30,000	120,000	85,000	59,804	61,400	60,247	55,000	63,250	61,250
Canada/International	5	4	3	20,000	47,308	45,230	61,248	35,661	56,185	45,776	38,706	60,624	60,000
All Other	213	98	70	20,000	20,000	100,000	110,000	47,163	53,178	49,888	45,000	50,000	46,750

* This table represents only full-time salaries and placements reported by type. Some individuals omitted placement information, rendering some information unusable. Comparison with other tables will show different numbers of total placements owing to completeness of the data reported by individuals and schools.

Table 8 / Placements and Full-Time Salaries of Reporting 2006 Graduates*

School	Total Placements	Salaries		Low Salary		High Salary		Average Salary			Median Salary		
		Women	Men	Women	Men	Women	Men	Women	Men	All	Women	Men	All
Alabama	9	8	1	$22,000	$22,000	$47,500	$22,000	$37,875	$22,000	$36,111	$38,750	$22,000	$37,500
Albany	16	11	3	24,960	30,000	56,000	50,000	39,994	42,000	41,063	38,500	46,000	40,186
British Columbia	19	17	2	32,980	40,518	74,000	45,230	46,443	42,874	46,068	45,230	42,874	45,230
Buffalo	44	32	6	24,500	32,000	55,000	45,000	38,692	37,833	38,491	38,000	37,500	38,000
Catholic University	20	15	5	38,000	30,000	60,000	46,000	46,041	37,200	43,831	45,000	39,000	44,000
Clarion	32	24	3	23,400	28,000	50,000	40,020	35,160	32,007	34,809	34,000	28,000	33,000
Dalhousie	15	10	5	34,922	28,268	52,762	61,248	43,071	44,891	43,678	42,349	47,308	42,578
Dominican	17	10	3	15,000	33,000	50,000	45,000	32,130	40,200	34,820	30,000	45,000	33,000
Drexel	22	17	4	29,000	31,000	70,000	50,000	44,020	40,250	43,266	42,750	40,000	41,750
Emporia	15	12	1	24,000	25,000	46,000	25,000	31,571	25,000	31,065	29,500	25,000	29,000
Florida State	18	11	6	16,600	38,700	53,000	55,000	35,798	44,117	38,734	35,000	41,000	38,700
Hawaii	14	8	3	28,000	40,000	67,000	50,000	40,813	43,667	41,591	39,250	41,000	40,500
Illinois	73	53	17	24,000	36,000	120,000	80,000	43,328	50,057	44,962	40,000	45,000	41,425
Indiana	62	52	8	22,000	15,248	56,000	62,400	36,791	38,183	36,980	37,000	39,558	37,440
Iowa	14	—	—	—	—	—	—	—	—	33,256	—	—	35,000
Kent State	60	40	11	21,000	20,000	62,000	50,000	37,570	36,097	37,252	36,500	34,000	36,000
Kentucky	31	23	8	20,000	31,605	53,000	47,000	32,818	38,451	34,272	31,583	37,500	33,000
Long Island	41	35	3	31,000	33,000	100,000	49,500	46,038	39,471	45,520	46,000	35,912	45,250
Louisiana State	22	20	1	28,000	33,000	48,000	33,000	36,021	33,000	35,610	36,000	33,000	35,500
Michigan	64	30	23	23,956	35,500	84,000	110,000	50,162	60,543	54,581	46,500	62,500	55,000
Missouri–Columbia	3	3	—	18,000	—	39,000	—	29,500	—	29,500	31,500	—	31,500

N.C. Central	20	13	5	21,000	31,000	55,000	50,000	37,512	38,820	37,875	36,000	37,500	36,550
N.C. Chapel Hill	21	15	4	31,000	33,500	62,400	72,000	42,301	53,125	44,580	42,000	53,500	43,000
N.C. Greensboro	47	30	14	20,000	20,000	62,000	55,000	35,772	36,079	35,869	35,808	34,500	35,308
North Texas	108	78	24	20,000	26,000	100,000	50,000	41,608	39,679	41,154	41,000	40,000	40,500
Oklahoma	11	8	1	24,000	40,000	57,000	40,000	33,400	40,000	34,225	31,000	40,000	31,500
Pittsburgh	42	33	9	24,000	15,000	53,500	51,000	37,610	38,488	37,790	38,500	39,450	38,500
Rhode Island	10	5	5	23,566	35,000	50,000	42,000	37,513	38,037	37,775	36,000	37,283	36,642
Rutgers	37	25	10	23,800	28,000	50,500	58,000	42,122	44,598	42,829	43,200	43,840	43,500
San José	110	76	14	23,500	28,000	98,000	85,000	45,757	46,685	45,901	45,000	43,500	45,000
Simmons	105	82	12	20,000	11,000	72,500	66,000	38,882	42,394	39,503	38,000	41,500	38,653
South Carolina	23	17	4	31,000	37,000	45,000	51,000	38,015	44,000	39,155	38,101	44,000	38,312
South Florida	47	38	9	22,307	30,000	58,000	45,000	36,036	37,925	36,333	36,492	37,500	36,602
Southern Conn.	29	26	2	12,000	37,350	50,000	43,800	36,955	40,575	37,214	38,500	40,575	38,500
St. John's	7	6	1	32,500	45,000	57,325	45,000	45,528	45,000	45,452	47,171	45,000	45,000
Syracuse	8	4	3	42,000	29,500	56,000	46,000	47,875	39,167	44,143	46,750	42,000	44,000
Tennessee	25	18	7	21,000	27,000	53,000	45,000	36,743	37,557	36,971	35,930	38,000	36,759
Texas (Austin)	32	26	5	24,000	30,000	58,000	80,000	41,281	51,400	42,913	39,500	45,000	40,000
Texas Woman's	24	19	1	19,000	31,000	50,000	31,000	38,722	31,000	38,336	42,000	31,000	42,000
UCLA	10	7	1	40,000	52,000	85,000	52,000	53,143	52,000	53,000	47,000	52,000	49,500
Washington	18	13	4	36,000	39,000	92,000	78,000	48,587	58,750	50,978	44,000	59,000	46,000
Wayne State	65	46	13	20,800	33,100	80,000	85,000	41,519	50,769	43,540	39,000	48,000	40,000
Wisc. (Madison)	56	30	8	25,000	27,040	67,000	45,000	41,550	37,609	40,720	40,000	39,250	40,000
Wisc. (Milwaukee)	16	10	5	28,000	28,000	67,000	46,000	42,900	35,060	40,287	42,000	32,000	41,000

* This table represents only placements and salaries reported as full-time. Some individuals or schools omitted some information, rendering information unusable. Comparisons with other tables will show different numbers of placement and salary.

(continued from page 401)

On a positive note, minority graduates in special libraries reported significant improvement in salaries. These salaries recovered from a drop in 2005, gaining $7,246 to reach an average of $49,500. The trend in salaries for minorities mirrors the overall trend in special libraries, whose salaries rose 6.1 percent. It is important to note that special library placements reported by minority graduates declined somewhat over the previous year.

Salaries for minorities took the largest hits in other agencies and school libraries, dipping approximately 17.5 percent from 2005 in other agencies; however, salaries there are still 9 percent above the overall annual averages. School library salaries had a less dramatic reversal at approximately 3.9 percent.

Location continues to matter for graduates reporting minority status. On a bright note, this group experienced salary gains in the Midwest, up 7.5 percent to $42,080. Following the pattern of the rest of the Southeast, salaries plummeted there by 8.8 percent. Canadian graduates reporting minority status had significantly higher salaries than all Canadian graduates, which may be due to the increased number of individuals claiming minority status.

Public libraries (36.4 percent) and academic libraries (29 percent) continue to be popular choices for minority graduates, and each type has seen modest salary growth. Salaries in public libraries rose by $1,368 (3.6 percent) for graduates reporting minority status, while average starting salaries in academic libraries surged 5.6 percent to $41,942 (approximately 7.1 percent higher than the overall average).

Gender Inequity Remains

Comparing average starting salaries for women and men continues to be an exercise in frustration. While women have seen positive improvement in salaries, finally topping $40,000, their salaries continue to lag approximately 6.5 percent behind salaries for men.

Proportionately, women comprise approximately 80 percent of the LIS work force. However, smaller percentages of women found jobs in academic libraries (73.6 percent women) and special libraries (76.7 percent) and with vendors (66 percent women) and other organizations (46 percent). Three of these four workplaces offer the top starting salaries (other agencies, vendors, and special libraries). So fewer women are finding positions in the higher paying organizations. This was especially noticeable in the other agencies, where women's starting salaries ($47,163) were 12.8 percent below those earned by their male counterparts ($53,178). The exception appeared in special libraries, where women ($45,606) had achieved salaries 17.8 percent higher than men ($37,482), as well as the average starting salary for all women (11.1 percent higher).

Despite the salary differentials, in 2006 men did not experience the stellar salary growth of the previous year. The average starting salary for men grew only 2.5 percent from 2005 compared to a 4.3 percent rise the year before. They experienced unexpected success in public libraries, where salaries rose by 4.7 percent.

Regional Boom or Bust?

This year's sleeper was the Southwest. With the inclusion of LIS programs that had not participated in the previous year and an increased number of respondents, salaries and placements showed health across library types. While placements across Texas were high, there were more in Colorado and Utah than have been reported in past years, making up a combined 17 percent of the total placements in the Southwest in 2006. Women in the Southwest experienced enormous salary growth, up 11.3 percent to $39,793; men's average annual salaries rose by 9.5 percent to $40,587. Similarly, salaries for jobs in public libraries, school libraries, and special libraries had spectacular jumps.

In special libraries, average annual salaries grew to $40,167 from $32,800 (approximately 18.3 percent). Even though the actual number of placements remained low, reported placements in special libraries more than doubled among the Southwest cohort. Another area contributing to the spectacular increases is "other organizations." Much like special libraries, while the overall number remained small, placements increased by 51 percent from the previous year, and salaries went up by more than 7.1 percent to $46,221.

Salaries in the Southeast suffered (down 3.2 percent) while reported placements increased (up 25 percent). Public and academic libraries had remarkable improvements in the number of jobs reported (increases of 42.1 percent and 38.6 percent, respectively). More graduates reported jobs in school libraries in the region also, increasing approximately 35 percent from 2005. Possible explanations for the salary dip include the continued fallout from the hurricanes and floods that have ravaged the Southern United States in recent years, eliminating jobs and funding for public institutions and negatively impacting tax bases in areas where the general population has shifted.

Defining the 'Other'

Over the past few surveys, there has been a steady rise in the number of LIS graduates who reported placements in other types of agencies and positions outside of libraries, with a spike this year, as noted. Graduates reporting these "other" jobs have found work in nonprofit organizations and agencies other than libraries, in private industry, and elsewhere, including bioengineering and independent consulting. This has implications for salary levels for these types of agencies. The nonprofit sector has the lowest salaries (at $42,117) on the scale, while, not surprisingly, private industry has the highest (at $59,025). In a follow-up survey, those who reported employment outside of the LIS profession in other agencies said that even though they are not in traditional library jobs, they do make use of the skills and competencies gained with the degree. One graduate described himself as being employed in the computer science field but applying information science theories and information organization principles. Another related her research skills to her responsibilities as a business analyst. The general consensus was that their education is transferable and has made them more flexible and in high demand outside of more traditional library environments.

LS or IS

There has been an ongoing suspicion that there is a significant difference between salaries for those individuals who find jobs in *information science* (IS) compared with those whose jobs are defined as *library science* (LS). The 2006 graduates were asked to explore how they define their positions in terms of either library science or information science. Of the 1,551 graduates who responded to the question, approximately 72 percent stated that their jobs were clearly LS, 12 percent claimed IS, and the remaining 16 percent described their positions as falling into other professional areas, such as business or higher education. Interestingly, 74 percent of the graduates describing their positions as IS are women, refuting previous assumptions that more men were accepting IS jobs.

The IS positions ranged from knowledge management and usability testing to information consulting and digital services. However, many of the more traditional positions, such as reference/information services and cataloging, fell under the IS label as well. Perhaps this is a function of the individual LIS program's philosophies (being an "I" school or an "L" school) rather than a function of the job itself. It may also be a product of the type of agency in which a graduate is employed, though many IS graduates landed in traditional library settings.

More significant than job title is the impact an IS or LS designation had on salaries. The average annual starting salary for graduates who identified their jobs as IS was $48,413 compared to $39,580 for LS jobs (an 18.2 percent variance). Salary differences were even more apparent when comparing women to men. In 2006 women who reported salaries for IS-related jobs had an average annual starting salary of $46,118, while men received $55,423 on average.

Is a Master's Degree Enough?

A random sample of *Library Journal* survey respondents were asked to participate in a very brief follow-up survey. Among the questions, they were asked to discuss the challenges they faced in finding their first professional LIS position. The most common issue reported was finding a job when they had only limited professional experience in libraries. Being in a profession with many career-changers (approximately 51 percent of graduates said LIS was not their first professional career), many LIS graduates bring unique and specialized skills on their résumés. However, despite extensive backgrounds in other fields, they had difficulty convincing employers that their lack of practical library experience would not inhibit their job performance. This might explain the increasing number of temporary professional positions that LIS graduates reported as a way to gain experience while seeking permanent professional employment. This challenge may also be seen in the length of the job search. Graduates agree that students need to make the most of every opportunity to volunteer in libraries and other information agencies as well as seek out fieldwork and internships that will provide additional experience.

Graduates were also asked to discuss what best prepared them for their first professional position. As in the past, they concurred that networking with professionals in the field was key, as was active participation in professional organizations. Some found working as a graduate assistant in the LIS department or the university library invaluable for gaining contacts and experience. Graduates readily discussed the relationship of their coursework to their first jobs, e.g., taking sufficient children and YA literature classes allowed them to be versatile in serving their young constituents.

The 2006 graduates generally felt knowledgeable about the profession as a whole and the specific positions they sought. For example, one graduate who wanted to become a cataloger took every cataloging/classification and information organization class available to build a strong theoretical background and participated in supervised fieldwork, which allowed him to garner practical experience as well. Another graduate summed it up this way: "I found that employers expected you to understand what they want you to do, and the more you know, the better you'll look. In other words, research doesn't stop with the degree."

One final challenge that several graduates discussed in the follow-up survey was related to location. Approximately 16 percent of the 2006 graduates indicated a move outside of their home region. As a group, graduates said that finding the ideal location, one where they were willing to move their families and where salaries were acceptable, was tricky. Searching for the right place was especially lengthy for graduates who wanted to move long distances and for those seeking nonlibrary jobs (the elusive "other") in nonmetropolitan areas.

Advice to Future Graduates

A final question on the follow-up survey—for advice they would give to future colleagues—elicited responses from the philosophical to the practical. But in general, graduates stressed a need to be able to parlay personal background into professional experience. They emphasized the need for experience in a library or information agency even if it's in the capacity of a volunteer or page. Additionally, they suggested polishing the professional persona before entering the job market. One advised, "Be sure your MySpace or other social networking Web pages are what you want future employers to see. The first thing a department head does when she gets a résumé is google the person." For those going the corporate route, another advised, "No visible tattoos! Before going to an interview with a reputable firm, take out the face piercings and nose rings. Dye your blue (purple, mauve, or green) hair something 'normal.' Invest in a professionally prepared résumé." Such professionalism extends to attitude, as expressed in the final piece of practical advice the 2006 graduates issued: "Show your administration that your job is more than just a 'job,' that it is your career."

Accredited Master's Programs in Library and Information Studies

This list of graduate programs accredited by the American Library Association is issued by the ALA Office for Accreditation. Regular updates and additional details appear on the Office for Accreditation's Web site at http://www.ala.org/ala/accreditation/lisdirb/lisdirectory.cfm. More than 200 institutions offering both accredited and nonaccredited programs in librarianship are included in the 60th edition of *American Library Directory* (Information Today, Inc., 2007–2008).

Northeast: Conn., D.C., Md., Mass., N.J., N.Y., Pa., R.I.

Catholic University of America, School of Lib. and Info. Science, 620 Michigan Ave. N.E., Washington, DC 20064. Kimberly Kelley, dean. Tel. 202-319-5085, fax 202-219-5574, e-mail cua-slis@cua.edu, World Wide Web http://slis.cua.edu. Admissions contact: Jeannine Marino. Tel. 202-319-5085, e-mail marino@cua.edu.

Clarion University of Pennsylvania, College of Education and Human Services, Dept. of Lib. Science, 210 Carlson Lib. Bldg., 840 Wood St., Clarion, PA 16214. Bernard F. Vavrek, chair. Tel. 866-272-5612, fax 814-393-2150, World Wide Web http://www.clarion.edu/libsci. Admissions contact: Lois Dulavitch. Tel. 866-272-5612, e-mail ldulavitch@clarion.edu.

Drexel University, College of Info. Science and Technology, 3141 Chestnut St., Philadelphia, PA 19104-2875. David E. Fenske, dean. Tel. 215-895-2474, fax 215-895-2494, e-mail info@ischool.drexel.edu, World Wide Web http://www.ischool.drexel.edu. Admissions contact: Matthew Lechtenburg. Tel. 215-895-1951.

Long Island University, Palmer School of Lib. and Info. Science, C. W. Post Campus, 720 Northern Blvd., Brookville, NY 11548-1300. Mary L. Westermann-Cicio, dean pro tem. Tel. 516-299-2866, fax 516-299-4168, e-mail palmer@cwpost.liu.edu, World Wide Web http://www.liu.edu/palmer. Admissions contact: Rosemary Chu. Tel. 516-299-2487, e-mail rchu@liu.edu.

Pratt Institute, School of Info. and Lib. Science, 144 W. 14 St., New York, NY 10011. Tula Giannini, dean. Tel. 212-647-7682, fax 202-367-2492, e-mail infosils@pratt.edu, World Wide Web http://www.pratt.edu/sils. Admissions contact: Claire Moore.

Queens College, City Univ. of New York, Grad. School of Lib. and Info. Studies, Rm. 254, Rosenthal Lib., 65-30 Kissena Blvd., Flushing, NY 11367-1597. Virgil L. P. Blake, dir. Tel. 718-997-3790, fax 718-997-3797, e-mail gc_gslis@qc.cuny.edu, World Wide Web http://www.qc.edu/gslis. Admissions contact: Roberta Brody. E-mail roberta_brody@qc.edu.

Rutgers University, Dept. of Lib. and Info. Science, School of Communication, Info., and Lib. Studies, 4 Huntington St., New Brunswick, NJ 08901-1071. Michael Lesk, chair. Tel. 732-932-7500 ext. 8955, fax 732-932-2644, e-mail scilsmls@scils.rutgers.edu, World Wide Web http://www.scils.rutgers.edu. Admissions contact: Ross Todd.

Saint John's University, College of Liberal Arts and Sciences, Div. of Lib. and Info. Science, 8000 Utopia Pkwy., Jamaica, NY 11439. Jeffery E. Olson, dir. Tel. 718-990-6200, fax 718-990-2071, e-mail dlis@stjohns.edu, World Wide Web http://www.stjohns.edu/libraryscience. Admissions contact: Deborah Martinez. Tel. 618-990-6209.

Simmons College, Grad. School of Lib. and Info. Science, 300 The Fenway, Boston, MA 02115. Michelle Cloonan, dean. Tel. 617-521-2800, fax 617-521-3192, e-mail gslis@simmons.edu, World Wide Web http://www.simmons.edu/gslis.

Southern Connecticut State University, School of Communication, Info., and Lib. Science, 501 Crescent St., New Haven, CT

06515. Josephine Sche, chair. Tel. 203-392-5781, fax 203-392-5780, e-mail ils@southernct.edu, World Wide Web http://www.southernct.edu/ils.

Syracuse University, School of Info. Studies, 343 Hinds Hall, Syracuse, NY 13244. Elizabeth Liddy, dean. Tel. 315-443-2911, fax 315-443-6886, e-mail ist@syr.edu, World Wide Web http://www.ist.syr.edu. Admissions contact: Scott Nicholson. Tel. 315-443-2911, e-mail mls@syr.edu.

University at Albany, State Univ. of New York, College of Computing and Info., Dept. of Info. Studies, Draper 113, 135 Western Ave., Albany, NY 12222. Terrence Maxwell, chair. Tel. 518-442-5110, fax 518-442-5367, e-mail infostudies@albany.edu, World Wide Web http://www.albany.edu/cci/informationstudies/index.shtml. Admissions contact: Frances Reynolds. E-mail reynolds@albany.edu.

University at Buffalo, State Univ. of New York, Graduate School of Educ., Lib. and Info. Studies, 534 Baldy Hall, Box 1020, Buffalo, NY 14260. Judith Robinson, chair. Tel. 716-645-2412, fax 716-645-3775, e-mail ub-lis@buffalo.edu, World Wide Web http://www.gse.buffalo.edu/programs/lis. Admissions contact: Radhika Suresh. Tel. 716-645-2110, e-mail gse-info@buffalo.edu.

University of Maryland, College of Info. Studies, 4105 Hornbake Lib. Bldg., College Park, MD 20742. Jennifer Preece, dean. Tel. 301-405-2033, fax 301-314-9145, World Wide Web http://www.clis.umd.edu. Admissions tel. 301-405-2033, e-mail lbscgrad@deans.umd.edu.

University of Pittsburgh, School of Info. Sciences, 135 N. Bellefield Ave., Pittsburgh, PA 15260. Richard C. Cox, chair. Tel. 800-672-9435, fax 412-624-5231, e-mail lisinq@mail.sis.pitt.edu, World Wide Web http://www.sis.pitt.edu. Admissions contact: Shabana Reza. Tel. 412-624-3988.

University of Rhode Island, Grad. School of Lib. and Info. Studies, Rodman Hall, 94 W. Alumni Ave., Kingston, RI 02881. Gale Eaton, dir. Tel. 401-874-2947, fax 401-874-4964, e-mail gslis@etal.uri.edu, World Wide Web http://www.uri.edu/artsci/lsc.

Southeast: Ala., Fla., Ga., Ky., La., Miss., N.C., S.C., Tenn., P.R.

Florida State University, College of Info., Shores Bldg., Tallahassee, FL 32306-2100. Larry Dennis, dean. Tel. 850-644-5775, fax 850-644-9763, e-mail grad@ci.fus.edu, World Wide Web http://www.ci.fsu.edu. Admissions contact: Delores Bryant. Tel. 850-645-3280.

Louisiana State University, School of Lib. and Info. Science, 267 Coates Hall, Baton Rouge, LA 70803. Beth Paskoff, dean. Tel. 225-578-3158, fax 225-578-4581, e-mail slis@lsu.edu, World Wide Web http://slis.lsu.edu. Admissions contact: LaToya Coleman Joseph. E-mail lcjoseph@lsu.edu.

North Carolina Central University, School of Lib. and Info. Sciences, P.O. Box 19586, Durham, NC 27707. Irene Owens, dean. Tel. 919-530-6485, fax 919-530-6402, World Wide Web http://www.nccuslis.org. Admissions contact: Tysha Jacobs. Tel. 919-530-7320.

University of Alabama, School of Lib. and Info. Studies, Box 870252, Tuscaloosa, AL 35487-0252. Elizabeth Aversa, dean. Tel. 205-348-4610, fax 205-348-3746, e-mail info@slis.ua.edu, World Wide Web http://www.slis.ua.edu. Admissions contact: Beth Riggs.

University of Kentucky, School of Lib. and Info. Science, 300 Little Lib., Lexington, KY 40506-0224. Timothy W. Sineath, dir. Tel. 859-257-8876, fax 859-257-4205, e-mail ukslis@uky.edu, World Wide Web http://www.uky.edu/CIS/SLIS. Admissions contact: Will Buntin. Tel. 859-257-3317, e-mail wjbun0@uky.edu.

University of North Carolina at Chapel Hill, School of Info. and Lib. Science, CB 3360, 100 Manning Hall, Chapel Hill, NC 27599-3360. José-Marie Griffiths, dean. Tel. 919-962-8366, fax 919-962-8071, e-mail info@ils.unc.edu, World Wide Web http://www.sils.unc.edu. Admissions contact: Lara Bailey.

University of North Carolina at Greensboro, Dept. of Lib. and Info. Studies, School of Educ., 349 Curry Bldg., Greensboro, NC 27402-6170. O. Lee Shiflett, chair. Tel.

336-334-3477, fax 336-334-5060, World Wide Web http://www.uncg.edu/lis. Admissions contact: Cindy Felts. E-mail cpfelts@uncg.edu.

University of Puerto Rico, Graduate School of Info. Sciences and Technologies, Box 21906, San Juan, PR 00931-1906. Nitza Hernández, dir. Tel. 787-763-6199, fax 787-764-2311, e-mail egcti@uprrp.edu, World Wide Web http://egcti.upr.edu. Admissions contact: Migdalia Dávila. Tel. 787-764-0000 ext. 3530, e-mail midavila @uprrp.edu.

University of South Carolina, College of Mass Communications and Info. Studies, School of Lib. and Info. Science, 1501 Greene St., Columbia, SC 29208. Samantha K. Hastings, dir. Tel. 803-777-3858, fax 803-777-7938, e-mail shasting@gwm. sc.edu, World Wide Web http://www. libsci.sc.edu. Admissions contact: Alice Hartzog. Tel. 800-304-3153, e-mail hartzoga @gwm.sc.edu.

University of South Florida, College of Arts and Sciences, School of Lib. and Info. Science, 4202 E. Fowler Ave., CIS 1040, Tampa, FL 33620. John N. Gathegi, dir. Tel. 813-974-3520, fax 813-974-6840, e-mail lis@cas.usf.edu, World Wide Web http://www.cas.usf.edu/lis. Admissions contact: Richard Austin. E-mail raustin@ cas.usf.edu.

University of Southern Mississippi, College of Educ. and Psychology, School of Lib. and Info. Science, 118 College Drive, No. 5146, Hattiesburg, MS 39406-0001. M. J. Norton, dir. Tel. 601-266-4228, fax 601-266-5774, e-mail slis@usm.edu, World Wide Web http://www.usm.edu/slis. Admissions tel. 601-266-5137, e-mail graduatestudies@usm.edu.

University of Tennessee, School of Info. Sciences, 451 Communication Bldg., Knoxville, TN 37996-0341. Edwin M. Cortez, dir. Tel. 865-974-2148, fax 865-974-4967, World Wide Web http://www.sis.utk.edu. Admissions contact: Tanya Arnold. E-mail tnarnold@utk.edu.

Valdosta State Univ., Dept. of Info. Studies, 1500 N. Patterson St., Valdosta, GA 31698-0133. Wallace Koehler, dir. Tel. 229-333-5966, fax 229-259-5055, e-mail mlis@valdosta.edu, World Wide Web http://www.valdosta.edu/mlis. Admissions contact: Sheila Peacock.

Midwest: Ill., Ind., Iowa, Kan., Mich., Mo., Ohio, Wis.

Dominican University, Grad. School of Lib. and Info. Science, 7900 W. Division St., River Forest, IL 60305. Susan Roman, dean. Tel. 708-524-6845, fax 708-524-6657, e-mail gslis@dom.edu, World Wide Web http://www.gslis.dom.edu. Admissions contact: Tracie D. Hall. Tel. 708-524-6848, e-mail thall@dom.edu.

Emporia State University, School of Lib. and Info. Management, 1200 Commercial, Campus Box 4025, Emporia, KS 66801. Gwen Alexander, dean. Tel. 620-341-5203, fax 620-341-5233, e-mail sliminfo @emporia.edu, World Wide Web http:// slim.emporia.edu. Admissions contact: Daniel Roland. Tel. 620-341-5064, e-mail slimapply@emporia.edu.

Indiana University, School of Lib. and Info. Science, LI 011, 1320 E. 10 St., Bloomington, IN 47405-3907. Blaise Cronin, dean. Tel. 812-855-2018, fax 812-855-6166, e-mail slis@indiana.edu, World Wide Web http://www.slis.indiana.edu. Admissions contact: Rhonda Spencer.

Kent State University, School of Lib. and Info. Science, Box 5190, Kent, OH 44242-0001. Richard E. Rubin, dir. Tel. 330-672-2782, fax 330-672-7965, e-mail inform@ slis.kent.edu, World Wide Web http:// www.slis.kent.edu. Admissions contact: Cheryl Tennant.

University of Illinois at Urbana-Champaign, Grad. School of Lib. and Info. Science, 501 E. Daniel St., Champaign, IL 61820-6211. John Unsworth, dean. Tel. 217-333-3280, fax 217-244-3302, e-mail apply@ lis.uiuc.edu, World Wide Web http://www. lis.uiuc.edu. Admissions contact: Valerie Youngen. Tel. 217-333-0734, e-mail vyoungen@uiuc.edu.

University of Iowa, School of Lib. and Info. Science, 3087 Main Lib., Iowa City, IA 52242-1420. James K. Elmborg, dir. Tel. 319-335-5707, fax 319-335-5374, e-mail slis@uiowa.edu, World Wide Web http://slis.uiowa.edu/~slisweb. Admissions contact: Kit Austin. E-mail caroline-austin@uiowa.edu.

University of Michigan, School of Info., 304 West Hall Bldg., 1085 S. University Ave., Ann Arbor, MI 48109-1092. Martha Pollack, dean. Tel. 734-763-2285, fax 734-764-2475, e-mail si.admissions@umich.edu, World Wide Web http://www.si.umich.edu. Admissions contact: Laura Elgas. E-mail lauramb@umich.edu.

University of Missouri, College of Educ., School of Info. Science and Learning Technologies, 303 Townsend Hall, Columbia, MO 65211. John Wedman, dir. Tel. 573-882-4546, fax 573-884-0122, e-mail sislt@missouri.edu, World Wide Web http://sislt.missouri.edu.

University of Wisconsin–Madison, College of Letters and Sciences, School of Lib. and Info. Studies, Rm. 4217, H. C. White Hall, 600 N. Park St., Madison, WI 53706. Louise S. Robbins, dir. Tel. 608-263-2900, fax 608-263-4849, e-mail uw-slis@slis.wisc.edu, World Wide Web http://www.slis.wisc.edu. Admissions contact: Barbara J. Arnold. Tel. 608-263-2909, e-mail bjarnold@wisc.edu.

University of Wisconsin–Milwaukee, School of Info. Studies, P.O. Box 413, Milwaukee, WI 53211. Johannes Britz, dean. Tel. 414-229-4707, fax 414-229-6699, e-mail info@sois.uwm.edu, World Wide Web http://www.uwm.edu/dept/sois.

Wayne State University, Lib. and Info. Science Program, 106 Kresge Lib., Detroit, MI 48202. Stephen T. Bajjaly, dir. Tel. 313-577-1825, fax 313-577-7563, e-mail asklis@wayne.edu, World Wide Web http://www.lisp.wayne.edu. Admissions contact: Matthew Fredericks. Tel. 313-577-2446, e-mail aj8416@wayne.edu.

Southwest: Ariz., Okla., Texas

Texas Woman's University, School of Lib. and Info. Studies, P.O. Box 425438, Denton, TX 76204-5438. Ling Hwey Jeng, dir. Tel. 940-898-2602, fax 940-898-2611, e-mail slis@twu.edu, World Wide Web http://www.twu.edu/cope/slis. Admissions contact: Brenda Mallory. E-mail bmallory@mail.wu.edu.

University of Arizona, School of Info. Resources and Lib. Science, 1515 E. First St., Tucson, AZ 85719. Jana Bradley, dir. Tel. 520-621-3565, fax 520-621-3279, e-mail sirls@email.arizona.edu, World Wide Web http://www.sir.arizona.edu. Admissions contact: Geraldine Fragoso.

University of North Texas, School of Lib. and Info. Sciences, Box 311068, Denton, TX 76203-1068. Herman L. Totten, dean. Tel. 940-565-2445, fax 940-565-3101, e-mail slis@unt.edu, World Wide Web http://www.unt.edu/slis. Admissions contact: LeAnne Coffey. Tel. 940-565-3562, e-mail coffey@unt.edu.

University of Oklahoma, School of Lib. and Info. Studies, College of Arts and Sciences, Rm. 120, 401 W. Brooks, Norman, OK 73019-6032. Kathy Latrobe, dir. Tel. 405-325-3921, fax 405-325-7648, e-mail slisinfo@ou.edu, World Wide Web http://www.ou.edu/cas/slis. Admissions contact: Maggie Ryan.

University of Texas at Austin, School of Info., 1 University Sta., D7000, Austin, TX 78712-0390. Andrew Dillon, dean. Tel. 512-471-3821, fax 512-471-3971, e-mail info@ischool.utexas.edu, World Wide Web http://www.ischool.utexas.edu. Admissions contact: Carla Criner. Tel. 512-471-5654, e-mail criner@ischool.utexas.edu.

West: Calif., Colo., Hawaii, Wash.

San José State University, School of Lib. and Info. Science, 1 Washington Sq., San José, CA 95192-0029. Ken Haycock, dir. Tel. 408-924-2490, fax 408-924-2476, e-mail office@slis.sjsu.edu, World Wide Web http://slisweb.sjsu.edu. Admissions contact: Scharlee Phillips. Tel. 408-924-2417, e-mail sphillip@slis.sjsu.edu.

University of California, Los Angeles, Graduate School of Educ. and Info. Studies, Dept. of Info. Studies, Box 951520, Los Angeles, CA 90095-1520. Anne Gilliland, chair. Tel. 310-825-8799, fax 310-206-3076, e-mail info@gseis.ucla.edu, World Wide Web http://is.gseis.ucla.edu. Admissions contact: Susan Abler. Tel. 310-825-5269, e-mail abler@gseis.ucla.edu.

University of Denver, Morgridge College of Educ., Lib. and Info. Science Program, JMAC Bldg., 2450 S. Vine St., Denver, CO 80208. Deborah S. Grealy, dir. Tel. 303-871-2747, fax 303-871-2709, World Wide Web http://www.du.edu/education/programs/lis. Admissions contact: Nick Heckart. E-mail nheckart@du.edu.

University of Hawaii, College of Natural Sciences, Lib. and Info. Science Program, 2550 McCarthy Mall, Honolulu, HI 96822. Andrew Wertheimer, chair. Tel. 808-956-7321, fax 808-956-3548, e-mail slis@hawaii.edu, World Wide Web http://www.hawaii.edu/slis. Admissions contact: Gail Morimoto.

University of Washington, The Info. School, 370 Mary Gates Hall, Box 352840, Seattle, WA 98195-2840. Harry Bruce, dean. Tel. 206-685-9937, fax 206-616-3152, e-mail info@ischool.washington.edu, World Wide Web http://www.ischool.washington.edu. Admissions contact: Admissions coordinator. Tel. 206-543-1794, e-mail mlis@ischool.washington.edu.

Canada

Dalhousie University, School of Info. Management, Kenneth C. Rowe Management Bldg., Halifax, NS B3H 3J5. Fiona Black, dir. Tel. 902-494-3656, fax 902-494-2451, e-mail sim@dal.ca, World Wide Web http://www.sim.management.dal.ca. Admissions contact: JoAnn Watson. Tel. 902-494-3656, e-mail mlis@dal.ca.

McGill University, Grad. School of Info. Studies, 3459 McTavish St., Montreal, PQ H3A 1Y1. France Bouthillier, dir. Tel. 514-398-4204, fax 514-398-7193, e-mail sis@mcgill.ca, World Wide Web http://www.mcgill.ca/sis. Admissions contact: Kathryn Hubbard.

Université de Montréal, École de Bibliothéconomie et des Sciences de l'Information, C.P. 6128, Succursale Centre-Ville, Montreal, QC H3C 3J7. Jean-Michel Salaun, dir. Tel. 514-343-6400, fax 514-343-5753, e-mail ebsiinfo@ebsi.umontreal.ca, World Wide Web http://www.ebsi.umontreal.ca. Admissions contact: Céline Lapierre. E-mail celine.lapierre@umontreal.ca.

University of Alberta, School of Lib. and Info. Studies, 3-20 Rutherford S., Edmonton, AB T6G 2J4. Anna Altmann, dir. Tel. 780-492-4578, fax 780-492-2430, e-mail slis@ualberta.ca, World Wide Web http://www.slis.ualberta.ca. Admissions contact: Joanne Hilger. Tel. 780-492-4140, e-mail joanne.hilger@ualberta.ca.

University of British Columbia, School of Lib., Archival, and Info. Studies, Ste. 301, 6190 Agronomy Rd., Vancouver, BC V6T 1Z3. Edie Rasmussen, dir. Tel. 604-822-2404, fax 604-822-6006, e-mail slais@interchange.ubc.ca, World Wide Web http://www.slais.ubc.ca. Admissions contact: Michelle Mallette. E-mail slaisad@interchange.ubc.ca.

University of Toronto, Faculty of Info. Studies, Rm. 211, 140 George St., Toronto, ON M5S 3G6. Brian Cantwell Smith, dean. Tel. 416-978-3202, fax 416-978-5762, e-mail inquire@fis.utoronto.ca, World Wide Web http://www.fis.utoronto.ca. Admissions contact: Judy Dunn. Tel. 416-978-3934, e-mail judy.dunn@utoronto.ca.

University of Western Ontario, Grad. Programs in Lib. and Info. Science, Faculty of Info. and Media Studies, Rm. 240, North Campus Bldg., 1151 Richmond St., London, ON N6A 5B7. Thomas Carmichael, dean. Tel. 519-661-4017, fax 519-661-3506, e-mail mlisinfo@uwo.ca, World Wide Web http://fims.uwo.ca. Admissions contact: Shelley Long.

Library Scholarship Sources

For a more complete list of scholarships, fellowships, and assistantships offered for library study, see *Financial Assistance for Library and Information Studies,* published annually by the American Library Association (ALA). The document is also available on the ALA Web site at http://www.ala.org/ala/hrdr/educprofdev/financialassistance.cfm.

American Association of Law Libraries. (1) A varying number of scholarships of a minimum of $1,000 for graduates of an accredited law school who are degree candidates in an ALA-accredited library school; (2) a varying number of scholarships of varying amounts for library school graduates working on a law degree, non-law graduates enrolled in an ALA-accredited library school, and law librarians taking a course relating to law librarianship; (3) the George A. Strait Minority Stipend of $3,500 for varying numbers of minority librarians working toward an advanced degree to further a law library career; and (4) a varying number of $500 scholarships for law librarians taking courses relating to law librarianship. For information, write to: Scholarship Committee, AALL, 53 W. Jackson Blvd., Suite 940, Chicago, IL 60604.

American Library Association. (1) The Marshall Cavendish Scholarship of $3,000 for a varying number of students who have been admitted to an ALA-accredited library school; (2) the David H. Clift Scholarship of $3,000 for a varying number of students who have been admitted to an ALA-accredited library school; (3) the Tom and Roberta Drewes Scholarship of $3,000 for a varying number of library support staff; (4) the Mary V. Gaver Scholarship of $3,000 for a varying number of individuals specializing in youth services; (5) the Miriam L. Hornback Scholarship of $3,000 for a varying number of ALA or library support staff; (6) the Christopher J. Hoy/ERT Scholarship of $5,000 for a varying number of students who have been admitted to an ALA-accredited library school; (7) the Tony B. Leisner Scholarship of $3,000 for a varying number of library support staff; (8) the

Cicely Phippen Marks Scholarship of $3,000 for a varying number of students admitted to an ALA-accredited program specializing in federal librarianship; (9) Spectrum Initiative Scholarships of $6,500 for a varying number of minority students admitted to an ALA-accredited library school. For information on all ALA scholarships, write to: ALA Scholarship Clearinghouse, 50 E. Huron St., Chicago, IL 60611. For information, write to: ALA Scholarship Clearinghouse, 50 E. Huron St., Chicago, IL 60611, or see http://www.ala.org/hrdr/scholarship.html.

ALA/American Association of School Librarians. The AASL School Librarians Workshop Scholarship of $3,000 for a candidate admitted to a full-time ALA-accredited MLS or school library media program. For information, write to: ALA Scholarship Clearinghouse, 50 E. Huron St., Chicago, IL 60611, or see http://www.ala.org/hrdr/scholarship.html.

ALA/Association for Library Service to Children. (1) The Bound to Stay Bound Books Scholarship of $6,500 each for four students who are U.S. or Canadian citizens, who have been admitted to an ALA-accredited program, and who will work with children in a library for one year after graduation; (2) the Frederic G. Melcher Scholarship of $6,000 each for two U.S. or Canadian citizens admitted to an ALA-accredited library school who will work with children in school or public libraries for one year after graduation. For information, write to: ALA Scholarship Clearinghouse, 50 E. Huron St., Chicago, IL 60611, or see http://www.ala.org/hrdr/scholarship.html.

ALA/Association of College and Research Libraries and the Institute for Scientific Information. (1) The ACRL Doctoral Dissertation Fellowship of $1,500 for a student who has completed all coursework, and submitted a dissertation proposal that has been accepted, in the area of academic librarianship; (2) the Samuel Lazerow Fellowship of $1,000 for a research, travel, or writing project in acquisitions or technical services in an academic or research library; (3) the ACRL and Coutts Nijhoff International West European Specialist Study Grant of up to 4,500 euros to pay travel expenses, room, and board for a ten-day trip to Europe for an ALA member (selection is based on proposal outlining purpose of trip). For information, write to: Megan Griffin, ALA/ACRL, 50 E. Huron St., Chicago, IL 60611.

ALA/Association of Specialized and Cooperative Library Agencies. Century Scholarship of up to $2,500 for a varying number of disabled U.S. or Canadian citizens admitted to an ALA-accredited library school. For information, write to: ALA Scholarship Clearinghouse, 50 E. Huron St., Chicago, IL 60611, or see http://www. ala.org/hrdr/scholarship.html.

ALA/International Relations Committee. The Bogle Pratt International Library Travel Fund grant of $1,000 for a varying number of ALA members to attend a first international conference. For information, write to: Michael Dowling, ALA/IRC, 50 E. Huron St., Chicago, IL 60611.

ALA/Library and Information Technology Association. (1) The LITA/Christian Larew Memorial Scholarship of $3,000 for a student who has been admitted to an ALA-accredited program in library automation and information science; (2) the LITA/OCLC Minority Scholarship in Library and Information Technology of $3,000 for a minority student admitted to an ALA-accredited program; (3) the LITA/LSSI Minority Scholarship of $2,500 for a minority student admitted to an ALA-accredited program. For information, write to: ALA Scholarship Clearinghouse, 50 E. Huron St., Chicago, IL 60611, or see http://www.ala.org/hrdr/scholarship.html.

ALA/Public Library Association. The Demco New Leaders Travel Grant Study Award of up to $1,500 for a varying number of PLA members with MLS degrees and five years or less experience. For information, write to: PLA Awards Program, ALA/PLA, 50 E. Huron St., Chicago, IL 60611.

American-Scandinavian Foundation. Fellowships and grants for 25 to 30 students, in amounts from $3,000 to $18,000, for advanced study in Denmark, Finland, Iceland, Norway, or Sweden. For information, write to: Exchange Division, American-Scandinavian Foundation, 58 Park Ave., New York, NY 10026.

Association for Library and Information Science Education (ALISE). A varying number of research grants of up to $2,500 each for members of ALISE. For information, write to: Association for Library and Information Science Education, Box 7640, Arlington, VA 22207.

Association of Jewish Libraries. The AJL Scholarship Fund offers up to two scholarships of $500 each for MLS students who plan to work as Judaica librarians. For information, write to: Lynn Feinman, 92nd St. Y Library, 1395 Lexington Ave., New York, NY 10128, e-mail lfeinman@92Y.org.

Association of Seventh-Day Adventist Librarians. The D. Glenn Hilts Scholarship of $1,200 for a member of the Seventh-Day Adventist Church in a graduate library program. For information, write to: Ms. Wisel, Association of Seventh-Day Adventist Librarians, Columbia Union College, 7600 Flower Ave., Takoma Park, MD 20912.

Beta Phi Mu. (1) The Sarah Rebecca Reed Scholarship of $2,000 for a person accepted in an ALA-accredited library program; (2) the Frank B. Sessa Scholarship of $1,250 for a Beta Phi Mu member for continuing education; (3) the Harold Lancour Scholarship of $1,500 for study in a foreign country relating to the applicant's work or schooling; (4) the Blanche E. Woolls Scholarship for School Library Media Service of $1,500 for a person accepted in an ALA-accredited library program; (5) the Doctoral Dissertation Scholarship of $2,000 for a person who has completed course work toward a doctorate; (6) the Eugene Garfield Doctoral Dissertation Scholarship of $3,000 for a person who has approval of a dissertation topic. For information, write to: Executive Director, Beta Phi Mu, Florida State University, SIS, Tallahassee, FL 32306-2100.

Canadian Association of Law Libraries. The Diana M. Priestly Scholarship of $2,500 for a student with previous law library experience or for entry to an approved Canadian law school or accredited Canadian library school. For information, write to: Janet Mass, Chair, CALL/ACBD Scholarship and Awards Committee, Gerard J. LaForest Law Library, University of New Brunswick, Bag Service 44999, Fredericton, NB E38 6C9.

Canadian Federation of University Women. (1) The Alice E. Wilson Award of $6,000 for six students enrolled in graduate studies in any field, with special consideration given to candidates returning to study after at least three years; (2) the Margaret McWilliams Pre-Doctoral Fellowship of $13,000 for a full-time student who has completed one full year of study at the doctoral level; (3) the CFUW Memorial Fellowship of $10,000 for a student enrolled in a master's program in science, mathematics, or engineering; (4) the Beverly Jackson Fellowship of $2,000 for a student over age 35 enrolled in graduate work at an Ontario University; (5) the 1989 Ecole Polytechnique Commemorative Award of $7,000 for a student enrolled in graduate studies relating particularly to women; (6) the Bourse Georgette LeMoyne award of $7,000 for graduate study at a Canadian university where one of the languages of administration and instruction is French; (7) the Dr. Marion Elder Grant Fellowship of $11,000 for a full-time student at the master's or doctoral level; (8) the Margaret Dale Philp Biennial Award of $3,000 for graduate studies in the humanities or social sciences. For information, write to: Fellowships Program Manager, Canadian Federation of University Women, 251 Bank St., Suite 305, Ottawa, ON K2P 1X3, Canada.

Canadian Library Association. (1) The World Book Graduate Scholarship in Library and Information Science of $2,500; (2) the CLA Dafoe Scholarship of $5,000; and (3) the H. W. Wilson Scholarship of $2,000—each scholarship is given to a Canadian citizen or landed immigrant to attend an accredited Canadian library school; (4) the Library Research and Development Grant of $1,000 for a member of the Canadian Library Association, in support of theoretical and applied research in library and information science. For information, write to: CLA Membership Services Department, Scholarships and Awards Committee, 328 Frank St., Ottawa, ON K2P 0X8, Canada.

Catholic Library Association. (1) The World Book, Inc., Grant of $1,500 divided among no more than three CLA members for continuing education in children's or school librarianship; (2) the Rev. Andrew L. Bouwhuis Memorial Scholarship of $1,500 for a student accepted into a graduate program in library science. For information, write to: Jean R. Bostley, SSJ, Scholarship Chair, Catholic Library Association, 100 North St., Suite 224, Pittsfield, MA 01201-5109.

Chinese American Librarians Association. (1) The Sheila Suen Lai Scholarship and (2) the C. C. Seetoo/CALA Conference Travel Scholarship each offer $500 to a Chinese descendant who has been accepted in an ALA-accredited program. For information, write to: MengXiong Liu, Clark Library, San José State University, 1 Washington Sq., San José, CA 95192-0028.

Church and Synagogue Library Association. The Muriel Fuller Memorial Scholarship of $200 (including texts) for a correspondence course offered by the association. Open to CSLA members only. For information, write to: CSLA, 2920 S.W. Dolph Court, Suite 3A, Portland, OR 97280-0357.

Council on Library and Information Resources. (1) The Rovelstad Scholarship in International Librarianship, to enable a student enrolled in an accredited LIS program to attend the IFLA Annual Conference; (2) the A. R. Zipf Fellowship in Information Management of $10,000, awarded annually to a U.S. citizen enrolled in graduate school who shows exceptional promise for leadership and technical achievement. For more information, write to: A. R. Zipf Fellowship, Council on Library and Information Resources, 1755 Massachusetts Ave. N.W., Suite 500, Washington, DC 20036.

Massachusetts Black Librarians' Network. Two scholarships of at least $500 and $1,000 for minority students entering an ALA-accredited master's program in library science with no more 12 semester hours completed toward a degree. For information, write to: Pearl Mosley, Chair, Massachusetts Black Librarians' Network, 17 Beech Glen St., Roxbury, MA 02119.

Medical Library Association. (1) The Cunningham Memorial International Fellowship of $3,500 for each of two health sciences librarians from countries other than the United States and Canada; (2) a scholarship of $5,000 for a person entering an ALA-accredited library program, with no more than one-half of the program yet to be completed; (3) a scholarship of $5,000 for a minority student for graduate study; (4) a varying number of Research, Development and Demonstration Project Grants of $100 to $1,000 for U.S. or Canadian citizens who are MLA members; (5) the MLA Doctoral Fellowship of $2,000 for doctoral work in medical librarianship or information science; (6) the Rittenhouse Award of $500 for a student enrolled in an ALA-accredited library program or a recent graduate working as a trainee in a library internship program; (7) Continuing Education Grants of $100 to $500 for U.S. or Canadian citizens who are MLA members. For information, write to: Professional Development Department, Medical Library Association, 65 E. Wacker Place, Suite 1900, Chicago, IL 60601-7298.

Mountain Plains Library Association. A varying number of grants of up to $600 each for MPLA members with at least two years of membership, for continuing education. For information, write to: Judy Zelenski, MPLA Executive Secretary, 14293 W. Center Drive, Lakewood, SD 80228.

Society of American Archivists. The Colonial Dames Awards, two grants of $1,200 each for specific types of repositories and collections. For information, write to: Debra Noland, Society of American Archivists, 521 S. Wells St., 5th fl., Chicago, IL 60607.

Southern Regional Education Board. A varying number of grants of varying amounts to cover in-state tuition for graduate or postgraduate study in an ALA-accredited library school for residents of various southern U.S. states (qualifying states vary year by year). For information, write to: Academic Common Market, c/o Southern Regional Education Board, 592 Tenth St. N.W., Atlanta, GA 30318-5790.

Special Libraries Association. (1) Three $6,000 scholarships for students interested in special-library work; (2) the Plenum Scholarship of $1,000 and (3) the ISI Scholarship of $1,000, each also for students interested in special-library work; (4) the Affirmative Action Scholarship of $6,000 for a minority student interested in special-library work; and (5) the Pharmaceutical Division Stipend Award of $1,200 for a student with an undergraduate degree in chemistry, life sciences, or pharmacy entering or enrolled in an ALA-accredited program. For information on the first four scholarships, write to: Scholarship Committee, Special Libraries Association, 1700 18th St. N.W., Washington, DC 20009-2508. For information on the Pharmaceutical Stipend, write to: Susan E. Katz, Awards Chair, Knoll Pharmaceuticals Science Information Center, 30 N. Jefferson St., Whippany, NJ 07981.

Library Scholarship and Award Recipients, 2007

Scholarships and awards are listed by organization.

American Association of Law Libraries (AALL)

AALL and West Group George A. Strait Minority Scholarships. *Winners:* Mary Godfrey Rickards, Clarence Robertson, Taciana Williams, Xiaomeng Zhang.

AALL Scholarships. *Winners:* (Library Degree for Law School Graduates) Caitlan Elwood, John Hadler, Louis Rosen, Jacob Sayward; (Library Degree for Non-Law School Graduates) Sara Balls, Kauren Seney, Katherine Sosnoff, Katharine Stockert.

Joseph L. Andrews Bibliographic Award. *Winners:* Michael Chiorazzi and Marguerite L. Most.

Marian Gould Gallagher Distinguished Service Award. To recognize extended and sustained service to law librarianship. *Winners:* Carol D. Billings, Roger F. Jacobs, Cossette T. Sun.

LexisNexis/John R. Johnson Memorial Scholarships. *Winners:* Valerie Bowen, David Dames, Christopher Hudson.

American Library Association (ALA)

ALA/Information Today Library of the Future Award ($1,500). For a library, consortium, group of librarians, or support organization for innovative planning for, applications of, or development of patron training programs about information technology in a library setting. *Donor:* Information Today, Inc. *Winner:* Alliance Second Life Library, East Peoria, Illinois, for development of a 3D virtual world library.

Leo Albert Spectrum Scholarship. To a designated Spectrum Scholarship recipient. *Donor:* Leo Albert. *Winner:* Caroline Caviness.

Hugh C. Atkinson Memorial Award ($2,000). For outstanding achievement (including risk taking) by academic librarians that has contributed significantly to improvements in library automation, management, and/or development or research. *Offered by:* ACRL, ALCTS, LAMA, and LITA divisions. *Winner:* James G. Neal.

Carroll Preston Baber Research Grant (up to $3,000). For innovative research that could lead to an improvement in library services to any specified group(s) of people. *Donor:* Eric R. Baber. *Winner:* Not awarded in 2007.

Beta Phi Mu Award ($1,000). For distinguished service in library education. *Donor:* Beta Phi Mu International Library Science Honorary Society. *Winner:* Barbara Immroth.

Bogle Pratt International Library Travel Fund Award ($1,000). To ALA member(s) to attend their first international conference. *Donors:* Bogle Memorial Fund and Pratt Institute School of Information and Library Science. *Winner:* Dora T. Ho.

W. Y. Boyd Literary Novel Award. *Winner:* See "Literary Prizes, 2007" in Part 5.

Calloway Marathon Spectrum Scholarship. To a designated Spectrum Scholarship recipient. *Donor:* Gregory Calloway and friends. *Winner:* Not awarded in 2007.

David H. Clift Scholarship ($3,000). To worthy U.S. or Canadian citizens enrolled in an ALA-accredited program toward an MLS degree. *Winner:* Kristen Allen.

Eileen Cooke State and Local James Madison Award. To recognize individuals or groups who have championed public access to government information. *Winner:* Patricia Glass Schuman, president, Neal-Schuman Publishers.

Melvil Dewey Medal. To an individual or group for recent creative professional achievement in library management, training, cataloging and classification, and the tools and techniques of librarianship.

Donor: OCLC/Forest Press. *Winner:* Sarah Thomas, director, Oxford University Library Services.

Tom and Roberta Drewes Scholarship ($3,000). To a library support staff member pursuing a master's degree. *Donor:* Quality Books. *Winner:* Christopher David Case.

EBSCO/ALA Conference Sponsorship Award (up to $1,000). To enable ten librarians to attend the ALA Annual Conference. *Donor:* EBSCO Subscription Services. *Winners:* Jennifer Brannock, Lisa Gann, Katy Herrick, Amy Hoseth, Kristie Morrison, Jessica Moyer, Lan Shen, Robbie Sittel, Alexandra Tyle, Jill Woolums.

Equality Award ($500). To an individual or group for an outstanding contribution that promotes equality in the library profession. *Donor:* Scarecrow Press. *Winners:* Gladys Smiley Bell, Kenneth A. Yamashita.

Elizabeth Futas Catalyst for Change Award ($1,000). To recognize and honor a librarian who invests time and talent to make positive change in the profession of librarianship. *Donor:* Elizabeth Futas Memorial Fund. *Winner:* Jenna Freedman.

Loleta D. Fyan Public Library Research Grant (up to $10,000). For projects in public library development. *Donor:* Fyan Estate. *Winner:* Not awarded in 2007.

Mary V. Gaver Scholarship ($3,000). To a student pursuing an MLS and specializing in youth services. *Winner:* Wendy Brown.

Louise Giles Spectrum Scholarship. To a designated Spectrum Scholarship recipient. *Donor:* Louise Giles. *Winner:* Phillippa Caldeira.

William R. Gordon Spectrum Scholarship. To a designated Spectrum Scholarship recipient. *Donor:* William R. Gordon and friends. *Winner:* Not awarded in 2007.

Ken Haycock Award ($1,000). For significant contribution to public recognition and appreciation of librarianship through professional performance, teaching, or writing. *Winner:* Mary Dempsey, commissioner, Chicago Public Library.

Honorary ALA Membership. *Honorees:* David Cohen, Alice L. Hagemeyer, Anita R. Schiller, Alphonse F. Trezza.

Miriam L. Hornback Scholarship ($3,000). To an ALA or library support staff person pursuing a master's degree in library science. *Winner:* Anna Lea Foote.

Paul Howard Award for Courage ($1,000). To a librarian, library board, library group, or an individual who has exhibited unusual courage for the benefit of library programs or services. *Donor:* Paul Howard Memorial Fund. *Winners:* George Christian, Peter Chase, Barbara Bailey, and Jan Nocek, four Connecticut librarians who defied the gag order provision of the USAPatriot Act when they received an FBI National Security Letter.

John Ames Humphry/OCLC/Forest Press Award ($1,000). To an individual for significant contributions to international librarianship. *Donor:* OCLC/Forest Press. *Winner:* Winston Tabb.

Tony B. Leisner Scholarship ($3,000). To a library support staff member pursuing a master's degree program. *Donor:* Tony B. Leisner. *Winner:* Elizabeth Aspen Walker.

Joseph W. Lippincott Award ($1,000). To a librarian for distinguished service to the profession. *Donor:* Joseph W. Lippincott III. *Winner:* Winston Tabb.

James Madison Award. To recognize efforts to promote government openness. *Winner:* Paul K. McMasters, former Freedom Forum First Amendment ombudsman.

Marshall Cavendish Excellence in Library Programming Award ($2,000). To recognize either a school library or public library that demonstrates excellence in library programming by providing programs that have community impact and respond to community need. *Winner:* Calgary (Alberta) Public Library for "It's Not a Crime to Read."

Marshall Cavendish Scholarship ($3,000). To a worthy U.S. or Canadian citizen to begin an MLS degree in an ALA-accredited program. *Winner:* Jill Golden.

Medical Library Association/National Library of Medicine Spectrum Scholarship. To a designated Spectrum Scholarship recipient or recipients. *Donor:* Medical Library Association. *Winners:* Seung-Hae Bang, Natalie Pulley.

Schneider Family Book Awards (three awards of $5,000). To authors or illustrators of books that embody artistic expressions of the disability experience for child and adolescent audiences. *Donor:* Katherine Schneider. *Winners:* See "Literary Prizes, 2007" in Part 5.

Scholastic Library Publishing Award (formerly the Grolier Foundation Award) ($1,000). For stimulation and guidance of reading by children and young people. *Donor:* Scholastic Library Publishing. *Winner:* Eliza T. Dresang.

Spectrum Doctoral Fellowships. To provide full tuition support and stipends to minority U.S. and Canadian LIS doctoral students. *Donors:* Institute of Museum and Library Services; University of Pittsburgh; University of California, Los Angeles; University of Wisconsin School of Library and Information Studies. *Winners:* Janet Ceja Alcalá, Tammy Mays, Liladhar Pendse, Elizabeth Rodriguez, J. Brenton Stewart, Vivian Wong.

Spectrum Initiative Scholarships ($6,500). Presented to minority students admitted to an ALA-accredited library school. *Donors:* ALA and Institute of Museum and Library Services. *Winners:* Sara Abdmishani, Raymundo Andrade, Lisa Ree Anfield, David Aponte, Aimee Yeong Babcock-Ellis, Rita Benitez, Gaurav Bhatnagar, Dana Lee Bing, Jennifer Blakely, Angela Bonds, Carmen Boston, RaShauna Brannon, Alice C. Brown, Norah A. Burns, Tina Chan, Stephen S. Chan, Lulu Chen, Linnae Ann-Marie Cintron, Henrique Balbino Coelho, Christine Cordova, Michael Sean Creedon, Yago Said Cura, Prisciliana Kristina Delgado, Heather Devine, Dan Tam Do, Khue Duong, Akunna Eneh, Rita Felton-Mitchell, Yesenia Figueroa, Jamey Frails, Blodine F. Francois, Sheneatha Frison, Brenda Garcia, Meseret Gebrekristos, Sarah Ann Geisler, Andrea Gibbs, Glynnis Gilbert, Janelle Gonzalez, Susan Hoang, Doreen Howson, Christine Jackson, Lynette Jackson, Robert L. Jones, Bergis Jules, Marc Levitt, Jenny Lockerby, Teresa Mares, Vanessa Tepsis Martin, Roshin Mathew, Edwin Maxwell, Shakema Miller, Michelle M. Miller, Andres Montejo, Claudia Moore, Martin A. Morales-Duran, Dolly Morse, Janice Murray, Sarah Beth Okner, Bijal Patel, Kimberly Patton, Annie Patrick, Richard S. Porter, Rona Razon, Francis Reyes, Jose Rivera, Amy Roberson, Megan Rucker, Oscar Rueda, Amina SaniKangiwa, Kristal Sergent, Helen Snowden, Joi Sorensen, Autumn Sullivan, Phuong Vu, Jason Yamashita.

Sullivan Award for Public Library Administrators Supporting Services to Children. To a library supervisor/administrator who has shown exceptional understanding and support of public library services to children. *Donor:* Peggy Sullivan. *Winner:* Keith Kuhn.

Howard M. and Gladys B. Teeple Spectrum Scholarship. To a designated Spectrum Scholarship recipient. *Donor:* Religion and Ethics Institute. *Winner:* Kathy Carroll.

Thomson Gale Group Financial Development Award ($2,500). To a library organization for a financial development project to secure new funding resources for a public or academic library. *Donor:* Thomson Gale Group. *Winner:* Not awarded in 2007.

Betty J. Turock Spectrum Scholarship. To a designated Spectrum Scholarship recipient. *Donor:* JTBC Foundation. *Winner:* Not awarded in 2007.

H. W. Wilson Library Staff Development Grant ($3,500). To a library organization for a program to further its staff development goals and objectives. *Donor:* H. W. Wilson Company. *Winner:* Lee County (Florida) Library System.

Women's National Book Association/Ann Heidbreder Eastman Grant ($750). To a librarian to take a course or participate in an institute devoted to aspects of publishing as a profession or to provide reimbursement for such study completed within the past year. *Winner:* Linda Moskovics.

World Book/ALA Goal Grant (up to $10,000). To ALA units for the advancement of public, academic, or school library service and librarianship through support of programs that implement the goals and priorities of ALA. *Donor:* World Book. *Winner:* Young Adult Library Services Association for "Improving Teen Services in Key States."

ALA/Allied Professional Association

SirsiDynix Award for Outstanding Achievement in Promoting Salaries and Status for Library Workers ($2,500). *Donor:* Sirsi-Dynix. *Winners:* Alachua County (Florida) Library District; Connie Vinita Dowell, dean, San Diego State University Library and Information Access Department; Theresa McMahan, director, Sullivan County (Tennessee) Library System.

American Association of School Librarians (AASL)

AASL/ABC-CLIO Leadership Grant (up to $1,750). For planning and implementing leadership programs at state, regional, or local levels to be given to school library associations that are affiliates of AASL. *Donor:* ABC-CLIO. *Winner:* Association for Indiana Media Educators.

AASL/Baker & Taylor Distinguished Service Award ($3,000). For outstanding contributions to librarianship and school library development. *Donor:* Baker & Taylor Books. *Winner:* Not awarded in 2007.

AASL Collaborative School Library Media Award ($2,500). For expanding the role of the library in elementary and/or secondary school education. *Donor:* Sagebrush Corporation. *Winner:* Renee Zorc, Daniel Wright Junior High School, Lincolnshire, Illinois.

AASL Crystal Apple Award. To an individual, individuals, or group for a significant impact on school libraries and students. *Winner:* Scholastic Library Publishing.

AASL Distinguished School Administrators Award ($2,000). For expanding the role of the library in elementary and/or secondary school education. *Donor:* ProQuest. *Winner:* Nathan S. Greenberg, Londonderry (New Hampshire) School District.

AASL/Frances Henne Award ($1,250). To a school library media specialist with five or fewer years in the profession to attend an AASL regional conference or ALA Annual Conference for the first time. *Donor:*

Greenwood Publishing Group. *Winner:* Jessica Klinker.

AASL/Highsmith Research Grant (up to $5,000). To conduct innovative research aimed at measuring and evaluating the impact of school library media programs on learning and education. *Donor:* Highsmith, Inc. *Winner:* Award discontinued in 2007.

AASL School Librarian's Workshop Scholarship ($3,000). To a full-time student preparing to become a school library media specialist at the preschool, elementary, or secondary level. *Donor:* Jay W. Toor, president, Library Learning Resources. *Winner:* Donna Mae Ohlgren.

Information Technology Pathfinder Award ($1,000 to the specialist and $500 to the library). To library media specialists for innovative approaches to microcomputer applications in the school library media center. *Donor:* Follett Software Company. *Winners:* (elementary) Holly Hartell, Pacolet (South Carolina) Elementary School; (secondary) Sheila C. Howard, North Atlanta (Georgia) High School.

Intellectual Freedom Award ($2,000). To a school library media specialist who has upheld the principles of intellectual freedom. *Donor:* ProQuest. *Winner:* Not awarded in 2007.

National School Library Media Program of the Year Award ($10,000 each in three categories). To school districts and single schools for excellence and innovation in outstanding library media programs. *Donor:* Follett Library Resources. *Winners:* (district) Norman (Oklahoma) Public Schools; (single schools) Harpeth Hall School, Nashville, Tennessee, and North Elementary School, Noblesville, Indiana.

Association for Library Collections and Technical Services (ALCTS)

ALCTS George Cunha and Susan Swartzburg Preservation Award ($1,250). To recognize cooperative preservation projects and/or individuals or groups that foster collaboration for preservation goals. *Donor:* LBI. *Winner:* To be awarded first in 2008.

ALCTS Presidential Citations for Outstanding Service. *Winners:* Jennifer Bowen, Beth Picknally Camden, Peggy Johnson, Glenn Patton, Julie Reese, Edward Swanson, Christine Taylor, Beacher Wiggins.

Hugh C. Atkinson Memorial Award. *See under* American Library Association.

Ross Atkinson Lifetime Achievement Award. To recognize the contribution of an ALCTS member and library leader who has demonstrated exceptional service to ALCTS and its areas of interest. *Donor:* EBSCO. *Winner:* Brian E. C. Schottlaender.

Paul Banks and Carolyn Harris Preservation Award ($1,500). To recognize the contribution of a professional preservation specialist who has been active in the field of preservation and/or conservation for library and/or archival materials. *Donor:* Preservation Technologies. *Winner:* Walter Henry.

Best of *LRTS* Award ($250). To the author(s) of the best paper published each year in the division's official journal. *Winners:* Jim Stemper and Susan Barribeau for "Perpetual Access to Electronic Journals: A Survey of One Academic Research Library's Licenses."

Blackwell's Scholarship Award ($2,000 scholarship to the U.S. or Canadian library school of the recipient's choice). To honor the author(s) of the year's outstanding monograph, article, or original paper in the field of acquisitions, collection development, and related areas of resource development in libraries. *Donor:* Blackwell's. *Winner (posthumously):* Ross Atkinson, Cornell University, for "Six Key Challenges for the Future of Collection Development"; *library school beneficiary:* Simmons College.

CSA/Ulrich's Serials Librarianship Award ($1,500). For leadership in serials-related activities. *Donor:* CSA. *Winner:* Julia Blixrud.

First Step Award (Wiley Professional Development Grant) ($1,500). For librarians new to the serials field to attend the ALA Annual Conference. *Donor:* John Wiley & Sons. *Winner:* Paula Webb.

Leadership in Library Acquisitions Award ($1,500). For significant contributions by an outstanding leader in the field of library acquisitions. *Donor:* Harrassowitz. *Winner:* Nancy Gibbs.

Margaret Mann Citation (and $2,000 to the U.S. or Canadian library school of the winning author's choice). To a cataloger or classifier for achievement in the areas of cataloging or classification. *Donor:* Online Computer Library Center. *Winner:* Robert Wolven.

Outstanding Collaboration Citation. For outstanding collaborative problem-solving efforts in the areas of acquisition, access, management, preservation, or archiving of library materials. *Winner:* CLOCKSS (Controlled Lots of Copies Keep Stuff Safe), Stanford University Libraries.

Esther J. Piercy Award ($1,500). To a librarian with no more than ten years' experience for contributions and leadership in the field of library collections and technical services. *Donor:* YBP Library Services. *Winner:* Robert L. Bothmann.

Sage Support Staff Travel Grants (up to $1,000). To enable support staff to attend an ALA Annual Conference. *Donor:* Sage Publications. *Winners:* Monica Claasen-Wilson, Julia Merkel, Audrey Pryce, Nancy Slate, LaShawn Wilson, Siu Min Yu.

Association for Library Service to Children (ALSC)

ALSC/Book Wholesalers, Inc. BWI Summer Reading Program Grant ($3,000). To an ALSC member for implementation of an outstanding public library summer reading program for children. *Donor:* Book Wholesalers, Inc. *Winner:* Santa Clara (California) City Library.

May Hill Arbuthnot Honor Lectureship. To an author, critic, librarian, historian, or teacher of children's literature who prepares a paper considered to be a significant contribution to the field of children's literature. *Winner:* David Macaulay.

Mildred L. Batchelder Award. *Winner:* See "Literary Prizes, 2007" in Part 5.

Louise Seaman Bechtel Fellowship ($4,000). For librarians with 12 or more years of professional-level work in children's library collections, to read and study at the Baldwin Library, University of Florida. *Donor:* Bechtel Fund. *Winner:* Charmette Kuhn-Kendrick.

Pura Belpré Award. *Winners:* See "Literary Prizes, 2007" in Part 5.

Bookapalooza Program Awards. To provide three libraries with a collection of materials that will help transform their collection. *Winners:* College Gate Elementary School Library, Anchorage, Alaska; Custer County School District Library, Westcliffe, Colorado; Creswell (Oregon) Library.

ALSC/Booklist/YALSA Odyssey Award. To the producer of the best audiobook for children and/or young adults available in English in the United States. *Sponsor: Booklist. Winner:* To be awarded first in 2008.

Bound to Stay Bound Books Scholarships (scholarships of $6,500 each). For men and women who intend to pursue an MLS or advanced degree and who plan to work in the area of library service to children. *Donor:* Bound to Stay Bound Books. *Winners:* Jessica Kerlin, Laura Knouff, Esther Mortensen, Jeanna Rex.

Randolph Caldecott Medal. *Winner:* See "Literary Prizes, 2007" in Part 5.

ALSC/Candlewick Press "Light the Way" Grant ($5,000). To a library conducting exemplary outreach to underserved populations, presented in honor of author Kate DiCamillo. *Donor:* Candlewick Press. *Winner:* To be awarded first in 2008.

Andrew Carnegie Medal. To the U.S. producer of the most distinguished video for children in the previous year. *Sponsor:* Carnegie Corporation of New York. *Winners:* Mo Willems and Weston Woods Studios for *Knuffle Bunny.*

Carnegie-Whitney Awards (up to $5,000). For the publication of bibliographic aids for research. *Donors:* James Lyman Whitney and Andrew Carnegie Funds. *Winners:* Carolyn Garnes, Nadean Meyer, Jie Tian and Mathew Mallard, Jocelyn Tipton, Young Adult Library Services Association.

Distinguished Service to ALSC Award ($1,000). To recognize significant contributions to, and an impact on, library services to children and/or ALSC. *Winner:* Caroline Ward.

Theodor Seuss Geisel Award. *Winner:* See "Literary Prizes, 2007" in Part 5.

Maureen Hayes Author/Illustrator Visit Award (up to $4,000). For an honorarium and travel expenses to enable a library talk to children by a nationally known author/illustrator. *Sponsor:* Simon & Schuster Children's Publishing. *Winners:* Betty Ranck, Lauren Miller.

Frederic G. Melcher Scholarship ($6,000). To two students entering the field of library service to children for graduate work in an ALA-accredited program. *Winners:* Rebecca Heckathorn, Cynthia Jablonka Simpson.

John Newbery Medal. *Winner:* See "Literary Prizes, 2007" in Part 5.

Penguin Young Readers Group Awards ($600). To children's librarians in school or public libraries with ten or fewer years of experience to attend the ALA Annual Conference. *Donor:* Penguin Young Readers Group. *Winners:* Rachel Martin Gould, Cheryl "Kay" Gooch, Sally L. Miculek, Suzanne Myers Harold.

Robert F. Sibert Medal. To the author of the most distinguished informational book for children published during the preceding year. *Donor:* Bound to Stay Bound Books. *Winner:* See "Literary Prizes, 2007" in Part 5.

Tandem Library Books Literature Program Award ($1,000 toward ALA Annual Conference attendance for the development of an outstanding reading or literature program for children. *Donor:* Tandem Library Books. *Winner:* Diane Williamson.

Laura Ingalls Wilder Medal. To an author or illustrator whose works have made a lasting contribution to children's literature. *Winner:* See "Literary Prizes, 2007" in Part 5.

Association for Library Trustees and Advocates (ALTA)

ALTA/Gale Outstanding Trustee Conference Grant Award ($750). *Donor:* Gale Research. *Winner:* Not awarded in 2007.

ALTA Literacy Award (citation). To a library trustee or an individual who, in a volunteer capacity, has made a significant contribution to addressing the illiteracy problem in the United States. *Winner:* Not awarded in 2007.

ALTA Major Benefactors Honor Award (citation). To individuals, families, or corporate bodies that have made major benefactions to public libraries. *Winner:* Not awarded in 2007.

Trustee Citations. To recognize public library trustees for individual service to library development on the local, state, regional, or national level. *Winners:* Jane Rowland, Patricia O. Norman.

Association of College and Research Libraries (ACRL)

ACRL Academic or Research Librarian of the Year Award ($5,000). For outstanding contribution to academic and research librarianship and library development. *Donor:* YBP Library Services. *Winner:* Lizabeth A. Wilson.

ACRL Distinguished Education and Behavioral Sciences Librarian Award ($1,000). To an academic librarian who has made an outstanding contribution as an education and/or behavioral sciences librarian through accomplishments and service to the profession. *Donor:* John Wiley & Sons. *Winner:* Patricia O'Brien Libutti.

ACRL Doctoral Dissertation Fellowship ($1,500). To a doctoral student in the field of academic librarianship whose research has potential significance in the field. *Donor:* Thomson Scientific. *Winner:* Jihyun Kim.

ACRL Special Presidential Recognition Award (plaque). To recognize an individual's special career contributions to ACRL and the library profession. *Winner:* Not awarded in 2007.

ACRL/WSS Award for Career Achievement in Women's Studies Librarianship. *Donors:* Greenwood Publishing Group and Routledge. *Winner:* Sandra A. River.

ACRL/WSS Award for Significant Achievement in Women's Studies Librarianship.

Winners: Jennifer Gilley, Kayo Denda, Jenna Freedman, Sharon Ladenson.

Hugh C. Atkinson Memorial Award. *See under* American Library Association.

Best Practices in Marketing @ your library Awards ($2,000). To recognize academic and research libraries that demonstrate outstanding best practices marketing programs. *Donor:* Springer. *Winners:* Not awarded in 2007.

Community College Learning Resources Leadership/Library Achievement Awards ($500). To recognize outstanding achievement in library programs or leadership. *Sponsor:* EBSCO Information Services. *Winners:* (leadership) David R. Dowell; (programs) Hagan Foundation Center for the Humanities, Spokane (Washington) Community College.

Coutts Nijhoff International West European Specialist Study Grant (up to 4,500 euros). Supports research pertaining to West European studies, librarianship, or the book trade. *Sponsor:* Coutts Nijhoff International. *Winner:* Thea Lindquist.

Miriam Dudley Instruction Librarian Award ($1,000). For the advancement of bibliographic instruction in a college or research institution. *Donor:* Elsevier Science. *Winner:* Debra L. Gilchrist.

Excellence in Academic Libraries Awards ($3,000). To recognize outstanding community college, college, and university libraries. *Donor:* Blackwell's Book Services. *Winners:* (community college) Hostos Community College/City University of New York Library; (college) Coates Library, Trinity University, San Antonio; (university) Georgia Institute of Technology Library and Information Center.

Haworth Press Distance Learning Librarian Conference Sponsorship Award ($1,200). To an ACRL member working in distance-learning librarianship in higher education. *Winner:* Anne Marie Casey.

Instruction Section Innovation Award ($3,000). To librarians or project teams in recognition of a project that demonstrates creative, innovative, or unique approaches to information literacy instruction or programming. *Donor:* LexisNexis. *Winner:*

Instructional Services Department, University of North Carolina at Chapel Hill.

Marta Lange/CQ Press Award ($1,000). To recognize an academic or law librarian for contributions to bibliography and information service in law or political science. *Donor:* CQ Press. *Winner:* Binh P. Le.

Samuel Lazerow Fellowship for Research in Acquisitions or Technical Services ($1,000). To foster advances in acquisitions or technical services by providing librarians a fellowship for travel or writing in those fields. *Sponsor:* Thomson Scientific. *Winner:* Not awarded in 2007.

Katharine Kyes Leab and Daniel J. Leab Exhibition Catalog Awards (citations). For the best catalogs published by American or Canadian institutions in conjunction with exhibitions of books and/or manuscripts. *Winners:* (division I–expensive) *No Other Appetite: Sylvia Plath, Ted Hughes, and the Blood Jet of Poetry,* Groller Club, and *Half-Life: 25 Years of Books by Barbara Tetenbaum and Triangular Press,* Multnomah County (Oregon) Library; (division II–moderately expensive) *Letters to Sala: A Young Woman's Life in Nazi Labor Camps,* New York Public Library; division III–inexpensive) *Maxwell Did It! Photographing the Atlantic City Boardwalk, 1920s–1950s,* Duke University, and *Ezra Pound in His Time and Beyond: The Influence of Pound on Twentieth-Century Poetry,* University of Delaware–Newark; (division IV–brochures) *A Tumultuous Assembly: Visual Poems of the Italian Futurists,* Getty Research Institute, Los Angeles; (division V–electronic exhibition) *Vanished Worlds, Enduring People: Cornell University's Native American Collection,* Cornell University.

Oberly Award for Bibliography in the Agricultural or Natural Sciences. Biennially, for the best English-language bibliography in the field of agriculture or a related science in the preceding two-year period. *Donor:* Eunice Rockwood Oberly Memorial Fund. *Winners:* University of Minnesota Libraries, University of Minnesota Department of Applied Economics, and American Agricultural Economics Association for *AgEcon Search.*

Ilene F. Rockman Instruction Publication of the Year Award ($3,000). To recognize an outstanding publication relating to instruction in a library environment in the past two years. *Sponsor:* Emerald Group. *Winners:* James K. Elmborg and Sheril Hook for "Centers for Learning: Writing Centers and Libraries in Collaboration" in *ACRL Publications in Librarianship* no. 58.

Association of Specialized and Cooperative Library Agencies (ASCLA)

ASCLA Cathleen Bourdon Service Award. To recognize an ASCLA personal member for outstanding service and leadership to the division. *Winner:* Not awarded in 2007.

ASCLA Century Scholarship (up to $2,500). For a library school student or students with disabilities admitted to an ALA-accredited library school. *Winner:* Cynthia Nugent.

ASCLA Exceptional Service Award. To recognize exceptional service to patients, the homebound, inmates, and to medical, nursing, and other professional staff in hospitals. *Winner:* Diana Reese, Colorado State Library.

ASCLA Leadership Achievement Award. To recognize leadership and achievement in the areas of consulting, multitype library cooperation, and state library development. *Winners:* Lee A. Logan and Kitty Pope, Alliance Library System, East Peoria, Illinois.

ASCLA Professional Achievement Award. To recognize professional achievement within the areas of consulting, networking, statewide service, and programs. *Winner:* Thomas J. Sanville, OhioLINK.

Francis Joseph Campbell Award. For a contribution of recognized importance to library service for the blind and physically handicapped. *Winner:* Sue O. Murdock.

KLAS/National Organization on Disability Award for Library Service to People with Disabilities ($1,000). To a library organization to recognize an innovative project to benefit people with disabilities. *Donor:* Keystone Systems. *Winner:* Braille Institute of Library Services.

Black Caucus of the American Library Association (BCALA)

BCALA Excellence in Librarianship Award. *Winner:* Sibyl E. Moses.

BCALA Trailblazer's Award. Presented once every five years in recognition of outstanding and unique contributions to librarianship. *Winner:* To be awarded next in 2010.

Ethnic and Multicultural Information and Exchange Round Table (EMIERT)

David Cohen/EMIERT Multicultural Award ($300). To recognize articles of significant research and publication that increase understanding and promote multiculturalism in North American libraries. *Donor:* Routledge. *Winner:* Not awarded in 2007.

Gale/EMIERT Multicultural Award ($1,000). For outstanding achievement and leadership in serving the multicultural/multiethnic community. *Donor:* Gale Research. *Winner:* Not awarded in 2007.

Exhibits Round Table (ERT)

Christopher J. Hoy/ERT Scholarship ($5,000). To an individual or individuals who will work toward an MLS degree in an ALA-accredited program. *Donor:* Family of Christopher Hoy. *Winner:* Schmitz Couillard.

Federal and Armed Forces Librarians Round Table (FAFLRT)

FAFLRT Achievement Award. For achievement in the promotion of library and information service and the information profession in the federal government community. *Winner:* Not awarded in 2007.

Adelaide del Frate Conference Sponsor Award ($1,000). To encourage library school students to become familiar with federal librarianship and ultimately seek work in federal libraries; for attendance at ALA Annual Conference and activities of the Federal and Armed Forces Librarians Round Table. *Winner:* Alba Scott.

Distinguished Service Award (citation). To honor a FAFLRT member for outstanding and sustained contributions to the association and to federal librarianship. *Winner:* Maria G. Pisa, National Agricultural Library.

Cicely Phippen Marks Scholarship ($1,500). To a library school student with an interest in working in a federal library. *Winner:* Allison L. Snell.

Gay, Lesbian, Bisexual, and Transgendered Round Table (GLBT)

Stonewall Book Awards. *Winners:* See "Literary Prizes, 2007" in Part 5.

Government Documents Round Table (GODORT)

James Bennett Childs Award. To a librarian or other individual for distinguished lifetime contributions to documents librarianship. *Winner:* August A. Imholtz, Jr.

Bernadine Abbott Hoduski Founders Award (plaque). To recognize documents librarians who may not be known at the national level but who have made significant contributions to the field of local, state, federal, or international documents. *Winner:* Thomas A. Stave.

LexisNexis Documents to the People Award ($3,000). To an individual, library, organization, or noncommercial group that most effectively encourages or enhances the use of government documents in library services. *Winner:* Cathy N. Hartman.

Newsbank/Readex Catharine J. Reynolds Award ($2,000). Grants to documents librarians for travel and/or study in the field of documents librarianship or area of study benefiting performance as documents librarians. *Donor:* Newsbank and Readex Corporation. *Winner:* Chi-Shiou Lin.

W. David Rozkuszka Scholarship ($3,000). To provide financial assistance to an individual who is currently working with government documents in a library while completing a master's program in library science. *Winner:* Michael Schmidt.

Intellectual Freedom Round Table (IFRT)

John Phillip Immroth Memorial Award for Intellectual Freedom ($500). For notable contribution to intellectual freedom fueled by personal courage. *Winner:* Not awarded in 2007.

Eli M. Oboler Memorial Award ($500). Biennially, to an author of a published work in English or in English translation dealing with issues, events, questions, or controversies in the area of intellectual freedom. *Winner:* Not awarded in 2007.

ProQuest/SIRS State and Regional Achievement Award ($1,000). To an innovative and effective intellectual freedom project covering a state or region during the calendar year. *Donor:* ProQuest Social Issues Resource Series (SIRS). *Winners:* "The Connecticut John Does"—librarians George Christian, Peter Chase, Barbara Bailey, and Janet Nocek—who challenged the constitutionality of National Security Letters issued under the USAPatriot Act.

Library Administration and Management Association (LAMA)

AIA/ALA Library Buildings Award. To recognize excellence in the architectural design and planning of libraries. *Sponsors:* LAMA and the American Institute of Architects. *Winners:* Gluckman Mayner Architects, Richärd + Bauer Architecture, P&T Architects and Engineers Ltd., Bohlin Cywinski Jackson, CO Architects, Ann Beha Architects, Polshek Partnership Architects LLP, Office dA, Patkau Architects.

Hugh C. Atkinson Memorial Award. *See under* American Library Association.

Diana V. Braddom Fundraising and Financial Development Section Scholarship ($1,000). To enable attendance at the ALA Annual Conference. *Donor:* Diana V. Braddom. *Winners:* JaEun Ku.

John Cotton Dana Library Public Relations Awards ($3,000). To libraries or library organizations of all types for public relations programs or special projects ended during the preceding year. *Donors:* H. W. Wilson Company and H. W. Wilson Foundation. *Winners:* Brooklyn (New York) Public Library, Douglas County (Colorado) Libraries, Huntsville-Madison County (Alabama) Public Library, Illinois State University–Normal, Ocean County

(New Jersey) Library, Office of Commonwealth (Pennsylvania) Libraries, Wyoming State Library.

LAMA/IDA Library Interior Design Awards. To recognize excellence in library interior design. *Sponsors:* LAMA Business and Equipment Section and the Interior Design Association. *Winners:* Not awarded in 2007.

LAMA Cultural Diversity Grant ($1,000). To support creation and dissemination of resources that will assist library administrators and managers in developing a vision and commitment to diversity. *Winner:* Not awarded in 2007.

LAMA Group Achievement Award. To honor LAMA committees or task forces, recognizing outstanding teamwork supporting the goals of LAMA. *Winners:* LAMA/International Interior Design Association Award Committee.

LAMA Leadership Award. *Winner:* Julie B. Todaro.

LAMA President's Award. *Winner:* American Institute of Architects.

LAMA/YBP Student Writing and Development Award ($1,000 grant to attend the ALA Annual Conference). *Donor:* YBP Library Services. *Winner:* Miriam Matteson for "Integrating Theory and Practice: The Role of the Professional Library Association."

Library and Information Technology Association (LITA)

Hugh C. Atkinson Memorial Award. *See under* American Library Association.

Ex Libris Student Writing Award ($1,000 and publication in *Information Technology and Libraries*). For the best unpublished manuscript on a topic in the area of libraries and information technology written by a student or students enrolled in an ALA-accredited library and information studies graduate program. *Donor:* Ex Libris. *Winner:* Timothy Dickey.

LITA/Brett Butler Entrepreneurship Award ($5,000). To recognize a librarian or library for demonstrating exemplary entrepreneurship by providing innovative products or services through the application of information technology. *Donor:* Thomson

Gale Group. *Winners:* Annette Bailey and Godmar Back, Virginia Tech University.

LITA/Christian Larew Memorial Scholarship ($3,000). To encourage the entry of qualified persons into the library and information technology field. *Sponsor:* Informata.com. *Winner:* Karin Dalziel.

LITA/Library Hi Tech Award ($1,000). To an individual or institution for a work that shows outstanding communication for continuing education in library and information technology. *Donor:* Emerald Press. *Winner:* Priscilla Caplan, Florida Center for Library Automation.

LITA/LSSI Minority Scholarship in Library and Information Science ($2,500). To encourage a qualified member of a principal minority group to work toward an MLS degree in an ALA-accredited program with emphasis on library automation. *Donor:* Library Systems and Services. *Winner:* Lydia C. Welhan.

LITA/OCLC Frederick G. Kilgour Award for Research in Library and Information Technology ($2,000 and expense-paid attendance at the ALA Annual Conference). To bring attention to research relevant to the development of information technologies. *Donor:* OCLC. *Winner:* Richard Pearce-Moses.

LITA/OCLC Minority Scholarship in Library and Information Technology ($3,000). To encourage a qualified member of a principal minority group to work toward an MLS degree in an ALA-accredited program with emphasis on library automation. *Donor:* OCLC. *Winner:* Heather Devine.

Library History Round Table (LHRT)

Phyllis Dain Library History Dissertation Award ($500). To the author of a dissertation treating the history of books, libraries, librarianship, or information science. *Winner:* Not awarded in 2007.

Donald G. Davis Article Award (certificate). For the best article written in English in the field of U.S. and Canadian library history. *Winner:* Not awarded in 2007.

Eliza Atkins Gleason Book Award. Presented every third year to the author of the best book in English in the field of library history. *Winner:* Carl Ostrowski for *Books,*

Maps, and Politics: A Cultural History of the Library of Congress, 1783–1861 (University of Massachusetts).

Justin Winsor Prize Essay ($500). To an author of an outstanding essay embodying original historical research on a significant subject of library history. *Winner:* Jean L. Preer for "Promoting Citizenship: Librarians Help Get Out the Vote in the 1952 Presidential Election."

Library Research Round Table (LRRT)

Ingenta Research Award (up to $6,000). To sponsor research projects about acquisition, use, and preservation of digital information; the award includes $1,000 to support travel to a conference to present the results of that research. *Sponsor:* Ingenta. *Winners:* Aaron Shrimplin, John Fink, Susan Hurst, and Kevin Messner, Miami University of Ohio Libraries.

Jesse H. Shera Award for Distinguished Published Research ($500). For a research article on library and information studies published in English during the calendar year. *Winners:* Gary Marchionini, Paul Solomon, Cheryl Davis, and Terrell Russell, University of North Carolina at Chapel Hill.

Jesse H. Shera Award for Support of Dissertation Research ($500). To recognize and support dissertation research employing exemplary research design and methods. *Winner:* Melissa Just, University of Southern California, Los Angeles.

Map and Geography Round Table (MAGERT)

MAGERT Honors Award. To recognize lifetime achievement and contributions to map and geography librarianship. *Winner:* Not awarded in 2007.

New Members Round Table (NMRT)

Shirley Olofson Memorial Award ($1,000). To an individual to help defray costs of attending the ALA Annual Conference. *Winner:* Marissa Ball.

Student Chapter of the Year Award. To an ALA student chapter for outstanding contributions to ALA. *Winner:* Library and Information Science Chapter, University of Arizona.

3M Professional Development Grant. To new NMRT members to encourage professional development and participation in national ALA and NMRT activities. *Donor:* 3M. *Winners:* Stacy Brown, John Meier, Danielle Pollock.

Office for Diversity

Achievement in Diversity Research Honor. To an ALA member who has made significant contributions to diversity research in the profession. *Winner:* Not awarded in 2007.

Diversity Research Grants ($2,500). To the authors of research proposals that address critical gaps in the knowledge of diversity issues within library and information science. *Winners:* Karen E. Downing, Allison M. Sutton, and Mark Winston and Allison Rainey.

Office for Information Technology Policy

L. Ray Patterson Copyright Award. To recognize an individual who supports the constitutional purpose of U.S. copyright law, fair use, and the public domain. *Sponsor:* Freedom to Read Foundation. *Winner:* Peter Jaszi.

Office for Intellectual Freedom

Freedom to Read Foundation Roll of Honor (citation): To recognize individuals who have contributed substantially to the foundation. *Winner:* Lucille C. Thomas.

Office for Literacy and Outreach Services

Jean E. Coleman Library Outreach Lecture. *Sponsor:* 15th of March, Inc. *Winners:* Anne E. Moore, Roland Hansen.

Diversity Fair Awards (total of $700). To outreach librarians for their institutions' diversity-in-action initiatives. *Winners:* (first place) Lori J. Wilcox; (second place) John Bradford; (third place) Linda Sperry.

Estela and Raúl Mora Award ($1,000 and plaque). For the most exemplary program celebrating Día de Los Niños/Día de Los Libros. *Winner:* Broward County (Florida) Library.

Public Information Office

Scholastic Library/Grolier National Library Week Grant ($5,000). To libraries or library associations of all types for a public awareness campaign in connection with National Library Week in the year the grant is awarded. *Sponsor:* Scholastic Library Publishing. *Winner:* Minoa (New York) Elementary School Library.

Public Library Association (PLA)

Advancement of Literacy Award (plaque). To a publisher, bookseller, hardware and/or software dealer, foundation, or similar group that has made a significant contribution to the advancement of adult literacy. *Donor: Library Journal. Winner:* Jacksonville (Florida) Public Library Foundation.

Baker & Taylor Entertainment Audio Music/Video Product Grant ($2,500 worth of audio music or video products). To help a public library to build or expand a collection of either or both formats. *Donor:* Baker & Taylor. *Winner:* L. D. Fargo Library, Lake Mills, Wisconsin.

Gordon M. Conable Award ($1,500). To a public library staff member, library trustee, or public library for demonstrating a commitment to intellectual freedom and the Library Bill of Rights. *Sponsor:* LSSI. *Winner:* Ken Verdoia.

Demco New Leaders Travel Grants (up to $1,500). To PLA members who have not attended a major PLA continuing-education event in the past five years. *Winners:* Lisë Chlebanowski, Janet Eldred, Susan Fisher, Terri Romberger.

EBSCO Excellence in Small and/or Rural Public Service Award ($1,000). Honors a library serving a population of 10,000 or less that demonstrates excellence of service to its community as exemplified by an overall service program or a special program of significant accomplishment. *Donor:*

EBSCO Information Services. *Winner:* Kenai (Alaska) Community Library.

Highsmith Library Innovation Award ($2,000). To recognize a public library's innovative achievement in planning and implementing a creative community service program. *Donor:* Highsmith. *Winner:* Athens-Clarke County (Georgia) Library.

Allie Beth Martin Award ($3,000). To honor a public librarian who has demonstrated extraordinary range and depth of knowledge about books or other library materials and has distinguished ability to share that knowledge. *Donor:* Baker & Taylor. *Winner:* Barry Trott.

PLA Grow Your Own @ your library Institutional Scholarship ($8,000). To public libraries for reimbursement of tuition costs of employees working toward an LIS degree at the undergraduate or graduate level. *Winners:* Dallas (Texas) Public Library; Palm Beach County (Florida) Library System; Chesterfield County (Virginia) Public Library; Hall County (Georgia) Library System; Davies County (Kentucky) Public Library; Northwest Regional Library, Belle Fourche, South Dakota; Dunham (New York) Public Library; Decorah (Iowa) Public Library; Upper Skagit (Washington) Library District.

Public Libraries Magazine Feature Writing Awards ($500 and $300). To public library employees for feature-length articles published during the preceding year. *Winners:* (first prize) Meagan Albright for "The Public Library's Responsibility to LGBT Communities—Recognizing, Representing, and Serving"; (second prize) Mary Cosper LeBoeuf for "Ill Winds: Hurricanes and Public Libraries Along the Gulf Coast."

Charlie Robinson Award ($1,000). Honors a public library director who, over a period of seven years, has been a risk taker, an innovator, and/or a change agent in a public library. *Donor:* Baker & Taylor. *Winner:* Sandra Feinberg.

Public Programs Office

Sara Jaffarian School Library Program Award ($4,000). To honor a K–8 school library that has conducted an exemplary program or program series in the humanities. *Donors:* Sara Jaffarian and ALA Cultural Communities Fund. *Winner:* Central Elementary School Library, Wilmette, Illinois.

Reference and User Services Association (RUSA)

ABC-CLIO Online History Award ($3,000). To recognize professional achievement in historical reference and librarianship. *Donor:* ABC-CLIO. *Winner:* Faith Jones, New York Public Library, for the Yizkor Books Project.

Atlas Mentoring Award (STARS) ($1,000). To a library practitioner new to the field of interlibrary loan, resource sharing, or electronic reserves, to attend an ALA Annual Conference. *Donor:* Atlas Systems. *Winner:* Danielle Cournoyer.

Virginia Boucher-OCLC Distinguished ILL Librarian Award ($2,000). To a librarian for outstanding professional achievement, leadership, and contributions to interlibrary loan and document delivery. *Winner:* Anne K. Beaubien.

Sophie Brody Medal. *Winner:* See "Literary Prizes, 2007" in Part 5.

Dartmouth Medal. For creating current reference works of outstanding quality and significance. *Donor:* Dartmouth College. *Winners:* Thomson Gale for *Encyclopaedia Judaica* (2006) and Cambridge University Press for *Historical Statistics of the United States—Earlier Times to the Present: Millennial Edition* (2006).

Dun & Bradstreet Award for Outstanding Service to Minority Business Communities ($2,000). *Donor:* Dun & Bradstreet. *Winner:* Liz Kudwa.

Dun & Bradstreet Public Librarian Support Award ($1,000). To support the attendance at the ALA Annual Conference of a public librarian who has performed outstanding business reference service. *Donor:* Dun & Bradstreet. *Winner:* Rachelle Miller.

Emerald Research Grant Award ($5,000). To an ALA member seeking support to conduct research in business librarianship. *Donor:* Emerald Group Publishing. *Winners:* Lisa G. O'Connor, Diane M. Owens, and Y. Diana Wu.

Genealogical Publishing Company/History Section Award ($1,500). To encourage and commend professional achievement in historical reference and research librarianship. *Donor:* Genealogical Publishing Company. *Winner:* Louis A. Vyhnanek.

MARS Recognition Certificate. For excellence in service to the Machine-Assisted Reference Section. *Winner:* LeiLani Freund.

Margaret E. Monroe Library Adult Services Award (citation). To a librarian for impact on library service to adults. *Winner:* Barry Trott.

Isadore Gilbert Mudge–R. R. Bowker Award ($5,000). For distinguished contributions to reference librarianship. *Donor:* R. R. Bowker. *Winner:* Barbara Bibel.

Reference Service Press Award ($2,500). To the author or authors of the most outstanding article published in *RUSQ* during the preceding two volume years. *Donor:* Reference Service Press. *Winners:* C. Brandi Borman and Pamela Jane McKenzie for "Trying to Help Without Getting in Their Faces: Public Library Staff Descriptions of Providing Consumer Health Information."

John Sessions Memorial Award (plaque). To a library or library system in recognition of work with the labor community. *Donor:* Department of Professional Employees, AFL/CIO. *Winner:* James B. Carey Library, Rutgers University.

Louis Shores–Greenwood Publishing Group Award ($3,000). To an individual, team, or organization to recognize excellence in reviewing of books and other materials for libraries. *Donor:* Greenwood Publishing Group. *Winner:* Katina Pathemos Strauch.

Thomson Financial Student Travel Award (BRASS) ($1,000). For a student or students enrolled in an ALA-accredited master's degree program to attend the ALA Annual Conference. *Donor:* Thomson Financial. *Winners:* Anthony B. Lin, Sylvia James.

Thomson Gale Award for Excellence in Business Librarianship ($3,000). To an individual for distinguished activities in the field of business librarianship. *Donor:* Thomson Gale. *Winner:* Sylvia James.

Thomson Gale Award for Excellence in Reference and Adult Services ($3,000). To a library or library system for developing an imaginative and unique library resource to meet patrons' reference needs. *Donor:* Thomson Gale. *Winner:* Springfield-Greene County (Missouri) Library.

Social Responsibilities Round Table (SRRT)

Coretta Scott King Awards. *Winners:* See "Literary Prizes, 2007" in Part 5.

Jackie Eubanks Memorial Award ($500). To honor outstanding achievement in promoting the acquisition and use of alternative media in libraries. *Donor:* SRRT Alternatives in Publication Task Force. *Winner:* Not awarded in 2007.

Young Adult Library Services Association (YALSA)

Alex Awards. *Winners:* See "Literary Prizes, 2007" in Part 5.

Baker & Taylor/YALSA Scholarship Grants ($1,000). To young adult librarians in public or school libraries to attend an ALA Annual Conference for the first time. *Donor:* Baker & Taylor. *Winners:* Christine Beaver, Dana Hutchins.

BWI/YALSA Collection Development Grant ($1,000). To YALSA members who represent a public library and work directly with young adults, for collection development materials for young adults. *Donor:* Book Wholesalers, Inc. *Winners:* Carrie Wuensch-Harden, Karen Odom.

Margaret A. Edwards Award ($2,000). *Winner:* See "Literary Prizes, 2007" in Part 5.

Great Book Giveaway (books, videos, CDs, and audiocassettes valued at a total of $25,000). *Winner:* New Orleans Public Library.

Frances Henne/VOYA Research Grant ($500 minimum). To provide seed money to an individual, institution, or group for a project to encourage research on library service to young adults. *Donor:* Scarecrow Press. *Winners:* Holly Anderton and Karen Brooks-Reese.

Michael L. Printz Award. *Winner:* See "Literary Prizes, 2007" in Part 5.

YALSA/Greenwood Publishing Group Service to Young Adults Achievement Award ($2,000). Awarded biennially to a YALSA member who has demonstrated unique and sustained devotion to young adult services. *Donor:* Greenwood. *Winner:* To be awarded first in 2008.

YALSA William C. Morris YA Debut Award. To a first-time author writing for young adults in the fiction, nonfiction, poetry, short story, or graphic work categories. *Donor:* William C. Morris Endowment. *Winner:* To be awarded first in 2008.

YALSA/Sagebrush Award ($1,000). For an exemplary young adult reading or literature program. *Donor:* Sagebrush Corporation. *Winner:* Joanna Peled.

American Society for Information Science and Technology (ASIS&T)

ASIS&T Award of Merit. For an outstanding contribution to the field of information science. *Winner:* Donald H. Craft.

ASIS&T Best Information Science Book. *Winner:* Not awarded in 2007.

ASIS&T Proquest Doctoral Dissertation Award ($1,000 plus expense-paid attendance at ASIS&T Annual Meeting). *Winner:* W. John MacMullen for "Contextual Analysis of Variation and Quality in Human-Curated Gene Ontology Annotations."

ASIS&T Research in Information Science Award. For a systematic program of research in a single area at a level beyond the single study, recognizing contributions in the field of information science. *Winner:* Ophir Freider.

ASIS&T Special Award. To recognize long-term contributions to the advancement of information science and technology and enhancement of public access to information and discovery of mechanisms for improved transfer and utilization of knowledge. *Winner:* Not awarded in 2007.

James M. Cretsos Leadership Award. *Winner:* Not awarded in 2007.

Watson Davis Award. For outstanding continuous contributions and dedicated service to the society. *Winner:* Paula Galbraith.

Thomson ISI Citation Analysis Research Grant. *Winner:* Philip M. Davis for his proposal "Does Free Access to Scholarly Articles Increase Readership and Citation Impact?"

Thomson ISI Doctoral Dissertation Proposal Scholarship. *Winner:* Philip Edwards for "Mapping Scholars' Decision Processes and Factors that Influence How They Publish and Distribute Their Work."

Thomson ISI Outstanding Information Science Teacher Award ($500). *Winner:* Peter Ingwersen.

John Wiley Best *JASIST* Paper Award. *Winner:* Catherine Blake and Wanda Pratt for "Collaborative Information Synthesis," Parts 1 and 2.

Art Libraries Society of North America (ARLIS/NA)

ARLIS/NA Conference Travel Award. *Winners:* Laura Schwartz, Elizabeth Berenz.

ARLIS/NA Internship Award. To provide financial support for students preparing for a career in art librarianship or visual resource librarianship. *Winner:* Martha González Palacios.

AskART Conference Attendance Award ($1,000). *Winner:* Christine Hennessey.

Andrew Cahan Photography Award ($1,000). To encourage conference participation of art information professionals in the field of photography. *Winner:* Karen Rinaldo.

Distinguished Service Award. To honor an individual whose exemplary service in art librarianship, visual resources curatorship, or a related field has made an outstanding national or international contribution to art information and/or art librarianship. *Winner:* Not awarded in 2007.

Melva J. Dwyer Award. To the creators of exceptional reference or research tools relating to Canadian art and architecture. *Winners:* Charles C. Hill, Johanne Lamoureux, Ian M. Thom, curators, National Gallery of Canada, for *Emily Carr: New Perspectives on a Canadian Icon* (Douglas & McIntyre).

Judith A. Hoffberg Student Award for Conference Attendance ($750). *Winner:* Sarah Carter.

Howard and Beverly Joy Karno Award ($1,000). To provide financial assistance to a professional art librarian in Latin America through interaction with ARLIS/NA members and conference participation. *Winners:* Christine Sala, Paula Gabbard.

Gerd Muehsam Award. To one or more graduate students in library science programs to recognize excellence in a graduate paper or project. *Winner:* Tang Li for "Developing a Shape-and-Composition CBIR Thesaurus for the Traditional Chinese Landscape."

Puvill Libros Award ($1,000). To encourage professional development of European art librarians through interaction with ARLIS/NA colleagues and conference participation. *Winners:* Anna Maria Poma-Swank, Michel Nijhoff.

Smithsonian American Art Museum Student Diversity Award for Conference Attendance ($750). *Winner:* Tang Li.

George Wittenborn Memorial Book Awards. See "Literary Prizes, 2007" in Part 5.

Worldwide Books Award for Electronic Resources. *Winners:* Jeanne Brown for Las Vegas Architects and Buildings Database, Susan Craig for Biographical Dictionary of Kansas Artists (Active Before 1945).

Worldwide Books Award for Publications. *Winner:* Martin Aurand for *The Spectator and the Topographical City* (University of Pittsburgh).

Association for Library and Information Science Education (ALISE)

ALISE Award for Teaching Excellence in the Field of Library and Information Science Education. *Winners:* Dania Bilal, Betsy Hearne.

ALISE/Eugene Garfield Doctoral Dissertation Award ($500). *Winner:* Kate Williams

for "Social Networks, Social Capital, and the Use of Information and Communications Technology in Socially Excluded Communities: A Study of Community Groups in Manchester, England."

ALISE/Linworth Youth Services Paper Award. *Winner:* Not awarded in 2007.

ALISE Pratt-Severn Faculty Innovation Award ($1,000). *Winner:* Not awarded in 2007.

ALISE Professional Contribution to Library and Information Science Education Award. *Winner:* Brooke E. Sheldon.

ALISE Research Grant Awards (one or more grants totaling $5,000): *Winners:* Eileen Abels, Denise Agosto, and Lorri Mon for "Remote Reference in Practice and the Classroom."

ALISE Service Award. *Winner:* Toni Carbo.

ALISE/Bohdan S. Wynar Research Paper Competition. For a research paper concerning any aspect of librarianship or information studies by a member of ALISE. *Winners:* Charles Hildreth and Selena Aytac for "Recent Library Practitioner Research: A Methodological Analysis and Critique."

ALISE/University of Washington Information School Youth Services Graduate Student Travel Award ($750). To support the costs associated with travel to and participation in the ALISE Annual Conference. *Winner:* To be awarded for the first time in 2009.

Dialog/ALISE Methodology Paper Competition ($500). *Winner:* Lokman Meho for "E-mail Interviewing in Qualitative Research: A Methodological Discussion."

Doctoral Students to ALISE Grant. To enable one or more promising LIS doctoral students to attend the ALISE Annual Conference. *Winners:* Maria Soudan, Rachel Fleming-May.

OCLC/ALISE Library and Information Science Research Grant (LISRG) Program. *Winners:* M. Asim Qayyum, Carlos Suarez, Balseiro Rio Piedras, and Tania Garcia-Ramos for "Investigating the User Needs and Preferences for a Specialized Environmental Library"; Melissa Gross and Don Latham for "Self-Views of Information Seeking Skills: Undergraduates' Understanding of What It Means to Be Information Literate."

Beta Phi Mu

Beta Phi Mu Award. *See under* American Library Association.

Eugene Garfield Doctoral Dissertation Fellowship. *Winner:* Donghua Tao.

Harold Lancour Scholarship for Foreign Study. For graduate study in a foreign country related to the applicant's work or schooling. *Winner:* Theodore Patrick Milas.

Sarah Rebecca Reed Scholarship. For study at an ALA-accredited library school. *Winner:* Erin Macauley.

Frank B. Sessa Scholarship for Continuing Professional Education. For continuing education for a Beta Phi Mu member. *Winner:* Not awarded in 2007.

Blanche E. Woolls Scholarship ($1,000). For a beginning student in school library media services. *Winner:* Lisa Ree Anfield.

Bibliographical Society of America (BSA)

BSA Fellowships. For scholars involved in bibliographical inquiry and research in the history of the book trades and in publishing history. *Winners:* Carlos Aguirre, Cécile Alduy, Renzo Baldasso, Frank Brannon, Christopher Cook, Kevin Curran, Michael Eisenberg, Jake Gibbs, Heidi Kaufman, John Meier, Katherine Scheil, Justin Tonra, Fei-Hsien Wang.

BSA New Scholars Program. *Selectees:* Christopher Hunter, Eli MacLaren, Thierry Rigogne.

William L. Mitchell Prize for Research on Early British Serials ($1,000). Awarded triennially for the best single work published in the previous three years. *Winner:* To be awarded next in 2009.

Justin G. Schiller Prize for Bibliographical Work on Pre-20th-Century Children's Books ($2,000). To encourage scholarship in the bibliography of historical children's books. *Winner:* Lawrence Darton for *The Dartons: An Annotated Check-List of Children's Books Issued by Two Publishing Houses 1787–1876* (Oak Knoll).

Canadian Library Association (CLA)

Olga B. Bishop Award ($200). To a library school student for the best paper on government information or publications. *Winner:* Not awarded in 2007.

CLA Award for the Advancement of Intellectual Freedom in Canada. *Winner:* Canadian Journalists for Free Expression.

CLA Elizabeth Dafoe Scholarship ($5,000). *Winner:* Debra Franke.

CLA/Ken Haycock Award for Promoting Librarianship ($1,000). To honor an individual for contributing significantly to the public recognition and appreciation of librarianship. *Winner:* Christiane Charette.

CLA/Information Today Award for Innovative Technology. *Donor:* Information Today, Inc. *Winner:* University of Lethbridge (Alberta) Library.

CLA Outstanding Service to Librarianship Award. *Donor:* R. R. Bowker. *Winner:* Larry Moore.

CLA Research and Development Grant ($1,000). *Winner:* Matthew Griffis for "Living History: The Survival of Carnegie Libraries in Ontario."

CLA Student Article Award. *Winner:* Melissa Poremba for "Resources You Can Count On @ your library."

CLA/3M Award for Achievement in Technical Services ($1,000). *Winner:* Kingston Frontenac Public Library for "RFP Application Mashup."

CLA/YBP Award for Outstanding Contribution to Collection Development and Management ($1,000). To recognize a CLA/ACB member who has made an outstanding local, national, or international contribution in the field of library collection development or management. *Sponsor:* YBP Library Services. *Winner:* To be awarded for the first time in 2008.

W. Kaye Lamb Award for Service to Seniors. *Winner:* Not awarded in 2007.

H. W. Wilson Scholarship ($2,000). *Winner:* Michele Collins.

World Book Graduate Scholarship in Library Science ($2,500). *Winner:* Nancy Black.

Canadian Association for School Libraries (CASL)

CASL National Book Service Teacher-Librarian of the Year Award. *Winner:* Mary Locke.

CASL Margaret B. Scott Award of Merit. For the development of school libraries in Canada. *Winners:* Susan Perkins, Joanie Proske, Kim Anderson, Jade Graber, Laurie Lewis.

CASL Angela Thacker Memorial Award. For outstanding contribution to teacher-librarianship. *Winner:* Marlene Asselin.

Chancellor Group Conference Grant. *Winner:* Not awarded in 2007.

Canadian Association of College and University Libraries (CACUL)

CACUL/Miles Blackwell Award for Outstanding Academic Librarian. *Sponsor:* Blackwell's. *Winner:* William B. Maes.

CACUL Innovation Achievement Award ($1,500). *Sponsor:* SirsiDynix. *Winner:* Library Service of the University of Quebec, Montreal, for Thésaurus RASUQAM.

CTCL Award for Outstanding College Librarian. *Winner:* Marie DeYoung.

CTCL Innovation Achievement Award. *Sponsor:* ProQuest. *Winner:* Augustana Campus Library, University of Alberta, for its information literacy program.

Canadian Association of Public Libraries (CAPL)

CAPL/Brodart Outstanding Public Library Service Award. *Winner:* Josephine Bryant.

Canadian Association of Special Libraries and Information Services (CASLIS)

CASLIS Award for Special Librarianship in Canada. *Winner:* Christine Corston.

Canadian Library Trustees Association (CLTA)

CLTA/Stan Heath Achievement in Literacy Award. For an innovative literacy program by a public library board. *Donor:* ABC Canada. *Winner:* Not awarded in 2007.

CLTA Merit Award for Distinguished Service as a Public Library Trustee. *Winner:* Sally Gibson.

Chinese-American Librarians Association (CALA)

CALA Distinguished Service Award. To a librarian who has been a mentor, role model, and leader in the fields of library and information science. *Winner:* Sha Li Zhang.

CALA President's Recognition Award. *Winners:* Xudong Jin and Guoqing Li, co-chairs of the CALA International Relations Committee.

CALA Scholarship of Library and Information Science ($1,000). *Winner:* Lian Lauren Sin.

CALA Special Award. *Winner:* Sally T. Tseng.

Sheila Suen Lai Scholarship ($500). *Winner:* Yi Ren.

C. C. Seetoo/CALA Conference Travel Scholarship ($500). For a student to attend the ALA Annual Conference and CALA program. *Winner:* Katherine Yanqing Sun.

Sally T. Tseng Professional Development Grant ($1,000). *Winners:* Xudong Jin, Guoqing Li, Haipeng Li.

Huang Tso-ping and Wu Yao-yu Scholarship Memorial Research Grant ($200): *Winner:* Xiaoai Ren.

Church and Synagogue Library Association (CSLA)

CSLA Award for Outstanding Congregational Librarian. For distinguished service to the congregation and/or community through devotion to the congregational library. *Winner:* Not awarded in 2007.

CSLA Award for Outstanding Congregational Library. For responding in creative and innovative ways to the library's mission of reaching and serving the congregation and/or the wider community. *Winner:* Faith Community Lutheran Library, Longmont, Colorado.

CSLA Award for Outstanding Contribution to Congregational Libraries. For providing inspiration, guidance, leadership, or resources to enrich the field of church or synagogue librarianship. *Winner:* Not awarded in 2007.

Helen Keating Ott Award for Outstanding Contribution to Children's Literature. *Winner:* Not awarded in 2007.

Pat Tabler Memorial Scholarship Award. *Winner:* Elaine Amromin, Temple Beth David Library, Sierra Madre, California.

Coalition for Networked Information

Paul Evan Peters Award. Awarded biennially to recognize notable and lasting international achievements relating to high-performance networks and the creation and use of information resources and services that advance scholarship and intellectual productivity. *Winner:* Not awarded in 2007.

Paul Evan Peters Fellowship ($2,500 a year for two years). Awarded biennially to a student pursuing a graduate degree in librarianship or the information sciences. *Winner:* Not awarded in 2007.

Council on Library and Information Resources (CLIR)

Mellon Fellowship Program for Dissertation Research in the Humanities in Original Sources (stipends of up to $20,000 to support dissertation research). *Winners:* Jeffrey Ahlman, Daniel Amsterdam, Peter Broadwell, Daniel Domingues de Silva, David Hunter, Rebecca Johnson, Ryan Kashanipour, Fabiola Lopez-Duran, Vanessa Mongey, Catherine Styer, Nu-Anh Tran, Uranchimeg Tsultem, Mari Webel.

Rovelstad Scholarship in International Librarianship. To enable a student enrolled in an accredited LIS program to attend the IFLA World Library and Information Congress. *Winner:* Lorraine Alison Dong.

A. R. Zipf Fellowship in Information Management ($5,000). To a student enrolled in graduate school who shows exceptional promise for leadership and technical achievement. *Winner:* Alvin K. Cheung.

Friends of Libraries USA (FOLUSA)

FOLUSA/Baker & Taylor Awards ($2,000). To friends groups that have distinguished themselves in support of their libraries. *Winners:* (large library; tie) Friends of the Leesburg (Florida) Library, Friends of the Minneapolis Public Library; (small library) Friends of the Mineola (Texas) Memorial Library.

FOLUSA Public Service Award. *Winner:* U.S. Sen. Susan Collins (R-Maine).

Bill and Melinda Gates Foundation

Access to Learning Award ($1 million). To public libraries or similar organizations outside the United States for innovative programs that provide the public free access to information technology. *Administered by:* International Network for the Availability of Scientific Publications. *Winner:* Northern Territory (Australia) Library Program for its Libraries and Knowledge Centers project.

Global Libraries Initiative Award ($1 million). *Winner:* International Federation of Library Associations and Institutions (IFLA).

International Federation of Library Associations and Institutions (IFLA)

Dr. Shawky Salem Conference Grant (up to $1,900). To enable an expert in library and information science who is a national of an Arab country to attend the IFLA Conference for the first time. *Winner:* Randa Al-Chidiac, University of Balamand Libraries, Lebanon.

Frederick Thorpe Individual Awards (up to £5,000 total). To librarians working in libraries for the blind. *Donor:* Ulverscroft Foundation. *Winners:* Hélène Kudzia of the Médiathèque de l'Association Valentin Haüy, Paris, £1,500 to spend 20 days at the Library of the Deutsche Blindenstudienanstalt, Marburg, Germany; Hosein Rohani Sadr of the National Library and Archives of Iran, £2,000 to study DAISY technology at the Swedish Library of Talking Books and Braille.

Frederick Thorpe Organizational Award (up to £15,000). To a library organization for development of service delivery to the visually impaired. *Winners:* Integrated Documentation System of the Cuyo National University, Mendoza, Argentina, £6,250; Centro para la Integración y el Desarrollo del Invidente, Lima, Peru, £10,000; Adaptive Technology Center for the Blind, Addis Ababa, Ethiopia, £5,000.

Medical Library Association (MLA)

Estelle Brodman Award for the Academic Medical Librarian of the Year. To honor significant achievement, potential for leadership, and continuing excellence at mid-career in the area of academic health sciences librarianship. *Winner:* Jan LaBeause.

Lois Ann Colaianni Award for Excellence and Achievement in Hospital Librarianship. To a member of MLA who has made significant contributions to the profession in the area of overall distinction or leadership in hospital librarianship. *Winner:* Ethel Madden.

Cunningham Memorial International Fellowships ($3,500). Six-month grant and travel expenses in the United States and Canada for one or more foreign librarians. *Winners:* Alison Kinengyere, Jin Cheng.

Louise Darling Medal. For distinguished achievement in collection development in the health sciences. *Winner:* Esther Carrigan.

Janet Doe Lectureship. *Winner:* Henry L. Lemkau, Jr. *Topic:* "Constants, Context and Change: The Pursuit of Purpose."

EBSCO/MLA Annual Meeting Grants (up to $1,000). *Winners:* Agnes Chikonzo, Ladonna Guillot, Maureen Knapp, Lauren Young.

Ida and George Eliot Prize. For an essay published in any journal in the preceding calendar year that has been judged most effective in furthering medical librarianship. *Donor:* Login Brothers Books. *Winner:* Not awarded in 2007.

Murray Gottlieb Prize. For the best unpublished essay submitted by a medical librarian on the history of some aspect of health sciences or a detailed description of a library exhibit. *Donors:* Ralph and Jo Grimes. *Winner:* Elizabeth Connor for "The Body Politic: The Contributions of Physician-Patriot Joseph Warren."

Hospital Libraries Section/MLA Professional Development Grants. *Winners:* Hella Bluhm-Stieber, Brenda Wong.

David A. Kronick Traveling Fellowship ($2,000). *Sponsor:* Bowden-Massey Foundation. *Winner:* Michele R. Tennant.

Joseph Leiter NLM/MLA Lectureship. *Winner:* Kent A. Smith.

Donald A. B. Lindberg Research Fellowship ($25,000). *Winner:* Michele R. Tennant.

Lucretia W. McClure Excellence in Education Award. To an outstanding educator in the field of health sciences librarianship and informatics. *Winner:* Renata Geer.

Majors/MLA Chapter Project of the Year Award. *Sponsor:* Majors Scientific Books. *Winner:* Upstate New York and Ontario Chapter of MLA for their survey on membership recruitment and retention in the Academy of Health Information Professionals at both the chapter and national levels.

MLA Continuing Education Awards. *Winners:* Rick Wallace, Alice Weber.

MLA Fellowships. *Winners:* Nancy Clemmons, Kathryn J. Hoffman, Sheldon Kotzin, James Shedlock, Patricia Thibodeau.

MLA President's Award. *Winner:* Beth M. Wescott.

MLA Research, Development, and Demonstration Project Grant ($100 to $1,000). *Winners:* Fern Cheek, Sally Harvey.

MLA Scholarship (up to $5,000). For graduate study at an ALA-accredited library school. *Winner:* Catherine Murch.

MLA Scholarship for Minority Students (up to $5,000). For graduate study at an ALA-accredited library school. *Winner:* Lisa Chow.

Marcia C. Noyes Award. For an outstanding contribution to medical librarianship. *Winner:* Betsy L. Humphreys.

Rittenhouse Award. For the best unpublished paper on medical librarianship submitted by a student enrolled in, or having been enrolled in, a course for credit in an ALA-accredited library school or a trainee in an internship program in medical librarianship. *Donor:* Rittenhouse Medical Bookstore. *Winner:* Susan Miller for "The Necessity of the Hospital Library to the Institution and Community It Serves."

Thomson Scientific/Frank Bradway Rogers Information Advancement Award ($500). For an outstanding contribution to knowledge of health science information delivery. *Winner:* Legacy Tobacco Documents Library.

Music Library Association

Carol June Bradley Award. To support studies that involve the history of music libraries or special collections. *Winner:* Gary Galván.

Vincent H. Duckles Award. For the best book-length bibliography or other research tool in music. *Winner:* Mary Lewis for *Antonio Gardano, Venetian Music Printer, 1538–1569* (Garland).

Dena Epstein Award for Archival and Library Research in American Music. To support research in archives or libraries internationally on any aspect of American music. *Winners:* Sarah Dorsey and R. Allen Lott.

Walter Gerboth Award. To members of MLA who are in the first five years of their professional library careers, to assist research-in-progress in music or music librarianship. *Winner:* Michelle Lynn Oswell.

Richard S. Hill Award, For the best article on music librarianship or article of a music-bibliographic nature. *Winner:* Jeremy L. Smith for "A Newly Discovered Edition of William Byrd's 'Psalmes, Sonets & Songs: Provenance and Significance'" in *Notes* 62, no. 2.

Eva Judd O'Meara Award. For the best review published in *Notes*. *Winner:* Ruth A. Solie for *George Grove, Music and Victorian Culture,* ed. by Michael Musgrave (Palgrave).

Special Achievement Award. To recognize extraordinary service to the profession of music librarianship over a relatively short period of time. *Winner:* Not awarded in 2007.

REFORMA (National Association to Promote Library and Information Services to Latinos and the Spanish-Speaking)

REFORMA scholarships ($1,500). To students who qualify for graduate study in library science and who are citizens or permanent residents of the United States. *Winners:* Lucía Acin-Andion, Rebecca Alcalá, Adriana Huertas, José Reyes, Angel Román.

K. G. Saur (Munich, Germany)

K. G. Saur Award for Best *LIBRI* Student Paper ($500). To author(s) to recognize the most outstanding article published in *LIBRI* during the preceding year. *Donor:* K. G. Saur Publishing. *Winner:* Joy L. Austria for "Developing Evaluation Criteria for Podcasts."

Society of American Archivists (SAA)

C. F. W. Coker Award for Description. *Winner:* Greg Bradsher.

Colonial Dames of America and Donna Cutts Scholarships (up to $1,200). To enable new archivists to attend the Modern Archives Institute of the National Archives and Records Administration. *Winners:* Claire-Lise Bénaud, Béatrice Colastin Skokan.

Council Exemplary Service Award. For outstanding service to SAA and the archives profession. *Winners:* Trudy Huskamp Peterson, Victoria Irons Walch.

Fellows' Ernst Posner Award. For an outstanding essay dealing with a facet of archival administration, history, theory, or methodology, published in *American Archivist. Winner:* A*CENSUS Working Group for "Special Section on Archival Census and Educational Needs Survey in the United States."

Philip M. Hamer and Elizabeth Hamer Kegan Award. For individuals and/or institutions that have increased public awareness of a specific body of documents. *Winner:* National Library of Medicine for "Profiles in Science."

Oliver Wendell Holmes Award. To enable overseas archivists already in the United States or Canada for training to attend the SAA annual meeting. *Winner:* Gerald Chaudron.

J. Franklin Jameson Award. For individuals and/or organizations that promote greater public awareness of archival activities and programs. *Winner: Chicago Tribune.*

Sister M. Claude Lane, O.P., Memorial Award. For a significant contribution to the field of religious archives. *Winner:* Roger M. Dahl.

Waldo Gifford Leland Prize. For writing of superior excellence and usefulness in the field of archival history, theory, or practice. *Winners:* Waverly Lowell and Tawny Ryan Nelb for *Architectural Records: Managing Design and Construction Records* (SAA).

Theodore Calvin Pease Award. For the best student paper. *Winner:* Elizabeth Snowden for "Our Archives, Our Selves: Documentation Strategy and the Re-Appraisal of Professional Identity."

Donald Peterson Student Scholarship Award (up to $1,000). To enable a student or recent graduate to attend the SAA Annual Meeting. *Winner:* Chela Scott Weber.

Harold T. Pinkett Minority Student Award. To encourage minority students to consider careers in the archival profession and promote minority participation in SAA. *Winners:* Janel Quirante, Bergis K. Jules.

Preservation Publication Award. To recognize an outstanding work published in North America that advances the theory or the practice of preservation in archival institutions. *Winner:* Heritage Preservation for *Field Guide to Emergency Response.*

SAA Fellows. Highest individual distinction awarded to a limited number of members for their outstanding contribution to the archival profession. *Honored*: R. Joseph Anderson, Laurie A. Baty, Jane Kenamore, Robert Sidney Martin, Christine Weideman, Joel F. Wurl.

SAA Spotlight Award. To recognize the contributions of individuals who work for the good of the profession and of archival collections, and whose work would not typically receive public recognition. *Winner:* Alan H. Stein.

Special Libraries Association (SLA)

Mary Adeline Connor Professional Development Scholarship (up to $6,000). For post-M.L.S. certificate or degree programs in any subject area, technological skill, or managerial expertise relevant to applicants' career needs and goals in special librarianship. *Winner:* Vaishali Jahagirdar.

John Cotton Dana Award. For exceptional support and encouragement of special librarianship. *Winner:* Gloria Zamora.

Diversity Leadership Development Award ($1,000 stipend). *Winners:* Blanca Chou, Cheryl Jacocks-Terrell, Debal C. Kar, Lina Ortega, Janet Todwong.

Dow Jones Leadership Award ($2,000). For excellence in special librarianship. *Winner:* Jane Kinney Meyers.

Hall of Fame Award. To a member or members of the association at or near the end of an active professional career for an extended and sustained period of distinguished service to the association. *Winners:* Paul Wasserman, Gary D. Wiggins.

SLA Affirmative Action Scholarship ($6,000). *Winner:* Terence L. Johnson.

SLA Fellows. *Honored:* Terri Brooks, Patricia Cia, Toby Pearlstein, Gail Stahl, Wei Wei.

SLA/LexisNexis Innovations in Technology Award ($1,000). *Winner:* Karen Huffman.

SLA Member Achievement Award. *Sponsors:* Thomson Scientific and Dialog. *Winner:* Sharon A. Lenius.

SLA Plenum Scholarship ($1,000). For graduate study leading to a Ph.D. from a recognized program in library science, information science, or related fields of study. *Winner:* Not awarded in 2007.

SLA Presidential Citations. For notable contributions that enhance the association or further its goals and objectives. *Winners:* Clare Hart, Jane Macoustra.

SLA Professional Award. *Sponsor:* Springer. *Winner:* SLA Military Librarians Division.

SLA Research Grants (incorporating the Steven I. Goldspiel Memorial Research Grant) (up to $25,000). *Winners:* Michael Fanning for "Impulse for Growth! Laying Foundations for SLA Membership Acquisition and Growth in Germany for 2008"; David Shumaker and Mary Talley for "Models of Embedded Librarianship: A Research Proposal."

SLA Student Scholarships ($1,000). For graduate study in librarianship leading to a master's degree in library or information science. *Winners:* Meghan Fahey, Julie May, Jennifer Rohan.

Rose L. Vormelker Award. *Winner:* Eileen Abels.

H. W. Wilson Company Award ($500). For the most outstanding article in the past year's *Information Outlook. Donor:* H. W. Wilson Company. *Winners:* Helen Clegg and Susan Montgomery of A. T. Kearney for "How to Write an RFP for Information Products" (June 2006).

Part 4
Research and Statistics

Library Research and Statistics

Research and Statistics on Libraries and Librarianship in 2007

Denise M. Davis

Director, Office for Research and Statistics, American Library Association

This year I thought I would take a slightly different approach to presenting research and statistics about libraries and librarianship. Recognizing that there is far more research being done than can be summarized here, I thought identifying some key topics and supporting research would be a more effective approach. Rather than presenting research by type of library, the research is presented topically. Five key topics emerged: funding, social networking and privacy, young adult services, effectiveness of school libraries, and general research methods used by the profession.

Topping the list in 2007 were problems with library funding—referendum failures, property tax revolts, reductions in funding to higher education, and continued erosion in school library support. While some libraries are experiencing funding growth, many are not. A study of this issue by the American Library Association (ALA), scheduled to be released in 2008, was still being completed when this report was prepared. It was difficult to find any published research in these areas except for a few tangential instances, primarily in the areas of assessment, evaluation, and secondary data analysis. Although these may certainly be used to articulate the need for adequate library funding, they do not evaluate funding per se. This is a call to researchers to begin looking at this issue more seriously.

Next was the use of social-networking utilities. An ever-growing concern regarding user privacy surfaced in the general literature and a few research articles are noted. Use of libraries and library services by young adults has been underrepresented in library research. Articles about services and trends exist in general library literature, but it was difficult to find a strong research study in this area. Therefore, a household survey done for ALA is noted to draw attention to this issue (another call to the research community).

Effectiveness of school libraries, always an area of interest, is highlighted through a doctoral dissertation that investigated school library programs in California.

Finally, this article will spotlight a few studies that looked more generally at research methods in librarianship.

Funding

Three research studies provide broad consideration of library funding concerns, especially in public libraries.

An interesting article on public library funding was published by Ignace Glorieux, Toon Kuppens, and Dieter Vanderboeck of the Vrije Universiteit Brussel—"Mind the Gap: Societal Limits to Public Library Effectiveness" (*Library & Information Science Research* 29(2) (June 2007), pp. 188–208 and online at http://www.sciencedirect.com). The authors assessed the impact and effectiveness of state-mandated public libraries in Belgium, and go so far as to define an effective library: "An effective library is defined here as a library that, given the context in which it operates, performs well in conditions on which it has no influence." The authors used standard output measures to assess effectiveness, as well as measures unique to Belgian libraries (e.g., membership fees), and used Belgian census demographic data to contextualize the findings. The study discovered findings in usage similar to patterns in U.S. public libraries, such as lower usage by males and higher educational attainment being an indicator of higher usage. Dissimilar to patterns in the United States, the study found that the number of registered users decreased in municipalities with higher levels of low-income residents. Using regression analysis, the authors found interesting borrowing and library use patterns by males, which were especially affected by the hours a library was open. Men were heavier users of nonprint collections such as DVDs and CDs. The authors raise interesting questions about attracting users to the library and the consequences of such activity as meeting demands for specific formats of materials. Descriptive statistics of the study findings are included in the article.

Technology Report Broadened

For the first time, the long-standing research by John Carlo Bertot and Charles McClure around Internet connectivity and services in public libraries introduced detailed technology-related expenditure questions to the 2007 ALA survey on library funding and technology. Led by ALA's Office for Research and Statistics, the 2007 study asked libraries about funding of public-access computing services. The final report, *Libraries Connect Communities: Public Library Funding and Technology Access Study 2006–2007 Report* (http://www.ala.org/ala/ors/0607report/0607report.htm) presents the findings of this research.

Building upon research conducted by ALA in 2006 regarding overall public library funding, the technology study solicited information on services funded by state agencies on public libraries' behalf, as well as library expenditures on technology-related staff and services and on the sources from which the funding was derived (local, state, federal, fines/fees, grants, and so forth). This level of finance detail does not exist in other national library data collection initiatives, and it represents the most current fiscal year actual and projected figures available on a national basis.

Responses became most interesting when analyzed by metropolitan status and by source of revenue. They aligned closely with the total distributions by expenditure categories (e.g., staff, collection, and other expenditures) as reported to the National Center for Education Statistics (NCES) in the E.D. Tabs publication *Public Libraries in the United States: Fiscal Year 2004* (http://www.nces.ed. gov/pubs2006/2006349.pdf). However, what is now known through the fiscal detail of the technology access study is that libraries reported applying fines/fees and donations to "other" expenditures by nearly a two-to-one ratio. It is in the "other" expenditure category that many technology expenditures occur. If this projection holds true, it suggests that libraries may not be in a position to rely on local tax support to fund technology, but are relying disproportionately on fines, fees, and fund raising to provide what have become basic library services.

Other concerns about funding libraries and technology-related services centered on basic building infrastructure, supporting online job searching and e-education, e-government services accessible through public libraries, and just keeping staff trained in using the technologies patrons demand.

Networks' Funding Role

"Library Networks, Cooperatives, and Consortia: A Definitional Study and Survey" investigated what organizations are helping libraries make the limited funding go further. Study findings and a searchable database of organization records is available on the project Web site (http://www.ala.org/ala/ors/lncc). Funded by the Institute of Museum and Library Services and ALA, the study confirmed a decline in the number of formally organized entities supporting libraries since the last such study (1996). Three key findings emerged from this project: Networks, cooperatives, and consortia primarily serve multiple types of libraries (e.g., public, academic, school, and special) rather than one particular type, and are regionally based; the longer the network or cooperative has been established, the more diverse its services to its member libraries; services to be provided over the coming two to three years varied dramatically depending upon the size of the membership of the network or cooperative.

More than 200 library networks, cooperatives, and consortia reported on current and future services, funding, and staffing. Services provided to members by more than 75 percent of responding networks and cooperatives included

- Communication among member libraries (directories, e-mail lists, newsletters, other publications)
- Resource sharing (reciprocal borrowing, cooperative collection development, union catalog, union list of serials, requesting mechanisms)
- General professional development, continuing education, or staff training
- General consulting/technical assistance
- Cooperative purchasing or group discounts

The highest priorities for the next two to three years for library networks and cooperative organizations included automation, networking, and other technology; courier document delivery; resource sharing; and general professional development/continuing education.

Social Networking and Privacy

Although primarily an article about the relationship between laws—specifically the Children's Online Privacy Protection Act (COPPA)—and Internet use, a study by Tracy Mitrano looks at how social networking utilities bump into individual privacy and federal laws ("A Wider World: Youth, Privacy, and Social Networking Technologies," *Educause Review,* November-December 2006, pp. 16–28). Mitrano, director of IT Policy and of the Computer Policy and Law program at Cornell, raises interesting questions regarding limits of privacy, regulatory requirements placed on technology developers of open space and social networking virtual environments, and privacy concerns from the user's perspective. Examples pepper the article, many coming from individuals themselves. What is adequate privacy? Is privacy contextual? Have we learned anything from earlier technology deployment? (The last is rhetorical, because Mitrano makes a reasoned argument that we are repeating old mistakes with new online utilities.) Perhaps the most revealing statement Mitrano makes relates to her not having an online presence in environments like Facebook; "I don't want someone else to own my or Cornell's intellectual property," she says, "or to collect, hold, or sell my personally identifiable information, nor do I want to be beholden to someone else's commercial interest."

Taking a slightly more scientific approach to understanding online privacy, Mike Z. Yao, Ronald E. Rice, and Kier Wallis conducted a survey of more than 400 undergraduates at a U.S. university ("Predicting User Concerns About Online Privacy," *Journal of the American Society for Information Science and Technology* 58(8), pp. 710–722). Drawing on previous research in the areas of privacy, efficacy, and Internet use, the authors formed a hypothesis path model and conducted their study to validate that online privacy concern path model.

Students taking part in the study were presented with a range of value scale statement sets to determine their perspectives on privacy. The assessment areas were need for privacy, generalized self-efficacy, beliefs in privacy rights, Internet use fluency, Internet use diversity, and concerns about online privacy (organizational privacy and general online privacy). Each scale utilized different response options, some were yes/no and others used Likert scales. A total of 83 questions were asked from the various scales, and one question was asked about perception of gender differences in concern over online privacy. A series of path models were developed depicting predictability of online privacy concerns. Comparing the hypothesis path model against the model formed from the study revealed some interesting findings. Interestingly, gender is irrelevant in an individual's perception of online privacy. Rather, the researchers concluded that "individuals' beliefs in privacy rights and the dispositional desire for privacy in general are the main factors determining concerns about privacy issues in the specific context of the Internet." (p. 719) A few limiting factors were identified by the researchers and should be considered when interpreting these study findings. One was the real-versus-perceived knowledge and fluency in using the Internet by study participants. Another was the study group—college students. Additional research in this area is needed, but this study certainly presents interesting findings to consider as we try to understand online privacy issues.

Young Adults

ALA initiated a household study regarding young adult use of public and school libraries. Conducted by Harris Interactive for ALA, "Youth Use of Public and School Libraries" (http://www.ala.org/ala/yalsa/HarrisYouthPoll.pdf) indicated that 56 percent had visited a public library and/or library Web site in the previous month, and 78 percent had visited a school library and/or Web site. Although borrowing books for personal or school assignments was the most highly ranked use of both public and school libraries, users were more likely to use the school library Web site for information and research and to study than the public library. About 25 percent of young adults indicated they would use school library computers more if the information they needed weren't blocked, and 32 percent if more-interesting books and activities or events were offered. About 38 percent indicated they would use the public library more if it were closer to where they live, and 26 percent would use it more if there were a space restricted to teenagers.

Effectiveness of School Libraries

Two noteworthy studies on the topic of school library effectiveness were a doctoral dissertation coauthored by Stacy Sinclair-Tarr and William Tarr, Jr. ("Using Large-Scale Assessments to Evaluate the Effectiveness of School Library Programs in California," OCLC record number 70262077, summary results published in *Phi Delta Kappan* 88(9), pp. 710–711), and a study by Barbara Immroth and W. Bernard Lukenbill ("Teacher-School Library Media Specialists Collaboration Through Social Marketing Strategies," *School Library Media Research* 10, 2007). The Immroth-Lukenbill article provides a valuable bibliography of references cited.

Research Methods for the Profession

Three research methods articles were particularly interesting.

The first is "U.S. Public Library Data: A Unified Field Theory" by Bob Molyneux (*Public Library Quarterly* 24(3), 3–19). This should be mandatory reading for LIS students or for anyone new to public library data. The overview of public library data reporting systems, including an OPAC vendor-developed utility (the SirsiDynix Normative Data Project), is very well done. It isn't that the author demystifies the data sets, but the data are put into meaningful context.

The second is "Inferential Statistics and Librarianship" by Juris Dilevko (*Library and Information Science Research* 29: 209–229), which is valuable for anyone interested in the predominant patterns in research methodology used by the library and information industry. In particular, the author analyzed the incidence of inferential statistics as a research method for articles published between 2001 and 2005. A purpose of the analysis was to determine whether librarians need skills—either passive or active knowledge—in inferential statistics to interpret research using this method. It was determined that about 14.5 percent of articles published in five LIS journals included inferential statistics or techniques.

Detailed analysis by journal title and type of descriptive or inferential statistics is provided and suggests that the shift toward more assessment-based performance measurement by libraries requires greater knowledge of inferential statistics.

The third article is Elizabeth C. Hamilton's "The Impact of Survey Data: Measuring Success" (*Journal of the American Society for Information Science and Technology* 58(2): 190–199). Focusing on the Canadian National Population Health Survey, Hamilton conducted citation analysis to investigate the impact and value of national social surveys and use of the data in further research or secondary analysis. This research is particularly pertinent to U.S. researchers as the government moves away from a detailed decennial census to annual sample social surveys administered through the American Community Survey (ACS). A strong bibliography accompanies the article.

Articles and Reports of Note

Building Effective, Sustainable, Practical Assessment, the proceedings of the Library Assessment Conference sponsored by the Association of Research Libraries in September 2006 in Charlottesville, Virginia, can be ordered as a print volume or downloaded as a pdf from the ARL Web site at http://libraryassessment.org/archive/index.shtml.

Some other articles and reports worthy of mention are:

- "Challenge of Rural People to Reduce Digital Divide in the Globalized World: Theory and Practice" by Hasan Akca, Murat Sayili, and Kemal Esengun, *Government Information Quarterly* 24(2), pp. 404–413, 2007
- "A Comparative Evaluation of Search Techniques for Query-by-Humming Using the MUSART Testbed" by Roger B. Tannenberg, William P. Birmingham, Bryan Pardo, Ning Hu, Colin Meek, and George Tzanetakis, *Journal of the American Society for Information Science and Technology* 58(5), pp. 687–701, 2007
- "Defining a Session on Web Search Engines" by Bernard J. Jansen, Amanda Spink, Chris Blakely, and Sherry Koshman, *Journal of the American Society for Information Science and Technology* 58(6), pp. 862–871, 2007
- "Social Capital and Public Libraries: The Need for research" by Andreas Varheim, *Library & Science Research* 29, pp. 416–428, 2007

Awards and Grants that Honor and Support Excellent Research

The professional library associations offer many awards and grants to recognize and encourage research. The 2007 awards and grants here are listed under the name of the sponsoring association, and in the case of ALA by the awarding division, in alphabetical order. More-detailed information about the prizes and prizewinners can be found at the association Web sites.

An award to honor the contributions of Mary Jo Lynch, former director of the ALA Office for Research and Statistics, was established by Beta Phi Mu's

Distinguished Lecture Program in 2005 and named the Mary Jo Lynch Distinguished Research Award. In 2007 the award, a funded lectureship, was presented to Beta Phi Mu's Beta Beta Epsilon Chapter at University of Wisconsin–Madison and to its Gamma Chapter at Florida State University.

More information about the award is available at http://www.beta-phi-mu.org/distinguished_lectures.html.

American Library Association

http://www.ala.org

Jesse H. Shera Award for Excellence in Published Research
Winners: Gary Marchionini, Paul Solomon, Cheryl Davis, and Terrell Russell.

Association of College and Research Libraries (ACRL)

http://www.ala.org/acrl

Doctoral Dissertation Fellowship
Winner: Jihyun Kim for "Faculty Self-Archiving Behavior: Methods and Factors Affecting the Decision to Self-Archive."

Coutts Nijhoff International West European Specialist Study Grant
Winner: Thea Lindquist for her proposal "From the Ashes: Identifying, Documenting, and Rebuilding the Herzogin Anna Amalia Bibliothek's Fruchtbringende Gesellschaft (Fruitbearing Society) Collections."

Ilene F. Rockman Instruction Publication of the Year Award
Winners: James K. Elmborg and Sheril Hook for "Centers for Learning: Writing Centers and Libraries in Collaboration" in *ACRL Publications in Librarianship* 58.

Library and Information Technology Association/OCLC

http://www.ala.org/lita

Frederick G. Kilgour Award for Research in Library and Information Technology
Winner: Richard Pearce-Moses.

American Society for Information Science and Technology

http://www.asis.org

Research in Information Science Award (formerly the ASIS&T Research Award)
Winner: Ophir Frieder.

ProQuest Doctoral Dissertation Award
Winner: W. John MacMullen for "Contextual Analysis of Variation and Quality in Human-Curated Gene Ontology Annotations."

Thomson ISI Citation Analysis Research Grant (formerly the ISI/ASIS&T Citation Analysis Research Grant)
Winner: Philip M. Davis for his proposal "Does Free Access to Scholarly Articles Increase Readership and Citation Impact?"

Thomson ISI Doctoral Dissertation Proposal Scholarship (formerly the ASIS&T/ISI Doctoral Dissertation Proposal Scholarship)

Winner: Philip Edwards for "Mapping Scholars' Decision Processes and Factors that Influence How They Publish and Distribute Their Work."

John Wiley Best JASIST Paper Award

Winners: Catherine Blake and Wanda Pratt for "Collaborative Information Synthesis, Part 1" and "Collaborative Information Synthesis, Part 2: Recommendations for Information Systems to Support Synthesis."

Association for Library and Information Science Education

http://www.alise.org

ALISE/Eugene Garfield Doctoral Dissertation Competition

Winner: Kate Williams for "Social Networks, Social Capital, and the Use of Information and Communications Technology in Socially Excluded Communities: A Study of Community Groups in Manchester, England."

ALISE Research Grant Competition

Winners: Eileen Abels, Denise Agosto, and Lorri Mon for "Remote Reference in Practice and the Classroom."

Medical Library Association

http://www.mlanet.org

Janet Doe Lectureship for 2008

Winner: Thomas G. Basler, Medical University of South Carolina–Charleston

Donald A. B. Lindberg Research Fellowship

Winner: Michele R. Tennant, AHIP, Health Science Center Libraries and Genetics Institute, University of Florida–Gainesville.

President's Award

Winner: Beth M. Wescott, National Network of Libraries of Medicine, Baltimore.

Old Data in New Files:
The Search for Causes and Trends

Robert E. Molyneux

The library world is awash with data collected in various ways and for various purposes. The history of the collection of data about libraries is a rich one.

Well known are the episodic large national surveys intended to assess the state of some aspect of libraries, such as the "Public Libraries and the Internet" report by John Carlo Bertot, Charles McClure, and others done through the Information and Use Management and Policy Institute (http://www.ii.fsu.edu/plinternet_reports. cfm) at Florida State University. Others have taken existing data from various sources and compared them—Adriano Balbi's seminal 1834 *A Statistical Essay on the Libraries of Vienna and the World* (McFarland, 1986) is an early look at library data and their many vagaries as he tried to assess which European libraries were the largest. Balbi's investigation led him to make observations about library data that are as fresh today as they were when he wrote them.

For the purposes of this discussion, we will concentrate on another subset of library data: those that have been collected systematically from a consistent set of libraries, on an annual basis, and over various periods of time, again for different purposes. Data collected for one purpose can be reused for another, and that is just what this article is about. We reuse these data to observe trends affecting libraries. There are a number of series published regularly, but this article focuses on four and of those four mentions one just briefly. These series were published annually and have been—or are in the process of being—recompiled into one large, longitudinal series.

Four Longitudinal Recompilations

These four series are

- The Gerould/Association of Research Libraries (ARL) data. This series was begun in 1907–1908 by James Thayer Gerould while he was at the University of Minnesota and continued by him when he moved to Princeton University. ARL was founded in 1932, and over the years the Gerould series morphed into the ARL data by a complicated process that need not concern us here. Today, ARL-whose members are the preeminent research libraries in the United States and Canada-maintains this series. This year marks the 100th anniversary of the series. The Gerould Statistics are available on the Web (http://fisher.lib.virginia.edu/libsites/gerould) and the entire series (Gerould and ARL together) is available from ARL (http://www.arl.org/stats/annualsurveys/arlstats/index.shtml). The first modern longitudinal recompilation of such a series was done on part of

Robert E. Molyneux has worked on compiling, documenting, and analyzing library data for more than 20 years and has taught a variety of library school classes dealing with the integration of computers and networking technology in libraries. He is vice president for product development at Equinox Software, Inc.

this long series by Kendon Stubbs and David Buxton: *Cumulated ARL University Library Statistics, 1962–1963 Through 1978–1979* (ARL, 1981). It included machine-readable data and professional documentation. More important, perhaps, was its infrastructure and insights which have informed subsequent longitudinal series, including the Gerould Statistics. Stubbs and Buxton's publication can be regarded as the first substantive advance in our understanding of the characteristics of library data since Balbi's 1834 work. It would be difficult to overestimate the importance of either work.

- The biennial Academic Library Statistics (ALS) compiled by the National Center for Education Statistics (NCES). This important series had not yet been recompiled into a longitudinal series at the time this report was prepared, but it should be by mid-2008. After languishing, this series is being revived and updated by NCES. Unlike the ARL data, which compile statistics on an influential but small set of libraries, the ALS data are a universe survey; questionnaires go out to all U.S. academic libraries NCES identifies, and the data are currently available for 1996, 1998, 2000, 2002, and 2004. For those not interested in trends in major research libraries but rather in analyzing trends in smaller academic libraries—for example, community college libraries or libraries at theological schools—this would be the series to examine. I am in the process of recompiling this series for longitudinal purposes (http://www.nclis.gov/statsurv/NCES/als/index.html). These data will be in the public domain. There are various series on smaller academic libraries, one that goes back to the 1930s. There have, in fact, been three separate series published by the American Library Association (ALA) and its Association of College and Research Libraries (ACRL), as well as others by other groups. These series are not dealt with here either because they do not exist in longitudinal form or are not available at this time.

- An annual series that reports universe data on each individual public library system in the United States (started in 1987) (available at http://www.nclis.gov/statsurv/NCES/pldf3/index.html).

- A second series containing summary data about characteristics of U.S. public libraries in the various states (best data since 1992), available at http://www.nclis.gov/statsurv/NCES/pusum/index.html.

The latter two public library series are compiled and published historically by NCES. In the future, the Institute of Museum and Library Services (IMLS) will manage the annual collection and publication of these data. Both of these series have been recompiled, and these longitudinal recompilations are in the public domain and are currently on the site of the National Commission on Library and Information Science (NCLIS). NCLIS will close in 2008, and these NCES/NCLIS data will need a new home.

These four series have the following characteristics: they are readily available for research use, are well documented, and three already have longitudinal recompilations.

What Are 'Longitudinal' Data?

It is an odd characteristic of these various annual cumulations that they are published and almost exclusively used as if no other years exist. Each year is published separately so that year-to-year changes are not immediately apparent. Longitudinal data, on the other hand, are organized so that trends can be analyzed.

These annual data are collected for several main purposes:

- *For budget justification.* This use is largely formulaic. "Last year, compared with other libraries in our peer group, we went up in rankings on these various measures. Alas, on these others, we fell. Give us more money."
- *For directory information.* To locate libraries with problems with similar configurations or collections. Library directors will use this information to call other directors to talk about how to handle these similar problems.
- *For planning.* If the funding authority wants the library to reach some level, what will it take? What does it take, for instance, for our library to be eligible to be a member of ARL?

These purposes have been enough to produce a number of annual data compilations, but it has to be conceded that these purposes are not sophisticated—not a surprising revelation in a non-numerate field like ours. There is essentially no analytical purpose to these numbers beyond those listed above, other than occasional lip service to the notion of trends even though there is no way to see them with the data as published. As a result the data show a static view of libraries even though libraries are actually dynamic institutions that respond to stimuli. If funding goes up, libraries spend more, buy more materials, and hire more people. If funding goes down, libraries cut back on expenditures, buy fewer materials, and employ fewer people. By examining only one year at a time, important trends and their causes are missed.

Longitudinal data, then, consist of data organized to examine trends. In the case of three of these data series, the annual data have been recompiled and an infrastructure added to aid trend analysis. Recompilation involves a number of tasks depending on the series. The early Gerould series reported data on "Leland Stanford Jr. University," which we commonly call "Stanford University" today. In the process of recompilation, then, institution name anomalies are resolved so that data from one institution can be examined readily. In the NCES data series discussed here, there is no variable for the year of reporting so this has to be added during recompilation. In the public library universe file, there have been four different variable names used over the years for the libraries' total expenditures so variable names are also resolved to one so that, in this example, one can readily examine changes in expenditure levels by whatever set of libraries are of interest. These examples are only the tip of the iceberg—this undertaking is complex. In addition to programming, ancillary files must be created to document these series so that they can be used by anyone interested and, then, finally, the data must be made available.

(text continues on page 458)

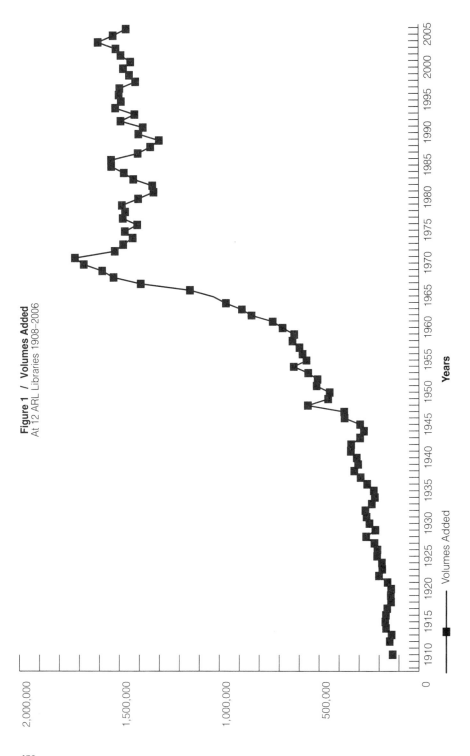

Figure 1 / Volumes Added
At 12 ARL Libraries 1908–2006

Volumes Added

Years

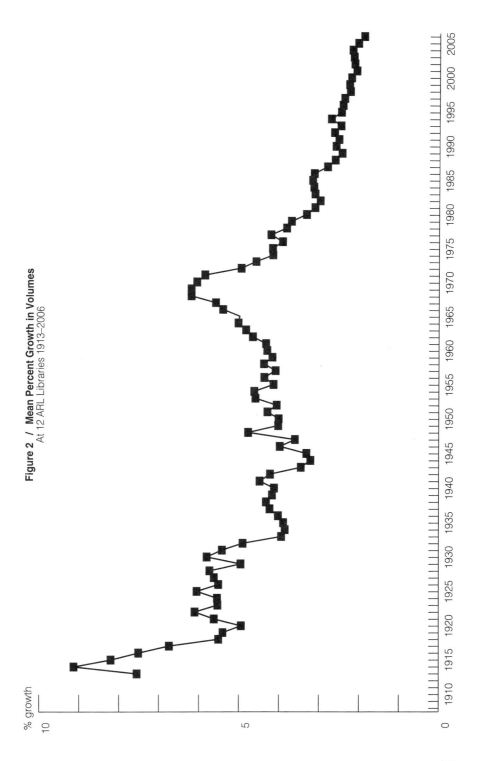

Figure 2 / Mean Percent Growth in Volumes
At 12 ARL Libraries 1913–2006

(continued from page 455)

A Look at the Data

The Gerould/ARL data, given their long duration, are first. It is a characteristic of these longitudinal files that the number of variables, and often the number of libraries, increase over time. The first year of the Gerould data had five variables ("Books in Library," "Added Last Year," "Spent for Books, Periodicals, and Binding," "Number Assistants," and "Total Salaries." There were 14 institutions reporting those variables, but two did not continue reporting, so that we have 12 libraries that have reported from 1907–1908 through 2005–2006. Today, there are 113 academic members of ARL.

Figure 1 shows the total number of volumes "added last year" at 12 libraries that have reported since the beginning. The chart shows a steady increase until the high in 1971 and a roughly steady state since then. During the latter period, of course, the model for these libraries was not so much what they hold but what they can access—and increasing digitization has affected a number of aspects, including what is a "volume."

Figure 2 presents this growth as a percent. Note that the first years of Gerould Statistics were biennial, so an annual percent increase cannot be calculated before 1913. This is a fascinating graph because it gives insight into the history of higher education in the United States through library data. The initial very high increases were the result of high growth at a few of the libraries. There is a steady decline over the period that reflects the fact that the volumes added each year are divided by an increasing book stock in the denominator. But we can see the effects of the Depression, World War II, and the oil shock of the early 1970s. Of course, with these graphs we are drawing pictures to get a sense of what is going on for subsequent analysis. It seems clear and makes sense to conclude that these important libraries reflect the health of the economy in general. They are institutions with national reach. And how could it be otherwise? Libraries get funding from taxes and/or from private donations and each will be higher when the economy is healthy and lower during bad economic times.

A similar analysis of trends in U.S. public libraries is forthcoming in *Public Library Quarterly* (26, nos. 3/4, 2007). There it is possible to see the dynamic response to faltering public library funding that began in the late 1990s through a series of charts and tables. That analysis was done on national-level data, but several states have different economic conditions and it is possible to analyze them separately.

Figure 3 shows circulations per capita in Oregon and in Hawaii over time. Oregon's figures are not the highest in the United States in the latest data—that honor goes to Ohio—nor are Hawaii's figures the lowest. These two were chosen because of the percent change over the entire period.

Figure 4 shows that, as a percentage, Oregon's circulations per capita increased by 67 percent while Hawaii's fell by 15 percent. These figures are at the extreme for public libraries by state, although the District of Columbia's libraries are in the same state summary series and they fell 43 percent. Only eight states showed declines in circulations per capita over the period.

(text continues on page 461)

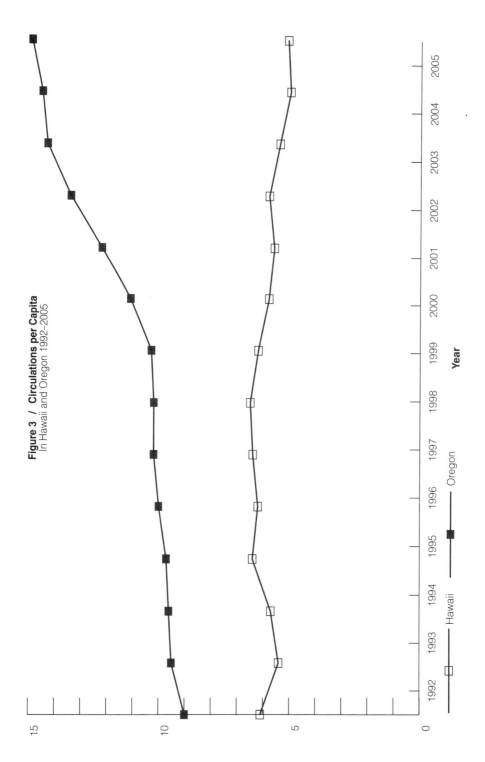

Figure 3 / Circulations per Capita
In Hawaii and Oregon 1992–2005

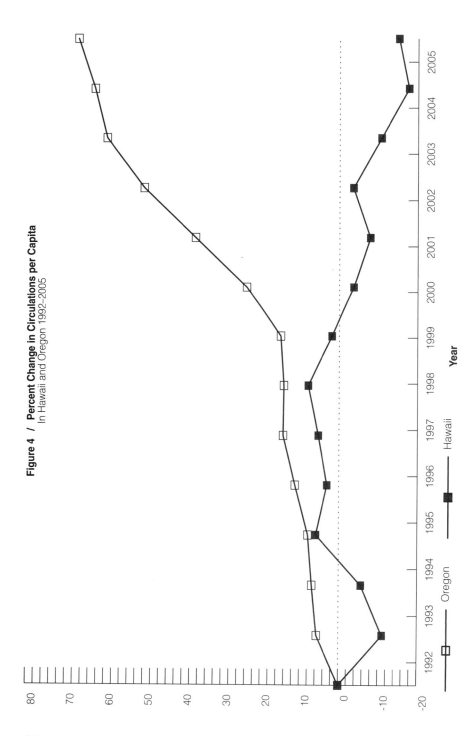

Figure 4 / Percent Change in Circulations per Capita
In Hawaii and Oregon 1992–2005

(continued from page 458)

Now we come to the point: we can learn many things from this kind of analysis. For instance: what works? What will make libraries better and minimize the effects of economic downturns? Which method of funding libraries will result in more circulations? And can we use these data and our understanding of causal relationships to do what analysts in almost all fields do: predict? That is, if we spend less (or more) on books and more (or less) on staff, will we know what the effect will be on circulations, as an example?

In the case of Hawaii, funding for public libraries fell over the period, while that for Oregon increased. That is scarcely a surprising revelation, but what was the cause of this different experience? With data from 50 states, plus a good bit of comparable data from Canadian libraries, what can we discover about funding and organizing libraries to make them better in good and in bad times?

What I have done here is use the data to draw pictures; this strategy does not replace the necessity for serious analysis, but these pictures do give hints about an analytical approach that will give us insights into what works; they also give us the ability to predict. One does not have to have tomorrow's data to have a pretty good idea of what to expect if one has an understanding of the relationships between the variables being measured. If library funding follows the economy, and we know the effect of that funding on other variables, then by watching the economy we can make predictions about future library funding and the effect this funding will have on the libraries themselves. That would be a useful ability to have.

Number of Libraries in the United States and Canada

Statistics are from *American Library Directory* (*ALD*) *2007–2008* (Information Today, Inc., 2007). Data are exclusive of elementary and secondary school libraries.

Libraries in the United States

Public Libraries	17,005 *
Public libraries, excluding branches	9,765 †
Main public libraries that have branches	1,411
Public library branches	7,240
Academic Libraries	3,749 *
Community college	1,167
Departmental	177
Medical	9
Religious	9
University and college	2,582
Departmental	1,409
Law	182
Medical	246
Religious	235
Armed Forces Libraries	302 *
Air Force	86
Medical	8
Army	143
Medical	29
Marine Corps	12
Navy	61
Law	1
Medical	13
Government Libraries	1,174 *
Law	404
Medical	164
Special Libraries (excluding public, academic, armed forces, and government)	7,881 *
Law	928
Medical	1,548
Religious	558
Total Special Libraries (including public, academic, armed forces, and government)	9,181
Total law	1,515
Total medical	2,017
Total religious	1,070
Total Libraries Counted(*)	30,111

Libraries in Regions Administered by the United States

Public Libraries	28*
Public libraries, excluding branches	10†
Main public libraries that have branches	3
Public library branches	18
Academic Libraries	37*
Community college	6
Departmental	3
Medical	0
University and college	31
Departmental	22
Law	3
Medical	2
Religious	1
Armed Forces Libraries	2*
Air Force	1
Army	1
Navy	0
Government Libraries	6*
Law	1
Medical	2
Special Libraries (excluding public, academic, armed forces, and government)	7*
Law	3
Medical	1
Religious	1
Total Special Libraries (including public, academic, armed forces, and government)	16
Total law	7
Total medical	5
Total religious	2
Total Libraries Counted(*)	80

Libraries in Canada

Public Libraries 2,035*	
Public libraries, excluding branches	809†
Main public libraries that have branches	130
Public library branches	1,226
Academic Libraries	342*
Junior college	84
Departmental	15
Medical	0
Religious	3

University and college	258
Departmental	177
Law	16
Medical	19
Religious	35
Government Libraries	309*
Law	35
Medical	5
Special Libraries (excluding public, academic, armed forces, and government)	982*
Law	109
Medical	183
Religious	26
Total Special Libraries (including public, academic, armed forces, and government)	1,095
Total law	160
Total medical	207
Total religious	95
Total Libraries Counted(*)	3,668

Summary

Total U.S. Libraries	30,111
Total Libraries Administered by the United States	80
Total Canadian Libraries	3,668
Grand Total of Libraries Listed	33,859

Note: Numbers followed by an asterisk are added to find "Total libraries counted" for each of the three geographic areas (United States, U.S.-administered regions, and Canada). The sum of the three totals is the "Grand total of libraries listed" in *ALD*. For details on the count of libraries, see the preface to the 60th edition of *ALD—Ed.*

† Federal, state, and other statistical sources use this figure (libraries *excluding* branches) as the total for public libraries.

Highlights of NCES and IMLS Surveys

Public Libraries

The following are highlights from the publication *Public Libraries in the United States, Fiscal Year 2005,* released in November 2007 by the National Center for Education Statistics (NCES). For more information on NCES surveys, see the article "National Center for Education Statistics Library Statistics Program" in Part 1.

- There were 9,198 public libraries (administrative entities) in the 50 states and the District of Columbia in fiscal year (FY) 2005.

- A total of 1,544 public libraries (17 percent) had one or more branch library outlets, with a total of 7,503 branch outlets in FY 2005. The total number of central library outlets was 9,040. The total number of stationary outlets (central library outlets and branch library outlets) was 16,543. Eight percent of public libraries had one or more bookmobile outlets, for a total of 825 bookmobiles.

- In FY 2005, 53 percent of public libraries were part of a municipal government, 15 percent were nonprofit association libraries or agency libraries, 14 percent were separate government units known as library districts, 10 percent were part of a county/parish, 3 percent had multijurisdictional legal basis under an intergovernmental agreement, 2 percent were part of a school district, 1 percent were part of a city/county, and 1 percent reported their legal basis as "other."

- Nationwide, library visits to public libraries totaled 1.4 billion, or 4.7 library visits per capita, in FY 2005.

- In FY 2005 total nationwide circulation of public library materials was 2.1 billion, or 7.2 materials circulated per capita. Among the 50 states and the District of Columbia, the highest circulation per capita was 15.0 (Ohio), and the lowest was 2.1 (District of Columbia).

- Nationwide, circulation of children's materials was 716.4 million, or 35 percent of total circulation.

- Attendance at children's programs was 54.6 million.

- Internet terminals available for public use in public libraries nationwide numbered 185,179 terminals, or 3.2 terminals per 5,000 population, in FY 2005. The average number of Internet terminals available for public use per stationary outlet was 11.2.

- Nationwide, public libraries had 815.6 million print materials in their collections, or 2.8 volumes per capita. By state, the number of print materials per capita ranged from 1.6 (Nevada) to 5.4 (Maine).

- Public libraries nationwide had 41.5 million audio materials, or 144.9 items per 1,000 population, and 39.7 million video materials, or 138.5 items per 1,000 population, in their collections in FY 2005.

- Public libraries had a total of 137,855 paid full-time-equivalent (FTE) staff in FY 2005. Librarians accounted for 33 percent of total FTE staff; 67 percent were in other positions. More than two-thirds of the librarians (68 percent) had master's degrees from programs of library and information studies accredited by the American Library Association (ALA-MLS degrees).
- Forty-six percent of all public libraries, or 4,254 libraries, had librarians with ALA-MLS degrees.
- In FY 2005, 81 percent of public libraries' total operating revenue of about $9.7 billion came from local sources, 10 percent from state sources, less than 1 percent from federal sources, and 8 percent from other sources, such as monetary gifts and donations, interest, library fines, fees, and grants.
- Total operating expenditures for public libraries were $9.1 billion in FY 2005. Of this, 66 percent was spent for paid staff and 13 percent for the library collection.
- Nationwide, the average per capita operating expenditure for public libraries was $31.65. By state, the highest average per capita operating expenditure was $56.62 (District of Columbia) and the lowest was $13.50 (Mississippi).

State Library Agencies

The following are highlights from *State Library Agency Report for FY 2006,* released in November 2007 by the Institute of Museum and Library Services (IMLS) Library Statistics Program. For more information on IMLS surveys, see the article "Institute of Museum and Library Services Library Programs" in Part 2.

Governance

- Nearly all state library agencies (48 states and the District of Columbia) were located in the executive branch of government, as of October 1, 2006. In two states (Arizona and Tennessee), the state library agency was located in the legislative branch. Of the state library agencies located in the executive branch, almost two-thirds (32 states) were part of a larger agency.
- Among state library agencies that were part of a larger agency on October 1, 2006, five (Louisiana, New Hampshire, New Mexico, North Carolina, and Utah) were located within a state department of cultural resources.

Allied Operations

- Allied operations are those for which state libraries provide services not ordinarily considered a state library agency function. These allied services may include maintaining state archives, managing state records, conducting legislative research for the state, or operating a museum or art gallery.

Ten state library agencies maintain the state archives or manage state records.

- State library agencies in 27 states hosted or provided funding for a State Center for the Book.

- State library agencies in four states (Arizona, California, Kansas, and Oklahoma) served as the primary state legislative research organization. The state history museum or art gallery was an allied operation of the Alaska, Arizona, and Connecticut state library agencies.

Electronic Services

- Most state library agencies (46 states and the District of Columbia) planned or monitored the development of electronic networks. State library agencies in 42 states and the District of Columbia operated electronic networks.

- State library agencies in 47 states and the District of Columbia supported the development of bibliographic databases via electronic networks, and state library agencies in 44 states and the District of Columbia supported the development of full-text or data files via electronic networks.

- Thirty-two state library agencies provided funds or facilitated their own digitization or digital programs or services. Other libraries or library cooperatives received financial support or the facilitation of digitization or digital programs or services in 31 states.

- All of the state library agencies, except Nevada and Washington, facilitated or subsidized electronic access to a union catalog, a list of titles of works, usually periodicals, in physically separate library collections. Nine state libraries offered union catalog access via a Telnet gateway, and three (Montana, New York, and Pennsylvania) provided union catalog access on CD-ROMs.

- Forty-nine state library agencies reported combined expenditures of $60.2 million for statewide database licensing. Of these states, Texas had the highest expenditure ($6.5 million) among states that reported expenditures for statewide database licensing. All state library agencies with such expenditures provided statewide database licensing services to public libraries and remote users in their states. At least two-thirds of state library agencies provided statewide database licensing services to all of the other user groups.

- For 16 state library agencies, 100 percent of their statewide database licensing expenditures came from federal sources. State funds accounted for 100 percent of six agencies' statewide database licensing expenditures (Alabama, Delaware, Minnesota, Missouri, North Carolina, and Wisconsin).

Internet Access

- All state library agencies facilitated library access to the Internet in one or more of the following ways: providing Internet training or consultation to state or local library staff or state library end users; providing direct funding to libraries for Internet access; providing equipment to libraries for Internet access; providing access to directories, databases, or online catalogs via the Internet; or managing a Web site, file server, bulletin boards, or electronic mailing lists.

- Of 45 state library agencies with Internet workstations available for public use, 815 were owned by the state library agencies and 16 were placed in the library by other agencies or groups.

Services to Public Libraries

- Public libraries serve all residents of a given community, district, or region, and typically receive financial support, in whole or part, from public funds. All state library agencies provided the following types of services to public libraries: administration of Library Services and Technology Act (LSTA) grants; collection of library statistics; library planning, evaluation, and research; and review of technology plans for the e-rate discount program.

- Nearly all state library agencies (47 to 50 agencies) provided consulting services, continuing education, interlibrary loan referral services, library legislation preparation or review, and summer reading program support.

- Services to public libraries provided by 40 to 45 state library agencies included literacy program support, reference referral services, state standards or guidelines, or statewide public relations or library promotion campaigns.

- Thirteen state library agencies reported accreditation of public libraries, and 22 state library agencies reported certification of public librarians in FY 2006.

Services to Academic Libraries

- Academic libraries are integral parts of colleges, universities, or other academic institutions for postsecondary education, organized and administered to meet the needs of students, faculty, and affiliated staff. In FY 2006 more than two-thirds of state library agencies (36 to 43 agencies) provided the following services to academic libraries: administration of LSTA grants, continuing education, interlibrary loan referral services, or reference referral services.

- In FY 2006 four state library agencies (California, Illinois, Montana, and New York) administered state aid to academic libraries.

- Thirty-one state library agencies provided consulting services, 26 provided union list development, and 24 provided statewide public relations/library promotion campaigns to academic libraries.

- In FY 2006 no state library agency reported accreditation of academic libraries. The state library agencies in Indiana, Massachusetts, New Mexico, and Washington reported certification of academic librarians.

Services to School Library Media Centers

- School library media centers (LMCs) are integral parts of the educational program of elementary and secondary schools, with materials and services that meet the curricular, information, and recreational needs of students, teachers, and administrators. More than two-thirds of state library agencies (37 to 40) provided administration of LSTA grants, continuing education, or interlibrary loan referral services to LMCs in FY 2006.

- In 2006 a total of 32 agencies provided reference referral services, 30 provided consulting services, and 26 provided statewide public relations/ library promotion campaigns to LMCs.

- The state library agencies for California, Illinois, and Montana administered state aid to school LMCs in FY 2006.

- No state library agencies reported accreditation of LMCs, but three state library agencies (Indiana, Massachusetts, and Pennsylvania) reported certification of library media specialists in FY 2006.

Services to Special Libraries

- Special libraries are located in business firms, professional associations, government agencies, or other organized groups. A special library may be maintained by a parent organization to serve a specialized clientele; or an independent library may provide materials or services, or both, to the public, a segment of the public, or other libraries. Special libraries include libraries in state institutions. The scope of special library collections and services is limited to the subject interests of the host or parent institution. In FY 2006 more than two-thirds of state library agencies (34 to 41 agencies) served special libraries through administration of LSTA grants, consulting services, continuing education, interlibrary loan referral, and reference referral services.

- Twenty-six state library agencies provided library planning, evaluation, and research to special libraries in FY 2006. Twenty-five provided union list development to special libraries.

- Six state library agencies (California, Illinois, Montana, New York, Rhode Island, and Washington) administered state aid to special libraries in FY 2006.

- In FY 2006 no state library agency accredited special libraries. The state library agencies for Indiana, Massachusetts, Oklahoma, and Washington reported certification of librarians in special libraries.

Services to Library Cooperatives

- Library cooperatives are groups of autonomous libraries joined by formal or informal agreements to perform various services cooperatively, such as resource sharing or communications. They include multitype library systems and public library systems, but not multiple outlets under the same administration. Two-thirds of state library agencies (34 agencies) administered LSTA grants to library systems in FY 2006.

- At least half of state library agencies (26 to 31 agencies) provided the following services to library cooperatives in FY 2006: consulting services, continuing education, interlibrary loan referral, library legislation preparation/ review, library planning, evaluation and research, and reference referral.
- Twenty-three state library agencies administered state aid to library cooperatives in FY 2006.
- Five state library agencies reported library cooperative accreditation, and seven reported certification of librarians of library cooperatives.

Outlets and User Groups

- State library service outlets have regular hours of service when state library staff are present to serve users.
- The state library, as part of its regular operation, pays the staff and all service costs. The main or central outlet is a single-unit library where the principal collections are located and handled. Other outlets have separate quarters, a permanent basic collection of books and/or other materials, permanent paid staff, and a regular schedule of hours open to users. In FY 2006 state library agencies reported a total of 121 service outlets—47 main or central outlets, 70 other outlets (excluding bookmobiles), and 4 bookmobiles.
- Washington had 16 state library agency outlets, and Tennessee had 13 state library agency outlets in FY 2006.
- Five different user groups received library services through state library agency outlets. In FY 2006 the user groups and the number of outlets were as follows: general public (81 outlets); state government employees (75 outlets); blind and physically handicapped individuals (58 outlets); residents of state correctional institutions (33 outlets); and residents of other state institutions (22 outlets).
- In FY 2006 New Mexico had four state library agency bookmobiles available to serve the general public, state government employees, and the blind and physically handicapped.

Public Service Hours

- Every state library agency except Hawaii offered public service hours in FY 2006. The number of hours at the main outlet that served the general public or state employees ranged from 60 hours a week in Tennessee to 32 hours a week in California.
- Six state library agencies (Alabama, Minnesota, Nebraska, New York, Rhode Island, and Wyoming) reported offering 40 public service hours per week at the main outlet for the general public or state government employees in FY 2006.
- Five state library agencies (Colorado, the District of Columbia, Hawaii, Idaho, and Maryland) did not offer public service hours at their main outlet in 2006.

Collections

- In FY 2006 the number of book and serial volumes held by state library agencies totaled 23.4 million. Two state library agencies each had book and serial volumes exceeding 2 million: New York had 2.7 million and Michigan had 2.4 million volumes. The number of books and serial volumes in the Connecticut, New Jersey, Texas, and Virginia state libraries exceeded 1 million. The state library agencies for Hawaii, Maryland, and the District of Columbia do not maintain collections.

- Thirty-seven state library agencies held a total of 27.2 million uncataloged government documents in FY 2006. The states with the largest collections of uncataloged government documents were California (4.5 million) and Illinois (3.4 million). Three other state library agencies had collections that exceeded 2 million uncataloged government documents: Arkansas (2.8 million), Oklahoma (2.7 million), and Ohio (2.4 million).

Service Transactions

- In FY 2006 there were 1.7 million visits to state library agencies. The states with the largest number of visits were Washington with 267,000 visits and Virginia with 254,000 visits.

- State library agencies reported 2.6 million circulations in FY 2006. Washington reported the most circulation transactions (765,000). Other states with circulations of 100,000 or more were Tennessee (432,000), Michigan (247,000), Virginia (232,000), Maine (203,000), and New Mexico (143,000).

- In FY 2006 state library agencies conducted 1.1 million reference transactions. Florida reported the most reference transactions (122,000).

- State library agencies provided 400,000 interlibrary loans in FY 2006. The four state libraries that provided the most interlibrary loans were Vermont (60,000), South Dakota (41,000), Maine (36,000), and New York (35,000).

- In FY 2006 state library agencies received 165,000 interlibrary loans. The five state library agencies that received the most interlibrary loans were Maine (28,000), Ohio and South Dakota (19,000 each), North Dakota (17,000), and Washington (15,000).

- Nationwide about 8,000 LSTA and state grants were awarded in FY 2006. The most grants (2,000) were awarded by the Illinois state library agency.

- State library agencies hosted 6,000 events in FY 2006. Those events were attended by 121,000 individuals.

- The three state library agencies that hosted the largest number of events in FY 2006 were New York (698), Texas (487), and California (457). The states with event attendance of more than 5,000 individuals were California (11,000), New York (7,300), Nebraska (7,000), Ohio (5,800), Illinois (5,600), and Texas (5,100).

Staff

- The total number of budgeted full-time-equivalent (FTE) positions in state library agencies was 3,500 as of October 1, 2006.
- On October 1, 2006, most of the budgeted FTE positions (52 percent) were in library services; 18 percent were in library development, 13 percent were in administration, and 16 percent were in such other services as allied operations.

Revenue

- Sources of state library agency revenue are the federal government, state government, and other sources, such as local, regional, or multijurisdictional sources, and fees for service or fines. State library agencies may receive income from private sources, such as foundations, corporations, friends of libraries groups, and individuals. In FY 2006 state library agencies reported total revenue of $1.1 billion. Most revenue was from state sources (82 percent), followed by federal sources (14 percent) and other sources (3 percent).
- In FY 2006 federal revenue to state library agencies totaled $158.8 million and state revenue was $906.5 million. California received the most federal revenue in 2006 ($16.6 million). Nine state library agencies received less that $1 million in federal revenue: Alaska, Delaware, the District of Columbia, Maine, North Dakota, South Dakota, Vermont, West Virginia, and Wyoming.
- Of the federal revenue to state library agencies in FY 2006, 97 percent consisted of LSTA funds. Thirty state library agencies directed all of the federal revenue to LSTA activities.
- Most of the $906.5 million in state revenue available in FY 2006 funded state aid to libraries. Thirty-one percent of state revenue supported state library agency operations. The remaining 6 percent of state revenue supported other activities, such as interagency transfers. Three states (Hawaii, New Hampshire, and South Dakota) and the District of Columbia targeted 100 percent of their state revenue to state library agency operations.

Expenditures

- State library agencies reported total expenditures of $1.1 billion in FY 2006, which came from state funds (82 percent), federal funds (15 percent), and funds from other sources (3 percent).
- In FY 2006 state library agencies' total expenditures averaged $3.66 per capita. The 10 agencies with total expenditures of less than $2 per capita were Arizona, California, Colorado, Indiana, Iowa, Missouri, Ohio, Oregon, Texas, and Washington.
- Revenue for operating expenditures is received from various public and private sources. Sixty-nine percent ($219.4 million) of FY 2006 operating expenditures came from state revenue.

- State library agencies' financial assistance to libraries is funded by federal, state, or other revenue sources; 89 percent of state revenue to state library agencies supported financial assistance to libraries in FY 2006.
- Total expenditures for financial assistance to libraries were $754.1 million in FY 2006. The states with the largest expenditures for financial assistance to libraries in FY 2006 were New York ($95.3 million) and Pennsylvania ($81.2 million).
- In five state library agencies (Louisiana, Maine, Michigan, New Mexico, and Virginia) 100 percent of the support for financial assistance to libraries in FY 2006 was from state revenue.
- In FY 2006 state library agencies reported capital outlay expenditures of $1.4 million. State revenue was the source of 67 percent of those capital outlay expenditures.
- Federal revenue represented 16 percent of state library agencies' capital outlay expenditures in FY 2006. Ten state library agencies had capital outlay expenditures from federal revenue: Arkansas, Florida, Idaho, Kansas, Kentucky, Mississippi, New Jersey, North Carolina, South Dakota, and Texas.
- Other expenditures are those not included in operating expenditures, financial assistance to libraries, or capital outlay. These other expenditures may include expenditures for allied operations, if the expenditures are from the state library agency budget. In FY 2006 state library agencies had $22.5 million in other expenditures.
- In FY 2006 most (61 percent) of state library agencies' other expenditures ($22.5 million) were supported by state revenue. Federal revenue supported 27 percent of state library agencies' other expenditures.
- Expenditures are categorized as total, operating expenditures, financial assistance to libraries, capital outlay, and other. Financial assistance to libraries represented the largest percentage of expenditures (69 percent). Operating expenditures accounted for 29 percent of total expenditures.
- Operating expenditures included salaries, wages, employee benefits, collection expenditures, and other operating expenditures. In FY 2006 state library agencies reported $318.4 million in operating expenditures.
- Salaries and wages accounted for 44 percent of the operating expenditures.
- Financial support to libraries included LSTA grants and all other funds distributed to libraries and library cooperatives if the funds are administered by the state library agency. In FY 2006 state library agency expenditures for financial support to libraries were $754.1 million.

Financial Assistance to Libraries

- State library agencies' total expenditures reported in FY 2006 for financial assistance to individual public libraries were $432.4 million, representing 57 percent of all expenditures for financial assistance to libraries.
- Library cooperatives serving only public libraries received $111.8 million in financial support from state library agencies in FY 2006. Fifteen per-

cent of all financial assistance to libraries was targeted to library cooperatives serving public libraries only.

- Per capita expenditures of state library agencies for financial assistance to libraries in FY 2006 were $1.44 for individual public libraries and 37 cents for library cooperatives serving only public libraries.
- In FY 2006 state library agencies' financial assistance to libraries from state sources totaled $669.8 million. Individual public libraries received $401.3 million of those state funds, representing 60 percent of state revenue for financial assistance for libraries.
- Per capita expenditures of state library agencies for financial assistance to libraries, from state sources, were $1.34 for individual public libraries and 34 cents for library cooperatives serving only public libraries.
- In FY 2006 state library agencies had expenditures of $157.3 million in LSTA funds for statewide services, grants, or LSTA administration. Most of the LSTA funds were targeted to statewide services (51 percent) or grants (46 percent).
- Library technology, connectivity, and services accounted for 55 percent of LSTA expenditures by state library agencies in FY 2006. Other activities that were targeted were services to persons having difficulty using libraries (19 percent) and services for lifelong learning (23 percent). LSTA administration accounted for less than 3 percent of all LSTA expenditures by state library agencies in FY 2006.

Library Acquisition Expenditures, 2006–2007: U.S. Public, Academic, Special, and Government Libraries

The information in these tables is taken from *American Library Directory (ALD) 2007–2008* (Information Today, Inc., 2007). The tables report acquisition expenditures by public, academic, special, and government libraries.

The total number of libraries in the United States and in regions administered by the United States listed in this 60th edition of *ALD* is 30,191, including 17,033 public libraries, 3,786 academic libraries, 7,888 special libraries, 304 armed forces libraries, and 1,180 government libraries.

Understanding the Tables

Number of libraries includes only those U.S. libraries in *ALD* that reported annual acquisition expenditures (2,379 public libraries, 900 academic libraries, 178 special libraries, 68 government libraries). Libraries that reported annual income but not expenditures are not included in the count. Academic libraries include university, college, and junior college libraries. Special academic libraries, such as law and medical libraries, that reported acquisition expenditures separately from the institution's main library are counted as independent libraries.

The amount in the *total acquisition expenditures* column for a given state is generally greater than the sum of the categories of expenditures. This is because the total acquisition expenditures amount also includes the expenditures of libraries that did not itemize by category.

Figures in *categories of expenditure* columns represent only those libraries that itemized expenditures. Libraries that reported a total acquisition expenditure amount but did not itemize are only represented in the total acquisition expenditures column.

Table 1 / Public Library Acquisition Expenditures

State	Number of Libraries	Total Acquisition Expenditures	Books	Other Print Materials	Periodicals/ Serials	Manuscripts & Archives	AV Equipment	AV Materials	Microforms	Electronic Reference	Preservation
Alabama	32	2,989,480	1,574,465	22,105	195,448	0	18,297	225,379	211,000	89,989	1,800
Alaska	12	865,880	109,145	7,500	16,588	0	0	15,079	0	11,515	0
Arizona	28	14,422,559	5,965,341	3,690,639	171,210	0	1	1,873,848	35,994	1,627,573	21,100
Arkansas	17	4,577,482	2,395,789	900	133,109	0	0	317,891	2,615	190,962	1,520
California	75	55,989,774	30,327,155	975,591	3,990,331	77,251	700	7,663,113	452,493	5,718,981	119,909
Colorado	30	15,031,933	9,338,306	50,360	804,708	0	500	1,621,888	4,381	1,191,077	3,950
Connecticut	72	12,054,596	4,412,219	573,894	803,604	1,000	17,200	757,546	120,313	863,466	15,795
Delaware	5	497,229	142,294	0	2,300	0	25,600	26,263	0	1,500	0
District of Columbia	0	0	0	0	0	0	1,000	0	0	0	0
Florida	42	29,584,215	10,613,903	494,781	2,834,164	1,500	42,100	4,823,213	93,804	1,741,046	2,000
Georgia	18	14,022,316	2,529,157	116,301	142,514	0	3,142	543,310	28,864	432,745	3,604
Hawaii	1	5,517,009	0	3,278,130	953,192	0	0	0	134,607	1,151,080	0
Idaho	17	752,061	167,833	515	19,241	0	3,800	24,970	0	589	1,500
Illinois	155	48,939,774	14,373,863	120,607	1,147,599	13,000	142,994	3,628,849	122,178	4,305,789	8,566
Indiana	156	30,578,149	10,991,759	622	1,376,964	0	299,172	3,280,789	199,281	1,353,918	69,905
Iowa	83	3,861,638	2,230,349	103,749	300,925	1,300	17,678	411,284	11,404	154,203	1,369
Kansas	45	9,121,064	2,802,385	21,166	872,670	15	26,379	829,176	5,132	682,285	300
Kentucky	26	7,043,213	1,535,339	26,629	114,076	0	3,231	814,828	11,806	214,333	1,200
Louisiana	13	5,563,202	2,847,874	4,000	419,052	3,000	151,405	755,103	38,200	240,706	0
Maine	51	1,856,094	982,134	1,350	178,240	2,100	6,350	123,599	21,200	37,731	51,000
Maryland	7	11,431,203	2,766,982	47,425	160,883	0	0	919,958	0	684,133	0
Massachusetts	130	13,861,365	5,388,870	87,546	642,075	500	30,041	1,459,572	83,982	591,123	7,323
Michigan	107	41,516,429	9,526,169	8,760	920,130	0	76,678	2,715,934	31,618	1,356,452	14,337
Minnesota	36	15,977,711	8,485,926	31,503	222,815	0	23,739	2,253,628	6,379	1,091,899	1,750

Categories of Expenditure (in U.S. dollars)

State											
Mississippi	7	2,170,018	516,260	0	1,142,998	0	1,795	145,392	9,957	69,101	2,596
Missouri	66	24,117,610	8,584,373	42,936	673,393	160	15,020	1,905,926	231,715	3,247,809	42,558
Montana	17	1,268,946	607,812	2,253	101,648	6,700	5,316	114,183	5,792	72,658	3,231
Nebraska	32	2,109,319	521,634	1,350	69,207	0	500	58,599	14,259	422,156	2,500
Nevada	4	1,423,042	100,000	0	9,000	0	0	13,000	0	18,000	0
New Hampshire	80	3,469,271	1,339,025	3,885	182,036	0	2,500	310,397	19,425	119,412	12,450
New Jersey	95	23,419,831	12,417,468	62,851	1,374,382	0	37,300	2,905,513	145,632	1,548,076	4,106
New Mexico	12	2,550,389	1,340,724	427	44,584	0	9,225	222,857	9,285	82,404	0
New York	157	32,711,228	13,891,075	317,071	4,084,308	5,500	219,824	2,836,322	269,370	1,809,661	71,453
North Carolina	30	11,072,075	6,553,075	85,696	213,636	0	24,840	617,319	22,952	457,490	413
North Dakota	15	1,470,154	632,133	59,000	70,870	0	32,000	98,881	3,600	91,637	1,000
Ohio	88	64,244,006	28,108,738	706,269	4,875,828	4,991	127,392	10,856,982	594,603	7,516,418	388,846
Oklahoma	11	9,172,239	4,944,451	4,968	866,531	0	0	1,172,585	4,800	734,257	0
Oregon	55	13,066,596	6,335,654	22,629	1,092,092	0	0	2,181,553	18,324	834,246	0
Pennsylvania	150	24,452,632	4,714,761	285,177	552,890	0	85,643	915,038	339,147	801,970	311,035
Rhode Island	13	2,359,452	1,319,546	16,268	146,584	0	1,846	255,368	16,760	311,451	7,974
South Carolina	20	13,254,955	8,053,611	23,400	459,189	6,000	195,091	1,821,701	2,592	1,489,294	13,862
South Dakota	18	2,175,277	1,441,687	108,728	152,264	530	395	278,406	13,980	161,241	0
Tennessee	25	6,281,928	3,380,165	269,170	196,195	0	9,000	232,247	0	181,591	723
Texas	98	21,751,254	8,252,768	30,444	1,010,334	0	11,112	1,678,232	81,954	730,267	5,507
Utah	13	3,134,123	1,773,072	1,400	117,363	245,000	19,900	479,869	10,650	114,385	72,000
Vermont	42	852,694	497,060	0	32,643	120	2,500	82,626	200	38,097	1,000
Virginia	33	17,023,028	5,393,057	58,007	675,000	43,000	0	1,187,515	127,873	801,044	737,072
Washington	28	35,102,568	5,206,093	65,442	298,526	0	54,265	1,590,588	23,124	714,024	15,084
West Virginia	14	2,741,296	1,499,539	83,175	84,195	0	5,000	186,986	11,310	627,361	7,412
Wisconsin	78	10,318,888	6,031,776	43,984	353,654	0	9,856	1,609,158	26,733	736,153	11,163
Wyoming	19	1,964,325	323,812	4,694	41,778	0	6,000	140,358	55	37,865	0
U.S. Virgin Islands	1	8,000	7,000	0	1,000	0	0	0	0	0	0
Totals	2,379	679,739,520	263,293,626	11,963,297	35,343,896	411,667	1,766,327	68,982,821	3,619,343	47,501,163	2,038,913
Estimated % of Acquisition Expenditures			38.73	1.76	5.2	0.06	0.26	10.15	0.53	6.99	0.3

Table 2 / Academic Library Acquisition Expenditures

State	Number of Libraries	Total Acquisition Expenditures	Books	Other Print Materials	Periodicals/ Serials	Manuscripts & Archives	AV Equipment	AV Materials	Microforms	Electronic Reference	Preservation
						Categories of Expenditure (in U.S. dollars)					
Alabama	18	15,357,939	15,357,939	15,357,939	15,357,939	15,357,939	15,357,939	15,357,939	15,357,939	15,357,939	15,357,939
Alaska	2	19,500	4,000	0	1,800	0	0	250	0	0	0
Arizona	11	4,264,604	827,804	67,581	752,060	17,979	400	106,597	53,952	1,284,638	16,099
Arkansas	8	11,530,824	1,954,258	363,500	6,338,165	0	130,600	110,508	214,399	2,216,844	128,657
California	68	58,885,629	12,832,702	319,206	20,605,898	2,000	90,989	591,402	1,090,118	12,241,875	931,525
Colorado	14	19,058,185	2,737,839	10,654	9,928,858	100,000	0	89,981	14,480	1,957,549	87,936
Connecticut	13	40,017,282	1,512,998	37,772	3,879,504	0	8,202	96,382	112,239	1,239,698	104,346
Delaware	3	8,335,891	30,000	0	8,000	0	0	0	0	0	0
District of Columbia	7	18,953,142	2,082,533	53,135	5,716,524	5,000	26,300	6,417	85,969	1,059,090	133,002
Florida	32	36,726,768	8,702,748	853,174	15,519,598	0	28,200	472,291	439,079	9,712,390	366,943
Georgia	22	17,842,509	1,593,650	2,000	5,084,778	0	10,872	112,924	1,770,788	809,993	105,895
Hawaii	4	775,133	157,285	500	199,325	0	3,000	21,836	40,614	107,026	19,000
Idaho	3	4,332,643	413,976	0	2,289,626	0	0	5,260	0	422,409	22,913
Illinois	41	32,716,523	3,189,496	25,991	6,798,988	3,000	198,754	317,808	207,186	2,537,445	153,252
Indiana	22	21,762,503	4,203,607	0	10,674,502	7,460	65,050	198,060	120,407	3,195,958	122,917
Iowa	22	26,485,165	3,409,049	250,035	10,909,236	0	36,139	100,190	105,709	1,892,441	132,239
Kansas	23	12,154,370	2,613,509	2,000	6,306,600	22,000	16,991	61,507	37,059	2,870,645	56,416
Kentucky	17	29,629,514	3,932,989	38,778	21,672,574	21,590	3,713	97,100	259,692	960,666	324,641
Louisiana	9	3,612,175	860,795	35,173	1,201,217	4,781	3,720	1,228	38,521	766,795	30,953
Maine	5	7,856,890	1,452,140	0	5,652,761	0	0	32,616	93,165	227,000	108,708
Maryland	13	10,017,460	1,327,065	1,400	2,986,631	9,884	15,000	115,794	85,282	1,401,742	67,730
Massachusetts	33	35,872,324	4,543,333	43,502	14,868,959	0	232,151	100,008	155,861	7,591,276	214,448
Michigan	33	22,612,025	2,727,375	137,537	4,767,581	26,000	32,000	114,229	224,868	4,833,620	126,918
Minnesota	17	12,022,692	2,139,256	0	4,048,690	0	49,179	203,977	80,503	2,253,418	105,198

State	#										
Mississippi	8	3,910,029	440,867	0	1,480,001	0	55,000	51,853	117,100	1,334,212	47,318
Missouri	21	29,023,938	1,356,700	908,719	2,373,478	2,678	5,181	112,201	189,943	2,520,897	227,853
Montana	6	643,817	284,234	0	228,583	0	10,000	6,000	3,000	102,000	10,000
Nebraska	8	11,024,816	528,358	101,451	1,266,527	0	51,400	96,220	91,505	383,100	51,713
Nevada	2	415,295	136,754	0	11,877	0	0	15,908	217	49,926	613
New Hampshire	6	7,720,276	1,173,680	0	4,099,060	0	740	1,584	25,075	1,173,916	74,484
New Jersey	17	11,848,471	1,532,761	114,617	3,804,248	7,000	22,576	125,395	73,514	1,604,181	25,135
New Mexico	8	6,525,763	77,280	0	1,700	0	20,000	24,000	0	5,000	0
New York	57	157,457,548	10,397,054	292,003	19,685,045	34,940	304,842	475,244	436,404	13,876,692	433,379
North Carolina	32	30,838,097	7,405,418	226,320	17,232,095	4,025	26,109	427,455	526,266	3,099,368	363,095
North Dakota	4	2,766,611	446,664	10,000	1,546,634	0	1,080	15,129	0	493,296	31,976
Ohio	34	30,894,732	6,516,616	95,771	8,793,931	2,461	89,293	252,735	304,959	4,916,502	330,596
Oklahoma	9	6,983,104	531,857	56,186	2,109,267	4,100	500	75,695	13,818	649,434	25,000
Oregon	22	29,788,071	1,552,071	27,980	3,666,989	0	54,282	84,012	2,264	892,793	110,055
Pennsylvania	37	34,871,198	5,394,059	177,216	10,401,308	34,000	80,907	311,537	495,773	3,994,246	330,884
Rhode Island	7	3,638,450	1,021,061	2,340	1,527,065	7,000	25,000	83,211	21,153	839,315	26,203
South Carolina	15	6,486,442	2,015,626	0	2,409,518	0	3,480	106,819	110,221	976,352	76,376
South Dakota	6	3,651,612	301,114	0	1,158,592	0	2,792	15,170	9,885	620,250	25,951
Tennessee	18	9,811,009	1,307,424	300	1,945,862	0	4,000	110,422	104,693	2,507,677	40,852
Texas	43	54,651,710	9,742,429	37,340	18,455,305	8,050	199,871	629,078	451,862	7,982,738	365,495
Utah	5	5,201,669	1,261,480	0	3,040,758	0	1,000	90,332	4,247	735,327	2,414
Vermont	7	1,785,773	414,601	500	638,496	3,000	7,000	34,444	13,335	350,760	16,666
Virginia	28	30,622,395	7,144,582	524,320	12,001,064	2,000	97,108	300,829	250,219	5,624,668	130,094
Washington	22	8,539,669	1,950,799	6,000	3,283,802	14,360	80,200	172,395	66,283	1,085,446	67,323
West Virginia	14	3,155,001	409,898	123,755	905,965	14,336	34,355	56,774	80,000	953,160	6,108
Wisconsin	17	10,423,613	2,607,828	3,127	6,294,548	918	2,878	200,767	171,392	969,927	103,841
Wyoming	2	3,133,203	248,823	0	2,703,875	0	0	0	0	0	0
U.S. Virgin Islands	5	4,222,100	212,000	1,000	278,800	5,000	23,300	18,500	0	176,000	2,500
Total	900	960,876,102	145,018,384	20,308,822	306,914,207	15,721,501	17,512,093	22,208,013	24,150,958	132,857,640	21,643,599
Estimated % of Acquisition Expenditures		15.09		2.11	31.94	1.64	1.82	2.31	2.51	13.83	2.25

Table 3 / Special Library Acquisition Expenditures

State	Number of Libraries	Total Acquisition Expenditures	Books	Other Print Materials	Periodicals/ Serials	Manuscripts & Archives	AV Equipment	AV Materials	Microforms	Electronic Reference	Preservation
Alabama	1	1,375	250	0	525	0	0	0	0	500	100
Alaska	0	0	0	0	0	0	0	0	0	0	0
Arizona	5	17,560	1,260	0	0	0	0	0	0	0	0
Arkansas	0	0	0	0	0	0	0	0	0	0	0
California	15	461,548	103,698	2,000	206,959	0	2,500	600	50	84,741	8,000
Colorado	2	25,270	7,000	0	1,000	0	0	2,000	0	0	0
Connecticut	0	0	0	0	0	0	0	0	0	0	0
Delaware	0	0	0	0	0	0	0	0	0	0	0
District of Columbia	4	902,078	139,130	0	57,871	0	0	261	25,000	13,000	504,877
Florida	6	102,900	50,350	1,000	36,800	0	0	0	0	7,500	3,300
Georgia	0	0	0	0	0	0	0	0	0	0	0
Hawaii	0	0	0	0	0	0	0	0	0	0	0
Idaho	0	0	0	0	0	0	0	0	0	0	0
Illinois	19	2,906,603	199,630	20,862	215,671	5,400	6,300	8,000	5,150	134,250	19,100
Indiana	3	49,225	37,725	0	120	500	0	0	3,780	0	1,500
Iowa	3	239,200	500	0	0	0	0	0	0	0	1,000
Kansas	3	43,849	4,162	4,000	2,587	0	0	0	0	0	100
Kentucky	1	17,500	11,000	0	6,500	0	0	0	0	0	0
Louisiana	1	25,000	5,000	1,000	7,000	5,000	2,000	500	2,000	500	2,000
Maine	1	1,797	1,673	0	0	0	0	0	0	0	124
Maryland	5	181,800	34,000	1,000	130,900	50	1,000	0	0	13,000	350
Massachusetts	8	1,696,380	383,592	50	106,600	0	0	7,000	0	348,400	27,100
Michigan	0	0	0	0	0	0	0	0	0	0	0
Minnesota	4	61,050	21,350	5,000	11,500	0	200	1,000	0	16,000	3,000

State											
Mississippi	0	0	0	0	0	0	0	0	0	0	0
Missouri	3	305,149	36,943	0	61,676	0	10,278	0	0	9,408	186,594
Montana	2	41,271	10,800	3,000	3,500	0	0	0	21,971	500	0
Nebraska	2	2,800	650	300	1,700	0	0	0	0	0	0
Nevada	1	1,000	0	0	0	0	0	0	0	0	0
New Hampshire	2	49,825	15,000	2,000	3,000	15,000	0	0	0	0	9,000
New Jersey	5	65,600	35,500	0	13,400	0	0	6,000	0	2,500	7,200
New Mexico	0	0	0	0	0	0	0	0	0	0	0
New York	26	601,440	155,312	3,050	273,487	23,000	5,400	11,462	1,000	70,125	20,820
North Carolina	0	0	0	0	0	0	0	0	0	0	0
North Dakota	1	3,500	0	0	1,500	2,000	0	0	0	0	0
Ohio	12	1,391,500	145,680	550	633,944	1,200	150	1,181	1,619	583,925	10,651
Oklahoma	4	63,767	7,300	400	28,100	2,500	15,000	0	0	8,500	1,317
Oregon	2	2,300	200	100	1,050	0	0	0	50	0	0
Pennsylvania	12	418,529	54,094	74,689	83,932	30,721	0	11,059	10,000	120,391	24,143
Rhode Island	1	50,895	32,695	0	8,000	0	0	0	0	0	10,200
South Carolina	1	29,600	14,000	0	5,000	0	0	6,000	3,000	0	0
South Dakota	0	0	0	0	0	0	0	0	0	0	0
Tennessee	3	36,500	15,000	2,500	9,000	0	500	3,000	0	6,500	0
Texas	9	1,086,839	45,324	45,992	27,674	500	167	622	0	115,000	500
Utah	1	75,000	5,000	5,000	10,000	0	5,000	0	0	50,000	0
Vermont	0	0	0	0	0	0	0	0	0	0	0
Virginia	5	609,602	139,395	13,100	44,000	42,492	43,000	15,960	4,200	27,500	106,000
Washington	1	2,000	1,000	0	0	0	0	0	0	0	0
West Virginia	2	236,000	9,000	0	125,000	0	0	500	0	101,500	0
Wisconsin	2	60,200	26,200	300	13,000	0	0	0	0	18,000	2,500
Wyoming	0	0	0	0	0	0	0	0	0	0	0
Total	178	11,866,452	1,749,413	185,893	2,130,996	128,363	91,495	75,145	77,820	1,731,740	949,476
Estimated % of Acquisition Expenditures			14.74	1.57	17.96	1.08	0.77	0.63	0.66	14.59	8

Table 4 / Government Library Acquisition Expenditures

State	Number of Libraries	Total Acquisition Expenditures	Books	Other Print Materials	Periodicals/ Serials	Manuscripts & Archives	AV Equipment	AV Materials	Microforms	Electronic Reference	Preservation
Alabama	0	0	0	0	0	0	0	0	0	0	0
Alaska	0	0	0	0	0	0	0	0	0	0	0
Arizona	1	228,291	0	0	0	0	0	0	0	14,049	0
Arkansas	0	0	0	0	0	0	0	0	0	0	0
California	12	2,514,335	742,550	23,400	816,138	0	9,300	6,551	30,831	321,770	9,236
Colorado	0	0	0	0	0	0	0	0	0	0	0
Connecticut	0	0	0	0	0	0	0	0	0	0	0
Delaware	0	0	0	0	0	0	0	0	0	0	0
District of Columbia	2	1,755,881	7,200	0	17,779	0	0	0	0	44,118	0
Florida	2	154,545	45,750	0	89,170	0	0	1,625	0	18,000	0
Georgia	0	0	0	0	0	0	0	0	0	0	0
Hawaii	0	0	0	0	0	0	0	0	0	0	0
Idaho	0	0	0	0	0	0	0	0	0	0	0
Illinois	1	22,500	0	0	0	0	0	0	0	0	0
Indiana	0	0	0	0	0	0	0	0	0	0	0
Iowa	0	0	0	0	0	0	0	0	0	0	0
Kansas	2	804,633	302,025	0	360,565	0	0	0	0	136,611	5,432
Kentucky	0	0	0	0	0	0	0	0	0	0	0
Louisiana	3	4,452,018	14,313	0	105,100	0	0	500	0	0	0
Maine	1	257,079	0	0	0	0	0	0	0	0	0
Maryland	4	9,556,755	523,000	19,800	5,147,850	0	0	7,700	0	2,416,225	31,050
Massachusetts	5	502,768	195,036	0	0	0	0	0	0	68,332	7,500
Michigan	2	75,509	39,909	10,000	12,000	0	500	6,100	0	7,000	0
Minnesota	2	137,500	21,000	0	61,500	0	0	0	0	55,000	0

Categories of Expenditure (in U.S. dollars)

State											
Mississippi	1	2,500	0	0	0	0	0	0	0	0	0
Missouri	0	0	0	0	0	0	0	0	0	0	0
Montana	1	260,000	0	0	0	0	0	0	0	0	0
Nebraska	0	0	0	0	0	0	0	0	0	0	0
Nevada	2	728,880	485,158	0	70,619	0	1,479	0	5,658	165,966	0
New Hampshire	1	70,000	0	0	0	0	0	0	0	0	0
New Jersey	0	0	0	0	0	0	0	0	0	0	0
New Mexico	0	0	0	0	0	0	0	0	0	0	0
New York	4	1,389,180	5,000	0	5,000	0	0	0	0	12,000	5,300
North Carolina	1	419,400	368,757	0	16,000	0	0	0	8,643	26,000	0
North Dakota	1	40,000	5,000	0	30,000	0	0	0	0	5,000	0
Ohio	2	220,596	134,836	0	17,600	0	7,500	1,000	0	42,460	0
Oklahoma	0	0	0	0	0	0	0	0	0	0	0
Oregon	2	60,800	14,000	0	35,000	0	1,000	5,000	0	0	0
Pennsylvania	8	1,236,596	712,100	0	500	0	0	0	0	120,733	6,000
Rhode Island	1	44,298	9,963	0	31,746	0	0	1,653	0	936	0
South Carolina	0	0	0	0	0	0	0	0	0	0	0
South Dakota	0	0	0	0	0	0	0	0	0	0	0
Tennessee	1	125,000	0	0	0	0	0	0	0	0	0
Texas	2	207,616	156,313	0	33,434	0	0	14,692	0	3,177	0
Utah	0	0	0	0	0	0	0	0	0	0	0
Vermont	0	0	0	0	0	0	0	0	0	0	0
Virginia	2	80,917	31,044	0	40,434	0	0	730	0	6,636	0
Washington	0	0	0	0	0	0	0	0	0	0	109
West Virginia	0	0	0	0	0	0	0	0	0	0	0
Wisconsin	2	124,000	34,000	0	67,000	0	0	0	0	22,000	1,000
Wyoming	0	0	0	0	0	0	0	0	0	0	0
Total	68	25,471,597	3,846,954	53,200	6,957,435	0	19,779	45,551	45,132	3,486,013	65,627
Estimated % of Acquisition Expenditures			15.10	0.21	27.31	0.00	0.08	0.18	0.18	13.69	0.26

Public Library State Rankings, 2005

State	Library Visits per Capita*	Reference Transactions per Capita	Circulation Transactions per Capita	Interlibrary Loans per 1,000 Population	Terminals per Outlet
Alabama	47	37	48	33	12
Alaska	22	48	35	25	46
Arizona	39	26	25	40	3
Arkansas	49	39	45	45	41
California	34	27	39	24	11
Colorado	10	9	6	21	20
Connecticut	7	8	15	14	26
Delaware	26	45	28	9	27
District of Columbia***	44	1	51	50	34
Florida	37	6	37	37	1
Georgia	41	18	44	34	4
Hawaii	33	40	41	51	29
Idaho	13	47	19	29	42
Illinois	16	4	17	6	8
Indiana	4	19	4	35	9
Iowa	17	46	12	23	47
Kansas	6	11	7	10	37
Kentucky	40	41	36	39	14
Louisiana	50	30	49	32	36
Maine	18	36	23	13	49
Maryland	24	7	11	30	2
Massachusetts	15	33	20	4	35
Michigan	28	31	30	8	18
Minnesota	23	24	10	12	28
Mississippi	51	50	50	47	39
Missouri	25	15	16	28	25
Montana	35	51	34	18	38
Nebraska	5	32	9	31	43
Nevada	36	43	33	38	23
New Hampshire	27	44	21	16	51
New Jersey	21	20	32	15	19
New Mexico	32	28	31	42	30
New York	19	5	22	7	21
North Carolina	38	10	38	49	10
North Dakota	29	38	24	22	48
Ohio	1	3	1	5	6
Oklahoma	31	35	27	36	31
Oregon	11	23	2	2	32
Pennsylvania	42	42	40	11	24
Rhode Island	14	22	29	3	16
South Carolina	43	12	42	46	7
South Dakota	9	25	13	19	45
Tennessee	48	34	47	48	22
Texas	46	13	43	43	5
Utah	3	2	3	44	17

State	Library Visits per Capita*	Reference Transactions per Capita	Circulation Transactions per Capita	Interlibrary Loans per 1,000 Population	Terminals per Outlet
Vermont	20	29	26	17	50
Virginia	30	17	18	41	13
Washington	2	16	5	27	15
West Virginia	45	49	46	26	44
Wisconsin	12	21	8	1	33
Wyoming	8	14	14	20	40

	Terminals per 5,000 Population**	Book and Serial Volumes per Capita	Audio Materials per 1,000 Population	Video Materials per 1,000 Population	Current Serials Subscriptions per 1,000 Population
Alabama	14	42	42	41	49
Alaska	11	21	20	5	5
Arizona	45	49	40	37	50
Arkansas	46	38	48	47	44
California	50	40	45	38	45
Colorado	32	33	16	13	26
Connecticut	20	10	12	6	7
Delaware	47	39	33	31	23
District of Columbia***	49	14	32	51	18
Florida	44	48	35	28	36
Georgia	28	50	51	50	51
Hawaii	48	34	21	46	42
Idaho	24	23	27	26	34
Illinois	9	18	5	8	17
Indiana	6	9	3	3	11
Iowa	7	13	10	10	2
Kansas	4	4	11	2	10
Kentucky	37	44	41	42	39
Louisiana	27	36	49	34	25
Maine	5	1	24	16	14
Maryland	39	31	14	30	29
Massachusetts	23	3	19	14	15
Michigan	16	22	22	25	20
Minnesota	21	24	25	24	28
Mississippi	42	45	50	45	47
Missouri	19	19	23	27	16
Montana	12	25	37	32	31
Nebraska	3	6	9	15	8
Nevada	51	51	36	29	43
New Hampshire	22	8	15	11	1
New Jersey	30	17	28	22	21
New Mexico	17	26	34	39	33
New York	29	16	4	20	4
North Carolina	35	46	46	49	41
North Dakota	15	11	29	23	19
Ohio	10	12	1	1	12

	Terminals per 5,000 Population**	Book and Serial Volumes per Capita	Audio Materials per 1,000 Population	Video Materials per 1,000 Population	Current Serials Subscriptions per 1,000 Population
Oklahoma	25	37	39	44	38
Oregon	33	28	7	17	27
Pennsylvania	36	35	17	33	32
Rhode Island	13	15	31	19	24
South Carolina	31	43	44	43	37
South Dakota	1	2	13	7	9
Tennessee	43	47	47	48	48
Texas	34	41	43	40	46
Utah	38	30	26	18	30
Vermont	2	7	8	12	3
Virginia	40	32	30	36	35
Washington	26	27	18	21	22
West Virginia	41	29	38	35	40
Wisconsin	18	20	6	4	6
Wyoming	8	5	2	9	13

	Paid FTE Staff per 25,000 Population	Paid FTE Librarians per 25,000 Population	ALA-MLS Librarians per 25,000 Population	Other Paid FTE Staff per 25,000 Population	Total Operating Income per Capita
Alabama	41	33	44	46	47
Alaska	30	30	25	26	16
Arizona	43	45	26	36	39
Arkansas	47	44	51	41	46
California	49	48	24	44	29
Colorado	14	27	15	9	9
Connecticut	5	7	2	10	8
Delaware	39	39	42	37	27
District of Columbia***	8	6	1	14	2
Florida	36	43	21	29	30
Georgia	48	51	34	40	44
Hawaii	33	36	11	25	40
Idaho	25	35	46	17	37
Illinois	7	14	9	5	4
Indiana	2	11	8	2	5
Iowa	19	4	29	39	28
Kansas	4	5	20	7	12
Kentucky	32	15	43	43	35
Louisiana	27	26	38	28	31
Maine	10	8	14	22	32
Maryland	17	18	18	16	13
Massachusetts	11	9	6	21	18
Michigan	24	23	12	23	15
Minnesota	28	32	23	24	21
Mississippi	34	28	50	32	51
Missouri	13	34	31	6	17

	Paid FTE Staff per 25,000 Population	Paid FTE Librarians per 25,000 Population	ALA-MLS Librarians per 25,000 Population	Other Paid FTE Staff per 25,000 Population	Total Operating Income per Capita
Montana	42	21	49	51	42
Nebraska	18	10	33	27	26
Nevada	44	49	41	35	22
New Hampshire	15	1	10	38	20
New Jersey	12	29	7	8	6
New Mexico	31	25	30	31	33
New York	6	17	4	4	3
North Carolina	46	50	32	33	43
North Dakota	40	22	45	49	45
Ohio	1	12	5	1	1
Oklahoma	35	20	40	42	36
Oregon	23	31	16	13	10
Pennsylvania	38	41	28	34	38
Rhode Island	9	16	3	12	14
South Carolina	37	42	22	30	41
South Dakota	16	13	36	18	25
Tennessee	50	47	48	45	49
Texas	51	46	35	47	48
Utah	29	40	39	19	23
Vermont	22	3	27	48	34
Virginia	26	37	19	15	24
Washington	20	38	13	11	7
West Virginia	45	24	47	50	50
Wisconsin	21	19	17	20	19
Wyoming	3	2	37	3	11

	State Income per Capita	Local Income per Capita	Other Income per Capita	Operating Expenditures per Capita	Collection Expenditures per Capita
Alabama	27	46	37	46	47
Alaska	24	13	33	15	29
Arizona	44	31	51	39	33
Arkansas	26	43	48	49	48
California	28	27	16	30	43
Colorado	47	7	20	9	6
Connecticut	36	10	5	8	11
Delaware	7	33	17	27	25
District of Columbia***	51	1	26	1	5
Florida	17	25	46	33	31
Georgia	9	47	49	42	45
Hawaii	2	51	31	37	16
Idaho	33	34	22	38	41
Illinois	12	2	10	4	2
Indiana	8	5	13	5	3
Iowa	30	24	25	26	22
Kansas	32	11	8	13	10

	State Income per Capita	Local Income per Capita	Other Income per Capita	Operating Expenditures per Capita	Collection Expenditures per Capita
Kentucky	20	29	38	41	37
Louisiana	19	28	32	32	42
Maine	42	36	4	28	35
Maryland	5	18	7	14	9
Massachusetts	21	17	14	16	14
Michigan	22	12	24	18	27
Minnesota	18	20	18	20	30
Mississippi	10	49	43	51	51
Missouri	29	14	12	21	8
Montana	37	39	27	44	40
Nebraska	38	22	39	24	17
Nevada	25	35	2	31	19
New Hampshire	49	15	23	19	21
New Jersey	23	4	21	6	12
New Mexico	13	30	47	34	18
New York	11	3	1	3	13
North Carolina	16	42	41	43	44
North Dakota	34	45	15	45	39
Ohio	1	40	9	2	1
Oklahoma	35	32	30	36	34
Oregon	41	8	19	10	20
Pennsylvania	4	44	11	35	38
Rhode Island	3	26	6	12	23
South Carolina	14	38	45	40	32
South Dakota	46	19	42	25	15
Tennessee	45	48	40	48	50
Texas	43	41	50	47	46
Utah	39	21	34	23	7
Vermont	48	37	3	29	36
Virginia	15	23	36	22	28
Washington	40	6	35	7	4
West Virginia	6	50	44	50	49
Wisconsin	31	16	28	17	24
Wyoming	50	9	29	11	26

	Staff Expenditures per Capita	Salary and Wages Expenditures per Capita	Average Rank	Rank of Ranks
Alabama	46	45	39.55	46
Alaska	15	17	23.23	25
Arizona	38	39	37.18	43
Arkansas	49	49	44.68	50
California	27	30	34.00	38
Colorado	12	12	16.95	11
Connecticut	5	3	10.68	5
Delaware	31	32	30.18	29
District of Columbia***	1	1	20.95	19

	Staff Expenditures per Capita	Salary and Wages Expenditures per Capita	Average Rank	Rank of Ranks
Florida	34	33	31.23	32
Georgia	41	43	39.27	45
Hawaii	39	27	33.32	35
Idaho	33	34	30.86	31
Illinois	6	5	8.55	3
Indiana	8	7	8.18	2
Iowa	24	25	21.91	23
Kansas	16	13	11.50	6
Kentucky	42	41	35.86	41
Louisiana	35	35	33.68	36
Maine	28	23	21.86	22
Maryland	13	14	17.23	14
Massachusetts	14	10	16.00	9
Michigan	20	21	20.95	19
Minnesota	19	19	22.32	24
Mississippi	51	51	43.95	49
Missouri	23	24	20.23	17
Montana	44	46	36.14	42
Nebraska	26	28	21.32	21
Nevada	30	31	33.95	37
New Hampshire	18	15	20.91	18
New Jersey	4	6	16.50	10
New Mexico	32	38	30.64	30
New York	3	4	9.95	4
North Carolina	43	42	38.05	44
North Dakota	47	44	33.09	34
Ohio	2	2	5.86	1
Oklahoma	36	36	34.32	39
Oregon	11	16	18.18	15
Pennsylvania	37	37	31.68	33
Rhode Island	10	8	14.91	7
South Carolina	40	40	34.95	40
South Dakota	22	22	20.09	16
Tennessee	48	48	45.36	51
Texas	45	47	40.91	47
Utah	25	29	24.50	27
Vermont	29	26	23.45	26
Virginia	21	20	26.27	28
Washington	9	9	17.18	13
West Virginia	50	50	41.27	48
Wisconsin	17	18	17.09	12
Wyoming	7	11	15.09	8

FTE = Full-time equivalent
*   Per capita is based on the unduplicated population of legal service areas.
** Average number of public-use terminals per 5,000 population.
***The District of Columbia, while not a state, is included in the state rankings. Special care should be using in comparing its data to state data.

Source: Compiled by Julia C. Miller from *Public Libraries in the United States: Fiscal Year 2005*, National Center for Education Statistics (2007).

Library Buildings 2007: Going, Going, Green

Bette-Lee Fox

Managing Editor, *Library Journal*

The year in architecture offered grand façades, creative collaborations, and calamities overcome and viewed as opportunities. The 168 public building projects and 21 academic facilities completed between July 1, 2006, and June 30, 2007, are truly allowing us to catch sight of the future.

One caveat before we plunge into the wealth of fascinating detail. For the third year, *Library Journal* has employed an online data collection tool. As wonderful as technology is, when it malfunctions, all heck breaks loose. Our apologies to any library whose project was submitted electronically but not reported here. We might just revert to paper forms in the future.

Sustaining a Good Thing

This year we are acknowledging "green" spaces. Many libraries reported here achieved Leadership in Energy and Environmental Design (LEED) certification—among them the William Wise Law Library at the University of Colorado–Boulder School of Law; the MacArthur Park Branch of Long Beach (California) Public Library; Broward County (Florida) South Regional/Broward Community College Library; the Harbor City-Harbor Gateway Branch of Los Angeles Public Library; and Portsmouth (New Hampshire) Public Library. Others incorporated sustainable design principles into their projects. Daylighting ("controlled admission of natural light through windows to reduce or eliminate electric lighting"), air quality upgrades, renewable resources, water reuse principles, low-voltage lighting fixtures, energy efficiency, and native plants are just a few of the checklist items for an eco-friendly facility.

The libraries sharing space are exhibiting their own brand of conservation, as costs and planning fall on multiple shoulders. Two branches of the Arlington County (Virginia) Public Library are cooperative community projects, one neighboring with Arlington's well-known Signature Theatre. The Cañada College Library and Resource Center in San Mateo, California, links to a community amphitheater. And speaking of theaters, the Kansas City (Missouri) Central Library's film vault was recast into a state-of-the-art screening room through a generous donation from the Stanley H. Durwood Foundation.

By the Numbers

The projects do seem to be getting larger and larger. The San Mateo Public Library Main library stands tall at $64.8 million, with plenty of parking below ground. The main and system headquarters of the Allen County Public Library in Fort Wayne, Indiana, is an impressive addition/remodel that totes up to $66.6

Adapted from *Library Journal*, December 2007

million. At more than $1.1 billion, the total outlay for all projects is the second highest *Library Journal* has ever recorded.

Fewer academic projects were submitted this year; maybe it was that techno glitch again. Still, our 21 projects feature some handsome support to our educational infrastructure. Some highlights are the Belk Library and Information Commons at Appalachian State University in Boone, North Carolina; the Beatley Library at Simmons College in Boston; and the Hill Library at North Carolina State University, Raleigh.

For libraries moving forward with building projects, green seems to be the color of choice with regard to both funding and design decision making. We are not abandoning our built libraries with the advent of the Internet but trying to make them more long-lasting, more environmentally sound, more responsible as community centers and civic innovators. Everyone else will be green with envy.

Table 1 / New Academic Library Buildings, 2007

Name of Institution	Project Cost	Gross Area (Sq. Ft.)	Sq. Ft. Cost	Construction Cost	Equipment Cost	Book Capacity	Architect
*Carol Grotnes Belk Library and Information Commons, Appalachian State University, Boone, NC	$37,485,000	221,000	$156.11	$34,500,000	$1,289,192	1,000,000	Pease Associates; Shepley Bulfinch...
Cañada College Library & Resource Center, San Mateo, CA	30,000,000	72,526	306.77	22,249,000	843,900	79,643	Noll & Tam
Hampden-Sydney College Library, VA	18,541,539	83,403	203.78	16,995,825	1,545,714	350,000	Marcellus, Wright, Cox
Roger & Peggy Madigan Library, Pennsylvania College of Technology, Williamsport	17,332,127	104,800	137.04	14,362,161	1,782,935	160,000	Murray Associates
Warren Library, Palm Beach Atlantic University, West Palm Beach, FL	17,100,000	54,538	313.54	17,100,000	0	350,000	Leo A. Daly
William A. Wise Law Library, University of Colorado at Boulder School of Law	n.a.	59,000	222.25	13,113,000	1,034,400	679,949	Centerbrook Architects; Davis Partnership
**Learning Resources Center, Ozarks Technical Community College, Richwood Valley Campus, MO	534,140	3,020	157	474,140	60,000	5,600	Hagerman New Urbanism

* For a continuation of the project, see Additions and Renovations.

** Library part of a larger college building of departments and classrooms.

n.a. = not available

Table 2 / Academic Library Buildings, Additions and Renovations, 2007

Name of Institution	Status	Project Cost	Gross Area (Sq. Ft.)	Sq. Ft. Cost	Construction Cost	Equipment Cost	Book Capacity	Architect
*Beatley Library, Simmons College, Boston	Total	$40,000,000	121,000	n.a.	n.a.	n.a.	240,000	Fletcher
	New	n.a.	n.a.	n.a.	n.a.	n.a.	n.a.	Harkness Cohen
	Renovated	n.a.	n.a.	n.a.	n.a.	n.a.	n.a.	Moneyhun
Library West, University of Florida, Gainesville	Total	n.a.	177,000	$136.68	$24,192,175	n.a.	1,250,000	Ross Barney
	New	n.a.	n.a.	n.a.	n.a.	n.a.	n.a.	Architects
	Renovated	n.a.	n.a.	n.a.	n.a.	n.a.	n.a.	
Daniel J. Evans Library, Evergreen State College, Olympia, WA	Total	16,345,750	119,382	99	11,853,500	$110,000	292,000	Studio Meng
	New	n.a.	34,681	n.a.	n.a.	n.a.	32,000	Strazzara
	Renovated	n.a.	84,701	n.a.	n.a.	n.a.	260,000	
**Carol Grotnes Belk Library and Information Commons, Appalachian State University, Boone, NC	Total	8,344,200	188,416	42	7,850,000	n.a.	n.a.	Shepley
	New	3,844,200	106,000	33.49	3,550,000	n.a.	0	Bulfinch....
	Renovated	4,500,000	82,416	52	4,300,000	n.a.	n.a.	Pease Assocs.
Grace Hauenstein Library, Aquinas College, Grand Rapids, MI	Total	7,300,000	49,998	103.59	5,179,084	400,000	120,000	Progressive AE
	New	n.a.	27,095	n.a.	n.a.	n.a.	n.a.	
	Renovated	n.a.	22,903	n.a.	n.a.	n.a.	n.a.	

* Multiuse project in conjunction with a multiuse building.

** Addition of parking facility and renovation of old library for academic purposes; see New Buildings for additional information.

n.a. = not available

Table 3 / Academic Library Buildings, Renovations Only, 2007

Name of Institution	Project Cost	Gross Area (Sq. Ft.)	Sq. Ft. Cost	Construction Cost	Equipment Cost	Book Capacity	Architect
D.H. Hill Library, North Carolina State University, Raleigh	$11,200,000	60,000	$130.99	$7,823,537	$400,000	n.a.	Meyer, Scherer, & Rockcastle
Estelle M. Black Library, Rock Valley College, Rockford, IL	5,514,852	60,104	81.36	4,889,852	625,000	102,780	Legat Architects
King Library Project/Writing Center, Miami University, Oxford, OH	4,533,700	85,000	44.12	3,750,000	684,000	100,000	BHDP Architecture
Wm. R. Perkins Library, Duke University, Durham, NC	4,086,000	31,000	128.58	3,986,000	100,000	30,000	Shepley, Bulfinch...
Buswell Memorial Library, Wheaton College, IL	2,213,000	37,000	49.14	1,818,000	395,000	n.a.	FGM Architects
Todd Wehr Memorial Library, Viterbo University, La Crosse, WI	989,606	27,392	28.2	772,483	217,123	80,000	Borton Construction
Special Collections Dept., Watkinson Library, Trinity College, Hartford, CT	546,529	3,000	122.51	367,527	73,546	n.a.	Charney Architects, LLC
University College Library, Broward Community College, Davie, FL	430,200	2,914	109.13	318,000	94,000	n.a.	Saltz Michelson
Du Bois Library, University of Massachusetts, Amherst	173,268	3,100	21.61	67,000	106,268	0	OFI Contract Interiors

n.a. = not available

Table 4 / New Public Library Buildings, 2007

Community	Pop. ('000)	Code	Project Cost	Const. Cost	Gross Sq. Ft.	Sq. Ft. Cost	Equip. Cost	Site Cost	Other Costs	Book Capacity	Federal Funds	State Funds	Local Funds	Gift Funds	Architect
Alabama															
Birmingham	6	B	n.a.	n.a.	8,100	n.a.	n.a.	n.a.	n.a.	20,000	$0	$0	$0	$0	Khafra Engineering
Fairhope	137	M	$7,925,183	$6,428,984	72,000	$85.72	$1,050,199	Owned	$446,000	10,815	543,683		4,300,000	3,081,500	Walcott Adams...
Alaska															
Homer	11	M	8,818,124	6,456,240	17,115	377.23	360,000	960,000	1,041,884	43,350	4,572,792	1,253,252	66,160	2,925,920	ECI/Hyer, Inc.
Arizona															
Avondale	75	O	7,537,053	6,233,870	31,000	201.09	839,360	344,000	119,823	65,670	0	0	7,537,053	0	Smithgroup
Gilbert	90	O	4,436,241	3,177,500	20,500	155.00	895,000	288,000	75,741	41,750	0	0	4,436,241	0	HDA
Phoenix	63	B	9,941,897	5,135,087	25,000	205.40	3,366,143	2,326	1,440,667	140,000	0	0	9,810,001	131,896	Line And Space, LLC
Arkansas															
Huntsville	14	M	281,036	234,989	2,848	82.51	19,441	Owned	26,606	20,000	0	156,523	103,395	21,118	Ken Shireman...
California															
Bonita	12	B	4,514,179	3,734,942	10,118	369.13	257,267	Owned	521,970	30,253	0	0	4,514,179	0	Dominy & Assocs.
Campo	3	B	989,783	721,158	2,490	289.62	49,137	Owned	219,488	12,034	310,000	0	679,783	0	Platt/Whitelaw
Corona	12	B	5,292,852	4,768,232	9,196	518.51	324,223	Owned	200,397	20,100	0	0	5,292,852	0	STK
Fairfield	24	B	7,360,000	4,960,000	15,000	330.67	960,000	Owned	1,440,000	47,000	0	4,100,385	3,259,615	0	Group 4 Architecture
Folsom	69	M	12,600,000	8,500,000	24,000	354.17	600,000	1,800,000	1,700,000	100,000	0	0	12,500,000	100,000	BSA Architects
Harbor City	68	B	10,135,000	6,800,000	14,650	464.16	235,000	2,300,000	800,000	40,000	0	5,712,764	4,422,236	100,000	Carde Ten Architects
Long Beach	57	B	13,098,322	8,395,156	16,155	519.66	867,326	1,255,122	2,580,718	63,000	0	6,366,733	5,419,467	1,312,122	CWA AIA, Inc.
Morgan Hill	36	M	19,000,000	12,400,000	28,000	442.86	250,000	Owned	6,350,000	n.a.	0	0	18,500,000	500,000	Noll & Tam
Oxnard	79	B	10,709,604	6,802,923	23,034	295.34	961,199	1,141,031	1,804,451	80,000	347,750	5,795,760	4,312,172	255,922	Roesling Nakamura...
San Diego	23	B	9,371,500	6,408,858	15,626	410.14	700,000	Owned	2,262,642	50,000	0	1,000,000	8,371,500	0	Coombs Architecture
San Diego	7	B	3,165,253	2,000,000	7,214	277.24	190,253	750,000	225,000	28,000	0	0	550,000	2,615,253	Fehlman La Barre
San José	55	B	12,301,355	9,246,282	28,000	330.22	450,035	Owned	2,605,038	134,166	0	0	12,226,355	75,000	Anderson Brulé Archs.
San José	39	B	10,507,634	8,120,854	21,500	377.71	314,748	Owned	2,072,032	111,006	0	0	10,457,634	55,000	Studios Architecture
San José	55	B	11,482,897	7,988,376	21,035	379.77	382,014	Leased	3,112,507	100,474	0	0	11,462,897	20,000	Aedis Architecture
San Leandro	30	B	6,760,000	4,140,000	9,740	425.05	500,000	500,000	1,620,000	n.a.	0	3,800,856	2,959,144	0	Group 4 Architecture
San Mateo*	96	M	64,482,714	46,649,688	166,898	279.51	4,481,632	1,700,000	11,651,394	360,000	0	20,000,000	36,369,119	8,113,595	EHDD Architecture
Stockton	40	O	2,279,000	1,508,000	7,000	215.43	175,000	Owned	596,000	40,000	0	0	2,229,000	50,000	Urban Ernst Design
Temecula	94	O	18,159,104	12,494,857	34,000	367.50	1,579,474	Owned	4,084,773	160,033	0	8,552,414	9,356,690	250,000	LPA
Yreka	2	B	1,027,439	811,011	3,300	245.76	72,150	15,000	129,278	9,081	179,927	533,635	13,533	300,344	Siskiyou Design Group

Symbol Code: B=Branch Library; BS=Branch and System Headquarters; M=Main Library; MS=Main and System Headquarters; S=System Headquarters; O=combined use space; n.a. =not available

Table 4 / New Public Library Buildings, 2007 *(cont.)*

Community	Pop. ('000)	Code	Project Cost	Const. Cost	Gross Sq. Ft.	Sq. Ft. Cost	Equip. Cost	Site Cost	Other Costs	Book Capacity	Federal Funds	State Funds	Local Funds	Gift Funds	Architect
Colorado															
Arvada	48	B	$10,706,598	$7,139,588	34,172	$208.93	$799,110	$1,200,000	$1,567,900	n.a.	$0	$0	$10,706,598	$0	RNL Design
Connecticut															
Willington	6	M	3,480,000	2,820,000	18,560	151.94	250,000	Owned	430,000	23,054	0	500,000	3,000,000	0	Kenyon & Cutler
Delaware															
Wilmington	74	B	6,830,000	5,370,000	18,000	298.34	363,000	Owned	1,100,000	50,000	0	2,660,000	2,870,000	1,300,000	RMJM Hillier
Florida															
Leesburg	50	M	8,330,892	6,962,237	41,971	165.88	709,143	Owned	659,512	n.a.	0	500,000	7,485,123	345,769	Harvard Jolly Inc.
Miami	32	M	3,933,686	2,445,349	7,500	326.05	927,711	560,626	0	4,900	0	0	3,933,686	0	Miami-Dade Cty.
Pembroke Pines	300	B	14,892,000	11,530,406	70,000	164.72	1,845,000	Leased	1,516,594	200,000	0	819,800	14,072,200	0	IBI Group; Harvard...
Ruskin	38	B	10,879,000	6,222,000	40,000	155.55	3,687,000	450,000	520,000	150,000	0	500,000	10,379,000	0	Gouldevans Assocs.
Illinois															
Moline	43	M	12,406,514	10,319,231	68,000	151.75	963,250	Owned	1,124,033	212,440	0	124,449	11,459,275	1,125,185	OPN Architects
Indiana															
Kendallville	17	M	8,200,000	6,100,000	50,000	122.00	470,000	Owned	1,630,000	90,000	0	0	6,400,000	1,800,000	Moake Park Group
Roselawn	3	B	2,518,385	1,978,240	12,070	163.90	143,172	140,000	256,973	50,000	0	0	2,503,385	15,000	Interdesign
West Lafayette	25	B	3,663,614	2,674,230	13,500	198.09	201,000	420,000	368,384	50,000	0	0	3,053,614	610,000	Troyer Group
Iowa															
Burlington	27	M	10,725,112	8,998,112	50,000	179.96	779,000	Owned	948,000	156,800	0	0	780,000	9,945,112	Leo A. Daly
Oelwein	7	M	2,935,567	1,970,136	14,700	134.02	389,333	295,164	280,934	n.a.	0	250,000	1,581,280	1,104,287	Novak Design
Kentucky															
Frankfort	48	M	9,905,248	8,247,261	39,290	209.91	742,831	344,438	570,718	200,000	0	0	9,755,248	150,000	Woollen, Molzan
Independence	151	B	9,256,159	7,119,048	39,000	182.54	952,434	742,535	442,142	91,363	0	0	9,056,159	200,000	Robert Ehmet Hayes
Louisiana															
Baton Rouge	29	B	4,471,963	3,632,607	14,000	259.47	438,317	84,000	317,039	58,580	0	7,262	4,471,963	0	Tipton Associates
Maryland															
Baltimore	70	B	10,100,000	8,600,000	30,318	283.65	1,000,000	Owned	500,000	n.a.	0	0	7,650,000	2,450,000	RMJM Hillier
Frederick	30	B	10,936,000	8,028,000	31,060	258.47	1,160,000	1,000,000	748,000	89,664	0	0	9,886,000	1,050,000	BMK Architects
Germantown	80	B	17,299,772	11,022,100	27,699	397.92	800,817	2,215,899	3,260,956	200,000	0	0	17,299,772	0	Lukmire Partnership
Prince Frederick	80	MS	7,950,000	6,400,000	28,000	228.57	550,000	600,000	400,000	n.a.	0	400,000	7,550,000	80,000	Grimm + Parker

Symbol Code: B=Branch Library; BS=Branch and System Headquarters; M=Main Library; MS=Main and System Headquarters; S=System Headquarters; O=combined use space; n.a.=not available

Location															
Rockville	60	BS	25,867,394	18,394,406	101,000	182.12	990,000	2,494,109	3,988,879	200,000	0	700,000	25,167,394	0	Grimm + Parker
Michigan															
Sand Lake	5	B	1,412,088	1,149,490	8,814	130.42	125,000	28,000	109,598	45,000	945,000	0	413,736	53,352	Andrus Architecture
Minnesota															
St. Paul	55	B	9,293,260	6,612,953	58,884	112.30	1,022,444	200,250	1,457,613	115,000	0	0	9,293,260	150,000	BKV Group
Mississippi															
Jackson	22	B	2,255,650	1,912,154	14,000	136.58	125,409	Owned	218,087	63,000	0	0	2,255,650	240,000	Cooke Douglass Farr...
Missouri															
Platte City	4	B	3,955,847	3,130,036	15,638	200.16	86,163	586,520	153,128	85,000	0	0	3,955,847	0	Tognascioli & Assocs.
Montana															
Bozeman	48	M	18,299,375	10,754,263	52,300	205.63	677,005	2,150,000	4,718,107	161,900	2,076,000	1,680,000	7,270,624	7,272,751	Overland; Studio-FORMA; Johnston
Nebraska															
Falls City	5	M	2,809,010	2,267,567	15,000	151.17	137,309	200,000	204,134	55,000	52,000	0	1,500,000	1,257,010	Clark Enersen
New Hampshire															
Portsmouth	21	M	9,578,327	7,703,600	39,542	194.82	844,033	Owned	1,030,694	150,000	99,000	0	8,916,419	562,908	Amsler Mashek...
New York															
Cambria Heights	24	B	7,950,000	4,950,000	18,000	275.00	400,000	Owned	2,600,000	56,732	0	0	7,950,000	0	Kostowgreenwood
Clifton Park	52	M	15,000,000	10,391,304	55,000	188.93	1,743,826	600,000	2,264,870	250,000	0	0	15,000,000	0	Woodward, Connor...
Cold Spring Harbor	9	M	13,125,000	8,500,000	24,000	354.17	575,000	2,450,000	1,600,000	120,000	0	0	9,900,000	3,225,000	Beatty Harvey
Long Island City	34	B	9,700,000	7,050,000	18,000	391.67	650,000	Owned	2,000,000	41,034	0	0	9,700,000	0	Helpern Architects
New York	45	B	5,933,622	4,533,348	11,450	395.93	212,939	Leased	1,187,335	32,655	0	0	5,933,622	0	Rogers Marvel
Ossining	33	M	15,900,000	12,600,000	48,000	262.50	700,000	Owned	2,600,000	120,000	0	120,000	15,800,000	0	Beatty Harvey
North Carolina															
Cary	70	B	10,071,632	5,928,146	29,480	201.09	829,353	Owned	3,314,133	149,000	0	0	10,071,632	0	Clearscapes
Columbus	19	MS	3,984,081	2,973,000	17,783	167.18	365,000	444,081	202,000	67,500	0	0	2,316,048	1,668,033	ADW Architects, PA
Holly Springs	20	B	3,193,980	1,705,281	8,100	210.53	265,703	319,966	903,030	72,876	0	0	3,193,980	0	Little Diversified
Ohio															
Canton	29	B	3,977,464	2,726,052	20,383	133.74	397,197	486,098	368,117	54,613	0	0	3,372,464	605,000	Meehan Architects
Canton	51	B	2,553,595	2,003,026	19,380	103.36	414,387	Leased	136,182	56,241	0	0	2,553,595	0	Meehan Architects
Wooster	114	M	13,147,704	8,062,842	49,000	164.55	411,600	3,104,916	1,568,346	190,000	0	0	9,061,759	4,085,945	Meehan Architects
Oregon															
Estacada	18	M	3,426,750	2,009,000	12,060	166.58	75,250	186,500	1,156,000	n.a.	0	0	2,200,000	1,226,750	SRG Partnership
La Grande	24	M	6,110,072	4,709,275	19,044	247.28	357,377	416,107	627,313	n.a.	0	350,000	2,605,719	3,199,353	OTAK Architects
Talent	7	B	1,284,904	915,062	7,068	129.47	118,168	Owned	251,674	n.a.	0	0	956,904	328,000	Skelton Straus Seibert
Tillamook	25	MS	5,254,459	3,865,660	30,000	128.86	360,000	450,000	578,799	n.a.	0	0	4,260,376	994,083	Richard Turi

Symbol Code: B=Branch Library; M=Main Library; MS=Main and System Headquarters; S=System Headquarters; BS=Branch and System Headquarters; O=combined use space; n.a.=not available

Table 4 / New Public Library Buildings, 2007 *(cont.)*

Community	Pop. ('000)	Code	Project Cost	Const. Cost	Gross Sq. Ft.	Sq. Ft. Cost	Equip. Cost	Site Cost	Other Costs	Book Capacity	Federal Funds	State Funds	Local Funds	Gift Funds	Architect
Texas															
El Paso	78	M	$4,680,000	$3,622,122	21,500	$168.47	$534,193	Owned	$523,685	90,000	$0	$0	$4,680,000	$0	Enviro Idea
Taylor	15	M	3,600,000	3,000,000	20,000	150.00	400,000	Owned	200,000	120,000	0	0	3,600,000	0	Komatsu Architecture
Virginia															
Glen Allen	68	B	13,400,000	8,615,038	40,300	213.77	3,895,336	Owned	889,626	120,000	0	0	13,400,000	0	PSA Dewberry
Hopewell	23	MS	7,510,000	6,500,000	36,000	180.56	480,000	30,000	500,000	90,000	0	0	7,510,000	0	Grimm + Parker
Lexington	4	B	819,950	563,400	5,200	108.35	101,000	10,500	145,050	25,000	575,000	0	0	286,525	Reynolds Architects
Richmond	55	B	15,840,000	9,708,734	53,000	183.16	4,078,199	Owned	2,053,067	180,000	0	0	15,840,000	0	PSA Dewberry
Shirlington**	205	B	13,200,000	n.a.	53,000	n.a.	798,456	Owned	1,100,000	60,000	0	0	13,200,000	0	Lukmire Partnership
Washington															
Burlington	8	M	5,970,178	4,022,656	21,629	185.98	804,260	Owned	1,143,262	n.a.	0	0	5,970,178	0	Lewis Architecture
Seattle	18	B	5,360,273	3,173,176	5,652	561.43	128,305	1,513,462	545,330	18,700	0	0	3,409,974	1,950,300	Weinstein Architects
Seattle	21	B	6,223,411	3,417,741	10,000	341.77	368,277	1,864,370	573,023	40,200	0	0	1,554,570	4,668,841	Miller/Hull
Seattle	4	B	3,174,941	2,005,144	5,019	399.51	135,537	446,047	588,213	18,700	0	0	3,147,663	27,279	Johnston Architects
West Virginia															
Center Point	3	B	84,014	70,581	1,344	52.52	8,923	Owned	4,510	600	0	57,975	26,039	0	none reported

* The San Mateo project consists of a three-story building, plus 2½ levels of underground parking; the latter skews the square-foot cost. Without the parking area, the square-foot cost is $401.08

** A joint community project, the center includes a 15,000 square-foot library along with a regional theater. Construction costs for the library alone are not available.

n.a. = not available

Symbol Code: B=Branch Library; BS=Branch and System Headquarters; M=Main Library; MS=Main and System Headquarters; S=System Headquarters; O=combined use space; n.a.=not available

Table 5 / Public Library Buildings, Additions and Renovations, 2007

Community	Pop. ('000)	Code	Project Cost	Const. Cost	Gross Sq. Ft.	Sq. Ft. Cost	Equip. Cost	Site Cost	Other Costs	Book Capacity	Federal Funds	State Funds	Local Funds	Gift Funds	Architect
Arizona															
Phoenix	0	S	$456,450	$256,000	15,550	$16.46	$200,450	Owned	$0	0	$0	$0	$456,450	$0	Phoenix Design One
Prescott	42	MS	6,019,235	4,955,970	38,000	130.42	600,000	Owned	463,265	140,000	0	50,000	4,541,235	1,428,000	Otwell & Assocs.
Arkansas															
Bryant	10	B	615,287	538,427	3,688	145.99	35,556	Owned	41,304	n.a.	0	0	615,975	3,000	Taggart, Foster...
Greenwood	20	M	40,850	32,210	5,700	5.65	8,640	Owned	0	60,000	0	0	40,850		none
Maumelle	15	B	1,528,234	1,268,605	3,535	358.87	147,111	Owned	112,518	20,000	0	0	1,528,234	0	Fennell Purifoy...
California															
Carmichael	81	B	7,089,362	5,006,723	20,690	241.99	500,000	Owned	1,582,639	105,000	0	0	6,800,000	300,000	Noll & Tam
Ripon	16	B	3,410,000	1,200,000	11,000	109.09	440,000	1,600,000	170,000	50,000	0	0	1,690,000	1,720,000	SKW & Assocs.
Rolling Hills Estates	1	O	42,610	6,600	1,500	4.40	36,010	Leased	0	800	0	0	0	42,670	none
San Francisco	45	B	2,033,000	1,043,000	9,580	108.87	523,000	Owned	467,000	n.a.	0	0	1,510,000	523,000	Fougeron Architecture
San Francisco	23	B	4,960,500	3,427,000	8,536	401.48	386,000	Owned	1,147,500	n.a.	0	0	4,574,500	386,000	Thomas Hacker Archs.
San Rafael	13	B	1,940,000	1,170,000	3,450	339.13	140,000	Owned	630,000	n.a.	180,000	1,288,893	231,107	240,000	Group 4 Architecture
Connecticut															
Essex	7	M	2,600,000	2,004,350	9,555	209.77	278,844	Owned	316,806	39,446	2,000,000	500,000	0	1,500,000	Best Joslin
New London	26	M	1,027,081	900,260	10,000	90.03	34,000	Owned	93,541	24,000	50,000	333,333	384,468	260,000	Lindsay Liebig Roche
Norwalk	21	B	4,267,156	3,679,046	11,057	332.73	155,000	Owned	433,110	37,000	0	500,000	3,767,046	200,000	Schoenhardt Arch.
District of Columbia															
Southeast Branch Library (For more on this renovation project, see *Library by Design*, a supplement to the September 15, 2007, issue of *Library Journal*.)															
Florida															
Century	7	B	489,949	330,322	3,000	110.11	113,300	Owned	46,327	10,000	0	0	376,649	113,300	Strobel & Hunter
Orlando	1,000	M	1,427,833	1,311,698	40,000	32.79	27,000	Owned	89,135	n.a.	0	0	1,427,833	0	HKS Architects
Georgia															
Cartersville	90	M	7,499,550	5,461,719	45,442	120.19	1,348,444	Owned	689,837	155,800	0	2,500,000	5,000,000	0	Jova/Daniels/Busby
Clayton	16	O	498,956	424,010	11,893	35.65	53,126	Owned	21,820	58,268	0	430,920	68,036	0	Bailey & Assocs.
Illinois															
Northlake	27	M	8,670,930	7,504,000	37,592	199.62	417,930	Owned	749,000	112,000	0	0	8,670,930	0	PSA-Dewberry
Wheaton	56	M	20,435,000	16,552,000	124,518	132.92	2,369,000	Owned	1,514,000	n.a.	0	0	20,435,000	12,248	Burnidge Cassell

Symbol Code: B=Branch Library; BS=Branch and System Headquarters; M=Main Library; MS=Main and System Headquarters; S=System Headquarters; O=combined use space; n.a.=not available

Table 5 / Public Library Buildings, Additions and Renovations, 2007 *(cont.)*

Community	Pop. ('000)	Code	Project Cost	Const. Cost	Gross Sq. Ft.	Sq. Ft. Cost	Equip. Cost	Site Cost	Other Costs	Book Capacity	Federal Funds	State Funds	Local Funds	Gift Funds	Architect
Indiana															
Bluffton	27	M	$3,550,000	$2,737,736	39,280	$69.70	$360,285	Owned	$451,979	n.a.	$0	$0	$3,526,402	$23,598	Design Collaborative
Fort Wayne	344	MS	66,667,730	49,937,909	367,000	136.07	6,068,588	840,296	9,820,937	n.a.	0	0	66,667,730	0	MSKTD: Gwathmey
Jeffersonville	58	M	7,899,892	6,466,713	47,000	137.59	826,447	Owned	606,732	300,000	0	0	7,899,892	0	Robert Kissinger
Lebanon	17	M	8,000,000	6,815,000	48,000	141.98	250,000	Owned	935,000	90,000	0	0	8,000,000	0	Odle McGuire Shook
Pendleton	22	M	5,407,122	4,254,615	28,080	151.52	307,305	110,000	735,202	n.a.	0	0	5,407,122	0	KR Montgomery
South Whitley	5	M	1,037,341	770,521	14,646	52.61	168,320	Owned	98,500	4,000	0	500,000	0	537,341	Searce Rudisel
Tipton	17	M	1,484,282	n.a.	24,500	n.a.	n.a.	Owned	99,980	n.a.	0	0	1,469,282	15,000	KR Montgomery
Iowa															
Des Moines	22	B	3,253,475	2,612,506	14,900	175.34	208,840	Owned	432,129	55,000	0	0	950,000	2,303,475	OPN Architects
Kansas															
Independence	14	M	3,864,326	2,988,259	23,100	129.36	476,714	Owned	399,353	n.a.	0	0	3,864,326	0	GLPM Architects
Kentucky															
Shepherdsville	73	M	2,228,869	2,010,000	16,000	125.63	72,896	Owned	145,973	6,400	0	0	2,184,913	147,087	Nolan & Nolan
Louisiana															
Tallulah	13	MS	72,410	64,642	8,673	7.45	0	Owned	7,768	150,000	0	0	72,410	0	McManus Consulting
Maryland															
Pikesville	45	B	3,553,597	2,857,735	21,500	132.92	324,992	Owned	370,870	106,000	0	0	3,534,597	19,000	Rubeling & Assocs.
Massachusetts															
Charlton	13	M	7,089,000	5,790,000	27,800	208.27	355,000	Owned	944,000	n.a.	0	2,417,814	3,627,000	1,050,000	J. Stewart Roberts
Florence	10	M	2,567,000	2,274,931	9,500	239.47	114,799	Owned	177,270	n.a.	150,000	1,204,000	511,000	702,500	Caolo & Bieniek
Great Barrington	8	M	4,324,525	3,506,877	13,625	257.39	246,431	Owned	571,217	n.a.	0	1,407,052	2,769,544	147,929	J. Stewart Roberts
Harvard	6	M	7,820,033	6,434,155	19,483	330.24	345,000	Leased	1,040,878	78,500	0	2,490,000	2,600,000	2,730,033	CBT Architects
Leominster	42	M	13,271,498	10,164,027	44,513	228.34	778,333	310,000	2,019,138	137,705	0	3,021,441	9,464,280	785,807	Beacon Architectural
New Salem	1	M	706,283	533,051	3,479	153.22	13,443	32,032	127,757	n.a.	225,000	286,530	183,153	11,600	Galante Architecture
Watertown	33	M	11,315,000	9,222,995	45,000	204.96	610,000	Owned	1,482,005	120,000	0	2,972,408	7,342,592	1,000,000	Lerner/Ladds + Bartels
Michigan															
E. Grand Rapids	10	B	4,500,000	3,820,000	27,700	137.91	316,400	Owned	363,600	125,000	0	0	3,500,000	1,000,000	Cox, Medendorp, Olson
Plymouth	37	M	3,727,000	2,622,000	52,000	50.42	755,000	Owned	350,000	275,000	0	0	3,672,000	55,000	Merritt McPherson…

Symbol Code: B=Branch Library; BS=Branch and System Headquarters; M=Main Library; MS=Main and System Headquarters; S=System Headquarters; O=combined use space; n.a.=not available

Location															Architect
Minnesota															
Minneapolis	20	B	4,680,710	3,297,210	17,000	193.95	508,000	Owned	875,500	65,000	0	140,870	4,328,340	211,500	KKE Architects
Minneapolis	32	B	4,501,375	3,297,210	32,600	101.14	530,000	Owned	674,165	57,000	0	141,583	4,183,000	176,792	KKE Architects
Stillwater	40	M	11,850,000	10,447,200	38,680	270.09	302,800	Owned	1,100,000	n.a.	0	150,000	6,400,000	5,300,000	Miller Dunwiddie
Missouri															
Annapolis	3	B	109,514	0	2,576	0.00	36,687	66,027	6,800	4,560	0	5,366	38,121	66,027	Randall Pierce
Kansas City	239	B	234,000	15,482	800	19.35	198,518	Leased	20,000	0	0	0	0	235,000	Helix Architecture
Montana															
Big Timber	3	M	1,300,000	1,100,000	4,000	275.00	80,000	Owned	120,000	27,050	0	0	0	1,300,000	A&E Architects, PC
New Jersey															
Parsippany	51	M	5,802,271	4,402,971	36,538	120.50	837,000	Owned	562,300	127,210	0	1,100,000	4,702,271	0	Beatty, Harvey
Somerset	60	M	8,180,000	6,700,000	36,000	186.11	450,000	Owned	1,030,000	157,000	0	1,117,000	6,963,000	100,000	Dennis Kowal
New York															
Babylon	12	M	4,850,000	3,500,000	17,500	200.00	75,000	Owned	1,275,000	100,000	0	0	4,850,000	0	Beatty, Harvey
Brooklyn	n.a.	B	755,000	480,000	6,939	69.17	62,000	Owned	213,000	n.a.	0	0	755,000	0	Louise Braverman
Greenlawn	18	M	8,239,254	6,231,059	38,264	162.84	969,853	Owned	1,038,342	168,660	0	0	8,239,254	0	Beatty, Harvey
Haverstraw	10	B	599,561	457,446	4,200	108.91	100,665	Owned	41,450	n.a.	0	144,928	461,000	0	Arcari + Iovino
New Hyde Park	23	M	9,110,000	4,743,000	26,000	182.42	550,000	1,861,000	1,956,000	80,000	0	0	9,110,000	0	Beatty, Harvey
New York	103	O	610,534	433,736	2,786	155.68	101,338	Owned	75,460	23,579	0	0	0	700,534	Sage & Coombe
Staten Island	187	O	319,760	212,414	2,000	106.21	31,173	Owned	76,173	9,500	0	0	0	319,760	Highland Assocs.
Syosset	34	O	14,479,775	11,609,719	64,200	180.84	899,775	Owned	1,970,281	300,000	0	9,000	14,469,925	850	Raymond Beeler
North Carolina															
Raleigh	150	B	9,637,330	4,641,242	30,747	150.95	742,293	3,066,087	1,187,708	204,761	198,000	0	9,439,330	0	Clearscapes
Raleigh	9	B	495,854	298,073	5,480	54.39	70,085	Leased	127,696	26,352	0	0	495,854	0	Cherry Huffman
Ohio															
Alliance	22	MS	2,425,300	1,982,991	21,545	92.04	181,833	Owned	260,476	244,110	0	0	2,425,300	0	Caplea Studios
Brecksville	31	B	1,814,970	551,643	15,215	36.26	425,153	Owned	838,174	91,950	0	0	1,814,970	0	Van Dyke Architects
Columbus	33	B	1,099,466	947,540	3,100	305.66	48,463	20,851	82,612	12,911	0	399,466	0	700,000	Design Group
Kent	34	M	15,046,319	11,577,878	55,000	210.51	1,296,994	Owned	2,171,447	n.a.	0	0	15,046,319	0	Burt Hill Kosar…
Metamora	7	M	217,030	183,918	1,500	122.61	6,030	Owned	27,082	n.a.	0	0	187,187	29,843	Munger Munger
New Concord	3	B	215,000	126,522	5,120	24.71	83,588	Owned	4,890	34,162	0	0	215,000	0	Kelly Architectural
Pemberville	9	M	795,454	698,409	9,100	76.75	11,355	Owned	85,690	3,245	0	0	798,899	0	ESA Assocs.; Vetter
Rocky River	21	M	3,294,041	2,523,676	39,594	63.73	207,970	Owned	562,395	n.a.	0	0	3,291,041	3,000	Van Dyke Architects
Oregon															
Hillsboro	158	MS	13,900,000	4,990,000	76,000	65.66	645,000	6,800,000	1,465,000	n.a.	0	0	12,900,000	1,000,000	LRS Architects

Symbol Code: B=Branch Library; BS=Branch and System Headquarters; M=Main Library; MS=Main and System Headquarters; S=System Headquarters; O=combined use space; n.a.=not available

501

Table 5 / Public Library Buildings, Additions and Renovations, 2007 *(cont.)*

Community	Pop. ('000)	Code	Project Cost	Const. Cost	Gross Sq. Ft.	Sq. Ft. Cost	Equip. Cost	Site Cost	Other Costs	Book Capacity	Federal Funds	State Funds	Local Funds	Gift Funds	Architect
Pennsylvania															
Pittsburgh	23	B	$2,137,145	$1,100,193	5,745	$191.50	$198,574	Owned	$838,378	31,000	$0	$400,000	$272,473	$1,464,672	Loysen + Kreuthmeier
Rhode Island															
Cumberland	32	M	763,640	661,914	4,945	133.86	50,766	Owned	50,960	n.a.	0	351,488	300,837	111,315	Saccoccio & Assocs.
South Carolina															
Greenville	36	B	680,359	457,574	12,050	37.97	115,345	Owned	107,440	6,180	0	0	680,359	0	Craig Gaulden Davis
Sumter	104	M	5,501,341	4,546,426	45,000	101.03	497,531	Owned	457,384	n.a.	0	0	5,501,341	0	James, Durant...
South Dakota															
Watertown	26	M	4,640,571	3,573,604	32,360	110.43	272,426	Owned	794,541	181,326	0	0	4,622,471	18,100	Architecture Inc.
Tennessee															
Knoxville	36	B	2,885,305	1,318,358	12,070	109.23	235,865	$1,200,000	131,082	45,000	0	0	2,885,305	0	Cockrill Design
Texas															
Austin	42	B	4,121,123	1,819,018	13,250	137.28	164,950	742,948	1,394,207	75,000	0	0	4,121,123	0	Nelsen Partners
El Paso	600	MS	10,100,000	6,600,000	101,000	65.35	5,000,000	Owned	3,000,000	n.a.	0	0	10,100,000	0	PSRBB
Lewisville	106	M	11,071,000	8,780,040	77,800	112.85	1,530,960	Owned	760,000	250,000	0	0	11,056,000	15,000	F & S Partners
Luling	5	M	250,000	250,000	2,170	115.21	0	Owned	0	n.a.	0	0	0	250,000	TSG Architects
Utah															
Garland	2	M	18,000	4,230	866	4.88	4,476	Owned	9,294	900	n.a.	7,000	4,000	7,000	none
Kaysville	25	B	218,008	160,802	5,415	29.70	47,607	Leased	9,599	65,000	0	0	218,008	0	CRS Assocs.
Virginia															
Arlington	205	O	5,100,000	n.a.	180	n.a.	618,360	Owned	3,500	n.a.	0	0	5,100,000	0	Gensler
Chesapeake	13	O	2,184,534	1,734,534	8,741	198.44	290,000	Owned	160,000	12,000	168,210	81,924	1,934,400	0	Rodriguez Ripley...
Washington															
Seattle	25	B	6,246,979	5,021,823	15,000	334.79	319,294	Owned	905,862	66,700	0	0	6,172,979	74,000	Olson Sundberg...
Seattle	30	B	6,784,252	5,634,314	16,493	341.62	248,685	Owned	901,253	66,700	0	0	4,228,053	2,556,199	Schacht Aslani Archs.
Wyoming															
Gillette	39	MS	2,025,849	1,537,000	44,985	34.17	293,849	Owned	195,000	200,000	0	0	2,015,565	10,284	Schutz Foss Archs.

n.a. = not available

Symbol Code: B=Branch Library; BS=Branch and System Headquarters; M=Main Library; MS=Main and System Headquarters; S=System Headquarters; O=combined use space; n.a.=not available

Table 6 / Public Library Buildings, Six-Year Cost Summary

	Fiscal 2002	Fiscal 2003	Fiscal 2004	Fiscal 2005	Fiscal 2006	Fiscal 2007
Number of new buildings	101	103	99	91	81	82
Number of ARRs*	111	92	102	94	79	86
Sq. ft. new buildings	2,144,185	2,340,374	3,178,027	2,349,670	2,050,087	2,245,929
Sq. ft. ARRs	2,351,100	1,725,902	2,096,243	1,530,382	1,505,326	2,300,619
New Buildings						
Construction cost	$303,284,460	$420,486,065	$655,261,309	$420,241,028	$421,856,723	$491,240,609
Equipment cost	44,985,041	51,738,413	72,422,017	57,152,920	51,541,695	60,666,368
Site cost	28,523,513	30,095,454	30,873,801	43,892,631	43,897,019	37,089,067
Other cost	48,115,515	69,981,113	157,419,044	75,384,007	90,240,356	105,271,399
Total—Project cost	429,787,571	573,531,535	916,026,171	596,670,586	611,502,793	705,543,661
ARRs—Project cost	358,658,087	263,624,575	326,410,267	235,915,173	293,982,768	426,681,990
New and ARR Project cost	$788,445,658	$837,156,110	$1,242,436,438	$832,585,759	$905,485,561	$1,132,225,651
Fund Sources						
Federal, new buildings	$5,395,598	$9,106,615	$3,765,492	$3,657,196	$9,733,136	$9,701,152
Federal, ARRs	5,197,596	6,482,225	6,202,088	3,692,293	4,150,883	2,971,210
Federal, total	$10,593,194	$15,588,840	$9,967,580	$7,349,489	$13,884,019	$12,672,362
State, new buildings	$13,745,400	$18,465,123	$115,846,277	$28,458,752	$26,218,139	$65,941,808
State, ARRs	18,874,053	16,090,024	24,889,690	12,816,996	28,803,122	23,951,016
State, total	$32,619,453	$34,555,147	$140,735,967	$41,275,748	$55,021,261	$89,892,824
Local, new buildings	$363,288,508	$507,445,956	$703,245,493	$537,391,416	$534,202,531	$560,754,782
Local, ARRs	312,253,572	207,977,217	237,027,037	193,115,934	236,808,805	369,691,281
Local, total	$675,542,080	$715,423,173	$940,272,530	$730,507,350	$771,011,336	$930,446,063
Gift, new buildings	$39,257,565	$39,094,374	$93,284,817	$27,464,751	$43,422,990	$71,784,153
Gift, ARRs	20,795,667	31,972,475	58,402,733	26,579,726	24,780,729	31,906,464
Gift, total	$60,053,232	$71,066,849	$151,687,550	$54,044,477	$68,203,719	$103,690,617
Total funds used	$778,807,959	$836,634,009	$1,242,663,627	$833,177,064	$908,120,335	$1,136,701,866

* ARR: Additions, Renovations, and Remodels

Book Trade Research and Statistics

Failures, Mergers, Technology, Harry Head 2007's Publishing News

Jim Milliot

Business and News Director, *Publishers Weekly*

The big publishing story of early 2007 had its start on the last business day of 2006 when Advanced Marketing Services (AMS) filed for bankruptcy. The major supplier of books to warehouse clubs and the parent company of distributor Publishers Group West (PGW), AMS did business with nearly every significant publisher. With AMS occupying such a crucial place in the industry, all parties involved moved quickly to find a resolution to the Chapter 11 filing. In the end, the company was basically divided in two and sold. Baker & Taylor acquired the majority of AMS's assets related to the warehouse clubs, paying approximately $72 million and using the assets to form Baker & Taylor Marketing Services. Several wholesalers, however, used AMS's problems to whittle away at its dominance of the warehouse market. Levy Home Entertainment took over distribution to BJ's, while Anderson Merchandisers, after testing distribution to about 100 Sam's Clubs, assumed distribution to all Sam's outlets in February 2008.

The fate of PGW's nearly 200 distribution clients was largely decided in March when the Perseus Books Group won bankruptcy court approval to acquire more than 100 distribution contracts that had been held by PGW. As part of the deal, Perseus paid publishers 75 percent of the money owed to them by PGW. Another distributor, National Book Network, picked up about 20 contracts, paying publishers the full amount they were owed, and other distributors signed a number of the remaining clients, providing most PGW publishers with a new distribution home by spring 2007. The quick action helped to prevent any PGW clients from filing for bankruptcy, although the disruption in cash flow led to the sale of a few companies.

Just as the dust from AMS's bankruptcy was cooling down in late spring, the hype surrounding the publication of *Harry Potter and the Deathly Hallows,* the final volume in the blockbuster Harry Potter series, began to heat up. The consumer media were filled with stories about the book, including speculation on how the series would end. U.S. publisher Scholastic was largely successful in preventing pirated copies from turning up in stores before the July 21 release date as it combatted bloggers and Internet sites that claimed to know how the book ended.

The publication of *Hallows* gave a much-needed boost to bookstore sales, which had been slightly down for the first half of 2007. The sales impact could have been much higher had traditional stores and online retailers not aggressively discounted the title. Few stores sold *Hallows* for the list price of $34.99, with many retailers using the book as a loss leader. Amazon, for example, acknowledged that it lost money on the title, which it offered at deep discounts, despite selling 2.5 million copies worldwide. The combination of the popularity of the series and the low price contributed to a record sales performance. Scholastic, which printed 14 million copies, reported that during the first ten days on sale *Hallows* sold 11.5 million copies; previously Scholastic had reported that the title had sold 8.3 million in its first 24 hours on sale. Barnes & Noble sold 2.1 million copies in the second quarter—400,000 through its Web site and 1.7 million through its stores.

A second publication story that made a splash in the mainstream media was the fall release of O. J. Simpson's *If I Did It*. After the original publisher, the ReganBooks imprint of HarperCollins, canceled the project following a public outcry against the book and TV project, the parents of murder victim Ron Goldman acquired the rights to the manuscript. When the major New York houses were reluctant to publish the title, the independent publisher Beaufort Books picked up the book, which sold more than 100,000 copies.

Big sales numbers were also generated when Oprah Winfrey relaunched her book club in January 2007 after putting it on hiatus after the James Frey fiasco in 2006. In January Winfrey picked Sidney Poitier's *The Measure of a Man: A Spiritual Autobiography,* which went on to sell about 900,000 copies.

In March the nation's second-largest bookstore chain, Borders, announced its long-awaited restructuring plan. Borders said it would sell most of its international operations, close several hundred underperforming Waldenbook outlets in the United States, and take back operation of its Web site from Amazon. The announcement was met with widespread approval from publishers.

Two of the country's largest publishers changed names in the year. Hachette, which acquired the Time Warner Trade Book group in 2006, changed the name of its Warner Books division to Grand Central Publishing. Holtzbrinck, headquartered in Germany, renamed its English-language holdings Macmillan. HarperCollins's HarperSanFrancisco division changed its name to HarperOne. The library services company Sagebrush Books renamed itself Tandem Library Group. Disney Publishing kept its name but lost its home, moving 175 employees from its Fifth Avenue Manhattan offices to new quarters in suburban White Plains.

Trends

Publishers and booksellers spent 2007 exploring ways to capitalize on technology. Late in the year, Amazon unveiled its long-awaited e-book reader, the Kindle. The device, priced at $399, allows customers to wirelessly download e-books, and Amazon had about 90,000 titles ready to read at launch. Demand quickly outpaced supply, and Amazon was still filling backorders in early 2008. Reflecting the importance of online retailing, Borders and Barnes & Noble both redesigned their Web sites. In the case of Borders, the redesign was the first step in taking back operation of the site from Amazon. Borders, which is one of several retailers selling the Sony Reader, expanded its relationship with the company, upping the number of stores in which it sells the device and making more titles available.

With digital downloads of spoken word audio increasing rapidly, eMusic, which sells music digital downloads, entered the spoken word field, offering digital downloads without digital rights management (DRM) protection in contrast to the digital download leader, Audible, which offers only titles with DRM. While sales of digital downloads of spoken word audio picked up in 2007, another technology that gained quick traction in 2007 was e-mailing book excerpts to personal digital assistants (PDAs), Blackberrys, and other devices, through a system developed by a startup called DailyLit. Two companies were launched in 2007 to deliver book content to mobile phones; Mobifusion started in January, delivering full text to cell phones, while Moka launched in the spring to send text messages of key book points to cell phones.

Publishers began to take more control over their digital operations in 2007. Random House and HarperCollins both began digital warehouses to store books in digital formats, and both publisher launched "widgets," book icons that can be put on other Web sites that contain information about the books. HarperCollins also invested in the company that helped it develop its digital warehouse, NewsStand, and began offering digital services to other publishers. Late in the year, Hachette signed with NewsStand to help it with its digital projects.

With print-on-demand (POD) becoming more important to traditional publishers, Simon & Schuster incensed authors when it changed the language in its contract to redefine when books can be called "out of print." Under the revision, S&S considered books to be in print as long as they were available in POD formats. Authors protested, arguing that unless S&S was actually selling printed books, rights should revert to them. A compromise was reached in which authors could request that once sales fell to certain thresholds they would get their rights back.

In a move to cut costs, a growing number of newspapers either reduced or eliminated book review coverage in 2007. Among the papers that made changes were the *Atlanta Journal Constitution,* the *Dallas Morning News,* the *Los Angeles Times,* and the *San Francisco Chronicle.* Reduction in the number of reviews was bad news for publishers, which also had to contend with a new National Endowment for the Arts study that, two years after its Reading at Risk report, found more declines in reading, particularly among young people.

New Ventures

The Scandinavian publisher Egmont Group announced late in 2007 that it was forming a New York-based children's publishing division to be led by industry veteran Elizabeth Law. Egmont USA, with distribution by Random House, will specialize in young adult and middle grades fiction.

The American children's book publisher Lerner Publishing opened a British division. HarperCollins teamed with the independent film house Sharp Independent to form Sharp Independent at HarperCollins, which will develop movies based on HarperCollins books.

New imprints opened during 2007 included Voice, formed by Hyperion and aimed at women over 35. John Wiley formed Fisher Investment Press to focus on financial titles. Pocket Books formed Karen Hunter Publishing, while Random House and Sylvan Learning formed the Sylvan Learning Books imprint aimed at students. Bantam Dell created Bantam Discovery to publish simultaneous editions of mass market and trade paperbacks. Book packager Weldon Owen formed a publishing imprint, Gold Street Press, which is being distributed by Ingram Publisher Services. NAL formed the Obsidian Mystery imprint to house all of its mystery titles. Rodale formed the Modern Times imprint to focus on political and current affairs books.

The year was the last for a number of companies. Despite the growth in digital downloads of spoken word audio, MediaBay closed after burning through millions of dollars in a failed attempt to transition from a traditional spoken word audio club to delivering digital downloads. After just a year in business, Koen-Levy Book Wholesalers, a division of Levy Home Entertainment, was closed. The small distributor Bookworld closed down in the fall, and the Christian retail chain Bible Factory Outlet filed for Chapter 7. Doubleday shut down its Morgan Road imprint, which it launched in 2004, after it had released only 17 titles.

Mergers and Acquisitions

The biggest acquisitions in 2007 were in the educational publishing segment, where the five largest deals were worth more than $13 billion. Thomson Corp. sold its Thomson Learning subsidiary to OMERs, a Canadian pension fund, and Apex Holdings, a large private equity firm, for $7.1 billion. Following the sale, Thomson Learning was renamed Cengage, and in December Cengage reached an agreement to buy the college division of Houghton Mifflin from Houghton Mifflin Riverdeep for $750 million.

The sale of Houghton Mifflin's college division came shortly after HM Riverdeep closed on its purchase of the American education, trade, and reference assets of Harcourt from Reed Elsevier. HM Riverdeep paid $4 billion for the Harcourt assets and immediately began integrating the companies that are now known as Houghton Mifflin Harcourt. Tony Lucki was appointed chairman and Gerald Hughes president and chief operating officer. Although the trade segment is a small part of Houghton Mifflin Harcourt, the impact of the merger was felt first in that unit when Gary Gentel, interim president of Houghton Mifflin trade group, was named head of the new Houghton Mifflin Harcourt Trade and Reference division, while Dan Farley, head of the Harcourt trade group, left the company at the end of January (2008). Houghton Mifflin Harcourt also announced that it was closing the Harcourt Trade office in San Diego by June 2008; the office had 65 employees, some of whom were offered the chance to relocate to Houghton Mifflin Harcourt offices in Boston and New York.

Earlier in the year, Reed Elsevier sold the Harcourt testing group and its international educational publishing division to Pearson for $950 million. Pearson also paid $477 million for the education company eCollege.

On the trade publishing side, the Perseus Book Group acquired the Avalon Publishing Group from owner Charlie Winton. As part of merging Avalon into

Perseus, Perseus closed the Carroll & Graf and Thunder's Mouth imprints and eliminated about 40 positions. Following his sale of Avalon, Winton, along with Jack Shoemaker, bought Shoemaker & Hoard from Perseus and formed Counterpoint LLC, adding Counterpoint Press and Soft Skull Press to the new Counterpoint. Soft Skull was one of the few distribution clients of PGW that were sold due in part to the bankruptcy of the distributor. Two other former PGW clients that were sold were Hugh Lauter Levin Associates, which was acquired by Rizzoli, and Inner Ocean, which was bought by New World Library.

In April 2007 Bertlesmann consolidated its position in the book club field, paying $150 million to buy out Time Warner's 50 percent stake in Bookspan. In the reorganization that followed, Bertelsmann eliminated 280 positions, 15 percent of the company's work force, and shut several specialized clubs. Eagle Publishing, owner of the Conservative Book Club, bought Bookspan's American Compass Book Club.

One of the more talked-about acquisitions in the year was Amazon's purchase of the independent spoken word audio publisher Brilliance Audio. The acquisition gave Amazon a presence in the production of audio content.

The online self-publishing market underwent some consolidation in 2007 when the private equity firm Bertram Capital bought two of the industry leaders, AuthorHouse and iUniverse. Cooper Square, a new publishing house formed by an unnamed equity firm and Rowman & Littlefield, made two acquisitions, buying T&N Children's Publishing and Northland Publishing.

In the reference and scholarly market, Taylor & Francis bought Haworth Press and Productivity Press, while John Wiley and Sons completed its $1.08 billion purchase of STM publisher Blackwell Publishing. On the manufacturing side, Donnelley completed its $1.3 billion purchase of Banta and then consolidated its position even further with the acquisition of Von Hoffman.

People

Jack Romanos retired as CEO of Simon & Schuster at the end of 2007 and was succeeded by Carolyn Reidy. In her first major appointments, Reidy promoted Michael Selleck to executive vice president, sales and marketing, while Dennis Eulau was named executive vice present of operations. Larry Norton, who had overseen sales, left the company at the end of the year. Internationally, Francois McHardy was named managing director of Simon & Schuster Australia, succeeding Jon Attenborough.

Random House had a number of executives depart during 2007. Early in the year Don Weisberg, executive vice president and COO North America, who ran the company's sales operation, resigned. Random did not directly replace Weisberg, appointing Deputy Chairman Ed Volini to oversee the sales group. Another longtime Random executive, Jackie Everly, resigned as senior vice president/associate publisher and executive director of marketing at Doubleday Broadway. Suzanne Hertz was promoted to succeed Everly. In June Sheryl Stebbins stepped down as vice president and publisher of Random House Value Publishing, and Susan Hettleman was named to supervise the unit. David Naggar, president of Random House Audio and Diversified Publishing, Random House Information, and Fodor's Travel groups, resigned late in the year. Nancy Miller, one-time editor-in-chief of Ballantine and most recently senior vice president and executive editor, left the company in October. Tim Ditlow, publisher of Random Audio's Listening Library division, left the company. Stephen Cobb was named president of the newly formed Doubleday Religious Publishing Group, which succeeded Doubleday Religion. Cobb was previously president of Colorado Springs-based WaterBrook Multnomah, which is now part of the new group. Bill Barry, who had been president of Doubleday Religion, resigned.

Steve Ross resigned as senior vice president and publisher of Crown to become president and publisher of HarperCollins's Collins U.S. division. He succeeded Joe Tessitore, who had resigned earlier in the year. Crown promoted Tina Constable from executive director of publicity to publisher of Crown, Crown Business, and Crown Forum. Late in the year, Harper hired Lisa Sharkey as senior vice president for creative development in a move that effectively replaced the ousted Judith Regan. Brian Murray, HarperCollins group president, was promoted to the newly created position of president of HarperCollins worldwide. At the company's religious division, Doug Lockhart resigned as president at the end of June and Maureen Girkins was named to succeed him starting in 2008.

Penguin appointed Amy Einhorn publisher of her own imprint within the Putnam group. Eamon Dolan left his post as editor-in-chief of Houghton Mifflin to join Penguin Press in a similar role. He succeeded Scott Moyers, who joined the Wylie Agency as director. Luke Dempsey was named to succeed Laureen Rowland as editor-in-chief of Hudson Street Press, while Cherise Davis was named editor-in-chief of Plume. Jeff Gomez, head of Internet marketing at Macmillan, was named senior director of online consumer sales and marketing.

Hachette named Beth Ford COO and executive vice president, while April Hattori was named director of communications. Deb Futter joined Hachette's Grand Central imprint as vice president and editor-in-chief of its hardcover division, filling a position left open when Amy Einhorn left to go to Penguin. Futter was deputy editorial director at Doubleday. Another ex-Doubleday employee, Michelle Rapkin, was named executive editor of Hachette's Center Street imprint. Amy Pierpont was named senior editor at Grand Central and editorial director of the company's romance imprint, Forever.

At McGraw-Hill, Philip Ruppel was promoted to president of McGraw-Hill Professional. Linda Cunningham left as editorial director of Meredith Books when the company ended its New York operation and exited the children's business. Jonathan Merkh was named publisher of Guidepost Books and Jennifer Willingham was appointed vice president of marketing.

Among the major personnel shifts at independent houses, Gary Krebs left AdamsMedia to become group publisher at Globe Pequot. Don Linn, former owner of Consortium, took over as president of the Taunton Press book group. Skyhorse Publishing named Herman Graf acquiring editor and Trish Hoard managing editor. Bill Krause was promoted to publisher of Llewellyn Worldwide. Neal Maillet was named publisher of Workman's Timber Press imprint.

As part of a major restructuring, Marcus Wilhelm resigned as head of Bookspan and was replaced by Stuart Goldfarb, who heads a combined books and music club operation, Bertelsmann Direct North America. Late in the year Hartmut Ostrowski took over as chairman and CEO of Bertelsmann.

Among major moves in children's publishing, Lisa Holton stepped down as head of Scholastic's trade and book fair divisions. Ellie Berger was named to succeed her as head of trade, while Alan Boyko was named president of book fairs. On the executive side, Maureen O'Connell, who had spent two years at Barnes & Noble, was named chief administrative officer as well as CFO, succeeding Mary Winston in the CFO role. Bill Boedeker was named director of children's publishing at Chronicle. Walter Lorraine, a 55-year veteran of Houghton Mifflin's children books, retired at the end of the year. Former Disney editor-in-chief-Brenda Bowen was hired by HarperCollins to launch her own children's books imprint. Liz Van Doren, editorial director of Harcourt's children's division, was one of five people to lose their jobs in a reorganization. Stephen Roxburgh was named publisher of Boyds Mills Press.

In retail, Borders named Robert Gruen executive vice president of marketing and merchandising, and Kenneth Armstrong was appointed executive vice president of U.S. stores, replacing Vin Altruda. Ric Vanzura, executive vice president for emerging technology and chief strategy officer, and Bill Nasshan, senior vice president of trade books, also left the company. Retail veteran Dick Lynch was appointed president of Borders's Paperchase division. Susan Harwood, CIO at Books-A-Million, was named to head Borders's technology efforts. In the independent sector, Andy Ross resigned as head of Cody's Books. Brian Elliott was promoted to CEO of online book retailer Alibris.

In distribution, Susan Reich was named president of a reorganized PGW July 30, while Arnie Wright was named president of Baker & Taylor.

Changes among literary agents included the appointment of longtime International Creative Management (ICM) agent Richard Abate to open an East Coast book division for Endeavor. Shawn Coyne, cofounder of the defunct Rugged Land, joined Endeavor as an agent. Veteran editor Dan Conaway joined Writers House.

In a major executive shift overseas, Richard Charkin resigned as CEO of Macmillan UK to become executive director of Bloomsbury.

Bestsellers

It was a good year for Khaled Hosseini in 2007 with two books enjoying long runs on *Publishers Weekly*'s bestsellers lists. His first title, *The Kite Runner,* spent 51 weeks on the trade paperback list, while his new title, *A Thousand Splendid Suns,* spent 31 weeks on the hardcover fiction list following its release in the spring. Mitch Albom's *For One More Day,* which had a long stay on the 2006 fiction list, hit the charts for 25 weeks in 2007. Only two debut authors made the bestseller chart in 2007—Joe Hill with *Heart-Shaped Box* and Sarah Addison Allen with *Garden Spells.* The prolific James Patterson had six titles make various lists, while Dean Koontz and Danielle Steel each had three titles reach bestsellerdom. The year's biggest seller, however, was in the children's category: *Harry Potter and the Deathly Hallows.*

In nonfiction, *The Secret* by newcomer Rhonda Byrne dominated the field, staying on the list for 50 weeks, with 29 of those weeks in the top spot. *You on a Diet: The Owner's Manual for Waist Management* by physicians Mehmet C. Oz and Michael F. Roizen spent 11 weeks at No. 1 and a total of 27 weeks on the list.

An analysis of how publishers fared in 2007 showed that Random House lost market share on both the hardcover and paperback lists. Random's titles accounted for 23.5 percent of all spots on the hardcover bestseller list in 2007, down from 28 percent in 2006. The company had 88 hardcovers hit the list in 2007 compared with 96 in 2006, and the number of weeks its books stayed on the list dropped to 373 from 495. Gaining market share was Simon & Schuster, with 54 titles hitting the hardcover list for 325 weeks, giving it a 20.4 percent share. Penguin, with 51 hardcover bestsellers, had a slight dip in market share to 14.9 percent, while HarperCollins's market share fell by 3.4 percent to 11.6 percent of the hardcover real estate. Harper's decline allowed Hachette Book Group to move past it into fourth place with an 11.8 percent share of the hardcover list with its 30 titles remaining on the list for 188 weeks.

The big winner on the paperback side was Penguin. Led by *The Kite Runner, The Memory Keeper's Daughter,* and *Eat, Pray, Love,* which together totaled 147 weeks on the trade paperback list, Penguin had 24.2 percent of the paperback bestseller spots, putting it at No. 1. Random House dropped 2.1 percent, giving it 23.5 percent of the trade list. Simon & Schuster and Hachette also dropped down the charts, holding a 10.4 percent and 8.4 percent share, respectively. Harper-Collins inched up to claim a 10.1 percent share. [For a detailed account of the 2007 bestsellers, see "Bestsellers of 2007" in Part 5—*Ed.*].

Prices of U.S. and Foreign Published Materials

Janet Belanger Morrow

Editor, ALA ALCTS Library Materials Price Index Editorial Board

The Library Materials Price Index (LMPI) Editorial Board of the American Library Association's Association for Library Collections and Technical Services' Publications Committee continues to monitor prices for a range of library materials from sources within North America and from other key publishing centers around the world.

During 2006 price increases for library materials were mixed, with four categories underperforming the U.S. Consumer Price Index (CPI). Periodicals significantly outperformed the CPI as usual, as did hardcover and academic books prices for the second year in a row. Over the past several years, books have started to exhibit some of the same inflationary activity seen in the serials industry, though not in the double digits through 2006. However, preliminary data for 2007 show a substantial increase in the CPI and trade paperbacks exhibiting a double-digit increase from 2006. CPI data are obtained from the Bureau of Labor Statistics Web site at http://www.bls.gov/cpi.

Two indexes have not been updated and are repeated from last year. Several factors have hampered index preparation in recent years. These include mergers and acquisitions in the publishing and distribution world that make it more difficult to determine what is published in a foreign country by "multinational" firms; the conversion of several key countries to the euro; and migrations by vendors to new internal systems. Several compilers are in active discussions with vendors to obtain data to revive their indexes.

	Percent Change				
Index	2003	2004	2005	2006	2007
CPI	1.9	3.3	3.4	2.5	4.1
Periodicals	8.2	6.5	7.8	7.3	n.a.
Serials services	7.2	7.1	n.a.	n.a.	n.a.
Hardcover books	n.a.	0.0	-3.60	5.14	0.36
Academic books	1.3	1.9	6.4	2.9	n.a.
College books	4.8	4.4	1.7	3.0	0.47
Mass market paperbacks	n.a.	0.0	0.80	1.27	0.47
Trade paperbacks	n.a.	0.0	5.72	0.83	12.72
Audiobooks	n.a.	0.0	15.67	-8.78	7.18
Newspapers	3.5	2.1	-0.9	1.8	-2.0

n.a. = not available

U.S. Published Materials

Tables 1 through 8B indicate average prices and price indexes for library materials published primarily in the United States. These indexes are U.S. Periodicals (Table 1), U.S. Serials Services (Table 2), U.S. Hardcover Books (Table 3),

North American Academic Books (Table 4), U.S. College Books (Table 5), U.S. Mass Market Paperback Books (Table 6), U.S. Paperbacks (Excluding Mass Market) (Table 7), and U.S. Daily Newspapers and International Newspapers (Tables 8A and 8B).

Periodical and Serial Prices

The LMPI Editorial Board and Swets Information Services jointly produce the U.S. Periodicals Price Index (USPPI) (Table 1). The subscription prices shown are publishers' list prices, excluding publisher discount or vendor service charges. This report includes 2005, 2006, and 2007 data indexed to the base year of 1984. Unfortunately, due to delays beyond the compiler's control, this index could not be updated in time for the publication deadline and is repeated from the previous edition.

Compiled by Brenda Dingley, this table shows that U.S. periodical prices, excluding Russian translations, increased by 7.2 percent from 2006 to 2007. This figure represents a 0.5 percent decrease in the overall rate of inflation from the 7.8 percent figure posted from 2005 to 2006. Including the Russian translation category, the single-year increase was only slightly lower, at 7.1 percent for 2007. This figure is 0.6 percent lower than the rate of 7.7 percent for the entire sample in 2006. In 2007, as in 2006, the overall greatest price increases were in the sciences, which averaged a 7.5 percent average overall increase in 2007. Unlike 2006, when the Home Economics category posted an increase of 11.8 percent, in 2007 no subject category showed the double-digit increases seen in previous years. The highest increase in 2007 was again in Home Economics, at 9.8 percent. Education posted the second highest increase at 9.3 percent, and the Political Sciences and Zoology categories posted the third-highest increase at 8.5 percent. Children's Periodicals, as usual, showed the lowest increase, at 0.3 percent.

More extensive reports from the periodicals price index have been published annually in the April 15 issue of *Library Journal* through 1992, in the May issue of *American Libraries* from 1993 to 2002, and in the October 2003 issue of *Library Resources and Technical Services.* The full reports for the 1999–2006 studies are available on the Web site of the Association for Collections and Library Technical Services (ALCTS) at the URL http://www.ala.org/ala/alcts/ divgroups/publicationsdiv/librarymaterials/librarymaterials.cfm. Future editions of the USPPI will also be posted on the ALCTS Web site as they are completed.

The U.S. Serials Services Index (Table 2) has not been updated recently and is current through 2004. A new compiler has been selected to work on this index and we hope to have it updated for next year's article. When last updated, compiler Nancy Chaffin noted that titles continued to experience migration from print to electronic format. As the index is built only of printed products, the e-only titles were dropped from the various subject indexes. As this trend continues, it becomes more difficult to identify new titles that are print subscriptions.

All areas of serials services saw increases in prices for 2004, with the highest a tie between General and Humanities and U.S. Documents (both at 11.3 percent) and the lowest (5.2 percent) in Science and Technology. The average increase was 7.1 percent for all subject categories. More extensive reports on

(text continues on page 520)

Table 1 / U.S. Periodicals: Average Prices and Price Indexes, 2005–2007

Index Base: 1984 = 100

Subject Area	1984 Average Price	2005 Average Price	2005 Index	2006 Average Price	2006 Index	2007 Average Price	2007 Index
U.S. periodicals excluding Russian translations	$54.97	$349.79	636.3	$377.08	686.0	$404.40	735.7
U.S. periodicals including Russian translations	72.47	449.69	620.5	484.18	668.1	518.55	715.6
Agriculture	24.06	141.46	587.9	148.86	618.7	159.51	663.0
Business and Economics	38.87	205.85	529.6	218.33	561.7	231.66	596.0
Chemistry and physics	228.90	1,879.56	821.1	2,045.12	893.5	2,189.67	956.6
Children's periodicals	12.21	28.62	234.4	28.63	234.5	28.71	235.2
Education	34.01	190.32	559.6	203.07	597.1	222.05	652.9
Engineering	78.70	552.02	701.4	592.99	753.5	634.85	806.7
Fine and applied arts	26.90	70.93	263.7	76.24	283.4	77.63	288.6
General interest periodicals	27.90	54.47	195.2	57.53	206.2	59.03	211.6
History	23.68	89.65	378.6	93.92	396.6	101.40	428.2
Home economics	37.15	171.03	416.7	191.25	466.0	210.05	511.8
Industrial arts	30.40	144.97	476.9	148.05	487.0	154.84	509.4
Journalism and communications	39.25	160.88	409.9	168.67	429.7	174.51	444.6
Labor and industrial relations	29.87	168.73	564.9	183.77	615.2	186.87	625.6
Law	31.31	120.95	386.3	126.25	403.2	133.46	426.2
Library and information sciences	38.85	136.99	352.6	145.61	374.8	154.73	398.3
Literature and language	23.02	80.39	349.2	87.54	380.3	91.80	398.8
Mathematics, botany, geology, general science	106.56	729.15	684.3	788.55	740.0	853.36	800.8
Medicine	125.57	962.83	766.8	1,034.83	824.1	1,113.97	887.1
Philosophy and religion	21.94	81.11	369.7	87.28	397.8	93.00	423.9
Physical education and recreation	20.54	69.77	339.7	72.82	354.5	76.28	371.4
Political science	32.43	189.87	585.5	205.29	633.0	222.77	686.9
Psychology	69.74	496.41	711.8	539.07	773.0	579.93	831.6
Russian translations	381.86	2,496.09	653.7	2,677.92	701.3	2,856.72	748.1
Sociology and anthropology	43.87	284.18	647.8	309.70	706.0	335.16	764.0
Zoology	78.35	680.81	868.9	745.61	951.6	809.07	1,032.6
Total number of periodicals							
Excluding Russian translations	3,731	3,728		3,728		3,728	
Including Russian translations	3,942	3,910		3,910		3,910	

Compiled by Brenda Dingley, University of Missouri, Kansas City, based on subscription information supplied by Swets Information Services.

Table 2 / U.S. Serials Services: Average Price and Price Indexes 2002–2004
Index Base: 1984 = 100

Subject Area	1984	2002		2003			2004		
	Average Price	Average Price	Index	Average Price	Percent Increase	Index	Average Price	Percent Increase	Index
U.S. serials services*	$295.13	$747.16	253.2	$800.74	7.2	271.3	$857.96	7.1	290.7
Business	437.07	849.65	194.4	911.89	7.3	208.6	975.45	7.0	223.2
General and humanities	196.55	569.02	289.5	596.50	4.8	303.5	663.75	11.3	337.7
Law	275.23	839.65	305.1	916.06	9.1	332.8	975.82	6.5	354.5
Science and technology	295.36	975.49	330.3	1,054.03	8.1	356.9	1,108.86	5.2	375.4
Social sciences	283.82	656.54	231.3	698.13	6.3	246.0	768.44	10.1	270.7
U.S. documents	97.37	202.60	208.1	189.05	-6.7	194.2	210.39	11.3	216.1
Total number of services	1,537	1,311		1,310			1,326		

Compiled by Nancy J. Chaffin, Arizona State University (West) from data suppled by the Faxon Company, publishers' list prices, and library acquisitions records.
The definition of a serial service has been taken from *American National Standard for Library and Information Services and Related Publishing Practices—Library Materials—Criteria for Price Indexes* (ANSI Z39.20 - 1983).
*Excludes Wilson Index; excludes Russian translations as of 1988.

Table 3 / U.S. Hardcover Books: Average Prices and Price Indexes, 2005–2007

Index Base: 2004 = 100

Category	2004 Average Price	2005 Volumes	2005 Average Price	2005 Index	2006 Volumes	2006 Average Price	2006 Index	2007 Volumes	2007 Average Price	2007 Index
Agriculture	$67.15	648	$57.61	85.8	581	$61.38	91.4	689	$72.16	107.5
Arts	71.72	3,463	61.15	85.3	3,951	77.22	107.7	4,146	74.72	104.2
Biography	47.39	1,624	47.25	99.7	1,623	51.77	109.2	1,664	51.72	109.1
Business	111.16	2,742	108.82	97.9	2,775	112.20	100.9	2,893	114.69	103.2
Education	96.83	1,112	90.99	94.0	1,303	97.05	100.2	1,267	104.30	107.7
Fiction	27.89	4,721	28.38	101.8	4,478	28.65	102.7	4,485	33.45	119.9
General works	99.82	2,356	92.13	92.3	2,281	96.57	96.7	2,134	114.85	115.1
Graphic novels	30.04	240	33.81	112.5	337	31.86	106.1	366	33.57	111.8
History	76.27	4,532	78.01	102.3	4,702	83.38	109.3	4,875	80.42	105.4
Home economics	29.75	1,336	30.55	102.7	1,375	29.84	100.3	1,324	27.95	93.9
Juveniles	24.71	14,774	26.21	106.1	14,457	26.24	106.2	14,885	28.49	115.3
Language	101.60	1,268	104.38	102.7	1,231	104.60	103.0	1,495	104.36	102.7
Law	144.75	1,281	145.60	100.6	1,411	162.06	112.0	1,424	153.37	106.0
Literature	93.48	1,866	109.23	116.8	1,892	94.99	101.6	2,269	99.33	106.3
Medicine	154.62	2,684	148.08	95.8	2,929	153.53	99.3	2,916	146.97	95.1
Music	75.20	408	76.87	102.2	390	76.57	101.8	474	74.23	98.7
Philosophy, psychology	102.96	2,085	89.34	86.8	2,405	83.11	80.7	2,428	82.03	79.7
Poetry, drama	37.88	470	41.81	110.4	380	44.76	118.2	431	46.55	122.9
Religion	65.20	2,653	58.65	90.0	2,583	66.81	102.5	2,564	69.37	106.4
Science	164.09	4,649	162.38	99.0	4,859	158.23	96.4	4,596	167.68	102.2
Sociology, economics	97.63	4,912	96.06	98.4	5,497	109.70	112.4	5,569	101.09	103.5
Sports, recreation	47.15	904	36.84	78.1	973	36.84	78.1	879	36.71	77.9
Technology	134.54	2,770	142.73	106.1	3,160	125.92	93.6	2,888	126.43	94.0
Travel	45.65	414	37.45	82.0	384	42.38	92.8	734	48.34	105.9
Totals	$78.72	63,912	$75.89	96.4	65,957	$79.79	101.4	67,395	$80.08	101.7

Compiled by Catherine Barr from data supplied by Baker & Taylor.

Table 4 / North American Academic Books: Average Prices and Price Indexes 2004–2006

(Index Base: 1989 = 100)

Subject Area	LC Class	1989 No. of Titles	1989 Average Price	2004 No. of Titles	2004 Average Price	2005 No. of Titles	2005 Average Price	2006 No. of Titles	2006 Average Price	2006 % Change 2005–2006	Index
Agriculture	S	897	$45.13	950	$72.88	971	$68.95	963	$65.14	-5.5	144.3
Anthropology	GN	406	32.81	332	57.88	377	62.04	368	67.94	9.5	207.1
Botany	QK	251	69.02	118	100.48	198	94.29	239	115.31	22.3	167.1
Business and economics	H	5,979	41.67	5,389	64.86	7,377	68.74	7,485	71.64	4.2	171.9
Chemistry	QD	577	110.61	411	172.45	533	187.38	484	176.72	-5.7	159.8
Education	L	1,685	29.61	2,354	47.47	2,787	51.30	3,011	56.86	10.8	192.0
Engineering and technology	T	4,569	64.94	4,503	102.95	5,832	105.58	5,666	98.67	-6.5	151.9
Fine and applied arts	M-N	3,040	40.72	3,332	48.82	4,215	48.16	4,652	52.77	9.6	129.6
General works	A	333	134.65	74	58.79	85	52.06	97	72.40	39.1	53.8
Geography	G	396	47.34	591	76.81	803	76.54	788	80.11	4.7	169.2
Geology	QE	303	63.49	184	99.06	191	104.50	203	100.12	-4.2	157.7
History	C-D-E-F	5,549	31.34	6,400	46.92	7,174	49.47	7,296	52.54	6.2	167.6
Home economics	TX	535	27.10	517	36.73	700	37.74	683	41.23	9.3	152.2
Industrial arts	TT	175	23.89	164	34.18	179	35.48	237	32.54	-8.3	136.2
Law	K	1,252	51.10	1,881	82.55	2,568	86.69	2,701	87.26	0.7	170.8
Library and information science	Z	857	44.51	454	65.61	489	69.93	479	62.89	-10.1	141.3

Subject	LC Class										
Literature and language	P	10,812	24.99	9,915	39.28	12,391	41.53	12,551	45.69	10.0	182.8
Mathematics and computer science	QA	2,707	44.68	2,926	76.67	3,552	82.41	3,365	76.47	-7.2	171.2
Medicine	R	5,028	58.38	4,670	76.72	6,226	83.45	6,550	85.21	2.1	146.0
Military and naval science	U-V	715	33.57	456	47.92	548	56.67	643	58.96	4.0	175.6
Philosophy and religion	B	3,518	29.06	4,713	49.97	5,636	53.31	5,745	59.32	11.3	204.1
Physical education and recreation	GV	814	20.38	993	41.44	1,179	38.26	1,226	41.23	7.8	202.3
Physics and astronomy	QB	1,219	64.59	916	106.92	1,273	105.76	1,285	104.67	-1.0	162.0
Political science	J	1,650	36.76	1,664	54.55	2,094	63.95	2,300	65.94	3.1	179.4
Psychology	BF	890	31.97	807	50.67	980	56.85	1,010	55.27	-2.8	172.9
Science (general)	Q	433	56.10	276	96.99	384	86.82	416	84.02	-3.2	149.8
Sociology	HM	2,742	29.36	3,639	50.65	4,513	53.47	4,856	60.55	13.2	206.2
Zoology	QH,L,P,R	1,967	71.28	1,482	100.49	2,129	104.04	2,235	107.34	3.2	150.6
Average for all subjects		59,299	$41.69	60,111	$61.50	75,384	$65.42	77,534	$67.29	2.9	161.4

Compiled by Stephen Bosch, University of Arizona from electronic data provided by Blackwell Book Services and YBP Library Services. The data represent all titles (hardcover, trade, and paperback books, as well as annuals and electronic books) treated for all approval plan customers serviced by the vendors. This table covers titles published or distributed in the United States and Canada during the calendar years listed.

This index does not include paperback editions. The inclusion of these items does impact pricing in the index.

(continued from page 514)
serials services pricing are available on the ALCTS Web site at http://www.ala.
org/ala/alcts/divgroups/publicationsdiv/librarymaterials/librarymaterials.cfm.

Book Prices

Tables 3 (Hardcover Books), 6 (Mass Market Paperbacks), and 7 (Other Paperbacks), prepared by Catherine Barr, are compiled from a new source this year—
book wholesaler Baker & Taylor—and are not directly comparable with previous
years' data, which came from R. R. Bowker's Books in Print. Differences in the
two databases have inevitably resulted in variations in totals and across categories. For this reason, the index base for these tables has been changed to 2004.
Each of the tables gives average prices for 2005, 2006, and 2007 (preliminary).
Refer to the 2007 *Bowker Annual* to find the average prices, indexed to a base
year of 1997, that were derived from the Books in Print database for the years
2004 and 2005, plus preliminary figures for 2006. This year we have also added
a new category—graphic novels—and a new table on audiobooks (Table 7A).

According to the new data, average book prices generally rose over the years
from 2004 through 2007 for all formats except audiobooks, which dipped from a
high of $40.45 in 2005 to $36.90 in 2006 (a fall of $3.55 or 8.78 percent) and
recovered to $39.55 in 2007 (an increase of $2.65 or 7.18 percent). Although the
new paperback prices are very close to those reported previously, those for hardcover show a substantial increase. The average price given for 2004 hardcovers,
for example, is now $78.72, a jump from the previous price of $61.32.

Average book prices for fiction rose in 2006 and 2007, apart from the audiobook sector, which showed a decrease of 3 percent in 2006 but rose 8.10 percent
in 2007. Hardcover fiction titles increased by less than 1 percent in 2006 but rose
by 16.75 percent in 2007. Mass market fiction increased 0.64 percent in 2006 and
1.11 percent in 2007, while trade and other paperbacks increased 4.48 percent in
2006 and 5.47 percent in 2007.

Prices for the other key area—children's and young adult books (juveniles)—were mixed in 2006 and 2007. Hardcover prices increased 0.11 percent
and 8.57 percent, respectively. Children's and YA mass market paperbacks rose
7.25 percent in 2006 but dropped 0.81 percent in 2007, while trade and other
paperback children's and YA titles fell for both years, by 3.73 percent in 2006
and by 1.26 percent in 2007.

The North American Academic Books Price Index (Table 4) is prepared by
Stephen Bosch. The average price of North American Academic Books in 2006
(Table 4) increased by 2.9 percent as compared with the 2005 average price. The
growth of electronic books is now influencing book prices. Starting in 2006 and
continuing into the foreseeable future, the major vendors have been very aggressive in adding electronic books to their offerings. In most academic settings
e-books are not cheaper than the print counterparts and a portion of the price
increase is due to the addition of the more expensive e-book versions. To be sure
that this is truly is the case, Bosch reports, "I redid the 2006 data using a file from
one vendor that included no electronic books, and the number of titles in the combined index dropped by 8,334 and the average price declined 5.5 percent. Due to

customer demands, vendors offer multiple platforms and pricing models for e-books; consequently there can be multiple prices for the same title. Since this is where the market is going, it is appropriate to have e-books in the index, but it is also good to know that this is a driver for price increases, not a price decrease at this time. Publishers are still very concerned that selling e-books to libraries will hurt overall sales, so pricing to libraries is higher than print pricing."

For the past two years the average prices have been trending higher (up 6.4 percent in 2005). In addition to the growth of e-books, there are some other factors that may help explain this increase. One vendor reported sharp increases in the prices for reprints, which jumped 22.5 percent (see http://www.blackwell. com/downloads/CC_2007_Introduction.pdf). Also, it was reported by YBP Library Services that their average price in 2006–2007 increased from the previous year by only 0.4 percent if cloth editions were the preferred version, but by 3.3 percent if paper were the preferred edition (see http://www.ybp.com/book_ price_update.html). As the index includes both paper and cloth, price rises in the paper editions are also a factor in the overall price increase.

The data used for this index are derived from all titles treated by Blackwell Book Services and by YBP in their approval plans during the calendar years listed. The index does include paperback editions as supplied by these vendors and the recent increases in the number and prices of paperbacks distributed as part of the approval plans have clearly influenced the prices reflected in the index figures. In addition, e-books are now being treated in approval plans and these are consequently part of the data reports and are in the index. The inclusion of both paperbacks and e-books has resulted in the numbers of titles increasing, as each will have a unique ISBN and is treated as a separate edition. So drivers for this price increase include general price inflation as well as increases from the inclusion of e-books that generally are more expensive than print counterparts. Many e-book pricing models add extra charges of as much as 50 percent to the retail price. Paperbacks and e-books will continue to be a part of this index, as they are included in the approval plan data and represent a viable part of the North American book market. The direct impact on inflation caused by hardback/paperback/ e-book pricing continues to be unquantifiable, but it is clear that the increases in overall price inflation for academic books during the past few years seem to correlate to increases in paperback numbers and now the impact of e-books. This may change, as publishers have started to "up" the size of paperbacks as well as the price, or as e-books find pricing levels closer to normal retail.

Analysis of the data as it is processed shows that the overlap titles that are excluded from the index tend to be more expensive than the unique titles processed by each vendor. This fact will tend to hold down the average prices in the index. In all cases, the average price of a book for each vendor is 4 percent to 6 percent higher than the aggregate average price. This shows that when the titles are combined in the aggregate index, the unique titles each vendor handles tend to be cheaper than the titles that overlap. This makes sense because publications from small publishers tend to be cheaper than those of mainstream publishers, and the small publishers will tend to make up more of the unique titles handled by each vendor. All vendors will carry the full title list from Macmillan or Oxford University Press, but a small regional press may not be supplied by all vendors.

Current trends reported by vendors indicate that increases are going to grow in 2007 and there should also be increases in the titles and formats available.

Price changes vary, as always, among subject areas. This year there were several double-digit increases in subject areas and several areas saw prices decrease. If you look at the top four areas for price increases, all broad subject areas are represented: General Works, Botany, Sociology, and Philosophy and Religion. Education and Literature are the other two areas the showed double-digit inflation. This is unusual, but e-books represented well over 10 percent in these categories and that was a contributing factor to the price increases.

It is good to remember that price indexes become less accurate at describing price changes the smaller the sample becomes. General Works is a small sampling and showed a 39.1 percent increase, but to then conclude that all books in the area increased 39.1 percent is not correct. This area has a small sample size of only 97 books and the inclusion of just a few large expensive items can have a major impact on prices for the category. As this area has a relatively small number of titles, but large numbers of expensive encyclopedic sets, prices will always be volatile. This year Library and Information Sciences prices dropped 10 percent. This category only has 479 titles and it only takes a handful of titles to push these numbers down. The smaller the sample size the greater the chance for variance caused by the inclusion or lack of a few expensive books.

This compilation of the U.S. College Books Price Index (Table 5), prepared by Frederick C. Lynden, contains price and indexing information for the years 2005 through 2007 (index base year of 1989), and also the percentage change between 2006 and 2007. The index is based on titles reviewed in *Choice* magazine, a publication of the Association for College and Research Libraries, a division of the American Library Association. Data for this index were compiled from 6,599 reviews of books published in *Choice* during 2007; expensive titles ($500 or more) were omitted from the analysis, thus the total number of titles reported is smaller. As with the Table 4 (North American Academic Books), this index includes some paperback prices; as a result, the average price of books is less than if only hardcover books were included.

For 2007 the overall average price for books in the Humanities, Sciences, and Social and Behavioral Sciences (including reference books) was $62.44, a negligible 0.47 percent increase over the average 2006 price of $62.15. Reference books continued to have the highest average price at $128.54 but the lowest percentage increase over the previous year, -6.1 percent. Without reference books included, the average 2007 book price was $57.15 or a 1.6 percent increase over the average 2006 price of $56.24.

The average 2007 price for Humanities titles increased by 1.8 percent over the previous year. The average price for Science and Technology titles decreased by more than 1 percent (1.4.), whereas the price for Social and Behavioral Sciences titles increased by 2.8 percent. Since 1989 there has been an overall book price increase of 54.1 percent when reference books are included. Calculated separately, reference books showed a 6 percent decrease over the previous year (2006). This figure is in line with past years so last year must have been an

(text continues on page 529)

Table 5 / U.S. College Books: Average Prices and Price Indexes 1989, 2005–2007
(Index Base for All Years: 1989=100)

Subject	1989 No. of Titles	1989 Avg. Price per Title	2005 No. of Titles	2005 Avg. Price per Title	2005 Indexed to 1989	2005 Indexed to 2004	2006 No. of Titles	2006 Avg. Price per Title	2006 Indexed to 1989	2006 Indexed to 2005	2007 No. of Titles	2007 Avg. Price per Title	2007 Indexed to 1989	2007 Indexed to 2006	2007 Percent Change 2006–2007
General	19	$40.19	n.a.	n.a.	n.a.	n.a.	n.a.	n.a.	n.a.	n.a.	n.a.	n.a.	n.a.	n.a.	n.a.
Humanities	21	32.33	64	$49.04	151.7	95.8	63	$55.45	171.5	113.1	61	$55.00	170.1	99.2	-0.8
Art and Architecture	276	55.56	145	52.26	94.1	98.2	155	53.26	95.9	101.9	152	57.55	103.6	108.1	8.1
Fine Arts	n.a.	n.a.	167	58.85	n.a.	98.4	182	58.48	n.a.	99.4	226	61.02	n.a.	104.3	4.3
Architecture	83	n.a.	83	54.62	n.a.	95.6	81	54.07	n.a.	99.0	75	57.00	n.a.	105.4	5.4
Photography	24	44.11	31	57.24	129.8	127.3	50	50.34	114.1	87.9	48	51.76	117.3	102.8	2.8
Communication	42	32.70	99	50.74	155.2	95.0	77	51.01	156.0	100.5	93	58.83	179.9	115.3	15.3
Language and Literature	110	35.17	86	56.85	161.6	94.5	71	62.81	178.6	110.5	95	54.88	156.0	87.4	-12.6
African and Middle Eastern	n.a.	n.a.	19	57.69	n.a.	107.8	15	56.18	n.a.	97.4	24	49.58	n.a.	88.3	-11.7
Asian and Oceanian	n.a.	n.a.	17	44.17	n.a.	87.4	26	56.21	n.a.	127.3	40	54.07	n.a.	96.2	-3.8
Classical	75	43.07	31	57.26	132.9	92.4	29	68.94	160.1	120.4	27	77.23	179.3	112.0	12.0
English and American	547	30.27	418	53.92	178.1	103.4	424	57.36	189.5	106.4	401	57.70	190.6	100.6	0.6
Germanic	38	32.18	38	63.44	197.1	111.3	23	64.99	202.0	102.4	29	61.66	191.6	94.9	-5.1
Romance	97	30.30	76	60.10	198.3	115.2	70	56.89	187.8	94.7	89	51.28	169.2	90.1	-9.9
Slavic	41	27.92	15	44.85	160.6	93.2	15	42.98	153.9	95.8	15	67.01	240.0	155.9	55.9
Other	63	25.09	n.a.	n.a.	n.a.	n.a.	n.a.	n.a.	n.a.	n.a.	n.a.	n.a.	n.a.	n.a.	n.a.
Performing Arts	20	29.41	22	35.10	119.3	90.4	18	71.31	242.5	203.2	25	50.55	171.9	70.9	-29.1
Film	82	33.00	109	43.95	133.2	83.5	118	52.00	157.6	118.3	133	52.44	158.9	100.8	0.8
Music	156	35.34	140	52.15	147.6	93.5	156	49.02	138.7	94.0	145	53.60	151.7	109.3	9.3
Theater and Dance	58	34.18	51	56.42	165.1	99.7	38	57.62	168.6	102.1	43	51.20	149.8	88.9	-11.1
Philosophy	185	37.25	178	49.01	131.6	98.2	164	60.13	161.4	122.7	187	58.64	157.4	97.5	-2.5
Religion	174	33.49	251	46.95	140.2	103.6	200	46.47	138.8	99.0	232	50.73	151.5	109.2	9.2
Total Humanities	2,009	$36.09	2,040	$52.37	145.1	99.5	1,975	$55.11	152.7	105.2	2140	$56.09	155.4	101.8	1.8
Science/Technology	99	$46.90	51	$46.65	99.5	118.5	57	$44.15	94.1	94.6	65	$46.46	99.1	105.2	5.2
History of Science and Technology	74	40.56	118	45.53	112.3	105.6	112	41.06	101.2	90.2	95	47.73	117.7	116.2	16.2

Table 5 / U.S. College Books: Average Prices and Price Indexes 1989, 2005–2007 *(cont.)*
(Index Base for All Years: 1989=100)

Subject	1989 No. of Titles	1989 Avg. Price per Title	2005 No. of Titles	2005 Avg. Price per Title	2005 Indexed to 1989	2005 Indexed to 2004	2006 No. of Titles	2006 Avg. Price per Title	2006 Indexed to 1989	2006 Indexed to 2005	2007 No. of Titles	2007 Avg. Price per Title	2007 Indexed to 1989	2007 Indexed to 2006	2007 Percent Change 2006–2007
Astronautics and Astronomy	22	50.56	43	50.93	100.7	90.8	50	54.56	107.9	107.1	71	50.37	99.6	92.3	-7.7
Biology	97	51.01	142	65.61	128.6	107.3	116	69.65	136.5	106.2	138	58.18	114.1	83.5	-16.5
Botany	29	63.91	63	57.47	89.9	97.6	54	73.06	114.3	127.1	48	55.62	87.0	76.1	-23.9
Zoology	53	49.21	97	65.55	133.2	98.8	71	66.16	134.4	100.9	76	76.36	155.2	115.4	15.4
Chemistry	21	70.76	73	121.84	172.2	106.8	60	110.55	156.2	90.7	76	116.67	164.9	105.5	5.5
Earth Science	34	79.44	52	82.73	104.1	123.9	46	61.15	77.0	73.9	54	79.63	100.2	130.2	30.2
Engineering	87	66.74	92	108.88	163.1	117.2	96	108.70	162.9	99.8	90	90.31	135.3	83.1	-16.9
Health Sciences	94	34.91	136	45.91	131.5	99.5	122	57.19	163.8	124.6	151	52.75	151.1	92.2	-7.8
Information and Computer Science	70	40.35	65	63.16	156.5	101.3	43	71.10	176.2	112.6	55	63.55	157.5	89.4	-10.6
Mathematics	60	48.53	90	73.39	151.2	111.7	93	70.90	146.1	96.6	90	65.38	134.7	92.2	-7.8
Physics	22	43.94	63	73.85	168.1	95.6	72	67.93	154.6	92.0	81	79.13	180.1	116.5	16.5
Sports and Physical Education	18	27.46	65	36.04	131.2	82.6	54	40.39	147.1	112.1	20	37.52	136.6	92.9	-7.1
Total Science/Technology	780	$49.54	1,150	$66.44	134.1	107.6	1046	$67.06	135.4	100.9	1,110	$66.15	133.5	98.6	-1.4
Social/Behavioral Sciences	92	$37.09	119	$50.19	135.3	104.5	103	$49.98	134.8	99.6	102	$60.65	163.5	121.3	21.3
Anthropology	96	39.94	132	56.13	140.5	103.1	130	57.11	143.0	101.7	96	67.55	169.1	118.3	18.3
Business, Management, and Labor	145	35.72	144	51.75	144.9	115.8	139	48.49	135.8	93.7	132	50.78	142.2	104.7	4.7
Economics	332	40.75	228	56.85	139.5	108.5	239	58.16	142.7	102.3	261	63.37	155.5	109.0	9.0
Education	71	34.50	175	49.02	142.1	108.3	169	53.52	155.1	109.2	159	51.75	150.0	96.7	-3.3
History, Geography, and Area Studies	59	42.10	108	46.11	109.5	86.9	137	54.99	130.6	119.3	105	49.33	117.2	89.7	-10.3
Africa	44	34.85	33	50.74	145.6	82.4	36	57.29	164.4	112.9	29	54.94	157.6	95.9	-4.1
Ancient History	n.a.	n.a.	45	60.48	n.a.	92.4	47	70.66	n.a.	116.8	57	71.50	n.a.	101.2	1.2

Asia and Oceania	76	34.75	74	56.91	163.8	105.6	81	53.67	154.4	94.3	83	56.04	161.3	104.4	4.4
Central and East. Europe	n.a.	n.a.	57	51.89	n.a.	96.4	53	51.67	n.a.	99.6	60	55.80	n.a.	108.0	8.0
Latin America and the Caribbean	42	37.23	69	52.20	140.2	101.7	61	56.17	150.9	107.6	56	52.06	139.8	92.7	-7.3
Middle East and North Africa	30	36.32	45	50.22	138.3	96.6	37	51.83	142.7	103.2	45	64.82	178.5	125.1	25.1
North America	349	30.56	380	40.79	133.5	96.4	396	40.51	132.6	99.3	406	42.53	139.2	105.0	5.0
United Kingdom	n.a.	n.a.	82	52.11	n.a.	91.4	73	58.14	n.a.	111.6	73	56.88	n.a.	97.8	-2.2
Western Europe	287	42.08	142	58.09	138.0	110.1	141	57.51	136.7	99.0	168	48.88	116.2	85.0	-15.0
Political Science	28	33.56	25	52.31	155.9	82.0	22	48.11	143.4	92.0	37	60.88	181.4	126.5	26.5
Comparative Politics	236	37.82	189	57.10	151.0	102.2	219	58.80	155.5	103.0	228	58.17	153.8	98.9	-1.1
International Relations	207	35.74	155	50.08	140.1	99.3	157	56.49	158.1	112.8	156	53.02	148.3	93.9	-6.1
Political Theory	59	37.76	70	48.71	129.0	87.8	57	55.68	147.5	114.3	60	60.41	160.0	108.5	8.5
U.S. Politics	212	29.37	178	44.80	152.5	96.3	158	48.94	166.6	109.2	160	46.88	159.6	95.8	-4.2
Psychology	179	36.36	116	54.47	149.8	98.4	122	59.00	162.3	108.3	130	59.19	162.8	100.3	0.3
Sociology	178	36.36	182	52.76	145.1	102.3	198	52.05	143.2	98.7	257	57.14	157.2	109.8	9.8
Total Social/Behavioral Sciences	2,722	$36.43	2,748	$50.94	139.8	100.6	2,775	$52.98	145.4	104.0	2,860	$54.46	149.5	102.8	2.8
Total General, Humanities, Science/Technology, Social Science (excl. Reference)	5,530	$38.16	5,938	$54.43	142.6	101.8	5,796	$56.24	147.4	103.3	6,110	$57.15	149.8	101.6	1.6
Reference	636	$61.02	n.a.	n.a.	n.a.	n.a.	n.a.	n.a.	n.a.	n.a.	n.a.	n.a.	n.a.	n.a.	n.a.
General	n.a.	n.a.	52	$86.72	n.a.	100.4	35	$92.25	n.a.	106.4	33	$136.26	n.a.	147.7	47.7
Humanities	n.a.	n.a.	137	125.31	n.a.	132.7	152	131.80	n.a.	105.2	139	114.51	n.a.	86.9	-13.1
Science and Technology	n.a.	n.a.	97	127.71	n.a.	113.6	73	147.50	n.a.	115.5	64	96.76	n.a.	65.6	-34.4
Social and Behavioral Sciences	n.a.	n.a.	267	128.65	n.a.	96.5	198	144.69	n.a.	112.5	253	143.28	n.a.	99.0	-1.0
Total Reference	636	$61.02	553	$123.72	202.8	108.2	458	$136.85	224.3	110.6	489	$128.54	210.7	93.9	-6.1
Grand Total (incl. Reference)	6,166	$40.52	6,491	$60.33	148.9	101.7	6,254	$62.15	153.4	103.0	6,599	$62.44	154.1	100.5	0.5

Compiled by Frederick C. Lynden.
n.a. = not available

Table 6 / U.S. Mass Market Paperbacks Average Per-Volume Prices, 2005–2007
Index Base: 2004 = 100

Category	2004 Average Prices	2005 Final Volumes	2005 Final Average Prices	2005 Final Index	2006 Final Volumes	2006 Final Average Prices	2006 Final Index	2007 Final Volumes	2007 Final Average Prices	2007 Final Index
Agriculture	n.a.	n.a.	n.a.	n.a.	n.a.	n.a.	n.a.	n.a.	n.a.	n.a.
Arts	$7.54	4	$8.23	109.2	3	$7.99	106.0	3	$8.64	114.6
Biography	7.79	21	7.77	99.7	13	7.76	99.6	10	7.89	101.3
Business	7.99	1	7.99	100.0	n.a.	n.a.	n.a.	n.a.	n.a.	n.a.
Education	n.a.	n.a.	n.a.	n.a.	n.a.	n.a.	n.a.	n.a.	n.a.	n.a.
Fiction	6.21	4,241	6.27	101.0	4,306	6.31	101.6	4,194	6.38	102.7
General works	7.18	107	7.50	104.5	129	7.71	107.4	105	7.44	103.6
Graphic novels	n.a.	2	8.47	n.a.	5	7.99	n.a.	n.a.	n.a.	n.a.
History	7.38	25	7.69	104.2	15	7.52	101.9	12	7.66	103.8
Home economics	7.24	4	6.37	88.0	3	7.66	105.8	2	7.75	107.0
Juveniles	5.95	524	5.79	97.3	467	6.21	104.4	442	6.16	103.5
Language	n.a.	1	6.99	n.a.	1	5.99	n.a.	4	6.24	n.a.
Law	7.99	n.a.	n.a.	n.a.	n.a.	n.a.	n.a.	n.a.	n.a.	n.a.
Literature	6.95	1	7.95	114.4	1	7.95	114.4	n.a.	n.a.	n.a.
Medicine	7.49	2	7.75	103.5	4	6.62	88.4	4	6.87	91.7
Music	7.95	1	7.95	100.0	n.a.	n.a.	n.a.	n.a.	n.a.	n.a.
Philosophy, psychology	7.36	9	10.74	145.9	20	7.38	100.3	11	7.88	107.1
Poetry, drama	6.28	27	6.09	97.0	8	6.21	98.9	5	6.37	101.4
Religion	7.61	4	11.21	147.3	6	7.49	98.4	2	6.99	91.9
Science	6.99	n.a.	n.a.	n.a.	1	7.99	114.3	n.a.	n.a.	n.a.
Sociology, economics	7.09	6	7.08	99.9	4	7.22	101.8	2	7.49	105.6
Sports, recreation	7.22	19	7.44	103.1	13	6.87	95.2	24	5.99	83.0
Technology	n.a.	n.a.	n.a.	n.a.	n.a.	n.a.	n.a.	n.a.	n.a.	n.a.
Travel	n.a.	n.a.	n.a.	n.a.	1	7.99	n.a.	n.a.	n.a.	n.a.
Total	$6.23	4,999	$6.28	100.8	5,000	$6.36	102.1	4,820	$6.39	102.6

Compiled by Catherine Barr from data supplied by Baker & Taylor. n.a. = not available

Table 7 / U.S. Paperbacks (Excluding Mass Market): Average Prices and Price Indexes, 2005–2007
Index Base: 2004 = 100

Category	2004 Average Price	2005 Final			2006 Final			2007 Final		
		Volumes	Average Price	Index	Volumes	Average Price	Index	Volumes	Average Price	Index
Agriculture	$26.82	914	$27.43	102.3	880	$29.13	108.6	815	$31.27	116.6
Arts	31.62	3,871	30.10	95.2	3,940	32.76	103.6	3,930	31.94	101.0
Biography	19.56	1,854	19.12	97.8	1,798	19.73	100.9	1,868	19.66	100.5
Business	50.66	6,294	62.81	124.0	5,264	66.61	131.5	9,865	82.57	163.0
Education	32.98	4,710	32.87	99.7	4,814	35.85	108.7	4,202	35.24	106.9
Fiction	15.28	8,113	15.41	100.9	8,042	16.10	105.4	8,434	16.98	111.1
General works	26.98	5,823	27.97	103.7	5,852	32.56	120.7	5,459	31.06	115.1
Graphic novels	12.97	2,178	13.17	101.5	2,189	13.72	105.8	2,365	15.08	116.3
History	28.96	5,650	32.56	112.4	5,830	31.67	109.4	6,272	32.24	111.3
Home economics	18.66	2,632	18.74	100.4	2,380	19.85	106.4	2,273	19.31	103.5
Juveniles	11.97	11,095	11.54	96.4	11,229	11.11	92.8	10,516	10.97	91.6
Language	40.78	3,215	46.39	113.8	2,899	43.33	106.3	2,509	42.03	103.1
Law	53.84	1,935	61.57	114.4	3,282	53.79	99.9	2,740	67.89	126.1
Literature	32.70	2,307	29.41	89.9	1,680	32.40	99.1	1,762	35.83	109.6
Medicine	56.69	3,396	62.53	110.3	3,652	60.96	107.5	3,582	69.28	122.2
Music	22.43	2,530	22.09	98.5	2,519	24.96	111.3	2,123	28.28	126.1
Philosophy, psychology	31.93	3,494	31.14	97.5	3,302	32.09	100.5	3,674	31.54	98.8
Poetry, drama	15.56	2,239	16.04	103.1	2,061	16.18	104.0	2,148	16.95	108.9
Religion	20.38	5,569	19.98	98.0	5,657	20.27	99.5	5,425	20.04	98.3
Science	57.40	3,832	62.06	108.1	3,730	60.12	104.7	3,528	63.80	111.1
Sociology, economics	34.48	7,020	38.43	111.5	6,716	38.44	111.5	7,265	42.86	124.3
Sports, recreation	19.74	2,433	18.62	94.3	2,492	19.20	97.3	2,232	19.16	97.1
Technology	62.36	5,558	61.00	97.8	5,171	58.90	94.5	4,727	60.04	96.3
Travel	17.35	2,156	18.89	108.9	2,818	18.96	109.3	3,313	20.74	119.5
Totals	$30.61	98,818	$32.36	105.7	98,197	$32.63	106.6	101,027	$36.78	120.2

Compiled by Catherine Barr from data supplied by Baker & Taylor.

Table 7A / U.S. Audiobooks: Average Prices and Price Indexes, 2005–2007
Index Base: 2004 = 100

Category	2004 Average Price	2005 Volumes	2005 Average Price	2005 Index	2006 Volumes	2006 Average Price	2006 Index	2007 Volumes	2007 Average Price	2007 Index
Agriculture	$16.47	4	$29.78	113.3	12	$30.13	182.9	17	$33.51	203.5
Arts	27.30	27	46.22	118.9	42	32.83	120.3	23	28.98	106.2
Biography	36.19	289	38.65	102.5	327	38.85	107.4	403	45.19	124.9
Business	31.33	137	43.13	111.8	205	40.06	127.9	263	33.45	106.8
Education	31.26	63	22.02	90.8	57	41.25	132.0	35	38.45	123.0
Fiction	38.71	2,904	41.61	102.9	3,018	40.36	104.3	3,582	43.63	112.7
General works	29.61	239	28.41	98.8	261	29.67	100.2	286	33.43	112.9
Graphic novels	n.a.	2	16.48	n.a.	n.a.	n.a.	n.a.	2	19.47	n.a.
History	33.42	195	41.50	108.1	313	40.55	121.3	487	48.24	144.3
Home economics	25.00	26	15.18	90.2	17	18.90	75.6	18	28.91	115.6
Juveniles	25.69	739	28.91	103.2	753	32.08	124.9	1,064	32.40	126.1
Language	48.05	643	71.35	123.3	385	41.58	86.5	285	39.05	81.3
Law	62.93	44	54.87	91.9	46	76.46	121.5	24	59.25	94.2
Literature	23.82	16	25.79	102.0	38	20.25	85.0	38	32.97	138.4
Medicine	82.18	6	159.96	177.8	18	54.46	66.3	19	61.24	74.5
Music	26.48	108	26.61	100.1	155	24.84	93.8	101	23.11	87.3
Philosophy, psychology	25.23	215	25.43	100.2	204	27.10	107.4	332	29.05	115.1
Poetry, drama	20.73	79	23.35	102.6	122	23.50	113.4	84	27.54	132.9
Religion	30.88	365	27.55	96.7	349	26.96	87.3	352	28.32	91.7
Science	34.41	34	38.64	104.2	49	33.25	96.6	47	38.20	111.0
Sociology, economics	31.29	86	39.01	107.7	163	30.95	98.9	218	40.22	128.5
Sports, recreation	31.99	37	29.95	98.0	41	36.27	113.4	64	36.91	115.4
Technology	43.56	10	47.88	104.3	8	31.88	73.2	10	35.46	81.4
Travel	21.62	13	41.91	120.3	13	22.35	103.4	45	44.22	204.5
Total	$34.97	6,281	$40.45	115.7	6,596	$36.90	105.5	7,799	$39.55	113.1

(continued from page 522)

aberration. There has been a steady increase in the overall prices of reference books, and since 1989, a 211 percent increase in the average price. The decline in the number of print reference books published in recent years may be a result of more online reference titles.

This year there are no appendixes listing data for non-book and higher-priced titles, which are excluded from the index. The author will supply this information upon request.

Newspaper Prices

The indexes for U.S. (Table 8A) and international (Table 8B) newspapers are compiled by Genevieve Owens and Wilba Swearingen. The international newspapers index shows a substantial increase of 15.8 percent while the U.S. dailies show a slight decrease of 2 percent. In 2007 both indexes showed increases. The slight decrease in domestic papers is attributable to publishers' attempts to remain competitive in a market where their major competition is now online. The steep increase in international newspapers is due to the ever-increasing cost of shipping. Data are provided with the assistance of EBSCO Subscription Services.

Prices of Other Media

The U.S. nonprint media index (former Table 9) does not appear this year. Those wishing historical information can find data for 1997 and 1998, indexed to a base of 1980, in the 2001 edition of the *Bowker Annual.* The database, compiled in previous years by Dana Alessi, collects information from titles reviewed in *Booklist, Library Journal, School Library Journal,* and *Video Librarian.*

The CD-ROM price inventory that formerly appeared as Table 10 has also been discontinued. As with U.S. Serials Services, many of the titles that were published in CD-ROM format have migrated to Web editions. Additionally, the changes from single workstation pricing to network pricing or site licenses made tracking of the prices for this category of material difficult.

Efforts to develop a price index for electronic journals are still under discussion, but many factors have hindered progress in this area, not the least of which are the continued volatility of pricing models, consortial pricing, and institution-specific package deals. The Association of Research Libraries is also considering ways to gather this important economic data for libraries.

Foreign Prices

Exchange rates were closely watched during 2007 and the dollar has not performed well against any of the monitored currencies. For the first time since 2004, the dollar lost ground against all four monitored currencies. This will undoubtedly cause some additional increases in prices for monographs and journals purchased from these areas, adding to the increases reported in the indexes.

Table 8A / U.S. Daily Newspapers:
Average Prices and Price Indexes, 1990–2008
Index Base: 1990 = 100

Year	Number of Titles	Average Price	Percent Change	Index
1990	165	$189.58	0.0	100.0
1991	166	198.13	4.5	104.5
1992	167	222.68	12.4	117.5
1993	171	229.92	3.3	121.3
1994	171	261.91	13.9	138.2
1995	172	270.22	3.2	142.5
1996	166	300.21	11.1	158.4
1997	165	311.77	3.9	164.5
1998	163	316.60	1.5	167.0
1999	162	318.44	0.6	168.0
2000	162	324.26	1.8	171.0
2001	160	330.78	2.0	174.5
2002	158	340.38	2.9	179.5
2003	156	352.65	3.6	186.0
2004	154	364.97	3.5	192.5
2005	154	372.64	2.1	196.6
2006	154	369.24	-0.9	194.8
2007	152	375.76	1.8	198.2
2008	149	368.30	-2.0	194.3

Compiled by Genevieve S. Owens, Williamsburg Regional Library, and Wilba Swearingen, Louisiana State University Health Sciences Center Library, New Orleans, from data supplied by EBSCO Information Services. We thank Kathleen Born of EBSCO for her assistance with this project.

Table 8B / International Newspapers:
Average Prices and Price Indexes, 1993–2008
Index Base: 1993 = 100

Year	Number of Titles	Average Price	Percent Change	Index
1993	46	$806.91	0.0	100.0
1994	46	842.01	4.3	104.3
1995	49	942.13	11.9	116.3
1996	50	992.78	5.4	123.0
1997	53	1,029.49	3.7	127.6
1998	52	1,046.72	1.7	129.7
1999	50	1,049.13	0.2	130.0
2000	50	1,050.88	0.2	130.2
2001	50	1,038.26	-1.2	128.7
2002	49	1,052.69	1.4	130.5
2003	46	1,223.31	16.2	151.6
2004	43	1,301.71	6.4	161.3
2005	47	1,352.23	3.9	167.6
2006	45	1,306.79	-3.4	161.9
2007	44	1,354.60	3.7	167.9
2008	40	1,568.71	15.8	194.4

Compiled by Genevieve S. Owens, Williamsburg Regional Library, and Wilba Swearingen, Louisiana State University Health Sciences Center Library, New Orleans, from data supplied by EBSCO Information Services. We thank Kathleen Born of EBSCO for her assistance with this project.

Dates	12/31/02*	12/31/03*	12/31/04**	12/31/05**	12/31/06**	12/30/07**
Canada	1.5592	1.2958	1.1880	1.1680	1.1720	.9990
Euro	0.9414	0.7913	0.7530	0.8470	0.7590	.6800
U.K.	0.6182	0.5478	0.5240	0.5820	0.5120	.4860
Japan	121.8900	106.2700	103.1100	117.9400	119.5300	110.8800

* Data from the regional Federal Reserve Bank of St. Louis (http://www.stls.frb.org/fred/data/exchange.html).

** Data from Financial Management Services. U.S. Treasury Department (http://fms.treas.gov/intn.html). The change is due to the Federal Reserve Bank of St. Louis no longer reporting Euro to U.S. and U.K. to U.S. rates.

The foreign price index that follows is British Academic Books (Table 9). Latin American Periodicals (Tables 10A and 10B) are being temporarily retired as we seek a new compiler; it has not been updated in more than four years. Tables showing prices for German academic books, German academic periodicals, and Dutch English-language periodicals have not been updated and are not included in this volume. Please refer to earlier editions of the *Bowker Annual* for historical information.

British Prices

The price index for British academic books (Table 9) is compiled by Curt Holleman from information supplied by Blackwell's Book Services. The average price in pounds of a British book went from £45.09 in 2006 to £46.39 in 2007, an increase of 2.9 percent. The average daily price of the pound against the dollar rose 8.6 percent. The cost for U.S. libraries of purchasing an average British book therefore rose about 11.7 percent in 2007 from 2006. Clearly, for U.S. libraries the cost of British books rose far more on account of the falling dollar than from the effects of inflation. The double-digit increase in the cost of each book was mitigated slightly by the small decrease in the total number of academic books published in the United Kingdom in 2007. Book production went from 13,400 to 13,065, a decrease of 2.6 percent in the course of a year.

Using the Price Indexes

Librarians are encouraged to monitor trends in the publishing industry and changes in economic conditions when preparing budget forecasts and projections. The ALA ALCTS Library Materials Price Index Editorial Board endeavors to make information on publishing trends readily available by sponsoring the annual compilation and publication of price data contained in Tables 1 to 9. The indexes cover newly published library materials and document prices and rates of percent changes at the national and international level. They are useful benchmarks against which local costs can be compared, but because they reflect retail prices in the aggregate, they are not a substitute for cost data that reflect the collecting patterns of individual libraries, and they are not a substitute for specific cost studies.

(text continues on page 534)

Table 9 / **British Academic Books: Average Prices and Price Indexes, 2005–2007**
Index Base: 1985 = 00; prices listed are pounds sterling

	1985		2005			2006			2007		
Subject Area	No. of Titles	Average Price	No. of Titles	Average Price	Index	No. of Titles	Average Price	Index	No. of Titles	Average Price	Index
General works	29	£30.54	26	£33.59	110.0	33	£43.04	140.9	34	39.86	130.5
Fine arts	329	21.70	603	29.94	138.0	456	32.68	150.6	457	32.12	148.0
Architecture	97	20.68	199	36.38	175.9	152	44.31	214.3	179	41.68	201.5
Music	136	17.01	134	38.44	226.0	141	37.73	221.8	181	42.49	249.8
Performing arts except music	110	13.30	290	31.42	236.2	277	36.60	275.2	271	40.05	301.1
Archaeology	146	18.80	129	40.87	217.4	104	39.61	210.7	107	48.71	259.1
Geography	60	22.74	55	50.01	219.9	29	50.50	222.1	35	56.10	246.7
History	1,123	16.92	1,198	36.02	212.9	1,031	40.54	239.6	1,077	40.91	241.8
Philosophy	127	18.41	359	43.54	236.5	388	45.45	246.9	385	46.90	254.8
Religion	328	10.40	601	40.00	384.6	667	40.85	392.8	684	40.93	393.6
Language	135	19.37	292	45.68	235.8	268	49.25	254.3	257	49.28	254.4
Miscellaneous Humanities	59	21.71	37	37.92	174.7	42	34.84	160.5	20	25.91	119.3
Literary texts	570	9.31	1,138	14.68	157.7	1,046	16.14	173.4	1,000	15.22	163.5
Literary Criticism	438	14.82	619	43.62	294.3	545	44.46	300.0	680	46.58	314.3
Law	188	24.64	674	63.17	256.4	614	62.42	253.3	683	67.41	273.6
Library Science and Book Trade	78	18.69	65	40.65	217.5	79	45.47	243.3	73	45.27	242.2
Mass communications	38	14.20	170	41.68	293.5	180	42.42	298.7	151	44.67	314.6
Anthropology and Ethnology	42	20.71	72	50.57	244.2	51	49.73	240.1	80	47.51	229.4
Sociology	136	15.24	276	47.74	313.3	238	50.55	331.7	239	49.86	327.2
Psychology	107	19.25	156	42.56	221.1	191	47.02	244.3	161	48.25	250.6
Economics	334	20.48	603	56.20	274.4	542	58.44	285.4	491	62.03	302.9
Political Science and Intl. Relations	314	15.54	879	46.23	297.5	813	48.23	310.4	839	50.23	323.2
Miscellaneous Social Sciences	20	26.84	33	65.90	245.5	33	54.06	201.4	43	60.37	224.9
Military Science	83	17.69	58	40.48	228.8	85	49.24	278.3	85	46.20	261.2
Sports and Recreation	44	11.23	131	37.23	331.5	143	38.48	342.7	103	39.86	354.9
Social Service	56	12.17	99	40.41	332.0	101	36.79	302.3	94	42.90	352.5
Education	295	12.22	429	38.92	318.5	449	44.54	364.5	425	45.59	373.1
Management and Business Administration	427	19.55	890	47.74	244.2	870	49.19	251.6	812	49.33	252.3
Miscellaneous Applied Social Studies	13	9.58	28	39.90	416.5	28	45.14	471.2	33	47.09	491.5
Criminology	45	11.45	150	43.17	377.0	134	44.37	387.5	141	44.22	386.2

Applied Inter-discip. Soc. Studies	254	14.17	595	47.20	333.1	581	50.61	357.2	563	52.30	369.1
General science	43	13.73	59	38.57	280.9	39	39.98	291.2	39	47.84	348.4
Botany	55	30.54	38	53.26	174.4	27	63.40	207.6	19	68.37	223.9
Zoology	85	25.67	51	59.64	232.3	42	51.95	202.4	35	52.38	204.1
Human Biology	35	28.91	45	50.65	175.2	35	52.25	180.7	27	49.59	171.5
Biochemistry	26	33.57	19	69.10	205.8	21	63.67	189.7	14	67.43	200.9
Miscellaneous Biological Sciences	152	26.64	138	54.08	203.0	130	57.76	216.8	117	54.79	205.7
Chemistry	109	48.84	70	69.91	143.1	60	64.10	131.2	54	87.53	179.2
Earth sciences	87	28.94	87	63.34	218.9	92	60.86	210.3	71	64.09	221.5
Astronomy	43	20.36	74	42.92	210.8	73	47.59	233.7	68	41.73	205.0
Physics	76	26.58	185	56.22	211.5	165	53.87	202.7	96	54.92	206.6
Mathematics	123	20.20	225	49.39	244.5	203	44.41	219.9	154	49.55	245.3
Computer Sciences	150	20.14	142	41.49	206.0	123	37.49	186.1	133	38.73	192.3
Inter-disciplinary Technical Fields	38	26.14	36	51.61	197.4	42	55.02	210.5	51	57.39	219.5
Civil Engineering	134	28.68	128	80.38	280.3	126	80.40	280.3	115	75.02	261.6
Mechanical Engineering	27	31.73	24	54.62	172.1	30	78.76	248.2	18	66.38	209.2
Electrical and Electronic Engineering	100	33.12	126	65.63	198.2	113	59.21	178.8	123	61.66	186.2
Materials Science	54	37.93	48	90.58	238.8	38	97.71	257.6	47	93.64	246.9
Chemical Engineering	24	40.48	30	77.60	191.7	21	79.59	196.6	15	72.93	180.2
Miscellaneous Technology	217	36.33	286	54.89	151.1	279	55.48	152.7	251	55.64	153.2
Food and Domestic Science	38	23.75	90	30.98	130.4	78	34.13	143.7	88	28.05	118.1
Non-clinical Medicine	97	18.19	181	43.80	240.8	234	38.64	212.4	178	47.78	262.7
General Medicine	73	21.03	87	50.53	240.2	65	54.02	256.9	53	55.00	261.5
Internal Medicine	163	27.30	185	60.74	222.5	185	57.74	211.5	149	60.01	219.8
Psychiatry and Mental Disorders	71	17.97	238	34.42	191.5	225	38.23	212.7	170	39.88	221.9
Surgery	50	29.37	57	67.95	231.4	58	62.31	212.2	37	69.51	236.7
Miscellaneous Medicine	292	22.08	318	49.31	223.3	274	51.28	232.2	289	51.50	233.2
Dentistry	20	19.39	17	34.86	179.8	19	51.41	265.1	15	49.23	253.9
Pharmacy*	n.a.	n.a.	5	29.79	n.a.	9	41.05	n.a.	9	73.21	na
Nursing	71	8	105	29.42	367.8	106	25.11	313.9	86	28.00	350.0
Agriculture and Forestry	78	23.69	63	48.47	204.6	56	47.95	202.4	52	57.94	244.6
Animal Husbandry and Vet. Medicine	34	20.92	59	43.88	209.8	53	48.59	232.3	46	55.67	266.1
Natural Resources and Conservation	58	22.88	50	60.39	263.9	62	57.10	249.6	60	52.74	230.5
Total, All Books (NT)	9,049	£19.07	14,260	£43.37	227.4	13,400	£45.09	236.4	13,065	£46.39	243.3

* New category introduced in 2001.
Last year's average price was £45.09 and the overall inflation rate is 2.9%.
n.a. = not available

(continued from page 531)

Differences between local prices and those found in national indexes arise partially because these indexes exclude discounts, service charges, shipping and handling fees, and other costs that the library might incur. Discrepancies may also relate to a library's subject coverage; mix of titles purchased, including both current and backfiles; and the proportion of the library's budget expended on domestic or foreign materials. These variables can affect the average price paid by an individual library, although the individual library's rate of increase may not differ greatly from the national indexes.

LMPI is interested in pursuing studies that would correlate a particular library's costs with the national prices. The group welcomes interested parties to its meetings at ALA Annual and Midwinter conferences.

The Library Materials Price Index Editorial Board consists of compilers Catherine Barr, Ajaye Bloomstone, Stephen Bosch, Nancy Chaffin, Brenda Dingley, Virginia Gilbert, Curt Holleman, Frederick Lynden, Genevieve Owens, and Wilba Swearingen, and editor Janet Belanger Morrow.

Book Title Output and Average Prices: 2004–2007

Catherine Barr
Contributing Editor

Constance Harbison
Baker & Taylor

American book title output continued to climb over the four-year period from 2004 to 2007, rising by 4.4 percent in 2005, just under 1 percent in 2006, and 2.4 percent in 2007.

The figures in this edition of the *Bowker Annual* were compiled by book wholesaler Baker & Taylor and are not directly comparable with previous years' data, which came from R. R. Bowker's *Books in Print*. Differences in the two databases have inevitably resulted in variations in totals and across categories. Book title output—and average prices—derived from the *Books in Print* database for the years 2004 and 2005, plus preliminary figures for 2006, can be found in the 2007 *Bowker Annual*.

This year we have also added a new table on Audiobooks (Table 6) and a new category—graphic novels—that appears in all tables except Table 6. The graphic novel category includes both fiction and nonfiction.

Output by Format and by Category

Output of hardcovers and paperbacks generally held steady or grew in 2007, with overall hardcover titles and editions increasing by 1,438 (2.18 percent) following a gain of 2,045 (3.2 percent) in 2006. Hardcovers priced at less than $81—nearly 70 percent of the hardcover market—increased by 1,157 titles (2.54 percent) in 2007 after falling by 149 (0.33 percent) in 2006. Mass market paperback output fell by 180 titles (3.6 percent) in 2007 but trade paperbacks registered an increase of 2,830 titles (2.88 percent). In 2006 mass market paperback output held steady (increasing 0.02 percent) while trade paperbacks fell by 621 titles or 0.63 percent. Output of audiobooks continued to rise in 2007, with a jump of 1,203 titles or 18.2 percent following the increase of 315 titles (5.02 percent) registered in 2006.

Fiction and juvenile books, two key categories, showed mixed results across formats in both 2007 and 2006. Trade paperback fiction grew by 392 titles in 2007 (4.87 percent), while mass market fiction fell by 112 titles (2.6 percent) and hardcover fiction (less than $81) fell by 111 titles (2.50 percent) after a drop of 237 titles (5.07 percent) in 2006. In 2007 books for juveniles (children's and young adult titles) made gains in hardcover (up 413 titles or 2.95 percent) but lost ground in trade paperbacks (down 713 titles or 6.35 percent). Both fiction and juveniles did well in audiobooks, accounting for 45.9 percent and 13.6 percent, respectively, of total audiobook output in 2007.

Graphic novels showed impressive increases of 39.74 percent in 2006 and 7.95 percent in 2007 in hardcover editions, and a solid increase of 8.04 percent in trade paperback editions in 2007.

Table 1 / American Book Production, 2004–2007

Category	2004 Final	2005 Final	2006 Final	2007 Preliminary
Agriculture	1,461	1,562	1,463	1,507
Arts	7,096	7,343	7,896	8,083
Biography	3,447	3,499	3,434	3,542
Business	7,852	9,114	8,106	12,815
Education	5,347	5,846	6,121	5,457
Fiction	15,723	17,079	16,921	17,205
General works	8,422	8,298	8,288	7,717
Graphic novels	1,826	2,420	2,531	2,733
History	10,854	10,209	10,547	11,162
Home economics	3,662	3,985	3,773	3,616
Juveniles	24,286	26,412	26,222	25,900
Language	3,980	4,500	4,136	4,013
Law	3,316	3,257	4,733	4,209
Literature	3,844	4,179	3,573	4,030
Medicine	5,874	6,098	6,646	6,551
Music	3,201	2,941	2,909	2,600
Philosophy, psychology	5,735	5,594	5,735	6,124
Poetry, drama	2,589	2,736	2,449	2,585
Religion	8,212	8,232	8,276	7,995
Science	8,177	8,498	8,609	8,173
Sociology, economics	11,854	11,946	12,236	12,852
Sports, recreation	3,519	3,360	3,484	3,138
Technology	8,478	8,335	8,343	7,624
Travel	2,164	2,571	3,206	4,049
Totals	160,919	168,014	169,637	173,680

The following nonfiction categories have shown overall strength over the past two years: arts (number of titles up 7.5 percent in 2006 and 2.4 percent in 2007); history (up 3.3 percent in 2006 and 5.8 percent in 2007), philosophy/psychology (up 2.5 percent and 6.8 percent, respectively), sociology/economics (up 2.4 percent and 5.0 percent, respectively), and travel (up a solid 24.7 percent in 2006 and 26.3 percent in 2007). Business titles shot up 58 percent in 2007 after falling 11 percent in 2006. Categories showing downward trends in new title output are general works (losing 0.1 percent in 2006 and 6.9 percent in 2007), home economics (down 5.3 percent in 2006 and 4.2 percent in 2007), language (losing 8.1 percent in 2006 and 3.0 percent in 2007), and music (down 1.1 percent in 2006 and 10.6 percent in 2007). The other categories show mixed results, up one year and down the next, or vice versa.

Average Book Prices

Overall average book prices (list prices) rose in 2006 and 2007 for all formats except audiobooks, which dipped from a high of $40.45 in 2005 to $36.90 in

(text continues on page 542)

Table 2 / Hardcover Average Per-Volume Prices, 2004–2007

Category	2004 Final			2005 Final			2006 Final			2007 Preliminary		
	Vols.	$ Total	Prices	Vols.	$ Total	Prices	Vols.	$ Total	Prices	Vols.	$ Total	Prices
Agriculture	635	$42,641.34	$67.15	648	$37,329.51	$57.61	581	$35,661.46	$61.38	689	49,718.08	72.16
Arts	3,325	238,484.97	71.72	3,463	211,752.58	61.15	3,951	305,103.19	77.22	4,146	309,789.36	74.72
Biography	1,607	76,149.66	47.39	1,624	76,731.25	47.25	1,623	84,017.68	51.77	1,664	86,057.93	51.72
Business	2,636	293,007.34	111.16	2,742	298,392.83	108.82	2,775	311,342.68	112.20	2,893	331,810.81	114.69
Education	1,087	105,253.84	96.83	1,112	101,184.56	90.99	1,303	126,460.94	97.05	1,267	132,154.05	104.30
Fiction	4,629	129,115.36	27.89	4,721	134,001.67	28.38	4,478	128,313.39	28.65	4,485	150,001.35	33.45
General works	2,351	234,673.19	99.82	2,356	217,069.67	92.13	2,281	220,272.43	96.57	2,134	245,092.40	114.85
Graphic novels	204	6,127.42	30.04	240	8,113.77	33.81	337	10,736.68	31.86	366	12,287.44	33.57
History	4,642	354,049.63	76.27	4,532	353,551.56	78.01	4,702	392,069.19	83.38	4,875	392,062.91	80.42
Home economics	1,264	37,609.94	29.75	1,336	40,817.49	30.55	1,375	41,032.30	29.84	1,324	37,001.40	27.95
Juveniles	13,242	327,212.02	24.71	14,774	387,288.02	26.21	14,457	379,384.85	26.24	14,885	424,012.09	28.49
Language	1,302	132,278.28	101.60	1,268	132,353.33	104.38	1,231	128,760.56	104.60	1,495	156,020.07	104.36
Law	1,444	209,017.53	144.75	1,281	186,513.22	145.60	1,411	228,661.28	162.06	1,424	218,395.39	153.37
Literature	1,869	174,705.93	93.48	1,866	203,823.30	109.23	1,892	179,720.56	94.99	2,269	225,373.26	99.33
Medicine	2,658	410,974.97	154.62	2,684	397,458.06	148.08	2,929	449,697.45	153.53	2,916	428,566.09	146.97
Music	485	36,469.98	75.20	408	31,361.14	76.87	390	29,862.89	76.57	474	35,186.03	74.23
Philosophy, psychology	2,179	224,339.21	102.96	2,085	186,280.13	89.34	2,405	199,881.75	83.11	2,428	199,158.02	82.03
Poetry, drama	468	17,726.79	37.88	470	19,649.00	41.81	380	17,008.04	44.76	431	20,061.97	46.55
Religion	2,667	173,884.75	65.20	2,653	155,594.04	58.65	2,583	172,561.45	66.81	2,564	177,867.39	69.37
Science	4,650	763,009.61	164.09	4,649	754,918.88	162.38	4,859	768,828.55	158.23	4,596	770,636.94	167.68
Sociology, economics	5,104	498,305.04	97.63	4,912	471,822.46	96.06	5,497	603,046.81	109.70	5,569	562,955.43	101.09
Sports, recreation	1,012	47,718.25	47.15	904	33,300.34	36.84	973	35,849.10	36.84	879	32,263.76	36.71
Technology	2,841	382,219.22	134.54	2,770	395,355.12	142.73	3,160	397,922.58	125.92	2,888	365,133.92	126.43
Travel	328	14,974.14	45.65	414	15,504.25	37.45	384	16,272.06	42.38	734	35,483.43	48.34
Totals	62,629	$4,929,948.41	$78.72	63,912	$4,850,166.18	$75.89	65,957	$5,262,467.87	$79.79	67,395	$5,397,089.52	$80.08

Table 3 / Hardcover Average Per-Volume Prices, Less Than $81, 2004–2007

Category	2004 Final			2005 Final			2006 Final			2007 Preliminary		
	Vols.	$ Total	Prices	Vols.	$ Total	Prices	Vols.	$ Total	Prices	Vols.	$ Total	Prices
Agriculture	480	$15,152.61	$31.57	509	$15,696.55	$30.84	430	$13,395.89	$31.15	468	$14,711.25	$31.43
Arts	2,724	121,492.80	44.60	2,922	131,454.03	44.99	3,239	147,344.00	45.49	3,354	156,650.20	46.71
Biography	1,458	45,791.29	31.41	1,465	45,634.30	31.15	1,463	45,759.88	31.28	1,473	47,161.39	32.02
Business	1,326	57,750.96	43.55	1,387	58,874.14	42.45	1,407	58,105.77	41.30	1,507	61,908.72	41.08
Education	593	30,323.20	51.14	619	30,025.36	48.51	763	39,771.11	52.12	710	39,417.74	55.52
Fiction	4,590	122,732.76	26.74	4,677	125,244.17	26.78	4,440	120,236.94	27.08	4,329	118,330.79	27.33
General works	1,827	51,074.96	27.96	1,840	53,279.28	28.96	1,768	50,574.30	28.61	1,623	47,651.31	29.36
Graphic novels	202	5,937.42	29.39	234	7,382.10	31.55	327	9,588.72	29.32	353	10,876.09	30.81
History	3,442	150,502.11	43.73	3,312	145,814.54	44.03	3,224	143,889.54	44.63	3,304	150,289.25	45.49
Home economics	1,230	32,712.87	26.60	1,290	34,632.29	26.85	1,338	35,236.80	26.34	1,300	34,453.58	26.50
Juveniles	12,868	259,669.38	20.18	14,254	281,615.92	19.76	14,002	277,322.34	19.81	14,415	295,398.35	20.49
Language	673	34,176.77	50.78	619	32,161.23	51.96	578	30,710.45	53.13	757	42,411.53	56.03
Law	576	29,891.28	51.89	332	17,355.46	52.28	328	18,188.15	55.45	348	18,815.81	54.07
Literature	1,148	58,043.24	50.56	1,086	55,566.30	51.17	1,096	57,593.39	52.55	1,265	68,785.18	54.38
Medicine	752	41,787.64	55.57	725	40,206.91	55.46	692	39,094.68	56.50	672	38,291.90	56.98
Music	333	14,270.93	42.86	287	10,972.32	38.23	253	10,700.64	42.30	318	13,416.57	42.19
Philosophy, psychology	1,301	58,564.35	45.01	1,295	60,532.88	46.74	1,403	65,239.37	46.50	1,405	67,603.12	48.12
Poetry, drama	441	13,316.29	30.20	430	13,294.11	30.92	346	11,061.90	31.97	372	11,962.57	32.16
Religion	2,057	63,966.39	31.10	2,092	62,382.29	29.82	1,908	60,383.34	31.65	1,860	60,095.94	32.31
Science	1,374	68,406.59	49.79	1,363	65,588.90	48.12	1,318	67,190.04	50.98	1,382	70,326.51	50.89
Sociology, economics	3,069	157,890.19	51.45	2,803	147,611.47	52.66	2,941	153,318.59	52.13	3,046	160,557.09	52.71
Sports, recreation	944	27,414.80	29.04	856	26,105.55	30.50	915	26,985.67	29.49	838	25,429.42	30.35
Technology	967	48,656.27	50.32	869	46,003.93	52.94	962	52,715.57	54.80	847	46,098.04	54.43
Travel	295	8,829.20	29.93	388	11,341.45	29.23	364	11,422.21	31.38	716	28,119.58	39.27
Totals	44,670	$1,518,354.30	$33.99	45,654	$1,518,775.48	$33.27	45,505	$1,545,829.29	$33.97	46,662	$1,628,761.93	$34.91

Table 4 / Mass Market Paperbacks Average Per-Volume Prices, 2004–2007

Category	2004 Final			2005 Final			2006 Final			2007 Preliminary		
	Vols.	$ Total	Prices	Vols.	$ Total	Prices	Vols.	$ Total	Prices	Vols.	$ Total	Prices
Agriculture	n.a.	n.a.	n.a.	n.a.	n.a.	n.a.	n.a.	n.a.	n.a.	n.a.	n.a.	n.a.
Arts	7	$52.81	$7.54	4	$32.92	$8.23	3	$23.97	$7.99	3	$25.93	$8.64
Biography	21	163.66	7.79	21	163.18	7.77	13	100.83	7.76	10	78.86	7.89
Business	1	7.99	7.99	1	7.99	7.99	n.a.	n.a.	n.a.	n.a.	n.a.	n.a.
Education	n.a.	n.a.	n.a.	n.a.	n.a.	n.a.	n.a.	n.a.	n.a.	n.a.	n.a.	n.a.
Fiction	4,001	24,917.11	6.23	4,245	27,200.91	6.41	4,401	44,783.93	10.18	4,286	44,100.13	10.29
General works	131	940.76	7.18	107	802.30	7.50	134	2,168.92	16.19	107	1,260.78	11.78
Graphic novels	n.a.	n.a.	n.a.	2	16.94	8.47	5	39.95	7.99	n.a.	n.a.	n.a.
History	38	280.62	7.38	25	192.20	7.69	15	112.85	7.52	12	91.88	7.66
Home economics	4	28.96	7.24	4	25.47	6.37	3	22.97	7.66	2	15.49	7.75
Juveniles	535	3,181.19	5.95	524	3,036.44	5.79	472	3,728.59	7.90	445	3,054.88	6.86
Language	n.a.	n.a.	n.a.	1	6.99	6.99	1	5.99	5.99	4	24.96	6.24
Law	2	15.98	7.99	n.a.	n.a.	n.a.	n.a.	n.a.	n.a.	n.a.	n.a.	n.a.
Literature	1	6.95	6.95	1	7.95	7.95	1	7.95	7.95	n.a.	n.a.	n.a.
Medicine	2	14.98	7.49	2	15.49	7.75	4	26.47	6.62	4	27.47	6.87
Music	1	7.95	7.95	1	7.95	7.95	n.a.	n.a.	n.a.	n.a.	n.a.	n.a.
Philosophy, psychology	4	29.43	7.36	9	96.67	10.74	20	147.50	7.38	11	86.69	7.88
Poetry, drama	20	125.56	6.28	27	164.31	6.09	8	49.64	6.21	5	31.83	6.37
Religion	4	30.43	7.61	4	44.84	11.21	6	44.92	7.49	2	13.98	6.99
Science	2	13.98	6.99	n.a.	n.a.	n.a.	1	7.99	7.99	n.a.	n.a.	n.a.
Sociology, economics	9	63.79	7.09	6	42.45	7.08	4	28.88	7.22	3	158.80	52.93
Sports, recreation	15	108.34	7.22	20	201.18	10.06	14	149.20	10.66	24	143.72	5.99
Technology	n.a.	n.a.	n.a.	n.a.	n.a.	n.a.	n.a.	n.a.	n.a.	n.a.	n.a.	n.a.
Travel	n.a.	n.a.	n.a.	n.a.	n.a.	n.a.	1	7.99	7.99	n.a.	n.a.	n.a.
Totals	4,798	$29,990.49	$6.25	5,004	$32,066.18	$6.41	5,106	$51,458.54	$10.08	4,918	$49,115.40	$16,371.80

n.a. = not available

Table 5 / Trade Paperback Average Per-Volume Prices, 2004–2007

Category	2004 Final			2005 Final			2006 Final			2007 Preliminary		
	Vols.	$ Total	Prices	Vols.	$ Total	Prices	Vols.	$ Total	Prices	Vols.	$ Total	Prices
Agriculture	826	$22,151.79	$26.82	914	$25,070.86	$27.43	880	$25,636.00	$29.13	815	$25,486.43	$31.27
Arts	3,762	118,947.21	31.62	3,871	116,517.43	30.10	3,940	129,081.38	32.76	3,930	125,539.27	31.94
Biography	1,819	35,572.20	19.56	1,854	35,444.77	19.12	1,798	35,482.63	19.73	1,868	36,716.45	19.66
Business	5,152	260,987.92	50.66	6,294	395,355.91	62.81	5,264	350,630.74	66.61	9,865	814,578.13	82.57
Education	4,249	140,146.76	32.98	4,710	154,804.57	32.87	4,814	172,560.22	35.85	4,202	148,058.09	35.24
Fiction	7,093	108,350.49	15.28	8,113	125,015.40	15.41	8,042	129,437.29	16.10	8,434	143,190.17	16.98
General works	5,927	159,894.43	26.98	5,823	162,888.43	27.97	5,852	190,518.51	32.56	5,459	169,550.58	31.06
Graphic novels	1,622	21,044.43	12.97	2,178	28,687.22	13.17	2,189	30,033.73	13.72	2,365	35,660.77	15.08
History	6,173	178,792.29	28.96	5,650	183,935.99	32.56	5,830	184,662.49	31.67	6,272	202,191.13	32.24
Home economics	2,389	44,590.34	18.66	2,632	49,335.73	18.74	2,380	47,253.03	19.85	2,273	43,893.36	19.31
Juveniles	10,440	124,974.19	11.97	11,095	128,040.38	11.54	11,229	124,717.06	11.11	10,516	115,310.57	10.97
Language	2,675	109,092.29	40.78	3,215	149,144.88	46.39	2,899	125,606.70	43.33	2,509	105,460.34	42.03
Law	1,826	98,318.58	53.84	1,935	119,135.40	61.57	3,282	176,526.51	53.79	2,740	186,011.22	67.89
Literature	1,974	64,559.01	32.70	2,307	67,840.66	29.41	1,680	54,428.36	32.40	1,762	63,128.49	35.83
Medicine	3,189	180,795.46	56.69	3,396	212,336.83	62.53	3,652	222,625.52	60.96	3,582	248,173.68	69.28
Music	2,711	60,820.44	22.43	2,530	55,893.60	22.09	2,519	62,867.48	24.96	2,123	60,035.23	28.28
Philosophy, psychology	3,546	113,222.14	31.93	3,494	108,789.33	31.14	3,302	105,973.64	32.09	3,674	115,895.14	31.54
Poetry, drama	2,101	32,684.26	15.56	2,239	35,920.06	16.04	2,061	33,340.52	16.18	2,148	36,410.73	16.95
Religion	5,525	112,581.45	20.38	5,569	111,293.82	19.98	5,657	114,650.58	20.27	5,425	108,703.51	20.04
Science	3,514	201,706.12	57.40	3,832	237,804.48	62.06	3,730	224,243.58	60.12	3,528	225,072.19	63.80
Sociology, economics	6,721	231,772.61	34.48	7,020	269,783.46	38.43	6,716	258,129.59	38.44	7,265	311,402.36	42.86
Sports, recreation	2,490	49,151.83	19.74	2,433	45,305.19	18.62	2,492	47,842.19	19.20	2,232	42,767.11	19.16
Technology	5,623	350,644.05	62.36	5,558	339,050.28	61.00	5,171	304,581.06	58.90	4,727	283,802.39	60.04
Travel	1,836	31,858.40	17.35	2,156	40,732.24	18.89	2,818	53,437.71	18.96	3,313	68,696.29	20.74
Totals	93,183	$2,852,658.69	$30.61	98,818	$3,198,126.92	$32.36	98,197	$3,204,266.52	$32.63	101,027	$3,715,733.63	$36.78

Table 6 / Audiobook Average Per-Volume Prices, 2004–2007

Category	2004 Final			2005 Final			2006 Final			2007 Preliminary		
	Vols.	$ Total	Prices	Vols.	$ Total	Prices	Vols.	$ Total	Prices	Vols.	$ Total	Prices
Agriculture	2	$32.94	$16.47	4	$119.13	$29.78	12	$361.60	$30.13	17	$569.60	$33.51
Arts	27	737.10	27.30	27	1,247.83	46.22	42	1,378.82	32.83	23	666.64	28.98
Biography	247	8,938.69	36.19	289	11,169.56	38.65	327	12,704.37	38.85	403	18,213.30	45.19
Business	147	4,605.54	31.33	137	5,909.03	43.13	205	8,212.51	40.06	263	8,797.89	33.45
Education	35	1,094.20	31.26	63	1,387.07	22.02	57	2,351.06	41.25	35	1,345.59	38.45
Fiction	2,878	111,412.74	38.71	2,904	120,833.85	41.61	3,018	121,820.65	40.36	3,582	156,277.28	43.63
General works	282	8,351.04	29.61	239	6,789.51	28.41	261	7,742.75	29.67	286	9,559.64	33.43
History	144	4,811.86	33.42	195	8,092.91	41.50	313	12,693.01	40.55	487	23,495.21	48.24
Home economics	1	25.00	25.00	26	394.75	15.18	17	321.33	18.90	18	520.31	28.91
Juveniles	641	16,465.09	25.69	739	21,364.02	28.91	753	24,159.03	32.08	1,064	34,471.20	32.40
Language	377	18,116.47	48.05	643	45,874.96	71.35	385	16,006.70	41.58	285	11,129.43	39.05
Law	14	881.00	62.93	44	2,414.45	54.87	46	3,517.32	76.46	24	1,421.94	59.25
Literature	22	524.13	23.82	16	412.57	25.79	38	769.57	20.25	38	1,252.87	32.97
Medicine	5	410.89	82.18	6	959.75	159.96	18	980.34	54.46	19	1,163.58	61.24
Music	168	4,447.96	26.48	108	2,874.12	26.61	155	3,849.70	24.84	101	2,334.10	23.11
Philosophy, psychology	250	6,307.07	25.23	215	5,467.09	25.43	204	5,527.75	27.10	332	9,644.37	29.05
Poetry, drama	102	2,114.22	20.73	79	1,844.45	23.35	122	2,867.57	23.50	84	2,312.98	27.54
Religion	436	13,464.44	30.88	365	10,056.89	27.55	349	9,409.79	26.96	352	9,966.97	28.32
Science	35	1,204.44	34.41	34	1,313.77	38.64	49	1,629.10	33.25	47	1,795.55	38.20
Sociology, economics	131	4,099.12	31.29	86	3,355.22	39.01	163	5,044.29	30.95	218	8,768.76	40.22
Sports, recreation	24	767.73	31.99	37	1,107.97	29.95	41	1,487.00	36.27	64	2,362.55	36.91
Technology	7	304.91	43.56	10	478.84	47.88	8	255.02	31.88	10	354.63	35.46
Travel	12	259.40	21.62	13	544.79	41.91	13	290.57	22.35	45	1,989.75	44.22
Total	5,987	$209,375.98	$34.97	6,279	$254,012.53	$40.45	6,596	$243,379.85	$36.90	7,797	$308,414.14	$39.56

(continued from page 536)

2006 (a fall of $3.55 or 8.78 percent) and recovered to $39.55 in 2007 (an increase of $2.65 or 7.18 percent). Increases for other formats ranged in 2006 from a low of 0.83 percent—27 cents—for trade paperbacks (Table 5) to a high of 5.14 percent—$3.90—for hardcovers (Table 2); in 2007 these two formats reversed positions, registering increases of 0.36 percent—29 cents—for hardcovers and 12.72 percent—$4.15—for trade paperbacks. Hardcovers priced at less than $81 (Table 3) rose by 70 cents (2.10 percent) in 2006 and 94 cents (2.77 percent) in 2007, and prices of mass market paperbacks (Table 4) increased by 8 cents (1.27 percent) and 3 cents (0.47 percent), respectively.

The average book prices for fiction rose in 2006 and 2007, apart from the audiobook sector, which showed a decrease of $1.25 (3 percent) in 2006 but rose $3.27 (8.10 percent) in 2007. Hardcover fiction titles priced at less than $81 increased 30 cents (1.12 percent) in 2006 and 25 cents (0.92 percent) in 2007. Mass market fiction increased 4 cents (0.64 percent) in 2006 and 7 cents (1.11 percent) in 2007, while trade fiction increased 69 cents (4.48 percent) in 2006 and 88 cents (5.47 percent) in 2007.

Prices for children's and young adult books (juveniles) were mixed in 2006 and 2007. Hardcover prices increased 5 cents (0.25 percent) and 68 cents (3.43 percent), respectively. Juvenile mass market paperbacks rose 42 cents (7.25 percent) in 2006 but dropped 5 cents (0.81 percent) in 2007, while trade paperback titles fell for both years, by 43 cents (3.73 percent) in 2006 and by 14 cents (1.26 percent) in 2007.

Book Sales Statistics, 2007: AAP Estimates

Association of American Publishers

Net sales by the U.S. publishing industry are estimated to have increased by 3.2 percent from 2006 to 2007 to a grand total of nearly $25 billion, according to figures released by the Association of American Publishers (AAP).

The AAP report, which uses data from the U.S. Bureau of the Census as well as sales data from 81 publishers, indicates a compound growth rate of 2.5 percent a year since 2002.

Trade sales of adult and juvenile books grew 3.0 percent from 2006 to $8.5 billion, at a compound growth rate of 3.6 percent. The strongest growth in this category came from adult hardbound books, whose sales rose 7.8 percent from 2006 to a total of $2.8 billion with a compound growth rate of 3.4 percent. Adult paperbound books rose by 0.2 percent from 2006 to nearly $2.3 billion with a compound growth rate of 4.0 percent.

Sales of hardbound titles for children and young adults (juvenile) fell by 0.5 percent to just over 2.0 billion; however paperbound saw an increase of 4.1 percent to nearly 1.4 billion from 2006. Over the longer term, juvenile books are performing well, with compound annual growth rates of 4.6 percent for hardbound and 2.1 percent for paperbound since 2002.

The estimates for hardbound and paperbound juvenile titles do not include the Harry Potter series, which began in 1997. According to AAP, the sales estimate without the series provides a better assessment of the growth of the market for juvenile books.

Audiobooks registered an increase of 19.8 percent from 2006 to a total of $218 million, at a compound growth rate of 8.8 percent per year, and 2007 was also a good year for religious books, which saw an increase of 5.2 percent compared with 2006 with $783 million in sales (compound growth was strong at 7.1 percent). E-books posted a 23.6 percent increase with $67 million in sales and a compound growth rate of 55.7 percent since 2002.

After an increase in 2006, mass market paperbacks saw a decline of 2.0 percent in 2007, dropping to $1.1 billion for a compound annual growth rate of minus 1.7 percent. Sales through book clubs fell by 2.8 percent from 2006 to $622 million.

Education titles had a solid year; sales of K–12 (el-hi) products rose by 2.7 percent to nearly $6.4 billion, with a compound growth rate of 1.9 percent. Higher education titles saw sales approaching $3.7 billion, up 6.5 percent on 2006 with a compound growth rate of 4.0 percent.

For more data on 2007 sales estimates, prepared by Management Practice, Inc., visit http://www.publishers.org/main/IndustryStats/indStats_02.htm. For additional information, contact Tina Jordan, AAP New York (212-255-0200 ext. 263, tjordan@publishers.org).

Table 1 / Estimated Book Publishing Industry Net Sales, 2002–2007
(figures in thousands of dollars)

	2002 Census $	2003 $	% Change from 2002	2004 $	% Change from 2003	2005 $	% Change from 2004	2006 $	% Change from 2005	2007 $	% Change from 2006	Compound Growth Rate 2002–2007
Trade (total)	7,144,188	6,872,190	-3.8	7,504,458	9.2	8,043,471	7.2	8,274,103	2.9	8,525,932	3.0	3.6
Adult hardbound	2,371,553	2,314,636	-2.4	2,460,458	6.3	2,495,175	1.4	2,597,477	4.1	2,800,080	7.8	3.4
Adult paperbound	1,876,620	1,865,360	-0.6	1,917,590	2.8	2,099,187	9.5	2,277,618	8.5	2,282,173	0.2	4.0
Juvenile hardbound	1,636,248	1,484,077	-9.3	1,902,587	28.2	2,100,456	10.4	2,058,447	-2.0	2,048,155	-0.5	4.6
Juvenile paperbound	1,259,767	1,208,117	-4.1	1,223,823	1.3	1,348,653	10.2	1,340,561	-0.6	1,395,524	4.1	2.1
Book clubs and mail order	852,384	775,669	-9.0	706,634	-8.9	659,290	-6.7	639,511	-3.0	621,605	-2.8	-6.1
Mass market paperback	1,216,710	1,196,026	-1.7	1,089,580	-8.9	1,091,759	0.2	1,141,980	4.6	1,119,140	-2.0	-1.7
Audiobooks	143,410	161,049	12.3	159,922	-0.7	206,299	29.0	182,162	-11.7	218,230	19.8	8.8
Religious	556,799	836,312	50.2	883,145	5.6	829,273	-6.1	744,687	-10.2	783,411	5.2	7.1
E-books	7,337	19,772	169.5	30,271	53.1	43,832	44.8	54,396	24.1	67,233	23.6	55.7
Professional	3,155,191	3,268,778	3.6	3,334,154	2.0	3,300,812	-1.0	3,376,731	2.3	3,474,656	2.9	1.9
El-hi (K–12 education)	5,795,044	5,939,920	2.5	5,945,860	0.1	6,570,175	10.5	6,189,105	-5.8	6,356,211	2.7	1.9
Higher education	3,025,029	3,133,930	3.6	3,190,341	1.8	3,359,429	5.3	3,453,493	2.8	3,677,970	6.5	4.0
All other	136,488	153,932	12.8	161,629	5.0	158,558	-1.9	140,641	-11.3	115,185	-18.1	-3.3
Total	22,032,580	22,357,578	1.5	23,005,994	2.9	24,262,898	5.5	24,196,809	-0.3	24,959,573	3.2	2.5

Source: Association of American Publishers

The International Book Market in Transition: U.S. Book Exports and Imports in 2007

Albert N. Greco

Senior Researcher
The Institute for Publishing Research
201-439-1839, e-mail angreco@aol.com

Classic economic theory states that a weak dollar will stimulate exports and dampen imports, issues analyzed in the published literature on exports and imports (Greco, 2005; Greco, Rodriguez, and Wharton, 2007; Delgado, Farinas, and Ruano, 2002; Wiedersheim-Paul, Olson, and Welch, 1978; Awokuse, 2008). The events of 2007 substantiated the validity of this long-held theory. With a weakened U.S. dollar, exports increased 9.6 percent while imports were up by nearly 7.4 percent. In 2006 the opposite was the case; exports inched up 2.84 percent while imports increased by 4.84 percent.

The important ratio of exports to imports (i.e., the ratio of exports as a percentage of total U.S. shipments) has been sagging since 1997, with only a modest uptick in 2005. Another small but significant increase (from 0.92 to 0.94) in this ratio was evident in 2007.

Table 1 / U.S. Trade in Books: 1970–2007
($ million)

Year	U.S. Book Exports	U.S. Book Imports	Ratio: U.S. Book Exports/Imports
1970	$174.9	$92.0	1.90
1975	269.3	147.6	1.82
1980	518.9	306.5	1.69
1985	591.2	564.2	1.05
1990	1,415.1	855.1	1.65
1995	1,779.5	1,184.5	1.50
1996	1,775.6	1,240.1	1.43
1997	1,896.6	1,297.5	1.46
1998	1,841.8	1,383.7	1.33
1999	1,871.1	1,441.4	1.30
2000	1,877.0	1,590.5	1.18
2001	1,712.3	1,627.8	1.05
2002	1,681.2	1,661.2	1.01
2003	1,693.6	1,755.9	0.96
2004	1,740.5	1,934.4	0.90
2005	1,894.3	2,026.3	0.93
2006	1,948.1	2,124.3	0.92
2007	2,135.2	2,281.3	0.94

Source: U.S. Department of Commerce, International Trade Administration. All totals are rounded off to one decimal point. Data for individual categories may not add to totals due to statistical rounding. Due to changes in the classification of "U.S. traded products" and what constitutes products classified as "books," data prior to 1990 are not strictly comparable to data beginning in 1990.

The equally important ratio of exports as a percentage of total U.S. shipments (i.e., total book revenues) topped the 7 percent mark (7.1 percent) for the first time since 2000 (when it stood at 7.6 percent), hopefully a harbinger for the industry.

Table 2 / U.S. Book Industry Shipments Compared with U.S. Book Exports: 1970–2007
($ million)

Year	Total Shipments	U.S. Book Exports	Exports as a Percent of Total Shipments
1970	$2,434.2	$174.9	7.2
1975	3,536.5	269.3	7.6
1980	6,114.4	518.9	8.5
1985	10,165.7	591.2	5.8
1990	14,982.6	1,415.1	9.4
1995	19,471.0	1,779.5	9.1
1996	20,285.7	1,775.6	8.8
1997	21,131.9	1,896.6	9.0
1998	22,507.0	1,841.8	8.2
1999	23,926.9	1,871.1	7.8
2000	24,749.0	1,877.0	7.6
2001	24,742.6	1,712.3	6.9
2002	25,270.2	1,681.2	6.7
2003	25,998.5	1,693.6	6.5
2004	26,450.9	1,740.5	6.6
2005	27,839.4	1,894.3	6.8
2006	28,782.2	1,948.1	6.8
2007	29,928.9	2,135.2	7.1

Source: U.S. Department of Commerce, International Trade Administration; and the Book Industry Study Group, Inc. (BISG). Due to changes in the classification of U.S. traded products and what constitutes products classified as "books," data prior to 1990 are not strictly comparable to data beginning in 1990. All totals are rounded off to one decimal point. Data for individual categories may not add to totals due to statistical rounding.

What happened in 2007 to reverse these downward spirals? What book categories experienced an increase in exports? More importantly, what can the book publishing industry do to strengthen its export strategies in order to offset the projected softness in domestic book sales in 2008?

Significance of Book Exports

Every four years, during U.S. presidential candidate debates, the issue of globalization is discussed in some detail. While most economists believe that globalization is ultimately beneficial in that it allows a country to concentrate on the manufacture of goods and/or provision of services where it has a competitive advantage, some believe that globalization has had a pernicious impact on jobs, wages, and national stability.

Table 3 / Top Ten Export Destinations for U.S. Books 1998–2007
($'000)

Country	1998	1999	2000	2001	2002	2003	2004	2005	2006	2007	Percent Change 2006–2007
Canada	807,583	807,541	756,667	727,698	742,619	776,441	812,833	866,173	918,250	962,509	4.8
United Kingdom	237,062	253,646	264,230	250,031	270,622	274,596	289,196	284,993	291,376	300,150	3.0
Japan	133,281	101,146	123,100	129,316	100,804	95,835	98,436	93,394	78,219	78,301	0.1
Australia	157,928	139,588	116,302	66,010	70,806	76,067	78,549	100,769	107,754	110,922	2.9
Mexico	58,770	65,599	73,886	63,804	64,938	68,132	66,087	102,658	71,316	79,685	11.7
Singapore	26,536	41,135	60,669	48,985	49,570	48,358	57,974	53,395	49,734	52,689	5.9
Germany	40,671	43,134	34,341	34,007	29,081	34,128	27,174	35,789	38,298	76,176	98.9
South Korea	16,106	24,627	36,793	35,499	29,131	24,698	26,670	38,557	33,432	44,400	32.8
China	17,224	12,414	12,019	10,711	11,739	15,491	18,110	16,532	25,777	29,715	15.3
India	12,286	11,954	14,430	15,992	19,513	16,807	18,967	22,497	21,757	40,022	84.0

Source: U.S. Department of Commerce, International Trade Administration.

Note: Individual shipments are excluded from the foreign trade data if valued under $2,500. All totals are rounded off to one decimal point. Data for individual categories may not add to totals due to statistical rounding.

The basic issues relating to globalization have been analyzed extensively. Goldberg and Knetter (1999), in an important paper, sought to measure the level of intensity in developed and emerging markets, issues also addressed by Cooper and Kleinschmidt (1985), Cavusgil and Zou (1994), and Baldwin and Gu (2003). Katsikeas and Morgan (1994) took a behavioral approach in seeking to understand perceptional views on exports. Sanghamitra, Roberts, and Tybout (2007) utilized an econometric analysis to ascertain market entry costs associated with exports. Gala's theoretical work (2008) on exchange rates will remain one of the major analyses of this complex issue.

The International Intellectual Property Alliance (2007) investigated the impact of book piracy on U.S. publishers. These firms lost at least $500 million to pirates, cutting into book exports and profit margins.

While the Book Industry Study Group's *Book Industry Trends 2007* contained datasets on domestic sales, exports and imports were analyzed, providing a useful overview of the export market for various book categories.

Market for U.S. Book Exports in 2007

For the past ten years, Canada has been the major export partner of the United States. In 2007 exports to Canada topped $962.5 million, up 4.8 percent from the previous year. Even though other nations posted impressive increases, notably Germany (up 98.9 percent in 2007), India (up 84 percent), South Korea (up 32.8 percent), and Mexico (up 11.7 percent), it is likely Canada will retain its position of importance for the foreseeable future. China, an important market that long avoided U.S. exports, was up an impressive 15.3 percent in 2007 (exports to China have increased 72.5 percent since 1998).

The United Kingdom was again the second largest export destination for U.S. books, and was up a modest 3.0 percent. Other important customers included Singapore (up 5.9 percent), Japan (up 0.1 percent), and Australia (up 2.9 percent).

For more than a decade, the top 25 nations accounted for the vast majority of all U.S. book exports. These countries purchased 93.2 percent of all exports, down slightly from 2006 (93.3 percent) and 2005 (94.0 percent). While this slippage is statistically not significant, the U.S. Department of Commerce might want to investigate what it could do to strengthen sales to these important top 25 nations as they have both the financial resources and the pivotal infrastructure needed to handle large quantities of U.S. books.

An investigation of specific book export categories revealed several anomalies. First, the Department of Commerce uses the "harmonious trade system" (HTS) for book categories. This means that textbooks and hardcover books are large aggregated categories, not allowing researchers to drill down to determine specific subcategory data (for example, college versus el-hi textbooks, or adult trade hardcover books versus university press hardcover books). Second, six of the eight book categories reported declines in unit exports. While industry experts cannot be surprised by the steep declines posted by dictionaries and thesauruses (down 38.2 percent) or encyclopedias (down 14.4 percent) because the information they contain is readily available online or otherwise available on home computers, the data on textbooks (down 21.6 percent) and professional

Table 4 / U.S. Book Exports to 25 Principal Countries: 2006–2007

Country	Value ($'000) 2006	Value ($'000) 2007	Percent Change 2006–2007
Canada	$918,250	$962,509	4.8
United Kingdom	291,376	300,150	3.0
Australia	107,754	110,922	2.9
Japan	78,219	78,301	0.1
Mexico	71,316	79,685	11.7
Singapore	49,734	52,689	5.9
Germany	38,298	76,176	98.9
South Korea	33,432	44,400	32.8
China	25,777	29,715	15.3
India	21,757	40,022	84.0
South Africa	21,172	18,627	-12.0
Philippines	19,131	18,883	-1.3
Hong Kong	17,844	19,722	10.5
Taiwan	16,144	18,663	15.6
Brazil	13,758	21,676	57.6
Netherlands	11,879	12,260	3.2
New Zealand	11,731	14,385	22.6
Belgium	11,113	13,852	24.6
Saudi Arabia	9,804	10,109	3.1
Malaysia	9,801	9,913	1.1
Sweden	8,765	10,544	20.3
Nigeria	7,970	11,635	46.0
United Arab Emirates	5483	9,999	82.4
Argentina	5084	13,461	164.8
Hungary	4428	11,038	149.3
Total, Top 25 Countries	$1,817,023	$1,989,336	9.9
All Others	$131,080	$145,858	5.6
Grand Total	$1,948,103	$2,135,195	9.6

Source: U.S. Department of Commerce, International Trade Administration. Note: Individual shipments are excluded from the foreign trade data if valued under $2,500. All totals are rounded off to one decimal point. Data for individual categories may not add to totals due to statistical rounding.

books (down 24.1 percent) must be viewed as unsettling in light of the valuable content of these books. Third, the unit data were more significant than the revenue tallies. While six of the eight categories posted increases in revenues, this was due to changes in wholesale prices rather than real increases in business. These issues merit investigation by the book industry as they reveal a weakening in unit sales, a trend that could pose serious problems in the coming years.

A detailed review of the major book categories revealed exceptionally uneven patterns in 2007.

Mass market paperbacks, long an important export book category, experienced declines in revenues in three markets—the United Kingdom, down 17.6 percent; South Africa, down 7.6 percent; and the Philippines, down 17.7 percent—but the slippage in units was evident in six countries, with the United

Table 5 / U.S. Exports of Books: 2007

Category	Value ($'000)	Percent Change 2006–2007	Units ('000)	Percent Change 2006–2007
Dictionaries and thesauruses	$3,792	21.8	533	-38.2
Encyclopedias	6,436	-6.1	750	-14.4
Art books	26,328	67.0	4,156	9.2
Textbooks	430,058	1.0	33,093	-21.6
Religious books	114,065	20.2	44,222	-4.4
Technical, scientific, and professional	560,938	17.3	37,391	-24.1
Hardcover books, n.e.s.	160,123	-1.6	20,190	-21.8
Mass market paperbacks	239,495	10.5	80,309	5.1

Source: U.S. Department of Commerce, International Trade Administration.

Note: Individual shipments are excluded from the foreign trade data if valued under $2,500.00. All totals are rounded off to one decimal point. Data for individual categories may not add to totals due to statistical rounding.

n.e.s. = not elsewhere specified

Table 6 / U.S. Exports of Mass Market Paperbacks (Rack Size): Top Ten Markets 2007

Country	Value ($'000)	Percent Change 2006–2007	Units ('000)	Percent Change 2006–2007
Canada	$125,864	10.9	46,969	15.2
United Kingdom	18,776	-17.6	5,424	-18.2
Japan	13,244	7.0	4,456	-24.7
Australia	11,197	77.0	4,149	26.9
South Africa	10,375	-7.6	2,318	-17.9
Philippines	9,278	-17.7	2,967	-24.1
Argentina	5,279	309.0	1,712	233.5
China	5,271	34.0	1,479	-10.2
Singapore	4,952	10.0	1,180	5.3
Brazil	4,661	4.3	940	-32.0

Source: U.S. Department of Commerce, International Trade Administration. All totals are rounded off to one decimal point. Data for individual categories may not add to totals due to statistical rounding.

Kingdom down 18.2 percent, Japan 24.7 percent, South Africa 17.9 percent, the Philippines 24.1 percent, China 10.2 percent, and Brazil 32 percent.

Exports in the technical, scientific, and professional sector posted incredibly impressive increases in revenues (Germany up 206.2 percent, Belgium up 22.6 percent, and Canada up 15.2 percent), although the declines of Australia (down 7 percent) and Japan (down 11.1 percent) were of concern. However, the declines in units (a pattern evident in far too many book categories in 2007) were unnerving: Mexico down 91 percent, Australia down 40.2 percent, the United Kingdom down 12.8 percent. This is one of the major book categories in the United States, and these unit statistics reveal a weakening in this market sector. Hopefully, this was a one-year anomaly.

Table 7 / U.S. Exports of Technical, Scientific, and Professional Books: Top Ten Markets 2007

Country	Value ($'000)	Percent Change 2006–2007	Units ('000)	Percent Change 2006–2007
Canada	$181,523	15.2	14,979	6.0
United Kingdom	100,504	16.0	4,136	-12.8
Germany	54,148	206.2	3,071	196.8
Australia	33,169	-7.0	2,273	-40.2
Japan	32,124	-11.1	1,404	-28.5
India	17,774	168.4	785	91.8
Mexico	15,726	-24.3	1,018	-91.0
Singapore	15,402	2.8	2,944	-3.2
Belgium	12,106	22.6	608	-7.2
China	11,769	10.7	641	-9.9

Source: U.S. Department of Commerce, International Trade Administration. All totals are rounded off to one decimal point. Data for individual categories may not add to totals due to statistical rounding.

Table 8 / U.S. Exports of Textbooks: Top Ten Markets 2007

Country	Value ($'000)	Percent Change 2006–2007	Units ('000)	Percent Change 2006–2007
United Kingdom	$88,402	-20.7	8,639	-35.8
Canada	101,849	11.9	6,270	7.7
Australia	38,347	-4.0	3,176	-27.0
South Korea	27,953	46.4	1,991	-2.7
Singapore	26,405	-0.4	2,958	-14.7
Japan	21,463	-0.3	1,219	-11.5
Mexico	11,896	29.9	1,043	-7.4
Taiwan	9,262	21.3	518	-28.5
India	8,445	39.3	631	6.7
Hong Kong	6,981	-20.3	370	-44.6

Source: U.S. Department of Commerce, International Trade Administration. All totals are rounded off to one decimal point. Data for individual categories may not add to totals due to statistical rounding.

Fortunately, religious books posted strong annual increases in revenues in nine key market countries (Australia up 32.8 percent, Nigeria 53.3 percent, Argentina 193.8 percent, Germany 245 percent, and South Africa 79.1 percent), although some unit softness was evident in Canada (down 30.9 percent) and Colombia (down 46.3 percent).

The textbook category was equally unsettling because U.S. educational content is considered "world class" in many fields, notably management, marketing, finance, and information technology. Steep revenue declines were recorded to the United Kingdom (down 20.7 percent) and to Hong Kong (down 20.3 percent). Unit sales dropped precipitously in seven markets, including the United Kingdom (down 35.8 percent), Singapore (14.7 percent), Japan (11.5 percent), Taiwan (28.5 percent), and Hong Kong (44.6 percent).

Table 9 / U.S. Exports of Religious Books: Top Ten Markets 2007

Country	Value ($'000)	Percent Change 2006–2007	Units ('000)	Percent Change 2006–2007
United Kingdom	$16,670	9.8	6,484	1.6
Australia	15,395	32.8	3,405	10.9
Canada	14,192	-10.2	4,209	-30.9
Nigeria	10,330	53.3	3,144	43.4
Mexico	9,122	10.7	4,173	-2.8
Argentina	6,409	193.8	4,605	309.3
Germany	3,526	245.0	1,384	323.4
South Africa	2,688	79.1	1,094	35.6
Colombia	2,206	4.3	635	-46.3
Philippines	2,068	11.0	884	6.4

Source: U.S. Department of Commerce, International Trade Administration. All totals are rounded off to one decimal point. Data for individual categories may not add to totals due to statistical rounding.

Hardbound books, a curious amalgamation of various book categories, sustained sharp declines in unit sales in five of the top ten markets, with unsettling results in three traditional markets: Canada (down 16.2 percent), Japan (down 56.7 percent), and the United Kingdom (down 30 percent). Declines were also seen in other major markets—Australia was down 29.8 percent and India 32.6 percent.

The situation in the revenue sector was almost as bleak, with three important markets all posting declines—the United Kingdom (down 33.9 percent), Australia (down 26.7 percent), and Japan (down 28.3 percent).

While several of these declines could be anomalies, the U.S. book industry needs to study the potential long-term impact of sales drops in the exceptionally important professional and textbook categories.

Table 10 / U.S. Exports of Hardbound Books 2007: Top Ten Markets 2007

Country	Value ($'000)	Percent Change 2006–2007	Units ('000)	Percent Change 2006–2007
Canada	$106,367	0.6	13,360	-16.2
United Kingdom	13,130	-33.9	1,989	-30.0
Australia	5,638	-26.7	716	-29.8
India	4,255	-8.2	721	-32.6
Singapore	2,757	178.3	417	37.0
Sweden	2,206	37.3	125	50.3
United Arab Emirates	2,168	249.2	146	138.2
South Korea	2,103	68.4	274	32.3
China	2,051	33.0	178	3.3
Japan	1,746	-28.3	195	-56.7

Source: U.S. Department of Commerce, International Trade Administration. All totals are rounded off to one decimal point. Data for individual categories may not add to totals due to statistical rounding.

The remaining three categories are rather small. Two of them—encyclopedias and serial installments and dictionaries and thesauruses—represent book categories adversely affected by computers supplying their functions, considerably lessening the demand for printed books. It is likely that in a few years these categories may be dropped from coverage in this study.

Table 11 / U.S. Exports of Encyclopedias and Serial Installments: Top Ten Markets 2007

Country	Value ($'000)	Percent Change 2006–2007	Units ('000)	Percent Change 2006–2007
Japan	$1,725	33.5	174	5.8
Canada	2,015	33.5	260	36.8
South Africa	316	-16.6	33	-36.5
Australia	312	-38.0	27	-42.9
Venezuela	254	58.1	13	-63.3
Mexico	240	-72.2	38	-75.9
Hong Kong	218	n.a.	25	n.a.
Taiwan	181	561.0	21	554.3
India	179	312.5	19	294.0
United Kingdom	141	-8.1	11	7.6

Source: U.S. Department of Commerce, International Trade Administration. All totals are rounded off to one decimal point. Data for individual categories may not add to totals due to statistical rounding.

n.a. = not available.

Table 12 / U.S. Exports of Dictionaries (Including Thesauruses): Top Ten Markets 2007

Country	Value ($'000)	Percent Change 2006–2007	Units ('000)	Percent Change 2006–2007
Canada	$1,375	40.4	179	15.9
Brazil	867	2,349.8	122	2,088.3
Mexico	426	-53.5	72	-86.1
South Korea	238	17.9	20	-10.9
Colombia	134	-17.4	21	48.0
India	80	n.a.	11	n.a.
Philippines	79	130.4	15	190.7
Germany	71	542.7	10	542.6
Costa Rica	53	-7.7	11	-6.4
Finland	52	n.a.	15	n.a.

Source: U.S. Department of Commerce, International Trade Administration. All totals are rounded off to one decimal point. Data for individual categories may not add to totals due to statistical rounding.

n.a. = not available.

Art and pictorial books have remained a slightly more robust export category, although the revenues and units are tiny when compared with the larger categories. It remains unclear how long this category will be covered in this study, although it will probably outlast the other two "marginal" book categories mentioned above.

Table 13 / U.S. Exports of Art and Pictorial Books: Top Ten Markets 2007

Country	Value ($'000)	Percent Change 2006–2007	Units ('000)	Percent Change 2006–2007
United Kingdom	$10,895	160.8	1,786	85.5
Georgia	2,935	39.3	500	39.3
Canada	2,446	49.9	313	-11.0
Germany	2,027	281.9	326	232.2
Netherlands	799	542.8	141	148.8
Colombia	679	3,989.3	117	2,445.3
Japan	630	128.5	93	34.0
Philippines	561	n.a.	37	n.a.
Mexico	518	46.8	67	-31.5
Australia	502	-41.9	76	-70.9

Source: U.S. Department of Commerce, International Trade Administration. All totals are rounded off to one decimal point. Data for individual categories may not add to totals due to statistical rounding.

n.a. = not available.

U.S. Book Imports, 2007

Two types of books are imported into the United States. In the first category are books that are printed and published abroad—perhaps scholarly books from the United Kingdom or religious books from Israel or Italy. Included in the second category are books printed abroad for U.S. publishers, perhaps juvenile books from Hong Kong or textbooks from China, and this category is growing. Many publishers of books that are not "time-sensitive" ("time-sensitive" books would include, for instance, bestsellers that might need a quick second or third printing) can reduce their costs for printing, paper, and binding (PPB), as well as some plant costs, and increase their profit margins by utilizing offshore printers. In some instances, a 50 percent PPB cost saving can be achieved with offshore printers, sparking increased demand for these foreign printing operations.

Since 2002 China has been the largest source of imported books, with a 12.5 percent increase in 2007 ($815.68 million compared with $724.7 million in 2006 when it was up 19.7 percent). The vast majority of books imported from China are titles printed abroad for U.S. publishers, a trend that is likely to grow at double-digit rates for the foreseeable future.

While Canada was a distant second as a source of imported books in 2006, it fell to third place (at $298.6 million, up 2.2 percent between 2006 and 2007). The United Kingdom's 16 percent increase in sales ($332.6 million in 2007 versus $286.6 million in 2006) pushed it ahead of Canada in 2007.

Hong Kong ($125.1 million in 2007, down 8.4 percent from $136.6 million in 2006) and Singapore ($115.6 million in 2006, $120.9 million in 2007, up 4.5 percent) again round out the top five.

Table 15 lists the top 25 nations that export books to the United States. Germany, Italy, Japan, South Korea, and Mexico again made the top ten, but in 2007 there were a few interesting developments.

Table 14 / Top Ten Import Sources of Books: 1998–2007
($'000)

Country	1998	1999	2000	2001	2002	2003	2004	2005	2006	2007	Percent Change 2006–2007
China	101,012	142,459	220,895	267,582	338,489	413,065	533,524	605,229	724,742	815,677	12.5
United Kingdom	314,290	278,252	317,660	303,897	267,853	287,972	304,619	307,517	286,624	332,579	16.0
Canada	215,825	221,462	229,045	243,689	251,085	275,053	289,423	281,120	292,273	298,633	2.2
Hong Kong	200,242	229,293	224,834	229,719	223,452	189,783	185,963	176,079	136,617	125,138	-8.4
Singapore	94,672	89,000	86,630	96,325	100,610	103,383	113,900	115,314	115,609	120,867	4.5
Germany	63,066	57,082	57,345	53,092	55,993	52,055	57,353	68,211	76,657	82,088	7.1
Italy	102,525	100,475	94,983	87,779	83,360	84,167	78,567	69,463	69,571	69,393	-0.3
Japan	58,775	55,087	59,268	49,956	47,198	45,277	48,726	50,765	63,822	88,062	38.0
South Korea	25,816	29,728	29,430	35,559	40,459	39,083	46,265	54,303	54,398	54252	-0.3
Mexico	17,404	22,748	24,656	19,272	18,627	21,828	22,627	40,956	47,089	32,380	-31.2

Source: U.S. Department of Commerce, International Trade Administration. All totals are rounded off to one decimal point. Data for individual categories may not add to totals due to statistical rounding.

First, while the annual results varied from 2006 (in some instances shifting downward), South America remained an important source of books, paced by Mexico, Colombia, Peru, and Brazil. Second, the Pacific Rim and Asia retained their position of importance, with impressive tallies by Japan, South Korea, India, Taiwan, and, of course, China. Low operating costs and unit manufacturing and PPB costs in these nations assure they will remain tied to the U.S. market. However, any protracted slowdown in the U.S. economy—clearly evident in the second half of 2007 and the first quarter of 2008—could have a modest impact on book manufacturing in many of these nations.

Table 15 / U.S. Book Imports from 25 Principal Countries:
2006–2007

Country	Value		Percent Change 2006–2007
	2006	2007	
China	$724,742	$815,677	12.5
United Kingdom	286,624	332,579	16.0
Canada	292,273	298,633	2.2
Hong Kong	136,617	125,138	-8.4
Singapore	115,609	120,867	4.5
Germany	76,657	82,088	7.1
Italy	69,571	69,393	-0.3
Japan	63,822	88,062	38.0
South Korea	54,398	54,252	-0.3
Mexico	47,089	32,380	-31.2
Spain	36,901	32,646	-11.5
France	31,006	25,562	-17.6
Colombia	22,102	36,274	64.1
Thailand	19,476	18,747	-3.7
Belgium	15,113	12,860	-14.9
India	14,222	16,439	15.6
Malaysia	14,011	13,816	-1.4
Israel	12,874	14,309	11.1
Taiwan	8,860	9,866	11.4
Netherlands	8,570	8,084	-5.7
Australia	6,828	6,811	-0.2
United Arab Emirates	6,748	6,075	-10.0
Peru	6,009	6,969	16.0
Brazil	5,994	5,882	-1.9
Sweden	5,527	5,526	0.0
Total: Top 25 Countries	$2,081,643	$2,238,936	7.6
All Others	$42,663	$42,338	-0.8
Grand Total:	$2,124,306	$2,281,275	7.4

Source: U.S. Department of Commerce, International Trade Administration. All totals are rounded off to one decimal point. Data for individual categories may not add to totals due to statistical rounding. Individual shipments are excluded from the foreign trade data if valued under $2,500.

As in previous years, hardcover books remained the largest and most significant import category in 2007, topping $725 million (up 10.3 percent; in 2006 the total was $657.2 million). Textbooks experienced an impressive 27.5 percent increase in revenues ($310.5 million; $243.5 million in 2006). Textbooks surged ahead of technical, scientific, and professional category ($275.8 million in 2007, $249.2 million the previous year). The religious books sector retained its status as the fourth-largest import category with a 16.1 percent increase in revenues in 2007 ($132.7 million, compared with $114.3 million in 2006). Unfortunately, mass market paperbacks sagged in the import sector, inching up barely 0.3 percent.

The remaining three categories sustained deep declines, again reinforcing the belief that they have become marginal book categories in both the import and the export arenas.

Table 16 / U.S. Imports of Books: 2006–2007

Category	Value ($'000)		Percent Change 2006–2007
	2006	2007	
Encyclopedias	$5,912	$3,110	-47.4
Textbooks	243,489	310,491	27.5
Religious books	114,254	132,687	16.1
Technical, scientific, and professional	249,248	275,844	10.7
Hardcover books, n.e.s.	657,237	725,052	10.3
Mass market paperbacks	108,524	108,883	0.3
Art and pictorial books	49,961	48,974	-2.8
Dictionaries and thesauruses	11,775	9,907	-15.9

Source: U.S. Department of Commerce, International Trade Administration. All totals are rounded off to one decimal point. Data for individual categories may not add to totals due to statistical rounding. Individual shipments are excluded from the foreign trade data if valued under $2,500.

n.e.s. = not elsewhere specified

Book Import Categories in 2007

Lower PPB costs abroad had a positive impact on textbook imports. Hardbound textbooks are weighty tomes (generally in excess of 300 pages) with expensive paper and binding, color illustrations, charts, and tables. While the United Kingdom maintained its hegemony in revenues (up 10 percent), it sustained a 5 percent decline in units in this category. China, on the other hand, posted impressive increases in both revenues (up 67.8 percent, sliding past Canada) and units (up 44.7 percent). If China maintains this pace, it will eclipse the United Kingdom as the primary source of imported textbooks. Canada's position has become weaker in recent years, something that must be of concern to Canadian printers, publishers, and governmental leaders.

A number of other countries increased their shipments to the United States, including Singapore (up a dramatic 57.9 percent in revenues and 96.6 percent in units) and several South American countries. Colombia was up 67.5 percent in revenues but showed a more modest rise of 4.6 percent in units, and Mexico experienced a 42.7 percent increase in revenues but a striking 243.2 percent increase in units. South America is now a well-entrenched and important offshore printing center. However, Europe remains the primary source of textbooks, with strong results tallied by Germany (up 52.9 percent in revenues and 41.6 percent in units), Spain (up 38.4 percent in revenues but off 22.8 percent in revenues), and Italy (with revenues up 46 percent and units 67.7 percent).

Surprisingly, India fell out of the top ten in 2007 (it ranked 13th in revenues, down 37.6 percent, and units were off by 47.7 percent, dropping India to 17th in this category). This was after an 80.6 percent increase in revenues and 10.6 percent in units in 2006. India has long been adversely affected by stringent bureaucratic policies that have sometimes weakened its ability to compete in certain manufacturing industries, a pattern evident in 2007.

Table 17 / U.S. Imports of Textbooks: Top Ten Markets 2007

Country	Value ($'000)	Percent Change 2006–2007	Units ('000)	Percent Change 2006–2007
United Kingdom	$78,678	10.0	3,274	-5.0
China	65,173	67.8	21,618	44.7
Canada	64,671	31.8	10,712	12.6
Hong Kong	32,904	4.9	6,953	-0.2
Singapore	14,402	57.9	4,852	96.6
Colombia	6,509	67.5	1,259	4.6
Mexico	6,084	42.7	2,722	243.2
Germany	5,289	52.9	273	41.6
Spain	4,887	38.4	392	-22.8
Italy	4,662	46.0	837	67.7

Source: U.S. Department of Commerce, International Trade Administration. All totals are rounded off to one decimal point. Data for individual categories may not add to totals due to statistical rounding.

Between 2002 and 2005, religious books (most of them printed—not published and printed—abroad) were the fastest-growing import category for the United States, often exceeding an annual growth rate in the 5 percent to 7 percent range. It is therefore not surprising that these books have emerged as a major import sector, but what has been unpredicted (at least since 2002) is the emergence of China as the largest foreign printer of religious books.

In 2006 China topped the $27.8 million plateau (up 26.8 percent), shipping more than 12 million units (an increase of 9.3 percent). South Korea was behind China in revenues ($21.51 million, down 8.5 percent), but its units surpassed China (14.2 million, down 5.7 percent). However, in 2007, while China posted another strong record in both revenues (up 8.7 percent, reaching $30.3 million) and units (up 7.6 percent at 12.98 million), South Korea inexplicably experienced declines in both revenues (down 7.1 percent to $20.0 million) and units (off 16.2 percent to 11.9 million). This put South Korea behind not only China but also Colombia, which turned in an impressive performance (up 155.3 percent in revenues and 20.5 percent in units).

The other nations traditionally active in this category include Israel (up 6.6 percent in revenues and 50.5 percent in units in 2007), and Belgium (down in both revenues, by 10.8 percent, and units, by 4 percent). The United Kingdom (especially in Bibles), Spain, and Mexico maintained sizable market shares, as did Hong King and Canada.

Table 18 / U.S. Imports of Bibles, Testaments, Prayer Books, and Other Religious Books: Top Ten Markets 2007

Country	Value ($'000)	Percent Change 2006–2007	Units ('000)	Percent Change 2006–2007
China	$30,306	8.7	12,977	7.6
Colombia	20,697	155.3	12,586	20.5
South Korea	19,990	-7.1	11,903	-16.2
Israel	11,857	6.6	3,436	50.5
Belgium	7,577	-10.8	2,965	-4.0
United Kingdom	4,395	-29.1	1,037	-15.5
Spain	3,734	-7.5	816	-6.2
Mexico	4,035	20.3	4,362	21.8
Hong Kong	3,432	7.2	7,122	222.8
Canada	3,280	15.6	6,297	426.8

Source: U.S. Department of Commerce, International Trade Administration. All totals are rounded off to one decimal point. Data for individual categories may not add to totals due to statistical rounding.

The United Kingdom and Canada have long dominated the technical, scientific, and professional book sector. However, China emerged as the largest source of these books for the U.S. market in 2007, accounting for $59.6 million (up 33.5 percent) and 10.5 million units (up 23.5 percent).

Japan and Germany have replaced both Canada and the United Kingdom in terms of revenues and units.

This book sector in 2007 posted four declines in revenues (Canada, the United Kingdom, Hong Kong, and Mexico) and seven declines in units (Germany, Canada, the United Kingdom, Hong Kong, France, Mexico, and Singapore). Additional declines, and potentially deep ones, are anticipated in the coming years as this sector has been moving rapidly toward electronic distribution of content, in reality the fastest conversion of print to electronic products of any major book category in the United States. It is likely that by 2009 or 2010, the concept of a "technical, scientific, and professional book unit" will become an anachronism since the publishers active in this field record dollars and not units.

China strengthened its already lofty position in the hardbound book sector with a 12.5 percent increase in revenues ($370.2 million) and an 18.2 percent growth rate in units (173.1 million units). The United Kingdom and Canada both experienced increases in revenues ($112.7 million and $34.5 million, respectively), but declines in units (18.1 percent and 7.8 percent, respectively). Unit decline patterns were also evident in Thailand, Japan, Spain, and Germany.

Many hardbound and mass market paperback books are "time sensitive" and publishers need to replenish orders for bestsellers quickly, so this category is unlikely to generate significant increases in imports unless the Canadian and Mexican printers can ratchet up their turnaround time for printing and shipping (more likely to occur if no negative changes in NAFTA are negotiated) in the coming years. The pattern in the mass market sector was also odd, with the same

Table 19 / U.S. Imports of Technical, Scientific, and Professional Books:
Top Ten Markets 2007

Country	Value ($'000)	Percent Change 2006–2007	Units ('000)	Percent Change 2006–2007
China	$59,605	33.5	10,511	23.5
Japan	54,979	77.0	946	0.0
Germany	44,244	9.3	1,922	-17.3
Canada	35,008	-12.9	6,167	-4.7
United Kingdom	27,801	-6.6	2,721	-8.3
Hong Kong	7,950	-23.0	2,505	-5.3
Italy	6,613	8.7	320	15.7
France	6,234	61.9	292	-5.4
Mexico	5,807	-55.7	3,766	-78.9
Singapore	4,613	-8.3	1,328	-1.5

Source: U.S. Department of Commerce, International Trade Administration. All totals are rounded off to one decimal point. Data for individual categories may not add to totals due to statistical rounding.

Table 20 / U.S. Imports of Hardbound Books: Top Ten Markets 2007

Country	Value ($'000)	Percent Change 2006–2007	Units ('000)	Percent Change 2006–2007
China	$370,191	12.5	173,097	18.2
United Kingdom	112,695	28.5	9,147	-18.1
Singapore	59,965	5.0	25,658	9.5
Hong Kong	34,157	-5.9	14,244	3.4
Italy	33,792	5.2	5,781	-10.3
Canada	34,477	8.1	7,136	-7.8
Thailand	10,097	-10.2	2,278	-30.8
Japan	10,784	7.1	3,235	-2.2
Spain	9,132	-20.5	1,618	-32.0
Germany	8,808	-11.5	1,040	-40.7

Source: U.S. Department of Commerce, International Trade Administration. All totals are rounded off to one decimal point. Data for individual categories may not add to totals due to statistical rounding.

six nations sustaining declines in revenues and units: Canada; Singapore; Hong Kong; Italy; Spain; and Mexico. China again maintained the top position in this sector even with relatively unimpressive increases (up 7.9 percent in revenues and 1.4 percent in units). The United Kingdom had a banner year, but the gap between that nation and China appears insurmountable.

The import pattern for encyclopedias and serial installments, dictionaries and thesauruses, and art books was precarious. It remains to be seen if they will be analyzed in the future.

Conclusions

Three book categories are in the process of transforming content from a "print only" to a "print and electronic" to an "electronic and print" business model.

Table 21 / U.S. Imports of Mass Market Paperbacks (Rack Size): Top Ten Markets 2007

Country	Value ($'000)	Percent Change 2006–2007	Units ('000)	Percent Change 2006–2007
China	$33,581	7.9	22,427	1.4
United Kingdom	24,793	64.5	7,163	104.9
Canada	22,254	-11.1	7,969	-38.1
Singapore	5,824	-37.2	5,242	-24.9
Hong Kong	3,994	-27.3	1,990	-39.0
Italy	3,926	-49.9	1,062	-51.7
Spain	2,887	-27.3	948	-32.7
Mexico	2,351	-12.4	906	-34.8
Japan	1,464	18.3	233	38.7
South Korea	1,346	59.2	1,235	193.5

Source: U.S. Department of Commerce, International Trade Administration. All totals are rounded off to one decimal point. Data for individual categories may not add to totals due to statistical rounding.

Table 22 / U.S. Imports of Encyclopedias and Serial Installments: Top Ten Markets 2007

Country	Value ($'000)	Percent Change 2006–2007	Units ('000)	Percent Change 2006–2007
China	$948	-54.1	289	-39.5
Mexico	623	-41.8	130	-26.0
Hong Kong	329	58.6	95	310.0
Canada	223	258.9	12	-49.1
Spain	203	-64.8	24	22.1
Singapore	194	-63.2	43	-36.7
Belgium	105	781.4	7	n.a.
Chile	74	n.a.	22	n.a.
United Arab Emirates	73	-39.9	45	-33.0
Italy	66	-64.5	18	-33.7

Source: U.S. Department of Commerce, International Trade Administration. All totals are rounded off to one decimal point. Data for individual categories may not add to totals due to statistical rounding. Calculations used two decimal points because of the size of the totals.

n.a. = not available

These categories are technical books and the educational book sectors (i.e., el-hi and college). The other major book categories (adult, juvenile, mass market paperbacks, and religious books) will move more slowly in the digital direction because of a variety of factors, including consumer preferences, technological issues, and financial concerns.

This technological metamorphosis will have far-reaching consequences throughout the vast book industry supply chain, including declines in the total number of textbooks and educational books printed abroad for U.S. publishers.

A few other substantive issues center on the state of the U.S. economy.

First, some economists put forward a theory that "decoupling" had occurred. In essence, many nations in Europe as well as Brazil, Russia, India, and China

Table 23 / U. S. Imports of Dictionaries and Thesauruses: Top Ten Markets 2007

Country	Value ($'000)	Percent Change 2006–2007	Units ('000)	Percent Change 2006–2007
United Kingdom	$2,198	4.4	526	3.0
Germany	1,731	3.1	441	-7.1
China	1,417	-1.4	676	-0.9
Italy	838	-48.0	249	-25.0
Spain	808	98.1	169	36.2
Canada	665	24.5	790	105.1
Hong Kong	413	-44.2	91	-69.5
Colombia	258	47.6	58	-6.8
Singapore	248	-32.0	71	-54.6
Poland	247	69.8	62	-32.7

Source: U.S. Department of Commerce, International Trade Administration. All totals are rounded off to one decimal point. Data for individual categories may not add to totals due to statistical rounding. Calculations used two decimal points because of the size of the totals.

Table 24 / U. S. Imports of Art and Pictorial Books (Minimum Value $5): Top Ten Markets 2007

Country	Value ($'000)	Percent Change 2006–2007	Units ('000)	Percent Change 2006–2007
Germany	$6,191	11.7	509	14.6
China	6,189	39.6	768	47.6
Italy	4,942	16.8	321	23.0
Hong Kong	2,225	22.1	243	17.3
United Kingdom	1,797	-0.3	126	-3.6
Singapore	1,391	42.1	132	21.2
France	1,075	-86.4	46	-16.6
Netherlands	793	6.2	44	11.3
Spain	787	-23.7	43	-30.3
South Korea	655	-4.9	87	-0.6

Source: U.S. Department of Commerce, International Trade Administration. All totals are rounded off to one decimal point. Data for individual categories may not add to totals due to statistical rounding. Calculations used two decimal points because of the size of the totals.

(the so-called BRIC countries) had decoupled their economies from dependence on the U.S. economy. However, the credit liquidity and mortgage events in the United States in the second half of 2007 and the first quarter of 2008 spread throughout the world, effectively calling into question whether decoupling had indeed occurred.

Second, because the U.S. economy slowed in the first half of 2008 and showed signs of continuing to do so in the second half, imports may increase as publishers seek to curb costs and increase margins with foreign printed books. Exports could conceivably increase dramatically if the U.S. dollar remains soft throughout 2008.

And third, this industry needs to pay more attention to collecting and analyzing basic, critical macroeconomic data that will assist U.S. publishers in exporting more books abroad.

References

Awokuse, Titus O. (2008). "Trade Openness and Economic Growth: Is Growth Export-Led or Import-Led?" *Applied Economics* 40:2 (January), 161–165.

Baldwin, John R., and Wulong Gu (2003). "Export-Market Participation and Productivity Performance in Canadian Manufacturing." *Canadian Journal of Economics* 36:3 (August), 634–657.

Book Industry Study Group, Inc. (2007). *Book Industry Trends 2007.*

Cavusgil, S. Tamer, and Shaoming Zou (1994). "Marketing Strategy—Performance Relationship: An Investigation of the Empirical Link in Export Market Ventures." *Journal of Marketing* 58:1 (January), 1–21.

Cooper, Robert G., and Elko J. Kleinschmidt (1985). "The Impact of Export Strategy on Export Sales Performance." *Journal of International Business Studies* 16:1 (Spring), 37–55.

Delgado, Miguel A., Jose C. Farinas, and Sonia Ruano (2002). "Firm Productivity and Export Markets: A Non-Parametric Approach." *Journal of International Economics* 57:2 (August), 397–422.

Gala, Paulo (2008). "Real Exchange Rate Levels and Economic Development: Theoretical Analysis and Economic Evidence." *Cambridge Journal of Economics* 32:2 (March), 273–289.

Goldberg, Pinelopi Koujianou, and Michael M. Knetter (1999). "Measuring the Intensity of Competition in Export Markets." *Journal of International Economics* 47:1 (February), 27–60.

Greco, A. N. (2005). *The Book Publishing Industry.* Lawrence Erlbaum Associates.

Greco, A. N., Clara E. Rodriguez, and Robert M. Wharton (2007). *The Culture and Commerce of Publishing in the 21st Century.* Stanford Business Books.

International Intellectual Property Alliance (2007). Appendix A: IIPA Special 301 Recommendations; Special 301 Report, Appendix B: Methodology. See http://www.iipa.com.

Katsikeas, Constantine S., and Robert E. Morgan (1994). "Differences in Perceptions of Exporting Problems Based on Firm Size and Export Market Experience." *European Journal of Marketing* 28:5, 17–35.

Sanghamitra, Das, Mark J. Roberts, and James R. Tybout (2007). "Market Entry Costs, Producer Heterogenity, and Export Dynamics." *Econometrica* 75: 3 (May), 837–873.

Wiedersheim-Paul, Finn, Hans C. Olson, and Lawrence S. Welch (1978). "Pre-Export Activity: The First Step in Internationalization." *Journal of International Business Studies* 9:1 (Spring-Summer), 47–58.

Number of Book Outlets
in the United States and Canada

The *American Book Trade Directory* (Information Today, Inc.) has been published since 1915. Revised annually, it features lists of booksellers, wholesalers, periodicals, reference tools, and other information about the U.S. and Canadian book markets. The data shown in Table 1, the most current available, are from the 2008–2009 edition of the directory.

The 20,339 stores of various types shown are located throughout the United States, Canada, and regions administered by the United States. "General" bookstores stock trade books and children's books in a general variety of subjects. "College" stores carry college-level textbooks. "Educational" outlets handle school textbooks up to and including the high school level. "Mail order" outlets sell general trade books by mail and are not book clubs; all others operating by mail are classified according to the kinds of books carried. "Antiquarian" dealers sell old and rare books. Stores handling secondhand books are classified as "used." "Paperback" stores have more than 80 percent of their stock in paperbound books. Stores with paperback departments are listed under the appropriate major classification ("general," "department store," "stationer," and so forth.). Bookstores with at least 50 percent of their stock on a particular subject are classified by subject.

Table 1 / Bookstores in the United States and Canada, 2007

Category	United States	Canada
Antiquarian General	876	81
Antiquarian Mail Order	345	12
Antiquarian Specialized	169	5
Art Supply Store	71	2
College General	3,255	178
College Specialized	123	9
Comics	220	25
Computer Software	2	0
Cooking	271	8
Department Store	1,610	3
Educational*	190	35
Federal Sites†	221	1
Foreign Language*	23	3
General	4,289	652
Gift Shop	155	7
Juvenile*	136	21
Mail Order General	142	15
Mail Order Specialized	435	22
Metaphysics, New Age, and Occult	172	24
Museum Store and Art Gallery	509	33
Nature and Natural History	39	7
Newsdealer	32	2
Office Supply	20	3

Table 1 / Bookstores in the United States and Canada, 2007 *(cont.)*

Category	United States	Canada
Other‡	2,273	403
Paperback§	124	5
Religious*	2,330	217
Self Help/Development	24	8
Stationer	5	4
Toy Store	44	20
Used*	451	78
Totals	18,456	1,883

* Includes Mail Order Shops for this topic, which are not counted elsewhere in this survey.

† National Historic Sites, National Monuments, and National Parks.

‡ Stores specializing in subjects or services other than those covered in this survey.

§ Includes Mail Order. Excludes used paperback bookstores, stationers, drugstores, or wholesalers handling paperbacks.

Review Media Statistics

Compiled by the staff of the *Bowker Annual*

Number of Books and Other Media Reviewed by Major Reviewing Publications 2006–2007

	Adult		Juvenile		Young Adult		Total	
	2006	2007	2006	2007	2006	2007	2006	2007
Booklist[1]	4,909	4,939	3,123	2,849	—	—	8,032	7,788
BookPage	714	n.a.	102	n.a.	47	n.a.	863	n.a.
Bulletin of the Center for Children's Books[2]	—	—	971	855	—	—	971	855
Chicago Sun Times	535	525	90	85	—	—	625	610
Chicago Tribune Sunday Book Section	600	500	275	250	25	100	900	850
Choice[3]	6,315	6,672	—	—	—	—	6,315	6,672
Horn Book Guide	—	—	3,446	3,421	1,092	751	4,536	4,172
Horn Book Magazine	1	3	316	297	95	79	411	379
Kirkus Reviews[4]	2,552	2,725	1,795	1,998	—	—	4,347	4,723
Library Journal[5]	6,100	6,166	—	—	—	—	6,100	6,166
Los Angeles Times	1,200	n.a.	—	—	—	—	1,200	n.a.
New York Times Sunday Book Review[4]	1,065	1,075	135	125	—	—	1,200	1,200
Publishers Weekly[6]	5,911	6,004	1,200	878	—	—	7,111	6,882
School Library Journal[4]	238	250	4,161	4,283	—	—	4,399	4,533
Washington Post Book World	1,500	1,200	150	100	50	50	1,700	1,350

n.a. = not available

1 All figures are for a 12-month period from September 1, 2006 to August 31, 2007 (vol. 103). YA books are included in the juvenile total. *Booklist* also reviewed 596 other media.

2 All figures are for 12-month period beginning September and ending July/August. YA books are included in the juvenile total. The *Bulletin* also reviewed 22 professional books.

3 All materials reviewed in *Choice* are scholarly publications intended for undergraduate libraries. *Choice* also reviewed 411 Internet sites, 9 CD-ROMs, and 1 DVD.

4 YA books are included in the juvenile total.

5 In addition, *Library Journal* reviewed 303 audiobooks, 403 DVDs/videos, 43 magazines, 304 books in Collection Development, and 59 online databases, and previewed 1,091 books in "Prepub Alert," "Prepub Mystery," and "Prepub Audio."

6 Of the total of 6,882 reviews, 1,090 were online only.

Part 5
Reference Information

Bibliographies

The Librarian's Bookshelf

Mary Ellen Quinn

Editor, *Booklist/Reference Books Bulletin,* American Library Association

Most of the books on this selective bibliography have been published since 2005; a few earlier titles are retained because of their continuing importance.

General Works

American Library Directory, 2008–2009. 2v. Information Today, Inc., 2008. $299.95.

Annual Review of Information Science and Technology (ARIST). Ed. by Blaise Cronin. Information Today, Inc., 2008. $124.95.

The Bowker Annual Library and Book Trade Almanac, 2008. Information Today, Inc., 2008. $199.95.

Encyclopedia of Library and Information Science. 2nd ed. Ed. by Miriam A. Drake. Marcel Dekker, 2003. $1,500. Also available online.

Library Literature and Information Science Index. H. W. Wilson, 1921–. Also available online, 1984–.

Library Literature and Information Science Retrospective: 1905–1983. H. W. Wilson (http://www.hwwilson.com/Databases/liblit _retro.htm).

The Oxford Guide to Library Research. 3rd ed. By Thomas Mann. Oxford University Press, 2005. Paper $18.95.

The Whole Library Handbook. 4th ed. Ed. by George Eberhart. American Library Association, 2006. Paper $42.

Academic Libraries

The Academic Library and the Net Gen Student: Making the Connection. By Susan Gibbons. American Library Association, 2007. Paper $45.

The Academic Library Manager's Forms, Policies, and Procedures Handbook with CD-ROM. By Rebecca Brumley. Neal-Schuman, 2007. Paper and CD-ROM $149.95.

Academic Library Trends and Statistics, 2005. Association of College and Research Libraries/American Library Association, 2006. 3 vols. $440.

ARL Statistics. Association of Research Libraries. Annual. 1962–. $120.

Beyond Survival: Managing Academic Libraries in Transition. By Elizabeth J. Wood and Rush Miller. Libraries Unlimited, 2006. Paper $45.

CLIP (College Library Information Packet) *Notes.* Association of College and Research Libraries/American Library Association, 1980–. Most recent volume is No. 38, 2007. $27.

Making a Difference: Leadership and Academic Libraries. By Peter Hernon and Nancy Rossiter. Libraries Unlimited, 2007. Paper. $45.

Real-Life Marketing and Promotion Strategies in College Libraries: Connecting with Campus and Community. Ed. by Barbara Whitney Petruzzelli. Haworth, 2006. Paper $22.95.

Revisiting Outcomes Assessment in Higher Education. Ed. by Peter Hermon, Robert E. Dugan, and Candy Schwartz. Libraries Unlimited, 2006. Paper $50.

SPEC Kits. Association of Research Libraries. 1973–. 10/yr. $285.

Administration and Personnel

Advances in Library Administration and Organization. Most recent volume is No. 23. Ed. by Edward D. Garten and Delmus E. Williams. Elsevier Science, 2006. $94.95.

Field Guide to Emergency Response. Heritage Preservation Trust, 2006. Paper $29.95.

Fundamentals of Library Supervision. By Joan Giesecke and Beth McNeil. American Library Association, 2005. Paper $48.

Human Resources for Results: The Right Person for the Right Job. By Jeanne Goodrich and Paula M. Singer. 2007. American Library Association, 2007. Paper $55.

Library and Information Center Management. 7th ed. By Robert D. Stueart and Barbara B. Moran. Libraries Unlimited, 2007. $70.

Library Board Strategic Guide: Going to the Next Level. By Ellen G. Moore and Patricia H. Fisher. Scarecrow, 2007. Paper $35.

Management Basics for Information Professionals. 2nd ed. By G. Edward Evans and Patricia Layzell Ward. Neal-Schuman, 2007. Paper $70.

The Neal-Schuman Directory of Public Library Job Descriptions. By Rebecca Brumley. Neal-Schuman, 2005. Paper and CD-ROM $125.

The New OPL Sourcebook: A Guide for Solo and Small Libraries. By Judith A. Siess. Information Today, Inc., 2006. Paper $39.50.

Putting Customers First. 40-minute video. Library Information Network, 2007. DVD or VHS $99.

Risk and Insurance Management Manual for Libraries. By Mary Breighner, William Payton, and Jeanne M. Drewes. Library Administration and Management Association/American Library Association, 2005. Paper $40.

Running a Small Library: A How-To-Do-It Manual. Ed. by John Moorman. Neal-Schuman, 2006. Paper $59.95.

Small Change, Big Problems: Detecting and Preventing Financial Misconduct in Your Library. By Herbert Snyder. American Library Association, 2006. Paper $40.

Strategic Planning and Management for Library Managers. By Joseph R. Matthews. Libraries Unlimited, 2005. Paper $42.

Supervising Staff: A How-To-Do-It Manual. By Marcia Trotta. Neal-Schuman, 2006. Paper $59.95.

Training Library Staff and Volunteers to Provide Extraordinary Customer Service. By Julie Todaro and Mark L. Smith. Neal-Schuman, 2006. Paper $65.

Buildings and Space Planning

Designing a School Library Media Center for the Future. By Rolf Erikson and Carolyn Markuson. American Library Association, 2007. Paper $45.

Library as Place: Rethinking Roles, Rethinking Space. Council on Library and Information Resources, 2005. Download pdf from http://www.clir.org/pubs/abstract/pub/29abst.html.

Library Furnishings: A Planning Guide. By Tish Murphy. McFarland, 2007. Paper $45.

Managing Your Library Construction Project. By Richard C. McCarthy. American Library Association, 2007. Paper $58.

The New Downtown Library. By Shannon Mattern. University of Minnesota, 2006. Paper $39.95.

Planning New and Remodeled Archival Facilities. By Thomas P. Wilsted. Society of American Archivists, 2007. Paper $49.

Cataloging and Classification

Authority Control in Organizing and Accessing Information: Definition and International Experience. Ed. by Arlene G. Taylor and Barbara B. Tillett. Haworth, 2005. Paper $34.95.

Catalog It: A Guide to Cataloging School Library Materials. 2nd ed. By Allison Kaplan and Ann Riedling. Linworth, 2006. Paper $44.95.

Cataloging and Organizing Digital Resources: A How-To-Do-It Manual for Librarians. By Anne M. Mitchell and Brian E. Surratt. Neal-Schuman, 2005. Paper $75.

Cataloging Correctly for Kids: An Introduction to the Tools. 4th ed. Ed. by Sheila S. Intner, Joanna F. Fountain, and Jane E. Gilchrist. American Library Association, 2005. Paper $38.

Cataloging Cultural Objects: A Guide to Describing Cultural Works and Their Images. By Murtha Baca, Patricia Harpring, Elisa Lanzi, Linda McRae, and Ann Whiteside. American Library Association, 2006. Paper $85.

Education for Library Cataloging: International Perspectives. Ed. by Dajin D. Sun and Ruth C. Carter. Haworth, 2006. Paper $49.95.

Introduction to Cataloging and Classification. 10th ed. By Arlene G. Taylor. Libraries Unlimited, 2006. Paper $50.

Knowledge Without Boundaries: Organizing Information for the Future. Ed. by Michael A. Chopey. Association for Library Collections and Technical Services/American Library Association, 2006. Paper $49.

Managing Electronic Records. Ed. by Julie McLeod and Catherine Hare. Facet, 2006. $89.95.

Metadata: A Cataloger's Primer. Ed. by Richard P. Smiraglia. Haworth, 2005. Paper $39.95.

Organizing Audiovisual and Electronic Resources for Access. 2nd ed. By Ingrid Hsieh-Yee. Libraries Unlimited, 2006. Paper $45.

Standard Cataloging for School and Public Libraries. 4th ed. By Sheila S. Intner and Jean Weihs. Libraries Unlimited, 2007. Paper $50.

Understanding Metadata. National Information Standards Organization (NISO), 2004. Free pdf download file from http://www.niso.org.

Children's and Young Adult Services and Materials

Children's Books: A Practical Guide to Selection. By Phyllis J. Van Orden and Sunny Strong. Neal-Schuman, 2007. Paper $59.95

Collection Management for Youth: Responding to the Needs of Learners. By Sandra Hughes-Hassell and Jacqueline C. Mancall. American Library Association, 2005. Paper $38.

Connecting with Reluctant Teen Readers: Tips, Titles, and Tools. By Patrick Jones. Neal-Schuman, 2006. Paper. $59.95.

Digital Inclusion, Teens, and Your Library: Exploring the Issues and Acting on Them. By Lesley S. J. Farmer. Libraries Unlimited, 2005. Paper $40.

Dynamic Youth Services Through Outcome-Based Planning and Evaluation. By Eliza T. Dresang, Melissa Gross, and Leslie Edmonds Holt. American Library Association, 2006. Paper $42.

Extreme Teens: Library Services to Nontraditional Young Adults. By Sheila B. Anderson. Libraries Unlimited, 2006. Paper $36.

Fiore's Summer Reading Program Handbook: A How-To-Do-It Manual. By Carole D. Fiore. Neal-Schuman, 2005. Paper $65.

Fundamentals of Children's Services. By Michael Sullivan. American Library Association, 2005. Paper $50.

The Guy-Friendly YA Library. By James Rollie Welch. Libraries Unlimited, 2007. Paper $40.

Library Teen Advisory Groups. By Diane P. Tuccillo. Scarecrow, 2005. $34.95.

The Newbery and Caldecott Awards: A Guide to the Medal and Honor Books. Association for Library Service to Children/American Library Association, 2007. Paper $19.

The Newbery/Printz Companion: Booktalk and Related Materials for Award Winners and Honor Books. By John T. Gillespie and Corinne J. Naden. 3rd ed. Libraries Unlimited, 2006. $75.

Outstanding Library Service to Children: Putting the Core Competencies to Work. By Rosanne Cerny, Penny Markey, and Amanda Williams. Association for Library

Services to Children/American Library Association, 2006. Paper $25.

Serving Young Teens and 'Tweens. Ed. by Sheila B. Anderson. Libraries Unlimited, 2006. $40.

Sizzling Summer Reading Programs for Young Adults. 2nd ed. By Katharine L. Kan. American Library Association, 2006. Paper $30.

The Teen-Centered Book Club: Readers into Leaders. By Bonnie Kunzel and Constance Hardesty. Libraries Unlimited, 2006. Paper $40.

Youth Information-Seeking Behavior II: Context, Theories, Models, and Issues. Ed. by Mary K. Chelton and Colleen Cool. Scarecrow, 2006. Paper $45.

Collection Development

Collection Development Issues in the Online Environment. Ed. by Di Su. Haworth, 2006. Paper $19.95.

The Collection Program in Schools: Concepts, Practices, and Information Sources. 4th ed. By Kay Bishop. Libraries Unlimited, 2007. Paper $50.

Graphic Novels: A Genre Guide to Comic Books, Manga, and More. By Michael Pawuk. Libraries Unlimited, 2006. $65.

The Kovacs Guide to Electronic Library Collection Development: Essential Core Subject Collections, Selection Criteria, and Guidelines. By Diane Kovacs and Kara L. Robinson. Neal-Schuman, 2004. Paper $125.

Copyright

Colleges, Code, and Copyright: The Impact of Digital Networks and Technological Controls on Copyright and the Dissemination of Information in Higher Education. Association of College and Research Libraries/American Library Association, 2005. Paper $28.

The Complete Copyright Liability Handbook for Librarians and Educators. By Thomas A. Lipinski. Neal-Schuman, 2006. Paper $125.

Copyright Catechism: Practical Answers to Everyday School Dilemmas. By Carol Simpson. Linworth, 2005. Paper $36.95.

Copyright for Schools: A Practical Guide. 4th ed. By Carol Simpson. Linworth, 2005. Paper $44.95.

Copyright Issues Relevant to Digital Preservation and Dissemination of Pre-1972 Commercial Sound Recordings by Libraries and Archives. By June M. Besek. Council on Library and Information Resources, 2006. Paper $20.

Copyright Law and the Distance Education Classroom. By Tomas A. Lipinski. Scarecrow, 2005. Paper $42.50.

Copyright Law for Librarians and Educators: Creative Strategies and Practical Solutions. 2nd ed. By Kenneth D. Crews. American Library Association, 2005. Paper $45.

Intellectual Property: Everything the Digital-Age Librarian Needs to Know. By Timothy Lee Wherry. American Library Association, 2007. Paper $50.

Intellectual Property Rights: A Critical History. By Christopher May and Susan K. Sell. Lynne Rienner, 2006. $55.

Reserves, Electronic Reserves, and Copyright: The Past and the Future. By Brice Austin. Haworth, 2005. Paper $19.95.

Distance Education

Going the Distance: Library Instruction for Remote Users. Ed. by Susan J. Clayton. Neal-Schuman, 2007. Paper. $65.

Libraries Without Walls 6: Evaluating the Distributed Delivery of Library Services. Ed. by Peter Brophy, Jenny Craven, and Margaret Markland. Facet, 2006. $125.

Supporting E-Learning: A Guide for Library and Information Managers. Ed. by Maxine Melling. Facet, 2005. $99.95.

The Electronic Library

Building an Electronic Resource Collection: A Practical Guide. By Stuart D. Lee and Frances Boyle. Facet, 2004. Paper $75.

The Changing Landscape for Electronic Resources: Content, Access, Delivery, and

Legal Issues. Ed. by Yem S. Fong and Suzanne M. Ward. Haworth, 2004. Paper $36.

Digital Library Development: The View from Kanazawa. Ed. by Deanna B. Marcum and Gerald George. Libraries Unlimited, 2006. Paper $68.

E-Metrics for Library and Information Professionals: How to Use Data for Managing and Evaluating Electronic Resource Collections. By Andrew White and Eric Djiva Kamal. Neal-Schuman, 2006. $75.

The Information Commons Handbook. By Donald Robert Beagle. Neal-Schuman, 2006. $125.

EScholarship: A LITA Guide. Ed. by Debra Shapiro. Library and Information Technology Association/American Library Association, 2005. Paper $32.

Licensing in Libraries: Practical and Ethical Aspects. Ed. by Karen Rupp-Serrano. Haworth, 2005. Paper $29.95.

The Whole Digital Library Handbook. Ed. by Diane Kresh. American Library Association, 2007. Paper $55.

Evaluation of Library Services

Demonstrating Results: Using Outcome Measurement in Your Library. By Rhea Joyce Rubin. American Library Association, 2006. Paper $55.

Evaluating the Impact of Your Library. By Sharon Markless and David Streatfield. Facet, 2006. $99.95.

The Evaluation and Measurement of Library Services. By Joseph R. Matthews. Libraries Unlimited, 2007. Paper $50.

Library Assessment in Higher Education. By Joseph R. Matthews. Libraries Unlimited, 2007. Paper $45.

Measuring for Results: The Dimensions of Public Library Effectiveness. By Joseph R. Matthews. Libraries Unlimited, 2004. Paper $44.

Measuring Your Library's Value: How to Do a Cost-Benefit Analysis for Your Public Library. By Donald S. Elliot, Glen E. Holt, Sterling W. Hayden, and Leslie Edmonds Holt. American Library Association, 2007. Paper $55.

Revisiting Outcomes Assessment in Higher Education. Ed. by Peter Hernon, Robert E. Dugan, and Candy Schwartz. Libraries Unlimited, 2006. Paper $50.

Fund-Raising

Big Book of Library Grant Money, 2007. American Library Association, 2007. Paper $275.

Getting Grants in Your Community. By Sally Gardner Reed and Beth Nawalinski. Friends of Libraries U.S.A., 2005. Paper and CD-ROM $40.

Grants for Libraries: A How-To-Do-It Manual and CD-ROM for Librarians. By Stephanie K. Gerding and Pamela H. MacKellar. Neal-Schuman, 2006. Paper and CD-ROM $99.95.

National Guide to Funding for Libraries and Information Services. 8th ed. Ed. by Jeffrey A. Falkenstein. The Foundation Center, 2005. Paper $125.

History

The Encyclopedia of the Library of Congress: For Congress, the Nation and the World. Ed. by John Y. Cole and Jane Aikin. Bernan, 2005. $125.

Libraries and Librarianship: Sixty Years of Challenge and Change, 1945–2005. By George Bobinski. Scarecrow, 2007. $40.

Library: An Unquiet History. By Matthew Battles. W. W. Norton, 2003. Paper $14.95.

Information Literacy

The Blue Book on Information Age Inquiry, Instruction, and Literacy. By Daniel Callison and Leslie Preddy. Libraries Unlimited, 2006. Paper $45.

Information Literacy Assessment: Standards-Based Tools and Assignments. By Teresa Y. Neely. Association of College and Research Libraries/American Library Association, 2006. Paper $42.

Information Literacy: Essential Skills for the Information Age. 2nd ed. By Michael B. Eisenberg, Carrie A. Lowe, and Kathleen

L. Spitzer. Libraries Unlimited, 2004. Paper $50.

Learning to Lead and Manage Information Literacy Instruction. By Esther S. Grassian and Joan R. Kaplowitz. Neal-Schuman, 2005. Paper and CD-ROM $75.

Proven Strategies for Building an Information Literacy Program. Ed. by Susan Carol Curzon and Lynn D. Lampert. Neal-Schuman, 2007. Paper $65.

Student Engagement and Information Literacy. Ed. by Craig Gibson. Association of College and Research Libraries/American Library Association, 2006. Paper $27.

Teaching Information Skills: Theory and Practice. By Jo Webb and Chris Powis. Facet, 2004. $99.95.

Information Science

Fundamentals of Information Studies: Understanding Information and Its Environment. By June Lester and Wallace C. Koehler, Jr. Neal-Schuman, 2007. Paper $65.

Introduction to Modern Information Retrieval. 2nd ed. By G. G. Chowdhury. Facet, 2004. Paper $89.95.

Spanning the Theory-Practice Divide in Library and Information Science. By Bill Crowley. Scarecrow, 2005. Paper $50.

Intellectual Freedom

Banned Books Resource Guide. Office for Intellectual Freedom/American Library Association, 2007. Paper $39.

Burning Books. By Haig Bosmajian. McFarland, 2006. $39.95.

Burning Books and Leveling Libraries: Extremist Violence and Cultural Destruction. By Rebecca Knuth. Praeger, 2006. $39.95.

IFLA/FAIFE World Report on Libraries and Intellectual Freedom. IFLA/FAIFE, 2005. Paper 27 euros.

The New Inquisition: Understanding and Managing Intellectual Freedom Challenges. By James LaRue. Libraries Unlimited, 2007. Paper $40.

Patriot Debates: Experts Debate the USA Patriot Act. Ed. by Stewart A. Baker and John Kavanagh. American Bar Association, 2005. Paper $29.95.

Privacy in the 21st Century: Issues for Public, School and Academic Libraries. By Helen R. Adams, Robert F. Bocher, Carol A. Gordon, and Elizabeth Barry-Kessler. Libraries Unlimited, 2005. Paper $40.

Interlibrary Loan, Document Delivery, and Resource Sharing

Interlibrary Loan and Document Delivery: Best Practices for Operating and Managing Interlibrary Loan Services in All Libraries. By Lee Andrew Hilyer. Haworth, 2006. Paper $19.95.

The Internet/Web

Archiving Websites: A Practical Guide for Information Management Professionals. By Adrian Brown. Facet, 2006. $99.95.

Creating Database-Backed Library Web Pages Using Open Source Tools. By Stephen R. Westman. American Library Association, 2006. Paper $48.

Knitting the Semantic Web. Ed. by Jane Greenberg and Eva Méndez. Haworth, 2007. $75.

Libraries and Google. Ed. by William Miller and Rita M. Pellen. Haworth, 2006. Paper $24.95.

Portals and Libraries. Ed. by Sarah C. Michalak. Haworth, 2006. Paper $29.95.

Web-Based Instruction: A Guide for Libraries. 2nd ed. By Susan Sharpless Smith. American Library Association, 2005. Paper $55.

XHTML and CSS Essentials for Library Web Design. By Michael Sauers. Neal-Schuman, 2006. Paper $75.

Knowledge Management

The Knowledge Entrepreneur. By Stan Skrzeszewski. Scarecrow, 2006. Paper $27.

What They Didn't Tell You About Knowledge Management. By Jay Liebowitz. Scarecrow, 2006. Paper $35.

Librarians and Librarianship

A Day in the Life: Career Options in Library and Information Science. Ed. by Priscilla K. Schontz and Richard A. Murray. Libraries Unlimited, 2007. $45.

Achieving Diversity: A How-To-Do-It Manual for Libraries. Ed. by Barbara I. Dewey and Loretta Parham. Neal-Schuman, 2006. Paper $65.

African American Librarians in the Far West: Pioneers and Trailblazers. Ed. by Binnie Tate Wilkin. Scarecrow, 2006. Paper $55.

The ALA-APA Salary Survey 2007: Librarian—Public and Academic. ALA-Allied Professional Association and the ALA Office for Research and Statistics. American Library Association, 2006. Paper $70.

The ALA-APA Salary Survey 2007: Non-MLS—Public and Academic. ALA-Allied Professional Association and the ALA Office for Research and Statistics. American Library Association, 2006. Paper $100.

ARL Annual Salary Survey, 2006–2007. Association of Research Libraries, 2007. Paper $150.

Introduction to the Library and Information Professions. By Roger C. Greer, Robert J. Grover, and Susan G. Fowler. Libraries Unlimited, 2007. Paper $60.

Last One Out Turn Off the Lights: Is This the Future of American and Canadian Libraries? Ed. by Susan E. Cleyle and Louise M. McGillis. Scarecrow, 2005. Paper $47.

Leadership Basics for Librarians and Information Professionals. By G. Edward Evans and Patricia Layzell Ward. Scarecrow, 2007. $40.

Librarianship and Information Science in the Islamic World, 1966–1999: An Annotated Bibliography. By Sterling Joseph Coleman, Jr. Scarecrow, 2005. Paper $62.

Libraries and the Fight Against HIV/AIDS, Poverty and Corruption. Ed. by Susanne Seidelin and Thomas Skov Jensen. IFLA, 2006. Paper 27 euros.

Library as Place: History, Community, and Culture. Ed. by John E. Buschman and Gloria J. Leckie. Libraries Unlimited, 2006. Paper $50.

Perspectives, Insights and Priorities: Seventeen Leaders Speak Freely of Librarianship. Ed. by Norman Horrocks. Scarecrow, 2005. Paper $26.95.

Résumé Writing and Interviewing Techniques That Work: A How-To-Do-It Manual for Librarians. By Robert R. Newlen. Neal-Schumann, 2006. Paper $55.

Rethinking Information Work: A Career Guide for Librarians and Other Information Professionals. By G. Kim Doherty. Libraries Unlimited, 2006. Paper $38.

The Romance of Libraries. By Madeleine Lefebvre. Scarecrow, 2006. Paper $27.

Sacred Stacks: The Higher Purpose of Libraries and Librarianship. By Nancy Kalikow Maxwell. American Library Association, 2006. Paper $32.

Unfinished Business: Race, Equity and Diversity in Library and Information Science Education. Ed. by Maurice B. Wheeler. Scarecrow, 2005. Paper $43.

Library 2.0

Blogging and RSS: A Librarian's Guide. By Michael Sauers. Information Today, Inc., 2006. Paper $29.50.

Gamers . . . In the Library?! By Eli Neilburger. American Library Association, 2007. Paper $42.

Library 2.0: A Guide to Participatory Library Service. By Michael E. Casey and Laura C. Savastinuk. Information Today, Inc., 2007. $29.50.

Library 2.0 and Beyond: Innovative Technologies and Tomorrow's Users. Ed. by Nancy Courtney. Libraries Unlimited, 2007. Paper $45.

Social Software in Libraries: Building Collaboration, Communication, and Community Online. By Meredith G. Farkas. Information Today, Inc., 2007. Paper $39.50.

Preservation

Capturing Analog Sound for Digital Presentation: Report of a Roundtable Discussion of Best Practices for Transferring Analog Discs and Tapes. 2006. Download pdf from http://www.clir.org/pubs/reports/

pub137/pub137.pdf, or $20 from Council on Library and Information Resources.

Photographs: Archival Care and Management. Rev. ed. By Mary Lynn Ritzenthaler and Diane Vogt-O'Connor. Society of American Archivists, 2006. $84.95.

Preparing for the Worst, Planning for the Best: Protecting Our Cultural Heritage from Disaster. Ed. by Johanna G. Wellheiser and Nancy E. Gwinn. K. G. Saur, 2005. 78 euros.

Preservation and Conservation for Libraries and Archives. By Nelly Balloffet and Jenny Hille. American Library Association, 2005. $125.

Protecting Your Library's Digital Sources: The Essential Guide to Planning and Preservation. By Miriam B. Kahn. American Library Association, 2004. Paper $45.

Public Libraries

Breaking the Mold: Innovative Libraries and Programs. 25-minute video. Library Video Network, 2007. DVD or VHS $99.

Cultural Programming for Libraries: Linking Libraries, Communities, and Culture. By Deborah A. Robertson. American Library Association, 2005. Paper $85.

Exemplary Public Libraries: Lessons in Leadership, Management and Service. By Joy M. Greiner. Libraries Unlimited, 2004. $50.

Hennen's Public Library Planner: A Manual and Interactive CD-ROM. By Thomas J. Hennen, Jr. Neal-Schuman, 2004. Paper and CD-ROM $125.

Introduction to Public Librarianship. By Kathleen de la Peña McCook. Neal-Schuman, 2004. Paper $59.95.

Public Library Data Service Statistical Report. Public Library Association/American Library Association, 2007. Paper $120.

The Public Library Manager's Forms, Policies and Procedures Handbook with CD-ROM. By Rebecca Brumley. Neal-Schuman, 2004. Paper with CD-ROM $125.

The Thriving Library: Successful Strategies for Challenging Times. By Marylaine

Block. Information Today, Inc., 2007. Paper $50.

Public Relations/Marketing

Blueprint for Your Library Marketing Plan: A Guide to Help You Survive and Thrive. By Patricia H. Fisher and Marseille M. Pride. American Library Association, 2005. Paper $50.

Going Places with Youth Outreach: Smart Marketing Strategies for Your Library. By Angela B. Pfeil. American Library Association, 2005. Paper $32.

Library Marketing That Works! By Suzanne Walters. Neal-Schuman, 2004. Paper and CD-ROM $65.

Library Public Relations, Promotions and Communication: A How-To-Do-It Manual. 2nd ed. By Lisa A. Wolfe. Neal-Schuman, 2005. Paper $65.

Marketing Your Library. By Peggy Barber and Linda Wallace. 20-minute video. Library Video Network, 2005. VHS or DVD $99.

Merchandising Strategies. 22-minute video. Library Video Network, 2005. VHS or DVD $120.

Readers' Advisory

Genreflecting: A Guide to Popular Reading Interests. 6th ed. By Diana Tixier Herald. Libraries Unlimited, 2005. $60.

I Need a Book: Reader's Advisory for Adults. 19-minute video. Library Services Network, 2006. VHS or DVD $99.

Nonfiction Readers' Advisory. By Neal Wyatt. American Library Association, 2007.

Readers' Advisory Service in the Public Library. By Joyce G. Saricks. American Library Association, 2005. Paper $38.

The Real Story: A Guide to Nonfiction Reading Interests. By Sarah Statz Cord. Libraries Unlimited, 2006. Paper $40.

Serving Teens Through Readers' Advisory. By Heather Booth. American Library Association, 2007. Paper $36.

The Teen Readers' Advisor. By RoseMary Honnold. Neal-Schuman, 2006. Paper $75.

Reference Services

Reference and Information Services in the Twenty-First Century: An Introduction. By Kay Ann Cassell and Uma Hiremath. Neal-Schuman, 2006. Paper $65.

The Reference Collection: From the Shelf to the Web. Ed. by William J. Frost. Haworth, 2006. Paper $34.95.

The Reference Librarian's Policies, Forms, Guidelines, and Procedures Handbook with CD-ROM. By Rebecca Brumley. Neal-Schuman, 2006. Paper and CD-ROM $125.

The Virtual Reference Desk: Creating a Reference Future. Ed. by R. David Lankes, Eileen G. Abels, Marilyn Domas White, and Saira N. Haque. Neal-Schuman, 2006. Paper $75.

School Libraries/Media Centers

Collaborating with Administrators and Educational Support Staff. By Lesley S. J. Farmer. Neal-Schuman, 2007. Paper $65.

District Library Administration: A Big Picture Approach. By Cynthia Anderson. Linworth, 2005. Paper $44.95.

Essential Documents for School Libraries: I've-Got-It! Answers to I-Need-It-Now! Questions. By Colleen MacDonell. Linworth, 2005. Paper $44.95.

Facilities Planning for School Library Media and Technology Centers. By Steven M. Baule. Linworth, 2007. Paper $39.95.

Leadership and the School Librarian: Essays from Leaders in the Field. Ed. by Mary Lankford. Linworth, 2006. Paper $44.95.

Less Is More: A Practical Guide to Weeding School Library Collections. By Donna J. Baumbach and Linda L. Miller. American Library Association, 2006. Paper $35.

Library 101: A Handbook for the School Library Media Specialist. By Claire Gatrell Stephens and Patricia Franklin. Libraries Unlimited, 2007. Paper $35.

New on the Job: A School Library Media Specialist's Guide to Success. By Ruth Toor and Hilda K. Weisburg. American Library Association, 2006. Paper $38.

Reference Skills for School Library Media Specialists: Tools and Tips. 2nd ed. By Ann Marlow Riedling. Linworth, 2005. Paper $44.95.

Reviving Reading: School Library Programming, Author Visits, and Books That Rock! By Alison M. G. Follos. Libraries Unlimited, 2006. Paper $32.

School Reform and the School Library Media Specialist. By Sandra Hughes-Hassell and Violet H. Harada. Libraries Unlimited, 2007. Paper $40.

Seven Steps to an Award-Winning School Library Program. By Ann M. Martin. Libraries Unlimited, 2005. Paper $35.

Technology and the School Library: A Comprehensive Guide for Media Specialists and Other Educators. By Odin L. Jurowski. Scarecrow, 2006. Paper $45.

The Whole School Library Handbook. Ed. by Blanche Woolls and David V. Loertscher. American Library Association, 2005. Paper $50.

Serials

E-Journals: A How-To-Do-It Manual for Building, Managing, and Supporting Electronic Journal Collection. By Donnelyn Curtis. Neal-Schuman, 2005. Paper $75.

Open Access Bibliography: Liberating Scholarly Literature with E-Prints and Open Access Journals. By Charles W. Bailey, Jr. 2005. Download pdf from http://info.lib.uh.edu/cwb/oab.pdf or $45 from Association of Research Libraries.

Serials in Libraries: Issues and Practices. By Steve Black. Libraries Unlimited, 2006. Paper $45.

Services for Special Groups

Adult Learners Welcome Here. By Margaret Crowley Weibel. Neal-Schuman, 2007. Paper $75.

¡Bienvenidos! ¡Welcome! A Handy Resource Guide for Marketing Your Library to Latinos. By Susannah Mississippi Byrd. American Library Association, 2005. Paper $22.

Bridging the Digital Divide in the Spanish-Speaking Community. Colorado State Library. Library Video Network, 2004. DVD $40.

Improving the Quality of Library Services for Students with Disabilities. Ed. by Peter Hernon. Libraries Unlimited, 2006. Paper $45.

Library Services to Indigenous Populations: Viewpoints and Resources. Ed. by Kelly Webster. American Library Association, 2005. Paper $23.

Library Services to the Incarcerated: Applying the Public Library Model in Correctional Facility Libraries. By Sheila Clark and Erica MacCreaigh. Libraries Unlimited, 2006. Paper $40.

Libros Esenciales: Building, Marketing, and Programming a Core Collection of Spanish Language Children's Materials. By Tim Wadham. Neal-Schuman, 2006. Paper $65.

Serving Latino Communities: A How-To-Do-It Manual. 2nd ed. By Camila Alire and Jacqueline Ayala. Neal-Schuman, 2007. Paper $59.95.

Serving New Immigrant Communities in the Library. By Sondra Cuban. Libraries Unlimited, 2007. Paper $40.

Still Struggling for Equality: American Public Library Services with Minorities. By Plummer Alston Jones, Jr. Libraries Unlimited, 2005. $70.

Try Your Hand at This: Easy Ways to Incorporate Sign Language Into Your Programs. By Kathy MacMillan. Scarecrow, 2006. Paper $32.

Technical Services

Community, Collaboration, and Collections: The Writings of Ross Atkinson. Ed. by Robert Alan and Bonnie MacEwan. Association for Library Collections and Technical Services/American Library Association, 2006. Paper $75.

From Catalog to Gateway: Charting a Course for Future Access. Ed. by Bill Sleeman and Pamela Bluh. Association for Library Collections and Technical Services/American Library Association, 2006. Paper $54.

In-House Book Binding and Repair. By Sharon McQueen. Scarecrow, 2005. Paper $37.

Innovative Redesign and Reorganization of Library Technical Services: Paths for the Future and Case Studies. Ed. by Bradford Lee Eden. Libraries Unlimited, 2004. Paper $50.

Integrating Print and Digital Resources in Library Collections. Ed. by Audrey Fenner. Haworth, 2006. Paper $29.95.

Teams in Library Technical Services. Ed. by Rosann Bazirjian and Rebecca Mugridge. Scarecrow, 2006. Paper $40.

Technology

Audio and Video Equipment Basics for Libraries. By Jim Farrington. Scarecrow, 2006. Paper $45.

Automation Primer for School Library Media Centers and Small Libraries. By Barbara Schultz-Jones. Linworth, 2006. Paper $39.95.

Directory of Library Automation Software, Systems, and Services, 2006–2007. Ed. by Pamela Cibbarelli. Information Today, Inc., 2006. Paper $89.

Information Tomorrow: Reflections on Technology and the Future of Public and Academic Libraries. Ed. by Rachel Singer Gordon. Information Today, Inc., 2007. Paper $35.

Listen Up! Podcasting for Schools and Libraries. By Linda W. Braun. Information Today, Inc., 2007. Paper $29.50.

The Neal-Schuman Library Technology Companion: A Basic Guide for Library Staff. By John Burke. Neal-Schuman, 2006. Paper $59.95.

Technologies for Education: A Practical Guide. 5th ed. By Ann E. Barron, Karen S. Ivers, Nick Lilavois, and Julie A. Wells. Libraries Unlimited, 2006. Paper $48.

Technology for Results: Developing Service-Based Plans. By Diane Mayo. American Library Association, 2005. Paper $55.

Technology Made Simple: An Improvement Guide for Small and Medium Libraries. By Kimberly Bolan and Robert Cullin. American Library Association, 2006. Paper $40.

Technology Planning: Preparing and Updating a Library Technology Plan. By Joseph R. Matthews. Libraries Unlimited, 2005. Paper $50.

Using PDAs in Libraries: A How-To-Do-It Manual. By Colleen Cuddy. Neal-Schuman, 2005. Paper $65.

Wireless Networking: A How-To-Do-It Manual for Libraries. By Louise E. Alcorn and Maryellen Mott Allen. Neal-Schuman, 2006. Paper $65.

Periodicals and Periodical Indexes

ARL
Acquisitions Librarian
Advanced Technology Libraries
Against the Grain
American Archivist
American Libraries
Behavioral and Social Sciences Librarian
Book Links
Booklist
Bookmobile and Outreach Services
The Bottom Line: Managing Library Finances
Cataloging and Classification Quarterly
Catholic Library World
Children and Libraries: The Journal of the Association for Library Services to Children
Choice
Church and Synagogue Libraries
Collection Management
College and Research Libraries
College and Undergraduate Libraries
Communicator (Librarians' Guild)
Community and Junior College Libraries
Computers in Libraries
FYI: The Journal for the School Information Professional
IFLA Journal

Information Outlook (formerly *Special Libraries*)
Information Technology and Libraries
Journal of Academic Librarianship
Journal of Education for Library and Information Science
Journal of Information Ethics
Journal of Interlibrary Loan, Document Delivery and Information Supply
Journal of Library Administration
Journal of the American Society for Information Science and Technology
Journal of the Medical Library Association
Knowledge Quest
Law Library Journal
Legal Reference Services Quarterly
Libraries & Culture
Library Administration and Management
Library Administrator's Digest
Library and Archival Security
Library and Information Science Research (*LIBRES*)
Library Hi-Tech News
Library Issues: Briefings for Faculty and Academic Administrators
Library Journal
Library Media Connection (formerly *Book Report* and *Library Talk*)
Library Quarterly
Library Resources and Technical Services
Library Technology Reports
Library Trends
Librarysparks
Medical Reference Services Quarterly
MultiMedia and Internet @ Schools
Music Library Association Notes
Music Reference Services Quarterly
NetConnect
New Review of Children's Literature and Librarianship
The One-Person Library
Portal: Libraries and the Academy
Progressive Librarian
Public Libraries
Public Library Quarterly
Reference and User Services Quarterly (formerly *RQ*)
Reference Librarian
Resource Sharing & Information Networks
RSR: Reference Services Review
Rural Libraries Journal

School Library Journal
School Library Media Research
Science & Technology Libraries
Searcher: The Magazine for Database Professionals
Serials Librarian
Serials Review
Technical Services Quarterly
Technicalities
Video Librarian
Voice of Youth Advocates (VOYA)
World Libraries
Young Adult Library Services

Blogroll

ALA TechSource (http://www.techsource.ala.org/blog).

blyberg.net. By John Blyberg (http://www.blyberg.net).

Free Range Librarian. By Karen G. Schneider (http://freerangelibrarian.com).

Librarian.net. By Jessamyn West (http://www.librarian.net).

Library Garden (http://librarygarden.blogspot.com).

Library Marketing—Thinking Outside the Book. By Jill Stover (http://library marketing.blogspot.com).

Library Voice. By Chad F. Boeninger (http://libraryvoice.com).

LibraryBytes. By Helene Blowers (http://www.librarybytes.com).

LibraryCrunch. By Michael Casey (http://www.librarycrunch.com).

The Medium Is the Message. By Eric Schnell (http://ericschnell.blogspot.com).

ResourceShelf. By Gary Price (http://www.resourceshelf.com).

The Shifted Librarian. By Jenny Levine (http://www.theshiftedlibrarian.com).

Stephen's Lighthouse. By Stephen Abram (http://stephenslighthouse.sirsi.com).

Tame the Web: Libraries and Technology. By Michael Stephens (http://tametheweb.com).

The Ubiquitous Librarian. By Brian S. Mathews (http://theubiquitouslibrarian.typepad.com).

Walt at Random. By Walt Crawford (http://walt.lishost.org).

Ready Reference

How to Obtain an ISBN

Andy Weissberg and Louise Timko

United States ISBN/SAN Agency

The International Standard Book Numbering (ISBN) system was introduced into the United Kingdom by J. Whitaker & Sons Ltd. in 1967 and into the United States in 1968 by R. R. Bowker. The Technical Committee on Documentation of the International Organization for Standardization (ISO TC 46) is responsible for the international standard.

The purpose of this standard is to "establish the specifications for the International Standard Book Number (ISBN) as a unique international identification system for each product form or edition of a monographic publication published or produced by a specific publisher." The standard specifies the construction of an ISBN, the rules for assignment and use of an ISBN, and all metadata associated with the allocation of an ISBN.

Types of monographic publications to which an ISBN may be assigned include printed books and pamphlets (in various product formats); electronic publications (either on the Internet or on physical carriers such as CD-ROMs or diskettes); educational/instructional films, videos, and transparencies; educational/instructional software; audiobooks on cassette or CD or DVD; braille publications; and microform publications.

Serial publications, printed music, and musical sound recordings are excluded from the ISBN standard as they are covered by other identification systems.

The ISBN is used by publishers, distributors, wholesalers, bookstores, and libraries, among others, in 217 countries and territories as an ordering and inventory system. It expedites the collection of data on new and forthcoming editions of monographic publications for print and electronic directories used by the book trade. Its use also facilitates rights management and the monitoring of sales data for the publishing industry.

The "new" ISBN consists of 13 digits. As of January 1, 2007, a revision to the ISBN standard was implemented in an effort to substantially increase the numbering capacity. The 10-digit ISBN identifier (ISBN-10) is now replaced by the ISBN 13-digit identifier (ISBN-13). All facets of book publishing are now expected to use the ISBN-13, and the ISBN agencies throughout the world are now issuing only ISBN-13s to publishers. Publishers with existing ISBN-10s need to convert their ISBNs to ISBN-13s by the addition of the EAN prefix 978 and recalculation of the new check digit:

ISBN-10: 0-8352-8235-X
ISBN-13: 978-0-8352-8235-2

When the inventory of the ISBN-10s has been exhausted, the ISBN agencies will start assigning ISBN-13s with the "979" prefix instead of the "978." There is no 10-digit equivalent for 979 ISBNs.

Construction of an ISBN

An ISBN currently consists of 13 digits separated into the following parts:

1 A prefix of "978" for an ISBN-10 converted to an ISBN-13
2 Group or country identifier, which identifies a national or geographic grouping of publishers
3 Publisher identifier, which identifies a particular publisher within a group
4 Title identifier, which identifies a particular title or edition of a title
5 Check digit, the single digit at the end of the ISBN that validates the ISBN-13

For more information regarding ISBN-13 conversion services provided by the U.S. ISBN Agency at R. R. Bowker, LLC, visit the ISBN Agency Web site at http://www.isbn.org, or contact the U.S. ISBN Agency at isbn-san@bowker.com.

Publishers requiring their ISBNs to be converted from the ISBN-10 to ISBN-13 format can use the U.S. ISBN Agency's free ISBN-13 online converter at http://isbn.org/converterpub.asp. Large list conversions can be requested by e-mailing isbnconversion@bowker.com. Publishers can also subscribe to view their ISBN online log book by accessing their personal account at http://www.bowkerlink.com.

Displaying the ISBN on a Product or Publication

When an ISBN is written or printed, it should be preceded by the letters ISBN, and each part should be separated by a space or hyphen. In the United States, the hyphen is used for separation, as in the following example: ISBN 978-0-8352-8235-2. In this example, 978 is the prefix that precedes the ISBN-13, 0 is the group identifier, 8352 is the publisher identifier, 8235 is the title identifier, and 2 is the check digit. The group of English-speaking countries, which includes the United States, Australia, Canada, New Zealand, and the United Kingdom, uses the group identifiers 0 and 1.

The ISBN Organization

The administration of the ISBN system is carried out at three levels—through the International ISBN Agency in the United Kingdom, through the national agencies, and through the publishing houses themselves. The International ISBN Agency, which is responsible for assigning country prefixes and for coordinating the worldwide implementation of the system, has an advisory panel that represents the International Organization for Standardization (ISO), publishers, and libraries. The International ISBN Agency publishes the *Publishers International ISBN Directory,* which is a listing of all national agencies' publishers with their assigned ISBN publisher prefixes. R. R. Bowker, as the publisher of *Books In Print* with its extensive and varied database of publishers' addresses, was the obvious place to initiate the ISBN system and to provide the service to the U.S. publishing industry. To date, the U.S. ISBN Agency has entered more than 180,000 publishers into the system.

ISBN Assignment Procedure

Assignment of ISBNs is a shared endeavor between the U.S. ISBN Agency and the publisher. Publishers can make online application through the ISBN Agency's Web site, or by phone or fax. After an application is received and processed by the agency, an ISBN Publisher Prefix is assigned, along with a computer-generated block of ISBNs that is mailed or e-mailed to the publisher. The publisher then has the responsibility to assign an ISBN to each title, keep an accurate record of each number assigned, and register each title in the *Books In Print* database at http://www.bowkerlink.com. It is the responsibility of the ISBN Agency to validate assigned ISBNs and keep a record of all ISBN publisher prefixes in circulation.

ISBN implementation is very much market-driven. Major distributors, wholesalers, retailers, and so forth recognize the necessity of the ISBN system and request that publishers register with the ISBN Agency. Also, the ISBN is a mandatory bibliographic element in the International Standard Bibliographical Description (ISBD). The Library of Congress Cataloging in Publication (CIP) Division directs publishers to the agency to obtain their ISBN prefixes.

Location and Display of the ISBN

On books, pamphlets, and other printed material, the ISBN shall be printed on the verso of the title leaf or, if this is not possible, at the foot of the title leaf itself. It should also appear on the outside back cover or on the back of the jacket if the book has one (the lower right-hand corner is recommended). The ISBN shall also appear on any accompanying promotional materials following the provisions for location according to the format of the material.

On other monographic publications, the ISBN shall appear on the title or credit frames and any labels permanently affixed to the publication. If the publication is issued in a container that is an integral part of the publication, the ISBN shall be displayed on the label. If it is not possible to place the ISBN on the item or its label, then the number should be displayed on the bottom or the back of the container, box, sleeve, or frame. It should also appear on any accompanying material, including each component of a multi-type publication.

Printing of ISBN in Machine-Readable Coding

All books should carry ISBNs in the EAN-13 bar code machine-readable format. All ISBN EAN-13 bar codes start with the EAN prefix 978 for books. As of January 1, 2007, all EAN bar codes should have the ISBN-13 appearing immediately above the bar code in eye-readable format, preceded by the acronym "ISBN." The recommended location of the EAN-13 bar code for books is in the lower right-hand corner of the back cover (see Figure 1).

Figure 1 / Printing the ISBN in Bookland/EAN Symbology

Five-Digit Add-On Code

In the United States, a five-digit add-on code is used for additional information. In the publishing industry, this code is used for price information. The lead digit of the five-digit add-on has been designated a currency identifier, when the add-on is used for price. Number 5 is the code for the U.S. dollar, 6 denotes the Canadian dollar, 1 the British pound, 3 the Australian dollar, and 4 the New Zealand dollar. Publishers that do not want to indicate price in the add-on should print the code 90000 (see Figure 2).

Figure 2 / Printing the ISBN Bookland/EAN Number in Bar Code with the Five-Digit Add-On Code

978 = ISBN Bookland/EAN prefix
5 = Code for U.S. $
2499 = $24.99

90000 means no information
in the add-on code

Reporting the Title and the ISBN

After the publisher reports a title to the ISBN Agency, the number is validated and the title is listed in the many R. R. Bowker hard-copy and electronic publications, including *Books in Print; Forthcoming Books; Paperbound Books in Print; Books in Print Supplement; Books Out of Print; Books in Print Online; Books in Print Plus-CD ROM; Children's Books in Print; Subject Guide to Children's Books in Print; Books Out Loud: Bowker's Guide to AudioBooks; Bowker's Complete Video Directory; Software Encyclopedia; Software for Schools;* and other specialized publications.

For an ISBN application and information, visit the ISBN Agency Web site at http://www.isbn.org, call the toll-free number 877-310-7333, fax 908-219-0188, or write to the United States ISBN Agency, 630 Central Ave., New Providence, NJ 07974.

How to Obtain an ISSN

National Serials Data Program
Library of Congress

In the early 1970s the rapid increase in the production and dissemination of information and an intensified desire to exchange information about serials in computerized form among different systems and organizations made it increasingly clear that a means to identify serial publications at an international level was needed. The International Standard Serial Number (ISSN) was developed and became the internationally accepted code for identifying serial publications.

The ISSN is an international standard, ISO 3297: 2007, as well as a U.S. standard, ANSI/NISO Z39.9. The 2007 edition of ISO 3297 expands the scope of the ISSN to cover continuing resources (serials, as well as updating databases, looseleafs, and some Web sites).

The number itself has no significance other than as a brief, unique, and unambiguous identifier. The ISSN consists of eight digits in Arabic numerals 0 to 9, except for the last—or check—digit, which can be an X. The numbers appear as two groups of four digits separated by a hyphen and preceded by the letters ISSN—for example, ISSN 1234-5679.

The ISSN is not self-assigned by publishers. Administration of the ISSN is coordinated through the ISSN Network, an intergovernmental organization within the UNESCO/UNISIST program. The network consists of national and regional centers, coordinated by the ISSN International Centre, located in Paris. Centers have the responsibility to register serials published in their respective countries.

Because serials are generally known and cited by title, assignment of the ISSN is inseparably linked to the key title, a standardized form of the title derived from information in the serial issue. Only one ISSN can be assigned to a title in a particular medium. For titles issued in multiple media—e.g., print, online, CD-ROM—a separate ISSN is assigned to each medium version. If a title change occurs or the medium changes, a new ISSN must be assigned. Centers responsible for assigning ISSNs also construct the key title and create an associated bibliographic record.

A significant new feature of ISO 3297: 2007 is the Linking ISSN (ISSN-L), a mechanism that enables collocation or linking among different media versions of a continuing resource. The ISSN-L will allow a unique designation (one of the existing ISSNs) to be applied to all media versions of a continuing resource while retaining the separate ISSN that pertains to each version. ISSN-L will facilitate search, retrieval, and delivery across all medium versions of a serial or other continuing resource for improved ISSN functionality in OpenURL linking, search engines, library catalogs, and knowledge bases. The new standard also supports interoperability by specifying the use of ISSN and ISSN-L with other systems such as DOI, OpenURL, URN, and EAN bar codes. Implementation of ISSN-L is expected in the latter part of 2008.

The ISSN International Centre handles ISSN assignments for international organizations and for countries that do not have a national center. It also maintains and distributes the collective ISSN database that contains bibliographic records corresponding to each ISSN assignment as reported by the rest of the network. The database contains more than 1 million ISSNs.

In the United States, the National Serials Data Program at the Library of Congress is responsible for assigning and maintaining the ISSNs for all U.S. serial titles. Publishers wishing to have an ISSN assigned should request an application form from the program, or download one from the program's Web site, and ask for an assignment. Assignment of the ISSN is free, and there is no charge for its use.

The ISSN is used all over the world by serial publishers to distinguish similar titles from each other. It is used by subscription services and libraries to manage files for orders, claims, and back issues. It is used in automated check-in systems by libraries that wish to process receipts more quickly. Copyright centers use the ISSN as a means to collect and disseminate royalties. It is also used as an identification code by postal services and legal deposit services. The ISSN is included as a verification element in interlibrary lending activities and for union catalogs as a collocating device. In recent years, the ISSN has been incorporated into bar codes for optical recognition of serial publications and into the standards for the identification of issues and articles in serial publications. Another recent use for the ISSN is as a linking mechanism in online systems where the ISSN can serve to connect catalog records or citations in abstracting and indexing databases with full-text journal content via OpenURL resolvers or reference linking services.

For further information about the ISSN or the ISSN Network, U.S. libraries and publishers should contact the National Serials Data Program, Library of Congress, Washington, DC 20540-4160 (telephone 202-707-6452, fax 202-707-6333, e-mail issn@loc.gov). ISSN application forms and instructions for obtaining an ISSN are also available via the Library of Congress World Wide Web site, http://www.loc.gov/issn.

Non-U.S. parties should contact the ISSN International Centre, 20 rue Bachaumont, 75002 Paris, France (telephone 33-1-44-88-22-20, fax 33-1-40-26-32-43, e-mail issnic@issn.org, World Wide Web http://www.ISSN.org).

How to Obtain an SAN

Andy Weissberg and Louise Timko

United States ISBN/SAN Agency

SAN stands for Standard Address Number. The SAN system, an American National Standards Institute (ANSI) standard, assigns a unique identification number that is used to positively identify specific addresses of organizations in order to facilitate buying and selling transactions within the industry. It is recognized as the identification code for electronic communication within the industry.

For purposes of this standard, the book industry includes book publishers, book wholesalers, book distributors, book retailers, college bookstores, libraries, library binders, and serial vendors. Schools, school systems, technical institutes, and colleges and universities are not members of this industry, but are served by it and therefore included in the SAN system.

The purpose of the SAN is to ease communications among these organizations, of which there are several hundreds of thousands that engage in a large volume of separate transactions with one another. These transactions include purchases of books by book dealers, wholesalers, schools, colleges, and libraries from publishers and wholesalers; payments for all such purchases; and other communications between participants. The objective of this standard is to establish an identification code system by assigning each address within the industry a unique code to be used for positive identification for all book and serial buying and selling transactions.

Many organizations have similar names and multiple addresses, making identification of the correct contact point difficult and subject to error. In many cases, the physical movement of materials takes place between addresses that differ from the addresses to be used for the financial transactions. In such instances, there is ample opportunity for confusion and errors. Without identification by SAN, a complex record-keeping system would have to be instituted to avoid introducing errors. In addition, problems with the current numbering system—such as errors in billing, shipping, payments, and returns—are significantly reduced by using the SAN system. The SAN also eliminates one step in the order fulfillment process: the "look-up procedure" used to assign account numbers. Previously a store or library dealing with 50 different publishers was assigned a different account number by each of the suppliers. The SAN solved this problem. If a publisher prints its SAN on its stationery and ordering documents, vendors to whom it sends transactions do not have to look up the account number, but can proceed immediately to process orders by SAN.

Libraries are involved in many of the same transactions as book dealers, such as ordering and paying for books and charging and paying for various services to other libraries. Keeping records of transactions—whether these involve buying, selling, lending, or donations—entails operations suited to SAN use. SAN stationery speeds up order fulfillment and eliminate errors in shipping, billing, and crediting; this, in turn, means savings in both time and money.

History

Development of the Standard Address Number began in 1968 when Russell Reynolds, general manager of the National Association of College Stores (NACS), approached R. R. Bowker and suggested that a "Standard Account Number" system be implemented in the book industry. The first draft of a standard was prepared by an American National Standards Institute (ANSI) Committee Z39 subcommittee, which was co-chaired by Russell Reynolds and Emery Koltay of Bowker. After Z39 members proposed changes, the current version of the standard was approved by NACS on December 17, 1979.

Format

The SAN consists of six digits plus a seventh *Modulus 11* check digit; a hyphen follows the third digit (XXX-XXXX) to facilitate transcription. The hyphen is to be used in print form, but need not be entered or retained in computer systems. Printed on documents, the Standard Address Number should be preceded by the identifier "SAN" to avoid confusion with other numerical codes (SAN XXXXXXX).

Check Digit Calculation

The check digit is based on *Modulus 11,* and can be derived as follows:

1. Write the digits of the basic number.   2 3 4 5 6 7
2. Write the constant weighting factors associated with
    each position by the basic number.   7 6 5 4 3 2
3. Multiply each digit by its associated weighting factor.   14 18 20 20 18 14
4. Add the products of the multiplications. $14 + 18 + 20 + 20 + 18 + 14 = 104$
5. Divide the sum by *Modulus 11* to find the remainder. $104 \div 11 = 9$
                                                                                      plus a remainder of 5
6. Subtract the remainder from the *Modulus 11* to generate the
    required check digit. If there is no remainder, generate a check
    digit of zero. If the check digit is 10, generate a check digit of X
    to represent 10, since the use of 10 would require an extra digit. $11 - 5 = 6$
7. Append the check digit to create the standard seven-digit
    Standard Address Number.   SAN 234-5676

SAN Assignment

R. R. Bowker accepted responsibility for being the central administrative agency for SAN, and in that capacity assigns SANs to identify uniquely the addresses of organizations. No SANs can be reassigned; in the event that an organization should cease to exist, for example, its SAN would cease to be in circulation entirely. If an organization using an SAN should move or change its name with no change in ownership, its SAN would remain the same, and only the name or address would be updated to reflect the change.

The SAN should be used in all transactions; it is recommended that the SAN be imprinted on stationery, letterheads, order and invoice forms, checks, and all other documents used in executing various book transactions. The SAN should always be printed on a separate line above the name and address of the organization, preferably in the upper left-hand corner of the stationery to avoid confusion with other numerical codes pertaining to the organization, such as telephone number, zip code, and the like.

SAN Functions

The SAN is strictly a Standard Address Number, becoming functional only in applications determined by the user; these may include activities such as purchasing, billing, shipping, receiving, paying, crediting, and refunding. It is the method used by Pubnet and PubEasy systems and is required in all electronic data interchange communications using the Book Industry Systems Advisory Committee (BISAC) EDI formats. Every department that has an independent function within an organization could have a SAN for its own identification.

For additional information or to make suggestions, write to ISBN/SAN Agency, R. R. Bowker, LLC, 630 Central Ave., New Providence, NJ 07974, call 908-219-0276, or fax 908-219-0188. The e-mail address is san@bowker.com. The SAN Web site for online applications is at http://www.isbn.org.

Distinguished Books

Notable Books of 2007

The Notable Books Council of the Reference and User Services Association, a division of the American Library Association, selected these titles for their significant contribution to the expansion of knowledge or for the pleasure they can provide to adult readers.

Fiction

Bloom, Amy. *Away.* Random House.

Carlson, Ron. *Five Skies.* Penguin Viking.

Chabon, Michael. *The Yiddish Policeman's Union.* HarperCollins.

Clarke, Brock. *An Arsonist's Guide to Writers' Homes in New England.* Algonquin.

Clinch, John. *Finn: A Novel.* Random House.

Englander, Nathan. *The Ministry of Special Cases.* Knopf.

Holthe, Tess Uriza. *The Five-Forty-Five to Cannes.* Crown.

Jones, Lloyd. *Mister Pip.* Dell.

McEwan, Ian. *On Chesil Beach.* Nan A. Talese.

Malouf, David. *The Complete Stories.* Pantheon.

Pettersen, Per. *Out Stealing Horses.* Graywolf.

Trevor, William. *Cheating at Canasta.* Penguin Viking.

Nonfiction

Ackerman, Diane. *The Zookeeper's Wife: A War Story.* W. W. Norton.

Angier, Natalie. *The Canon.* Houghton Mifflin.

Ayres, Ian. *Super Crunchers.* Bantam.

Godwin, Peter. *When a Crocodile Eats the Sun.* Little Brown.

Groopman, Jerome. *How Doctors Think.* Houghton Mifflin.

Howell, Georgina. *Gertrude Bell: Queen of the Desert, Shaper of Nations.* Farrar, Straus & Giroux.

Isaacson, Walter. *Einstein: His Life and Universe.* Simon & Schuster.

Kingsolver, Barbara. *Animal, Vegetable, Miracle: A Year of Food Life.* HarperCollins.

Margonelli, Lisa. *Oil on the Brain.* Doubleday.

Weisman, Alan. *The World Without Us.* St. Martins.

Poetry

Bosselaar, Laure-Anne. *A New Hunger.* Ausable.

Kennedy, X. J. *In a Prominent Bar in Secaucus.* Johns Hopkins.

Best Books for Young Adults

Each year a committee of the Young Adult Library Services Association (YALSA), a division of the American Library Association, compiles a list of the best fiction and nonfiction appropriate for young adults ages 12 to 18. Selected on the basis of each book's proven or potential appeal and value to young adults, the titles span a variety of subjects as well as a broad range of reading levels.

Fiction

Alexie, Sherman. *The Absolutely True Diary of a Part-Time Indian* (illus. by Ellen Forney). Little, Brown (978-0-3160-1368-0).

Alexie, Sherman. *Flight.* Grove/Atlantic Black Cat (978-0-8021-7037-8).

Anderson, Laurie Halse. *Twisted.* Penguin (978-0-670-06101-3).

Asher, Jay. *Thirteen Reasons Why.* Penguin (978-1-59514-171-2).

Brande, Robin. *Evolution, Me, and Other Freaks of Nature.* Random (978-0-375-94349-2).

Brooks, Martha. *Mistik Lake.* Farrar, Straus & Giroux (978-0-374-34985-1).

Burgess, Melvin. *Bloodsong.* Simon & Schuster (978-1-4169-3616-9).

Cameron, Peter. *Someday This Pain Will Be Useful to You.* Farrar, Straus & Giroux (978-0-374-30989-3).

Carey, Janet Lee. *Dragon's Keep.* Harcourt (978-0-15-205926-2).

Carey, Mike. *The Re-Gifters* (illus. by Sonny Liew and Mark Hempel). DC Comics (978-1-4012-0303-0).

Cassidy, Anne. *Looking for JJ.* Harcourt (978-0-15-206190-6).

Castellucci, Cecil. *Beige.* Candlewick (978-0-7636-3066-9).

Clarke, Judith. *One Whole and Perfect Day.* Front Street (978-1-932425-95-6).

Compestine, Ying Chang. *Revolution Is Not a Dinner Party.* Henry Holt (978-0-8050-8207-4).

Cross, Shauna. *Derby Girl.* Henry Holt (978-0-8050-8023-0).

Cullen, Lynn. *I Am Rembrandt's Daughter.* Bloomsbury (978-1-59990-046-9).

Dowd, Siobhan. *A Swift Pure Cry.* Random House (978-0-385-75108-7).

Downham, Jenny. *Before I Die.* Random House (978-0-385-75155-1).

Doyle, Larry. *I Love You, Beth Cooper.* (illus. by Evan Dorkin). HarperCollins (978-0-06-123617-4).

Ellis, Ann Dee. *This Is What I Did.* Little, Brown (978-0-316-01363-5).

Felin, M. Sindy. *Touching Snow.* Atheneum (978-1-4169-1795-3).

Friesen, Gayle. *For Now.* Kids Can (978-1-55453-133-2).

Gipi. *Notes for a War Story.* Spectrum. Roaring Brook (978-1-59643-261-1).

Grey, Christopher. *Leonardo's Shadow: Or, My Astonishing Life as Leonardo da Vinci's Servant.* Simon & Schuster (978-1-4169-0543-1).

Hale, Shannon. *Book of a Thousand Days* (illus. by James Noel Smith). Bloomsbury (978-1-59990-051-3).

Hemphill, Stephanie. *Your Own, Sylvia: A Verse Portrait of Sylvia Plath.* Random House (978-0-375-83799-9).

Hinds, Gareth. *Beowulf.* Candlewick (978-0-7636-3022-5).

Hornby, Nick. *Slam.* Penguin (978-0-399-25048-4).

Hosseini, Khaled. *A Thousand Splendid Suns.* Penguin (978-1-59448-950-1).

Jenkins, A. M. *Repossessed.* HarperCollins (978-0-06-083568-2).

Jocelyn, Marthe. *How It Happened in Peach Hill.* Random House (978-0-375-83701-2).

Johnston, Tony. *Bone by Bone by Bone.* Roaring Brook (978-1-59643-113-3).

Jones, Lloyd. *Mister Pip.* Dell (978-0-385-34106-6).

Key, Watt. *Alabama Moon.* Farrar, Straus & Giroux (978-0-374-30184-2).

Klass, David. *Firestorm.* Farrar, Straus & Giroux (978-0-374-32307-3).

Knox, Elizabeth. *Dreamquake: Book Two of the Dreamhunter Duet.* Farrar, Straus & Giroux (978-0-374-31854-3).

Koertge, Ron. *Strays.* Candlewick (978-0-7636-2705-8).

Lanagan, Margo. *Red Spikes.* Random House (978-0-375-84320-4).

Landy, Derek. *Skulduggery Pleasant.* HarperCollins (978-0-06-123115-5).

Lat. *Town Boy.* Roaring Brook (978-1-59643-331-1).

Lockhart, E. *Dramarama.* Hyperion (978-0-7868-3815-8).

Lyga, Barry. *The Astonishing Adventures of Fanboy and Goth Girl.* Houghton Mifflin (978-0-618-72392-8).

Lyga, Barry. *Boy Toy.* Houghton Mifflin (978-0-618-72393-5).

McCaughrean, Geraldine. *The White Darkness.* HarperCollins (978-0-06-089035-3).

MacCready, Robin Merrow. *Buried.* Penguin (978-0-525-47724-2).

Marillier, Juliet. *Wildwood Dancing.* Random House (978-0-375-83364-9).

Mieville, China. *Un Lun Dun.* Random House (978-0-345-49516-7).

Miller, Sarah. *Miss Spitfire: Reaching Helen Keller.* Simon & Schuster (978-1-4169-2542-2).

Moore, Perry. *Hero.* Hyperion (978-1-4231-0195-6).

Murdock, Catherine Gilbert. *The Off Season.* Houghton Mifflin (978-0-618-68695-7).

Myers, Walter Dean. *What They Found: Love on 145th Street.* Random House (978-0-385-32138-9).

Olmstead, Robert. *Coal Black Horse.* Algonquin (978-1-56512-521-6).

Peet, Mal. *Tamar: A Novel of Espionage, Passion, and Betrayal.* Candlewick (978-0-7636-3488-9).

Resau, Laura. *Red Glass.* Random House (978-0-385-73466-0).

Resau, Laura. *What the Moon Saw.* Random House (978-0-385-73343-4).

The Restless Dead: Ten Original Stories of the Supernatural (ed. by Deborah Noyes). (978-0-7636-2906-9).

Rowling, J. K. *Harry Potter and the Deathly Hallows* (illus. by Mary GrandPré). Scholastic (978-0-545-01022-1).

Schmidt, Gary D. *The Wednesday Wars.* Clarion (978-0-618-72483-3).

Sedgwick, Marcus. *My Swordhand Is Singing.* Random House (978-0-375-84689-2).

Selznick, Brian. *The Invention of Hugo Cabret: A Novel.* Scholastic (978-0-439-81378-5).

Shakespeare, William. *Romeo and Juliet* (adapted by Richard Appignanesi, illus. by Sonia Leong). Abrams (978-0-8109-9325-9).

Sharenow, Robert. *My Mother the Cheerleader.* HarperCollins (978-0-06-114896-5).

Shusterman, Neal. *Unwind.* Simon & Schuster (978-1-4169-1204-0).

Smith, Roland. *Peak.* Harcourt (978-0-15-202417-8).

Sonnenblick, Jordan. *Notes from the Midnight Driver.* Scholastic (978-0-439-75779-9).

St. James, James. *Freak Show.* Penguin (978-0-525-47799-0).

Tan, Shaun. *The Arrival.* Scholastic (978-0-439-89529-3).

Thompson, Kate. *The New Policeman.* HarperCollins (978-0-06-117427-8).

Wallace, Rich. *One Good Punch.* Random House (978-0-375-81352-8).

Weinheimer, Beckie. *Converting Kate.* Penguin (978-0-670-06152-5).

Wiess, Laura. *Such a Pretty Girl.* Simon & Schuster (978-1-4165-2183-9.

Wizner, Jake. *Spanking Shakespeare.* Random House (978-0-375-84086-9).

Zarr, Sara. *Story of a Girl.* Little, Brown (978-0-316-01453-3).

Zevin, Gabrielle. *Memoirs of a Teenage Amnesiac.* Farrar, Straus & Giroux (978-0-374-34946-2).

Nonfiction

Beah, Ishmael. *A Long Way Gone: Memoirs of a Boy Soldier.* Farrar, Straus & Giroux (978-0-374-10523-5).

Crisler, Curtis L. *Tough Boy Sonatas* (illus. by Floyd Cooper). Boyds Mills (978-1-932425-77-2).

The Deep: The Extraordinary Creatures of the Abyss (ed. by Claire Nouvian). University of Chicago (978-0-226-59566-5).

Fradin, Judith Bloom, and Dennis Brindell Fradin. *Jane Addams: Champion of Democracy.* Clarion (978-0-618-50436-7).

Helfer, Andrew. *Malcolm X: A Graphic Biography* (illus. by Randy Duburke). Farrar, Straus & Giroux (978-0-8090-9504-9).

Marrin, Albert. *The Great Adventure: Theodore Roosevelt and the Rise of Modern America.* Penguin (978-0-525-47659-7).

Polly, Matthew. *American Shaolin: Flying Kicks, Buddhist Monks, and the Legend of Iron Crotch: An Odyssey in the New China.* Penguin (978-1-59240-262-5).

Raddatz, Martha. *The Long Road Home: A Story of War and Family.* Penguin (978-0-399-15382-2).

Reef, Catherine. *e.e. cummings: a poet's life.* Clarion (978-0-618-56849-9).

Sis, Peter. *The Wall: Growing Up Behind the Iron Curtain.* Farrar, Straus & Giroux (978-0-374-34701-7).

Tammet, Daniel. *Born on a Blue Day: Inside the Extraordinary Mind of an Autistic Savant.* Simon & Schuster (978-1-4165-3507-2).

Quick Picks for Reluctant Young Adult Readers

The Young Adult Library Services Association, a division of the American Library Association, annually chooses a list of outstanding titles that will stimulate the interest of reluctant teen readers. This list is intended to attract teens who, for whatever reason, choose not to read.

The list, compiled by an 11-member committee, includes fiction and nonfiction titles published from late 2006 through 2007.

Fiction

Adams, Lenora. *Baby Girl.* Simon & Schuster (978-1-4169-2512-5).

Anderson, Laurie Halse. *Twisted.* Penguin (978-0-670-061013).

Aronson, Sarah. *Head Case.* Roaring Brook (978-1-59643-214-7).

Asher, Jay. *Thirteen Reasons Why.* Penguin (978-1-5951-4-1712).

Barnes, Jennifer Lynn. *Tattoo.* Random (978-0-385-903639).

Blank, Jessica. *Almost Home.* Hyperion (978-1-4231-0642-5).

Brewer, Heather. *The Chronicles of Vladimir Tod: Eighth Grade Bites.* Penguin (978-0-5254-7-8119).

Cast, P. C., and Kristen Cast. *Marked: The House of Night, Book 1.* St. Martin's (978-0-312-36026-9).

Cast, P. C., and Kristen Cast. *Betrayed: The House of Night, Book 2.* St. Martin's (978-0-312-36028-3).

Castellucci, Cecil. *Beige.* Candlewick (978-0-7636-3066-9).

Cooney, Caroline B. *Diamonds in the Shadow.* Random House (978-1-4000-7423-5).

Cross, Shauna. *Derby Girl.* Henry Holt (978-0-8050-8023-0).

Crutcher, Chris. *Deadline.* HarperCollins (978-0-06-085089-0).

Davis, Mark, Mike Davis, and Brandon Schultz. *Blokhedz: Book 1 of Genesis.* Simon & Schuster (978-1-4165-4073-1).

De la Cruz, Melissa. *Masquerade.* Hyperion (978-0-78683-8936).

Erskine, Kathryn. *Quaking.* Penguin (978-0-399-24774-3).

Fields, Terri. *Holdup.* Roaring Brook (978-1-59643-219-2).

Flinn, Alex. *Beastly.* HarperCollins (978-0-06-087416-2).

Fullerton. Alma. *Walking on Glass.* HarperCollins (978-0-06-077851-2).

Gonzalez, Julie. *Ricochet.* Random House (978-0-3857-3228-4).

Grant, Vicki. *I.D.* Orca (978-1-55143-694-4).

Gratz, Alan. *Something Rotten: A Horatio Wilkes Mystery.* Penguin (978-0-8037-3216-2).

Halpern, Julie. *Get Well Soon.* Fiewel & Friends (978-0-312-36795-4).

Harazin, S. A. *Blood Brothers.* Random House (978-0-3857-3364-9).

Harmon, Michael. *Skate.* Random House (978-0-375-97516-5).

Harvey, Sarah N. *Bull's Eye.* Orca (978-1-55143-679-1).

Henderson, J. A. *Bunker 10.* Harcourt (978-0-15-206240-8).

Hopkins, Ellen. *Glass.* Simon & Schuster (978-1-4169-4090-6).

Hopkins, Ellen. *Impulse.* Simon & Schuster (978-1-4169-0356-9).

Jacobs, Deborah Lynn. *Choices.* Roaring Brook (978-1-59643-217-8).

Johnston, Jeffry W. *Fragments.* Simon & Schuster (978-1-4169-2486-9).

Knowles, Jo. *Lessons from a Dead Girl.* Candlewick (978-0-7636-3279-3).

Koertge, Ron. *Strays.* Candlewick (978-0-7636-2705-8).

Lane, Dakota. *The Secret Life of It Girls.* Simon & Schuster (978-1-4169-1492-1).

Lubar, David. *True Talents.* Tom Doherty (978-0-7653-0977-8).

Lynn, Erin. *Demon Envy.* Penguin (978-0-425-21737-5).

Mackler, Carolyn. *Guyaholic: The Story of Finding, Flirting, Forgetting . . . and the*

Boy Who Changes Everything. Candlewick (978-0-7636-2537-5).

McClintock, Norah. *Bang.* Orca (978-1-55143-654-8).

McClintock, Norah. *Down.* Orca (978-1-55143-766-8).

McKayhan, Monica. *Indigo Summer.* Harlequin (978-0-373-83075-6).

McNab, Andy, and Robert Rigby. *Avenger.* Penguin (978-0-399-24685-2).

Mead, Richelle. *Vampire Academy.* Penguin (978-1-59414-174-3).

Myers, Walter Dean. *What They Found: Love on 145th Street.* Random House (978-0385-3218-9).

Nance, Andrew, and Colin Polhemus (illus.). *Daemon Hall.* Henry Holt (978-0-8050-8171-8).

Plummer, Louise. *Finding Daddy.* Random House (978-0-385-70392-1).

Pow, Tom. *Captives.* Roaring Brook (978-1-59643-201-7).

Reinhardt, Dana. *Harmless.* Random House (978-0-385-74699-1).

Ryan, Darlene. *Responsible.* Orca (978-1-55143-685-2).

Schreiber, Mark. *Star Crossed.* Llewelyn (978-0-7387-1001-3).

Sewell, Earl. *Keysha's Drama.* Harlequin (978-0-373-83079-3).

Shakespeare, William, Richard Appignasi, and Sonia Leong (illus.). *Manga Shakespeare: Romeo and Juliet.* Abrams (978-0-8109-9325-2).

Shaw, Susan. *Safe.* Penguin (978-0-525-47829-4).

Showalter, Gena. *Oh My Goth.* Simon & Schuster (978-1-4165-2474-8).

Shusterman, Neal. *Unwind.* Simon & Schuster (978-1-4169-1204-0).

Sitomer, Alan L. *Homeboyz.* Hyperion (978-1-4231-0030-0).

Smith, Roland. *Peak.* Harcourt (978-0-15-202417-8).

Sones, Sonya. *What My Girlfriend Doesn't Know.* Simon & Schuster (978-0-689-87602-8).

St. James, James. *Freak Show.* Penguin (978-0-525-47799-0).

Stone, Jeff. *Crane.* Random House (978-09375-83077-8).

Strasser, Todd. *Boot Camp.* Simon & Schuster (978-1-4169-0848-7).

Sweeney, Joyce. *Headlock.* Henry Holt (978-0-8050-8018-6).

Tullson, Diane. *The Darwin Expedition.* Orca (978-155143-676-0).

Van Diepen, Allison. *Snitch.* Simon & Schuster (978-1-4169-5030-1).

Vande Velde, Vivian. *Remembering Raquel.* Harcourt (978-0-15-205976-7).

Velez, Ivan. *Dead High Yearbook.* Penguin (978-0-525-47783-9).

Volponi, Paul. *Rucker Park Setup.* Penguin (978-0-670-06130-3).

Vrettos, Adrienne Maria. *Sight.* Simon & Schuster (978-1-4169-0657-5).

Wasserman, Robin. *Chasing Yesterday: Book 1, The Awakening.* Scholastic (978-0-439-93338-4).

Watson, C. G. *Quad.* Penguin (978-1-59514-138-5).

Wiess, Laura. *Such a Pretty Girl.* Simon & Schuster (978-1-58180-847-6).

Zarr, Sara. *Story of a Girl.* Little, Brown (978-0-316-01453-3).

Nonfiction

50 Cent. *50 x 50: 50 Cent in His Own Words.* Simon & Schuster (978-1-4165-4471-5).

Alvarado, Melissa, Hope Meng, and Melissa Rannels, with Matthew Carden (illus.). *Subversive Seamster: Transform Thrift Store Threads into Street Couture.* Taunton (978-1-59514-171-2).

Aranzi, Aronzo. *The Bad Book.* Vertical (978-1-93223469-5).

Ash, Russell. *Firefly's World of Facts.* Firefly (978-1-55407-313-9).

Bey, Dawoud. *Class Pictures.* Aperture (978-1-59711-043-3).

Blakeney, Faith and Justina, and Ellen Schultz. *99 Ways to Cut, Sew and Deck Out Your Denim.* Crown (978-0-307-35170-8).

Carlowicz, Michael. *Moon.* Abrams (978-0-8109-9307-5).

Chryssicas, Mary Kaye. *Breathe: Yoga for Teens.* Dorling Kindersley (978-0-756-62661-7).

Cooper, Robbie. *Alter Ego: Avatars and Their Creators.* Chris Boot (978-1-905712-02-1).

Dingle, Adrian, with Simon Basher (illus.). *The Periodic Table: Elements with Style.* Houghton Mifflin (978-0-7534-6085-6).

Editors of *CosmoGirl! Cosmogirl! Make It Yourself: 50 Fun and Funky Projects.* Sterling (978-158816-624-1).

Editors of *Inside Cheerleading. Cheerleading: From Tryouts to Championships.* Rizzoli (978-0-7893-1565-6).

Editors of *Seventeen* Magazine. *Seventeen Real Girl, Real Life Stories: True Crime.* Sterling (978-1-58816-648-1).

Everhart, Mike. *Sea Monsters: Prehistoric Monsters of the Deep.* National Geographic (978-1-4262-0085-4).

Gee, Joshua. *Encyclopedia Horrifica.* Scholastic (978-0-4399-2-2555).

Golus, Carrie. *Tupac Shakur.* Lerner (978-0-8225-6609-0).

Grahame-Smith, Seth. *How to Survive a Horror Movie: All the Skills to Dodge the Kills.* Chronicle (978-1-59474-179-1).

Grandits, John. *Blue Lipstick: Concrete Poems.* Clarion (978-0-618-56860-4).

Greenfield, Lauren. *Thin.* Chronicle (978-0-8118-5633-1).

Grody, Steve, and James Prigoff. *Graffiti L.A.: Street Style and Art.* Abrams (978-0-8-1099-2986).

Handy, Roger, and Karin Elsener. *Found Photos: Rear Ends.* Abrams (978-0-8109-0926-7).

Harrington, Jane. *Extreme Pets.* Scholastic (978-0-439-82948-9).

Hess, Nina. *A Practical Guide to Monsters.* Wizards of the Coast (978-0-7869-4809-3).

Jamal, Joseph. *Tupac Shakur Legacy.* Simon & Schuster (978-0-7432-92603).

Lee, John. *Street Scene.* F&W (978-1-158180-847-6).

Lewry, Fraser, and Tom Ryan. *Kittenwar.* Chronicle (978-0-8118-5980-6).

Pardes, Bronwen. *Doing It Right: Making Smart, Safe and Satisfying Choices About Sex.* Simon & Schuster (978-1-4169-1823-X).

Pearce, Fred. *Earth: Then and Now.* Firefly (978-1-55407-298-9).

Pearson, Felicia "Snoop," and David Ritz. *Grace After Midnight: A Memoir.* Grand Central (978-0-446-19518-8).

Rogge, Hannah, and Adrian Buckmaster (illus.). *Save This Shirt!* Stewart, Tabori and Chang (978-1-58479-584-1).

Salant, James. *Leaving Dirty Jersey: A Crystal Meth Memoir.* Simon & Schuster (978-1-4169-3629-9).

Shivack, Nadia. *Inside Out: Portrait of an Eating Disorder.* Simon & Schuster (978-0-689-85216-9).

Simonson, Louise. *DC Comics Covergirls.* Rizzoli (978-0-7893-1544-1).

Smedman, Lisa. *From Boneshakers to Choppers: The Rip-Roaring History of Motorcycles.* Annick (978-1-55451-016-0).

Thalia. *Belleza! Lessons in Lipgloss and Happiness.* Chronicle (978-0-8118-5829-8).

Warren, Frank. *A Lifetime of Secrets: A PostSecret Book.* HarperCollins (978-0-06123860-4).

Willett, Edward. *Jimi Hendrix: Kiss the Sky.* Enslow (978-0-7660-2449-6).

Yoshinaga, Masayuki. *Gothic and Lolita.* Phaidon (978-0-7148-4785-6).

Audiobooks for Young Adults

Each year a committee of the Young Adult Library Services Association, a division of the American Library Association, compiles a list of the best audiobooks for young adults ages 12 to 18. The titles are selected for their teen appeal and recording quality, and because they enhance the audience's appreciation of any written work on which the recordings may be based. While the list as a whole addresses the interests and needs of young adults, individual titles need not appeal to this entire age range but rather to parts of it.

Nonfiction

Mao's Last Dancer, by Li Cunxin, read by Paul English. Bolinda Audio, 8 hours and 55 minutes, 8 discs (978-1-74093-820-4).

Fiction

An Abundance of Katherines, by John Green, read by Jeff Woodman. Brilliance Audio, 7 hours, 6 discs (978-1-4233-2451-5).

Before I Die, by Jenny Downham, read by Charlotte Parry. Listening Library, 7 hours and 10 minutes, 6 discs (978-0-7393-6288-4).

The Black Tattoo, by Sam Enthoven, read by John Lee. Listening Library, 13 hours and 57 minutes, 11 discs (978-0-7393-3675-5).

Bloody Jack, Being an Account of the Curious Adventures of Mary "Jacky" Faber, Ship's Boy, by L. A. Meyer, read by Katherine Kellgren. Listen and Live Audio, 8 hours, 6 discs (978-1-59316-094-4).

Cupid, by Julius Lester, read by Stephen McKinley Henderson. Listening Library, 5 hours and 37 minutes, 5 discs (978-0-7393-4850-5).

Evolution, Me, and Other Freaks of Nature, by Robin Brande, read by Kaili Vernoff. Listening Library, 6 hours and 25 minutes, 5 discs (978-0-375-84349-5).

Forever in Blue, by Ann Brashares, read by Angela Goethals. Listening Library, 9 hours and 3 minutes, 7 discs (978-0-7393-4845-1).

Harry Potter and the Deathly Hallows, by J. K. Rowling, read by Jim Dale. Listening Library, 21 hours and 40 minutes, 17 discs (978-0-7393-6041-5) or 12 cassettes (978-0-7393-6040-8).

I Am the Messenger, by Markus Zusak, read by Marc Aden Gray. Listening Library, 8 hours and 40 minutes, 7 discs (978-0-7393-3692-2).

Jazz, by Walter Dean Myers, narrated by James "D-Train" Williams and Vaneese Thomas. Live Oak Media, 43 minutes (978-1-4301-0022-5).

Life as We Knew It, by Susan Beth Pfeffer, read by Emily Bauer. Listening Library, 9 hours, 7 discs (978-0-7393-3683-0).

Mimus, by Lilli Thal, read by Maxwell Caulfield. Listening Library, 12 hours and 28 minutes, 10 discs (978-0-7393-4865-9).

The Off Season, by Catherine Gilbert Murdock, read by Natalie Moore. Listening Library, 6 hours, 5 discs (978-0-7393-5106-2).

Peak, by Roland Smith, read by Ramon de Ocampo. Recorded Books, 7 hours and 30 minutes, 6 discs (978-1-4281-6356-0) or 6 cassettes (978-1-4281-6351-5).

The Rules of Survival, by Nancy Werlin, read by Daniel Passer. Listening Library, 9 hours and 8 minutes, 5 discs (978-0-7393-5115-4).

Samurai Shortstop, by Alan Gratz, read by Arthur Morey. Listening Library, 7 hours and 21 minutes, 6 discs (978-0-7393-3624-3).

Skulduggery Pleasant, by Derek Landy, read by Rupert Degas. HarperChildren's Audio, 7 hours and 30 minutes (978-0-06-134104-5).

Soul Eater: Chronicles of Ancient Darkness, Book 3, by Michelle Paver, read by Ian

McKellen, Recorded Books, 6 hours and 45 minutes, 6 discs (978-1-4281-4609-9) or 6 cassettes (978-1-4281-4604-4).

Thirteen Reasons Why, by Jay Asher, read by Joel Johnstone and Debra Wiseman. Listening Library, 6 hours and 15 minutes, 5 discs (978-0-7393-6122-1).

Treasure Island, by Robert Louis Stevenson, read by Alfred Molina. Listening Library, 7 hours (978-0-7393-5083-6).

Wintersmith, by Terry Pratchett, read by Stephen Briggs. HarperChildren's Audio, 8 hours and 30 minutes, 7 discs (978-0-06-123336-4).

The Reading List

Established in 2007 by the Reference and User Services Association (RUSA), a division of the American Library Association, this list highlights outstanding genre fiction that merits special attention by general adult readers and the librarians who work with them.

RUSA's Reading List Council, which consists of ten librarians who are experts in readers' advisory and collection development, selects books in eight categories: Adrenaline (suspense, thrillers, and action adventure), Fantasy, Historical Fiction, Horror, Mystery, Romance, Science Fiction, and Women's Fiction.

Adrenaline

The Second Objective by Mark Frost (Hyperion).

Fantasy

The Name of the Wind by Patrick Rothfuss (Daw).

Historical Fiction

The Religion by Tim Willocks (Farrar, Straus & Giroux).

Horror

The Heart-Shaped Box by Joe Hill (William Morrow).

Mystery

Mistress of the Art of Death by Ariana Franklin (Putnam).

Romance

Natural Born Charmer by Susan Elizabeth Phillips (Morrow).

Science Fiction

In War Times by Kathleen Ann Goonan (Tor).

Women's Fiction

Garden Spells by Sarah Addison Allen (Bantam).

Notable Children's Books

A list of notable children's books is selected each year by the Notable Children's Books Committee of the Association for Library Service to Children, a division of the American Library Association. Recommended titles are selected by children's librarians and educators based on originality, creativity, and suitability for children. [See "Literary Prizes, 2007" later in Part 5 for Caldecott, Newbery, and other award winners—*Ed.*]

Books for Younger Readers

Agee, Jon. *Nothing.* Illus. Hyperion (978-0-7868-3694-9).

Bang-Campbell, Monika. *Little Rat Makes Music.* Illus. by Molly Bang. Harcourt (978-0-15-205305-5).

Broach, Elise. *When Dinosaurs Came with Everything.* Illus. by David Small. Simon & Schuster (978-0-689-86922-8).

Brown, Monica. *My Name Is Gabito: The Life of Gabriel García Márquez / Me Llamo Gabito: La Vida de Gabriel García Márquez.* Illus. by Raúl Colón. Luna Rising (978-0-87358-908-6).

Coffelt, Nancy. *Fred Stays with Me!* Illus. by Tricia Tusa. Little, Brown (978-0-316-88269-9).

Cole, Brock. *Good Enough to Eat.* Illus. Farrar, Straus & Giroux (978-0-374-32737-8).

Deedy, Carmen Agra. *Martina the Beautiful Cockroach: A Cuban Folktale.* Illus. by Michael Austin. Peachtree (978-1-56145-399-3).

Dillon, Leo, and Diane Dillon. *Mother Goose Numbers on the Loose.* Illus. Harcourt (978-0-15-205676-6).

Floca, Brian. *Lightship.* Illus. Simon & Schuster (978-1-4169-2436-4).

Global Fund for Children. *Global Babies.* Illus. Charlesbridge (978-1-58089-174-5).

Gonzalez, Maya Christina. *My Colors, My World / Mis Colores, Mi Mundo.* Illus. Children's (978-0-89239-221-6).

Graham, Bob. *Dimity Dumpty: The Story of Humpty's Little Sister.* Illus. Candlewick (978-0-7636-3078-2).

Gravett, Emily. *Orange Pear Apple Bear.* Illus. Simon & Schuster (978-1-4169-3999-3).

Harrington, Janice N. *The Chicken-Chasing Queen of Lamar County.* Illus. by Shelley Jackson. Farrar, Straus & Giroux (978-0-374-31251-0).

Henkes, Kevin. *A Good Day.* Illus. Greenwillow (978-0-06-114018-1).

Here's a Little Poem: A Very First Book of Poetry. Ed. by Jane Yolen and Andrew Fusek Peters. Illus. by Polly Dunbar. Candlewick (978-0-7636-3141-3).

Isadora, Rachel. *Yo, Jo!* Illus. Harcourt (978-0-15-205783-1).

Lunde, Darrin. *Hello, Bumblebee Bat.* Illus. by Patricia J. Wynne. Charlesbridge (978-1-57091-374-7).

McKissack, Patricia C. *The All-I'll-Ever-Want Christmas Doll.* Illus. by Jerry Pinkney. Schwartz & Wade (978-0-375-83759-3).

Montes, Marisa. *Los Gatos Black on Halloween.* Illus. by Yuyi Morales. Henry Holt (978-0-8050-7429-1).

Morales, Yuyi. *Little Night.* Illus. Roaring Brook (978-1-59643-088-4).

Perkins, Lynne Rae. *Pictures from Our Vacation.* Illus. Greenwillow (978-0-06-085097-5).

Pinkney, Jerry. *Little Red Riding Hood.* Illus. Little, Brown (978-0-316-01355-0).

Sayre, April Pulley. *Vulture View.* Illus. by Steve Jenkins. Holt (978-0-8050-7557-1).

Seeger, Laura Vaccaro. *Dog and Bear: Two Friends, Three Stories.* Illus. Roaring Brook (978-1-59643-053-2).

Seeger, Laura Vacarro. *First the Egg.* Illus. Roaring Brook (978-1-59643-272-7).

Thompson, Lauren. *Ballerina Dreams: A True Story.* Illus. by James Estrin. Feiwel & Friends (978-0-312-37029-9).

Wheeler, Lisa. *Jazz Baby.* Illus. by R. Gregory Christie. Harcourt (978-0-15-202522-9).

Willems, Mo. *Knuffle Bunny Too: A Case of Mistaken Identity.* Illus. Hyperion (978-1-4231-0299-1).

Willems, Mo. *There Is a Bird on Your Head!* Illus. Hyperion (978-1-4231-0686-9).

Middle Readers

Bishop, Nic. *Nic Bishop Spiders.* Illus. Scholastic (978-0-439-87756-5).

Dowson, Nick. *Tracks of a Panda.* Illus. by Yu Rong. Candlewick (978-0-7636-3146-8).

Giblin, James Cross. *The Many Rides of Paul Revere.* Illus. Scholastic (978-0-439-57290-3).

Goscinny, René. *Nicholas and the Gang.* Illus. by Jean-Jacques Sempé. Trans. from French by Anthea Bell. Phaidon (978-0-7148-4788-7).

Hest, Amy. *Remembering Mrs. Rossi.* Illus. by Heather Maione. Candlewick (978-0-7636-2163-6).

Judge, Lita. *One Thousand Tracings: Healing the Wounds of World War II.* Illus. Hyperion (978-1-4231-0008-9).

Kobayashi, Issa. *Today and Today.* Illus. by G. Brian Karas. Scholastic (978-0-439-59078-5).

Lehman, Barbara. *Rainstorm.* Illus. Houghton (978-0-618-75639-1).

Levine, Ellen. *Henry's Freedom Box: A True Story from the Underground Railroad.* Illus. by Kadir Nelson. Scholastic (978-0-439-77733-9).

Lewin, Ted. *At Gleason's Gym.* Illus. Roaring Brook (978-1-59643-231-4).

Mora, Pat. *Yum! ¡Mmmm! ¡Que Rico! Americas' Sproutings.* Illus. by Rafael López. Lee & Low (978-1-58430-271-1).

Park, Linda Sue. *Tap Dancing on the Roof.* Illus. by Istvan Banyai. Clarion (978-0-618-23483-7).

Ray, Deborah Kogan. *Down the Colorado: John Wesley Powell, the One-Armed Explorer.* Illus. Farrar (978-0-374-31838-3).

Richter, Jutta. *The Cat: Or, How I Lost Eternity.* Illus. by Rotraut Susanne Berner. Trans. from German by Anna Brailovsky. Milkweed (978-1-57131-676-9).

Schlitz, Laura Amy. *The Bearskinner: A Tale of the Brothers Grimm.* Illus. by Max Grafe. Candlewick (978-0-7636-2730-0).

Selznick, Brian. *The Invention of Hugo Cabret.* Illus. Scholastic (978-0-439-81378-5).

Stewart, Trenton Lee. *The Mysterious Benedict Society.* Little, Brown (978-0-316-05777-6).

Varon, Sara. *Robot Dreams.* Illus. Roaring Brook (978-1-59643-108-9).

Older Readers

Alexander, Lloyd. *The Golden Dream of Carlo Chuchio.* Henry Holt (978-0-8050-8333-0).

Alexander, Elizabeth, and Marilyn Nelson. *Miss Crandall's School for Young Ladies and Little Misses of Color.* Illus. by Floyd Cooper. Boyds Mills (978-1-59078-456-3).

Bausum, Ann. *Muckrakers: How Ida Tarbell, Upton Sinclair, and Lincoln Steffens Helped Expose Scandal, Inspire Reform, and Invent Investigative Journalism.* Illus. National Geographic (978-1-4263-0137-7).

Barakat, Ibtisam. *Tasting the Sky: A Palestinian Childhood.* Farrar, Straus & Giroux (978-0-374-35733-7).

Bernier-Grand, Carmen T. *Frida: ¡Viva la Vida! Long Live Life!* Illus. Marshall Cavendish (978-0-7614-5336-9).

Burns, Loree Griffin. *Tracking Trash: Flotsam, Jetsam, and the Science of Ocean Motion.* Illus. Houghton (978-0-618-58131-3).

Compestine, Ying Chang. *Revolution Is Not a Dinner Party.* Henry Holt (978-0-8050-8207-4).

Curtis, Christopher Paul. *Elijah of Buxton.* Scholastic (978-0-439-02344-3).

Engle, Margarita. *The Poet Slave of Cuba: A Biography of Juan Francisco Manzano.* Illus. by Sean Qualls. Henry Holt (978-0-8050-7706-3).

Freedman, Russell. *Who Was First? Discovering the Americas.* Illus. Clarion (978-0-618-66391-0).

Gore, Al. *An Inconvenient Truth: The Crisis of Global Warming.* Illus. Viking (978-0-670-06272-0).

Grandits, John. *Blue Lipstick: Concrete Poems.* Clarion (978-0-618-56860-4).

Holm, Jennifer. *Middle School Is Worse Than Meatloaf: A Year Told Through Stuff.* Illus. by Elicia Castaldi. Simon & Schuster (978-0-689-85281-7).

Krull, Kathleen. *Marie Curie: Giants of Science No. 4.* Illus. by Boris Kulikov. Viking (978-0-670-05894-5).

Miyabe, Miyuki. *Brave Story.* Trans. from Japanese by Alexander O. Smith. VIZ Media (978-1-4215-1196-2).

Neri, G. *Chess Rumble.* Illus. by Jesse Joshua Watson. Lee & Low (978-1-58430-279-7).

Rowling, J. K. *Harry Potter and the Deathly Hallows.* Scholastic (978-0-545-01022-1).

Schlitz, Laura Amy. *Good Masters! Sweet Ladies! Voices from a Medieval Village.* Illus. by Robert Byrd. Candlewick (978-0-7636-1578-9).

Schmidt, Gary. *The Wednesday Wars.* Clarion (978-0-618-72483-3).

Sís, Peter. *The Wall: Growing Up Behind the Iron Curtain.* Illus. Farrar, Straus & Giroux (978-0-374-34701-7).

Tan, Shaun. *The Arrival.* Illus. Scholastic (978-0-439-89529-3).

Thompson, Kate. *The New Policeman.* Greenwillow (978-0-06-117427-8).

Wells, Rosemary. *Red Moon at Sharpsburg.* Viking (978-0-670-03638-7).

Williams, Marcia. *Chaucer's Canterbury Tales.* Illus. Candlewick (978-0-7636-3197-0).

Woodson, Jacqueline. *Feathers.* Putnam (978-0-399-23989-2).

Wynne-Jones, Tim. *Rex Zero and the End of the World.* Farrar, Straus & Giroux (978-0-374-33467-3).

All Ages

Bryan, Ashley. *Let It Shine: Three Favorite Spirituals.* Illus. Simon & Schuster (978-0-689-84732-5).

Prelutsky, Jack. *Good Sports: Rhymes About Running, Jumping, Throwing, and More.* Illus. by Chris Raschka. Knopf (978-0-375-83700-5).

Prévert, Jacques. *How to Paint the Portrait of a Bird.* Illus. and trans. by Mordicai Gerstein. Roaring Brook (978-1-59643-215-4).

Notable Recordings for Children

This list of notable recordings for children was selected by the Association for Library Service to Children, a division of the American Library Association. Recommended titles are chosen by children's librarians and educators on the basis of their originality, creativity, and suitability.

Black Duck. Listening Library, 5 hours and 30 minutes. Elementary–middle school. Narrator David Ackroyd leads a trip back to New England's rum-running days.

Bloody Jack, Being an Account of the Curious Adventures of Mary "Jacky" Faber, Ship's Boy. Listen and Live Audio, 8 hours. Middle school–YA. Katherine Kellgren tells the story of an 18th century London girl who stows away aboard a ship.

Cave of the Dark Wind. Brilliance Audio, 2 hours. Elementary. Jim Dale reads this sequel to *Peter and the Starcatchers.*

Clementine. Recorded Books. 1 hour and 30 minutes. Elementary. Sara Pennypacker's story is narrated by Jessica Almasy.

A Crooked Kind of Perfect. Listening Library, 3 hours and 17 minutes. Elementary. Zoe achieves keyboard fame in Tai Alexandra Ricci's reading of Linda Urban's book.

Dooby Dooby Moo. Weston Woods, 13 minutes. Beginning readers. Randy Travis tells the story of Duck and his barnyard friends as they plan to enter the county fair talent show.

"Dream." Lyric Partners, 47 minutes. Preschool. Mae Robertson performs a collection of lullabies.

Epossumondas Saves the Day. Recorded Books, 15 minutes. Beginning readers. A little possum stars as the hero of this bayou tale.

Every Child Deserves a Lifetime: Songs from the For Our Children Series. Shout! Factory, 55 minutes. All ages. An eclectic collection of songs performed by well-known musicians.

Harry Potter and the Deathly Hallows. Listening Library, 21 hours and 40 minutes. Middle school–YA. Jim Dale is the narrator as Harry faces the greatest challenges of his life.

Hattie Big Sky. Listening Library, 8 hours and 30 minutes. Middle school–YA. Kirsten Potter narrates this tale set in Montana in the early 20th century.

The Higher Power of Lucky. Listening Library, 3 hours and 38 minutes. Elementary–middle school. Ten-year-old Lucky seeks her "higher power" in this award-winning story.

If a Tree Falls at Lunch Period. Listening Library, 4 hours and 16 minutes. Middle school. Fitting in and friendship are the themes of this story by Gennifer Choldenko, told by Ariadne Meyers and Francois Battiste.

The Invention of Hugo Cabret. Scholastic Audiobooks, 2 hours and 51 minutes. Middle school. Jeff Woodman tells the story of 12-year-old orphan Hugo Cabret who believes he will see his future if he can fix the mechanical man that so fascinated his father.

Jazz. Live Oak Media, 43 minutes. Beginning readers. James "D-Train" Williams and Vaneese Thomas narrate this work by Walter Dean Myers on the history of jazz, told through a series of poems.

The Librarian from the Black Lagoon. Weston Woods, 8 minutes. Beginning readers. A reading of Mike Thaler's picture book about rumors, exaggerations, and the school library.

Lilly's Big Day. Live Oak Media, 14 minutes. Beginning readers. Lilly has her heart set on being the flower girl at her teacher's wedding in this reading by Laura Hamilton of Kevin Henkes's book.

Marley: A Dog Like No Other. HarperChildren's Audio, 4 hours. Elementary. Neil Patrick Harris narrates this children's adaptation of *Marley and Me,* a story about a man and his canine best friend.

The Rules of Survival. Listening Library, 6 hours and 8 minutes. Middle school–YA. Daniel Passer tells Nancy Werlin's story of teenage Matthew's harrowing journey to find a safe haven from his abusive mother.

Skulduggery Pleasant. HarperChildren's Audio, 7 hours and 30 minutes. Middle school–YA. An award-winning mystery tale by Derek Landy, told by Rupert Degas.

Seven Blind Mice. Weston Woods, 9 minutes. Beginning readers. B. D. Wong tells Ed Young's tale about seven blind mice who discover that wisdom comes from seeking the whole.

Treasure Island. Listening Library, 7 hours and 9 minutes. Middle school–YA. Alfred Molina narrates Robert Louis Stevenson's pirate classic.

A Very Brave Witch. Weston Woods, 5 minutes. Beginning readers. A read-along Halloween picture book with a musical background.

The Wednesday Wars. Scholastic Audiobooks, 7 hours and 28 minutes. Middle school. Joel Johnstone tells the story of Holling Hoodhood's seventh grade year at Camillo Junior High in 1967.

Welcome to Camden Falls. Scholastic Audiobooks, 4 hours and 27 minutes. Elementary. Ann M. Martin's noteworthy book about young sisters who have to move to a new town following their parents' death is read by Ariadne Meyers.

Notable Children's Videos

These titles are selected by a committee of the Association for Library Service to Children, a division of the American Library Association. Recommendations are based on originality, creativity, and suitability for young children.

Becoming an Organized Student. Human Relations Media, 20 minutes. Ages 10–14.

Big Brown Bear's Up and Down Day. Nutmeg Media, 24 minutes. Ages 2–6.

Dooby Dooby Moo. Weston Woods Studios, 10 minutes. Ages 3–8.

Finding Daddy: A Story of the Great Depression. Nutmeg Media, 17 minutes. Ages 5–10.

Getting to Know the World's Greatest Artists: Andy Warhol. Getting to Know, Inc., 24 minutes. Ages 8–14.

Huffing: The Latest Facts about Inhalant Abuse. Human Relations Media, 20 minutes. Ages 10 and up.

I Hate English! Nutmeg Media, 15 minutes. Ages 5–9.

John, Paul, George and Ben. Weston Woods Studios, 13 minutes. Ages 6–10.

Jump In! Freestyle Edition. Buena Vista Home Entertainment, 85 minutes. Ages 10–13.

Just Yell Fire: Empowering Girls to Protect Themselves. Just Yell Fire/Maggie Jessup, 45 minutes. Ages 11–19.

Leonardo, the Terrible Monster. Weston Woods Studios, 8 minutes. Ages 3–8.

The Librarian from the Black Lagoon Weston Woods Studios, 9 minutes. Ages 5–8.

Max's Words. Weston Woods Studios, 10 minutes. Ages 4–9.

Nightmare at School. National Film Board of Canada, 9 minutes. Ages 8–14.

Now and Ben: The Modern Inventions of Benjamin Franklin. Spoken Arts, 13 minutes. Ages 8–12.

Rosa. Weston Woods Studios, 14 minutes. Ages 5–10.

Seven Blind Mice. Weston Woods Studios, 7 minutes. Ages 4–8.

A Very Brave Witch. Weston Woods Studios, 7 minutes. Ages 3–8.

Wallace's Lists. Weston Woods Studios, 15 minutes. Ages 4–8.

Water Detectives. National Film Board of Canada, 12 minutes. Ages 8–14.

Great Interactive Software for Kids

This list is chosen by a committee of the Association for Library Service to Children, a division of the American Library Association. Titles are chosen on the basis of their originality, creativity, and suitability for children.

1701 AD. Aspyr Media (http://www.aspyr. com). Ages 10 and up. Players strategize in the golden age of exploration while building, trading, exploring, and battling on land and sea. Windows.

Anime Studio. E-Frontier (http://www.e-frontier.com). Ages 10 and up. A complete animation program for creating anime and cartoons for print, video, Web design, fine art, comics, and education. Windows and Mac.

Big Brain Academy. Nintendo (http://www. nintendo.com). All ages. Fifteen games, three difficulty levels, intended to stimulate thinking skills.

Collage Machine. ProtoZone Interactives (http://www.protozone.net). All ages. Users create collages from hundreds of included images, letters, and numbers. Options allow dragging, dropping, resizing, drawing, or importing digital photos. Windows and Mac.

Crazy Machines 1.5. Viva-Media (http:// www.viva-media.com). Elementary. An improved and expanded version of the original game, offering even more odd contraptions and gadgets to build. Windows and Mac.

KaleidoDraw. ProtoZone Interactives (http:// www.protozone.net). All ages. Users create endless kaleidoscopic effects as they explore the art and science of patterns and symmetry. The created pictures can be saved or printed. Windows and Mac.

KaleidoPix. ProtoZone Interactives (http:// www.protozone.net). All ages. Choosing from more than 60 set patterns, creating new ones, or using personal pictures, users create unique kaleidoscopes. Windows and Mac.

Nancy Drew: The Creature of Kapu Cave. Her Interactive (http://www.herinteractive. com). Ages 10 and up. Nancy goes to Hawaii as a research assistant to an eccentric entomologist and is soon involved in a mystery involving bugs and a secret research laboratory. She enlists the help of the Hardy Boys, who are on the island investigating a mystery of their own. Various puzzles lead to solving the interlocking stories.

Sid Meier's Railroads. Firaxis (http://firaxis. com). All ages. Train buffs and aspiring businesspeople will enjoy exploring a world of model and real-life railroads. Fifteen historic and fictional scenarios, five difficulty levels, and multiplayer options make for variety. Windows.

Snapshot Adventures: Secret of Bird Island. Large Animal Games (http://www.large animal.com). All ages. Photographing birds of many species provides clues to the whereabouts of a missing grandfather. Windows.

Bestsellers of 2007

Hardcover Bestsellers: They're Back—Again and Again

Daisy Maryles

Executive Editor, *Publishers Weekly*

What a difference a year makes? Well, very little, when the topic is bestsellers. In hardcover fiction, the 2007 chart toppers—James Patterson, Janet Evanovich, Nicholas Sparks, Dean Koontz and Patricia Cornwell—were also the sales leaders in 2006 and 2005. Sue Grafton and David Baldacci scored in the top 15 in 2007 and in 2005. In fact, the only new name on the 2007 hardcover fiction list with sales of more than 200,000 was Donald McCaig, with *Rhett Butler's People*. But to earn the ranking of No. 16 on the annual chart, he wrote about a well-known literary figure from one of the all-time bestsellers. And debut novelists barely made a dent in 2007 annual sales.

Patterson had the most success in 2007. He landed five books in the top 15, with combined sales of more than 4.4 million. In 2006 and 2005 he had four books in the top 15. Khaled Hosseini also had a stellar year, leading the fiction charts with his second novel, *A Thousand Splendid Suns*. His debut, *The Kite Runner*, was the 2007 trade paper bestseller.

Familiarity breeds success; that held true for many of the nonfiction top sellers, too. Two books by doctors Roizen and Oz were in the top 15. Kevin Trudeau, Joel Osteen, Suze Orman, Paula Deen, and Guinness World Records were also back again in lead positions.

Still, there were many newbies in nonfiction. The bestselling hardcover book of 2007, *The Secret*, boasted sales of more than 4.5 million and dominated the top spot on the charts for 29 weeks. Three of the top ten 2007 bestsellers were from Collins, and they were all first-timers: altogether, *The Dangerous Book for Boys, The Daring Book for Girls* and *Deceptively Delicious* sold about 4.7 million copies, enough for HarperCollins to post gains in the second quarter ended December 31.

Religion and politics are comfortable bestseller bedfellows, and 2007 had a plethora of books in these categories. Religious leaders Joel Osteen, T. D. Jakes, and Max Lucado were in the top 30. Thomas Nelson, the largest religion publisher in the United States, had the largest number of books with sales of 100,000 or more—14 in 2007 compared to its previous high of 10 in 2006. Popular political topics among 2007 bestsellers included the Supreme Court—a memoir by Clarence Thomas and Jeffrey Toobin's *The Nine: Inside the Secret World of the Supreme Court*—and books by former presidents Ronald Reagan, Bill Clinton, and Jimmy Carter (and by presidential hopeful Barack Obama).

Cooking and fitness continued to be bestseller favorites. Paula Deen had three 2007 bestsellers with combined sales of more than 1 million. Other well-known cooks among the 100,000+ crowd included Martha Stewart, Giada De Laurentiis, Jamie Oliver, and Alice Waters. And after all that good eating, we turn to diet and fitness; there was hardly a week in the course of 2007 that the

Adapted from *Publishers Weekly*, March 24, 2008

Publishers Weekly 2007 Bestsellers

FICTION

1. **A Thousand Splendid Suns** by Khaled Hosseini. Riverhead (5/07) 2,201,865
2. **Playing for Pizza** by John Grisham. Doubleday (9/07) #1,445,000
3. **Double Cross** by James Patterson. Little, Brown (11/07) 1,428,974
4. **The Choice** by Nicholas Sparks. Grand Central (9/07) 1,200,809
5. **Lean Mean Thirteen** by Janet Evanovich. St. Martin's (6/07) 1,116,828
6. **Plum Lovin'** by Janet Evanovich. St. Martin's (1/07) 1,080,686
7. **Book of the Dead** by Patricia Cornwell. Putnam (10/07) 1,027,000
8. **The Quickie** by James Patterson and Michael Ledwidge. Little, Brown (7/07) 795,736
9. **The 6th Target** by James Patterson and Maxine Paetro. Little, Brown (5/07) 769,460
10. **The Darkest Evening of the Year** by Dean Koontz. Bantam (11/07) #740,000
11. **Step on a Crack** by James Patterson and Michael Ledwidge. Little, Brown (2/07) 732,702
12. **You've Been Warned** by James Patterson and Howard Roughan. Little, Brown (9/07) 724,713
13. **T Is for Trespass** by Sue Grafton. Putnam (12/07) 716,582
14. **Stone Cold** by David Baldacci. Grand Central (11/07) 670,590
15. **Nineteen Minutes** by Jodi Picoult. Atria Books (3/07) 609,000

NONFICTION

1. **The Secret** by Rhonda Byrne. Atria/Beyond Words (11/06) *4,590,000
2. **The Dangerous Book for Boys** by Conn and Hal Iggulden. Collins (5/07) 1,900,000
3. **Deceptively Delicious** by Jessica Seinfeld. Collins (10/07) 1,800,000
4. **You: Staying Young—The Owner's Manual for Extending Your Warranty** by Michael F. Roizen, M.D., and Mehmet C. Oz, M.D. Free Press (10/07) 1,451,945
5. **I Am America (and So Can You!)** by Stephen Colbert. Grand Central (10/07) 1,422,876
6. **Become a Better You: 7 Keys to Improving Your Life Every Day** by Joel Osteen. Free Press (10/07) 1,181,173
7. **The Daring Book for Girls** by Andrea J. Buchanan & Miriam Peskowitz. Collins (10/07) 1,000,000
8. **You: On a Diet—The Owner's Manual for Waist Management** by Michael F. Roizen, M.D., and Mehmet C. Oz, M.D. Free Press (10/06) *998,324
9. **Guinness World Records 2008.** Guinness World Records (8/07) 980,000
10. **The Weight Loss Cure 'They' Don't Want You to Know About** by Kevin Trudeau. Alliance (4/07) 825,913
11. **Quiet Strength: The Principles, Practices and Priorities of a Winning Life** by Tony Dungy with Nathan Whitaker. Tyndale House (07/07) 820,124
12. **Women & Money: Owning the Power to Control Your Destiny** by Suze Orman. Spiegel & Grau (2/07) 753,618
13. **A Long Way Gone: Memoirs of a Boy Soldier** by Ishmael Beah. Farrar, Straus & Giroux/Sarah Crichton (2/07) 611,435
14. **Clapton** by Eric Clapton. Broadway (9/07) 600,756
15. **Christmas with Paula Deen: Recipes and Stories from My Favorite Holiday** by Paula Deen. Simon & Schuster (10/07) #580,000

---

* All sales figures reflect books sold in calendar year 2007.

Sales figures were submitted to *Publishers Weekly* in confidence, for use in placing titles on the lists. Numbers shown are rounded down to indicate relationship to sales figures for other titles.

Note: Rankings are determined by sales figures provided by publishers; the numbers generally reflect reports of copies "shipped and billed" in calendar year 2007. Publishers were instructed to adjust sales figures to include returns through January 31, 2007. Publishers did not at that time know what total returns would be—indeed, the majority of returns occur after that cutoff date—so none of these figures should be regarded as final net sales. (Dates in parentheses indicate month and year of publication.)

hardcover top 15 did not include at least one title on these topics, more often two. Four of the top 15 titles advocated healthy eating.

Of course, famous names and personalities were strong in nonfiction. Stephen Colbert amused readers with his *I Am America (and So Can You!)* and claimed the No. 5 spot for bestselling nonfiction last year; Eric Clapton hit the right chord with his memoir—it was the No. 14 nonfiction title. Steve Martin's *Born Standing Up* took the No. 22 slot for the year. Tom Brokaw, Ken Burns, Wayne W. Dyer, James Cramer, and many others wrote books that did well and benefited from media exposure.

The Usual Disclaimer

As in previous years, all the calculations in this article are based on shipped-and-billed figures supplied by publishers for new books issued in 2006 and 2007 and reflect only 2007 domestic trade sales. Figures for all books listed with a number symbol (#) were submitted to *Publishers Weekly* in confidence, for use only in placing titles on the lists. Numbers are rounded down to indicate their sales relationship to other titles.

The Fiction Runners-Up

16. *Rhett Butler's People* by Donald McCaig. St. Martin's (606,304)
17. *High Noon* by Nora Roberts. Putnam (592,735)
18. *Blaze* by Richard Bachman. Scribner (581,000)
19. *World Without End* by Ken Follett. Dutton (552,165)
20. *Sisters* by Danielle Steel. Delacorte (505,000)
21. *The Chase* by Clive Cussler. Putnam (478,195)
22. *The Children of Hurin* by J. R .R. Tolkien. Houghton Mifflin (462,000)
23. *Protect and Defend* by Vince Flynn. Atria (451,000)
24. *Home to Holly Springs* by Jan Karon. Viking (450,110)
25. *Simple Genius* by David Baldacci. Grand Central (449,089)
26. *I Heard That Song Before* by Mary Higgins Clark. Simon & Schuster (#440,000)
27. *The Almost Moon* by Alice Sebold. Little, Brown (432,837)
28. *Invisible Prey* by John Sandford. Putnam (415,239)
29. *For One More Day* by Mitch Albom. Hyperion (410,565)
30. *Innocent in Death* by J. D. Robb. Putnam (396,530)

300,000+

Creation in Death by J. D. Robb. Putnam (395,080)

The Navigator by Clive Cussler with Paul Kemprecos. Putnam (364,764)

Shopaholic & Baby by Sophie Kinsella. Dial (360,000)

Double Take by Catherine Coulter. Putnam (355,565)

Dark of the Moon by John Sandford. Putnam (354,117)

200,000+

The Overlook by Michael Connelly. Little, Brown (298,784)

Confessor by Terry Goodkind. Tor (280,644)

Where Angels Go by Debbie Macomber. Mira (266,433)

The Christmas Promise by Donna Van Liere. St. Martin's (266,167)

The Venetian Betrayal by Steve Berry. Ballantine (262,875)

Kingdom Come: The Final Victory by Tim LaHaye and Jerry B. Jenkins. Tyndale House (259,792)

Play Dirty by Sandra Brown. Simon & Schuster (#257,000)

Robert Ludlum's The Bourne Betrayal by Eric Van Lustbader. Grand Central (256,993)

Pandora's Daughter by Iris Johansen. St. Martin's (252,859)

Drop Dead Beautiful by Jackie Collins. St. Martin's (6/07) #251,363 (4)

Shadow Dance by Julie Garwood. Ballantine (251,294)

Everlasting by Kathleen E. Woodiwiss. Morrow (250,000)

Fresh Disasters by Stuart Woods. Putnam (249,715)

The Yiddish Policemen's Union by Michael Chabon. HarperCollins (245,465)

The Harlequin by Laurell K. Hamilton. Berkley (245,155)

Shoot Him If He Runs by Stuart Woods. Putnam (243,787)

The Secret Servant by Daniel Silva. Putnam (240,925)

The Hunters by W. E. B. Griffin. Putnam (230,589)

Third Degree by Greg Iles. Scribner (220,000)

The Boleyn Inheritance by Philippa Gregory. Touchstone (211,046)

Bones to Ashes by Kathy Reichs. Scribner (210,000)

The Woods by Harlan Coben. Dutton (209,525)

Obsession by Jonathan Kellerman. Ballantine (202,241)

Critical by Robin Cook. Putnam (200,592)

The Last Summer (of You and Me) by Ann Brashares. Riverhead (200,129)

Whitethorn Woods by Maeve Binchy. Knopf (200,000)

The Judas Strain by James Rollins. Morrow (200,000)

150,000+

The Penny by Joyce Meyer and Deborah Bedford. FaithWords (197,945)

The Wheel of Darkness by Douglas Preston and Lincoln Child. Grand Central (197,324)

Dead Heat by Dick Francis and Felix Francis. Putnam (188,078)

Devil May Cry by Sherrilyn Kenyon. St. Martin's (183,257)

Someone to Love by Jude Deveraux. Atria (179,000)

Dark Possession by Christine Feehan. Berkley (175,737)

On Chesil Beach by Ian McEwan. Doubleday/Nan A. Talese (175,186)

Bridge of Sighs by Richard Russo. Knopf (175,000)

Heart-Shaped Box by Joe Hill. Morrow (175,000)

You Suck: A Love Story by Christopher Moore. Morrow (175,000)

Mark's Story by Tim LaHaye and Jerry B. Jenkins. Putnam (174,501)

A Lick of Frost by Laurell K. Hamilton. Ballantine (173,240)

High Profile by Robert B. Parker. Putnam (173,003)

Now & Then by Robert B. Parker. Putnam (171,005)

The Alexandria Link by Steve Berry. Ballantine (168,790)

The Double Agents by W. E. B. Griffin and William E. Butterworth, IV. Putnam (164,208)

Back on Blossom Street by Debbie Macomber. Mira (162,960)

The Ravenscar Dynasty by Barbara Taylor Bradford. St. Martin's (160,883)

Run by Ann Patchett. HarperCollins (159,345)

The Good Husband of Zebra Drive by Alexander McCall Smith. Pantheon (158,039)

Pontoon: A Novel of Lake Wobegon by Garrison Keillor. Viking (150,075)

The Burnt House by Faye Kellerman. Morrow (150,000)

Natural Born Charmer by Susan Elizabeth Phillips. Morrow (150,000)

The Blue Zone by Andrew Gross. Morrow (150,000)

125,000+

Body Surfing by Anita Shreve. Little, Brown (147,488)

Rant: An Oral Biography of Buster Casey by Chuck Palahniuk. Doubleday (146,554)

The Sleeping Doll by Jeffery Deaver. Simon & Schuster (#145,700)

White Lies by Jayne Ann Krentz. Putnam (145,105)

Skin by Ted Dekker. Thomas Nelson (143,616)

Exile by Richard North Patterson. Holt (141,538)

The Double Bind by Chris Bohjalian. Crown/Shaye Areheart (138,906)

Spare Change by Robert B. Parker. Putnam (137,432)

The Bone Garden by Tess Gerritsen. Ballantine (136,806)

The Heir by Barbara Taylor Bradford. St. Martin's (135,090)

Exit Ghost by Philip Roth. Houghton Mifflin (134,767)

Up Close and Dangerous by Linda Howard. Ballantine (134,161)

Peony in Love by Lisa See. Random House (134,129)

Loving Frank by Nancy Horan. Ballantine (132,203)

The Tin Roof Blowdown by James Lee Burke. Simon & Schuster (#128,000)

The First Commandment by Brad Thor. Atria Books (127,000)

The Cat Who Had 60 Whiskers by Lilian Jackson Braun. Putnam (125,806)

Pearl Harbor: A Novel of December 8th by Newt Gingrich and William R. Forstchen. St. Martin's/Thomas Dunne (125,440)

Sweet Revenge by Diane Mott Davidson. Morrow (125,000)

The Christmas Pearl by Dorothea Benton Frank. Morrow (125,000)

Justice Denied by J. A. Jance. Morrow (125,000)

Innocent as Sin by Elizabeth Lowell. Morrow (125,000)

The Land of Mango Sunsets by Dorothea Benton Frank. Morrow (125,000)

Absolute Fear by Lisa Jackson. Kensington (125,000)

100,000+

The River Knows by Amanda Quick. Putnam (123,925)

Falling Man by Don DeLillo. Scribner (121,000)

The Fifth Vial by Michael Palmer. St. Martin's (120,240)

Spook Country by William Gibson. Putnam (118,635)

Sandworms of Dune by Brian Herbert and Kevin J. Anderson. Tor (116,647)

Tree of Smoke by Denis Johnson. Farrar, Straus & Giroux (115,825)

White Night by Jim Butcher. Roc (115,137)

The Race by Richard North Patterson. Holt (114,639)

Daddy's Girl by Lisa Scottoline. HarperCollins (114,514)

The Watchman by Robert Crais. Simon & Schuster (#113,800)

Family Tree by Barbara Delinsky. Doubleday (113,706)

Sugar Daddy by Lisa Kleypas. St. Martin's (110,691)

Power Play by Joseph Finder. St. Martin's (110,346)

The Sanctuary by Raymond Khoury. Dutton (110,000)

Away by Amy Bloom. Random House (108,296)

All Together Dead by Charlaine Harris. Ace (105,414)

Up in Honey's Room by Elmore Leonard. Morrow (105,000)

Up Close and Personal by Fern Michaels. Kensington (105,000)

Deep Storm by Lincoln Child. Doubleday (104,978)

The Lady in Blue by Javier Sierra. Atria (103,000)

The Elves of Cintra by Terry Brooks. Del Rey (102,891)

The Abstinence Teacher by Tom Perrotta. St. Martin's (102,640)

Sleeping with Strangers by Eric Jerome Dickey. Dutton (102,639)

The Quest by Wilbur Smith. St. Martin's/Thomas Dunne (102,002)

The Brief Wondrous Life of Oscar Wao by Junot Díaz. Riverhead (101,164)

Hand of Evil by J. A. Jance. Touchstone (100,576)

Heartsick by Chelsea Cain. St. Martin's (100,546)

The Gatecrasher by Madeleine Wickham. St. Martin's (100,253)

What the Dead Know by Laura Lippman. Morrow (100,000)

Love & Lies by Kimberla Lawson Roby. Morrow (100,000)

Strike Force by Dale Brown. Morrow (100,000)

When Day Breaks by Mary Jane Clark. Morrow (100,000)

The Nonfiction Runners-Up

16. *Reposition Yourself* by T. D. Jakes. Atria (564,000)

17. *BOOM! Voices of the Sixties—Personal Reflections on the '60s and Today* by Tom Brokaw. Random House (549,594)

18. *3:16: The Numbers of Hope* by Max Lucado. Thomas Nelson (543,477)

19. *I Feel Bad About My Neck: And Other Thoughts on Being a Woman* by Nora Ephron. Knopf (500,000)

20. *Einstein: His Life and Universe* by Walter Isaacson. Simon & Schuster (#494,000)

21. *An Inconvenient Book* by Glenn Beck. Threshold Editions (462,717)

22. *Born Standing Up* by Steve Martin. Scribner (441,000)

23. *The War: An Intimate History* by Geoffrey C. Ward and Ken Burns. Knopf (425,000)

24. *Change Your Thoughts Change Your Life: Living the Wisdom of the Tao* by Wayne W. Dyer. Hay House (410,693)

25. *Good Dog. Stay.* by Anna Quindlen. Random House (401,728)

26. *Giving: How Each of Us Can Change the World* by Bill Clinton. Knopf (400,000)

27. *Lone Survivor* by Marcus Luttrell with Patrick Robinson. Little, Brown (393,565)

28. *The Reagan Diaries* by Ronald Reagan. HarperCollins (388,149)

29. *Jim Cramer's Stay Mad for Life* by James Cramer. Simon & Schuster (#382,000)

30. *Rescuing Sprite* by Mark Levin. Pocket Books (374,112)

300,000+

Paula Deen: It Ain't All About the Cookin' by Paula Deen. Simon & Schuster (#366,000)

God Is Not Great: How Religion Poisons Everything by Christopher Hitchens. Twelve (359,232)

Be the Pack Leader by Cesar Millan and Melissa Jo Peltier. Harmony (347,931)

Think Big and Kick Ass in Business and Life by Donald J. Trump and Bill Zanker. Collins (346,000)

The 4-Hour Workweek by Timothy Ferriss. Crown (332,272)

Everyday Pasta by Giada De Laurentiis. Clarkson Potter (318,601)

It's All About Him: Finding the Love of My Life by Denise Jackson with Ellen Vaughn. Thomas Nelson (317,000)

Where Have All the Leaders Gone? by Lee Iacocca. Scribner (310,000)

200,000+

If Democrats Had Any Brains, They'd Be Republicans by Ann Coulter. Crown Forum (290,978)

My Grandfather's Son: A Memoir by Clarence Thomas. HarperCollins (283,202)

Jeff Foxworthy's Redneck Dictionary III: Learning to Talk More Gooder Fastly by Jeff Foxworthy. Villard (282,973)

Freakonomics, Revised Edition by Steven D. Levitt and Stephen J. Dubner. Morrow (275,000)

Marley & Me by John Grogan. Morrow (275,000)

Somebody's Gotta Say It by Neal Boortz. Morrow (275,000)

Animal, Vegetable, Miracle: A Year of Food Life by Barbara Kingsolver. HarperCollins (272,939)

The Total Money Makeover: A Proven Plan for Financial Success by Dave Ramsey. Thomas Nelson (272,000)

The Nine: Inside the Secret World of the Supreme Court by Jeffrey Toobin. Doubleday (263,667)

The Coldest Winter: America and the Korean War by David Halberstam. Hyperion (260,068)

The Audacity of Hope by Barack Obama. Crown (259,525)

A Family Christmas by Caroline Kennedy. Hyperion (259,208)

I Dare You: Embrace Life with Passion by Joyce Meyer. FaithWords (253,135)

Kids Are Americans Too by Bill O'Reilly. Morrow (250,000)

The Power of Simple Prayer: How to Talk with God About Everything by Joyce Meyer. FaithWords (244,466)

Now, Discover Your Strengths by Marcus Buckingham and Donald O. Clifton. Free Press (239,966)

Come On People: On the Path from Victims to Victors by Bill Cosby and Alvin F. Poussaint, M.D. Thomas Nelson (237,000)

The Diana Chronicles by Tina Brown. Doubleday (232,580)

Heaven Is Real: Lessons on Earthly Joy by Don Piper and Cecil Murphey. Berkley Praise (230,977)

Mother Teresa: Come Be My Light by Mother Teresa and Brian Kolodiejchuk. Doubleday (227,030)

Power to the People by Laura Ingraham. Regnery (220,000)

In an Instant: A Family's Journey of Love and Healing by Lee and Bob Woodruff. Random House (217,829)

1776: The Illustrated Edition by David McCullough. Simon & Schuster (#208,000)

The World Without Us by Alan Weisman. St. Martin's/Thomas Dunne (201,252)

Plato and a Platypus Walk into a Bar: Understanding Philosophy Through Jokes by Thomas Cathcart and Daniel Klein. Abrams Image (200,000)

150,000+

The Black Swan: The Impact of the Highly Improbable by Nassim Nicholas Taleb. Random House (199,784)

New Day, New You: 365 Devotions for Enjoying Everyday Life by Joyce Meyer. FaithWords (195,372)

The Proper Care and Feeding of Marriage by Laura Schlessinger. HarperCollins (189,856)

Infidel by Ayaan Hirsi Ali. Free Press (189,667)

The Intellectual Devotional: American History by David S. Kidder and Noah D. Oppenheim. Rodale (182,896)

Celebrity Detox (The Fame Game) by Rosie O'Donnell. Grand Central (182,270)

How Doctors Think by Jerome Groopman, M.D. Houghton Mifflin (182,069)

Our Dumb World by The Onion. Little, Brown (177,059)

You Can Run But You Can't Hide by Duane "Dog" Chapman. Hyperion (175,882)

Facing Your Giants by Max Lucado. Thomas Nelson (175,122)

Slash by Slash with Anthony Bozza. Harper Entertainment (175,000)

If I Did It: Confessions of the Killer by the Goldman Family. Beaufort (170,695)

Spiritual Connections: How to Find Spirituality Throughout All the Relationships in Your Life by Sylvia Browne. Hay House (169,833)

At the Center of the Storm: My Years at the CIA by George Tenet. HarperCollins (167,386)

The Best Life Diet by Bob Greene. Simon & Schuster (#162,000)

The 12 Second Sequence by Jorge Cruise. Crown (161,715)

The Art of Simple Food by Alice Waters. Clarkson Potter (161,683)

The Book of General Ignorance by John Mitchinson and John Lloyd. Harmony (161,463)

Louder than Words: A Mother's Journey in Healing Autism by Jenny McCarthy. Dutton (161,090)

Made to Stick: Why Some Ideas Survive and Others Die by Chip Heath and Dan Heath. Random House (161,053)

Musicophilia: Tales of Music and the Brain by Oliver Sacks. Knopf (160,000)

Things I Overheard While Talking to Myself by Alan Alda. Random House (158,344)

The Heroin Diaries by Nikki Sixx. Pocket Books (156,754)

The Martha Stewart Living Cookbook: The New Classics by *Martha Stewart Living* magazine. Clarkson Potter (153,428)

21 Pounds in 21 Days by Roni DeLuz with James Hester. Collins (153,000)

The Intellectual Devotional by David S. Kidder and Noah D. Oppenheim. Rodale (152,817)

Cook with Jamie: My Guide to Making You a Better Cook by Jamie Oliver. Hyperion (152,024)

Paula Deen Celebrates: Best Dishes and Best Wishes for the Best Times of Your Life by Paula Deen. Simon & Schuster (#151,000)

Bad Dogs Have More Fun by John Grogan. Vanguard Press (150,651)

A Lifetime of Secrets by Frank Warren. Morrow (150,000)

125,000+

Starting Your Best Life Now by Joel Osteen. FaithWords (149,587)

Don't Bet Against Me!: Beating the Odds Against Breast Cancer and in Life by Deanna Favre with Angela Hunt. Tyndale House (148,808)

Secret Societies: And How They Affect Our Lives Today by Sylvia Browne. Hay House (143,625)

The Spectrum by Dean Ornish, M.D. Ballantine (143,310)

Scriptures and Meditations for Your Best Life Now by Joel Osteen. FaithWords (143,070)

Day of Reckoning: How Hubris, Ideology, and Greed Are Tearing America Apart by Patrick J. Buchanan. St. Martin's/Thomas Dunne (142,586)

Do You! 12 Laws to Access the Power in You to Achieve Happiness and Success by Russell Simmons and Chris Morrow. Gotham (141,256)

The Vixen Diaries by Karrine Steffans. Grand Central (140,706)

Go Put Your Strengths to Work: Six Powerful Steps to Achieve Outstanding Performance by Marcus Buckingham. Free Press (140,574)

Love & Respect: The Love She Most Desires, the Respect He Desperately Needs by Emerson Eggerichs. Thomas Nelson (139,891)

Basic Black by Cathie Black. Crown Business (139,806)

Wonderful Tonight by Pattie Boyd and Penny Junor. Harmony (139,500)

What's Your Poo Telling You? by Anish Sheth, M.D., and Josh Richman. Chronicle (137,707)

Legacy of Ashes: The History of the CIA by Tim Weiner. Doubleday (137,640)

The Abs Diet for Women by David Zinczenko with Ted Spiker. Rodale (136,861)

The Day of Battle: The War in Sicily and Italy 1943–1944 by Rick Atkinson. Holt (131,309)

Law of Attraction by Michael J. Losier. Grand Central (129,878)

The Conscience of a Liberal by Paul Krugman. W. W. Norton (127,216)

Fair Game: My Life as a Spy, My Betrayal by the White House by Valerie Plame Wilson. Simon & Schuster (#126,000)

Golf My Own Damn Way: A Real Guy's Guide to Chopping Ten Strokes Off Your

Score by John Daly with Glen Waggoner. HarperCollins (125,536)

Grace (Eventually) by Anne Lamott. Riverhead (125,000)

100,000+

What Got You Here Won't Get You There by Marshall Goldsmith with Mark Reiter. Hyperion (123,732)

Get Out of That Pit: Straight Talk About God's Deliverance by Beth Moore. Thomas Nelson (123,184)

The Journey: Living by Faith in an Uncertain World by Billy Graham. Thomas Nelson (121,969)

Presidential Courage: Brave Leaders and How They Changed America, 1789–1989 by Michael Beschloss. Simon & Schuster (#118,900)

Every Day Deserves a Chance by Max Lucado. Thomas Nelson (118,863)

Just a Guy: Notes from a Blue Collar Life by Bill Engvall with Alan Eisenstock. St. Martin's (118,245)

Beyond the White House by Jimmy Carter. Simon & Schuster (#116,000)

The No Asshole Rule: Building a Civilized Workplace and Surviving One That Isn't by Robert I. Sutton. Business Plus (115,954)

Mother Angelica's Little Book of Life Lessons and Everyday Spirituality by Raymond Arroyo. Doubleday (115,809)

The Year of Living Biblically: One Man's Humble Quest to Follow the Bible as Literally as Possible by A. J. Jacobs. Simon & Schuster (#113,000)

The God Delusion by Richard Dawkins. Houghton Mifflin (110,336)

From My Heart to Yours: Life Lessons on Faith, Family and Friendship by Robin McGraw. Thomas Nelson (109,769)

Crazies to the Left of Me, Wimps to the Right: How One Side Lost Its Mind and the Other Lost Its Nerve by Bernard Goldberg. HarperCollins (107,579)

Epicenter: Why the Current Rumblings in the Middle East Will Change Your Future by Joel C. Rosenberg. Tyndale House (106,538)

Mannheim Steamroller Christmas: The Season for Joy by Chip Davis. Thomas Nelson (106,022)

Landmines in the Path of the Believer by Charles F. Stanley. Thomas Nelson (105,531)

Schulz and Peanuts: A Biography by David Michaelis. Harper (105,323)

Talent Is Never Enough by John C. Maxwell. Thomas Nelson (104,971)

Write It When I'm Gone by Thomas M. DeFrank. Putnam (104,867)

The Shock Doctrine: The Rise of Disaster Capitalism by Naomi Klein. Holt/Metropolitan (104,299)

Power, Faith and Fantasy by Michael B. Oren. W. W. Norton (103,734)

The Astonishing Power of Emotions by Esther and Jerry Hicks. Hay House (103,653)

The Truth War: Fighting for Certainty in an Age of Deception by John D. MacArthur. Thomas Nelson (102,659)

Thank You Power: Making the Science of Gratitude Work for You by Deborah Norville. Thomas Nelson (102,336)

Reading Judas: The Gospel of Judas and the Shaping of Christianity by Elaine Pagels and Karen L. King. Viking (102,041)

Broken Government by John W. Dean. Viking (102,032)

Martha Stewart's Homekeeping Handbook by Martha Stewart. Clarkson Potter (101,359)

The Zookeeper's Wife by Diane Ackerman. W. W. Norton (101,136)

Big Papi: My Story of Big Dreams and Big Hits by David Ortiz with Tony Massarotti. St. Martin's (101,210)

Cesar's Way by Cesar Millan and Melissa Jo Peltier. Harmony (101,096)

Outrage by Dick Morris and Eileen McGann. HarperCollins (100,977)

Signs of Life by David Jeremiah. Thomas Nelson (100,847)

Look Me in the Eye by John Elder Robison. Crown (100,230)

Teach Like Your Hair's on Fire by Rafe Esquith. Viking (100,112)

Tim Gunn: A Guide to Quality, Taste and Style by Tim Gunn and Kate Maloney. Abrams Image (100,000)

Paperback Bestsellers: Familiar Faces to the Fore

Dermot McEvoy
Senior Editor, *Publishers Weekly*

Well, to paraphrase Richard Nixon, you won't have sudoku to kick around anymore. After years in the forefront, not a single sudoku title was submitted to *Publishers Weekly* (*PW*) for the 2007 paperback bestsellers. But the good news is that all the other paperback favorites that readers have come to love over the years—familiar novelists and cookbook authors and movie/television tie-ins—are back in abundance. As a sign of the political and economic times, there are also sightings of a bestselling presidential candidate and books by several financial gurus with answers for a shaky economy.

Paperback remains the domain of genre fiction; romance, thriller, and supernatural all find a well-earned place among 2007's bestselling titles. Some of the names change over the years, but they remain familiar ones nonetheless. In years past, Sandra Brown, Michael Crichton, or Ken Follett have dominated; this year, those icons had only a book each on the list. But others stepped into the breach. Tops in 2007 in terms of number of titles on the list was Jodi Picoult, with an amazing ten titles and combined sales of 2,040,649. Nora Roberts had seven, for a total of 5,568,661 sold. James Patterson weighed in with six (3,933,949); Janet Evanovich had four bestsellers (4,150,000); and three for Clive Cussler (1,751,629) and Fern Michaels (2,014,000). Literary cachet was provided by Cormac McCarthy, whose *The Road* and his movie tie-in *No Country for Old Men* both made the list, combining to sell 1,681,592 copies.

Rachael Ray remains the queen of cookbook authors. Although there were rumors that her syndicated television show might be cancelled, there will still be plenty of Ray on the various shows she has on the Food Network. Ray placed three titles on *PW*'s bestseller lists in 2007, with a combined total sales of 1,071,801 copies. *Rachael Ray: Just in Time* was the biggest seller, at 703,681 copies, for publisher Clarkson Potter. Paula Deen, another Food Network stalwart, also benefited from extensive exposure, and her *Lady & Sons Savannah Country* sold 181,904 copies for Random House. Strangely, the author who came in second to Ray in total foodie sales was Phyllis Pellman Good, who does not have a TV show. Her Fix-It and Forget-It series of cookbooks sold 546,950 copies in 2007.

If book sales are a barometer of the national mood, then Sen. Barack Obama should be on his way to the White House. In 2007 his two memoirs, *The Audacity of Hope* and *Dreams from My Father,* sold 439,658 copies for Three Rivers. Neither John McCain nor Hillary Clinton made the list.

With the financial markets in trouble, it is a little surprising (or is it?) to see that only three well-known financial gurus made the list. Robert Kiyosaki's *Rich Dad, Poor Dad* sold 323,937 for Grand Central, while Suze Orman's *The Money Book for the Young, Fabulous, and Broke* netted 280,368 for Riverhead. The "Latte Factor" man, David Bach, sold 188,080 copies of *Start Late, Finish Rich* for Broadway. This may be an important area for publishers in 2008.

Movie and television tie-ins still have a tremendous impact on paperback sales, sometimes propelling backlist titles to the front again. In 2007 a total of 13 tie-ins sold an overall total of more than 3,800,000 copies. Movie tie-ins were led by *The Nanny Diaries* by Nicola Kraus and Emma McLaughlin, which sold nearly 800,000 copies in both trade paper and mass market. Other heavy sellers were *Freedom Writers Diary* by Erin Gruwell, *The Mist* by Stephen King, and *I Am Legend* by Richard Matheson.

Listed below are trade paperbacks and mass market titles published in 2006 and 2007; the rankings are based only on 2007 sales. To qualify, trade paperbacks had to have sold more than 100,000 copies in 2007; for mass markets, sales of more than 500,000 were required. A single asterisk (*) indicates the book was published in 2006; a double asterisk (**) means the book was published earlier but either remained or reappeared on *PW*'s bestseller charts in 2007. These reappearances are most often movie tie-ins. A pound symbol (#) indicates that the shipped-and-billed figure was rounded down to the nearest 5,000 to indicate the books' sales relationship to other titles—the actual figures were given to *PW* in confidence, for use only in placing titles on these lists.

Trade Paperbacks

1 Million+

Eat, Pray, Love by Elizabeth Gilbert. Rep. Penguin (4,274,804)

**The Kite Runner* by Khaled Hosseini. Rep. Riverhead (2,022,041)

Water for Elephants by Sara Gruen. Rep. Algonquin (1,450,000)

The Road by Cormac McCarthy. Rep. Vintage (1,364,722)

**The Memory Keeper's Daughter* by Kim Edwards. Rep. Penguin (1,362,585)

The Pillars of the Earth by Ken Follett. Rep. NAL (1,310,419)

Love in the Time of Cholera by Gabriel García Márquez. Rep. Vintage (1,298,554)

#***90 Minutes in Heaven* by Don Piper and Cecil Murphey. Orig. Revell (1,273,000)

Jerusalem Countdown by John Hagee. Revised. Frontline (1,200,000)

***Middlesex* by Jeffrey Eugenides. Rep. Picador (1,000,000)

***Measure of a Man* by Sidney Poitier. Orig. HarperOne (1,000,000)

750,000+

***Skinny Bitch* by Rory Freedman and Kim Barnouin. Orig. Running Press (987,000)

Into the Wild by Jon Krakauer. Rep. Anchor (918,234)

Three Cups of Tea by Greg Mortenson and David Oliver Relin. Rep. Penguin (843,390)

500,000+

The 5th Horseman by James Patterson and Maxine Paetro. Rep. Grand Central (707,340)

**Night* by Elie Wiesel. Orig. Hill & Wang/ FSG (705,053)

Rachael Ray: Just in Time by Rachael Ray. Orig. Clarkson Potter (703,681)

***What to Expect When You're Expecting* by Heidi Murkoff, Arlene Eisenberg, and Sandee Hathaway. Revised. Workman (696,134)

Blink by Malcolm Gladwell. Rep. Little, Brown (630,376)

***The Alchemist* by Paulo Coelho. Orig. HarperOne (603,000)

**The Pursuit of Happyness* by Chris Gardner and Quiny Troupe. Rep. Amistad (600,000)

Dear John by Nicholas Sparks. Rep. Grand Central (576,173)

The Five Love Languages by Gary Chapman. Rep. Moody (562,337)

***Atonement* by Ian McEwan. Rep. Anchor (562,124)

Suite Française by Irène Némirovsky. Rep. Vintage (530,353)

The Purpose Driven Life by Rick Warren. Rep. Zondervan (525,000)

Your Best Life Now by Joel Osteen. Rep. FaithWords (503,350)

250,000+

***The Five People You Meet in Heaven* by Mitch Albom. Rep. Hyperion (481,183)

**#*The Wisdom of Menopause* by Christiane Northrup, M.D. Revised. Bantam (475,000)

***My Sister's Keeper* by Jodi Picoult. Rep. Washington Square (457,000)

***Tuesdays with Morrie* by Mitch Albom. Rep. Broadway (450,000)

**Snow Flower and the Secret Fan* by Lisa See. Rep. Random (447,035)

***What to Expect the First Year* by Heidi Murkoff, Arlene Eisenberg, and Sandee Hathaway. Revised. Workman (404,370)

The Year of Magical Thinking by Joan Didion. Rep. Vintage (402,276)

***1,000 Places to See Before You Die* by Patricia Schultz. Orig. Workman (402,271)

*The Glass Castle by Jeanette Walls. Rep. Scribner (396,000)

1,000 Places to See in the USA and Canada Before You Die by Patricia Schultz. Orig. Workman (394,846)

The Emperor's Children by Claire Messud. Rep. Vintage (389,695)

*Love Walked In by Marisa de los Santos. Rep. Plume (380,000)

***Running with Scissors* by Augusten Burroughs. Rep. Picador (375,000)

The World Is Flat by Thomas Friedman. Rep. Picador (375,000)

***The Tipping Point* by Malcolm Gladwell. Rep. Little, Brown (370,716)

Baby Proof by Emily Giffin. Rep. Griffin (350,000)

***The Secret Life of Bees* by Sue Monk Kidd. Rep. Penguin (333,901)

***Their Eyes Were Watching God* by Zora Neale Hurston. Rep. Harper (333,511)

The Omnivore's Dilemma by Michael Pollan. Rep. Penguin (330,189)

Skinny Bitch in the Kitch by Rory Freedman and Kim Barnouin. Orig. Running Press (325,000)

***Rich Dad, Poor Dad* by Robert T. Kiyosaki with Sharon L. Lechter. Orig. Grand Central (323,937)

Everyday Food by *Martha Stewart Living* magazine. Orig. Clarkson Potter (321,217)

**The Inheritance of Loss* by Kiran Desai. Rep. Grove (320,800)

Stumbling on Happiness by Daniel Gilbert. Rep. Vintage (319,902)

#**The Constant Princess* by Philippa Gregory. Rep. Touchstone (318,000)

No Country for Old Men by Cormac McCarthy. Rep. Vintage (316,870)

The Parting by Beverly Lewis. Orig. Bethany House (315,478)

The Best Life Diet by Bob Greene. Rep. Simon & Schuster (309,596)

***Battlefield of the Mind* by Joyce Meyer. Orig. FaithWords (303,636)

Fix-It and Forget-It 5-Ingredient Favorites by Phyllis Pellman Good. Orig. Good Books (302,200)

The Nanny Diaries by Nicola Kraus and Emma McLaughlin Griffin (300,000)

Life Picture Puzzle by the editors of *Life*. Orig. Life (292,369)

Mayflower by Nathaniel Philbrick. Rep. Penguin (287,481)

**Wicked by Gregory Maguire. Rep. Harper (281,431)

The Thirteenth Tale by Diane Setterfield. Rep. Washington Square (281,000)

The Guy Not Taken by Jennifer Weiner. Rep. Washington Square (281,000)

The Money Book for the Young, Fabulous, and Broke by Suze Orman. Rep. Riverhead (280,368)

***The Miracle Ball Method* by Elaine Petrone. Orig. Workman (279,098)

Plain Truth by Jodi Picoult. Rep. Washington Square (278,000)

Irish Hearts by Nora Roberts. Reissue. Silhouette (264,000)

The Freedom Writers Diary by the Freedom Writers with Erin Gruwell. Movie tie-in. Broadway (255,846)

*The Tenth Circle by Jodi Picoult. Rep. Washington Square (255,000)

***The Audacity of Hope* by Barack Obama. Rep. Three Rivers (252,819)

Caring for Your Baby and Young Child by American Academy of Pediatrics. Revised. Bantam (250,000)

100,000+

Don't Make a Black Woman Take Off Her Earrings by Tyler Perry. Rep. Riverhead (245,226)

**Fix-It and Forget-It Cookbook* by Dawn J. Ranck and Phyllis Pellman Good. Orig. Good Books (244,750)

#*The Boleyn Inheritance* by Philippa Gregory. Rep. Touchstone (242,000)

Cesar's Way by Cesar Millan and Melissa Jo Peltier. Rep. Three Rivers (236,701)

Summer Pleasures by Nora Roberts. Reissue. Silhouette (236,000)

#**The 7 Habits of Highly Effective People* by Stephen R. Covey. Rep. Free Press (235,000)

Labyrinth by Kate Mosse. Rep. Berkley (230,646)

**The Curious Incident of the Dog in the Night-Time* by Mark Haddon. Rep. Vintage (228,969)

**The Devil in the White City* by Erik Larson. Rep. Vintage (228,663)

Table for Two by Nora Roberts. Reissue. Silhouette (226,000)

Extreme Fat Smash Diet by Ian K. Smith, M.D. Orig. Griffin (225,000)

Nature Girl by Carl Hiaasen. Rep. Grand Central (222,340)

Sanctuary by Nora Roberts. Reissue. Berkley (220,602)

Sunrise by Karen Kingsbury. Orig. Tyndale (220,265)

**Something Blue* by Emily Giffin. Orig. Griffin (220,000)

Thirteen Moons by Charles Frazier. Rep. Random (215,850)

Healthy Aging by Andrew Weil, M.D. Rep. Anchor (212,533)

Ever After by Karen Kingsbury. Orig. Zondervan (210,250)

Summer by Karen Kingsbury. Orig. Tyndale (206,078)

Rise and Shine by Anna Quindlen. Rep. Random (203,917)

**I Hope They Serve Beer in Hell* by Tucker Max. Orig. Citadel (200,000)

Can't Wait to Get to Heaven by Fannie Flagg. Rep. Ballantine (199,153)

Life Original Picture Puzzle by the editors of *Life*. Orig. Life (197,441)

Forever by Karen Kingsbury. Orig. Tyndale (195,574)

Just Beyond the Clouds by Karen Kingsbury. Orig. Center Street (191,283)

**A Raisin in the Sun* by Lorraine Hansberry. TV tie-in. Vintage (191,115)

The Sneaky Chef by Missy Chase Lapine. Orig. Running Press (190,000)

Start Late Finish Rich by David Bach. Rep. Broadway (188,080)

**Rachael Ray Express Lane Meals* by Rachael Ray. Orig. Clarkson Potter (187,633)

Charlie Wilson's War by George Crile. Movie tie-in. Grove (187,473)

**Dreams from My Father* by Barack Obama. Rep. Three Rivers (186,839)

What Is the What by Dave Eggers. Rep. Vintage (185,778)

Blue Shoes and Happiness by Alexander McCall Smith. Rep. Anchor (185,687)

**The Lady & Sons Savannah Country Cookbook* by Paula Deen. TV tie-in. Random (181,904)

**Rachael Ray 365: No Repeats* by Rachael Ray. Orig. Clarkson Potter (180,487)

**The Pact* by Jodi Picoult. Rep. Harper-Perennial (179,170)

**Perfect Match* by Jodi Picoult. Rep. Washington Square (175,000)

#*The 6 Most Important Decisions You'll Ever Make* by Sean Covey. Orig. Touchstone (175,000)

**The Lovely Bones* by Alice Sebold. Rep. Back Bay (172,461)

**Salem Falls* by Jodi Picoult. Rep. Washington Square (172,000)

**Vanishing Acts* by Jodi Picoult. Rep. Washington Square (170,000)

**What to Expect the Toddler Years* by Heidi Murkoff, Arlene Eisenberg, and Sandee Hathaway. Orig. Workman (166,316)

The Gathering by Anne Enright. Orig. Grove/Black Cat (166,225)

The Life and Times of the Thunderbolt Kid by Bill Bryson. Rep. Broadway (165,836)

Fiasco by Thomas E. Ricks. Rep. Penguin (164,227)

Wish You Well by David Baldacci. Rep. Grand Central (163,540)

Special Topics in Calamity Physics by Marisha Pessl. Rep. Penguin (163,362)

Come Back by Claire and Mia Fontaine. Rep. HarperPerennial (162,193)

*Wild at Heart by John Eldredge. Rep. Nelson (161,952)

Evening by Susan Minot. Rep. Vintage (161,218)

Chicken Soup for the New Mom's Soul by Jack Canfield, et al. Orig. HCI (161,167)

Possible Side Effects by Augusten Burroughs. Rep. Picador (160,000)

Robert Ludlum's The Arctic Event by James H. Cobb (series created by Robert Ludlum). Orig. Grand Central (156,148)

Chosen by a Horse by Susan Richards. Rep. Harvest (155,781)

Chicken Soup for the Soul: Celebrating Mothers and Daughters by Jack Canfield, et al. Orig. HCI (154,351)

Lost and Found by Carolyn Parkhurst. Rep. Back Bay (154,172)

**Mere Christianity by C. S. Lewis. Rep. HarperOne (154,000)

*Fifty Reasons Why Jesus Came to Die by John Piper. Orig. Crossway (152,900)

**One Hundred Years of Solitude by Gabriel García Márquez. Rep. HarperPerennial (152,878)

A Man Without a Country by Kurt Vonnegut. Rep. Random (151,537)

The Secrets of a Fire King by Kim Edwards. Rep. Penguin (151,302)

*1776 by David McCullough. Rep. Simon & Schuster (150,415)

Lost & Found by Jacqueline Sheehan. Orig. Avon (150,000)

Culture Warrior by Bill O'Reilly. Rep. Broadway (147,227)

Manhunt by James L. Swanson. Rep. HarperPerennial (145,951)

**Captivating by John and Stasi Eldredge. Rep. Thomas Nelson (143,987)

**Wicked by Gregory Maguire. Tie-in edition. Harper (143,820)

**The Zombie Survival Guide by Max Brooks. Rep. Three Rivers (143,684)

In Defense of Israel by John Hagee. Orig. Frontline (142,000)

**How to Grill by Steven Raichlen. Orig. Workman (141,684)

*Snow by Orhan Pamuk. Rep. Vintage (141,683)

**A People's History of the United States by Howard Zinn. Rep. HarperPerennial (141,174)

#Veil of Roses by Laura Fitzgerald. Orig. Bantam (140,000)

**Mountains Beyond Mountains by Tracy Kidder. Rep. Random (139,514)

Are You Smarter than a Fifth Grader? by Michael Benson. Orig. HarperEntertainment (136,492)

Dispatches from the Edge by Anderson Cooper. Rep. Harper (134,975)

*The Worst Hard Time by Timothy Egan. Rep. Mariner (134,890)

*Keeping Faith by Jodi Picoult. Rep. HarperPerennial (134,479)

You Are Captivating by Stasi Eldredge. Orig. Nelson (133,839)

Digging to America by Anne Tyler. Rep. Ballantine (132,577)

World War Z by Max Brooks. Rep. Three Rivers (132,549)

*#The History of Love by Nicole Krauss. Rep. Norton (132,100)

*Son of a Witch by Gregory Maguire. Rep. Harper (132,030)

**Men Are from Mars, Women Are from Venus by John Gray. Rep. Harper (131,892)

*Saving Fish from Drowning by Amy Tan. Rep. Ballantine (131,693)

Fast Food Nation by Eric Schlosser. Rep. HarperPerennial (131,286)

Whistling in the Dark by Lesley Kagen. Orig. NAL (130,570)

The Silver Palate Cookbook 25th Anniversary Edition by Julee Rosso and Sheila Lukins with Michael McLaughlin. Orig. Workman (130,025)

Heart of Texas: Vol. 2 by Debbie Macomber. Rep. Mira (129,707)

Happiness Sold Separately by Lolly Winston. Rep. Grand Central (128,203)

Everyman by Philip Roth. Rep. Vintage (128,092)

Heart of Texas: Vol. 1 by Debbie Macomber. Rep. Mira (128,009)

The Looming Tower by Lawrence Wright. Rep. Vintage (127,321)

Confessions of a Video Vixen by Karrine Steffans. Orig. Amistad (127,000)

Wisdom of Our Fathers by Tim Russert. Rep. Random (125,398)

Simpsons Comics Beach Blanket Bongo by Matt Groening. Orig. Harper (125,099)

A Dirty Job by Christopher Moore. Rep. Harper (125,060)

**#*Slaughterhouse-Five* by Kurt Vonnegut. Rep. Dial (125,000)

**#*Women's Bodies, Women's Wisdom* by Christiane Northrup, M.D. Revised. Bantam (125,000)

In the Company of the Courtesan by Sarah Dunant. Rep. Random (124,444)

Eye Contact by Cammie McGovern. Rep. Penguin (123,540)

***The Screwtape Letters* by C. S. Lewis. Rep. HarperOne (122,000)

#*Blind Side* by Michael Lewis. Rep. Norton (121,000)

Absurdistan by Gary Shteyngart. Rep. Random (120,615)

**A Whole New Mind* by Daniel Pink. Rep. Riverhead (120,014)

**The Fat Smash Diet* by Ian K. Smith, M.D. Orig. Griffin (120,000)

Thunderstruck by Erik Larson. Rep. Three Rivers (119,679)

The Biggest Loser Fitness Program. Orig. Rodale (118,308)

P.S., I Love You by Cecelia Ahern. Movie tie-in. Hyperion (117,906)

***The Poisonwood Bible* by Barbara Kingsolver. Rep. HarperPerennial (117,014)

***Confessions of an Ugly Stepsister* by Gregory Maguire. Rep. Harper (116,521)

The Volumetrics Eating Plan by Barbara Rolls. Rep. Harper (116,125)

**The Book of Useless Information* by Noel Botham. Orig. Perigee (115,283)

**#*The American Academy of Pediatrics New Mother's Guide to Breastfeeding* by American Academy of Pediatrics. Orig. Bantam (115,000)

The Redemption of Sarah Cain by Beverly Lewis. Movie tie-in. Bethany (114,773)

**1491* by Charles C. Mann. Rep. Vintage (113,189)

**The Mermaid Chair* by Sue Monk Kidd. Rep. Penguin (113,043)

Savannah Breeze by Mary Kay Andrews. Rep. Harper (112,140)

A Spot of Bother by Mark Haddon. Rep. Vintage (111,605)

***Reading Lolita in Tehran* by Azar Nafisi. Rep. Random (111,362)

Chicken Soup for the American Idol Soul by Jack Canfield et al. Orig. HCI (111,006)

***Mercy* by Jodi Picoult. Rep. Washington Square (111,000)

The Green Book by Elizabeth Rogers and Thomas M. Kostigen. Orig. Three Rivers (110,613)

**#*Confessions of a Shopaholic* by Sophie Kinsella. Rep. Dial (110,000)

**#*Cat's Cradle* by Kurt Vonnegut. Rep. Dial (110,000)

***Plain Truth* by Jodi Picoult. Rep. Washington Square (109,000)

Porn for Women by Susan Anderson. Orig. Chronicle (107,894)

**An Inconvenient Truth* by Al Gore. Rep. Rodale (107,742)

The Space Between Us by Thrity Umrigar. Rep. HarperPerennial (107,672)

A Thousand Tomorrows by Karen Kingsbury. Rep. Center Street (106,591)

Abundance by Sena Jeter Naslund. Rep. HarperPerennial (104,596)

The Best American Short Stories 2007 edited by Stephen King. Orig. Houghton Mifflin (103,047)

Kabul Beauty School by Deborah Rodriguez. Rep. Random (102,719)

**The Joy Luck Club* by Amy Tan. Rep. Penguin (102,573)

**Team of Rivals* by Doris Kearns Goodwin. Rep. Simon & Schuster (102,161)

The Rising Tide by Jeff Shaara. Rep. Ballantine (100,774)

**Darkly Dreaming Dexter* by Jeff Lindsay. TV tie-in. Vintage (100,441)

**Smashed* by Koren Zailckas. Rep. Penguin (100,382)

Love over Scotland by Alexander McCall Smith. Orig. Anchor (100,123)

My Life in France by Julia Child. Rep. Anchor (100,102)

Anybody Out There? by Marian Keyes. Rep. Avon (100,000)

Big Boned by Meg Cabot. Orig. Avon (100,000)

Changing Faces by Kimberla Lawson Roby. Rep. Avon (100,000)
Queen of Babble by Meg Cabot. Rep. Avon (100,000)

Almanacs, Atlases, and Annuals

Calorie King Calorie, Fat and Carbohydrate Counter 2007 by Allen Borushek. Family Health Publications (600,000)
The World Almanac and Book of Facts 2008 edited by C. Alan Joyce. Annual. World Almanac (425,000)
*The World Almanac and Book of Facts 2007 edited by Ken Park. Annual. World Almanac (390,000)
J. K. Lasser's Your Income Tax 2008 by J. K. Lasser Institute. Orig. Wiley. (200,000)
The Old Farmer's Almanac 2007. Annual. Yankee (190,000)
*What Color Is Your Parachute? 2007 by Richard Nelson Bolles. Revision. Ten Speed (161,000)

Mass Market

2 Million+

Blood Brothers by Nora Roberts. Orig. Jove (2,247,730)

1 Million+

Cross by James Patterson. Rep. Grand Central (1,831,296)
Angels Fall by Nora Roberts. Rep. Jove (1,655,329)
Judge & Jury by James Patterson and Andrew Gross. Rep. Grand Central (1,653,623)
Beach Road by James Patterson and Peter de Jonge. Rep. Grand Central (1,645,810)
Honeymoon by James Patterson and Howard Roughan. Rep. Grand Central (1,638,139)
Next by Michael Crichton. Rep. Harper (1,600,000)
Twelve Sharp by Janet Evanovich. Rep. St. Martin's (1,500,000)
At Risk by Patricia Cornwell. Rep. Berkley (1,445,075)
The Collectors by David Baldacci. Rep. Grand Central (1,286,410)

Two Little Girls in Blue by Mary Higgins Clark. Rep. Pocket (1,231,500)
True Believer by Nicholas Sparks. Rep. Grand Central (1,205,824)
Echo Park by Michael Connelly. Rep. Grand Central (1,068,053)
At First Sight by Nicholas Sparks. Rep. Grand Central (1,035,993)
Dead Watch by John Sandford. Rep. Berkley (1,005,314)
Hot Stuff by Janet Evanovich. Orig. St. Martin's (1,000,000)

750,000+

Wild Fire by Nelson DeMille. Rep. Grand Central (994,995)
74 Seaside Avenue by Debbie Macomber. Orig. Mira (971,329)
Born in Death by J. D. Robb. Rep. Berkley (955,073)
Treasure of Khan by Clive Cussler. Rep. Berkley (945,407)
Shadow Dance by Julie Garwood. Rep. Ballantine (932,058)
Ricochet by Sandra Brown. Rep. Pocket (906,000)
Innocent in Death by J. D. Robb. Rep. Berkley (895,194)
Motor Mouth by Janet Evanovich. Reissue. Harper (850,000)
The Ruins by Scott Smith. Rep. Vintage (835,321)
Gone by Jonathan Kellerman. Rep. Ballantine (816,792)
Polar Shift by Clive Cussler. Rep. Berkley (805,489)
Wife for Hire by Janet Evanovich. Revision. Harper (800,000)
The Bancroft Strategy by Robert Ludlum Rep. St. Martin's (800,000)
The Book of Fate by Brad Meltzer. Rep. Grand Central (788,365)
The Alexandria Link by Steve Berry. Rep. Ballantine (757,377)
The Black Order by James Rollins. Rep. Harper (750,000)

500,000+

The Divide by Nicholas Evans. Rep. Signet (740,077)

Someone to Love by Jude Deveraux. Rep. Pocket (734,000)

Golden Buddha by Clive Cussler and Craig Dirgo. Rep. Berkley (733,094)

Lisey's Story by Stephen King. Rep. Pocket (730,000)

Hide and Seek by Fern Michaels. Orig. Zebra (720,000)

Irish Dreams by Nora Roberts. Reissue. Silhouette (719,000)

Morning Comes Softly by Debbie Macomber. Rep. Avon (700,000)

The Secret Diaries of Miss Miranda Cheever by Julia Quinn. Orig. Avon (700,000)

The Marriage Game by Fern Michaels. Rep. Pocket (689,000)

Susannah's Garden by Debbie Macomber. Rep. Mira (686,435)

Promise Me by Harlan Coben. Rep. Signet (675,735)

Santa Cruise by Mary Higgins Clark and Carol Higgins Clark. Rep. Pocket (663,150)

Wicked by Gregory Maguire. Rep. Harper (650,000)

Exile by Richard North Patterson. Rep. St. Martin's (650,000)

Country Brides by Debbie Macomber. Rep. Mira (647,549)

Wizard's Daughter by Catherine Doulter. Orig. Jove (640,972)

Almost Dead by Lisa Jackson. Orig. Zebra (640,000)

Shiver by Lisa Jackson. Rep. Zebra (630,000)

Free Fall by Fern Michaels. Orig. Zebra (605,000)

Dakota Born by Debbie Macomber. Rep. Mira (601,453)

Dream Hunter by Sherilyn Kenyon. Orig. St. Martin's (600,000)

The Wrong Hostage by Elizabeth Lowell. Rep. Avon (600,000)

The Ravenscar Dynasty by Barbara Taylor Bradford. Rep. St. Martin's (600,000)

Mine Till Midnight by Lisa Kleypas. Orig. St. Martin's (600,000)

The Book of the Dead by Douglas Preston and Lincoln Child. Rep. Grand Central (592,400)

Fresh Disasters by Stuart Woods. Rep. Signet (575,775)

True Evil by Greg Iles. Rep. Pocket (571,000)

The Mist by Stephen King. Movie tie-in. Signet (560,902)

What Price Love? by Stephanie Laurens. Rep. Avon (550,000)

Dirty Blonde by Lisa Scottoline. Rep. Harper (550,000)

All Night Long by Jayne Ann Krentz. Rep. Jove (546,660)

Dark Celebration by Christine Feehan. Rep. Jove (545,957)

Crisis by Robin Cook. Rep. Berkley (543,348)

The Suspect by John Lescroart. Rep. Signet (540,876)

Short Straw by Stuart Woods. Rep. Signet (540,516)

Safe Harbor by Christine Feehan. Orig. Jove (540,393)

Act of Treason by Vince Flynn. Rep. Pocket (538,000)

The Templar Legacy by Steve Berry. Rep. Ballantine (526,230)

Dead Wrong by J. A. Jance. Rep. Harper (525,000)

Jeff Foxwothy's Redneck Dictionary II by Jeff Foxworthy. Rep. Ballantine (522,944)

Deadly Game by Christine Feehan. Orig. Jove (520,822)

Tom Clancy's Splinter Cell: Fallout by David Michaels. Orig. Berkley (518,622)

Dead of Night by J. D. Robb et al. Orig. Jove (515,194)

Capital Crimes by Jonathan Kellerman. Rep. Ballantine (513,239)

I Am Legend by Richard Matheson. Movie tie-in. Tor (511,361)

Web of Evil by J. A. Jance. Rep. Pocket (509,200)

The Mephisto Club by Tess Gerritsen. Rep. Ballantine (506,511)

Second Sight by Amanda Quick. Rep. Jove (503,412)

The Nanny Diaries by Nicola Kraus and Emma McLaughlin. Movie tie-in. St. Martin's (500,000)

Don't Look Down by Jennifer Crusie and Bob Mayer. Rep. St. Martin's (500,000)

Traitor by Stephen Coonts. Rep. St. Martin's (500,000)

More than Friends by Barbara Delinsky. Rep. Avon (500,000)

Full of Grace by Dorothea Benton Frank. Rep. Avon (500,000)

What Came Before He Shot Her by Elizabeth George. Rep. Harper (500,000)

The Shape Shifter by Tony Hillerman. Rep. Harper (500,000)

Beyond Seduction by Stephanie Laurens. Orig. Avon (500,000)

The Taste of Innocence by Stephanie Laurens. Rep. Avon (500,000)

Proof Positive by Phillip Margolin. Rep. Harper (500,000)

Children's Bestsellers: Farewell to Harry

Diane Roback

Senior Editor, Children's Books, *Publishers Weekly*

"I shall not look upon his like again," said Hamlet of his departed father, a sentiment that children (and adults) all over the world might express about the end of the Harry Potter saga. Publishers and especially booksellers would surely concur. *Harry Potter and the Deathly Hallows,* the seventh and final volume in J. K. Rowling's record-setting series, went on sale on July 21 and became the fastest-selling book ever. It sold 13.1 million copies in the United States last year, more than ten times that of its closest competitor in children's books, and two and a half times the sales for the adult nonfiction top seller, Rhonda Byrne's *The Secret.* In all, Scholastic sold just under 19 million Harry Potter books in 2007—quite a swan song year for the boy wizard.

Speaking of swans, Harry may be over, but 2007 was a huge year for Bella Swan, heroine of Stephenie Meyer's Twilight series. The latest installment, *Eclipse,* kicked the franchise into high gear, selling 1.1 million copies. And in 2007 the series sold 3 million copies combined, compared with 389,000 in 2006.

Also, you may not recognize the name Greg Heffley, but you may know him through his journal, *Diary of a Wimpy Kid,* which shot to the top of many bestsellers lists last year. With a sequel just out and five titles planned in all, we'll undoubtedly be hearing from the wimpy one in the future.

Notable in hardcover frontlist were followups to previous hits, including the concluding volume in the Sisterhood of the Traveling Pants series; another Maximum Ride title from James Patterson; the final collaboration between Bill Martin, Jr. and Eric Carle; and a new Fancy Nancy title. Also making appearances in the top ten: an adaptation for kids of John Grogan's *Marley & Me* and a picture book based on the song "Puff, the Magic Dragon."

The total number of hardcover frontlist titles was down compared to the previous year; 79 titles sold more than 100,000 copies in 2007, compared to 94 titles in 2006. Hardcover backlist stayed even: 66 titles sold above the 150,000-copy mark in 2007 vs. 64 in 2006. Paperback frontlist took a hit: 69 titles above 150,000 last year vs. 84 in 2006. And the paperback backlist was down just slightly: 85 titles above 150,000 compared with 91 in 2006.

In hardcover backlist, after the No. 1 title (Stephenie Meyer's *New Moon*), it's the usual assortment of tried-and-true titles: the *Goodnight Moon* board book, Dr. Seuss classics, *The Very Hungry Caterpillar, The Poky Little Puppy,* and so on. Nine of the top 20 titles, in fact, were written by Dr. Seuss. Some backlist sales are slipping a bit: *Goodnight Moon* sold 200,000 fewer copies than in 2006, the *Guess How Much I Love You* board book was down 100,000 copies, and Lemony Snicket sales were much lower, reflecting the end of that series in 2006.

The Newbery and Caldecott winners for last year racked up some healthy numbers: *The Higher Power of Lucky* sold 131,379 copies and *Flotsam* 142,471.

The paperback frontlist category continued to be dominated by series and tie-ins. The first Maximum Ride title sold just under a million copies, followed by the novelization of *High School Musical 2*. Other franchises represented include His Dark Materials, the Clique series, Hannah Montana, Pirates of the Caribbean, Narnia, and Dora the Explorer. Notable stand-alones in this category are the reissue of *A Wrinkle in Time* (400,000 copies), Mike Lupica's *Heat,* and the paperback editions of *The Book Thief* by Markus Zusak and *Princess Academy* by Shannon Hale.

Potter and Pullman were the big draws in paperback backlist: five of the six backlist Harry Potter titles were in the top ten (the sixth was No. 11), and *The Golden Compass* topped the chart with 1.3 million copies sold, thanks to December's movie. The other two His Dark Materials books did well, too, selling a combined 1.3 million backlist copies, and the omnibus edition in frontlist added another half a million. *Bridge to Terabithia* also came out as a movie last year, sparking sales of 500,000 copies. Newer franchises like Twilight, Eragon, and Percy Jackson had robust showings, and the ever-present staples stayed strong, including *The Outsiders, The Giver, Speak,* and *Charlie and the Chocolate Factory.*

Children's Hardcover Frontlist

300,000+

1. *Harry Potter and the Deathly Hallows* by J. K. Rowling, illus. by Mary GrandPré. Scholastic/Levine (13,114,692)
2. *Eclipse* by Stephenie Meyer. Little, Brown/Tingley (1,112,660)
3. *Forever in Blue: The Fourth Summer of the Sisterhood* by Ann Brashares. Delacorte (770,600)
4. *Diary of a Wimpy Kid* by Jeff Kinney. Abrams/Amulet (720,028)
5. *Maximum Ride: Saving the World and Other Extreme Sports* James Patterson. Little, Brown (590,875)
6. *Baby Bear, Baby Bear, What Do You See?* Bill Martin, Jr., illus. by Eric Carle. Holt (445,414)
7. *Fancy Nancy and the Posh Puppy* by Jane O'Connor, illus. by Robin Preiss Glasser. HarperCollins (399,046)
8. *Bad Dog, Marley!* by John Grogan, illus. by Richard Cowdrey. HarperCollins (390,148)
9. *Puff, the Magic Dragon* by Peter Yarrow and Lenny Lipton, illus. by Eric Puybaret. Sterling (375,000)
10. *Dragon of the Red Dawn* (Magic Tree House No. 37) by Mary Pope Osborne, illus. by Sal Murdocca. Random (355,521)
11. *The Three Snow Bears* by Jan Brett. Putnam (354,421)

12. *The Titan's Curse* (Percy Jackson and the Olympians No. 3) by Rick Riordan. Hyperion/Miramax (350,000)

13. *Diary of a Fly* by Doreen Cronin, illus. by Harry Bliss. HarperCollins/Cotler (323,336)

14. *Junie B., First Grader: Dumb Bunny* by Barbara Park, illus. by Denise Brunkus. Random (310,468)

15. *Disney High School Musical: All Access.* Disney (300,000).

200,000+

16. *Dog* by Matthew Van Fleet, photos by Brian Stanton. Simon & Schuster/Wiseman (261,813)

17. *Monday with a Mad Genius* (MTH No. 38) by Mary Pope Osborne, illus. by Sal Murdocca. Random (258,043)

18. *The Chronicles of Narnia Pop-up* by C. S. Lewis, illus. by Robert Sabuda. HarperCollins (251,520)

19. *Star Wars: A Pop-Up Guide to the Galaxy* by Matthew Reinhart. Orchard (248,918)

20. *Ana's Story* by Jenna Bush. HarperCollins (244,269)

21. *Marley* by John Grogan. Collins (233,270)

22. *Olivia Helps with Christmas* by Ian Falconer. Atheneum (224,446)

23. *Gallop!* by Rufus Butler Seder. Workman (223,007)

24. *The Invention of Hugo Cabret* by Brian Selznick. Scholastic (218,742)

25. *Eric Carle's ABC* by Eric Carle. Grosset & Dunlap (215,488)

26. *Beyond the Spiderwick Chronicles: The Nixie's Song* by Tony DiTerlizzi and Holly Black. Simon & Schuster (210,086)

27. *Mythology* by Lady Hestia Evans. Candlewick (207,725)

28. *Disney Bedtime Favorites.* Disney (202,000)

100,000+

29. *Slam* by Nick Hornby. Putnam (198,030)

30. *Physik* (Septimus Heap No. 3) by Angie Sage, illus. by Mark Zug. HarperCollins/Tegen (190,169)

31. *Disney Pirates of the Caribbean: From Ship to Shore.* Disney (190,000)

32. *Someday* by Alison McGhee, illus. by Peter H. Reynolds. Atheneum (181,002)

33. *Disney Princess: Enchanted Fashions* by Lara Bergen. Disney (180,000)

34. *Baby's First Book* by Garth Williams. Golden (178,533)

35. *Snakehead* (Alex Rider Adventures) by Anthony Horowitz. Philomel (177,825)

36. *Pirates: Most Wanted* by John Matthews. Atheneum (175,839)

37. *Disney Princess: Happily Ever After Stories.* Disney (175,000)

38. *Disney Pirates of the Caribbean: The Secret Files of the East India Trading Company* by Sir Thomas Faye. Disney (175,000)

39. *Extras* (Uglies No. 4) by Scott Westerfeld. Simon Pulse (172,615)

40. *Brown Bear, Brown Bear, What Do You See?* (40th Anniversary edition) by Bill Martin, Jr., illus. by Eric Carle. Holt (169,687)

41. *Summer Ball* by Mike Lupica. Philomel (162,189)

42. *The Alchemyst* by Michael Scott. Delacorte (151,863)

43. *Disney Pirates of the Caribbean: At World's End: The Movie Storybook* by T. T. Sutherland. Disney (150,000)

44. *Disney Bunnies: Goodnight, Thumper!* by Kitty Richards. Disney (150,000)

45. *Peter and the Secret of Rundoon* by Ridley Pearson and Dave Barry. Disney Editions (150,000)

46. *Disney High School Musical East High Yearbook* by Emma Harrison. Disney (150,000)

47. *Pirates Don't Change Diapers* by Melinda Long, illus. by David Shannon. Harcourt (148,348)

48. *Warriors* by James Harpur. Atheneum (146,621)

49. *What's Wrong, Little Pookie?* (board book) by Sandra Boynton. Random House/Corey (146,385)

50. *Harry Potter and the Deathly Hallows Deluxe Edition* by J. K. Rowling, illus. by Mary GrandPré. Scholastic/Levine (144,742)

51. *Biscuit's Pet & Play Halloween* by Alyssa Satin Capucilli, illus. by Dan Andreasen. HarperFestival (144,276)

52. *Gossip Girl: It Had to Be You* by Cecily von Ziegesar. Little, Brown/Poppy (137,274)

53. *Pilgrims of Rayne* (Pendragon No. 8) by D. J. MacHale. Simon & Schuster (137,068)

54. *Warriors Super Edition: Firestar's Quest* by Erin Hunter, illus. by Gary Chalk. HarperCollins (135,983)

55. *Warriors: Power of Three—No.1: The Sight* by Erin Hunter. HarperCollins (133,820)

56. *Vampyre: The Terrifying Lost Journal of Dr. Cornelius Van Helsing* by Dr. Cornelius Van Helsing and Gustav deWolff. HarperCollins (133,671)

57. *The Boys' Book* by Dominique Enright and Guy Macdonald, illus. by Nikalas Catlow. Scholastic Nonfiction (124,793)

58. *Shrek the Third: The Movie Storybook* by Alice Cameron, illus. by Larry Navarro. HarperEntertainment (123,155)

59. *The Story of Jesus* by Jane Werner Watson, illus. by Jerry Smath. Golden Inspirational (123,109)

60. *The Girls' Book* by Juliana Foster, illus. by Amanda Enright. Scholastic Nonfiction (119,708)

61. *Love, Stargirl* by Jerry Spinelli. Knopf (115,570)

62. *Charlie Bone and the Beast* by Jenny Nimmo. Orchard (115,524)

63. *Disney Pirates of the Caribbean: The Black Pearl—A Pop-Up Pirate Ship.* Disney (115,000)

64. *How Do Dinosaurs Go to School?* by Jane Yolen, illus. by Mark Teague. Scholastic/Blue Sky (114,466)

65. *Merry Christmas, Mouse!* by Laura Numeroff, illus. by Felicia Bond. HarperFestival (113,541)

66. *The Alphabet from A to Y with Bonus Letter Z!* by Steve Martin and Roz Chast. Doubleday/Flying Dolphin (113,190)

67. *Knuffle Bunny Too: A Case of Mistaken Identity* by Mo Williams. Hyperion (110,000)

68. *The Absolutely True Diary of a Part-Time Indian* by Sherman Alexie. Little, Brown (108,651)

69. *Ratatouille.* Random/Disney (108,426)

70. *The Icebound Land* (Ranger's Apprentice No. 3). John Flanagan. Philomel (106,602)

71. *Sesame Street Guess Who, Elmo!* by Wendy Wax. Reader's Digest (106,542)

72. *The Lost Files of Nancy Drew* by Carolyn Keene. Grosset & Dunlap (106,122)

73. *The Wrath of Mulgrath: Movie Tie-In Edition* (The Spiderwick Chronicles No. 5) by Tony DiTerlizzi and Holly Black. Simon & Schuster (106,012)

74. *Have Yourself a Furry Little Christmas* by Naomi Kleinberg, illus. by Louis Womble. Random (105,235)

75. *Dinomummy* by Dr. Phil Manning. Kingfisher (103,411)

76. *Great Joy* by Kate DiCamillo, illus. by Bagram Ibatoulline. Candlewick (102,450)

77. *Jingle Bell Christmas* (The Backyardigans) by Catherine Lukas. Simon Spotlight (101,443)

78. *Disney Fairies: Fairy Haven and the Quest for the Wand* by Gail Carson Levine. Disney (100,000)

79. *Mickey Mouse Clubhouse: 5+1 Makes More Fun* by Sheila Sweeney Higginson. Disney (100,000)

Children's Hardcover Backlist

300,000+

1. *New Moon* by Stephenie Meyer. Little, Brown/Tingley, 2006 (820,604)

2. *Goodnight Moon* (board book) by Margaret Wise Brown, illus. by Clement Hurd. HarperFestival, 1991 (611,540)

3. *Hop on Pop* by Dr. Seuss. Random, 1963 (503,927)

4. *Dr. Seuss's ABC* by Dr. Seuss. Random, 1960 (484,000)

5. *The Poky Little Puppy* by Janette Sebring Lowrey. Golden, 2001 (470,258)

6. *The Cat in the Hat* by Dr. Seuss. Random, 1957 (445,330)

7. *Green Eggs and Ham* by Dr. Seuss. Random, 1960 (412,841)

8. *Are You My Mother?* by P. D. Eastman. Random, 1960 (394,528)

9. *Oh, the Places You'll Go!* by Dr. Seuss. Random, 1990 (391,455)

10. *Cars Little Golden Book* by Ben Smiley, illus. by Scott Tilley and Jean-Paul Orpinas. Golden/Disney, 2006 (391,250)

11. *The Very Hungry Caterpillar* (board book) by Eric Carle. Philomel, 1994 (383,142)

12. *Fox in Socks* by Dr. Seuss. Random, 1965 (350,346)

13. *Mr. Brown Can Moo, Can You?* (board book) by Dr. Seuss. Random, 1996 (343,111)

14. *Harry Potter and the Sorcerer's Stone* by J. K. Rowling, illus. by Mary GrandPré. Scholastic/Levine, 1996 (335,931)

15. *Harry Potter and the Order of the Phoenix* by J. K. Rowling, illus. by Mary GrandPré. Scholastic/Levine, 1996 (311,040)

16. *Guess How Much I Love You* (board book) by Sam McBratney, illus. by Anita Jeram. Candlewick, 1996 (309,125)

200,000+

17. *Go, Dog. Go!* by P. D. Eastman. Random, 1961 (296,484)

18. *Harry Potter and the Half-Blood Prince* by J. K. Rowling, illus. by Mary GrandPré. Scholastic/Levine, 1996 (295,339)

19. *Harry Potter and the Chamber of Secrets* by J. K. Rowling, illus. by Mary GrandPré. Scholastic/Levine, 1996 (287,543)

20. *One Fish, Two Fish, Red Fish, Blue Fish* by Dr. Seuss. Random, 1960 (281,079)

21. *Horton Hatches the Egg* by Dr. Seuss. Random, 1940 (275,488)

22. *I Love You Through and Through* by Bernadette Rossetti Shustak, illus. by Caroline Jayne Church. Scholastic/Cartwheel, 2005 (274,645)

23. *Harry Potter and the Prisoner of Azkaban* by J. K. Rowling, illus. by Mary GrandPré. Scholastic/Levine, 1996 (265,638)

24. *Harry Potter and the Goblet of Fire* by J. K. Rowling, illus. by Mary GrandPré. Scholastic/Levine, 1996 (257,880)

25. *Cars: Mater and the Ghost Light* Golden/Disney, 2006 (255,170)

26. *Put Me in the Zoo* by Robert Lopshire. Random, 1960 (249,223)

27. *Moo Baa La La La* (board book) by Sandra Boynton. Little Simon, 1995 (244,902)

28. *On the Night You Were Born* by Nancy Tillman. Feiwel and Friends, 2006 (234,133)

29. *Thomas and the Big, Big Bridge* by Rev. W. Awdry. Golden, 2003 (233,021)

30. *Ten Apples Up on Top!* by Dr. Seuss writing as Theo. LeSieg. Random, 1961 (229,895)

31. *The Giving Tree* by Shel Silverstein. HarperCollins, 1964 (229,660)
32. *Fisher Price Little People Let's Go to the Zoo!* by Ellen Weiss. Reader's Digest, 2006 (227,854)
33. *Cars (Read Aloud Board Book)* Random/Disney, 2006 (226,873)
34. *Fancy Nancy* by Jane O'Connor, illus. by Robin Preiss Glasser. Harper-Collins, 2005 (221,545)
35. *How the Grinch Stole Christmas!* by Dr. Seuss. Random, 1957 (220,088)
36. *Twilight* by Stephenie Meyer. Little, Brown/Tingley, 2005 (203,729)
37. *Yertle the Turtle* by Dr. Seuss. Random, 1958 (200,032)
38. *Disney Princess Collection* Disney, 2006 (200,000)
39. *Disney/Pixar Storybook Collection.* Disney, 2006 (200,000)
40. *Baby Einstein: Mirror Me!* by Julie Aigner-Clark. Hyperion, 2002 (200,000)

150,000+

41. *The Field Guide* (The Spiderwick Chronicles No. 1) by Tony DiTerlizzi and Holly Black. Simon & Schuster, 2003 (198,072)
42. *Barnyard Dance!* (board book) by Sandra Boynton. Workman, 1993 (195,410)
43. *Thomas Breaks a Promise* Illus. by Richard Courtney. Golden, 2006 (192,857)
44. *Dora's Rainbow Egg Hunt* by Kirsten Larson, illus. by Steven Savitsky. Simon Spotlight, 2006 (191,535)
45. *Scuffy the Tugboat* by Gertrude Crampton, illus. by Tibor Gergely. Golden, 2001 (191,460)
46. *Where Do Kisses Come From?* by Maria Fleming. Golden, 2006 (188,775)
47. *The Going-to-Bed Book* (board book) by Sandra Boynton. Little Simon, 1995 (180,252)
48. *Where the Sidewalk Ends* (30th anniversary edition) by Shel Silverstein. HarperCollins, 2003 (180,099)
49. *My Little Golden Book About God* by Eloise Wilkin. Golden Inspirational, 2000 (176,925)
50. *The Foot Book* (board book) by Dr. Seuss. Random, 1996 (174,897)
51. *Snuggle Puppy* (board book) by Sandra Boynton. Workman, 2003 (172,514)
52. *Fisher Price My Little People Farm* by Doris Tomaselli. Reader's Digest, 1997 (171,349)
53. *The Runaway Bunny* (board book) by Margaret Wise Brown, illus. by Clement Hurd. HarperFestival, 1991 (169,679)
54. *Six by Seuss* by Dr. Seuss. Random, 1991 (168,662)
55. *Where Is Baby's Belly Button?* by Karen Katz. Little Simon, 2000 (167,940)
56. *Good Night, Gorilla* (board book) by Peggy Rathmann. Putnam, 1996 (167,714)

57. *The End* (A Series of Unfortunate Events No. 13) by Lemony Snicket, illus. by Brett Helquist. HarperCollins, 2006 (167,328)
58. *My First Counting Book* by Lilian Moore. Golden, 2001 (166,965)
59. *Tails* by Matthew Van Fleet. Harcourt/Red Wagon, 2003 (166,043)
60. *The Shy Little Kitten* by Cathleen Schurr. Golden, 2004 (163,908)
61. *The Jolly Barnyard* by Annie North Bedford, illus. by Tibor Gergely. Golden, 2004 (162,283)
62. *My Very First Book of Colors* (board book) by Eric Carle. Philomel, 2005 (157,403)
63. *The Saggy Baggy Elephant* by Kathryn Jackson, illus. by Gustaf Tenggren. Golden, 1999 (156,088)
64. *Belly Button Book!* (board book) by Sandra Boynton. Workman, 2005 (152,437)
65. *Cars: Out for a Spin.* Disney, 2006 (150,000)
66. *Disney Storybook Collection.* Disney, 2006 (150,000)

100,000+

67. *Tawny Scrawny Lion.* Golden, 2001 (149,002)
68. *Flotsam* by David Wiesner. Clarion, 2006 (142,471)
69. *Santa Claus.* Rod Green, illus. by Carol Wright, Simon Danher, and Jon Lucas. Atheneum, 2006 (140,820)
70. *Mouse Cookies & More* by Laura Numeroff, illus. by Felicia Bond. HarperCollins/Geringer, 2006 (139,326)
71. *Big Red Barn* by Margaret Wise Brown, illus. by Felicia Bond. HarperFestival, 1995 (139,172)
72. *The Seeing Stone* (The Spiderwick Chronicles No. 2) by Tony DiTerlizzi and Holly Black. Simon & Schuster, 2003 (136,498)
73. *There's a Wocket in My Pocket!* (board book) by Dr. Seuss. Random, 1996 (134,634)
74. *Tootle* by Gertrude Crampton. Golden, 2001 (131,945)
75. *The Higher Power of Lucky* by Susan Patron. Atheneum/Jackson, 2006 (131,379)
76. *Disney Princess: Dress-Up.* Disney, 2004 (130,000)
77. *Toes, Ears, and Nose!* (board book) by Marion Dane Bauer, illus. by Karen Katz. Little Simon, 2002 (129,773)
78. *The Little Red Hen* by J. P. Miller. Golden, 2001 (129,611)
79. *The Monster at the End of This Book* by Jon Stone, illus. by Michael Smollin. Golden, 1999 (129,264)
80. *Fairyopolis* inspired by Cicely Mary Barker. Frederick Warne, 2005 (127,508)
81. *Dora's Christmas Adventure* by Christine Ricci, illus. by Piero Piluso. Simon Spotlight, 2006 (127,025)
82. *The Little Mermaid.* Golden/Disney, 1999 (126,966)

83. *Jungle Colors* (The Backyardigans) by Nancy Parent, illus. by Susan Hall. Simon Spotlight, 2005 (126,899)
84. *So Big!* by Anna Jane Hays, illus. by Christopher Moroney. Random, 2003 (125,099)
85. *The Golden Compass* (hardcover and deluxe) by Philip Pullman. Knopf, 1996 (125,096)
86. *Hand, Hand, Fingers, Thumb* (board book) by Al Perkins. Random, 1998 (123,434)
87. *The Happy Man and His Dump Truck* illus. by Tibor Gergely. Golden, 2005 (122,638)
88. *Dora's Halloween Adventure* by Sarah Willson, illus. by Steven Savitsky. Simon Spotlight, 2003 (122,489)
89. *How I Became a Pirate* by Melinda Long, illus. by David Shannon. Harcourt, 2003 (122,366)
90. *Counting Kisses* by Karen Katz. Little Simon, 2002 (120,909)
91. *A Blessing from Above* by Patricia Henderson, illus. by Elizabeth Edge. Golden, 2004 (119,762)
92. *The Fire Engine Book* by Tibor Gergely. Golden, 2001 (119,758)
93. *Dr. Ernest Drake's Dragonology* by Dugald A. Steer. Candlewick, 2003 (119,400)
94. *Pinkalicious* by Elizabeth Kann and Victoria Kann. HarperCollins, 2006 (117,506)
95. *Where the Wild Things Are* by Maurice Sendak. HarperCollins, 1963 (117,301)
96. *The Little Red Caboose* by Marian Potter. Golden, 2000 (117,220)
97. *I Can Read with My Eyes Shut!* by Dr. Seuss. Random, 1978 (117,149)
98. *The Secret of the Old Clock* (Nancy Drew No. 1) by Carolyn Keene. Grosset & Dunlap, 1930 (116,717)
99. *The Three Little Pigs.* Golden/Disney, 2004 (116,447)
100. *A Hatful of Seuss* by Dr. Seuss. Random, 1997 (114,599)
101. *Oh, the Thinks You Can Think!* by Dr. Seuss. Random, 1975 (113,205)
102. *Baby Einstein: Alphabooks* by Julie Aigner-Clark. Hyperion, 2005 (110,000)
103. *I'm a Big Sister* by Joanna Cole, illus. by Maxie Chambliss. HarperCollins, 1997 (109,506)
104. *If You Give a Mouse a Cookie* by Laura Numeroff, illus. by Felicia Bond. HarperCollins/Geringer, 1985 (108,602)
105. *Guess How Much I Love You* by Sam McBratney, illus. by Anita Jeram. Candlewick, 1995 (107,475)
106. *The Night Before Christmas* by Clement C. Moore, illus. by Mary Engelbreit. HarperCollins, 2002 (106,747)
107. *I Love It When You Smile* by Sam McBratney, illus. by Charles Fuge. HarperCollins, 2006 (105,808)
108. *Clap Your Hands* (board book). Random, 2002 (105,271)

109. *I'm a Big Brother* by Joanna Cole, illus. by Maxie Chambliss. Harper-Collins, 1997 (104,168)

110. *The Lorax* by Dr. Seuss. Random, 1971 (103,348)

111. *Noah's Ark* by Barbara Shook Hazen, illus. by Mircea Catusanu. Golden, 2003 (102,489)

112. *Baby Animals* by Garth Williams. Golden, 2004 (102,362)

113. *Christmas in the Manger* (board book) by Nola Buck, illus. by Felicia Bond. HarperFestival, 1998 (102,215)

114. *Dora's Valentine Day Adventure* by Christine Ricci. Simon Spotlight, 2006 (101,355)

115. *Lucinda's Secret* (The Spiderwick Chronicles No. 3) by Tony DiTerlizzi and Holly Black. Simon & Schuster, 2003 (100,704)

116. *The Wrath of Mulgrath* (The Spiderwick Chronicles No. 5) by Tony DiTerlizzi and Holly Black. Simon & Schuster, 2004 (100,140)

117. *Summer of the Sea Serpent* (Magic Tree House No. 31) by Mary Pope Osborne, illus. by Sal Murdocca. Random, 2004 (100,028)

118. *Blizzard of the Blue Moon* (MTH No. 36) by Mary Pope Osborne, illus. by Sal Murdocca. Random, 2006 (100,003)

Children's Paperback Frontlist

300,000+

1. *Maximum Ride: School's Out—Forever* by James Patterson. Little, Brown (999,753)

2. *Disney High School Musical 2: The Junior Novel* by N. B. Grace. Disney (675,000)

3. *Eldest* by Christopher Paolini. Knopf (650,919)

4. *His Dark Materials Omnibus* by Philip Pullman. Knopf (538,044)

5. *Disney High School Musical: Stories from East High: Battle of the Bands* by N. B. Grace. Disney (500,000)

6. *Mad for Miley: An Unauthorized Biography* by Lauren Alexander. Price Stern Sloan (425,571)

7. *It's Not Easy Being Mean* (Clique) by Lisi Harrison. Little, Brown/Poppy (410,133)

8. *Pirates of the Caribbean: At World's End* (junior novel) by T. T. Sutherland. Disney (410,000)

9. *A Wrinkle in Time* (The Time Quintet) by Madeleine L'Engle. Square Fish (398,498)

10. *Sealed with a Diss* (Clique) by Lisi Harrison. Little, Brown/Poppy (380,182)

11. *Disney High School Musical: Stories from East High—Wildcat Spirit* by Catherine Hapka. Disney (380,000)

12. *Hannah Montana: Truth or Dare* by M. C. King. Disney (380,000)

13. *Disney High School Musical: Stories from East High—Poetry in Motion* by Alice Alfonsi. Disney (350,000)

14. *Spider-Man 3: Spider-Man's New Suit* by N. T. Raymond. HarperEntertainment (341,987)

15. *Spider-Man 3: Meet the Heroes and Villains* by Harry Lime, illus. by Steven Gordon. HarperTrophy (331,786)

16. *Mythic Vision: The Making of Eragon* by Mark Cotta Vaz. Knopf (313,880)

17. *Disney High School Musical: Stories from East High—Crunch Time* by N. B. Grace. Disney (300,000)

18. *Hannah Montana: Hold on Tight* by Laurie McElroy. Disney (300,000)

200,000+

19. *Junie B., First Grader: Aloha-Ha-Ha* by Barbara Park, illus. by Denise Brunkus. Random (271,924)

20. *Sea of Monsters* (Percy Jackson and the Olympians No. 2) by Rick Riordan. Hyperion/Miramax (250,000)

21. *Hannah Montana: Nightmare on Hannah Street* by Laurie McElroy. Disney (250,000)

22. *Don't You Forget About Me* (Gossip Girl) by Cecily von Ziegesar. Little, Brown/Poppy (245,812)

23. *It's Sharing Day!* by Kirsten Larson, illus. by Ron Zalme. Simon Spotlight (238,976)

24. *Shrek the Third: Friend and Foes* by Catherine Hapka, illus. by Steven Gordon. HarperTrophy (238,442)

25. *Shrek the Third Mad Libs* by Roger Price and Leonard Stern. Price Stern Sloan (234,147)

26. *Dora Saves Mermaid Kingdom!* Michael Teitelbaum. Simon Spotlight (232,955)

27. *The Bad Beginning* (A Series of Unfortunate Events No. 1) by Lemony Snicket, illus. by Brett Helquist. HarperTrophy (231,658)

28. *Spider-Man 3: The Junior Novel* by Jasmine Jones. HarperEntertainment (226,110)

29. *Hannah Montana: Crush-Tastic!* by Beth Beechwood. Disney (225,000)

30. *The Reptile Room* (A Series of Unfortunate Events No. 2) by Lemony Snicket, illus. by Brett Helquist. HarperTrophy (217,013)

31. *Shrek the Third: Royally Wrong* by Annie Auerbach. HarperTrophy (215,306)

32. *Dora Helps Diego!* by Laura Driscoll, illus. by Tom Mangano. Simon Spotlight (213,394)

33. *Transformers: Optimus Prime Versus Megatron* by Sadie Chesterfield. HarperEntertainment (212,518)

34. *Shrek the Third: The Junior Novel* by Kathleen Weidner Zoehfeld. Harper-Entertainment (211,879)

35. *The Chronicles of Narnia Movie Tie-In Edition: Prince Caspian* by C. S. Lewis, illus. by Pauline Baynes. HarperEntertainment (211,558)

36. *Meet Julie* by Megan McDonald. American Girl (210,714)

37. *Transformers: Meet the Deceptions* by Jennifer Frantz, illus. by Guido Guidi. HarperTrophy (208,422)

38. *Unforgettable* (It Girl) by Cecily von Ziegesar. Little, Brown/Poppy (205,933)

39. *Prilla and the Butterfly Lie* (Disney Fairies) by Kitty Richards. Random/Disney (203,681)

40. *Transformers: The Junior Novel* by S. G. Wilkens. HarperEntertainment (203,457)

150,000+

41. *Heat* by Mike Lupica. Puffin (192,857)

42. *Ballerina Princess.* Random/Disney (189,934)

43. *Diego's Egg Quest* by Cynthia Stierle. Simon Spotlight (188,435)

44. *Barbie as the Island Princess: A Storybook* by Mary Man-Kong. Random (185,427)

45. *Barbie Fairytopia: Magic* by Mary Man-Kong. Golden (185,234)

46. *Meet the Robinsons: Keep Moving Forward* by Katherine Emmons, illus. by Ron Husband. HarperEntertainment (184,002)

47. *Transformers: Meet the Autobots* by Jennifer Frantz, illus. by Guido Guidi. HarperTrophy (182,737)

48. *The Book Thief* by Markus Zusak. Knopf (180,465)

49. *Diego and Papi to the Rescue* by Wendy Wax, illus. by John Hom. Simon Spotlight (178,011)

50. *Hannah Montana: Seeing Green* by M. C. King. Disney (175,000)

51. *Disney High School Musical Poster Book.* Disney (175,000)

52. *Shrek the Third: A Good King Is Hard to Find* by Catherine Hapka, illus. by Steven Gordon. HarperTrophy (174,343)

53. *Princess Academy* by Shannon Hale. Bloomsbury (173,000)

54. *Ark Angel* (Alex Rider Adventures) by Anthony Horowitz. Puffin (170,096)

55. *Hatchet* by Gary Paulsen. Aladdin (170,000)

56. *Night of the New Magic* (Magic Tree House No. 35) by Mary Pope Osborne. Random (167,785)

57. *The Big Cheese* (Ratatouille). Random/Disney (167,307)

58. *The Berenstain Bears and the Big Spelling Bee* by Jan and Mike Berenstain. HarperFestival (166,857)

59. *An Inconvenient Truth* by Al Gore. Viking (166,021)

60. *Shrek the Third: Fiona's Fairy-Tale Five* by Annie Auerbach. Harper-Entertainment (163,551)

61. *Tink, North of Never Land* (Disney Fairies) by Kiki Thorpe. Random/Disney (162,799)

62. *Thomas' Milkshake Muddle.* Random (160,075)

63. *Oh, Brother!* (Ratatouille). Random (159,815)

64. *Harry and His Bucket Full of Dinosaurs Uh-Oh!* by Schuyler Hooke, illus. by Art Mawhinney. Random (157,611)

65. *Barbie as the Island Princess* by Daisy Alberto. Random (155,733)

66. *Pirates of the Caribbean: At World's End—Saving Jack Sparrow* by T. T. Sutherland. Disney (155,000)

67. *Pirates of the Caribbean: At World's End—Singapore!* by T. T. Sutherland. Disney (155,000)

68. *Diego's Animal Science Book* by Kara McMahon. Simon Spotlight (151,361)

69. *ttfn* by Lauren Myracle. Abrams/Amulet (150,774)

Children's Paperback Backlist

300,000+

1. *The Golden Compass* (various editions) by Philip Pullman. Random, 1998 (1,337,680)

2. *Twilight* by Stephenie Meyer. Little, Brown/Tingley, 2006 (879,120)

3. *Harry Potter and the Half-Blood Prince* by J. K. Rowling, illus. by Mary GrandPré. Scholastic/Levine, 2006 (825,072)

4. *Harry Potter and the Order of the Phoenix* by J. K. Rowling. Scholastic/Levine, 2004 (778,564)

5. *Harry Potter and the Sorcerer's Stone* by J. K. Rowling. Scholastic/Levine, 1999 (696,188)

6. *The Subtle Knife* (various editions) by Philip Pullman. Random, 2001 (669,458)

7. *The Amber Spyglass* (various editions) by Philip Pullman. Random, 2002 (651,149)

8. *The Outsiders* by S. E. Hinton. Puffin, 1997 (566,229)

9. *Harry Potter and the Chamber of Secrets* by J. K. Rowling, illus. by Mary GrandPré. Scholastic/Levine, 2000 (562,835)

10. *Harry Potter and the Goblet of Fire* by J. K. Rowling. Scholastic/Levine, 2002 (556,799)

11. *Harry Potter and the Prisoner of Azkaban* by J. K. Rowling, illus. by Mary GrandPré. Scholastic/Levine, 2001 (548,512)

12. *Old, New, Red, Blue!* Random/Disney, 2006 (434,954)

13. *The Giver* by Lois Lowry. Laurel-Leaf, 1999 (423,368)

14. *Love You Forever* by Robert Munsch, illus. by Sheila McGraw. Firefly, 1986 (397,532)

15. *Dinosaurs Before Dark* (Magic Tree House No. 1) by Mary Pope Osborne, illus. by Sal Murdocca. Random, 1992 (390,463)

16. *The Lightning Thief* (Percy Jackson and the Olympians No. 1) by Rick Riordan. Hyperion/Miramax, 2006 (375,000)

17. *Hannah Montana: Keeping Secrets* by Beth Beechwood. Disney, 2006 (350,000)

18. *Disney High School Musical Junior Novel* by N. B. Grace. Disney, 2006 (350,000)

19. *Eragon* by Christopher Paolini. Knopf, 2005 (348,537)

20. *Cars: Driving Buddies.* Random/Disney, 2006 (314,801)

21. *Where the Wild Things Are* by Maurice Sendak. HarperCollins, 1988 (304,844)

22. *The Care and Keeping of You* by Valorie Schaefer, illus. by Norm Bendell. American Girl, 1998 (300,788)

23. *Hannah Montana: Face-off* by Alice Alfonsi. Disney, 2006 (300,000)

200,000+

24. *Mummies in the Morning* (MTH No. 3) by Mary Pope Osborne, illus. by Sal Murdocca. Random, 1993 (299,260)

25. *What Is a Princess?* Random/Disney, 2004 (293,601)

26. *Speak* by Laurie Halse Anderson. Puffin, 2001 (293,010)

27. *Hannah Montana: Super Sneak* by Laurie McElroy. Disney, 2006 (290,000)

28. *Pirates Past Noon* (MTH No. 4) by Mary Pope Osborne, illus. by Sal Murdocca. Random, 1994 (289,218)

29. *Bridge to Terabithia* by Katherine Paterson. HarperTrophy, 1987 (285,361)

30. *The Knight at Dawn* (MTH No. 2) by Mary Pope Osborne, illus. by Sal Murdocca. Random, 1993 (281,572)

31. *Tales of a Fourth Grade Nothing* by Judy Blume. Puffin, 2003 (273,233)

32. *Amelia Bedelia* by Peggy Parish, illus. by Fritz Siebel. HarperTrophy, 1992 (252,217)

33. *The Lion, the Witch and the Wardrobe* by C. S. Lewis. HarperTrophy, 1994 (248,045)

34. *Danny and the Dinosaur* Syd Hoff. HarperTrophy, 1992 (247,357)

35. *Thomas Goes Fishing* by Rev. W. Awdry, illus. by Richard Courtney. Random, 2005 (237,012)

36. *Biscuit* by Alyssa Satin Capucilli, illus. by Pat Schories. HarperTrophy, 1997 (235,457)

37. *Charlie and the Chocolate Factory* by Roald Dahl, illus. by Quentin Blake. Puffin, 1998 (234,252)

38. *The Trouble with Tink* (Disney Fairies) by Kiki Thorpe. Random/Disney, 2006 (228,894)

39. *Uglies* (Uglies No. 1) by Scott Westerfeld. Simon Pulse, 2005 (228,018)

40. *Junie B. Jones and the Stupid Smelly Bus* (Junie B. Jones No. 1) by Barbara Park, illus. by Denise Brunkus. Random, 1992 (226,653)

41. *Junie B. Jones and a Little Monkey Business* (Junie B. Jones No. 2) by Barbara Park, illus. by Denise Brunkus. Random, 1993 (222,931)

42. *Afternoon on the Amazon* (MTH No. 6) by Mary Pope Osborne, illus. by Sal Murdocca. Random, 1995 (216,769)

43. *Bridge to Terabithia* (movie tie-in) by Katherine Paterson. HarperEntertainment, 2006 (213,429)

44. *Prince Caspian* by C. S. Lewis. HarperTrophy, 1994 (202,009)

45. *Frog and Toad Are Friends* by Arnold Lobel. HarperTrophy, 1979 (201,489)

150,000+

46. *Maximum Ride: The Angel Experiment* by James Patterson. Little, Brown, 2006 (199,813)

47. *Holes* by Louis Sachar. Yearling and Laurel-Leaf, 2000 (197,863)

48. *Night of the Ninjas* (MTH No. 5) by Mary Pope Osborne, illus. by Sal Murdocca. Random, 1995 (196,006)

49. *Dolphins at Daybreak* (MTH No. 9) by Mary Pope Osborne, illus. by Sal Murdocca. Random, 1997 (194,202)

50. *Maniac Magee* by Jerry Spinelli. Little, Brown, 1999 (192,178)

51. *Superfudge* by Judy Blume. Puffin, 2003 (191,737)

52. *The Clique* by Lisi Harrison. Little, Brown/Poppy, 2004 (190,084)

53. *James and the Giant Peach* by Roald Dahl, illus. by Quentin Blake. Puffin, 1998 (185,411)

54. *Go, Baby Jaguar!* (Go, Diego, Go!) by Kirsten Larson, illus. by Art Mawhinney. Simon Spotlight, 2006 (181,850)

55. *Inkheart* by Cornelia Funke. Scholastic/Chicken House, 2005 (178,190)

56. *Sealed with a Kiss* (Disney Princess) by Melissa Lagonegro. Random/Disney, 2005 (177,774)

57. *Junie B. Jones and Some Sneaky Peeky Spying* (Junie B. Jones No. 4) by Barbara Park, illus. by Denise Brunkus. Random, 1994 (177,752)

58. *The Tale of Despereaux* by Kate DiCamillo, illus. by Timothy Basil Ering. Candlewick, 2006 (177,650)

59. *Midnight on the Moon* (MTH No. 8) by Mary Pope Osborne, illus. by Sal Murdocca. Random, 1996 (177,057)

60. *Cars: Thunder and Lightning*. Random/Disney, 2006 (175,835)

61. *Pop Bottle Science* by Lynn Brunelle. Workman, 2004 (175,223)

62. *Number the Stars* by Lois Lowry. Yearling and Laurel-Leaf, 1990 (174,580)

63. *Junie B. Jones and Her Big Fat Mouth* (Junie B. Jones No. 3) by Barbara Park, illus. by Denise Brunkus. Random, 1993 (169,517)

64. *Island of the Blue Dolphins* by Scott O'Dell. Yearling and Laurel-Leaf, 1971 (166,840)

65. *Hatchet* by Gary Paulsen. Aladdin, 2006 (165,436)

66. *Where the Red Fern Grows* by Wilson Rawls. Yearling and Laurel-Leaf, 1997 (163,751)

67. *Junie B., First Grader: Toothless Wonder* (Junie B. Jones No. 20) by Barbara Park, illus. by Denise Brunkus. Random, 2003 (163,177)

68. *Thomas' ABC Book* based on the stories of Rev. W. Awdry. Random, 1998 (161,628)

69. *Pretties* (Uglies No. 2) by Scott Westerfeld. Simon Pulse, 2005 (161,160)

70. *Beck and the Great Berry Battle* (Disney Fairies) by Laura Driscoll. Random/Disney (160,840)

71. *Rani in the Mermaid Lagoon* (Disney Fairies) by Lisa Papademetriou. Random/Disney, 2006 (160,021)

72. *Because of Winn-Dixie* by Kate DiCamillo. Candlewick, 2001 (159,950)

73. *Sunset of the Sabertooth* (MTH No. 7) by Mary Pope Osborne, illus. by Sal Murdocca. Random, 1996 (158,096)

74. *Dora Climbs Star Mountain* by Alison Inches. Simon Spotlight, 2006 (157,204)

75. *Biscuit Goes to School* by Alyssa Satin Capucilli, illus. by Pat Schories. HarperTrophy, 2003 (156,500)

76. *Dora's Easter Basket.* by Sarah Willson, illus. by Susan Hall. Simon Spotlight, 2003 (156,374)

77. *Puppy Takes a Bath* (Dora the Explorer) by Christine Ricci, illus. by Tom Mangano. Simon Spotlight, 2006 (156,326)

78. *Junie B. Jones and the Yucky Blucky Fruitcake* (Junie B. Jones No. 5) by Barbara Park, illus. by Denise Brunkus. Random, 1995 (156,157)

79. *The Magician's Nephew* by C. S. Lewis. HarperTrophy, 1994 (155,880)

80. *Best Friends for Never* (Clique No. 2) by Lisi Harrison. Little, Brown/Poppy, 2004 (154,597)

81. *Hoot* by Carl Hiaasen. Knopf and Yearling, 2004 (154,467)

82. *A Masterpiece for Bess* (Disney Fairies) by Lara Bergen. Random/Disney, 2006 (152,355)

83. *Into the Wild* (Warriors No. 1) by Erin Hunter. HarperTrophy, 2003 (152,337)

84. *Charlotte's Web* by E. B. White, illus. by Garth Williams. HarperTrophy, 1974 (151,841)

85. *The Chronicles of Narnia* by C. S. Lewis. HarperTrophy, 2001 (150,658)

Literary Prizes, 2007

Compiled by the Staff of the *Bowker Annual*

Alex Awards. To the authors of ten books published for adults that have high potential appeal to teenagers. *Sponsor:* Margaret Alexander Edwards Trust and *Booklist. Winners: The Book of Lost Things* by John Connolly (Simon & Schuster); *The Whistling Season* by Ivan Doig (Harcourt); *Eagle Blue: A Team, a Tribe, and a High School Basketball Season in Arctic Alaska* by Michael D'Orso (Bloomsbury); *Water for Elephants* by Sara Gruen (Algonquin); *Floor of the Sky* by Pamela Carter Joern (University of Nebraska); *Color of the Sea* by John Hamamura (Thomas Dunne); *The Blind Side: Evolution of a Game* by Michael Lewis (Norton); *Black Swan Green* by David Mitchell (Random House); *The World Made Straight* by Ron Rash (Henry Holt); *The Thirteenth Tale* by Diane Setterfield (Simon & Schuster).

Ambassador Book Awards: To honor an exceptional contribution to the interpretation of life and culture in the United States. *Offered by:* English-Speaking Union of the United States. *Winners:* (American Studies) Timothy Egan for *The Worst Hard Time: The Untold Story of Those Who Survived the Great American Dust Bowl* (Houghton Mifflin); (autobiography) Donald Antrim for *The Afterlife: A Memoir* (Farrar, Straus & Giroux); (biography) Debby Applegate for *The Most Famous Man in America: The Biography of Henry Ward Beecher* (Doubleday); (current affairs) Thomas E. Ricks for *Fiasco: The American Military Adventure in Iraq* (Penguin); (fiction) Amy Hempel for *The Collected Stories of Amy Hempel* (Scribner); (poetry) Louise Glück for *Averno* (Farrar, Straus & Giroux); (lifetime achievement) Garry Wills.

American Academy of Arts and Letters Awards in Literature. To honor writers of exceptional accomplishment in any genre. *Offered by:* American Academy of Arts and Letters. *Winners:* Joan Acocella, Charles D'Ambrosio, Barbara Ehrenreich, David Markson, Robert Morgan, Joan Silbert, William T. Vollman, Dean Young.

American Academy of Arts and Letters Rome Fellowships. For a one-year residency at the American Academy in Rome for young writers of promise. *Offered by:* American Academy of Arts and Letters. *Winners:* Junot Diaz, Sarah Manguso.

American Book Awards. For literary achievement by people of various ethnic backgrounds. *Offered by:* Before Columbus Foundation. *Winners:* Daniel Cassidy for *How the Irish Invented Slang: The Secret Language of the Crossroads* (CounterPunch); Michael Eric Dyson for *Come Hell or High Water: Hurricane Katrina and the Color of Disaster* (Basic); Rigoberto Gonzalez for *Butterfly Boy: Memories of a Chicano Mariposa* (University of Wisconsin Press); Reyna Grande for *Across a Hundred Mountains* (Atria Books); Ernestine Hayes for *Blonde Indian: An Alaska Native Memoir* (University of Arizona); Patricia Klindienst for *The Earth Knows My Name: Food, Culture and Sustainability in the Gardens of Ethnic Americans* (Beacon); Gary Panter for *Jimbo's Inferno* (Fantagraphics); Jeffrey F. L. Partridge for *Beyond Literary Chinatown* (University of Washington); Judith Roche for *Wisdom of the Body* (Black Heron); Kali Vanbaale for *The Space Between* (River City).

Rudolfo and Patricia Anaya Premio Aztlan Literary Prize. To honor a Chicano or Chicana fiction writer who has published no more than two books. *Offered by:* University of New Mexico. *Winner:* Reyna Grande.

Hans Christian Andersen Awards. To an author and an illustrator whose body of work has made an important and lasting contribution to children's literature. *Offered by:* International Board of Books for Young People (IBBY). *Winners:* To be awarded next in 2008.

Anthony Awards. For superior mystery writing. *Offered by:* Boucheron World Mystery Convention. *Winners:* (best mystery novel) Laura Lippman for *No Good Deeds* (Harper); (best first novel) Louise Penny for *Still Life* (St. Martin's).

Bakeless Literary Publication Prizes. For promising new writers. *Offered by:* Bread Loaf Writers' Conference of Middlebury College. *Winners:* (fiction) Steven Wingate for *Wifeshopping* (Mariner); (creative nonfiction) Dustin Beall Smith for *Only Endless Consequence* (Mariner); (poetry) Aaron Baker for *Mission Work* (Mariner).

Bancroft Prizes ($10,000). For books of exceptional merit and distinction in American history, American diplomacy, and the international relations of the United States. *Offered by:* Columbia University. *Winners:* Robert D. Richardson for *William James: In the Maelstrom of American Modernism* (Houghton Mifflin); Jack Temple Kirby for *Mockingbird Song: Ecological Landscapes of the South* (University of North Carolina).

Barnes & Noble Discover Great New Writers Awards. To honor a first novel and a first work of nonfiction by American authors. *Offered by:* Barnes & Noble, Inc. *Winners:* (fiction) Ben Fountain for *Brief Encounters with Che Guevara* (HarperCollins); (nonfiction) Eric Blehm for *The Last Season* (HarperCollins).

Margaret L. Batchelder Award. For an American publisher of a children's book originally published in a foreign country and subsequently published in English in the United States. *Offered by:* American Library Association, Association for Library Service to Children. *Winner:* Delacorte Press for *The Pull of the Ocean* by Jean-Claude Mourlevat, translated from French by Y. Maudet.

Pura Belpré Awards. To a Latino/Latina writer and illustrator whose work portrays, affirms, and celebrates the Latino cultural experience in an outstanding work of literature for children and youth. *Offered by:* American Library Association, Association for Library Service to Children. *Winners:* To be awarded next in 2008.

Curtis Benjamin Award. To an outstanding individual within the U.S. publishing industry who has shown exceptional innovation and creativity in the field of publishing. *Offered by:* Association of American Publishers. *Winner:* Not awarded in 2007.

Helen B. Bernstein Award. For excellence in journalism. *Offered by:* New York Public Library. *Winner:* Lawrence Wright for *The Looming Tower: Al Qaeda and the Road to 9/11* (Knopf).

Black Caucus of the American Library Association (BCALA) Literary Awards. *Winners:* (fiction) Marita Golden for *After* (Doubleday); (nonfiction) U.S. Sen. Barack Obama for *The Audacity of Hope: Thoughts on Reclaiming the American Dream* (Crown); (outstanding contribution to publishing) Thomas Battle and Donna Wells for *Legacy: Treasures of Black History* (National Geographic).

James Tait Black Memorial Prize (United Kingdom). To recognize literary excellence in biography and fiction. *Offered by:* University of Edinburgh. *Winners:* (fiction) Cormac McCarthy for *The Road* (Picador); (nonfiction) Byron Rogers for *The Man Who Went into the West: The Life of R. S. Thomas* (Aurum).

Book Sense Book of the Year Awards. To honor titles that member stores most enjoyed handselling during the past year. *Offered by:* American Booksellers Association. *Winners:* (fiction) Sara Gruen for *Water for Elephants* (Algonquin); (nonfiction) Nora Ephron for *I Feel Bad About My Neck and Other Thoughts on Being a Woman* (Knopf); (children's literature) Markus Zusak for *The Book Thief* (Knopf); (children's illustrated) Isabella Hatkoff, Craig Hatkoff, and Paul Kahumbu for *Owen and Mzee: The True Story of a Remarkable Friendship* (photos by Peter Greste) (Scholastic).

Boston Globe/Horn Book Awards. For excellence in children's literature. *Winners:* (fiction and poetry) M. T. Anderson for *The Astonishing Life of Octavian Nothing, Traitor to the Nation. Vol. 1, The Pox Party* (Candlewick); (nonfiction) Nicholas Debon for *The Strongest Man in the World* (Groundwood); (picture book) Laura Vaccaro Seeger for *Dog and Bear: Two Friends, Three Stories* (Roaring Brook).

W. Y. Boyd Literary Novel Award. To honor a novel set in a period when the United States was at war. *Offered by:* American Library Association. *Winner:* Robert J.

Mrazek for *The Deadly Embrace: A Novel of World War II* (Viking).

Michael Braude Award. For light verse. *Offered by:* American Academy of Arts and Letters. *Winner:* To be awarded next in 2008.

Bridport International Creative Writing Prizes (United Kingdom) (£5,000). For poetry and short stories. *Offered by:* Bridport Arts Centre. *Winners:* (poetry) Christopher Buehlman for "Wanton"; (short story) Graham Mort for "The Prince."

Sophie Brody Medal. For the U.S. author of the most distinguished contribution to Jewish literature for adults published in the preceding year. *Offered by:* Reference and User Services Association, American Library Association, Brodart Foundation. *Winner:* Daniel Mendelsohn for *The Lost: A Search for Six of Six Million* (Harper-Collins).

Randolph Caldecott Medal. For the artist of the most distinguished picture book. *Offered by:* American Library Association, Association for Library Service to Children. *Winner:* David Wiesner for *Flotsam* (Clarion).

California Book Awards. To California residents to honor books of fiction, nonfiction, and poetry published in the previous year. *Offered by:* Commonwealth Club of California. *Winners:* (poetry) Ishmael Reed for *New and Collected Poems, 1964–2006* (Carroll & Graf); (fiction) Ngugi wa Thiong'o for *Wizard of the Crow* (Pantheon); (nonfiction) Michael Pollan for *The Omnivore's Dilemma* (Penguin).

John W. Campbell Memorial Award. For science fiction writing. *Offered by:* Center for the Study of Science Fiction. *Winner:* Ben Bova for *Titan* (Tor).

Canadian Library Association Amelia Frances Howard-Gibbon Illustrator's Award. *Winner:* Leslie Elizabeth Watts (illustrator and author) for *The Baabaasheep Quartet* (Fitzhenry & Whiteside).

Canadian Library Association Book of the Year for Children *Winner:* Hadley Dyer for *Johnny Kellock Died Today* (Harper-Collins).

Canadian Library Association Young Adult Canadian Book Award. *Winner:* William Bell for *The Blue Helmet* (Doubleday).

CILIP Carnegie Medal (United Kingdom). For the outstanding children's book of the year. *Offered by:* CILIP: The Chartered Institute of Library and Information Professionals (formerly the Library Association). *Winner:* Meg Rosoff for *Just in Case* (Penguin).

CILIP Kate Greenaway Medal (United Kingdom). For children's book Illustration. *Offered by:* CILIP: The Chartered Institute of Library and Information Professionals. *Winner:* Mini Grey for *The Adventures of the Dish and the Spoon* (Jonathan Cape).

Chicago Tribune Literary Prize. For a lifetime of literary achievement by an author whose body of work has had great impact on American society. *Offered by: Chicago Tribune. Winner:* E. L. Doctorow.

Chicago Tribune Heartland Prize for Fiction ($7,500). *Offered by: Chicago Tribune. Winner:* Robert Olmstead for *Coal Black Horse* (Algonquin).

Chicago Tribune Heartland Prize for Nonfiction ($7,500). *Offered by: Chicago Tribune. Winner:* Orville Vernon Burton for *The Age of Lincoln* (Hill and Wang).

Chicago Tribune Nelson Algren Award ($5,000). For short fiction. *Offered by: Chicago Tribune. Winner:* Heather E. Goodman for "His Dog."

Chicago Tribune Young Adult Literary Prize. To recognize a distinguished literary career. *Winner:* Gary Paulsen.

Arthur C. Clarke Award (United Kingdom). For the best science fiction novel published in the United Kingdom. *Offered by:* British Science Fiction Association. *Winner:* M. John Harrison for *Nova Swing* (Gollancz).

David Cohen Prize (United Kingdom). Awarded biannually to a living British writer, novelist, poet, essayist, or dramatist in recognition of an entire body of work written in the English language. *Offered by:* David Cohen Family Charitable Trust. *Winner:* Dereck Mahon.

Matt Cohen Award (Canada). To a Canadian author whose life has been dedicated to writing as a primary pursuit, for a body of work. *Offered by:* Writers' Trust of Canada. *Winner:* Marie-Claire Blais.

Commonwealth Writers' Prize (United Kingdom). To reward and encourage new Commonwealth fiction and ensure that works of merit reach a wider audience outside their country of origin. *Offered by:* Commonwealth Institute. *Winners:* (best book) Lloyd Jones for *Mister Pip* (Dial); (best first book) D. Y. Béchard for *Vandal Love* (Anchor Canada).

Costa Book Awards (United Kingdom). For literature of merit that is readable on a wide scale. *Offered by:* Booksellers Association of Great Britain and Costa Coffee. *Winners:* (novel) A. L. Kennedy for *Day* (Knopf); (first novel) Catherine O'Flynn for *What Was Lost* (Henry Holt); (biography) Simon Sebag Montefiore for *Young Stalin* (Knopf).

Benjamin H. Danks Award ($20,000). To a promising young playwright. *Offered by:* American Academy of Arts and Letters. *Winner:* Adam Rapp.

Philip K. Dick Award. For a distinguished science fiction paperback published in the United States. *Offered by:* Norwescon. *Winner:* Chris Moriarty for *Spin Control* (Bantam).

Margaret A. Edwards Award ($2,000). To an author whose book or books have provided young adults with a window through which they can view their world and which will help them to grow and to understand themselves and their role in society. *Donor:* School Library Journal. *Winner:* Lois Lowry for *The Giver* (Houghton Mifflin, 1993).

Will Eisner Comic Industry Awards. *Winners:* (best anthology) Bill Willingham, et al., for *Fables: 2001 Nights of Snowfall* (Vertigo/DC); (best reality-based work) Alison Bechdel for *Fun Home* (Houghton Mifflin); (best graphic album, reprint) Darwyn Cooke for *Absolute DC: The New Frontier* (DC); (best U.S. Edition of International Material) Jason for *The Left Bank Gang* (Fantagraphics); (best U.S. edition of international material) Garon Tsuchiya and Nobuaki Minegishi for *Old Boy* (Dark Horse Manga); (special recognition) Hope Larson for *Gray Horses* (Oni); (best writer) Ed Brubaker; (best continuing series) Grant Morrison and Frank Quitely for "All Star Superman" (DC); (best continuing series) Paul Pope for "Batman: Year 100" (DC).

Marian Engel Award (Canada). To a female writer in mid-career for a body of work. *Offered by:* Writers' Trust of Canada. *Winner:* Caroline Adderson.

Clifton Fadiman Medal for Excellence in Fiction. To honor the most memorable book by an American author who deserves rediscovery and wider readership. *Offered by:* Mercantile Library of New York. *Winner:* Lore Segal for *Other People's Houses* (New Press).

Timothy Findley Award (Canada). To a male Canadian author in mid-career for a body of work. *Offered by:* Writers' Trust of Canada. *Winner:* Douglas Glover.

E. M. Forster Award ($15,000). To a young writer from England, Ireland, Scotland, or Wales, for a stay in the United States. *Offered by:* American Academy of Arts and Letters. *Winner:* Jez Butterworth.

Forward Prizes (United Kingdom). For poetry. *Offered by:* The Forward. *Winners:* (best collection, £10,000) Sean O'Brien for *The Drowned Book* (Macmillan); (best first collection, £5,000) Daljit Nagra for *Look We Have Coming To Dover!* (Faber and Faber); (best single poem, £1,000) Alice Oswald for "Dunt."

Benjamin Franklin Awards. To recognize excellence in independent publishing. *Offered by:* PMA—The Independent Book Publishers Association. *Winners:* (fiction) Douglas Light for *East Fifth Bliss* (Behler); (children's picture book) Laurie Friedman and Lynne Avril Cravath, illustrator, for *Love, Ruby Valentine* (Carolrhoda); (juvenile/young adult fiction) Hanna Jansen and Elizabeth D. Crawford for *Over a Thousand Hills I Walk with You* (Carolrhoda); (juvenile/young adult nonfiction) *Young Person's Career Skills Handbook* (JIST); (nature/environment) Lee Fedder for *John James Audubon and "The Birds of America"* (Huntington Library); (science/environment) George T. Jefferson and Lowell Lindsay, editors, for *Fossil Treasures of the Anza-Borrego*

Desert (Sunbelt); (multicultural) Lemuel A. Moyé for *Face to Face with Katrina Survivors: A First Responder's Tribute* (Open Hand); (religion) Simcha Weinstein for *Up, Up, and Oy Vey: How Jewish History, Culture and Values Shaped the Comic Book Superhero* (Leviathan); (best first book, fiction) Larry Sager for *No Guns, No Knives, No Personal Checks: The Tales of a San Francisco Cab Driver* (Everett Madison); (best first book, nonfiction) TJ Fisher, Roy F. Guste, Jr., and Louis Sahuc for *Orleans Embrace with the Secret Gardens of the Vieux Carre* (Morgana); (best first book, children's/young adult) Kaza Kingsley and Melvyn Grant for *Erec Rex: The Dragon's Eye* (Firelight); (mystery/suspense) John McEvoy for *Riders Down* (Poisoned Pen); (gay/lesbian) Lars Clausen for *Straight into Gay America* (Soulscapers); (recreation/sports) Cecilia "Pudge" Kleinkauf for *River Girls: Flyfishing for Young Women* (Johnson); (health/wellness) Jackson Hunsicker for *Turning Heads: Portraits of Grace, Inspiration and Possibilities* (Press On Regardless); (history/political) Diane Rapaport for *New England Court Records: A Research Guide for Genealogists and Historians* (Quill Pen); (humor) Colin Murphy and Donal O'Dea for *The Feckin' Book of Everything Irish* (O'Brian); (psychology/self-help) Pierce J. Howard for *The Owner's Manual for the Brain* (Bard).

Josette Frank Award (formerly the Children's Book Award). For a work of fiction in which children or young people deal in a positive and realistic way with difficulties in their world and grow emotionally and morally. *Offered by:* Bank Street College of Education and the Florence M. Miller Memorial Fund. *Winners:* Sara Pennypacker and Marla Frazee, illustrator, for *Clementine* (Hyperion), Christian Burch for *The Manny Files* (Athenium).

French-American Foundation Translation Prize. For a translation or translations from French into English of a work of fiction and nonfiction. *Offered by:* French-American Foundation. *Winners:* (fiction) Sandra Smith for Irène Némirovsky's *Suite Française* (Vintage); (nonfiction) Bruce Fink for Jacques Lacan's *Écrits* (W. W. Norton).

Frost Medal. To recognize achievement in poetry over a lifetime. *Offered by:* Poetry Society of America. *Winner:* John Hollander.

Lewis Galantiere Award. For a literary translation into English from any language other than German. *Offered by:* American Translators Association. *Winner:* To be awarded next in 2008.

Galaxy British Book Awards. *Offered by: Publishing News. Winners:* (Borders Book of the Year) Conn and Hal Iggulden for *The Dangerous Book for Boys* (HarperCollins); (Reader's Digest Author of the Year) Richard Dawkins; (Book People Lifetime Achievement Award) John Grisham; (Richard and Judy Best Read of the Year) Jed Rubenfeld for *The Interpretation of Murder* (Henry Holt); (Amazon.co.uk Biography of the Year) Peter Kay for *The Sound of Laughter* (Century); (WHSmith Children's Book of the Year) Ricky Gervais for *Flanimals of the Deep* (Faber & Faber); (BCA Crime Thriller of the Year) Ian Rankin for *The Naming of the Dead* (Orion); (Waterstone's Newcomer of the Year) Victoria Hislop for *The Island* (Harper); (Sainsbury's Popular Fiction Award) Marian Keyes for *Anybody Out There?* (Avon); (Tesco Sports Book of the Year) Steven Gerrard for *Gerrard: My Autobiography* (Bantam); (Play.com TV and Film Book of the Year) Lauren Weisberger for *The Devil Wears Prada* (HarperCollins); (deciBel Writer of the Year, for a writer of African, Caribbean, or Asian descent) Jackie Kay for *Wish I Was Here* (Picador).

Theodor Seuss Geisel Medal. For the best book for beginning readers. *Offered by:* American Library Association, Association for Library Service to Children. *Winner:* Laura McGee Kvasnosky for *Zelda and Ivy: The Runaways* (Candlewick).

Giller Prize (Canada) (C$40,000). For the best novel or short story collection written in English. *Offered by:* Giller Prize Foundation and Scotiabank. *Winner:* Elizabeth Hay for *Late Nights on Air* (McClelland & Stewart).

Golden Kite Awards. For children's books. *Offered by:* Society of Children's Book Writers and Illustrators. *Winners:* (fiction) Tony Abbott for *Fire Girl* (Little, Brown); (nonfiction) Russell Freedman for *The Adventures of Marco Polo* (Scholastic); (picture book text) Walter Dean Myers for *Jazz,* illustrated by Christopher Myers (Holiday House); (picture book illustration) Larry Day for *Not Afraid of Dogs,* written by Susanna Pitzer (Walker).

Governor General's Literary Awards (Canada). For works, in English and in French, of fiction, nonfiction, poetry, drama, and children's literature, and for translation. *Offered by:* Canada Council for the Arts. *Winners:* (fiction, English) Michael Ondaatje for *Divisadero* (McClelland & Stewart); (fiction, French) Sylvain Trudel for *La Mer de la Tranquillité* (Les Éditions Les Allusifs); (poetry, English) Don Domanski for *All Our Wonder Unavenged* (Brick); (poetry, French) Serge Patrice Thibodeau for *Seul On Est* (Éditions Perce-Neige); (drama, English) Colleen Murphy for *The December Man* (Playwrights Canada); (drama, French) Daniel Danis for *Le Chant du Dire-Dire* (Leméac Éditeur); (nonfiction, English) Karolyn Smardz Frost for *I've Got a Home in Glory Land: A Lost Tale of the Underground Railroad* (Thomas Allen); (nonfiction, French) Annette Hayward for *La Querelle du Régionalisme au Québec (1904–1931): Vers l'Autonomisation de la Littérature Québécoise* (Éditions du Nordir); (children's literature–text, English) Iain Lawrence for *Gemini Summer* (Random House); (children's literature–text, French) François Barcelo for *La Fatigante et le Fainéant* (Soulières Editeur); (children's literature–illustration, English) Duncan Weller for *The Boy from the Sun* (Simply Read); (children's literature–illustration, French) Geneviève Côté for *La Petite Rapporteuse de Mots* (text by Danielle Simard) (Les Éditions Les 400 Coups); (translation, into English) Nigel Spencer, for *Augustino and the Choir of Destruction* by Marie-Claire Blais (House of Anansi); (translation, into French) Lori Saint-Martin and Paul Gagné for *Last*

Notes and Other Stories by Tamas Dobozy (Les Éditions Les Allusifs).

Griffin Poetry Prizes (Canada). To a living Canadian poet or translator and a living poet or translator from any country, which may include Canada. *Offered by:* Griffin Trust. *Winners:* (Canadian) Don McKay for *Strike/Slip* (McClelland & Stewart); (international) Charles Wright for *Scar Tissue* (Farrar, Straus & Giroux); (lifetime recognition award) Tomas Tranströmer.

Gryphon Award. To recognize a noteworthy work of fiction or nonfiction for younger children. *Offered by:* The Center for Children's Books. *Winner:* Matteo Pericoli for *The True Story of Stellina* (Knopf).

Guardian Children's Fiction Prize (United Kingdom) (£1,500). For an outstanding children's novel. *Offered by: The Guardian. Winner:* Jenny Valentine for *Finding Violet Park* (HarperCollins).

Guardian First Book Award (United Kingdom) (£10,000). For recognition of a first book. *Offered by: The Guardian. Winner:* Dinaw Mengestu for *Children of the Revolution* (Jonathan Cape).

O. B. Hardison, Jr. Poetry Prize. To a U.S. poet who has published at least one book in the past five years, and has made important contributions as a teacher, and is committed to furthering the understanding of poetry. *Offered by:* Folger Shakespeare Library. *Winner:* David Wojahn.

Harvey Awards. *Winners:* (best original graphic album) Brian K. Vaughan and Niko Henrichon for *Pride of Baghdad* (DC); best anthology) *Flight, Vol. 3* (Ballantine); (special award for excellence in presentation) Alan Moore and Melindie Gebbie for *Lost Girls* (Top Shelf); (best writer) Ed Brubaker; (best artist) Frank Quietly.

R. R. Hawkins Award. For the outstanding professional/scholarly work of the year. *Offered by:* Association of American Publishers. *Winner:* Martin A. Nowak for *Evolutionary Dynamics: Exploring the Equations of Life* (Harvard University).

Heartland Prizes. To recognize an outstanding work of fiction and an outstanding work of nonfiction, each about people and places in America's heartland. *Offered by:*

Chicago Tribune. Winners: (fiction) Robert Olmstead for *Coal Black Horse* (Algonquin); (nonfiction) Orville Vernon Burton for *The Age of Lincoln* (Hill and Wang).

Ernest Hemingway Foundation Award. For a distinguished work of first fiction by an American. *Offered by:* PEN New England. *Winner:* Ben Fountain for *Brief Encounters With Che Guevara* (HarperCollins).

O. Henry Awards. To honor the year's best short stories published in American and Canadian magazines and written by American or Canadian authors. *Winners:* William Trevor for "The Room" in the *New Yorker;* Charles Lambert for "The Scent of Cinnamon" in *One Story;* Justine Dymond for "Cherubs" in *Massachusetts Review;* Eddie Chuculate for "Galveston Bay, 1826" in *Manoa;* Vu Tran for "The Gift of Years" in *Fence;* Richard McCann for "The Diarist" in *Bloom;* Joan Silber for "War Buddies" in *Land Grant College Review;* Tony D'Souza for "Diamilla" in *Tin House;* Yannick Murphy for "In a Bear's Eye" in *McSweeney's Quarterly;* Rebecca Curtis for "Summer, with Twins" in *Harper's;* Brian Evenson for "Mudder Tongue" in *McSweeney's Quarterly;* Sana Krasikov for "Companion" in the *New Yorker;* Bay Anapol for "A Stone House" in *Manoa;* Jan Ellison for "The Company of Men" in *New England Review;* Adam Haslett for "City Visit" in the *Atlantic Monthly;* Christine Schutt for "The Duchess of Albany" in *Noon;* Andrew Foster Altschul for "A New Kind of Gravity" in *StoryQuarterly;* Ariel Dorfman for "Gringos" in *Subtropics;* Susan Straight for "El Ojo de Agua" in *Zoetrope;* Alice Munro for "The View from Castle Rock" in the *New Yorker.*

William Dean Howells Medal. In recognition of the most distinguished novel published in the preceding five years. *Offered by:* American Academy of Arts and Letters. *Winner:* To be awarded next in 2010.

Hugo Awards. For outstanding science fiction writing. *Offered by:* World Science Fiction Convention. *Winners:* (best novel) Vernor Vinge for *Rainbows End* (Tor); (best nonfiction book) Julie Phillips (ed.) for *James Tiptree, Jr.: The Double Life of Alice B. Sheldon* (St. Martin's); (best novella) Robert Reed for "A Billion Eves" in *Asimov's,* October/November 2006; (best novelette) Ian McDonald for "The Djinn's Wife" in *Asimov's,* July 2006; (best short story) Timothy Pratt for "Impossible Dreams" in *Asimov's* July 2006.

Hurston/Wright Legacy Awards. To writers of African American descent for a book of fiction, a book of first fiction, a book of nonfiction, and a book of poetry. *Offered by:* Hurston/Wright Foundation and Borders Books. *Winners:* (fiction) Edward P. Jones for *All Aunt Hagar's Children* (Amistad); (first fiction) Aminatta Forna for *Ancestor Stones* (Bloomsbury); (nonfiction) Wangari Maathai for *Unbowed: A Memoir* (Anchor); (poetry) Patricia Smith for *Teahouse of the Almighty* (Coffee House).

Ignatz Awards. To recognize outstanding achievement in comics and cartooning. *Offered by:* SPX cartooning and comics festival. *Winners:* (outstanding artist) Jaime Hernandez for *Love & Rockets* (Fantagraphics); (outstanding anthology or collection) Kevin Huizenga for *Curses* (Drawn & Quarterly); (outstanding graphic novel) Anders Nilsen for *Don't Go Where I Can't Follow* (Drawn & Quarterly); (outstanding series) Kazimir Strzepek for "Mourning Star" (Bodega Distribution); (outstanding comic) Adrian Tomine for *Optic Nerve No. 11* (Drawn & Quarterly).

IMPAC Dublin Literary Award (Ireland). For a book of high literary merit, written in English or translated into English. *Offered by:* IMPAC Corp. and the City of Dublin. *Winner:* Per Petterson and Anne Born (translator, from Norwegian) for *Out Stealing Horses* (Vintage).

IRA Children's and Young Adult Book Awards. For first or second books in any language published for children or young adults. *Offered by:* International Reading Association. *Winners:* (primary, fiction) Mark Rogalski for *Tickets to Ride: An Alphabetical Amusement* (Running Press); (primary, nonfiction) Frank Keating for *Theodore* (Simon & Schuster); (intermediate, fiction) Joyce Moyer Hostetter for

Blue (Boyds Mills); (intermediate, nonfiction) Carla Kilough McClafferty for *Something Out of Nothing* (Farrar, Straus & Giroux); (young adult, fiction) Christopher Grey for *Leonardo's Shadow: Or, My Astonishing Life as Leonardo da Vinci's Servant* (Simon & Schuster); (young adult, nonfiction) Margarita Engle for *The Poet Slave of Cuba: A Biography of Joan Francisco Manzano* (Henry Holt).

Rona Jaffe Writers' Awards. To identify and support women writers of exceptional talent in the early stages of their careers. *Offered by:* Rona Jaffe Foundation. *Winners:* Elif Batuman, Sarah Braunstein, Robin Ekiss, Alma García, Jennifer Grotz, Holly Goddard Jones.

Jerusalem Prize (Israel). To a writer whose works best express the theme of freedom of the individual in society. *Offered by:* Jerusalem International Book Fair. *Winner:* Leszek Kolakowski.

Jewish Cultural Achievement Awards in the Arts Literary Award. *Offered by:* National Foundation for Jewish Culture. *Winner:* Not awarded in 2007.

Samuel Johnson Prize for Nonfiction (United Kingdom). For an outstanding work of nonfiction. *Offered by:* British Broadcasting Corporation. *Winner:* Rajiv Chandrasekaran for *Imperial Life in the Emerald City: Inside Iraq's Green Zone* (Bloomsbury).

Sue Kaufman Prize for First Fiction ($5,000). For a first novel or collection of short stories. *Offered by:* American Academy of Arts and Letters. *Winner:* Tony D'Souza for *Whiteman* (Harvest).

Ezra Jack Keats Awards. For children's picture books. *Offered by:* New York Public Library and the Ezra Jack Keats Foundation. *Winners:* (new writer award) Kelly Cunnane for *For You Are a Kenyan Child,* illustrated by Ana Juan (Athenium); (new illustrator award) Kristen Balouch for *Mystery Bottle* (Hyperion).

Coretta Scott King Awards. For works that promote the cause of peace and brotherhood. *Offered by:* American Library Association, Social Responsibilities Roundtable. *Winners:* (author) Sharon Draper for *Copper Sun* (Simon & Schuster); (illustrator) Kadir Nelson for *Moses: When Harriet Tubman Led Her People to Freedom,* written by Carole Boston Weatherford (Hyperion).

Coretta Scott King/John Steptoe Award for New Talent. To offer visibility to a writer or illustrator at the beginning of a career. *Sponsor:* Coretta Scott King Book Award Committee. *Winner:* Traci L. Jones for *Standing Against the Wind* (Farrar, Straus & Giroux).

Kiriyama Pacific Rim Book Prizes. For a book of fiction or a book of nonfiction that best contributes to a fuller understanding among the nations and peoples of the Pacific Rim. *Offered by:* Kiriyama Pacific Rim Institute. *Winner:* (fiction) Haruki Murakami for *Blind Willow, Sleeping Woman,* translated by Phillip Gabriel and Jay Rubin (Knopf); (nonfiction) Greg Mortenson and David Oliver Relin for *Three Cups of Tea: One Man's Mission to Promote Peace . . . One School at a Time* (Penguin).

Robert Kirsch Award for Lifetime Achievement. To a living author whose residence or focus is the American West, and whose contributions to American letters clearly merit body-of-work recognition. *Offered by: Los Angeles Times. Winner:* William Kittredge.

Lambda Literary Awards. To honor outstanding lesbian, gay, bisexual, and transgendered (LGBT) literature. *Offered by:* Lambda Literary Foundation. *Winners:* (anthology) Greg Herren and Paul J. Willis, eds., for *Love, Bourbon Street* (Alyson); (arts and culture) Lillian Faderman and Stuart Timmons for *Gay L. A.: A History of Sexual Outlaws, Power Politics, and Lipstick Lesbians* (Basic); (bisexual) Michael Szymanski and Nicole Kristal for *The Bisexual's Guide to the Universe* (Alyson); (children's, young adult) David Levithan and Billy Merrell, eds., for *The Full Spectrum* (Random House), Julie Anne Peters for *Between Mom and Jo* (Little Brown); (drama/theater) Tim Miller for *1001 Beds* (University of Wisconsin); (humor) Joe Keenan for *My Lucky Star* (Little Brown); (nonfiction) Lillian Faderman and Stuart Timmons for *Gay L. A.: A History of Sexual Outlaws, Power Politics, and Lipstick Lesbians* (Basic), Marcia Gallo for *Different Daughters* (Carroll & Graf); (LGBT studies) Horace Griffin for *Their Own Receive Them Not* (Pilgrim); (science fiction/fantasy/horror) Neal Drinnan for *Izzy and Eve* (Green Candy); (spirituality) Michael McColly for *The After-Death Room* (Soft Skull); (transgendered) Susan Stryker and Stephen Whittle, eds., for *The Transgender Studies Reader* (Routledge); (lesbian fiction) Sarah Waters for *The Night Watch* (Riverhead); (lesbian romance) Georgia Beers for *Fresh Tracks* (Bold Strokes); (lesbian mystery) Laurie R. King for *The Art of Detection* (Bantam); (lesbian poetry) Sina Queyras for *Lemon Hound* (Coach House); (lesbian memoir/biography) Alison Bechdel for *Fun Home* (Houghton Mifflin); (lesbian erotica) Laurinda D. Brown for *Walk Like a Man* (Q-Boro); (lesbian debut fiction) Ellis Avery for *The Teahouse Fire* (Riverhead); (gay fiction) Robert Westfield for *Suspension* (Harper Perennial); (gay romance) Rob Byrnes for *When the Stars Come Out* (Kensington); (gay mystery) Garry Ryan for *The Lucky Elephant Restaurant* (NeWest); (gay poetry) Jim Elledge for *A History of My Tattoo* (Stonewall); (gay memoir/biography) Bernard Cooper for *The Bill From My Father* (Simon & Schuster); (gay erotica) Jeff Mann for *A History of Barbed Wire* (Suspect Thoughts); (gay debut fiction) Robert Westfield for *Suspension* (Harper Perennial).

Harold Morton Landon Translation Award. For a book of verse translated into English by a single translator. *Offered by:* Academy of American Poets. *Winners:* Robert Fagles for *The Aeneid* by Virgil (Viking), Susanna Nied for *It* by Inger Christensen (New Directions).

Lannan Foundation Literary Awards. To recognize writers who have made significant contributions to English-language literature. *Offered by:* Lannan Foundation. *Winners:* (lifetime achievement) Anne Stevenson; (fiction) A. L. Kennedy, Susan Straight; (nonfiction) Mike Davis.

Lannan Foundation Literary Fellowships. To recognize young and mid-career writers of distinctive literary merit who demonstrate potential for continued outstanding work. *Offered by:* Lannan Foundation. *Winners:* Paula Gunn Allen, Daniel Alarcón, Edie Meidav, Dinaw Mengestu, Sineád Morrissey, Jeremy Scahill.

James Laughlin Award. To commend and support a second book of poetry. *Offered by:* Academy of American Poets. *Winner:* Brenda Shaughnessy for *Human Dark with Sugar* (Copper Canyon).

Ruth Lilly Poetry Prize. To a U.S. poet in recognition of lifetime achievement. *Offered by:* The Poetry Foundation. *Winner:* Lucille Clifton.

Astrid Lindgren Award (Sweden). In memory of Astrid Lindgren to honor outstanding children's literature and efforts to promote it. *Offered by:* Government of Sweden. *Winner:* Banco del Libro of Venezuela.

Locus Awards. For science fiction writing. *Offered by:* Locus Publications. *Winners:* (best novel) Vernor Vinge for *Rainbows End* (Tor); (best fantasy novel) Ellen Kushner for *The Privilege of the Sword* (Bantam Spectra); (best first novel) Naomi Novik for *Temeraire: His Majesty's Dragon/Throne of Jade/Black Powder* (Del Rey, Voyager); (best young adult) Terry Pratchett for *Wintersmith* (Harper); (best novella) Charles Stross for "Missile Gap" (One Million A.D.).

Los Angeles Times Book Prizes. To honor literary excellence. *Offered by: Los Angeles Times. Winners:* (biography) Neal Gabler for *The Triumph of the American Imagination* (Knopf); (current interest) Ian Buruma for *Murder in Amsterdam: The Death of Theo van Gogh and the Limits of Tolerance* (Penguin); (fiction) A. B. Yehoshua for *A Woman in Jerusalem,* translated from Hebrew by Hillel Halkin (Harcourt); (history) Lawrence Wright for *The Looming Tower: Al-Qaeda and the Road to 9/11* (Knopf); (mystery/thriller) Michael Connelly for *Echo Park* (Little, Brown); (poetry) Frederick Seidel for *Ooga-Booga* (Farrar, Straus & Giroux); (science and technology) Eric R. Kandel for *In Search of Memory: The Emergence of a New Science of Mind* (W. W. Norton); (young adult fiction) Coe Booth for *Tyrell* (Scholastic); (Art Seidenbaum Award for First

Fiction) Alice Greenway for *White Ghost Girls* (Grove).

Amy Lowell Poetry Travelling Scholarship. For a U.S. poet to spend one year outside North America in a country the recipient feels will most advance his or her work. *Offered by:* Amy Lowell Poetry Travelling Scholarship. *Winner:* David Roderick.

Anthony J. Lukas Prizes. For nonfiction writing that demonstrates literary grace, serious research, and concern for an important aspect of American social or political life. *Offered by:* Columbia University Graduate School of Journalism and the Nieman Foundation. *Winners:* (book prize) David Maraniss for *They Marched into Sunlight: War and Peace, Vietnam and America, October 1967* (Simon & Schuster); (history prize) Rebecca Solnit for *River of Shadows: Eadweard Muybridge and the Technological Wild West* (Viking); (work-in-progress) John Bowe for *Slavery Inc.*, to be published by Random House.

James Madison Book Award. To honor books representing excellence in bringing knowledge and understanding of American history to children ages 5 to 14. *Offered by:* Lynne Cheney. *Winner:* Joan Dash for *A Dangerous Engine: Benjamin Franklin, from Scientist to Diplomat,* illustrated by Duöan Petricic (Farrar, Straus & Giroux).

Man Asian Literary Prize ($10,000 plus $3,000 for translator, if applicable). For an Asian novel as yet unpublished in English. *Offered by:* Man Group. *Winners:* Jiang Rong and Howard Goldblatt (translator, from Chinese) for *Wolf Totem* (Penguin).

Man Booker International Literary Prize (United Kingdom). For a significant contribution to world literature. *Offered by:* Man Group. *Winner:* Chinua Achebe.

Man Booker Prize for Fiction (United Kingdom). For the best novel written in English by a Commonwealth author. *Offered by:* Booktrust and the Man Group. *Winner:* Anne Enright for *The Gathering* (Cape).

Lenore Marshall Poetry Prize. For an outstanding book of poems published in the United States. *Offered by:* Academy of American Poets. *Winner:* Alice Notley for *Grave of Light: New and Selected Poems 1970–2005* (Wesleyan).

Addison M. Metcalf Award. To a young writer of great promise. *Offered by:* American Academy of Arts and Letters. *Winner:* Suji Kwock Kim.

Vicky Metcalf Award for Children's Literature (Canada). To a Canadian writer of children's literature for a body of work. *Offered by:* George Cedric Metcalf Foundation. *Winner:* Kenneth Oppel.

Gustavus Myers Awards. For outstanding books that extend understanding of the root causes of bigotry. *Offered by:* Gustavus Myers Center for the Study of Bigotry and Human Rights in North America. *Winners:* Kenny Frie for *The History of My Shoes and the Evolution of Darwin's Theory* (Carroll & Graf); Saidiya Hartman for *Lose Your Mother: A Journey Along the Atlantic Slave Route* (Farrar, Straus & Giroux); INCITE! Women of Color Against Violence, eds., for *The Revolution Will Not Be Funded: Beyond the Non-Profit Industrial Complex* (South End); Sara Littlecrow-Russell for *The Secret Powers of Naming* (University of Arizona); Tina Lopes and Barb Thomas for *Dancing on Live Embers: Challenging Racism in Organizations* (Between the Lines); Micki McElya for *Clinging to Mammy: The Faithful Slave in Twentieth-Century America* (Harvard University); Steven Salaita for *Anti-Arab Racism in the USA: Where It Comes From and What It Means for Politics Today* (Pluto); Alex Sanchez for *Getting It* (Simon & Schuster); Chip Smith for *The Cost of Privilege: Taking on the System of White Supremacy and Racism* (Camino); Harriet A. Washington for *Medical Apartheid: The Dark History of Medical Experimentation on Black Americans from Colonial Times to the Present* (Doubleday).

Midwest Booksellers Choice Awards. *Offered by:* Midwest Booksellers Association. *Winners:* (fiction) Sara Gruen for *Water for Elephants* (Algonquin); (nonfiction) Michael Perry for *Truck: A Love Story* (HarperCollins); (poetry) Ted Kooser for *The Blizzard Voices* (University of Nebraska); (children's picture book) Kevin Henkes for *A Good Day* (HarperCollins); (children's literature) Catherine Gilbert

Murdock for *Dairy Queen* (Houghton Mifflin).

Moonbeam Children's Book Awards. To honor the year's best children's books, authors, and illustrators. *Offered by:* Jenkins Group and Independent Publisher Online. *Winners:* (board book) Fran Hodgkins and Laura J. Bryant, illustrator, for *If You Were My Baby: A Wildlife Lullaby* (Dawn); (alphabet/counting book) Claudia McGehee for *A Woodland Counting Book* (University of Iowa); (pop-up/cut-out) Jason O'Malley and Bruce Foster for *Halloween at the Zoo: A Pop-Up Trick-or-Treat Experience* (Jumping Jack); (activity book) Pam Abrams and Melissa Punch, photographer, for *Gadgetology: Kitchen Fun with Your Kids* (Harvard Common); (book with music/theatrical) Steve Van Zandt with the Banana Slug String Band and Katherine Zecca, illustrator, for *River Song* (Dawn); (audiobook) *The One and Only Shrek!* by William Steig, read by Meryl Streep and Stanley Tucci (Audio Renaissance); (picture book, preschool) Amy and Ashleigh Kieliszewski and Twila Jefferson, illustrator, for *Ashleigh's Fairies* (Ashleigh Marie); (picture book, ages 4 to 8) Janet Ruth Heller and Ben Hodson, illustrator, for *How the Moon Regained Her Shape* (Sylvan Dell); (picture book, all ages) Peggy Moss, Dee Dee Tardif, and Alissa Imre Geis, illustrator, for *Our Friendship Rules* (Tilbury House); (juvenile fiction, early reader) Sandra J. Philipson and Jenny Campbell, illustrator, for *Forever Home* (Chagrin River); (pre-teen fiction, intermediate) Karen Pavlicin for *Perch, Mrs. Sackets, and Crow's Nest* (Alma Little); (young adult fiction) Sheryl McFarlane *The Smell of Paint* (Fitzhenry & Whiteside); (young adult fiction, mature issues) Maureen Hull for *The View From a Kite* (Nimbus); (nonfiction, picture book) Jennifer Elder and Marc Thomas, illustrator, for *Autistic Planet* (Jessica Kingsley); (nonfiction, young adult) Marv Wolfman, Mario Ruiz, and William J. Rubin for *Homeland: The Illustrated History of the State of Israel* (Nachshon); (multicultural, picture book) Deirdre McLaughlin Mercier for *Yesterday We Had a Hurricane (Ayer*

Tuvimos un Huracán) (Bumble Bee); (multicultural fiction) Ellen S. Jaffe for *Feast of Lights* (Sumach); (multicultural nonfiction) Donald F. Montileaux, illustrator, for *Tatanka and the Lakota People: A Creation Story* (South Dakota State Historical Society); (comic/graphic novel) Shaun Tan for *The Arrival* (Hachette Livre Australia); (religion/spirituality) Sally Lloyd-Jones and Jago, illustrator, for *The Jesus Storybook Bible* (Zonderkidz); (holiday) Merrily Kutner and Ethan Long, illustrator, for *The Zombie Night Café* (Holiday House); (book with merchandise) Ellen Bryant Lloyd and Carol Schwartz, illustrator, for *Freckles and the Great Beach Rescue* (Butterfly Creations); (best first book) Michael DiLorenzo for *Adventures with Jonny: Let's Go Fishing!* (Running Moose); (best illustrator) Becky Kelly for *Heavenly Skies and Lullabies* (Llumina); (best book promoting world peace and human tolerance) Carrie Brown-Wolf for *Soul Sunday: A Family's Guide to Exploring Faith and Teaching Tolerance* (TEO Summit); (best book promoting environmental awareness) Sarah Stiles Bright and Gustav Moore, illustrator, for *Wind Bird: Gift of the Mist* (Maine Lakes Conservancy Institute); (best book promoting awareness of childhood disease or special needs) Dina Zeckhausen and Brian Boyd, illustrator, for *Full Mouse, Empty Mouse: A Tale of Food and Feelings* (Magination).

National Book Awards. For the best books of the year published in the United States. *Offered by:* National Book Foundation. *Winners:* (fiction) Denis Johnson for *Tree of Smoke* (Farrar, Straus & Giroux); (nonfiction) Tim Weiner for *Legacy of Ashes: The History of the C.I.A.* (Doubleday); (poetry) Robert Hass for *Time and Materials* (HarperCollins); (young people's literature) Sherman Alexie for *The Absolutely True Diary of a Part-Time Indian* (Little, Brown).

National Book Critics Circle Awards. For literary excellence. *Offered by:* National Book Critics Circle. *Winners:* (fiction) Kiran Desai for *The Inheritance of Loss* (Atlantic Monthly); (nonfiction) Simon

Schama for *Rough Crossings: Britain, the Slaves and the American Revolution* (Ecco); (biography) Julie Phillips for *James Tiptree, Jr.: The Double Life of Alice B. Sheldon* (St. Martin's); (criticism) Lawrence Weschler for *Everything That Rises: A Book of Convergences* (McSweeney's); (poetry) Troy Jollimore for *Tom Thomson in Purgatory* (Intuit House); (memoir/autobiography) Daniel Mendelsohn for *The Lost: A Search for Six of Six Million* (HarperCollins); (Nora Balakian Citation for Excellence in Reviewing) Steven Kellman; (Ivan Sandrof Lifetime Achievement Award) John Leonard.

National Book Foundation Literarian Award for Outstanding Service to the American Literary Community. *Offered by:* National Book Foundation. *Winner:* Terry Gross.

National Book Foundation Medal for Distinguished Contribution to American Letters. To a person who has enriched the nation's literary heritage over a life of service or corpus of work. *Offered by:* National Book Foundation. *Winner:* Joan Didion.

National Translation Award. To honor a translator whose work has made the most valuable contribution to literary translation into English. *Offered by:* American Literary Translators Association. *Winner:* Joel Agee for *Friedrich Dürrenmatt: Selected Writings* (University of Chicago).

NCTE Orbis Pictus Award. For outstanding nonfiction for children. *Offered by:* National Council of Teachers of English. *Winner:* Sy Montgomery for *Quest for the Tree Kangaroo: An Expedition to the Cloud Forest of New Guinea* (Houghton).

Nebula Awards. For science fiction writing. *Offered by:* Science Fiction and Fantasy Writers of America. *Winners:* (best novel) Jack McDevitt for *Seeker* (Ace); (best novella) James Patrick Kelly for "Burn" (Tachyon); (best novelette) Peter S. Beagle for "Two Hearts" (F&SF); (Andre Norton Award for Young Adult Science Fiction and Fantasy) Justine Larbalestier for *Magic or Madness* (Razorbill); (grand master) James Gunn.

Nereus Writers' Trust Nonfiction Prize (Canada). *Offered by:* Writers' Trust and Nereus Financial. *Winner:* Dragan Todorovic for *The Book of Revenge: A Blues for Yugoslavia* (Random House).

Nestlé Children's Book Prizes (formerly Smarties Book Prizes) (United Kingdom). To encourage high standards and to stimulate interest in books for children. *Offered by:* Nestlé UK Ltd. *Winners:* (9–11 years) Matt Haig for *Shadow Forest* (Bodley Head); (6–8 years) Chris Riddell for *Ottoline and the Yellow Cat* (Macmillan); (5 and younger) Sean Taylor and Nick Sharratt, illustrator, for *When a Monster is Born* (Orchard).

John Newbery Medal. For the most distinguished contribution to literature for children. *Offered by:* American Library Association, Association for Library Service to Children. *Winner:* Susan Patron for *The Higher Power of Lucky*, illustrated by Matt Phelan (Simon & Schuster).

Nimrod/Hardman Katherine Anne Porter Award. To a prose writer of demonstrated achievement. *Offered by:* American Academy of Arts and Letters. *Winner:* Carol Roh-Spaulding.

Nobel Prize in Literature (Sweden). For the total literary output of a distinguished career. *Offered by:* Swedish Academy. *Winner:* Doris Lessing.

Flannery O'Connor Awards for Short Fiction. For collections of short fiction. *Offered by:* University of Georgia Press. *Winners:* Peter LaSalle for *Tell Borges If You See Him* (University of Georgia); Anne Panning for *Super America* (University of Georgia); Margot Singer for *The Pale of Settlement* (University of Georgia).

Scott O'Dell Award. For historical fiction. *Offered by:* Bulletin of the Center for Children's Books, University of Chicago. *Winner:* Ellen Klages for *The Green Glass Sea* (Viking).

Orange Broadband Prize for Fiction (United Kingdom). For the best novel written by a woman and published in the United Kingdom. *Offered by:* Orange plc. *Winner:* Chimamanda Ngozi Adichie for *Half of a Yellow Sun* (Knopf).

Orange Broadband Award for New Writers (United Kingdom). For a first novel or short story collection written by a woman and published in the United Kingdom.

Offered by: Orange plc. *Winner:* Karen Connelly for *The Lizard Cage* (Harvill Secker).

Pegasus Awards. For outstanding works of poetry. *Offered by:* The Poetry Foundation. (Neglected Master Award, $50,000), for the life's work of a significant but under-recognized American poet. *Winner:* Anne Stevenson; (Emily Dickinson First Book Award, $10,000), to a writer over the age of 50 who has never published a book. *Winner:* Brian Culhane; (Randall Jarrell Award in Poetry Criticism, $10,000). *Winner:* Herbert Leibowitz; (Verse Drama Prize, $10,000) to honor a living poet who has written a previously unpublished, outstanding original verse drama in English. *Winner:* John Surowiecki.

PEN/Saul Bellow Award for Achievement in American Fiction. To a distinguished living American author of fiction. *Offered by:* PEN American Center. *Winner:* Philip Roth.

PEN Award for Poetry in Translation. For a book-length translation of poetry from any language into English and published in the United States. *Offered by:* PEN American Center. *Winner:* David Hinton for his translation from Chinese of *The Selected Poems of Wang Wei* (New Directions).

PEN Beyond Margins Awards. For book-length writings by authors of color, published in the United States during the current calendar year. *Offered by:* PEN American Center. *Winners:* Chimamanda Ngozi Adichie for her novel *Half of a Yellow Sun;* Ernest Hardy for his essay collection *Blood Beats, Vol. 1;* Harryette Mullen for her poetry anthology *Recyclopedia;* Alberto Ríos for his poetry collection *Theater of Night.*

PEN/Robert Bingham Fellowship. To a writer whose first novel or short story collection represents distinguished literary achievement and suggests great promise. *Offered by:* PEN American Center. *Winner:* Janna Levin for *A Madman Dreams of Turing Machines* (Knopf).

PEN Book-of-the-Month Club Translation Prize. For a book-length literary translation from any language into English. *Offered by:* PEN American Center. *Win-ner:* Sandra Smith for her translation from French of Irène Némirovsky's *Suite Française* (Knopf).

PEN/Faulkner Award for Fiction. To honor the best work of fiction published by an American. *Winner:* Philip Roth for *Everyman* (Houghton Mifflin).

PEN/John Kenneth Galbraith Award. To a distinguished book of general nonfiction. *Offered by:* PEN American Center. *Winner:* James Carroll for *House of War* (Houghton Mifflin).

PEN/Nora Magid Award. To honor a magazine editor whose high literary standards and taste have contributed significantly to the excellence of the publication he or she edits. *Offered by:* PEN American Center. *Winner:* Bradford Morrow, editor of *Conjunctions.*

PEN/Malamud Award. To an author who has demonstrated long-term excellence in short fiction. *Offered by:* PEN American Center. *Winner:* Elizabeth Spencer.

PEN/Nabokov Award. To celebrate the accomplishments of a living author whose body of work, either written in or translated into English, represents achievement in a variety of literary genres. *Offered by:* PEN American Center. *Winner:* Not awarded in 2007.

PEN/Phyllis Naylor Working Writer Fellowship. *Offered by:* PEN American Center. *Winner:* Diane Les Becquets.

PEN/Joyce Osterweil Award for Poetry. To recognize a new and emerging American poet. *Offered by:* PEN American Center. *Winner:* Peter Covino for *Cut Off the Ears of Winter* (New Issues).

PEN/Laura Pels Foundation Awards for Drama. To recognize a master American dramatist and an American playwright in mid-career. *Offered by:* PEN American Center. *Winners:* (dramatist) A. R. Gurney; (playwright) Naomi Iizuka.

PEN Prison Writing Awards. To provide support and encouragement to prison inmates whose writing shows merit or promise. *Offered by:* PEN American Center. *Winners:* (fiction) Clifford Barnes for "Confessions of a Jack-Off Artist;" (poetry) Steven Bulleit for "Doing Time;" (nonfiction) J. E. Wantz for "Feeling(s) Cheated;"

(memoir) Christina MacNaughton for "Just Another Death"; (drama) Keith Sanders for "A Time to Forget."

PEN Translation Fund grants. To promote the publication and reception of translated world literature in English. *Winners:* Susan Bernofsky for her translation from German of Robert Walser's 1908 novel *The Assistant* (New Directions); Jennifer Hayashida for her translation from Swedish of *Clockwork of Flowers: Explanations and Poems* by Fredrik Nyberg; Wen Huang for his translation from Chinese of *Farewell to Jiabiangou,* a collection of short stories by Yang Xianhui; Ha-yun Jung for her translation from Korean of *A Lone Room,* a novel by Shin Kyong-sook; Sara Khalili for her translation from Farsi of *Seasons of Purgatory,* a selection of short stories by Shahriar Mandanipour; Paul Olchváry for his translation from Hungarian of *The Ninth,* a novel by Ferenc Barnás; Bill Porter (Red Pine) for his translation from classical Chinese of an anthology of the poems of Wei Ying-wu (Copper Canyon); Katherine Silver for her translation from Spanish of *Senselessness* by Horacio Castellanos Moya (New Directions); Christopher Southward for his translation from Japanese of *Acacia,* short stories by Hitonari Tsuji; Alyson Waters for her translation from French of *The Colors of Infamy,* a novel by Albert Cossery.

PEN/Voelcker Award for Poetry. To an American poet at the height of his or her powers. *Offered by:* PEN American Center. *Winner:* Not awarded in 2007.

Maxwell E. Perkins Award. To honor an editor, publisher, or agent who has discovered, nurtured, and championed writers of fiction in the United States. *Offered by:* Mercantile Library of New York. *Winner:* Drenka Willen.

Edgar Allan Poe Awards. For outstanding mystery, suspense, and crime writing. *Offered by:* Mystery Writers of America. *Winners:* (novel) Jason Goodwin for *The Janissary Tree* (Farrar, Straus & Giroux); (first novel by an American author) Alex Berenson for *The Faithful Spy* (Random House); (paperback original) Naomi Hirahara for *Snakeskin Shamisen* (Bantam

Dell); (critical/biographical) E. J. Wagner for *The Science of Sherlock Holmes: From Baskerville Hall to the Valley of Fear* (Wiley); (fact crime) James L. Swanson for *Manhunt: The 12-Day Chase for Lincoln's Killer* (HarperCollins); (best young adult) Robin Merrow MacCready for *Buried* (Penguin); (best juvenile) Andrew Clements for *Room One: A Mystery or Two* (Simon & Schuster); (grand master) Stephen King; (Simon & Schuster–Mary Higgins Clark Award) Fiona Mountain for *Bloodline* (St. Martin's).

Michael L. Printz Award. For excellence in literature for young adults. *Offered by:* American Library Association, Young Adult Library Services Association. *Winner:* Gene Luen Yang for the graphic novel *American Born Chinese* (Roaring Brook).

V. S. Pritchett Memorial Prize (United Kingdom) (£1,000). For a previously unpublished short story. *Offered by:* Royal Society of Literature. *Winner:* Gabriela Blandy for "The Buck."

Prix Goncourt (France). For "the best imaginary prose work of the year." *Offered by:* Société des Gens des Lettres. *Winner:* Gilles Leroy for *Alabama Song* (Gallimard).

Pulitzer Prizes in Letters. To honor distinguished work by American writers, dealing preferably with American themes. *Offered by:* Columbia University Graduate School of Journalism. *Winners:* (fiction) Cormac McCarthy for *The Road* (Knopf); (history) Gene Roberts and Hank Klibanoff for *The Race Beat* (Knopf); (biography) Debby Applegate for *The Most Famous Man in America* (Doubleday); (poetry) Natasha Trethewey for *Native Guard* (Houghton Mifflin); (general nonfiction) Lawrence Wright for *The Looming Tower* (Knopf).

Quill Awards. To honor excellence in book publishing. *Offered by:* Reed Business Information and the NBC Universal Television Stations. *Winners:* (debut author of the year) Diane Setterfield for *The Thirteenth Tale* (Atria); (general fiction) Cormac McCarthy for *The Road* (Knopf); (romance) Nora Roberts for *Angels Fall*

(Putnam); (religion/spirituality) Stephen Prothero for *Religious Literacy: What Every American Needs to Know—and Doesn't* (Harper); (graphic novel) Scott McCloud for *Making Comics: Storytelling Secrets of Comics, Manga, and Graphic Novels* (Harper); (poetry) Kevin Young for *For the Confederate Dead* (Knopf); (cooking) Irma S. Rombauer, Marion Rombauer Becker, and Ethan Becker for *Joy of Cooking: 75th Anniversary Edition* (Scribner); (health/self-improvement) Jerome Groopman, M.D., for *How Doctors Think* (Houghton Mifflin); (biography/memoir) Walter Isaacson for *Einstein: His Life and Universe* (Simon & Schuster); (sports) Michael Weinreb for *The Kings of New York: A Year Among the Geeks, Oddballs, and Geniuses Who Make Up America's Top High School Chess Team* (Gotham); (humor) Amy Sedaris for *I Like You: Hospitality Under the Influence* (Warner); (history/current events/politics) Al Gore for *The Assault on Reason* (Penguin); (business) Robert I. Sutton for *The No Asshole Rule: Building a Civilized Workplace and Surviving One That Isn't* (Grand Central); (mystery/suspense) Laura Lippman for *What the Dead Know* (William Morrow); (science fiction/fantasy/horror) Patrick Rothfuss for *The Name of the Wind (The Kingkiller Chronicle: Day One)* (DAW); (children's picture books) David Wiesner for *Flotsam* (Houghton Mifflin); children's chapter books/middle grade) Brian Selznick for *The Invention of Hugo Cabret* (Scholastic); (young adult/teen) Patricia McCormick for *Sold* (Hyperion); (best audiobook) *To Kill a Mockingbird* by Harper Lee, read by Sissy Spacek (Caedmon Audio).

Raiziss/De Palchi Translation Award. For a translation into English of a significant work of modern Italian poetry by a living translator. *Offered by:* Academy of American Poets. *Winner:* Adria Bernardi for *Small Talk* by Rafaello Baldini.

Rea Award for the Short Story. To honor a living writer who has made a significant contribution to the short story as an art form. *Offered by:* Dungannon Foundation. *Winner:* Stuart Dybek.

Arthur Rense Poetry Prize. To an exceptional poet. *Offered by:* American Academy of Arts and Letters. *Winner:* To be awarded next in 2008.

John Llewellyn Rhys Prize (United Kingdom) (£5,000). For a work of literature by a British or Commonwealth author 35 or younger and published in the United Kingdom. *Offered by:* Booktrust. *Winner:* Sarah Hall for *The Carhullan Army* (Faber & Faber).

Rita Awards. *Offered by:* Romance Writers of America. *Winners:* (best traditional romance) Barbara Hannay for *Claiming His Family* (Harlequin); (best long contemporary romance) Lori Handeland for *The Mommy Quest* (Harlequin); (best romantic novella) Roxanne St. Claire for "'Tis the Silly Season" in *A NASCAR Holiday* (Harlequin); (best short historical romance) Betina Krahn for *The Book of True Desires* (Berkley); (best contemporary single title) Caridad Ferrer for *Adiós to My Old Life* (Pocket Books); (best long historical romance) Julia Quinn for *On the Way to the Wedding* (Avon); (best short contemporary romance) Jessica Bird for *From the First* (Harlequin); (best paranormal romance) Kresley Cole for *A Hunger Like No Other* (Pocket Books); (best romantic suspense) Annie Solomon for *Blackout* (Warner); (best inspirational romance) Tamera Alexander for *Revealed* (Bethany House); (best novel with strong romantic elements) Jennifer Ashley, writing as Laurien Gardner, for *A Lady Raised High: A Novel of Anne Boleyn* (Jove); (best first book) Tracy Anne Warren for *The Husband Trap* (Ballantine); (lifetime achievement) Linda Lael Miller.

Rodda Book Award. To recognize a book that exhibits excellence in writing and has contributed significantly to congregational libraries through promotion of spiritual growth. The award is given to books for adults, young adults, and children on a three-year-rotational basis. *Offered by:* Church and Synagogue Library Association. *Winner:* (young adult) Caroline B. Cooney for *A Friend At Midnight* (Delacourt).

Rogers Writers' Trust Fiction Prize (Canada). To a Canadian author of a novel or short story collection. *Offered by:* Rogers Communications. *Winner:* Kenneth J. Harvey for *Inside* (Random House).

Sami Rohr Prize for Jewish Literature ($100,000). *Offered by:* Family of Sami Rohr. *Winner:* Tamar Yellin for *The Genizah at the House of Shepher* (Toby).

Richard and Hinda Rosenthal Foundation Award ($5,000). For a work of fiction that is a considerable literary achievement though not necessarily a commercial success. *Offered by:* American Academy of Arts and Letters. *Winner:* Dana Spiotta for *Eat the Document* (Scribner).

Royal Society of Literature/Jerwood Awards for Nonfiction (United Kingdom). For authors engaged on their first major commissioned works of nonfiction. *Offered by:* Royal Society of Literature. *Winners:* Andrew Stott for a biography of the Regency clown Joseph Grimaldi, to be published by Canongate; Rachel Campbell-Johnston, for a biography of the artist Samuel Palmer, to be published by Bloomsbury; Daniel Swift for *A Terrible Fury,* on the bombing campaigns of World War II, to be published by Hamish Hamilton.

Royal Society of Literature Ondaatje Prize. For a distinguished work of fiction, nonfiction or poetry, evoking the spirit of a place. *Offered by:* Royal Society of Literature. *Winner:* Hisham Matar for his novel *In the Country of Men* (Dial).

Juan Rulfo International Latin American and Caribbean Prize (FIL Literature Prize) (Mexico) ($100,000). For lifetime achievement in any literary genre. *Offered by:* Juan Rulfo International Latin American and Caribbean Prize Committee. *Winner:* Fernando del Paso.

John Sargent, Sr. First Novel Prize. *Offered by:* Mercantile Library Center for Fiction. *Winner:* Junot Diaz for *The Brief Wondrous Life of Oscar Wao* (Riverhead/Penguin).

Schneider Family Book Awards. To honor authors and illustrators for books that embody artistic expressions of the disability experience of children and adolescents. *Offered by:* American Library Association.

Winners: (ages 0–10) Peter Seeger, Paul DuBois Jacobs, and R. Gregory Christie (illustrator) for *The Deaf Musicians* (Putnam); (ages 11–13) Cynthia Lord for *Rules* (Scholastic); (ages 13–18) Louis Sachar for *Small Steps* (Delacorte).

Shelley Memorial Award. To a poet living in the United States who is chosen on the basis of genius and need. *Offered by:* Poetry Society of America. *Winner:* Kimiko Hahn.

Robert F. Sibert Award. For the most distinguished informational book for children. *Offered by:* American Library Association, Association for Library Service to Children. *Winner:* Catherine Thimmesh for *Team Moon: How 400,000 People Landed Apollo 11 on the Moon* (Houghton).

WHSmith Literary Award: To the author whose book makes, in the opinion of the judges, the most significant contribution to literature. *Offered by:* WHSmith, plc. *Winner:* J. K. Rowling for *Harry Potter and the Half-Blood Prince* (Scholastic).

Spur Awards. *Offered by:* Western Writers of America. *Winners:* (best long novel) Elizabeth Crook for *The Night Journal* (Viking/Penguin); (best short novel) Tony Hillerman for *The Shape Shifter* (HarperCollins); (best original paperback novel) Dusty Richards for *The Horse Creek Incident* (Jove); (best first novel) Alan Geoffrion for *Broken Trail* (Fulcrum); (best nonfiction–historical) Hampton Sides for *Blood and Thunder: An Epic of the American West* (Doubleday); (best nonfiction–contemporary): Dennis L. Swibold for *Copper Chorus: Mining, Politics and the Montana Press, 1889–1959* (Montana Historical Society); (best nonfiction–biography) Kingsley M. Bray for *Crazy Horse: A Lakota Life* (University of Oklahoma); (best juvenile fiction) Joseph Bruchac for *Geronimo* (Scholastic); (best juvenile nonfiction) Jeff C. Young for *Bleeding Kansas and the Violent Clash Over Slavery in the Heartland* (Enslow); (poetry) Laurie Wagner Buyer for *Across the High Divide* (Ghost Road); (audiobook) Michael Johnson for *Healing Shine* (Season of Harvest).

Wallace Stevens Award. To recognize outstanding and proven mastery in the art of poetry. *Offered by:* Academy of American Poets. *Winner:* Charles Simic.

Bram Stoker Awards. For superior horror writing. *Offered by:* Horror Writers Association. *Winners:* (best novel) Stephen King for *Lisey's Story* (Scribner); (best first novel) Jonathan Maberry for *Ghost Road Blues* (Pinnacle); (best anthology) (tie) Joe Lansdale, ed., for *Retro Pulp Tales* (Subterranean) and John Skipp, ed., for *Mondo Zombie* (Cemetery Dance); (best nonfiction) (tie) Michael Largo for *Final Exits: The Illustrated Encyclopedia of How We Die* (Harper) and Kim Paffenroth for *Gospel of the Living Dead: George Romero's Visions of Hell on Earth* (Baylor); (best poetry collection) Bruce Boston for *Shades Fantastic* (Gromagon); (lifetime achievement) Thomas Harris.

Stonewall Book Awards. *Offered by:* Gay, Lesbian, Bisexual, and Transgendered Round Table, American Library Association. *Winners:* (Barbara Gittings Literature Award) Andrew Holleran for *Grief* (Hyperion); (Israel Fishman Nonfiction Award) Alison Bechdel for *Fun Home: A Family Tragicomic* (Houghton Mifflin).

The Story Prize. For a collection of short fiction. *Offered by: Story* magazine. *Winner:* Mary Gordon for *The Stories of Mary Gordon* (Pantheon).

Tanizaki Prize (Japan). Winner: Ogawa Yoko for *Meena's March.*

Charles Taylor Prize for Literary Nonfiction (Canada). To honor a book of creative nonfiction widely available in Canada and written by a Canadian citizen or landed immigrant. *Offered by:* Charles Taylor Foundation. *Winner:* Rudy Weibe for *Of This Earth: A Mennonite Boyhood in the Boreal Forest* (Knopf).

Sydney Taylor Children's Book Awards. For a distinguished contribution to Jewish children's literature. *Offered by:* Association of Jewish Libraries. *Winners:* (younger readers) Sarah Gershman for *The Bedtime Sh'ma: A Good Night Book,* illustrated by Kristina Swarner (EKS); (older readers) Sid Fleischman for *The Entertainer and the Dybbuk* (HarperCollins); (teen readers) Sonia Levitin for *Strange Relations* (Knopf).

Dylan Thomas Prize (United Kingdom) (£60,000). Awarded biennially for the year's best eligible commercially published work of literature. *Offered by:* David Cohen Family Charitable Trust and the Arts Council of England. *Winner:* Not awarded in 2007.

Thriller Awards. *Offered by:* International Thriller Writers. *Winners:* (best novel) Joseph Finder for *Killer Instinct* (St. Martin's); (best first novel) Nick Stone for *Mr. Clarinet* (HarperCollins); (best paperback original) P. J. Parrish for *An Unquiet Grave* (Pinnacle).

Thurber Prize. For a humorous book of fiction or nonfiction. *Offered by:* Thurber House. *Winner:* Joe Keenan for *My Lucky Star* (Back Bay).

Betty Trask Prize (United Kingdom). To a Commonwealth writer under the age of 35 for a "romantic or traditional" first novel. *Offered by:* Society of Authors. *Winner:* Will Davis for *My Side of the Story* (Bloomsbury).

Kate Tufts Discovery Award. For a first or very early book of poetry by an emerging poet. *Offered by:* Claremont Graduate School. *Winner:* Eric McHenry for *Potscrubber Lullabies* (Waywiser).

Kingsley Tufts Poetry Award. For a book of poetry by a mid-career poet. *Offered by:* Claremont Graduate School. *Winner:* Rodney G. Jones for *Salvation Blues: 100 Poems, 1985–2005* (Houghton Mifflin).

Harold D. Vursell Memorial Award ($10,000). To a writer whose work merits recognition for its prose style. *Offered by:* American Academy of Arts and Letters. *Winner:* Amy Hempel.

George Washington Book Prize. To recognize published works about George Washington or the founding era. *Offered by:* Washington College and the Gilder Lehman Institute of American History. *Winner:* Charles Rappleye for *Sons of Providence: The Brown Brothers, the Slave Trade, and the American Revolution* (Simon & Schuster).

Whitbread Literary Awards (United Kingdom). See Costa Book Awards.

Whiting Writers' Awards ($50,000). For emerging writers of exceptional talent and promise. *Offered by:* Mrs. Giles Whiting Foundation. *Winners:* (fiction) Ben Fountain, Brad Kessler, Dalia Sofer; (nonfiction) Carlo Rotella, Peter Trachtenberg, Jack Turner; (plays) Sheila Callaghan, Tarell Alvin McCraney; (poetry) Paul Guest, Cate Marvin.

Walt Whitman Award. To a U.S. poet who has not published a book of poems in a standard edition. *Offered by:* Academy of American Poets. *Winner:* Sally Van Doren for *Sex at Noon Taxes* (LSU Press).

Laura Ingalls Wilder Award. For an author or illustrator whose books have made a substantial and lasting contribution to children's literature. *Offered by:* American Library Association, Association for Library Service to Children. *Winner:* James Marshall.

Robert H. Winner Memorial Award. To a mid-career poet over 40 who has published no more than one book of poetry. *Offered by:* Poetry Society of America. *Winner:* Charlene Fix.

L. L. Winship Award. For a book of fiction, poetry, or creative nonfiction with a New England subject or written by a New England author. *Offered by:* PEN New England. *Winners:* (fiction) K. C. Frederick for *Inland* (Permanent); (poetry) Louise Glück for *Averno* (Farrar, Straus & Giroux); (nonfiction) Sebastian Junger for *A Death in Belmont* (W. W. Norton).

George Wittenborn Memorial Book Awards. To North American art publications that represent the highest standards of content, documentation, layout, and format. *Offered by:* Art Libraries Society of North America (ARLIS/NA). *Winners:* John Oliver Hand, Catherine A. Metzger, and Ron Spronk for *Prayers and Portraits: Unfolding the Netherlandish Diptych* (Yale University); Mike Cowdrey, Ned Martin, and Jody Martin for *American Indian Horse Masks* (Hawk Hill).

Thomas Wolfe Award. To honor writers with distinguished bodies of work. *Offered by:* Thomas Wolfe Society and University of North Carolina at Chapel Hill. *Winner:* Reynolds Price.

Helen and Kurt Wolff Translator's Prize. For an outstanding translation from German into English, published in the United States. *Offered by:* Goethe Institut Inter Nationes, Chicago. *Winner:* Peter Constantine for *Der Vogel Ist ein Rabe* (*The Bird Is a Raven*) by Benjamin Leberts (Knopf).

World Fantasy Convention Awards. For outstanding fantasy writing. *Offered by:* World Fantasy Convention. *Winners:* (novel) Gene Wolfe for *Soldier of Sidon* (Tor); (novella) Jeffrey Ford for "Botch Town" in *The Empire of Ice Cream* (Golden Gryphon); (short fiction) M. Rickert for *Journey Into the Kingdom* (Farrar, Straus & Giroux); (anthology), Ellen Datlow and Terri Windling, eds., for *Salon Fantastique* (Thunder's Mouth); (collection) M. Rickert for *Map of Dreams* (Golden Gryphon); (lifetime achievement) Betty Ballantine, Diana Wynne Jones.

Writers' Trust of Canada/McClelland & Stewart Journey Prize (Canada). To a new, developing Canadian author for a short story or an excerpt from a novel-in-progress. *Offered by:* McClelland & Stewart and James A. Michener. *Winner:* Heather Birrell for "BriannaSusannaAlana," published in *New Quarterly.*

Young Lions Fiction Award. For a novel or collection of short stories by an American under the age of 35. *Offered by:* Young Lions of the New York Public Library. *Winner:* Olga Grushin for *The Dream Life of Sukhanov* (Putnam).

Morton Dauwen Zabel Award. To a progressive and experimental writer. *Offered by:* American Academy of Arts and Letters. *Winner:* Not awarded in 2007.

Charlotte Zolotow Award. To the author of the best children's picture book published in the United States in the previous year. *Offered by:* Cooperative Children's Book Center, University of Wisconsin–Madison. *Winner:* Peter McCarty for *Moon Plane* (Henry Holt).

Part 6
Directory of Organizations

Directory of Library and Related Organizations

Networks, Consortia, and Other Cooperative Library Organizations

United States

Alabama

Alabama Health Libraries Association Inc. (ALHeLa), Baugh Biomedical Lib., Mobile 36688-0002. SAN 372-8218. Tel. 251-460-6893, fax 251-460-7638. *Head, Collection Management.* Ellen N. Sayed.

Jefferson County Hospital Librarians Association, Brookwood Medical Center, Birmingham 35209. SAN 371-2168. Tel. 205-877-1131, fax 205-877-1267.

Library Management Network, Inc. (LMN), 2132 Sixth Ave. S.E., Ste. 106, Decatur 35601. SAN 322-3906. Tel. 256-308-2529, fax 256-308-2533. *System Coord.* Charlotte Moncrief.

Marine Environmental Sciences Consortium, Dauphin Island Sea Lab, Dauphin Island 36528. SAN 322-0001. Tel. 251-861-2141, fax 251-861-4646, e-mail disl@disl.org. *Dir.* George Crozier.

Network of Alabama Academic Libraries, c/o Alabama Commission on Higher Education, Montgomery 36104. SAN 322-4570. Tel. 334-242-2211, fax 334-242-0270. *Dir.* Sue O. Medina.

Alaska

Alaska Library Network (ALN), 344 W. 3 Ave., Ste. 125, Anchorage 99501. SAN 371-0688. Tel. 907-269-6570, fax 907-269-6580, e-mail aslanc@eed.state.ak.us.

Arizona

Maricopa County Community College District/Library Technology Services, 2411 W. 14th St., Tempe 85281-6942. SAN 322-0060. Tel. 480-731-8774, fax 480-731-8787. *Dir. of Technology* Thom Saudargas.

Arkansas

Arkansas Area Health Education Center Consortium (AHEC), Sparks Regional Medical Center, Fort Smith 72901-4992. SAN 329-3734. Tel. 479-441-5337, fax 479-441-5339. *Dir.* Grace Anderson.

Arkansas Independent Colleges and Universities, 1 Riverfront Place, Ste. 610, North Little Rock 72114. SAN 322-0079. Tel. 501-378-0843, fax 501-374-1523. *Pres.* Kearney E. Dietz.

Northeast Arkansas Hospital Library Consortium, 223 E. Jackson, Jonesboro 72401. SAN 329-529X. Tel. 870-972-1290, fax 870-931-0839. *Dir.* Karen Crosser.

South Arkansas Film Coop., c/o Malvern-Hot Spring County Lib., Malvern 72104. SAN 321-5938. Tel. 501-332-5441, fax 501-332-6679, e-mail hotspringcountylibrary@yahoo.com. *Dir.* Tammy Carter.

California

Bay Area Library and Information Network (BayNet), 1462 Cedar St., Berkeley 94702.

SAN 371-0610. Tel. 510-525-4726, fax 510-525-4726, e-mail infobay@baynetlibs. org. *Admin. Officer* Rose Falanga.

Berkeley Information Network (BIN), Berkeley Public Lib., Berkeley 94704. Tel. 510-981-6166; 510-981-6150, fax 510-981-6246. *In Charge* Jane Cantlebury.

Califa, 32 W. 25 Ave., Ste. 201, San Mateo 94403. Tel. 650-572-2746, fax 650-349-5089, e-mail califa@califa.org. *Exec. Dir.* Linda Crowe.

Central Association of Libraries (CAL), 605 N. El Dorado St., Stockton 95202-1999. SAN 322-0125. Tel. 209-937-8649, fax 209-937-8292, e-mail 4999@ci.stockton. ca.us. *Dir.* Darla Gunning.

Claremont University Consortium (CUC), 800 Dartmouth Ave., Claremont 91711. Tel. 909-621-8150, fax 909-621-8681. *Chief Exec. Officer* Brenda Barham Hill.

Consortium for Open Learning, 333 Sunrise Ave., No. 229, Roseville 95661-3480. SAN 329-4412. Tel. 916-788-0660, fax 916-788-0696, e-mail cdl@calweb.com. *Operations Mgr.* Sandra Scott-Smith.

Consumer Health Information Program and Services (CHIPS), County of Los Angeles Public Lib., Carson 90745. SAN 372-8110. Tel. 310-830-0909, fax 310-834-4097. *Libn.* Scott A. Willis.

Gold Coast Library Network, 3437 Empresa Drive, Ste. C, San Luis Obispo 93401-7355. Tel. 805-543-6082, fax 805-543-9487. *Admin.* Maureen Theobald.

Hewlett-Packard Library Information Network, 1501 Page Mill Rd., Palo Alto 94304. SAN 375-0019. Tel. 650-857-3091, fax 650-852-8187. *Dir.* Eugenie Prime.

Kaiser Permanente Library System—Southern California Region (KPLS), Health Sciences Lib., Riverside 92505. SAN 372-8153. Tel. 951-353-3659, fax 951-353-3262. *Dir.* William Paringer.

Metropolitan Cooperative Library System (MCLS), 3675 E. Huntington Drive, Ste. 100, Pasadena 91107. SAN 371-3865. Tel. 626-683-8244, fax 626-683-8097, e-mail mclshq@mcls.org. *Interim Exec. Dir.* Laurel Patric.

Mountain Valley Library System (MVLS), 55 E St., Santa Rosa 95404. Tel. 707-544-0142, fax 707-544-8411 ext. 101. *Exec. Dir.* Annette Milliron.

National Network of Libraries of Medicine— Pacific Southwest Region (NN/LM PSR), Louise M. Darling Biomedical Lib., Los Angeles 90095-1798. SAN 372-8234. Tel. 310-825-1200, fax 310-825-5389, e-mail psr-nnlm@library.ucla.edu. *Dir.* Judy Consales.

Nevada Medical Library Group (NMLG), Barton Memorial Hospital Lib., South Lake Tahoe 96150. SAN 370-0445. Tel. 530-542-3000 ext. 2903, fax 530-541-4697. *In Charge* Laurie Anton.

Northern California Association of Law Libraries (NOCALL), PMB 336, San Francisco 94105. SAN 323-5777. E-mail admin@nocall.org. *Pres.* Prano Amjadi.

Northern California Consortium of Psychology Libraries (NCCPL), Alliant International Univ., Rudolph Hurwich Lib., San Francisco 94133. SAN 371-9006. Tel. 415-955-2156, e-mail nccpl-i@jfku.edu; nccpl-d@jfku.edu. *Pres.* Deanna Gage.

OCLC Western Service Center, 3281 E. Guasti Rd., Ste. 560, Ontario 91761. SAN 370-0747. Tel. 909-937-3300, fax 909-937-3384. *Dir.* Pamela Bailey.

Peninsula Libraries Automated Network (PLAN), 2471 Flores St., San Mateo 94403-4000. SAN 371-5035. Tel. 650-358-6714, fax 650-358-6715. *Database Mgr.* Susan Yasar.

Research Libraries Group, Inc. (RLG), 2029 Stierlin Ct., Ste. 100, Mountain View 94043-4684. SAN 322-0206. Fax 650-964-0943, e-mail ric@rlg.org. *Pres./CEO* James Michalko.

San Bernardino, Inyo, Riverside Counties United Library Services (SIRCULS), 3581 Mission Inn Ave., Riverside 92501-3377. SAN 322-0222. Tel. 951-369-7995, fax 951-784-1158, e-mail sirculs@inlandlib. org. *Exec. Dir.* Kathleen F. Aaron.

San Francisco Biomedical Library Network (SFBLN), H. M. Fishbon Memorial Lib., San Francisco 94115. SAN 371-2125. Tel. 415-885-7378, e-mail fishbon@itsa.ucfs. edu.

Santa Clarita Interlibrary Network (SCIL-NET), Powell Lib., Santa Clarita 91321. SAN 371-8964. Tel. 661-259-3540, fax 661-222-9159. *Libn.* John Stone.

Serra Cooperative Library System, 820 E. St., San Diego 92101. SAN 372-8129. Tel. 619-232-1225, fax 619-696-8649, e-mail serral@serralib.org. *ILL/Document Delivery Services* Ralph DeLauro.

Substance Abuse Librarians and Information Specialists (SALIS), P.O. Box 9513, Berkeley 94709-0513. SAN 372-4042. Tel. 510-597-3440, fax 510-985-6459, e-mail salis@salis.org. *Exec. Dir.* Andrea L. Mitchell.

Colorado

Automation System Colorado Consortium (ASCC), c/o Delta Public Lib., Delta 81416. Tel. 970-874-9630. *Technology Consultant* Connie Wolfrom.

Bi-State Academic Libraries (BI-SAL), c/o Marycrest International Univ., Denver 80236-2711. SAN 322-1393. Tel. 563-326-9254, fax 563-326-9250. *Libn.* Mary Edwards.

Bibliographical Center for Research, Rocky Mountain Region (BCR), 14394 E. Evans Ave., Aurora 80014-1478. SAN 322-0338. Tel. 303-751-6277, fax 303-751-9787, e-mail admin@bcr.org. *Exec. Dir.* David H. Brunell.

Colorado Alliance of Research Libraries, 3801 E. Florida Ave., Ste. 515, Denver 80210. SAN 322-3760. Tel. 303-759-3399, fax 303-759-3363. *Exec. Dir.* Alan Charnes.

Colorado Association of Law Libraries, P.O. Box 13363, Denver 80201. SAN 322-4325. Tel. 303-492-7312, fax 303-713-6218. *Pres.* Dan Cordova.

Colorado Council of Medical Librarians (CCML), P.O. Box 101058, Denver 80210-1058. SAN 370-0755. Tel. 303-837-7375, fax 303-837-7977. *Pres.* Joyce Condon.

Colorado Library Consortium (CLiC), 770 W. Hampden Ave., Ste. 340, Englewood 80110. SAN 371-3970. Tel. 303-422-1150, fax 303-431-9752. *Dir.* Valerie Horton.

Connecticut

Bibliomation, 32 Crest Rd, Middlebury 06762. Tel. 203-577-4076, fax 203-577-4077. *Chief Exec. Officer* Mike Simonds.

Capital Area Health Consortium, 270 Farmington Ave., Ste. 352, Farmington 06032-1994. SAN 322-0370. Tel. 860-676-1110, fax 860-676-1303, e-mail info@cahc.org. *Pres.* Karen Goodman.

Connecticut Library Consortium, 234 Court St., Middletown 06457-3304. SAN 322-0389. Tel. 860-344-8777, fax 860-344-9199, e-mail clc@ctlibrarians.org. *Exec. Dir.* Christine Bradley.

Council of State Library Agencies in the Northeast (COSLINE), Connecticut State Lib., Hartford 06106. SAN 322-0451. Tel. 860-757-6510, fax 860-757-6503.

CTW Library Consortium, Olin Memorial Lib., Middletown 06459-6065. SAN 329-4587. Tel. 860-685-3889, fax 860-685-2661. *System Libn.* Alan E. Hagyard.

Hartford Consortium for Higher Education, 950 Main St., Ste. 314, Hartford 06103. SAN 322-0443. Tel. 860-906-5016, fax 860-906-5118. *Exec. Dir.* Rosanne Druckman.

LEAP, 110 Washington Ave., North Haven 06473. SAN 322-4082. Tel. 203-239-1411, fax 203-239-9458. *Exec. Dir.* Diana Sellers.

Libraries Online, Inc. (LION), 100 Riverview Center, Ste. 252, Middletown 06457. SAN 322-3922. Tel. 860-347-1704, fax 860-346-3707. *Exec. Dir.* Joan Gillespie.

Library Connection, Inc., 599 Matianuck Ave., Windsor 06095-3567. Tel. 860-298-5322, fax 860-298-5328. *Exec. Dir.* George Christian.

North Atlantic Health Sciences Libraries, Inc. (NAHSL), Medial Lib. CB-3, Hartford 06102. SAN 371-0599. Tel. 508-856-6099, fax 508-856-5899. *Chair* Edward Donnald.

Delaware

Central Delaware Library Consortium, Dover Public Lib., Dover 19901. SAN 329-3696. Tel. 302-736-7030, fax 302-736-5087. *Dir.* Sheila B. Anderson.

Delaware Library Consortium (DLC), Delaware Academy of Medicine, Wilmington 19806. SAN 329-3718. Tel. 302-656-6398, fax 302-656-0470, e-mail library@delamed.org. *In Charge* Gail P. Gill.

District of Columbia

Computer Sciences Corporation/ERIC Project, 655 15th St. N.W., Ste. 500, Washington 20005. SAN 322-161X. Tel. 202-741-4200, fax 202-628-3205. *Dir.* Lawrence Henry.

Council for Christian Colleges and Universities, 321 Eighth St. N.E., Washington 20002. SAN 322-0524. Tel. 202-546-8713, fax 202-546-8913, e-mail council@cccu.org. *Pres.* Paul R. Corts.

District of Columbia Area Health Science Libraries (DCAHSL), American College of Obstetrics and Gynecology Resource Center, Washington 20024. SAN 323-9918. Tel. 202-863-2518, fax 202-484-1595, e-mail resources@acog.org. *Dir.* Mary A. Hyde.

EDUCAUSE, 1150 18th St. N.W., Ste. 1010, Washington 20036. SAN 371-487X. Tel. 202-872-4200, fax 202-872-4318. *Pres.* Brian Hawkins.

FEDLINK/Federal Library and Information Network, c/o Federal Lib. and Info. Center Committee, Washington 20540-4935. SAN 322-0761. Tel. 202-707-4800, fax 202-707-4818, e-mail flicc@loc.gov. *Exec. Dir.* Roberta I. Shaffer.

Interlibrary Users Association (IUA), c/o Urban Institute Lib., Washington 20037. SAN 322-1628. Tel. 202-261-5534, fax 202-223-3043. *Pres.* Nancy Minter.

Library of Congress, National Library Service for the Blind and Physically Handicapped (NLS), 1291 Taylor St. N.W., Washington 20542. SAN 370-5870. Tel. 202-707-5100, fax 202-707-0712, e-mail nls@loc.gov. *Dir.* Frank Kurt Cylke.

OCLC CAPCON Service Center, 1990 M St. N.W., Ste. 200, Washington 20036-3430. SAN 321-5954. Tel. 202-331-5771, fax 202-331-5788, e-mail oclccapcon@oclc.org. *Exec. Dir.* Irene M. Hoffman.

Transportation Research Board, 500 Fifth St. N.W., Washington 20001. SAN 370-582X.

Tel. 202-334-2990, fax 202-334-2527. *Dir.* Barbara Post.

Veterans Affairs Library Network (VALNET), Lib. Programs Office 19E, Washington 20420. SAN 322-0834. Tel. 202-273-8523, fax 202-273-9386. *Network Services* Ginny DuPont.

Washington Theological Consortium, 487 Michigan Ave. N.E., Washington 20017-1585. SAN 322-0842. Tel. 202-832-2675, fax 202-526-0818, e-mail wtconsort@aol.com. *Dir.* John Crossin.

Florida

Central Florida Library Cooperative (CFLC), 431 E. Horatio Ave., Ste. 230, Maitland 32751. SAN 371-9014. Tel. 407-644-9050, fax 407-644-7023. *Exec. Dir.* Marta Westall.

College Center for Library Automation (CCLA), 1753 W. Paul Dirac Drive, Tallahassee 32310. Tel. 850-922-6044, fax 850-922-4869, e-mail servicedesk@cclaflorida.org. *Exec. Dir.* Richard Madaus.

Consortium of Southeastern Law Libraries (COSELL), Lawton Chiles Legal Info. Center, Gainesville 32611. SAN 372-8277. Tel. 352-273-0710, fax 352-392-5093.

Florida Center for Library Automation (FCLA), 5830 N.W. 39 Ave., Gainesville 32606. Tel. 352-392-9020, fax 352-392-9188. *Dir.* James Corey.

Florida Library Information Network, R. A. Gray Bldg., Tallahassee 32399-0250. SAN 322-0869. Tel. 850-245-6600, fax 850-245-6744, e-mail library@dos.state.fl.us. *Circulation* Linda Pulliam.

Miami Health Sciences Library Consortium (MHSLC), Medical Lib. (142D), Miami VA Healthcare System, Miami 33125-1624. SAN 371-0734. Tel. 305-575-3187, fax 305-575-3118, e-mail vhamialibrary@va.gov. *Pres.* Devica Samsundar.

Northeast Florida Library Information Network (NEFLIN), 2233 Park Ave., Ste. 402, Orange Park 32073. Tel. 904-278-5620, fax 904-278-5625, e-mail office@neflin.org. *Exec. Dir.* Brad Ward.

Okaloosa County Public Library Cooperative (OCPLC), 204B N. Partin Drive, Niceville 32578. Tel. 850-609-5102, fax 850-609-5103. *Coord.* Robert Gorin.

Panhandle Library Access Network (PLAN), Five Miracle Strip Loop, Ste. 8, Panama City Beach 32407-3850. SAN 370-047X. Tel. 850-233-9051, fax 850-235-2286. *Exec. Dir.* William P. Conniff.

SEFLIN—Southeast Florida Library Information Network, Inc., Wimberly Lib., Office 452, Boca Raton 33431. SAN 370-0666. Tel. 561-208-0984, fax 561-208-0995. *Exec. Dir.* Tom Sloan.

Southwest Florida Library Network (SWFLN), Bldg. 3, Unit 7, Fort Myers 33913. Tel. 239-225-4225, fax 239-225-4229. *Exec. Dir.* Barbara J. Stites.

Tampa Bay Library Consortium, Inc., 1202 Tech Blvd., Ste. 202, Tampa 33619. SAN 322-371X. Tel. 813-740-3963, fax 813-628-4425.

Tampa Bay Medical Library Network (TABAMLN), Robert Arthur Williams Lib., Orlando 32803. SAN 322-0885. Tel. 407-303-7747 ext. 9878, fax 407-303-9622. *Pres.* Deanna Stevens.

Georgia

Association of Southeastern Research Libraries (ASERL), c/o SOLINET, Atlanta 30309-2955. SAN 322-1555. Tel. 404-892-0943, fax 404-892-7879. *Exec. Dir.* John Burger.

Atlanta Health Science Libraries Consortium, Fran Golding Medical Lib. at Scottish Rite, Atlanta 30342-1600. Tel. 404-785-2157, fax 404-785-2155. *Pres.* Kate Daniels.

Atlanta Regional Council for Higher Education (ARCHE), 50 Hurt Plaza, Ste. 735, Atlanta 30303-2923. SAN 322-0990. Tel. 404-651-2668, fax 404-651-1797, e-mail arche@atlantahighered.org. *Pres.* Michael Gerber.

Georgia Interactive Network for Medical Information (GAIN), c/o Medical Lib., Mercer Univ., Macon 31207. SAN 370-0577. Tel. 478-301-2515, fax 478-301-2051. *Dir.* Jan H. LaBeause.

Georgia Online Database (GOLD), c/o Public Lib. Services, Atlanta 30345-4304. SAN 322-094X. Tel. 404-235-7200, fax 404-235-7201. *Lib. Services Mgr.* Elaine Hardy.

Metro Atlanta Library Association (MALA), c/o Atlanta Fulton Public Lib.—ILC, Atlanta 30303-1089. SAN 378-2549. Tel.

404-730-1733, fax 404-730-1988. *Pres.* Rick L. Wright.

Southeastern Library Network (SOLINET), 1438 W. Peachtree St. N.W., Ste. 200, Atlanta 30309-2955. SAN 322-0974. Tel. 404-892-0943, fax 404-892-7879. *Exec. Dir.* Kate Nevins.

SWGHSLC, Colquitt Regional Medical Center Health Sciences Lib., Moultrie 31776. SAN 372-8072. Tel. 229-890-3460, fax 229-891-9345. *Libn.* Susan Leik.

Hawaii

Hawaii Library Consortium (HLC), 1020 Mawawaii St., Kapolei 96707. Tel. 808-693-7050, fax 808-693-7062, e-mail hlcboard-1@hawaii.edu. *Pres.* Richard Burns.

Hawaii-Pacific Chapter of the Medical Library Association (HPC-MLA), 1301 Punchbowl St., Honolulu 96813. SAN 371-3946. Tel. 808-547-4300, fax 808-547-4019. *Chair* Mabel Trafford.

Idaho

Canyon Owyhee Library Group, Ltd., 1407 Homedale Rd., Caldwell 83607. Tel. 208-454-9253 ext. 301, fax 208-455-9872. *Media Specialist* Marlene Earnest.

Cooperative Information Network (CIN), 8385 N. Government Way, Hayden 83835-9280. SAN 323-7656. Tel. 208-772-5612, fax 208-772-2498, e-mail hay@cin.kcl.org. *Fiscal Agent* John W. Hartung.

Gooding County Library Consortium, c/o Gooding H.S., Gooding 83330. SAN 375-0094. Tel. 208-934-4831, fax 208-934-4347. *Head Libn.* Cora Caldwell.

Grangeville Cooperative Network, c/o Grangeville Centennial Lib., Grangeville 83530-1729. SAN 375-0108. Tel. 208-983-0951, fax 208-983-2336, e-mail library@grangeville.us. *Dir.* Linda L. Ruthruff.

Idaho Health Information Association (IHIA), Kootenai Medical Center, WT Wood Medical Lib., Coeur d'Alene 83814. SAN 371-5078. Tel. 208-666-3498, fax 208-666-2948. *Dir.* Marcie Horner.

Library Consortium of Eastern Idaho, 457 Broadway, Idaho Falls 83402. SAN 323-7699. Tel. 208-612-8450, fax 208-529-1467. *System Admin.* Roger Evans.

LYNX Consortium, c/o Boise Public Lib., Boise 83702-7195. SAN 375-0086. Tel. 208-384-4238, fax 208-384-4025, e-mail askalibrarian@cityofboise.org. *Dir.* Stephen Cottrell.

Illinois

Alliance Library System, 600 High Point Lane, East Peoria 61611. SAN 371-0637. Tel. 309-694-9200, fax 309-694-9230. *Exec. Dir.* Kitty Pope.

American Theological Library Association (ATLA), 250 S. Wacker Drive, Ste. 1600, Chicago 60606-5889. SAN 371-9022. Tel. 312-454-5100, fax 312-454-5505, e-mail atla@atla.com. *Exec. Dir.* Dennis A. Norlin.

Areawide Hospital Library Consortium of Southwestern Illinois (AHLC), c/o St. Elizabeth Hospital Health Science Lib., Belleville 62222. SAN 322-1016. Tel. 618-234-2120, fax 618-222-4614.

Association of Chicago Theological Schools, Krauss-McCormick Lib., Chicago 60615. SAN 370-0658. Tel. 773-256-0735, fax 773-256-0737. *Dir.* Christine Wenderoth.

Capital Area Consortium, Decatur Memorial Hospital—Health Science Lib., Decatur 62526. Tel. 217-876-2940, fax 217-876-2945. *Coord.* Karen Stoner.

Center for Research Libraries, 6050 S. Kenwood, Chicago 60637-2804. SAN 322-1032. Tel. 773-955-4545, fax 773-955-4339. *Pres.* Bernard F. Reilly.

Chicago and South Consortium, Governors State Univ. Lib., University Park 60466. SAN 322-1067. Tel. 708-534-5000 ext. 5142, fax 708-534-8454.

Chicago Area Museum Librarians (CAML), c/o Lib., The Field Museum, Chicago 60605-2496. SAN 371-392X. Tel. 312-665-7887, fax 312-665-7839. *Chair, Reference Services.* Christine Giannoni.

Committee on Institutional Cooperation, 1819 S. Neil St., Ste. D, Champaign 61820. Tel. 217-333-8475, fax 217-244-7127, e-mail cic@uiuc.edu. *Dir.* Mark Sandler.

Consortium of Academic and Research Libraries in Illinois (CARLI), Lib. and Info. Science Bldg., Ste. 228, Champaign 61820-6211. SAN 322-3736. Tel. 217-

244-7593, fax 217-244-7596. *Exec. Dir.* Susan Singleton.

Council of Directors of State University Libraries in Illinois (CODSULI), Southern Illinois Univ. School of Medicine Lib., Springfield 62702-4910. SAN 322-1083. Tel. 217-545-9884, fax 217-545-0988.

East Central Illinois Consortium, Carle Foundation Hospital Lib., Urbana 61801. SAN 322-1040. Tel. 217-383-3456, fax 217-383-3452. *Mgr.* Gerald Dewitt.

Fox Valley Health Science Library Consortium, Provena St. Joseph Hospital Medical Lib., Elgin 60123. SAN 329-3831. Tel. 847-695-3200, fax 847-888-3532.

Heart of Illinois Library Consortium, 511 N.E. Greenleaf, Peoria 61603. SAN 322-1113. *Chair* Leslie Menz.

Illinois Library and Information Network (ILLINET), c/o Illinois State Lib., Springfield 62701-1796. SAN 322-1148. Tel. 217-782-2994, fax 217-785-4326. *Dir.* Anne Craig.

Illinois Office of Educational Services, 2450 Foundation Dr., Ste. 100, Springfield 62703-5464. SAN 371-5108. Tel. 217-786-3010, fax 217-786-3020, e-mail oesiscc@siu.edu.

LIBRAS, Inc., North Park Univ., Chicago 60625-4895. SAN 322-1172. Tel. 773-244-5584, fax 773-244-4891, e-mail rmwilliams @noctrl.edu. *Pres.* Sally Anderson.

Metropolitan Consortium of Chicago, Chicago School of Professional Psychology, Chicago 60610. SAN 322-1180. Tel. 312-329-6633, fax 312-644-6075. *Coord.* Margaret White.

National Network of Libraries of Medicine—Greater Midwest Region (NN-LM GMR), c/o Lib. of Health Sciences, Univ. of Illinois, Chicago 60612-4330. SAN 322-1202. Tel. 312-996-2464, fax 312-996-2226, e-mail gmr@uic.edu. *Acting Dir.* Carol Scherrer.

Quad Cities Libraries in Cooperation (Quad-LINC), 220 W. 23 Ave., Coal Valley 61240. SAN 373-093X. Tel. 309-799-3155 ext. 3254, fax 309-799-7916. *Assistant Dir., Technical Services and Automation* Position currently open.

System Wide Automated Network (SWAN), c/o Metropolitan Lib. System, Burr Ridge

60527-5783. Tel. 630-734-5000, fax 630-734-5050. *Dir. of Automation and Technology Services* Dean Bryan.`

Indiana

American Zoo and Aquarium Association (AZA-LSIG), Indianapolis Zoo, Indianapolis 46222. SAN 373-0891. Tel. 317-630-5110, fax 317-630-5114.

Central Indiana Health Science Libraries Consortium, Indiana Univ. School of Medicine Lib., Indianapolis 46202. SAN 322-1245. Tel. 317-274-8358, fax 317-274-4056. *Contact* Elaine Skopelja.

Collegiate Consortium Western Indiana, c/o Cunningham Memorial Lib., Terre Haute 47809. SAN 329-4439. Tel. 812-237-3700, fax 812-237-3376. *Dean of Lib.* Myrna McCallister.

Evansville Area Library Consortium, 3700 Washington Ave., Evansville 47750. SAN 322-1261. Tel. 812-485-4151, fax 812-485-7564. *Coord.* Jane Saltzman.

Indiana Cooperative Library Services Authority (INCOLSA), 6202 Morenci Trail, Indianapolis 46268-2536. SAN 322-1296. Tel. 317-298-6570, fax 317-328-2380.

Indiana State Data Center, Indiana State Lib., Indianapolis 46204-2296. SAN 322-1318. Tel. 317-232-3733, fax 317-232-3728. *Coord.* Frank H. Wilmot.

Northeast Indiana Health Science Libraries Consortium (NEIHSL), Univ. of Saint Francis Health Sciences Lib., Fort Wayne 46808. SAN 373-1383. Tel. 260-434-7453, fax 260-434-7695. *Coord.* Lauralee Aven.

Northwest Indiana Health Science Library Consortium, c/o N.W. Center for Medical Education, Gary 46408-1197. SAN 322-1350. Tel. 219-980-6852; 219-980-6709, fax 219-980-6524; 219-980-6566. *Libn.* Felicia A. Young.

Iowa

Consortium of College and University Media Centers (CCUMC), Iowa State Univ., Ames 50011-3243. SAN 322-1091. Tel. 515-294-1811, fax 515-294-8089, e-mail ccumc@ccumc.org. *In Charge* Mary Anderson.

Consortium of User Libraries (CUL), Lib. for the Blind and Physically Handicapped, Des Moines 50309-2364. Tel. 515-281-1333, fax 515-281-1378; 515-281-1263. *Pres.* Karen Keninger.

Dubuque Area Library Information Consortium, c/o N.E. Iowa Community College, Burton Payne Lib., Peosta 52068. Tel. 563-556-5110 ext. 269, fax 563-557-0340. *Coord.* Deb Seiffert.

Iowa Private Academic Library Consortium (IPAL), c/o Buena Vista Univ. Lib., Storm Lake 50588. SAN 329-5311. Tel. 712-749-2127, 712-749-2203, fax 712-749-2059, e-mail library@bvu.edu. *Univ. Libn.* Jim Kennedy.

Linn County Library Consortium, Russell D. Cole Lib., Mount Vernon 52314. SAN 322-4597. Tel. 319-895-4259. *Pres.* Aileen Chang-Matus.

Polk County Biomedical Consortium, c/o Des Moines Area Community College, Ankeny Campus, Ankeny 50021. SAN 322-1431. Tel. 515-964-6573, fax 515-965-7126. *In Charge* Diane Messersmith.

Quad City Area Biomedical Consortium, Great River Medical Center Lib., West Burlington 52655. SAN 322-435X. Tel. 319-768-4075, fax 319-768-4080. *Coord.* Judy Hawk.

Sioux City Library Cooperative (SCLC), c/o Sioux City Public Lib., Sioux City 51101-1203. SAN 329-4722. Tel. 712-255-2933 ext. 251, fax 712-279-6432. *Chair* Peg Brady.

State of Iowa Libraries Online (SILO), State Lib. of Iowa, Des Moines 50319. SAN 322-1415. Tel. 515-281-4105, fax 515-281-6191. *State Libn.* Mary Wegner.

Kansas

Associated Colleges of Central Kansas, 210 S Main St., McPherson 67460. SAN 322-1474. Tel. 620-241-5150, fax 620-241-5153.

Dodge City Library Consortium, c/o Central Elementary School, Dodge City 67801. SAN 322-4368. Tel. 620-227-1601, fax 620-227-1721. *Chair* Linda Zupancic.

Kansas Regents Library Database Consortium (RLDC), c/o Gail Underwood, Licensing Specialist, Lawrence 66045-7544. Tel. 785-864-3059, e-mail rldc@ku.edu. *Chair* Beth Turtle.

Statewide Resource Sharing, 300 S.W. 10 Ave., Rm. 343 N., Topeka 66612-1593. SAN 329-5621. Tel. 785-296-3875, fax 785-296-6650. *Dir.* Eric Hansen.

Kentucky

Association of Independent Kentucky Colleges and Universities (AIKCU), 484 Chenault Rd., Frankfort 40601. SAN 322-1490. Tel. 502-695-5007, fax 502-695-5057. *Pres.* Gary S. Cox.

Eastern Kentucky Health Science Information Network (EKHSIN), c/o Camden-Carroll Lib., Morehead 40351. SAN 370-0631. Tel. 606-783-6860, fax 606-784-2178. *Dir., Medical Lib.* Katy W. Roe.

Kentuckiana Metroversity, Inc., 109 E. Broadway, Louisville 40202. SAN 322-1504. Tel. 502-897-3374, fax 502-895-1647.

Kentucky Health Science Libraries Consortium, VA Medical Center, Lib. Services 142D, Louisville 40206-1499. SAN 370-0623. Tel. 502-287-6240, fax 502-287-6134. *Head Libn.* Gene M. Haynes.

Kentucky Virtual Library (KVL), 1024 Capital Center Dr., Ste. 320, Frankfort 40601. Tel. 502-573-1555, fax 502-573-0222, e-mail kyvl@ky.gov. *Dir.* Enid Wohlstein.

Theological Education Association of Mid America (TEAM-A), Southern Baptist Theological Seminary, Louisville 40280. SAN 377-5038. Tel. 502-897-4807, fax 502-897-4600. *Dir., Info. Resources* Ken Boyd.

Louisiana

Central Louisiana Medical Center Library Consortium (CLMLC), VA Medical Center 142D, Alexandria 71306. Tel. 318-619-9102, fax 318-619-9144, e-mail clmlc@yahoo.com. *Coord.* Miriam J. Brown.

Health Sciences Library Association of Louisiana (HSLAL), Tulane Health Sciences Lib., New Orleans 70112-2632.

SAN 375-0035. Tel. 504-988-2404, fax 504-988-2412. *Chair* Susan Dorsey.

Loan SHARK, State Lib. of Louisiana, Baton Rouge 70802. SAN 371-6880. Tel. 225-342-4920; 225-342-4918, fax 225-219-4725. *Head, Access Services* Kytara A. Gaudin.

Louisiana Government Information Network (LaGIN), c/o State Lib. of Louisiana, Baton Rouge 70802. SAN 329-5036. Tel. 225-342-4920, e-mail lagin@pelican.state.lib.la.us. *Coord.* Virginia Smith.

New Orleans Educational Telecommunications Consortium, 2 Canal St., Ste. 2038, New Orleans 70130. SAN 329-5214. Tel. 504-524-0350, fax 504-524-0327, e-mail noetc_inc@excite.com. *Exec. Dir.* Michael Adler.

Louisiana Library Network (LOUIS), Office Computing Services, Louisiana State Univ., Baton Rouge 70803. *Exec. Dir.* Ralph Boe.

Maine

Health Science Library Information Consortium (HSLIC), 211 Marginal Way, No. 245, Portland 04101. SAN 322-1601. Tel. 207-871-4081. *Chair* John Hutchinson.

Maryland

Library Video Network (LVN), 320 York Rd., Towson 21204. SAN 375-5320. Tel. 410-887-2090, fax 410-887-2091, e-mail lvn@bcpl.net. *Mgr.* Carl Birkmeyer.

Maryland Association of Health Science Librarians (MAHSL), Suburban Hospital Medical Lib., Bethesda 20814. SAN 377-5070. Tel. 301-896-3199. *Co-Pres.* Brittany Rice.

Maryland Interlibrary Loan Organization (MILO), c/o Enoch Pratt Free Lib., Baltimore 21201-4484. SAN 343-8600. Tel. 410-396-5498, fax 410-396-5837, e-mail milo@epfl.net. *Mgr.* Emma E. Beaven.

National Network of Libraries of Medicine (NN-LM), National Lib. of Medicine, Bethesda 20894. SAN 373-0905. Tel. 301-496-4777, fax 301-480-1467. *Dir.* Angela Ruffin.

National Network of Libraries of Medicine—Southeastern Atlantic Region (NNLM-

SEA), Univ. of Maryland Health Sciences and Human Services Lib., Baltimore 21201-1512. SAN 322-1644. Tel. 410-706-2855, fax 410-706-0099. *Dir.* Mary J. Tooey.

Regional Alcohol and Drug Abuse Resource Network (RADAR), National Clearinghouse for Alcohol and Drug Info., Rockville 20852. SAN 377-5569. Tel. 301-468-2600, fax 301-468-6433, e-mail info@health.org. *Coord.* Marion Pierce.

U.S. National Library of Medicine (NLM), 8600 Rockville Pike, Bethesda 20894. SAN 322-1652. Tel. 301-594-5983, fax 301-402-1384, e-mail custserv@nlm.nih.gov. *Chief, Public Services* Eve Marie LaCroix.

Washington Research Library Consortium (WRLC), 901 Commerce Dr., Upper Marlboro 20774. SAN 373-0883. Tel. 301-390-2031, fax 301-390-2020. *Exec. Dir.* Lizanne Payne.

Massachusetts

Boston Biomedical Library Consortium (BBLC), c/o Percy R. Howe Memorial Lib., Boston 02115. SAN 322-1725. Tel. 617-262-5200, fax 617-262-4021.

Boston Library Consortium, Inc., McKim Bldg., Boston 02117. SAN 322-1733. Tel. 617-262-0380, fax 617-262-0163. *Exec. Dir.* Barbara G. Preece.

Boston Regional Library System (BRLS), c/o Boston Public Lib., Boston 02117. Tel. 617-859-2380, fax 617-424-8617, e-mail brl@bpl.org. *Regional Admin.* Michael Colford.

Cape Libraries Automated Materials Sharing (CLAMS), 270 Communication Way, Unit 4E-4F, Hyannis 02601. SAN 370-579X. Tel. 508-790-4399, fax 508-771-4533. *Exec. Dir.* Monica Grace.

Catholic Library Association, 100 North St., Ste. 224, Pittsfield 01201-5109. SAN 329-1030. Tel. 413-443-2252, fax 413-442-2252, e-mail cla@cathla.org. *Exec. Dir.* Jean R. Bostley, SSJ.

Central and Western Massachusetts Automated Resource Sharing (C/W MARS), 67 Millbrook St., Ste. 201, Worcester 01606. SAN 322-3973. Tel. 508-755-3323 ext. 30, fax 508-755-3721. *Exec. Dir.* Joan Kuklinski.

Cooperating Libraries of Greater Springfield (CLIC), Springfield College, Springfield 01109. SAN 322-1768. Tel. 413-748-3502, fax 413-748-3631. *Dir.* Andrea Taupier.

Fenway Libraries Online (FLO), c/o Wentworth Inst. of Technology, Boston 02115. SAN 373-9112. Tel. 617-442-2384, fax 617-442-1519. *Dir.* Walter Stine.

Fenway Library Consortium, Univ. of Massachusetts, Boston 02125. SAN 327-9766. Tel. 617-521-2741; 617-573-8536, fax 617-521-3093. *Dir.* David Ortiz.

Massachusetts Health Sciences Libraries Network (MAHSLIN), Brigham and Women's Hospital, Boston 02115. SAN 372-8293. Tel. 617-525-6787, fax 617-975-0890. *Pres.* Anne Fladger.

Merrimack Valley Library Consortium, 123 Tewksbury St., Andover 01810. SAN 322-4384. Tel. 978-475-7632, fax 978-475-7179. *Exec. Dir.* Lawrence Rungren.

Massachusetts Regional Library System (METROWEST), 135 Beaver St., Waltham 02452. Tel. 781-398-1819, fax 781-398-1821. *Admin.* Sondra H. Vandermark.

Minuteman Library Network, 10 Strathmore Rd, Natick 01760-2419. SAN 322-4252. Tel. 508-655-8008, fax 508-655-1507. *Exec. Dir.* Susan McAlister.

National Network of Libraries of Medicine—New England Region (NN-LM NER), Univ. of Massachusetts Medical School, Shrewsbury 01545-2732. SAN 372-5448. Tel. 508-856-5979, fax 508-856-5977. *Dir.* Elaine Martin.

NELINET, 153 Cordaville Rd, Southborough 01772. SAN 322-1822. Tel. 508-460-7700 ext. 1934, fax 508-460-9455. *Exec. Dir.* Arnold Hirshon.

North of Boston Library Exchange (NOBLE), 26 Cherry Hill Dr., Danvers 01923. SAN 322-4023. Tel. 978-777-8844, fax 978-750-8472. *Exec. Dir.* Ronald A. Gagnon.

Northeast Consortium of Colleges and Universities in Massachusetts (NECCUM), Northern Essex Community College, Haverhill 01830. SAN 371-0602. Tel. 978-556-3400, fax 978-556-3738. *Dir.* Linda Hummel-Shea.

Northeastern Consortium for Health Information (NECHI), Lowell General Hospital

Health Science Library, Lowell 01854. SAN 322-1857. Tel. 978-937-6247, fax 978-937-6855. *Libn.* Donna Beales.

SAILS, Inc., 547 W. Groves St., Ste. 4, Middleboro 02346. SAN 378-0058. Tel. 508-946-8600, fax 508-946-8605. *Pres.* Robin Glasser.

Southeastern Massachusetts Consortium of Health Science Libraries (SEMCO), South Shore Hospital, South Weymouth 02190. SAN 322-1873. Tel. 781-340-8528, fax 781-331-0834. *Dir.* Kathy McCarthy.

Southeastern Massachusetts Regional Library System (SEMLS), 10 Riverside Drive, Lakeville 02347. Tel. 508-923-3531, fax 508-923-3539, e-mail semls@semls.org. *Admin.* Cynthia A. Roach.

West of Boston Network (WEBNET), Horn Lib., Babson College, Babson Park 02457. SAN 371-5019. Tel. 781-239-4308, fax 781-239-5226. *Pres.* Lynn Triplett.

Western Massachusetts Health Information Consortium, Baystate Medical Center Health Sciences Lib., Springfield 01199. SAN 329-4579. Tel. 413-794-1291, fax 413-794-1978. *Pres.* Karen Dorval.

Michigan

Berrien Library Consortium, c/o William Hessel Lib., Lake Michigan College, Benton Harbor 49022-1899. SAN 322-4678. Tel. 269-927-8605, fax 269-927-6656. *Pres.* Diane Baker.

Detroit Area Consortium of Catholic Colleges, c/o Sacred Heart Seminary, Detroit 48206. SAN 329-482X. Tel. 313-883-8500, fax 313-868-6440. *Dir.* Herman Peterson.

Detroit Area Library Network (DALNET), c/o Wayne State Univ., Detroit 48202. Tel. 313-577-6789, fax 313-577-1231. *Dir.* Steven Bowers.

Kalamazoo Consortium for Higher Education (KCHE), Kalamazoo College, Kalamazoo 49006. SAN 329-4994. Tel. 269-337-7220, fax 269-337-7219. *Pres.* Eileen B. Wilson-Oyelaran.

Lakeland Library Cooperative, 4138 Three Mile Rd. N.W., Grand Rapids 49534. SAN 308-132X. Tel. 616-559-5253, fax 616-

559-4329. *Interim Dir.* Martha Seaman McKee.

The Library Network (TLN), 13331 Reeck Rd., Southgate 48195-3054. SAN 370-596X. Tel. 734-281-3830, fax 734-281-1817. *Interim Dir.* Tammy Turgeon.

Michigan Association of Consumer Health Information Specialists (MACHIS), Bronson Methodist Hospital, Kalamazoo 49007. SAN 375-0043. Tel. 269-341-8627, fax 269-341-8828. *Dir.* Marge Kars.

Michigan Health Sciences Libraries Association (MHSLA), 1407 Rensen St., Ste. 4, Lansing 48910. SAN 323-987X. *Pres.* Patricia Martin.

Michigan Library Consortium (MLC), 1407 Rensen St., Ste. 1, Lansing 48910-3657. SAN 322-192X. Tel. 517-394-2420, fax 517-394-2096, e-mail reception@mlcnet. org. *Associate Dir.* Ruth Dukelow.

Northland Interlibrary System (NILS), 316 E. Chisholm St., Alpena 49707. SAN 329-4773. Tel. 989-356-1622, fax 989-354-3939. *Interim Dir.* Christine Johnson.

PALnet, 1040 W. Bristol Rd., Flint 48507. Tel. 810-766-4070. *Dir.* Stephanie C. John.

Southeastern Michigan League of Libraries (SEMLOL), Lawrence Technological Univ., Southfield 48075. SAN 322-4481. Tel. 248-204-3000, fax 248-204-3005. *Treas.* Gary Cocozzoli.

Southwest Michigan Library Cooperative (SMLC), 305 Oak St., Paw Paw 49079. SAN 371-5027. Tel. 269-657-4698, fax 269-657-4494. *Dir.* Alida L. Geppert.

Suburban Library Cooperative (SLC), 44750 Delco Blvd., Sterling Heights 48313. SAN 373-9082. Tel. 586-286-5750, fax 586-286-8951. *Interim Dir., System Libn.* Kristen Valyi-Hax.

Upper Peninsula of Michigan Health Science Library Consortium, c/o Marquette Health System Hospital, Marquette 49855. SAN 329-4803. Tel. 906-225-3429, fax 906-225-3524. *In Charge* Janis Lubenow.

Upper Peninsula Region of Library Cooperation, Inc., 1615 Presque Isle Ave., Marquette 49855. SAN 329-5540. Tel. 906-228-7697, fax 906-228-5627. *In Charge* Suzanne Dees.

Valley Library Consortium, 3210 Davenport Ave., Saginaw 48602-3495. Tel. 989-497-0925, fax 989-497-0918. *Exec. Dir.* Karl R. Steiner.

Minnesota

Capital Area Library Consortium (CALCO), c/o Minnesota Dept. of Transportation, Lib. MS155, Saint Paul 55155. SAN 374-6127. Tel. 651-296-5272, fax 651-297-2354. *Libn.* Shirley Sherkow.

Central Minnesota Libraries Exchange (CMLE), Miller Center, Rm. 130-D, Saint Cloud 56301-4498. SAN 322-3779. Tel. 320-255-2950, fax 320-654-5131, e-mail cmle@stcloudstate.edu. *Dir.* Patricia A. Post.

Community Health Science Library, c/o Saint Francis Medical Center, Breckenridge 56520. SAN 370-0585. Tel. 218-643-7542, fax 218-643-7452. *Dir.* Kristi Kaseman.

Cooperating Libraries in Consortium (CLIC), 1619 Dayton Ave., Ste. 204, Saint Paul 55104. SAN 322-1970. Tel. 651-644-3878, fax 651-644-6258. *Dir.* Karen Docherty.

Metronet, 1619 Dayton Ave., Ste. 314, Saint Paul 55104. SAN 322-1989. Tel. 651-646-0475, fax 651-649-3169, e-mail information @metrolibraries.net. *Exec. Dir.* Tom Shaughnessy.

Metropolitan Library Service Agency (MELSA), 1619 Dayton Ave., No. 314, Saint Paul 55104-6206. SAN 371-5124. Tel. 651-645-5731, fax 651-649-3169, e-mail melsa@melsa.org. *Exec. Dir.* Chris D. Olson.

MINITEX Library Information Network, Univ. of Minnesota–Twin Cities, 15 Andersen Lib., Minneapolis 55455-0439. SAN 322-1997. Tel. 612-624-4002, fax 612-624-4508. *Dir.* William DeJohn.

Minnesota Library Information Network (MnLINK), Univ. of Minnesota–Twin Cities, Minneapolis 55455-0439. Tel. 612-624-8096, fax 612-624-4508. *Info. Specialist* Nick Banitt.

Minnesota Theological Library Association (MTLA), c/o Bethel Seminary Lib., Saint Paul 55112. SAN 322-1962. Tel. 651-638-

6184, fax 651-638-6006. *Pres.* Sandy Oslund.

North Country Library Cooperative, 5528 Emerald Ave., Mountain Iron 55768-2069. SAN 322-3795. Tel. 218-741-1907, fax 218-741-1908. *Dir.* Linda J. Wadman.

Northern Lights Library Network, 103 Graystone Plaza, Detroit Lakes 56501-3041. SAN 322-2004. Tel. 218-847-2825, fax 218-847-1461, e-mail nloffice@nlln.org. *Dir.* Ruth Solie.

SMILE (Southcentral Minnesota Inter-Library Exchange), 1400 Madison Ave., No. 622, Mankato 56001. SAN 321-3358. Tel. 507-625-7555, fax 507-625-4049, e-mail smile@tds.lib.mn.us. *Dir.* Nancy Katharine Steele.

Southeastern Libraries Cooperating (SELCO), 2600 19th St. N.W., Rochester 55901-0767. SAN 308-7417. Tel. 507-288-5513, fax 507-288-8697. *Exec. Dir.* Ann B. Hutton.

Southwest Area Multicounty Multitype Interlibrary Exchange (SAMMIE), 109 S. 5 St., Ste. 30, Marshall 56258. SAN 322-2039. Tel. 507-532-9013, fax 507-532-2039, e-mail info@sammie.org. *Dir.* Robin Chaney.

Twin Cities Biomedical Consortium (TCBC), c/o Fairview Univ. Medical Center, Minneapolis 55455. SAN 322-2055. Tel. 612-273-6595, fax 612-273-2675. *Chair* Michael Scott.

Valley Medical Network, Lake Region Hospital Lib., Fergus Falls 56537. SAN 329-4730. Tel. 218-736-8158, fax 218-736-8731. *In Charge* Connie Schulz.

West Group, P.O. Box 64526, Saint Paul 55164-0526. SAN 322-4031. Tel. 651-687-7000, fax 651-687-5614, e-mail west. customer.service@thomson.com.

Mississippi

Central Mississippi Library Council (CMLC), c/o Millsaps College Lib., Jackson 39210. SAN 372-8250. Tel. 601-974-1070, fax 601-974-1082. *Admin./Treas.* Tom Henderson.

Mississippi Electronic Libraries Online (MELO), Mississippi State Board for Community and Junior Colleges, Jackson 39211. Tel. 601-432-6518, fax 601-432-

6363, e-mail melo@colin.edu. *Dir.* Audra Kimball.

Missouri

Greater Western Library Alliance (GWLA), 5109 Cherry St., Kansas City 64110. Tel. 816-926-8765, fax 816-926-8790. *Exec. Dir.* Adrian Alexander.

Health Sciences Library Network of Kansas City (HSLNKC), Univ. of Missouri–Kansas City Health Sciences Lib., Kansas City 64108-2792. SAN 322-2098. Tel. 816-235-1880, fax 816-235-6570. *Dir.* Peggy Mullaly-Quijas.

Kansas City Library Consortium (KCLC), 14 W. 10 St., Kansas City 64105. Fax 816-701-3464, e-mail kclcsupport@kclibrary. org. *Dir.* Donna Whitner.

Kansas City Metropolitan Library and Information Network, 15624 E. 24 Hwy., Independence 64050. SAN 322-2101. Tel. 816-521-7257, fax 816-461-0966. *Exec. Dir.* Susan Burton.

Kansas City Regional Council for Higher Education, Park Univ., Parkville 64152-3795. SAN 322-211X. Tel. 816-741-2816, fax 816-741-1296. *Dir.* Gloria Brady.

Library Systems Service, Bernard Becker Medical Lib., Washington Univ., Saint Louis 63110. SAN 322-2187. Tel. 314-362-7080, 314-362-2774, fax 314-454-6606. *Dir.* Paul Schoening.

Missouri Library Network Corp (MLNC), 8045 Big Bend Blvd., Ste. 202, Saint Louis 63119-2714. SAN 322-466X. Tel. 314-918-7222, fax 314-918-7727. *Acting Dir.* Tracy Byerly.

Saint Louis Regional Library Network, 341 Sappington Rd., Saint Louis 63122. SAN 322-2209. Tel. 314-395-1305.

Montana

Montana Library Network, Montana State Lib., Helena 59620-1800. Tel. 406-444-5431, fax 406-444-0581. *Dir.* Bruce Newell.

Nebraska

ICON Library Consortium, Univ. of Nebraska, McGoogan Lib. of Medicine, Omaha 68198-6705. Tel. 402-559-7099, fax 402-559-5498.

Lincoln Health Sciences Library Group (LHSLG), Univ. of Nebraska–Lincoln, Lincoln 68588-4100. SAN 329-5001. Tel. 402-472-2554, fax 402-472-5131.

NEBASE, c/o Nebraska Lib. Commission, Lincoln 68508-2023. SAN 322-2268. Tel. 402-471-2045, fax 402-471-2083.

Southeast Nebraska Library System, 5730 R. St., Ste. C-1, Lincoln 68505. SAN 322-4732. Tel. 402-467-6188, fax 402-467-6196.

Nevada

Desert States Law Library Consortium, Wiener-Rogers Law Lib., William S. Boyd School of Law, Las Vegas 89154-1080. Tel. 702-895-2404, fax 702-895-2416. *In Charge* Roberta Studwell.

Information Nevada, Interlibrary Loan Dept., Nevada State Lib. and Archives, Carson City 89701-4285. SAN 322-2276. Tel. 775-684-3328, fax 775-684-3330. *Contact* Hope Williams.

New Hampshire

Carroll County Library Cooperative, c/o Madison Lib., Madison 03849. SAN 371-8999. Tel. 603-367-8545, fax 603-367-4479, e-mail librarian@madison.lib.nh.us.

GMILCS, Inc., 1701B Hooksett Rd, Hooksett 03106. Tel. 603-485-4286, fax 603-485-4246, e-mail helpdesk@gmilcs.org. *System Admin.* Marilyn Borgendale.

Health Science Libraries of New Hampshire and Vermont, Lakes Region General Hospital, Laconia 03246. SAN 371-6864. Tel. 603-527-2837, fax 603-527-7197.

Hillstown Cooperative, 3 Meetinghouse Rd., Bedford 03110. SAN 371-3873. Tel. 603-472-2300, fax 603-472-2978.

Librarians of the Upper Valley Coop. (LUV Coop), 1173 U.S. Rte. 4, Canaan 03741. SAN 371-6856. Tel. 603-523-9650, e-mail canaantownlibrary@hotmail.com. *In Charge* Amy Thurber.

Merri-Hill-Rock Library Cooperative, c/o Sandown Public Lib., Sandown 03873-0580. SAN 329-5338. Tel. 603-887-3428, fax 603-887-0590, e-mail sandownlibrary

@comcast.net. *Dir., Lib. Services* Diane Heer.

New England Law Library Consortium (NELLCO), 9 Drummer Rd, Keene 03431. SAN 322-4244. Tel. 603-357-3385, fax 603-357-2075. *Exec. Dir.* Tracy L. Thompson.

New Hampshire College and University Council, 3 Barrell Court, Ste. 100, Concord 03301-8543. SAN 322-2322. Tel. 603-225-4199, fax 603-225-8108. *Exec. Dir.* Thomas R. Horgan.

Nubanusit Library Cooperative, c/o Peterborough Town Lib., Peterborough 03458. SAN 322-4600. Tel. 603-924-8040, fax 603-924-8041.

Scrooge and Marley Cooperative, 695 Main St., Laconia 03246. SAN 329-515X. Tel. 603-524-4775. *Chair* Randy Brough.

New Jersey

Basic Health Sciences Library Network (BHSL), Overlook Hospital Health Science Lib., Summit 07902. SAN 371-4888. Tel. 908-522-2886, fax 908-522-2274. *Coord.* Pat Regenberg.

Bergen Passaic Health Sciences Library Consortium, c/o Englewood Hospital and Medical Center, Health Sciences Lib., Englewood 07631. SAN 371-0904. Tel. 201-894-3069, fax 201-894-9049, e-mail lia.sabbagh@ehmc.com.

Burlington Libraries Information Consortium (BLINC), 5 Pioneer Blvd., Westampton 08060. Tel. 609-267-9660, fax 609-267-4091, e-mail hq@bcls.lib.nj.us. *Assistant Dir.* Molly Connor.

Central Jersey Regional Library Cooperative (CJRLC), 4400 Rte. 9 S., Ste. 3400, Freehold 07728-4232. SAN 370-5102. Tel. 732-409-6484, fax 732-409-6492. *Exec. Dir.* Connie S. Paul.

Central New Jersey Health Science Libraries Consortium (CNJHSLA), Saint Francis Medical Center Medical Lib., Trenton 08629. SAN 370-0712. Tel. 609-599-5068, fax 609-599-5773. *Libn.* Donna Barlow.

Consortium of Foundation Libraries, Robert Wood Johnson Foundation, Princeton 08543. SAN 322-2462. Tel. 609-452-8701. *Chair* Hinda Greenberg.

Cosmopolitan Biomedical Library Consortium (CBLC), Overlook Hospital Medical Lib., Summit 07902. SAN 322-4414. Tel. 908-522-2699. *In Charge* Vicki Sciuk.

Health Sciences Library Association of New Jersey (HSLANJ), Saint Michael's Medical Center, Newark 07102. SAN 370-0488. Tel. 973-877-5471, fax 973-877-5378. *Dir.* Larry Dormer.

Highlands Regional Library Cooperative, 66 Ford Rd., Ste. 124, Denville 07834. SAN 329-4609. Tel. 973-664-1776, fax 973-664-1780. *Exec. Dir.* Joanne P. Roukens.

INFOLINK/Eastern New Jersey Regional Library Cooperative, Inc., 44 Stelton Rd., Ste. 330, Piscataway 08854. SAN 371-5116. Tel. 732-752-7720, fax 732-752-7785. *Exec. Dir.* Cheryl O'Connor.

Integrated Information Solutions, 600 Mountain Ave., Rm. 6A-200, Murray Hill 07974. SAN 329-5400. Tel. 908-582-4840, fax 908-582-3146, e-mail libnet@library.lucent.com. *Mgr.* M. E. Brennan.

Libraries of Middlesex Automation Consortium (LMxAC), 1030 Saint George, Ste. 203, Avenel 07001. SAN 329-448X. Tel. 732-750-2525, fax 732-750-9392.

Monmouth-Ocean Biomedical Information Consortium (MOBIC), Community Medical Center, Toms River 08755. SAN 329-5389. Tel. 732-557-8117, fax 732-557-8354. *Libn.* Reina Reisler.

Morris Automated Information Network (MAIN), c/o Morris County Lib., 30 East Hanover Ave., Whippany 07981. SAN 322-4058. Tel. 973-631-5353, fax 973-631-5366. *Network Admin.* Ellen L. Sleeter.

Morris-Union Federation, 214 Main St., Chatham 07928. SAN 310-2629. Tel. 973-635-0603, fax 973-635-7827.

New Jersey Health Sciences Library Network (NJHSN), Overlook Hospital Lib., Summit 07902. SAN 371-4829. Tel. 908-522-2886, fax 908-522-2274. *In Charge* Patricia Regenberg.

New Jersey Library Network, Lib. Development Bureau, Trenton 08608. SAN 372-8161. Tel. 609-984-3293, fax 609-633-3963.

South Jersey Regional Library Cooperative, Paint Works Corporate Center, Gibbsboro 08026. SAN 329-4625. Tel. 856-346-

1222, fax 856-346-2839. *Exec. Dir.* Karen Hyman.

Virtual Academic Library Environment (VALE), William Paterson Univ. Lib., Wayne 07470-2103. Tel. 973-720-3179, fax 973-720-3171. *Chair* Judy Cohn.

New Mexico

Alliance for Innovation in Science and Technology Information (AISTI), 369 Montezuma Ave., No. 156, Santa Fe 87501. E-mail info@aisti.org. *Chair* Margaret Alexander.

Estacado Library Information Network (ELIN), 509 N. Shipp, Hobby 88240. Tel. 505-397-9328, fax 505-397-1508. *System Admin.* Cristine Adams.

New Mexico Consortium of Academic Libraries, Dean's Office, Albuquerque 87131-0001. SAN 371-6872. Tel. 505-277-5057, fax 502-277-7196. *Dean* Camila Alire.

New Mexico Consortium of Biomedical and Hospital Libraries, Albuquerque Regional Medical Center/Lib., Albuquerque 87102. SAN 322-449X. Tel. 505-727-8291, fax 505-727-8190, e-mail medicall@sjhs.org. *Libn.* Marian Frear.

New York

Academic Libraries of Brooklyn, Long Island Univ. Lib.-LLC 517, Brooklyn 11201. SAN 322-2411. Tel. 718-488-1081, fax 718-780-4057. *Dean* Constance Woo.

Associated Colleges of the Saint Lawrence Valley, SUNY Potsdam, Potsdam 13676-2299. SAN 322-242X. Tel. 315-267-3331, fax 315-267-2389. *Exec. Dir.* Anneke J. Larrance.

Brooklyn-Queens-Staten Island-Manhattan-Bronx Health Sciences Librarians (BQSIMB), 121 DeKalb Ave., Brooklyn 11201. SAN 370-0828. Tel. 718-630-7200, fax 718-630-8918. *Pres.* Luda Dolinsky.

Capital District Library Council for Reference and Research Resources, 28 Essex St., Albany 12206. SAN 322-2446. Tel. 518-438-2500, fax 518-438-2872. *Exec. Dir.* Jean K. Sheviak.

Central New York Library Resources Council (CLRC), 6493 Ridings Rd., Syracuse 13206-1195. SAN 322-2454. Tel. 315-

446-5446, fax 315-446-5590, e-mail mclane @clrc.org. *Exec. Dir.* Michael J. McLane.

Connect NY, Rochester Institute of Technology, Rochester 14623. Tel. 585-475-2050. *Dir. of Technology* Chris Lerch.

Council of Archives and Research Libraries in Jewish Studies (CARLJS), 330 Seventh Ave., 21st fl., New York 10001. SAN 371-053X. Tel. 212-629-0500, fax 212-629-0508, e-mail nfjc@jewishculture.org. *Associate Dir.* Dana Schneider.

Library Association of Rockland County (LARC), P.O. Box 917, New City 10956-0917. Tel. 845-352-5700 ext. 251. *Pres.* Fred Sandner.

Library Consortium of Health Institutions in Buffalo (LCHIB), 155 Abbott Hall, SUNY at Buffalo, Buffalo 14214. SAN 329-367X. Tel. 716-829-3900 ext. 143, fax 716-829-2211. *Exec. Dir.* Martin E. Mutka.

Long Island Library Resources Council (LILRC), Melville Lib. Bldg., Ste. E5310, Stony Brook 11794-3399. SAN 322-2489. Tel. 631-632-6650, fax 631-632-6662. *Dir.* Herbert Biblo.

Medical and Scientific Libraries of Long Island (MEDLI), c/o Palmer School of Lib. and Info. Science, Brookville 11548. SAN 322-4309. Tel. 516-299-2866; 516-299-4110, fax 516-299-4168. *Pres.* Mary Westermann-Cicio.

Medical Library Center of New York, 5 E. 102 St., New York 10029. SAN 322-3957. Tel. 212-427-1630, fax 212-876-6697. *Dir.* Lois Weinstein.

Metropolitan New York Library Council (METRO), 57 E. 11 St., 4th fl., New York 10003-4605. SAN 322-2500. Tel. 212-228-2320, fax 212-228-2598. *Exec. Dir.* Dottie Hiebing.

National Network of Libraries of Medicine—Middle Atlantic Region (NN-LM MAR), New York Academy of Medicine, New York 10029-5293. Tel. 212-822-7396, fax 212-534-7042, e-mail rml1@nyam.org. *Associate Dir.* Naomi Adelman.

New York State Higher Education Initiative (NYSHEI), 22 Corporate Woods Blvd., Albany 12211-2350. Fax 518-432-4346. *Exec. Dir.* Sharon Bonk.

Northeast Foreign Law Libraries Cooperative Group, Columbia Univ. Lib., New York

10027. SAN 375-0000. Tel. 212-854-1411, fax 212-854-3295. *Coord.* Silke Sahl.

Northern New York Library Network, 6721 US Hwy. 11, Potsdam 13676. SAN 322-2527. Tel. 315-265-1119, fax 315-265-1881, e-mail info@nnyln.org. *Exec. Dir.* John J. Hammond.

Nylink, 74 N. Pearl St., 5th fl., Albany 12207. SAN 322-256X. Tel. 518-443-5444, fax 518-432-4346, e-mail nylink@nylink.org. *Exec. Dir.* Mary-Alice Lynch.

Research Library Association of South Manhattan, Bobst Lib., New York Univ., New York 10012. SAN 372-8080. Tel. 212-998-2477, fax 212-995-4366. *Dean of Lib.* Carol Mandel.

Rochester Regional Library Council, 390 Packetts Landing, Fairport 14450. SAN 322-2535. Tel. 585-223-7570, fax 585-223-7712, e-mail rrlc@rrlc.org. *Exec. Dir.* Kathleen M. Miller.

South Central Regional Library Council, Clinton Hall, Ithaca 14850. SAN 322-2543. Tel. 607-273-9106, fax 607-272-0740, e-mail scrlc@lakenet.org. *Exec. Dir.* Jean Currie.

Southeastern New York Library Resources Council (SENYLRC), 21 S. Elting Corners Rd., Highland 12528-2805. SAN 322-2551. Tel. 845-883-9065, fax 845-883-9483. *Exec. Dir.* John L. Shaloiko.

SUNYConnect, Office of Lib. and Info. Services, Albany 12246. Tel. 518-443-5577, fax 518-443-5358. *Assistant Provost for Lib. and Info. Services* Carey Hatch.

United Nations System Electronic Information Acquisitions Consortium (UNSEIAC), c/o Dag Hammarskjold Lib., Rm. L-166A, New York 10017. SAN 377-855X. Tel. 212-963-7440, fax 212-963-2608. *Head Libn.* Linda Stoddart.

Western New York Library Resources Council, 4455 Genesee St., Buffalo 14225. SAN 322-2578. Tel. 716-633-0705, fax 716-633-1736. *Exec. Dir.* Sheryl Knab.

North Carolina

Cape Fear Health Sciences Information Consortium, c/o Ervin J. Biggs Lib., Lumberton 28358. SAN 322-3930. Tel. 910-671-5046, fax 910-671-5337.

Dialog Corp, 11000 Regency Pkwy., Ste. 10, Cary 27511. SAN 322-0176. Tel. 919-462-8600, fax 919-468-9890.

North Carolina Area Health Education Centers, Univ. of North Carolina Health Science Lib., CB 7585, Chapel Hill 27599-7585. SAN 323-9950. Tel. 919-962-0700. *Dir.* Diana McDuffee.

North Carolina Community College System, 200 W. Jones St., Raleigh 27603-1379. SAN 322-2594. Tel. 919-807-7100, fax 919-807-7164. *Admin. Dir.* Sharon Rasazo.

North Carolina Library and Information Network, State Lib. of North Carolina, Raleigh 27601-2807. SAN 329-3092. Tel. 919-807-7400, fax 919-733-8748. *State Libn.* Mary L. Boone.

Northwest AHEC Library at Hickory, Catawba Medical Center, Hickory 28602. SAN 322-4708. Tel. 828-326-3662, fax 828-326-3484. *Dir.* Karen Lee Martinez.

Northwest AHEC Library at Salisbury, c/o Rowan Regional Medical Center, Salisbury 28144. SAN 322-4589. Tel. 704-210-5069, fax 704-636-5050.

Northwest AHEC Library Information Network, Wake Forest Univ. School of Medicine, Winston-Salem 27157-1049. SAN 322-4716. Tel. 336-713-7009, fax 336-713-7028. *Senior Libn.* Julie Richardson.

Southeastern Chapter of the American Association of Law Libraries (SEAALL), Univ. of North Carolina at Chapel Hill, Chapel Hill 27599. *Pres.* Anne Klinefelter.

Triangle Research Libraries Network, Wilson Lib., Chapel Hill 27514-8890. SAN 329-5362. Tel. 919-962-8022, fax 919-962-4452. *Admin. Services* Patti Pittman.

Western North Carolina Library Network (WNCLN), D. Hiden Ramsey Lib., Univ. of North Carolina at Asheville, Asheville 28804. SAN 376-7205. Tel. 828-232-5095, fax 828-232-5137. *Dir.* Mark A. Stoffan.

North Dakota

Central Dakota Library Network, Morton Mandan Public Lib., Mandan 58554-3149. SAN 373-1391. Tel. 701-667-5365. *Dir.* Kelly Steckler.

Mid-America Law School Library Consortium (MALSLC), Univ. of North Dakota

School of Law, Grand Forks 58202. SAN 371-6813. Tel. 701-777-2535, fax 701-777-2219. *Chair* Gary Gott.

Tri-College University Libraries Consortium, 650 NP Ave., Fargo 58102. SAN 322-2047. Tel. 701-231-8170, fax 701-231-7205.

Ohio

Association of Christian Librarians (ACL), P.O. Box 4, Cedarville 45314. Tel. 937-766-2255, fax 937-766-5499, e-mail web master@acl.org; info@acl.org. *Exec. Dir.* Nancy J. Olson.

Central Ohio Hospital Library Consortium, 127 S. Davis Ave., Columbus 43222. SAN 371-084X. Tel. 614-234-5214, fax 614-234-1257. *Dir.* Rebecca Ayers.

Christian Library Consortium (CLC), c/o ACL, Cedarville 45314. Tel. 937-766-2255, fax 937-766-5499, e-mail info@acl. org. *Coord.* Beth Purtee.

Cleveland Area Metropolitan Library System (CAMLS), 20600 Chagrin Blvd., Ste. 500, Shaker Heights 44122-5334. SAN 322-2632. Tel. 216-921-3900, fax 216-921-7220. *Exec. Dir.* Michael G. Snyder.

Columbus Area Library and Information Council of Ohio (CALICO), c/o Westerville Public Lib., Westerville 43081. SAN 371-683X. Tel. 614-882-7277, fax 614-882-5369.

Consortium of Popular Culture Collections in the Midwest (CPCCM), c/o Popular Culture Lib., Bowling Green 43403-0600. SAN 370-5811. Tel. 419-372-2450, fax 419-372-7996. *In Charge* Nancy Down.

Five Colleges of Ohio, 102 Allen House, Gambier 43022. Tel. 740-427-5377, fax 740-427-5390. *Chair* Mark Huddleston.

Molo Regional Library System, 123 N. Bridge St., Newcomerstown 43832-1093. SAN 322-2705. Tel. 330-364-8535, fax 330-364-8537.

NEOUCOM Council of Associated Hospital Librarians, Oliver Ocasek Regional Medical Info. Center, Rootstown 44272. SAN 370-0526. Tel. 330-325-6616; 330-325-6600, fax 330-325-0522. *Dir.* Thomas C. Atwood.

Northeast Ohio Regional Library System/ NEO-RLS, 4445 Mahoning Ave. N.W.,

Warren 44483. SAN 322-2713. Tel. 330-847-7744, fax 330-847-7704, e-mail nola @nolanet.org. *Interim Exec. Dir.* Kristen Pool.

Northwest Library District (NORWELD), 181 1/2 S. Main St., Bowling Green 43402. SAN 322-273X. Tel. 419-352-2903, fax 419-353-8310. *Dir.* Allan Gray.

OCLC Online Computer Library Center, 6565 Frantz Rd., Dublin 43017-3395. SAN 322-2748. Tel. 614-764-6000, fax 614-718-1017, e-mail oclc@oclc.org. *Pres./CEO* Jay Jordan.

Ohio Health Sciences Library Association (OHSLA), c/o Fordham Health Sciences, Dayton 45435. Tel. 937-775-3837, fax 937-775-2232. *Pres.* Ximena Chrisagis.

Ohio Library and Information Network (Ohio-LINK), 2455 N. Star Rd., Ste. 300, Columbus 43221. SAN 374-8014. Tel. 614-728-3600, fax 614-728-3610, e-mail info@ohio link.edu. *Exec. Dir.* Thomas J. Sanville.

Ohio Network of American History Research Centers, Ohio Historical Society Archives/ Lib., Columbus 43211-2497. SAN 323-9624. Tel. 614-297-2510, fax 614-297-2546, e-mail ohsref@ohiohistory.org. *Research* Louise Jones.

Ohio Public Library Information Network (OPLIN), 2323 W. 5 Ave., Columbus 43204. Tel. 614-728-5252, fax 614-728-5256, e-mail support@oplin.org. *Exec. Dir.* Stephen Hedges.

OHIONET, 1500 W. Lane Ave., Columbus 43221-3975. SAN 322-2764. Tel. 614-486-2966, fax 614-486-1527. *Exec. Dir./ CEO* Michael P. Butler.

Rural Ohio Valley Health Sciences Library Network (ROVHSLN), Highland District Hospital, Hillsboro 45133. *Chair* Louis Mays.

Southeast Regional Library System (SERLS), 252 W. 13 St., Wellston 45692. SAN 322-2756. Tel. 740-384-2103, fax 740-384-2106, e-mail dirserls@oplin.org. *Dir.* Marion J. Cochran.

Southwestern Ohio Council for Higher Education, 3155 Research Blvd., Ste. 204, Dayton 45420-4015. SAN 322-2659. Tel. 937-258-8890, fax 937-258-8899, e-mail soche@soche.org.

State Assisted Academic Library Council of Kentucky (SAALCK), c/o SWON Libs., Cincinnati 45241. SAN 371-2222. Tel. 513-751-4422, fax 513-751-0463, e-mail saalck@saalck.org. *Exec. Dir.* Anne Abate.

SWON Libraries, 10815 Indeco Drive, Ste. 200, Cincinnati 45241-2926. SAN 322-2675. Tel. 513-751-4422, fax 513-751-0463, e-mail info@swonlibraries.org. *Exec. Dir.* Anne K. Abate.

Theological Consortium of Greater Columbus (TCGC), Trinity Lutheran Seminary, Columbus 43209-2334. Tel. 614-384-4646, fax 614-238-0263, e-mail voyager@www.tcgcohio.org. *Lib. Systems Mgr.* Ray Olson.

Oklahoma

Greater Oklahoma Area Health Sciences Library Consortium (GOAL), Mercy Memorial Health Center–Resource Center, Ardmore 73401. SAN 329-3858. Tel. 580-220-6625, fax 580-220-6599. *Pres.* Catherine Ice.

Oklahoma Health Sciences Library Association (OHSLA), Univ. of Oklahoma—HSC Bird Health Science Lib., Oklahoma City 73190. SAN 375-0051. Tel. 405-271-2285 ext. 48755, fax 405-271-3297. *Dir.* Clinton M. Thompson.

Oregon

Chemeketa Cooperative Regional Library Service, c/o Chemeketa Community College, Salem 97305-1453. SAN 322-2837. Tel. 503-399-5105, fax 503-399-7316, e-mail cocl@chemeketa.edu. *Coord.* Linda Cochrane.

Coastal Resource Sharing Network (CRSN), c/o Tillamook County Lib., Tillamook 97141. Tel. 503-842-4792, e-mail webmaster@beachbooks.org. *Pres.* Sara Charlton.

Coos County Library Service District, Tioga 104, 1988 Newmark, Coos Bay 97420. SAN 322-4279. Tel. 541-888-7260, fax 541-888-7285. *Dir.* Mary Jane Fisher.

Gorge LINK Library Consortium, c/o Hood River County Lib., Hood River 97031. Tel. 541-387-4659, 541-386-2535, fax 541-386-3835, e-mail gorge.link@co.

hood-river.or.us. *System Admin.* Jayne Guidinger.

Library Information Network of Clackamas County, 16239 S.E. McLoughlin Blvd., Ste. 208, Oak Grove 97267-4654. SAN 322-2845. Tel. 503-723-4888, fax 503-794-8238. *Mgr.* Joanna Rood.

Orbis Cascade Alliance, 1501 Kincaid, No. 4, Eugene 97401-4540. SAN 377-8096. Tel. 541-346-1832, fax 541-346-1968, e-mail orbcas@uoregon.edu. *Chair* Susan Barnes Whyte.

Oregon Health Sciences Libraries Association (OHSLA), Oregon Health and Science Univ. Lib., Portland 97239-3098. SAN 371-2176. Tel. 503-494-3462, fax 503-494-3322, e-mail library@ohsu.edu. *Dir.* James Morgan.

PORTALS (Portland Area Library System), P.O. Box 19000, Portland 97219. Tel. 503-977-4571, fax 503-977-4977. *Coord.* Roberta Richards.

Southern Oregon Library Federation, c/o Klamath County Lib., Klamath Falls 97601. SAN 322-2861. Tel. 541-882-8894, fax 541-882-6166. *Dir.* Andy Swanson.

Southern Oregon Library Information System (SOLIS), 724 S. Central Ave., Ste. 112, Medford 97501. Tel. 541-772-2141, fax 541-772-2144, e-mail solis_97501@yahoo.com. *System Admin.* Sylvia Lee.

Washington County Cooperative Library Services, 111 N.E. Lincoln St., MS No. 58, Hillsboro 97124-3036. SAN 322-287X. Tel. 503-846-3222, fax 503-846-3220. *Mgr.* Eva Calcagno.

Pennsylvania

Associated College Libraries of Central Pennsylvania, c/o Commonwealth Libs., Harrisburg 17126-1745. Tel. 717-783-5968, fax 717-783-2070. *Pres.* Caryn Carr.

Berks County Library Association (BCLA), Albright College Lib., Reading 19612-5234. SAN 371-0866. Tel. 610-921-7212. *Pres.* Joan King.

Central Pennsylvania Consortium (CPC), Dickinson College, Carlisle 17013-2896. SAN 322-2896. Tel. 717-245-1515, fax 717-245-1807, e-mail cpc@dickinson.edu.

Central Pennsylvania Health Sciences Library Association (CPHSLA), Memorial Medical Center Health Sciences Lib., Johnstown 15905. SAN 375-5290. Tel. 814-534-9413, fax 814-534-3244. *Pres.* Kris Kalina.

Cooperating Hospital Libraries of the Lehigh Valley Area, Estes Lib., Saint Luke's Hospital, Bethlehem 18015. SAN 371-0858. Tel. 610-954-3407, fax 610-954-4651. *Chair* Sharon Hrabina.

Delaware Valley Information Consortium (DEVIC), St. Mary Medical Center Medical Lib., Langhorne 19047. Tel. 215-710-2012, fax 215-710-4638. *Dir.* Rita Haydar.

Eastern Mennonite Associated Libraries and Archives (EMALA), 2215 Millstream Rd, Lancaster 17602. SAN 372-8226. Tel. 717-393-9745, fax 717-393-8751. *Chair* Edsel Burdge.

Erie Area Health Information Library Cooperative (EAHILC), UPMC Northwest Medical Lib., Seneca 16346-2130. SAN 371-0564. Tel. 814-437-7000 ext. 5331, fax 814-437-4538, e-mail nwmc@mail.cosmosbbs.com. *Chair* Ann L. Lucas.

Greater Philadelphia Law Library Association (GPLLA), P.O. Box 335, Philadelphia 19105-0335. SAN 373-1375. E-mail gpllal@hslc.org. *Pres.* Jeffrey W. Kreiling.

Health Sciences Libraries Consortium/Access PA/HSLC/Access PA, 3600 Market St., Ste. 550, Philadelphia 19104-2646. SAN 323-9780. Tel. 215-222-1532, fax 215-222-0416, e-mail support@hslc.org. *Exec. Dir.* Joseph C. Scorza.

Interlibrary Delivery Service of Pennsylvania (IDS), c/o Bucks County IU, No. 22, Doylestown 18901. SAN 322-2942. Tel. 215-348-2940 ext. 1620, fax 215-348-8315, e-mail ids@bucksiu.org. *Admin. Dir.* Beverly J. Carey.

Keystone Library Network, Dixon Univ. Center, Harrisburg 17110-1201. Tel. 717-720-4088, fax 717-720-4453. *Coord.* Mary Lou Sowden.

Laurel Highlands Health Science Library Consortium, 116 Luna Lane, Johnstown 15904. SAN 322-2950. Tel. 814-341-0242, fax 814-266-8230. *Dir.* Heather W. Brice.

Lehigh Valley Association of Independent Colleges, 130 W. Greenwich St., Bethlehem 18018. SAN 322-2969. Tel. 610-625-

7888, fax 610-625-7891. *Exec. Dir.* Tom A. Tenges.

Montgomery County Library and Information Network Consortium (MCLINC), 301 Lafayette St., 2nd fl., Conshohocken 19428. Tel. 610-238-0580, fax 610-238-0581, e-mail webmaster@mclinc.org. *System Admin.* Miriam Phillips.

Northeastern Pennsylvania Library Network, c/o Marywood Univ. Lib., Scranton 18509-1598. SAN 322-2993. Tel. 570-348-6260, fax 570-961-4769. *Dir.* Catherine H. Schappert.

Northwest Interlibrary Cooperative of Pennsylvania (NICOP), Edinboro Univ. of Pennsylvania, Edinboro 16444. SAN 370-5862. Tel. 814-732-2779, fax 814-732-2883. *Dir.* Donald Dilmore.

PALINET, 3000 Market St., Ste. 200, Philadelphia 19104-2801. SAN 322-3000. Tel. 215-382-7031, fax 215-382-0022, e-mail palinet@palinet.org. *Exec. Dir.* Catherine C. Wilt.

Pennsylvania Library Association, 220 Cumberland Pkwy., Ste. 10, Mechanicsburg 17055. Tel. 717-766-7663, fax 717-766-5440. *Pres.* Mary Garm.

Philadelphia Area Consortium of Special Collections Libraries (PACSCL), The Historical Society of Pennsylvania, Philadelphia 19107. SAN 370-7504. Tel. 215-985-1445, fax 215-985-1446, e-mail info@pacscl.org. *Chair* David Moltke-Hansen.

Southeastern Pennsylvania Theological Library Association (SEPTLA), c/o Lancaster Theological Seminary, Lancaster 17603. SAN 371-0793. Tel. 717-290-8755. *Chair* Marsha Blake.

State System of Higher Education Library Cooperative (SSHELCO), c/o Bailey Lib., Slippery Rock 16057. Tel. 724-738-2630, fax 724-738-2661. *Dir.* Philip Tramdack.

Susquehanna Library Cooperative (SLC), James V. Brown Lib., Williamsport 17701. SAN 322-3051. Tel. 570-326-0536. *Chair* John B. Pitcher.

Tri-State College Library Cooperative (TCLC), c/o Rosemont College Lib., Rosemont 19010-1699. SAN 322-3078. Tel. 610-525-0796, fax 610-525-1939, e-mail tclc@hslc.org. *Coord.* Ellen Gasiewski.

Rhode Island

Cooperating Libraries Automated Network— CLAN (Rhode Island), 600 Sandy Lane, Warwick 02886. SAN 329-4560. Tel. 401-738-2200, fax 401-736-8949. *Chair* Susan Reed.

Library of Rhode Island (LORI), c/o Office of Lib. and Info Services, Providence 02908-5870. SAN 371-6821. Tel. 401-222-2726, fax 401-222-4195. *Lib. Services Dir.* Anne Parent.

South Carolina

Charleston Academic Libraries Consortium (CALC), Trident Tech College, Learning Resource Centers, Charleston 29406-4607. SAN 371-0769. Tel. 843-574-6088, fax 843-574-6484. *Chair* Drucie Gullion.

Columbia Area Medical Librarians' Association (CAMLA), Professional Lib., Columbia 29201. SAN 372-9400. Tel. 803-898-1735, fax 803-898-1712. *Coord.* Neeta N. Shah.

Partnership Among South Carolina Academic Libraries (PASCAL), c/o Thomas Cooper Lib., Columbia 29208. Tel. 803-777-1327, fax 803-777-2818. *Exec. Dir.* Rick Moul.

South Carolina AHEC, c/o Medical Univ. of South Carolina, Charleston 29425. SAN 329-3998. Tel. 843-792-4431, fax 843-792-4430. *Exec. Dir.* David Garr.

South Carolina State Library/South Carolina Library Network, 1430 and 1500 Senate St., Columbia 29201. SAN 322-4198. Tel. 803-734-8666, fax 803-734-8676, e-mail webadm@leo.scsl.state.sc.us. *Dir., Info. Services* Mary Morgan.

South Dakota

South Dakota Library Network (SDLN), 1200 University, Unit 9672, Spearfish 57799-9672. SAN 371-2117. Tel. 605-642-6835, fax 605-642-6472. *Dir.* Gary Johnson.

Tennessee

Association of Memphis Area Health Science Libraries (AMAHSL), c/o Methodist Healthcare Nursing Lib., Memphis 38104. SAN 323-9802. Tel. 901-726-8862, fax 901-726-8807. *Libn.* Denise Fesmire.

Consortium of Southern Biomedical Libraries (CONBLS), Meharry Medical College, Nashville 37208. SAN 370-7717. Tel. 615-327-6728, fax 615-327-6448. *Acting Dir.* Marvelyn E. Thompson.

Knoxville Area Health Sciences Library Consortium (KAHSLC), Univ. of Tennessee Medical Center, Knoxville 37920. SAN 371-0556. Tel. 865-544-9525, fax 865-544-9527. *In Charge* Martha Earl.

Mid-Tennessee Health Science Librarians Association, VA Medical Center, Nashville 37212. SAN 329-5028. Tel. 615-327-4751 ext. 5523, fax 615-321-6336.

Tennessee Health Science Library Association (THeSLA), Holston Valley Medical Center Health Sciences Lib., Kingsport 37660. SAN 371-0726. Tel. 423-224-6870, fax 423-224-6014, e-mail sharon_m_brown@wellmont.org.

Tri-Cities Area Health Sciences Libraries Consortium, East Tennessee State Univ., James H. Quillen College of Medicine, Johnson City 37614. SAN 329-4099. Tel. 423-439-6252, fax 423-439-7025. *Dir.* Biddanda Ponnappa.

Wolf River Library Consortium, c/o Germantown Community Lib., Germantown 38138-2815. Tel. 901-757-7323, fax 901-756-9940. *Dir.* Sue Loper.

Texas

Abilene Library Consortium, 1222 N. 5 St., Abilene 79601. SAN 322-4694. Tel. 325-672-7081, fax 325-672-7084. *Exec. Dir.* Robert Gillette.

Amigos Library Services, Inc., 14400 Midway Rd., Dallas 75244-3509. SAN 322-3191. Tel. 972-851-8000, fax 972-991-6061, e-mail amigos@amigos.org. *Exec. Dir.* Bonnie Juergens.

Council of Research and Academic Libraries (CORAL), P.O. Box 290236, San Antonio 78280-1636. SAN 322-3213.

Del Norte Biosciences Library Consortium, El Paso Community College, El Paso 79998. SAN 322-3302. Tel. 915-831-4149, fax 915-831-4639. *Coord.* Becky Perales.

Harrington Library Consortium, 413 E. 4
Ave., Amarillo 79101. SAN 329-546X.
Tel. 806-378-6037, fax 806-378-6038.
Dir. Donna Littlejohn.
Health Libraries Information Network (Health
LINE), UT Southwestern Medical Center
Lib., Dallas 75390-9049. SAN 322-3299.
Tel. 214-648-2626, fax 214-648-2826.
Assistant V.P. for Libs. and Media Centers
Laurie Thompson.
Houston Area Library Automation Network
(HALAN), Houston Public Lib., Houston
77002. Tel. 832-393-1313, fax 832-393-
1427, e-mail website@hpl.lib.tx.us. *Chief*
Karen Williams.
Houston Area Research Library Consortium
(HARLiC), c/o Univ. of Houston Libs.,
Houston 77204-2000. SAN 322-3329. Tel.
713-743-9807, fax 713-743-9811. *Pres.*
Dana Rooks.
National Network of Libraries of Medicine—
South Central Region (NN/LM SCR), c/o
HAM-TMC Lib., Houston 77030-2809.
SAN 322-3353. Tel. 713-799-7880, fax
713-790-7030, e-mail nnlm-scr@exch.
library.tmc.edu. *Dir.* Elizabeth K. Eaton.
Northeast Texas Library System (NETLS),
625 Austin St., Garland 75040-6365. SAN
370-5943. Tel. 972-205-2566, fax 972-
205-2767. *Dir.* Claire Bausch.
South Central Academic Medical Libraries
Consortium (SCAMeL), c/o Lewis Lib.–
UNTHSC, Fort Worth 76107. SAN 372-
8269. Tel. 817-735-2380, fax 817-735-
5158.
Texas Council of Academic Libraries, Texas
Lib. Assn., Austin 78746-6763. SAN 322-
337X. *Pres.* Mark Tucker.
Texnet, P.O. Box 12927, Austin 78711. SAN
322-3396. Tel. 512-463-5406, fax 512-
936-2306, e-mail ill@tsl.state.tx.us.

Utah

Forest Service Library Network, Rocky
Mountain Research Sta., Ogden 84401.
SAN 322-032X. Tel. 801-625-5445, fax
801-625-5129, e-mail rmrs_library@fs.
fed.us. *Network Leader* Carol Ayer.
National Network of Libraries of Medicine—
MidContinental Region (NN-LM MCR),
Spencer S. Eccles Health Science Lib.,
Univ. of Utah, Salt Lake City 84112-5890.

SAN 322-225X. Tel. 801-587-3412, fax
801-581-3632. *Dir.* Wayne J. Peay.
Utah Academic Library Consortium (UALC),
Univ. of Utah, Salt Lake City 84112-0731.
SAN 322-3418. Tel. 801-581-3386; 801-
581-6594, fax 801-585-3033. *Dir.* Rita
Reusch.
Utah Health Sciences Library Consortium,
c/o Spencer S. Eccles Health Science Lib.,
Univ. of Utah, Salt Lake City 84112. SAN
376-2246. Tel. 801-588-2430.

Vermont

Vermont Resource Sharing Network, c/o
Vermont Dept. of Libs., Montpelier 05609-
0601. SAN 322-3426. Tel. 802-828-3261,
fax 802-828-2199. *Dir., Lib. Services* Mar-
jorie Zunder.

Virgin Islands

VILINET/Virgin Islands Library and Information Network, c/o Div. of Libs., Archives,
and Museums, Saint Thomas 00802. SAN
322-3639. Tel. 340-773-5715, fax 340-
773-3257. *Dir.* Wallace Williams.

Virginia

American Indian Higher Education Consortium (AIHEC), 121 Oronoco St., Alexandria 22314. SAN 329-4056. Tel. 703-838-
0400, fax 703-838-0388, e-mail aihec@
aihec.org. *Pres.* James Shanley.
Defense Technical Information Center, 8725
John J. Kingman Rd., Ste. 1948, Fort
Belvoir 22060-6218. SAN 322-3442. Tel.
703-767-9100, fax 703-767-9183. *Acting
Admin.* Paul Ryan.
Lynchburg Area Library Cooperative, Randolph College, Lynchburg 24503. SAN
322-3450. Tel. 434-947-8133, fax 434-
947-8134. *Instructional Services Libn.,
Reference Services* Patricia DeMars.
Lynchburg Information Online Network
(LION), 2315 Memorial Ave., Lynchburg
24503. SAN 374-6097. Tel. 434-381-
6311, fax 434-381-6173. *Dir.* John G. Jaf-
fee.
NASA Libraries Information System—NASA
Galaxie, NASA Langley Research Center,
MS 185-Technical Lib., Hampton 23681-

2199. SAN 322-0788. Tel. 757-864-2356, fax 757-864-2375, e-mail tech-library@larc.nasa.gov. *Branch Mgr.* Carolyn L. Helmetsie.

Richmond Academic Library Consortium (RALC), Virginia Commonwealth Lib., Richmond 23284-2033. SAN 322-3469. Tel. 804-828-1107, fax 804-828-1105. *Officer* John E. Ulmschneider.

Southside Virginia Library Network (SVLN), Longwood Univ., Farmville 23909-1897. SAN 372-8242. Tel. 434-395-2633, fax 434-395-2453. *Dir.* Wendell Barbour.

Southwestern Virginia Health Information Librarians (SWVAHILI), Carilion Health Sciences Lib., Roanoke 24033. SAN 323-9527. Tel. 540-981-8039, fax 540-981-8666, e-mail kdillon@carilion.com. *Chair* Kelly Near.

United States Army Training and Doctrine Command (TRADOC)/Library Program Office, U.S. Army HQ TRADOC, Fort Monroe 23651. SAN 322-418X. Tel. 757-788-2909, fax 757-788-2931. *Dir.* Janet Scheitle.

Virginia Independent College and University Library Association, c/o Mary Helen Cochran Lib., Sweet Briar 24595. SAN 374-6089. Tel. 434-381-6138, fax 434-381-6173. *Dir.* John Jaffee.

Virginia Tidewater Consortium for Higher Education (VTC), 1417 43rd St., Norfolk 23529-0293. SAN 329-5486. Tel. 757-683-3183, fax 757-683-4515, e-mail lgdotolo@aol.com. *Pres.* Lawrence G. Dotolo.

Virtual Library of Virginia (VIVA), George Mason Univ., Fairfax 22030. Tel. 703-993-4652, fax 703-993-4662. *Chair* Ralph Alberico.

Washington

Cooperating Libraries in Olympia (CLIO), Evergreen State College Lib. L2300, Olympia 98505. SAN 329-4528. Tel. 360-867-6260, fax 360-867-6790. *Dean, Lib. Services* Lee Lyttle.

Inland NorthWest Health Sciences Libraries (INWHSL), P.O. Box 10283, Spokane 99209-0283. SAN 370-5099. Tel. 509-324-7344, fax 509-324-7349. *Treas.* Robert Pringle.

National Network of Libraries of Medicine— Pacific Northwest Region (NN-LM PNR), Univ. of Washington, Seattle 98195-7155. SAN 322-3485. Tel. 206-543-8262, fax 206-543-2469, e-mail nnlm@u.washington.edu. *Dir.* Sherrilynne S. Fuller.

Palouse Area Library Information Services (PALIS), c/o Neill Public Lib., Pullman 99163. SAN 375-0132. Tel. 509-334-3595, fax 509-334-6051. *Dir.* Andriette Pieron.

VALNet, Asotin County Lib., Clarkston 99403. SAN 323-7672. Tel. 509-758-5454, fax 509-751-1460, e-mail admin.acl@valnet.org. *Dir.* Jennifer Ashby.

Washington Idaho Network (WIN), Gonzaga Univ., Spokane 99258. Tel. 509-323-6545, fax 509-324-5398, e-mail winsupport@gonzaga.edu. *Pres.* Eileen Bell-Garrison.

West Virginia

Huntington Health Science Library Consortium, Marshall Univ. Health Science Libs., Huntington 25701-3655. SAN 322-4295. Tel. 304-691-1753, fax 304-691-1766. *Dir.* Edward Dzierzak.

Mid-Atlantic Law Library Cooperative (MALLCO), College of Law Lib., Morgantown 26506-6135. SAN 371-0645. Tel. 304-293-7775; 304-293-7641, fax 304-293-6020. *In Charge* Camille M. Riley.

Wisconsin

Arrowhead Health Sciences Library Network, Wisconsin Indianhead Technical College, Shell Lake 54817. SAN 322-1954. Tel. 715-468-2815 ext. 2298, fax 715-468-2599. *Coord.* Judy Lyons.

Fox River Valley Area Library Consortium (FRVALC), Moraine Park Technical College, Fond Du Lac 54935. SAN 322-3531. Tel. 920-924-3112; 920-922-8611, fax 920-924-3117. *In Charge* Charlene Pettit.

Fox Valley Library Council, c/o OWLS, Appleton 54911. SAN 323-9640. Tel. 920-832-6190, fax 920-832-6422. *Pres.* Joy Schwarz.

Library Council of Southeastern Wisconsin, Inc., 814 W. Wisconsin Ave., Milwaukee 53233-2309. SAN 322-354X. Tel. 414-

271-8470, fax 414-286-2798, e-mail lcomm
@execpc.com. *Exec. Dir.* Susie M. Just.

Network of Illinois Learning Resources in
Community Colleges (NILRC), P.O. Box
120, Blanchardville 53516. Tel. 608-523-
4094, fax 608-523-4072. *Exec. Dir.* John
W. Berry.

North East Wisconsin Intertype Libraries,
Inc. (NEWIL), 515 Pine St., Green Bay
54301. SAN 322-3574. Tel. 920-448-
4412, fax 920-448-4420. *Coord.* Terrie
Howe.

Northwestern Wisconsin Health Science
Library Consortium, Dr. Joseph F. Smith
Medical Lib., Wausau Hospital, Wausau
54401. Tel. 715-847-2184, fax 715-847-
2183. *In Charge* Jan Kraus.

South Central Wisconsin Health Science
Library Consortium, c/o Fort Healthcare
Medical Lib., Fort Atkinson 53538. SAN
322-4686. Tel. 920-568-5194, fax 920-
568-5195. *Coord.* Carrie Garity.

Southeastern Wisconsin Health Science
Library Consortium, Veteran's Admin.
Center Medical Lib., Milwaukee 53295.
SAN 322-3582. Tel. 414-384-2000 ext.
42342, fax 414-382-5334. *Dir.* Janice
Curnes.

Southeastern Wisconsin Information Technology Exchange, Inc. (SWITCH), 6801
N. Yates Rd., Milwaukee 53217-3985.
SAN 371-3962. Tel. 414-351-2423, fax
414-228-4146. *Coord.* William A. Topritz-
hofer.

University of Wisconsin System School Library Education Consortium (UWSSLEC),
Graduate and Continuing Education, Univ.
of Wisconsin–Whitewater, Whitewater
53190. Tel. 262-472-1463; 262-472-5208,
fax 262-472-5210, e-mail lenchoc@uww.
edu. *Co-Dir.* E. Anne Zarinnia.

Wisconsin Area Research Center Network/
ARC Network, Wisconsin Historical Society, Madison 53706. SAN 373-0875. Tel.
608-264-6477, fax 608-264-6486. *Head,
Public Services* Richard Pifer.

Wisconsin Library Services (WILS), 728
State St., Rm. 464, Madison 53706-1494.
SAN 322-3612. Tel. 608-263-4981, 608-
263-4962, fax 608-262-6067, 608-263-
3684. *Dir.* Kathryn Schneider Michaelis.

Wisconsin Public Library Consortium
(WPLC), c/o South Central Lib. System,
Madison 53718. *Dir.* Phyllis Davis.

Wisconsin Valley Library Service (WVLS),
300 N. 1 St., Wausau 54403. SAN 371-
3911. Tel. 715-261-7250, fax 715-261-
7259. *Dir.* Heather Ann Eldred.

WISPALS Library Consortium, c/o Gateway
Technical College, Kenosha 53144-1690.
Tel. 262-564-2602, fax 262-564-2787.
Coord. Meredith Atkinson.

Wyoming

Western Council of State Libraries, Inc.,
Supreme Court and State Lib. Bldg.,
Cheyenne 82002. SAN 322-2314. Tel.
307-777-5911. *Pres.* Lesley Boughton.

WYLD Network, c/o Wyoming State Lib.,
Cheyenne 82002-0060. SAN 371-0661.
Tel. 307-777-6339, fax 307-777-6289.
State Libn. Lesley Boughton.

Canada

Alberta

Alberta Association of College Librarians
(AACL), Lakeland College—Learning
Resources Centre, Vermillion T9X 1K5.
SAN 370-0763. Tel. 780-853-8468, fax
780-853-8662. *Acting Dir.* Greg Michaud.

The Alberta Library (TAL), 6-14, 7 Sir Win-
ston Churchill Sq., Edmonton T5J 2V5.
Tel. 780-414-0805, fax 780-414-0806.
Exec. Dir. Lucy Pana.

NEOS Library Consortium, Cameron Lib.,
5th fl., Edmonton T6G 2J8. Tel. 780-492-
0075, fax 780-492-8302. *Mgr.* Margaret
Law.

British Columbia

British Columbia Academic Health Council
(BCAHC), 402-1770 W. 7 Ave., Vancouver V6J 4Y6. Tel. 604-739-3910 ext. 228,
fax 604-739-3931, e-mail info@bcahc.ca.
Chief Exec. Officer George Eisler.

British Columbia College and Institute
Library Services, Langara College Lib.,
Vancouver V5Y 2Z6. SAN 329-6970. Tel.

604-323-5639, fax 604-323-5544, e-mail cils@langara.bc.ca. *Dir.* Mary Anne Epp.

British Columbia Electronic Library Network (BC ELN), WAC Bennett Lib., 7th fl., Simon Fraser Univ., Burnaby V5A 1S6. Tel. 778-782-7003, fax 778-782-3023, e-mail office@eln.bc.ca. *Exec. Dir.* Anita Cocchia.

Council of Prairie and Pacific University Libraries (COPPUL), 2005 Sooke Rd., Victoria V9B 5Y2. Tel. 250-391-2554, fax 250-391-2556, e-mail coppul@royalroads.ca. *Exec. Dir.* Alexander Slade.

Electronic Health Library of British Columbia (e-HLbc), c/o Bennett Lib., Burnaby V5A 1S6. Tel. 778-782-5440, fax 778-782-3023, e-mail info@ehlbc.ca. *Coord.* JoAnne Newyear-Ramirez.

Public Library InterLINK, c/o Kingsway Branch, Burnaby Public Lib., Burnaby V5E 1G3. SAN 318-8272. Tel. 604-517-8441, fax 604-517-8410, e-mail plilink@moon.bcpl.gov.bc.ca. *Operations Mgr.* Rita Avigdor.

Manitoba

Manitoba Government Libraries Council (MGLC), c/o Instructional Resources Unit, Winnipeg R3G 0T3. SAN 371-6848. Tel. 204-945-7833, fax 204-945-8756. *Chair* John Tooth.

Manitoba Library Consortium, Inc. (MLCI), c/o Lib. Administration, Univ. of Winnipeg, Winnipeg R3B 2E9. SAN 372-820X. Tel. 204-786-9801, fax 204-783-8910. *Chair* Mark Leggott.

New Brunswick

Maritimes Health Libraries Association (MHLA-ABSM), c/o Region 7 Hospital Corp., Miramich E1V 3G5. SAN 370-0836. Tel. 506-623-3215, fax 506-623-3280. *Libn.* Nancy McAllister.

Nova Scotia

NOVANET, 1550 Bedford Hwy., No. 501, Bedford B4A 1E6. SAN 372-4050. Tel. 902-453-2470, fax 902-453-2369, e-mail office@novanet.ns.ca. *Info. Technology* Dylan Boudreau.

Ontario

Bibliocentre, 31 Scarsdale Rd., North York M3B 2R2. SAN 322-3663. Tel. 647-722-9300, fax 647-722-9301. *Exec. Dir.* Janice Hayes.

Canadian Association of Research Libraries (Association des Bibliothèques de Recherche du Canada), Morisset Hall, Rm. 238, Ottawa K1N 9A5. SAN 323-9721. Tel. 613-562-5385, fax 613-562-5195, e-mail carladm@uottawa.ca. *Exec. Dir.* Timothy Mark.

Canadian Health Libraries Association (CHLA-ABSC), 39 River St., Toronto M5A 3P1. SAN 370-0720. Tel. 416-646-1600, fax 416-646-9460, e-mail info@chla-absc.ca. *Pres.* Penny Logan.

Canadian Research Knowledge Network (CRKN), Morisset Hall, Rm. 236, Ottawa K1N 6N5. Tel. 613-562-5357, fax 613-562-5329. *Exec. Dir.* Deb deBruijn.

Consortium of Ontario Academic Health Libraries (COAHL), Health Sciences Lib., Hamilton C8N 3Z5. Tel. 905-525-9140. *Chair* Dianne Kharouba.

Consortium of Ontario Libraries (COOL), 111 Peter St., Ste. 902, Toronto M5V 2H1. Tel. 416-961-1669, fax 416-961-5122. *Dir.* Barbara Franchetto.

Hamilton and District Health Library Network, c/o St. Joseph's Hospital, Hamilton L8N 4A6. SAN 370-5846. Tel. 905-522-1155 ext. 3410. *Coord.* Jean Maragno.

Health Science Information Consortium of Toronto, c/o Gerstein Science Info. Center, Univ. of Toronto, Toronto M5S 1A5. SAN 370-5080. Tel. 416-978-6359, fax 416-971-2637. *Exec. Dir.* Position currently open.

Ontario Council of University Libraries (OCUL), 130 Saint George St., Toronto M5S 1A5. Tel. 416-946-0578, fax 416-978-6755. *Exec. Dir.* Kathy Scardellato.

Ontario Health Libraries Association (OHLA), c/o Lakeridge Health, Oshawa L1G 2B9. SAN 370-0739. Tel. 905-576-8711 ext. 3334, fax 905-721-4759.

Ontario Library Consortium (OLC), Owen Sound and North Grey Union Public Lib., Owen Sound N4K 4K4. *Pres.* Judy Armstrong.

Parry Sound and Area Access Network, c/o Parry Sound Public Lib., Parry Sound P2A 1E3. Tel. 705-746-9601, fax 705-746-9601, e-mail pslib@zeuter.com. *Chair* Laurine Tremaine.

Perth County Information Network (PCIN), c/o Stratford Public Lib., Stratford N5A 1A2. Tel. 519-271-0220, fax 519-271-3843, e-mail webmaster@pcin.on.ca. *CEO* Sam Coglin.

Shared Library Services (SLS), Shared Lib. Services, South Huron Hospital, Exeter N0M 1S2. SAN 323-9500. Tel. 519-235-4002 ext. 249, fax 519-235-4476, e-mail shha.sls@shha.on.ca. *Libn.* Linda Wilcox.

Southwestern Ontario Health Libraries and Information Network (SOHLIN), South Huron Hospital, Exeter N0M 1S2. Tel. 519-235-5168, fax 519-235-4476. *Pres.* Linda Wilcox.

Toronto Health Libraries Association (THLA), 3409 Yonge St., Toronto M4N 2L0. SAN 323-9853. Tel. 416-485-0377, fax 416-485-6877, e-mail medinfoserv@rogers.com. *Pres.* Michelle Arbuckle.

Toronto School of Theology, 47 Queen's Park Crescent E., Toronto M5S 2C3. SAN 322-452X. Tel. 416-978-4039, fax 416-978-7821. *Chair* Lorna Young.

Quebec

Association des Bibliothèques de la Santé Affiliées a l'Université de Montréal (ABSAUM), c/o Health Library Univ., Montreal H3C 3J7. SAN 370-5838. Tel. 514-343-6826, fax 514-343-2350. *Dir.* Diane Raymond.

Canadian Heritage Information Network (CHIN), 15 Eddy St., 4th fl., Gatineau K1A 0M5. SAN 329-3076. Tel. 819-994-1200, fax 819-994-9555, e-mail service@chin.gc.ca. *Mgr.* Patricia Young.

National Library and Information-Industry Associations, United States and Canada

American Association of Law Libraries

Executive Director, Kate Hagan
53 W. Jackson Blvd., Ste. 940, Chicago, IL 60604
312-939-4764, fax 312-431-1097, e-mail khagan@aall.org
World Wide Web http://www.aallnet.org

Object

The American Association of Law Libraries (AALL) is established for educational and scientific purposes. It shall be conducted as a nonprofit corporation to promote and enhance the value of law libraries to the public, the legal community, and the world; to foster the profession of law librarianship; to provide leadership in the field of legal information; and to foster a spirit of cooperation among the members of the profession. Established 1906.

Membership

Memb. 5,000+. Persons officially connected with a law library or with a law section of a state or general library, separately maintained. Associate membership available for others. Dues (Indiv.) $208; (Retired) $52; (Student) $52. Year. July 1–June 30.

Officers

Pres. Ann T. Fessenden, U.S. Court of Appeals, 8th Circuit Lib., 22.300 U.S. Courthouse, 111 S. 10 St., St. Louis, MO 63102. Tel. 314-244-2660, fax 314-244-2675, e-mail ann_fessenden@ca8.uscourts.gov; *V.P.* James E. Duggan; *Secy.* Darcy Kirk; *Treas.* David S. Mao; *Past Pres.* Sarah G. Holterhoff.

Executive Board

Steven P. Anderson, Janice E. Henderson, Lyonette Louis-Jacques, Cornell H. Winston, Sally Wise.

American Library Association

Executive Director, Keith Michael Fiels
50 E. Huron St., Chicago, IL 60611
800-545-2433, 312-280-1392, fax 312-440-9374
World Wide Web http://www.ala.org

Object

The mission of the American Library Association (ALA) is to provide leadership for the development, promotion, and improvement of library and information services and the profession of librarianship in order to enhance learning and ensure access to information for all. Founded 1876.

Membership

Memb. (Indiv.) 60,983; (Inst.) 3,480; (Corporate) 266; (Total) 64,729 (as of July 12, 2007). Any person, library, or other organization interested in library service and librarians. Dues (Indiv.) 1st year, $60; 2nd year, $90; 3rd year and later, $120; (Trustee and Assoc. Memb.) $54; (Lib. Support Staff) $42; (Student) $30; (Foreign Indiv.) $72; (Other) $42; (Inst.) $110 and up, depending on operating expenses of institution.

Officers (2007–2008)

Pres. Loriene Roy, Professor, School of Info., Univ. of Texas at Austin, 1 University Sta., D7000, Austin, TX 78712-0390. Tel. 512-471-3959, fax 512-471-3971, email loriene@ischool.utexas.edu; *Pres.-Elect* Jim Rettig, Univ. Libn., Boatwright Memorial Lib., Univ. of Richmond, 28 Westhampton Way, Richmond, VA 23173. Tel. 804-289-8456, fax 804-287-1840, e-mail jrettig@richmond.edu; *Immediate Past Pres.* Leslie B. Burger, Dir., Princeton Public Lib., 65 Witherspoon St., Princeton, NJ 08542-3214. Tel. 609-924-8822 ext. 253, fax 609-924-7937, e-mail lburger@princetonlibrary.org; *Treas.* Rod Hersberger, Dean, Univ. Lib., California State University–Bakersfield, Walter W. Stiern Lib., 9001 Stockdale Hwy.,

Bakersfield, CA 93311-1022. Tel. 661-564-3042, fax 661-654-3238, e-mail rhersberger @csub.edu.

Executive Board

Francis J. Buckley, Jr. (2008), Mario M. Gonzalez (2009), Terri G. Kirk (2009), Charles E. Kratz, Jr. (2010), June A. Pinnell-Stephens (2008), Larry Romans (2010), Patricia H. Smith (2008), Roberta A. Stevens (2009).

Endowment Trustees

Daniel J. Bradbury, Robert R. Newlen, John Vitali; *Exec. Board Liaison* Rod Hersberger; *Staff Liaison* Gregory L. Calloway.

Divisions

See the separate entries that follow: American Assn. of School Libns.; Assn. for Lib. Collections and Technical Services; Assn. for Lib. Service to Children; Assn. for Lib. Trustees and Advocates; Assn. of College and Research Libs.; Assn. of Specialized and Cooperative Lib. Agencies; Lib. Admin. and Management Assn.; Lib. and Info. Technology Assn.; Public Lib. Assn.; Reference and User Services Assn.; Young Adult Lib. Services Assn.

Publications

ALA Handbook of Organization (ann.).

American Libraries (11 a year; memb.; organizations $60; foreign $70; single copy $6).

Book Links (6 a year; U.S. $39.95; foreign $46; single copy $8).

Booklist (22 a year; U.S. and possessions $94.50; foreign $110; single copy $6).

Round Table Chairpersons

(ALA staff liaison in parentheses)

Continuing Library Education Network and Exchange. Pat Traviss (Darlena Davis).

Ethnic and Multicultural Information Exchange. Myra Appel (Satia M. Orange).

Exhibits. Kathy Young (Deidre I. Ross).

Federal and Armed Forces Libraries. Janet M. Scheitle (Reginald Scott).

Gay, Lesbian, Bisexual, Transgendered. K. R. Roberto, Mary Callaghan Zunt (Satia M. Orange).

Government Documents. Bill Sleeman (Reginald Scott).

Intellectual Freedom. J. Douglas Archer (Nanette Perez).

International Relations. Joan S. Weeks (Delin R. Guerra).

Library History. Mary Niles-Maack (Letitia Earvin).

Library Instruction. Vibiana Bowman (Darlena Davis).

Library Research. John C. Bertot (Letitia Earvin).

Library Support Staff Interests. Sandra L. Olson (Darlena Davis).

Map and Geography. Pete Reehling (Danielle M. Alderson).

New Members. Nanette Wargo Donohue (Kimberly Sanders).

Social Responsibilities. Alison Lewis (Satia M. Orange).

Staff Organizations. Leon S. Bey (Darlena Davis).

Video. John Stephen Brantley (Danielle M. Alderson).

Committee Chairpersons

(ALA staff liaison in parentheses)

Accreditation (Standing). Richard E. Rubin (Karen L. O'Brien).

American Libraries Advisory (Standing). Jennifer Cargill (Leonard Kniffel).

Appointments (Standing). Jim Rettig (Lois Ann Gregory-Wood).

Awards (Standing). Lizbeth Bishoff (Cheryl Malden).

Budget Analysis and Review (Standing). Marilyn L. Hinshaw (Gregory L. Calloway).

Chapter Relations (Standing). Thomas Kevin Cherry (Michael P. Dowling).

Committee on Committees (Elected Council Committee). Jim Rettig (Lois Ann Gregory-Wood).

Conference Committee (Standing). Barbara W. Cole (Deidre I. Ross).

Conference Program Coordinating Team. Sarah E. Hamrick (Deidre I. Ross).

Constitution and Bylaws (Standing). Thaddeus P. Bejnar (JoAnne M. Kempf).

Council Orientation (Standing). Joseph M. Eagan (Lois Ann Gregory-Wood).

Diversity (Standing). Valerie P. Bell (Karen Letarte).

Education (Standing). Kenley E. Neufeld (Lorelle R. Swader).

Election (Standing). Nann Blaine Hilyard (Al Companio).

Human Resource Development and Recruitment (Standing). Vicki Varner Burger (Lorelle R. Swader).

Information Technology Policy Advisory. Dottie R. Hiebing (Frederick W. Weingarten).

Intellectual Freedom (Standing). Kenton L. Oliver (Judith F. Krug).

International Relations (Standing). Blanche Woolls (Michael P. Dowling).

Legislation (Standing). Camila A. Alire (Lynne E. Bradley).

Literacy (Standing). Sandra O. Newell (Dale P. Lipschultz).

Literacy and Outreach Services Advisory (Standing). Constance Lynn Purcell (Satia M. Orange).

Membership (Standing). Dora T. Ho (John F. Chrastka, Cathleen Bourdon).

Organization (Standing). Melora Ranney Norman (Lois Ann Gregory-Wood).

Orientation, Training, and Leadership Development. Donna O. Dziedzic (Lorelle Swader).

Policy Monitoring (Standing). Janet Swan Hill (Lois Ann Gregory-Wood).

Professional Ethics (Standing). Candace D. Morgan (Judith F. Krug).

Public and Cultural Programs Advisory (Standing). Deborah L. Jacobs (Deborah Anne Robertson).

Public Awareness (Standing). Judith A. Gibbons (Mark R. Gould).

Publishing (Standing). Sara McLaughlin (Donald E. Chatham).

Research and Statistics (Standing). Rochelle Logan (Denise M. Davis).

Resolutions. Peter McDonald (Lois Ann Gregory-Wood).

Rural, Native, and Tribal Libraries of All Kinds. David C. Ongley (Satia M. Orange).

Scholarships and Study Grants. Julie Brewer (Lorelle R. Swader).

Status of Women in Librarianship (Standing). ShinJoung Yeo (Lorelle R. Swader).

Web Site Advisory. Billie Peterson-Lugo (Robert P. Carlson, Sherri L. Vanyek).

Joint Committee Chairpersons

ALA/SAA/AAM: American Library Association–Society of American Archivists–American Association of Museums. Christian Yves Dupont (ALA); Deborra Richardson (SAA); Holly Witchey (AAM); Mary W. Ghikas (ALA staff liaison).

Association of American Publishers–ALA. To be announced (AAP); Leslie Burger (ALA); Keith Michael Fiels (ALA staff liaison).

Children's Book Council–ALA. Carole Fiore (ALA); To be announced (CBC); Diane Foote (ALA staff liaison).

American Association of School Librarians

Executive Director, Julie A. Walker
50 E. Huron St., Chicago, IL 60611
312-280-4382, 800-545-2433 ext. 4382, fax 312-280-5276
E-mail aasl@ala.org, World Wide Web http://www.aasl.org

Object

The mission of the American Association of School Librarians (AASL) is to advocate excellence, facilitate change, and develop leaders in the school library media field. AASL works to ensure that all members of the field collaborate to provide leadership in the total education program; participate as active partners in the teaching/learning process; connect learners with ideas and information, and prepare students for lifelong learning, informed decision making, a love of reading, and the use of information technologies.

Established in 1951 as a separate division of the American Library Association.

Membership

Memb. 9,900+. Open to all libraries, school library media specialists, interested individu-

als, and business firms with requisite membership in ALA.

Officers 2007–2008

Pres. Sara Kelly Johns; *Pres.-Elect* Ann M. Martin; *Treas.* Dennis J. LeLoup; *Past Pres.* Cyndi A. Phillip.

Board of Directors

Patricia T. Bauer, Nancy Dickinson, Jim Hayden, Marilyn Z. Joyce, Karen R. Lemmons, Eloise M. Long, Catherine E. Marriott, Robbie Leah Nickel, Sylvia K. Norton, Janice C. Ostrom, Floyd Clark Pentlin, Ann E. Petersen, Barbara J. Ray, Julie A. Walker (ex officio), Hilda K. Weisburg, Paul K. Whitsitt.

Publications

AASL Hotlinks (mo.; electronic, memb.).
Knowledge Quest (5 a year; memb.; non-memb. $40) (Online as *KQWeb* at http://www.ala.org/aasl/kqweb. *Ed.* Debbie Abilock. E-mail kq@abilock.net.
School Library Media Research (nonsubscription electronic publication available to memb. and nonmemb. at http://www.ala.org/aasl/slmr. *Eds.* Jean Donham. E-mail Jdonham@cornellcollege.edu; Carol L. Tilley. E-mail ctilley@uiuc.edu.

Committee Chairpersons

AASL/ACRL Joint Information Literacy Committee. Drucie Gullion, Judi Repman.
AASL/ALSC/YALSA Interdivisional Committee on School/Public Library Cooperation. Gail Bush.
AASL/ELMS Executive Committee. Allison G. Kaplan.
AASL/ISS Executive Committee. Alison Ernst.
AASL/SPVS Executive Committee. Charlie Makela.
Advocacy. Deb Logan.
Affiliate Assembly. Jay Bansbach.
Alliance for Association Excellence. Dennis LeLoup.
American University Press Book Selection. Judith McGowan.
Annual Conference 2008. Anita Vance.
Appointments. Merlyn Miller.
Blog Editorial Board. Alice Yucht.
Bylaws and Organization. Cassandra Barnett.
Collaborative School Library Media Award. Joanne M. Proctor.
Intellectual Freedom. Helen Adams.
Knowledge Quest Editorial Board. Debbie Abilock.
Legislation. Robert Roth.
National Institute, 2008. Anita Vance.
NCATE Coordinating Committee. Elizabeth Haynes.
Nominating. Donna Helvering.

Professional Development Coordinating Committee. Ken Stewart.
Promotion and Marketing Special Committee. Connie Champlin.
Publications. Don Adcock.
Research/Statistics. Nancy Everhart.
SLMR Electronic Editorial Board. Jean Donham, Carol Tilley.
Web Site Resource Guides Editorial Board. Donna Nix.

Task Force Chairpersons

AASL 2.0. Joyce Valenza.
Best List for Teacher Resources. Pam Berger.
Guidelines Editing. Bonnie Grimble.
No Child Left Behind. J. Linda Williams.
Quantitative Measurers. Nancy Dickinson.
School Library Media Month. Melissa Johnston.
Standards and Guidelines Implementation. Susan Ballard.
State Department Inquiry. Merlyn Miller.

Awards Committees and Chairpersons

ABC/CLIO Leadership Grant. Shauna Yusko.
Awards. Leslie Forsman.
Distinguished School Administrator Award. Linda Teel.
Distinguished Service Award. Valerie A. Edwards.
Frances Henne Award. Glenda Smith Rowe.
Information Technology Pathfinder Award. Melissa England Gardner.
Innovative Reading Grant. Elizabeth B. Massee.
Intellectual Freedom Award. Linda Weatherspoon.
National School Library Media Program of the Year Award. Fran Roscello.
Research Grant. Lesley Farmer.
School Librarians Workshop Scholarship. Ora R. Hall.

American Library Association
Association for Library Collections and Technical Services

Executive Director, Charles Wilt
50 E. Huron St., Chicago, IL 60611
800-545-2433 ext. 5030, fax 312-280-5033
E-mail cwilt@ala.org
World Wide Web http://www.ala.org/alcts

Object

The Association for Library Collections and Technical Services (ALCTS) envisions an environment in which traditional library roles are evolving. New technologies are making information more fluid and raising expectations. The public needs quality information anytime, anyplace. ALCTS provides frameworks to meet these information needs.

ALCTS provides leadership to the library and information communities in developing principles, standards, and best practices for creating, collecting, organizing, delivering, and preserving information resources in all forms. It provides this leadership through its members by fostering educational, research, and professional service opportunities. ALCTS is committed to quality information, universal access, collaboration, and life-long learning.

Standards: Develop, evaluate, revise, and promote standards for creating, collecting, organizing, delivering, and preserving information resources in all forms.

Best practices: Research, develop, evaluate, and implement best practices for creating, collecting, organizing, delivering, and preserving information resources in all forms.

Education: Assess the need for, sponsor, develop, administer, and promote educational programs and resources for life-long learning.

Professional development: Provide opportunities for professional development through research, scholarship, publication, and professional service.

Interaction and information exchange: Create opportunities to interact and exchange information with others in the library and information communities.

Association operations: Ensure efficient use of association resources and effective delivery of member services.

Established 1957; renamed 1988.

Membership

Memb. 5,150. Any member of the American Library Association may elect membership in this division according to the provisions of the bylaws.

Officers (2007–2008)

Pres. Pamela M. Bluh, Thurgood Marshall Law Lib., Univ. of Maryland, 501 W. Fayette St., Baltimore, MD 21201. Tel. 410-706-2736, fax 410-706-2372, e-mail pbluh@umaryland.edu; *Pres.-Elect* Dina Giambi, Univ. of Delaware Lib., 181 S. College Ave., Newark, DE 19717. Tel. 302-831-2829, fax 302-831-1046, e-mail dinag@udel.edu; *Past Pres.* Bruce Chr. Johnson, Cataloging Distribution Service, Lib. of Congress, Washington, DC 20540-0001. Tel. 202-707-1652, fax 202-707-3959, e-mail bjoh@loc.gov; *Councilor* Diane Dates Casey, Governors State Univ. Lib., 1 University Pkwy., University Park, IL 60466. Tel. 708-534-4110, fax 708-534-4564, e-mail d-casey@govst.edu.

Address correspondence to the executive director.

Board of Directors

Pamela Bluh, Beth Picknally Camden, Lynda Clendenning, Diane Dates Casey, Dina Giambi, Nancy Gibbs, Andrew Hart, Carol

Hryciw-Wing, Bruce Chr. Johnson, Cheryl Kern-Simirenko, Betty Landesman, Mary Charles Lasater, Reeta Sinha, Dale Swensen, Kay Walter, Daisy Waters, Mary Beth Weber, Charles Wilt.

Publications

ALCTS Newsletter Online (bi-mo.; free; posted at http://www.ala.org/alcts). *Ed.* Mary Beth Weber, Cataloging Dept., Rutgers Univ. Libs., 47 Davidson Rd, Piscataway, NJ 08854. Tel. 732-445-0500, fax 732-445-5888, e-mail mbfecko@rci.rutgers.edu.
Library Resources and Technical Services (q.; memb.; nonmemb. $75). *Ed.* Peggy Johnson, Univ. of Minnesota Libs., 499 Wilson Lib., 309 19th Ave. S., Minneapolis, MN 55455. Tel. 612-624-2312, fax 612-626-9353, e-mail m-john@tc.umn.edu.

Section Chairpersons

Acquisitions. Lynda Clendenning.
Cataloging and Classification. Mary Charles Lasater.
Collection Management and Development. Betty Landesman.
Continuing Resources. Daisy Waters.
Preservation and Reformatting. Andrew Hart.

Committee Chairpersons

Hugh C. Atkinson Memorial Award (ALCTS/ACRL/LAMA/LITA). Diane Bisom.
Ross Atkinson Lifetime Achievement Award Jury. Mary Case.
Paul Banks and Carolyn Harris Preservation Award Jury. Rebecca Ryder.
Best of *LRTS* Award Jury. Randy Roeder.

Blackwell's Scholarship Award Jury. Kathleen Brown.
Budget and Finance. Reeta Sinha.
Education. Christine DeZelar-Tiedman.
Fund Raising. Susan Davis.
International Relations. Sha Li Zhang.
Leadership Development. Betsy Simpson.
LRTS Editorial Board. Peggy Johnson.
Membership. Natalie Sommerville.
Nominating. Rosann Bazirjian.
Organization and Bylaws. Dale Swensen.
Outstanding Collaboration Citation Jury. Gracemary Smulewitz.
Esther J. Piercy Award Jury. Eleanor Cook.
Planning. Nancy Gibbs.
Program. Tim Strawn.
Publications. Norm Medeiros.

Discussion Groups

Authority Control (ALCTS/LITA). Edward Swanson.
Automated Acquisitions/In-Process Control Systems. Marsha Garman.
Creative Ideas in Technical Services. Linda Lomker.
Electronic Resources. Luiz Mendes.
MARC Formats (ALCTS/LITA). Naomi Young.
Newspapers. Errol Somay.
Out of Print. John Riley.
Role of the Professional in Academic Research Technical Service Departments. Ruth Fischer.
Scholarly Communications. Cynthia Krolikowski, Lila Ohler.
Technical Services Administrators of Medium-Sized Research Libraries. Roberta Winjum.
Technical Services Directors of Large Research Libraries. Lisa German.
Technical Services Workflow Efficiency. Bob Schatz.

American Library Association
Association for Library Service to Children

Executive Director, Diane Foote
50 E. Huron St., Chicago, IL 60611
312-280-2162, 800-545-2433 ext. 2162, fax 312-280-5271
E-mail dfoote@ala.org, World Wide Web http://www.ala.org/alsc

Object

The Association for Library Service to Children (ALSC) is interested in the improvement and extension of library services to children in all types of libraries, and is responsible for the evaluation and selection of book and nonbook materials for—and the improvement of techniques of—library services to children from preschool through eighth grade or junior high school age, when such materials or techniques are intended for use in more than one type of library. Founded 1901.

Membership

Memb. 4,113. Open to anyone interested in library services to children. For information on dues, see ALA entry.

Address correspondence to the executive director.

Officers

Pres. Jane B. Marino; *V.P./Pres.-Elect* Pat Scales; *Past Pres.* Kathleen T. Horning; *Fiscal Officer* Sue Zeigler; *Division Councilor* Linda Perkins.

Directors

Thom Barthelmess, Mary Fellows, Starr LaTronica, Kate McClelland, Penny Markey, Elizabeth Orsburn, Tim Wadham, Judy Zuckerman.

Publications

Children and Libraries: The Journal of the Association for Library Service to Children (q.; memb.; nonmemb. $40; foreign $50).
ALSConnect (q., electronic; memb. Not available by subscription.)

Committee Chairpersons

AASL/ALSC/YALSA Interdivisional Committee on School/Public Library Cooperation. Gail Bush.
ALA-CBC Joint Committee. Carole Fiore.
ALSC/Booklist/YALSA Odyssey Award Selection 2008. Mary Burkey.
ALSC BWI Summer Reading Grant. Mary R. Voors.
Arbuthnot Honor Lecture 2008. Deborah Stevenson.
Award Eligibility Task Force. Carolyn Brodie.
Mildred L. Batchelder Award 2008. Lucinda Ware.
Bechtel Fellowship. Denise Agosto.
Pura Belpré Award 2008. Rita Pino Vargas.
Budget. Andrew Medlar.
Randolph Caldecott Award 2008. Karen Breen.
Andrew Carnegie Award 2008. Wendy Woodfill.
Children and Libraries Advisory Committee. Rosanne Cerny.
Children and Technology. Christopher Borawski.
Distinguished Service Award 2008. Steven Herb.
Early Childhood Programs and Services. Rachel Payne.

Early Literacy Task Force. To be announced.

Education. Emily Chandler.

Theodor Seuss Geisel Award 2008. Cynthia Woodruff.

Great Interactive Software for Kids. Ann Crewdson.

Great Web Sites. Karen Lemmons, Becki Bishop.

Maureen Hayes Award. Floyd Dickman.

Intellectual Freedom. Sharon Senser.

International Relations. Elizabeth Heidemann.

Legislation. Jeanne Lamb.

Liaison with National Organizations. Rebecca Purdy, Stephanie Shauck.

Library Service to Special Population Children and Their Caregivers. Martha Simpson.

Local Arrangements (Anaheim). To be announced.

Managing Children's Services. Leslie Molnar.

Member Mentoring Task Force. Susan Birkett.

Membership. Carol Durusau.

National Planning of Special Collections. Melissa Schutt.

John Newbery Award 2008. Nina Lindsay.

Nominating 2008. Gretchen Wronka.

Notable Children's Books. Caroline Ward.

Notable Children's Recordings. To be announced.

Notable Children's Videos. Kathy Krasniwiecz.

Oral History. Susan Veltfort.

Organization and Bylaws. Lisa Sizemore, Amanda Moss.

Penguin Young Readers Group Award. Alison O'Reilly.

Preconference Planning. Carol Fiore.

Program Coordinating. Doris Gebel.

Public Awareness. Stephanie Bange.

Quicklist Consulting. Steven Engelfried, Lucia Gonzalez, Linda Williams.

Research and Development. Crystal Faris.

Charlemae Rollins President's Program 2008. Linda Ernst, Viki Ash.

Scholarships. B. Allison Gray.

School Age Programs and Service. Shilo Pearson.

Robert F. Sibert Award 2008. Kate Houston Mitchoff.

Tandem Library Books Literature Program Award. April Roy.

Laura Ingalls Wilder Award 2008. Cathryn Mercier.

American Library Association
Association for Library Trustees and Advocates

Executive Director (acting), Sally Gardner Reed
50 E. Huron St., Chicago, IL 60611-2795
312-280-2160, 800-545-2433 ext. 2161, fax 312-280-3256
E-mail sreed@folusa.org
World Wide Web http://www.ala.org/alta

Object

The Association for Library Trustees and Advocates (ALTA) was founded in 1890 as the American Library Trustee Association. It is the only division of the American Library Association dedicated to promoting and ensuring outstanding library service through educational programs that develop excellence in trusteeship and actions that advocate access to information for all. ALTA represents library trustees, advocates, volunteers, and friends throughout the United States and Canada. It became an ALA division in 1961.

In 2008 ALTA is working with Friends of Libraries U.S.A. (FOLUSA) to determine whether these two organizations should join together to become a single division within ALA.

Membership

Memb. 1,200. Open to all interested persons and organizations. For dues and membership year, see ALA entry.

Officers (2007–2008)

Pres. Donald L. Roalkvam. E-mail droalkva @allstate.com; *1st V.P./Pres.-Elect* Margaret

J. Danhof. E-mail pdanhof@yahoo.com; *2nd V.P.* Rose E. Mosley. E-mail rose.mosley@ ssa.gov; *Councilor* Shirley Bruursema. E-mail libsabsarg@aol.com; *Past Pres.* Anne D. Sterling. E-mail nimbleleap@aol.com.

Publication

The Voice (q.; memb.).

American Library Association
Association of College and Research Libraries

Executive Director, Mary Ellen K. Davis
50 E. Huron St., Chicago, IL 60611-2795
312-280-2523, 800-545-2433 ext. 2523, fax 312-280-2520
E-mail acrl@ala.org, World Wide Web http://www.ala.org/acrl

Object

The Association of College and Research Libraries (ACRL) leads academic and research librarians and libraries in advancing learning and scholarship. Founded 1938.

Membership

Memb. 13,411. For information on dues, see ALA entry.

Officers

Pres. Julie B. Todaro, Dean, Lib. Services, Rio Grande Campus, Austin Community College, 1212 Rio Grande, Austin, TX 78701-1710. Tel. 512-223-3071, fax 512-223-3431, e-mail jtodaro@austincc.edu; *Pres.-Elect* Erike C. Linke, Assoc. Dean, Univ. Libs., Carnegie Mellon Univ., 5000 Forbes Ave., Pittsburgh, PA 15213-3890. Tel. 412-268-7800, fax 412-268-2793, e-mail el08@ andrew.cmu.edu; *Past Pres.* Pamela Snelson, College Libn., Shadek-Fackenthal Lib., Franklin and Marshall College, P.O. Box 3003, Lancaster, PA 17604-3003. Tel. 717-291-3896, fax 717-291-4160, e-mail pamela.

snelson@fandm.edu; *Budget and Finance Chair* Theresa S. Byrd, Dir. of Libs., Ohio Wesleyan Univ., 43 Rowland Ave., Delaware, OH 43015-2333. Tel. 740-368-3246, fax 740-368-3222, e-mail fsbyrd@ owu.edu; *ACRL Councilor* Locke J. Morrisey, Head, Collections/Reference and Research Services, Gleeson Lib., Univ. of San Francisco, San Francisco, CA 94117-1080. Tel. 415-422-5399, e-mail morrisey@ usfca.edu.

Board of Directors

Officers; Janis M. Bandelin, Mary M. Carr, Elizabeth A. Dupuis, Lori A. Goetsch, Lynne O. King, Michael J. LaCroix, Debbie L. Malone, Karen A. Williams.

Publications

Choice (12 a year; $315; foreign $365–$435). *Ed.* Irving Rockwood.

Choice Reviews-on-Cards ($390; foreign $440–$520).

ChoiceReviews.Online 2.0 ($385).

College & Research Libraries (*C&RL*) (6 a year; memb.; nonmemb. $70). *Ed.* William Gray Potter.
College & Research Libraries News (11 a year; memb.; nonmemb. $46). *Ed.* David Free.
Publications in Librarianship (formerly *ACRL Monograph Series*) (occasional). *Ed.* Charles A. Schwartz.
RBM: A Journal of Rare Books, Manuscripts, and Cultural Heritage (s. ann.; $42). *Ed.* Richard Clement.

A full list of other publications and rates is available from the ACRL office.

Committee and Task Force Chairpersons

AASL/ACRL Information Literacy (interdivisional). Drucilla A. Gullion, Judi Repman.
Academic/Research Librarian of the Year Award. Cynthia K. Steinhoff.
Advocacy Coordinating. Carol Ann Hughes.
Appointments. Daniel R. Lee.
Hugh C. Atkinson Memorial Award. Diane B. Bisom.
Blog Advisory Board. Steven J. Bell.
Budget and Finance. Theresa S. Byrd.
Bylaws. Wilbur A. Stolt.
Choice Editorial Board. John P. Schmitt.
Colleagues. Frank A. d'Andraia, Julia M. Gelfand.
College & Research Libraries Editorial Board. William Gray Potter.
College & Research Libraries News Editorial Board. Lucia Snowhill.
Copyright. Becky S. Albitz.
Council of Liaisons. Frances J. Maloy.
Doctoral Dissertation Fellowship. Nancy H. Seamans.
Effective Practices Review Committee. Bonnie L. Tijerina.
Ethics. Lori J. Phillips.
Excellence in Academic Libraries Award (Nominations). Patricia A. Kreitz.
Excellence in Academic Libraries Award (Selection). Camila A. Alire.
Friends Fund. Lisa M. Browar.

Government Relations. W. Lee Hisle.
Information Literacy Advisory. Jennifer L. Dorner.
Institute for Information Literacy Executive. Stephanie Michel.
Intellectual Freedom. Julianne P. Hinz, Suzan Parker.
International Relations. Lesley Mutinta Moyo, Ravindra N. Sharma.
E. J. Josey Spectrum Scholar Mentor. Tyrone Heath Cannon.
Samuel Lazerow Fellowship. Richard Bradberry.
Leadership Recruitment and Nomination. Thomas Kirk.
Marketing Academic and Research Libraries. Frank A. D'Andraia.
Membership Advisory. Susanna D. Boylston.
National Conference Executive Committee, Seattle, 2009. Lizabeth Wilson.
New Publications Advisory. Jamie W. Gill.
Presidential Initiative Steering, Anaheim, 2008. Pat Hawthorne, Patricia H. Smith.
President's Program Planning Committee, Chicago, 2009. To be announced.
Professional Development Coordinating. Trevor A. Dawes.
Publications Coordinating. Daren Callahan.
Publications in Librarianship Editorial Board. Charles A. Schwartz.
Racial and Ethnic Diversity. Michele L. Saunders.
RBM Editorial Board. Richard W. Clement.
Research. Scott Walter.
Resources for College Libraries Editorial Board. Brian E. Coutts.
Scholarly Communications. John Ober, Joyce L. Ogburn.
Standards and Accreditation. William N. Nelson.
Statistics. Shawn P. Calhoun.
Status of Academic Librarians. Carolyn H. Allen.

Discussion Group Chairpersons

Alliances for New Directions in Teaching/Learning. Mark Horan.
Australian-Canadian-New Zealand Studies. Margaret Brill.
Balancing Baby and Book. Frances J. Maloy.

Consumer and Family Studies. Neosha A. Mackey.

Electronic Reserves. Laureen Esser.

Electronic Text Centers. Robert H. Scott.

Fee-Based Information Service Centers in Academic Libraries. To be announced.

Information Commons. Scott B. Mandernack, Michael Whitchurch.

Libraries and Information Science. Roxy A. Zimmerman.

Library Development. Charlene Baldwin.

Media Resources. Johan Oberg.

MLA International Bibliography. Liorah Anne Golomb.

New Members. Merinda Kaye Hensley.

Partnership Librarians. Ruth E. Kifer.

Personnel Administrators and Staff Development Officers. John A. Lehner, Angela J. Wright.

Philosophical, Religious, and Theological Studies. Richard Terry Chaffin.

Popular Cultures. Diane C. Kachmar.

Regional Campus Libraries. Darby Syrkin, Alica C. White.

Scholarly Communications. Kimberly Douglas.

Senior Administrators. Faye C. Backie, Roxanne Jeanine Selberg.

Sports and Recreation. Mila C. Su.

Team-Based Organizations. Robert Patrick Mitchell.

Undergraduate Libraries. Leah G. McGinnis, Jill Morrison McKinstry.

Section Chairpersons

African-American Studies Librarians. Carmelita N. Pickett.

Anthropology and Sociology. Katharine A. Whitson.

Arts. Eric A. Kidwell.

Asian, African, and Middle Eastern. Muhammad Al-Faruque.

College Libraries. Steven J. Bell.

Community and Junior College Libraries. Kenley E. Neufeld.

Distance Learning. William Thomas Denny.

Education and Behavioral Sciences. Penny M. Beile.

Instruction. Jean S. Caspers.

Law and Political Science. Kelly S. Janousek.

Literatures in English. Zofia Lesinska.

Rare Books and Manuscripts. Christian Yves Dupont.

Science and Technology. Barbara M. MacAlpine.

Slavic and East European. George Spencer.

University Libraries. Cheryl A. Middleton.

Western European Studies. Sarah G. Wenzel.

Woman's Studies. Jennifer R. Gilley.

American Library Association
Association of Specialized and Cooperative Library Agencies

Executive Director, Barbara Macikas
50 E. Huron St., Chicago, IL 60611-2795
312-280-4398, 800-545-2433 ext. 4398, fax 312-280-5273
World Wide Web http://www.ala.org/ascla

Object

Represents state library agencies, specialized library agencies, multitype library cooperatives, and independent librarians. Within the interests of these types of library organizations, the Association of Specialized and Cooperative Library Agencies (ASCLA) has specific responsibility for

1. Development and evaluation of goals and plans for state library agencies, specialized library agencies, and multitype library cooperatives to facilitate the implementation, improvement, and extension of library activities designed to foster improved user services, coordinating such activities with other appropriate ALA units

2. Representation and interpretation of the role, functions, and services of state library agencies, specialized library agencies, multitype library cooperatives, and independent librarians within and outside the profession, including contact with national organizations and government agencies

3. Development of policies, studies, and activities in matters affecting state library agencies, specialized library agencies, multitype library cooperatives, and independent librarians relating to (a) state and local library legislation, (b) state grants-in-aid and appropriations, and (c) relationships among state, federal, regional, and local governments, coordinating such activities with other appropriate ALA units

4. Establishment, evaluation, and promotion of standards and service guidelines relating to the concerns of this association

5. Identifying the interests and needs of all persons, encouraging the creation of services to meet these needs within the areas of concern of the association, and promoting the use of these services provided by state library agencies, specialized library agencies, multitype library cooperatives, and independent librarians

6. Stimulating the professional growth and promoting the specialized training and continuing education of library personnel at all levels in the areas of concern of this association and encouraging membership participation in appropriate type-of-activity divisions within ALA

7. Assisting in the coordination of activities of other units within ALA that have a bearing on the concerns of this association

8. Granting recognition for outstanding library service within the areas of concern of this association

9. Acting as a clearinghouse for the exchange of information and encouraging the development of materials, publications, and research within the areas of concern of this association

Membership

Memb. 900+.

Board of Directors (2007–2008)

Pres. Barbara Mates; *Pres.-Elect* Carol Ann Desch; *Past Pres.* Marilyn M. Irwin; *Dirs.-at-Large* Annette Milliron, Glennor Loy Shirley; *Div. Councilor* Kendall French Wiggin.

Publication

Interface (q.; memb.; single copies $7). *Ed.* Sara G. Laughlin, 1616 Treadwell Lane, Bloomington, IN 47408. Tel. 812-334-8485.

Committee Chairpersons

Accessibility Assembly. Simon J. M. Healey.
Accessibility for Electronic Media (ad hoc). William Reed.
Awards. Kathleen B. Hegarty.
Legislation. Barratt Wilkins.
Membership Promotion. Kathleen Allen O'Connor.
Nominating. Rahye L. Puckett.
Planning and Budget. Carol Ann Desch, Marilyn M. Irwin.
President's Program. Robin Hewitt Rousu.
Publications. Rhea Joyce Rubin.
Standards Review. Jeannette P. Smithee.

American Library Association
Library Administration and Management Association

Executive Director, Kerry Ward
50 E. Huron St., Chicago, IL 60611
312-280-5032, 800-545-2433 ext. 5032, fax 312-280-5033
E-mail kward@ala.org, World Wide Web http://www.ala.org/lama

Object

The Library Administration and Management Association (LAMA) Strategic Plan (2006–2010), adopted by its board of directors in January 2006, sets out the following:

Mission: The Library Administration and Management Association encourages and nurtures current and future leaders, and develops and promotes outstanding leadership and management practices.

Vision: LAMA will be the foremost organization developing present and future leaders in library and information services.

Image: LAMA is a welcoming community where aspiring and experienced leaders from all types of libraries, as well as those who support libraries, come together to gain skills in a quest for excellence in library management, administration, and leadership.

In addition,

- LAMA will be an organization in which value to its members drives decisions

- LAMA will expand and strengthen leadership and management expertise at all levels for all libraries

- LAMA will facilitate professional development opportunities to enhance leadership and management

- LAMA will be the preeminent professional organization that develops and supports library leaders and managers

Established 1957.

Membership

Memb. 4,800.

Officers (July 2007–June 2008)

Pres. W. Bede Mitchell; *V.P.* Molly Raphael; *Secy.* Emily A. Bergman; *Dirs.-at-Large* Cathy C. Miesse, Gina Millsap; *Div. Councilor* Sue H. MacTavish; *Past Pres.* Andrea Lapsley.

Address correspondence to the executive director.

Publications

Library Administration and Management (q.; memb.; nonmemb. $65; foreign $75). *Ed.* Gregg Sapp.

LEADS from LAMA (approx. biweekly; electronic; free). To subscribe, send to listproc@ala.org the message *subscribe lamaleads [first name last name]*.

Committee Chairpersons

Budget and Finance. Teri R. Switzer.
Continuing Education. Roderick MacNeil.
Cultural Diversity Grants. Sylvia Y. Sprinkle-Hamlin.
Editorial Advisory Board. Paul M. Anderson.
Financial Advancement. Desiree L. Webber.
Leadership Development. Catherine R. Friedman.
Marketing Communications. Marcia G. Schneider.
Membership. Donna J. Capelle-Cook.
Mentoring. Janine Golden.
Nominating. Thomas E. Schneiter.
Organization. Mary Frances Burns.
President's Program. Ann H. Hamilton.
Program. Frank R. Allen.
Publishing. Judith A. Adams-Volpe.
Recognition of Achievement. Elaine Ross Cline.
Strategic Planning Implementation. Anne Edwards.
Web Site Advisory Board. Virginia C. Branch.

American Library Association
Library and Information Technology Association

Executive Director, Mary C. Taylor
50 E. Huron St., Chicago, IL 60611
312-280-4267, 800-545-2433
E-mail mtaylor@ala.org, World Wide Web http://www.ala.org/lita

Object

As a center of expertise about information technology, the Library and Information Technology Association (LITA) leads in exploring and enabling new technologies to empower libraries. LITA members use the promise of technology to deliver dynamic library collections and services.

LITA educates, serves, and reaches out to its members, other ALA members and divisions, and the entire library and information community through its publications, programs, and other activities designed to promote, develop, and aid in the implementation of library and information technology.

Membership

Memb. 4,333.

Officers (2007–2008)

Pres. Mark Beatty; *V.P./Pres.-Elect* Andrew Pace; *Past Pres.* Bonnie Postlethwaite.

Directors

Officers; Mary Alice Ball, David W. Bretthauer, Michelle L. Frisque, Susan Logue, Andrew K. Pace, Jonathan Edward Rothman, Debra S. Shapiro, Karen J. Starr; *Councilor* Colby Riggs; *Bylaws and Organization* Clara Ruttenberg; *Exec. Dir.* Mary C. Taylor.

Publication

Information Technology and Libraries (*ITAL*) (q.; memb.; nonmemb. $55; single copy $20). *Ed.* Marc Truitt. For information or to send manuscripts, contact the editor.

Committee Chairpersons

Assessment and Research. Diane Bisom and Bonnie Postlethwaite.
Budget Review. Bonnie Postlethwaite.
Bylaws and Organization. Clara Ruttenberg.
Committee Chair Coordinator. Scott P. Muir.
Education. Barbara L. Spivey.
Executive. Mark Beatty.
International Relations. Teri Sierra.
ITAL Editorial Board. Marc Truitt.
Legislation and Regulation. Susan Jacobson.
LITA/Brett Butler Entrepreneurship Award. Nancy N. Colyar.
LITA/Endeavor Student Writing Award. Adrienne I. Lim.
LITA/Library Hi Tech Award. Linda D. Miller.
LITA/LSSI and LITA/OCLC Minority Scholarships. Gail Herrera.
LITA National Forum 2008. Dale Poulter.
LITA/OCLC Kilgour Award. Patricia R. Harris.
LITA/Christian Larew Scholarship. Kristin A. Antelman.
Membership Development. Lorre B. Smith.
Nominating. Patrick J. Mullin.
Program Planning. Gail P. Clement.
Publications. Dan K. Marmion.
Technology and Access. Beatrice Nichols.
TER Board. Martin R. Kalfatovic.
Top Technology Trends. Maurice York.
Web Coordinating. David Altenhof.

Interest Group Coordinators

Authority Control in the Online Environment (LITA/ALCTS). Edward Swanson.

Blogs, Interactive Media, Groupware, and Wikis. Jason Griffey.
Digital Library Technologies. Tyra Grant.
Distance Learning. Lauren Marie Pressley.
Electronic Resources Management (LITA/ALCTS). Elizabeth Stewart-Marshall.
Emerging Technologies. Joseph B. Ford.
Heads of Library Technology. Michelle Martin Robertson.
Imagineering. Catherine Wagner.
Interest Groups Coordinator. Matthew M. Calsada.

Internet Resources and Services. Joseph Fisher.
JPEG 2000 in Archives and Libraries. Peter Murray.
Library Consortia Automated Systems. Jon Mark Bolthouse.
Next Generation Catalog. Thomas P. Dowling.
Open Source Systems. Chris Strauber.
Public Libraries Technology. Paul Keith.
RFID Technology. Lynne A. Jacobsen.
Standards. Jacqueline E. Radebaugh.

American Library Association
Public Library Association

Executive Director, Greta K. Southard
50 E. Huron St., Chicago, IL 60611
312-280-5752, 800-545-2433 ext. 5752, fax 312-280-5029
E-mail pla@ala.org, World Wide Web http://www.pla.org

The Public Library Association (PLA) has specific responsibility for

1. Conducting and sponsoring research about how the public library can respond to changing social needs and technical developments

2. Developing and disseminating materials useful to public libraries in interpreting public library services and needs

3. Conducting continuing education for public librarians by programming at national and regional conferences, by publications such as the newsletter, and by other delivery means

4. Establishing, evaluating, and promoting goals, guidelines, and standards for public libraries

5. Maintaining liaison with relevant national agencies and organizations engaged in public administration and human services, such as the National Association of Counties, the Municipal League, and the Commission on Postsecondary Education

6. Maintaining liaison with other divisions and units of ALA and other library organizations, such as the Association for Library and Information Science Education and the Urban Libraries Council

7. Defining the role of the public library in service to a wide range of user and potential user groups

8. Promoting and interpreting the public library to a changing society through legislative programs and other appropriate means

9. Identifying legislation to improve and to equalize support of public libraries

PLA enhances the development and effectiveness of public librarians and public library services. This mission positions PLA to

• Focus its efforts on serving the needs of its members

• Address issues that affect public libraries

• Commit to quality public library services that benefit the general public

The goals of PLA are:

Advocacy and recognition. Public libraries will be recognized as the destination for a wide variety of valuable services and their funding will be a community priority.

A literate nation. PLA will be a valued partner of public library initiatives to create a nation of readers.

Staffing and recruitment. Public libraries will be recognized as exciting places to work and will be staffed by skilled professionals who are recognized as information experts, are competitively paid, and reflect the demographics of their communities.

Training and knowledge transfer. PLA will be nationally recognized as the leading source for continuing education opportunities for public library staff and trustees.

Membership

Memb. 10,000+. Open to all ALA members interested in the improvement and expansion of public library services to all ages in various types of communities.

Officers (2007–2008)

Pres. Jan Sanders, Pasadena Public Lib., 285 E. Walnut St., Pasadena, CA 91101. Tel. 626-744-4066, e-mail jsanders@cityof pasadena.net; *Pres.-Elect* Carol Sheffer, Queens Lib., 89-11 Merrick Blvd., Jamaica, NY 11432-5242. Tel. 718-990-0818, e-mail csheffer@queenslibrary.org; *Past Pres.* Susan H. Hildreth, California State Lib., P.O. Box 942837, Sacramento, CA 94237-0001. Tel. 916-654-0174, fax 916-654-0064, e-mail shhildreth@comcast.net.

Publication

Public Libraries (bi-mo.; memb.; nonmemb. $50; foreign $60; single copy $10). *Managing Ed.* Kathleen Hughes, PLA, 50 E. Huron St., Chicago, IL 60611. E-mail khughes@ala.org.

Cluster Chairpersons

Issues and Concerns Steering Committee. Carolyn A. Anthony.

Library Development Steering Committee. Alan Harkness.

Library Services Steering Committee. Marcellus Turner.

Committee Chairs

Issues and Concerns Cluster

Intellectual Freedom. Barbara J. Pickell.
International Relations. Lorraine M. Jackson.
Legislation. Theresa Maguire.
Public Policy in Public Libraries. Kathryn Robinson.
Recruitment of Public Librarians. To be announced.
Research and Statistics. Larry Nash White.
Staffing Issues. Anne T. Haimes.

Library Development Cluster

Branch Libraries. Paula L. Settoon.
Marketing Public Libraries. Bonnie L. Young.
Metropolitan Libraries. Fred J. Gitner.
Practical Applications of Technology in Public Libraries. Brian K. Auger.
Public Library Systems. Kimberlee A. De-Nero-Ackroyd.
Rural Library Services. Dwight Emlyn McInvaill.
Small and Medium-Sized Libraries. Kimberly Bolan.
Technology in Public Libraries. William H. Ptacek.

Library Services Cluster

Adult Continuing and Independent Learning Services. Marshall Alex Shore.
Audiovisual. Adele Bellinger.
Basic Education and Literacy Services. Dinah L. O'Brien.
Career and Business Services. Barbara A. Spruill.
Cataloging Needs of Public Libraries. Sally Gildea Smith.
Community Information Services. To be announced.

Reader's Advisory. Madlyn Schneider.

Services to Elementary-School-Age Children and Their Caregivers. Louise C. Lareau.

Services to Preschool Children and Their Caregivers. Penny Neef.

Business Committees

Annual Conference Coordinating Committee 2008. Mark L. Smith.

Annual Conference Coordinating Committee 2009. Kathleen S. Reif.

Awards. Eloise May.

Budget and Finance. Clara Nalli Bohrer.

Bylaws and Organization. Nann Blaine Hilyard.

Leadership Task Force. Luis Herrera.

National Conference 2008. Raymond Santiago.

National Conference (Program) 2008. Jane S. Eickhoff.

National Conference 2010. Kay K. Runge.

National Conference 2010 (Program). Jo Ann Pinder.

Nominating Committee 2008. Daniel L. Walters.

Nominating Committee 2009. Susan Hildreth.

Nominating Committee 2010. Jan W. Sanders.

Membership. Danis E. Kreimeier.

PLA Partners. Thomas A. Shepley.

President's Events 2008 and National Conference 2010. Elizabeth E. Bingham.

President's Events 2009. Sara Dallas.

Publications, Electronic Communications Advisory. To be announced.

Publications, PLA Monographs. Deborah Grodinsky.

Publications, Public Libraries Advisory. Bessie Condos.

Publications, Statistical Report Advisory. Mary E. Monaghan.

Publications, University Press Books for Public Libraries. Christina Maria Beaird.

American Library Association
Reference and User Services Association

President, David A. Tyckoson
50 E. Huron St., Chicago, IL 60611-2795
312-280-4398, 800-545-2433 ext. 4398, fax 312-280-5273
E-mail rusa@ala.org, World Wide Web http://www.ala.org/rusa

Object

The Reference and User Services Association (RUSA) is responsible for stimulating and supporting in every type of library the delivery of reference/information services to all groups, regardless of age, and of general library services and materials to adults. This involves facilitating the development and conduct of direct service to library users, the development of programs and guidelines for service to meet the needs of these users, and assisting libraries in reaching potential users.

The specific responsibilities of RUSA are

1. Conduct of activities and projects within the association's areas of responsibility

2. Encouragement of the development of librarians engaged in these activities and stimulation of participation by members of appropriate type-of-library divisions

3. Synthesis of the activities of all units within the American Library Association that have a bearing on the type of activities represented by the association

4. Representation and interpretation of the association's activities in contacts outside the profession

5. Planning and development of programs of study and research in these areas for the total profession

6. Continuous study and review of the association's activities

Membership

Memb. 5,363.

Officers (July 2007–June 2008)

Pres. David A. Tyckoson; *Pres.-Elect* Neal Wyatt; *Secy.* Naomi Lederer; *Past Pres.* Diana D. Shonrock.

Directors-at-Large

Linda Friend; Mary Allison Hollerich; Cynthia R. Levine; Mary M. D. Parker; Joseph A. Thompson, Jr.; Gary W. White; *Councilor* Pamela C. Sieving; *Ed.* Diane M. Zabel; *Ex Officio* Daniel C. Mack; *Exec. Dir.* Barbara A. Macikas.

Publication

RUSQ (q.; memb. $25 (included in dues), U.S. $65, foreign memb. $75, single copies $25). *Ed.* Diane M. Zabel.

Section Chairpersons

Business Reference and Services. Judith Faust.
Collection Development and Evaluation. Barry Trott.
History. Agnes Haigh Widder.
Machine-Assisted Reference. Mary M. Mintz.

Reference Services. Lisa R. Horowitz.
Sharing and Transforming Access to Resources. Margaret W. Ellingson.

Committee Chairpersons

Access to Information. Karen Jung.
AFL/CIO Joint Committee on Library Services to Labor Groups. Pamela Wilson.
Awards Coordinating. Jessica Moyer.
Conference Program. Mary L. Radford.
Conference Program Coordinating. David M. Hovde.
Membership. Joseph Yue.
Margaret E. Monroe Adult Services Award. Jennifer W. Mahnken.
Isadore Gilbert Mudge Award. Michael Whitchurch.
Nominating. Kathleen Mattews Kluegel.
Organization. Theodora T. Haynes.
Planning and Finance. Diana D. Shonrock.
Professional Development. Rebecca Jackson.
Publications. Cynthia R. Levine, Sara E. Williams.
Reference Services Press Award. Julia M. Gelfand.
John Sessions Memorial Award. Jannie R. Cobb.
Standards and Guidelines. Charles B. Thurston.
Thomson Gale Research Award for Excellence in Reference and Adult Services. Kathy L. Tomajko.
White House Conference on Aging (task force). Allan Martin Kleiman.

American Library Association
Young Adult Library Services Association

Executive Director, Beth Yoke
50 E. Huron St., Chicago, IL 60611
312-280-4390, 800-545-2433 ext. 4390
fax 312-280-5276
E-mail yalsa@ala.org
World Wide Web http://www.ala.org/yalsa
Blog http://blogs.ala.org/yalsa.php, MySpace page http://www.myspace.com/yalsa
Wiki http://wikis.ala.org/yalsa

Object

In every library in the nation, quality library service to young adults is provided by a staff that understands and respects the unique informational, educational, and recreational needs of teenagers. Equal access to information, services, and materials is recognized as a right, not a privilege. Young adults are actively involved in the library decision making process. The library staff collaborates and cooperates with other youth-serving agencies to provide a holistic, community-wide network of activities and services that support healthy youth development. To ensure that this vision becomes a reality, the Young Adult Library Services Association (YALSA)

1. Advocates extensive and developmentally appropriate library and information services for young adults ages 12 to 18

2. Promotes reading and supports the literacy movement

3. Advocates the use of information and communications technologies to provide effective library service

4. Supports equality of access to the full range of library materials and services, including existing and emerging information and communications technologies, for young adults

5. Provides education and professional development to enable its members to serve as effective advocates for young people

6. Fosters collaboration and partnerships among its individual members with the library community and other groups involved in providing library and information services to young adults

7. Influences public policy by demonstrating the importance of providing library and information services that meet the unique needs and interests of young adults

8. Encourages research and is in the vanguard of new thinking concerning the provision of library and information services for youth

Membership

Memb. 5,700. Open to anyone interested in library services, literature, and technology for young adults. For information on dues, see ALA entry.

Officers

Pres. Paula Brehm-Heeger. E-mail paula brehmheeger@fuse.net; *V.P./Pres.-Elect* Sarah Debraski. E-mail slcornish@gmail. com; *Past Pres.* Judy Nelson. E-mail jnelson @piercecountylibrary.org; *Division Councilor* Christine Allen. E-mail callen@rusd. k12.ca.us; *Fiscal Officer* Amy Alessio. E-mail aalessio@stdl.org.

Directors

Nick Buron. E-mail nick.h.buron@queens library.org; Michele Gorman. E-mail comix librarian@aol.com; Mary Hastler (ex officio). E-mail mhastler@bcpl.net; Erin V. Helmrich. E-mail helmriche@aadl.org; Maria

Gentle. E-mail mgentl@arlingtonva.us; Kimberly Anne Patton. E-mail kpatton@lawrence.lib.ks.us; Sara Ryan (ex officio). E-mail ryansara@gmail.com; Dawn Rutherford. E-mail drutherford@sno-isle.org.

Publication

Young Adult Library Services (q.) (memb.; nonmemb. $50; foreign $60). *Ed.* Valerie Ott.

AIIM—The Enterprise Content Management Association

President, John F. Mancini
1100 Wayne Ave., Ste. 1100, Silver Spring, MD 20910
800-477-2446, 301-587-8202, fax 301-587-2711
E-mail aiim@aiim.org, World Wide Web http://www.aiim.org
European Office: The IT Centre, 8 Canalside, Lowesmoor Wharf, Worcester WR1 2RR,
England. Tel. 44-1905-727600, fax 44-1905-727609, e-mail info@aiim.org.uk

Object

AIIM is an international authority on enterprise content management, the tools and technologies that capture, manage, store, preserve, and deliver content in support of business processes. Founded in 1943 as the Association for Information and Image Management.

Officers

Chair Jan Andersson, ReadSoft AB; *V. Chair* Robert W. Zagami, DataBank IMX; *Treas.* Lynn Fraas, Crown Partners; *Past Chair* Don McMahan.

Publication

AIIM E-DOC Magazine (bi-mo.; memb.).

American Indian Library Association (AILA)

President, Janice Rice, Univ. of Wisconsin–Madison.
World Wide Web http://www.ailanet.org

Object

To improve library and information services for American Indians.

Founded 1979; affiliated with American Library Association 1985.

Membership

Any person, library, or other organization interested in working to improve library and information services for American Indians may become a member.

Dues (Inst.) $30; (Indiv.) $15; (Student) $10.

Officers (July 2007–June 2008)

Pres. Janice Rice, College Lib., Rm. 2201, Helen C. White Hall, 600 N. Park St., Univ. of Wisconsin–Madison, Madison, WI 53706. E-mail jrice@library.wisc.edu; *V.P./Pres.-Elect* Susan Hanks. E-mail shanks@library.ca.gov; *Secy.* Holly Tomren. E-mail htomren@uci.edu; *Treas.* Joan Howland. E-mail howla001@umn.edu; *Past. Pres.* Carlene Engstrom. E-mail carlene_engstrom@skc.edu.

Publication

AILA Newsletter (q.).

Committee Chairs

Bylaws and Constitution. Stephanie Joseph.

Children's Literature Award. Naomi Caldwell.

Communications and Publications. Liana Juliano.

Development and Fund Raising. Richenda Wilkinson, Liana Juliano.

Nominating. Kelly Webster, Joan Howland.

Programming. Carlene Engstrom.

Scholarship Review Board. Joan Howland, Lotsee Patterson.

Subject Access and Classification. Kelly Webster, Jacquie Samples.

American Merchant Marine Library Association

(An affiliate of United Seamen's Service)
Executive Director, Roger T. Korner
635 Fourth Ave., Brooklyn, NY 11232
Tel. 718-369-3818, e-mail ussammla@ix.netcom.com
World Wide Web http://uss-ammla.com

Object

Provides ship and shore library service for American-flag merchant vessels, the Military Sealift Command, the U.S. Coast Guard, and other waterborne operations of the U.S. government. Established 1921.

Officers (2007–2008)

Pres. Edward R. Morgan; *V.P.s* Thomas J. Bethel, John M. Bowers, Capt. Timothy A. Brown, James Capo, David Cockroft, Ron Davis, Capt. Remo Di Fiore, John Halas, Rene Lioeanjie, George E. Murphy, Capt. Gregorio Oca, Michael Sacco, John J. Sweeney; *Secy.* Donald E. Kadlac; *Treas.* William D. Potts; *Gen. Counsel* John L. DeGurse, Jr.; *Exec. Dir.* Roger T. Korner.

American Society for Information Science and Technology

Executive Director, Richard B. Hill
1320 Fenwick Lane, Ste. 510, Silver Spring, MD 20910
301-495-0900, fax 301-495-0810, e-mail asis@asis.org
World Wide Web http://www.asis.org

Object

The American Society for Information Science and Technology (ASIS&T) provides a forum for the discussion, publication, and critical analysis of work dealing with the design, management, and use of information, information systems, and information technology.

Membership

Memb. (Indiv.) 3,500; (Student) 800; (Inst.) 250. Dues (Indiv.) $140; (Student) $40; (Inst.) $650 and $800.

Officers

Pres. Nancy Roderer, Johns Hopkins Univ.; *Pres.-Elect* Donald O. Case, Univ. of Kentucky; *Treas.* Vicki Gregory, Univ. of South Florida; *Past Pres.* Edie Rasmussen, Univ. of British Columbia.

Address correspondence to the executive director.

Board of Directors

Dirs.-at-Large Suzie Allard, Donald Case, Efthimis Efthimiadis, Katherine McCain, Beata Panagopoulos, Victor Rosenberg, K. T. Vaughan, Julian Warner; Barbara Wildemuth; *Deputy Dirs.* Amy Wallace, Shelly Warwick; *Exec. Dir.* Richard B. Hill.

Publications

Advances in Classification Research, vols. 1–10. Available from Information Today, Inc., 143 Old Marlton Pike, Medford, NJ 08055.

Annual Review of Information Science and Technology. Available from Information Today, Inc.

ASIS&T Thesaurus of Information Science and Librarianship. Available from Information Today, Inc.

Bulletin of the American Society for Information Science and Technology. Available from ASIS&T.

Covert and Overt: Recollecting and Connecting Intelligence Service and Information Science, ed. by Robert V. Williams and Ben-Ami Lipetz. Available from Information Today, Inc.

Editorial Peer Review: Its Strengths and Weaknesses by Ann C. Weller. Available from Information Today, Inc.

Electronic Publishing: Applications and Implications, ed. by Elisabeth Logan and Myke Gluck. Available from Information Today, Inc.

Evaluating Networked Information Services: Techniques, Policy and Issues by Charles R. McClure and John Carlo Bertot. Available from Information Today, Inc.

From Print to Electronic: The Transformation of Scientific Communication by Susan Y. Crawford, Julie M. Hurd, and Ann C. Weller. Available from Information Today, Inc.

Historical Information Science: An Emerging Unidiscipline by Lawrence J. McCrank. Available from Information Today, Inc.

Historical Studies in Information Science, ed. by Trudi Bellardo Hahn and Michael Buckland. Available from Information Today, Inc.

The History and Heritage of Scientific and Technological Information Systems, ed. by W. Boyd Rayward and Mary Ellen Bowden. Available from Information Today, Inc.

Information and Emotion: The Emergent Affective Paradigm in Information Behavior Research and Theory, ed. by Diane

Nahl and Dania Bilal. Available from Information Today, Inc.

Information Management for the Intelligent Organization: The Art of Environmental Scanning, 2nd edition, by Chun Wei Choo. Available from Information Today, Inc.

Information Representation and Retrieval in the Digital Age by Heting Chu. Available from Information Today, Inc.

Intelligent Technologies in Library and Information Service Applications by F. W. Lancaster and Amy Warner. Available from Information Today, Inc.

Introductory Concepts in Information Science by Melanie J. Norton. Available from Information Today, Inc.

Journal of the American Society for Information Science and Technology. Available from John Wiley and Sons, 605 Third Ave., New York, NY 10016.

Knowledge Management for the Information Professional, ed. by T. Kanti Srikantaiah and Michael Koenig. Available from Information Today, Inc.

Knowledge Management: The Bibliography, compiled by Paul Burden. Available from Information Today, Inc.

Proceedings of ASIS&T Annual Meetings. Available from Information Today, Inc.

Scholarly Publishing: The Electronic Frontier, ed. by Robin P. Peek and Gregory B. Newby. Available from MIT Press, Cambridge, Massachusetts.

Statistical Methods for the Information Professional by Liwen Vaughan. Available from Information Today, Inc.

Theories of Information Behavior, ed. by Karen E. Fisher, Sanda Erdelez, and Lynne E. F. McKechnie. Available from Information Today, Inc.

The Web of Knowledge: A Festschrift in Honor of Eugene Garfield, ed. by Blaise Cronin and Helen Barsky Atkins. Available from Information Today, Inc.

Committee Chairpersons

Awards and Honors. Robin Peek.
Budget and Finance. Vicki L. Gregory.
Constitution and Bylaws. William Edgar.
Education. Prudence Dalrymple.
Leadership Development. Debora Barreau.
Membership. Caryn Anderson.
Nominations. Edie Rasmussen.
Publications and Scholarly Communications. Samantha Hastings.
Standards. Marcia Zeng.

American Theological Library Association

300 S. Wacker Dr., Ste. 2100, Chicago, IL 60606-6701
Tel. 888-665-2852, 312-454-5100, fax 312-454-5505
E-mail atla@atla.com, World Wide Web http://www.atla.com/atlahome.html

Mission Statement

The mission of the American Theological Library Association (ATLA) is to foster the study of theology and religion by enhancing the development of theological and religious libraries and librarianship. In pursuit of this mission, the association undertakes

• To foster the professional growth of its members, and to enhance their ability to serve their constituencies as administrators and librarians

• To advance the profession of theological librarianship, and to assist theological librarians in defining and interpreting the proper role and function of libraries in theological education

• To promote quality library and information services in support of teaching, learning, and research in theology, religion, and related disciplines and to create such tools and aids (including publications) as may be helpful in accomplishing this

- To stimulate purposeful collaboration among librarians of theological libraries and religious studies collections, and to develop programmatic solutions to information-related problems common to those librarians and collections

Membership

(Inst.) 265; (International Inst.) 13; (Indiv.) 492; (Student) 67; (Lifetime) 90; (Affiliates) 71.

Officers

Pres. Martha Lund Smalley, Research Services Libn., Yale Univ. Divinity School Lib., 409 Prospect St., New Haven, CT 06511. Tel. 203-432-6374, fax 203-432-3906, e-mail martha.smalley@yale.edu; *V.P.* David R. Stewart, Dir. of Lib. Services, Luther Seminary, 2481 Como Ave., St. Paul, MN 55108. Tel. 651-641-3592, fax 651-641-3280, e-mail dstewart@luthersem.edu; *Secy.* Roberta A. Schaafsma, Assoc. Dir., Duke Univ. Divinity School Lib., Box 90972, Durham, NC 27708-0972. Tel. 919-660-3491, fax 919-681-7594, e-mail roberta.schaafsma@duke.edu.

Directors

Carrisse Mickey Berryhill, Eileen Crawford, M. Patrick Graham, Duane Harbin, Cait Kokolus, Saundra Lipton, Allen W. Mueller, James C. Pakala, Laura Wood.

Publications

ATLA Indexes in MARC Format (2 a year).

ATLA Religion Database on CD-ROM, 1949–.

ATLA Religion Database: Ten Year Subset on CD-ROM, 1993–.

Biblical Studies on CD-ROM (ann.).

Catholic Periodical and Literature Index on CD-ROM (ann.).

Index to Book Reviews in Religion (ann.).

Newsletter (q.; memb.; nonmemb. $55). *Ed.* Sara Corkery.

Old Testament Abstracts on CD-ROM (ann.).

Proceedings (ann.; memb.; nonmemb. $55). *Ed.* Sara Corkery.

Religion Index One: Periodicals (2 a year).

Research in Ministry: An Index to Doctor of Ministry Project Reports (ann.), print and online.

Archivists and Librarians in the History of the Health Sciences

President, Micaela Sullivan-Fowler
Curator/History of the Health Sciences Librarian, Ebling Library
University of Wisconsin at Madison, 720 S. Highland Ave., Madison, WI 53705
608-262-2402, e-mail msullivan@library.wisc.edu
World Wide Web http://www.library.ucla.edu/libraries/biomed/alhhs

Object

This association was established exclusively for educational purposes, to serve the professional interests of librarians, archivists, and other specialists actively engaged in the librarianship of the history of the health sciences by promoting the exchange of information and by improving the standards of service.

Membership

Memb. 170. Dues $15 (Americas), $21 (other countries).

Officers

Pres. Micaela Sullivan-Fowler; *Pres.-Elect* Lisa A. Mix. E-mail lisa.mix@library.ucsf.

edetu; *Secy./Treas.* Brooke Fox. E-mail ebf2@musc.edu; *Membs.-at-Large* Toby A. Appel, Judy M. Chellnick, K. Garth Huston, Jr., Tim L. Pennycuff.

Publication

The Watermark (q.; memb.). *Ed.* Eric v.d. Luft, Gegensatz Press, 108 Deborah Lane, North Syracuse, NY 13212-1931. Tel. 315-464-4585, e-mail ericvdluft@verizon.net.

ARMA International—The Association for Information Management Professionals

Executive Director, Marilyn Bier
13725 W. 109 St., Ste. 101, Lenexa, KS 66215
888-301-3324, 913-341-3808, fax 913-341-3742
E-mail hq@arma.org, World Wide Web http://www.arma.org

Object

To advance the practice of records and information management as a discipline and a profession; to organize and promote programs of research, education, training, and networking within that profession; to support the enhancement of professionalism of the membership; and to promote cooperative endeavors with related professional groups.

Membership

Annual dues $150 for international affiliation (student/retired $25). Chapter dues vary.

Officers (July 2007–June 2008)

Pres. Carol E. B. Choksy, IRAD Consulting, 4103 Gold Grove Rd., Greenwood, IN 46143. Tel. 317-294-8329; *Pres.-Elect* John Frost, IBM Corp., 12408 John Simpson Court, Austin, TX 78732. Tel. 877-622-9929; *Chair* Susan McKinney, Records and Info. Manage-ment, Univ. of Minnesota, 502 Morrill Hall, 100 Church St. S.E., Minneapolis 55455. Tel. 612-625-3497; *Treas.* Patrick J. Cunningham, Motorola, Inc., 1303 E. Algonquin Rd., Schaumburg, IL 60196. Tel. 847-576-5469; *Past Pres.* Susan McKinney, Univ. of Minnesota, 502 Morrill Hall, 100 Church St. S.E., Minneapolis MN 55455. Tel. 612-625-3497.

Directors

Sharon Alexander-Gooding, Douglas Allen, Beth Chiaiese, Galina Datskovsky, Nicholas De Laurentis, Pamela Duane, Michael Langstone, Deborah Marshall, Bonnie Nadler, Daryll Prescott, Gita Werapitiya, Jesse Wilkins.

Publication

Information Management Journal (bi-mo.). *Managing Ed.* Mike Harrington.

Art Libraries Society of North America (ARLIS/NA)

Executive Director, Elizabeth Clarke
38 Steffler Drive, Guelph, ON N1G 3N5
519-827-1506, fax 519-827-1825, e-mail eclarke33@rogers.com
World Wide Web http://www.arlisna.org

Object

To foster excellence in art librarianship and visual resources curatorship for the advancement of the visual arts. Established 1972.

Membership

Memb. 1,100. Dues (Inst./Business Affiliate) $145; (Indiv.) $85; (Student) $45; (Retired/Unemployed) $45; (Sustaining) $250; (Sponsor) $500; (Overseas) $65. Year. Jan. 1–Dec. 31. Membership is open to all those interested in visual librarianship, whether they be professional librarians, students, library assistants, art book publishers, art book dealers, art historians, archivists, architects, slide and photograph curators, or retired associates in these fields.

Officers

Pres. Deborah K. Ultan Boudewyns, 170B Wilson Lib., Univ. of Minnesota, 309 19th Ave S., Minneapolis, MN 55455. Tel. 612-625-6438, e-mail ultan004@umn.edu; *V.P./Pres.-Elect* Ken Soehner, Thomas J. Watson Lib., Metropolitan Museum of Art, 1000 Fifth Ave., New York, NY 10028. Tel. 212-570-3934, fax 212-570-3847, e-mail ken.soehner@metmuseum.org; *Secy.* Rebecca Price, 2396 Duderstadt Center, Ann Arbor, MI 48109-2094. Tel. 734-647-2094, e-mail rpw@umich.edu; *Treas.* Fran Scott, Architecture Lib., Greene Bldg., Rm. 309, Rensselaer Research Libs, Rensselaer Polytechnic Institute, 110 Eighth St., Troy, NY 12180-3590. Tel. 518-276-6312, fax 518-276-6753, e-mail scottf2@rpi.edu; *Past Pres.* Ann Baird Whiteside, Rotch Lib. of Architecture and Planning, MIT, Rm. 7-238, 77 Massachusetts Ave., Cambridge, MA 02139. Tel. 617-258-5594, fax 617-253-9331, e-mail awhites@mit.edu.

Address correspondence to the executive director.

Publications

ARLIS/NA Update (bi-mo.; memb.).

Art Documentation (2 a year; memb., subscription).

Handbook and List of Members (ann.; memb.).

Occasional Papers (price varies).

Miscellaneous others (request current list from headquarters).

Committee Chairpersons

ARLIS/NA and VRA Summer Educational Institute for Visual Resources and Image Management. Amy Lucker, Karin Whalen, Eileen Fry, Jeanne Keefe.

Awards. Susan Moon.

Cataloging Advisory. Kay Teel.

Development. Jon Evans.

Distinguished Service Award. Betsy Peck-Learned.

Diversity. Vanessa Kam, Laurel Bliss.

Finance. Lynda White.

International Relations. Kristen Regina.

Membership. Rachel Resnik.

Gerd Muehsam Award. Tony White.

Nominating. Carole Ann Fabian.

Professional Development. Tom Caswell.

Public Policy. Tim Shipe.

Publications. Roger Lawson.

Research Awards. Alan Michelson, Hannah Bennett.

Standards. Aprille Nace.

Travel Awards. Jennifer Parker.

George Wittenborn Award. Margaret Culbertson.

Asian/Pacific American Librarians Association (APALA)

Executive Director, Gerardo ("Gary") Colmenar
World Wide Web http://www.apalaweb.org

Object

To provide a forum for discussing problems and concerns of Asian/Pacific American librarians; to provide a forum for the exchange of ideas by Asian/Pacific American librarians and other librarians; to support and encourage library services to Asian/Pacific American communities; to recruit and support Asian/Pacific American librarians in the library/information science professions; to seek funding for scholarships in library/information science programs for Asian/Pacific Americans; and to provide a vehicle whereby Asian/Pacific American librarians can cooperate with other associations and organizations having similar or allied interests. Founded 1980; incorporated 1981; affiliated with American Library Association 1982.

Membership

Open to all librarians and information specialists of Asian/Pacific descent working in U.S. libraries and information centers and other related organizations, and to others who support the goals and purposes of APALA. Asian/Pacific Americans are defined as people residing in North America who self-identify as Asian/Pacific American. Dues (Inst.) $50; (Indiv.) $20; (Students/Unemployed Librarians) $10.

Officers (July 2007–June 2008)

Pres. Buenaventura ("Ven") B. Basco, Univ. of Central Florida Libs. E-mail bbasco@mail.ucf.edu; *V.P./Pres.-Elect* Michelle Baildon, MIT Humanities Lib. E-mail baildon@mit.edu; *Secy.* Suhasini L. Kumar, Carlson Lib., Univ. of Toledo. E-mail Skumar@utnet.utoledo.edu; *Treas.* Sherise Kimura, Gleeson Lib., Univ. of San Francisco. E-mail kimura@usfca.edu; *Past Pres.* Ben Wakashige, National American Univ. E-mail bwakashige@national.edu.

Publication

APALA Newsletter (q.).

Committee Chairs

Awards. Dora Ho.
Constitution and Bylaws. Thaddeus Bejnar.
Finance and Fund Raising. Sherise Kimura.
Membership and Recruitment. Michelle Baildon.
Newsletter and Publications. Suhasini Kumar, Gary Colmenar.
Nomination. Ben Wakashige.
Program. Ven Basco.
Publicity. Angela Boyd, Maria Carpenter.
Research and Travel. Alanna Aiko Moore.
Scholarships. Ganga Dakshinamurti, Laura Park.
Web. Holly Yu.

Association of Academic Health Sciences Libraries

Executive Director, Marlis Korber
2150 N. 107 St., Ste. 205, Seattle, WA 98133
206-367-8704, fax 206-367-8777
E-mail aahsl@sbims.com, World Wide Web http://www.aahsl.org

Object

The Association of Academic Health Sciences Libraries (AAHSL) is composed of the directors of libraries of more than 140 accredited U.S. and Canadian medical schools belonging to the Association of American Medical Colleges. Its goals are to promote excellence in academic health science libraries and to ensure that the next generation of health practitioners is trained in information-seeking skills that enhance the quality of healthcare delivery, education, and research. Founded 1977.

Membership

Memb. 140+. Regular membership is available to nonprofit educational institutions operating a school of health sciences that has full or provisional accreditation by the Association of American Medical Colleges. Regular members shall be represented by the chief administrative officer of the member institution's health sciences library. Associate membership (and nonvoting representation) is available to organizations having an interest in the purposes and activities of the association.

Officers (2007–2008)

Pres. Linda Watson, Health Sciences Libs., Univ. of Minnesota–Twin Cities; *Pres.-Elect* Julia Sollenberger, Univ. of Rochester Medical Center; *Secy./Treas.* Paul Schoening, Bernard Becker Medical Lib., Washington Univ. School of Medicine; *Past Pres.* Elaine Martin, Lamar Soutter Lib., Univ. of Massachusetts.

Directors

Jim Bothmer, Health Science Lib., Creighton Univ.; Mary Ryan, Univ. of Arkansas for Health Sciences Lib.; Pat Thibodeau, Medical Center Lib., Duke Univ.

Association of Independent Information Professionals (AIIP)

8550 United Plaza Blvd., Ste. 1001, Baton Rouge, LA 70809
225-408-4400, fax 225-408-4422, e-mail info@aiip.org
World Wide Web http://www.aiip.org

Object

AIIP's members are owners of firms providing such information-related services as online and manual research, document delivery, database design, library support, consulting, writing, and publishing. The objectives of the association are

- To advance the knowledge and understanding of the information profession
- To promote and maintain high professional and ethical standards among its members
- To encourage independent information professionals to assemble to discuss common issues

- To promote the interchange of information among independent information professionals and various organizations
- To keep the public informed of the profession and of the responsibilities of the information professional

Membership

Memb. 650+.

Officers (2007–2008)

Pres. Crystal Sharp, CD Sharp Info. Systems. Tel. 519-495-2889, e-mail crystal@cdsharp.com; *Pres.-Elect* Jane John, On Point Research. Tel. 207-373-1755; *Secy.* Mark Goldstein, International Research Center. Tel. 602-470-0389; *Treas.* Maryanne Nasiatka, Blue Lion Media. Tel. 734-454-0926.

Publications

Connections (q.).
Membership Directory (ann.).
Professional Paper series.

Association of Jewish Libraries

P.O. Box 1118, Teaneck, NJ 07666
212-725-5359, e-mail ajlibs@osu.edu
World Wide Web http://www.jewishlibraries.org

Object

The Association of Jewish Libraries (AJL) promotes Jewish literacy through enhancement of libraries and library resources and through leadership for the profession and practitioners of Judaica librarianship. The association fosters access to information, learning, teaching, and research relating to Jews, Judaism, the Jewish experience, and Israel.

Goals

- Maintain high professional standards for Judaica librarians and recruit qualified individuals into the profession

- Facilitate communication and exchange of information on a global scale

- Encourage quality publication in the field in all formats and media

- Stimulate publication of high-quality children's literature

- Facilitate and encourage establishment of Judaica library collections
- Enhance information access for all through application of advanced technologies
- Publicize the organization and its activities in all relevant venues
- Stimulate awareness of Judaica library services among the public at large
- Promote recognition of Judaica librarianship within the wider library profession
- Encourage recognition of Judaica library services by other organizations and related professions
- Ensure continuity of the association through sound management, financial security, effective governance, and a dedicated and active membership

Membership

Memb. 1,100. Dues $50; (Student/Retired) $30. Year. July 1–June 30.

Officers (July 2006–June 2008)

Pres. Laurel S. Wolfson, Hebrew Union College–Jewish Institute of Religion; *V.P./Pres.-Elect* Susan Dubin, Off-the-Shelf Lib. Services; *V.P. Memb.* Joseph Galron, Ohio State Univ., Columbus; *V.P. Publications* Deborah Stern, Reconstructionist Rabbinical College; *Treas.* Schlomit Schwarzer; *Recording Secy.* Elana Gensler, West Hempstead (New York) Public Lib.; *Corresponding Secy.* Rachel K. Glasser, Yavneh Academy; *Past Pres.* Ronda Rose, Temple Emanuel, Beverly Hills.

Address correspondence to the association.

Publications

AJL Newsletter (q.). *Ed.* Libby K. White, Baltimore Hebrew Univ., 5800 Park Heights Ave., Baltimore, MD 21215.
Judaica Librarianship (irreg.). *Ed.* Zachary M. Baker, Green Lib. 321, ASRG, Stanford Univ. Libs., Stanford, CA 94305-6004.

Division Presidents

Research Libraries, Archives, and Special Libraries. Elliot H. Gertel, Univ. of Michigan.
Synagogue, School, and Center Libraries. Etta D. Gold, Temple Beth Am, Miami.

Association of Research Libraries

Executive Director, Duane E. Webster
21 Dupont Circle N.W., Ste. 800, Washington, DC 20036
202-296-2296, fax 202-872-0884
E-mail arlhq@arl.org, World Wide Web http://www.arl.org

Object

The Association of Research Libraries (ARL) influences the changing environment of scholarly communication and the public policies that affect research libraries and the diverse communities they serve. ARL pursues this mission by advancing the goals of its member research libraries, providing leadership in public and information policy to the scholarly and higher education communities, fostering the exchange of ideas and expertise, and shaping a future environment that leverages its interests with those of allied organizations.

Membership

Memb. 123. Membership is institutional. Dues: $22,444 for 2008.

Officers

Pres. Marianne Gaunt, Rutgers Univ.; *V.P./Pres.-Elect* Thomas C. Leonard, Univ. of California, Berkeley; *Past Pres.* Sherrie Schmidt, Arizona State Univ.

Board of Directors

Barbara Dewey, Univ. of Tennessee; Brinley Franklin, Univ. of Connecticut; Marianne Gaunt, Rutgers Univ.; Tom Leonard, Univ. of California, Berkeley; Charles B. Lowry, Univ. of Maryland; Carol A. Mandel, New York Univ.; Dana C. Rooks, Univ. of Houston; Sherrie Schmidt, Arizona State Univ.; Winston Tabb, Johns Hopkins Univ.; Karin Trainer, Princeton Univ.; Paul Wiens, Queens Univ.; Jennifer Younger, Univ. of Notre Dame.

Publications

ARL: A Bimonthly Report on Research Library Issues and Actions from ARL, CNI, and SPARC (bi-mo.).
ARL Academic Health Sciences Library Statistics (ann.).
ARL Academic Law Library Statistics (ann.).
ARL Annual Salary Survey (ann.).
ARL Preservation Statistics (ann.).
ARL Statistics (ann.).
SPEC Kits (6 a year).

Committee and Work Group Chairpersons

Diversity Initiatives. Karin Trainer, Princeton Univ.
Fair Use and Related Exemptions. Mary Case, Univ. of Illinois, Chicago.
Membership. Marilyn Sharrow, Univ. of California, Davis.
Public Policies Affecting Research Libraries. Sarah Michalak, Univ. of North Carolina, Chapel Hill.
Research, Teaching, and Learning. Barbara Dewey, Univ. of Tennessee.
Scholarly Communication. Jim Neal, Columbia Univ.
Special Collections Working Group, Alice Prochaska, Yale Univ.
Statistics and Assessment. Colleen Cook, Texas A&M Univ.

ARL Membership

Nonuniversity Libraries

Boston Public Lib., Canada Inst. for Scientific and Technical Info., Center for Research Libs., Lib. and Archives Canada, Lib. of Congress, National Agricultural Lib., National Lib. of Medicine, New York Public Lib., New York State Lib., Smithsonian Institution Libs.

University Libraries

Alabama; Albany (SUNY); Alberta; Arizona; Arizona State; Auburn; Boston College; Boston Univ.; Brigham Young; British Columbia; Brown; Buffalo (SUNY); California, Berkeley; California, Davis; California, Irvine; California, Los Angeles; California, Riverside; California, San Diego; California, Santa Barbara; Case Western Reserve; Chicago; Cincinnati; Colorado; Colorado State; Columbia; Connecticut; Cornell; Dartmouth; Delaware; Duke; Emory; Florida; Florida State; George Washington; Georgetown; Georgia; Georgia Inst. of Technology; Guelph; Harvard; Hawaii; Houston; Howard; Illinois, Chicago; Illinois, Urbana-Champaign; Indiana; Iowa; Iowa State; Johns Hopkins; Kansas; Kent State; Kentucky; Laval; Louisiana State; Louisville; McGill; McMaster; Manitoba; Maryland; Massachusetts; Massachusetts Inst. of Technology; Miami (Florida); Michigan; Michigan State; Minnesota; Missouri; Montreal; Nebraska, Lincoln; New Mexico; New York; North Carolina; North Carolina State; Northwestern; Notre Dame; Ohio; Ohio State; Oklahoma; Oklahoma State; Oregon; Pennsylvania; Pennsylvania State; Pittsburgh; Princeton; Purdue; Queen's (Kingston, Ontario); Rice; Rochester; Rutgers; Saskatchewan; South Carolina; Southern California; Southern Illinois; Stony Brook (SUNY); Syracuse; Temple; Tennessee; Texas; Texas A&M; Texas Tech; Toronto; Tulane; Utah; Vanderbilt; Virginia; Virginia Tech; Washington; Washington (Saint Louis): Washington State; Waterloo; Wayne State; Western Ontario; Wisconsin; Yale; York.

Association of Vision Science Librarians

Chair 2008–2009, Cindy Hutchison, Director of Library Services, New England College of
Optometry, 424 Beacon St., Boston MA 02115
E-mail hutchisonc@neco.edu
World Wide Web http://spectacle.berkeley.edu/~library/AVSL.HTM

Object

To foster collective and individual acquisition and dissemination of vision science information, to improve services for all persons seeking such information, and to develop standards for libraries to which members are attached. Founded 1968.

Membership

Memb. (U.S.) 62; (International) 50.

Publications

Core List of Audio-Visual Related Serials.
Guidelines for Vision Science Libraries.
Opening Day Book, Journal and AV Collection—Visual Science.
Publication Considerations in the Age of Electronic Opportunities.
Standards for Vision Science Libraries.
Union List of Vision-Related Serials (irreg.).

Meetings

Annual meeting held in the fall, midyear mini-meeting with the Medical Library Association in the spring.

Beta Phi Mu
(International Library and Information Studies Honor Society)

Executive Director, Christie Koontz
College of Information, Florida State University, Tallahassee, FL 32306-2100
850-644-3907, fax 850-644-9763
E-mail ckoontz@ci.fsu.edu, World Wide Web http://www.beta-phi-mu.org

Object

To recognize distinguished achievement in and scholarly contributions to librarianship, information studies, or library education, and to sponsor and support appropriate professional and scholarly projects relating to these fields. Founded at the University of Illinois in 1948.

Membership

Memb. 26,000. Open to graduates of library school programs accredited by the American Library Association who fulfill the following requirements: complete the course requirements leading to a fifth year or other advanced degree in librarianship with a scholastic average of 3.75 where A equals 4 points (this provision shall also apply to planned programs of advanced study beyond the fifth year that do not culminate in a degree but that require full-time study for one or more academic years) and rank in the top 25 percent of their class; and receive a letter of recommendation from the faculty of their respective library schools attesting to their professional promise.

Officers

Pres. Nancy Zimmerman, School of Lib. and Info. Science, Univ. of South Carolina, 1501 Green St., Columbia, SC 29208; *V.P./Pres.-Elect* Sue Stroyan, Milner Lib., Illinois State Univ., Campus Box 8900, Normal, IL 61700-8900; *Treas.* David Whisenant, College Center for Library Automation, 1753 W. Paul Dirac Dr., Tallahassee, FL 32310; *Exec. Dir.* Christie Koontz, College of Info., Florida State Univ., Tallahassee, FL 32306-2100. Tel. 850-644-3907, fax 850-644-9763, e-mail betaphimuinfoadmin.fsu.edu.

Directors

Dirs. Timothy Sineath, Blanche Woolls, Mark Wendt, Kathleen Strauss, Eloise May, Ron Miller; *Dirs.-at-Large* Marie L. Radford, Sue Searing.

Publications

Beta Phi Mu Monograph Series. Book-length scholarly works based on original research in subjects of interest to library and information professionals. Available from Greenwood Press, 88 Post Rd. W., Box 5007, Westport, CT 06881-9990.

Chapbook Series. Limited editions on topics of interest to information professionals.

Newsletter (electronic only). *Ed.* Harla J. Frank.

Chapters

Alpha. Univ. of Illinois, Grad. School of Lib. and Info. Science; *Beta.* (Inactive) Univ. of Southern California, School of Lib. Science; *Gamma.* Florida State Univ., School of Lib. and Info. Studies; *Delta.* (Inactive) Loughborough College of Further Educ., School of Libnship., Loughborough, England; *Epsilon.* Univ. of North Carolina, School of Lib. Science; *Zeta.* Atlanta Univ., School of Lib. and Info. Studies; *Theta.* Pratt Inst., Grad. School of Lib. and Info. Science; *Iota.* Catholic Univ. of America, School of Lib. and Info. Science; Univ. of Maryland, College of Lib. and Info. Services; *Kappa.* (Inactive). Western Michigan Univ., School of Libnship.; *Lambda.* Univ. of Oklahoma, School of Lib. Science; *Mu.* Univ. of Michigan, School of Lib. Science; *Xi.* Univ. of Hawaii, Grad. School of Lib. Studies; *Omicron.* Rutgers Univ., Grad. School of Lib. and Info. Studies; *Pi.* Univ. of Pittsburgh, School of Lib. and Info. Science; *Rho.* Kent State Univ., School of Lib. Science; *Sigma.* Drexel Univ., School of Lib. and Info. Science; *Tau.* (Inactive) State Univ. of New York at Genesee, School of Lib. and Info. Science; *Upsilon.* (Inactive) Univ. of Kentucky, College of Lib. Science; *Phi.* Univ. of Denver, Grad. School of Libnship. and Info. Mgt.; *Chi.* Indiana Univ., School of Lib. and Info. Science; *Psi.* Univ. of Missouri at Columbia, School of Lib. and Info. Sciences; *Omega.* (Inactive) San José State Univ., Div. of Lib. Science; *Beta Alpha.* Queens College, City College of New York, Grad. School of Lib. and Info. Studies; *Beta Beta.* Simmons College, Grad. School of Lib. and Info. Science; *Beta Delta.* State Univ. of New York at Buffalo, School of Info. and Lib. Studies; *Beta Epsilon.* Emporia State Univ., School of Lib. Science; *Beta Zeta.* Louisiana State Univ., Grad. School of Lib. Science; *Beta Eta.* Univ. of Texas at Austin, Grad. School of Lib. and Info. Science; *Beta Theta.* (Inactive) Brigham Young Univ., School of Lib. and Info. Science; *Beta Iota.* Univ. of Rhode Island, Grad. Lib. School; *Beta Kappa.* Univ. of Alabama, Grad. School of Lib. Service; *Beta Lambda.* North Texas State Univ., School of Lib. and Info. Science; Texas Woman's Univ., School of Lib. Science; *Beta Mu.* Long Island Univ., Palmer Grad. Lib. School; *Beta Nu.* Saint John's Univ., Div. of Lib. and Info. Science; *Beta Xi.* North Carolina Central Univ., School of Lib. Science; *Beta Omicron.* (Inactive) Univ. of Tennessee at Knoxville, Grad. School of Lib. and Info. Science; *Beta Pi.* Univ. of Arizona, Grad. Lib. School; *Beta Rho.* Univ. of Wisconsin at Milwaukee, School of Lib. Science; *Beta Sigma.* (Inactive) Clarion State College, School of Lib. Science; *Beta Tau.* Wayne State Univ., Div. of Lib. Science; *Beta Upsilon.* (Inactive) Alabama A&M Univ., School of Lib. Media; *Beta Phi.* Univ.

of South Florida, Grad. Dept. of Lib., Media, and Info. Studies; *Beta Psi.* Univ. of Southern Mississippi, School of Lib. Service; *Beta Omega.* Univ. of South Carolina, College of Libnship.; *Beta Beta Alpha.* Univ. of California, Los Angeles, Grad. School of Lib. and Info. Science; *Beta Beta Gamma.* Rosary College, Grad. School of Lib. and Info. Science; *Beta Beta Delta.* Univ. of Cologne, Germany; *Beta Beta Epsilon.* Univ. of Wisconsin at Madison, Lib. School; *Beta Beta Lambda* Univ. of Washington, Seattle; *Beta Beta Zeta.* Univ. of North Carolina, Greensboro, Dept. of Lib. Science and Educational Technology; *Beta Beta Theta.* Univ. of Iowa, School of Lib. and Info. Science; *Beta Beta Iota.* State Univ. of New York, Univ. at Albany, School of Info. Science and Policy; *Beta Beta Kappa.* Univ. of Puerto Rico, Grad. School of Info. Sciences and Technologies; *Pi Lambda Sigma.* Syracuse Univ., School of Info. Studies.

Bibliographical Society of America

Executive Secretary, Michèle E. Randall
P.O. Box 1537, Lenox Hill Station, New York, NY 10021
212-452-2710 (tel./fax), e-mail bsa@bibsocamer.org
World Wide Web http://www.bibsocamer.org

Object

To promote bibliographical research and to issue bibliographical publications. Organized 1904.

Membership

Memb. 1,200. Dues (Indiv.) $65; (Sustaining) $250; (Contributing) $100; (Student) $20); (Inst.) $75. Year. Jan.–Dec.

Officers

Pres. John Neal Hoover. E-mail jhoover@umsl.edu; *V.P.* Claudia Funke. E-mail ccf6@columbia.edu; *Secy.* David R. Whitesell. E-mail whitesel@fas.harvard.edu; *Treas.* G. Scott Clemons. E-mail scott.clemons@bbh.com; *Past Pres.* John Bidwell. E-mail jbidwell@morganlibrary.org.

Council

(2008) William Baker, Patricia Fleming, James May, Deirdre C. Stam; (2009) Anthony Bliss, John Neal Hoover, Barbara Shailor, Daniel Slive; (2010) Eugene S. Flam, James N. Green, Arthur L. Schwarz, Carolyn L. Smith.

Publication

Papers of the Bibliographical Society of America (q.; memb.). *Ed.* Trevor Howard-Hill, Thomas Cooper Lib., Univ. of South Carolina, Columbia, SC 29208. Tel./fax 803-777-7046, e-mail ralphcrane@msn.com.

Black Caucus of the American Library Association

President, Wanda Brown
Z. Smith Reynolds Lib., Wake Forest University, Winston-Salem, NC 27109.
Tel. 336-758-5094, fax 336-758-4652, e-mail brownw@wfu.edu
World Wide Web http://www.bcala.org

Mission

The Black Caucus of the American Library Association (BCALA) serves as an advocate for the development, promotion, and improvement of library services and resources to the nation's African American community, and provides leadership for the recruitment and professional development of African American librarians. Founded in 1970.

Membership

Membership is open to any person, institution, or business interested in promoting the development of library and information services for African Americans and other people of African descent and willing to maintain good financial standing with the organization. The membership is currently composed of librarians and other information professionals, library support staff, libraries, publishers, authors, vendors, and other library-related organizations in the United States and abroad. Dues (Corporate) $200; (Institutional) $60; (Regular) $45; (Student) $10.

Officers

Pres. Wanda Brown. E-mail brownw@wfu.edu; *V.P./Pres.-Elect* Karolyn S. Thompson. Tel. 601-266-5111, fax 601-266-4410, e-mail karolyn.thompson@usm.edu; *Secy.* Jennifer Lang. Tel. 609-258-5476, fax 609-258-0441, e-mail lang@princeton.edu; *Treas.* Stanton F. Biddle. E-mail treasurer@bcala.org; *Past Pres.* Andrew P. Jackson (Sekou Molefi Baako). E-mail andrew.p.jackson@queens library.org.

Executive Board

Talia Abdullah; Vivian Bordeaux; Lisa Boyd; Jannie Cobb; Denyvetta Davis; Sharon Epps; S. D. Harris; Gerald Holmes; Julius Jefferson, Jr.; Alys Jordan; Jerome Offord, Jr.; Sylvia Sprinkle-Hamlin; Dorothy Ann Washington; Kelvin Watson; Teri B. Weil.

Publication

BCALA Newsletter (bi-mo; memb.). *Interim Ed.* S. D. Harris, e-mail sdh.newsletter@bcala.org.

Committee Chairpersons

Affiliated Chapters. Sylvia Sprinkle-Hamlin, Lainey Westbrooks.
Affirmative Action. Jane Moore McGinn, Howard F. McGinn.
Awards. ayo dayo, Billie Walker.
Budget/Audit. Jos N. Holman, Bobby Player.
Constitution and Bylaws. Brenda Hunter, Billy Beal.
Fund Raising. Sam Morrison, Kelvin Watson.
History. Sibyl E. Moses.
International Relations. Lavonda K. Broadnax, Allene F. Hayes.
E. J. Josey Scholarship. Rochelle Ballard, Michael C. Walker.
Literary Awards. John Page, Joel White.
Membership. Gladys Smiley Bell, Rudolph Clay.
Newsletter. S. D. Harris.
Nominations/Elections. Andrew P. Jackson.
Programs. Karolyn S. Thompson.
Public Relations. Valerie Bell, Rose T. Dawson.

Recruitment and Professional Development. LeRoy ("Lee") LaFleur.
Services to Children of Families of African Descent. Karen Lemmons, S. D. Harris.
Technology Advisory. H. Jamane Yeager.
John C. Tyson Memorial Scholarship. Em Claire Knowles.

Awards

BCALA Literary Awards.
BCALA Trailblazer's Award.
DEMCO/ALA Black Caucus Award for Excellence in Librarianship.
Distinguished Service Award.
E. J. Josey Scholarship Award.
Smiley Student Fund.
John Tyson Award.

Canadian Association for Information Science (CAIS) (L'Association Canadienne des Sciences de l'Information)

President, Gloria Leckie
Faculty of Information and Media Studies, University of Western Ontario
North Campus Building, Rm. 240E, London, ON N6A 5B7
Tel. 519-661-2111 ext. 88505, fax 519-661-3506, World Wide Web http://www.cais-acsi.ca

Object

To promote the advancement of information science in Canada and encourage and facilitate the exchange of information relating to the use, access, retrieval, organization, management, and dissemination of information.

Membership

Institutions and individuals interested in information science and involved in the gathering, organization, and dissemination of information (such as information scientists, archivists, librarians, computer scientists, documentalists, economists, educators, journalists, and psychologists) and who support CAIS's objectives can become association members. Dues (Inst.) $165; (Personal) $75; (Senior) $40; (Student) $40.

Directors

Pres. Gloria Leckie, Univ. of Western Ontario; *V.P.* Joan Bartlett, McGill Univ.; *Treas.* Ali Shiri, Univ. of Alberta; *Dir., Communications* Haidar Moukdad, Dalhousie Univ.; *Dir., Membership* Clément Arsenault, Univ. de Montréal; *Secy.* Kimiz Dalkir, McGill Univ.; *Past Pres.* Lisa Given, Univ. of Alberta.

Publication

Canadian Journal of Information and Library Science. Ed. Heidi Julien, Univ. of Alberta.

Canadian Library Association (CLA)

Executive Director, Don Butcher
328 Frank St., Ottawa, ON K2P 0X8
613-232-9625 ext. 306, fax 613-563-9895
E-mail dbutcher@cla.ca, World Wide Web http://www.cla.ca

Object

CLA is its members' advocate and public voice, educator, and network. It builds the Canadian library and information community by promoting, developing, and supporting library and information services and advancing today's information professionals, through cooperation with all who share its values. The association represents Canadian librarianship to the federal government and media, carries on international liaison with other library associations and cultural agencies, offers professional development programs, and supports such core library values as intellectual freedom and access to information, particularly for disadvantaged populations. Founded in 1946, CLA is a nonprofit voluntary organization governed by an elected executive council.

Membership

Memb. (Indiv.) 2,000; (Inst.) 460. Open to individuals, institutions, and groups interested in librarianship and in library and information services.

Officers

Pres. Alvin Schrader, Professor, Univ. of Alberta School of Lib. and Info. Studies; *V.P./Pres.-Elect* Ken Roberts, Hamilton Public Lib.; *Treas.* Theresa Tomchyshyn, Dept. of National Defense Communications Security Establishment.

Publications

Feliciter: Linking Canada's Information Professionals (6 a year; magazine/journal).
CLA Digest (bi-weekly; electronic newsletter).

Divisions

Canadian Association for School Libraries (CASL).
Canadian Association of College and University Libraries (CACUL).
Canadian Association of Public Libraries (CAPL).
Canadian Association of Special Libraries and Information Services (CASLIS).
Canadian Library Trustees Association (CLTA).

Catholic Library Association

Executive Director, Jean R. Bostley, SSJ
100 North St., Ste. 224, Pittsfield, MA 01201-5109
413-443-2252, fax 413-442-2252, e-mail cla@cathla.org
World Wide Web http://www.cathla.org

Object

The promotion and encouragement of Catholic literature and library work through cooperation, publications, education, and information. Founded 1921.

Membership

Memb. 1,000. Dues $45–$300. Year. July–June.

Officers (2007–2009)

Pres. Catherine M. Fennell, Gertrude Kistler Memorial Lib., Rosemont College, 1400 Montgomery Ave., Rosemont, PA 19010; *V.P./Pres.-Elect* Nancy K. Schmidtmann, 174 Theodore Dr., Coram, NY 11727; *Past Pres.* Kenneth O'Malley, CP, Paul Bechtold Lib., Catholic Theological Union, 5401 S. Cornell Ave., Chicago, IL 60615-5698.

Address correspondence to the executive director.

Executive Board

Officers; John R. Edson, Hamburg Public Lib., 102 Buffalo St., Hamburg, NY 14075. E-mail edsonj@buffalolib.org; Jean Elvekrog, 401 Doral Ct., Waunakee, WI 53597. E-mail jelvekrog@tds.net; Anne LeVeque, Research Libn., Washington, D.C. E-mail anne.leveque@gmail.com; Malachy R. McCarthy, Claretian Missionaries Archives, 205 W. Monroe St., Chicago, IL 60606. E-mail malachym@claretians.org; Frances O'Dell, OSF, Barry Univ. Lib., 11300 N.E. 2 Ave., Miami Shores, FL 33161. E-mail fodell@mail.barry.edu; Annette B. Thibodeaux, Archbishop Chapelle H.S., 8800 Veterans Blvd., Metairie, LA 70003. E-mail annettet3@cox.net.

Publications

Catholic Library World (q.; memb.; nonmemb. $60). *General Ed.* Mary E. Gallagher, SSJ; *Catholic Periodical and Literature Index* (*CLPI*) (q.; $400 calendar year; abridged ed., $125 calendar year; *CPLI* online, inquire). *Ed.* Kathleen Spaltro.

Center for the Study of Rural Librarianship

Department of Library Science, Clarion University of Pennsylvania,
840 Wood St., Clarion, PA 16214.
Tel. 814-393-2014, fax 814-393-2150, e-mail vavrek@clarion.edu or csrl@clarion.edu
World Wide Web http://www.clarion.edu/rural

Object

The Center for the Study of Rural Librarianship (CSRL) is a research, publishing, consultative, and continuing education facility established in the Department of Library Science at Clarion University of Pennsylvania in 1978. Its mission is to extend knowledge relative to the nature and role of rural and small libraries worldwide, whose defining characteristics are a limited budget and a diverse clientele. CSRL is concerned with the development and use of information technology in rural communities, and its recent endeavors include library outreach and, particularly, bookmobile services in the United States and overseas.

Its objectives are

- To stimulate imaginative thinking relative to rural library services
- To identify problems endemic with library services—for those currently being served and those who are not yet served
- To provide consultative services in designing new service patterns in rural libraries
- To conduct and/or coordinate research relative to identifiable library problems
- To stimulate continuing education
- To coordinate physical and human resources which could be lent to analyze library services
- To collect data relevant to the needs of rural libraries

Two professional associations are affiliated with CSRL: the Association for Rural and Small Libraries and the Association of Bookmobile and Outreach Services.

The Association for Rural and Small Libraries (ARSL) (http://www.webjunction. org/arsl) includes members among public, school, small urban branch, special, corporate, and small academic libraries. The association's mission is to provide a network of people and materials to support rural and small library staff, volunteers, and trustees to integrate the library thoroughly with the life and work of the community it serves.

The Association of Bookmobile and Outreach Services (ABOS) (http://www.abos-outreach.org) encompasses libraries of all types. The association's mission is to support and encourage government officials, library administrators, trustees, and staff in the provision of quality bookmobile and outreach services to meet diverse community information and programming needs.

Membership in ARSL and ABOS and attendance at their annual conferences are open to all individuals and institutions seeking to champion rural libraries and outreach services. Both associations are supported by CSRL in cooperation with the H. W. Wilson Foundation.

Publications

CSRL has published the journal *Rural Libraries* since 1980 and the journal *Bookmobile and Outreach Services* since 1998. Both are printed twice yearly, with annual subscription rates of $20 for domestic and $30 for international subscribers. Back copies are available at $10 each, and selected full-text articles are available at http://www.clarion.edu/rural. CSRL also publishes a variety of monographs, bibliographies, and other resources.

CSRL maintains listservs for ARSL and ABOS to provide forums for discussion, sharing of best practices and success stories, relevant library news, and professional networking.

Chief Officers of State Library Agencies (COSLA)

Director, Tracy Tucker
201 E. Main St., Ste. 1405, Lexington, KY 40507
859-514-9151, fax 859-514-1966, e-mail ttucker@amrms.com, World Wide Web
http://www.cosla.org

Object

To provide a means of cooperative action among its state and territorial members, to strengthen the work of the respective state and territorial agencies, and to provide a continuing mechanism for dealing with the problems faced by the heads of these agencies, which are responsible for state and territorial library development.

Membership

COSLA is an independent organization of the men and women who head the state and territorial agencies responsible for library development. Its membership consists solely of the top library officers of the 50 states, the District of Columbia, and the territories, variously designated as state librarian, director, commissioner, or executive secretary.

Officers (2006–2008)

Pres. J. Gary Nichols, State Libn., Maine State Lib., 64 State House Sta., Augusta, ME 04333-0064. Tel. 207-287-5600, fax 207- 287-5615, e-mail gary.nichols@maine.gov; *V.P./Pres.-Elect* Susan McVey, Dir., State of Oklahoma Dept. of Libs., 200 N.E. 18 St., Oklahoma City, OK 73105-3298. Tel. 405- 521-2502, fax 405-521-1077, e-mail smcvey @oltn.odl.state.ok.us; *Secy.* Rebecca Mitchell, Dir., State of Alabama Public Lib. Services, 6030 Monticello Drive, Montgomery, AL 36130-0001. Tel. 334-213-3901, fax 334-213-3993, e-mail rmitchell@apls.state.al.us; *Treas.* Annie Norman, Dir. and State Libn., State of Delaware Div. of Libs./State Lib., 43 S. DuPont Hwy., Dover, DE 19901-7430. Tel. 302-739-4748, fax 302-739-6787, e-mail norman@lib.de.us; *Past Pres.* GladysAnn Wells, Dir., State Lib. of Arizona, State Capitol, 1700 W. Washington, Rm. 200, Phoenix, AZ 85007-2812. Tel. 602-542-4035, fax 602- 542-4972, e-mail gawells@lib.az.us; *Dirs.* Ann Joslin, State Libn., Idaho Commission for Libs., 325 W. State St., Boise, ID 83702- 6055. Tel. 208-334-2150, fax 208-334-4016, e-mail ann.joslin@libraries.idaho.gov; Rod Wagner, Dir., State of Nebraska Lib. Commission, The Atrium, 1200 N St., Ste. 120, Lincoln, NE 68508-2023. Tel. 402-471-4001, fax 402-471-2083, e-mail rwagner@nlc.state. ne.us; *Assn. Dir.* Tracy Tucker. Tel. 859-514- 9210, e-mail ttucker@amrms.com.

Chinese American Librarians Association (CALA)

Executive Director, Shixing Wen
E-mail shixingwen@yahoo.com
World Wide Web http://www.cala-web.org

Object

To enhance communications among Chinese American librarians as well as between Chinese American librarians and other librarians; to serve as a forum for discussion of mutual problems and professional concerns among Chinese American librarians; to promote Sino-American librarianship and library services; and to provide a vehicle whereby Chinese American librarians can cooperate with other associations and organizations having similar or allied interests.

Membership

Memb. 1,100+ Open to anyone who is interested in the association's goals and activities. Dues (Regular) $30; (International/Student/Nonsalaried) $15; (Inst.) $100; (Affiliated) $100; (Life) $300.

Officers

Pres. Dora Ho. E-mail dora4ala@yahoo.com; *V.P./Pres.-Elect* Sha Li Zhang. E-mail slzhang@uncg.edu; *Treas.* Maggie Wang. E-mail wang_maggie@hotmail.com; *Past Pres.* Haipeng Li. E-mail haipeng.li@oberlin.edu.

Publications

Journal of Library and Information Science (2 a year; memb.; nonmemb. $15).
Membership Directory (memb.).
Newsletter (2 a year; memb.; nonmemb. $10). *Ed.* Shuyong Jiang.

Committee Chairpersons

Awards. Jiun Kuo.
Constitution and Bylaws. Harriet Ying.
Finance. Esther Lee.
International Relations. Guoqing Li, Lisa Zhao.
Membership. Hong Wang.

Church and Synagogue Library Association

2920 S.W. Dolph Ct., Ste. 3A, Portland, OR 97219
503-244-6919, 800-542-2752, fax 503-977-3734
E-mail CSLA@worldaccessnet.com, World Wide Web http://www.cslainfo.org

Object

The Church and Synagogue Library Association (CSLA) provides educational guidance in the establishment and maintenance of congregational libraries.

Its purpose is to act as a unifying core for church and synagogue libraries; to provide the opportunity for a mutual sharing of practices and problems; to inspire and encourage a sense of purpose and mission among church and synagogue librarians; to study and guide the development of church and synagogue librarianship toward recognition as a formal branch of the library profession. Founded 1967.

Membership

Memb. 1,800. Dues (Inst.) $200; (Affiliated) $100; (Congregational) $60 ($65 foreign); (Indiv.) $40 ($45 foreign).

Officers (July 2007–July 2008)

Pres. Craig Kubic; *Pres.-Elect* J. Theodore Anderson; *2nd V.P.* Judy Birch; *Treas.* Bill Anderson; *Admin.* Judith Janzen; *Past Pres.* Maryann Barth; *Ed., Church and Synagogue Libraries* Mark Olson, 1225 Dandridge St., Fredricksburg, VA 22401; *Book Review Ed.* Monica Tenney, 399 Blenheim Rd., Columbus, OH 43214-3219. E-mail motenney@aol.com.

Executive Board

Officers; committee chairpersons.

Publications

Bibliographies (1–5; price varies).
Church and Synagogue Libraries (bi-mo.; memb.; nonmemb. $45; Canada $55).
CSLA Guides (1–20; price varies).

Committee Chairpersons

Awards. Kay Mowery.
Conference. Pat Shufeldt, Rod McClendon.
Library Services. Esther Beirbaum.
Nominations and Elections. Jane Hope.
Publications. Alice Hamilton.

Coalition for Networked Information

Executive Director, Clifford A. Lynch
21 Dupont Circle, Ste. 800, Washington, DC 20036
202-296-5098, fax 202-872-0884
E-mail info@cni.org, World Wide Web http://www.cni.org

Mission

The Coalition for Networked Information (CNI) is an organization to advance the transformative promise of networked information technology for the advancement of scholarly communication and the enrichment of intellectual productivity.

Membership

Memb. 228. Membership is institutional. Dues $6,400. Year. July–June.

Steering Committee

Richard P. West, California State Univ. (*Chair*); Kenneth Hamma, J. Paul Getty Trust; Brian L. Hawkins, EDUCAUSE; Timothy Lance, NYSERNet; Ronald L. Larsen, EDUCAUSE; Richard E. Luce, ARL; Clifford A. Lynch, CNI; Diana G. Oblinger, EDUCAUSE; Brian E. C. Schottlaender, Univ. of California, San Diego; Donald J. Waters, Andrew W. Mellon Foundation; Duane E. Webster, Assn. of Research Libs.; Karin Wittenborg, ARL.

Publication

CNI-Announce (subscribe by e-mail to cni-announce-subscribe@cni.org).

Council on Library and Information Resources

1755 Massachusetts Ave. N.W., Ste. 500, Washington, DC 20036-2124
202-939-4750, fax 202-939-4765
World Wide Web http://www.clir.org

Object

In 1997 the Council on Library Resources (CLR) and the Commission on Preservation and Access (CPA) merged and became the Council on Library and Information Resources (CLIR). CLIR's mission is to expand access to information, however recorded and preserved, as a public good. CLIR identifies and defines the key emerging issues related to the welfare of libraries and the constituencies they serve, convenes the leaders who can influence change, and promotes collaboration among the institutions and organizations that can achieve change. The council's interests embrace the entire range of information resources and services from traditional library and archival materials to emerging digital formats. It assumes a particular interest in helping institutions cope with the accelerating pace of change associated with the transition into the digital environment.

CLIR is an independent, nonprofit organization. While maintaining appropriate collaboration and liaison with other institutions and organizations, the council operates independently of any particular institutional or vested interests. Through the composition of its board, it brings the broadest possible perspective to bear upon defining and establishing the priority of the issues with which it is concerned.

Board

CLIR's Board of Directors currently has 15 members.

Officers

Chair Paula T. Kaufman; *Pres.* Charles Henry. E-mail chenry@clir.org; *Treas.* Herman Pabbruwe.

Address correspondence to headquarters.

Publications

Annual Report.
CLIR Issues (bi-mo.).
Technical reports.

Council on Library/Media Technicians

President, Jackie Hite
E-mail jmhite0@dia.mil
World Wide Web http://colt.ucr.edu

The Council on Library/Media Technicians (COLT), an affiliate of the American Library Association, is an international organization that works to address the issues and concerns of library and media support staff personnel.

Since 1967 COLT has addressed issues covering such areas as technical education, continuing education, certification, job description uniformity, and the more elusive goals of gaining recognition and respect for the professional work that its members do.

Objectives

COLT's objectives are

- To function as a clearinghouse for information relating to library support staff personnel
- To advance the status, employment, and certification of library staff
- To promote effective communication and cooperation with other organizations whose purposes and objectives are similar to those of COLT

COLT's Web site, http://colt.ucr.edu, provides information on library technician pro-

grams, a speaker exchange listing for help in organizing workshops and conferences, bibliographies on needed resources, and jobline resource links.

COLT holds an annual conference, generally immediately preceding the American Library Association Annual Conference.

Membership

Membership is open to all library employees. Dues (Inst.) $70 ($95 foreign); (Indiv.) $45 ($70 foreign); (Student) $35. Year Jan.–Dec.

Officers (2007–2008)

Pres. Jackie Hite. E-mail jmhite0@dia.mil; *V.P./Pres.-Elect.* Chris Egan. E-mail egan@rand.org; *Secy.* Robin Martindill. E-mail rmartind@sdccd.edu; *Treas.* Stan Cieplinski. E-mail stan.cieplinski@domail.maricopa.edu; *Past Pres.* Jackie Lakatos. E-mail jlakatos@lemontlibrary.org; *Exec. Dir.* Margaret Barron, PMB 168, 28262 Chardon Rd., Willoughby Hills, OH 44092.

Federal Library and Information Center Committee

Executive Director, Roberta I. Shaffer
Library of Congress, Washington, DC 20540-4935
202-707-4800, World Wide Web http://www.loc.gov/flicc

Object

The Federal Library and Information Center Committee (FLICC) makes recommendations on federal library and information policies, programs, and procedures to federal agencies and to others concerned with libraries and information centers. The committee coordinates cooperative activities and services among federal libraries and information centers and serves as a forum to consider issues and policies that affect federal libraries and information centers, needs and priorities in providing information services to the government and to the nation at large, and efficient and cost-effective use of federal library and information resources and services. Furthermore, the committee promotes improved access to information, continued development and use of the Federal Library and Information Network (FEDLINK), research and development in the application of new technologies to federal libraries and information centers, improvements in the management of federal libraries and information centers, and relevant education opportunities. Founded 1965.

Membership

Libn. of Congress, Dir. of the National Agricultural Lib., Dir. of the National Lib. of Medicine, Dir. of the National Lib. of Educ., representatives of each of the cabinet-level executive departments, and representatives of each of the following agencies: National Aeronautics and Space Admin., National Sci-

ence Foundation, Smithsonian Institution, U.S. Supreme Court, National Archives and Records Admin., Admin. Offices of the U.S. Courts, Defense Technical Info. Center, Government Printing Office, National Technical Info. Service (Dept. of Commerce), Office of Scientific and Technical Info. (Dept. of Energy), Exec. Office of the President, Dept. of the Army, Dept. of the Navy, Dept. of the Air Force, and chair of the FEDLINK Advisory Council. Fifteen additional voting member agencies are selected on a rotating basis by the voting members of FEDLINK. These rotating members serve three-year terms. One representative of each of the following agencies is invited as an observer to committee meetings: Government Accountability Office, General Services Admin., Joint Committee on Printing, National Commission on Libs. and Info. Science, Office of Mgt. and Budget, Office of Personnel Mgt., and U.S. Copyright Office.

Officers

Chair James H. Billington, Libn. of Congress; *Chair Designate* Deanna Marcum, Assoc. Libn. for Lib. Services, Lib. of Congress; *Exec. Dir.* Roberta I. Shaffer.

Address correspondence to the executive director.

Publication

FEDLINK Technical Notes (every other month).

Federal Publishers Committee

Chair, John Ward
International Trade Administration, Washington, DC 20230
202-482-5489, fax 202-482-5819
E-mail john.ward@mail.doc.gov

Object

To foster and promote effective management of data development and dissemination in the federal government through exchange of information, and to act as a focal point for federal agency publishing.

agencies, and corporations, as well as independent organizations concerned with federal government publishing and dissemination. Some key federal government organizations represented are the Joint Committee on Printing, Government Printing Office, National Technical Info. Service, National Commission on Libs. and Info. Science, and the Lib. of Congress.

Membership

Memb. 500. Membership is available to persons involved in publishing and dissemination in federal government departments,

Publication

Guide to Federal Publishing (occasional).

Friends of Libraries U.S.A. (FOLUSA)

Executive Director, Sally Gardner Reed
1420 Walnut St., Ste. 450, Philadelphia, PA 19102-4017
800-936-5872, 215-790-1674, fax 215-545-3821
E-mail friends@folusa.org, World Wide Web http://www.folusa.org

Object

Friends of Libraries U.S.A. (FOLUSA), established in 1979 as a committee of the Library Administration and Management Association of the American Library Association, is a national nonprofit organization providing networking opportunities and educational support for local friends-of-libraries groups, trustees, and library foundations. Membership includes more than 3,000 friends groups, boards of trustees, foundations, libraries, and individuals.

FOLUSA provides consulting services, training, and workshops at the regional, state, and national levels focusing on developing friends groups, boards of trustees, and foundations, for fund raising, effective relation-

ships, and advocacy. It works with library lay support groups to enhance their efforts as advocates, volunteers, program and community-outreach catalysts, and as fund-raisers in support of their local and state libraries.

Membership

Membership is open to all friends of libraries groups, libraries, and individuals who support libraries. Dues (Indiv.) $35 up; (Small Libs., budgets under $1 million) $50; (Large Libs., budgets over $1 million) $100; (Small Friends Groups, fewer than 100 members) $40; (Medium Friends Groups, 100 to 499 members) $65; (Large Friends Groups, 500+ members) $100. "All-in-one" memberships are available that include membership for the library administration, the friends, the trustees, and the foundation for one price. Dues in this category are (Small Libs., budgets under $1 million) $100; (Medium Libs., budgets between $1 million and $10 million) $175; (Large Libs., budgets over $10 million) $200.

In 2008 FOLUSA is working with the board of the Association of Library Trustee and Advocates (ALTA), a division of the American Library Association (ALA), to determine whether to join together to create a new division of ALA.

Officers (2007–2008)

Pres. John Carson; *V.P./Pres.-Elect* Peggy Barber; *Secy.* Robin Hoklotubbe; *Treas.* Laura Salmon; *Past Pres.* Mary K. Dodge.

Directors

Peggy Barber, George Coe, Rodrigue Gauvin, Agnes Griffen, Charles Hanson, Samuel Huang, Cherine Janzen, Ed McBride, Jeana Mays-Browne, Peter Pearson, Veronda Pitchford, Lana Porter, Barbara Prentice, Doug Roesemann, Robert Rotello, Kay Runge, Susan Schmidt, Margaret Schuster, Kathryn Suarez, Alan Walker, David Warren, Joe Weed.

Publications

NewsUpdate, (bi-mo.)
Making Our Voices Heard: Citizens Speak Out for Libraries
Getting Grants in Your Community
101+ Great Ideas for Libraries and Friends

Medical Library Association

Executive Director, Carla Funk
65 E. Wacker Place, Ste. 1900, Chicago, IL 60601-7298
312-419-9094, fax 312-419-8950
E-mail info@mlahq.org, World Wide Web http://www.mlanet.org

Object

MLA, a nonprofit educational organization, is composed of health sciences information professionals with more than 4,700 members worldwide. Through its programs and services, MLA provides lifelong educational opportunities, supports a knowledge base of health information research and works with a global network of partners to promote the importance of quality information for improved health to the healthcare community and the public.

Membership

Memb. (Inst.) 850+; (Indiv.) 3,600+. Institutional members are medical and allied scientific libraries. Individual members are people who are (or were at the time membership was established) engaged in professional library or bibliographic work in medical and allied scientific libraries or people who are interested in medical or allied scientific libraries. Dues (Student) $40; (Emeritus) $55; (International) $110; (Indiv.) $165; and (Inst.) $255–$600, based on the number of the library's periodicals subscriptions. Members may be affiliated with one or more of MLA's 23 special interest sections and 14 regional chapters.

Officers

Pres. Mark E. Funk. E-mail mefunk@mail. med.cornell.edu; *Pres-Elect* Mary L. Ryan. E-mail ryanmaryl@uams.edu; *Past Pres.* Jean P. Shipman. E-mail jpshipma@vcu.edu.

Directors

Margaret Bandy (2008), Gary A. Freiberger (2010), Craig C. Haynes (2008), T. Scott Plutchak (2009), Paula Raimondo (2010), Tovah Reis (2008), Connie Schardt (2008), Laurie L. Thompson (2010), Linda Walton (2009).

Publications

Journal of the Medical Library Association (q.; $163).

MLA News (10 a year; $58).

Miscellaneous (request current list from association headquarters).

Music Library Association

8551 Research Way, Ste. 180, Middleton, WI 53562
608-836-5825, World Wide Web http://www.musiclibraryassoc.org

Object

To promote the establishment, growth, and use of music libraries; to encourage the collection of music and musical literature in libraries; to further studies in musical bibliography; to increase efficiency in music library service and administration; and to promote the profession of music librarianship. Founded 1931.

Membership

Memb. 1,274. Dues (Inst.) $125; (Indiv.) $90; (Retired or Associate) $60; (Paraprofessional) $45; (Student) $35. Year. July 1–June 30.

Officers

Pres. Philip R. Vandermeer, Music Lib., Wilson Lib. CB3906, Univ. of North Carolina–Chapel Hill, Chapel Hill 27514. Tel. 919-966-1113, fax 919-843-0418, e-mail vanderme@email.unc.edu; *Past Pres.* Bonna J. Boettcher. E-mail bjb57@cornell.edu; *Rec. Secy.* Karen Little. E-mail klittle@louisville.edu; *Treas./Exec. Secy.* Brad Short. E-mail short@wustl.edu.

Members-at-Large

(2007–2008) David Gilbert, Rebecca Littman, Jean Morrow; (2008–2009) George Boziwick, Eunice Schroeder, Holling Smith-Borne.

Publications

MLA Index and Bibliography Series (irreg.; price varies).
MLA Newsletter (q.; memb.).
MLA Technical Reports (irreg.; price varies).
Music Cataloging Bulletin (mo.; $25).
Notes (q.; indiv. $85; inst. $100).

National Association of Government Archives and Records Administrators (NAGARA)

90 State St., Albany, NY 12207
518-463-8644, fax 518-463-8656
E-mail nagara@caphill.com, World Wide Web http://www.nagara.org

Object

Founded in 1984, NAGARA is a growing nationwide association of local, state, and federal archivists and records administrators, and others interested in improved care and management of government records. NAGARA promotes public awareness of government records and archives management programs, encourages interchange of information among government archives and records management agencies, develops and implements professional standards of government records and archival administration, and encourages study and research into records management problems and issues.

Membership

Most NAGARA members are federal, state, and local archival and records management agencies.

Officers

Pres. Mary Beth Herkert, Archives Div., Offices of the Secy. of State, 800 Summer St. N.E., Salem, OR 97310. Tel. 503-373-0701, fax 503-373-0953, e-mail mary.e.herkert@state.or.us; *V.P.* Tracey Berezansky, Alabama Dept. of Archives and History, P.O. Box 300100, Montgomery, AL 36130-0100. Tel.

334-353-4604, fax 334-353-4321, e-mail tracey.berezansky@archiveds.alabama.gov; *Secy.* Caryn Wojcik, Michigan Historical Center, 3405 N. Martin Luther King, Jr. Blvd., Lansing, MI 48909. Tel. 517-335-8222, fax 517-335-9418, e-mail wojcikc@michigan.gov; *Treas.* John Stewart, National Archives and Records Admin., Great Lakes Region, 7358 S. Pulaski Rd., Chicago, IL 60629-5898. Tel. 773-581-7816, fax 312-886-7883, e-mail john.stewart@nara.gov.

Directors

Paul Bergeron, City of Nashua (New Hampshire); Jelain Chubb, Missouri State Archives; Bonnie Curtin, Federal Trade Commission; Nancy Fortna, National Archives and Records Admin., Washington, D.C.; Sandy Hart, McKinney, Texas; Adam Jansen, Washington State Digital Archives; Kay Lanning Minchew, Troup County (Georgia) Archives.

Publications

Clearinghouse (q.; memb.).
Crossroads (q.; memb.).
Government Records Issues (series).
Preservation Needs in State Archives.
Program Reporting Guidelines for Government Records Programs.

National Church Library Association

Executive Director, Susan Benish
275 S. Third St., Ste. 101A, Stillwater, MN 55082
651-430-0770, e-mail info@churchlibraries.org
World Wide Web http://www.churchlibraries.org

Object

The National Church Library Association (NCLA, formerly the Lutheran Church Library Association) is a nonprofit organization that serves the unique needs of congregational libraries and those who manage them. NCLA provides inspiration, solutions, and support to church librarians in the form of printed manuals and guidelines, booklists, the quarterly journal *Libraries ALIVE,* national conferences, a mentoring program, online support, and personal advice. Regional chapters operate throughout the country.

Membership

Memb. 800 churches, 100 personal. Dues $40, $55. Year. Jan.–Jan.

Officers

Pres. Karen Gieseke; *V.P.* vacant; *Secy.* Rachel Riensche; *Treas.* Terry Maroney; *Past Pres.* Barbara Livdahl.

Address correspondence to the executive director.

Directors

Deanna Gordon, Doreen Knudson, Chris Magnusson, Violet Russell, Carol Spaulding, Sandra Thornby.

Publication

Libraries ALIVE (q.; memb.).

Committee Chairpersons

Advisory. Mary Jordan.
Librarian Resources. Marlys Johnson.

National Federation of Advanced Information Services

Executive Director, Bonnie Lawlor
1518 Walnut St., Ste. 1004, Philadelphia, PA 19102
215-893-1561, fax 215-893-1564
E-mail nfais@nfais.org
World Wide Web http://www.nfais.org

Object

The National Federation of Advanced Information Services (NFAIS) is an international nonprofit membership organization composed of leading information providers. Its membership includes government agencies, nonprofit scholarly societies, and private-sector businesses. NFAIS is committed to promoting the value of authoritative content. It serves all groups that create, aggregate, organize, or facilitate access to such information. In order to improve members' capabilities and to contribute to their ongoing success, NFAIS provides opportunities for education, advocacy, and a forum in which to address common interests. Founded 1958.

Membership

Memb. 60. Full members are organizations whose main focus is any of the following activities: information creation, organization, aggregation, dissemination, access, or retrieval. Organizations are eligible for associate member status if they do not meet the qualifications for full membership.

Officers (2007–2008)

Pres. Kevin Bouley; *Pres.-Elect* David Brown; *Treas.* Barbara Dobbs Mackenzie; *Secy.* Judith Russell; *Past Pres.* Linda Beebe.

Directors

Terence Ford, David Gillikin, Ellen Herbst, Keith MacGregor, Janice Mears, Lucian Parziale, Judith Russell, Rafael Sidi.

Staff

Exec. Dir. Bonnie Lawlor. E-mail blawlor@nfais.org; *Dir., Planning and Communications* Jill O'Neill. E-mail jilloneill@nfais.org; *Customer Service* Margaret Manson. E-mail mmanson@nfais.org.

Publications

For a detailed list of NFAIS publications, see the NFAIS Web site.

National Information Standards Organization

Managing Director, Todd Carpenter
1 N. Charles Ave., Ste. 1905, Baltimore, MD 21201
301-654-2512, fax 410-685-5278
E-mail nisohq@niso.org, World Wide Web http://www.niso.org

Object

NISO, the National Information Standards Organization, a nonprofit association accredited by the American National Standards Institute (ANSI), identifies, develops, maintains, and publishes technical standards to manage information in our changing and ever-more-digital environment. NISO standards apply both traditional and new technologies to the full range of information-related needs, including discovery, retrieval, repurposing, storage, metadata, business information, and preservation.

Experts from the information industry, libraries, systems vendors, and publishing participate in the development of NISO standards. The standards are approved by the consensus body of NISO's voting membership, which consists of nearly 80 voting members representing libraries, publishers, vendors, government, associations, and private businesses and organizations. In addition, approximately 25 libraries are NISO Library Standards Alliance members. NISO is supported by its membership and corporate grants. NISO is a nonprofit educational organization. NISO is accredited by ANSI and serves as the U.S. Technical Advisory Group to ISO/TC 46 Information and Documentation.

Membership

Memb. Approx. 80. Open to any organization, association, government agency, or company willing to participate in and having substantial concern for the development of NISO standards. Libraries support NISO as members of the Library Standards Alliance.

Officers

Chair James Neal, 517 Butler Lib., Columbia Univ., 535 W. 114 St., New York, NY 10027. Tel. 212-854-2247, fax 212-854-4972, e-mail jneal@columbia.edu; *V. Chair/Chair-Elect* to be announced; *Immediate Past Chair* Carl Grant, President, Co-Founder, CARE Affiliates, 4445 Pearman Rd., Blacksburg, VA 24060. Tel. 540-529-7885, fax 540-557-1210, e-mail carl@care-affiliates.com; *Treas.* Winston Tabb, Milton S. Eisenhower Lib., Johns Hopkins Univ., 3400 N. Charles St., Baltimore, MD 21218. Tel. 410-516-8328, fax 410-516-5080, e-mail wtabb@jhu.edu.

Directors

Nancy Davenport, Lorcan Dempsey, John Erickson, John Harwood, Michael Jensen, Chuck Koscher, Oliver Pesch, Bruce Rosenblum.

Publications

Information Standards Quarterly (U.S. $120/year, foreign $150, back issues $40/each).

NISO Newsline (free monthly e-letter released on the first Wednesday of each month. See the NISO Web site for details on subscribing and archived issues).

For additional NISO publications, see the article "National Information Standards Organization (NISO) Standards" later in Part 6.

NISO published standards are available free of charge as downloadable pdf files from the NISO Web site (http://www.niso.org). Standards in hard copy are available for sale on the Web site. The *NISO Annual Report* is available on request.

Patent and Trademark Depository Library Association

World Wide Web http://www.ptdla.org

Object

The Patent and Trademark Depository Library Association (PTDLA) provides a support structure for the 84 patent and trademark depository libraries (PTDLs) affiliated with the U.S. Patent and Trademark Office (USPTO). The association's mission is to discover the interests, needs, opinions, and goals of the PTDLs and to advise USPTO in these matters for the benefit of PTDLs and their users, and to assist USPTO in planning and implementing appropriate services. Founded in 1983 as the Patent Depository Library Advisory Council; name changed to Patent and Trademark Depository Library Association in 1988; became an American Library Association affiliate in 1996.

Membership

Open to any person employed in a patent and trademark depository library whose responsibilities include the patent collection. Affiliate membership is also available. Dues $25.

Officers (2007–2008)

Pres. Leena Lalwani. E-mail llalwani@umich.edu; *V.P./Pres.-Elect* Karon King. E-mail karon.king@lib.state.ia.us; *Secy.* Jim Miller. E-mail jimiller2@umd.edu; *Treas.* Dawn Rohan. E-mail drohan@state.wy.us; *Past Pres.* Jan Comfort. E-mail comforj@clemson.edu.

Regional Representatives

Region 1, Leonard Adams. E-mail len.adams@library.umass.edu; Region 2, Connie Wu. E-mail conniewu@rci.rutgers.edu; Region 3, Marion Armour-Gemmen. E-mail marmour@wvu.edu; Region 4, Jan Comfort. E-mail comforj@clemson.edu; Region 5, Robert Klein. E-mail patents@mdpls.org; Region 6, Esther Crawford. E-mail crawford@rice.edu; Region 7, Ran Raider. E-mail ran.raider@wright.edu; Region 8, Nancy Spitzer. E-mail spitzer@engr.wisc.edu; Region 9, Suzanne Holcombe. E-mail sholcom@okstate.edu; Region 10, Walt Johnson. E-mail wjohnson@mplib.org; Christina Byrne. E-mail cbyrne@u.washington.edu; Region 11, Sam Kushner. E-mail kushners@lvccld.org; Region 12, Kristine Ogilvie. E-mail kogilvie@library.ca.org.

Publication

Intellectual Property Journal of the PTDLA. Electronic at http://www.ptdla.org/ipjournal.html. *Eds.* Claudine Jenda, Auburn Univ. Libs., 231 Mell St., Auburn, AL 36849-5606. Tel. 334-844-1658, e-mail jendaca@auburn.edu; Andrew Wohrley, Auburn Univ. Libs. Tel. 334-844-4461, e-mail wohrlaj@auburn.edu; Esther Crawford, Fondren Lib., Rice Univ., P.O. Box 1892, Houston, TX 77251-1892. Tel. 713-348-6212, crawford@rice.edu.

REFORMA (National Association to Promote Library and Information Services to Latinos and the Spanish-Speaking)

President, Mario A. Ascencio
National Office Manager, Sandra Rios Balderrama
P.O. Box 4386, Fresno, CA 93744
Tel. 480-734-4460, e-mail reformaoffice@riosbalderrama.com
World Wide Web http://www.reforma.org

Object

Promoting library services to the Spanish-speaking for more than 38 years, REFORMA, an affiliate of the American Library Association, works in a number of areas to promote the development of library collections to include Spanish-language and Latino-oriented materials; the recruitment of more bilingual and bicultural professionals and support staff; the development of library services and programs that meet the needs of the Latino community; the establishment of a national network among individuals who share its goals; the education of the U.S. Latino population in regard to the availability and types of library services; and lobbying efforts to preserve existing library resource centers serving the interest of Latinos.

Membership

Memb. 800+. Any person who is supportive of the goals and objectives of REFORMA.

Officers

Pres. Mario A. Ascencio, George Mason Univ. Libs., 4400 University Drive, MSN 2FL, Fairfax, VA 22030-4444. Tel. 703-993-3720, fax 703-993-2494, e-mail mascenci@gmu.edu; *Pres.-Elect* Luis Chaparro; *Secy.* Delores Carlito; *Treas. (interim)* Robin Imperial; *Memb.-at-Large* Siobhan Champ-Black-well; *Past Pres.* Roxana Benavides; *Chapter Reps.* Loida Garcia-Febo, Maria Kramer, Laura Maldonado-Hastert.

Committees

Pura Belpré Award. Rita Pino.
Children's and Young Adult Services. Lucia Gonzalez.
Education. To be appointed.
Finance. Ana-Elba Pavón.
International Relations. Patrick Sullivan.
Legislative. Carol Brey-Casiano.
Membership. Robin Imperial.
Mora Award. Roberto Zapata.
Nominations. Ana-Elba Pavón.
Organizational Development. Yolanda Valentín.
Public Relations. Selina Gómez-Beloz.
Recruitment and Mentoring. Toni Anaya, Alberto Herrera.
Translations. Armando Trejo.

Publication

REFORMA Newsletter (s. ann; memb.).

Meetings

General membership and board meetings take place at the American Library Association Midwinter Meeting and Annual Conference.

Society for Scholarly Publishing

Executive Director, Francine Butler
10200 W. 44 Ave., Ste. 304, Wheat Ridge, CO 80033
303-422-3914, fax 303-422-8894
E-mail ssp@resourcecenter.com, World Wide Web http://www.sspnet.org

Object

To draw together individuals involved in the process of scholarly publishing. This process requires successful interaction of the many functions performed within the scholarly community. The Society for Scholarly Publishing (SSP) provides the leadership for such interaction by creating opportunities for the exchange of information and opinions among scholars, editors, publishers, librarians, printers, booksellers, and all others engaged in scholarly publishing.

Executive Committee

Pres. Sue Kesner, Copyright Clearance Center. E-mail skesner@copyright.com; *Pres.-Elect* October Ivins, Ivins eContent Solutions. E-mail october.ivins@mindspring.com; *Past Pres.* Judy Luther, Informed Strategies. E-mail judy.luther@informedstrategies.com; *Secy./Treas.* Ray Fastiggi, Rockefeller Univ. Press. E-mail fastigg@rockefeller.edu.

Membership

Memb. 800. Open to all with an interest in the scholarly publishing process and dissemination of information. Dues (Indiv.) $130; (Libn.) $75; (Early Career) $75; (New Student) $30; (Supporting) $1,200; (Sustaining) $2,900. Year. Jan. 1–Dec. 31.

Meetings

An annual meeting is held in late May/early June; the location changes each year. SSP also conducts several seminars throughout the year and a Top Management Roundtable each fall.

Society of American Archivists

Executive Director, Nancy Perkin Beaumont
17 N. State St., Ste. 1425, Chicago, IL 60602
312-922-0140, fax 312-347-1452, e-mail nbeaumont@archivists.org
World Wide Web http://www.archivists.org

Object

Provides leadership to ensure the identification, preservation, and use of records of historical value. Founded 1936.

Membership

Memb. 5,035. Dues (Indiv.) $77–$216, graduated according to salary; (Assoc.) $77, domestic; (Student) $44; (Inst.) $247; (Sustaining) $484.

Officers (2007–2008)

Pres. Mark A. Greene, American Heritage Center, Univ. of Wyoming, 2111 Willett Drive, P.O. Box 3924, Laramie, WY 82071-3924. Tel. 307-766-2474, fax 307-766-5511, e-mail mgreene@uwyo.edu; *V.P.* Frank

Boles, Clarke Historical Library, Central Michigan Univ., Park 142, Mount Pleasant, MI 48859. Tel. 517-774-3352, 989-774-3965, e-mail boles1fj@cmich.edu; *Treas.* Ann Russell, Northeast Document Conservation Center, 100 Brickstone Sq., 4th fl., Andover, MA 01810-1494. Tel. 978-470-1010, fax 978-475-6021, e-mail annr@nedcc.org.

Staff

Exec. Dir. Nancy Perkin Beaumont; *Dir., Memb. and Technical Services* Brian P.

Doyle; *Publishing Dir.* Teresa Brinati; *Educ. Dir.* Solveig DeSutter; *Dir., Finance and Administration* Thomas Jurczak.

Publications

American Archivist (q.; $85; foreign $90). *Ed.* Mary Jo Pugh; *Managing Ed.* Teresa Brinati. Books for review and related correspondence should be addressed to the managing editor.

Archival Outlook (bi-mo.; memb.). *Ed.* Teresa Brinati.

Software and Information Industry Association (SIIA)

1090 Vermont Ave. N.W., Washington, DC 20005
Tel. 202-289-7442, fax 202-289-7097
World Wide Web http://www.siia.net

Membership

Memb. 520 companies. Formed January 1, 1999, through the merger of the Software Publishers Association (SPA) and the Information Industry Association (IIA). Open to companies involved in the creation, distribution, and use of software, information products, services, and technologies. For details on membership and dues, see the SIIA Web site.

Staff

Pres. Kenneth Wasch. E-mail kwasch@siia.net.

Officers

Chair Robert Merry, Congressional Quarterly; *V. Chair* Stuart Udell, Penn Foster; *Secy./Treas.* Larry Snowhite, Houghton Mifflin.

Board of Directors

Cindy Braddon, McGraw-Hill; Jim Parkinson, Sun Microsystems; Alan Scott, Dow Jones; Joseph Fitzgerald, Symantec; Kathy Hurley, Pearson; Steven Manzo, Reed Elsevier; Bernard McKay, Intuit; Robert Merry, Congressional Quarterly; Jack Sabo, New York Board of Trade; Tim Sheehy, IBM; Larry Snowhite, Houghton Mifflin; Fred Hawrysh, Thomson; Stuart Udell, Penn Foster; Tom Rabon, Red Hat; Ken Wasch, SIIA.

SPARC

Executive Director, Heather Joseph
21 Dupont Circle, Ste. 800, Washington, DC 20036
202-296-2296, fax 202-872-0884
E-mail sparc@arl.org
World Wide Web http://www.arl.org/sparc

SPARC, the Scholarly Publishing and Academic Resources Coalition, is an international alliance of academic and research libraries working to correct imbalances in the scholarly publishing system. Developed by the Association of Research Libraries, SPARC has become a catalyst for change. Its pragmatic focus is to stimulate the emergence of new scholarly communication models that expand the dissemination of scholarly research and reduce financial pressures on libraries. Action by SPARC in collaboration with stakeholders—including authors, publishers, and libraries—builds on the unprecedented opportunities created by the networked digital environment to advance the conduct of scholarship.

SPARC's role in stimulating change focuses on

- Advocating policy changes that advance the potential of technology to advance scholarly communication and that explicitly recognize that dissemination is an essential, inseparable component of the research process

- Educating stakeholders about the problems facing scholarly communication and the opportunities for change

- Incubating real-world demonstrations of business and publishing models that advance changes benefiting scholarship and academe

SPARC is a visible advocate for changes in scholarly communication that benefit more than the academic community alone. Founded in 1997, SPARC has expanded to represent more than 800 academic and research libraries in North America, Britain, Europe, and Japan.

Membership

SPARC membership is open to North American and international academic and research institutions and consortia that share an interest in creating a more open and diverse marketplace for scholarly communication. Dues are scaled by membership type and budget. For more information, visit SPARC's Web site at http://www.arl.org/sparc, SPARC Europe at http://www.sparceurope.org, or SPARC Japan at http://www.nii.ac.jp/sparc.

Publications

The Right to Research: The Student Guide to Opening Access to Scholarship (2008), part of a campaign to engage students on the issue of research access.

Author Rights (2006), an educational initiative and introduction to the SPARC Author Addendum, a legal form that enables authors of journal articles to modify publishers' copyright transfer agreements and allow authors to keep key rights to their articles.

Open Access News Blog, daily updates on the worldwide movement for open access to science and scholarship, written by Peter Suber and cosponsored by SPARC.

SPARC Open Access Newsletter, a monthly roundup of developments relating to open access publishing written by Peter Suber.

SPARC e-news, SPARC's bimonthly newsletter featuring SPARC activities, an industry roundup, upcoming workshops and events, and articles relating to developments in scholarly communication.

Sponsorships for Nonprofit Scholarly and Scientific Journals: A Guide to Defining and Negotiating Successful Sponsorships (2005), a resource for nonprofit publishers.

A more complete list of SPARC publications, including brochures, articles, and guides, is available at http://www.arl.org/sparc.

Special Libraries Association (SLA)

Chief Executive Officer, Janice R. Lachance
331 S. Patrick St., Alexandria, VA 22314
703-647-4900, fax 703-647-4901
E-mail sla@sla.org, janice@sla.org
World Wide Web http://www.sla.org

Mission

To advance the leadership role of the association's members in putting knowledge to work for the benefit of decision makers in corporations, government, the professions, and society; to shape the destiny of our information- and knowledge-based society.

Membership

Memb. 11,000. Dues (Organizational) $650; (Indiv.) $99–$160; (Student/Retired) $35.

Officers (January 2008–December 2009)

Pres. Stephen Abram. E-mail Stephen.abram @sirsidynix.com; *Pres.-Elect* Gloria Zamora. E-mail gzamora@andia.gov; *Treas.* Sylvia R. James. E-mail dajames@11daymer.freeserve. co.uk; *Chapter Cabinet Chair* Libby Trudell. E-mail libby.trudell@thomson.com; *Chapter Cabinet Chair-Elect* Susan Fifer Canby. E-mail sfiferca@ngs.org; *Div. Cabinet Chair* Robyn C. Frank. E-mail robynfranksp@ comcast.net; *Div. Chapter Chair-Elect* Tom Rink. E-mail rink@suok.edu; *Past Pres.*

Rebecca B. Vargha. E-mail vargha@ils.unc. edu.

Directors

Officers; Kate L. Arnold, Deb Hunt, Tamika McCollough, Cindy Romaine, Roberto Sarmiento, Ty Webb.

Publication

Information Outlook (mo.) (memb., nonmemb. $125/yr.)

Committee Chairpersons

Awards and Honors. Pam Rollo.
Bylaws. James Manasco.
Cataloging. John Gallwey.
Diversity Leadership Development. Stephanie D. Tolson.
Professional Development. Roberta Brody.
Public Policy. Neil Infield.
Public Relations. Jill Strand.
Research. Eileen Abels.
Technical Standards. J. David Martin.

Theatre Library Association (TLA)

c/o The New York Public Library for the Performing Arts,
40 Lincoln Center Plaza, New York, NY 10023
World Wide Web http://tla.library.unt.edu

Object

To further the interests of collecting, preserving, and using theater, cinema, and performing arts materials in libraries, museums, and private collections. Founded 1937.

Membership

Memb. 325. Dues (Indiv.) $20–$30, (Inst.) $40. Year. Jan. 1–Dec. 31.

Officers

Pres. Martha S. LoMonaco, Fairfield Univ.; *V.P.* Kenneth Schlesinger, Lehman College, CUNY; *Exec. Secy.* David Nochimson, Fashion Inst. of Technology; *Treas.* Angela Weaver, Univ. of Washington.

Executive Board

Pamela Bloom, Susan Brady, Phyllis Dircks, James Fisher, Beth Kerr, Stephen Kuehler, Mark Maniak, Susan Mosakowski, Tobin Nellhaus, Karen Nickeson, Catherine Ritchie, Ellen Truax; *Honorary* Marian Seldes; *Historian* Louis A. Rachow; *Legal Counsel* Georgia Harper; *Past Pres.* Kevin Winkler.

Publications

Broadside (3 per yr.; memb.).
Performing Arts Resources (occasional; memb.).
Membership Directory (annual; memb.). *Ed.* David Nochimson.

Committee Chairpersons

Conference Planning. Kenneth Schlesinger.
Membership. Angela Weaver.
Nominating. Kevin Winkler.
Professional Award. Maryann Chach, Phyllis Dircks, Don B. Wilmeth.
Publications. Robert W. Melton.
Strategic Planning. Kenneth Schlesinger.
TLA/Freedley Awards. Stephen M. Vallillo.

Urban Libraries Council (ULC)

President, Martín Gómez
125 S. Wacker Drive, Suite 1050, Chicago, IL 60606
312-676-0999, fax 312-676-0950
E-mail info@urbanlibraries.org
World Wide Web http://www.urbanlibraries.org

Object

To strengthen the public library as an essential part of urban life; to identify and make known the opportunities for urban libraries; to facilitate the exchange of ideas and programs of member libraries and other libraries; to develop programs that enable libraries to act as a focus of community development and to supply the informational needs of the new urban populations; to conduct research and educational programs that will benefit urban libraries and to solicit and accept grants, contributions, and donations essential to their implementation.

Current major projects supported by grant funding from a variety of sources include Librarians for America's Neighborhoods and the Executive Leadership Institute (both funded by grants from the Institute of Museum and Library Services), and the Gates Foundation-funded report "Making Cities Stronger: Public Library Contributions to Local Economic Development." ULC is a 501(c)(3) not-for-profit corporation based in the state of Illinois.

ULC's Foresight 2020 initiative, being launched this year, is teaching libraries how to spot trends and adapt quickly, putting them in a proactive mode regardless of how their environment changes.

Membership

Membership is open to public libraries serving populations of 100,000 or more located in a Standard Metropolitan Statistical Area and corporations specializing in library-related materials and services. The organization also offers corporate and associate memberships.

Officers (2007–2008)

Chair Charles Higueras, San Francisco Public Lib., 100 Larkin St., San Francisco, CA 94102; *V. Chair/Chair-Elect* Patrick Losinski, Columbus Metropolitan Lib., 96 South Grant, Columbus, OH 43215; *Secy./Treas.* Raymond Santiago, Miami-Dade Public Lib., 101 W. Flagler St., Miami, FL 33130; *Past Chair* Mary Dempsey, Chicago Public Lib., 400 S. State St., Chicago, IL 60605.

Officers serve one-year terms, members of the executive board two-year terms. New officers are elected and take office at the summer annual meeting of the council.

Executive Board

Susan W. Adams. E-mail bereasue@sbcglobal.net; Ginnie Cooper. E-mail ginnie.cooper@dc.gov; Mary A. Dempsey. E-mail mdempsey@chipublib.org; Charles Higueras. E-mail chigueras@vbnarch.com; John Kretzmann. E-mail j-kretzmann@northwestern.edu; Okeima Lawrence. E-mail okeima@mailcity.com; Wai-Fong Lee. E-mail wflee@sccd.ctc.edu; Jane Light. E-mail jane.light@sjlibrary.org; Patrick Losinski. E-mail plosinski@columbuslibrary.org; Robert Martin. E-mail rmartin2@mail.twu.edu; Dennis B. Martinez. E-mail dmartinez@dennis martinez.com; Clement Alexander Price. E-mail caprice@andromeda.rutgers.edu; Dot Ridings. E-mail dridings@aol.com; Raymond Santiago. E-mail santiagor@mdpls.org; Rivkah Sass. E-mail rsass@omahapubliclibrary.org; Keith B. Simmons. E-mail ksimmons@bassberry.com.

Key Staff

Pres.-CEO Martín Gómez; *Chief Operating Officer* Rick J. Ashton; *Senior V.P., Program and Development* Danielle Patrick Milam; *V.P. Finance* Angela Goodrich; *V.P. Membership and Communications* Veronda J. Pitchford.

State, Provincial, and Regional Library Associations

The associations in this section are organized under three headings: United States, Canada, and Regional. Both the United States and Canada are represented under Regional associations.

United States

Alabama

Memb. 1,200. Term of Office. Apr. 2007–Apr. 2008. Publication. *The Alabama Librarian* (q.).

Pres. Theresa C. Trawick, Lurleen B. Wallace Community College, MacArthur Campus, P.O. Drawer 910, Opp 36467. Tel. 334-493-5368, e-mail ttrawick@lbwcc.edu; *Pres.-Elect* Eve Engle Kneeland, Auburn Public Lib., 479 E. Thach Ave., Auburn 36839. Tel. 334-501-3196; *Secy.* Susan Nelson, Hueytown Elementary, 112 Forest Rd., Hueytown 35023-2112. Tel. 205-379-4100; *Treas.* Paul O. Blackmon, Alabama Southern Community College, P.O. Box 2000, Thomasville 36784. Tel. 334-636-9642 ext. 646; *Past Pres.* Bettye Forbus, Houston-Love Memorial Lib., P.O. Box 1369, Dothan 36302. Tel. 334-793-9767.

Address correspondence to the association, 9154 Eastchase Pkwy., Ste. 418, Montgomery 36117. Tel. 334-414-0113, e-mail administrator@allanet.org.

World Wide Web http://allanet.org.

Alaska

Memb. 450+. Publication. *Newspoke* (bi-mo.).

Pres. Jane Fuerstenau. E-mail ifjef@uaa.alaska.edu; *V.P.–Committees* David Ongley. E-mail david.ongley@tuzzy.org; *V.P.–Conference* James Huesmann. E-mail ffjlh3@uaf.edu; *Secy.* Joyce McCombs. E-mail delta library@wildak.net; *Treas.* Diane Ruess. E-mail ffder@uaf.edu; *Past Pres.* Joseph D'Elia. E-mail jdelia@city.kodiak.ak.us; *Exec. Officer* Mary Jennings. E-mail maryj@gci.net.

Address correspondence to the secretary, Alaska Lib. Assn., P.O. Box 81084, Fairbanks 99708. Fax 877-863-1401, e-mail akla@akla.org.

World Wide Web http://www.akla.org.

Arizona

Memb. 1,000. Term of Office. Nov. 2007–Nov. 2008. Publication. *AzLA Newsletter* (mo.).

Pres. Angela Creel-Erb, Arizona Western College, 2020 S. Ave. 8E, Yuma 85365. Tel. 928-344-7776, e-mail angie.creel-erb@azwestern.edu; *Pres.-Elect* Denise C. Keller, Pinal County Lib. Dist., P.O. Box 2974, Florence 85232. Tel. 520-866-6457, fax 520-866-6533, e-mail denise.keller@co.pinal.az.us; *Secy.* Mary Hartz Musgrave, Oro Valley Public Lib. E-mail mhartz@orovalley.net; *Treas.* Linda Renfro, Blue Ridge Unified School Dist. Tel. 928-368-6119, e-mail lrenfro@brusd.k12.az.us; *Past Pres.* Ann Dutton Ewbank, Fletcher Lib., Arizona State Univ. Tel. 602-543-8527, e-mail ann.ewbank@asu.edu; *Exec. Dir.* Debbie Hanson. Tel. 480-609-3999, e-mail admin@azla.org.

Address correspondence to the executive director, AzLA, 1030 E. Baseline Rd., Ste. 105-1025, Tempe 85283.

World Wide Web http://www.azla.org.

Arkansas

Memb. 600. Term of Office. Jan.–Dec. 2008. Publication. *Arkansas Libraries* (bi-mo.).

Pres. Deborah Hall, Arkansas State Lib., 1 Capitol Mall, Little Rock 72201. Tel. 501-682-2845, fax 501-682-1899, e-mail dhall@asl.lib.ar.us; *V.P./Pres.-Elect* Jerrie Townsend, Phillips Community College, 2807 Hwy. 165 S., Box A, Stuttgart 72160. Tel. 870-673-4201 ext. 1818, e-mail jtownsend@pccua.edu; *Secy./Treas.* Jamie Melson, Main Lib., Central Arkansas Lib. System, 100 Rock St., Little Rock 72201. Tel. 501-918-3074, fax 501-376-1830, e-mail jamiem@cals.lib.ar.us; *Past Pres.* Ashley Burris, Lawrence County Lib., 1315 W. Main St.,

Walnut Ridge, 72476. Tel. 870-886-3222, fax 870-886-9520, e-mail akburris@hotmail. com; *Exec. Admin.* Barbara Martin, P.O. Box 958, Benton 72018-0958. Tel. 501-860-7585, fax 501-776-9709, e-mail arlib2@sbcglobal. net.

Address correspondence to the executive administrator.

World Wide Web http://www.arlib.org.

California

Memb. 2,500. Publication. *Clarion* (s. ann.).

Pres. Monique le Conge, Richmond Public Lib. Tel. 510-620-6555, e-mail monique_ leconge@ci.richmond.ca.us; *V.P./Pres.-Elect* Barbara Roberts, Palm Springs Public Lib. Tel. 760-322-8375, e-mail Barbara.Roberts@ palmsprings-ca.gov; *Treas.* Annette Milliron DeBacker, North Bay Cooperative Lib. System. Tel. 707-544-0142, e-mail annetnbc@ sonic.net; *Past Pres.* Margaret Todd, County of Los Angeles Public Lib. Tel. 562-940- 8400, e-mail mdtodd@gw.colapl.org; *Exec. Dir./Secy.* Susan E. Negreen, California Lib. Assn., 717 20th St., Ste. 200, Sacramento 95814. Tel. 916-447-8541 ext. 2, fax 916- 447-8394, e-mail snegreen@cla-net.org.

Address correspondence to the executive director.

World Wide Web http://www.cla-net.org.

Colorado

Memb. 1,100. Publication. *Colorado Libraries* (q.). *Co-Eds.* Janet Lee, Dayton Memorial Lib., Regis Univ., 3333 Regis Blvd., D-20, Denver 80221. Tel. 303-458-3552, fax 303- 964-5143, e-mail jlee@regis.edu; Eileen Dumas, Aurora Public Lib., 14949 E. Alameda Pkwy., Aurora 80012. Tel. 303-739-6637, fax 303-739-6579, e-mail edumas@ci.aurora. co.us.

Pres. Martin Garnar. Tel. 303-964-5459, e-mail mgarnar@regis.edu; *V.P./Pres.-Elect* Jody Howard. Tel. 303-859-1242, e-mail jodyhoward@comcast.net; *Secy.* Sharon Morris. Tel. 303-866-6946, e-mail morris_s @cde.state.co.us; *Treas.* Shannon Cruthers. Tel. 303-556-6701, e-mail shannon.cruthers @cudenver.edu; *Past Pres.* Beth Wrenn- Estes. Tel. 303-322-2430, e-mail bwestes@ mac.com; *Exec. Dir.* Kathleen Noland, Col-

orado Association of Libs., 12081 W. Alameda Pkwy., No. 427, Lakewood 80228. Tel. 303-463-6400, e-mail kathleen@cal-webs.org.

Address correspondence to the executive director.

World Wide Web http://www.cal-webs.org.

Connecticut

Memb. 1,000+. Term of Office. July 2007– June 2008. Publication. *Connecticut Libraries* (11 a year). *Ed.* David Kapp, 4 Llynwood Drive, Bolton 06040. Tel. 203-647-0697, e- mail dkapp@aol.com.

Pres. Carl Antonucci, Capital CC, Hartford. Tel. 860-906-5021, e-mail cantonucci @ccc.commnet.edu; *V.P./Pres.-Elect* Kathy Leeds, Wilton Lib. Assn. Tel. 203-762-7196, fax 203-834-1166, e-mail kathy_leeds@ wiltonlibrary.org; *Treas.* Jan Fisher, Bridgeport Public Lib., Bridgeport 06604. Tel. 203- 576-7777, fax 203-333-0253, e-mail jfisher@ bridgeportpubliclibrary.org; *Past Pres.* Barbara Bailey, Welles-Turner Memorial Lib., Glastonbury. Tel. 860-652-7717, fax 860- 652-7721, e-mail bailey@glastct.org; *Coord.* Pam Najarian, Connecticut Lib. Assn., P.O. Box 75, Middletown 06457. Tel. 860-346- 2444, fax 860-344-9199, e-mail cla@ct librarians.org.

Address correspondence to the coordinator.

World Wide Web http://www.ctlibrary association.org.

Delaware

Memb. 219. Term of Office. Apr. 2007–Apr. 2008. Publication. *DLA Online Bulletin* (online only).

Pres. Lynne Haines, Sussex Dept. of Libs., 22215 S. DuPont Hwy., P.O. Box 589, Georgetown 19947. Tel. 302-855-7890, fax 302-855-7895, e-mail lhaines@lib.de.us; *V.P.* Rebecca Knight, Univ. of Delaware Libs., 181 S. College Avenue, Newark 19717. Tel. 302-831-1730, fax 302-831-1631, e-mail knight@udel.edu; *Secy.* Sonja Brown, Delaware Div. of Libs., 43 S. DuPont Hwy., Dover 19901. Tel. 302-739-4748 ext. 120, fax 302-739-6787, e-mail: sonja.brown@state.de. us; *Treas.* Michael Gutierrez, Univ. of Delaware Libs., 181 S. College Ave., Newark 19717-5267. Tel. 302-831-6076, fax 302-

831-1631, e-mail mgutierr@udel.edu; *Past Pres.* Paul Anderson, Univ. of Delaware Libs., 181 S. College Ave., Newark 19717. Tel. 302-831-2231, fax 302-831-2231, e-mail pa@udel.edu.

Address correspondence to the association, Box 816, Dover 19903-0816. E-mail dla@dla.lib.de.us.

World Wide Web http://www2.lib.udel.edu/dla-crld/index.htm.

District of Columbia

Memb. 300+. Term of Office. July 2007–June 2008. Publication. *Intercom* (mo.).

Pres. Barbara Folensbee-Moore. Tel. 301-587-3674, e-mail bfolensbee-moore@morgan lewis.com; *V.P./Pres.-Elect* M-J Oboroceanu; *Secy.* Colleen Semitekol; *Treas.* Carol Bursik; *Past Pres.* Elaine Cline.

Address correspondence to the association, Box 14177, Benjamin Franklin Sta., Washington 20044. Tel. 202-872-1112.

World Wide Web http://www.dcla.org.

Florida

Memb. (Indiv.) 1,400+. Term of Office. April 2007–March 2008. Publication. *Florida Libraries* (s. ann.). *Ed.* Gloria Colvin, Florida State Univ. Libs. E-mail gpcolvin@yahoo.com.

Pres. Charles Parker, Tampa Bay Lib. Consortium, 1201 Tech Blvd., Ste. 202, Tampa 33619. Tel. 813-622-8252, e-mail cparker@tblc.org; *V.P./Pres.-Elect* Mercedes Clement, Daytona Beach Community College, 1200 W. International Speedway Blvd., Daytona Beach 32120. Tel. 386-506-3440, e-mail clemenm@dbcc.edu; *Secy.* Barbara Stites, Florida Gulf Coast Univ., 10501 FGCU Blvd. S., Fort Myers 33965-7602. Tel. 954-360-1380, e-mail bstites@fgcu.edu; *Treas.* Carol Russo, Hollywood Branch Lib., Broward County Lib., 2600 Hollywood Blvd., Hollywood 33020. Tel. 954-926-2432, e-mail crusso@browardlibrary.org; *Past Pres.* Sol Hirsch, Alachua County Lib. District, 401 E. University Ave., Gainesville 32601. Tel. 352-334-3910, e-mail shirsch@aclib.us; *Exec. Dir.* Ruth O'Donnell, 3509 Trillium Court, Tallahassee 32312. Tel. 850-

668-6911, e-mail flaexecutivedirector@comcast.net.

Address correspondence to the executive director.

World Wide Web http://www.flalib.org.

Georgia

Memb. 1,080. Publication. *Georgia Library Quarterly. Ed.* Susan Cooley, Sara Hightower Regional Lib., 205 Riverside Pkwy., Rome 30161. Tel. 706-236-4621, fax 706-236-4631, e-mail cooleys@mail.floyd.public.lib.ga.us.

Pres. JoEllen Ostendorf, Troup-Harris-Coweta Regional Lib., 115 Alford St., La-Grange 30240. Tel. 706-882-7784 ext. 12, e-mail jostendorf@thclibrary.net; *1st V.P./Pres.-Elect* Betty Paulk. E-mail bpaulk@valdosta.edu; *2nd V.P.* Elaine Yontz. E-mail eyontz@valdosta.edu; *Secy.* Cheryl Rogers. E-mail cheryl@uncleremus.org; *Treas.* Carol Stanley. E-mail cstanley@athenstech.edu; *Past Pres.* Bob Fox. E-mail bob.fox@library.gatech.edu.

Address correspondence to the president, c/o Georgia Lib. Assn., Box 793, Rex 30273-0793.

World Wide Web http://gla.georgialibraries.org.

Hawaii

Memb. 320. Publication. *HLA Newsletter* (3 a year).

Pres. Douglas Bates, Brigham Young Univ.–Hawaii. Tel. 808-675-3851, e-mail batesd@byuh.edu; *V.P.* Jane Barnwell, Pacific Resources for Educ. and Learning; *Secy.* Loraine Oribio, Tokai Univ. E-mail loribio@tokai.edu; *Treas.* Lea Domingo, Univ. of Hawaii at Manoa. E-mail lead@hawaii.edu; *Past Pres.* Keiko Okuhara, Univ. of Hawaii at Manoa. E-mail keikooku@hawaii.edu.

Address correspondence to the president.

Idaho

Memb. 500. Term of Office. Oct. 2007–Oct. 2008.

Pres. Sandra Shropshire, E. M. Oboler Lib., Idaho State Univ., P.O. Box 8089, Pocatello 83209-8089. Tel. 208-282-2671, e-mail shrosand@isu.edu; *V.P./Pres.-Elect* Susan Tabor-Boesch, Wood River Middle School, 900 N. 2 Ave., Hailey 83333. Tel. 208-578-5030 ext. 2323, e-mail staborboesch @blaineschools.org; *Secy.* Jody Vestal, Boise Public Lib., 715 S. Capitol Blvd., Boise 83702. Tel. 208-562-4034, e-mail jvestal@ cityofboise.org; *Treas.* Steve Poppino, College of Southern Idaho, 315 Falls Ave., Twin Falls 83383-1238. Tel. 208-732-6504, fax 208-732-3087, e-mail spoppino@csi.edu; *Past Pres.* Tamra Hawley-House, Boise Public Lib., 715 S. Capitol Blvd., Boise 83702. Tel. 208-384-4200, fax 208-384-4025, e-mail thawley@cityofboise.org.

Address correspondence to the association, P.O. Box 8533, Moscow 83844.

World Wide Web http://www.idaho libraries.org.

Illinois

Memb. 3,000. Term of Office. July 2007–July 2008. Publication. *ILA Reporter* (bimo.).

Pres. Bradley F. Baker, Ronald Williams Lib., Northeastern Illinois Univ., 5500 N. St. Louis Ave., Chicago 60625-4625. Tel. 773-442-4470, fax 773-442-4531, e-mail b-baker@neiu.edu; *V.P./Pres.-Elect* Donna Dziedzic, Naperville Public Lib., 200 W. Jefferson, Naperville 60540. Tel. 630-961-4100 ext. 151, fax 630-637-6149, e-mail ddziedzic @naperville-lib.org; *Treas.* Jamie Bukovac, Indian Prairie Public Lib., 401 Plainfield Rd., Darien 60561. Tel. 630-887-8760, fax 630-887-1018, e-mail bukovacj@indianprairie library.org; *Past Pres.* Tamiye Meehan, Indian Trails Public Lib., 355 S. Schoenbeck Rd., Wheeling 60090. Tel. 847-459-4100 ext. 202, fax 847-459-4760, e-mail tmeehan@indian trailslibrary.org; *Exec. Dir.* Robert P. Doyle, 33 W. Grand Ave., Ste. 301, Chicago 60610-4306. Tel. 312-644-1896, fax 312-644-1899, e-mail doyle@ila.org.

Address correspondence to the executive director.

World Wide Web http://www.ila.org.

Indiana

Memb. 3,000+. Term of Office. March 2007–April 2008. Publication. *Indiana Libraries* (s.

ann.). *Ed.* Alberta Davis Comer, Cunningham Memorial Lib., Indiana State Univ., 650 Sycamore St., Terre Haute 47809. E-mail acomer@isugw.indstate.edu.

Pres. Carl A. Harvey, II, North Elementary, 440 N. 10 St., Noblesville 46060-2099. Tel. 317-773-0482, fax 317-776-6274, e-mail carl_harvey@mail.nobl.k12.in.us; *V.P.* Cheryl Truesdell, Helmke Lib., Indiana Univ. Purdue Univ.–Fort Wayne, 2101 E. Coliseum Blvd., Fort Wayne 46805. Tel. 260-481-6506, fax 260-481-6509, e-mail truesdel@ ipfw.edu; *Secy.* Janet Pfadt, Fox Hill Elementary, 802 Fox Hill Drive, Indianapolis 46228-1476. Tel. 317-259-5371, fax 317-259-5383, e-mail jpfadt@msdwt.k12.in.us; *Treas.* jan Gillespie, 2118 Main St., Anderson 46016. Tel. 765-529-0362 ext. 333, fax 765-521-3581, e-mail jang@nchcpl.lib.in.us; *Past Pres.* Jane Myers, 109 Ulen Blvd., Lebanon 46052. Tel. 765-482-0621, e-mail myers.jane @sbcglobal.net; *Exec. Dir.* Linda Kolb. E-mail lkolb@ilfonline.org.

Address correspondence to Indiana Lib. Federation, 941 E. 86 St., Ste. 260, Indianapolis 46240. Tel. 317-257-2040, fax 317-257-1389, e-mail ilf@indy.net.

World Wide Web http://www.ilfonline.org.

Iowa

Memb. 1,700. Term of Office. Jan.–Dec. Publication. *The Catalyst* (bi-mo.). *Ed.* Laurie Hews.

Pres. Barbara Peterson, Council Bluffs Public Lib., 400 Willow Ave., Council Bluffs 51503. Tel. 712-323-7553, fax 712-323-1269, e-mail bpeterson@cbpl.lib.ia.us; *V.P./ Pres.-Elect* Ellen Neuhaus, Rod Lib., Univ. of Northern Iowa, 1227 W. 27 St., Cedar Falls 50613. Tel. 319-273-3739, fax 319-273-2913, e-mail ellen.neuhaus@uni.edu; *Secy.* Marilyn Murphy, Busse Center Lib., Mount Mercy College, 1330 Elmhurst Drive N.E., Cedar Rapids 52402. Tel. 319-363-8213 ext. 1244, fax 319-363-9060, e-mail marilyn@mtmercy.edu; *Past Pres.* Sheryl Bissen, Grinnell College Libs., 1111 Sixth Ave., Grinnell 50112. Tel. 641-269-3359, fax 641-269-4283, e-mail bissen@grinnell.edu; *Exec. Dir.* Laurie Hews. Tel. 515-273-5322, fax 515-309-4576, e-mail executivedirector@ iowalibraryassociation.org.

Address correspondence to the association, 3636 Westown Pkwy., Ste. 202, West Des Moines 50266.

World Wide Web http://www.iowalibrary association.org.

Kansas

Memb. 1,500. Term of Office. July 2007– June 2008. Publication. *KLA Newsletter* (q.).

Pres. Carla Kaiser, Basehor Community Lib., 2812 N. 155 St., Basehor 66007. Tel. 913-724-2828; *1st V.P.* Laura Loveless, Kansas City Public Lib.; *2nd V.P.* Denise Smith, Stanton County Lib.; *Secy.* Gina Millsap, Topeka Shawnee County Lib., 1020 S.W. Washburn, Topeka 66604. Tel. 785-580-4400; *Past Pres.* Rosanne Siemens, Kansas Lib. Assn.

Address correspondence to the executive director.

World Wide Web http://skyways.lib.ks.us/ KLA.

Kentucky

Memb. 1,900. Term of Office. Oct. 2007– Oct. 2008. Publication. *Kentucky Libraries* (q.).

Pres. Fannie Cox, Ekstrom Lib., Univ. of Louisville, Louisville 40292. Tel. 502-852-2705, e-mail fmcox@louisville.edu; *V.P./ Pres.-Elect* Debbe Oberhausen, Crescent Hill Branch, Louisville Free Public Lib., 2762 Frankfort Ave., Louisville 40206. Tel. 502-574-1793, e-mail debra.oberhausen@lfpl.org; *Secy.* Darlah Zweifel, Meade County H.S., 938 Old State Rd., Brandenburg 40108. Tel. 270-442-7515 ext. 4522, e-mail darlah. zweifel@meade.kyschools.us; *Past Pres.* Laura Davison, Univ. of Kentucky Medical Center Lib., Lexington 40526-0298. Tel. 859-323-6138, fax 859-323-1040, e-mail davison@email.uky.edu; *Exec. Secy.* Tom Underwood, 1501 Twilight Trail, Frankfort 40601. Tel. 502-223-5322, fax 502-223-4937, e-mail info@kylibasn.org.

Address correspondence to the executive secretary.

World Wide Web http://www.kylibasn.org.

Louisiana

Memb. 1,100+. Term of Office. July 2007– June 2008. Publication. *Louisiana Libraries* (q.). *Ed.* Vivian Solar. Tel. 225-647-8924, fax 225-644-0063, e-mail vsolar@state.lib.la. us.

Pres. Melissa Elrod. Tel. 318-865-7949, fax 318-865-5041, e-mail melrod@cadddo. k12.la.us; *1st V.P./Pres.-Elect* Melissa Hymel. Tel. 225-638-7593, fax 225-638-9847, e-mail mkhymel@yahoo.com; *Past Pres.* Beth Paskoff. Tel. 225-578-1480, fax 225-578-4581, e-mail bpaskoff@lsu.edu; *Exec. Dir.* Beverly Laughlin. Tel. 337-550-7890, fax 337-550-7846, e-mail office@llaonline.org.

Address correspondence to Louisiana Lib. Assn., 421 S. 4 St., Eunice 70535.

World Wide Web http://www.llaonline.org.

Maine

Memb. 950. Term of Office. (Pres., V.P.) July 2007–July 2008. Publication. *MLA-To-Z* (q., online).

Pres. Rich Boulet, Blue Hill Public Lib., P.O. Box 824, Parker Point Rd., Blue Hill 04614. Tel. 207-374-5515, fax 207-374-5254, e-mail rboulet@bluehill.lib.me.us; *V.P./Pres.-Elect* Molly Larson, Rockport Public Lib., P.O. Box 8, Rockport 04856. Tel. 207-236-3642, e-mail mlarson@ rockport.lib.me.us; *Secy.* Diane Jones, Camden Public Lib., 55 Main St., Camden 04843. Tel. 207-236-3440, fax 207-236-6673, e-mail dsjones@camden.lib.me.us; *Treas.* Alisia Wygant, Colby College, 155 Goose Pecker Ridge, Montville 04941. Tel. 207-859-5146, e-mail arwygant@colby.edu; *Past Pres.* Nikki Maounis, Rockland Public Lib., 80 Union St., Rockland 04841. Tel. 207-594-0310, fax 207-594-0333, e-mail nmaounis@ rockland.me.us; *Exec. Secy.* Edna Comstock, Empowerment Enterprises, 331 State St., Augusta 04330.

Address correspondence to the association, 31 State St., Augusta 04330. Tel. 207-441-1410, e-mail empoweredna@gwi.net.

World Wide Web http://mainelibraries.org.

Maryland

Memb. 1,300. Term of Office. July 2007–July 2008. Publications. *Happenings* (mo.), *The Crab* (q.).

Pres. Marion Francis, Anne Arundel County Public Lib. Tel. 410-222-7234, e-mail mfrancis@aacpl.net; *1st V.P./Pres.-Elect* Darrell Batson. Frederick County Public Lib. Tel. 301-600-1613, e-mail dbatson@fredcomd.net; *Past Pres.* Michael Gannon, Anne Arundel County Public Lib.; *Exec. Dir.* Margaret Carty.

Address correspondence to the association, 1401 Hollins St., Baltimore 21223. Tel. 410-947-5090, fax 410-947-5089, e-mail mla@mdlib.org.

World Wide Web http://mdlib.org.

Massachusetts

Memb. (Indiv.) 1,000; (Inst.) 100. Term of Office. July 2007–June 2008. Publication. *Bay State Libraries* (4 a year).

Pres. Kimberly Lynn. Tel. 978-623-8400, fax 978-623-8407, e-mail klynn@mhl.org; *V.P./Pres.-Elect* Richard Callaghan. Tel. 781-275-9440, fax 781-275-3590, e-mail rcallaghan@minlib.net; *Secy.* Gianna Gifford. Tel. 617-521-2777, fax 617-521-3093, e-mail gianna.gifford@simmons.edu; *Treas.* Nora Blake. Tel. 413-665-5511, fax 413-665-6776, e-mail nblake@masscat.org; *Past Pres.* Kathy Glick Weil. Tel. 617-796-1400, fax 617-965-8457, e-mail glickweil@minlib.net; *Exec. Mgr.* Elizabeth Hacala, Massachusetts Lib. Assn., P.O. Box 535, Bedford 01730. Tel. 781-275-7729, fax 781-998-0393, e-mail mlaoffice@masslib.org.

Address correspondence to the executive manager.

World Wide Web http://www.masslib.org.

Michigan

Memb. (Indiv.) 1,900+. Term of Office. July 2007–June 2008 Publications. *Michigan Librarian Newsletter* (6 a year), *Michigan Library Association Forum* (s. ann., online).

Pres. Josie Parker, Ann Arbor District Lib.; *Pres.-Elect* Kathy Irwin, Univ. of Michigan–Dearborn Lib.; *Secy.* Faye Backie, Michigan State Univ.; *Treas.* Gail Parsons,

Public Libs. of Saginaw; *Past Pres.* Leah Black, Michigan State Univ.

Address correspondence to Gretchen Couraud, Exec. Dir., Michigan Lib. Assn., 1407 Rensen St., Ste. 2, Lansing 48910. Tel. 517-394-2774 ext. 224, e-mail couraudg@mlcnet.org.

World Wide Web http://www.mla.lib.mi.us.

Minnesota

Memb. 900. Term of Office. (Pres., Pres.-Elect) Jan.–Dec. 2008.

Pres. Wendy Wendt, Marhall-Lyon County Lib., Marshall 56258. Tel. 507-537-7003, e-mail wendyw@marshalllyonlibrary.org; *Pres.-Elect* Ken Behringer. E-mail ken.behringer@co.dakota.mn.us; *Secy.* Carla Urban-Dewey. E-mail dewey002@umn.edu; *Treas.* Robin Chaney. E-mail robin@sammie.org; *Past Pres.* Heidi Hoks. E-mail heidih@grrl.lib.mn.us.

Address correspondence to the association, 1619 Dayton Ave., Ste. 314, Saint Paul 55104. Tel. 877-867-0982 (toll-free), 651-641-0982, fax 651-641-3169, e-mail mla office@mnlibraryassociation.org.

World Wide Web http://www.mnlibrary association.org.

Mississippi

Memb. 600. Term of Office. Jan.–Dec. 2008. Publication. *Mississippi Libraries* (q.).

Pres. Jeff Slagell, Roberts-LaForge Lib., Delta State Univ. Tel. 662-846-4441, e-mail jslagell@deltastate.edu; *V.P./Pres.-Elect* Jan Willis, Elizabeth Jones Lib. Tel. 662-841-9029, e-mail jwillis@li.lib.ms.us; *Secy.* Judy Card, First Regional Lib. Tel. 662-429-4439 ext.120, e-mail jcard@first.lib.ms.us; *Treas.* Amanda Powers, Mitchell Memorial Lib., Mississippi State Univ. Tel. 662-325-7677, e-mail apowers@library.msstate.edu; *Past Pres.* Catherine A. Nathan, First Regional Lib. System. Tel. 662-429-4439, e-mail cnathan@first.lib.ms.us; *Exec. Secy.* Mary Julia Anderson, P.O. Box 13687, Jackson 39236-3687. Tel. 601-981-4586, fax 601-981-4501, e-mail info@misslib.org.

Address correspondence to the executive secretary.

World Wide Web http://www.misslib.org/index.php.

Missouri

Memb. 800+. Term of Office. Jan.–Dec. 2008. Publication. *MO INFO* (bi-mo.). *Ed.* Margaret Booker.

Pres. Karen Hayden, Little Dixie Regional Libs., 111 N. 4 St., Moberly 65270. Tel. 660-263-4426, fax 660-263-4024, e-mail khayden @little-dixie.lib.mo.us; *Pres.-Elect* Kimberlee Ried, National Archives and Records Admin., 2312 E. Bannister Rd., Kansas City 64131. Tel. 816-268-8072, fax 816-268-8037, e-mail kimberlee.ried@nara.gov; *Secy.* Joy Dufrain, Scenic Regional Lib.–Warren County, 340 Hwy. WW, Wright City 63390. Tel. 636-922-8474, fax 636-922-8524, e-mail jdufrain@stchas.edu; *Treas.* Ray Hall, Mexico–Audrain County Lib. Dist., 305 W. Jackson, Mexico 65265. Tel. 573-581-4939, e-mail cinnamonrabbit@real.more.net; *Past Pres.* Karen Horny, Missouri State Univ. Libs., 901 S. National Ave., Springfield 65897. Tel. 417-836-4525, fax 417-836-4764, e-mail karenhorny@missouristate.edu; *Exec. Dir.* Margaret Booker, Missouri Lib. Assn., 3212-A LeMone Industrial Blvd., Columbia 65201. Tel. 573-449-4627, fax 573-449-4655, e-mail mla001@more.net.

Address correspondence to the executive director.

World Wide Web http://www.molib.org.

Montana

Memb. 600. Term of Office. July 2007–June 2008. Publication. *Montana Library Focus* (bi-mo.).

Pres. Honore Bray, Missoula Public Lib., P.O. Box 21, Hall 59837. Tel. 406-258-3860, fax 406-728-5900, e-mail hbray@mtlib.org; *Pres.-Elect* Della Dubbe, Glacier County Lib. Tel. 406-873-4572, e-mail glibrary@ northentel.net; *Past Pres.* Lynn McKinney, Billings Senior H.S., 1001 Babcock Blvd., Billings 59105. Tel. 406-247-2217, fax 406-255-3610, e-mail mckinney1@billings.k12. mt.us; *Exec. Dir.* Debra Kramer, Montana Lib. Assn., P.O. Box 1085, Manhattan 59741.

Tel. 406-670-8449, e-mail cdmkramer@ hotmail.com.

Address correspondence to the executive director.

World Wide Web http://www.mtlib.org.

Nebraska

Term of Office. Jan.–Dec. 2008. Publication. *Nebraska Library Association Quarterly* (*NLAQ*) (q.). *Ed.* John Bernardi. E-mail bernardj@omahapubliclibrary.org.

Pres. Lisa Olivigni, Crete Public Lib. E-mail lolivigni@crete-ne.gov. E-mail lolivigni @crete-ne.gov; *V.P./Pres.-Elect* Pam Bohmfalk, Hastings Public Lib. E-mail pbohmfal@ hastings.lib.ne.us; *Secy.* Diana Johnson, Stromsburg Public Lib. E-mail stromsburgpl @alltel.net; *Treas.* Julie Hector, Lincoln City Libs. E-mail j.hector@lincolnlibraries.org; *Past Pres.* Beth Goble, Nebraska Lib. Commission. E-mail bgoble@nlc.state.ne.us; *Exec. Dir.* Kathleen Thomsen, 1901 W. F St., North Platte 69101-4955. E-mail katet323@ msn.com

Address correspondence to the executive director.

World Wide Web http://www.nebraska libraries.org.

Nevada

Memb. 450. Term of Office. Jan.–Dec. 2008. Publication. *Nevada Libraries* (q.).

Pres. Denise Gerdes, Las Vegas–Clark County Lib. Dist. E-mail nlapres2008@ yahoo.com or gerdesd@lvccld.org; *V.P./ Pres.-Elect* Jeanette Hammons, Elko County Lib. E-mail jmhammon@clan.lib.nv.us; *Treas.* Susan D. Williams, Virtual Lib., Las Vegas–Clark County Lib. Dist. E-mail williamssd@lvccld.org; *Past Pres.* Debbie Jacobs, Clayton Middle School Lib., Washoe County School Dist., 1295 Wyoming Ave., Reno 89503. Tel. 775-746-5860, e-mail djacobs@washoe.k12.nv.us; *Exec. Secy.* Robbie DeBuff. E-mail rjdebuff@hotmail. com.

Address correspondence to the executive secretary.

World Wide Web http://www.nevada libraries.org.

New Hampshire

Memb. 700. Publication. *NHLA News* (q.).

Pres. Amy Thurber, Canaan Town Lib., 1173 U.S. Rte. 4, P.O. Box 368, Canaan 03714. Tel. 603-523-9650, e-mail athurber@ canaanlibrary.org; *V.P./Pres.-Elect* Steve Butzel, Nashua Public Lib., 2 Court St., Nashua 03060. Tel. 603-5898-4647, e-mail steven.butzel@nashualibrary.org; *Secy.* Sue Hoadley, Pelham Public Lib., 24 Village Green, Pelham 03016. Tel. 603-635-7581, e-mail shoadley@pelhamweb.com; *Treas.* Carl Heidenblad, Nesmith Lib., P.O. Box 60, Windham 03087. Tel. 603-432-7154, e-mail cheidenblad@library.windham.nh.us; *Past Pres.* Annie Donahue, Manchester Lib., Univ. of New Hampshire, 400 Commercial St., Manchester 03101. Tel. 603-641-4173, e-mail annie.donahue@unh.edu.

Address correspondence to the association, c/o LGC, P.O. Box 617, Concord 03302-0617.

World Wide Web http://webster.state.nh.us/nhla.

New Jersey

Memb. 1,700. Term of Office. July 2007–June 2009. Publication. *New Jersey Libraries Newsletter* (mo.).

Pres. Michele Reutty, Oakland Public Lib., 2 Municipal Plaza, Oakland 07436. Tel. 201-337-3742, fax 201-337-0261, e-mail reutty@bccls.org; *V.P.* Heidi Lynn Cramer, Newark Public Lib., Washington St., P.O. Box 630, Newark 07101. Tel. 973-733-7837, fax 973-733-8539, e-mail hcramer@npl.org; *2nd V.P.* Nancy Madacsi, Taylor Lib., Centenary College, 400 Jefferson St., Hackettstown 07840. Tel. 908-852-1400 ext. 2345, fax 908-850-9528, e-mail madacsin@ centenarycollege.edu; *Secy.* Jennifer Lang, 66 Witherspoon St., No. 231, Princeton 08542. Tel. 609-258-5476, fax 609-258-0441, e-mail lang@princeton.edu; *Treas.* Keith McCoy, Roselle Public Lib., 104 W. 4 Ave., Roselle 07203. Tel. 908-245-5809, fax 908-298-8881, e-mail wkmccoy@lmxac.org; *Past Pres.* Joan Bernstein, Mount Laurel Lib., 100 Walt Whitman Ave., Mount Laurel 08054. Tel. 856-234-7319 ext. 303, fax 856-234-6916, e-mail jeb@mtlaurel.lib.nj.us;

Exec. Dir. Patricia Tumulty, NJLA, P.O. Box 1534, Trenton 08607. Tel. 609-394-8032, fax 609-394-8164, e-mail ptumulty@njla.org.

Address correspondence to the executive director.

World Wide Web http://www.njla.org.

New Mexico

Memb. 550. Term of Office. Apr. 2007–Apr. 2008. Publication. *New Mexico Library Association Newsletter* (6 a year).

Pres. Louise Hoffmann. E-mail hoffmannl @sanjuancollege.edu; *V.P.* Cassandra Osterloh. E-mail cassandra.osterloh@gmail.com; *Secy.* Phyllis Reed. E-mail phyllisreed@ voruidoso.com; *Treas.* Clyde Henderson. E-mail chenderson@navajotech.edu.

Address correspondence to the association, Box 26074, Albuquerque 87125. Tel. 505-400-7309, fax 505-891-5171, e-mail admin@ nmla.org.

World Wide Web http://www.nmla.org.

New York

Memb. 3,000. Term of Office. Oct. 2007–Oct. 2008. Publication. *NYLA Bulletin* (6 a year). *Ed.* Michael J. Borges.

Pres. Rosina Alaimo. Tel. 716-626-8846, e-mail rosella@att.net; *Pres.-Elect* Josh Cohen. Tel. 845-471-6060 ext. 17, e-mail jcohen@midhudson.org; *Treas.* Ed Falcone. Tel. 914-375-7951, e-mail efalcone@ypl.org; *Past Pres.* Rachel Baum. Tel. 518-248-1781, e-mail RachelRBaum@gmail.com; *Exec. Dir.* Michael J. Borges. E-mail director@ nyla.org.

Address correspondence to the executive director, New York Lib. Assn., 252 Hudson Ave., Albany 12210. Tel. 800-252-6952 (toll-free), 518-432-6952, fax 518-427-1697, e-mail director@nyla.org.

World Wide Web http://www.nyla.org.

North Carolina

Memb. 1,100. Term of Office. Oct. 2007–Oct. 2009. Publications. *North Carolina Library Association E-news* (bi-mo.). *Ed.* Marilyn Schuster, Local Documents/Special Collections, Univ. of North Carolina–Charlotte. E-mail mbschust@email.uncc.edu;

North Carolina Libraries Online (2 a year). *Ed.* Ralph Lee Scott, Joyner Lib., ECU, Greenville 27858. Tel. 252-328-0265, e-mail scottr@ecu.edu.

Pres. Phil Barton, Rowan Public Lib., 714 Brookmont Ave., Salisbury 28146-7293. Tel. 704-633-5462, e-mail pbarton2@carolina.rr. com; *V.P./Pres.-Elect* Sherwin Rice, Bladen Community College, P.O. Box 266, Dublin 28332. Tel. 910-879-5641, e-mail srice@ bladen.cc.nc.us; *Secy.* Caroline Walters, 1110 W. Murray Ave., Durham 27704. Tel. 919-962-6402, e-mail carolinejwalters@verizon. net; *Treas.* Andrea Tullos, Orange County Lib., P.O. Box 8181, Hillsboro 27278. Tel. 919-245-2529, e-mail tullos.andrea@gmail. com; *Past Pres.* Robert Burgin, North Carolina Central Univ., 307 Swiss Lake Drive, Cary 27513. Tel. 919-462-0134, fax 919-380-8074, e-mail rburgin@mindspring.com *Admin. Asst.* Kim Parrott, North Carolina Lib. Assn., 1811 Capital Blvd., Raleigh 27604. Tel. 919-839-6252, fax 919-839-6253, e-mail nclaonline@ibiblio.org.

Address correspondence to the administrative assistant.

World Wide Web http://www.nclaonline. org.

North Dakota

Memb. (Indiv.) 400; (Inst.) 18. Term of Office. Sept. 2007–Sept. 2008. Publication. *The Good Stuff* (q.). *Ed.* Marlene Anderson, Bismarck State College Lib., Box 5587, Bismarck 58506-5587. Tel. 701-224-5578.

Pres. Donna James, Allen Memorial Lib., Valley City State Univ., 101 College St. S.W., Valley City 58072-4098. Tel. 701-845-7275, fax 701-845-7437, e-mail donna.james @vcsu.edu; *Pres.-Elect* Phyllis Ann K. Bratton, Raugust Lib., Jamestown College, 6070 College Lane, Jamestown 58405-0002. Tel. 701-252-3467 ext. 2433, fax 701-253-4318, e-mail pbratton@jc.edu; *Secy.* Laurie L. McHenry, Chester Fritz Lib., Univ. of North Dakota, P.O. Box 14626, Grand Forks 58208-4626. Tel. 701-777-2919, fax 701-777-3319, e-mail lauriemchenry@mail.und.nodak.edu; *Treas.* Michael Safratowich, Harley French Lib. of the Health Sciences, Univ. of North Dakota, Box 9002, Grand Forks 58202-9002. Tel. 701-777-2602, fax 701-777-4790, e-mail

msafrat@medicine.nodak.edu; *Past Pres.* Beth Postema, Fargo Public Lib., 102 N. 3 St., Fargo 58102. Tel. 701-241-1491, fax 701-241-8581, e-mail bpostema@cityof fargo.com.

Address correspondence to the president.

World Wide Web http://www.ndla.info.

Ohio

Memb. 3,400+. Term of Office. Jan.–Dec. 2008. Publication. *Access* (11 a year).

Pres. Margaret Danziger, Toledo–Lucas County Public Lib., Toledo 43624-1614. Tel. 419-259-5260, e-mail mdanziger@toledo library.org; *V.P./Pres.-Elect* Scott Shafer, Lima Public Lib., 650 W. Market St., Lima 45801. Tel. 419-228-5113, e-mail shafers@ limalibrary.com; *Past Pres.* Cindy Lombardo, Tuscarawas County Public Lib., New Philadelphia; *Exec. Dir.* Douglas S. Evans.

Address correspondence to the executive director, OLC, 2 Easton Oval, Ste. 525, Columbus 43219-7008. Tel. 614-416-2258, fax 614-416-2270, e-mail olc@olc.org.

World Wide Web http://www.olc.org.

Oklahoma

Memb. (Indiv.) 1,000; (Inst.) 60. Term of Office. July 2007–June 2008. Publication. *Oklahoma Librarian* (bi-mo.). *Ed.* Janet Croft. E-mail jcroft@ou.edu.

Pres. Jan Bryant. E-mail ljanbryant@eok. lib.ok.us; *V.P./Pres.-Elect* Kathy Latrobe. E-mail klatrobe@ou.edu; *Secy.* Alden Street. E-mail astreet@pls.lib.ok.us; *Treas.* Sarah Robbins. E-mail srobbins@ou.edu; *Past Pres.* Pat Weaver-Meyers. E-mail plweaver meyers@noble.org; *Exec. Dir.* Kay Boies, 300 Hardy Drive, Edmond 73013. Tel. 405-525-5100, fax 405-525-5103, e-mail kboies@ sbcglobal.net.

Address correspondence to the executive director.

World Wide Web http://www.oklibs.org.

Oregon

Memb. (Indiv.) 1,000+. Publications. *OLA Hotline* (bi-w.), *OLA Quarterly.*

Pres. Sarah Beasley, Portland State Univ. Tel. 503-725-3688, e-mail beasleys@pdx.edu

V.P./Pres.-Elect Mary Ginnane, Eugene Public Lib. E-mail mary.j.ginnane@ci.eugene.or.us; *Secy.* Brandon Barnett, Multnomah County Lib. E-mail wooga@q7.com; *Treas.* Shirley Roberts, Eastern Oregon Univ. E-mail sroberts@eou.edu; *Past Pres.* Aletha Bonebrake, Baker County Public Lib. Tel. 541-523-6419, e-mail alethaboneb@msn.com.

Address correspondence to Oregon Lib. Assn., P.O. Box 2042, Salem 97308. Tel. 503-370-7019, e-mail olaweb@olaweb.org, World Wide Web http://www.olaweb.org.

Pennsylvania

Memb. 1,800. Term of Office. Jan.–Dec. 2008. Publication. *PaLA Bulletin* (10 a year).

Pres. Mary Garm, Lackawanna County Lib. System. E-mail garm@albright.org; *1st V.P.* Joe Fennewald, Penn State–Hazleton. E-mail jaf23@psu.edu; *2nd V.P.* Carrie Turner, Cheltenham Twp. Public Lib. E-mail cturner@mclinc.org; *Treas.* Jo Ellen Kenney, Carnegie Lib. of McKeesport. E-mail kenneyj@einetwork.net; *Past Pres.* Janice Trapp, J. V. Brown Lib. E-mail jtrapp@jvbrown.edu; *Exec. Dir.* Glenn R. Miller, Pennsylvania Lib. Assn., 220 Cumberland Pkwy., Ste. 10, Mechanicsburg 17055. Tel. 717-766-7663, fax 717-766-5440, e-mail glenn@palibraries.org.

Address correspondence to the executive director.

World Wide Web http://www.palibraries.org.

Rhode Island

Memb. (Indiv.) 350+; (Inst.) 50+. Term of Office. June 2007–June 2009. Publication. *Rhode Island Library Association Bulletin.*

Pres. Christopher La Roux, Greenville Public Lib., 573 Putnam Pike, Greenville 02828. Tel. 401-949-3630, e-mail president@rilibraryassoc.org; *V.P./Pres.-Elect* Laura Marlane, Central Falls Free Public Lib., 205 Central St., Central Falls 02863. Tel. 401-727-7440, e-mail vicepresident@rilibrary assoc.org; *Secy.* Hope Houston, Office of Lib. and Info. Services, 1 Capitol Hill, Providence 02908. Tel. 401-222-5770, e-mail secretary@rilibraryassoc.org; *Treas./Past*

Pres. Cindy Lunghofer, East Providence Public Lib., 41 Grove Ave., East Providence 02914. Tel. 401-434-2453, e-mail book_n@yahoo.com.

World Wide Web http://www.rilibrary assoc.org.

South Carolina

Memb. 550+. Term of Office. Jan.–Dec. 2008. Publication. *News and Views.*

Pres. Curtis R. Rogers, South Carolina State Lib., 1430 Senate St., Columbia 29211. Tel. 803-734-8928, fax 803-734-8676, e-mail crogers@statelibrary.sc.gov; *1st V.P./Pres.-Elect* Libby Young, Furman Univ., 10 W. Earle St., Greenville 29609. Tel. 864-294-2260, fax 864-294-3004, e-mail libby.young@furman.edu; *2nd V.P.* Rayburne Turner, Otranto Rd. Branch, Charleston County Public Lib., 2261 Otranto Rd., North Charleston 29406. Tel. 843-572-4094, fax 843-572-4190, e-mail turner@ccpl.org; *Secy.* Karen Brown, Thomas Cooper Lib., Univ. of South Carolina, Columbia 29208. Tel. 803-777-4267, fax 803-777-4661, e-mail kwbrown@gwm.sc.edu; *Treas.* Jeronell ("Nell") Bradley, Florence Darlington Technical College. Tel. 843-661-8032, e-mail jeronell.bradley@fdtc.edu; *Past Pres.* Quincy Pugh, Richland County Public Lib., 1431 Assembly St., Columbia 29201. Tel. 803-929-3449, fax 803-929-3448, e-mail qpugh@richland.lib.sc.us; *Exec. Secy.* Gabrielle Barnes, South Carolina Lib. Assn., P.O. Box 1763, Columbia 29202. Tel. 803-252-1087, e-mail scla@capconsc.com.

Address correspondence to the executive secretary.

World Wide Web http://www.scla.org.

South Dakota

Memb. (Indiv.) 428; (Inst.) 66. Term of Office. Oct. 2007–Oct. 2008. Publication. *Book Marks* (bi-mo.).

Pres. Robin Schrupp, Grant County Public Lib., Milbank. E-mail gclibrary21@hotmail.com; *V.P./Pres.-Elect* Nancy Sabbe, Madison Public Lib., Madison. E-mail nsabbe@sdln.net; *Recording Secy.* Judith Howard, Augustana College. E-mail judith.

howard@augie.edu; *Past Pres.* Greta Chapman, Rapid City Public Lib. E-mail gchapman @rcplib.org; *Exec. Secy./Treas.* Brenda Hemmelman. E-mail bkstand@rap.midco.net.

Address correspondence to the executive secretary, SDLA, Box 1212, Rapid City 57709-1212. Tel. 605-343-3750, e-mail bkstand@rap.midco.net.

World Wide Web http://www.sdlibrary association.org.

Tennessee

Memb. 734. Term of Office. July 2007–June 2008. Publications. *Tennessee Librarian* (q.), *TLA Newsletter* (bi-mo.) (both online only at http://www.tnla.org).

Pres. Jane Pinkston, Tennessee State Lib. and Archives, 403 Seventh Ave. N., Nashville 37243. E-mail jane.pinkston@state.tn. us; *V.P./Pres.-elect* Sue Szostak. E-mail sszostak@mscc.edu; *Recording Secy.* Virginia Cairns. E-mail virginia-cairns@utc.edu; *Past Pres.* Pat Thompson. E-mail pat. thompson@state.tn.us; *Exec. Dir.* Annelle R. Huggins, Tennessee Lib. Assn., Box 241074, Memphis 38124. Tel. 901-485-6952, e-mail ahuggins@midsouth.rr.com.

Address correspondence to the executive director.

World Wide Web http://tnla.org.

Texas

Memb. 7,300. Term of Office. Apr. 2007–Apr. 2008. Publications. *Texas Library Journal* (q.), *TLACast* (9 a year).

Pres. Steve Brown, North Richland Hills Public Lib. E-mail sbrown@nrhtx.com; *Pres.-Elect* Melody S. Kelly, Univ. of North Texas. E-mail mkelly@library.unt.edu; *Treas.* Janet Key, Tarrant County College. E-mail janet.key@tccd.edu; *Past Pres.* Jana Knezek. Tel. 210-522-8190, fax 210-706-8974, e-mail janaknezek@nisd.net; *Exec. Dir.* Patricia H. Smith, TXLA, 3355 Bee Cave Rd., Ste. 401, Austin 78746-6763. Tel. 512-328-1518, fax 512-328-8852, e-mail pats@txla.org.

Address correspondence to the executive director.

World Wide Web http://www.txla.org.

Utah

Memb. 650. Term of Office. May 2007–May 2008. Publication. *Utah Libraries News* (bi-mo.) (online at http://www.ula.org/newsletter).

Pres. Dorothy Horan, Family History Lib., 50 E. North Temple, COB 3, Salt Lake City 84602. Tel. 801-240-6125, e-mail horandm@ ldschurch.org; *V.P./Pres.-Elect* Steve Decker, Cedar City Public Lib., Cedar City 84720. Tel. 435-586-6661 ext. 1001, fax 435-865-7280, e-mail dsteve@cedarcity.org; *Past Pres.* Julie Williamsen, 5720 Harold B. Lee Lib., Brigham Young Univ., Provo 84602. Tel. 801-422-6763, e-mail julie_williamsen @byu.edu; *Exec. Secy.* Ranny Lacanienta, 2820 Harold B. Lee Lib., Brigham Young Univ., Provo 84602. Tel. 801-422-6278, fax 801-422-0466, e-mail ranny@byu.edu or admin@ula.org.

Address correspondence to the executive secretary.

World Wide Web http://www.ula.org.

Vermont

Memb. 400. Publication. *VLA News* (6 a year).

Pres. Barbara Doyle-Wilch, Middlebury College Lib., 110 Storrs Ave., Middlebury 05753. Tel. 802-443-5490, e-mail bdoylewi @middlebury.edu; *V.P./Pres.-Elect* Judah S. Hamer, 1571 Rte. 30, Cornwall 05753. Tel. 802-443-1860, e-mail jshamer@gmail.com; *Secy.* Brenda Ellis, Middlebury College Lib., 110 Storrs Ave. Middlebury 05753. Tel. 802-443-5497, e-mail bellis@middlebury.edu; *Treas.* Donna Edwards, Samuel Read Hall Lib., Lyndon State College, P.O. Box 919, Lyndonville 05851. Tel. 802-626-6447, fax 802-626-6331, e-mail donna.edwards@lsc. vsc.edu; *Past Pres.* Lisa von Kann, St. Johnsbury Athenaeum, 1171 Main St., St. Johnsbury 05819. Tel. 802-748-8291, e-mail lvkann@stjathenaeum.org.

Address correspondence to VLA, Box 803, Burlington 05402.

World Wide Web http://www.vermont libraries.org.

Virginia

Memb. 1,100+. Term of Office. Oct. 2007–Oct. 2008. Publications. *Virginia Libraries* (q.); *VLA Newsletter* (10 a year).

Pres. Donna Cote, Central Rappahannock Regional Lib., 1201 Caroline St., Fredericksburg 22401. Tel. 540-372-1160, e-mail dcote@crrl.org; *V.P./Pres.-Elect* Robin Benke, UVA–Wise, 116 Dotson Ave., Wise 24293. Tel. 276-328-0151, e-mail rbenke@virginia.edu; *2nd V.P.* Caryl Gray, Univ. Libs., Virginia Tech, 304 Fincastle Drive, Blacksburg 24060. Tel. 540-231-9229, e-mail cegray@vt.cdu; *Secy.* Laurie Roberts, Tazewell County Public Lib., P.O. Box 929, Tazewell 24651. Tel. 276-988-2541, e-mail lroberts@tcplweb.org; *Treas.* Matt Todd, Northern Virginia Community College, 3001 N. Beaugard St., Alexandria 22331. Tel. 703-845-6033, e-mail mtodd@nvcc.edu; *Exec. Dir.* Linda Hahne, P.O. Box 8277, Norfolk 23503-0277. Tel. 757-583-0041, fax 757-583-5041, e-mail lhahne@coastalnet.com.

Address correspondence to the executive director.

World Wide Web http://www.vla.org.

Washington

Memb. 1,200. Term of Office. Apr. 2007–Apr. 2009. Publication. *ALKI* (3 a year). *Ed.* Margaret Thomas, Box 43165, Olympia WA 98504. Tel. 360-481-1250, e-mail alkieditor@wla.org.

Pres. Martha Parsons, WSU Energy Program Lib., 925 Plum St. S.E., Olympia 98501. Tel. 360-956-2159, fax 360-236-2159, e-mail parsonsm@energy.wsu.edu; *V.P./Pres.-Elect* Tim Mallory, Timberland Regional Lib., 415 Tumwater Blvd. S.W., Tumwater 98501. Tel. 360-704-4502, fax 360-586-6838, e-mail tmallory@trlib.org; *Secy.* Nancy Slote, Capitol Hill Lib., 425 Harvard Ave. E., Seattle 98102. Tel. 206-684-4715, fax 206-733-9538, e-mail nancy.slote@spl.org; *Treas.* Priscilla Ice, Spokane Valley Lib., 12004 E. Main, Spokane 99206. Tel. 509-893-8451, fax 509-893-8478, e-mail pice@scld.org; *Past Pres.* Carolynne Myall, John F. Kennedy Lib., Eastern Washington Univ., 816 F St., Cheney 99004. Tel. 509-359-6967, fax 509-359-2476, e-mail cmyall

@ewu.edu; *Assn. Coord.* Gail E. Willis, 4016 First Ave. N.E., Seattle 98105-6502. Tel. 206-545-1529, fax 206-545-1543, e-mail washla@wla.org.

Address correspondence to the association coordinator.

World Wide Web http://www.wla.org.

West Virginia

Memb. 650+. Term of Office. Dec. 2007–Nov. 2008. Publication. *West Virginia Libraries* (6 a year). *Ed.* Pam Coyle, Martinsburg Public Lib., 101 W. King St., Martinsburg 25401 Tel. 304-267-8933, e-mail pcoyle@martin.lib.wv.us.

Pres. Barbara LaGodna, Evansdale Lib., WVU, P.O. Box 6105, Morgantown 26505. Tel. 304-293-9748, e-mail blagodna@wvu.edu; *1st V.P./Pres.-Elect* Brian Raitz, Parkersburg and Wood County Public Lib., 3100 Emerson Ave., Parkersburg 26104-2414. Tel. 304-420-4587 ext. 11, e-mail raitzb@parklib.wv.us; *2nd V.P.* Sarah Cranstoun, Summersville Public Lib., 6201 Webster Rd., Summersville 26651. Tel. 304-872-0844, e-mail sarach@mail.mln.lib.wv.us; *Secy.* Martha Yancey, Evansdale Lib., WVU, P.O. Box 6105, Morgantown 26506-6105. Tel. 304-293-5039, e-mail myancey@wvu.edu; *Treas.* Beth Royall, Evansdale Lib., WVU, P.O. Box 6105, Morgantown 26506-6105. Tel. 304-293-9755, e-mail beth.royall@mail.wvu.edu; *Past Pres.* Ann Farr, Greenbrier County Public Lib., 301 Courtney Drive, Lewisburg 24901. Tel. 304-647-7568, e-mail farrann@mail.mln.lib.wv.us.

Address correspondence to the president.

World Wide Web http://www.wvla.org.

Wisconsin

Memb. 1,800. Term of Office. Jan.–Dec. Publication. *WLA Newsletter* (q.).

Pres. Pat Chevis, Stoughton Public Lib., 304 S. 4 St., Stoughton 53589. E-mail pchevis@scls.lib.wi.us; *Pres.-Elect* Walter Burkhalter, Mid-Wisconsin Federated Lib. System, 112 Clinton St., Horicon 53032. E-mail wburkh@mwfls.org; *Secy.* Tasha Saecker, Elisha D. Smith Public Lib., 440 First St., Menasha 54952-3191. E-mail saecker@menashalibrary.org; *Treas.* Jan Berg, DeForest Public Lib., 203 Library St., DeForest 53532. E-mail bergjd@scls.lib.wi.us; *Past Pres.* Becca Berger, Door County Lib., 107 S. 4 Ave., Sturgeon Bay 54235. E-mail rberger@mail.nfls.lib.wi.us; *Exec. Dir.* Lisa K. Strand, Wisconsin Lib. Assn., 5250 E. Terrace Drive, Ste. A1, Madison 53718-8345. Tel. 608-245-3640, fax 608-245-3646, e-mail strand@scls.lib.wi.us., e-mail strand@scls.lib.wi.us.

Address correspondence to the association. World Wide Web http://www.wla.lib.wi.us.

Wyoming

Memb. 450+. Term of Office. Oct. 2007–Oct. 2008.

Pres. Brian Greene, Wyoming State Lib. Tel. 307-777-6339, fax 307-777-6289, e-mail bgreen@state.wy.us; *V.P./Pres.-Elect* Cynthia Twing, Johnson County Public Lib. Tel. 307-684-5546, fax 307-684-7888, e-mail ctwing@will.state.wy.us; *Recording Secy.* Meg Martin, Wyoming State Law Lib. Tel. 307-777-8564, e-mail mmartin@courts.state. wy.us; *Past Pres.* Ara Anderson, Campbell County Public Lib. System. Tel. 307-687-9210, fax 307-686-4009, e-mail aanderson@will.state.wy.us; *Exec. Secy.* Laura Grott, Box 1387, Cheyenne 82003. Tel. 307-632-7622, fax 307-638-3469, e-mail grottski@aol.com.

Address correspondence to the executive secretary. World Wide Web http://www.wyla.org.

Canada

Alberta

Memb. 500. Term of Office. May 2007–Apr. 2008. Publication. *Letter of the LAA* (4 a year).

Pres. Della Paradis, Northern Alberta Institute of Technology, TR170, 11762 106 St., Edmonton T5G 2R1. E-mail dellap@nait.ca; *V.P.* Karla Palichuk, Alberta Lib. 6-14, 7 Sir Winston Churchill Sq., Edmonton T5J 2V5. E-mail kpalichuk@thealberta library.ab.ca; *2nd V.P.* Marianne Graff, Yellowhead Regional Lib., Box 400, 433 King St., Spruce Grove T7X 2Y1. E-mail mgraff@

yrl.ab.ca; *Treas.* Melanie Johnson, 3523-114A St., Edmonton T6J 1N2. E-mail siljohn @telusplanet.net; *Past Pres.* Anne Carr-Wiggin, NEOS Lib. Consortium, Ring House No. 1, Univ. of Alberta, Edmonton T6G 2E1. E-mail anne.carr-wiggin@ualberta.ca; *Exec. Dir.* Christine Sheppard, 80 Baker Crescent N.W., Calgary T2L 1R4. Tel. 403-284-5818, fax 403-282-6646, e-mail christine.sheppard @shaw.ca.

Address correspondence to the executive director. World Wide Web http://www.laa.ca.

British Columbia

Memb. 820. Term of Office. April 2007–April 2008. Publication. *BCLA Reporter.* Ed. Ted Benson.

Pres. Deborah Thomas, Burnaby Public Lib., 7252 Kingsway, Burnaby V5E 1G3. E-mail deborah.thomas@bpl.bc.ca; *V.P./Pres.-Elect* Lynne Jordon, Greater Victoria Public Lib., 735 Broughton St., Victoria V8W 3H2. E-mail ljordon@gvpl.ca; *Treas.* Katy Nelson, McPherson Lib., Univ. of Victoria, P.O. Box 1800, STN CSC., Victoria V8W 3H5. E-mail katnel@uvic.ca; *Past Pres.* Inba Kehoe, McPherson Lib., Univ. of Victoria, P.O. Box 1800, STN CSC., Victoria V8W 3H5. E-mail ikehoe@uvic.ca; *Exec. Dir.* Michael Burris.

Address correspondence to the association, 900 Howe St., Ste. 150, Vancouver V6Z 2M4. Tel. 604-683-5354, fax 604-609-0707, e-mail office@bcla.bc.ca. World Wide Web http://www.bcla.bc.ca.

Manitoba

Memb. 500+. Term of Office. May 2007–May 2008. Publication. *Newsline* (mo.).

Pres. H. Rainer Schira, John E. Robbins Lib., Brandon Univ., 270 18th St., Brandon R7A 6A9. Tel. 204-727-7463, fax 204-726-1072, e-mail schirar@brandonu.ca; *V.P.* Carolyn Minor, Millennium Lib., 251 Donald St., Winnipeg R3C 3P5. Tel. 204-986-4206, e-mail northwest@hotmail.com; *Secy.* Lori Giles-Smith, Neil John Maclean Health Sciences Lib., 770 Bannatyne Ave., Winnipeg R3E 0W3. Tel. 204-789-3344, fax 204-789-3922, e-mail lori_giles-smith@umanitoba.ca; *Treas.* Bonita ("Bunny") Cobb, Manitoba

Lib. Assn., 606-100 Arthur St., Winnipeg R3B 1H3. Tel. 204-943-4567, fax 204-942-155, e-mail gbcobb@shaw.ca; *Past Pres.* Betty Braaksma, Elizabeth Dafoe Lib., Univ. of Manitoba, Winnipeg R3T 2N2. Tel. 204-474-7193, fax 204-474-7597, e-mail braaksma @cc.umanitoba.ca.

Address correspondence to the association, 606-100 Arthur St., Winnipeg R3B 1H3. Tel. 204-943-4567, fax 204-942-1555, e-mail manitobalibrary@gmail.com.

World Wide Web http://www.mla.mb.ca.

Ontario

Memb. 5,200+. Term of Office. Jan. 2008–Jan. 2009. Publications. *Access* (q.); *Teaching Librarian* (3 a year).

Pres. Sam Coghlan. E-mail scoghlan@ city.stratford.on.ca; *V.P./Pres.-Elect* Peggy Thomas. E-mail peggy.thomas@tel.tdsb.on. ca; *Treas.* Sonia Lewis. E-mail sonia.lewis@ kpl.org; *Past Pres.* Esther Rosenfeld. E-mail esther.rosenfeld@sympatico.ca; *Exec. Dir.* Shelagh Paterson. E-mail spaterson@ accessola.com.

Address correspondence to the association, 50 Wellington St. E., Ste. 201, Toronto M5E 1C8. Tel. 416-363-3388, fax 416-941-9581, e-mail info@accessola.com.

World Wide Web http://www.accessola. com.

Quebec

Memb. (Indiv.) 109; (Inst.) 17; (Commercial) 2. Term of Office. May 2007–April 2008. Publication. *ABQLA Bulletin* (3 a year).

Pres. Janine West. E-mail jwwest@cote-saint-luc.qc.ca; *V.P.* Lisa Milner; *Exec. Secy./Secy./Treas.* Janet Ilavsky, Box 1095, Pointe-Claire H9S 4H9. Tel. 514-697-0146, e-mail abqla@abqla.qc.ca; *Past Pres.* Mary Jane O'Neill. E-mail oneillmj@ville.pointe-claire.qc.ca.

Address correspondence to the executive secretary.

World Wide Web http://www.abqla.qc.ca.

Saskatchewan

Memb. 225. Term of Office. May 2007–May 2008. Publication. *Forum* (4 a year).

Pres. Amy Rankin, RCMP Resource Centre, P.O. Box 6500, Regina S4P 3J7. Tel. 306-780-5824, fax 306-780-7599, e-mail arankin-library@hotmail.com; *V.P.* Erin O. Romanyshyn, Saskatoon Public Lib., 311 23rd St. E., Saskatoon S7K 0J6. Tel. 306-975-7608, fax 306-975-7521, e-mail e. romanyshyn@saskatoonlibrary.ca; *Treas.* Chris Pepin, Bureau of Statistics, Saskatchewan Finance, 9th fl., 2350 Albert St., Regina. Tel. 306-787-6335, fax 306-787-6311, e-mail cpepin@finance.gov.sk.ca; *Past Pres.* Carol Shepstone, Univ. of Saskatchewan Lib., 145 Murray Bldg., 3 Campus Drive, Saskatoon S7N 5A4. Tel. 306-966-5960, fax 306-966-6040, e-mail carol. shepstone@usask.ca; *Exec. Dir.* Judith Silverthorne, 2010 Seventh Ave., No. 15, Regina S4R 1C2. Tel. 306-780-9413, fax 306-780-9447, e-mail slaexdir@sasktel.net.

Address correspondence to the executive director.

World Wide Web http://www.lib.sk.ca/sla.

Regional

Atlantic Provinces: N.B., N.L., N.S., P.E.

Memb. (Indiv.) 200+; (Inst.) 26. Term of Office. May 2006–May 2007. Publications. *APLA Bulletin* (bi-mo.), *Membership Directory* (ann.).

Pres. Ivan Douthwright, George A. Rawlyk Lib., Atlantic Baptist Univ., P.O. Box 6004, Moncton, NB E1C 9L7. Tel. 506-863-6443, fax 506-858-9694, e-mail ivan. douthwright@abu.nb.ca; *V.P./Pres.-Elect* Donna Bourne-Tyson, Mount Saint Vincent Univ., 166 Bedford Hwy., Halifax, NS B3M 2J6. Tel. 902-457-6108, fax 902-457-6445, e-mail donna.bourne-tyson@msvu.ca; *Secy.* Collette Saunders, Patrick Power Lib., Saint Mary's Univ., Halifax, NS B3H 3C3. Tel. 902-491-6287, fax 902-420-5561, e-mail collette.saunders@smu.ca; *Treas.* Ewa Piorko, CBC Radio Halifax Music Lib., 5600 Sackville St., Halifax, NS B3J 1L2. Tel. 902-420-4404, fax 902-420-4192, e-mail apla_ executive@yahoo.ca; *Past Pres.* Jennifer Richard, Vaughan Memorial Lib., Acadia Univ., Wolfville, NS B4P 2R6. Tel. 902-585-

1403, fax 902-585-1748, e-mail jennifer. richard@acadiau.ca.

Address correspondence to Atlantic Provinces Lib. Assn., c/o School of Info. Mgt., Faculty of Mgt., Kenneth C. Rowe Mgt. Bldg., 6100 University Ave., Halifax, NS B3H 3J5.

World Wide Web http://www.apla.ca.

Mountain Plains: Ariz., Colo., Kan., Mont., Neb., Nev., N.Dak., N.M., Okla., S.Dak., Utah, Wyo.

Memb. 820. Term of Office. May 2006–May 2008. Publications. *MPLA Newsletter* (bimo.), *Ed./Advertising Mgr.* Judy Zelenski, 14293 W. Center Drive, Lakewood, CO 80228. Tel. 303-985-7795, e-mail mpla_execsecretary@operamail.com.

Pres. Wayne Hanway, Southeastern Public Lib. System, 401 N. 2 St., McAlester, OK 74501. Tel. 918-426-0456, fax 918-423-0550, e-mail whanway@sepl.lib.ok.us; *V.P./Pres.-Elect* Robert Banks, Topeka and Shawnee County Public Lib., 1515 S.W. 10 Ave., Topeka, KS 66604. Tel. 785-580-4481, fax 785-580-4496, e-mail rbanks@mail.tscpl.org; *Recording Secy.* David Alexander, I. D. Weeks Lib., Univ. of South Dakota, 414 E. Clark St., Vermillion, SD 57007. Tel. 605-677-6078, fax 605-677-5488, e-mail david. alexander@usd.edu; *Past Pres.* Sharon Osenga, Meridian Lib. System, 3519 Second Ave., Kearney, NE 68847. Tel. 308-234-2087, fax 308-234-4040, e-mail sosenga@frontiernet. net; *Exec. Secy.* Judy Zelenski, 14293 W. Center Drive, Lakewood, CO 80228. Tel. 303-985-7795, e-mail mpla_execsecretary@operamail.com.

Address correspondence to the executive secretary, Mountain Plains Lib. Assn.

World Wide Web http://www.mpla.us.

New England: Conn., Maine, Mass., N.H., R.I., Vt.

Memb. (Indiv.) 1,300; (Inst.) 100. Term of Office. Nov. 2007–Oct. 2008. Publication. *New England Libraries* (bi-mo.). *Ed.* David Bryan, 157 S. Orleans Rd., Orleans, MA 02653. Tel. 508-240-2357, e-mail publications manager@nelib.org.

Pres. Kristin M. Jacobi, J. Eugene Smith Lib., Eastern Connecticut State Univ., 83 Windham St., Willimantic, CT 06226. Tel. 860-465-4508, fax 860-465-5523, e-mail president@nelib.org; *V.P./Pres.-Elect* Mary Ann Tricarico, New England Institute of Art, Brookline, Massachusetts. E-mail vice president@nelib.org; *Secy.* Marija Sanderling, Lane Memorial Lib., 2 Academy Ave., Hampton, NH 03842. Tel. 603-926-3368, fax 603-926-1348, e-mail secretary@nelib.org; *Treas.* Kerry Cronin, Rye Public Lib., 581 Washington Rd., Rye, NH 03870. Tel. 603-964-8401, fax 603-964-7065, e-mail treasurer @nelib.org; *Past Pres.* Susan Raskin Abrams, Newton Free Lib., 330 Homer St., Newton Center, MA 02459-1429. Tel. 617-796-1370, fax 617-964-9549, e-mail pastpresident@nelib.org; *Exec. Secy.* Peter Blaisdell, New England Lib. Assn., P.O. Box 709, Marblehead, MA 01945. Tel. 781-631-1578, fax 781-631-1579, e-mail executivesecretary@nelib.org.

Address correspondence to the executive secretary.

World Wide Web http://www.nelib.org.

Pacific Northwest: Alaska, Idaho, Mont., Ore., Wash., Alberta, B.C.

Memb. (Active) 550; (Subscribers) 100. Term of Office. Aug. 2007–Aug. 2008. Publication. *PNLA Quarterly. Ed.* Mary Bolin, 319A Love Lib., Univ. of Nebraska, P.O. Box 881140, Lincoln, NE 68588-4100. Tel. 402-472-4281, e-mail mbolin2@unl.edu.

Pres. Kathy Waston, Marshall Public Lib., 113 S. Garfield, Pocatello, ID 83204. Tel. 208-232-1263 ext. 30, fax 208-232-9266, e-mail kwatson@marshallpl.org; *V.P.* Susannah Price, BPL, 715 Capitol Blvd., Boise, ID 83702-7195. Tel. 208-384-4026, e-mail sprice@cityofboise.org; *Secy.* Brent Roberts, Montana State Univ.–Billings. E-mail broberts @msubillings.edu; *Treas.* Katie Cargill, Eastern Washington Univ. Libs., 816 F St., Cheney, WA 99004. Tel. 509-359-2385, fax 509-359-2476, e-mail kcargill@mail.ewu. edu; *Past Pres.* Jason Openo, Salem Public Lib., P.O. Box 14810, 585 Liberty St. S.E., Salem, OR 97309. Tel. 503-588-6183, fax 503-588-6055, e-mail jopeno@cityofsalem. net.

Address correspondence to the president, Pacific Northwest Lib. Assn.

World Wide Web http://www.pnla.org.

Southeastern: Ala., Ark., Fla., Ga., Ky., La., Miss., N.C., S.C., Tenn., Va., W.Va.

Memb. 500. Term of Office. Nov.–Oct. Publication. *The Southeastern Librarian* (q.). *Ed.* Perry Bratcher, 503A Steely Lib., Northern Kentucky Univ., Highland Heights, KY 41099. Tel. 859-572-6309, fax 859-572-6181, e-mail bratcher@nku.edu.

Pres. Faith A. Line, Sumter County Lib., 111 N. Harvin St., Sumter, SC 29150. Tel. 803-773-7273, e-mail linef@infoave.net; *1st V.P./Pres.-Elect* Kathleen R. T. Imhoff, Lexington (Kentucky) Public Lib. Tel. 859-231-5599, e-mail kimhoff@lexpublib.org; *Secy.* Gordon N. Baker, Clayton State Univ. Tel. 678-466-4325, e-mail gordonbaker@clayton.edu; *Treas.* William N. Nelson, Augusta State Univ. Lib. Tel. 706-737-1745, fax 706-667-4415, e-mail wnelson@aug.edu; *Past Pres.* Judith A. Gibbons, Kentucky Dept. for Libs. and Archives. Tel. 502-564-8300, fax 502-564-5773, e-mail judith.gibbons@ky.gov.

Address correspondence to Southeastern Lib. Assn., P.O. Box 950, Rex, GA 30273-0950. Tel. 678-466-4325, fax 770-961-3712, e-mail bob.fox@library.gatech.edu.

World Wide Web http://sela.jsu.edu.

State and Provincial Library Agencies

The state library administrative agency in each of the U.S. states will have the latest information on its state plan for the use of federal funds under the Library Services and Technology Act (LSTA). The directors and addresses of these state agencies are listed below.

Alabama

Rebecca Mitchell, Dir., Alabama Public Lib. Service, 6030 Monticello Dr., Montgomery 36130. Tel. 334-213-3902, fax 334-213-3993, e-mail rmitchell@apls.state.al.us.

Alaska

Kathryn H. Shelton, Dir., Alaska Dept. of Educ., Div. of Libs., Archives, and Museums, Box 110571, Juneau 99811-0571. Tel. 907-465-2911, fax 907-465-2151, e-mail kay_shelton@eed.state.ak.us.

Arizona

GladysAnn Wells, State Libn., Arizona State Lib., Archives and Public Records, Ste. 200, 1700 W. Washington, Phoenix 85007-2896. Tel. 602-926-4035, fax 602-542-4972, e-mail gawells@lib.az.us.

Arkansas

Carolyn Ashcraft, State Libn., Arkansas State Lib., 1 Capitol Mall, 5th fl., Little Rock 72201-1081. Tel. 501-682-1526, fax 501-682-1899, e-mail cashcraf@asl.lib.ar.us.

California

Susan Hildreth, State Libn., California State Lib., P.O. Box 942837, Sacramento 94237-0001. Tel. 916-654-0174, fax 916-654-0064, e-mail shildreth@library.ca.gov.

Colorado

Eugene Hainer, State Libn., Colorado State Lib., Rm. 309, 201 E. Colfax Ave., Denver 80203. Tel. 303-866-6733, fax 303-866-6940, e-mail hainer_g@cde.state.co.us.

Connecticut

Kendall F. Wiggin, State Libn., Connecticut State Lib., 231 Capitol Ave., Hartford 06106. Tel. 860-757-6510, fax 860-757-6503, e-mail kwiggin@cslib.org.

Delaware

Anne Norman, Dir. and State Libn., Div. of Libs., 43 S. DuPont Hwy., Dover 19901. Tel. 302-739-4748 ext. 126, fax 302-739-6787, e-mail annie.norman@state.de.us.

District of Columbia

Ginnie Cooper, Chief Libn., District of Columbia Public Lib., 901 G St. N.W., Washington 20001. Tel. 202-727-1101, fax 202-727-1129, e-mail ginnie.cooper@dc.gov.

Florida

Judith Ring, State Libn., Div. of Lib. and Info., R. A. Gray Bldg., 500 S. Bronough St., Tallahassee 32399-0250. Tel. 850-245-6604, fax 850-488-2746, e-mail jring@dos.state.fl.us.

Georgia

Lamar Veatch, State Libn., Georgia Public Lib. Service, 1800 Century Place, Ste. 150, Atlanta 30345-4304. Tel. 404-235-7200, fax 404-235-7201, e-mail lveatch@state.lib.ga.us.

Hawaii

Jo Ann Schindler, State Libn., Hawaii State Public Lib. System, 44 Merchant St., Honolulu 96813. Tel. 808-586-3704, fax 808-586-3715, e-mail joann@librarieshawaii.org.

Idaho

Ann Joslin, State Libn., Idaho Commission for Libs., 325 W. State St., Boise 83713. Tel. 208-334-2150, fax 208-334-4016, e-mail ann.joslin@libraries.idaho.gov.

Illinois

Anne Craig, Dir., Illinois State Lib., Gwendolyn Brooks Bldg., 300 S. 2 St., Springfield 62701-1796. Tel. 217-524-4200, fax 217-785-6062, e-mail acraig@ilsos.net.

Indiana

Roberta L. Brooker, Dir., Indiana State Lib., 140 N. Senate Ave., Indianapolis 46204. Tel. 317-232-3692, fax 317-232-0002, e-mail rbrooker@statelib.lib.in.us.

Iowa

Mary Wegner, State Libn., State Lib. of Iowa, 1112 E. Grand Ave., Des Moines 50319. Tel. 515-281-4105, fax 515-281-6191, e-mail mary.wegner@lib.state.ia.us.

Kansas

Christie Pearson Brandau, State Libn., Kansas State Lib., 300 S.W. 10 Ave., Topeka 66612-1593. Tel. 785-296-3296, fax 785-296-6650, e-mail christieb@kslib.info.

Kentucky

Wayne Onkst, State Libn./Commissioner, Kentucky Dept. for Libs. and Archives, 300 Coffee Tree Rd., Frankfort 40602-0537. Tel. 502-564-8300 ext. 312, fax 502-564-5773, e-mail wayne.onkst@ky.gov.

Louisiana

Rebecca Hamilton, State Libn., State Lib. of Louisiana, 701 N. 4 Ave., P.O. Box 131, Baton Rouge 70821-0131. Tel. 225-342-4923, fax 225-219-4804, e-mail rhamilton@crt.state.la.us.

Maine

J. Gary Nichols, State Libn., Maine State Lib., 64 State House Sta., Augusta 04333-0064. Tel. 207-287-5600, fax 207-287-5615, e-mail gary.nichols@maine.gov.

Maryland

Irene Padilla, Asst. State Superintendent for Libs., Maryland State Dept. of Educ., 200 W. Baltimore St., Baltimore 21201. Tel. 410-767-0435, fax 410-333-2507, e-mail ipadilla@msde.state.md.us.

Massachusetts

Robert C. Maier, Dir., Massachusetts Board of Lib. Commissioners, 648 Beacon St., Boston 02215. Tel. 617-725-1860 ext. 249, fax 617-421-9833, e-mail robert.maier@state.ma.us.

Michigan

Nancy Robertson, State Libn., Lib. of Michigan, 702 W. Kalamazoo, P.O. Box 30007, Lansing 48909-7507. Tel. 517-373-5504, fax 517-373-4480, e-mail nrobertson@michigan.gov.

Minnesota

Suzanne Miller, State Libn., Lib Development and Services, Minnesota Dept. of Educ., 1500 Hwy. 36 W., Roseville 55113-4266. Tel. 651-582-8722, fax 651-582-8897, e-mail suzanne.miller@state.mn.us.

Mississippi

Sharman Bridges Smith, Exec. Dir., Mississippi Lib. Commission, 3881 Eastwood Dr., Jackson 39211. Tel. 601-432-4039, fax 601-432-4480, e-mail sharman@mlc.lib.ms.us.

Missouri

Margaret Conroy, Dir., Missouri State Lib., 600 W. Main, P.O. Box 387, Jefferson City 65102-0387. Tel. 573-751-2751, fax 573-751-3612, e-mail margaret.conroy@sos.mo.gov.

Montana

Darlene Staffeldt, State Libn., Montana State Lib., 1515 E. 6 Ave., P.O. Box 201800, Helena 59620-1800. Tel. 406-444-3115, fax 406-444-0266, e-mail dstaffeldt@mt.us.

Nebraska

Rodney G. Wagner, Dir., Nebraska Lib. Commission, Ste. 120, 1200 N St., Lincoln 68508-2023. Tel. 402-471-2045, fax 402-471-2083, e-mail rwagner@nlc.state.ne.us.

Nevada

Daphne DeLeon, Admin., Nevada State Lib. and Archives, 100 N. Stewart St., Carson City 89710-4285. Tel. 775-684-3315, fax 775-684-3311, e-mail dodeleon@clan.lib.nv.us.

New Hampshire

Michael York, State Libn., New Hampshire State Lib., 20 Park St., Concord 03301. Tel. 603-271-2392, fax 603-271-6826, e-mail myork@library.state.nh.us.

New Jersey

Norma E. Blake, State Libn., New Jersey State Lib., P.O. Box 520, Trenton 08625-0520. Tel. 609-278-2640, fax 609-292-2746, e-mail nblake@njstatelib.org.

New Mexico

Susan Oberlander, State Libn., New Mexico State Lib., 1209 Camino Carlos Rey, Santa Fe 87505-6980. Tel. 505-476-9762, fax 505-476-9761, e-mail oberlanders@stlib.state.nm.us.

New York

Janet M. Welch, State Libn./Asst. Commissioner for Libs., New York State Lib., 10C34 Cultural Educ. Center, Albany 12230. Tel. 518-474-5930, fax 518-486-6880, e-mail jwelch2@mail.nysed.gov.

North Carolina

Mary L. Boone, State Libn., State Lib. of North Carolina, 4640 Mail Service Center, 109 E. Jones St., Raleigh 27699-4640. Tel. 919-807-7410, fax 919-733-8748, e-mail mary.boone@ncmail.net.

North Dakota

Doris Ott, State Libn., North Dakota State Lib., Dept. 250, 604 E. Boulevard Ave., Bismarck 58505-0800. Tel. 701-328-2492, fax 701-328-2040, e-mail dott@nd.us.

Ohio

Jo Budler, State Libn., State Lib. of Ohio, 274 E. 1 Ave., Columbus 43201. Tel. 614-644-7061, fax 614-466-3584, e-mail jbudler@sloma.state.ohio.us.

Oklahoma

Susan McVey, Dir., Oklahoma Dept. of Libs., 200 N.E. 18 St., Oklahoma City 73105. Tel. 405-522-3173, fax 405-525-7804, e-mail smcvey@oltn.odl.state.ok.us.

Oregon

Jim Scheppke, State Libn., Oregon State Lib., 250 Winter St. N.E., Salem 97310-0640. Tel. 503-378-4367, fax 503-585-8059, e-mail jim.b.scheppke@state.or.us.

Pennsylvania

Mary Clare Zales, Deputy Secy. of Educ./ Commissioner of Libs., Office of Commonwealth Libs., 333 Market St., Harrisburg 17105. Tel. 717-787-2646, fax 717-772-3265, e-mail mzales@state.pa.us.

Rhode Island

Howard Boksenbaum, Chief of Lib. Services, Office of Lib. and Info. Services, 1 Capitol Hill, Providence 02908-5803. Tel. 401-222-3153, fax 401-222-4195, e-mail howardbm@olis.ri.gov.

South Carolina

David S. Goble, State Libn., South Carolina State Lib., P.O. Box 11469, Columbia 29211. Tel. 803-734-8656, fax 803-734-8676, e-mail dgoble@statelibrary.sc.gov.

South Dakota

Dorothy M. Liegl, State Libn., South Dakota State Lib., 800 Governors Dr., Pierre 57501-

2294. Tel. 605-773-3131, fax 605-773-6962, e-mail dorothy.liegl@state.sd.us.

Tennessee

Jeanne D. Sugg, State Libn./Archivist, Tennessee State Lib. and Archives, 403 Seventh Ave. N., Nashville 37243-0312. Tel. 615-741-7996, fax 615-532-9293, e-mail jeanne.sugg@state.tn.us.

Texas

Peggy D. Rudd, Dir./Libn., Texas State Lib. and Archives Commission, P.O. Box 12927, Austin 78711-2927. Tel. 512-463-5460, fax 512-463-5436, e-mail peggy.rudd@tsl.state.tx.us.

Utah

Donna Jones Morris, State Libn./Dir., Utah State Lib. Div., 250 N. 1950 W., Salt Lake City 84115-7901. Tel. 801-715-6770, fax 801-715-6767, e-mail dmorris@utah.gov.

Vermont

Sybil Brigham McShane, State Libn., Vermont Dept. of Libs., 109 State St., Montpelier 05609-0601. Tel. 802-828-3265, fax 802-828-2199, e-mail sybil.mcshane@dol.state.vt.us.

Virginia

Sandra G. Treadway, Libn. of Virginia, Lib. of Virginia, 800 E. Broad St., Richmond 23219. Tel. 804-692-3535, fax 804-692-3594, e-mail sandra.treadway@lva.virginia.gov.

Washington

Jan Walsh, State Libn., Washington State Lib., P.O. Box 42460, Olympia 98504-2460. Tel. 360-704-5253, fax 360-586-7575, e-mail jwalsh@secstate.wa.gov.

West Virginia

James D. Waggoner, Secy., West Virginia Lib. Commission, 1900 Kanawha Blvd. E., Charleston 25305-0620. Tel. 304-558-2041,

fax 304-558-2044, e-mail waggoner@wvlc.lib.wv.us.

Wisconsin

Richard Grobschmidt, State Libn., Asst. Superintendent, Div. for Libs. and Community Learning, Dept. of Public Instruction, P.O. Box 7841, Madison 53707-7841. Tel. 608-266-2205, fax 608-267-1052, e-mail richard.grobschmidt@dpi.state.wi.us.

Wyoming

Lesley Boughton, State Libn., Wyoming State Lib., 516 S. Greeley Hwy., Cheyenne 82002. Tel. 307-777-5911, fax 307-777-6289, e-mail lbough@state.wy.us.

American Samoa

Cheryl Morales, Territorial Libn., Feleti Barstow Public Lib., P.O. Box 997687, Pago Pago, AS 96799. Tel. 684-633-5816, fax 684-633-5823, e-mail feletibarstow@yahoo.com.

Federated States of Micronesia

Nena S. Nena, Secy., Dept. of Health, Educ., and Social Affairs, FSM Div. of Educ., P.O. Box PS 70, Pallikir, Pohnpei, FM 96941. Tel. 691-320-2643, fax 691-320-5263, e-mail nsnena@mail.fm.

Guam

Shirley Souza, Acting Dir./Territorial Libn., Guam Public Lib. System, 254 Martyr St., Hagatna 96910. Tel. 671-475-4753, fax 671-477-9777.

Northern Mariana Islands

Erlinda Naputi, Acting State Libn., Joeten-Kiyu Public Lib., Box 501092, Saipan, MP 96950. Tel. 670-235-7324, fax 670-235-7550, e-mail naputi@saipan.com.

Palau

Mario Katosang, Minister of Educ., Republic of Palau, Box 7080, Koror, PW 96940. Tel.

680-488-1464, fax 680-488-1465, e-mail mariok@palaumoe.net.

Puerto Rico

Aura M. Rodriguez Ramos, Dir., Lib. Services and Info. Program, P.O. Box 190759, San Juan, PR 00919-0759. Tel. 787-754-1120, fax 787-754-0843, e-mail rodriguezram@de.gobierno.pr.

Republic of the Marshall Islands

Amram Mejbon, Acting Secy., Internal Affairs, Alele Inc., P.O. Box 629, Majuro, MH 96960. Tel. 692-625-8240, fax 692-625-3226, e-mail alele@ntamar.net.

Virgin Islands

Robert S. Mathes, Commissioner, Dept. of Planning and Natural Resources, Div. of Libs, Archives, and Museums, Terminal Bldg., Cyril E. King Airport., St. Thomas, VI 00802. Tel. 340-774-3320, fax 340-775-5706.

Canada

Alberta

Bonnie Gray, Mgr., Public Lib. Services, Alberta Municipal Affairs and Housing, 803 Standard Life Centre, 10405 Jasper Ave., Edmonton T5J 4R7. Tel. 780-415-0295, fax 780-415-8594, e-mail bonnie.gray@gov.ab.ca.

British Columbia

Maureen Woods, Dir., Public Lib. Services Branch, Ministry of Community, Aboriginal and Women's Services, 800 Johnson St., Victoria BC V8W 1N3. Tel. 250-356-1791, fax 250-953-3225, e-mail maureen.woods@gems8.gov.bc.ca.

Manitoba

Sylvia Nicholson, Dir., Public Lib. Services, Manitoba Dept. of Culture, Heritage and Tourism, Unit 200, 1525 First St. S., Brandon

R7A 7A1. Tel. 204-726-6590, e-mail pls@gov.mb.ca.

New Brunswick

Sylvie Nadeau, Exec. Dir., New Brunswick Public Lib. Service, 250 King St., Place 2000, P.O. Box 6000, Fredericton E3B 5H1. Tel. 506-453-2354, fax 506-444-4064, e-mail Sylvie.Nadeau@gnb.ca. World Wide Web http://www.gnb.ca/publiclibraries.

Newfoundland and Labrador

David Norman, Exec. Dir., Provincial Info. Resources and Lib. Board, 48 St. George's Ave., Stephenville A2N 1K9. Tel. 709-737-3964, fax 709-643-0925, e-mail dnorman@publib.nf.ca, World Wide Web http://www.nlpubliclibraries.ca.

Northwest Territories

Alison Hopkins, Territorial Libn., NWT Lib. Services, 75 Woodland Dr., Hay River X0E 1G1. Tel. 867-874-6531, fax 867-874-3321, e-mail Alison_Hopkins@gov.nt.ca. World Wide Web http://www.nwtpls.gov.nt.ca.

Nova Scotia

Jennifer Evans, Dir., Nova Scotia Provincial Lib., Ste. 2015, 100 Main St., Dartmouth B2X 1R5. Tel. 902-424-2455, fax 902-424-0633, e-mail evansjl@gov.ns.ca.

Nunavut

Ron Knowling, Mgr., Lib. Policy, Baker Lake Headquarters, Nunavut Public Lib. Services, Box 270, Baker Lake X0C 0A0. Tel. 867-793-3326, fax 867-793-3332, e-mail rknowling@gov.nu.ca.

Ontario

Suzanne Rowe-Knight, Mgr., Libraries, Programs and Services Branch, Ontario Government Ministry of Culture, 400 University Ave., 4th fl., Toronto M7A 2R9. Tel. 416-314-7342, fax 416-314-7635, e-mail suzanne.roweknight@ontario.ca.

Prince Edward Island

Allan Groen, Provincial Libn., Province of Prince Edward Island, P.O. Box 7500, Morell COA 1S0. Tel. 902-961-7320, fax 902-961-7322, e-mail ajgroen@gov.pe.ca.

Quebec

Serge Bernier, Dir., Direction des Arts, des Bibliothèques, et des Industries Culturelles, Bloc A, 3e étage, Quebec G1R 5G5. Tel. 418-691-3137, e-mail serge.bernier@stat. gouv.qc.ca.

Saskatchewan

Joylene Campbell, Provincial Libn., Saskatchewan Learning, 1945 Hamilton St., Regina S4P 2C8. Tel. 306-787-2972, fax 306-787-2029, e-mail jcampbell@library. gov.sk.ca.

Yukon Territory

Julie Ourom, Dir., Public Libs., Community Development Div., Dept. of Community Services, Box 2703, Whitehorse Y1A 2C6. Tel. 867-667-5447, fax 867-393-6333, e-mail julie.ourom@gov.yk.ca.

State School Library Media Associations

Alabama

Children's and School Libns. Div., Alabama Lib. Assn. Memb. 650. Publication. *The Alabama Librarian* (q.).

Chair Deidra Brewer, Highland Park/Webster Elementary, Muscle Shoals. E-mail dbrewer@mscs.k12.al.us; *V. Chair/Chair-Elect* Barbara Curry, Autauga-Prattville Public Lib., 254 Doster St., Prattville 36067. E-mail bcurry@appl.info; *Secy.* Dorothy Hunt, MacMillan International Academy, 25 Covington St., Montgomery 36104. E-mail jahunt62@knology.net; *Past Chair* Jessica E. Platt, Zelia Stephens Early Childhood Center, Alabama State Univ., 1100 Tuscaloosa St., Montgomery 36101. E-mail ernstwhile@yahoo.com; *Assn. Admin.* Carol Lee, Professional Services Group, 400 S. Union St., Ste. 140, Montgomery 36104. Tel. 334-263-1272, fax 334-265-1281, e-mail mdginc@bellsouth.net.

Address correspondence to the association administrator.

World Wide Web http://allanet.org.

Alaska

Alaska Assn. of School Libns. Memb. 200+. Term of Office. Mar. 2008–Mar. 2009. Publication. *Puffin* (3 a year). *Ed.* Laura Guest. E-mail laura.guest@matsuk12.us.

Pres. Lynn Ballam, North Pole Middle School. E-mail lballam@mac.com; *Pres.-Elect* Suzanne Metcalfe, Diamond H.S., Anchorage. E-mail metcalfe_suzanne@asdk12.org; *Secy.* Kari Sagel, Blatchley Middle School, Sitka. E-mail sagelk@mail.ssd.k12.ak.us; *Treas.* Janet Madsen, West Valley H.S., Fairbanks. E-mail jmadsen@northstar.k12.ak.us; *Past Pres.* Erika Drain. E-mail erikad@mehs.us.

World Wide Web http://www.akla.org/akasl.

Arizona

Teacher-Libn. Div., Arizona Lib. Assn. Memb. 1,000. Publication. *AZLA Newsletter.*

Chair Sally Roof, Madison Meadows Middle School. Tel. 602-664-7640, e-mail sroofhoff@cox.net; *Co-Chairs-Elect* Jean Kilker, 160 E. Estero Lane, Litchfield Park 85340. Tel. 602-764-2134 or 623-935-1464, e-mail jkilker@phxhs.k12.az.us or jlkilk@earthlink.net; Kerrita Westrick, Verrado Middle School, 553 Plaza Circle, Litchfield Park 85340. Tel. 623-547-1324 or 623-935-1911, e-mail kerrlita@cox.net or westrick@lesd.k12.az.us; *Past Chair* Linda Renfro, Blue Ridge Unified School Dist. Tel. 928-368-6119, e-mail lrenfro@brusd.k12.az.us.

Address correspondence to the chairperson.

World Wide Web http://www.azla.affiniscape.com.

Arkansas

Arkansas Assn. of Instructional Media. Term of Office. Apr. 2007–April 2008.

Pres. Devona Pendergrass. E-mail dpendergrass@mtnhome.k12.ar.us; *Pres.-Elect* Lori Bush. E-mail lori.bush@lh.k12.ar.us; *Secy.* Glenda Jenkins. E-mail gjenkins@indian.dsc.k12.ar.us; *Treas.* Lawanda Dale. E-mail dalelj@yahoo.com; *Past Pres.* Evelyn McFadden. E-mail emcfadden@sdale.org.

Address correspondence to the president.

World Wide Web http://aaim.k12.ar.us.

California

California School Lib. Assn. Memb. 2,200. Publication. *CSLA Journal* (2 a year); *CSLA Bulletin* (9 a year).

Pres. Sandra Yoon, Bakersfield City ESD, 1300 Baker St., Bakersfield 93305. Tel. 661-631-4808, e-mail yoons@bcsd.com; *Past Pres.* Martha Rowland, 5735 47th Ave., Sacramento 95824. Tel. 916-643-9091, e-mail martha-rowland@sac-city.k12.ca.us; *Exec. Dir.* Linda Jewett, 1001 26th St., Sacramento 95816. Tel. 916-447-2684, fax 916-447-2695, e-mail jewettl@pacbell.net.

Address correspondence to the executive director.

World Wide Web http://www.schoolibrary.org.

Colorado

Colorado Assn. of School Libns. Memb. 300+. Term of Office. Nov. 2007–Oct. 2009. *Pres.* Su Eckhardt, 10930 W. Powers Ave., Littleton 80127. Tel. 303-979-7799, fax 970-245-7854, e-mail sueckhardt@earthlink.net; *V.P./Pres.-Elect* Susan Gilbert, Clear Lake Middle School. Tel. 720-542-4606, e-mail gilbert.susan@comcast.net; *Past Pres.* Mary Katherine Katzer, Marmot Lib. Network, 123 N. 7 St., Ste. 302, Grand Junction 81501. Tel. 970-242-3331 ext. 13, fax 970-245-7854, e-mail mk@marmot.org; *Secy.* Nancy White, Academy School Dist. 20, 1110 Chapel Hill Drive, Colorado Springs 80904. Tel. 719-234-1362, e-mail nwhite@asd20.org; *Exec. Dir.* Kathleen Sagee Noland, Colorado Assn. of School Libns., 12081 W. Alameda Pkwy., No. 427, Lakewood 80228. Tel. 303-463-6400, fax 303-798-2485, e-mail kathleen@cal-webs.org or executivedirector@cal-webs.org.

World Wide Web http://www.cal-webs.org.

Connecticut

Connecticut Assn. of School Libns. (formerly Connecticut Educational Media Assn.). Memb. 550. Term of Office. July 2007–June 2008. Publication. *CEMA Gram* (mo.).

Pres. Janet Roche. E-mail rochefamily 1023@comcast.net; *V.P.* David Bilmes. E-mail bilmesd@new-milford.k12.ct.us; *Recording Secy.* Christopher Barlow. E-mail christophbarlow@sbcglobal.net; *Treas.* Sewell Pruchnik. E-mail spruchnik@snet.net; *Admin. Secy.* Anne Weimann, 25 Elmwood Ave., Trumbull 06611. Tel. 203-372-2260, E-mail anneweimann@gmail.com.

Address correspondence to the administrative secretary.

World Wide Web http://www.ctcema.org.

Delaware

Delaware School Lib. Media Assn., Div. of Delaware Lib. Assn. Memb. 100+. Term of Office. May 2007–May 2008. Publications. *DSLMA Newsletter* (online; irreg.); column

in *DLA Bulletin* (3 a year) (online at http://www.dla.lib.de.us/bulletin.shtml).

Pres. Jane Stewart, W. B. Simpson Elementary, 5 Old North Rd., Camden 19934. E-mail jane.stewart@cr.k12.de.us; *V.P./Pres.-Elect* Barb Fitzpatrick, Lulu M. Ross Elementary, 310 Lovers Lane, Milford 19963; *Secy.* Carole Carpenter, Milford H.S., 1019 N. Walnut St., Milford 19763. E-mail ccarpent@mail.milford.k12.de.us; *Past Pres.* Jamie Alascia, William Henry Middle School, 65 Carver Rd., Dover 19904. Tel. 302-672-1620, e-mail dslmapresident@yahoo.com.

Address correspondence to the president.

World Wide Web http://www.udel.edu/erc/dslma.

District of Columbia

District of Columbia Assn. of School Libns. Memb. 35. Publication. *Newsletter* (4 a year).

Pres. André Maria Taylor. E-mail diva librarian2@aol.com.

Address correspondence to Virginia Moore, 330 10th St. N.E., Washington DC 20002. Tel. 301-502-4203.

Florida

Florida Assn. for Media in Education. Memb. 1,450. Term of Office. Nov. 2007–Oct. 2008. Publication. *Florida Media Quarterly. Ed.* Pat Dedicos. E-mail dedicosp@education central.org.

Pres. Miriam Needham. E-mail miriam.needham@marion.k12.fl.us; *V.P.* Belinda Vose. E-mail belinda.vose@marion.k12.fl.us; *Pres.-Elect* Deb Svec. E-mail dsvec@bellsouth.net; *Secy.* Gail Przeclawski. E-mail przeclg@ocps.net; *Treas.* Sherie Bargar. E-mail bargars@osceola.k12.fl.us.

Address correspondence to FAME, 2563 Capital Medical Blvd., Tallahassee 32308. E-mail info@floridamedia.org.

World Wide Web http://www.florida media.org.

Georgia

Georgia Lib. Assn., School Lib. Media Div. *Chair* Tim Wojcik, Our Lady of Mercy Catholic H.S. Tel. 770-461-2202, e-mail wojcikt@bellsouth.net; *Chair-Elect* Judi

Repman, Georgia Southern Univ. Tel. 912-681-5394, e-mail jrepman@georgiasouthern. edu; *Secy.* Brian W. Jones, Forest Park H.S. Tel. 404-362-3890; *Past Chair* Pam Nutt, Moore Elementary. Tel. 770-229-3756, e-mail pnutt@spalding.k12.ga.us.

World Wide Web http://gla.georgia libraries.org/div_media.htm.

Georgia Lib. Media Assn. Memb. 700+. Term of Office. Jan. 2008–Jan. 2009.

Pres. Rosalind L. Dennis. E-mail rosalind_ l_dennis@fc.dekalb.k12.ga.us; *V.P.* Sherry Grove. E-mail sgrove@dougherty.k12.ga.us; *Secy.* Kathleen Disney. E-mail kathleen_ r_disney@fc.dekalb.k12.ga.us; *Treas.* Rebecca Amerson. E-mail rebecca.amerson@ cherokee.k12.ga.us; *Past Pres.* Donna Milner. E-mail donnamilner@yahoo.com.

World Wide Web http://www.glma-inc. org.

Hawaii

Hawaii Assn. of School Libns. Memb. 200+. Term of Office. June 2007–July 2008. Publication. *HASL Newsletter* (4 a year).

Pres. Linda Marks, Kalihi Uka Elementary. E-mail flcadiz@aol.com; *V.P., Programming* Lynette Kam, Moanalua Elementary. E-mail lynette_kam@notes.k12.hi.us; *V.P., Membership* Deb Peterson, Cooke Lib., Punahou. E-mail dpeterson@punahou.edu; *Recording Secy.* Ruth Bradford, Farrington H.S.; *Corresponding Secy.* Audrey Aono, Mokapu Elementary. E-mail audrey_aono@ notes.k12.hi.us; *Treas.* Ardith Fujii, Kalihi Kai Elementary. E-mail ardith_fujii@notes. k12.hi.us; *Past Pres.* Loraine Hotoke, Liholiho Elementary. E-mail loraine_hotoke@ notes.k12.hi.us.

Address correspondence to the association, Box 235019, Honolulu 96823.

World Wide Web http://hasl.ws.

Idaho

Educational Media Div., Idaho Lib. Assn. Term of Office. Oct. 2007–Oct. 2009. Publication. Column in *Idaho Librarian* (q.).

Chair Glynda Pflieger, Melba School District. E-mail gpflieger@melbaschools.org.

Address correspondence to the chairperson.

World Wide Web http://www.idaho libraries.org.

Illinois

Illinois School Lib. Media Assn. Memb. 1,100. Term of Office. July 2007–June 2008. Publications. *ISLMA News* (4 a year); *ISLMA Membership Directory* (ann.); *Linking for Learning: The Illinois School Library Media Program Guidelines; Powerful Libraries Make Powerful Learners: The Illinois Study.*

Pres. Jane A. Sharka, 0N655 Winfield Scott Drive, Winfield 60190. Tel. 630-668-6554, e-mail jane@sharka.org; *Pres-Elect* Randee Hudson, Millburn School, 18550 W. Millburn Rd., Wadsworth 60083. Tel. 847-356-8331, fax 847-356-9722, e-mail rhudson @millburn24.net; *Past Pres.* Becky Robinson, Galesburg H.S., 1135 W. Fremont St., Galesburg 61401. Tel. 309-343-4146, fax 309-343-7122, e-mail brobinson@galesburg 205.org; *Exec. Secy.* Kay Maynard, ISLMA, P.O. Box 598, Canton 61520. Tel. 390-649-0911, fax 309-649-0916, e-mail islma@ islma.org.

World Wide Web http://www.islma.org.

Indiana

Assn. for Indiana Media Educators. Publications. *Focus on Indiana Libraries* (mo.); *Indiana Libraries* (q.).

Pres. John McDonald, Connersville Middle School, 1900 Grand Ave., Connersville 47331-2236. Tel. 765-825-1139, fax 765-827-4346, e-mail mcdonald@fayette.k12. in.us; *Pres.-Elect* Robyn Young, Avon H.S., 7575 Oriole Way, Avon 46123. Tel. 317-272-2586 ext. 3015, fax 317-272-4155, e-mail ryoung@avon.k12.in.us; *Secy.* Beth Slightom, Fall Creek Valley Middle School, Indianapolis 46236. Tel. 317-823-5490, fax 317-823-5497, e-mail bethslightom@msdlt. k12.in.us; *Treas.* Kristen Borrelli, Yost Elementary, 100 W. Beam St., Chesterton 46304. Tel. 219-983-3640, e-mail kristen.borrelli@ duneland.k12.in.us; *Past Pres.* Kimberly Carr, Burris Laboratory School, Muncie 47306. Tel. 765-285-2342, fax 765-285-2342, e-mail 01kcarr@bsu.edu.

Address correspondence to the association, 941 E. 86 St., Ste. 260, Indianapolis 46240. Tel. 317-257-2040, fax 317-257-1389, e-mail ilf@indy.net.

World Wide Web http://www.ilfonline. org/AIME.

Iowa

Iowa Assn. of School Libns. Memb. 192. Term of Office. Jan.–Jan. Publication. *IASL Journal* (online, 4 a year). *Co-Eds.* Karla Krueger. E-mail karla.krueger@uni.edu; Becky Johnson. E-mail bcjohnson@cr.k12. ia.us.

Pres. Julie Larson. E-mail larson.julie@ iccsd.k12.ia.us; *V.P./Pres.-Elect* Cheryl Carruthers. E-mail ccarruthers@aea267.k12.ia. us; *Secy./Treas.* Diane Brown. E-mail ddbrown@muscatine.k12.ia.us; *Past Pres.* Denise Rehmke. E-mail rehmke.denise@ iccsd.k12.ia.us.

Address correspondence to the president.
World Wide Web http://www.iasl-ia.org.

Kansas

Kansas Assn. of School Libns. Memb. 600. Term of Office. Aug. 2007–July 2008. Publication. *KASL News* (online; q.).

Pres. Laura Soash. Tel. 316-794-4260, e-mail lnsoash@yahoo.com; *Pres.-Elect* Cindy Pfeiffer. Tel. 620-235-3240, e-mail cpfeiffer @usd250.org; *Secy.* Kaylyn Keating. E-mail kaylynk@usd475.com; *Treas.* Anita Brozik. Tel. 316-788-8500 ext. 251, e-mail abrozik @usd260.com; *Past Pres.* Martha House. Tel. 620-767-5149, e-mail mhouse@cgrove 417.org; *Exec. Secy.* Judith Eller, 8517 W. Northridge, Wichita 67205. Tel. 316-773-6723, e-mail judell8517@sbcglobal.net.

Address correspondence to the executive secretary.

World Wide Web http://www.skyways. org/KASL.

Kentucky

Kentucky School Media Assn. Memb. 620. Term of Office. Oct. 2007–Oct. 2008. Publication. *KSMA Newsletter* (q.).

Pres. Evie Topcik, Louisville Collegiate School, 2427 Glenmary Ave., Louisville

40204. E-mail evtop@loucol.com; *Pres.-Elect* Fred Tilsley, Sandgap Elementary, P.O. Box 320, Sandgap 40481. E-mail fred.tilsley @jackson.kyschools.us; *Secy.* Crystal Smallwood, P.O. Box 246, Dorton 41520. Tel. 606-639-9842, e-mail crystal.smallwood@ pike.kyschools.us; *Treas.* Mary Alice Hunt. E-mail maryalicehunt@bellsouth.net; *Past Pres.* Darlah Zweifel, Meade County H.S., 938 Old State Rd., Brandenburg 40108. E-mail darlah@bbtel.com.

Address correspondence to the president.
World Wide Web http://www.kysma.org.

Louisiana

Louisiana Assn. of School Libns. Memb. 250. Term of Office. July 2007–June 2008.

Pres. Peggy Wheelis. Tel./fax 318-338-2267, e-mail wheelis@bayou.com.

Address correspondence to the association, c/o Louisiana Lib. Assn., 421 S. 4 St., Eunice 70535. Tel. 337-550-7890, fax 337-550-7846, e-mail office@llaonline.org.

World Wide Web http://www.llaonline. org/sig/lasl.

Maine

Maine School Lib. Assn. Memb. 350. Term of Office. May 2005–May 2008. Publication. *Maine Entry* (with the Maine Lib. Assn.; q.).

Pres. Jeff Small, Cony H.S., Augusta. E-mail jsmall@augustaschools.org; *V.P.* Peggy Becksvoort, Falmouth Middle School. E-mail pbecks@fps.k12.me.us; *Secy.* Joyce Lewis, Winslow H.S. E-mail jlucas@winslowk12. org; *Treas.* Donna Chale, Warsaw Middle School. E-mail dchale@warsaw-ms.sad53. k12.me.us; *Past Pres.* Terri Caouette, Lincoln Middle School. E-mail tcaouette@ yahoo.com; *Exec. Secy.* Edna Comstock. E-mail empoweredna@gwi.net.

Address correspondence to the president.
World Wide Web http://www.maslibraries. org.

Maryland

Maryland Assn. of School Libns. (formerly Maryland Educational Media Organization). Term of Office. July 2007–June 2009.

Pres. Beth Shapiro, Towson H.S., Baltimore County. E-mail eshapiro@bcps.org; *Secy.* Patricia Goff, Kenwood H.S., Baltimore County. E-mail pgoff@bcps.org; *Treas.* Sandra Bicksler, Professional Lib., Anne Arundel County. E-mail sbicksler@aacps. org; *Past Pres.* Dorothy P. D'Ascanio, Jackson Road Elementary, 900 Jackson Rd., Silver Spring 20904. E-mail dorothy_p._ d'ascanio@fc.mcps.k12.md.us.

Address correspondence to the association, Box 21127, Baltimore 21228.

World Wide Web http://maslmd.org.

Massachusetts

Massachusetts School Lib. Assn. Memb. 800. Term of Office. June 2007–May 2008. Publication. *Media Forum* (online, q.).

Pres. Sandy Kelly, Carlisle Elementary. Tel. 978-369-6550 ext. 314; *Secy.* Carol Klatt, Northeast Elementary, Waltham. Tel. 781-314-5747, e-mail klattc@k12.waltham. ma.us; *Treas.* Barbara Andrews. Tel. 617-610-3792, e-mail bandrews4@rcn.com; *Exec. Dir.* Kathy Lowe, MSLA, P.O. Box 658, Lunenburg 01462. Tel. 978-582-6967, e-mail klowe@maschoolibraries.org.

Address correspondence to the executive director.

World Wide Web http://www.maschoo libraries.org.

Michigan

Michigan Assn. for Media in Education. Memb. 1,200. Term of Office. Jan.–Dec. 2008. Publications. *Media Spectrum* (2 a year); *MAME Newsletter* (4 a year).

Pres. Judy Hauser, Oakland Schools, 2111 Pontiac Lake Rd., Waterford 48328. Tel. 248-209-2371, fax 248-209-2538, e-mail judy.hauser@oakland.k12.mi.us; *Pres.-Elect* Kathleen McBroom, Dearborn Public Schools, 18700 Audette, Dearborn 48124. Tel. 313-827-3078, fax 313-827-3132, e-mail mcbroom @dearborn.k12.mi.us; *Secy.* Margy Barile, Haslett Public Schools, 5450 Marsh Rd., Haslett 48840. E-mail barilema@haslett.k12. mi.us; *Treas.* Bruce Popejoy, East Jackson Community Schools, 4340 Walz Rd., Jackson 49201. Tel. 517-764-6010, fax 517-764-

6081, e-mail mameexhibits@aol.com; *Past Pres.* Josephine Kirkbride, Chippewa Hills School Dist., 350 E. Wheatland Ave., Remus 49340. Tel. 989-967-8230, e-mail jkirkbride @chsd.us; *Exec. Dir.* Roger Ashley, MAME, 1407 Rensen, Ste. 3, Lansing 48910. Tel. 517-394-2808, fax 517-394-2096, e-mail ashley mame@aol.com.

Address correspondence to the executive director.

World Wide Web http://www.mame.gen. mi.us.

Minnesota

Minnesota Educational Media Organization. Memb. 700. Term of Office. July 2007–July 2008. Publications. *Minnesota Media*; *MEM-Orandum*; *MTNews*.

Pres. Gary Ganje, Dist. 742 Media Services, 115 13th Ave., South St. Cloud 56301. Tel. 320-252-8770, e-mail gary.ganje@ isd742.org; *Pres.-Elect* Leslie Yoder, St. Paul Public Schools, 1930 Como Ave., St. Paul 55108. Tel. 651-603-4923, e-mail leslie. yoder@spps.org; *Secy./Admin. Asst.* Deanna Sylte, P.O. Box 130555, Roseville 55113. Tel. 651-771-8672, e-mail admin@memoweb. org; *Treas.* Margaret Meyer, 4371 107th Ave., Clear Lake 55319. Tel. 763-261-6324, e-mail mmeyer@becker.k12.mn.us; *Past Co.-Pres.* Gina Light, Eagle Creek Elementary, 6855 Woodware, Shakopee 55379. Tel. 952-496-5943, e-mail gmlight@chaska.net; Barb Theirl, Anoka-Hennepin, 2727 N. Ferry St., Anoka 55303. Tel. 763-506-1334, e-mail barbara.theirl@anoka.k12.mn.us.

World Wide Web http://memoweb.org.

Mississippi

School Section, Mississippi Lib. Assn. Memb. 1,300.

Chair Diane B. Willard, Franklin Junior H.S. Tel. 601-384-2878, e-mail dwillard@ fcsd.k12.ms.us; *Exec. Secy.* Mary Julia Anderson.

Address correspondence to School Section, Mississippi Lib. Assn., P.O. Box 13687, Jackson 39236-3687. Tel. 601-981-4586, fax 601-981-4501, e-mail info@misslib.org.

World Wide Web http://www.misslib.org.

Missouri

Missouri Assn. of School Libns. Memb. 1,000. Term of Office. June 2007–JUNE 2008. Publication. *Connections* (q.).

Pres. Dea Borneman. E-mail deaborneman @missouristate.edu; *1st V.P./Pres.-Elect* Gayla Strack. E-mail gayla.strack@raytown schools.org; *2nd V.P.* Maggie Newbold. E-mail mnewbold@fz.k12.mo.us; *Secy.* Michelle Schmitt. E-mail mschmitt@ladue.k12.mo.us; *Treas.* Curtis Clark. E-mail msmediacenter @harrisonville.k12.mo.us; *Past Pres.* Linda Weatherspoon. E-mail lweather@catnet.gen. mo.us.

Address correspondence to the association, 606 Dix Rd., Jefferson City 65109. Tel. 573-893-4155, fax 573-632-6678, e-mail masl_org@earthlink.net.

World Wide Web http://www.maslonline. org.

Montana

Montana School Lib. Media Div., Montana Lib. Assn. Memb. 200+. Publication. *FOCUS* (published by Montana Lib. Assn.) (q.).

Exec. Dir., Montana Lib. Assn. Debra Kramer, 169 W. River Rock Rd., Belgrade 59714. Tel. 406-670-8446, e-mail debkmla @hotmail.com.

World Wide Web http://www.mtlib.org/ slmd/slmd.html.

Nebraska

Nebraska Educational Media Assn. Memb. 370. Term of Office. July 2007–June 2008. Publication. *NEMA News* (q.).

Pres. Judy A. Henning. E-mail judy. henning@kearneypublic.org; *Pres.-Elect* Robin Schrack. E-mail rschrack@esu3.org; *Secy.* Carrie Turner. E-mail carrieturner@ westside66.org; *Treas.* Lynne Wragge. E-mail lynnewragge@hotmail.com; *Past Pres.* Pamela Springer. E-mail pspringer@paplv. esu3.org; *Exec. Secy.* Anne Kalkowski. E-mail nemacontact@gmail.com.

Address correspondence to the executive secretary.

World Wide Web http://myweb.unomaha. edu/~lgilbert/NEMAsite/index.html.

Nevada

Nevada School and Children's Libs. Section, Nevada Lib. Assn. Memb. 120.

Chair Florica Hagendorn; *Exec. Secy.* Robbie DeBuff. E-mail rjdebuff@hotmail. com.

Address correspondence to the executive secretary.

World Wide Web http://www.nevada libraries.org/publications/handbook/nscls.html.

New Hampshire

New Hampshire Educational Media Assn., Box 418, Concord 03302-0418. Memb. 265. Term of Office. June 2007–June 2008. Publication. *Online News* (fall, winter, spring; online and print).

Pres. Sharon Silva, Mastricola Upper Elementary, 26 Baboosic Lake Rd., Merrimack 03054. Tel. 603-424-6221, e-mail sharon. silva@merrimack.k12.nh.us; *V.P.* vacant; *Recording Secy.* Melissa Moore, Northwood Elementary, 511 First N.H. Turnpike, Northwood 03290-6206. Tel. 603-942-5488 ext. 313, e-mail mmoore@northwood.k12.nh.us; *Treas.* Jeff Kent, Eastman School, 15 Shawmut St., Concord 03301. Tel. 603-225-0858, e-mail jkent@csd.k12.nh.us; *Past Pres.* Diane Beaman, Laconia, NH 03246. Tel. 603-524-8468, e-mail deaman@metrocast. net.

Address correspondence to the president.

World Wide Web http://www.nhema.net.

New Jersey

New Jersey Association of School Librarians (NJASL). Memb. 1,100. Term of Office. Aug. 2007–July 2008. Publication. *Bookmark* (mo.).

Pres. Leslie Blatt, Dr. William H. Horton School, 291 N. 7 St., Newark 07107. Tel. 973-268-5286, e-mail mrsles@aol.com; *Pres.-Elect* Angela Crockett, Paterson Public School 24, 482-507 Market St., Paterson 07501. Tel. 973-321-1000 ext. 22453, fax 973-321-0247, e-mail lmc24@paterson.k12. nj.us.

Address correspondence to the president, NJASL, Box 610, Trenton 08607. Tel. 609-394-8032.

World Wide Web http://www.njasl.org.

New York

School Lib. Media Section, New York Lib. Assn., 252 Hudson St., Albany 12210. Tel. 518-432-6952. Memb. 880. Term of Office. Oct. 2007–Oct. 2008. Publications. *SLMS-Gram* (q.); participates in *NYLA Bulletin* (mo. except July and Aug.).

Pres. Marie Barron. E-mail mbarron@cccsd.org; *Pres.-Elect* Carole Kupelian. E-mail carolek@twcny.rr.com; *Secy.* Pauline Herr. E-mail pherr@acsdny.org; *Treas.* Patty Martire. E-mail pmartire@mtmorriscsd.org; *Past Pres.* Sally Daniels. E-mail sallydaniels@twcny.rr.com.

World Wide Web http://www.nyla.org

North Carolina

North Carolina School Lib. Media Assn. Memb. 1,180+. Term of Office. Oct. 2007–Oct. 2008.

Pres. Trudy Moss, Watauga H.S., 400 High School Dr., Boone 28607. Tel. 828-264-2407, fax 828-264-9030, e-mail mosst@watauga.k12.nc.us; *V.P./Pres.-Elect* Deb Christensen, Union County Public Schools, Central Academy of Technology and Arts, 600 Brewer Dr., Monroe 28112. Tel. 704-296-3088, fax 704-296-3090, e-mail deb.christensen@ucps.k12.nc.us; *Secy.* Walter Carmichael, Vienna Elementary, 1975 Chickasha Rd., Pfafftown 27040. Tel. 336-945-5163, e-mail wcarmichael@wsfcs.k12.nc.us; *Treas.* Libby Oxenfeld, Guilford County Schools, 120 Franklin Blvd., Greensboro 27401. Tel. 336-370-2310, fax 336-370-2363, e-mail oxenfee@gcsnc.com; *Past Pres.* Jackie Pierson, Winston-Salem/Forsyth County Schools, 1605 Miller St., Winston-Salem 27101. Tel. 336-727-2373, e-mail jpierson@triad.rr.com.

Address correspondence to the president.
World Wide Web http://www.ncslma.org.

North Dakota

School Lib. and Youth Services Section, North Dakota Lib. Assn. Memb. 100. Term of Office. Sept. 2007–Sept. 2008. Publication. *The Good Stuff* (q).

Chair Kathy Berg, 152 Riverside Park Rd., Bismarck 58504-5332. Tel. 701-323-4567, fax 701-250-4099, e-mail kathy_berg@bismarckschools.org.

Address correspondence to the chairperson.

Ohio

Ohio Educational Lib. Media Assn. Memb. 1,000. Term of Office. Jan.–Dec. 2008. Publication. *Ohio Media Spectrum* (q.).

Pres. Kathy Halsey. E-mail khalsey@canalwin.k12.oh.us; *V.P.* Marie Sabol. E-mail sabolm@hudson.edu; *Secy.* Susan Yutsey. E-mail syutzey@uaschools.org; *Treas.* Cynthia DuChane. E-mail duchane@infohio.org; *Past Pres.* Vicky Schmarr. E-mail schmarrv@aol.com; *Dir. of Services* Kate Brunswick, 17 S. High St., Ste. 200, Columbus 43215. Tel. 614-221-1900, fax 614-221-1989, e-mail kate@assnoffices.com.

Address correspondence to the director of services.

World Wide Web http://www.oelma.org.

Oklahoma

Oklahoma Assn. of School Lib. Media Specialists. Memb. 300+. Term of Office. July 2007–June 2008. Publication. *Oklahoma Librarian.*

Pres. Priscilla Allen. E-mail pdallen@okcps.org; *Pres.-Elect* Sally Rice. E-mail sbratton@norman.k12.ok.us; *Secy.* Nancy Remus. E-mail nremus@ba.k12.ok.us; *Treas.* Tina Ham. E-mail hamti@tulsaschools.org; *Past Pres.* Stephanie McDaniel Brucks. E-mail mcdanst@tulsaschools.org.

Address correspondence to the president, c/o Oklahoma Lib. Assn., 300 Hardy Drive, Edmond 73013. Tel. 405-348-0506.

World Wide Web http://www.oklibs.org/oaslms.

Oregon

Oregon Educational Media Assn. Memb. 600. Term of Office. July 2007–June 2008. Publication. *OEMA Newsletter* (online).

Pres. Gregory Lum. E-mail glum@jesuitportland.org; *Pres.-Elect* Merrie Olson. E-mail lolson43@msn.com; *Secy.* Jenny Takeda. E-mail jenny_takeda@beavton.k12.or.us; *Treas.* Victoria McDonald. E-mail vmcdonald @lshigh.org; *Past Pres.* Allen Kopf. E-mail kopf@umatilla.k12.or.us; *Exec. Dir.* Jim Hayden, Box 277, Terrebonne 97760. Tel./ fax 541-923-0675, e-mail j23hayden@aol. com.

Address correspondence to the executive director.

World Wide Web http://www.oema.net.

Pennsylvania

Pennsylvania School Libns. Assn. Memb. 1,400+. Term of Office. July 2007–June 2008. Publication. *Learning and Media* (q.).

Pres. Margaret Foster. E-mail mfoster@ northallegheny.org; *V.P./Pres.-Elect* Nancy H. G. Smith. E-mail nanka5@comcast.net; *Secy.* Connie Burlingame. E-mail cbgame@ empireaccess.net; *Treas.*Connie Roupp. E-mail croupp@stny.rr.com; *Past Pres.* Anita Vance. E-mail alv@lion.crsd.k12.pa.us.

Address correspondence to the president.

World Wide Web http://www.psla.org.

Rhode Island

Rhode Island Educational Media Assn. Memb. 350+. Term of Office. June 2007–May 2008.

Pres. Jacqueline Lamoureux. E-mail jackie lam@cox.net; *V.P.* Barbara Ashby. E-mail gjwl@aol.com; *Secy.* Beth Grabbert. E-mail bgrabbert@cpsed.net; *Treas.* Jane Vincelette. E-mail jwv@cox.net; *Past Pres.* Phyllis Humphrey. E-mail rid04893@ride.ri.net.

Address correspondence to the association, Box 470, East Greenwich 02818.

World Wide Web http://www.ri.net/ RIEMA.

South Carolina

South Carolina Assn. of School Libns. Memb. 1,100. Term of Office. June 2007–May 2008. Publication. *Media Center Messenger* (4 a year).

Pres. Kitt Lisenby. E-mail lisenbyk@kcsd. k12.sc.us; *V.P./Pres.-Elect* Valerie Byrd Fort. E-mail val_byrd@yahoo.com; *Secy.* Carole McGrath. E-mail cmcgrath@hampton1.k12.

sc.us; *Treas.* Stephen Reed. E-mail screed3103 @aol.com; *Past Pres.* Ida Thompson. E-mail trt255@bellsouth.net.

Address correspondence to the president.

World Wide Web http://www.scasl.net.

South Dakota

South Dakota School Lib. Media Assn., Section of the South Dakota Lib. Assn. and South Dakota Education Assn. Memb. 140+. Term of Office. Oct. 2007–Oct. 2008.

Chair Jean Dietrich, Custer Schools. E-mail jdiedtrich@csd.k12.sd.us.

Tennessee

Tennessee Assn. of School Libns. Memb. 450. Term of Office. Jan.–Dec. 2008. Publication. *Footnotes* (q.).

Pres. Lynn Caruthers, Marvin Wright Elementary, 4717 Derryberry Lane, Spring Hill 37174. E-mail lcaruth@charter.net; *V.P./Pres.-Elect* Bruce Hester, Northeast Middle School, 3703 Trenton Rd., Clarksville 37040. E-mail bruce.hester@cmcss.net; *Secy.* Andre Crafford, Collierville Middle School, 146 College St., Collierville 38017. E-mail acrafford@scsk12.org; *Treas.* Carol Burr, Goodlettsville Elementary, 514 Donald St., Goodlettsville 37072. E-mail carol.burr@ mnps.org; *Past Pres.* Margaret Hausauer, Kenwood Elementary, 1101 Peachers Mill Rd., Clarksville 37042. E-mail margaret. hausauer@cmcss.net.

Address correspondence to the president.

World Wide Web http://www.korrnet.org/ tasl.

Texas

Texas Assn. of School Libns. (Div. of Texas Lib. Assn.). Memb. 4,000+. Term of Office. Apr. 2007–Apr. 2008. Publication. *Media Matters* (3 a year).

Chair MaryJo Humphreys, Round Rock ISD. Tel. 512-424-6102, e-mail maryjohum @yahoo.com; *Chair-Elect* Jackie Chetzron, Richardson ISD. Tel. 469-593-1624, e-mail jackie.chetzron@risd.org; *Secy.* Leigh Ann Jones, Frisco ISD. Tel. 469-633-6843, e-mail jonesl@friscoisd.org; *Past Chair* Maribel

Castro, St. John's Middle School, Houston. Tel. 713-850-0222 ext. 236, e-mail serial reader@gmail.com.

Address correspondence to Texas Lib. Assn., 3355 Bee Cave Rd., Ste. 401, Austin 78746. Tel. 512-328-1518, fax 512-328-8852, e-mail tla@txla.org.

World Wide Web http://www.txla.org/groups/tasl.

Utah

Utah Educational Lib. Media Assn. Memb. 512. Term of Office. Mar. 2007–Feb. 2008. Publication. *UELMA Newsletter* (q.).

Pres. Michael Goodman, Mount Jordan Middle School, 9360 S. 300 E., Sandy 84070. Tel. 801-412-2071, fax 801-412-2055, e-mail mlgcsg@msn.com; *Pres.-Elect* Debbie Naylor, Lehi H.S., 180 N. 500 E., Lehi 84043. Tel. 801-768-7000 ext. 337, fax 801-768-7007, e-mail dnaylor@alpine.k12.ut.us; *Secy.* Kathy Minson, Joel P. Jensen Middle School, 8105 S. 3200 W., West Jordan 84088. Tel. 801-412-2870, fax 801-412-2875, e-mail kathryn.minson@jordan.k12.ut.us; *Past Pres.* Cindy Mitchell, South Jordan Middle School, 10245 S. 2700 W., South Jordan 84095. Tel. 801-412-2917, fax 801-412-2930, e-mail cindy.mitchell@jordan.k12.ut.us; *Exec. Dir.* Larry Jeppesen, Cedar Ridge Middle School, 65 N. 200 W., Hyde Park 84318. Tel. 435-563-6229, fax 435-563-3915, e-mail larry.jeppesen@cache.k12.ut.us.

Address correspondence to the executive director.

World Wide Web http://www.uelma.org.

Vermont

Vermont School Lib. Assn. (formerly Vermont Educational Media Assn.). Memb. 243. Term of Office. May 2007–May 2008. Publication. *VSLA News* (q.).

Pres. Jean Fournier, Grace Stuart Orcutt Lib., St. Johnsbury Academy, St. Johnsbury 05819. E-mail jfournier@stjacademy.org; *Pres.-Elect* Susan Monmaney, Main Street Middle School, 170 Main St., Montpelier 05602. E-mail susanm@mpsvt.org; *Secy.* Dollinda Lund, Lyndon Institute Lib., Lyndon Center 05850. E-mail dollinda.lund @lyndoninstitute.org; *Treas.* Donna Smyth, Proctor Elementary, Proctor 05765. E-mail donna.smyth@rcsu.org; *Past Pres.* Anne L. Gallivan, Barstow Memorial School, Chittenden 05737. E-mail agallivan@barstow.k12.vt.us.

Address correspondence to the president.

World Wide Web http://vsla.info.

Virginia

Virginia Educational Media Assn. Memb. 1,700. Term of Office. (Pres., Pres.-Elect) Oct. 2007–Nov. 2008 (other officers 2 years in alternating years). Publication. *Mediagram* (q.).

Pres. Nancy Silcox, Samuel W. Tucker Elementary, Alexandria. E-mail nancy.silcox @acps.k12.va.us; *Pres.-Elect* Terrill Britt, G. A. Treakle Elementary, Chesapeake. E-mail britttwe@cps.k12.va.us; *Secy.* Janice Raspen, Conway Elementary, Stafford County. E-mail jraspen@staffordschools.net; *Treas.* Kathy Meredith, Tomahawk Elementary, Hampton. E-mail kmeredith@campbell.k12.va.us; *Past Pres.* Laurel Morgan, Lake Taylor Middle School, Norfolk. E-mail lmorgan @nps.k12.va.us; *Exec. Dir.* Jean Remler. Tel. 703-764-0719, fax 703-272-3643, e-mail jremler@pen.k12.va.us.

Address correspondence to the association, Box 2743, Fairfax 22031-0743.

World Wide Web http://vema.gen.va.us.

Washington

Washington Lib. Media Assn. Memb. 1,450+. Term of Office. October–October. Publication. *The Medium* (3 a year).

Pres. Linda Collins. E-mail lcollins@upsd.wednet.edu; *Pres.-Elect* Dave Sonnen. E-mail wlmadave@gmail.com; *V.P.* Linda King. E-mail winesapple@aol.com; *Secy.* Lorrie Monprode. E-mail monprodel@monroe.wednet.edu; *Treas.* Kate Pankiewicz. E-mail kate.pankiewicz@shorelineschools.org; *Past Pres.* Marianne Hunter. E-mail mhunter @nthurston.k12.wa.us.

Address correspondence to the association, Box 50194, Bellevue 98015-0194. E-mail wlma@wlma.org.

World Wide Web http://www.wlma.org.

West Virginia

School Lib. Div., West Virginia Lib. Assn. Memb. 50. Term of Office. Nov. 2007–Nov. 2008. Publication. *WVLA School Library News* (5 a year).

Co-Chairs Karen Figgatt, Dunbar Intermediate School, 1300 Myers Ave., Dunbar 25064. Tel. 304-766-1570, e-mail kfiggatt@kcs. kana.k12.wv.us; Celene Seymour, Marshall Univ. Graduate College, 100 Angus E. Peyton Drive, South Charleston 25303-1600. Tel. 304-746-8901, e-mail seymour@ marshall.edu.

Address correspondence to the chairpersons.

Wisconsin

Wisconsin Educational Media and Technology Assn. Memb. 1,100+. Publication. *WEMTA Dispatch* (q.).

Pres. Annette Smith. E-mail arsmith@ centurytel.net; *Pres.-Elect* Jo Ann Carr. E-mail carr@education.wisc.edu; *Secy.* Vicki Santacroce. E-mail vsantacrose@ ashwaubenon.k12.wi.us; *Treas.* Sandy Heiden. E-mail sheiden@seymour.k12.wi.us; *Past Pres.* Kate Bugher. E-mail kbugher@ madison.k12.wi.us.

Address correspondence to Courtney Rounds, WEMA Assn. Mgr., P.O. Box 206, Boscobel 53805. Tel. 608-375-6020, e-mail wemtamanager@hughes.net.

World Wide Web http://www.wemaonline. org.

Wyoming

School Lib. Media Personnel Section, Wyoming Lib. Assn. Memb. 90+. Term of Office. Oct. 2007–Oct. 2008. Publications. *WLA Newsletter*; *SSLMP Newsletter*.

Chair Sheryl Fanning, Cheyenne East H.S., E-mail fannings@laramie1.k12.wy.us; *Chair-Elect* Peggy Jording, Newcastle Schools. E-mail jordingp@weston1.k12.wy.us; *Secy.* Lori Clark-Erickson, Jackson Hole H.S. E-mail lclark-erickson@teton1.k12.wy.us. Address correspondence to the chairperson.

International Library Associations

International Association of Agricultural Information Specialists

Peter Ballantyne, President
P.O. Box 63, Lexington, KY 40588-0063
E-mail peter.ballantyne@iaald.org
World Wide Web http://www.iaald.org

Object

The International Association of Agricultural Information Specialists (IAALD) facilitates professional development of and communication among members of the agricultural information community worldwide. Its goal is to enhance access to and use of agriculture-related information resources. To further this mission, IAALD will promote the agricultural information profession, support professional development activities, foster collaboration, and provide a platform for information exchange. Founded 1955.

Membership

Memb. 400+. Dues (Inst.) US$110; (Indiv.) US$50.

Officers

Pres. Peter Ballantyne (Netherlands). E-mail peter.ballantyne@iaald.org; *1st V.P.* Stephen Rudgard (Italy). E-mail stephen.rudgard@iaald.org; *2nd V.P.* Dorothy Mukhebi (Uganda). E-mail dorothy.mukhebi@iaald.org; *Secy.-Treas.* Toni Greider (USA). E-mail toni.greider@iaald.org.

Publication

Agricultural Information Worldwide (memb.).

International Association of Law Libraries

Jules Winterton, President
P.O. Box 5709, Washington, DC 20016-1309
World Wide Web http://www.iall.org

Object

The International Association of Law Libraries (IALL) is a worldwide organization of librarians, libraries, and other persons or institutions concerned with the acquisition and use of legal information emanating from sources other than their jurisdictions, and from multinational and international organizations.

IALL's basic purpose is to facilitate the work of librarians who must acquire, process, organize, and provide access to foreign legal materials. IALL has no local chapters but maintains liaison with national law library associations in many countries and regions of the world.

Membership

More than 800 members in more than 50 countries on five continents.

Officers

Pres. Jules Winterton, Institute of Advanced Legal Studies, Univ. of London, 17 Russell Sq., London WCIB 5DR, England. Tel. 44-20-7862-5884, fax 44-20-7862-5850, e-mail julesw@sas.ac.uk; *1st V.P.* Richard Danner, Duke Univ. School of Law, Box 90361, Durham, NC 27708-0361. Tel. 919-613-7115, fax 919-613-7237, e-mail danner@law.duke.edu; *2nd V.P.* Halvor Kongshavn, Law Lib., Bergen Univ. Lib., N-5020 Bergen, Norway. Tel. 47-55-58-95-25, fax 47-55-58-95-22, e-mail halvor.kongshavn@ub.uib.no; *Secy.* Jennefer Aston, Bar Council of Ireland, P.O. Box 4460, Dublin 7, Ireland. Tel. 353-1-817-5121, fax 353-1-817-5151, e-mail jaston@iol.ie; *Treas.* Ann Morrison, Dalhousie Law School, 6061 University Ave., Halifax, Nova Scotia B3H 4H9, Canada. Tel. 902-494-2640/6301, fax 902-494-6669, e-mail ann.morrison@dal.ca; *Past Pres.* Holger Knudsen, Max-Planck-Institut für Ausländisches und Internationales Privatrecht, Mittelweg 187, D-20148, Hamburg, Germany. Tel. 49-40-41900-226, fax 49-40-41900-288, e-mail knudsen@mpipriv.de.

Board Members

Amanda Barratt, Brand Van Zyl Law Lib., Univ. of Cape Town, South Africa; Ruth Bird, Bodleian Law Lib., Oxford Univ., England; Barbara Garavaglia, Univ. of Michigan Law Lib.; Ligita Gjortlere, Riga Graduate School of Law Lib., Riga, Latvia; Petal Kinder, High Court of Australia Lib., Canberra; Xinh Luu, Univ. of Virginia Law Lib.; Uma Narayan, Nishith Desai Assoc., Mumbai, India; Anita Soboleva, JURIX (Jurists for Constitutional Rights and Freedoms), Moscow, Russia.

Publication

International Journal of Legal Information (3 a year; US$60 indiv.; US$95 institutions).

International Association of Music Libraries, Archives and Documentation Centres

c/o Roger Flury, IAML Secretary General
Music Room, National Library of New Zealand
Box 1467, Wellington 6001, New Zealand
Tel. 64-4-474-3039, fax 64-4-474-3035, e-mail secretary@iaml.info
World Wide Web http://www.iaml.info

Object

The object of the International Association of Music Libraries, Archives and Documentation Centres (IAML) is to promote the activities of music libraries, archives, and documentation centers and to strengthen the cooperation among them; to promote the availability of all publications and documents relating to music and further their biblio-graphical control; to encourage the development of standards in all areas that concern the association; and to support the protection and preservation of musical documents of the past and the present.

Membership

Memb. 2,000.

Board Members

Pres. Martie Severt, MCO Muziekbiblio-theek, Postbus 125, NL-1200 AC Hilversum, Netherlands. E-mail m.severt@mco.nl; *V.P.s* James P. Cassaro, Theodore M. Finney Music Lib., Univ. of Pittsburgh, B28 Music Bldg., Pittsburgh, PA 15260. Tel. 412-624-4130, fax 412-624-4180, e-mail cassaro+@pitt.edu; Jon Bagues, ERESBIL, Archivo Vasco de la Música C/ Alfonso XI, 2, Código postal 20100-Errenteria Guipuzcoa, Euskal Herria, Spain. Tel. 34-943-000-868, fax 34-943-529-706, e-mail jbagues@eresbil.com; Aurika Gergeleziu, Fine Arts Information Centre, National Lib. of Estonia, Tönismägi 2, EE15189 Tallinn, Estonia. Tel. 372-6307-159, fax 372-6311-410, e-mail aurika@nlib.ee; Jutta Lambrecht, WDR D&A/Recherche Leitung Musik und Notenarchiv, Appellhofplatz 1, D-50667 Cologne, Germany. Tel. 49-0-221-220-3376, fax 49-0-221-220-9217, e-mail jutta.lambrecht@wdr.de; *Treas.* Kathryn Adamson, Royal Academy of Music, Marylebone Rd., London NW1 5HT, England. Tel. 44-0-20-7873-7321, e-mail K.Adamson@ram.ac.uk; *Past Pres.* Massimo Gentili-Tedeschi, Biblioteca Nazionale Braidense, Ufficio Ricerca Fondi Musicali, via Conservatorio 12, I-20122 Milan, Italy. Tel. 39-02-7601-1822, fax 39-02-7600-3097.

Publication

Fontes Artis Musicae (4 a year; memb.). *Ed.* Maureen Buja, Naxos Digital Services Ltd., Level 11, Cyberport 1, 100 Cyberport Rd., Hong Kong. Tel. 852-2993-5635.

Professional Branches

Archives and Documentation Centres. John Shepard, Blanche and Irving Laurie Music Lib., Rutgers Univ., 8 Chapel Drive, New Brunswick, NJ 08901-8527, USA.
Broadcasting and Orchestra Libraries. Jutta Lambrecht, Westdeutscher Rundfunk, Dokumentation und Archive, Appellhofplatz 1, D-50667 Cologne, Germany.
Libraries in Music Teaching Institutions. Anne Le Lay, Médiathèque Musicale de Paris, Service de Documentation, 8 porte Saint-Eustache, Forum des Halles, 75045 Paris Cedex, France.
Public Libraries. Hanneke Kuiper, Public Lib., Oosterdoksstraat 143, 1011 DK Amsterdam, Netherlands.
Research Libraries. Joachim Jaenecke, Staatsbibliothek, 10102 Berlin, Germany.

International Association of School Librarianship

Karen Bonanno, Executive Secretary
P.O. Box 83, Zillmere, Qld. 4034, Australia
Fax 617-3633-0570, e-mail iasl@kb.com.au
World Wide Web http://www.iasl-online.org

Object

The mission of the International Association of School Librarianship (IASL) is to provide an international forum for those interested in promoting effective school library programs as viable instruments in the educational process. The association provides guidance and advice for the development of school library programs and the school library pro-fession. IASL works in cooperation with other professional associations and agencies.

The objectives of IASL are to advocate the development of school libraries throughout all countries; to encourage the integration of school library programs into the instructional and curriculum development of the school; to promote the professional preparation and continuing education of school library personnel; to foster a sense of community among school librarians in all parts of the world; to foster and extend relationships between school librarians and other professionals connected with children and youth; to foster research in the field of school librarianship and the integration of its conclusions with pertinent knowledge from related fields; to promote the publication and dissemination of information about successful advocacy and program initiatives in school librarianship; to share information about programs and materials for children and youth throughout the international community; and to initiate and coordinate activities, conferences, and other projects in the field of school librarianship and information services. Founded 1971.

Membership

Memb. Approximately 600.

Officers and Executive Board

Pres. James Henri, Hong Kong; *V.P.s* Barbara Combes, Australia; Lesley Farmer, USA; Diljit Singh, Malaysia; *Treas.* Anne Lockwood, Australia; *Dirs.* (to be appointed), Africa–Sub-Sahara; Lourense Das, Europe; Marlene Asselin, Canada; Blanche Woolls, USA; June Wall, Oceania; Angel Leung Yuet Ha, East Asia; Colleen MacDonell, International Schools; Katharina B. L. Berg, Latin America/Caribbean; Jagtar Singh, Asia; Michelle Fitzgerald, North Africa/Middle East.

Publications

Selected papers from proceedings of annual conferences:

22nd Annual Conference, 1993, Adelaide, Australia. *Dreams and Dynamics.* US$15.

23rd Annual Conference, 1994, Pittsburgh. *Literacy: Traditions, Cultures, Technology.* US$15.

24th Annual Conference, 1995, Worcester, England. *Sustaining the Vision.* US$15.

25th Annual Conference, 1996, Ocho Rios, Jamaica. *School Libraries Imperatives for the 21st Century.* US$15.

29th Annual Conference, 2000, Malmo, Sweden. *Information Literacy: Key to the Future.* US$15.

31st Annual Conference, 2002, Petaling Jaya, Malaysia. *School Libraries for a Knowledge Society.* US$30.

32nd Annual Conference, 2003, Durban, South Africa. *School Libraries: Breaking Down Barriers.* US$30.

33rd Annual Conference, 2004, Dublin, Ireland. *From Aesop to E-Book: The Story Goes On.* US$30.

34th Annual Conference, 2005, Hong Kong. *Information Leadership in a Culture of Change.* US$20.

35th Annual Conference, 2006, Lisbon, Portugal. *The Multiple Faces of Literacy: Reading. Knowing. Doing.* US$20.

36th Annual Conference, 2007, Taipei, Taiwan. *Cyberspace, D-world, E-learning: Giving Libraries and Schools the Cutting Edge.* US$20.

International Association of Technological University Libraries

President, Maria Heijne, Postbus 98, 2600 MG Delft, Netherlands
World Wide Web http://www.iatul.org

Object

The object of the International Association of Technological University Libraries (IATUL) is to provide a forum where library directors can meet to exchange views on matters of current significance in the libraries of universities of science and technology. Research projects identified as being of sufficient interest may be followed through by working parties or study groups.

Membership

Ordinary, associate, sustaining, and honorary. Membership fee 75–150 euros a year, sustaining membership 500 euros a year. Memb. 239 (in 42 countries).

Officers and Executives

Pres. Maria Heijne, Postbus 98, 2600 MG Delft, Netherlands. E-mail M.A.M.Heijne@library.tudelft.nl; *Secy.* Paul Sheehan, Dublin City Univ. Lib., Dublin 9, Ireland. E-mail paul.sheehan@dcu.ie; *Treas.* Reiner Kallenborn, Munich Technical Univ. Lib., Arcisstrasse 21, Munich 80230, Germany. E-mail kallenborn@ub.tum.de; *Past Pres.* Gaynor Austen, Queensland Univ. Technology Lib., GPO Box 2434, Brisbane, Qld. 4001, Australia. E-mail g.austen@qut.edu.au.

Publication

IATUL Proceedings on CD-ROM (ann.).

International Council on Archives

David Leitch, Secetary-General Designate
60 rue des Francs-Bourgeois, 75003 Paris, France
Tel. 33-1-40-27-63-06, fax 33-1-42-72-20-65, e-mail ica@ica.org
World Wide Web http://www.ica.org

Object

The mission of the International Council on Archives (ICA) is to establish, maintain, and strengthen relations among archivists of all lands, and among all professional and other agencies or institutions concerned with the custody, organization, or administration of archives, public or private, wherever located. Established 1948.

Membership

Memb. Approximately 1,800 (representing about 180 countries and territories).

Officers

Deputy Secy.-Gen. Perrine Canavaggio; *Office Mgr.* Annick Carteret.

Publications

Comma (memb.). (CD-ROM only since 2005).
Flash (3 a year; memb.).
Guide to the Sources of the History of Nations (Latin American Series, 11 vols. pub.; Africa South of the Sahara Series, 20 vols. pub.; North Africa, Asia, and Oceania Series: 15 vols. pub.).

Guide to the Sources of Asian History (English-language series [India, Indonesia, Korea, Nepal, Pakistan, Singapore], 14 vols. pub.; National Language Series [Indonesia, Korea, Malaysia, Nepal, Thailand], 6 vols. pub.; other guides, 3 vols. pub.).

International Federation of Film Archives

Secretariat, 1 rue Defacqz, B-1000 Brussels, Belgium
Tel. 32-2-538-3065, fax 32-2-534-4774, e-mail info@fiafnet.org
World Wide Web http://www.fiafnet.org

Object

Founded in 1938, the International Federation of Film Archives (FIAF) brings together not-for-profit institutions dedicated to rescuing films and any other moving-image elements considered both as cultural heritage and as historical documents.

FIAF is a collaborative association of the world's leading film archives whose purpose has always been to ensure the proper preservation and showing of motion pictures. A total of 141 archives in more than 70 countries collect, restore, and exhibit films and cinema documentation spanning the entire history of film.

FIAF seeks to promote film culture and facilitate historical research, to help create new archives around the world, to foster training and expertise in film preservation, to encourage the collection and preservation of documents and other cinema-related materials, to develop cooperation between archives, and to ensure the international availability of films and cinema documents.

Officers

Pres. Eva Orbanz; *Secy.-Gen.* Meg Labrum; *Treas.* Patrick Loughney; *Membs.* Jan-Erik Billinger, Vittorio Boarini, Sylvia Frank, Luca Giuliani, Lise Gustavson, Eric Le Roy, Carlos Magalhães, Hisashi Okajima, Vladimir Opela, Iván Trujillo Bolio.

Address correspondence to Christian Dimitriu, senior administrator, c/o FIAF Secretariat. E-mail info@fiafnet.org.

Publications

Journal of Film Preservation.

International Index to Film Periodicals.

FIAF International Filmarchive database (OVID).

FIAF International Index to Film Periodicals (ProQuest).

For additional FIAF publications, see http://www.fiafnet.org.

International Federation of Library Associations and Institutions

Peter Johan Lor, Secretary-General
P.O. Box 95312, 2509 CH The Hague, Netherlands
Tel. 31-70-314-0884, fax 31-70-383-4827
E-mail ifla@ifla.org, World Wide Web http://www.ifla.org

Object

The object of the International Federation of Library Associations and Institutions (IFLA) is to promote international understanding, cooperation, discussion, research, and development in all fields of library activity, including bibliography, information services, and the education of library personnel, and to provide a body through which librarianship can be represented in matters of international interest. Founded 1927.

Officers and Governing Board

Pres. Claudia Lux, Zentral- und Landesbibliothek, Berlin; *Pres.-Elect* Ellen Tise, Univ. of Stellenbosch, South Africa; *Treas.* Gunnar Sahlin, National Lib. of Sweden, Stockholm; *Governing Board* Helena R. Asamoah-Hassan, Kwame Nkrumah Univ. of Science and Technology, Kumasi, Ghana; Barbara J. Ford, Univ. of Illinois at Urbana-Champaign; Premila Gamage, Institute of Policy Studies, Colombo, Sri Lanka; Nancy E. Gwinn, Smithsonian Inst. Lib., Washington, D.C.; Torny Kjekstad, Baerum Bibliotek, Sandvika, Norway; Trine Kolderup Flaten, Bergen Public Lib., Bergen, Norway; Patrice Landry, Swiss National Lib., Bern; Bob McKee, CILIP, London; Danielle Mincio, Bibliothèque Cantonale et Universitaire, Lausanne, Switzerland; Ingrid Parent, Lib. and Archives Canada, Ottawa; Pascal Sanz, Bibliothèque Nationale de France, Paris; Réjean Savard, Univ. de Montréal-EBSI, Montreal; Barbara Schleihagen, Deutscher Bibliotheksverband e.V., Berlin; Joaquín Selgas Gutiérrez, Biblioteca de Castilla-La Mancha, Toledo, Spain; Lynn F. Sipe, Univ. of Southern California, Los Angeles; Anna Maria Tammaro, Univ. of Parma, Fiesole, Italy; Steve W. Witt, Center for Global Studies, Univ. of Illinois; Zhang Xiaolin, Lib. of Chinese Academy of Sciences, Beijing; *Secy.-Gen.* Peter Johan Lor; *Coord. Professional Activities* Sjoerd M. J. Koopman.

Publications

IFLA Annual Report.
IFLA Directory (bienn.).
IFLA Journal (4 a year).
IFLA Professional Reports.
IFLA Publications Series.
International Cataloguing and Bibliographic Control (q.).
International Preservation News.

American Membership

American Assn. of Law Libs.; American Lib. Assn.; Assn. for Lib. and Info. Science Educ.; Assn. of Research Libs.; International Assn. of Agricultural Info. Specialists; International Reading Assn.; Medical Lib. Assn.; Special Libs. Assn. *Institutional Membs.* There are 126 libraries and related institutions that are institutional members or consultative bodies and sponsors of IFLA in the United States (out of a total of 1,119), and 104 personal affiliates (out of a total of 290).

International Organization for Standardization

Alan Bryden, Secretary-General
ISO Central Secretariat, 1, ch. de la Voie-Creuse, Case postale 56,
CH-1211 Geneva 20, Switzerland
41-22-749-01-11, fax 41-22-733-34-30, e-mail central@iso.org
World Wide Web http://www.iso.org

Object

The International Organization for Standardization (ISO) is a worldwide federation of national standards bodies, founded in 1947, at present comprising 157 members, one in each country. The object of ISO is to promote the development of standardization and related activities in the world with a view to facilitating international exchange of goods and services, and to developing cooperation in the spheres of intellectual, scientific, technological, and economic activity. The scope of ISO covers international standardization in all fields except electrical and electronic engineering standardization, which is the responsibility of the International Electrotechnical Commission (IEC). The results of ISO technical work are published as International Standards.

Officers

Pres. Håkan Murby, Sweden; *V.P. (Policy)* George Arnold, USA; *V.P. (Technical Management)* Ziva Patir, Israel.

Technical Work

The technical work of ISO is carried out by some 190 technical committees. These include:

ISO/TC 46–Information and documentation (Secretariat, Association Française de Normalization, 11 ave. Francis de Pressensé, 93571 Saint-Denis La Plaine, Cedex, France). Scope: Standardization of practices relating to libraries, documentation and information centers, indexing and abstracting services, archives, information science, and publishing.

ISO/TC 37–Terminology and language and content resources (Secretariat, INFOTERM, Aichholzgasse 6/12, 1120 Vienna, Austria, on behalf of Österreichisches Normungsinstitut). Scope: Standardization of principles, methods, and applications relating to terminology and other language and content resources in the contexts of multilingual communication and cultural diversity.

ISO/IEC JTC 1–Information technology (Secretariat, American National Standards Institute, 25 W. 43 St., 4th fl., New York, NY 10036). Scope: Standardization in the field of information technology.

Publications

ISO Annual Report.

ISO CataloguePlus on CD-ROM (combined catalog of published standards and technical work program) (ann.).

ISO Focus (11 a year).

ISO International Standards.

ISO Management Systems (bi-mo.).

ISO Memento (ann.).

ISO Online information service on World Wide Web (http://www.iso.org).

Foreign Library Associations

The following is a list of regional and national library associations around the world. A more complete list can be found in *International Literary Market Place* (Information Today, Inc.).

Regional

Africa

Standing Conference of Eastern, Central, and Southern African Lib. and Info. Assns., c/o Zambia Lib. Assn., P.O. Box 32379, Lusaka 10101, Zambia. Tel. 260-966-72-9464, e-mail benson.njobvu@gmail.com, World Wide Web http://www.scecsal.org/ssecret.html. *Chair* Benson Njobvu; *Secy.* Muntinta Beene Nabuyanda.

The Americas

Asociación de Bibliotecas Universitarias, de Investigación e Institucionales del Caribe (ACURIL) (Assn. of Caribbean Univ., Research, and Institutional Libs.), Box 23317, UPR Sta., San Juan, PR 00931-3317. Tel. 787-790-8054, 787-764-0000, e-mail acuril@rrpac.upr.clu.edu, World Wide Web http://acuril.uprrp.edu/que.htm. *Pres.* Pedro Padilla-Rosa, Biblioteca de Derecho, Universidad de Puerto Rico. E-mail ppadilla@law.upr.edu; *V.P.* Adele Merritt-Bernard. E-mail merritt_adele@hotmail.com; *Exec. Secy.* Oneida Rivera de Ortiz, Biblioteca Regional del Caribe y Estudios Latinoamericanos, Sistema de Bibliotecas, Universidad de Puerto Rico, P.O. Box 23317, San Juan 00931. Tel. 787-764-0000 ext. 7916, e-mail acurilsec@yahoo.com.

Seminar on the Acquisition of Latin American Lib. Materials (SALALM), c/o *Exec. Secy.* Hortensia Calvo, SALALM Secretariat, Latin American Lib., 422 Howard Tilton Memorial Lib., 7002 Freret St., New Orleans, LA 70118-5549. Tel. 504-247-1366, fax 504-247-1367, e-mail salalm@tulane.edu, World Wide Web http://www.library.cornell.edu/colldev/salalmhome.html. *Pres.* Molly Molloy, New Mexico State Univ.

Asia

Congress of Southeast Asian Libns. (CONSAL), c/o *Secy.-Gen.* Le Thuy Duong, National Lib. of Vietnam, 31 Trang Thi St., Hanoi, Vietnam. Tel. 844-824-8870, fax 844-825-3357, e-mail dzuong@gmail.com, World Wide Web http://www.consal.org.sg.

The Commonwealth

Commonwealth Lib. Assn., Univ. of the West Indies, Bridgetown Campus, Learning Resources Center, P.O. Box 144, Mona, Kingston 7, Jamaica. Tel. 876-927-0083, fax 876-927-1926, e-mail nkpodo@uwimonal.edu.jm. *Exec. Secy.* Norma Amenu-Kpodo.

Standing Conference on Lib. Materials on Africa, Commonwealth Secretariat, Marlborough House, Pall Mall, London SW1Y 5HX, England. Tel. 020-7747-6168, fax 020-7747-6164, e-mail scolma@hotmail.com, World Wide Web http://www.lse.ac.uk/library/scolma. *Chair* Barbara Spina, School of Oriental and African Studies, Univ. of London, Thornhaugh St., Russell Sq., London WC1H 0XG, England. Tel. 020-7898-4157, fax 020-7898-4159, e-mail bs24@soas.ac.uk; *Secy.* Ros Buck, Oxfam, John Smith Dr., Cowley, Oxford OX4 2JY, England. Tel. 01865-473757, e-mail rbuck@oxfam.org.uk.

Europe

Ligue des Bibliothèques Européennes de Recherche (LIBER) (Assn. of European Research Libs.), c/o Susan Vejlsgaard, Asst. Secy., LIBER Secretariat, Royal Lib., P.O. Box 21, 2104 Copenhagen K, Denmark. Tel. 45-33-93-62-22, fax 45-33-91-95-96, e-mail sv@kb.dk, World Wide Web http://www.libereurope.eu.

National

Argentina

Asociación de Bibliotecarios Graduados de la República Argentina (ABGRA) (Assn. of Graduate Libns. of Argentina), Tucumán 1424, 8 piso D, C1050AAB Buenos Aires. Tel./fax 11-4371-5269, e-mail info@ abgra.org.ar, World Wide Web http:// www.abgra.org.ar. *Pres.* Ana Maria Peruchena Zimmermann; *Exec. Secy.* Rosa Emma Monfasani.

Australia

Australian Lib. and Info. Assn., Box 6335, Kingston, ACT 2604. Tel. 2-6215-8222, fax 2-6282-2249, e-mail enquiry@alia.org. au, World Wide Web http://www.alia.org. au. *Pres.* Dagmar Schmidmaier; *Exec. Dir.* Sue Hutley.

Australian Society of Archivists, c/o Queensland State Archives, P.O. Box 1397, Sunnybank Hills, Qld. 4109. Tel. 7-3131-7777, fax 7-3131-7764, e-mail info@ archives.qld.gov.au, World Wide Web http://www.archivists.org.au. *Pres.* Kathryn Dan; *Secy.* Fiona Burn.

National and State Libs. Australasia, c/o State Lib. of Victoria, 328 Swanston St., Melbourne, Vic. 3000. Tel. 3-8664-7512, fax 3-9639-4737, e-mail nsla@slv.vic.gov. au, World Wide Web http://www.casl.org. au. *Chief Exec. Officer* Anne-Marie Schwirtlich.

Austria

Österreichische Gesellschaft für Dokumentation und Information (Austrian Society for Documentation and Info.), c/o Wirtschaftuniversitaet Wien, Augasse 9, 1090 Vienna. Tel. 1-31336-5107, fax 01-31336-905107, e-mail oegdi@termnet.at, World Wide Web http://www.oegdi.at. *Pres.* Gerhard Richter.

Vereinigung Österreichischer Bibliothekarinnen und Bibliothekare (Assn. of Austrian Libns.), Voralberg State Lib., Fluherstr. 4, 6900 Bregenz. E-mail voeb@uibk.ac.at, World Wide Web http://www.univie.ac.at/ voeb/php. *Pres.* Harald Weigel; *Secy.* Ortwin Heim.

Bangladesh

Lib. Assn. of Bangladesh, Central Public Lib. Bldg., Shahbagh, Ramma, Dhaka 1000. Tel. 2-863-1471, e-mail msik@icddrb.org. *Pres.* M. Shamsul Islam Khan; *Gen. Secy.* Kh. Fazlur Rahman.

Barbados

Lib. Assn. of Barbados, P.O. Box 827E, Bridgetown, Saint Michael. *Pres.* Shirley Yearwood; *Secy.* Hazelyn Devonish.

Belgium

Archief- en Bibliotheekwezen in België (Belgian Assn. of Archivists and Libns.), Keizershaan 4, 1000 Brussels. Tel. 2-519-5351, fax 2-519-5533, e-mail wouter.bracke@ kbr.be. *Gen. Secy.* Wouter Bracke.

Association Belge de Documentation/ Belgische Vereniging voor Documentatie (Belgian Assn. for Documentation), chaussée de Wavre 1683, Waversesteenweg, B-1160 Brussels. Tel. 2-675-58-62, fax 2-672-74-46, e-mail info@abd-bvd.be, World Wide Web http://www.abd-bvd.be. *Pres.* Paul Heyvaert; *Secy.* Christopher Boon.

Association Professionnelle des Bibliothécaires et Documentalistes (Assn. of Libns. and Documentation Specialists), 30 rue Rêve d'Or, 7100 La Louvière. Tel. 71-61-43-35, fax 71-61-16-34, e-mail biblio. hainaut@skynet.be, World Wide Web http://www.a-p-b-d.be. *Pres.* Laurence Boulanger; *Secy.* Laurence Hennaux.

Vlaamse Vereniging voor Bibliotheek-, Archief-, en Documentatiewezen (Flemish Assn. of Libns., Archivists, and Documentalists), Statiestraat 179, B-2600 Berchem, Antwerp. Tel. 3-28-14457, e-mail vvbad@ vvbad.be, World Wide Web http://www. vvbad.be/node/116. *Pres.* Geert Puype; *Exec. Dir.* Marc Storms.

Belize

Belize Lib. Assn., c/o Central Lib., Bliss Inst., P.O. Box 287, Belize City. Tel. 2-7267, fax 2-34246. *Pres.* H. W. Young; *Secy.* Robert Hulse.

Bolivia

Asociación Boliviana de Bibliotecarios (Bolivian Lib. Assn.), c/o Efrain Virreria Sanchez, Casilla 992, Cochabamba. Tel. 64-1481. *Dir.* Gunnar Mendoza.

Centro Nacional de Documentacion Cientifica y Tecnologica (National Scientific and Technological Documentation Center), Av. Mariscal Santa Cruz 1175, Esquina c Ayacucho, Bolivia. Tel. 02-359-583, fax 02-359-586, e-mail iiicndct@huayna. umsa.edu.bo, World Wide Web http://www.Bolivian.com/industrial/cndct. *Contact* Ruben Valle Vera.

Bosnia and Herzegovina

Drustvo Bibliotekara Bosne i Hercegovine (Libns. Society of Bosnia and Herzegovina), Zmaja od Bosne 8B, 71000 Sarajevo. Tel. 33-275-312, fax 33-218-431, e-mail nubbih@nub.ba, World Wide Web http://www.nub.ba. *Pres.* Nevenka Hajdarovic.

Botswana

Botswana Lib. Assn., Box 1310, Gaborone. Tel. 31-355-2295, fax 31-357-291, World Wide Web http://www.bla.0catch.com. *Chair* Bobana Badisang; *Secy.* Peter Tshukudu.

Brazil

Associação dos Arquivistas Brasileiros (Assn. of Brazilian Archivists), Av. Presidente Vargas 1733, Sala 903, 20210-030 Rio de Janiero RJ. Tel. 21-2507-2239, fax 21-3852-2541, e-mail aab@aab.org.br, World Wide Web http://www.aab.org.br. *Pres.* Lucia Maria Vellosode Oliveira; *Secy.* Laura Regina Xavier.

Brunei Darussalam

Persatuan Perpustakaan Kebangsaan Negara Brunei (National Lib. Assn. of Brunei), Perpustakaan Universiti Brunei Darussalam, Jalan Tungku Link Gadong BE 1410. Tel. 2-223-060, fax 2-235-472, e-mail chieflib@lib.ubd.edu.bn, World Wide

Web http://www.ppknbd.org.bn. *Pres.* Puan Nellie bte Dato Paduka Haji Sunny.

Cameroon

Association des Bibliothécaires, Archivistes, Documentalistes et Muséographes du Cameroun (Assn. of Libns., Archivists, Documentalists, and Museum Curators of Cameroon), B.P. 4609, Yaoundé, Nlongkak Centre Province. Tel. 222-6362, fax 222-4785, e-mail abadcam@yahoo.fr. *Pres.* Hilaire Omokolo.

Canada

Bibliographical Society of Canada/La Société Bibliographique du Canada, P.O. Box 575, Postal Sta. P, Toronto, ON M5S 2T1. E-mail mcgaughe@yorku.ca, World Wide Web http://www.library.utoronto.ca/bsc. *Pres.* David McKnight; *Secy.* Greta Golick.

Canadian Assn. of Research Libraries/Association des Bibliothèques de Recherche du Canada (CARL/ABRC), Morisset Hall, 65 University St., Ste. 239, Ottawa, ON K1N 9A5. Tel. 613-562-5385, fax 613-562-5195, e-mail carladm@uottawa.ca, World Wide Web http://www.carl-abrc.ca. *Pres.* Leslie Weir, Chief Libn., Univ. of Ottawa Library Network, 65 University St., Ottawa ON K1N 9A5. E-mail lweir@uottawa.ca.

Chile

Colegio de Bibliotecarios de Chile AG (Chilean Lib. Assn.), Diagonal Paraguay 383, Torre 11 of. 122, 6510017 Santiago. Tel. 2-222-56-52, fax 2-635-50-23, e-mail cbc@bibliotecarios.cl, World Wide Web http://www.bibliotecarios.cl. *Pres.* Marcia Marinovic Simunovic; *Secy.* Ana Maria Pino Yanez.

China

China Society for Lib. Science, 33 Zhongguancun (S), Beijing 100081. Tel. 10-6841-9270, fax 10-6841-9271, e-mail ztxhmsc@pulicf.nlc.gov.cn, World Wide Web http://www.nlc.gov.cn. *Secy.-Gen.* Gulian Li; *Pres.* Liu Deyou.

Colombia

Asociación Colombiana de Bibliotecólogos y Documentalistas (Colombian Assn. of Libns. and Documentalists), Carrera 50, 27-70, Modulo 1 Nivel 4, Bloque C, Colceincias, Bogotá. Tel. 1-360-3077, World Wide Web http://www.ascolbi.org/acerca.htm. *Pres.* Carlos Alberto Zapata.

Congo (Republic of)

Direction Générale des Services de Bibliothèques, Archives, et Documentation (Directorate of Lib., Archives, and Documentation Services), Bibliothèque Nationale Populaire, BP 1489, Brazzaville. Tel. 833-485, fax 832-253.

Costa Rica

Asociación Costarricense de Bibliotecarios (Costa Rican Assn. of Libns.), Apdo. 3308, San José. Tel. 234-9989, e-mail info@cesdepu.com, World Wide Web http://www.cesdepu.com. *Secy.-Gen.* Rodolfo Saborio Valverde.

Côte d'Ivoire

Association pour le Développement de la Documentation, des Bibliothèques et Archives de la Côte d'Ivoire (Assn. for the Development of Info, Libs., and Archives of Ivory Coast), c/o Bibliothèque Nationale, BPV 180, Abidjan. Tel. 32-38-72. *Secy.-Gen.* Cangah Guy; *Dir.* Ambroise Agnero.

Croatia

Hrvatsko Knjiznicarsko Drustvo (Croatian Lib. Assn.), c/o Nacionalna i sveucilisna knjiznica, Hrvatske bratske zajednice 4, 10000 Zagreb. Tel./fax 1-615-93-20, e-mail hkd@nsk.hr, World Wide Web http://www.hkdrustvo.hr. *Pres.* Zdenka Sviben. E-mail z.sviben@kqz.hr; *Secy.* Isabella Mauro. E-mail isabella.mauro@kqz.hr.

Cuba

Lib. Assn. of Cuba, c/o Biblioteca Maximo Gomez, Calle Parado No. 205, 10100 Havana. Tel. 7-8620-9783, fax 7-8812-428, e-mail ascubi@bnjm.cu. *Pres.* Margarita Bellas Vilarino; *Dir.* Marta Terry González.

Cyprus

Kypriakos Synthesmos Vivliothicarion (Lib. Assn. of Cyprus), P.O. Box 1039, 1434 Nicosia. Tel. 22-404-849. *Pres.* Costas D. Stephanov; *Secy.* Paris G. Rossos.

Czech Republic

Svaz Knihovníku Informačních Pracovníkú Ceské Republiky (Assn. of Lib. and Info. Professionals of the Czech Republic), National Lib., Klementinum 190, 11001 Prague 1. Tel. 2-2166-3111, e-mail vit.richter@nkp.cz, World Wide Web http://www.nkp.cz. *Pres.* Vit Richter.

Denmark

Arkivforeningen (Archives Society), c/o Landsarkivet for Sjaelland, Jagtvej 10, 22 Copenhagen N. Tel. 31-39-35-20, fax 33-15-32-39. *Pres.* Tyge Krogh; *Secy.* Charlotte Steinmark.

Danmarks Biblioteksforening (Danish Lib. Assn.), Vesterbrogade 20/5, 1620 Copenhagen V. Tel. 33-25-09-35, fax 33-25-79-00, e-mail wv@dbf.dk, World Wide Web http://www.dbf.dk. *Dir.* Winnie Vitzansky.

Danmarks Forskningsbibliotheksforening (Danish Research Lib. Assn.), c/o Statsbiblioteket, Universitetsparken 8000, Århus C. Tel. 45-89-46-22-07, fax 45-89-46-22-20, e-mail df@statsbiblioteket.dk, World Wide Web http://www.dfdf.dk. *Pres.* Claus Vesterager Pedersen; *Secy.* Hanne Dahl.

Dansk Musikbiblioteksforening (Assn. of Danish Music Libs.), Nordjysk Musikkonservatorium, Ryesgade 52, 9000 Aalborg. Tel. 33-47-43-16, fax 33-47-47-10, e-mail dmbf@kb.dk, World Wide Web http://www.dmbf.nu. *Pres.* Ole Bisbjerg; *Secy.-Gen* Jane Mariegaard.

Kommunernes Skolebiblioteksforening (Assn. of Danish School Libs.), Krimsveg 29B 1, DK-2300 Copenhagen S. Tel. 33-11-13-91, fax 33-11-13-90, e-mail komskol-

bib@ksbf.dk, World Wide Web http://
www.ksbf.dk. *Chief Exec.* Paul Erik
Sorensen.

Dominican Republic

Asociación Dominicana de Bibliotecarios
(Dominican Assn. of Libns.), c/o Bibliote-
ca Nacional, Cesar Nicolás Penson 91,
Plaza de la Cultura, Pichincha, Santo
Domingo. Tel. 809-688-4086, fax 809-
688-5841, e-mail biblioteca.nacional@
dominicana.com. *Pres.* Prospero J. Mella-
Chavier; *Secy.-Gen.* V. Regús.

Ecuador

Asociación Ecuatoriana de Bibliotecarios
(Ecuadoran Lib. Assn.), c/o Casa de la
Cultura Ecuatoriana Benjamin Carrión,
Ave. 12 de Octubre 555, Quito. Tel. 2528-
840, fax 2223-391, e-mail asoebfp@
hotmail.com. *Pres.* Wilson Vega; *Dir.*
Laura de Crespo.

Egypt

Egyptian Assn. for Lib. and Info. Science,
c/o Dept. of Archives, Libnship., and Info.
Science, Faculty of Arts, Univ. of Cairo,
Cairo. Tel. 2-567-6365, fax 2-572-9659.
Pres. S. Khalifa; *Secy.* Hosam El-Din.

El Salvador

Asociación de Bibliotecarios de El Salvador
(El Salvador Lib. Assn.), Apdo. 2923, San
Salvador. Tel. 216-312, fax 225-0278.
Pres. Carmen Salinas de Salinas.

Asociación General de Archivistas de El Salvador (Assn. of Archivists of El Salvador),
Edificio Comercial San Fancisco No. 214,
Ga. C Ote y 2a Ave. Nte, San Salvador.
Tel. 222-94-18, fax 281-58-60, e-mail
agnes@agn.gob.sv, World Wide Web
http://www.agn.gob.sv.

Ethiopia

Ye Ethiopia Betemetshaft Serategnoch Mah-
ber (Ethiopian Lib. and Info. Assn.), Box
30530, Addis Ababa. Tel. 1-511-344, fax
1-552-544. *Pres.* Mulugeta Hunde; *Secy.*
Girma Makonnen.

Finland

Suomen Kirjastoseura (Finnish Lib. Assn.),
Runeberginkatu 15 A 23, 00100 Helsinki.
Tel. 9-6221-340, fax 9-6221-466, e-mail
fla@fla.fi, World Wide Web http://
kirjastoseura.kaapeli.fi. *Pres.* Tarja Cron-
berg.

France

Association des Archivistes Français (Assn.
of French Archivists), 9 rue Montcalm, F-
75018 Paris. Tel. 1-46-06-39-44, fax 1-46-
06-39-52, e-mail secretariat@archivistes.
org, World Wide Web http://www.
archivistes.org. *Pres.* Henri Zuber; *Secy.*
Agnès Dejob.

Association des Bibliothécaires Français
(Assn. of French Libns.), 31 rue de Chab-
rol, F-75010 Paris. Tel. 1-55-33-10-30, fax
1-55-30-10-31, e-mail abf@abf.asso.fr,
World Wide Web http://www.abf.asso.fr.
Pres. Gérard Briand; *Gen. Secy.* Jean-
François Jacques.

Association des Professionnels de l'Information et de la Documentation (Assn. of Info.
and Documentation Professionals), 25 rue
Claude Tillier, F-75012 Paris. Tel. 1-43-
72-25-25, fax 1-43-72-30-41, e-mail adbs
@adbs.fr, World Wide Web http://www.
adbs.fr. *Pres.* Florence Wilhelm.

Germany

Arbeitsgemeinschaft der Spezialbibliotheken
(Assn. of Special Libs.), c/o Herder-Insti-
tute eV, Bibliothek, Gisonenweg 5-7,
35037 Marburg. Tel. 6421-91-78-41, fax
6421-184-139, World Wide Web http://
www.aspb.de. *Chair* Juergen Warmbrunn.
E-mail warmbrunn@herder-institut.de;
Secy. Jadwiga Warmbrunn.

Berufsverband Information Bibliothek (Assn.
of Info. and Lib. Professionals), Bielefeld
Univ. Lib., P.O. Box 10021, 33502 Bielefeld. Tel. 521-106-4032, fax 521-106-
4052, World Wide Web http://www.bib-
info.de. *Pres.* Susanne Riedel.

Deutsche Gesellschaft für Informationswis-
senschaft und Informationspraxis eV (German Society for Info. Science and Practice), Hanauer Landstr. 151-153, 60314

Frankfurt-am-Main 1. Tel. 69-43-03-13, fax 69-490-90-96, e-mail mail@dgi-info. de, World Wide Web http://www.dgd.de. *Pres.* Gabriele Beger.

Deutscher Bibliotheksverband eV (German Lib. Assn.), Strasse des 17 Juni 114, 10623 Berlin. Tel. 30-39-00-14-80, fax 30-39-00-14-81, e-mail dbv@bibliotheksverband.de, World Wide Web http://www.bibliotheks verband.de. *Pres.* Gudrun Heute-Bluhm; *Chair* Gabriele Beger.

VdA—Verband Deutscher Archivarinnen und Archivare (Assn. of German Archivists), Woerthstr. 3, 36037 Fulda. Tel. 661-29-109-72, fax 661-29-109-74, e-mail info@vda.archiv.net, World Wide Web http://www.vda.archiv.net. *Chair* Robert Kretzschmar.

Verein Deutscher Bibliothekare eV (Society of German Libns.), Universitaetsstr. 22, 86159 Augsburg. Tel. 821-598-5361, fax 821-598-5407, e-mail info@vdb-online.de, World Wide Web http://www.vdb-online. org. *Chair* Ulrich Hohoff.

Ghana

Ghana Lib. Assn., Box 4105, Accra. Tel. 21-516-0122, fax 21-021-60358, e-mail gibassocitionat@yahoo.com. *Pres.* Helena Asamoah-Hassan; *Secy.* A. W. K. Insaidoo.

Greece

Enosis Hellinon Bibliothekarion (Greek Lib. Assn.), 4 Skoulenion St., 105 61 Athens. Tel. 210-322-6625. *Pres.* K. Xatzopoulou; *Gen. Secy.* E. Kalogeraky.

Guyana

Guyana Lib. Assn., c/o National Lib., 76-77 Church and Main Sts., Georgetown. Tel. 0226-2690, fax 0226-2699, e-mail natlib @sdnp.org.gy, World Wide Web http:// www.natlib.gov.gy. *Pres.* Ivor Rodriguez; *Secy.* Gwyneth George.

Honduras

Asociación de Bibliotecarios y Archiveros de Honduras (Assn. of Libns. and Archivists of Honduras), 11a Calle, 1a y 2a Avdas., No. 105, Comayagüela DC, Tegucigalpa.

Pres. Francisca de Escoto Espinoza; *Secy.-Gen.* Juan Angel R. Ayes.

Hong Kong

Hong Kong Lib. Assn., GPO 10095, Hong Kong. E-mail hkla@hkla.org.hk, World Wide Web http://www.hklib.org. *Pres.* Michael Robinson.

Hungary

Magyar Könyvtárosok Egyesülete (Assn. of Hungarian Libns.), Hold u 6, H-1054 Budapest. Tel./fax 1-311-8634, e-mail mke@oszk.hu, World Wide Web http:// www.mke.oszk.hu. *Pres.* Bakos Klara; *Exec. Secy.* Eva Jaki.

Iceland

Upplysing—Felag bokasafns-og upplysing afraeoa (Information—the Icelandic Lib. and Info. Science Assn.), Lagmuli 7, 108 Reykjavik. Tel. 553-7290, fax 588-9239, e-mail upplysing@bokis.is, World Wide Web http://www.bokis.is. *Pres.* H. A. Hardarson; *Secy.* A. Agnarsdottir.

India

Indian Assn. of Academic Libns., c/o Jawaharlal Nehru Univ. Lib., New Mehrauli Rd., New Delhi 110067. Tel. 11-683-1717. *Secy.* M. M. Kashyap.

Indian Assn. of Special Libs. and Info. Centres, P-291, CIT Scheme 6M, Kankurgachi, Kolkata 700054. Tel. 33-334-9651, e-mail iaslic19@iaslic1955.org, World Wide Web http://www.iaslic1955.org. *Publisher* J. M. Das.

Indian Lib. Assn., A/40-41, Flat 201, Ansal Bldg., Mukerjee Nagar, Delhi 110009. Tel. 11-326-4748, e-mail ilanet1@nda.vsnl.net. in. *Pres.* Kalpana Dasgsupta.

Indonesia

Ikatan Pustakawan Indonesia (Indonesian Lib. Assn.), Jalan Merdeka Selatan No. 11, 10110 Jakarta, Pusat. Tel./fax 21-385-5729, e-mail mahmudin@lib.itb.ac.id, World Wide Web http://ipi.pnri.go.id. *Pres.* S. Kartosdono.

Iraq

Arab Archivists Institute, c/o National Centre of Archives, National Lib. Bldg., P.O. Box 594, Bab-Al-Muaddum, Baghdad. Tel. 1-416-8440. *Dir.* Salim Al-Alousi.

Ireland

Cumann Leabharlann Na h-Eireann (Lib. Assn. of Ireland), 53 Upper Mount St., Dublin. Tel. 1-6120-2193, fax 1-6121-3090, e-mail president@libraryassociation. ie, World Wide Web http://www.library association.ie. *Pres.* Ruth Flanagan.

Israel

Israel Libns. and Info. Specialists Assn., Israel 9 Beit Hadfus St., Givaat Shaul, Jerusalem. Tel. 2-658-9515, fax 2-625-1628, e-mail icl@icl.org.il, World Wide Web http://www.icl.org.il. *Pres.* Benjamin Schachter.

Israel Society of Libs. and Info. Centers, P.O. Box 28273, 91282 Jerusalem. Tel./fax 2-624-9421, e-mail asmi@asmi.org.il, World Wide Web http://www.asmi.org.il. *Chair* Shoshana Langerman.

Italy

Associazione Italiana Biblioteche (Italian Lib. Assn.), C.P. 2461, 00185 Rome. Tel. 6-446-3532, fax 6-444-1139, e-mail aib@ aib.it, World Wide Web http://www.aib.it. *Pres.* Mauro Guerrini; *Secy.* Marcello Sardelli.

Jamaica

Lib. and Info. Assn. of Jamaica., P.O. Box 125, Kingston 5. Tel./fax 876-927-1614, e-mail liajapresident@yahoo.com, World Wide Web http://www.liaja.org.jm. *Pres.* David Drysdale.

Japan

Joho Kagaku Gijutsu Kyokai (Info. Science and Technology Assn.), Sasaki Bldg., 7 Koisikawa-2, Bunkyo-ku, Tokyo 112-0002. Tel. 3-3813-3791, fax 3-3813-3793, e-mail infosta@infosta.or.jp, World Wide

Web http://www.infosta.or.jp. *Pres.* T. Gondoh; *Gen. Mgr.* Yukio Ichikawa.

Nihon Toshokan Kyokai (Japan Lib. Assn.), 1-11-14 Shinkawa, Chuo-ku, Tokyo 104 0033. Tel. 3-3523-0811, fax 3-3523-0841, e-mail info@jla.or.jp, World Wide Web http://www.jla.or.jp. *Secy.-Gen.* Reiko Sakagawa.

Senmon Toshokan Kyogikai (Japan Special Libs. Assn.), c/o Japan Lib. Assn., Bldg. F6, 1-11-14 Shinkawa Chuo-ku, Tokyo 104-0033. Tel. 3-3537-8335, fax 3-3537-8336, e-mail jsla@jsla.or.jp, World Wide Web http://www.jsla.or.jp. *Pres.* Kousaku Inaba; *Exec. Dir.* Fumihisa Nakagawa.

Jordan

Jordan Lib. Assn., P.O. Box 6289, Amman. Tel./fax 6-462-9412, e-mail info@jorla. org, World Wide Web http://www.jorla. org. *Pres.* Anwar Akroush; *Secy.* Yousra Abu Ajamieh.

Kenya

Kenya Lib. Assn., Box 46031, 00100 Nairobi. Tel. 2-72480-4541, fax 2-811-455, e-mail gitachir@yahoo.com, World Wide Web http://www.klas.or.ke. *Chair* Rosemary Gitachu; *Secy.* Esther K. Obachi.

Korea (Republic of)

Korean Lib. Assn., 60-1, Banpo-dong, Seocho-gu, Seoul 137-702. Tel. 2-535-4868, fax 2-535-5616, e-mail klanet@hitel.net, World Wide Web http://www.korla.or.kr. *Pres.* Ki Nam Shin; *Exec. Dir.* Won Ho Jo.

Korea (Democratic People's Republic of)

Lib. Assn. of the Democratic People's Republic of Korea, P.O. Box 200, Pyongyang. E-mail kyokoi@jaspul.org.

Laos

Association des Bibliothécaires Laotiens (Lao Lib. Assn.), c/o Direction de la Bibliothèque Nationale, Ministry of Info. and Culture, B.P. 704, Vientiane. Tel. 21-21-

2452, fax 21-21-2408, e-mail bailane@laotel.com.

Latvia

Lib. Assn. of Latvia, Latvian National Lib., Kr. Barona 14, 2 Stavs, 205 telpa, 1423 Riga. Tel. 371-728-7620, fax 371-728-0851, e-mail lnb@lbi.lnb.lv, World Wide Web http://www.lnb.lv. *Pres.* Aldis Abele.

Lebanon

Lebanese Lib. Assn., c/o American Univ. of Beirut, Univ. Lib./Serials Dept., Box 11-0236, Beirut. Tel. 1-350-000, fax 1-351-706, World Wide Web http://www.aub.edu.lb. *Pres.* Fawz Abdalleh; *Exec. Secy.* Rudaynah Shoujah.

Lesotho

Lesotho Lib. Assn., Private Bag A26, Maseru. Tel./fax 340-601, e-mail mmc@doc.isas.nul.ls. *Chair* S. M. Mohai; *Secy.* N. Taole.

Lithuania

Lithuanian Libns. Assn., Sv. Ignoto 6-108, LT-2600, Vilnius. Tel./fax 2-750-340, e-mail lbd@vpu.lt, World Wide Web http://www.lbd.lt. *Pres.* Vida Garunkstyte.

Luxembourg

Assn. Luxembourgeoise des Bibliothécaires, Archivistes, et Documentalistes (ALBAD) (Luxembourg Assn. of Libns., Archivists, and Documentalists), c/o National Lib. of Luxembourg, 37 Blvd. Roosevelt, L-2450 Luxembourg. Tel. 352-22-97-55-1, fax 352-47-56-72, e-mail jean-marie.reding@bnl.etat.lu, World Wide Web http://www.albad.lu.

Macedonia

Bibliotekarsko Drustvo na Makedonija (Union of Libns.' Assns. of Macedonia), P.O. Box 566, 91000 Skopje. Tel. 91-226-846, fax 91-232-649, e-mail bdm@bdm.org.mk, World Wide Web http://www.nubsk.edu.mk. *Pres.* Zorka Cekicevska; *Secy.* Nada Karadzoska.

Malawi

Malawi Lib. Assn., Box 429, Zomba. Tel. 50-522-222, fax 50-523-225, e-mail d.b.v.phiri@unima.wn.apc.org. *Chair* Geoffrey F. Salanje; *Secy.-Gen.* Stanley Gawani.

Malaysia

Persatuan Perpustakaan Malaysia (Lib. Assn. of Malaysia), 232 Jalan Tun Razak, 50572 Kuala Lumpur. Tel. 3-2687-1700, fax 3-2694-2490, e-mail pnmweb@pnm.my, World Wide Web http://www.pnm.my. *Pres.* Chew Wing Foong; *Secy.* Leni Abdul Latif.

Mali

Association Malienne des Bibliothécaires, Archivistes et Documentalistes (Mali Assn. of Libns., Archivists, and Documentalists), Bibliothèque Nationale du Mali, B.P. 159, Bamako. Tel. 22-49-63. *Dir.* Mamadou Konoba Keiita.

Malta

Malta Lib. and Info. Assn. (MaLIA), c/o Univ. of Malta Lib., Msida MSD 2080. Tel. 2132-2054, e-mail info@malia-malta.org, World Wide Web http://www.malia-malta.org. *Chair* Robert Mizzi.

Mauritania

Association Mauritanienne des Bibliothécaires, Archivistes et Documentalistes (Mauritanian Assn. of Libns., Archivists, and Documentalists), c/o Bibliothèque Nationale, B.P. 20, Nouakchott. *Pres.* O. Diouwara; *Secy.* Sid'Ahmed Fall dit Dah.

Mauritius

Mauritius Lib. Assn., c/o The British Council, Royal Rd., P.O. Box 111, Rose Hill. Tel. 454-9550, fax 454-9553, e-mail ielts@mu.britishcouncil.org, World Wide Web http://www.britishcouncil.org/mauritius. *Pres.* K. Appadoo; *Secy.* S. Rughoo.

Mexico

Asociación Mexicana de Bibliotecarios (Mexican Assn. of Libns.), Apdo. 12-800, Administración Postal Mundial, 03001 México DF 06760. Tel. 155-55-75-33-96, fax 155-55-75-11-35, e-mail correo@ambac.org.mx, World Wide Web http://www.ambac.org.mx. *Pres.* Felipe Becerril Torres; *Secy.* Elias Cid Ramirez.

Myanmar

Myanmar Lib. Assn., c/o National Lib., Government Offices, Kannar Rd., Yangon. Tel. 1-272-058, fax 01-532-927. *Pres.* U Khin Maung Tin; *Secy.* U Thein Shwe.

Nepal

Pravidhik Jagat (Nepal Lib. Assn.), GPO 2773, Kathmandu. Tel. 331-316. *Contact* Rudra Prasad Dulal.

The Netherlands

Nederlandse Vereniging voor Beroepsbeoefenaren in de Bibliotheek-Informatie-en Kennissector (Netherlands Assn. of Libns., Documentalists, and Info. Specialists), NVB-Nieuwegracht 15, 3512 LC Utrecht. Tel. 30-231-1263, fax 30-231-1830, e-mail nvbinfo@wxs.nl, World Wide Web http://www.nvbonline.nl. *Pres.* J. S. M. Savenije.

New Zealand

New Zealand Library Assn. (Lib. and Info. Assn. of New Zealand Aotearoa) (LIANZA), P.O. Box 12-212, Wellington 6144. Tel. 4-473-5834, fax 4-499-1480, e-mail office@lianza.org.nz, World Wide Web http://www.lianza.org.nz. *Pres.* Vye Perrone.

Nicaragua

Asociación Nicaraguense de Bibliotecarios y Profesionales a Fines (Nicaraguan Assn. of Libns.), Apdo. 3257, Managua. *Exec. Secy.* Susana Morales Hernández.

Nigeria

Nigerian Lib. Assn., c/o National Lib. Assn., Sanusi Dantata House, Business Central District, Garki District, Abuja 900001. Tel. 8055-365245, fax 9-234-6773, e-mail info@nla-ng.org, World Wide Web http://www.nla-ng.org. *Pres.* A. O. Banjo; *Secy.* D. D. Bwayili.

Norway

Arkivarforeningen (Assn. of Archivists), Postboks 4015, Ulleval Sta., N-0806 Oslo. Tel. 2202-2657, fax 2223-7489, e-mail synne.stavheim@riksarkivaren.dep.no, World Wide Web http://www.arkivarforeningen. no.

Norsk Bibliotekforening (Norwegian Lib. Assn.), Malerhaugveien 20, N-0661 Oslo. Tel. 2324-3430, fax 2267-2368, e-mail nbf@norskbibliotekforening.no, World Wide Web http://www.norskbibliotekforening. no. *Dir.* Berit Aaker.

Pakistan

Pakistan Lib. Assn., c/o Pakistan Inst. of Development Economics, P.O. Box 1091, Islamabad 44000. Tel. 51-921-4523, fax 51-922-1375, e-mail nlpiba@isb.paknet. com.pk, World Wide Web http://www.nlp.gov.pk. *Pres.* Sain Malik; *Secy.-Gen.* Atta Ullah.

Panama

Asociación Panameña de Bibliotecarios (Panama Lib. Assn.), c/o Biblioteca Interamericana Simón Bolivar, Estafeta Universitaria, Panama City. *Pres.* Bexie Rodriguez de León.

Paraguay

Asociación de Bibliotecarios Universitarios del Paraguay (Assn. of Paraguayan Univ. Libns.), Universidad Nacional de Asuncion, Casilla 910, 2064 Asunción. Tel. 21-507-080, fax 21-213-734. *Pres.* Gloria Ondina Ortiz; *Secy.* Celia Villamayor de Diaz.

Peru

Asociación de Archiveros del Perú (Peruvian Assn. of Archivists), Av. Manco Capacc No. 1180, tercer piso, La Victoria. Tel. 1-472-8729, fax 1-472-7408, e-mail contactos @adapperu.com, World Wide Web http://www.adapperu.org. *Pres.* Juan Antonio Espinoza Morante.

Asociación Peruana de Bibliotecarios (Peruvian Assn. of Libns.), Bellavista 561 Miraflores, Apdo. 995, Lima 18. Tel. 1-474-869. *Pres.* Martha Fernandez de Lopez; *Secy.* Luzmila Tello de Medina.

Philippines

Assn. of Special Libs. of the Philippines, Rm. 301, National Lib. Bldg., T. M. Kalaw St., 2801 Ermita, Manila. Tel. 2-893-9590, fax 2-893-9589, e-mail vvt126_ph@yahoo. com. *Pres.* Valentina Tolentino; *Secy.* Socorro G. Elevera.

Bibliographical Society of the Philippines, National Lib. of the Philippines, T. M. Kalaw St., 1000 Ermita, Manila. Tel. 2-583-252, fax 2-502-329, e-mail amb@nlp. gov.ph, World Wide Web http://www. nlp.gov.ph. *Chief* Leticia D. A. Tominez.

Philippine Libns. Assn., Rm. 301, National Lib. of the Philippines, T. M. Kalaw St., 1000 Ermita, Manila. Tel. 2-525-9401, fax 02-523-0068, e-mail dojlib@hotmail.com. *Pres.* Fe Angela M. Verzosa.

Poland

Stowarzyszenie Bibliotekarzy Polskich (Polish Libns. Assn.), al Niepodleglosci 213, 02-086 Warsaw. Tel. 22-608-28-24, fax 22-825-53-49, e-mail biurozgsbp@wp.pl, World Wide Web http://ebib.info. *Pres.* Elzbieta Stefanczyk; *Secy.-Gen.* Maria Burchard.

Portugal

Associação Portuguesa de Bibliotecários, Arquivistas e Documentalistas (Portuguese Assn. of Libns., Archivists, and Documentalists), R. Morais Soares, 43C, 1 Dt, 1900-341 Lisbon. Tel. 21-816-19-80, fax 21-815-45-08, e-mail bad@apbad.pt, World Wide Web http://www.apbad.pt. *Pres.* Antonio Jose de Pina Falcao.

Puerto Rico

Sociedad de Bibliotecarios de Puerto Rico (Society of Libns. of Puerto Rico), P.O. Box 22898, Universidad de Puerto Rico, San Juan 00931-2898. Tel./fax 787-764-0000, World Wide Web http://www. geocities.com/sociedadsbpr. *Pres.* Sonia Ibarra; *Secy.* Doris E. Rivera Marrero.

Russia

Rossiiskaya Bibliotechnaya Assotsiatsiya (Russian Lib. Assn.), 18 Sadovaya St., St. Petersburg 191069. Tel. 812-118-85-36, fax 812-110-58-61, e-mail rba@nlr.ru, World Wide Web http://www.rba.ru. *Pres.* Vladimir N. Zaitsev; *Exec. Secy.* Maya Shaparneva.

Senegal

Association Sénégalaise des Bibliothécaires, Archivistes et Documentalistes (Senegalese Assn. of Libns., Archivists, and Documentalists), Université Cheikh Anta Diop de Dakar, BP 3252, Dakar. Tel. 221-864-27-73, fax 221-824-23-79, e-mail asbad200@hotmail.com, World Wide Web http://www.ebad.ucad.sn/sites_heberges/as bad/index.htm. *Pres.* Djibril Ndiaye; *V.P.* Khady Kane Touré; *Secy.-Gen.* Bernard Dione.

Serbia and Montenegro

Jugoslovenski Bibliografsko Informacijski Institut, Terazije 26, 11000 Belgrade. Tel. 11-687-836, fax 11-687-760, e-mail yubin @jbi.bg.ac.yu, World Wide Web http:// www.jbi.bg.ac.yu. *Dir.* Radomir Glavicki.

Sierra Leone

Sierra Leone Assn. of Archivists, Libns., and Info. Scientists, 7 Percival St., Freetown. Tel. 22-22-0758. *Pres.* Deanna Thomas.

Singapore

Lib. Assn. of Singapore, National Lib. Board, 100 Victoria St., No. 14-01, Singapore 188064. Tel. 6749-7990, fax 6749-7480, e-mail lassec@las.org.sg, World Wide Web http://www.las.org.sg. *Pres.* Ngian Lek Choh.

Slovenia

Zveza Bibliotekarskih Druötev Slovenije (Union of Assns. of Slovene Libns.), Turjaöka 1, 1000 Ljubljana. Tel. 01-20-01-193, fax 01-42-57-293, e-mail zveza-biblio.ds-nuk@quest.arnes.si, World Wide Web http://www.zbds-zveza.si. *Pres.* Melita Ambrozic.

South Africa

Lib. and Info. Assn. of South Africa, P.O. Box 1598, Pretoria 0001. Tel. 12-337-6129, fax 12-337-6108, e-mail liasa@liasa.org.za, World Wide Web http://www.liasa.org.za. *Pres.* Tommy Matthee; *Secy.* Naomi Haasbroek.

Spain

Asociación Española de Archiveros, Bibliotecarios, Museólogos y Documentalistas (Spanish Assn. of Archivists, Libns., Curators, and Documentalists), Recoletos 5, 3 izquierda, interior, 28001 Madrid. Tel. 91-575-17-27, fax 91-578-16-15, e-mail anabad@anabad.org, World Wide Web http://www.anabad.org. *Pres.* Julia M. Rodriguez Barrero.

Sri Lanka

Sri Lanka Lib. Assn., Professional Center, 275/75 Bauddhaloka Mawatha, Colombo 7. Tel./fax 11-258-9103, e-mail slla@slltnet.lk, World Wide Web http://www.slla.org.lk. *Pres.* Piyadasa Ranasinge.

Swaziland

Swaziland Lib. Assn., Box 2309, Mbabane. Tel. 404-2633, fax 404-3863, e-mail sdnationalarchives@realnet.co.sz, World Wide Web http://www.swala.sz. *Chair* Faith Mkhonta; *Secy.* Jabulile Dlamini.

Sweden

Svensk Biblioteksförening (Swedish Lib. Assn.), Saltmätargatan 3A, P.O. Box 3127, S-103 62 Stockholm. Tel. 8-545-132-30, fax 8-545-132-31, e-mail info@biblioteksforeningen.org, World Wide Web http://www.biblioteksforeningen.org. *Secy.-Gen.* Niclas Lindberg.

Svensk Förening för Informationsspecialister (Swedish Society for Info. Specialists), Box 55580, S-102 04 Stockholm. Tel. 8-678-23-20, fax 8-678-23-01, e-mail kansliet@sfis.nu, World Wide Web http://www.sfis.nu. *Pres.* Margareta Nelke.

Svenska Arkivsamfundet (Swedish Assn. of Archivists), Stockholms stadsarkiv, Box 22063, S-104 22 Stockholm. Tel. 46-197-000, fax 46-197-070, e-mail info@arkivsamfundet.org, World Wide Web http://www.arkivsamfundet.org. *Pres.* Berndt Fredriksson.

Switzerland

Association des Bibliothèques et Bibliothécaires Suisses/Vereinigung Schweizerischer Bibliothekare/Associazione dei Bibliotecari Svizzeri (Assn. of Swiss Libs. and Libns.), Hallestr. 58, CH-3012 Bern. Tel. 31-382-42-40, fax 31-382-46-48, e-mail bbs@bbs.ch, World Wide Web http://www.bbs.ch. *Gen. Secy.* Barbara Kraeuchi.

Schweizerische Vereinigung für Dokumentation/Association Suisse de Documentation (Swiss Assn. of Documentation), Schmidgasse 4, Postfach 6301, CH-6301 Zug. Tel. 41-726-45-05, fax 41-726-45-09, e-mail svd-asd@hispeed.ch, World Wide Web http://www.svd-asd.org. *Pres.* Urs Naegeli.

Verein Schweizer Archivarinnen und Archivare (Assn. of Swiss Archivists), Schweizerisches Bundesarchiv, Brunngasse 60, CH-3003 Bern. Tel. 31-312-72-72, e-mail vsa-aas@smueller.ch, World Wide Web http://www.vsa-aas.org. *Pres.* Andreas Kellerhals.

Taiwan

Lib. Assn. of China, c/o National Central Lib., 20 Chungshan S. Rd., Taipei 100-01. Tel. 2-2331-2475, fax 2-2370-0899. *Pres.* Huang Shih-wson; *Secy.-Gen.* Teresa Wang Chang.

Tanzania

Tanzania Lib. Assn., P.O. Box 33433, Dar es Salaam. Tel. 255-744-296-134, e-mail tla_tanzania@yahoo.com, World Wide Web http://www.tla.or.tz. *Chair* Alli Mcharazo.

Thailand

Thai Lib. Assn., 1346 Akarnsongkrau Rd. 5, Klongchan, Bangkapi, 10240 Bangkok. Tel. 02-734-9022, fax 02-734-9021, e-mail tla2497@yahoo.com, World Wide Web http://tla.or.th. *Pres.* Chutima Sacchanand; *Exec. Secy.* Suwadee Vichetpan.

Trinidad and Tobago

Lib. Assn. of Trinidad and Tobago, Box 1275, Port of Spain. Tel. 868-687-0194, e-mail secretary@latt.org.tt. *Pres.* Lillibeth S. V. Ackbarali; *Secy.* Sally Anne Montserin.

Tunisia

Association Tunisienne des Documentalistes, Bibliothécaires et Archivistes (Tunisian Assn. of Documentalists, Libns., and Archivists), Centre de Documentation Nationale 8004, rue Kheredinne Pacha, 1002 Tunis, Tel. 651-924. *Pres.* Ahmed Ksibi.

Turkey

Türk Kütüphaneciler Derneği (Turkish Libns. Assn.), Necatibey Caddesi Elgun Sok 8/8, Kizilay/Ankara. Tel. 312-230-13-25, fax 312-232-04-53, e-mail tkd.dernek@gmail. com, World Wide Web http://www. kutuphaneci.org.tr. *Pres.* Ali Fuat Kartal; *Secy.* Hakan Anameric.

Uganda

Uganda Lib. and Info. Assn., P.O. Box 8147, Kampala. Tel. 141-256-77-467698. *Editor* Matthew Lubuulwa. E-mail nlubuulwa@ yahoo.com.

Ukraine

Ukrainian Lib. Assn., Lesia Ukrainka Kyiv Public Lib., Turgenivska Str. 83/85, 04050 Kyiv. E-mail pashkovavs@yahoo.com, World Wide Web http://www.uba.org.ua. *Pres.* Valentyna S. Pashkova.

United Kingdom

ASLIB, the Assn. for Info. Management, Holywell Centre, 1 Phipp St., London EC2A 4PS, England. Tel. 20-7613-3031, fax 20-7613-5080, e-mail aslib@aslib. com, World Wide Web http://www.aslib. co.uk. *Dir.* R. B. Bowes.

Bibliographical Society, Institute of English Studies, Senate House, Rm. 306, Malet St., London WC1E 7HU, England. Tel. 20-7611-7244, fax 20-7611-8703, e-mail secretary@bibsoc.org.uk, World Wide Web http://www.bibsoc.org.uk/bibsoc. htm. *Pres.* Elisabeth Leedham-Green.

Chartered Inst. of Lib. and Info. Professionals (CILIP) (formerly the Lib. Assn.), 7 Ridgmount St., London WC1E 7AE, England. Tel. 20-7255-0500, fax 20-7255-0505, e-mail info@cilip.org.uk, World Wide Web http://www.cilip.org.uk. *Chief Exec.* Bob McKee.

School Lib. Assn., Unit 2, Lotmead Business Village, Lotmead Farm, Wanborough, Swindon, Wilts. SN4 0UY, England. Tel. 1793-791-787, fax 1793-791-786, e-mail info@sla.org.uk, World Wide Web http:// www.sla.org.uk. *Pres.* Gervase Phinn; *Chief Exec.* Kathy Lemaire.

Scottish Lib. and Info. Council, 1st fl., Bldg. C, Brandon Gate, Leechlee Rd., Hamilton ML3 6AU, Scotland. Tel. 1698-458-888, fax 1698-283-170, e-mail slic@slainte.org. uk, World Wide Web http://www.slainte. org.uk. *Dir.* Elaine Fulton.

Society of Archivists, Prioryfield House, 20 Canon St., Taunton, Somerset TA1 1SW, England. Tel. 1823-327-030, fax 1823-371-719, e-mail societyofarchivists@archives.org.uk, World Wide Web http://www.archives.org.uk. *Chair* Peter Anderson; *Exec. Secy.* Patrick Cleary.

Society of College, National, and Univ. Libs (SCONUL) (formerly Standing Conference of National and Univ. Libs.), 102 Euston St., London NW1 2HA, England. Tel. 20-7387-0317, fax 20-7383-3197, e-mail info@sconul.ac.uk, World Wide Web http://www.sconul.ac.uk. *Exec. Secy.* Toby Bainton.

Welsh Lib. Assn., Lib., Univ. of Wales, Singleton Park, Swansea SA3 4RJ, Wales. Tel. 1792-295-174, fax 1792-295-851. *Pres.* Andrew Green. E-mail andrew.green@llgc.org.uk.

Uruguay

Agrupación Bibliotecológica del Uruguay (Uruguayan Lib. and Archive Science Assn.), Cerro Largo 1666, 11200 Montevideo. Tel. 2-400-57-40. *Pres.* Luis Alberto Musso.

Asociación de Bibliotecólogos del Uruguay, Eduardo V. Haedo 2255, P.O. Box 1315, 11000 Montevideo. Tel./fax 2-4099-989, e-mail abu@adinet.com.uy, World Wide Web http://www.abu.net.uy. *Pres.* Eduardo Correa.

Vatican City

Biblioteca Apostolica Vaticana, Cortile del Belvedere, 00120 Vatican City, Rome. Tel. 6-6987-9402, fax 6-6988-4795, e-mail bav@vatlib.it, World Wide Web http://bav.vatican.va/en/v_home_bav/home_bav.shtml. *Prefect* H.E. Raffaele Farina.

Venezuela

Colegio de Bibliotecólogos y Archivólogos de Venezuela (Venezuelan Lib. and Archives Assn.), Apdo. 6283, Caracas. Tel. 212-572-1858. *Pres.* Elsi Jimenez de Diaz.

Vietnam

Hòi Thu-Vien Viet Nam (Vietnamese Lib. Assn.), National Lib. of Vietnam, 31 Trang Thi, 10000 Hanoi. Tel. 4-8254-927, fax 4-8-253-357, e-mail info@nlv.gov.vn, World Wide Web http://www.nlv.gov.vn.

Zaire

Association Zaïroise des Archivistes, Bibliothécaires et Documentalistes (Zaire Assn. of Archivists, Libns., and Documentalists), BP 805, Kinshasa X1. Tel. 012-30123. *Exec. Secy.* E. Kabeba-Bangasa.

Zambia

Zambia Lib. Assn., Great East Rd. Campus, P.O. Box 32379, 10101 Lusaka. Tel. 966-72-9464. *Chair* Benson Njobvu. E-mail bensonnjobvu@gmail.com.

Zimbabwe

Zimbabwe Lib. Assn., P.O. Box 3133, Harare. Tel. 4-692-741. *Chair* Driden Kunaka; *Hon. Secy.* Albert Masheka.

Directory of Book Trade and Related Organizations

Book Trade Associations, United States and Canada

For more extensive information on the associations listed in this section, see the annual edition of *Literary Market Place* (Information Today, Inc.).

AIGA—The Professional Assn. for Design (formerly the American Institute of Graphic Arts), 164 Fifth Ave., New York, NY 10010. Tel. 212-807-1990, fax 212-807-1799, e-mail info@aiga.org, World Wide Web http://www.aiga.org. *Pres.* Sean Adams, AdamsMorioka, 8484 Wilshire Blvd., Ste. 600, Beverly Hills, CA 90211. Tel. 323-966-5990, e-mail sean_a @adamsmorioka.com; *Exec. Dir.* Richard Grefe. E-mail grefe@aiga.org.

American Booksellers Assn., 200 White Plains Rd., Tarrytown, NY 10591. Tel. 800-637-0037, 914-591-2665, fax 914-591-2720, World Wide Web http://www. bookweb.org. *Pres.* Russ Lawrence, Chapter One Book Store, 252 Main St., Hamilton, MT 59840-2552. Tel. 406-363-5220, fax 406-363-5003, e-mail russ@chapter1 bookstore.com; *V.P./Secy.* Gayle Shanks, Changing Hands Bookstore, 6428 S. McClintock Dr., Tempe, AZ 85283. Tel. 480-730-1142, fax 480-730-1196, e-mail gayleshanks@msn.com; *Chief Exec. Officer* Avin Mark Domnitz. E-mail avin@ bookweb.org.

American Literary Translators Assn. (ALTA), Univ. of Texas–Dallas, Box 830688, Mail Sta. JO51, Richardson, TX 75083-0688. Tel. 972-883-2093, fax 972-883-6303, e-mail jdickey@utdallas.edu, World Wide Web http://www.utdallas.edu/alta. *Pres.* Jim Kates. *V.P.* Barbara Harshav; *Secy.*

Susan Harris; *Admin. Asst.* Lindy Jolly. E-mail lindy.jolly@utdallas.edu.

American Medical Publishers Committee (AMPC), c/o Sara Firestone, Dir., Professional/Scholarly Publishing Div., Assn. of American Publishers, 71 Fifth Ave., New York, NY 10003-3004. Tel. 212-255-0200 ext. 257, fax 212-255-7007, e-mail sfirestone@publishers.org.

American Printing History Assn., Box 4519, Grand Central Sta., New York, NY 10163-4519. World Wide Web http://www. printinghistory.org. *Pres.* Paul Romaine. *Exec. Secy.* Stephen Crook. E-mail sgcrook @printinghistory.org.

American Society of Indexers, 10200 W. 44 Ave., Ste. 304, Wheat Ridge, CO 80033. Tel. 303-463-2887, fax 303-422-8894, e-mail info@asindexing.org, World Wide Web http://www.asindexing.org/site. *Pres.* Carolyn Weaver. E-mail president@as indexing.org; *V.P./Pres.-Elect* Fred Leise; *Secy.* Enid Zafran; *Exec. Dir.* Francine Butler.

American Society of Journalists and Authors, 1501 Broadway, Ste. 302, New York, NY 10036. Tel. 212-997-0947, fax 212-937-3215, e-mail director@asja.org, World Wide Web http://www.asja.org. *Pres.* Bob Bittner. E-mail prez@asja.org; *Exec. Dir.* Alexandra Owens.

American Society of Magazine Editors, 810 Seventh Ave., 24th fl., New York, NY 10019. Tel. 212-872-3735, e-mail asme@

magazine.org, World Wide Web http://www.magazine.org. *Pres.* Nina Link. E-mail president@magazine.org; *Exec. Dir.* Marlene Kahan.

American Society of Media Photographers, 150 N. 2 St., Philadelphia, PA 19106. Tel. 215-451-2767, fax 215-451-0880, e-mail mopsik@asmp.org, World Wide Web http://www.asmp.org. *Exec. Dir.* Eugene Mopsik.

American Society of Picture Professionals, 117 S. Saint Asaph St., Alexandria, VA 22314. Tel. 703-299-0219, fax 703-299-9910, e-mail cathy@aspp.com, World Wide Web http://www.aspp.com. *Pres.* Eileen Flanagan; *Exec. Dir.* Cathy D.-P. Sachs.

American Translators Assn., 225 Reinekers Lane, Ste. 590, Alexandria, VA 22314. Tel. 703-683-6100, fax 703-683-6122, e-mail ata@atanet.org, World Wide Web http://www.atanet.org. *Pres.* Jiri Stejskal; *Pres.-Elect* Nicholas Hartmann; *Secy.* Virginia Perez Santalla; *Treas.* Peter Krawutschke; *Exec. Dir.* Walter W. Bacak, Jr. E-mail walter@atanet.org.

Antiquarian Booksellers Assn. of America, 20 W. 44 St., 4th fl., New York, NY 10036-6604. Tel. 212-944-8291, fax 212-944-8293, e-mail inquiries@abaa.org, World Wide Web http://www.abaa.org. *Pres.* David Lilburne, Antipodean Books, Maps, and Prints; *V.P.* Stuart Bennett, Stuart Bennett Rare Books; *Exec. Dir.* Susan Benne. E-mail hq@abaa.org.

Assn. of American Publishers, 71 Fifth Ave., New York, NY 10003. Tel. 212-255-0200, fax 212-255-7007. *Washington Office* 50 F St. N.W., Washington, DC 20001-1564. Tel. 202-347-3375, fax 202-347-3690. *Pres./CEO* Patricia S. Schroeder; *V.P.s* Allan Adler, Tina Jordan, Barbara Meredith; *Dir., Communications and Public Affairs* Judith Platt; *Exec. Dir., School Div.* Jay Diskey; *Exec. Dir., Higher Education* Bruce Hildebrand; *Exec. Dir., International Copyright Enforcement* Patricia Judd; *Chair* Richard Sarnoff, Random House.

Assn. of American Univ. Presses, 71 W. 23 St., Ste. 901, New York, NY 10010. Tel. 212-989-1010, e-mail info@aaupnet.org,

World Wide Web http://aaupnet.org. *Pres.* Sanford Thatcher, Penn State Univ. Press; *Pres.-Elect* Alex Holzman, Temple Univ. Press; *Exec. Dir.* Peter J. Givler. E-mail pgivler@aaupnet.org.

Assn. of Authors' Representatives, 76A 9th Ave., No. 312, New York, NY 10036. World Wide Web http://aar-online.org.

Assn. of Booksellers for Children (ABC), 6538 Collins Ave., No. 168, Miami Beach, FL 33141. Tel. 617-390-7759, fax 617-344-0540, e-mail kristen@abfc.com, World Wide Web http://www.abfc.com. *Exec. Dir.* Kristen McLean.

Assn. of Canadian Publishers, 174 Spadina Ave., Ste. 306, Toronto, ON M5T 2C2. Tel. 416-487-6116, fax 416-487-8815, World Wide Web http://www.publishers.ca. *Pres.* Jack Wayne, Canadian Scholars' Press, 180 Bloor St. W., Ste. 801, Toronto, ON M5S 2V6. Tel. 416-929-2774 ext. 23, fax 416-929-1926, e-mail jwayne@cspi.org; *V.P.* Rodger Touchie, Heritage Group, Ste 301, 3555 Outrigger Rd., Nanoose Bay, BC V9P 9K1. Tel. 250-468-5328, fax 250-468-5318, e-mail publisher@heritagehouse.ca; *Exec. Dir.* Carolyn Wood. Tel. 416-487-6116 ext. 222, e-mail carolyn_wood@canbook.org.

Assn. of Educational Publishers (AEP), 510 Heron Dr., Ste. 201, Logan Township, NJ 08085. Tel. 856-241-7772, fax 856-241-0709, e-mail mail@edpress.org, World Wide Web http://www.aepweb.org. *Pres.* Rachelle Cracchiolo; *Pres.-Elect* Richard Casabonne; *V.P.* Suzanne I. Barchers; *Treas.* Neal Goff; *CEO/Exec. Dir.* Charlene F. Gaynor. E-mail cgaynor@aepweb.org.

Authors Guild, 31 E. 32 St., 7th fl., New York, NY 10016. Tel. 212-563-5904, fax 212-564-5363, e-mail staff@authorsguild.org. *Pres.* Roy Blount, Jr.; *V.P.s* Judy Blume, James B. Stewart; *Treas.* Peter Petre; *Secy.* Pat Cummings.

Book Industry Study Group, 370 Lexington Ave., Ste. 900, New York, NY 10017. Tel. 646-336-7141, fax 646-336-6214, e-mail info@bisg.org, World Wide Web http://www.bisg.org. *Co-Chairs* Andrew Weber, Random House; Dominique Raccah, Source

books; *Exec. Dir.* Michael Healy. E-mail
michael@bisg.org.

Book Manufacturers' Institute, 2 Armand
Beach Drive, Ste. 1B, Palm Coast, FL
32137. Tel. 386-986-4552, fax 386-986-
4553, e-mail info@bmibook.com, World
Wide Web http://www.bmibook.org. *Pres.*
Ken Fultz, Mazer Corp.; *V.P./Pres.-Elect*
James F. Conway, III, Courier Corp.;
Treas. John R. Paeglow, I.B.T. Global;
Exec. V.P./Secy. Bruce W. Smith. Address
correspondence to the executive vice pres-
ident.

Bookbuilders of Boston, 49 Hawley Rd., Sci-
tuate, MA 02066. Tel. 781-378-1361, fax
419-821-2171, e-mail office@bbboston.
org, World Wide Web http://www.
bbboston.org. *Pres.* Marty Rabinowitz; *1st
V.P.* Kelly Bower; *2nd V.P.* William Henry;
Treas. Scott Payne; *Clerk* Meredith Nadler.

Bookbuilders West, 9328 Elk Grove Blvd.,
Ste. 105-250, Elk Grove, CA 95624. Tel.
415-670-9564, e-mail operations@book
builders.org, World Wide Web http://
www.bookbuilders.org. *Pres.* Michele Bis-
son Savoy, Quebecor World; *Secy.* Pam
Augspurger, Univ. of California Press;
Treas. Michael O'Brien, Laserwords U.S.

Canadian Booksellers Assn., 789 Don Mills
Rd., Ste. 700, Toronto, ON M3C 1T5. Tel.
416-467-7883, fax 416-467-7886, e-mail
enquiries@cbabook.org, World Wide Web
http://www.cbabook.org. *Pres.* Eleanor
LeFave, Mable's Fables, Toronto. E-mail
lefave1@sympatico.ca; *V.P.* Nancy Frater,
BookLore, Orangeville, Ontario; *Exec.
Dir.* Susan Dayus. E-mail sdayus@cba
book.org.

Canadian ISBN Agency, c/o Published Heritage, Library and Archives Canada, 395
Wellington St., Ottawa, ON K1A 0N4.
Tel. 819-994-6872, fax 819-997-7517, e-
mail isbn@lac-bac.gc.ca, World Wide
Web http://www.collectionscanada.ca/
isbn/index-e.html.

Canadian Printing Industries Association,
151 Slater St., Ste. 1110, Ottawa, ON K1P
5H3. Tel. 613-236-7208, fax 613-232-
1334, e-mail belliott@cpia-aci.ca, World
Wide Web http://www.cpia-aci.ca. *Pres.*
Bob Elliott; *Chair* Sean Murray.

Catholic Book Publishers Assn., 8404 James-
port Dr., Rockford, IL 61108. Tel. 815-
332-3245, e-mail cbpa3@aol.com, World
Wide Web http://cbpa.org. *Pres.* Jill Kurtz;
Exec. Dir. Terry Wessels.

Chicago Book Clinic, 5443 N. Broadway,
Ste. 101, Chicago, IL 60640. Tel. 773-
561-4150, fax 773-561-1343, e-mail
chgobookclinic@aol.com, World Wide
Web http://www.chicagobookclinic.org.
Pres. Jen Thomas, Ecological Fibers, 9704
Prairie Lane, Belvidere, IL 61008. Tel.
847-630-0244, e-mail jthomas@fibermark.
com; *V.P.* Dawn Weinfurtner, Friesens
Corp., 8809 Riley Rd., Wonder Lake, IL
60097. Tel. 815-653-9485, fax 815-575-
1186, e-mail dawnw@friesens.com; *Admin.*
Kevin G. Boyer. E-mail kgboyer@ix.
netcom.com.

Children's Book Council, 12 W. 37 St., 2nd
fl., New York, NY 10018-7480. Tel. 212-
966-1990, fax 212-966-2073, World Wide
Web http://www.cbcbooks.org. *Chair*
Simon Boughton; *V. Chair/Chair-Elect*
Doug Whiteman; *Secy.* Brenda Bowen;
Treas. Suzanne Murphy.

Copyright Society of the USA, 352 Seventh
Ave., Ste. 739, New York, NY 10001.
World Wide Web http://www.csusa.org.
Pres. Helene Blue; *V.P./Pres.-Elect* Karen
Frank; *Secy.* Gloria Phares; *Treas.* Corey
Field; *Admin.* Amy Nickerson. E-mail
amy@csusa.org.

Council of Literary Magazines and Presses,
154 Christopher St., Ste. 3C, New York,
NY 10014. Tel. 212-741-9110, fax 212-
741-9112, e-mail info@clmp.org, World
Wide Web http://www.clmp.org. *Pres.* Ira
Silverberg; *V.P.* Nicole Dewey; *Exec. Dir.*
Jeffrey Lependorf. E-mail jlependorf@
clmp.org.

Educational Paperback Assn., Box 1399, East
Hampton, NY 11937. Tel. 631-329-3315,
e-mail edupaperback@aol.com, World
Wide Web http://www.edupaperback.org.
Pres. Neil Jaffe; *V.P.* Dan Walsh; *Treas.*
Anne Sterling; *Exec. Secy.* Marilyn Abel.

Evangelical Christian Publishers Assn., 9633
S. 48 St., Ste. 140, Phoenix, AZ 85044.
Tel. 480-966-3998, fax 480-966-1944, e-
mail info@ecpa.org, World Wide Web
http://www.ecpa.org. *Pres./CEO* Mark W.

Kuyper; *Chair* Mike Hyatt, Thomas Nelson Publishers.

Graphic Artists Guild, 32 Broadway, Ste. 1114, New York, NY 10004. Tel. 212-791-3400, fax 212-792-0333, e-mail admin @gag.org, World Wide Web http://www. gag.org. *Pres.* John Schmelzer. E-mail president@gag.org; *Admin. Dir.* Patricia McKiernan. E-mail admin@gag.org.

Great Lakes Booksellers Assn., c/o *Exec. Dir.* Jim Dana, Box 901, 208 Franklin St., Grand Haven, MI 49417. Tel. 616-847-2460, fax 616-842-0051, e-mail glb@ books-glba.org, World Wide Web http:// www.books-glba.org. *Pres.* Nicola Rooney, Nicola's Books, Ann Arbor, Michigan. E-mail nicolasbooks@sbcglobal.net; *V.P.* Carol Besse, Carmichael's Bookstore, Louisville, Kentucky. E-mail csbesse@ bellsouth.net; *Past Pres.* Sue Boucher, Lake Forest Book Store, Lake Forest, Illinois. E-mail lfbooks@aol.com.

Guild of Book Workers, 521 Fifth Ave., New York, NY 10175. Tel. 212-292-4444, e-mail communications@guildofbook workers.allmail.net, World Wide Web http://palimpsest.stanford.edu/byorg/gbw. *Pres.* James Reid-Cunningham. E-mail president@guildofbookworkers.allmail. net; *V.P.* Andrew Huot. E-mail vice president@guildofbookworkers.allmail. net.

Horror Writers Assn., 244 Fifth Ave., Ste. 2767, New York, NY 10001. E-mail hwa @horror.org, World Wide Web http:// www.horror.org. *Pres.* Deborah LeBlanc. E-mail president@horror.org.

IAPHC—The Graphic Professional Resource Network (formerly the International Assn. of Printing House Craftsmen), 7042 Brooklyn Blvd., Minneapolis, MN 55429. Tel. 800-466-4274, 763-560-1620, fax 763-560-1350, World Wide Web http://www. iaphc.org. *Pres./CEO* Kevin Keane. E-mail kkeane1069@aol.com; *Exec. V.P.* Lesley Addy. E-mail director@iaphc.org.

International Standard Book Numbering U.S. Agency, 630 Central Ave., New Providence, NJ 07974. Tel. 877-310-7333, fax 908-219-0188, e-mail isbn-san@bowker. com, World Wide Web http://www.isbn.

org. *General Mgr.* Andy Weissberg; *ISBN/ SAN Senior Ed.* Louise Timko.

Jewish Book Council, 520 Eighth Ave., Fourth fl., New York, NY 10010. Tel. 212-201-2920, fax 212-532-4952, e-mail jbc@jewishbooks.org, World Wide Web http://www.jewishbookcouncil.org. *Pres.* Lawrence J. Krule; *Exec. Dir.* Carolyn Starman Hessel.

Library Binding Institute, 4300 S. U.S. Hwy. 1, No. 203-296, Jupiter, FL 33477. Tel. 561-745-6821, fax 561-775-0089, e-mail info@lbibinders.org, World Wide Web http://www.lbibinders.org. *Pres.* Gerrit Dykhouse, Wallaceburg Bookbinding, 95 Arnold St., Wallaceburg, ON N8A 3P3, Canada. Tel. 519-627-3552, fax 519-627-6922, e-mail gdykhouse@wbmbindery. com; *Exec. Dir.* Debra Nolan. E-mail dnolan@lbibinders.org.

Magazine Publishers of America, 810 Seventh Ave., 24th fl., New York, NY 10019. Tel. 212-872-3700, e-mail mpa@ magazine.org, World Wide Web http:// www.magazine.org. *Pres./CEO* Nina Link. Tel. 212-872-3710, e-mail president@ magazine.org.

Midwest Independent Publishers Assn., Box 581432, Minneapolis, MN 55458-1432. Tel. 651-917-0021, World Wide Web http://www.mipa.org. *Pres.* Pat Morris, Ricochet Frog Press. E-mail patmorris@ comcast.net.

Miniature Book Society. World Wide Web http://www.mbs.org. *Pres.* Julian Edison. E-mail jiestl@mac.com; *V.P.* Peter Thomas. E-mail peteranddonna@cruzio.com; *Secy.* Janet King. E-mail kking@midohio.net; *Treas.* Kathy King. E-mail kking@ midohio.net; *Past Pres.* Eileen Cummings. E-mail inkydew@aol.com.

Minnesota Book Publishers Roundtable. *Pres.* Alison Vandenberg, Hazelden Publishing, P.O. Box 176, 15251 Pleasant Valley Rd., Center City, MN 55012. Tel. 651-213-4567, e-mail avandenberg@ hazelden.org. World Wide Web http:// www.publishersroundtable.org.

Mountains and Plains Independent Booksellers Assn., 19 Old Town Sq., Ste. 238, Fort Collins, CO 80524. Tel. 970-484-5856, fax 970-407-1479, e-mail info@

mountainsplains.org, World Wide Web http://www.mountainsplains.org.

National Assn. for Printing Leadership, 75 W. Century Rd., Paramus, NJ 07652. Tel. 800-642-6275, 201-634-9600, fax 201-986-2976, e-mail info@napl.org, World Wide Web http://www.napl.org. *Pres./ CEO* Joseph P. Truncale.

National Assn. of College Stores, 500 E. Lorain St., Oberlin, OH 44074-1294. Tel. 800-622-7498, 440-775-7777, fax 440-775-4769, e-mail info@nacs.org, World Wide Web http://www.nacs.org. *CEO* Brian Cartier. E-mail bcartier@nacs.org.

National Coalition Against Censorship (NCAC), 275 Seventh Ave., New York, NY 10001. Tel. 212-807-6222, fax 212-807-6245, e-mail ncac@ncac.org, World Wide Web http://www.ncac.org. *Exec. Dir.* Joan E. Bertin. E-mail bertin@ncac. org.

New Atlantic Independent Booksellers Assn. (NAIBA), 2667 Hyacinth St., Westbury, NY 11590. Tel. 516-333-0681, fax 516-333-0689, e-mail info@naiba.com. World Wide Web http://www.newatlanticbooks. com. *Pres.* Joe Drabyak, Chester County Book Co., 975 Paoli Pike, West Chester, PA 19380. Tel. 610-696-1661, fax 610-429-9006, e-mail jdrabyak@ccbmc.com; *Exec. Dir.* Eileen Dengler.

New England Independent Booksellers Assn., 297 Broadway, Arlington, MA 02474. Tel. 781-316-2988, fax 781-316-2605, e-mail steve@neba.org, World Wide Web http:// www.newenglandbooks.org. *Pres.* Judy Crosby; *V.P.* Mitch Gaslin; *Treas.* Dick Hermans; *Exec. Dir.* Steve Fischer.

New York Center for Independent Publishing (formerly the Small Press Center), 20 W. 44 St., New York, NY 10036. Tel. 212-764-7021, fax 212-840-2046, e-mail info @smallpress.org, World Wide Web http:// www.nycip.org. *Exec. Dir.* Karin Taylor.

North American Bookdealers Exchange, Box 606, Cottage Grove, OR 97424. Tel./fax 541-942-7455, e-mail nabe@book marketingprofits.com, World Wide Web http://bookmarketingprofits.com. *Dir.* Al Galasso.

Northern California Independent Booksellers Assn., The Presidio, 1007 General Ken-nedy Ave., Box 29169, San Francisco, CA 94129. Tel. 415-561-7686, fax 415-561-7685, e-mail office@nciba.com, World Wide Web http://www.nciba.com. *Pres.* Nick Setka; *V.P.* Judy Wheeler; *Exec. Dir.* Hut Landon.

Pacific Northwest Booksellers Assn., 214 E. 12 Ave., Eugene, OR 97401-3245. Tel. 541-683-4363, fax 541-683-3910, e-mail infopnba.org, World Wide Web http:// www.pnba.org. *Pres.* Paul Hanson, Eagle Harbor Book Co., 157 Winslow Way E., Bainbridge Island, WA 98110-2425. Tel. 206-842-5332, fax 206-842-0320; e-mail paulh@eagleharborbooks.com; *Exec. Dir.* Thom Chambliss.

PEN American Center, Div. of International PEN, 588 Broadway, Ste. 303, New York, NY 10012. Tel. 212-334-1660, fax 212-334-2181, e-mail pen@pen.org, World Wide Web http://www.pen.org. *Pres.* Francine Prose; *V.P.* Billy Collins; *Exec. Dir.* Michael Roberts. E-mail mroberts@ pen.org.

Periodical and Book Assn. of America, 481 Eighth Ave., Ste. 826, New York, NY 10001. Tel. 212-563-6502, fax 212-563-4098, e-mail info@pbaa.net, World Wide Web http://www.pbaa.net. *Pres.* Robert Kerekes. E-mail bob.kerekes@meredith. com; *Chair* William Michalopoulos. E-mail wmichalopoulos@hfmus.com; *Exec. Dir.* Lisa W. Scott. E-mail lscott@pbaa.net or lisawscott@hotmail.com.

PMA, the Independent Book Publishers Assn. (formerly Publishers Marketing Assn.), 627 Aviation Way, Manhattan Beach, CA 90266. Tel. 310-372-2732, fax 310-374-3342, e-mail info@pma-online. org, World Wide Web http://www.pma-online.org. *Pres.* Florrie Binford Kichler; *Exec. Dir.* Terry Nathan.

Romance Writers of America, 16000 Stueb-ner Airline Dr., Ste. 140, Spring, TX 77379. Tel. 832-717-5200, fax 832-717-5201, e-mail info@rwanational.org, World Wide Web http://www.rwanational.org. *Pres.* Sherry Lewis. E-mail president@ rwanational.org; *Pres.-Elect* Diane Persh-ing. E-mail diane@dianepershing.com; *Exec. Dir.* Allison Kelley. E-mail akelley @rwanational.org.

Science Fiction and Fantasy Writers of America, P.O. Box 877, Chestertown, MD 21620. E-mail execdir@sfwa.org, World Wide Web http://www.sfwa.org. *Pres.* Michael Capobianco; *V.P.* Andrew Burt; *Treas.* Susan Linville; *Secy.* Alma Alexander; *Exec. Dir.* Jane Jewell.

Small Publishers Assn. of North America (SPAN), 1618 W. Colorado Ave., Colorado Springs, CO 80904. Tel. 719-475-1726, e-mail span@spannet.org, World Wide Web http://www.spannet.org. *Exec. Dir.* Scott Flora.

Society of Children's Book Writers and Illustrators (SCBWI), 8271 Beverly Blvd., Los Angeles, CA 90048. Tel. 323-782-1010, fax 323-782-1892, e-mail scbwi@scbwi.org, World Wide Web http://www.scbwi.org. *Pres.* Stephen Mooser. E-mail stephen mooser@scbwi.org; *Exec. Dir.* Lin Oliver.

Society of Illustrators (SI), 128 E. 63 St., New York, NY 10021. Tel. 212-838-2560, fax 212-838-2561, e-mail info@society illustrators.org, World Wide Web http://www.societyillustrators.org.

Society of National Association Publications (SNAP), 8405 Greensboro Dr., Ste. 800, McLean, VA 22102. Tel. 703-506-3285, fax 703-506-3266, e-mail snapinfo@snaponline.org, World Wide Web http://www.snaponline.org. *Pres.* Anne Zender. E-mail anne.zender@ahima.org; *V.P.* Kathleen Rakestraw.

Southern Independent Booksellers Alliance, 3806 Yale Ave., Columbia, SC 29205. Tel. 800-331-9617, 803-779-0118, fax 803-779-0113, e-mail info@sibaweb.com, World Wide Web http://www.sibaweb.com. *Pres.* Karin Wilson, Page & Palette, Fairhope, Alabama.

Technical Assn. of the Pulp and Paper Industry, 15 Technology Pkwy. S., Norcross, GA 30092 (P.O. Box 105113, Atlanta, GA 30348). Tel. 770-446-1400, fax 770-446-6947, World Wide Web http://www.tappi.org. *Pres.* Larry N. Montague; *Chair* Mark R. McCollister; *V. Chair* Jeff Siegel.

Western Writers of America, c/o Paul A. Hutton, MSC06 3770, 1 Univ. of New Mexico, Albuquerque, NM 87131-0001. E-mail wwa@unm.edu, World Wide Web http://www.westernwriters.org. *Pres.* Cotton Smith; *V.P.* Johnny D. Boggs; *Exec. Dir.* Paul A. Hutton.

Women's National Book Assn., c/o Susannah Greenberg Public Relations, P.O. Box 237, FDR Station, New York, NY 10150. Tel./fax 212-208-4629, e-mail publicity@bookbuzz.com, World Wide Web http://www.wnba-books.org. *Pres.* Laurie Beckelman, Prentice Associates, 160 Tea Rock Lane, Marshfield, MA 02050. Tel. 781-834-8002, e-mail lbeckelman@aol.com; *V.P./Pres.-Elect* Joan Gelfand, 2261 Market St., No. 164, San Francisco, CA 94114. Tel. 415-665-9292, e-mail joangelfand@pacbell.net; *Secy.* Michele Leber, 1805 Crystal Dr., No. 911, Arlington, VA 22202-4420. Tel. 703-920-2010, fax 703-979-6372, e-mail michele.leber@comcast.net; *Treas.* Amy Barden, 3101 Ravensworth, Alexandria, VA 22302. Tel. 703-578-4023, e-mail amyb3cat@yahoo.com.

International and Foreign Book Trade Associations

For Canadian book trade associations, see the preceding section, "Book Trade Associations, United States and Canada." For a more extensive list of book trade organizations outside the United States and Canada, with more detailed information, consult *International Literary Market Place* (Information Today, Inc.), which also provides extensive lists of major bookstores and publishers in each country.

International

African Publishers' Network, BP 3429, Abidjan 01, Côte d'Ivoire. Tel. 202-11801, fax 202-11803, e-mail apnetes@yahoo.com, World Wide Web http://www.freewebs.com/africanpublishers. *Chair* Mamadou Aliou Sow; *Exec. Secy.* Akin Fasemore.

Afro-Asian Book Council, 4835/24 Ansari Rd., Daryaganj, New Delhi 110002, India. Tel. 11-2325-8865, fax 11-2326-7437, e-mail afro@aabcouncil.org. *Secy.-Gen.* Sukumar Das; *Dir.* Saumya Gupta.

Centre Régional pour la Promotion du Livre en Afrique (Regional Center for Book Promotion in Africa), P.O. Box 1646, Yaoundé, Cameroon. Tel. 22-4782. *Secy.* William Moutchia.

Centro Régional para el Fomento del Libro en América Latina y el Caribe (CERLALC) (Regional Center for Book Promotion in Latin America and the Caribbean), Apdo. Aéreo 57348, Bogotá 2, Colombia. Tel. 1-212-6056, fax 1-255-4614, e-mail libro@cerlalc.com, World Wide Web http://www.cerlalc.com. *Dir.* Carmen Barvo.

Federation of European Publishers, rue Montoyer 31, Boîte 8, 1000 Brussels, Belgium. Tel. 2-770-11-10, fax 2-771-20-71, e-mail info@fep-fec.eu, World Wide Web http://www.fep-fee.be. *Pres.* Jonas Modig; *Dir.-Gen.* Anne Bergman-Tahon.

International Assn. of Scientific, Technical, and Medical (STM) Publishers, Prama House, 267 Banbury Rd., Oxford OX2 7HT, England. Tel. 1865-339-321, fax 1865-339-325, e-mail info@stm-assoc.org, World Wide Web http://www.stm-assoc.org. *Chair* Jerry Cowhig; *CEO* Michael Mabe.

International Board on Books for Young People (IBBY), Nonnenweg 12, CH-4003 Basel, Switzerland. Tel. 61-272-29-17, fax 61-272-27-57, e-mail ibby@ibby.org, World Wide Web http://www.ibby.org. *Admin. Dir.* Elizabeth Page.

International Booksellers Federation, chaussée de Charleroi 51b, Boîte 1, 1060 Brussels, Belgium. Tel. 2-223-49-40, fax 2-223-49-38, e-mail ibf.booksellers@skynet.be, World Wide Web http://www.ibf-booksellers.org. *Pres.* Eric Hardin; *Dir.* Françoise Dubruille.

International League of Antiquarian Booksellers, 400 Summit Ave., Saint Paul, MN 55102. Tel. 800-441-0076, 612-290-0700, fax 612-290-0646, e-mail info@ilab-lila.com, World Wide Web http://www.ilab.org. *Pres.* Michael Steinbach; *Secy.-Gen.* Arnoud Gerits.

International Publishers Assn. (Union Internationale des Editeurs), ave. de Miremont 3, CH-1206 Geneva, Switzerland. Tel. 22-346-3018, fax 22-347-5717, e-mail secretariat@internationalpublishers.org, World Wide Web http://www.ipa-uie.org. *Pres.* Ana Maria Cabanellas; *Secy.-Gen.* Jens Bammel.

National

Argentina

Cámara Argentina del Libro (Argentine Book Assn.), Avda. Belgrano 1580, 4 piso, 1093 Buenos Aires. Tel. 1-4381-8383, fax 1-4381-9253, e-mail cal@editores.org.ar, World Wide Web http://www.editores.org.ar. *Pres.* Carlos de Santos; *Dir.* Norberto J. Pou.

Fundación El Libro (Book Foundation), Hipolito Yrigoyen 1628, 5 piso, 1089 Buenos Aires. Tel. 11-4374-3288, fax 11-4375-0268, e-mail fundacion@el-libro. com.ar, World Wide Web http://www.el-libro.com.ar. *Pres.* Carlos Alberto Pazos; *Dir.* Marta V. Diaz.

Australia

Australian and New Zealand Assn. of Antiquarian Booksellers, 604 High St., Prahran, Vic. 3181. Tel. 3-9525-1649, fax 3-9529-1298, e-mail admin@anzaab.com, World Wide Web http://www.anzaab.com. *Pres.* Lovella Kerr.

Australian Booksellers Assn., 828 High St., Unit 9, Kew East, Vic. 3102. Tel. 3-9859-7322, fax 3-9859-7344, e-mail mail@aba. org.au, World Wide Web http://www.aba. org.au. *Pres.*Tim Peach; *Exec. Dir.* Celia Pollock.

Australian Publishers Assn., 60/89 Jones St., Ultimo, NSW 2007. Tel. 2-9281-9788, fax 2-9281-1073, e-mail apa@publishers.asn. au, World Wide Web http://www. publishers.asn.au. *Chief Exec.* Maree McCaskill.

Austria

Hauptverband des Österreichischen Buchhandels (Austrian Publishers and Booksellers Assn.), Grünangergasse 4, A-1010 Vienna. Tel. 1-512-15-35, fax 1-512-84-82, e-mail hvb@buecher.at, World Wide Web http://www.buecher.at. *Pres.* Alexander Potyka.

Verband der Antiquare Österreichs (Austrian Antiquarian Booksellers Assn.), Grünangergasse 4, A-1010 Vienna. Tel. 1-512-15-35, fax 1-512-84-82, e-mail sekretariat@ hvb.at, World Wide Web http://www. antiquare.at.

Belarus

National Book Chamber of Belarus, 11 Masherow Ave., 220600 Minsk, Belarus. Tel. 172-235-839, fax 172-235-825, e-mail palata@palata.belpak.minsk.by. *Contact* Anatoli Voronko.

Belgium

Vlaamse Boekverkopersbond (Flemish Booksellers Assn.), Te Buelaerlei 37, 2140 Borgerhout. Tel. 03-287-66-90, fax 3-281-22-40, e-mail vbb@boek.be, World Wide Web http://www.boek.be. *Gen. Secy.* Luc Tessens.

Bolivia

Cámara Boliviana del Libro (Bolivian Booksellers Assn.), Calle Capitan Ravelo No. 2116, 682 La Paz. Tel. 2-44-4239, fax 2-44-1523, e-mail cabolib@ceibo.entelnet. bo. *Pres.* Rolando Condori Salinas.

Brazil

Cámara Brasileira do Livro (Brazilian Book Assn.), Cristiano Viana 91, 05411-000 Sao Paulo-SP. Tel. /fax 11-3069-1300, e-mail cbl@cbl.org.br, World Wide Web http:// www.cbl.org.br. *Pres.* Oswaldo Siciliano; *Gen. Mgr.* Aloysio T. Costa.

Sindicato Nacional dos Editores de Livros (Brazilian Publishers Assn.), Rue da Ajuda 35-18 andar, 20040-000 Rio de Janeiro-RJ. Tel. 21-2533-0399, fax 21-2533-0422, e-mail snel@snel.org.br, World Wide Web http://www.snel.org.br. *Pres.* Paulo Roberto Rocco.

Chile

Cámara Chilena del Libro AG (Chilean Assn. of Publishers, Distributors, and Booksellers), Av. Libertador Bernardo O'Higgins 1370, Oficina 501, Santiago. Tel. 56-2-698-9519, fax 56-2-698-9226, e-mail prolibro@tie.cl, World Wide Web http:// www.camlibro.cl. *Pres.* Eduardo Castillo Garcia.

Colombia

Cámara Colombiana del Libro (Colombian Book Assn.), Calle 40, No. 21-31, Bogotá DC. Tel. 1-288-6188, fax 1-287-3320, e-mail camlibro@camlibro.com.co, World Wide Web http://www.camlibro.com.co.

Czech Republic

Svaz českých knihkupců a nakladatelů (Czech Publishers and Booksellers Assn.), Jana Masaryka 56, 120 00 Prague 2. Tel. 2-24-219-944, fax 2-24-219-942, e-mail sckn@sckn.cz, World Wide Web http://www.sckn.cz. *Chair* Jitka Undeova.

Denmark

Danske Boghandlerforening (Danish Booksellers Assn.), Siljangade 6 3, DK 2300 Copenhagen S. Tel. 32-54-22-55, fax 32-54-00-41, e-mail ddb@bogpost.dk, World Wide Web http://www.bogguide.dk. *Pres.* Jesper Moller; *Dir.* Olaf Winslow.

Danske Forlaeggerforening (Danish Publishers Assn.), Skindergade 7 st tv, DK 1159 Copenhagen K. Tel. 33-15-66-88, fax 33-15-65-88, e-mail danishpublishers@danishpublishers.dk, World Wide Web http://www.danskeforlag.dk. *Pres.* Peter Mollerup; *Dir.* Marie Svane.

Ecuador

Cámara Ecuatoriana del Libro, Núcleo de Pichincha, Avda. Eloy Alfaro, N29-61 e Inglaterra piso N 9, Quito. Tel. 2-553-311, fax 2-553-314, e-mail celnp@hoy.net, World Wide Web http://celibro.org.ec. *Pres.* Luis Mora Ortega.

Egypt

General Egyptian Book Organization, P.O. Box 235, Cornich El-Nil, Ramlat Boulaq, Cairo. Tel. 202-2577-5109, fax 202-2764-276, e-mail info@egyptianbook.org.eg, World Wide Web http://www.egyptianbook.org.eg/en. *Chair* Nasser El Ansary.

Estonia

Estonian Publishers Assn., Roosikrantsi 6, 10119 Tallinn. Tel. 2-644-9866, fax 2-641-1443, e-mail astat@eki.ee, World Wide Web http://www.estbook.com. *Dir.* A. Trummal.

Finland

Kirjakauppaliitto Ry (Booksellers Assn. of Finland), Fredrikinkatu 47, 00100 Helsinki. Tel. 9-6859-9110, fax 9-6859-9119, e-mail toimisto@kirjakauppaliitto.fi, World Wide Web http://www.kirjakauppaliitto.fi. *Pres.* Stig-Bjorn Nyberg; *Dir.* Olli Erakivi.

Suomen Kustannusyhdistys (Finnish Book Publishers Assn.), P.O. Box 177, 00121 Helsinki. Tel. 9-2287-7250, fax 9-612-1226, e-mail veikko.sonninen@skyry.net, World Wide Web http://www.skyry.net. *Dir.* Veikko Sonninen.

France

Cercle de la Librairie (Circle of Professionals of the Book Trade), 35 rue Grégoire-de-Tours, F-75006 Paris. Tel. 1-44-41-28-00, fax 1-44-41-28-65, e-mail commercial@electre.com, World Wide Web http://www.electre.com. *Pres.* Charles Henri Flammarion.

Fédération Française des Syndicats de Libraires (FFSL) (French Booksellers Assn.), 43 rue de Châteaudun, F-75009 Paris. Tel. 1-42-82-00-03, fax 1-42-82-10-51. *Pres.* Jean-Luc Dewas.

France Edition, 115 blvd. Saint-Germain, F-75006 Paris. Tel. 1-44-41-13-13, fax 1-46-34-63-83, e-mail info@franceedition.org, World Wide Web http://www.franceedition.org. *Pres.* Liana Levi; *Dir.-Gen.* Jean-Guy Boin. *New York Branch* French Publishers Agency, 853 Broadway, Ste. 1509, New York, NY 10003-4703. Tel./fax 212-254-4540, World Wide Web http://frenchpubagency.com.

Syndicat National de la Librairie Ancienne et Moderne (National Assn. of Antiquarians and Modern Booksellers), 4 rue Gît-le-Coeur, F-75006 Paris. Tel. 1-43-29-46-38, fax 1-43-25-41-63, e-mail slam-livre@wanadoo.fr, World Wide Web http://www.slam-livre.fr. *Pres.* Alain Marchiset.

Syndicat National de l'Edition (National Union of Publishers), 115 blvd. Saint-Germain, F-75006 Paris. Tel. 1-44-41-40-50, fax 1-44-41-40-77, World Wide Web http://www.snedition.fr. *Pres.* Serge Eyrolles.

Union des Libraires de France (Union of French Booksellers), 40 rue Grégoire-de-Tours, F-75006 Paris. Tel./fax 1-43-29-88-79. *Pres.* Eric Hardin; *Gen. Delegate* Marie-Dominique Doumenc.

Germany

Börsenverein des Deutschen Buchhandels e.V. (Stock Exchange of German Booksellers), Grosser Hirschgraben 17-21, 60313 Frankfurt-am-Main. Tel. 69-1306-0, fax 69-1306-201, e-mail info@boev.de, World Wide Web http://www.boersenverein.de. *Gen. Mgr.* Harald Heker.

Verband Deutscher Antiquare e.V. (German Antiquarian Booksellers Assn.), Geschäftsstelle, Norbert Munsch, Seeblick 1, 56459 Elbingen. Tel. 6435-909-147, fax 6435-909-148, e-mail buch@antiquare.de, World Wide Web http://www.antiquare.de. *Pres.* Eberhard Koestler.

Ghana

University Bookshop (formerly West African University Booksellers Assn.), Univ. of Ghana, P.O. Box 25, Legon. Tel./fax 21-500-398, unibks@ug.gn.apc.org. *Mgr.* Emmanuel K. H. Tonyigah.

Greece

Hellenic Federation of Publishers and Booksellers, 73 Themistocleous St., 106 83 Athens. Tel. 2103-300-924, fax 2133-301-617, e-mail poev@otenet.gr. *Pres.* Georgios Dardanos.

Hungary

Magyar Könyvkiadók és Könyvterjesztök Egyesülése (Assn. of Hungarian Publishers and Booksellers), Kertesz u 41, 1073 Budapest. Tel. 1-343-25-40, fax 1-343-25-41, e-mail mkke@mkke.hu, World Wide Web http://www.mkke.hu. *Pres.* István Bart; *Secy.-Gen.* Péter Zentai.

Iceland

Félag Islenskra Bókaútgefenda (Icelandic Publishers Assn.), Baronsstig 5, 101 Reykjavik. Tel. 511-8020, fax 511-5020, e-mail baekur@simnet.is, World Wide Web http://www.bokatidindi.is.

India

Federation of Indian Publishers, Federation House, 18/1-C Institutional Area, Aruna Asaf Ali Marg, New Delhi 110067. Tel. 11-2696-4847, fax 11-2686-4054, e-mail fip1@satyam.net.in, World Wide Web http://www.fiponweb.com. *Pres.* Shri Anand Bhushan.

Indonesia

Ikatan Penerbit Indonesia (Assn. of Indonesian Book Publishers), Jl. Kalipasir 32, Jakarta 10330. Tel. 21-314-1907, fax 21-314-6050, e-mail sekretariat@ikapi.or.id, World Wide Web http://www.ikapi.or.id. *Pres.* Arselan Harahap; *Secy.-Gen.* Robinson Rusdi.

Ireland

CLE: The Irish Book Publishers Assn., 25 Denzille Lane, Dublin 2. Tel. 1-639-4868, e-mail info@publishingireland.com, World Wide Web http://www.publishingireland.com. *Pres.* Tony Farmar.

Israel

Book and Printing Center, Israel Export Institute, 29 Hamered St., P.O. Box 50084, Tel Aviv 61500. Tel. 3-514-2830, fax 3-514-2902, e-mail export-institute@export.gov.il or pama@export.gov.il, World Wide Web http://www.export.gov.il. *Dir.-Gen.* Yechiel Assia.

Book Publishers Assn. of Israel, P.O. Box 20123, 61201 Tel Aviv. Tel. 3-561-4121, fax 3-561-1996, e-mail info@tbpai.co.il, World Wide Web http://www.tbpai.co.il. *Managing Dir.* Amnon Ben-Shmuel; *Chair* Racheli Edelman.

Italy

Associazione Italiana Editori (Italian Publishers Assn.), Via delle Erbe 2, 20121 Milan. Tel. 2-86-46-3091, fax 2-89-01-0863, e-mail aie@aie.it, World Wide Web http://www.aie.it. *Dir.* Ivan Cecchini.

Associazione Librai Antiquari d'Italia (Antiquarian Booksellers Assn. of Italy), Via del Parione 11, 50123 Florence. Tel. 55-282-635, fax 55-214-831, e-mail alai@alai.it, World Wide Web http://www.alai.it. *Pres.* Umberto Pregliasco.

Jamaica

Booksellers' Assn. of Jamaica, P.O. Box 80, Kingston. Tel. 876-922-5883, fax 876-922-4743. *Pres.* Keith Shervington.

Japan

Antiquarian Booksellers' Association of Japan, 29 San-ei-cho, Shinjuku-ku, Tokyo 160-0008. Tel. 3-3357-1411, fax 3-3351-5855, e-mail abaj@abaj.gr.jp, World Wide Web http://www.abaj.gr.jp. *Pres.* Yoshio Nakao.

Japan Assn. of International Publications (formerly Japan Book Importers Assn.), Chiyoda Kaikan 21-4, Nihonbashi 1-chome, Chuo-ku, Tokyo 103-0027. Tel. 3-3271-6901, fax 3-3271-6920, e-mail jaip@poppy.ocn.ne.jp, World Wide Web http://www.jaip.gr.jp. *Chair* Seishiro Murata; *Secy.-Gen.* Hiroshi Takahashi.

Japan Book Publishers Assn., 6 Fukuromachi, Shinjuku-ku, Tokyo 162-0828. Tel. 3-3268-1301, fax 3-3268-1196, e-mail rd@jbpa.or.jp, World Wide Web http://www.jbpa.or.jp. *Pres.* Kunizo Asakura; *Exec. Dir.* Tadashi Yamashita.

Kenya

Kenya Publishers Assn., P.O. Box 42767, Nairobi 00100. Tel. 20-375-2344, fax 20-375-4076, e-mail kenyapublishers@wananchi.com, World Wide Web http://www.kenyabooks.org. *Exec. Secy.* Lynnette Kariuki.

Korea (Republic of)

Korean Publishers Assn., 105-2 Sagan-dong, Jongro-gu, Seoul 110-190. Tel. 82-2-735-2701-4, fax 82-2-738-5414, e-mail kpa@kpa21.or.kr, World Wide Web http://eng.kpa21.or.kr/main/index.htm.

Latvia

Latvian Publishers Assn., Brivibas iela 109, LV-1001 Riga. Tel. 371-728-2392, fax 371-728-0549, e-mail lga@gramatizdeveji.lv, World Wide Web http://www.gramatizdeveji.lv. *Pres.* Ingrida Vaverniece; *Exec. Dir.* Dace Pugaca.

Lithuania

Lithuanian Publishers Assn., Ave. Jaksto 22-13, 01105 Vilnius. Tel./fax 5-261-7740, e-mail lla@centras.lt, World Wide Web http://www.lla.lt. *Pres.* Arvydas Andrijauskas.

Malaysia

Malaysian Book Publishers' Assn., No. 39 Jln. Nilam 1/2, Subang Sq., Subang High-Tech Industrial Park Batutiga, 40000 Shah Alam, Selangor. Tel. 3-5637-9044, fax 3-5637-9043, e-mail inquiry@cerdik.com.my, World Wide Web http://www.mabopa.com.my. *Pres.* Ng Tieh Chuan.

Mexico

Cámara Nacional de la Industria Editorial Mexicana (Mexican Publishers' Assn.), Holanda No. 13, CP 04120, Mexico 21. Tel. 5-6-88-24-34, fax 5-6-04-31-47, e-mail cepromex@caniem.com, World Wide Web http://www.caniem.com. *Co-Pres.* A. H. Gayosso, J. C. Cramerez.

The Netherlands

KVB—Koninklijke Vereeniging van het Boekenvak (formerly Koninklijke Vereeniging ter Bevordering van de Belangen des Boekhandels) (Royal Dutch Book Trade Assn.), Postbus 15007, 1001 MA Amsterdam. Tel. 20-624-02-12, fax 20-620-88-71, e-mail nbb@boekbond.nl, World Wide Web http://www.kvb.nl. *Exec. Dir.* C. Verberne.

Nederlands Uitgeversverbond (Royal Dutch Publishers Assn.), Postbus 12040, 1100 AA Amsterdam. Tel. 20-43-09-150, fax 20-43-09-179, e-mail info@nuv.nl, World Wide Web http://www.nuv.nl. *Pres.* Henk J. L. Vonhoff.

Nederlandsche Vereeniging van Antiquaren (Netherlands Assn. of Antiquarian Booksellers), Prisengracht 15, 2512 EW The Hague. Tel. 070-364-98-40, fax 070-364-33-40, e-mail kok@xs4all.nl, World Wide Web http://nvva.nl. *Pres.* Ton Kok.

Nederlandse Boekverkopersbond (Dutch Booksellers Assn.), Prins Hendriklaan 72, 3721 AT Bilthoven. Tel. 030-228-79-56, fax 030-228-45-66, e-mail nbb@boekbond.nl, World Wide Web http://www.boekbond.nl. *Pres.* D. Anbeek; *Exec. Secy.* A. C. Doeser.

New Zealand

Booksellers New Zealand, Box 13-248, Wellington. Tel. 4-478-5511, fax 4-478-5519, e-mail enquiries@booksellers.co.nz, World Wide Web http://www.booksellers.co.nz. *Chair* Tony Moores; *Chief Exec.* Alice Heather.

Nigeria

Nigerian Publishers Assn., GPO Box 2541, Ibadan. Tel. 2-241-4427, fax 2-241-3396, e-mail nigpa@skannet.com or nigpa@steineng.net. *Pres.* V. Nwankwo.

Norway

Norske Bokhandlerforening (Norwegian Booksellers Assn.), Øvre Vollgate 15, 0158 Oslo 1. Tel. 22-00-75-80, fax 22-33-38-30, e-mail dnf@forleggerforeningen.no, World Wide Web http://www.forleggerforeningen.no. *Dir.* Kristin Cecilie Slordahl.

Norske Forleggerforening (Norwegian Publishers Assn.), Øvre Vollgate 15, 0158 Oslo 1. Tel. 22-00-75-80, fax 22-33-38-30, e-mail dnf@forleggerforeningen.no, World Wide Web http://www.forleggerforeningen.no. *Contact* Kristin Cecilie Slordahl.

Peru

Cámara Peruana del Libro (Peruvian Publishers Assn.), Av. Abancay 4ta cuadra, Lima. Tel. 1-428-7690, fax 1-427-7331, e-mail dn@binape.gob.pe, World Wide Web http://www.binape.gob.pe. *Pres.* Julio Cesar Flores Rodriguez; *Exec. Dir.* Dra Loyda Moran Bustamente.

Philippines

Philippine Educational Publishers Assn., 84 P. Florentino St., Sta. Mesa Heights, Quezon City. Tel. 2-712-4106, fax 2-731-3448, e-mail dbuhain@cnl.net, World Wide Web http://nbdb.gov.ph/publindust.htm. *Pres.* Dominador D. Buhain.

Poland

Polskie Towarzystwo Wydawców Ksiazek (Polish Society of Book Editors), ul. Mazowiecka 2/4, 00-048 Warsaw. Tel. 22-826-72-71, fax 22-826-07-35. *Pres.* Janusz Fogler; *Gen. Secy.* Donat Chruscicki.

Stowarzyszenie Ksiegarzy Polskich (Assn. of Polish Booksellers), ul. Mokotowska 4/6, 00-641 Warsaw. Tel. 22-252-874, World Wide Web http://www.bookweb.org/orgs/1322.html. *Pres.* Tadeusz Hussak.

Portugal

Associação Portuguesa de Editores e Livreiros (Portuguese Assn. of Publishers and Booksellers), Av. dos Estados Unidas da America 97, 6 Esq., 1700-167 Lisbon. Tel. 21-843-51-80, fax 21-848-93-77, e-mail apel@apel.pt, World Wide Web http://www.apel.pt. *Pres.* António Baptista Lopes.

Russia

Publishers Assn., ul. B. Nikitskaya 44, 121069 Moscow. Tel. 495-202-1174, fax 495-202-3989, e-mail aski@rol.ru, World Wide Web http://www.aski.ru. *Dir.* V. Shibaev.

Rossiiskaya Knizhnaya Palata (Russian Book Chamber), ul. Ostozhenka d ya, 119034 Moscow. Tel. 495-291-12-78, fax 495-291-96-30, e-mail bookch@postman.ru, World Wide Web http://www.bookchamber.ru.

Serbia and Montenegro

Association of Yugoslav Publishers and Booksellers, P.O. Box 883, 11000 Belgrade. Tel. 11-2642-533, fax 11-2686-539, e-mail ognjenl@eunet.yu. *Dir.*Zivadin Mitrovic; *Mgr.* Marina Radojicic.

Singapore

Singapore Book Publishers Assn., c/o Cannon International, Block 86, Marine Parade Central No. 03-213, Singapore 440086. Tel. 6344-7801, fax 6344-0897, e-mail twcsbpa@singnet.com.sg. *Pres.* K. P. Siram; *Dir.* Tan Wu Cheng.

Slovenia

Zdruzenie Zaloznikov in Knjigotrzcev Slovenije Gospodarska Zbornica Slovenije (Assn. of Publishers and Booksellers of Slovenia), Dimiceva 13, SI 1504 Ljubljana. Tel. 1-5898-474, fax 1-5898-100, e-mail info@gzs.si, World Wide Web http://www.gzs.si. *Pres.* Milan Matos.

South Africa

Publishers Assn. of South Africa, Centre for the Book, P.O. Box 15277, Vlaeberg 8018. Tel. 21-426-2728, fax 21-426-1733, e-mail pasa@publishsa.co.za, World Wide Web http://www.publishsa.co.za. *Mgr.* Samantha Faure; *Admin.* Desiree Murdoch.

South African Booksellers Assn. (formerly Associated Booksellers of Southern Africa), P.O. Box 870, Bellville 7530. Tel. 21-945-1572, fax 21-945-2169, e-mail saba@sabooksellers.com, World Wide Web http://sabooksellers.com. *Pres.* Guru Redhi; *Secy.* Peter Adams.

Spain

Federación de Gremios de Editores de España (Federation of Spanish Publishers Assns.), Cea Bermúdez 44-2 Dcha, 2003 Madrid. Tel. 915-345-195, fax 915-352-625, e-mail fgee@fge.es, World Wide Web http://www.federacioneditores.org. *Pres.* D. Emiliano Martinez; *Exec. Dir.* Antonio Ma Avila.

Sri Lanka

Sri Lanka Assn. of Publishers, 112 S. Mahinda Mawatha, Colombo 10. Tel. 11-269-5773, fax 11-269-5663, e-mail dayawansa jay@hotmail.com, World Wide Web http://www.lankahands.com. *Dir.* Dayawansa Jayakody; *Gen. Secy.* Gamini Wijesuriya.

Sudan

Sudanese Publishers Assn., c/o Institute of African and Asian Studies, Khartoum Univ., P.O. Box 321, Khartoum 11115. Tel. 11-778-0031, fax 11-770-358, e-mail makkawi@sudanmail.net. *Dir.* Abel Rahim Makkawi.

Sweden

Svenska Förläggareföreningen (Swedish Publishers Assn.), Drottninggatan 97, S-11360 Stockholm. Tel. 8-736-19-40, fax 8-736-19-44, e-mail info@forlaggareforeningen. se, World Wide Web http://www. forlaggareforeningen.se. *Dir.* Kristina Ahlinder.

Switzerland

Association Suisse des Éditeurs de Langue Française (ASELF) (Swiss Assn. of English-Language Publishers), 2 ave. Agassiz, 1001 Lausanne. Tel. 21-319-71-11, fax 21-319-79-10, e-mail pschibli@centrezational. cl, World Wide Web http://www. culturactif.ch/editions/asef1.htm. *Secy. Gen.* Philippe Schibli.

Schweizerischer Buchhandler- und Verleger-Verband (Swiss German-Language Booksellers and Publishers Assn.), Alderstr. 40, Postfach, 8034 Zurich. Tel. 044-421-36-00, fax 044-421-36-18, e-mail sbvv@swiss books.ch, World Wide Web http://www. swissbooks.ch. *Exec. Dir.* Martin Jann.

Thailand

Publishers and Booksellers Assn. of Thailand, 947/158-159 Moo 12, Bang Na-Trad Rd., Bang Na, Bangkok 10260. Tel. 2-954-9560-4, fax 2-954-9565-6, e-mail info@

pubat.or.th, World Wide Web http://www. pubat.or.th.

Uganda

Uganda Publishers and Booksellers Assn., P.O. Box 7732, Kampala. Tel. 41-259-163, fax 41-251-160, e-mail mbd@infocom.co. ug. *Contact* Martin Okia.

United Kingdom

Antiquarian Booksellers Assn., Sackville House, 40 Piccadilly, London W1J 0DR, England. Tel. 20-7439-3118, fax 20-7439-3119, e-mail admin@aba.org.uk, World Wide Web http://www.aba.org.uk. *Pres.* Jonathan Potter; *Admins.* Philippa Gibson, Deborah Stratford.

Assn. of Learned and Professional Society Publishers, 8 Rickford Rd., Nailsea, North Somerset RS48 4PY, England. Tel. 1275-858-837, World Wide Web http://www. alpsp.org/ngen_public. *Chief Exec.* Ian Russell.

Booktrust, 45 East Hill, Wandsworth, London SW18 2QZ, England. Tel. 20-8516-2972, fax 20-8516-2978, World Wide Web http://www.booktrust.org.uk.

Educational Publishers Council, 29B Montague St., London WC1B 5BW, England. Tel. 20-7691-9191, fax 20-7691-9199, e-mail mail@publishers.org.uk, World Wide Web http://www.publishers.org.uk. *Chair* Kate Harris; *Dir.* Graham Taylor.

Publishers Assn., 29B Montague St., London WC1B 5BW, England. Tel. 20-7691-9191, fax 20-7691-9199, e-mail mail@publishers. org.uk, World Wide Web http://www. publishers.org.uk. *Pres.* Mike Boswood; *Chief Exec.* Simon Juden.

Scottish Book Trust, Sandeman House, Trunk's Close, 55 High St., Edinburgh EH1 1SR, Scotland. Tel. 131-524-0160, fax 131-524-0161, e-mail info@scottish booktrust.com, World Wide Web http://

www.scottishbooktrust.com. *Chief Exec. Officer* Marc Lambert.

Scottish Publishers Assn., Scottish Book Centre, 137 Dundee St., Edinburgh EH11 1BG, Scotland. Tel. 131-228-6866, fax 131-228-3220, e-mail enquiries@scottish books.org, World Wide Web http://www. scottishbooks.org. *Dir.* Lorraine Fannin; *Chair* Janis Adams.

Welsh Books Council (Cyngor Llyfrau Cymru), Castell Brychan, Aberystwyth, Ceredigion SY23 2JB, Wales. Tel. 1970-624-151, fax 1970-625-385, e-mail castell brychan@wbc.org.uk, World Wide Web http://www.cllc.org.uk. *Dir.* Gwerfyl Pierce Jones.

Uruguay

Cámara Uruguaya del Libro (Uruguayan Publishers Assn.), Juan D. Jackson 1118, 11 200 Montevideo. Tel. 82-41-57-32, fax 82-41-18-60, e-mail camurlib@adinet. com.uy. *Pres.* Ernesto Sanjines.

Venezuela

Cámara Venezolana del Libro (Venezuelan Publishers Assn.), Av. Andrés Bello, Edificio Centro Andrés Bello, Torre Oeste 11, piso 11, of. 112-0, Caracas 1050. Tel. 212-793-1347, fax 212-793-1368, e-mail cave libro@cantv.net. *Dir.* M. P. Vargas.

Zambia

Booksellers and Publishers Assn. of Zambia, Box 31838, Lusaka. Tel. 1-255-282, fax 1-255-195, e-mail bpaz@zamnet.zm, World Wide Web http://africanpublishers.org. *Exec. Dir.* Basil Mbewe.

Zimbabwe

Zimbabwe Book Publishers Assn., P.O. Box 3041, Harare. Tel./fax 4-754-256, e-mail engelbert@collegepress.co.zw.

National Information Standards Organization (NISO) Standards

Information Retrieval

Z39.2-1994 (R2001)	Information Interchange Format
Z39.47-1993 (R2003)	Extended Latin Alphabet Coded Character Set for Bibliographic Use (ANSEL)
Z39.50-2003	Information Retrieval (Z39.50) Application Service Definition and Protocol Specification
Z39.53-2001	Codes for the Representation of Languages for Information Interchange
Z39.64-1989	(R2002) East Asian Character Code for Bibliographic Use
Z39.76-1996	(R2002) Data Elements for Binding Library Materials
Z39.84-2005	Syntax for the Digital Object Identifier
Z39.88-2004	The OpenURL Framework for Context-Sensitive Services
Z39.89-2003	The U.S. National Z39.50 Profile for Library Applications

Library Management

Z39.7-2004	Information Services and Use: metrics and statistics for libraries and information providers—Data Dictionary
Z39.20-1999	Criteria for Price Indexes for Print Library Materials
Z39.71-2006	Holdings Statements for Bibliographic Items
Z39.73-1994 (R2001)	Single-Tier Steel Bracket Library Shelving
Z39.83-2002	Circulation Interchange—Part 1: Protocol (NCIP)
Z39.83-2002	Circulation Interchange—Part 2: Protocol Implementation Profile 1

Preservation and Storage

Z39.32-1996 (R2002)	Information on Microfiche Headers
Z39.48-1992 (R2002)	Permanence of Paper for Publications and Documents in Libraries and Archives
Z39.62-2000	Eye-Legible Information on Microfilm Leaders and Trailers and on Containers of Processed Microfilm on Open Reels
Z39.74-1996 (R2002)	Guides to Accompany Microform Sets
Z39.77-2001	Guidelines for Information About Preservation Products
Z39.78-2000 (R2006)	Library Binding

Z39.79-2001   Environmental Conditions for Exhibiting Library and
                     Archival Materials
Z39.87-2006   Data Dictionary—Technical Metadata for Digital Still
                     Images

Publishing and Information Management

Z39.9-1992 (R2001)   International Standard Serial Numbering (ISSN)
Z39.14-1997 (R2002) Guidelines for Abstracts
Z39.18-2005   Scientific and Technical Reports—Preparation,
                     Presentation, and Preservation
Z39.19-2005   Guidelines for the Construction, Format, and Management
                     of Monolingual Controlled Vocabularies
Z39.23-1997 (R2002) Standard Technical Report Number Format and Creation
Z39.26-1997 (R2002) Micropublishing Product Information
Z39.29-2005   Bibliographic References
Z39.41-1997 (R2002) Printed Information on Spines
Z39.43-1993 (R2006) Standard Address Number (SAN) for the Publishing
                     Industry
Z39.56-1996 (R2002) Serial Item and Contribution Identifier (SICI)
Z39.82-2001   Title Pages for Conference Publications
Z39.85-2001   Dublin Core Metadata Element Set
Z39.86-2005   Specifications for the Digital Talking Book
ANSI/NISO/ISO   Electronic Manuscript Preparation and Markup
12083-1995 (R2002)

In Development/NISO Initiatives

NISO examines new areas for standardization, reports, and best practices on a
continuing basis to support its ongoing standards development program. NISO
working groups are exploring these areas:

- Exchange of Serial Subscription Information Serials JWP—(NISO and
  EDItEUR)
- License Expression—(NISO, DLF, EDItEUR, and PLS)
- Metasearch Initiative—Access Management, Collection Description, and
  Search/Retrieve
- RFID for Library Applications
- Shared E-Resource Understanding (SERU)
- Standardized Usage Statistics Harvesting Initiative (SUSHI)
- Versions of Journal Articles (NISO and ALPSP)

NISO Technical Reports, Recommended Practices, and Other Publications

Best Practices for Designing Web Services in the Library Context (RP-2006-01)
Environmental Guidelines for the Storage of Paper Records (TR01-1995)
Guidelines for Indexes and Related Information Retrieval Devices (TR02-1997)

Guidelines to Alphanumeric Arrangement and Sorting of Numerals and Other Symbols (TR03-1999)

Information Standards Quarterly (*ISQ*) (NISO quarterly newsletter)

A Framework of Guidance for Building Good Digital Collections

The RFP Writer's Guide to Standards for Library Systems

Metadata Demystified: A Guide for Publishers

Networked Reference Services: Question/Answer Transaction Protocol (TR04-2006)

NISO Metasearch XML Gateway Implementers Guide (RP-2006-02)

NISO Newsline (free monthly e-newsletter)

Ranking of Authentication and Access Methods Available to the Metasearch Environment (RP-2005-01)

Search and Retrieval Citation Level Data Elements (RP-2005-03)

Search and Retrieval Results Set Metadata (RP-2005-02)

Understanding Metadata

Up and Running: Implementing Z39.50—Proceedings of a Symposium Sponsored by the State Library of Iowa

Z39.50: A Primer on the Protocol

Z39.50 Implementation Experiences

Workshop reports and white papers are available on the NISO Web site at http://www.niso.org/standards/std_resources.html.

For more information, contact NISO, 4733 Bethesda Ave., Suite 300, Bethesda, MD 20814. Tel. 301-654-2512, fax 301-654-1721, e-mail nisohq@niso.org, World Wide Web http://www.niso.org.

Calendar, 2008–2014

The list below contains information on association meetings or promotional events that are, for the most part, national or international in scope. State and regional library association meetings are also included. To confirm the starting or ending date of a meeting, which may change after the *Bowker Annual* has gone to press, contact the association directly. Addresses of library and book trade associations are listed in Part 6 of this volume. For information on additional book trade and promotional events, see *Literary Market Place* and *International Literary Market Place,* published by Information Today, Inc., and other library and book trade publications such as *Library Journal, School Library Journal,* and *Publishers Weekly. American Libraries,* published by the American Library Association, maintains an online calendar at http://www.ala.org/ala/alonline/calendar/calendar.cfm. An Information Today events calendar can be found at http://www.infotoday.com/calendar.shtml.

2008

June

1–4	Academic Library Advancement and Development Network Conference	Austin, TX
5–7	Canadian Assn. for Information Science	Vancouver, BC
5–7	London Antiquarian Book Fair	London, England
5–8	North American Serials Interest Group	Phoenix, AZ
14–17	Cape Town Book Fair	Cape Town, South Africa
14–17	Special Libraries Assn.	Seattle, WA
19–20	Forbidden Fruit: The Censorship of Literature and Information for Young People	Southport, England
26–7/2	American Library Assn. Annual Conference	Anaheim, CA
29–7/2	International Society for Technology in Education	San Antonio, TX

July

1–5	Ligue des Bibliothèques Européennes de Recherche (LIBER)	Istanbul, Turkey
10–13	Tokyo International Book Fair	Tokyo, Japan
12–16	American Assn. of Law Libraries	Portland, OR
20–22	Church and Synagogue Library Assn.	Greenville, SC

July 2008 *(cont.)*

20–25	International Assn. of Music Libraries, Archives, and Documentation Centres	Naples, Italy
28–31	International Reading Association World Congress	San José, Costa Rica

August

3–6	International Assn. of School Librarianship	Berkeley, CA
4–6	Assn. of Research Libraries Library Assessment Conference	Seattle, WA
6–9	Pacific Northwest Library Assn.	Post Falls, ID
10–15	IFLA World Library and Information Congress	Quebec City, QC
14–16	Nevada Library Assn.	Las Vegas
14–17	Americas Conference on Information Systems (AMCIS 2008)	Toronto, ON
23–31	Society of American Archivists	San Francisco
24–27	World Conference on Agricultural Information	Tokyo, Japan

September

1–4	Beijing International Book Fair	Beijing, China
3–8	Moscow International Book Fair	Moscow, Russia
4–5	Ninth European Conference on Knowledge Management	Southampton, England
11–13	Madrid International Book Fair	Madrid, Spain
14–16	Assn. of Information and Dissemination Centers	Boston
14–18	Ninth International Conference on Music Information Retrieval	Philadelphia
18–20	Assn. for Library Service to Children National Institute	Salt Lake City
18–21	REFORMA	El Paso, TX
19–21	International Antiquarian Book Fair of Brussels	Brussels, Belgium
22–23	Web Search University	Washington, DC
23–26	Illinois Library Assn.	Chicago
24–26	South Dakota Library Assn.	Chamberlain
25–28	Göteborg International Book Fair	Göteborg, Sweden
26–28	First World Summit on the Knowledge Society	Athens, Greece

October

1–3	Missouri Library Assn.	St. Louis
1–4	Idaho Library Assn.	Idaho Falls
1–4	Kentucky Library Assn./Kentucky School Media Assn./Southeastern Library Assn./Assn. of Research Libraries	Louisville

1–4	Wyoming Library Assn.	Casper
5–7	Arkansas Library Assn.	Little Rock
8–10	Minnesota Library Assn.	Twin Cities
13–15	International Information Management Assn.	San Diego, CA
15–17	Georgia Library Assn.	Athens
15–17	Iowa Library Assn.	Dubuque
15–17	Nebraska Library Assn./Nebraska Educational Media Assn.	Lincoln
15–19	Frankfurt Book Fair	Frankfurt, Germany
16–17	Internet Librarian International	London, England
16–17	Maryland Association of School Librarians	Ellicott City
16–19	Library and Information Technology Assn.	Cincinnati
19–21	New England Library Assn.	Manchester, NH
20–22	Internet Librarian	Monterey, CA
20–23	ARMA International	Las Vegas
21–24	Michigan Library Assn.	Kalamazoo
21–24	South Carolina Library Assn.	Greenville
22–24	Ohio Educational Library Media Assn.	Columbus
23–24	International Conference on Knowledge Management	Columbus, OH
23–24	Maine Library Assn.	Bethel
23–24	Virginia Library Assn.	Williamsburg
24–29	American Society for Information Science and Technology	Columbus, OH
29–31	North Carolina School Library Media Assn.	Winston-Salem

November

1–9	27th Istanbul Book Fair	Istanbul, Turkey
2–3	Massachusetts School Library Assn.	Sturbridge
4–7	Wisconsin Library Assn.	Middleton
5–7	Michigan Assn. for Media in Education	Dearborn
5–8	New York Library Assn.	Saratoga Springs
6–8	Colorado Assn. of Libraries	Denver
6–8	Virginia Educational Media Assn.	Richmond
7–9	LiberBerlin (antiquarian book fair)	Berlin, Germany
7–9	Young Adult Literature Symposium (YALSA)	Nashville, TN
9–12	Pennsylvania Library Assn.	Valley Forge
14–16	Boston International Antiquarian Book Fair	Boston
14–17	California Library Assn.	San José
17–18	SPARC Institutional Repositories Meeting	Baltimore
18–20	Indiana Library Federation	Indianapolis
19–21	Minnesota Library Association Conference	Bloomington
20–23	California School Library Assn.	Sacramento
21–23	Oslo Book Fair	Oslo, Norway
29–7/12	Guadalajara International Book Fair	Guadalajara, Mexico

December 2008

3–5	West Virginia Library Assn.	White Sulphur Springs
8–9	International Conference on Gray Literature	Amsterdam, Netherlands
8–10	Arizona Library Assn.	Glendale
14–16	International Conference on Information Systems (ICIS 2008)	Paris, France

2009

January

20–22	Information Online 2009	Sydney, Australia
20–23	Assn. for Library and Information Science Education (ALISE)	Denver
23–28	American Library Assn. Midwinter Meeting	Denver

February

4–9	Taipei International Book Exhibition	Taipei, Taiwan
8–11	CODEX International Book Fair	Berkeley, CA
13–15	California International Antiquarian Book Fair	San Francisco
15–20	Jerusalem International Book Fair	Jerusalem, Israel

March

12–15	Assn. of College and Research Libraries	Seattle, WA
17–22	Abu Dhabi International Book Fair	Abu Dhabi
22–24	Wisconsin Educational Media and Technology Assn.	Madison
28–4/4	Texas Library Assn.	Houston

April

1–3	Kansas Library Assn./Mountain Plains Library Assn.	Wichita
8–10	Tennessee Library Assn.	Nashville
19–21	Missouri Assn. of School Librarians	Osage Beach
20–22	London Book Fair	London, England
23–25	American Society of Indexers	Portland, OR

May

29–31	BookExpo America	New York

June

5–7	London Antiquarian Book Fair	London, England
13–18	Special Libraries Assn.	Washington, DC

July

9–15	American Library Assn. Annual Conference	Chicago

October

1–3	LITA National Forum	Salt Lake City
6–9	Illinois Library Assn.	Peoria
7–9	Minnesota Library Assn.	Duluth
14–18	Frankfurt Book Fair	Frankfurt, Germany
18–20	New England Library Assn.	Hartford, CT
18–21	Pennsylvania Library Assn.	Harrisburg
20–23	Wisconsin Library Assn.	Appleton
21–23	Iowa Library Assn.	Des Moines
21–23	Ohio Library Council	Cleveland

November

4–7	Michigan Library Assn.	Lansing
4–8	American Assn. of School Librarians	Charlotte, NC
19–21	Virginia Educational Media Assn.	Roanoke
19–22	California School Library Assn.	Ontario

2010

January

15–20	American Library Assn. Midwinter Meeting	Boston

March

23–27	Public Library Assn.	Portland, OR

April

4–6	Wisconsin Educational Media and Technology Assn.	Wisconsin Dells
7–9	Kansas Library Assn.	Wichita
13–16	Texas Library Assn.	San Antonio
18–20	Missouri Assn. of School Librarians	Osage Beach
19–21	London Book Fair	London, England

June

24–30	American Library Assn. Annual Conference	New York

October

6–8	Minnesota Library Assn.	Rochester
12–14	Iowa Library Assn.	Coralville
17–19	New England Library Assn.	Sturbridge, MA

2011

January

28–2/2   American Library Assn. Midwinter Meeting   San Diego

April

6–8   Kansas Library Assn.   Topeka
7–10   Assn. of College and Research Libraries   Philadelphia
12–15   Texas Library Assn.   Austin

June

23–29   American Library Assn. Annual Conference   New Orleans

October

5–7   Minnesota Library Assn.   Twin Cities

2012

January

20–25   American Library Assn. Midwinter Meeting   Dallas, TX

April

17–20   Texas Library Assn.   Houston

June

21–27   American Library Assn. Annual Conference   Anaheim, CA

2013

January

25–30   American Library Assn. Midwinter Meeting   Seattle, WA

April

4–7   Assn. of College and Research Libraries   Indianapolis, IN
8–11   Texas Library Assn.   San Antonio

June

20–26   American Library Assn. Annual Conference   Washington, DC

2014

January

24–29   American Library Assn. Midwinter Meeting   Philadelphia

April

8–11   Texas Library Assn.   Dallas

June

26–2/7   American Library Assn. Annual Conference   Las Vegas

Acronyms

A

AAAS. American Association for the Advancement of Science

AALL. American Association of Law Libraries

AAP. Association of American Publishers

AASL. American Association of School Librarians

ABA. American Booksellers Association

ABFFE. American Booksellers Foundation for Free Expression

ACAP. Automated Content Access Protocol

ACRL. Association of College and Research Libraries

ACS. American Community Survey

AgNIC. Agriculture Network Information Center

AIIP. Association of Independent Information Professionals

AILA. American Indian Library Association

AJL. Association of Jewish Libraries

ALA. American Library Association

ALCTS. Association for Library Collections and Technical Services

ALIC. Archives Library Information Center

ALISE. Association for Library and Information Science Education

ALS. National Center for Education Statistics, Academic Libraries Survey

ALSC. Association for Library Service to Children

ALTA. Association for Library Trustees and Advocates

AMMLA. American Merchant Marine Library Association

AMS. Advanced Marketing Services

APALA. Asian/Pacific American Librarians Association

ARC. National Archives and Records Administration, Archival Research Catalog

ARL. Association of Research Libraries

ARLIS/NA. Art Libraries Society of North America

ASCLA. Association of Specialized and Cooperative Library Agencies

ASIS&T. American Society for Information Science and Technology

ATLA. American Theological Library Association

B

BCALA. Black Caucus of the American Library Association

BEA. BookExpo America

BSA. Bibliographical Society of America

C

CAIS. Canadian Association for Information Science

CALA. Chinese American Librarians Association

CALEA. Communications Assistance for Law Enforcement Act

CAP. Canada, Community Access Program

CAPL. Canadian Association of Public Libraries

CARL. Canadian Association of Research Libraries

CASL. Canadian Association for School Libraries

CASLIS. Canadian Association of Special Libraries and Information Services

CCC. Copyright Clearance Center

CCIA. Computer and Communications Industry Association

CD-ROM. Compact Disc Read-Only Memory

CDNL. Conference of Directors of National Libraries

CGP. U.S. Government Printing Office, *Catalog of Government Publications*

CLA. Canadian Library Association; Catholic Library Association

CLTA. Canadian Library Trustees Association

CNI. Coalition for Networked Information

CNIB. Canadian National Institute for the Blind

CNRI. Corporation for National Research Initiatives

COLT. Council on Library/Media Technicians

COPA. Child Online Protection Act

COPPA. Children's Online Privacy Protection Act

COSLA. Chief Officers of State Library Agencies

CSLA. Church and Synagogue Library Association

CSRL. Center for the Study of Rural Librarianship

D

DLF. Digital Library Federation

DMCA. Digital Millennium Copyright Act

DOE. Education, U.S. Department of

DRM. Digital rights management

DTB. Digital talking book (DTB) technology

DTIC. Defense Technical Information Center

E

EAR. National Technical Information Service, Export Administration Regulations

EMIERT. American Library Association, Ethnic and Multicultural Information and Exchange Round Table

EPA. Environmental Protection Agency

ERIC. Educational Resources Information Center

ERMI. Digital Library Federation, E-Resources Management Initiative

F

FAFLRT. American Library Association, Federal and Armed Forces Librarians Round Table

FBI. Federal Bureau of Investigation

FDLP. U.S. Government Printing Office, Federal Depository Library Program

FDsys. U.S. Government Printing Office, Federal Digital System

FEDRIP. National Technical Information Service, FEDRIP (Federal Research in Progress Database)

FIAF. International Federation of Film Archives

FISA. Foreign Intelligence Surveillance Act

FLICC. Federal Library and Information Center Committee

FOIA. Freedom of Information Act

FOLUSA. Friends of Libraries U.S.A.

FPC. Federal Publishers Committee

G

GLBT. American Library Association, Gay, Lesbian, Bisexual, and Transgendered Round Table

GLIN. Global Legal Information Network

GODORT. American Library Association, Government Documents Round Table

GPO. Government Printing Office

GRC. National Technical Information Service, GOV.Research Center

GST. Canada, Goods and Services Tax

GWAS. National Center for Biotechnology Information, Genome-Wide Association Studies (GWAS) project

H

HTS. Book trade, harmonious trade system

I

IAALD. International Association of Agricultural Information Specialists

IACs. Defense Technical Information Center, Information Analysis Centers

IALL. International Association of Law Libraries

IAML. International Association of Music Libraries, Archives and Documentation Centres

IASL. International Association of School Librarianship

IATUL. International Association of Technological University Libraries

IFLA. International Federation of Library Associations and Institutions

IFRT. American Library Association, Intellectual Freedom Round Table

ILL/DD. Interlibrary loan/document delivery

ILS. Government Printing Office, Integrated Library System

IMLS. Institute of Museum and Library Services

IRDW. Association of Research Libraries, Initiative to Recruit a Diverse Work Force

ISBN. International Standard Book Number

ISCAP. Interagency Security Classification Appeals Panel

ISO. International Organization for Standardization

ISOO. Information Security Oversight Office

ISSN. International Standard Serial Number

L

LAC. Library and Archives Canada

LAMA. Library Administration and Management Association

LCA. Library Copyright Alliance

LCDP. Association of Research Libraries, Leadership and Career Development Program

LHRT. American Library Association, Library History Round Table

LIS. Library/information science

LITA. Library and Information Technology Association

LJ. Library Journal

LOVE. Livingston Organization for Values in Education

LRRT. American Library Association, Library Research Round Table

LSP. National Center for Education Statistics, Library Statistics Program

LSTA. Library Services and Technology Act

M

MAGERT. American Library Association, Map and Geography Round Table

METS. Digital Library Federation, Metadata Encoding and Transmission Standard

MLA. Medical Library Association; Music Library Association

N

NAGARA. National Association of Government Archives and Records Administrators

NAL. National Agricultural Library

NARA. National Archives and Records Administration

NCES. National Center for Education Statistics

NCLA. National Church Library Association

NCLB. No Child Left Behind

NCLIS. National Commission on Libraries and Information Science

NDC. National Declassification Center

NDIIPP. National Digital Information Infrastructure and Preservation Program

NDNP. Newspapers, National Digital Newspaper Program

NEH. National Endowment for the Humanities

NFAIS. NFAIS (National Federation of Advanced Information Services)

NIH. National Institutes of Health

NISO. National Information Standards Organization

NLE. National Library of Education

NLM. National Library of Medicine

NMRT. American Library Association, New Members Round Table

NNA. National Newspaper Association

NSF. National Science Foundation

NSL. National Security Letters

NTIS. National Technical Information Service

O

OCA. Open Content Alliance

OGIS. National Archives and Records Administration, Office of Government Information Services
OJS. Software programs, Open Journal Systems (OJS) software
ORC. Internet/Web, Online Resource Center

P

PIDB. Public Interest Declassification Board
PIRG. Public Interest Research Group
PLA. Public Library Association
PMC. PubMedCentral
PRISM. Association of American Publishers, PRISM (Partnership for Research Integrity in Science and Medicine)
PTDLA. Patent and Trademark Depository Library Association
PURLs. Software programs, Persistent Uniform Resource Locators
PW. Publishers Weekly

R

RIAA. Recording Industry Association of America
RUSA. Reference and User Services Association

S

SAA. Society of American Archivists
SAN. Standard Address Number
SASS. National Center for Education Statistics, Library Statistics Program, Schools and Staffing Survey
SBU. Government information, access to, Sensitive But Unclassified
SCI. Scholarly Communications Institute
SERU. Association of Research Libraries, Simplified e-Resource Understanding
SIIA. Software and Information Industry Association

SKILLS. Strengthening Kids' Interest in Learning and Libraries Act
SLA. Special Libraries Association
SPARC. SPARC (Scholarly Publishing and Academic Resources Coalition)
SRIM. National Technical Information Service, Selected Research in Microfiche
SRRT. American Library Association, Social Responsibilities Round Table
SSP. Society for Scholarly Publishing
STINET. Scientific and Technical Information Network
STM. Scientific, Technical, and Medical (STM)

T

TBPA. Taiwan Book Publishers Association
TLA. Theatre Library Association

U

ULC. Urban Libraries Council

V

VHP. History, Veterans History Project

W

WNC. World News Connection
WSIS. World Summit on the Information Society
WTO. World Trade Organization

Y

YALSA. Young Adult Library Services Association
YPG. Association of American Publishers, Young to Publishing Group

Index of Organizations

Please note that many cross-references refer to entries in the Subject Index.

A

Adobe, 220
AdSense, 59
Advanced Marketing Services (AMS), 505
AGRICOLA (Agricultural OnLine Access), 95–96, 119–120
Agriculture Network Information Center (AgNIC), 91
Agriculture, U.S. Department of (USDA) pomological watercolor collection, 93–94
See also National Agricultural Library
AGRIS (Agricultural Science and Technology database), 120
AIIM—The Enterprise Content Management Association, 703
Allied Professional Association, 422
Amazon.com, 50, 200, 506, 509
  Kindle, 506
  Perfect 10 v. Amazon, 58–60, 232
American Anthropological Association, 29
American Association for the Advancement of Science (AAAS), 28
American Association of Law Libraries (AALL), 415, 419, 683
American Association of School Librarians (AASL), 388, 686–687
  awards, 422
  scholarships, 415
  65 percent solution, 180
American Booksellers Association (ABA), 221–227
  ABACUS, 222
  Book Sense program, 224–225, 640
  conferences, 221, 222, 223
  educational programs, 222–223
  Emerging Leaders Project, 224
  Web site, 222–223

American Booksellers Foundation for Free Expression (ABFFE), 226–227
American Folklife Center, 79, 84
American Indian Library Association (AILA), 703–704
American Library Association (ALA), 177–192, 684–703
  advocacy, 180
  awards, 192, 419–433, 451
  Banned Books Week, 181
  conferences, 178, 179, 183–184, 187, 245, 271, 322
  Diversity, Office for, 430
  employment Web site, 386
  Ethnic and Multicultural Information and Exchange Round Table (EMIERT) awards, 427
  Exhibits Round Table awards, 427
  exhibits, touring, 185
  Federal and Armed Forces Librarians Round Table (FAFLRT) awards, 427
  funding, study of, 445
  Gay, Lesbian, Bisexual, and Transgendered Round Table (GLBT), 427
  Government Documents Round Table (GODORT) awards, 427
  grants, 190, 416
  Graphics READ CDs, 188–189
  highlights, 179–181
  Information Technology Policy, Office for; awards, 430
  Intellectual Freedom Round Table (IFRT), 427–428, 430
  Internet connectivity, 446
  leadership, 190
  Libraries Connect Communities . . . , 446
  Library History Round Table (LHRT) awards, 429

Subject Index

Please note that many cross-references refer to entries in the Index of Organizations.

Archives *(cont.)*
  open archives initiative, 163
  See also Archives Library Information Center; Library and Archives Canada; National Archives and Records Administration
Arizona
  humanities councils, 347
  library associations, 745
  networks and cooperative library organizations, 659
  school library media associations, 767
Arkansas
  humanities councils, 347
  library associations, 745–746
  networks and cooperative library organizations, 659
  school library media associations, 767
Armed forces, libraries, number of, 462(table), 463(table)
Arriba Soft Corp., Kelly v., 59
Art books
  U.S. exports, 553, 554(table)
  U.S. imports, 557(table), 560
Associations, *see* Book trade, associations; Library associations and agencies *and* names of specific associations
Atkins, Gorran v., 203
Atlases, bestselling, 621
The Audacity of Hope (Obama), 615
Audiobooks, 195, 535
  average prices, 528(table), 541(table)
  best books for children, 602–603
  best books for young adults, 598–599
  online, 81
  sales, 543–544, 544(table)
Audiovisual materials
  acquisition expenditures
    academic libraries, 478–479(table)
    government libraries, 482–483(table)
    public libraries, 476–477(table)
    special libraries, 480–481(table)
  Library of Congress preservation activities, 76–78
  Webcasting of sound recordings, 328
  See also Audio-Visual Conservation Center
Author rights, 230, 246, 507
Avery, Paul, 30
Awards, 419–441, 639–656
  AALL, 419
  AAP, 209–210, 212, 217, 218, 219
  ACRL, 451

ALA, 192, 419–433, 451
ALISE, 266, 434–435, 452
ARLIS/NA, 433–434
ASIS, 433, 451–452
Beta Phi Mu, 435
Book Sense, 640
BSA, 435
CALA, 436
Caldecott Medal, 187, 624, 641
CLA, 287, 435–436
CLIR, 437
Coalition for Networked Information, 437
CSLA, 436–437
FLICC, 135
FOLUSA, 272–273, 437
Benjamin Franklin, 642–643
Gates Foundation, 437
IFLA, 279–280, 437–438
IMLS, 359
LHRT, 429
LITA, 451
MLA, 438–439
National Book Awards, 649
Newbery Medal, 187, 624, 650
Nobel Prize in Literature, 650
PEN, 651–652
Present Company (Merwin), 84
Pulitzer Prizes in Letters, 652
REFORMA, 439
for research, 450–452
SAA, 439–440
K. G. Saur, 439
SLA, 308, 440–441
YALSA, 191, 432–433
See also Books, best books; Grants *and* names of specific awards *or* organizations

B

Bach, David, 615
Balbi, Adriano, 453
Baldacci, David, 606
Banned Books Week, 181
Beach Music (Conroy), 204
Belgium, 446
Bestsellers, 511–512, 606–638
  almanacs, atlases, annuals, 621
  children's books, 623–638
  cookbooks, 606
  fiction, 607, 608–611
  hardcover, 606–614

College and research libraries *(cont.)*
  future directions, 182
  number of, 462(table), 463(table)
  open access, 29, 244
  placement sources, online, 388–389
  role of library, 234–236
  salary comparison, 402–403(table)
  SPARC campus education, 247
  state library agency-provided services, 468
  statistics, 144–145, 454, 456–457(table)
  STINET, 163
  University Publishing in a Digital Age, 228
  See also Association of College and
      Research Libraries; Association of
      Research Libraries; Communications
      Assistance for Law Enforcement Act;
      Council on Library and Information
      Resources; National Center for Educa-
      tion Statistics
College Cost Reduction Act, 315, 334–338
Colorado
  humanities councils, 347
  library associations, 746
  networks and cooperative library organiza-
      tions, 681
  school library media associations, 768
Communications Assistance for Law
    Enforcement Act (CALEA), 234
Computers
  software, *see* Software programs
  See also CD-ROM; Networks and network-
      ing
Conferences and seminars
  AAP, 197, 212, 219–220
  ABA, 221, 222, 223
  ACRL, 187
  ALA, 178, 179, 183–184, 187, 204, 245,
      271, 322
  ALISE, 265–267
  ARL, 237, 239, 240, 241–242, 450
  calendar of events, 817–823
  CDNL, 276
  CLIR, 250, 251, 252
  DLF, 250, 257
  DTIC, 156, 162
  European Commission, Scientific Publish-
      ing in the European Research Area, 30
  FLICC, 139
  FOLUSA, 271
  IFLA, 183, 275–276
  IMLS, 380–382
  Library of Congress, 84–85

LITA, 188
NNA, 217
NSF, 30
PLA, 188
Scholarly Publishing Conference, 29
SLA, 308–309
SPARC, 247
WSIS, 276–277
See also as subhead, e.g., American Library
    Association, conferences; Conference
    of Directors of National Libraries
Congress; online guide to House/Senate
    members, 115
Congressional Record, 114
Connecticut
  humanities councils, 347
  library associations, 746
  networks and cooperative library organiza-
      tions, 681
  school library media, associations, 768
Conroy, Pat, 204
Conservation and preservation, *see* Preserva-
    tion
Cookbooks, 606, 615
Copyright Act, 56
  amendments, *see* Digital Millennium Copy-
      right Act
  misleading copyright notices, 317
  Section 108 Study Group, 47–48, 233,
      316–317
Copyright and copyright law, 46–54, 232
  AAP activities, 196–197
  antipiracy activities, 207
  bibliography for librarians, 572
  Canadian, 296–297
  Chinese issues, 207
  collective works, 48–49
  digital copyright, *see* Digital rights man-
      agement
  Educational Fair Use Today, 56, 232
  fair use, 52–53, 56–64, 231–232, 316, 328
    Bill Graham Archives v. *Dorling Kinders-
        ley,* 60–62
    Blanch v. *Koons,* 57–58
    decisions, significance of, 62–64
    Kelly v. *Arriba Soft Corp.,* 59
    Perfect 10 v. *Amazon.com,* 58–60
  filtering, 51, 200, 317–320
  international protection, 207–209, 317
  Internet archive, 52
  Japanese, 209

O

Obama, Barack (Sen.), 606, 615
O'Brien, Timothy, 202
O'Brien, Trump v., 202
Ohio
  humanities council, 349
  library associations, 753
  networks and cooperative library organizations, 674–675
  school library media associations, 773
Oklahoma
  humanities council, 349
  library associations, 753
  networks and cooperative library organizations, 675
  school library media associations, 773
Oliver, Jamie, 606
Open access, 321–322
  to federal agency records, 331–334
  genome data, 104
  journals, 28–30
  scholarly publishing and, 28–33
OPEN Government Act, 331–332
Oregon
  humanities council, 349, 773–774
  library associations, 753–754
  library circulation, 458, 459(table), 460(table), 461
  networks and cooperative library organizations, 675
  school library media associations, 773–774
Orman, Suze, 606, 615
Orphan works, 52, 197, 278
  legislation, 316
Osteen, Joel, 606
Oz, Metmet C., 511, 606

P

Paperback books, 535–536
  almanacs/atlases/annuals, 621
  bestsellers, 615–621
    children's, 632–638
    mass market, 621–623
    trade, 616–621
  exports, mass market paperbacks, 549–550, 550(table)
  imports, mass market paperbacks, 557(table), 559–560, 561(table)
  prices and price indexes, 521, 527(table)

  U.S. mass market, averages, 526(table), 539(table)
  U.S. trade, averages, 540(table)
  sales, 544(table)
  See also Association of American Publishers, Trade Publishing
Patterson, James, 511, 606, 615, 623, 624
Peer-to-peer technology, 320
Pennsylvania
  humanities council, 349
  library associations, 754
  networks and cooperative library organizations, 675–676
  school library media associations, 774
Perfect 10, Inc. v. *Visa International Service Association,* 50
Perfect 10 v. *Amazon.com,* 58–60, 232
Periodicals and serials
  acquisition expenditures
    academic libraries, 478–479(table)
    government libraries, 482–483(table)
    public libraries, 476–477(table)
    special libraries, 480–481(table)
  antitrust issues in journal publishing, 246
  bibliography for librarians, 577, 579–580
  e-journals, 29, 229
  exports (U.S.), 553(table)
  imports (U.S.), 560, 561(table)
  online employment sources, 390
  open access to scholarly journals, 28–30, 325
  preservation, 229
  prices and price indexes, 514, 515(table), 520
    U.S., average, 516(table)
  See also International Standard Serial Number; Newspapers
Philippines, 208–209
Photographs, 48
Picoult, Jodi, 615
Placement and recruitment
  AAP activities, 198–199
  ALA activities, 386
  ALISE, 266
  ARL activities, 236–238
  career development, 374–375(table)
  diversity, 401, 406
  Internet employment sources, 199, 385–391
    American Libraries, 386
    blogs, 391
    employment agencies/commercial services, 390